The Conscious Reader

The
Conscious Reader

TENTH EDITION

CAROLINE SHRODES
Late, The Union Institute

MICHAEL SHUGRUE
The College of Staten Island of the City University of New York

MARC DIPAOLO
Alvernia College

CHRISTIAN J. MATUSCHEK

PEARSON
Longman

New York San Francisco Boston
London Toronto Sydney Tokyo Singapore Madrid
Mexico City Munich Paris Cape Town Hong Kong Montreal

Senior Sponsoring Editor: Virginia L. Blanford
Marketing Manager: Alexandra Smith
Senior Supplements Editor: Donna Campion
Production Manager: Ellen MacElree
Project Coordination, Text Design, and Electronic Page Makeup: Electronic
    Publishing Services Inc., NYC
Senior Cover Designer/Manager: Nancy Danahy
Cover Image: Lit doorway near Picasso Museum, Ciutat Vella area, Barcelona,
    Spain. Altrendo/Getty Images, Inc.
Photo Researcher: Linda Sykes
Manufacturing Buyer: Lucy Hebard
Printer and Binder: R. R. Donnelley & Sons Company
Cover Printer: Phoenix Color Corp.

For permission to use copyrighted material, grateful acknowledgment is made to
the copyright holders on pp. 913–921, which are hereby made part of this
copyright page.

Library of Congress Cataloging-in-Publication Data

The conscious reader / [edited by] Caroline Shrodes ... [et al.].— 10th ed.
    p. cm.
    Includes index.
    ISBN 0-321-36604-2
    1. College readers. I. Shrodes, Caroline.
    PE1122.C586 2006
    808'.0427—dc22

                                                      2005018403

Please visit us at http://www.ablongman.com/shrodes

ISBN 0-321-36604-2

2 3 4 5 6 7 8 9 10—DOC—08 07 06

BRIEF CONTENTS

Art and Composition   2

The Search for Self   20

Personal Relationships: Parents and Children   98

Personal Relationships: Men and Women   188

The Cultural Tradition: Popular Culture   270

The Cultural Tradition: Art, the Artist, and Society   354

Science, the Environment, and the Future   462

Freedom and Human Dignity   570

Globalism, Nationalism, and Cultural Identity   684

The Examined Life: Education   798

v

DETAILED CONTENTS

Art and Composition

The Search for Self

NOTEBOOK

PERSONAL REMINISCENCES

FICTION

POETRY

Personal Relationships: Parents and Children

NOTEBOOK

PERSONAL REMINISCENCES

ESSAYS

FICTION

Personal Relationships: Men and Women

NOTEBOOK

PERSONAL REMINISCENCES

ESSAYS

FICTION

POETRY

∾∾∾∾∾

The Cultural Tradition: Popular Culture

NOTEBOOK

PERSONAL REMINISCENCES

ESSAYS

POETRY

∾∾∾∾∾

The Cultural Tradition: Art, the Artist, and Society

NOTEBOOK

Science, the Environment,
and the Future

Freedom and Human Dignity

FICTION

POETRY

Globalism, Nationalism, and Cultural Identity

NOTEBOOK

PERSONAL REMINISCENCES

ESSAYS

POETRY

D R A M A

෴

The Examined Life: Education

N O T E B O O K

P E R S O N A L   R E M I N I S C E N C E S

E S S A Y S

F I C T I O N

P O E T R Y

RHETORICAL CONTENTS

The following arrangement of expository essays suggests ways in which readers can approach the selections. The classifications are not rigid, and many selections might fit as easily into one category as into another.

ANALYSIS

ARGUMENT AND PERSUASION

COMPARISON / CONTRAST

DEFINITION

NARRATION

PREFACE

...the unexamined life is not worth living.

—PLATO, *The Apology*

The tenth edition of *The Conscious Reader* contains many refreshing, exciting enrichments. The "Notebook" at the beginning of each section introduces the ideas and techniques developed therein and includes texts that complement and illuminate one another. A new section, "Globalism, Nationalism, and Cultural Identity," reflects current educational, social, and moral concerns regarding the relationship between the individual, national governments, and the world. This edition also grants more attention to the interrelatedness of texts, topics, and images.

The expanded, all-new portfolio of color and black-and-white images includes eight pages of color artwork in the "Art and Composition" section and more than thirty black-and-white pictures spread throughout the book. Discussion questions and writing assignments marked by this symbol, ℅, create pedagogical links between the pictures and the accompanying texts.

Voices in this edition include a rich representation of Poets Laureate, Nobel Laureates, established and contemporary literary figures, and distinguished commentators, as well as several essays and stories that were specially commissioned for *The Conscious Reader* and have never before seen print. These include a student's interpretation of a contemporary short story (offered as a model for future student work) and an essay on music appreciation that includes musical notation.

More than two-thirds of the readings in this book are nonfiction prose, primarily exposition or argument. Some of the essays are personal and readily comprehensible and provide models for early writing assignments. Others, which are more complex, should help students develop the ability to reason abstractly. The selections engage the readers' interests by virtue of their style and their focus on issues of universal concern. They reflect the continuity between past and present and serve as a catalyst to the readers' self-expression, to help sharpen their perceptions and widen their sympathies.

Consciousness heightened through reading develops effective writing, and the act of writing fosters self-definition. As students extend awareness by reading, they become increasingly conscious of the reservoir of memories and experiences from which to draw and the variety of forms and techniques that give shape to their writing.

Each selection has a headnote and suggestions for discussion and writing to help students explore multiple levels of understanding. The suggestions invite students to pay careful attention to thought and structure and to compare their experience with the vision of life expressed in the selections. Exploring cultural patterns both similar and alien to their own should encourage a continuing dialectic in classroom discussion as well as in writing.

If there is a dominant theme in these readings, it is that neither understanding of the past nor projections of the future can eliminate conflict from our lives and that opposing forces in the self and society are a part of the human condition. Indeed, it is vital that these forces contend. For it is primarily through conscious recognition and expression of these conflicting forces that we may find our way to a tolerance of ambiguity and to an increased freedom of choice.

◌◌◌◌◌

Instructor's Manual
Companion Web site

The Instructor's Manual accompanying *The Conscious Reader,* prepared by Dominic Delli Carpini of York College of Pennsylvania, is designed to be helpful without being intrusive. Its primary goals are to help instructors select readings that will fit the design and aims of their course to expand upon the text's suggestions for discussion and writing in ways geared more toward instructors than students, and to give instructors some inroads toward discussing the rhetoric and style of each piece. The manual treats nonfiction essays, imaginative literature, and visual images as examples of the skillful use of language and art from which students-writers can learn a good deal.

The Instructor's Manual also suggests ways that the readings can work together, crossing boundaries of genre in ways well suited to composition courses and helping student to forge connections in style as well as theme.

The Companion Web site to accompany *The Conscious Reader,* Tenth Edition (http://www.ablongman.com/shrodes), also written by Dominic Delli Carpini, offers a wealth of resources for both student and instructors.

Students can access detailed summaries, discussion and writing exercises, Web explorations, and annotated Web links for further study. Instructors will find a sample syllabus, useful Web links, and the Instructor's Manual available for download.

Acknowledgments

We extend our thanks to Virginia Blanford for her gracious, artful, and expert editorial guidance.

We thank Rebecca Gilpin for constant, good-natured assistance.

We thank Brian DiPaolo for his research, writing, and editorial skills.

We thank Don Bachardy, one of America's premiere portrait artists, and James P. White, Executive Director of the Christopher Isherwood Foundation, for their enthusiastic support and original contributions to the Search for Self Notebook and color art section.

We thank John Pence for offering the support of the John Pence Gallery in researching and securing permissions for works of art.

We thank Jörn Jacob Rohwer for his imaginative research into the life of Zarah Leander for the Parents and Children Notebook.

Thanks to the following reviewers:

Sarah T. D'Angelantonio, Franklin Pierce College

Nicole Dean, California State University, Fullerton

Rebecca Fisher, Holyoke Community College

Ellen Lansky, Inver Hills Community College

Amy Lawlor, Pasadena City College

Ronda K. Mehrer, Black Hills State University

Lisa Shuchter, Fairfield University

Derek Soles, Drexel University

Tom Veale, U. S. Military Academy, West Point

Laura Wadenpfuhl, New Jersey City University

M. F. S., M. D., AND C. J. M.

The Conscious Reader

Art and Composition

Being interested in a specific person, not a generic one, and having no 'ideal' image in my head, male or female, my aim is to explore physical and psychological terrain unknown to me. Rather than a perfect specimen, I search for the unexpected and often find it in what seem at first to be ordinary, unspectacular-looking individuals.

The experience of sitting, of being alone with another person while looking intently at him or her, often for several hours, is like no other I know. [It is] a true collaboration.

—DON BACHARDY

Works of art, in my opinion, are the only objects in the material universe to possess internal order, and that is why, though I don't believe that only art matters, I do believe in Art for Art's sake.

—E. M. FORSTER, "Art for Art's Sake"

Picasso at Work, Villa la Californie
DAVID DOUGLAS DUNCAN, 1957

Harry Ransom Humanities Research Center, The University of Texas at Austin

‭ ‬ ∾∾∾∾

MIKEL GLASS

I Once Was Lost, Oil on canvas, 1996

Mikel Glass, born in 1962 in Boston, MA, is a graduate of the New York Academy of Arts. Glass has exhibited with institutions such as the Hirschl and Adler Gallery, New York, NY; the John Pence Gallery, San Francisco, CA; and Gallery Albert Benamou, Paris, France. During the past fifteen years, Glass has explored a wide range of artistic genres including still life, portraiture, and history painting. A realistic painter, Glass produces work that can be described not only as classically balanced but also as particularly unsettling, borrowing compositions from other artists and then subverting them into something else altogether, or constructing rigorous still lifes that resemble historic panoramas or depict fruits and vegetables in hilarious, mad ballets. His online portfolios showcase Glass' impressive range as well as his relentless quest to close the divide between traditional and contemporary expression through explorations of his own subconscious.

Suggestions for Discussion

1. Explore Glass' painting carefully, and then catalogue the unusual array of sights that the artist spreads out before you. Which details in *I Once Was Lost* strike you as most interesting? Why do you think this is so?

2. What might the relationships among these objects be? Do the objects in this picture present themselves to you as if they were characters in a narrative? If so, what is their story?

3. Glass states: *"Ideally, painting for me is a vehicle for exploring the subconscious mind, using objects and people symbolically and metaphorically as visual medium. Irony and humor are welcome by-products of this process. . . . I subscribe to the idea of using art to explore one's inner workings, yet as a realist I also believe that those emotions can be conveyed using recognizable form."* The painter has chosen the title. In what way does *I Once Was Lost* illuminate the picture for you?

Suggestion for Writing

Write a short narrative using Mikel Glass' visionary or dreamlike painting as an illustration. Be just as imaginative in your story as Glass is in his painting. Or, if you can imagine *I Once Was Lost* as the backdrop of a theater piece, become the playwright and formulate the plot.

❦❦❦

DON BACHARDY

Self-portrait, Nov. 6, 2003,
Acrylic on paper

ALBRECHT DÜRER

Self-portrait in Furcoat,
Oil on panel, 1500

Don Bachardy, born in Los Angeles, CA, in 1934, is one of the major contemporary American portrait painters, often sought out by celebrities
among others because of his particular style and often striking choice of
color. Bachardy studied at the Chouinard Art Institute, Los Angeles, and
the Slade School of Art, London, and has published several collections of
his work, including *One Hundred Drawings* (1983), *Drawings of the Male
Nude* (1985), and *Stars in My Eyes* (1999). Bachardy also contributed illustrations to *Short Cuts: The Screenplay* by Robert Altman (1993) and is the
subject of a documentary, *The Eyes of Don Bachardy.* His work resides in
the permanent collections of the Metropolitan Museum of Art in New
York, the Henry E. Huntington Library, the Smithsonian Institution, and
the National Portrait Gallery in London, England.

Albrecht Dürer, born in 1471 in Nuremberg, Germany, as the third of
eighteen children, was a painter, wood carver, engraver, printmaker,
goldsmith, and mathematician. He is best known for his religious-
themed woodcuts in series, including *The Apocalypse* (1498), two series
on the crucifixion of Christ—*The Great Passion* (1498–1510) and *The
Little Passion* (1510–11)—and for his individual prints such as *Knight,
Death, and the Devil* (1513) and *Melancholia I* (1514). Perhaps the
most widely reproduced and best known of Dürer's works is a grey and
white brush drawing on blue-grounded paper entitled *Hands of the
Apostle,* generally known as *The Praying Hands.* Dürer is widely
regarded as the greatest artist of the Northern Renaissance. He died in
Nuremberg in 1528.

Suggestions for Discussion

1. At a glance, how do the men depicted strike you? What do you see in the images that might account for this reaction?

2. Now take a closer look at both the self-portraits. Pay attention to the choice of color, composition (how much of the body is actually displayed), and the use of light. Carefully examine the facial expressions, especially the eyes. Examine their postures, clothing, and hairstyles. How does the presentation of self differ? How is it similar?

3. According to Don Bachardy, *"The breakneck speed that working from life often demands can give the drawing or painting a rawness or unfinished look disturbing to some. To hide these telltale effects of a live confrontation seems to me wrong. On occasion, they should be flaunted. If a drawing or painting is done spontaneously, it should look spontaneous."* With this in mind, look again at Bachardy's portrait of himself. Do you see any reflection of his written statement in his painting? Now consider Dürer's portrait in comparison. Does it seem "unfinished" or "raw" in any way? Why or why not?

4. In this most celebrated of his self-portraits, Albrecht Dürer paints himself as a 28-year-old, when he was already renowned throughout Europe. His posture would have been familiar to most onlookers at the time (you may have seen similar depictions or iconographies in a museum or a church); Dürer clearly idealized his own portrait and thereby evoked a popular iconography of Christ. A practicing believer, he may have wanted to convey that an artist's creativity is God-given. Bachardy, on the other hand, states: *"The picture is pretty much doing itself. I'm just like a servant who mixes the paint and dips the brush. And sometimes I have a kind employer."* Bachardy painted himself at age 69. Compare the different statements of self, Dürer's painted one and Bachardy's written one. Do they differ? Do they intersect? How?

Suggestion for Writing

Try to imagine a meeting between Don Bachardy and Albrecht Dürer at the ages they are in their portraits. What might they say to one another about their callings as artists? How might they share their vision? Would they understand each other? Take into account the different time periods and cultures in which they lived as well as the difference in their ages. Invent a brief background story and write the dialogue. You may want to act out the encounter in class.

ERNESTO THAYAHT

The Great Helmsman, Oil on canvas, 1939

JEFFREY AARONSON

Rockefeller Center, Archival giclée print, 2002

Ernesto Thayaht (1893–1959) was an Italian of Anglo-Swiss parentage who worked as an illustrator, decorator, painter, sculptor, goldsmith, and garment maker. His piece, *The Great Helmsman,* both characterizes Thayaht's style as a futuristic painter and illustrates Italy's political landscape under Il Duce, Benito Mussolini, who was also at times referred to as "The Great Helmsman."

Jeffrey Aaronson (b. 1955) is an American digital photographer and photojournalist who has captured on film celebrities, the natural wonders of the world, and human rights crises for periodicals such as *Vanity Fair, Time,* the *New York Times,* and the *Smithsonian.* This 2002 image was shot on the streets of New York and printed by Aaronson without digital manipulation.

Suggestion for Discussion

Compare and contrast the two images, paying special attention to the figures—their faces, chests, hands and legs, and their body language. Take into account their different cultural backgrounds and the different period of time.

Suggestion for Writing

Both figures are heroes of their time, fighting an apparent evil of their time, one in history and one in fiction. Both can serve as symbols, one for fascism, the other for popular culture. Reflect on the various roles of heroes in our society, their need to be heroes and our need for heroes. What makes the hero a hero? If one person is identified as a hero, then what are all the others? Losers? Villains? Sheep? Ordinary or average? Who makes these classifications and why? Respond to these questions in an essay.

CRCRCRCR

ANTHONY WAICHULIS

Orchestrating the Drama, Oil on panel, 2003

DAMIEN HIRST

Autopsy with Brain, Oil on canvas, 2003

Pennsylvania native Anthony Waichulis (b. 1972) is a photographer and painter who often chooses as his subjects typically American objects and memorabilia such as currency, game pieces, and baseball cards.

Damien Hirst, born in 1965 in Bristol, England, is perhaps best known for artistically rendered dead animals, medical paraphernalia, and smokers, and he frequently chooses empty, confined spaces as settings for his work.

Suggestion for Discussion

Why do you think we have chosen to juxtapose these two paintings? What connections do you see? What disconnections do you sense? Pay attention to style, subject, color, and the feelings being evoked.

Suggestions for Writing

1. How real are these images of skulls and brains to you? What makes them real? Do they differ from each other? Does the media used make a difference—that is, would you feel differently seeing these images in a movie on TV or a report on the news? Discuss these questions in writing.

2. Hirst's artwork has stirred up controversy from time to time. Does his work here disturb or offend you? Does Waichulis' work? Where do you think that artwork that challenges the viewer should best be displayed? Should it be limited to museums? Schools? College textbooks? Some argue that art is no good if people are not willing to hang it in their living room. Do you agree? Write an argument based on your responses to these questions.

TOBY GARD

Lara Croft, Tomb Raider, Computer Graphic

ARTEMISIA GENTILESCHI

Judith and Her Maidservant, Oil on canvas, ca. 1625–27

Lara Croft was created by a software company, EIDOS, as the heroine of their *Indiana-Jones*-inspired computer game series *Tomb Raider.* The character has appeared in several comic books and in two live-action films, played by Angelina Jolie.

Roman-born Artemisia Gentileschi (1593–1652) was the oldest child of the well-known painter Orazio Gentileschi. Trained by her father early on, she soon demonstrated great skill at painting and continued her studies under a friend of her father, Agostino Tassi, after being rejected by several art academies. Orazio eventually accused Tassi of raping his daughter, instigating a highly publicized, seven-month trial in 1612 (an event depicted in the 1998 French film, *Artemisia).* Several of her works, including *Judith Slaying Holofernes,* ca. 1612–13, *Female Martyr,* ca. 1615, *The Penitent Magdalene,* ca. 1617–20, or *Judith and Her Maidservant,* ca. 1625–27, can be seen as cathartic and symbolic attempts to deal with the physical and psychic pain of her rape. A specialist in historical and religious paintings during a period when such lofty topics were deemed beyond the abilities of women artists, Gentileschi is now viewed as one of the most accomplished of the Early Baroque artists, following in the footsteps of Caravaggio but bringing a unique feminine perspective to her art.

Suggestion for Discussion

Compare and contrast both images. Pay attention to details, including the setting, the persons involved, activities, posture, light, and so on.

Suggestion for Writing

1. According to Amy-Jill Levine, a New Testament studies scholar at Vanderbilt University Divinity School, Judith is *like Wonder Woman, only Jewish.* Reflect on the artistic representations of female heroism seen here in the portraits of Croft and Judith and on Levine's comment about Judith. You may also want to read Gloria Steinem's essay on *Wonder Woman* in the Popular Culture section of this book. Formulate your own opinion on heroic figures, female stereotypes, and your view of yourself as a woman or a man in relation to women. Synthesize your views in an essay.

2. The *Book of Judith* is part of the Catholic version of the Bible. It is considered apocryphal, or non-canonical, by protestant churches and the Jewish community. Look up the book of Judith online through the New American Bible (www.usccb.org/nab/bible/index.htm) and read Chapter 13, Verses 1 to 10, about how the two powerful "sheroes" have beheaded the aggressor. Then look again at Artemisia's illustration of the scene and reread the headnote about the artist. Now reflect on the following quotes:

> "For if through identification with her Judith and Abra [the maidservant] the artist Artemisia found a liberating courage inspired by a heroic model, identification also permitted her to apply to her own life experience to liberate Judith from the confining stereotypes of heroine and seductress, and to imbue her with human complexity."
>
> Mary D. Garrard, art historian

> "Art is like medicine—it can heal. Yet I've always been amazed at how many people believe in medicine but don't believe in art, without questioning either."
>
> Damien Hirst, artist

Both statements reflect on the notion of transformation and healing. Respond to either quote in an essay.

I Once Was Lost
Oil on canvas, 1996

MIKEL GLASS
John Pence Gallery, San Francisco, CA

11

Self-portrait, Nov. 6, 2003
Acrylic on paper

DON BACHARDY

Don Bachardy, Santa Monica, CA

Self-portrait in Furcoat
Oil on panel, 1500

ALBRECHT DÜRER

Alte Pinakothek, Munich/Scala/Art Resource, NY

The Great Helmsman
Oil on canvas, 1939

ERNESTO THAYAHT

Mitchell Wolfson Jr. Collection,
Fondazione Colombo, Genoa, Italy

Rockefeller Center
Archival giclée print, 2002

JEFFREY AARONSON

Jeffrey Aaronson/Network Aspen

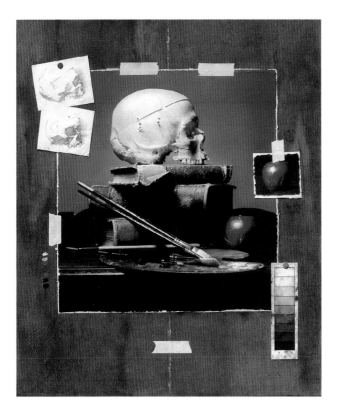

**Orchestrating
the Drama**
Oil on panel, 2003

ANTHONY
WAICHULIS

John Pence Gallery,
San Francisco, CA

Autopsy with Brain
Oil on canvas, 2003

DAMIEN HIRST

Prudence Cuming Associates.
Copyright the artist.

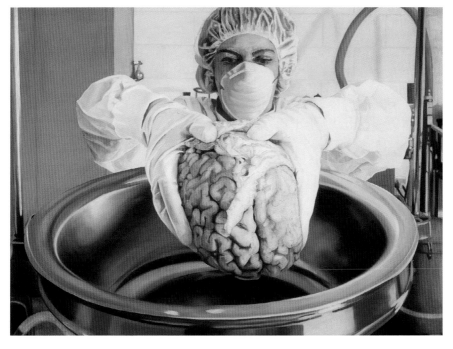

Lara Croft, Tomb Raider
Computer Graphic

TOBY GARD

Judith and Her Maidservant
Oil on canvas, ca. 1625–27

ARTEMISIA GENTILESCHI

The Detroit Institute of Arts

17

The Mystery Play, 1994

GRANT MORRISON, JON J. MUTH

ɷɷɷɷ

GRANT MORRISON, JON J. MUTH

The Mystery Play, 1994

The Mystery Play (1994) is a graphic novel produced for DC Comics' *Vertigo* imprint collaboratively by writer Grant Morrison and artist Jon J. Muth. A comic book artist since the early 1980s, Muth is best known for contributing to writer J. M. DeMatteis' series *Moonshadow* and Neil Gaiman's *Sandman.* His artwork is widely considered delicate, sophisticated, and artistically mature. Morrison made a name for himself as a comic book writer crafting the scripts to offbeat titles such as *Doom Patrol* and *Animal Man* before becoming one of the most respected writers of contemporary mainstream superhero comic books. He has written acclaimed stories for *Batman, Superman,* the *Justice League,* and *X-Men,* and is the creator and writer of the comic books *The Invisibles* and *The New Adventures of Hitler.*

Suggestions for Discussion

1. The accompanying image reproduces a full page of *The Mystery Play,* which merges words and images; it is a complete narrative that uses a traditional comic book format. You may have enjoyed other comic books or comic strips in your childhood—in fact, you may still. Focus on the text and illustrations reproduced here. Think in terms of your own familiarity with comic books, as well as in terms of literature and art. Does this fit your expectations for a comic book? For a work of literature? For a work of art? Why or why not?

2. *The Mystery Play* is a captivating crime story. Think about various media: a mystery story told out loud, written as a novel, created as a comic book, or shot as a film. Draw on your own experience in thinking about how the difference in format impacts the experience of the narrative. Do you prefer one format over another? Why might a writer or artist choose one or another way of telling a story?

Suggestion for Writing

Should comic books and graphic novels be considered serious literature? Should they be analyzed, reviewed, and evaluated as we might a novel or a poem? Pick your side of this question and state your arguments.

The Search for Self

As I dance, whirling and joyous, happier than I've ever been in my life, another bright-faced dancer joins me.... The other dancer has obviously come through all right, as I have done. She is beautiful, whole and free. And she is also me.

—ALICE WALKER, "Beauty: When the Other Dancer Is the Self"

I had always had a pretty good opinion of myself as a writer. But, during those first days with Bergmann, it was lowered considerably.

—CHRISTOPHER ISHERWOOD, "Prater Violet"

Untitled, from My Generation
TOBIAS PRASSE
Tobias Prasse Photography

Untitled, from My Generation
TOBIAS PRASSE
Tobias Prasse/Zefa-Corbis

NOTEBOOK

CHRISTOPHER ISHERWOOD

Prater Violet

Born in Cheshire, England, Christopher Isherwood (1904–1986) taught English in Germany during the early 1930s. His experiences there became the basis for *The Berlin Stories* (1946), a collection of fiction that inspired the musical *Cabaret*. Isherwood moved to California in 1939 and later underwent a conversion to Hinduism. With the publication of his 1976 memoir *Christopher and His Kind*, he established himself as a major figure in the gay rights movement. The following selection is taken from his autobiographical novel *Prater Violet* (1945), a satire of the film industry.

I had always had a pretty good opinion of myself as a writer. But, during those first days with Bergmann, it was lowered considerably. I had flattered myself that I had imagination, that I could invent dialogue, that I could develop a character. I had believed that I could describe almost anything, just as a competent artist can draw you an old man's face, or a table, or a tree.

Well, it seemed that I was wrong.

The period is early twentieth century, some time before the 1914 war. It is a warm spring evening in the Vienna Prater. The dancehalls are lighted up. The coffee houses are full. The bands blare. Fireworks are bursting above the trees. The swings are swinging. The round-abouts are revolving. There are freak shows, gypsies telling fortunes, boys playing the concertina. Crowds of people are eating, drinking beer, wandering along the paths beside the river. The drunks sing noisily. The lovers, arm in arm, stroll whispering in the shadow of the elms and the silver poplars.

There is a girl named Toni, who sells violets. Everybody knows her, and she has a word for everybody. She laughs and jokes as she offers the flowers. An officer tries to kiss her; she slips away from him good-humoredly. An old lady has lost her dog; she is sympathetic. An indignant, tyrannical gentleman is looking for his daughter; Toni knows where she is, and with whom, but she won't tell.

Then, as she wanders down the alleys carrying her basket, light-hearted and fancy-free, she comes face to face with a handsome boy in the dress of a student. He tells her, truthfully, that his name is Rudolf. But he is not what he seems. He is really the Crown Prince of Borodania.

All this I was to describe. "Do not concern yourself with the shots," Bergmann had told me. "Just write dialogue. Create atmosphere. Give the camera something to listen to and look at."

I couldn't. I couldn't. My impotence nearly reduced me to tears. It was all so simple, surely? There is Toni's father, for instance. He is fat and jolly, and he has a stall where he sells *Wiener Wuerstchen*. He talks to his customers. He talks to Toni. Toni talks to the customers. They reply. It is all very gay, amusing, delightful. But what the hell do they actually say?

I didn't know. I couldn't write it. That was the brutal truth—I couldn't draw a table. I tried to take refuge in my pride. After all, this was movie work, hack work. It was something essentially false, cheap, vulgar. It was beneath me. I ought never to have become involved in it, under the influence of Bergmann's dangerous charm, and for the sake of the almost incredible twenty pounds a week which Imperial Bulldog was prepared, quite as a matter of course, to pay me. I was betraying my art. No wonder it was so difficult.

Nonsense. I didn't really believe that, either. It isn't vulgar to be able to make people talk. An old man selling sausages isn't vulgar, except in the original meaning of the word, "belonging to the common people." Shakespeare would have known how he spoke. Tolstoy would have known. I didn't know because, for all my parlor socialism, I was a snob. I didn't know how anybody spoke, except public-school boys and neurotic bohemians.

I fell back, in my despair, upon memories of other movies. I tried to be smart, facetious. I made involved, wordy jokes. I wrote a page of dialogue which led nowhere and only succeeded in establishing the fact that an anonymous minor character was having an affair with somebody else's wife. As for Rudolf, the incognito Prince, he talked like the lowest common denominator of all the worst musical comedies I had ever seen. I hardly dared to show my wretched attempts to Bergmann at all.

He read them through with furrowed brows and a short profound grunt; but he didn't seem either dismayed or surprised. "Let me tell you something. Master," he began, as he dropped my manuscript casually into the wastepaper basket, "the film is a symphony. Each movement is written in a certain key. There is a note which has to be chosen and struck immediately. It is characteristic of the whole. It commands the attention."

Sitting very close to me, and pausing only to draw long breaths from his cigarette, he started to describe the opening sequence. It was astounding.

Everything came to life. The trees began to tremble in the evening breeze, the music was heard, the roundabouts were set in motion. And the people talked. Bergmann improvised their conversation, partly in German, partly in ridiculous English; and it was vivid and real. His eyes sparkled, his gestures grew more exaggerated, he mimicked, he clowned. I began to laugh. Bergmann smiled delightedly at his own invention. It was all so simple, so effective, so obvious. Why hadn't I thought of it myself?

Bergmann gave me a little pat on the shoulder. "It's nice, isn't it?"

"It's wonderful! I'll note that down before I forget."

Immediately, he was very serious. "No, no, It is wrong. All wrong. I only wanted to give you some idea. . .No, that won't do. Wait. We must consider. . ."

Clouds followed the sunshine. Bergmann scowled grimly as he passed into philosophical analysis. He gave me ten excellent reasons why the whole thing was impossible. They, too, were obvious. Why hadn't I thought of them? Bergmann sighed. "It's not so easy. . ." He lit another cigarette. "Not so easy," he muttered. "Wait. Wait. Let us see. . ."

He rose and paced the carpet, breathing hard, his hands folded severely behind his back, his face shut against the outside world, implacably, like a prison door. Then a thought struck him. He stopped, amused by it. He smiled.

"You know what my wife tells me when I have these difficulties? 'Friedrich,' she says, 'Go and write your poems. When I have cooked the dinner, I will invent this idiotic story for you. After all, prostitution is a woman's business.'"

That was what Bergmann was like on his good days; the days when I was Alyosha Karamazov, or, as he told Dorothy, like Balaam's ass, "who *once* said a marvelous line." My incompetence merely stimulated him to more brilliant flights of imagination. He sparkled with epigrams, he beamed, he really amazed himself. On such days, we suited each other perfectly. Bergmann didn't really need a collaborator at all. But he needed stimulation and sympathy; he needed someone he could talk German to. He needed an audience.

His wife wrote to him every day, Inge two or three times a week. He read me extracts from their letters, full of household, theatrical and political gossip; and these led to anecdotes, about Inge's first concert, about his mother-in-law, about German and Austrian actors, and the plays and films he had directed. He would spend a whole hour describing how he had produced *Macbeth* in Dresden, with masks, in the style of a Greek tragedy. A morning would go by while he recited his poems, or told me of his last days in Berlin, in the spring of that year, when the Storm Troopers were roving the streets like bandits, and his wife had saved him from several dangerous situations by a quick answer or a joke. Although Bergmann was an Austrian, he had been advised to give up his job and leave Germany in a hurry. They had lost most of their money in consequence. "And so, when Chatsworth's offer came, you see, I could not afford to refuse. There was no alternative. I had my doubts about this artificial Violet, from the very first. Even across half of Europe, it didn't smell so good. . . .Never mind, I said to myself. Here is a problem. Every problem has its solution. We will do what we can. We will not despair. Who knows? Perhaps, after all, we shall present Mr. Chatsworth with a charming nosegay, a nice little surprise."

Bergmann wanted all my time, all my company, all my attention. During those first weeks, our working day steadily increased in length, until I had to make a stand and insist on going home to supper. He seemed determined to possess me utterly. He pursued me with questions, about my friends, my interests, my habits, my love life. The weekends, especially, were the object of his endless, jealous curiosity. What did I do? Whom did I see? Did I live like a monk? "Is it Mr. W.H. you seek, or the Dark Lady of the Sonnets?" But I was equally obstinate. I wouldn't tell him. I teased him with smiles and hints.

Foiled, he turned his attention to Dorothy. Younger and less experienced, she was no match for his inquisitiveness. One morning, I arrived to find her in tears. She rose abruptly and hurried into the next room. "She has her struggle," Bergmann told me, with a certain grim satisfaction. "It's not so easy." Dorothy, it appeared, had a boy friend, an older man, who was married. He didn't seem able to make up his mind which of the two women he liked better; just now, he had gone back to his wife. His name was Clem. He was a car salesman. He had taken Dorothy to Brighton for weekends. Dorothy also had a lover of her own age, a radio engineer, nice and steady, who wanted to marry her. But the radio engineer lacked glamour; he couldn't compete with the fatal appeal of Clem, who wore a little black mustache.

Bergmann's interest in all this was positively ghoulish. In addition, he knew everything about Dorothy's father, another sinister influence, and about her aunt, who worked at an undertaker's, and was having an affair with her brother-in-law. At first, I could hardly believe that Dorothy had really brought herself to reveal such intimate details, and suspected Bergmann of having invented the whole story. She seemed such a shy, reserved girl. But soon they were actually speaking of Clem in my presence. When Dorothy cried, Bergmann would pat her on the shoulder, like God Himself, and murmur, "That's all right, my child. Nothing to do. It will pass."

He was fond of lecturing me on Love. "When a woman is awakened, when she gets the man she wants, she is amazing, amazing. You have no idea. . . Sensuality is a whole separate world. What we see on the outside, what comes up to the surface—it's nothing. Love is like a mine. You go deeper and deeper. There are passages, caves, whole strata. You discover entire geological eras. You find things, little objects, which enable you to reconstruct her life, her other lovers, things she does not even know about herself, things you must never tell her that you know. . .

"You see," Bergmann continued, "women are absolutely necessary to a man; especially to a man who lives in ideas, in the creation of moods and thoughts. He needs them, like bread. I do not mean for the coitus; that is not so important, at my age. One lives more in the fantasy. But one needs their aura, their ambience, their perfume. Women always recognize a man who wants this thing from them. They feel it at once, and they come to him, like horses." Bergmann paused, grinning. "You see, I am an old Jewish Socrates who preaches to the Youth. One day, they will give me the hemlock."

In the hot little room, our life together seemed curiously isolated. The three of us formed a self-contained world, independent of London, of Europe, of 1933. Dorothy, the representative of Woman, did her best to keep the home in some kind of order, but her efforts were not very successful. Her schemes for arranging Bergmann's huge litter of papers only caused worse confusion. As he could never describe exactly what it was that he was looking for, she could never tell him where she had put it. This sent him into frenzies of frustration. "Terrible, terrible. This definitely kills me. Too idiotic for words." And he would relapse into grumpy silence.

Then there was the problem of meals. The house had a restaurant service, theoretically. It could produce bitter coffee, very strong black tea, congealed eggs, sodden toast and a gluey chop, followed by some nameless kind of yellow pudding. The food took an almost incredible time to arrive. As Bergmann said, when you ordered breakfast, it was best to ask for what you wanted at lunch, because it would be four hours before you got it. So we lived chiefly on cigarettes.

At least twice a week, there was a Black Day. I would enter the flat to find Bergmann in complete despair. He hadn't slept all night, the story was hopeless, Dorothy was crying. The best way of dealing with this situation was to make Bergmann come out with me to lunch. Our nearest restaurant was a big gloomy place on the top floor of a department store. We ate early, when there were very few other customers, sitting together at a table in the darkest corner, next to a rather sinister grandfather clock, which reminded Bergmann of the story by Edgar Allan Poe.

"It ticks every moment," he told me. "Death comes nearer. Syphilis. Poverty. Consumption. Cancer discovered too late. My art no good, a failure, a damn flop. War. Poison gas. We are dying with our heads together in the oven."

And then he would begin to describe the coming war. The attack on Vienna, Prague, London and Paris, without warning, by thousands of planes, dropping bombs filled with deadly bacilli; the conquest of Europe in a week; the subjugation of Asia, Africa, the Americas; the massacre of the Jews, the execution of intellectuals, the herding of non-Nordic women into enormous state brothels; the burning of paintings and books, the grinding of statues into powder; the mass sterilization of the unfit, mass murder of the elderly, mass conditioning of the young; the reduction of France and the Balkan countries to wilderness, in order to make national parks for the Hitler Jugend; the establishment of Brown Art, Brown Literature, Brown Music, Brown Philosophy, Brown Science and the Hitler Religion, with its Vatican at Munich and its Lourdes at Berchtesgaden: a cult based upon the most complex system of dogmas concerning the real nature of the Fuehrer, the utterances of *Mein Kampf,* the ten thousand Bolshevist heresies, the sacrament of Blood and Soil, and upon elaborate rituals of mystic union with the Homeland, involving human sacrifice and the baptism of steel.

"All these people," Bergmann continued, "will be dead. All of them. . . No, there is one. . ." He pointed to a fat, inoffensive man sitting alone in a distant corner. "He will survive. He is the kind that will do anything, anything to be allowed to live. He will invite the conquerors to his home, force his wife to cook for them and serve the dinner on his bended knees. He will denounce his mother. He will offer his sister to a common soldier. He will act as a spy in prisons. He will spit on the Sacrament. He will hold down his daughter while they rape her. And, as a reward for this, he will be given a job as bootblack in a public lavatory, and he will lick the dirt from people's shoes with his tongue. . ." Bergmann shook his head sadly. "Too bad. I do not envy him."

This kind of talk had a strange effect on me. Like all my friends, I said I believed that a European war was coming soon. I believed it as one believes that one will die, and yet I didn't believe. For the coming war was as unreal to me as death itself. It was unreal because I couldn't imagine anything beyond it; I refused to imagine anything; just as a spectator refuses to imagine what is behind the scenery in a theatre. The outbreak of war, like the moment of death, crossed my perspective of the future like a wall; it marked the instant, total end of my imagined world. I thought about this wall from time to time, with acute depression and a flutter of fear at the solar plexus. Then, again, I forgot or ignored it. Also, just as when one thinks of one's own death, I secretly whispered to myself, "Who knows? Maybe we shall get around it somehow. Maybe it will never happen."

Bergmann's apocalyptic pictures of universal doom made the prospect of war more unreal than ever, and so they never failed to cheer me up. I suppose they worked like that for him, too; probably that was why he dwelt upon them so gleefully. And, while he was in the midst of the horrors, his glance around the room generally discovered a girl or woman who interested him, and diverted the stream of his imagination toward more agreeable subjects.

His favorite was the manageress of the restaurant, a handsome blonde with a very sweet motherly smile, about thirty years old. Bergmann approved of her highly. "I have only to look at her," he told me, "to know that she is satisfied. Deeply satisfied. Some man has made her happy. For her, there is no longer any search. She has found what we are all looking for. She understands all of us. She does not need books, or theories, or philosophy, or priests. She understands Michelangelo, Beethoven, Christ, Lenin—even Hitler. And she is afraid of nothing, nothing. . . .Such a woman is my religion."

The manageress would always have a special smile for Bergmann when we came in; and, during the meal, she would walk over to our table and ask if everything was all right. "Everything is all right, my darling," Bergmann would reply; "thanks to God, but chiefly to you. You restore our confidence in ourselves."

I don't know exactly what the manageress made of this, but she smiled, in an amused, kindly way. She really was very nice. "You see?" Bergmann would turn to me, after she had gone. "We understand each other perfectly."

And so, our confidence restored by *das ewige Weibliche,* we went back refreshed to tend the poor little *Prater Violet,* wilting in the suffocating atmosphere of our flat.

Suggestions for Discussion

1. Describe the relationship between the narrator and Bergmann.

2. What is Dorothy's dilemma, and how do the two men treat her?

3. How does Isherwood's story depict the process of writing a screenplay and making a film? How might this process differ from the creative process Isherwood employed in writing for his own satisfaction and for publication?

Suggestion for Writing

Like Aryeh Lev Stollman's *Die Grosse Liebe* (p. 100), Isherwood's story contrasts the romanticism of motion pictures made during the Nazi regime with the brutal realities of a world at war. What do both stories say about the relationship between the films of the World War II era, their target audiences, and the moviemakers who produced these films? Write an essay examining the topic.

J A M E S   P.   W H I T E

Influences

A Guggenheim Fellowship winner, James White is the executive director of the Christopher Isherwood Foundation. He edited *A Christopher Isherwood Reader* (1989) and is the author of *Birdsong* (1995). The following scene is a fictionalized account of an afternoon White spent with

Sketch of James P. White, Feb. 9, 1980, ink on paper, Don Bachardy, Santa Monica, CA.

the cancer-stricken Isherwood in Santa Monica, California, shortly before Isherwood's death in 1986. Like Isherwood's *Prater Violet* (reprinted in this Notebook), White's story is autobiographical fiction. Isherwood is identified by his middle names, William Bradshaw, and the character of Jake is a composite of White and Isherwood's longtime partner, artist Don Bachardy. Bachardy's portrait of White, rendered during the time period this story takes place, accompanies the selection.

At 5:30 when Jake arrived at William's, Eric's truck was parked beside the Volkswagen in the carport. Eric had turned out to be the perfect nurse for William. Jake went down the steps and entered the house, flowers from the garden arranged in a big blue pot set in the center of the coffee table. The blinds were open, light filling up the room. Eric stood in the kitchen doorway, grinning, drying his hands on a dishtowel.

"How is he?" Jake asked.

"He was sleeping a minute ago," Eric said. "He's expecting you."

Jake nodded and started down the hallway, the walls on either side covered with drawings and paintings. As he approached William's bedroom, he hesitated. A seriousness molded the room even before Jake entered. He saw William lying in his pajamas, his face grimacing. Obviously he couldn't find a comfortable position in bed. He looked up at Jake. "Shit! Oh shit!" he said.

Jake was afraid of making William worse by helping wrong, by moving his body in a painful direction.

Eric appeared at once, hurried past, and putting his arms around William, adjusted his position a little. A notch. "There," he said. "Better?"

"Much," William said.

"I'm making soup," Eric said. He brought the aroma of onions on his Khaki shirt and jeans. Jake had had no idea that Eric was such a good cook.

"He even got me to eat earlier," William said.

Eric left and Jake perched on the edge of the bed.

William didn't feel like talking. His eyes closed. He appeared to be sleeping.

Several minutes later, Jake heard the phone ringing twice in the back room, then listened as Eric took a message. As Eric passed by, along the halfway, he said, "That's the tenth person to call today."

Jake stood up and walked around the bed to the glass door overlooking the ocean. The water was almost turquoise. He glanced back at William.

William suddenly looked up at him. "Oh, Jake," he said. "Is it sunny outside?"

"Would you like to sit on the terrace?"

"Very much."

But how does he get there? Jake thought as he went into the kitchen to tell Eric. Eric was humming at the stove. He was adding salt to a bubbling pot of soup.

"He wants to sit on the terrace," Jake said. "Is that OK?"

"Of course," Eric said. He turned down the flame on the burner, then followed Jake back down the hallway. In the bedroom Eric said to William, "Put your arms around my neck and trust me. I'll go very easy and if you don't make any sudden moves, it won't hurt."

The flesh on William's arms sagged as he encircled Eric's horse-like neck. Then Eric lifted and William's eyes widened, but yes, he was on his feet. Eric's arm wrapped around his waist and supported him.

"Good!" Eric continued to the wooden deck, high above the ground and just outside the bedroom. The bright ocean made Jake close his eyes; it sparkled like an uncovered light bulb. Jake pulled out one of the wrought iron chairs with pillow seats at the table.

"All right, I'll let you down easy, but I won't let go until you're comfortable. Okay?" He knelt down, settling William onto the seat.

William reached out to the table and steadied himself. "Very good," he said.

Eric stood up, his hands free. "If you want anything, just call out. I can hear you from the kitchen."

"Yes, love," William said.

Jake stretched, the sunlight comfortable, then he sat down.

"I've been thinking about my mother today," William said. "She cared only about what others thought about her and us. To the last minute of her life, appearances were most important. What I wrote about was distasteful to her. After people got to know who I was, she was okay with it. Toward the end of her life, no one could work for her because she accused everyone who worked for her of stealing."

William fell silent. A moment later, he said, "I also was thinking of my nanny. She really loved me. Starting life with that wonderful woman was a blessing."

"I felt that love you felt with your nanny twice," Jake said. "First with my grandmother. She had to be big and fat she was so filled with love. I remember how she patted me right here, on the knee when she sat by me or how she put her arm around me. She would have done anything for me. And my son—when he was a kid, before he went to college, I knew he loved me as much as he could."

"Imagine," William said. "Ohhh! Shit!"

Jake rose. In one second, Eric appeared, hurrying to the deck, bringing a pillow, helping William position himself. It was as if he'd been watching. "You need to eat something," Eric said.

"No, love. It makes me sick to think of it."

"I have just cut up a fresh orange. I'll bring a few slices. See if you can suck on them."

"All right," William said.

"Is the pain any better?" Jake asked.

"Yes." William's white face was chalky, his eyes watery.

"It's so beautiful out here," Jake said. He noticed a bird singing, then another, flying low, its voice entirely different. Sunlight patterned the table and the deck and the air occasionally blew against his shirt. "This is the first time I've really noticed how many different flowers you have," Jake said. He saw William was interested. "Those purple Bougainvillaea, my god, they're beautiful."

"Yes, they're something."

"And those little orange flowers growing out of their own pot. We had them in Texas when I grew up."

"Oh yes?"

"And the Birds of Paradise. We only saw photographs of them. And the air," Jake said.

"I often sleep with the glass door to my bedroom open. But the light is powerful in the morning and wakes me if I do."

"Look at the ocean," Jake said. It was like he couldn't keep the view inside his head because it had so many beautiful parts. The sunlight had brightness, the breeze a slight warmth, the flowers different smells and colors.

"Ohhh! God!"

Jake stood up, but waited for Eric, who came instantly. Eric put his arms around William's shoulders and held, then righted them. "Better?"

"Yes. Thank you, love. But no oranges."

Eric left.

William looked directly at Jake. He waited until Eric was out of hearing. "The angel of death," William said.

Yes he is, Jake thought, but did not answer. The aroma of healthy soup drifted in from the kitchen.

"The angel of my death," William said.

"Nonsense."

"I've left directions for there to be no burial," William said. "I'm leaving my body to the medical school of UCLA for whatever purpose they want. I want no memorial service. You can go through all the papers the second I'm dead."

"Yes," Jake said.

"And anything you think one should not see, file." He coughed. "Would you get me water, Jake?"

Jake hurried from the room. The entire house seemed to be under Eric's supervision. The windows in the kitchen and the tile floor were just cleaned. Not a dirty dish was in sight and the soup still simmered in a big stainless container on the gas stove.

Jake took the glass of water to William and asked, "Do you want some, now?"

William spread his lips and Jake carefully tilted the glass then took it away. William swallowed and drew in a deep breath. "Thank you," he said.

Jake decided to mention death, in case William wanted to talk about it. "Are you afraid of dying?" Jake asked, as he sat down.

"I don't know," William said. "Are you?"

William's eyes closed, his lips smiling. Sunlight was patterned on his forehead.

"When I was sick in New York once," Jake said, "a good friend told me he thought I was going to die and I got upset. I was 30. I hadn't thought for a minute that I was. But I was sick. I remember how hostile I felt toward him."

"Yes, we all know what's coming."

The phone began to ring and Jake heard Eric call out, "Could you get it?"

Jake hurried into the bedroom, then the hallway and into the office. He picked up the receiver on the fifth ring.

"Is William Bradshaw there?"

"He can't come to the phone. Can I take a message?"

"This is William Perkins at Warner's. Would you leave a message that I called?"

"Of course. I'm ready," Jake took down the name and number. Then he hung up and realized he stood alone in the office for the first time. The chaise lounge had sunken places where William frequently lay. The typewriter had a sheet of paper in the carriage, a checkbook lay on the surface of the desk—all these must have been in use just a few days ago.

Jake walked over and read the paragraph on the typed sheet. From what he could tell it was part of the novel William worked on.

He heard Eric and turned around, the message in his hand.

"He's waiting for you," Eric said. "Are you hungry yet?"

"Is there anything I can do to help?" Jake asked. "I'll eat later."

Jake hurried back outside. William was not in pain and was smiling. Jake sat down. "What was W.H. Auden like?" he asked.

"I've written about him. He was eccentric and brilliant."

"Why didn't you write poetry?"

"You don't write poetry when W.H. Auden is your closest friend," William said.

Jake smiled. "You knew Virginia Woolf?"

"Yes. She published my first book. I liked her very much."

"Did you know her husband?"

"Leonard? Yes, of course. I knew them all, Jake."

"It is amazing how many people you've known."

"I've been lucky." William said. "You're talking about the famous ones. They're the only ones you could know about. But there were so many others, Jake. Such people—I couldn't begin to tell you about them."

Jake nodded in agreement.

"The people." William said, and his expression changed.

Jake saw that William wanted to cry. He was trying with all his strength to hold back the tears. "Jake—."

Jake didn't know what to do. William was the hero, the strong one. Jake got up and walked closer to him. Jake put his arms around him. He could feel William's head shake, just a little; he was crying. Jake held him gently.

"Oh Jake," William said, "the people that I've known—they've touched me. They've touched me."

His voice was so moving that Jake could not speak. Holding William as he would a flower or a bird or anything fragile, he felt William's touch, and knew exactly what William meant.

Then William leaned back and Jake let go. For a moment, neither spoke. A bird flying just above the tops of the trees let out a high, repetitive sound.

"I want you to taste the soup," Eric said, coming onto the terrace. "It's delicious." He carried two bowlfuls. Eric's profile was like a general's, strong forehead, nose, chin. Eric set down the soup.

Jake tried the soup first. "It's wonderful, Eric," he said.

William tasted it and approved.

"All right," Eric said. "Have one more."

William opened his mouth, then swallowed the soup Eric gave him.

"One more, please."

"No."

"Just try. Only one more."

William ate one more spoonful. Then he leaned his head back, his eyes closed.

"No more sun," Eric said. He lifted William easily from the chair and helped him into the bedroom.

Jake stayed on the terrace several minutes as he finished his soup. Then he took the dishes into the kitchen and went past the dining room into the living area. He sat on one of the plush velvet chairs while William rested. Jake had eaten a lot and the strong light flowing through the living room windows made him groggy. He closed his eyes. He nodded off.

Instantly he was driving along a freeway, at night, and cars coming in the opposite lane had their lights on. Stores along the highway were bright. As Jake drove he blinked, because of the glaring lights. Then he tried to open his eyes and couldn't. He tried hard to see, but his eyelids were sealed shut. Finally he got them open, yet could not see. He realized he was experiencing blindness and in the middle of the darkness was a light and the glare was all he saw. The car was speeding, others were coming, and he was about to crash.

He woke up with a start, aware he had been sleeping. He closed his eyes and a moment later, he fell back to sleep. This time in his dream he was lying in a bed. He tried to get out of the bed, but he felt paralyzed. He could not move his arms or legs and when he tried to breathe, he began to suffocate. No organ in his body was functioning.

When he awoke again, he felt the reassuring softness of the chair and the heat of the light against his face. The images vanished. Something about his dreams made a deeper impression than most and he did not know why. He thought about the blindness, then about being paralyzed. They had to do with death. For a few seconds he tried to calm down. Then he got up and started down the hallway to William's bedroom, hoping that William could sleep.

Suggestions for Discussion

1. Describe the relationship between Jake and William Bradshaw.

2. Since this work is autobiographical fiction, how much should the reader assume really happened, and how much is artistic license? What might this piece reveal to us about the real-life Isherwood?

Suggestions for Writing

1. The scene in *Prater Violet* features a character based on the young Isherwood acting as an apprentice figure to an older artist and businessman. White's story reverses Isherwood's role, placing a fictionalized version of the writer in the position of mentor at the end of his life. Compare these two visions of Isherwood in a brief essay. Reflect on how age and the roles of the mentor and student define a person.

2. White's piece parallels scenes and themes from the film *Gods and Monsters* (1998) and the book it is based on, Christopher Bram's *Father of Frankenstein* (1995). Watch the film or read the novel, and note the similarities and differences between the portrayals of Isherwood and dying filmmaker James Whale.

PERSONAL REMINISCENCES

ANNIE DILLARD

So This Was Adolescence

Annie Dillard (b. 1945), a contributing editor to *Harper's,* won a Pulitzer Prize in 1975 for *Pilgrim at Tinker Creek.* Her recent works include *For the Time Being, The Writing Life,* and *Teaching a Stone to Talk.* "So This Was Adolescence" is a selection from her 1987 book, *An American Childhood.* In this excerpt, Dillard experiences adolescence as an identity crisis. She describes her behavior with graphic imagery and questions whether she might "lose the world forever, that I had so loved."

When I was fifteen, I felt it coming; now I was sixteen, and it hit.

My feet had imperceptibly been set on a new path, a fast path into a long tunnel like those many turnpike tunnels near Pittsburgh, turnpike tunnels whose entrances bear on brass plaques a roll call of those men who died blasting them. I wandered witlessly forward and found myself going down, and saw the light dimming; I adjusted to the slant and dimness, traveled further down, adjusted to greater dimness, and so on. There wasn't a whole lot I could do about it, or about anything. I was going to hell on a handcart, that was all, and I knew it and everyone around me knew it, and there it was.

I was growing and thinning, as if pulled. I was getting angry, as if pushed. I morally disapproved most things in North America, and blamed my innocent parents for them. My feelings deepened and lingered. The swift moods of early childhood—each formed by and suited to its occasion— vanished. Now feelings lasted so long they left stains. They arose from nowhere, like winds or waves, and battered at me or engulfed me.

When I was angry, I felt myself coiled and longing to kill someone or bomb something big. Trying to appease myself, during one winter I whipped my bed every afternoon with my uniform belt. I despised the spectacle I made in my own eyes—whipping the bed with a belt, like a creature demented!—and I often began halfheartedly, but I did it daily after school as a desperate discipline, trying to rid myself and the innocent world of my wildness. It was like trying to beat back the ocean.

Sometimes in class I couldn't stop laughing; things were too funny to be borne. It began then, my surprise that no one else saw what was so funny.

I read some few books with such reverence I didn't close them at the finish, but only moved the pile of pages back to the start, without breathing, and began again. I read one such book, an enormous novel, six times that way—closing the binding between sessions, but not between readings.

On the piano in the basement I played the maniacal "Poet and Peasant Overture" so loudly, for so many hours, night after night, I damaged the piano's keys and strings. When I wasn't playing this crashing overture, I played boogie-woogie, or something else, anything else, in octaves—otherwise, it wasn't loud enough. My fingers were so strong I could do push-ups with them. I played one piece with my fists. I banged on a steel-stringed guitar till I bled, and once on a particularly piercing rock-and-roll downbeat I broke straight through one of Father's snare drums.

I loved my boyfriend so tenderly, I thought I must transmogrify into vapor. It would take spectroscopic analysis to locate my molecules in thin air. No possible way of holding him was close enough. Nothing could cure this bad case of gentleness except, perhaps, violence: maybe if he swung me by the legs and split my skull on a tree? Would that ease this insane wish to kiss too much his eyelids' outer corners and his temples, as if I could love up his brain?

I envied people in books who swooned. For two years I felt myself continuously swooning and continuously unable to swoon; the blood drained from my face and eyes and flooded my heart; my hands emptied, my knees unstrung, I bit at the air for something worth breathing—but I failed to fall, and I couldn't find the way to black out. I had to live on the lip of a waterfall, exhausted.

When I was bored I was first hungry, then nauseated, then furious and weak. "Calm yourself," people had been saying to me all my life. Since early childhood I had tried one thing and then another to calm myself, on those few occasions when I truly wanted to. Eating helped; singing helped. Now sometimes I truly wanted to calm myself. I couldn't lower my shoulders; they seemed to wrap around my ears. I couldn't lower my voice although I could see the people around me flinch. I waved my arm in class till the very teachers wanted to kill me.

I was what they called a live wire. I was shooting out sparks that were digging a pit around me, and I was sinking into that pit. Laughing with Ellin at school recess, or driving around after school with Judy in her jeep, exultant, or dancing with my boyfriend to Louis Armstrong across a polished diningroom floor, I got so excited I looked around wildly for aid; I didn't know where I should go or what I should do with myself. People in books split wood.

When rage or boredom reappeared, each seemed never to have left. Each so filled me with so many years' intolerable accumulation it jammed the space behind my eyes, so I couldn't see. There was no room left even on my surface to live. My rib cage was so taut I couldn't breathe. Every cubic centimeter of atmosphere above my shoulders and head was heaped with last straws. Black hatred clogged my very blood. I couldn't peep, I couldn't wiggle or blink; my blood was too mad to flow.

For as long as I could remember, I had been transparent to myself, unselfconscious, learning, doing, most of every day. Now I was in my own way; I myself was a dark object I could not ignore. I couldn't remember how to forget myself. I didn't want to think about myself, to reckon myself in, to deal with myself every livelong minute on top of everything else—but swerve as I might, I couldn't avoid it. I was a boulder blocking my own path. I was a dog barking between my own ears, a barking dog who wouldn't hush.

So this was adolescence. Is this how the people around me had died on their feet—inevitably, helplessly? Perhaps their own selves eclipsed the sun for so many years the world shriveled around them, and when at last their inescapable orbits had passed through these dark egoistic years it was too late, they had adjusted.

Must I then lose the world forever, that I had so loved? Was it all, the whole bright and various planet, where I had been so ardent about finding myself alive, only a passion peculiar to children, that I would outgrow even against my will?

Suggestions for Discussion

1. What "hit" the author when she was sixteen?

2. How does the metaphor of the tunnel and her movement in it relate to the author's sense of self? How does it relate to her description of what follows?

3. What details of her attitudes and behavior tell you about Annie Dillard's experience of adolescence?

4. What evidence is brought forward that the author was "what they called a live wire"?

5. What does the author mean by being "transparent" to herself? How is that state contrasted with her being in her own way?

6. What images contribute to the reader's understanding of Dillard's sense of crisis?

7. In what sense is Dillard's final questioning a logical conclusion to what has preceded in her narrative?

Suggestions for Writing

1. Recount some of your adolescent experiences and indicate how they related to your sense of self.

2. Draw a portrait of an adolescent you know by examining her/his attitudes and behavior.

3. Compare Dillard's experience of adolescence with that of other writers in this section.

ᒍᑌᒍᑌᒍᑌ

GREG GRAFFIN

Anarchy in the Tenth Grade

Greg Graffin (b. 1965) has been part of the punk group Bad Religion since its inception. He has a master's degree in geology from UCLA and has completed a doctoral thesis in zoology at Cornell University entitled "Evolution, Monism, Atheism, and the Naturalist World-View." Utilizing his knowledge of arts and sciences, Graffin has continued to advocate the importance of diversity and creative evolution in both modern biology and modern music. In this article, Graffin explains why being a punk made him a man.

In 1976, I moved with my mom and brother to the San Fernando Valley in Los Angeles. Like millions of other victims of divorce in the '70s, I had to deal with the fact that my father was now living far away (in Racine, Wisconsin) and that I would not get to see him as much.

This pain was compounded by the bewildering alienation I felt entering the Los Angeles Unified School District, a landscape unlike anything I'd ever experienced in my eleven years of life. I had dark brown, fluffy, wavy hair—unfeatherable, impossible to mold into the cool rock'n'roll hairdos that were so popular. We didn't have a lot of money, so I wore velour kids' shirts from Kmart and corduroys and cheap shoes from Payless. I rode a Sears ten-speed that was heavy and sluggish and that couldn't jump or skid, and I had a totally uncool powder blue plastic skateboard with noisy, open-bearing wheels. I thought the beach was a place to go swimming, not a symbol for a way of life.

People asked me, "Dude! …Do you party?" It took me about six months to realize it was a synonym for getting high. I did not know what a bong was or why someone would call it bitchin'. All I knew was that there was some weird secret about all this, and I was not one of those who were welcome to the information. Kids moved up the social ladder by revealing their knowledge of rock'n'roll and sharing their covert collections of black beauties, Quaaludes, and joints. If you partook, you were one of them; if not, you were a second-class loser.

I shriveled under this pressure. Unable to compete yet unwilling to shut down, I became friends with a particular class of people labeled geeks, nerds, dorks, wimps, and pussies (or worse, wussies). We hung out together after school and did creative things, but the greatest way to alleviate my suffering was with music. We had an old spinet piano that I would bang on while I sung songs I learned by ear.

I wanted to have a musical identity, like my peers at school, but I wasn't inspired by the bands that formed the fabric of this burnout drug culture: Led Zeppelin, Rush, Kiss, Journey, Foreigner, Styx, Lynyrd Skynyrd. Luckily, by the time I was fourteen I had discovered "Rodney on the Roq" (on station KROQ), and the local bands he played proved there was an entire community of people who used music to share their alienation and confusion. It also proved that you didn't have to be a virtuoso or signed to a major record label in order to be played on the radio. The music he played was gloriously vulgar, and inspiring in its simplicity.

I wanted to be a part of this group of social and musical misfits. I "went punk" at fifteen. I cut my wavy hair very short, dyed it pitch-black, and made my own T-shirts. I was determined to send in a tape to Rodney. I was introduced by a fellow wussy to the guys who would become Bad Religion. By the end of that same year, 1980, we had made our first record and Rodney had played it.

Usually this would make anyone a hero at his high school, but I was seen as the enemy. There were three punkers at school. And all of us got our asses kicked because of our musical preference. This scared me, but at the same time it made me feel powerful. It made me realize how frail most of the conformists really were, how easily they could be pushed to the point where they lost control. I found great solace in the community of other punkers from other schools, all with similar stories of oppression and abuse. We didn't just look different, we thought different. We wanted to confront the people or institutions that seemed unjust instead of establishing an institution from which we could exclude others (which, sadly, is what many punkers really want). I began to feel that there was a way to deal with my disillusionment: through questioning and challenging, not conforming and accepting.

This stance made me more insightful about human interaction, but it also made me more cynical and less compassionate toward those who weren't punk, and this definitely hampered my ability to have intimate relationships. We punkers bonded over our collective turmoil, not our individual desires or feelings. Maybe this is why so many of my friends got hooked on hard drugs, and some killed themselves. My punk friends did not practice true understanding, we only exhibited tolerance within our sect.

This shortcoming naturally extended to women. They dressed similarly, had similar hairstyles, and even slam-danced with us boys, but "women's issues" were not on our discussion agenda. Both sexes were too busy being stalwart and tough and equal. I was proud of my egalitarian view. Unfortunately, it gave me an excuse not to address the differences between the sexes. To this day, I am tolerant when women express themselves but bad at understanding their needs. This has interfered with my close friendships with women and undermined my ability to be a good husband.

When I was a teenager, sex was part of punk's shock-value system. Girls walked around in fishnet stockings and ripped-up dresses and it turned me on. We were all just trying to be cool. We were too young to have sex, and without parents around to stop us, it became more an act of rebellion and experimentation than an expression of affection or intimacy. And of course that behavior has come back to haunt me. It's exactly what I'm trying to unlearn now that I want to have a normal, loving relationship.

I got married at twenty-three, to a woman who wasn't punk but who shared some of my views of the world. We met in a college course called "The Intellectual History of the United States." Going to college was not exactly a punk gesture, but I thought it might be a place where dissenting voices were applauded. Yet I found that the university was as replete with the pressure to conform as my high school was. But thanks to my adviser's insistence that I had original research ideas, I was able to continue and receive a master of science in geology. I went on expeditions to the wilds of the western U.S., Mexico, and the lowland rain forests of Bolivia, and I worked for the L.A. County Museum. After that I went on to a Ph.D. program.

Today, I have a more sophisticated view of my surroundings. I own a house, I have insurance, I make financial decisions. I have a four-year-old boy and a girl who's two. I am raising them not to be bullies, not to pick on other kids the way I was picked on. I have no problem being an authority figure to them now, and as they grow up I hope to teach them not to fear authority, but to understand and question its inner logic.

Fatherhood has given me new insights into the world, just as geology, organismic biology, music, and travel do. This plurality insures my individuality. And learning to be an individual was the best gift I got from growing up punk. Last year, more people bought punk-rock records, tapes, CDs,

T-shirts, stickers, and concert tickets than ever before. As in any capitalist situation, the punk market is shifting away from its original intent. It is becoming a product category in which selling subcultural mystique is more important than giving a voice to its artists. It's no wonder there are a bunch of "punk police" out there monitoring whether bands like Bad Religion fit their stereotype of authenticity. It is also a shining example of how easy it is to follow the party line and champion a bandwagon mentality—which only motivates me to keep fighting for originality.

For sixteen years now—half my life—I have been a member of this strange subculture, and I have come to realize that there are both liberal and conservative wings of it. It is an inane task to try and define punk universally. A sixteen-year-old girl from an affluent religious family who shows up to church with her green Mohawk and FUCK JESUS shirt is punk. But so is a forty-two-year-old biology professor who claims that Charles Darwin's ideas were wrong. These people have never heard of nor met each other, and yet what links them is their challenge to institutions and to dogmatic thinking. Whether this is genetic or learned is unknown. But I feel a kinship with everyone who shares these traits.

Suggestions for Discussion

1. What was Graffin's original motivation for going punk?

2. Why does being seen as the enemy give Graffin a sense of his own power?

3. Graffin asserts that what links punkers at any age or stage is "their challenge to institutions and to dogmatic thinking." Using this definition, can you think of significant historical figures who might be characterized as punk?

Suggestions for Writing

1. Graffin found a way of "belonging" through establishing a musical identity. What strategies did you employ in high school? What identity did you adopt? Write a first-person account of this experience.

2. The attitudes he developed as a punker later made it difficult for the author to develop appropriate intimate relationships. Are there attitudes you developed as an adolescent that you now struggle to overcome? Try presenting this in an essay describing how you moved between different time periods in your life.

3. Graffin feels a special kinship with those who question and challenge, rather than conform and accept. How would you characterize the people with whom you feel a special bond? Write an essay about your intellectual or moral "family."

NANCY MAIRS

On Being a Cripple

Nancy Mairs (b. 1943) was born in California and received degrees from Wheaton College and the University of Arizona, where she earned her M.F.A. and Ph.D. Her professional career has been spent as an editor, professor, and writer. She writes in a variety of genres, including essays, poetry, autobiography, and fiction. Mairs's books include *In All the Rooms of the Yellow House* (1984), for which she received the Poetry Award from the Western States Art Foundation; *Remembering the Bone House* (1989); *Carnal Acts* (1990); *Voice Lessons* (1994); *Waist-High in the World* (1996); and *A Troubled Guest: Life and Death Stories* (2001). In the selection that follows, from *Plaintext* (1986), Mairs shares the experience of dealing with a chronic, crippling disease in the midst of the demanding richness of personal, family, and professional life.

> *To escape is nothing. Not to escape is nothing.*
>
> —Louise Bogan

The other day I was thinking of writing an essay on being a cripple. I was thinking hard in one of the stalls of the women's room in my office building, as I was shoving my shirt into my jeans and tugging up my zipper. Preoccupied, I flushed, picked up my book bag, took my cane down from the hook, and unlatched the door. So many movements unbalanced me, and as I pulled the door open I fell over backward, landing fully clothed on the toilet seat with my legs splayed in front of me: the old beetle-on-its-back routine. Saturday afternoon, the building deserted, I was free to laugh aloud as I wriggled back to my feet, my voice bouncing off the yellowish tiles from all directions. Had anyone been there with me, I'd have been still and faint and hot with chagrin. I decided that it was high time to write the essay.

First, the matter of semantics. I am a cripple. I choose this word to name me. I choose from among several possibilities, the most common of which are "handicapped" and "disabled." I made the choice a number of years ago, without thinking, unaware of my motives for doing so. Even now, I'm not sure what those motives are, but I recognize that they are complex and not entirely flattering. People—crippled or not—wince at the word "cripple," as they do not at "handicapped" or "disabled." Perhaps I want them to wince. I want them to see me as a tough customer, one to whom the fates/gods/viruses have not been kind, but who can face the brutal truth of her existence squarely. As a cripple, I swagger.

But, to be fair to myself, a certain amount of honesty underlies my choice. "Cripple" seems to me a clean word, straightforward and precise. It has an honorable history, having made its first appearance in the Lindis-farne Gospel in the tenth century. As a lover of words, I like the accuracy with which it describes my condition: I have lost the full use of my limbs. "Disabled," by contrast, suggests an incapacity, physical or mental. And I certainly don't like "handicapped," which implies that I have deliberately been put at a disadvantage, by whom I can't imagine (my God is not a Handicapper General), in order to equalize chances in the great race of life. These words seem to me to be moving away from my condition, to be widening the gap between word and reality. Most remote is the recently coined euphemism "differently abled," which partakes of the same seman-tic hopefulness that transformed countries from "undeveloped" to "under-developed," then to "less developed," and finally to "developing" nations. People have continued to starve in those countries during the shift. Some realities do not obey the dictates of language.

Mine is one of them. Whatever you call me, I remain crippled. But I don't care what you call me, so long as it isn't "differently abled," which strikes me as pure verbal garbage designed, by its ability to describe anyone, to describe no one. I subscribe to George Orwell's thesis that "the slovenli-ness of our language makes it easier for us to have foolish thoughts." And I refuse to participate in the degeneration of the language to the extent that I deny that I have lost anything in the course of this calamitous disease; I refuse to pretend that the only differences between you and me are the var-ious ordinary ones that distinguish any one person from another. But call me "disabled" or "handicapped" if you like. I have long since grown accus-tomed to them; and if they are vague, at least they hint at the truth. More-over, I use them myself. Society is no readier to accept crippledness than to accept death, war, sex, sweat, or wrinkles. I would never refer to another per-son as a cripple. It is the word I use to name only myself.

I haven't always been crippled, a fact for which I am soundly grateful. To be whole of limb is, I know from experience, infinitely more pleasant and useful than to be crippled; and if that knowledge leaves me open to bitter-ness at my loss, the physical soundness I once enjoyed (though I did not enjoy it half enough) is well worth the occasional stab of regret. Though never any good at sports, I was a normally active child and young adult. I climbed trees, played hopscotch, jumped rope, skated, swam, rode my bicycle, sailed. I despised team sports, spending some of the wretchedest after-noons of my life sweaty and humiliated, behind a field-hockey stick and under a basketball hoop. I tramped alone for miles along the bridle paths that webbed the woods behind the house I grew up in. I swayed through countless dim hours in the arms of one man or another under the scattered shot of light from mirrored balls, and gyrated through countless more as Tab Hunter and Johnny Mathis gave way to the Rolling Stones, Creedence Clearwater Revival, Cream. I walked down the aisle. I pushed baby carriages, changed tires in the rain, marched for peace.

When I was twenty-eight I started to trip and drop things. What at first seemed my natural clumsiness soon became too pronounced to shrug off. I consulted a neurologist, who told me that I had a brain tumor. A battery of tests, increasingly disagreeable, revealed no tumor. About a year and a half later I developed a blurred spot in one eye. I had, at last, the episodes "disseminated in space and time" requisite for a diagnosis: multiple sclero-sis. I have never been sorry for the doctor's initial misdiagnosis, however. For almost a week, until the negative results of the tests were in, I thought that I was going to die right away. Every day for the past nearly ten years, then, has been a kind of gift. I accept all gifts.

Multiple sclerosis is a chronic degenerative disease of the central ner-vous system, in which the myelin that sheathes the nerves is somehow eaten away and scar tissue forms in its place, interrupting the nerves' signals. Dur-ing its course, which is unpredictable and uncontrollable, one may lose vision, hearing, speech, the ability to walk, control of bladder and/or bow-els, strength in any or all extremities, sensitivity to touch, vibration, and/or pain, potency, coordination of movements—the list of possibilities is lengthy and yes, horrifying. One may also lose one's sense of humor. That's the easiest to lose and the hardest to survive without.

In the past ten years, I have sustained some of these losses. Characteristic of MS are sudden attacks, called exacerbations, followed by remissions, and these I have not had. Instead, my disease has been slowly progressive. My left leg is now so weak that I walk with the aid of a brace and a cane; and for dis-tances I use an Amigo, a variation on the electric wheelchair that looks rather like an electrified kiddie car. I no longer have much use of my left hand. Now my right side is weakening as well. I still have the blurred spot in my right eye. Overall, though, I've been lucky so far. My world has, of necessity, been cir-cumscribed by my losses, but the terrain left me has been ample enough for me to continue many of the activities that absorb me: writing, teaching, rais-ing children and cats and plants and snakes, reading, speaking publicly about MS and depression, even playing bridge with people patient and honorable enough to let me scatter cards every which way without sneaking a peek.

Lest I begin to sound like Pollyanna, however, let me say that I don't like having MS. I hate it. My life holds realities—harsh ones, some of them—

that no right-minded human being ought to accept without grumbling. One of them is fatigue. I know of no one with MS who does not complain of bone-weariness; in a disease that presents an astonishing variety of symptoms, fatigue seems to be a common factor. I wake up in the morning feeling the way most people do at the end of a bad day, and I take it from there. As a result, I spend a lot of time *in extremis* and, impatient with limitation, I tend to ignore my fatigue until my body breaks down in some way and forces rest. Then I miss picnics, dinner parties, poetry readings, the brief visits of old friends from out of town. The offspring of a puritanical tradition of exceptional venerability, I cannot view these lapses without shame. My life often seems a series of small failures to do as I ought.

I lead, on the whole, an ordinary life, probably rather like the one I would have led had I not had MS. I am lucky that my predilections were already solitary, sedentary, and bookish—unlike the world-famous French cellist I have read about, or the young woman I talked with one long afternoon who wanted only to be a jockey. I had just begun graduate school when I found out something was wrong with me, and I have remained, interminably, a graduate student. Perhaps I would not have if I'd thought I had the stamina to return to a full-time job as a technical editor; but I've enjoyed my studies.

In addition to studying, I teach writing courses. I also teach medical students how to give neurological examinations. I pick up freelance editing jobs here and there. I have raised a foster son and sent him into the world, where he has made me two grandbabies, and I am still escorting my daughter and son through adolescence. I go to Mass every Saturday. I am a superb, if messy, cook. I am also an enthusiastic laundress, capable of sorting a hamper full of clothes into five subtly differentiated piles, but a terrible housekeeper. I can do italic writing and, in an emergency, bathe an oil-soaked cat. I play a fiendish game of Scrabble. When I have the time and the money, I like to sit on my front steps with my husband, drinking Amaretto and smoking a cigar, as we imagine our counterparts in Leningrad and make sure that the sun gets down once more behind the sharp childish scrawl of the Tucson Mountains.

This lively plenty has its bleak complement, of course, in all the things I can no longer do. I will never run again, except in dreams, and one day I may have to write that I will never walk again. I like to go camping, but I can't follow George and the children along the trails that wander out of a campsite through the desert or into the mountains. In fact, even on the level I've learned never to check the weather or try to hold a coherent conversation: I need all my attention for my wayward feet. Of late, I have begun to catch myself wondering how people can propel themselves without canes. With only one usable hand, I have to select my clothing with care not so much for style as for ease of ingress and egress, and even so, dressing can be laborious.

I can no longer do fine stitchery, pick up babies, play the piano, braid my hair. I am immobilized by acute attacks of depression, which may or may not be physiologically related to MS but are certainly its logical concomitant.

These two elements, the plenty and the privation, are never pure, nor are the delight and wretchedness that accompany them. Almost every pickle that I get into as a result of my weakness and clumsiness—and I get into plenty—is funny as well as maddening and sometimes painful. I recall one May afternoon when a friend and I were going out for a drink after finishing up at school. As we were climbing into opposite sides of my car, chatting, I tripped and fell, flat and hard, onto the asphalt parking lot, my abrupt departure interrupting him in mid-sentence. "Where'd you go?" he called as he came around the back of the car to find me hauling myself up by the door frame. "Are you all right?" Yes, I told him, I was fine, just a bit rattly, and we drove off to find a shady patio and some beer. When I got home an hour or so later, my daughter greeted me with "What have you done to yourself?" I looked down. One elbow of my white turtleneck with the green froggies, one knee of my white trousers, one white kneesock were blood-soaked. We peeled off the clothes and inspected the damage, which was nasty enough but not alarming. That part wasn't funny: The abrasions took a long time to heal, and one got a little infected. Even so, when I think of my friend talking earnestly, suddenly, to the hot thin air while I dropped from his view as though through a trap door, I find the image as silly as something from a Marx Brothers movie.

I may find it easier than other cripples to amuse myself because I live propped by the acceptance and the assistance and, sometimes, the amusement of those around me. Grocery clerks tear my checks out of my checkbook for me, and sales clerks find chairs to put into dressing rooms when I want to try on clothes. The people I work with make sure I teach at times when I am least likely to be fatigued, in places I can get to, with the materials I need. My students, with one anonymous exception (in an end-of-the-semester evaluation) have been unperturbed by my disability. Some even like it. One was immensely cheered by the information that I paint my own fingernails; she decided, she told me, that if I could go to such trouble over fine details, she could keep on writing essays. I suppose I became some sort of bright-fingered muse. She wrote good essays, too.

The most important struts in the framework of my existence, of course, are my husband and children. Dismayingly few marriages survive the MS test, and why should they? Most twenty-two- and nineteen-year-olds, like George and me, can vow in clear conscience, after a childhood of chicken-pox and summer colds, to keep one another in sickness and in health so long as they both shall live. Not many are equipped for catastrophe: the dismay, the depression, the extra work, the boredom that a degenerative disease can insinuate into a relationship. And our society, with its emphasis on fun and its association of fun with physical performance, offers little encouragement for a whole spouse to stay with a crippled partner. Children experience similar stresses when faced with a crippled parent, and they are more helpless, since parents and children can't usually get divorced. They hate, of course, to be different from their peers, and the child whose mother is tacking down the aisle of a school auditorium packed with proud parents like a Cape Cod dinghy in a stiff breeze jolly well stands out in a crowd. Deprived of legal divorce, the child can at least deny the mother's disability, even her existence, forgetting to tell her about recitals and PTA meetings, refusing to accompany her to stores or church or the movies, never inviting friends to the house. Many do.

But I've been limping along for ten years now, and so far George and the children are still at my left elbow, holding tight. Anne and Matthew vacuum floors and dust furniture and haul trash and rake up dog droppings and button my cuffs and bake lasagne and Toll House cookies with just enough grumbling so I know that they don't have brain fever. And far from hiding me, they're forever dragging me by racks of fancy clothes or through teeming school corridors, or welcoming gaggles of friends while I'm wandering through the house in Anne's filmy pink babydoll pajamas. George generally calls before he brings someone home, but he does just as many dumb thankless chores as the children. And they all yell at me, laugh at some of my jokes, write me funny letters when we're apart—in short, treat me as an ordinary human being for whom they have some use. I think they like me. Unless they're faking….

Faking. There's the rub. Tugging at the fringes of my consciousness always is the terror that people are kind to me only because I'm a cripple. My mother almost shattered me once, with that instinct mothers have— blind, I think, in this case, but unerring nonetheless—for striking blows along the fault-lines of their children's hearts, by telling me, in an attack on my selfishness, "We all have to make allowances for you, of course, because of the way you are." From the distance of a couple of years, I have to admit that I haven't any idea just what she meant, and I'm not sure that she knew either. She was awfully angry. But at the time, as the words thudded home, I felt my worst fear, suddenly realized. I could bear being called selfish: I am. But I couldn't bear the corroboration that those around me were doing in fact what I'd always suspected them of doing, professing fondness while silently putting up with me because of the way I am. A cripple. I've been a little cracked ever since.

Along with this fear that people are secretly accepting shoddy goods comes a relentless pressure to please—to prove myself worth the burdens I impose, I guess, or to build a substantial account of goodwill against which I may write drafts in times of need. Part of the pressure arises from social expectations. In our society, anyone who deviates from the norm had better find some way to compensate. Like fat people, who are expected to be jolly, cripples must bear their lot meekly and cheerfully. A grumpy cripple isn't playing by the rules. And much of the pressure is self-generated. Early on I vowed that, if I had to have MS, by God I was going to do it well. This is a class act, ladies and gentlemen. No tears, no recriminations, no faint-heartedness.

One way and another, then, I wind up feeling like Tiny Tim, peering over the edge of the table at the Christmas goose, waving my crutch, piping down God's blessing on us all. Only sometimes I don't want to play Tiny Tim. I'd rather be Caliban, a most scurvy monster. Fortunately, at home no one much cares whether I'm a good cripple or a bad cripple as long as I make vichyssoise with fair regularity. One evening several years ago, Anne was reading at the dining-room table while I cooked dinner. As I opened a can of tomatoes, the can slipped in my left hand and juice spattered me and the counter with bloody spots. Fatigued and infuriated, I bellowed, "I'm so sick of being crippled!" Anne glanced at me over the top of her book. "There now," she said, "do you feel better?" "Yes," I said, "yes, I do." She went back to her reading. I felt better. That's about all the attention my scurviness ever gets.

Because I hate being crippled, I sometimes hate myself for being a cripple. Over the years I have come to expect—even accept—attacks of violent self-loathing. Luckily, in general our society no longer connects deformity and disease directly with evil (though a charismatic once told me that I have MS because a devil is in me) and so I'm allowed to move largely at will, even among small children. But I'm not sure that this revision of attitude has been particularly helpful. Physical imperfection, even freed of moral disapprobation, still defies and violates the ideal, especially for women, whose confinement in their bodies as objects of desire is far from over. Each age, of course, has its ideal, and I doubt that ours is any better or worse than any other. Today's ideal woman, who lives on the glossy pages of dozens of magazines, seems to be between the ages of eighteen and twenty-five; her hair has body, her teeth flash white, her breath smells minty, her underarms are dry; she has a career but is still a fabulous cook, especially of meals that take less than twenty minutes to prepare; she does not ordinarily appear to have a husband or children; she is trim and deeply tanned; she jogs, swims, plays tennis, rides a bicycle, sails, but does not bowl; she travels widely, even to out-of-the-way places like Finland and Samoa, always in the company of the ideal man, who possesses a nearly identical set of characteristics. There are a few exceptions. Though usually white and often blonde, she may be black, Hispanic, Asian, or Native American, so long as she is unusually sleek. She may be old, provided she is selling a laxative or is Lauren Bacall. If she is selling a detergent, she may be married and have a flock of strikingly messy children. But she is never a cripple.

Like many women I know, I have always had an uneasy relationship with my body. I was not a popular child, largely, I think now, because I was peculiar: intelligent, intense, moody, shy, given to unexpected actions and inexplicable notions and emotions. But as I entered adolescence, I believed myself unpopular because I was homely: my breasts too flat, my mouth too wide, my hips too narrow, my clothing never quite right in fit or style. I was not, in fact, particularly ugly, old photographs inform me, though I was well off the ideal; but I carried this sense of self-alienation with me into adulthood, where it regenerated in response to the depredations of MS. Even with my brace I walk with a limp so pronounced that, seeing myself on the videotape of a television program on the disabled, I couldn't believe that anything but an inchworm could make progress humping along like that. My shoulders droop and my pelvis thrusts forward as I try to balance myself upright, throwing my frame into a bony S. As a result of contractures, one shoulder is higher than the other and I carry one arm bent in front of me, the fingers curled into a claw. My left arm and leg have wasted into pipe-stems, and I try always to keep them covered. When I think about how my body must look to others, especially to men, to whom I have been trained to display myself, I feel ludicrous, even loathsome.

At my age, however, I don't spend much time thinking about my appearance. The burning egocentricity of adolescence, which assures one that all the world is looking all the time, has passed, thank God, and I'm generally too caught up in what I'm doing to step back, as I used to, and watch myself as though upon a stage. I'm also too old to believe in the accuracy of self-image. I know that I'm not a hideous crone, that in fact, when I'm rested, well dressed, and well made up, I look fine. The self-loathing I feel is neither physically nor intellectually substantial. What I hate is not me but a disease.

I am not a disease.

And a disease is not—at least not singlehandedly—going to determine who I am, though at first it seemed to be going to. Adjusting to a chronic incurable illness, I have moved through a process similar to that outlined by Elizabeth Kübler-Ross in *On Death and Dying*. The major difference—and it is far more significant than most people recognize—is that I can't be sure of the outcome, as the terminally ill cancer patient can. Research studies indicate that, with proper medical care, I may achieve a "normal" life span. And in our society, with its vision of death as the ultimate evil, worse even than decrepitude, the response to such news is, "Oh well, at least you're not going to *die*." Are there worse things than dying? I think that there may be.

I think of two women I know, both with MS, both enough older than I to have served as models. One took to her bed several years ago and has been there ever since. Although she can sit in a high-backed wheelchair, because she is incontinent she refuses to go out at all, even though incontinence pants, which are readily available at any pharmacy, could protect her from embarrassment. Instead, she stays at home and insists that her husband, a small quiet man, a retired civil servant, stay there with her except for a quick weekly foray to the supermarket. The other woman, whose illness was diagnosed when she was eighteen, a nursing student engaged to a young doctor, finished her training, married her doctor, accompanied him to Germany when he was in the service, bore three sons and a daughter, now grown and gone. When she can, she travels with her husband; she plays bridge, embroiders, swims regularly; she works, like me, as a symptomatic-patient instructor of medical students in neurology. Guess which woman I hope to be.

At the beginning, I thought about having MS almost incessantly. And because of the unpredictable course of the disease, my thoughts were always terrified. Each night I'd get into bed wondering whether I'd get out again the next morning, whether I'd be able to see, to speak, to hold a pen between my fingers. Knowing that the day might come when I'd be physically incapable of killing myself, I thought perhaps I ought to do so right away, while I still had the strength. Gradually I came to understand that the Nancy who might one day lie inert under a bedsheet, arms and legs paralyzed, unable to feed or bathe herself, unable to reach out for a gun, a bottle of pills, was not the Nancy I was at present, and that I could not presume to make decisions for that future Nancy, who might well not want in the least to die. Now the only provision I've made for the future Nancy is that when the time comes—and it is likely to come in the form of pneumonia, friend to the weak and the old—I am not to be treated with machines and medications. If she is unable to communicate by then, I hope she will be satisfied with these terms.

Thinking all the time about having MS grew tiresome and intrusive, especially in the large and tragic mode in which I was accustomed to considering my plight. Months and even years went by without catastrophe (at least without one related to MS), and really I was awfully busy, what with George and children and snakes and students and poems, and I hadn't the time, let alone the inclination, to devote myself to being a disease. Too, the richer my life became, the funnier it seemed, as though there were some connection between largesse and laughter, and so my tragic stance began to waver until, even with the aid of a brace and cane, I couldn't hold it for very long at a time.

After several years I was satisfied with my adjustment. I had suffered my grief and fury and terror, I thought, but now I was at ease with my lot. Then one summer day I set out with George and the children across the desert for a vacation in California. Part way to Yuma I became aware that my right leg felt funny. "I think I've had an exacerbation," I told George. "What shall we do?" he asked. "I think we'd better get the hell to California," I said, "because I don't know whether I'll ever make it again." So we went on to San Diego and then to Orange, and up the Pacific Coast Highway to Santa Cruz, across to Yosemite, down to Sequoia and Joshua Tree, and so back over the desert to home. It was a fine two-week trip, filled with friends and fair weather, and I wouldn't have missed it for the world, though I did in fact make it back to California two years later. Nor would there have been any point in missing it, since in MS, once the symptoms have appeared, the neurological damage has been done, and there's no way to predict or prevent that damage.

The incident spoiled my self-satisfaction, however. It renewed my grief and fury and terror, and I learned that one never finishes adjusting to MS. I don't know now why I thought one would. One does not, after all, finish adjusting to life, and MS is simply a fact of my life—not my favorite fact, of course—but as ordinary as my nose and my tropical fish and my yellow Mazda station wagon. It may at any time get worse, but no amount of worry or anticipation can prepare me for a new loss. My life is a lesson in losses. I learn one at a time.

And I had best be patient in the learning, since I'll have to do it like it or not. As any rock fan knows, you can't always get what you want. Particularly when you have MS. You can't, for example, get cured. In recent years researchers and the organizations that fund research have started to pay MS some attention even though it isn't fatal; perhaps they have begun to see that life is something other than a quantitative phenomenon, that one may be very much alive for a very long time in a life that isn't worth living. The researchers have made some progress toward understanding the mechanism of the disease: It may well be an autoimmune reaction triggered by a slow-acting virus. But they are nowhere near its prevention, control, or cure. And most of us want to be cured. Some, unable to accept incurability, grasp at one treatment after another, no matter how bizarre: megavitamin therapy, gluten-free diet, injections of cobra venom, hypothermal suits, lymphocytopharesis, hyperbaric chambers. Many treatments are probably harmless enough, but none are curative.

The absence of a cure often makes MS patients bitter toward their doctors. Doctors are, after all, the priests of modern society, the new shamans, whose business is to heal, and many an MS patient roves from one to another, searching for the "good" doctor who will make him well. Doctors too think of themselves as healers, and for this reason many have trouble dealing with MS patients, whose disease in its intransigence defeats their aims and mocks their skills. Too few doctors, it is true, treat their patients as whole human beings, but the reverse is also true. I have always tried to be gentle with my doctors, who often have more at stake in terms of ego than I do. I may be frustrated, maddened, depressed by the incurability of my disease, but I am not diminished by it, and they are. When I push myself up from my seat in the waiting room and stumble toward them, I incarnate the limitation of their powers. The least I can do is refuse to press on their ten-derest spots.

This gentleness is part of the reason that I'm not sorry to be a cripple. I didn't have it before. Perhaps I'd have developed it anyway—how could I know such a thing?—and I wish I had more of it, but I'm glad of what I have. It has opened and enriched my life enormously, this sense that my frailty and need must be mirrored in others, that in searching for and shaping a stable core in a life wrenched by change and loss, change and loss, I must recognize the same process, under individual conditions, in the lives around me. I do not deprecate such knowledge, however I've come by it.

All the same, if a cure were found, would I take it? In a minute. I may be a cripple, but I'm only occasionally a loony and never a saint. Anyway, in my brand of theology God doesn't give bonus points for a limp. I'd take a cure; I just don't need one. A friend who also has MS startled me once by asking, "Do you ever say to yourself, 'Why me, Lord?'" "No, Michael, I don't," I told him, "because whenever I try, the only response I can think of is 'Why not?'" If I could make a cosmic deal, who would I put in my place? What in my life would I give up in exchange for sound limbs and a thrilling rush of energy? No one. Nothing. I might as well do the job myself. Now that I'm getting the hang of it.

Suggestions for Discussion

1. Why does Mairs prefer the word "cripple" to "handicapped" or "disabled" to describe her condition?

2. How does she characterize the plenty, the privation of her life?

3. What does she mean by "I'd take a cure; I just don't need one"?

Suggestions for Writing

1. Mairs asserts that her multiple sclerosis is only one part of her multifaceted self: "What I hate is not me but a disease. I am not a disease." Write about how people tend instead to identify with things that have happened to them or with aspects of themselves. Use an example from your own experience to support this idea.

2. "My life is a lesson in losses. I learn one at a time." What does this convey about Mairs's attitude toward life? How would you handle a life-long "crisis"?

3. Examine the role of humor as a survival tool. Use examples from the essay and your own experience to explore the topic.

ᘱᘯᘱᘯᘱᘯ

JORGE LUÍS BORGES

Borges and I

Translated by Andrew Hurley

Jorge Luís Borges (1899–1986), Argentine poet, short-story writer, essay-ist, critic, and university professor, was best known for his esoteric short fiction. He received little recognition in America until the publication in 1968 of English translations of *Ficciónes, Labyrinths*, and *The Aleph and Other Stories*. In this short piece, published in 1962, the writer speaks of his dual nature, the self who surrenders everything to the creative Borges so that he can weave his tales and poems.

It's Borges, the other one, that things happen to. I walk through Buenos Aires and I pause—mechanically now, perhaps—to gaze at the arch of an entryway and its inner door; news of Borges reaches me by mail, or I see his name on a list of academics or in some biographical dictionary. My taste runs to hourglasses, maps, seventeenth-century typefaces, etymologies, the taste of coffee, and the prose of Robert Louis Stevenson; Borges shares those preferences, but in a vain sort of way that turns them into the accoutrements of an actor. It would be an exaggeration to say that our relationship is hos-tile—I live, I allow myself to live, so that Borges can spin out his literature, and that literature is my justification. I willingly admit that he has written a number of sound pages, but those pages will not save *me*, perhaps because the good in them no longer belongs to any individual, not even to that other man, but rather to language itself, or to tradition. Beyond that, I am doomed—utterly and inevitably—to oblivion, and fleeting moments will be all of me that survives in that other man. Little by little, I have been turn-ing everything over to him, though I know the perverse way he has of dis-torting and magnifying everything. Spinoza believed that all things wish to go on being what they are—stone wishes eternally to be stone, and tiger, to be tiger. I shall endure in Borges, not in myself (if, indeed, I am anybody at all), but I recognize myself less in his books than in many others', or in the tedious strumming of a guitar. Years ago I tried to free myself from him, and I moved on from the mythologies of the slums and outskirts of the city to games with time and infinity, but those games belong to Borges now, and I shall have to think up other things. So my life is a point-counterpoint, a kind of fugue, and a falling away—and everything winds up being lost to me, and everything falls into oblivion, or into the hands of the other man.

I am not sure which of us it is that's writing this page.

Suggestions for Discussion

1. Who is the speaker?

2. What is his relationship to and attitude toward Borges, the writer?

3. With what details are the dual aspects of his personality made clear? Define them.

4. How does he substantiate his belief that he is "doomed—utterly and inevitably—to oblivion"?

5. On the basis of this brief sketch, what conclusions are you invited to draw about the creative process and about the sources and subject matter of Borges's art?

Suggestions for Writing

1. Read a number of Borges's short stories and analyze the basis of their appeal.

2. The concept of the double appears frequently in literature. Write a sketch of a character in literature (Conrad's "The Secret Sharer," Melville's "Bartleby the Scrivener," Dostoevsky's "The Double," Poe's "William Wilson") who might be described as having a double.

3. Record your daily activities and thoughts for a week, paying no attention to mechanics or organization. Then select one of the journal items for full and logical development.

A L I C E   W A L K E R

Beauty: When the Other Dancer Is the Self

Alice Walker (b. 1944) has received numerous awards for her fiction; *The Color Purple* (1982), a best-selling novel, was nominated for the Book Critics Circle Award and received the American Book Award, the Candace Award of the National Coalition of 100 Black Women, and a

Pulitzer Prize. She has also published two collections of short stories, *You Can't Keep a Good Woman Down* (1981) and *In Love and Trouble* (1985). *Alice Walker Banned* (1996), *By the Light of My Father's Smile* (1998), and *Now Is the Time to Open Your Heart* (2004) comprises some of her recent publications. *In Search of Our Mother's Gardens: Woman- ist Prose* (1983) includes this reminiscence of the effect a traumatic injury to her eye had on her self-image.

It is a bright summer day in 1947. My father, a fat, funny man with beautiful eyes and a subversive wit, is trying to decide which of his eight children he will take with him to the county fair. My mother, of course, will not go. She is knocked out from getting most of us ready: I hold my neck stiff against the pressure of her knuckles as she hastily completes the braid- ing and then be-ribboning of my hair.

My father is the driver for the rich old white lady up the road. Her name is Miss Mey. She owns all the land for miles around, as well as the house in which we live. All I remember about her is that she once offered to pay my mother thirty-five cents for cleaning her house, raking up piles of her mag- nolia leaves, and washing her family's clothes, and that my mother—she of no money, eight children, and a chronic earache—refused it. But I do not think of this in 1947. I am two and a half years old. I want to go everywhere my daddy goes. I am excited at the prospect of riding in a car. Someone has told me fairs are fun. That there is room in the car for only three of us doesn't faze me at all. Whirling happily in my starchy frock, showing off my biscuit-polished patent-leather shoes and lavender socks, tossing my head in a way that makes my ribbons bounce, I stand, hands on hips, before my father. "Take me, Daddy," I say with assurance; "I'm the prettiest!"

Later, it does not surprise me to find myself in Miss Mey's shiny black car, sharing the back seat with the other lucky ones. Does not surprise me that I thoroughly enjoy the fair. At home that night I tell the unlucky ones all I can remember about the merry-go-round, the man who eats live chick- ens, and the teddy bears, until they say: that's enough, baby Alice. Shut up now, and go to sleep.

It is Easter Sunday, 1950. I am dressed in a green, flocked, scalloped- hem dress (handmade by my adoring sister, Ruth) that has its own smooth satin petticoat and tiny hot-pink roses tucked into each scallop. My shoes, new T-strap patent leather, again highly biscuit-polished. I am six years old and have learned one of the longest Easter speeches to be heard that day, totally unlike the speech I said when I was two: "Easter lilies / pure and white / blos- som in / the morning light." When I rise to give my speech I do so on a great wave of love and pride and expectation. People in the church stop rustling their new crinolines. They seem to hold their breath. I can tell they admire my dress, but it is my spirit, bordering on sassiness (womanishness), they secretly applaud.

"That girl's a little *mess*," they whisper to each other, pleased.

Naturally I say my speech without stammer or pause, unlike those who stutter, stammer, or, worst of all, forget. This is before the word "beautiful" exists in people's vocabulary, but "Oh, isn't she the cutest thing!" frequently floats my way. "And got so much sense!" they gratefully add…for which thoughtful addition I thank them to this day.

It was great fun being cute. But then, one day, it ended.

I am eight years old and a tomboy. I have a cowboy hat, cowboy boots, checkered shirt and pants, all red. My playmates are my brothers, two and four years older than I. Their colors are black and green, the only difference in the way we are dressed. On Saturday nights we all go to the picture show, even my mother; Westerns are her favorite kind of movie. Back home, "on the ranch," we pretend we are Tom Mix, Hopalong Cassidy, Lash LaRue (we've even named one of our dogs Lash LaRue); we chase each other for hours rustling cattle, being outlaws, delivering damsels from distress. Then my parents decide to buy my brothers guns. These are not "real" guns. They shoot "BBs," copper pellets my brothers say will kill birds. Because I am a girl, I do not get a gun. Instantly I am relegated to the position of Indian. Now there appears a great distance between us. They shoot and shoot at everything with their new guns. I try to keep up with my bow and arrows.

One day while I am standing on top of our makeshift "garage"—pieces of tin nailed across some poles—holding my bow and arrow and looking out toward the fields, I feel an incredible blow in my right eye. I look down just in time to see my brother lower his gun.

Both brothers rush to my side. My eye stings, and I cover it with my hand. "If you tell," they say, "we will get a whipping. You don't want that to happen, do you?" I do not. "Here is a piece of wire," says the older brother, picking it up from the roof; "say you stepped on one end of it and the other flew up and hit you." The pain is beginning to start. "Yes," I say. "Yes, I will say that is what happened." If I do not say this is what happened, I know my brothers will find ways to make me wish I had. But now I will say anything that gets me to my mother.

Confronted by our parents we stick to the lie agreed upon. They place me on a bench on the porch and I close my left eye while they examine the right. There is a tree growing from underneath the porch that climbs past the railing to the roof. It is the last thing my right eye sees. I watch as its trunk, its branches, and then its leaves are blotted out by the rising blood.

I am in shock. First there is intense fever, which my father tries to break using lily leaves bound around my head. Then there are chills: my mother tries to get me to eat soup. Eventually, I do not know how, my parents learn what has happened. A week after the "accident" they take me to see a doctor. "Why did you wait so long to come?" he asks, looking into my eye and shaking his head. "Eyes are sympathetic," he says. "If one is blind, the other will likely become blind too."

This comment of the doctor's terrifies me. But it is really how I look that bothers me most. Where the BB pellet struck there is a glob of whitish scar tissue, a hideous cataract, on my eye. Now when I stare at people—a favorite pastime, up to now—they will stare back. Not at the "cute" little girl, but at her scar. For six years I do not stare at anyone, because I do not raise my head.

Years later, in the throes of a mid-life crisis, I ask my mother and sister whether I changed after the "accident." "No," they say, puzzled. "What do you mean?"

What do I mean?

I am eight, and, for the first time, doing poorly in school, where I have been something of a whiz since I was four. We have just moved to the place where the "accident" occurred. We do not know any of the people around us because this is a different county. The only time I see the friends I knew is when we go back to our old church. The new school is the former state penitentiary. It is a large stone building, cold and drafty, crammed to overflowing with boisterous, ill-disciplined children. On the third floor there is a huge circular imprint of some partition that has been torn out.

"What used to be here?" I ask a sullen girl next to me on our way past it to lunch.

"The electric chair," says she.

At night I have nightmares about the electric chair, and about all the people reputedly "fried" in it. I am afraid of the school, where all the students seem to be budding criminals.

"What's the matter with your eye?" they ask, critically.

When I don't answer (I cannot decide whether it was an "accident" or not), they shove me, insist on a fight.

My brother, the one who created the story about the wire, comes to my rescue. But then brags so much about "protecting" me, I become sick.

After months of torture at the school, my parents decide to send me back to our old community, to my old school. I live with my grandparents and the teacher they board. But there is no room for Phoebe, my cat. By the time my grandparents decide there is room, and I ask for my cat, she cannot be found. Miss Yarborough, the boarding teacher, takes me under her wing, and begins to teach me to play the piano. But soon she marries an African—a "prince," she says—and is whisked away to his continent.

At my old school there is at least one teacher who loves me. She is the teacher who "knew me before I was born" and bought my first baby clothes. It is she who makes life bearable. It is her presence that finally helps me turn on the one child at the school who continually calls me "one-eyed bitch." One day I simply grab him by his coat and beat him until I am satisfied. It is my teacher who tells me my mother is ill.

My mother is lying in bed in the middle of the day, something I have never seen. She is in too much pain to speak. She has an abscess in her ear. I stand looking down on her, knowing that if she dies, I cannot live. She is being treated with warm oils and hot bricks held against her cheek. Finally a doctor comes. But I must go back to my grandparents' house. The weeks pass but I am hardly aware of it. All I know is that my mother might die, my father is not so jolly, my brothers still have their guns, and I am the one sent away from home.

"You did not change," they say.

Did I imagine the anguish of never looking up?

I am twelve. When relatives come to visit I hide in my room. My cousin Brenda, just my age, whose father works in the post office and whose mother is a nurse, comes to find me. "Hello," she says. And then she asks, looking at my recent school picture, which I did not want taken, and on which the "glob," as I think of it, is clearly visible, "You still can't see out of that eye?"

"No," I say, and flop back on the bed over my book.

That night, as I do almost every night, I abuse my eye. I rant and rave at it, in front of the mirror. I plead with it to clear up before morning. I tell it I hate and despise it. I do not pray for sight. I pray for beauty.

"You did not change," they say.

I am fourteen and baby-sitting for my brother Bill, who lives in Boston. He is my favorite brother and there is a strong bond between us. Understanding my feelings of shame and ugliness he and his wife take me to a local hospital, where the "glob" is removed by a doctor named O. Henry. There is still a small bluish crater where the scar tissue was, but the ugly white stuff is gone. Almost immediately I become a different person from the girl who does not raise her head. Or so I think. Now that I've raised my head I win the boyfriend of my dreams. Now that I've raised my head I have plenty of friends. Now that I've raised my head classwork comes from my lips as faultlessly as Easter speeches did, and I leave high school as valedictorian, most popular student, and *queen,* hardly believing my luck. Ironically, the girl who was voted most beautiful in our class (and was) was later shot twice through the chest by a male companion, using a "real" gun, while she was pregnant. But that's another story in itself. Or is it?

"You did not change," they say.

It is now thirty years since the "accident." A beautiful journalist comes to visit and to interview me. She is going to write a cover story for her magazine that focuses on my latest book. "Decide how you want to look on the cover," she says. "Glamorous, or whatever."

Never mind "glamorous," it is the "whatever" that I hear. Suddenly all I can think of is whether I will get enough sleep the night before the photography session: if I don't, my eye will be tired and wander, as blind eyes will.

At night in bed with my lover I think up reasons why I should not appear on the cover of a magazine. "My meanest critics will say I've sold out," I say. "My family will now realize I write scandalous books."

"But what's the real reason you don't want to do this?" he asks.

"Because in all probability," I say in a rush, "my eye won't be straight."

"It will be straight enough," he says. Then, "Besides, I thought you'd made your peace with that."

And I suddenly remember that I have.

I remember:

I am talking to my brother Jimmy, asking if he remembers anything unusual about the day I was shot. He does not know I consider that day the last time my father, with his sweet home remedy of cool lily leaves, chose me, and that I suffered and raged inside because of this. "Well," he says, "all I remember is standing by the side of the highway with Daddy, trying to flag down a car. A white man stopped, but when Daddy said he needed somebody to take his little girl to the doctor, he drove off."

I remember:

I am in the desert for the first time. I fall totally in love with it. I am so overwhelmed by its beauty, I confront for the first time, consciously, the meaning of the doctor's words years ago: "Eyes are sympathetic. If one is blind, the other will likely become blind too." I realize I have dashed about the world madly, looking at this, looking at that, storing up images against the fading of the light. *But I might have missed seeing the desert!* The shock of that possibility—and gratitude for over twenty-five years of sight—sends me literally to my knees. Poem after poem comes—which is perhaps how poets pray.

on sight

I am so thankful I have seen
The Desert
And the creatures in the desert
And the desert Itself.

The desert has its own moon
Which I have seen
With my own eye.

There is no flag on it.

Trees of the desert have arms
All of which are always up
That is because the moon is up
The sun is up
Also the sky
The stars
Clouds
None with flags.

If there *were* flags, I doubt
the trees would point.
Would you?

But mostly, I remember this:

I am twenty-seven, and my baby daughter is almost three. Since her birth I have worried about her discovery that her mother's eyes are different from other people's. Will she be embarrassed? I think. What will she say? Every day she watches a television program called "Big Blue Marble." It begins with a picture of the earth as it appears from the moon. It is bluish, a little battered-looking, but full of light, with whitish clouds swirling around it. Every time I see it I weep with love, as if it is a picture of Grandma's house. One day when I am putting Rebecca down for her nap, she suddenly focuses on my eye. Something inside me cringes, gets ready to try to protect myself. All children are cruel about physical differences, I know from experience, and that they don't always mean to be is another matter. I assume Rebecca will be the same.

But no-o-o-o. She studies my face intently as we stand, her inside and me outside her crib. She even holds my face maternally between her dimpled little hands. Then, looking every bit as serious and lawyerlike as her father, she says, as if it may just possibly have slipped my attention: "Mommy, there's a *world* in your eye." (As in, "Don't be alarmed, or do anything crazy.") And then, gently, but with great interest: "Mommy, where did you *get* that world in your eye?"

For the most part, the pain left then. (So what, if my brothers grew up to buy even more powerful pellet guns for their sons and to carry real guns themselves. So what, if a young "Morehouse man" once nearly fell off the steps of Trevor Arnett Library because he thought my eyes were blue.) Crying and laughing I ran to the bathroom, while Rebecca mumbled and sang herself off to sleep. Yes indeed, I realized, looking into the mirror. There was a world in my eye. And I saw that it was possible to love it: that in fact, for all it had taught me of shame and anger and inner vision, I did love it. Even to see it drifting out of orbit in boredom, or rolling up out of fatigue, not to mention floating back at attention in excitement (bearing witness, a friend has called it), deeply suitable to my personality, and even characteristic of me.

   That night I dream I am dancing to Stevie Wonder's song "Always" (the name of the song is really "As," but I hear it as "Always"). As I dance, whirling and joyous, happier than I've ever been in my life, another bright-faced dancer joins me. We dance and kiss each other and hold each other through the night. The other dancer has obviously come through all right, as I have done. She is beautiful, whole and free. And she is also me.

Suggestions for Discussion

1. How does the author use detail to portray herself at various ages? To portray her mother?

2. What changes in her personality and view of herself take place in the several age periods that Walker describes?

3. The line "you did not change" recurs. What is its relation to the narrative in the several scenes?

4. What is the significance of the repeated reference to raising her head at various stages of the author's development?

5. How does Walker equate prayer with poetry?

6. How does her daughter's comment on her eye affect her attitude?

7. What does the title signify?

Suggestions for Writing

1. Write a series of short vignettes illustrating how you viewed yourself and/ or others viewed you at various stages of your development.

2. Describe the ways in which a traumatic episode in your childhood or that of a person close to you has affected your attitudes or behavior.

~~~~~~~~~

ZORA NEALE HURSTON

How It Feels to Be Colored Me

Zora Neale Hurston (1891–1960) is now recognized as one of the truly innovative voices in twentieth-century American letters. Born in Florida, she began college while working as a domestic. She was ultimately able to go on to Howard University, a leading center of black scholarship, and to Barnard College, where she earned her B.A., and finally to Columbia University, where she did graduate work. She was a student of the anthropologist Franz Boas, who urged her to study Southern black folklore. In the twenties and thirties, she was a major figure in the Harlem Renaissance, but she ultimately died unknown and in poverty. During her career, she was a journalist, professor, librarian, folklorist, but above all,

Mound Bayou, Mississippi, 1976, Alex Webb/Magnum Photos, Inc.

she was a writer. Five of her books were published during her lifetime, the most prominent being *Mules and Men* (1935), for which she won the Anisfield-Wolf Award; *Their Eyes Were Watching God* (1937); and *Dust Track on a Road* (1942). Since 1985, a number of collections of her work have been published, the most recent being *Mule Bone: A Comedy of Negro Life* (1991); *Collected Essays, Volumes 1 and 2; Complete Short Stories; Complete Plays; Folklore, Memories, and Other Writings* (1995); and *Sweat* (1996). Here we see Hurston, despite her difficult experiences, at her most upbeat and affirmative, refusing the role of victim.

I am colored but I offer nothing in the way of extenuating circumstances except the fact that I am the only Negro in the United States whose grandfather on the mother's side was *not* an Indian chief.

I remember the very day that I became colored. Up to my thirteenth year I lived in the little Negro town of Eatonville, Florida. It is exclusively a colored town. The only white people I knew passed through the town going to or coming from Orlando. The native whites rode dusty horses, the Northern tourists chugged down the sandy village road in automobiles. The town knew the Southerners and never stopped cane chewing when they passed. But the Northerners were something else again. They were peered at cautiously from behind curtains by the timid. The more venturesome would come out on the porch to watch them go past and got just as much pleasure out of the tourists as the tourists got out of the village.

The front porch might seem a daring place for the rest of the town, but it was a gallery seat to me. My favorite place was atop the gate-post. Proscenium box for a born first-nighter. Not only did I enjoy the show, but I didn't mind the actors knowing that I liked it. I usually spoke to them in passing. I'd wave at them and when they returned my salute, I would say something like this: "Howdy-do-well-I-thank-you-where-you-goin'?" Usually the automobile or the horse paused at this, and after a queer exchange of compliments, I would probably "go a piece of the way" with them, as we say in farthest Florida. If one of my family happened to come to the front in time to see me, of course negotiations would be rudely broken off. But even so, it is clear that I was the first "welcome-to-our-state" Floridian, and I hope the Miami Chamber of Commerce will please take notice.

During this period, white people differed from colored to me only in that they rode through town and never lived there. They liked to hear me "speak pieces" and sing and wanted to see me dance the parse-me-la, and gave me generously of their small silver for doing these things, which seemed strange to me for I wanted to do them so much that I needed bribing to stop. Only they didn't know it. The colored people gave no dimes. They deplored any joyful tendencies in me, but I was their Zora nevertheless. I belonged to them, to the nearby hotels, to the county—everybody's Zora.

But changes came in the family when I was thirteen, and I was sent to school in Jacksonville. I left Eatonville, the town of the oleanders, as Zora. When I disembarked from the river-boat at Jacksonville, she was no more. It seemed that I had suffered a sea change. I was not Zora of Orange County any more, I was now a little colored girl. I found it out in certain ways. In my heart as well as in the mirror, I became a fast brown—warranted not to rub nor run.

But I am not tragically colored. There is no great sorrow dammed up in my soul, nor lurking behind my eyes. I do not mind at all. I do not belong to the sobbing school of Negrohood who hold that nature somehow has given them a lowdown dirty deal and whose feelings are all hurt about it. Even in the helter-skelter skirmish that is my life, I have seen that the world is to the strong regardless of a little pigmentation more or less. No, I do not weep at the world—I am too busy sharpening my oyster knife.

Someone is always at my elbow reminding me that I am the grand-daughter of slaves. It fails to register depression with me. Slavery is sixty years in the past. The operation was successful and the patient is doing well, thank you. The terrible struggle that made me an American out of a poten-tial slave said "On the line!" The Reconstruction said "Get set!"; and the gen-eration before said "Go!" I am off to a flying start and I must not halt in the stretch to look behind and weep. Slavery is the price I paid for civilization, and the choice was not with me. It is a bully adventure and worth all that I have paid through my ancestors for it. No one on earth ever had a greater chance for glory. The world to be won and nothing to be lost. It is thrilling to think—to know that for any act of mine, I shall get twice as much praise or twice as much blame. It is quite exciting to hold the center of the national stage, with the spectators not knowing whether to laugh or to weep.

The position of my white neighbor is much more difficult. No brown specter pulls up a chair beside me when I sit down to eat. No dark ghost thrusts its leg against mine in bed. The game of keeping what one has is never so exciting as the game of getting.

I do not always feel colored. Even now I often achieve the unconscious Zora of Eatonville before the Hegira. I feel most colored when I am thrown against a sharp white background.

For instance at Barnard. "Beside the waters of the Hudson" I feel my race. Among the thousand white persons, I am a dark rock surged upon, overswept by a creamy sea. I am surged upon and overswept, but through it all, I remain myself. When covered by the waters, I am; and the ebb but reveals me again.

Sometimes it is the other way around. A white person is set down in our midst, but the contrast is just as sharp for me. For instance, when I sit in the drafty basement that is The New World Cabaret with a white person, my color comes. We enter chatting about any little nothing that we have in common and are seated by the jazz waiters. In the abrupt way that jazz orchestras have, this one plunges into a number. It loses no time in circumlocutions, but gets right down to business. It constricts the thorax and splits the heart with its tempo and narcotic harmonies. This orchestra grows rambunctious, rears on its hind legs and attacks the tonal veil with primitive fury, rending it, clawing it until it breaks through to the jungle beyond. I follow those heathen—follow them exultingly. I dance wildly inside myself; I yell within, I whoop; I shake my assegai above my head, I hurl it true to the mark *yeeeeooww!* I am in the jungle and living in the jungle way. My face is painted red and yellow and my body is painted blue. My pulse is throbbing like a war drum. I want to slaughter something—give pain, give death to what, I do not know. But the piece ends. The men of the orchestra wipe their lips and rest their fingers. I creep back slowly to the veneer we call civilization with the last tone and find the white friend sitting motionless in his seat, smoking calmly.

"Good music they have here," he remarks, drumming the table with his fingertips.

Music! The great blobs of purple and red emotion have not touched him. He has only heard what I felt. He is far away and I see him but dimly across the ocean and the continent that have fallen between us. He is so pale with his whiteness then and I am so colored.

At certain times I have no race, I am *me*. When I set my hat at a certain angle and saunter down Seventh Avenue, Harlem City, feeling as snooty as the lions in front of the Forty-Second Street Library, for instance. So far as my feelings are concerned, Peggy Hopkins Joyce on the Boule Mich with her gorgeous raiment, stately carriage, knees knocking together in a most aristocratic manner, has nothing on me. The cosmic Zora emerges. I belong to no race nor time. I am the eternal feminine with its string of beads.

I have no separate feeling about being an American citizen and colored. I am merely a fragment of the Great Soul that surges within the boundaries. My country, right or wrong.

Sometimes, I feel discriminated against, but it does not make me angry. It merely astonishes me. How *can* any deny themselves the pleasure of my company! It's beyond me.

But in the main, I feel like a brown bag of miscellany propped against a wall. Against a wall in company with other bags, white, red and yellow. Pour out the contents, and there is discovered a jumble of small things priceless and worthless. A first-water diamond, an empty spool, bits of broken glass, lengths of string, a key to a door long since crumbled away, a rusty knifeblade, old shoes saved for a road that never was and never will be, a nail bent under the weight of things too heavy for any nail, a dried flower or two, still a little fragrant. In your hand is the brown bag. On the ground before you is the jumble it held—so much like the jumble in the bags, could they be emptied, that all might be dumped in a single heap and the bags refilled without altering the content of any greatly. A bit of colored glass more or less would not matter. Perhaps that is how the Great Stuffer of Bags filled them in the first place—who knows?

Suggestions for Discussion

1. When does Hurston cease to be Zora of Orange County and become a little colored girl?

2. What does the author mean when she says, "Slavery is the price I paid for civilization"? Do you agree with her?

3. Sometimes Zora feels "cosmic," like "a fragment of the Great Soul," "the eternal feminine." How do these feelings relate to how she understands race?

Suggestions for Writing

1. Hurston describes herself as a "brown bag of miscellany propped against a wall." If someone was to empty the bag that is *you*, what would that person find?

2. When did you become aware of how you appeared to the outside world? Did you change because of this? Describe.

3. In the photograph on p. 63, Alex Webb presents another *Colored Me*. In what ways is the image similar to, and in what ways is it different from, the image that Zora Neale Hurston portrays of herself? Pay particular attention to gestures, facial expressions, and the focus of the photograph. What story do you find in the photograph, beyond the obvious?

FICTION

꧁ꩅ꧂

ERNEST HEMINGWAY

Indian Camp

Ernest Hemingway (1899–1961), novelist and short-story writer, began his career as a reporter and during World War I served with an ambulance unit in France and Italy. After the war, he lived in Paris as a correspondent for the Hearst papers. During the Spanish Civil War, he went to Spain as a war correspondent. His works include the collections of short stories *In Our Time* (1925), *Men Without Women* (1927), and *The Fifth Column and the First 49 Stories* (1938); and the novels *The Sun Also Rises* (1926), *A Farewell to Arms* (1929), *For Whom the Bell Tolls* (1940), and *The Old Man and the Sea* (1952), which was awarded a Pulitzer Prize. In 1954 he received the Nobel Prize for Literature. Posthumously published works include *Islands in the Stream* (1970), *The Garden of Eden* (1986), and *The Complete Short Stories of Ernest Hemingway: The Finca Vigia Edition* (1998), which boasted seven new tales. "Indian Camp," from the collection *In Our Time,* is a story of initiation in which a boy is exposed to a violent birth and death.

At the lake shore there was another rowboat drawn up. The two Indians stood waiting.

Nick and his father got in the stern of the boat and the Indians shoved it off and one of them got in to row. Uncle George sat in the stern of the camp rowboat. The young Indian shoved the camp boat off and got in to row Uncle George.

The two boats started off in the dark. Nick heard the oarlocks of the other boat quite a way ahead of them in the mist. The Indians rowed with quick choppy strokes. Nick lay back with his father's arm around him. It was cold on the water. The Indian who was rowing them was working very hard, but the other boat moved further ahead in the mist all the time.

"Where are we going, Dad?" Nick asked.

"Over to the Indian camp. There is an Indian lady very sick."

"Oh," said Nick.

Across the bay they found the other boat beached. Uncle George was smoking a cigar in the dark. The young Indian pulled the boat way up on the beach. Uncle George gave both the Indians cigars.

They walked up from the beach through a meadow that was soaking wet with dew, following the young Indian who carried a lantern. Then they went into the woods and followed a trail that led to the logging road that ran back into the hills. It was much lighter on the logging road as the timber was cut away on both sides. The young Indian stopped and blew out his lantern and they all walked on along the road.

They came around a bend and a dog came out barking. Ahead were the lights of the shanties where the Indian bark-peelers lived. More dogs rushed out at them. The two Indians sent them back to the shanties. In the shanty nearest the road there was a light in the window. An old woman stood in the doorway holding a lamp.

Inside on a wooden bunk lay a young Indian woman. She had been trying to have her baby for two days. All the old women in the camp had been helping her. The men had moved off up the road to sit in the dark and smoke out of range of the noise she made. She screamed just as Nick and the two Indians followed his father and Uncle George into the shanty. She lay in the lower bunk, very big under a quilt. Her head was turned to one side. In the upper bunk was her husband. He had cut his foot very badly with an ax three days before. He was smoking a pipe. The room smelled very bad.

Nick's father ordered some water to be put on the stove, and while it was heating he spoke to Nick.

"This lady is going to have a baby, Nick," he said.

"I know," said Nick.

"You don't know," said his father. "Listen to me. What she is going through is called being in labor. The baby wants to be born and she wants it to be born. All her muscles are trying to get the baby born. That is what is happening when she screams."

"I see," Nick said.

Just then the woman cried out.

"Oh, Daddy, can't you give her something to make her stop screaming?" asked Nick.

"No. I haven't any anaesthetic," his father said. "But her screams are not important. I don't hear them because they are not important."

The husband in the upper bunk rolled over against the wall.

The woman in the kitchen motioned to the doctor that the water was hot. Nick's father went into the kitchen and poured about half of the water out of the big kettle into a basin. Into the water left in the kettle he put several things he unwrapped from a handkerchief.

"Those must boil," he said, and began to scrub his hands in the basin of hot water with a cake of soap he had brought from the camp. Nick watched his father's hands scrubbing each other with the soap. While his father washed his hands very carefully and thoroughly, he talked.

"You see, Nick, babies are supposed to be born head first but sometimes they're not. When they're not they make a lot of trouble for everybody. Maybe I'll have to operate on this lady. We'll know in a little while."

When he was satisfied with his hands he went in and went to work.

"Pull back that quilt, will you, George?" he said. "I'd rather not touch it."

Later when he started to operate Uncle George and three Indian men held the woman still. She bit Uncle George on the arm and Uncle George said, "Damn squaw bitch!" and the young Indian who had rowed Uncle George over laughed at him. Nick held the basin for his father. It all took a long time.

His father picked the baby up and slapped it to make it breathe and handed it to the old woman.

"See, it's a boy, Nick," he said. "How do you like being an interne?"

Nick said, "All right." He was looking away so as not to see what his father was doing.

"There. That gets it," said his father and put something into the basin. Nick didn't look at it.

"Now," his father said, "there's some stitches to put in. You can watch this or not, Nick, just as you like. I'm going to sew up the incision I made."

Nick did not watch. His curiosity had been gone for a long time.

His father finished and stood up. Uncle George and the three Indian men stood up. Nick put the basin out in the kitchen.

Uncle George looked at his arm. The young Indian smiled reminiscently.

"I'll put some peroxide on that, George," the doctor said.

He bent over the Indian woman. She was quiet now and her eyes were closed. She looked very pale. She did not know what had become of the baby or anything.

"I'll be back in the morning," the doctor said, standing up. "The nurse should be here from St. Ignace by noon and she'll bring everything we need."

He was feeling exalted and talkative as football players are in the dressing room after a game.

"That's one for the medical journal, George," he said. "Doing a Caesarean with a jack-knife and sewing it up with nine-foot, tapered gut leaders."

Uncle George was standing against the wall, looking at his arm.

"Oh, you're a great man, all right," he said.

"Ought to have a look at the proud father. They're usually the worst sufferers in these little affairs," the doctor said. "I must say he took it all pretty quietly."

He pulled back the blanket from the Indian's head. His hand came away wet. He mounted on the edge of the lower bunk with the lamp in one hand and looked in. The Indian lay with his face toward the wall. His throat had been cut from ear to ear. The blood had flowed down into a pool where his body sagged the bunk. His head rested on his left arm. The open razor lay, edge up, in the blankets.

"Take Nick out of the shanty, George," the doctor said.

There was no need of that. Nick, standing in the door of the kitchen, had a good view of the upper bunk when his father, the lamp in one hand, tipped the Indian's head back.

It was just beginning to be daylight when they walked along the logging road back toward the lake.

"I'm terribly sorry I brought you along, Nickie," said his father, all his post-operative exhilaration gone. "It was an awful mess to put you through."

"Do ladies always have such a hard time having babies?" Nick asked.

"No, that was very, very exceptional."

"Why did he kill himself, Daddy?"

"I don't know, Nick. He couldn't stand things, I guess."

"Do many men kill themselves, Daddy?"

"Not very many, Nick."

"Do many women?"

"Hardly ever."

"Don't they ever?"

"Oh, yes. They do sometimes."

"Daddy?"

"Yes."

"Where did Uncle George go?"

"He'll turn up all right."

"Is dying hard, Daddy?"

"No, I think it's pretty easy, Nick. It all depends."

They were seated in the boat, Nick in the stern, his father rowing. The sun was coming up over the hills. A bass jumped, making a circle in the water. Nick trailed his hand in the water. It felt warm in the sharp chill of the morning.

In the early morning on the lake sitting in the stern of the boat with his father rowing, he felt quite sure that he would never die.

Suggestions for Discussion

1. How is the emotional tension of the story built up by the descriptive details of the journey to the Indian camp and the arrival at the shanties?

2. Inside the hut, what images of sight, sound, and smell take you into the heart of the scene?

3. What is the effect of the rather cold, scientific attitude of the doctor-father? Of his laconic explanations to his son interspersed with details of action? Note the verbs he uses.

4. What do Uncle George and the young Indian observers contribute to the reader's rising sense of horror?

5. How are you prepared for the suicide of the husband?

6. Comment on the irony of the concluding conversation and the significance of the experience in Nick's emotional growth and awareness of life and death.

7. Explain the final sentence.

8. By specific reference to the text, support the view that this is primarily a story of Nick's initiation.

Suggestions for Writing

1. Discuss the story as a commentary on the condition of Indians in rural areas or on reservations today.

2. Write about an early experience in which you learned about birth or death or violence.

SANDRA CISNEROS

Hips

Sandra Cisneros (b. 1954) is an author and a poet of Mexican and Chicana descent whose work often centers on feminism, religion, love, and oppression. She was born in Chicago, graduated from Loyola University in 1976, and earned an M.F.A. in creative writing from the University of Iowa in 1978. Her work has seen publication in *Glamour,* the *New York Times,* the *Village Voice,* and *Revista Chicano-Riquena.* Cisneros's books include *Bad Boys* (1980), *My Wicked, Wicked Ways* (1987), *Woman Hollering Creek and Other Stories* (1991), *Loose Woman* (1994), and *Caramelo* (2002). The following scene, like many of its fellows in *The House on Mango Street* (1984), is a semiautobiographical story told in a lyric style.

I like coffee, I like tea.
I like the boys and the boys like me.
Yes, no, maybe so. Yes, no, maybe so…

One day you wake up and they are there. Ready and waiting like a new Buick with the keys in the ignition. Ready to take you where?

They're good for holding a baby when you're cooking, Rachel says, turning the jump rope a little quicker. She has no imagination.

You need them to dance, says Lucy. If you don't get them you may turn into a man. Nenny says this and she believes it. She is this way because of her age.

That's right, I add before Lucy or Rachel can make fun of her. She is stupid alright, but she *is* my sister.

But most important, hips are scientific, I say repeating what Alicia already told me. It's the bones that let you know which skeleton was a man's when it was a man and which a woman's.

They bloom like roses, I continue because it's obvious I'm the only one who can speak with any authority; I have science on my side. The bones just one day open. Just like that. One day you might decide to have kids, and then where are you going to put them? Got to have room. Bones got to give.

But don't have too many or your behind will spread. That's how it is, says Rachel whose mama is as wide as a boat. And we just laugh.

What I'm saying is who here is ready? You gotta be able to know what to do with hips when you get them, I say making it up as I go. You gotta know how to walk with hips, practice you know—like if half of you wanted to go one way and the other half the other.

That's to lullaby it, Nenny says, that's to rock the baby asleep inside you. And then she begins singing *seashells, copper bells, eevy, ivy, o-ver.*

I'm about to tell her that's the dumbest thing I've ever heard, but the more I think about it…

You gotta get the rhythm, and Lucy begins to dance. She has the idea, though she's having trouble keeping her end of the double-dutch steady.

It's gotta be just so, I say. Not too fast and not too slow. Not too fast and not too slow.

We slow the double circles down to a certain speed so Rachel who has just jumped in can practice shaking it.

I want to shake like hoochi-coochie, Lucy says. She is crazy.

I want to move like heebie-jeebie, I say picking up on the cue.

I want to be Tahiti. Or *merengue*. Or electricity. Or *tembleque!*

Yes, *tembleque.* That's a good one.

And then it's Rachel who starts it:

Skip, skip,
snake in your hips.

Wiggle around
and break your lip.

Lucy waits a minute before her turn. She is thinking. Then she begins:

The waitress with the big fat hips
who pays the rent with taxi tips…
says nobody in town will kiss her on the lips
because…
because she looks like Christopher Columbus!
Yes, no, maybe so. Yes, no, maybe so.

She misses on *maybe so*. I take a little while before my turn, take a breath, and dive in:

Some are skinny like chicken lips.
Some are baggy like soggy Band-Aids
after you get out of the bathtub.
I don't care what kind I get.
Just as long as I get hips.

Everybody getting into it now except Nenny who is still humming *not a girl, not a boy, just a little baby*. She's like that.

When the two arcs open wide like jaws Nenny jumps in across from me, the rope tick-ticking, the little gold earrings our mama gave her for her First Holy Communion bouncing. She is the color of a bar of naphtha laundry soap, she is like the little brown piece left at the end of the wash, the hard little bone, my sister. Her mouth opens. She begins:

My mother and your mother were washing clothes.
My mother punched your mother right in the nose.
What color blood came out?

Not that old song, I say. You gotta use your own song. Make it up, you know? But she doesn't get it or won't. It's hard to say which. The rope turning, turning, turning.

Engine, engine number nine,
running down Chicago line.
If the train runs off the track
do you want your money back?
Do you want your MONEY back?
Yes, no, maybe so. Yes, no, maybe so…

I can tell Lucy and Rachel are disgusted, but they don't say anything because she's *my* sister.

Yes, no, maybe so. Yes, no, maybe so…

Nenny, I say, but she doesn't hear me. She is too many light-years away. She is in a world we don't belong to anymore. Nenny. Going. Going.

Y-E-S spells yes and out you go!

Suggestions for Discussion

1. What are hips? Name three of the theories presented by the girls in this story.
2. Why does the narrator believe that she has to prepare for hips and know how to use them?
3. Why does this tale include the lyrics to several jump rope songs?

Suggestion for Writing

How did you first begin to understand the changes that your body would go through when you reached puberty? Write a semiautobiographical story based on your recollections.

∾∾∾∾

D A M O N   F.   M A R B U T

Get Lost

In two novels, *Ordinary Madness* and *Maxwell Hume,* Southern writer Damon F. Marbut (b. 1978) has written about coming of age in contemporary America. In "Get Lost," he uses the devices of the journey and the sexual encounter to explore the confusions of young adulthood, the search for sexual identity, and the need to pursue the life of the writer.

I sat in a bar in downtown Mobile, Saturday before Valentine's, staring back and forth from a scotch and a collection of poems. Rod McKuen, a favorite of my mother's when she lived in San Diego during the late 1960s—

in her tattered copies were remarks and questions, guidelines for my younger self to navigate the pages. But the book I'd found at a flea market that afternoon lacked any trace of her ink. I thought of her young, drinking Chianti on a California beach. The late afternoon was turning gray with the clouds, and I along with it. I paid my rude server, Marcie, and walked two blocks west to where I'd parked beside the Cathedral. I hopped in the car, denim jacket in the back seat, drove over Bankhead Tunnel and to the exit that would send me toward Pascagoula. I didn't stop for gas: I had fifty dollars cash and no toothbrush. But that wasn't important. New Orleans gets you there when it wants you badly enough. It can even sense when it's you who does the wanting.

The road from Mobile to New Orleans is a short one. My drive was a series of unimportant thoughts here and there between the sleepy industrial mills along the coast of Mississippi, a few cigarettes and studying the quick passage of highway paint lines beneath my ten-year-old Jeep. In Gulfport I stopped for beer at the Texaco where I'd broken down years earlier in my Explorer. The battery had exploded. I hadn't stopped for beer that night, but rather, chips and a soda to help my stomach make it comfortably ahead to Louisiana to where my mind had already raced. But it was nearly eight o'clock that Saturday when I screwed the cap on the last of the beers, tossed it in back and turned off the highway on to Canal Street.

I checked into the Marriott while leaving the Jeep running outside with hazard lights on. After a brief conversation with Alberta at the front desk, I was set for a smoking room on the fortieth floor. A dabbler in poetry, she suggested a few bars for spoken word. I thanked her and returned to my car, swung it around to valet and reentered through the lobby and to the elevators. My room was small, quiet and cold. They usually are. I found an ashtray on the white bathroom counter and moved to the window, slid back the thick curtains and lit a cigarette. Canal Street ran perpendicular to my side of the hotel; I was on top of it, never having known before how long and illuminated it is from merely driving it. I remembered hovering over La Grange the last time I flew to New York, how from elevated heights things reveal, more clearly, their pure and uncomplicated faces. Bourbon Street, a few blocks down, would have exuded misconception, even from my view on the fortieth. I didn't have to see past the hotels that separated us to understand it. After I finished the cigarette I checked my pockets and left the room for the city below.

The streets of the French Quarter are always Bourbon Street, just a more or less severe interpretation, all one mass of moving bodies, despondent vagrants, frozen mimes at intersections, the smell of things going wrong. Like in the blues clubs of Chicago, it's getting lost; to sit alongside other searching people is to feel that disconnection together. That was the substitution I'd left Mobile for, escaping the chaos of graduate school, sixty-hour workweeks and little, if any, time to write. No chances at love either, not any form of it. I snuck into a small restaurant on a side street once I'd made it to Bourbon, had a glass of wine and a bowl of alligator soup with Charlie, the pale-skinned bartender with sunken eyes and practiced smile, and then smoked a cigarette after paying out. For the first time in a long while I felt unobtrusive and forgettable; it was good to move along so unimportantly.

I walked further past open blues bars, bars with live tribute bands, small daiquiri stands, bistros, convenience stores with cigarettes still overpriced from Mardi Gras; the more popular places point themselves out as one moves along in the shuffle. Unmistakable, the crowds of enthusiasts swarm in huddles on the sidewalk and spill into the street. Commonly it's a bar with loud music and exposed breasts on a karaoke stage. I passed such an estab-lishment with disinterest and found myself in front of a jazz bar one block down. A determined, unfriendly man with a feather in his hat stood by the door and asked if I was interested. I nodded yes and, before I could thank him, I was briskly led by the upper arm like a punished child toward a seat near the stage front, tightly wedged between a couple in Maple Leaf sports-wear and a young man sitting alone in a suit. There were about sixty patrons directly in front of the trumpet player, Sharif. The rest sat stage right in front of wide doors that led into a courtyard. I started a tab with an older woman who seemed distracted and unhappy. She brought my double scotch shortly and I offered her a smile. She accepted only my card.

During breaks in songs, Sharif re-introduced his band that consisted of a drummer, a stand-up bass player, a pianist and an older gentleman on the alto sax and clarinet. The drummer spent most of his time watching his reflection in the mirror that surrounded the stage from his side all the way around to the back of the piano. Two couples at a nearby table laughed and pointed. I studied them studying him for a while, ordered another scotch, exchanged a few words with the Canadian couple who remained crammed together with me through to the following set, and then realized for the first time that evening that the couples were in town for the Valentine's Day weekend. I'd grown used to forgetting the holiday. The sound of Sharif's trumpet increased and rose to a volume loud enough for me to safely think about love and then quickly finish my drink.

After a few more scotches the band called it a night. I signed my tab and reentered Bourbon, the wave of people swelling in the street. It was near 11:30. The temperature had dropped in the two hours I'd been inside. I crossed the street head-on into Zydeco music roaring from two adjacent souvenir shops. A woman dressed as a corpse bride worked the next corner, frozen still with her arms propped above her head. When a passerby dropped money into the small cardboard box at her feet she would unfreeze and flap her wing-like arms and bare a set of sharp, eroding teeth before returning once more to stillness. I wanted the absinthe bar I'd heard about from a friend a couple weeks earlier. I ducked into a voodoo shop a block or so before the gay bars and asked directions from a young man with a shaved head who, after giving a brief history of absinthe and the difference between what was available in the States and the genuine product in Europe, pointed me toward Pirate's Alley two blocks over.

Once at the end of Pirate's Alley I walked into a small corner bar with tiny, unoccupied café tables outside and used the bathroom. The man at the voodoo shop had mentioned the word "vampire" concerning the bar's name, so in feeling dislocated I exited and walked the block. After a few minutes I returned to the head of the alley and stopped a man passing on the other side of the cobbled walkway.

"Vampire bar? I can tell you exactly where it is. You don't suppose I can have one of those cigarettes?"

"No problem."

I noticed as I extracted my lighter and pack from the inside of my jacket pocket that he carried a large piece of unwrapped prime rib. Both hands were covered in a thick film. I cupped the cigarette as I lit it for him, though he nonetheless put one of his hands over mine out of habit. With the same hand, he patted my shoulder.

"There's this bar called 'The Dungeon' two blocks down from this street here," he said, pointing over my shoulder. "And then down one. Right on the left."

"'The Dungeon'?"

"That's where all the rock stars hang out. All the multi-millionaires go spend all their money. It's the place you wanna go, man."

"It's just that I'm looking for an absinthe bar. Maybe with 'vampire' in the name."

"The Dungeon, man," he said, shifting to his other foot. "I'm telling you."

"Do they serve absinthe?"

"It's where the rock stars hang out."

"Right. But I was told there's an absinthe bar in Pirate's Alley. Is that it right there?" I pointed to the corner bar I'd stopped in moments earlier. An illumined sidewalk sign, thirty feet away, advertised itself as the previous home of William Faulkner. I looked down at the meat, sagging heavily from his fingers.

"You said it."

"Does it have something to do with vampires?"

"Vampires?" he asked, turning away. "You go to 'The Dungeon.' You'll thank me. Hey, man, I kindly appreciate the smoke."

As he made the top of the alley he bit from the meat and disappeared around the corner.

I returned to the bar, noticing a sign over the restroom that read, *One drink minimum to piss here.* It explained the bartender's earlier stare. He was an older man, more friendly as the drinks came and my wallet went. I ordered an absinthe and an Abita Amber, the latter of which I sipped while watching the sugar being melted, the liquor pouring, the six Aussies at a nearby table looking on with exuberance, raising their absinthe glasses to me, the newcomer. I found a corner table between the open doors and lit a cigarette.

After my second absinthe and third beer a group of young men entered from the opposite side of the bar. One wore a cowboy hat. He was thin and slightly muscular, wearing a ragged t-shirt and a handsome smile. A taller, thinner man stood to his left but I couldn't make his face. The black-haired boy in a blue silk shirt was beautiful. I could see him completely, perhaps through the drinks, from the time he came in and leaned into the bar. I needed to hear his voice. It's interesting how lonely I was letting solitude feel. I thought it was what I wanted. So after another cigarette I moved to the right of the cowboy to order another, and in minutes we were introducing ourselves. They were performers in a Broadway tour of *Grease* in town for the weekend. Michael was the one in blue, Woody in the hat. The other, a concerned-looking fellow, had messy hair and a serious pair of eyes. I cannot remember his name. After a while Michael and I bought each other a drink and stood closer as the first moments of our conversation became an hour.

"Do you smoke?" I asked, pulling a cigarette from my pack.

"No, but I'll go outside with you."

The bartender had closed the doors to keep out the cold. The polite thing was to not light up inside, because the bar was small and easily filled by the few patrons. Michael followed me out. After a mutual game of avoiding the inevitable he pushed himself into me and we kissed, two strangers together in a cold alley filled with Faulkner and distant music. I never had that smoke.

Back inside, Michael's friends chided us and said they were leaving to seek girls at a busier bar a few blocks away. I told them goodbye and shook their hands while Michael leaned in against my ear, whispering suggestions. It was the first time in years I recognized the feel of someone's smile against my neck. People may say they don't come to New Orleans expecting it, that touch. Not specifically that. But everyone wants it; everyone hopes it's what they can drive away with and remember.

Michael's matinee show featured Frankie Avalon, and the cast and ensemble had to be at call just after noon the following day. It was nearly three-thirty a.m., so I signed out and thanked the bartender. Michael finished his drink and smiled a tired smile as he kissed my temple. In the wild quickness of how moments give themselves away in the Quarter, we held hands from the alley all the way to Canal Street. After all, it was the weekend for love. And once we were forty floors up at the Marriot, I watched through the window the ever-moving city, as well as Michael undressing behind me. He clicked the bedside lamp and, once his fingertips found the small of my back, we collapsed together.

Periodically through the night I woke to the warm sweat of his chest blending with that from my back. It's a warmth that would have made me uncomfortable had it not come from such desirable and fleeting affection. I'd had a long run of near misses before and I learned how to identify, with lightning speed, when it is the love comes and goes. A person innately senses the potential for esteem, whether it's given or received. I'd written him my phone number, but I might have slept better knowing I'd never hear from him again. It was the kind of reckless love I felt I needed. I wanted to be a coward and avoid the investment of emotion. The mystery of the perfect moment would have given way to my usual, destructive analysis. But in the late morning when we rose from bed, there was a somber air about our upcoming departure. The night had been far too right to leave it without celebration. So with morning breath we kissed randomly, hurriedly, laughing during dips into our clothes from the floor. In the elevator we made a middle-aged couple visibly uncomfortable, our arms locked together as the floor levels blinked sleepily from the fortieth to the lobby. Michael was running late and left as I stood in line to check out. We exchanged smiles as he rounded the corner toward the front door. Mine likely held most of the longing between us. My back ached from restless sleep, from being attentive to his needs for comfort and my desire to stay awake to press my lips against his back as his breath fell, rose and fell again. His eyes, across the marble flooring and amidst the loudness of the arriving guests, were what I saw last.

The valet took a while to retrieve my Jeep. I wished it were stolen so I could have made the performance, to stand outside the stage door, to watch Michael exit still glowing from the show. After a while, though, I noticed a blur of white paint hurl itself down the second floor ramp and there was my Jeep. I tipped the man the last of my cash and hit Canal back to the interstate, lighting a cigarette and cracking the windows. A jazz station picked up with static on the radio. I turned it up as loud as my old speakers could manage as I blended with the eastbound traffic and put the city in the rearview.

The road from New Orleans is a long one. It's consumed by memories just made, memories that keep themselves when too important to risk being forgotten. I haven't found it difficult to leave before. But leaving the day before Valentine's was a return to my old life, even if two hours away, a life I'd lamented for its void of passion, its lack of immediacy. Footsteps are traced on the way to Alabama, what to do once there and why it is one goes back. Work, bills, friendships, talks in bars with poets and addicts. It's easy to find a reason to leave Mobile; the return is where the heart breaks over what can only be carried back in the mind.

I pulled in front of my house just after two-thirty. I lived with Matthew, a close friend since high school, and his girlfriend. Her black car was in the driveway.

"I haven't seen you in a week," Karen called from the couch as I stepped inside. Orson, our sheepdog, stretched by the dining room table and stood.

"Hi, sweetheart," I said to her, running a hand over Orson's head as he walked beside me.

"Coffee's on."

"Thanks." I set my jacket on an old sofa we kept in the front library, passed by Karen in the living room and went into the kitchen.

"You work tonight?"

"Tuesday." I poured a cup and pressed my palms around the mug. The neighbors were working on their roof out in the sun on the other side of our kitchen window. Beat from the drive, the thinking and the attempts not to, I took a slow sip.

"I've got news," Karen said, suddenly behind me.

"Yeah?" I turned to her.

"Matt proposed at dinner."

She told me the story with her usual, beautiful smile, the elation I envied that always accompanied her stories. We hugged beside the refrigerator. She cursed me for how little we saw of each other and Orson slumped to the ground, dissatisfied with being ignored. After a while Karen returned to the couch and I went to my room and shut the door.

I sat at my desk and pushed aside the stacks of paper I'd yet to edit and send to New York by deadline. Everything in the room was a new greeting, a new reminder that there were things left to do. The only thought that arose, though, was Michael's sweat becoming mine somewhere between the white sheets of a New Orleans hotel. It was a matter of time for the recollection of his face to disappear under the swarm of all that lay ahead in Mobile. And I was desperate to feel a deep happiness for Matt and Karen, but I couldn't seem to shake a weary exhilaration of my own. Love still had its plans. Confused and exhausted, I turned on my computer and began to type.

Suggestions for Discussion

1. What details bring New Orleans to life?
2. What do you think the narrator means when he says, "love still had its plans"?
3. Why is the narrator desperate to feel a deep happiness for Matt and Karen?

Suggestion for Writing

Do you believe that the narrator finds the escape, adventure, and love that he is looking for? Cite specific events from the story.

POETRY

T. S. ELIOT

The Love Song of J. Alfred Prufrock

Thomas Stearns Eliot (1888–1965) was born in St. Louis, was educated at
Harvard University, and studied in Paris and Oxford. He settled in England
in 1914 and became a British subject in 1927. His most influential poem,
The Waste Land, was published in 1922, followed by *The Hollow Men*
(1925), *Poems: 1909–1925* (1925), and *Poems: 1909–1935* (1936). His criticism includes *The Use of Poetry and the Use of Criticism* (1933), *Essays
Ancient and Modern* (1936), *Notes Toward the Definition of Culture* (1948),
and *To Criticize the Critic* (1965). His best-known poetic dramas are *Murder
in the Cathedral* (1935), *The Family Reunion* (1939), and *The Cocktail Party*
(1950). Prufrock's opposed selves in this dramatic monologue, published
in 1917, are separated from each other, the one exploring the idea of human
involvement and the other observing it in comfortable isolation.

*S'io credesse che mia risposta fosse
A persona che mai tornasse al mondo,
Questa fiamma staria senza piu scosse.
Ma perciocche giammai di questo fondo
Non torno vivo alcun, s'i'odo il vero,
Senza tema d'infamia ti rispondo.*

["If I believed that my answer would be to one
who would ever return to the world, this flame
would shake no more; but since no one ever
returns alive from this depth, if what I hear is
true, I answer you without fear of infamy."
—*Dante's Inferno,* XXVII, 61–66]

Let us go then, you and I,
When the evening is spread out against the sky
Like a patient etherised upon a table;
Let us go, through certain half-deserted streets,
The muttering retreats

Of restless nights in one-night cheap hotels
And sawdust restaurants with oyster-shells:
Streets that follow like a tedious argument
Of insidious intent
To lead you to an overwhelming question…
Oh, do not ask, "What is it?"
Let us go and make our visit.

In the room the women come and go
Talking of Michelangelo.

The yellow fog that rubs its back upon the window-panes,
The yellow smoke that rubs its muzzle on the window-panes
Licked its tongue into the corners of the evening,
Lingered upon the pools that stand in drains,
Let fall upon its back the soot that falls from chimneys,
Slipped by the terrace, made a sudden leap,
And seeing that it was a soft October night,
Curled once about the house, and fell asleep.

And indeed there will be time
For the yellow smoke that slides along the street,
Rubbing its back upon the window-panes;
There will be time, there will be time
To prepare a face to meet the faces that you meet;
There will be time to murder and create,
And time for all the works and days of hands
That lift and drop a question on your plate;
Time for you and time for me,
And time yet for a hundred indecisions,
And for a hundred visions and revisions,
Before the taking of a toast and tea.

In the room the women come and go
Talking of Michelangelo.

And indeed there will be time
To wonder, "Do I dare?" and, "Do I dare?"
Time to turn back and descend the stair,
With a bald spot in the middle of my hair—
[They will say: "How his hair is growing thin!"]
My morning coat, my collar mounting firmly to the chin,
My necktie rich and modest, but asserted by a simple pin—
[They will say: "But how his arms and legs are thin!"]
Do I dare
Disturb the universe?

In a minute there is time
For decisions and revisions which a minute will reverse.

    For I have known them all already, known them all:—
Have known the evenings, mornings, afternoons,
I have measured out my life with coffee spoons;
I know the voices dying with a dying fall
Beneath the music from a farther room.
    So how should I presume?

    And I have known the eyes already, known them all—
The eyes that fix you in a formulated phrase,
And when I am formulated, sprawling on a pin,
When I am pinned and wriggling on the wall,
Then how should I begin
To spit out all the butt-ends of my days and ways?
    And how should I presume?

    And I have known the arms already, known them all—
Arms that are braceleted and white and bare
[But in the lamplight, downed with light brown hair!]
Is it perfume from a dress
That makes me so digress?
Arms that lie along a table, or wrap about a shawl.
    And should I then presume?
    And how should I begin?

    Shall I say, I have gone at dusk through narrow streets
And watched the smoke that rises from the pipes
Of lonely men in shirt-sleeves, leaning out of windows?…
    I should have been a pair of ragged claws
Scuttling across the floors of silent seas.

    And the afternoon, the evening, sleeps so peacefully!
Smoothed by long fingers,
Asleep…tired…or it malingers,
Stretched on the floor, here beside you and me.
Should I, after tea and cakes and ices,
Have the strength to force the moment to its crisis?
But though I have wept and fasted, wept and prayed,
Though I have seen my head [grown slightly bald] brought in upon a platter,
I am no prophet—and here's no great matter;
I have seen the moment of my greatness flicker,
And I have seen the eternal Footman hold my coat, and snicker,
And in short, I was afraid.

    And would it have been worth it, after all,

After the cups, the marmalade, the tea,
Among the porcelain, among some talk of you and me,
Would it have been worth while,
To have bitten off the matter with a smile,
To have squeezed the universe into a ball
To roll it toward some overwhelming question,
To say: "I am Lazarus, come from the dead.
Come back to tell you all, I shall tell you all"—
If one, settling a pillow by her head,
    Should say: "That is not what I meant at all.
    That is not it, at all."

    And would it have been worth it, after all,
Would it have been worth while,
After the sunsets and the dooryards and the sprinkled streets,
After the novels, after the teacups, after the skirts that trail along the floor—
And this, and so much more?—
It is impossible to say just what I mean!
But as if a magic lantern threw the nerves in patterns on a screen:
Would it have been worth while
If one, settling a pillow or throwing off a shawl,
And turning toward the window, should say:
"That is not it at all,
That is not what I meant, at all."

No! I am not Prince Hamlet, nor was meant to be;
Am an attendant lord, one that will do
To swell a progress, start a scene or two,
Advise the prince; no doubt, an easy tool,
Deferential, glad to be of use,
Politic, cautious, and meticulous;
Full of high sentence, but a bit obtuse;
At times, indeed, almost ridiculous—
Almost, at times, the Fool.

[handwritten margin note: Ref. to Polonias has he really articulated any significant or is he like Polonias]

    I grow old...I grow old...
I shall wear the bottoms of my trousers rolled.

    Shall I part my hair behind? Do I dare to eat a peach?
I shall wear white flannel trousers, and walk upon the beach.
I have heard the mermaids singing, each to each.

[handwritten margin note: Ref. to the sirens.]

    I do not think that they will sing to me.

    I have seen them riding seaward on the waves
Combing the white hair of the waves blown back
When the wind blows the water white and black.

We have lingered in the chambers of the sea
By sea-girls wreathed with seaweed red and brown
Till human voices wake us, and we drown.

Suggestions for Discussion

1. Who are "you and I"?

2. What evidence can you find in the structural development of the poem to support the view that one self in the dramatic monologue acts out the conflict and the other assumes the role of observer? Cite lines from the poem in which shifts in mood and tone occur. How does the poem achieve dramatic unity?

3. Contrast the images of Prufrock's interior world with those of the external world. How does their recurring juxtaposition illuminate the doubleness of the speaker and contribute to tone? How is sensory experience used to convey the circularity of the dialogue with self? Why are the images of the etherized patient, the staircase, winding streets, cat, and fog especially appropriate dramatic symbols of the speaker's state of mind? Trace the use of sea imagery. How does it function differently in the metaphor of the crab and the vision of the mermaids? How do both relate to theme and tone? What do the allusions to John the Baptist, Lazarus, and Hamlet have in common?

4. Distinguish between the dramatic and the lyric elements. How is the mock heroic used to satirize both speaker and society? Study the effects of repetition on rhythm, tone, and meaning. How do the stanzas and the typographical breaks mark the shifts in tone? Discuss the relationship of tone to syntax, refrain, internal rhyme, diction, tempo, and melody. Comment on the irony in the title.

5. How does time function in the poem? How does the shift in tense from present to present perfect and future provide a key to the poem's resolution? What form does the speaker's recognition take? By what means does the poet evoke sympathy for Prufrock, who is psychically impotent to establish an intimate human relationship? To what do you attribute Prufrock's rejection of human encounter? What part does his self-mockery play in our response to him? Does the poem move beyond pathos and self-mockery?

6. In what respect may the poem be viewed as an expression of a search for self?

Suggestions for Writing

1. Write a character study of Prufrock in which you refer directly to the poem.

2. Write a dialogue in which your interior self is counterpointed against your social self or persona.

≈≈≈≈

DYLAN THOMAS

The Force That Through the Green Fuse Drives the Flower

Dylan Thomas (1914–1953) was born in Wales. He was a newspaper reporter for a time and worked for the BBC during World War II. He gained recognition as a lyric poet in his twenties and grew in popularity until his death while on a lecture tour in the United States. His *Collected Poems* appeared in 1953. A collection of his stories, sketches, and essays, *Quite Early One Morning,* was published in 1954; a group of stories and essays, *A Prospect of the Sea,* in 1955; and a verse play, *Under Milk Wood,* in 1954. The poet views natural forces as both destructive and life-giving; this poem, published in 1934, is an expression of his sense of the energy, both creative and destructive, that runs through all things.

Weathered features on Woodlawn Cemetery, 1997. © Christian J. Matuschek – Photography.

The force that through the green fuse drives the flower
Drives my green age; that blasts the roots of trees
Is my destroyer.
And I am dumb to tell the crooked rose
My youth is bent by the same wintry fever.

The force that drives the water through the rocks
Drives my red blood; that dries the mouthing streams
Turns mine to wax.
And I am dumb to mouth unto my veins
How at the mountain spring the same mouth sucks.

The hand that whirls the water in the pool
Stirs the quicksand; that ropes the blowing wind
Hauls my shroud sail.
And I am dumb to tell the hanging man
How of my clay is made the hangman's lime.

The lips of time leech to the fountain head;
Love drips and gathers, but the fallen blood
Shall calm her sores.
And I am dumb to tell a weather's wind
How time has ticked a heaven round the stars.

And I am dumb to tell the lover's tomb
How at my sheet goes the same crooked worm.

Suggestions for Discussion

1. What images suggest the relationship the poet sees between the world of nature and that of human passions?

2. How does the poet express the sense that the energy that runs through all things is both creator and destroyer? How does the two-line refrain at the end of each stanza relate this theme to the voice of the poet?

Suggestion for Writing

What images depict contrasting forces of life and death? How does the diction convey the sense of sexual energy?

DENISE LEVERTOV

In Mind

Denise Levertov (1923–1997) was born in England and came to the United States as a young woman. A poet and essayist, Levertov had a career that included work as an editor, a translator, and a professor, with a brief stint in nursing during World War II. She held four honorary degrees and won numerous awards for her poetry. These include most recently the Bobst and Shelley Prizes. Author of twenty-one volumes of poetry, Levertov's recent publications include *A Door in the Hive* (1989), *Evening Train* (1992), *New and Selected Essays* (1992), and *Tesserae: Memories and Suppositions* (1996). In the poem that follows, published in 1964, she presents portraits of two very different women who inhabit her mind.

> There's in my mind a woman
> of innocence, unadorned but
>
> fair-featured, and smelling of
> apples or grass. She wears
>
> a utopian smock or shift, her hair
> is light brown and smooth, and she
>
> is kind and very clean without
> ostentation—
>   but she has
> no imagination.
>   And there's a
> turbulent moon-ridden girl
>
> or old woman, or both,
> dressed in opals and rags, feathers
>
> and torn taffeta,
> who knows strange songs—
>
> but she is not kind.

Suggestions for Discussion

1. Each of the women Levertov describes possesses something that the other lacks. Does one woman "make up" for the other?

2. Are the women in Levertov's mind separate women? Or are they both part of the author's secret self, each part of the whole?

3. To which woman figure are you more drawn? Why?

Suggestions for Writing

1. Imagine this poem as a scene in a play. What kind of dialogue would emerge between the two characters?

2. How would you cast the play? Who would role-play each character?

3. Imagine the characters described as men. What would be the masculine equivalents of the two women Levertov describes?

ANNE SEXTON

Her Kind

Anne Sexton (1928–1974) taught and lectured widely, but she was above all a poet. Recipient of three honorary degrees and numerous fellowships, she was also awarded, among others, the Shelley and Pulitzer Prizes. Of her many books the best known are *To Bedlam and Part Way Back* (1960), from which the following poem is taken; *All My Pretty Ones* (1962); *Live or Die* (1966); *Transformations* (1971); and *The Death Notebooks* (1974). In "Her Kind," we see another portrayal of the complex and multiple nature of human personality.

I have gone out, a possessed witch,
haunting the black air, braver at night;
dreaming evil, I have done my hitch
over the plain houses, light by light:
lonely thing, twelve-fingered, out of mind.

A woman like that is not a woman, quite.
I have been her kind.

I have found the warm caves in the woods,
filled them with skillets, carvings, shelves,
closets, silks, innumerable goods;
fixed the suppers for the worms and the elves:
whining, rearranging the disaligned.
A woman like that is misunderstood.
I have been her kind.

I have ridden in your car, driver,
waved my nude arms at villages going by,
learning the last bright routes, survivor
where your flames still bite my thigh
and my ribs crack where your wheels wind.
A woman like that is not ashamed to die.
I have been her kind.

Suggestions for Discussion

1. Who is "I" in this poem?

2. What is meant by the phrase "her *kind*?" What *kind* of woman is the speaker relating to? What metaphors does Sexton use to describe the women (or woman?) evoked in this poem? How do these characterizations of womanhood relate to how society has understood and portrayed women?

3. Why is the protagonist described as "not a woman, quite," "misunderstood," "not ashamed to die"?

Suggestions for Writing

1. If you were to think of yourself in terms of a number of different characters or *personae,* what would they be? How would they relate to one another?

2. What are some of the stereotypes our culture has used to describe men? Have these had an impact on how men in our culture behave? Explain.

MARIANNE MOORE

The Mind Is an Enchanting Thing

Marianne Moore (1887–1972) was born in Missouri. She graduated from Bryn Mawr College and went on to teach at an Indian school, work in the New York Public Library, and edit *The Dial* (1925–1929). Her early poems were published in 1921, her *Collected Poems* in 1951. She was also the author of *Predilections* (1955), a volume of critical essays; a poetic translation of La Fontaine's *Fables* (1954); and a collection of poetry, *Tell Me, Tell Me* (1967). The following poem is from *Collected Poems;* the symbols of enchantment are drawn from nature, science, and art.

is an enchanted thing
    like the glaze on a
katydid-wing
        subdivided by sun
        till the nettings are legion.
Like Gieseking playing Scarlatti;

like the apteryx-awl
    as a beak, or the
kiwi's rain-shawl
        of haired feathers, the mind
        feeling its way as though blind,
walks along with its eyes on the ground.

It has memory's ear
    that can hear without
having to hear.
        Like the gyroscope's fall,
        truly unequivocal
because trued by regnant certainty,

it is a power of
     strong enchantment. It
is like the dove-
       neck animated by
       sun; it is memory's eye;
it's conscientious inconsistency.

It tears off the veil; tears
     the temptation, the
mist the heart wears,
       from its eyes,—if the heart
       has a face; it takes apart
dejection. It's fire in the dove-neck's

iridescence; in the
     inconsistencies
of Scarlatti.
       Unconfusion submits
       its confusion to proof; it's
not a Herod's oath that cannot change.

Suggestions for Discussion

1. The symbols of the poem derive from nature, art, and science. Identify them.

2. How do the similes contribute to the theme of enchantment? What paradoxes do you find, and how do they underscore the central theme?

THEODORE ROETHKE

The Waking

American poet Theodore Roethke (1908–1963) won the Pulitzer Prize for Poetry in 1953 for *The Waking: Poems, 1933–1953*. He received the Bollingen Award for Poetry in 1958, and a collection of his poems, *Words for the Wind,* was published in 1958. He taught during the last years of his life at the University of Washington, and *The Far Field* was published posthumously in 1964. In the following poem, from *The Collected Poems of Theodore Roethke* (1966), Roethke shows that among the many modes of learning, it is possible to learn "by going where I have to go."

> I wake to sleep, and take my waking slow.
> I feel my fate in what I cannot fear.
> I learn by going where I have to go.
>
> We think by feeling. What is there to know?
> I hear my being dance from ear to ear.
> I wake to sleep, and take my waking slow.
>
> Of those so close beside me, which are you?
> God bless the Ground! I shall walk softly there,
> And learn by going where I have to go.
>
> Light takes the Tree; but who can tell us how?
> The lowly worm climbs up a winding stair;
> I wake to sleep, and take my waking slow.
>
> Great Nature has another thing to do
> To you and me; so take the lively air,
> And, lovely, learn by going where to go.
>
> This shaking keeps me steady. I should know.
> What falls away is always. And is near.
> I wake to sleep, and take my waking slow.
> I learn by going where I have to go.

Suggestions for Discussion

1. Relate the title to the substance of the poem.
2. What are the modes of learning? Cite specific passages.
3. How does the use of paradox contribute to tone and substance? Comment on the rhythm, rhyme scheme, repetition of refrain, imagery, and diction.

Suggestion for Writing

Examine your own processes of learning and comment on their relative effectiveness.

CARL DENNIS

The God Who Loves You

Carl Dennis (b. 1939) is the author of seven books of poetry, including *Ranking the Wishes* (1997) and the Pulitzer Prize–winning *Practical Gods* (2001), which is the source for the following poem. He is also an English professor at the State University of New York at Buffalo and has been part of Warren Wilson College's creative writing faculty. Honored with fellowships from the Guggenheim Foundation and the National Endowment for the Arts, Dennis has also earned the Ruth Lily Prize in 2000 for his contribution to American poetry.

It must be troubling for the god who loves you
To ponder how much happier you'd be today
Had you been able to glimpse your many futures.
It must be painful for him to watch you on Friday evenings
Driving home from the office, content with your week—
Three fine houses sold to deserving families—
Knowing as he does exactly what would have happened
Had you gone to your second choice for college,
Knowing the roommate you'd have been allotted
Whose ardent opinions on painting and music
Would have kindled in you a lifelong passion.
A life thirty points above the life you're living
On any scale of satisfaction. And every point
A thorn in the side of the god who loves you.
You don't want that, a large-souled man like you
Who tries to withhold from your wife the day's disappointments
So she can save her empathy for the children.
And would you want this god to compare your wife
With the woman you were destined to meet on the other campus?
It hurts you to think of him ranking the conversation
You'd have enjoyed over there higher in insight
Than the conversation you're used to.
And think how this loving god would feel

Knowing that the man next in line for your wife
Would have pleased her more than you ever will
Even on your best days, when you really try.
Can you sleep at night believing a god like that
Is pacing his cloudy bedroom, harassed by alternatives
You're spared by ignorance? The difference between what is
And what could have been will remain alive for him
Even after you cease existing, after you catch a chill
Running out in the snow for the morning paper,
Losing eleven years that the god who loves you
Will feel compelled to imagine scene by scene
Unless you come to the rescue by imagining him
No wiser than you are, no god at all, only a friend
No closer than the actual friend you made at college,
The one you haven't written in months. Sit down tonight
And write him about the life you can talk about
With a claim to authority, the life you've witnessed,
Which for all you know is the life you've chosen.

Suggestions for Discussion

1. What is the difference between you and the character "you" being addressed in this poem?

2. Is this a religious poem? What function does god perform? What kind of god is being discussed?

3. Why does this poem end with an urging to write a letter?

Suggestion for Writing

Go ahead and write the letter that Carl Dennis wants you to.

Personal Relationships: Parents and Children

Be careful what you give children, for sooner or later, you are sure to get it back.

—BARBARA KINGSOLVER, "Somebody's Baby"

A selfish love seldom respects the rights of the beloved to be an autonomous person.

—THOMAS MERTON, "Love Can Be Kept Only By Being Given Away"

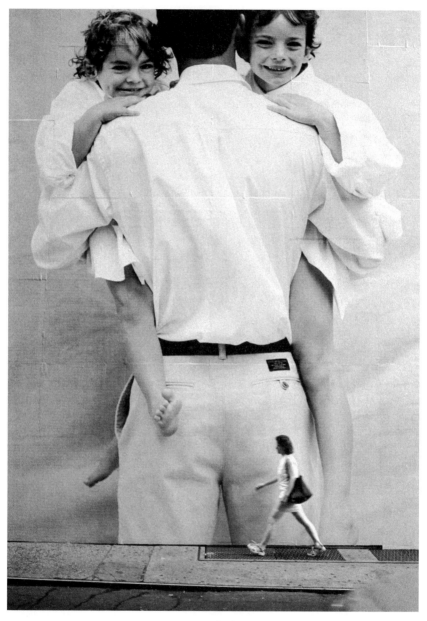

From New York Frames

VEIT METTE, 1993

© Veit Mette/Fotobuero, 1993

NOTEBOOK

A R Y E H   L E V   S T O L L M A N

Die Grosse Liebe

Canadian-raised Aryeh Lev Stollman is a neuroradiologist at Mount Sinai Medical Center in New York. The son of a rabbi, Stollman often infuses his work with elements of Jewish heritage. His novels include *The Far Euphrates* (1997), which won the Wilbur and Lambda awards, and *The Illuminated Soul* (2002), winner of *Hadassah Magazine*'s Harold U. Ribalow Prize. The following piece, from Stollman's 2003 short story collection *The Dialogues of Time and Entropy,* concerns the relationship between a son and his mother, a woman with a secret from her past in Nazi Germany.

"*The Great Love* was her best movie. I felt so happy watching her, no matter how many times I saw it."

As always in our house, when my mother described the movie in which her favorite actress starred, she spoke the language of her Berlin youth. Not the jumbled clacking of the crowded Scheunenviertel, noisy with the unsteady tongues of immigrants, but the soft, cultivated tones of the beautiful Grunewald, its grand villas overflowing with art and books and music, its gardens, its lawns sweeping down to quiet lakes.

When she pronounced the film's title—*Die Grosse Liebe*—it sounded to me, a boy born and growing up in the vast present tense of Ontario, so unlike the marvelous emotion it was meant to convey. Despite the gentle refinement of my mother's voice, that sublime sentiment—that grand passion—seemed almost grating and unpleasant. The dense language of my home, the elaborate syntax of my patents' distant, and to me, unknown lives, suddenly became vaguely unsettling.

The revelation that my mother even had a *Lieblingsschauspielerin*—a favorite actress—was a complete surprise and came on the evening after my father's funeral. My mother had never spoken of actors or movies before. As far as I knew, neither of my parents ever went to the movies, although I was allowed to do so. And except for one other occasion, the days leading up to my father's funeral were the only times I could remember my mother leaving the vicinity of our house. She had never gone shopping or out for a walk. I cannot recall her ever taking me to school. I never thought to question this behavior. I had simply accepted it as an aspect of her personality. It was never discussed or explained, and I was rather comforted by her generally quiet and steady presence in my childhood world.

I was only twelve at the time of my father's unexpected death and bewildered by my mother's strange disclosure. She had never been very talkative. But she had, on that exceptional night in my life, suddenly opened a hidden door and—I could not know it then—would permanently and just as abruptly close it again.

"I saw *The Great Love* maybe fifty times the year it premiered. That was the year I stayed with the Retters. Herr Retter took me to his theater, the Gloria Palace, whenever I was sad and needed to get away. I learned every song by heart." My mother smiled and caressed one slender hand with the other. "Sometimes I helped with the projector. I was very mechanical." Here my mother paused and frowned. "The Retters had a daughter my age. Ingrid had dark brown eyes and long black hair. She was a big chatterbox and caused a lot of trouble. *I* was the one with blue eyes and blond hair." My mother gently smoothed a lock of this same hair from her forehead, shook her head, and smiled again. "Of course, like most girls we dreamed of being actresses."

When my mother described the movie in which her favorite actress starred, and whose songs she had memorized, we were sitting together on the living room sofa. The last visitor, an old woman neighbor, had just left. My parents had kept mainly to themselves, and there had been few guests at the house after the funeral. Those who did make the visit included several neighbors, the old woman among them, and some business acquaintances who knew my father from his jewelry store. The old woman had silently helped my mother put away the food that had been set up on the dining room sideboard and then clean up the kitchen. Before she left she took my mother's hand: "I'm very sorry, dear. It's a terrible tragedy. But God is the true judge and we must learn to accept His will." My mother looked at her blankly and said, "Thank you."

Years later, when my mother herself was gravely ill, I took a leave from college to take care of her. She would not allow herself to be admitted to a hospital or permit strangers into the house. I asked her about the old woman. I wondered whatever became of her. My mother lifted her head off her pillow and gave me a surprised look. "Oh, no. There was never such a person that day."

"But there was, Mother. She was our neighbor. I even remember what she said—"

"No, you must be mistaken. And now, Joseph, I'm quite tired."

But I know I was not mistaken and the old woman really did exist. Recently, however, now that I am well into my forties, approaching the ages when my parents died, and I think back to this late exchange with my mother, I find myself increasingly alarmed. I can no longer conjure up a single one of the old woman's features. Did she have a long or short nose? What was the color of her eyes? How did she wear her hair? I recall only a sense of her frail, ghostly movements, the vague disruption of the still atmosphere of our house, and her parting words. The details of our house on that day I remember vividly—the carved oak sideboard in the dining room where the food had been set out on silver platters, the speckled green tiles on the kitchen floor over which the old woman passed, and the claret moiré fabric with which the living room sofa was upholstered.

"In *The Great Love* she played a beautiful singer named Hanna. Oma—whom you never met—was named Hanna, too." My mother had rarely referred to my grandparents except to say proudly that they had been *angesehene Leute*—highly educated and cultured people. Her father, she once told me, had composed art songs in the style of Hugo Wolf, and no doubt would have been famous had he not died, as she put it, *so vorzeitig*—so prematurely. "If you had been a girl, I would have certainly named you Hanna."

The night she told me about her favorite actress in her favorite movie, my mother never looked directly at me. Her eyes skimmed the top of my head and watched the pale blue walls of our living room as if she might be seeing the very same movie, projected there by memory's light. My initial unease at her elaborate reminiscence gave way to an odd comfort and excitement in hearing her talk to me at length as she might have with my father, even if she was in her own world. I had never before considered the mystery of my mother's youth and was now fascinated. I listened carefully and quietly.

While I was growing up, my parents' extreme personal reserve never seemed odd; rather, their conversations seemed dignified and appropriate. In their leisure they read books, or listened to records, mostly lieder and opera. We never went away on vacations. Often they spoke about my father's jewelry store. In the background I would hear references to "a wedding ring with six quadrillions" or "the young woman who bought the emerald pheasant brooch." Several nights a week my mother would go over the store receipts. She sat quietly at a small mahogany secretary in the den. A stack of papers would be piled neatly in front of her while she tapped her forehead with the eraser end of a pencil.

Somehow I grew up understanding that one did not ask questions of a personal nature, even to one's parents. I knew that surrounding every human being was a sacred wall of dignity and privacy. My parents never asked questions such as, "What are you thinking, Joseph?" or, "What did you do today?" They never entered my room without knocking. "*Joseph, darf ich eintreten?*" my mother would say if she needed to do any cleaning. As far as I could tell she never entered my room when I was out of the house.

And I am still taken aback, unsettled, observing people who talk too much, chatter, ask question after question.

My mother told the story of *The Great Love* in extensive detail. After her death, I would increasingly find myself reviewing in my mind's eye the scene of my mother's greatest confidence. When I tried to review this night in my mind, I would realize to my great dismay that I had forgotten some small detail, some tangential plot line my mother described, and with it, I felt, some irretrievable clue to her life. Sometimes I would experience physical symptoms when my memory failed me. I would break out in a sweat, breathe rapidly, or feel dizzy. And now, years later, the memory of my mother's description is further clouded by my persistent and pathetic attempts to patch up those gaps, to move through the doorway she had so briefly opened that evening.

The plot of *The Great Love* was—with its predictable twists and turns, period clichés, and movieland formulas—fairly simple. And it was of little interest to me at the time.

Paul, a handsome air force pilot on twenty-four hours' leave, attends one of Hanna's sold-out concerts in Berlin. That night, after the concert, during an air raid, fate brings them together in an underground shelter. They fall in love. But love is not easy in wartime. The next day, Paul had to go on a dangerous mission. Three weeks later, when he safely returns on furlough, they plan to marry right away, but an unexpected order comes in from the High Command. Paul must once again leave abruptly. Meanwhile Hanna, disappointed but still hopeful and understanding, goes on with her life and travels to Paris for her next concert.

"In Paris, Hanna stood onstage in the ballroom of a splendid palace, in front of hundreds of soldiers, many of whom were wounded." My mother sighed. "I kept thinking to myself, Did such places like that ballroom still exist in this crazy world? Yes. Yes. Of course they did! They must. It was an absolutely enchanting scene.

"Hanna wore a black velvet gown with a silver leaf embroidered near the top. Like so." My mother traced an arc across her own bust with her hand. "Hanna was so elegant, so charming, so warm. She stood onstage before a small orchestra. Her accompanist, a sweet older man, played the piano. She sang a wonderful song about how life had its ups and downs but in the end everything would turn out wonderful. And how she knew that one day her beloved, her soul mate, would return."

There were tears in my mother's eyes. I had never before seen my mother cry. She had not cried earlier that day at my father's small funeral, not had she cried when she came into my room the week before, her face very pale and drawn: "I have very bad news, Joseph. Papi was found dead in his store. We now must survive together."

I asked her only one question that night we sat together on the living room sofa.

"Did Father see it?"

My mother seemed startled by my interruption. "Oh, no. Papi was in a different hiding place. We weren't married yet." My mother dabbed her wet eyes with a handkerchief. The tears had stopped. "Papi was afraid to go outdoors to come to the theater. Someone might see him and catch him. But once when I was able to go to him, I told him about it. At first he was annoyed. He thought it all foolish, vulgar. Not something I should have been interested in. 'They are wicked people' he said. 'It's only a love story,' I said. Then Papi said he was sorry and listened, just to amuse me."

After my mother's death, on my first visit to Berlin, I watched *The Great Love* over and over, perhaps five times, all afternoon and evening, at a revival theater on the Kurfürstendamm. Each time I had the strange feeling that my mother was telling me the story as I watched it. Finally the manager came over to me and asked if something was the matter. I said I had come all the way from Canada to see this movie. He shook his head and walked away muttering. "*Noch ein verrückter Fan*—another crazy fan!"

After that a new memory emerged of my mother and her favorite actress in *The Great Love*. It was, I knew from the start, a false memory, but so insistent in nature that even now hardly a week goes by without its coming to mind as if it had actually happened.

In this false memory which has occurred to me ever since I first went to Berlin and saw *The Great Love* myself, my mother gets up from the sofa where she sat with me that night after my father's funeral. She stands up and begins to sing in the voice of her favorite actress. It is that woman's voice but darker and deeper, a voice that hovers between the Earth and the heavenly firmament, singing of miracles to be:

"*Ich weiss, es wird einmal ein Wunder geschehn. . .*
und ich weiss, dass wir uns wiedersehn!"

But in reality, my mother had been sitting the whole time. She never sang any lyrics. And I never in my life heard my mother sing.

Our house stood on a quiet street at the outskirts of town, and though modest in size, it was densely furnished with sofas and chairs, various mahogany and oak side tables, étagères, and lamps. Except for the kitchen, heavy draperies hung on the windows of every room, including the bedrooms. My mother kept the house meticulously clean. Though she never left the vicinity of the house, and had very little interaction with other people, she always dressed very elegantly, even lavishly. She subscribed to several fashion magazines to keep up with the latest styles. She ordered expensive fabrics from a store in Toronto and made her clothes herself.

Often when she was working in her sewing room she would call me over. "See, Joseph, this is a very fine silk, touch it. Feel its weight. Chinese silk is better than Indian. Please hold it out for me so I can see it better," or "This cotton comes from Egypt, the land of Nefertiti, the best cotton in the world."

My mother was also particular about her thick blond hair, which she brushed back from her high forehead and kept gently waved at the temples so it framed her oval face.

My father was always appreciative of my mother's efforts. "Ute, you are very beautiful tonight," or "How elegant you are, Ute." he would say when he came home from work.

"*Danke,* Albert."

My father did the household shopping on his way home from work. From time to time he brought my mother cosmetics, stockings, and even shoes.

Only once, before my father died, can I remember my mother leaving our house. One holiday. I believe it was Yom Kippur or Rosh Hashonah, when I was eight or nine, my father insisted we all go to the synagogue in town. I did not understand why, because we had never attended synagogue before and no one ever expressed an interest in doing so. I can still see my mother adjusting a small feathered hat atop her blond hair. The hat had a delicate transparent veil that hung in front of her eyes. Before we left the house, she glanced in the hallway mirror. She seemed pleased with her appearance. We drove into town for services. While we walked up the synagogue steps, my mother moved with an uncharacteristic awkwardness, constantly looking down at her shoes. I thought she was afraid of stumbling. At home my mother walked very erectly, her tall slender figure moving gracefully.

In the synagogue I stood between my parents and listened to the unfamiliar melancholy singing. I felt sad and bored. My mother leaned sideways and tugged discreetly on my father's sleeve. We moved out in single file from the crowded pew while the singing continued. Later, when we returned home, she looked at my father. She was pale and trembling.

"*Bitte, Albert, nie mehr.*"

"*Ja, Ute, nie mehr. Nie.*"

And we never did attend synagogue again.

When I asked her about that episode before she died, she said, "No. I never went into a synagogue, even as a child. We were never observant. Maybe you went with your father. Perhaps your father took you once. He was very nostalgic."

In my boyhood I began a beautiful and, I did not fully realize then, an extremely valuable gemstone collection. I stored my treasures in a velvet-lined leather case that I hid under my bed. This collection was gently but persistently encouraged by my father. Over time he presented me with many precious and semiprecious stones: an oval-cut ruby, a sapphire cabochon, a violet garnet. "For your birthday," he would say, or, "For your report card." My mother would nod and add, "You must always keep the pretty things Papi gives you. You can take them wherever you go."

"They are like having *Lösegeld*," my father once said.

"What?" I had never heard that word.

My mother looked sternly at my father.

"Oh, nothing," he said. Later I looked the word up. It meant ransom.

Often I would study my collection under the jeweler's loupe he had given me, which I kept on the desk in my bedroom. He had shown me how to scan a stone's surface and, in the case of a transparent stone, its depths. "A small flaw is a big tragedy if you're a jewel," he was fond of saying.

Once in elementary school, I came home and told my parents that my French teacher, Madame Dejarlais, thought I had an extraordinary gift for languages and that this might be useful in choosing a career for myself. She was right—after college I took a position in Toronto as a translator for a Canadian corporation that was expanding its business in Europe. My mother smiled pleasantly. She was sewing a hem on a dress.

My father said, "That is very good news, Joseph. We are happy to hear it."

My mother looked up from her work. "Yes, of course. We are very happy to hear it."

The next day my father gave me a two-carat marquise-cut emerald, the last gift I received from him. My mother said, "You must always keep the things Papi gives you."

After Paul safely fulfilled his mission, the one he was called to by the High Command, the one that postponed his marriage, he was given three weeks' leave. He traveled to Rome to surprise Hanna, who was rehearsing for her latest engagement. They were joyously reunited and decided to marry that very night. Suddenly, as they were making their plans, the phone rang. An officer friend asked him to help by joining a new and dangerous mission. This time it was not an order but a request. Paul instantly agreed to volunteer.

My mother's voice rose angrily as she described Hanna's reaction. "'Must you go *volunteer* and leave me just like that when we are about to marry! Without so much as an order! What about us? What about our marriage? Is that so unimportant? I cannot, I will not endure this any longer!'"

Then my mother's voice softened. She understood Paul's side as well. "Paul tried to reason with her. It was wartime and he had his responsibilities. 'And what is it you cannot endure,' he asked her, 'when so many awful things are happening in the world?'"

"But Hanna remained stubborn and so they broke off their engagement. Paul, dutifully, left on his mission. After he was gone. Hanna sat down and cried."

The morning after my father's funeral my mother knocked early on my bedroom door. *"Joseph, darf ich eintreten?"*

My mother was wearing a sky blue satin dress with long sleeves. There were white cuffs at her wrists and white buttons up the front of the dress. I remembered seeing the shimmering fabric when she was working on it in her sewing room, but I had never imagined the finished product. She appeared especially glamorous to me that day, like one of the models in the glossy magazines to which she subscribed.

"I will be back in the evening." She looked at me to see if I understood and then added. "I cannot sell Papi's store. He loved it too much."

I was puzzled, not because of the sudden and astonishing discarding of what clearly was some form of phobia. I never thought in such psychological terms when I was a child. I was puzzled mainly because it was three miles downtown to my father's store and my mother did not drive. I could not picture her, dressed in white-trimmed, sky blue satin, walking that distance, or for that matter, traveling on a bus, though it would have been simple to do so.

"I must go now, Joseph. The taxi is waiting."

For the next two years she went back and forth by taxi from our house to the store. She did not, as far as I knew, go anywhere else. I believe the store must have been for her an extension of our home. I took over from my father and did all the food shopping. My mother would give me a list with the brand names she preferred. Sometimes she asked me to buy certain cosmetics or stockings as my father had done for her. In her spare time she continued to order material from Toronto and make her own clothes.

My mother turned out to be a skilled businesswoman and was good with customers. She still sold jewelry as my father had, but she expanded her merchandise to include fine gifts, such as crystal and silver. Though at home she continued speaking to me in German, her English was much better than I had realized, and her accent diminished over the time she worked in the store. Occasionally I would catch her at home with her sewing, repeating some English word out loud until she was satisfied with her pronunciation. Once she caught me watching her. She smiled. "A good actress must adjust her accent for a new role."

My mother continued my father's custom of building up my gemstone collection. On the first anniversary of his death, she gave me a one-and-three-quarter-carat round-cut diamond. I examined it that night under my loupe. I scrutinized its brilliant surface table, the glittering facets of its crown and pavilion. Its depths were flawless and fine white. My mother asked if she could enter my room. She took the loupe and examined the diamond herself.

"Yes, it is really an excellent stone. You must keep it with all the things Papi gave you."

Sometimes after school or on Saturdays I helped my mother at the store. One day, near the second anniversary of my father's death, a short, dark-haired woman came into the store. No other customers were present. The woman wore expensive clothing, large sunglasses, and many rings on her fingers. She walked around the store, browsing. She looked at me, then my mother. My mother smiled. "May I help you, please?"

The woman answered in German. "Yes. Would you show me those bracelets?"

"*Natürlich.*" My mother leaned over to open the display counter.

The woman took off her sunglasses and glared at the blond hair on my mother's bent-over head. "Feuchtman," she whispered. "Feuchtman." It took me a moment to realize the woman was saying my mother's maiden name. My mother had rarely mentioned it. My mother looked up. She smiled. "*Wie, bitte?*" To this day I don't think my mother actually heard or understood that the woman had just called her name. Suddenly the woman whirled around, her scrawny arm outstretched, her fist slamming into my mother's jaw with surprising force. One of my mother's teeth flew out, clattered across the glass top of the display cabinet and then fell to the floor.

My mother stood up. Blood gleamed at the corner of her mouth. She was so startled that she did not even bring up a hand to feel the damage on her face.

"*Petzmaul! Verräterin!*" The woman spat at my mother. "Bitch! Traitor! You are worse than they were! The evil informer-girl is finally caught!"

The woman ran out of the store and disappeared. I heard a car speeding off but I was too shocked to run out and look for the license plate. I did not even move from where I was standing.

Finally my mother spoke. Her voice was altered because her lower jaw was now swollen. I could barely make out what she said. When she spoke she did not look directly at me. Her eyes skimmed the top of my head as they did the evening after my father's funeral, when she watched the pale blue walls of our living room and told me about her favorite actress in her favorite movie. She whispered.

"Oh, no. No, no. She is completely mistaken. I would never have worked for them even if they tortured me. I would never turn anyone in. How could I? . . . I had to do something to save your father. . . .No. No. I myself was hiding the whole time, first with the Retters. . ." She became silent. She wiped her mouth, then felt her jaw, opening and closing it slowly. She smoothed her blond hair back with both hands. She took in a deep breath and looked directly at me. "Well, no bones are broken. There is no need to see a doctor. You know I do not go to doctors. Why are you shaking?"

A week later she put the store up for sale.

According to city records, the Grunewald house, where my mother grew up, was destroyed during the war. Now, in its place, are pretty garden apartments with cobblestone trails meandering down to a small lake. The house of my mother's favorite movie actress in nearby Dahlem, across the street from a forest park, is now a retirement home.

A few years after my first visit, my company established a permanent office in Berlin. I requested a transfer. I thought of renting one of the garden apartments where my mother's house once stood, but none was available. Instead I found an apartment south of the Tiergarten and have lived here almost as long as my parents lived in Canada. At night, from my small balcony. I can see far across the lights of the Kurfürstendamm into the vast city. In *The Great Love*, Hanna had a balcony, too. In one scene she stands there with Paul looking out at the sparkling night sea of Berlin. "It is like a fairy tale," she says sighing.

"No," Paul answers her. "It is lovelier than a fairy tale."

I don't think it would be an exaggeration to say I have seen *The Great Love* more than fifty times. When I first moved to Berlin I would see it anytime it was playing at the revival houses, which was surprisingly often. Later, when it became available on video, I began watching it at home. I have also seen my mother's favorite actress in her other movies: *To New Shores, In the Open Air, Homeland*. But I found these other movies boring and never went to see any of them a second time.

My wife never asks me questions about this peculiar obsession of mine. She thinks only that I am a crazy fan. There are so many other people here who are fascinated with my mother's favorite actress. She is a great cult figure. If you go to the clubs you are bound to find someone dressed up like her, singing her songs. "Could Love Be a Sin?" or "My Life for Love." My wife is glad I have not come to that. *"Ich bin sehr dankbar dafür!"* she says. I am thankful for other things. Though we have now lived together for many years, she does not ask me about my family, nor do I ask about hers. I like to think of our life together as in the present, so long as the present maintains its own sense of privacy. Even in *The Great Love*, Paul and Hanna do not ask each other questions of a personal nature.

Lately, now that I am approaching the ages of my parents' premature deaths, when I recall my mother on the night of my father's funeral. I see us sitting on the claret moiré sofa as *The Great Love* is projected on the pale blue walls of our living room. We are watching it together. My mother takes my hand and smiles. She is enjoying herself so much and she hopes I am, too.

After Hanna and Paul break up. Paul leaves on his new mission, the dangerous mission for which he has nobly volunteered. Hanna remains in Rome rehearsing for her big concert.

Her concert is, of course, an amazing success. As she walks triumphantly offstage, she is handed a telegram. "Captain Paul Wendland has been wounded but only slightly. He is in an infirmary in the mountains." As Hanna returns to the stage and takes her bow, she whispers to her accompanist that she must leave that very night.

"Hanna, when will you return?" he asks sadly, for he is obviously in love with her, too.

"*Nie.*"

My mother recited this "Never" with the same restrained tone of conviction, the precise note of love and hope that I later witnessed each time I watched her favorite actress in her favorite movie.

Finally Hanna arrives at an infirmary somewhere in the Alps. Snow-covered mountain peaks are all around. She rushes over to Paul, who is sitting on the terrace, one arm in a sling. "Perhaps, Hanna, we can try again to get married." He laughingly points to his bandaged arm. "This time I really have three weeks' sick leave!"

Hanna smiles. She takes his hand. "And after the three weeks are over?"

Paul looks up and she looks up, too. Overhead, the sky is so wide and breathtaking. Here and there, glorious shafts of sunlight break through the billowing clouds. And suddenly, in the distance, a squadron of planes appears. And there, of course, to those wondrous heavens, Paul must return. That is where his duty lies.

"Paul turned and looked into Hanna's eyes," my mother told me. "Their faces were so beautiful, so full of happiness, it gave me goose bumps. And then Hanna nodded. Yes. Yes. She would marry him."

And then my mother turned and looked directly at me for the first time on that extraordinary night in my life. I trembled ever so slightly at the unbearable tenderness of her look. "If I had been them," my mother said, rising from the sofa. "I would gladly have sacrificed all of heaven for love."

Suggestions for Discussion

1. Based on the clues given in the story, how might one reconstruct the mother's past in Nazi Germany and the ethical dilemma she faced?

2. What does the film *Die Grosse Liebe* ("The Great Love") mean to the narrator, and what does it mean to his mother?

3. Stollman withholds certain information in the story. For example, he leaves passages in German untranslated and does not identify the Swedish Zarah Leander as the mother's favorite actress. What effect do these omissions have on the story and the reader?

Suggestion for Writing

Read the accompanying work of literary criticism on *Die Grosse Liebe* by Ursula Melendi. What meaning does she find in the story, and how does her interpretation compare with yours?

Images of Zarah Leander, collage with colored pencil, artist unknown. ©2005 Paul
Seller/Filmmuseum, Potsdam.

URSULA MELENDI

All of Heaven for Love

Born and raised in Bielefeld, Germany, Ursula Melendi earned a master's degree in English from the College of Staten Island, CUNY, as a mature student. She is a member of three book clubs and a former director of the United States Soccer Federation. The following essay is her interpretative analysis of Aryeh Lev Stollman's *Die Grosse Liebe.*

On the eve of his father's funeral service, twelve-year-old Joseph experiences a solitary moment when his mother's elevated emotions unexpectedly open a window to her previously well-guarded past. The reality of death and loss is temporarily replaced by the glow of his mother's young adult memories of her favorite romantic movie. "I saw *The Great Love* maybe fifty times the year it premiered," she admits with tear-filled eyes. Although his mother's unconventional behavior and her sudden emotional outpour are somewhat unsettling to Joseph, he awakens to a new level of understanding by gaining insight into the formerly unexplored chasms of her young mind.

Perhaps inspired by the fictional romance between a famous singer and a Luftwaffe pilot during World War II, Aryeh Lev Stollman's *Die Grosse Liebe** intricately weaves together places, events and experiences and ties the present to the past in a most touching and thought-provoking story. We are not exposed to the entire plot at one time, but gather bits and pieces of information through intermittent recollections, reflections and experiences of his characters. Stollman does not project a particular point of view, but lets the reader delve into the psyche of his characters and draw conclusions.

"*The Great Love* was her best movie. I felt so happy watching it," Joseph's mother reveals, speaking of the movie's heroine. It is not surprising that Ute's strong emotional attachment to her favorite love story and its glamorous female star was formed during a time when her immediate world was dominated by the heart-break of persecution and separation from loved ones.

Ute's most admirable character trait would most certainly be her ability to adjust to the changing demands of the world around her. "Herr Retter took me to his theater. . .whenever I was sad and needed to get away," she

---

*"Die Grosse Liebe" is part of a collection of short stories entitled *The Dialogues of Time and Entropy* (New York: Riverhead Books, 2003) 43–62.

confides. Living in hiding and being exposed to the overwhelming anxiety and fear generated by the senselessness of the Nazi movement fostered a sense of hopelessness and lethargy in most people; Ute, however, turns to and is empowered by the realm of illusion and escapist dreams. "Like most girls, we dreamed of being actresses," she admits to her son. Whether it is the romance between the movie's protagonists, Hanna and Paul, her admiration for the popular female singer, her rebellion against confining forces, or all of these, she is able to create another, more congenial world within her own narrow and precarious existence.

At a later date, we find Ute leading a seemingly conventional life as a wife and mother in Ontario, where her husband, Alfred, maintains a jewelry business. However, a closer look from the periphery of her new existence reveals her emotional and physical disassociation from the outside world. The windows of all rooms are covered with "heavy draperies," and she never ventures beyond the confines of her home, leaving her husband to shop for household items, "cosmetics, stockings, and even shoes."

While Joseph distinctly remembers having attended at least one partial Holy Day service with his parents at the local synagogue, his mother gently denies ever having had any connection to her religion. We wonder if her denial is a conscious deep-rooted fear of persecution or an unconscious suppression of conflicts within. Perhaps Ute has been immersed in her estrangement from the outside world so deeply and for so long that it has become a permanent mindset. Is her home another hiding place, a refuge and a place of protection from the evils of the outside world? Whatever the case may be, her surroundings are not characterized by melancholy, sadness or passive resignation, but by quiet harmony and creativity. Ute's homemaking talents flourish in her self-imposed isolation, and she dresses "elegantly, even lavishly" in the latest fashions which are hand-tailored by her and evoke her husband's praise and admiration.

Given Ute's flexible nature, it is not surprising that, after Alfred's sudden and unexpected death, she ventures out of her home to assume the responsibility of continuing her husband's business. Adversity, negative influences and years of detachment have not stifled her self confidence and her determination to adapt to her changed circumstances. "A good actress must adjust her accent for a new role," she points out when Joseph observes her trying to improve her English pronunciation.

Revealing untapped talents in not only maintaining her business but also in expanding it, Ute commutes back and forth to the store until a mysterious woman with a strong desire to humiliate and an almost murderous hatred enters her flourishing business one day, physically attacks her and unmasks her as a traitor.

We are unprepared for a disclosure of this nature, but recall that Mr. Retter's daughter, "a big chatterbox" who "caused a lot of trouble," had "dark brown eyes and long black hair," whereas Ute's blue eyes and blonde hair were considered more desirable Aryan traits. Is there a connection between Ingrid with her long black hair and the aggressive dark-haired woman? If the intruder's accusation is true, we wonder if Ute's involvement consisted of a single ill-considered act or a series of betrayals, and if she participated willingly or unwillingly.

The agressor addresses Joseph's mother as "Feuchtman," her maiden name; "feucht" meaning damp, neither wet nor dry, but something in between. Her maiden name could be indicative of a human being divided within herself. Ute says, "I would never turn anyone in," yet, in the same breath, "I had to do something to save your father."

We are reminded that both, Alfred and Ute, placed particular emphasis on Joseph's collection of precious stones. "You must always keep the pretty things Papi gives you. You can take them wherever you go," his mother admonished him as a youngster, referring to diamonds, rubies and emeralds as symbols of power, ransom money, if necessary. Was Ute able to extricate herself or her future husband from a life-threatening situation by implicating others or by using the bargaining power of precious jewels?

It is impossible to envision anyone's reaction to threatening circumstances; nevertheless, it is somewhat disconcerting to draw a connection between the individual accused of having incriminated her own kind and the woman who so tenderly shared her treasured memories. "If I had been them, I would gladly have sacrificed all of heaven for love," Ute admits longingly, referring to the young lovers of her favorite romance. Based on her and Alfred's reserved external demeanor we surmise that their approach to romance was sober, even unemotional perhaps. Alfred considered *Die Grosse Liebe* unconventional and felt it offended his sense of propriety. Ute has succumbed to conventional expectations and abandoned her romantic dreams in the process. Given the nature of her confinement as a young woman, we assume that she was first and foremost concerned with freedom and safety, finding contentment in a marriage based on respect rather than emotion, on commitment instead of passion. Her attitude is remarkable, however, as she has adjusted with grace and dignity to that which cannot be changed.

Joseph's passion for repeatedly watching *Die Grosse Liebe* might be interpreted as an obsession; in fact, he is labeled "another crazy fan" by the manager of a Berlin movie theater. For him, however, the memory of that spark of extraordinary emotion on his mother's part becomes a cherished reminiscence. He clings to the hours of shared confidence, of momentary recognition and unexpected interaction and is enveloped by the comfortable fuzziness of that experience which also serves as a mechanism to cloud his reality. He wavers between reality and illusion and both become intertwined when, in his mind's eye, he perceives his mother as the movie star, even hears her "sing in the voice of her favorite actress." Like Ute, he hoards his precious memory like a treasured object and keeps it hidden even from his wife who is an integral part of his life.

Aryeh Stollman's technique can be compared to that of a stone mason who slowly and carefully places building block upon building block until the desired effect has been achieved. His occasional use of German, always translated, sets his characters apart and adds to their uniqueness, making them come alive as they emerge from the world around them. This technique has also been employed by the author in his earlier novel *The Far Euphrates* (1997). Stollman skillfully weaves fragments of information into the narrative and into his characters' dialogues, especially Ute's. *Die Grosse Liebe* evokes a stream of reactions and questions which leave us with powerful impressions.

Suggestions for Discussion

1. What is the central thesis of this essay?

2. How does Melendi construct and organize her argument?

3. How can studying this essay teach a student to write more effectively?

Suggestions for Writing

1. Write your own essay in response to *Die Grosse Liebe.*

2. Using Melendi's work as a model, write an essay about another work of fiction from *The Conscious Reader.*

PERSONAL REMINISCENCES

～～～～～

THOMAS LYNCH

The Way We Are

Thomas Lynch (b. 1948) is a poet, essayist, and a funeral director from Milford, MI. He has written three collections of poetry *(Skating with Heather Grace, Grimalkin & Other Poems,* and *Still Life in Milford),* as well as *The Undertaking* (1997), *Bodies in Motion and at Rest* (2000), and *Booking Passage: We Irish and Americans* (2005). Lynch has also contributed essays and poems to the *Los Angeles Times,* the *New York Times, Esquire, Newsweek, Harper's,* the *New Yorker,* and other publications. In the excerpt that follows, Lynch works to free his son from the curse of alcoholism and wrestles with the limits of his power as a father to bring his own child peace of mind.

Which, godhelpus, maybe is the way my son is now—frightened and angry, stuck between egomania and inferiority complex, sick and tired, dead drunk. If his thirst is like mine he won't be able to talk his way out of it, think his way out of it, read or write or run his way out of it, lie or cheat or buy his way out of it. The only victory is in an admission of defeat. The only weapon is surrender.

Still, the father in me—the take-charge, I'll handle it, you can count on me, master of our destiny fellow—wants to fix it for him. Protecting and providing, that's what dads do. I've always been pretty good at scripts and I've got one for him with a happy ending if only he'll just learn the lines by heart and do exactly what I tell him to do.

Years back—it was the autumn of his freshman year in high school—when his grades went to hell and his smile disappeared and the music in our house got dark, I took him out of school one morning and said I was taking him to find out what the matter was. I said I thought there must be something very wrong to account for all the changes I could see. Maybe a tumor or a loose screw or maybe, because it ran in our family, drink and drugs and addictions. I told him we wouldn't quit until we found out what accounted for the darkness that had descended on his life and times. No diagnostic stone would be unturned.

So we started with the drug and alcohol assessment, which turned up, unremarkably, positive. He was fourteen and trying anything that came his way. So I explained how it was like diabetes or an allergy and he should know that he was in danger because of his family history. A beer for him, a joint, whatever pills or powders were going round, might do more damage than

116

"experimenting"—which is what we parents tell ourselves our sons and daughters are always doing.

By midwinter things had gone from bad to worse. I tried my best to ignore the obvious—his lackluster grades, the long hours in his room, the distance he began to keep, the smell of alcohol that was always on him. One night he came home besotted and muddy. He had passed out in the park, in a puddle. How he kept from drowning, how he crawled home, remains a mystery. The next morning I took him to a treatment center that one of my brothers had been to before. They took him in for thirteen days, detoxed him, told him that he was alcoholic, and told us he should get long-term care, that his alcoholism was chronic, acute and full-blown. There would be no cure, but with treatment he might get into a pattern of recovery that would allow him to live without using in a using world. We all wept. Inquiries were made. An adolescent treatment center was found. It was at a hospital on the south side of Cleveland and was named for a saint I'd never heard of before. My son said if I made him go he'd kill himself. There was a calm in his voice that said he wasn't bluffing. I said he was killing himself already. I said I'd buried lots of boys for lots of fathers. I said if I was going to have to be like those poor hollow men, standing in the funeral home with my darling son in a casket, while neighbors and friends and family gathered to say they wished there was something they could say or do, I told him, if he was going to be dead either way, at least he wouldn't die of my denial, my ignorance, my unwillingness to deal with the way we are. I said if he killed himself I would miss him terribly, I would never forget him and always love him and I'd hate to outlive him but I'd survive. And I'd call someone before I'd drink about it.

Calling this bet broke something inside.

Every Friday for three months I'd drive down and get him, bring him home for two nights and take him back Sunday in the afternoon. The turkey vultures and red-tailed hawks hovering over the Ohio Turnpike are all I remember of those travels now. It was a summer lost to our disease. Everywhere I looked was the shadow of death. But he survived it and came home and got a sponsor and started going to AA meetings and the darkness seemed to lift from him. His grades were good, his music improved, he was painting, writing, smiling again. He started dating. For all of a year he went on like this and I got to thinking it had all been worth it, the driving and the money and all the madness, because he was fixed, better, thriving again. He was living the life he was supposed to live. So when the old signs started up again I didn't see them. I didn't want to see them. I'd quit looking. I kept wanting to see him according to the script I'd written in which all these demons were behind him, before he had anything more to lose.

It was halfway through his third year of high school when I told him I couldn't ignore the obvious anymore. I couldn't live with a using alcoholic. It was making me crazy, all the pretense and worry. I asked him to go back into treatment, or take up an outpatient program, or return to his AA meetings, anything besides relapsing again. He refused. I told him I couldn't live with him. He called his mother. She came and got him.

In the best of all cases, he would have had to move to her side of the state, lose his drinking buddies, find a new school and new buyers and suppliers, pay the price for his drinking on demand. Instead, his mother got him an apartment here in town so he could stay in the same school, hang out at the old haunts and have fewer of the parental hoops to jump through.

It is nearly impossible for any divorced parent to bypass the opportunity to save a child from the other parent. Rescue is what parents are good at. And if a son or daughter needs rescuing from the same asshole that you couldn't live with, well, who's to blame them? Of course, the children pay dearly for such second opinions, in discipline avoided, diluted rules, old wars and old divisions redeclared. By the time most parents have evolved beyond such temptations, their children are married and parents on their own.

One night in midwinter I found him passed out in a snowbank on Main Street. He was drunk, frozen, full of remorse, mumbling things like "You shouldn't have to see me like this." I called his mother and said she could come and get him. She took him to the hospital because we didn't know what he might have taken. Or if he had frostbite. Or if his shivering was a seizure. When the emergency room pronounced him out of danger, she called the number my wife had given her. It was another treatment center. She buckled on her courage and took him there.

He spent twelve days in that drunk tank. He came out and returned more or less immediately to his relapse, only this time he tried to "manage" it better. His mother, wanting to be helpful, hopeful, trusting, because she loves him, signed for his driver's license and bought him a car. He got picked up for stealing wine from the grocer's, busted for possession of beer in the park, lost one job and then another, dented the car in a parking lot. Otherwise we saw little of him. The high school gave him a diploma. He lost his driver's license and got a year's probation.

On the strength of his portfolio he got admitted to a posh art school, and because I wanted badly to believe, because I wanted badly to say, in spite of everything I knew to the contrary, maybe talent and promise and art could overcome disease, maybe he had outgrown it, I paid his tuition, room and board, and watched and waited and said my prayers. One weekend he got picked up for driving drunk without a valid license and spent the night in jail. His grades at first were not great and then they disappeared. He spent another weekend in jail for his crimes and got another year's probation.

When he asked to move home this summer from the dormitory at the art school I said I would not live with a using drunk. He said he understood. That's the way we talk. I couldn't say I wouldn't live with him. He couldn't say he wouldn't drink again.

In the space between what we didn't say, my stupid hope and his sickness flourished. I wanted to remember him the way he was. And wanting it so bad, I welcomed him, half-hoping some of the lost months of his lost years would return. But they are gone and the summer has gone from bad to worse. He's tried so hard to keep from being a bother. He tries to come home after we've gone to bed. Some nights he calls and says he's staying with friends and some nights he falls asleep on the couch downstairs. He holds his breath and kisses us. He says he loves us. He really doesn't want me to worry. He doesn't want to bother me with his drinking. He doesn't want to disturb my remembrances and I want to remember the way he was and I know he wouldn't want people seeing him like this because really that's not him anymore, there on the couch, at four-thirty in the early morning, neither sleeping nor dead but somewhere in between with no clear indication of which way he's going.

Putting him out of my house is like sending a child to chemotherapy. It hurts so bad to think I cannot save him, protect him, keep him out of harm's way, shield him from pain. What good are fathers if not for these things? Why can't he be a boy again, safe from these perils and disasters? Lately I'm always on the brink of breaking. But remembering the way he was begins by dealing with the way he is, which is sick, sick to death, with something that tells him he's "not so bad"—that jail and joblessness and loneliness and blackouts are all within the "normal" range. His thirst puts him utterly beyond my protection but never outside the loop of my love. If he is going to die on a couch some night, of alcohol poisoning or from choking on his own puke, or burned up from a cigarette he passed out smoking; or if he drives his car into a bridge abutment or over some edge from which there is no return; or if he gets so crazy with pain and fear he puts a pistol in his mouth, Oh my God, the best I can manage is not my couch, not my car, not my pistol, Oh my God. If I cannot save him, I will not help him die, or welcome his killer in my home.

What I've learned from my sobriety, from the men and women who keep me sober, is how to pray. Blind drunks who get sober get a kind of blind faith—not so much a vision of who God is, but who God isn't, namely me.

When I was a child all of my prayers sounded like "Gimme, Gimme." I wanted a Jerry Mahoney puppet, to fly like Superman, and for my brothers and sisters to be adopted by other kindly parents and leave me and my mother and father alone. I got none of these things. These prayers were never answered.

When I was my son's age, I'd always begin with "Show me, Lord." I wanted a sign. I wanted God to prove Himself or Herself or Itself to me. In this I was a typical youth, full of outrage and arrogance and bravado. Nothing ever happened. I never saw a statue move or lightning strike or heard any voices that I couldn't account for. The ones I prayed to be blighted thrived. The proofs I prayed for never appeared. None of these prayers were ever answered.

For years, twenty of them anyway, as a new husband, new parent, new funeral director in town, as a social drinker and a working poet, I'd pray, albeit infrequently, "Why me, God?" The more I drank, the more I prayed it. Why do I have to work harder, longer, for less thanks or wages? Why does that magazine publish only brunettes or professors or free verse or the famous? Why can't I sleep in or get a break or win the lotto? Why would any woman leave a man like me? And when my inventory of "why me's" was exhausted, I would ask on behalf of my fellow man. Why did cars crash, planes fall out of the sky, bad things happen to good people? Why, if Anyone's in charge, did children die? Or folks go homeless? Or others get away with murder? I was carping daily, a victim of my all too often self-inflicted wounds. The silence out of heaven to these questions was real. Why wasn't God listening? I wanted to know. And before I'd agree to step one foot in heaven, I had a list of things I wanted explanations for.

There's a reason we are given two ears and one mouth.

Someone told me that I should just say "Thanks," and that all my prayers should begin that way and never stray far from the notion that life was a gift to be grateful for. I began by giving thanks for my family, for the blessings to my household, the gifts of my children. Then the daylight and the nightfall and the weather. Then the kindness you could see in humankind, their foibles and their tender mercies. I could even be grateful for the ex-wife, the tax man, the gobshites who run the world and ruin everything. The more I mouthed my thanks for them, the less they bothered me. There's another thing to be thankful for. I could be thankful even for this awful illness—cunning, baffling and powerful—that has taught me to weep and laugh out loud and better and for real. And thankful that, of all the fatal diseases my son might have gotten, he got one for which there is this little sliver of a hope that if he surrenders, he'll survive. Whatever happens, God will take care of him.

And every time I say it, the prayer gets answered. Someone, out of the blue, every day—maybe my wife or someone at the office or the guy in the line at the airport or something in a letter that came in the mail, or something in the lives of my sons or daughter—someone gives out with a sign or wonder in the voice of God, in some other voice than mine, to answer my prayer. Every day, every time, never fails, if I just say "Thanks," I'll get the answer, before the darkness comes—"You're welcome," it says. "You're welcome."

Suggestions for Discussion

1. What does Lynch's history with alcoholism teach him about his son's battle with the sickness?

2. How does this piece explore the human capacity for both denial and acceptance?

3. How does Lynch's relationship to God affect his relationship with his son?

Suggestion for Writing

Have you ever been presented with an insolvable problem? How have you dealt with your powerlessness in this instance? Explain.

JUDITH ORTIZ COFER

Casa: A Partial Remembrance of a Puerto Rican Childhood

Judith Ortiz Cofer (b. 1952) is a native of Puerto Rico who immigrated to the United States as a small child. Educated in Florida and Georgia, where she still resides, she attended Oxford University as a Scholar of the English Speaking Union, and participated in the prestigious Bread Loaf Writers' Conference at Middlebury College. A teacher of creative writing at the university level, she has received several awards for her poetry, including grants from the Witter Bynner Foundation and the National Endowment for the Arts. Her publications include *The Line of the Sun* (1989), *Silent Dancing* (1990), *The Year of Our Revolution* (1998), *Woman in Front of the Sun: On Becoming a Writer* (2000), and *The Meaning of Consuelo* (2003). In this selection, published in 1990, she shows the reader how knowledge, of a kind not found in books, is passed from generation to generation through the medium of storytelling.

At three or four o'clock in the afternoon, the hour of *café con leche,* the women of my family gathered in Mamá's living room to speak of important things and retell familiar stories meant to be overheard by us young girls, their daughters. In Mamá's house (everyone called my grandmother Mamá) was a large parlor built by my grandfather to his wife's exact specifications so that it was always cool, facing away from the sun. The doorway was on the side of the house so no one could walk directly into her living room. First they had to take a little stroll through and around her beautiful garden where prize-winning orchids grew in the trunk of an ancient tree she had hollowed out for that purpose. This room was furnished with several mahogany rocking chairs, acquired at the births of her children, and one intricately carved rocker that had passed down to Mamá at the death of her own mother.

It was on these rockers that my mother, her sisters, and my grandmother sat on these afternoons of my childhood to tell their stories, teaching each other, and my cousin and me, what it was like to be a woman, more specifically, a Puerto Rican woman. They talked about life on the island, and life in *Los Nueva Yores,* their way of referring to the United States from New York City to California: the other place, not home, all the same. They told real-life stories though, as I later learned, always embellishing them with a little or a lot of dramatic detail. And they told *cuentos,* the morality and cautionary tales told by the women in our family for generations: stories that became a part of my subconscious as I grew up in two worlds, the tropical island and the cold city, and that would later surface in my dreams and in my poetry.

One of these tales was about the woman who was left at the altar. Mamá liked to tell that one with histrionic intensity. I remember the rise and fall of her voice, the sighs, and her constantly gesturing hands, like two birds swooping through her words. This particular story usually would come up in a conversation as a result of someone mentioning a forthcoming engagement or wedding. The first time I remember hearing it, I was sitting on the floor at Mamá's feet, pretending to read a comic book. I may have been eleven or twelve years old, at that difficult age when a girl was no longer a child who could be ordered to leave the room if the women wanted freedom to take their talk into forbidden zones, nor really old enough to be considered a part of their conclave. I could only sit quietly, pretending to be in another world, while absorbing it all in a sort of unspoken agreement of my status as silent auditor. On this day, Mamá had taken my long, tangled mane of hair into her ever-busy hands. Without looking down at me and with no interruption of her flow of words, she began braiding my hair, working at it with the quickness and determination that characterized all her actions. My mother was watching us impassively from her rocker across the room. On her lips played a little ironic smile. I would never sit still for *her* ministrations, but even then, I instinctively knew that she did not possess Mamá's matriarchal power to command and keep everyone's attention. This was never more evident than in the spell she cast when telling a story.

"It is not like it used to be when I was a girl," Mamá announced. "Then, a man could leave a girl standing at the church altar with a bouquet of fresh flowers in her hands and disappear off the face of the earth. No way to track him down if he was from another town. He could be a married man, with maybe even two or three families all over the island. There was no way to know. And there were men who did this. Hombres with the devil in their flesh who would come to a pueblo, like this one, take a job at one of the haciendas, never meaning to stay, only to have a good time and to seduce the women."

The whole time she was speaking, Mamá would be weaving my hair into a flat plait that required pulling apart the two sections of hair with little jerks that made my eyes water; but knowing how grandmother detested whining and *boba* (sissy) tears, as she called them, I just sat up as straight and stiff as I did at La Escuela San Jose, where the nuns enforced good posture with a flexible plastic ruler they bounced off of slumped shoulders and heads. As Mamá's story progressed, I noticed how my young Aunt Laura lowered her eyes, refusing to meet Mamá's meaningful gaze. Laura was seventeen, in her last year of high school, and already engaged to a boy from another town who had staked his claim with a tiny diamond ring, then left for Los Nueva Yores to make his fortune. They were planning to get married in a year.

Mamá had expressed serious doubts that the wedding would ever take place. In Mamá's eyes, a man set free without a legal contract was a man lost. She believed that marriage was not something men desired, but simply the price they had to pay for the privilege of children and, of course, for what no decent (synonymous with "smart") woman would give away for free.

"María La Loca was only seventeen when it happened to her." I listened closely at the mention of this name. María was a town character, a fat middle-aged woman who lived with her old mother on the outskirts of town. She was to be seen around the pueblo delivering the meat pies the two women made for a living. The most peculiar thing about María, in my eyes, was that she walked and moved like a little girl though she had the thick body and wrinkled face of an old woman. She would swing her hips in an exaggerated, clownish way, and sometimes even hop and skip up to someone's house. She spoke to no one. Even if you asked her a question, she would just look at you and smile, showing her yellow teeth. But I had heard that if you got close enough, you could hear her humming a tune without words. The kids yelled out nasty things at her, calling her La Loca, and the men who hung out at the bodega playing dominoes sometimes whistled mockingly as she passed by with her funny, outlandish walk. But María seemed impervious to it all, carrying her basket of *pasteles* like a grotesque Little Red Riding Hood through the forest.

María La Loca interested me, as did all the eccentrics and crazies of our pueblo. Their weirdness was a measuring stick I used in my serious quest for a definition of normal. As a Navy brat shuttling between New Jersey and the pueblo, I was constantly made to feel like an oddball by my peers, who made fun of my two-way accent: a Spanish accent when I spoke English, and when I spoke Spanish I was told that I sounded like a *Gringa*. Being the outsider had already turned my brother and me into cultural chameleons. We developed early on the ability to blend into a crowd, to sit and read quietly in a fifth story apartment building for days and days when it was too bitterly cold to play outside, or, set free, to run wild in Mamá's realm, where she took charge of our lives, releasing Mother for a while from the intense fear for our safety that our father's absences instilled in her. In order to keep us from harm when Father was away, Mother kept us under strict surveillance. She even walked us to and from Public School No. 11, which we attended during the months we lived in Paterson, New Jersey, our home base in the states. Mamá freed all three of us like pigeons from a cage. I saw her as my liberator and my model. Her stories were parables from which to glean the *Truth*.

"María La Loca was once a beautiful girl. Everyone thought she would marry the Méndez boy." As everyone knew, Rogelio Méndez was the richest man in town. "But," Mamá continued, knitting my hair with the same intensity she was putting into her story, "this *macho* made a fool out of her and ruined her life." She paused for the effect of her use of the word "macho," which at that time had not yet become a popular epithet for an unliberated man. This word had for us the crude and comical connotation of "male of the species," stud; a *macho* was what you put in a pen to increase your stock.

I peeked over my comic book at my mother. She too was under Mamá's spell, smiling conspiratorially at this little swipe at men. She was safe from Mamá's contempt in this area. Married at an early age, an unspotted lamb, she had been accepted by a good family of strict Spaniards whose name was old and respected, though their fortune had been lost long before my birth. In a rocker Papá had painted sky blue sat Mamá's oldest child, Aunt Nena. Mother of three children, stepmother of two more, she was a quiet woman who liked books but had married an ignorant and abusive widower whose main interest in life was accumulating wealth. He too was in the mainland working on his dream of returning home rich and triumphant to buy the *finca* of his dreams. She was waiting for him to send for her. She would leave her children with Mamá for several years while the two of them slaved away in factories. He would one day be a rich man, and she a sadder woman. Even now her life-light was dimming. She spoke little, an aberration in Mamá's house, and she read avidly, as if storing up spiritual food for the long winters that awaited her in Los Nueva Yores without her family. But even Aunt Nena came alive to Mamá's words, rocking gently, her hands over a thick book in her lap.

Her daughter, my cousin Sara, played jacks by herself on the tile porch outside the room where we sat. She was a year older than I. We shared a bed and all our family's secrets. Collaborators in search of answers, Sara and I discussed everything we heard the women say, trying to fit it all together like a puzzle that, once assembled, would reveal life's mysteries to us. Though she and I still enjoyed taking part in boys' games—chase, volleyball, and even *vaqueros,* the island version of cowboys and Indians involving cap-gun battles and violent shoot-outs under the mango tree in Mamá's backyard—we loved best the quiet hours in the afternoon when the men were still at work, and the boys had gone to play serious baseball at the park. Then Mamá's house belonged only to us women. The aroma of coffee perking in the kitchen, the mesmerizing creaks and groans of the rockers, and the women telling their lives in *cuentos* are forever woven into the fabric of my imagination, braided like my hair that day I felt my grandmother's hands teaching me about strength, her voice convincing me of the power of storytelling.

That day Mamá told how the beautiful María had fallen prey to a man whose name was never the same in subsequent versions of the story; it was Juan one time, José, Rafael, Diego, another. We understood that neither the name nor any of the *facts* were important, only that a woman had allowed love to defeat her. Mamá put each of us in María's place by describing her wedding dress in loving detail: how she looked like a princess in her lace as she waited at the altar. Then, as Mamá approached the tragic denouement of her story, I was distracted by the sound of my Aunt Laura's violent rocking. She seemed on the verge of tears. She knew the fable was intended for her. That week she was going to have her wedding gown fitted, though no firm date had been set for the marriage. Mamá ignored Laura's obvious discomfort, digging out a ribbon from the sewing basket she kept by her rocker while describing María's long illness, "a fever that would not break for days." She spoke of a mother's despair: "that woman climbed the church steps on her knees every morning, wore only black as a *promesa* to the Holy Virgin in exchange for her daughter's health." By the time María returned from her honeymoon with death, she was ravished, no longer young or sane. "As you can see, she is almost as old as her mother already," Mamá lamented while tying the ribbon to the ends of my hair, pulling it back with such force that I just knew I would never be able to close my eyes completely again.

"That María's getting crazier every day." Mamá's voice would take a lighter tone now, expressing satisfaction, either for the perfection of my braid, or for a story well told—it was hard to tell. "You know that tune María is always humming?" Carried away by her enthusiasm, I tried to nod, but Mamá still had me pinned between her knees.

"Well, that's the wedding march." Surprising us all, Mamá sang out, "Da, da, dara...da, da, dara." Then lifting me off the floor by my skinny shoulders, she would lead me around the room in an impromptu waltz— another session ending with the laughter of women, all of us caught up in the infectious joke of our lives.

Suggestions for Discussion

Relate each of the following quotations to the selection you have just read.

1. "It was on these rockers that my mother, her sisters, and my grandmother sat on these afternoons of my childhood to tell their stories, teaching each other, and my cousin and me, what it was like to be a woman, more specifically, a Puerto Rican woman."

2. "Collaborators in search of answers, Sara and I discussed everything we heard the women say, trying to fit it all together like a puzzle that, once assembled, would reveal life's mysteries to us."

3. "We understood that neither the name nor any of the *facts* were important, only that a woman had allowed love to defeat her."

Suggestions for Writing

1. Children learn much of their culture from eavesdropping on the adult world. Describe a time when you had this experience.

2. Cofer distinguishes between "facts" and "themes." Truth in storytelling has far more to do with one than the other. Write a story in which this is manifest.

ESSAYS

THE KORAN

Sura 12. Joseph

Muslim religious tradition holds that the Koran is the infallible Word of God chronicled by the prophet Mohammed, who lived between 570 and 632 A.D. The Koran and its *surahs,* revealed to Mohammed by the Angel Gabriel, remains the cornerstone of the Arab way of life to this day. The following *surah,* the twelfth in the series, tells the story of Joseph, who is a figure of religious significance to the Christian and Jewish faiths as well as an important personage in the Muslim faith.

[MECCA]

In the Name of God, the Compassionate, the Merciful

Alif lām rā. These are the verses of the Glorious Book. We have revealed the Koran in the Arabic tongue so that you may grow in understanding.

In revealing this Koran We will recount to you the best of narratives, though before it you were heedless.

Joseph said to his father: "Father, I dreamt of eleven stars and the sun and the moon; I saw them prostrate themselves before me."

"My son," he replied, "say nothing of this dream to your brothers, lest they plot evil against you: Satan is the sworn enemy of man. You shall be chosen by your Lord. He will teach you to interpret visions, and will perfect His favour to you and to the house of Jacob, as He perfected it to your fore-fathers Abraham and Isaac before you. Your Lord is wise and all-knowing."

Surely in Joseph and his brothers there are signs for doubting men.

They said to each other: "Joseph and his brother are dearer to our father than ourselves, though we are many. Truly, our father is much mistaken. Let us slay Joseph, or cast him away in some far-off land, so that we may have no rivals in our father's love, and after that be honourable men."

One of them said: "Do not slay Joseph; but if you must, rather cast him into a dark pit. Some caravan will take him up."

126

They said to their father: "Why do you not trust us with Joseph? Surely we wish him well. Send him with us tomorrow, that he may play and enjoy himself. We will take good care of him."

He replied: "It would much grieve me to let him go with you; for I fear lest the wolf should eat him when you are off your guard."

They said: "If the wolf could eat him despite our numbers, then we should surely be lost!"

And when they took Joseph with them, they decided to cast him into a dark pit. We revealed to him, saying: "You shall tell them of all this when they will not know you."

At nightfall they returned weeping to their father. They said: "We went off to compete together and left Joseph with our packs. The wolf devoured him. But you will not believe us, though we speak the truth." And they showed him their brother's shirt, stained with false blood.

"No!" he cried. "Your souls have tempted you to evil. Sweet patience! God alone can help me bear the loss you speak of."

And a caravan passed by, who sent their water-bearer to the pit. And when he had let down his pail, he cried: "Rejoice! A boy!"

They concealed him as part of their merchandise. But God knew what they did. They sold him for a trifling price, for a few pieces of silver. They cared nothing for him.

The Egyptian who bought him said to his wife: "Be kind to him. He may prove useful to us, or we may adopt him as our son."

Thus We established Joseph in the land, and taught him to interpret dreams. God has power over all things, though most men may not know it. And when he reached maturity We bestowed on him wisdom and knowledge. Thus We reward the righteous.

His master's wife sought to seduce him. She bolted the doors and said: "Come!"

"God forbid!" he replied. "My lord has treated me with kindness. Wrongdoers never prosper."

She made for him, and he himself would have succumbed to her had he not been shown a sign from his Lord. Thus did We shield him from wantonness, for he was one of Our faithful servants.

They both rushed to the door. She tore his shirt from behind. And at the door they met her husband.

She cried: "Shall not the man who wished to violate your wife be thrown into prison or sternly punished?"

Joseph said: "It was she who attempted to seduce me."

"If his shirt is torn from the front," said one of her people, "she is speaking the truth and he is lying. If it is torn from behind, then he is speaking the truth and she is lying."

And when her husband saw Joseph's shirt rent from behind, he said to her: "This is but one of your tricks. Your cunning is great indeed! Joseph, say no more about this. Woman, ask pardon for your sin. You have done wrong."

In the city women were saying: "The Prince's wife has sought to seduce her servant. She has conceived a passion for him. It is clear that she has gone astray."

When she heard of their intrigues, she invited them to a banquet at her house. To each she gave a knife, and ordered Joseph to present himself before them. When they saw him, they were amazed at him and cut their hands, exclaiming: "God preserve us! This is no mortal, but a gracious angel."

"This is the man," she said, "on whose account you blamed me. I sought to seduce him, but he was unyielding. If he declines to do my bidding, he shall be thrown into prison and shall be held in scorn."

"Lord," said Joseph, "sooner would I go to prison than give in to their advances. Shield me from their cunning, or I shall yield to them and lapse into folly."

His Lord heard his prayer and warded off their wiles from him. He hears all and knows all.

Yet for all the evidence they had seen, they thought it right to jail him for a time.

Two young men entered the prison with him. One of them said: "I dreamt that I was pressing grapes." And the other said: "I dreamt that I was carrying a loaf upon my head, and that the birds came and ate of it. Tell us the meaning of these dreams, for we can see you are a virtuous man."

Joseph replied: "I can interpret them long before they are fulfilled. Whatever food you are provided with, I can divine for you its meaning, even before it reaches you. This knowledge my Lord has given me, for I have left the faith of those that disbelieve in God and deny the life to come. I follow the faith of my forefathers, Abraham, Isaac, and Jacob. We will serve no idols besides God. Such is the grace which God has bestowed on us and on all mankind. Yet most men do not give thanks.

"Fellow-prisoners! Are sundry gods better than God, the One, the One who conquers all? Those you serve besides Him are nothing but names which you and your fathers have devised and for which God has revealed no sanction. Judgement rests only with God. He has commanded you to worship none but Him. That is the true faith: yet most men do not know it.

"Fellow-prisoners, one of you will serve his lord with wine. The other will be crucified, and the birds will peck at his head. This is the answer to your question."

And Joseph said to the prisoner who he knew would be freed: "Remember me in the presence of your lord."

But Satan made him forget to mention Joseph to his lord, so that he stayed in prison for several years.

The king said: "I saw seven fatted cows which seven lean ones devoured; also seven green ears of corn and seven others dry. Tell me the meaning of this vision, my nobles, if you can interpret visions."

They replied: "It is but a medley of dream; nor are we skilled in the interpretation of dreams."

Thereupon the man who had been freed remembered Joseph after all that time. He said: "I shall tell you what it means. Give me leave to go."

He said to Joseph: "Tell us, man of truth, of the seven fatted cows which seven lean ones devoured; also of the seven green ears of corn and the other seven which were dry: so that I may go back to my masters and inform them."

He replied: "You shall sow for seven consecutive years. Leave in the ear the corn you reap, except a little which you may eat. Then there shall follow seven hungry years which will consume all but little of what you have stored. Then there will come a year of abundant rain, in which the people will press the grape."

The king said: "Bring this man before me."

But when the envoy came to him, Joseph said: "Go back to your master and ask him about the women who cut their hands. My master knows their cunning."

The king questioned the women, saying: "What made you attempt to seduce Joseph?"

"God forbid!" they replied. "We know no evil of him."

"Now the truth must come to light," said the Prince's wife. "It was I who sought to seduce him. He has told the truth."

"From this," said Joseph, "my lord will know that I did not betray him in his absence, and that God does not guide the work of the treacherous. Not that I am free from sin: man's soul is prone to evil, except his to whom God has shown mercy. My Lord is forgiving and merciful."

The king said: "Bring him before me. I will choose him for my own."

And when he had spoken with him, the king said: "You shall henceforth dwell with us, honoured and trusted."

Joseph said: "Give me charge of the granaries of the realm. I shall husband them wisely."

Thus did We establish Joseph in the land, and he dwelt there as he pleased. We bestow Our mercy on whom We will, and never deny the righteous their reward. Better is the reward of the life to come for those who believe in God and keep from evil.

Joseph's brothers arrived and presented themselves before him. He recognized them, but they knew him not. And when he had given them their provisions, he said: "Bring me your other brother from your father. Do you not see that I give just measure and am the best of hosts? If you do not bring him, you shall have no corn, nor shall you come near me again."

They replied: "We will endeavour to fetch him from his father. This we will surely do."

Joseph said to his servants: "Put their money into their packs, so that they may find it when they return to their people. Perchance they will come back."

When they returned to their father, they said: "Father, corn is henceforth denied us. Send our brother with us and we shall have our measure. We will take good care of him."

He replied: "Am I to trust you with him as I once trusted you with his brother? But God is the best of guardians: and of all those that show mercy He is the most merciful."

When they opened their packs, they discovered that their money had been returned to them. "Father," they said, "what more can we desire? Here is our money paid back to us. We will buy provisions for our people and take good care of our brother. We shall receive an extra camel-load; a camel-load should be easy enough."

He replied: "I will not let him go with you until you promise in God's name to bring him back to me, unless the worst befall you."

And when they had given him their pledge, he said: "God is the witness of your oath. My sons, enter the town by different gates. If you do wrong, I cannot ward off from you the wrath of God: judgement is His alone. In Him I have put my trust. In Him alone let the faithful put their trust."

And when they entered as their father had bade them, his counsel availed them nothing against the decree of God. It was but a wish in Jacob's soul which he had thus fulfilled. He was possessed of knowledge which We had given him, though most men have no knowledge.

When they went in to Joseph, he embraced his brother, and said: "I am your brother. Do not grieve at what they did."

And when he had given them their provisions, he hid a drinking-cup in his brother's pack.

Then a crier called out after them: "Travellers, you are thieves!"

They turned back and asked: "What have you lost?"

"We miss the king's drinking-cup," he replied. "He that brings it shall have a camel-load of corn. I pledge my word for it."

"In God's name," they cried, "you know we did not come to do evil in this land. We are no thieves."

The Egyptians said: "What penalty shall be his who stole it, if you prove to be lying?"

They replied: "He in whose pack the cup is found shall be your bondsman. Thus we punish the wrongdoers."

Joseph searched their bags before his brother's, and then took out the cup from his brother's bag.

Thus We directed Joseph. By the king's law he had no right to seize his brother: but God willed otherwise. We exalt in knowledge whom We will: but above those that have knowledge there is One more knowing.

They said: "If he has stolen—know then that a brother of his has committed theft before him."

But Joseph kept his secret and revealed nothing to them. He said: "Your deed was worse. God best knows the things you speak of."

They said: "Noble prince, this boy has an aged father. Take one of us, instead of him. We can see you are a generous man."

He replied: "God forbid that we should take any but the man with whom our property was found: for then we should be unjust."

When they despaired of him, they went aside to confer in private. The eldest said: "Have you forgotten that your father took from you a pledge in God's name, and that long ago you did your worst with Joseph. I will not stir from this land until my father gives me leave or God makes known to me His judgement: He is the best of judges. Return to your father and say to him: 'Father, your son has committed a theft. We testify only to what we know. How could we guard against the unforeseen? Inquire at the city where we lodged, and from the caravan with which we travelled. We speak the truth.' "

"No!" cried their father. "Your souls have tempted you to evil. But I will have sweet patience. God may bring them all to me. He alone is all-knowing and wise." And he turned away from them, crying: "Alas for Joseph!" His eyes went white with grief and he was oppressed with silent sorrow.

His sons exclaimed: "In God's name, will you not cease to think of Joseph until you ruin your health and die?"

He replied: "I complain to God of my sorrow and sadness. He has made known to me things that you know not. Go, my sons, and seek news of Joseph and his brother. Do not despair of God's spirit; none but unbelievers despair of God's spirit."

And when they went in to him, they said: "Noble prince, we and our people are scourged with famine. We have brought but little money. Give us some corn, and be charitable to us: God rewards the charitable."

"Do you know," he replied, "what you did to Joseph and his brother? You are surely unaware."

They cried: "Can you indeed be Joseph?"

"I am Joseph," he answered, "and this is my brother. God has been gracious to us. Those that keep from evil and endure with fortitude, God will not deny them their reward."

"By the Lord," they said, "God has exalted you above us all. We have indeed been guilty."

He replied: "None shall reproach you this day. May God forgive you: Of all those who show mercy, He is the most merciful. Take this shirt of mine and throw it over my father's face: he will recover his sight. Then return to me with all your people."

When the caravan departed their father said: "I feel the breath of Joseph, though you will not believe me."

"In God's name," said those who heard him, "it is but your old illusion."

And when the bearer of good news arrived, he threw Joseph's shirt over the old man's face, and he regained his sight. He said: "Did I not tell you that God has made known to me what you know not?"

His sons said: "Father, implore forgiveness for our sins. We have indeed done wrong."

He replied: "I shall implore my Lord to forgive you. He is forgiving and merciful."

And when they went in to Joseph, he embraced his parents and said: "Welcome to Egypt, safe, if God wills!"

He helped his parents to a couch, and they all fell on their knees and prostrated themselves before him.

"This," said Joseph to his father, "is the meaning of my old vision: my Lord has fulfilled it. He has been gracious to me. He has released me from prison and brought you out of the desert after Satan had stirred up strife between me and my brothers. My lord is gracious to whom He will. He alone is all-knowing and wise.

"Lord, You have given me authority and taught me to interpret dreams. Creator of the heavens and the earth, my Guardian in this world and in the hereafter. Allow me to die in submission, and admit me among the righteous."

That which We have now revealed to you is a tale of the unknown. You were not present when Joseph's brothers conceived their plans and schemed against him. Yet strive as you may, most men will not believe.

You shall demand of them no recompense for this. It is an admonition to all mankind.

Many are the marvels of the heavens and the earth; yet they pass them by and pay no heed to them. The greater part of them believe in God only if they can worship other gods besides Him.

Are they confident that God's scourge will not fall upon them, or that the Hour of Doom will not overtake them unawares, without warning?

Say: "This is my path. With sure knowledge I call on you to have faith in God, I and all my followers. Glory be to God! I am no idolater."

Nor were the apostles whom We sent before you other than mortals inspired by Our will and chosen from among their people.

Have they not travelled in the land and seen what was the end of those who disbelieved before them? Better is the world to come for those that keep from evil. Can you not understand?

And when at length Our apostles despaired and thought they were denied, Our help came down to them, delivering whom We pleased. The evil-doers could not be saved from Our scourge. Their annals point to a moral to men of understanding.

This is no invented tale, but a confirmation of previous scriptures, an explanation of all things, a guide and a blessing to true believers.

Suggestions for Discussion

1. How does this story deal with the issue of sibling rivalry?

2. How does the master's wife behave toward Joseph? What motivates her character?

3. How is Joseph's connection to divine powers a gift? How might it be called a curse?

Suggestions for Writing

1. Another version of this tale appears in the Book of Genesis (chapters 37 to 50) in the Hebrew Scriptures, also known as The Old Testament. How do the two versions of the tale differ and how are they similar? Write an essay in which you compare and contrast them.

2. As a creative exercise, rewrite the Joseph story from the perspective of one of the supporting characters, or one of the Joseph's principle antagonists.

BARBARA KINGSOLVER

Somebody's Baby

Barbara Kingsolver (b. 1955) is a naturalist and a writer with a background in biology who has homes in southern Arizona and in the Appalachian mountains. A poet, essayist, and novelist, she is the author of a short-story collection, *Homeland* (1989) as well as the novels *The Bean Trees* (1988), *Animal Dreams* (1990), *Pigs in Heaven* (1993), *The Poisonwood Bible* (1998), and *Prodigal Summer* (2001). The following piece first appeared in the 1995 book *High Tide in Tucson: Essays from Now or Never.*

As I walked out the street entrance to my newly rented apartment, a guy in maroon high-tops and a skateboard haircut approached, making kissing noises and saying, "Hi, gorgeous." Three weeks earlier, I would have assessed the degree of malice and made ready to run or tell him to bug off, depending. But now, instead, I smiled, and so did my four-year-old daughter, because after dozens of similar encounters I understood he didn't mean me but *her*.

This was not the United States.

For most of the year my daughter was four we lived in Spain, in the warm southern province of the Canary Islands. I struggled with dinner at midnight and the subjunctive tense, but my only genuine culture shock reverberated from this earthquake of a fact: people there like kids. They don't just say so, they *do*. Widows in black, buttoned-down CEOs, purple-sneakered teenagers, the butcher, the baker, all would stop on the street to have little chats with my daughter. Routinely, taxi drivers leaned out the window to shout "*Hola, guapa!*" My daughter, who must have felt my conditioned flinch, would look up at me wide-eyed and explain patiently, "I *like* it that people think I'm pretty." With a mother's keen myopia I would tell you, absolutely, my daughter is beautiful enough to stop traffic. But in the city of Santa Cruz, I have to confess, so was every other person under the height of one meter. Not just those who conceded to be seen and not heard. Whenever Camille grew cranky in a restaurant (and really, what do you expect at midnight?) the waiters flirted and brought her little presents, and nearby diners looked on with that sweet, wistful gleam of eye that I'd thought diners reserved for the dessert tray. What I discovered in Spain was a culture that held children to be its meringues and éclairs. My own culture, it seemed to me in retrospect, tended to regard children as a sort of toxic-waste product: a necessary evil, maybe, but if it's not our own we don't want to see it or hear it or, God help us, smell it.

If you don't have children, you think I'm exaggerating. But if you've changed a diaper in the last decade you know exactly the toxic-waste glare I mean. In the U.S. I have been told in restaurants: "We come here to get *away* from kids." (This for no infraction on my daughter's part that I could discern, other than being visible.) On an airplane I heard a man tell a beleaguered woman whose infant was bawling (as I would, to clear my aching ears, if I couldn't manage chewing gum): "If you can't keep that thing quiet, you should keep it at home."

Air travel, like natural disasters, throws strangers together in unnaturally intimate circumstances. (Think how well you can get to know the bald spot of the guy reclining in front of you.) Consequently airplanes can be a splendid cultural magnifying glass. On my family's voyage from New York to Madrid we weren't assigned seats together. I shamelessly begged my neighbor—a forty-something New Yorker traveling alone—if she would take my husband's aisle seat in another row so our airweary and plainly miserable daughter could stretch out across her parents' laps. My fellow traveler snapped, "No, I have to have the window seat, just like you *had* to have that baby."

As simply as that, a child with needs (and ears) became an inconvenient *thing,* for which I was entirely to blame. The remark left me stunned and, as always happens when someone speaks rudely to me, momentarily guilty: yes, she must be right, conceiving this child was a rash, lunatic moment of selfishness, and now I had better be prepared to pay the price.

In the U.S.A., where it's said that anyone can grow up to be President, we parents are left pretty much on our own when it comes to the Presidents-in-training. Our social programs for children are the hands-down worst in the industrialized world, but apparently that is just what we want as a nation. It took a move to another country to make me realize how thoroughly I had accepted my nation's creed of every family for itself. Whenever my daughter crash-landed in the playground, I was startled at first to see a sanguine, Spanish-speaking stranger pick her up and dust her off. And if a shrieking bundle landed at *my* feet, I'd furtively look around for the next of kin. But I quickly came to see this detachment as perverse when applied to children, and am wondering how it ever caught on in the first place.

My grandfathers on both sides lived in households that were called upon, after tragedy struck close to home, to take in orphaned children and raise them without a thought. In an era of shortage, this was commonplace. But one generation later that kind of semipermeable household had vanished, at least among the white middle class. It's a horrifying thought, but predictable enough, that the worth of children in America is tied to their dollar value. Children used to be field hands, household help, even miners and factory workers—extensions of a family's productive potential and so, in a sense, the property of an extended family. But *precious* property, valued and coveted. Since the advent of child-labor laws, children have come to hold an increasingly negative position in the economy. They're spoken of as a responsibility, a legal liability, an encumbrance—or, if their unwed mothers are on welfare, a mistake that should not be rewarded. The political shuffle seems to be about making sure they cost us as little as possible, and that their own parents foot the bill. Virtually every program that benefits children in this country, from *Sesame Street* to free school lunches, has been cut back in the last decade—in many cases, cut to nothing. If it takes a village to raise a child, our kids are knocking on a lot of doors where nobody seems to be home.

Taking parental responsibility to extremes, some policymakers in the U.S. have seriously debated the possibility of requiring a license for parenting. I'm dismayed by the notion of licensing an individual adult to raise an individual child, because it implies parenting is a private enterprise, like selling liquor or driving a cab (though less lucrative). I'm also dismayed by what it suggests about innate fitness or nonfitness to rear children. Who would devise such a test? And how could it harbor anything but deep class biases? Like driving, parenting is a skill you learn by doing. You keep an eye out for oncoming disasters, and know when to stop and ask for directions. The skills you have going into it are hardly the point.

The first time I tried for my driver's license, I flunked. I was sixteen and rigid with panic. I rolled backward precariously while starting on a hill; I misidentified in writing the shape of a railroad crossing sign; as a final disqualifying indignity, my VW beetle—borrowed from my brother and apparently as appalled as I—went blind in the left blinker and mute in the horn. But nowadays, when it's time for a renewal, I breeze through the driver's test without thinking, usually on my way to some other errand. That test I failed twenty years ago was no prediction of my ultimate competence as a driver, anymore than my doll-care practices (I liked tying them to the back of my bike, by the hair) were predictive of my parenting skills (heavens be praised). Who really understands what it takes to raise kids? That is, until after the diaper changes, the sibling rivalries, the stitches, the tantrums, the first day of school, the overpriced-sneakers standoff, the first date, the safe-sex lecture, and the senior prom have all been negotiated and put away in the scrapbook?

While there are better and worse circumstances from which to launch offspring onto the planet, it's impossible to anticipate just who will fail. One of the most committed, creative parents I know plunged into her role through the trapdoor of teen pregnancy; she has made her son the center of her life, constructed a large impromptu family of reliable friends and neighbors, and absorbed knowledge like a plant taking sun. Conversely, some of the most strained, inattentive parents I know are well-heeled professionals, self-sufficient but chronically pressed for time. Life takes surprising turns. The one sure thing is that no parent, ever, has turned out to be perfectly wise and exhaustively provident, 1,440 minutes a day, for 18 years. It takes help. Children are not commodities but an incipient world. They thrive best when their upbringing is the collective joy and responsibility of families, neighborhoods, communities, and nations.

It's not hard to figure out what's good for kids, but amid the noise of an increasingly antichild political climate, it can be hard to remember just to go ahead and do it: for example, to vote to raise your school district's budget, even though you'll pay higher taxes. (If you're earning enough to pay taxes at all, I promise, the school needs those few bucks more than you do.) To support legislators who care more about afterschool programs, affordable health care, and libraries than about military budgets and the Dow Jones industrial average. To volunteer time and skills at your neighborhood school and also the school across town. To decide to notice, rather than ignore it, when a neighbor is losing it with her kids, and offer to baby-sit twice a week. This is not interference. Getting between a ball player and a ball is interference. The ball is inanimate.

Presuming children to be their parents' sole property and responsibility is, among other things, a handy way of declaring problem children to be someone else's problem, or fault, or failure. It's a dangerous remedy; it doesn't change the fact that somebody else's kids will ultimately be in your face demanding *now* with interest what they didn't get when they were smaller and had simpler needs. Maybe in-your-face means breaking and entering, or maybe it means a Savings and Loan scam. Children deprived— of love, money, attention, or moral guidance—grow up to have large and powerful needs.

Always there will be babies made in some quarters whose parents can't quite take care of them. Reproduction is the most invincible of all human goals; like every other species, we're only here because our ancestors spent millions of years refining their act as efficient, dedicated breeders. If we hope for only sane, thoughtful people to have children, we can wish while we're at it for an end to cavities and mildew. But unlike many other species we are social, insightful, and capable of anticipating our future. We can see, if we care to look, that the way we treat children—*all* of them, not just our own, and especially those in great need—defines the shape of the world we'll wake up in tomorrow. The most remarkable feature of human culture is its capacity to reach beyond the self and encompass the collective good.

It's an inspiring thought. But in mortal fact, here in the U.S. we are blazing a bold downhill path from the high ground of "human collective," toward the tight little den of "self." The last time we voted on a school-budget override in Tucson, the newspaper printed scores of letters from readers incensed by the very possibility: "I don't have kids," a typical letter writer declared, "so why should I have to pay to educate other people's offspring?" The budget increase was voted down, the school district progressed from deficient to desperate, and I longed to ask that miserly nonfather just *whose* offspring he expects to doctor the maladies of his old age.

If we intend to cleave like stubborn barnacles to our great American ethic of every nuclear family for itself, then each of us had better raise and educate offspring enough to give us each day, in our old age, our daily bread. If we don't wish to live by bread alone, we'll need not only a farmer and a cook in the family but also a home repair specialist, an auto mechanic, an accountant, an import-export broker, a forest ranger, a therapist, an engineer, a musician, a poet, a tailor, a doctor, and at least three shifts of nurses. If that seems impractical, then we can accept other people's kids into our lives, starting now.

It's not so difficult. Most of the rest of the world has got this in hand. Just about any country you can name spends a larger percentage of its assets on its kids than we do. Virtually all industrialized nations have better schools and child-care policies. And while the U.S. grabs headlines by saving the occasional baby with heroic medical experiments, world health reports (from UNESCO, USAID, and other sources) show that a great many other parts of the world have lower infant mortality rates than we do—not just the conspicuously prosperous nations like Japan and Germany, but others, like Greece, Cuba, Portugal, Slovenia—simply because they attend better to all their mothers and children. Cuba, running on a budget that would hardly keep New York City's lights on, has better immunization programs and a higher literacy rate. During the long, grim haul of a thirty-year economic blockade, during which the United States has managed to starve Cuba to a ghost of its hopes, that island's child-first priorities have never altered.

Here in the land of plenty a child dies from poverty every fifty-three minutes, and TV talk shows exhibit teenagers who pierce their flesh with safety pins and rip off their parents every way they know how. All these punks started out as somebody's baby. How on earth, we'd like to know, did they learn to be so isolated and selfish?

My second afternoon in Spain, standing in a crowded bus, as we ricocheted around a corner and my daughter reached starfishwise for stability, a man in a black beret stood up and gently helped her into his seat. In his weightless bearing I caught sight of the decades-old child, treasured by the manifold mothers of his neighborhood, growing up the way leavened dough rises surely to the kindness of bread.

I thought then of the woman on the airplane, who was obviously within her rights to put her own comfort first, but whose withheld generosity gave my daughter what amounted to a sleepless, kicking, squirming, miserable journey. As always happens when someone has spoken to me rudely, I knew exactly what I should have said: Be careful what you give children, for sooner or later you are sure to get it back.

Suggestions for Discussion

1. According to Kingsolver, how are children treated differently in the United States from the way they are treated abroad?

2. In Kingsolver's view, how might children's "value" be calculated economically?

3. Why does Kingsolver object to the proposal that one might need a license to become a parent?

Suggestion for Writing

Is Kingsolver correct in her view that Americans undervalue and mistreat children? Respond to points she makes in her essay, either agreeing or disagreeing with them, and reinforce your argument by incorporating research and personal experiences of your own.

FICTION

∾∾∾∾∾

EDWIDGE DANTICAT

Selection from Breath, Eyes, Memory

Edwidge Danticat (b. 1969) is a Haitian-born author who immigrated to the United States at age 12 and published her first writings at 14. A winner of a James Milchener Fellowship, Danticat was also nominated for the National Book Award in 1995 for her short-story collection *Krik? Krak!* Among her other books are *Farming of Bones* (1998), *After the Dance* (2002), *Behind the Mountains* (2002), and *The Dew Breaker* (2004). Danticat earned a bachelor's degree in literature from Barnard College and a master of fine arts degree from Brown University. Her graduate thesis was published as *Breath, Eyes, Memory.* The following controversial passage, reprinted from that 1994 book, shocked many of her fellow Haitian-Americans with its depiction of regular virginity "tests" performed on women.

I asked my grandmother if I could cook supper for us that night.

Tante Atie offered to take me to a private vendor where food was cheaper than the *maché.* She put the leeches in some clean water and we started down the road.

"What are you making for us?" she asked.

"Rice, black beans, and herring sauce," I said.

"Your mother's favorite meal."

"That's what we cooked most often."

We followed a footpath off the road, down to a shallow stream. An old mule was yanking water vines from the edge of the stream while baby crabs freely dashed around its nostrils.

A woman filled a calabash a few feet from where my sandals muddied the water. Tante Atie chatted with the women as she went by. Some young girls were sitting barechested in the water, the sun casting darker shadows into their faces. Their hands squirted blackened suds as they pounded their clothes with water rocks.

A dusty footpath led us to a tree-lined cemetery at the top of the hill. Tante Atie walked between the wooden crosses, collecting the bamboo skeletons of fallen kites. She stepped around the plots where empty jars, conch shells, and marbles served as grave markers.

"Walk straight," said Tante Atie, "you are in the presence of family."

She walked around to each plot, and called out the names of all those who had been buried there. There was my great-grandmother, Beloved Martinelle Brigitte. Her sister, My First Joy Sophilus Gentille. My grandfather's sister, My Hope Atinia Ifé, and finally my grandfather, Charlemagne Le Grand Caco.

Tante Atie named them all on sight.

"Our family name, Caco, it is the name of a scarlet bird. A bird so crimson, it makes the reddest hibiscus or the brightest flame trees seem white. The Caco bird, when it dies, there is always a rush of blood that rises to its neck and the wings, they look so bright, you would think them on fire."

From the cemetery, we took a narrow footpath to the vendor's hut. On either side of us were wild grasses that hissed as though they were full of snakes.

We walked to a whitewashed shack where a young woman sold rice and black beans from the same sisal mat where she slept with her husband.

In the yard, the husband sat under the shade of a straw parasol with a pipe in his mouth and a demijohn at his feet. He was pounding small nails into leather straps and thin layers of polished wood to make sandals.

The hammering echoed in my head until I reached the cane fields. The men were singing about a woman who flew without her skin at night, and when she came back home, she found her skin peppered and could not put it back on. Her husband had done it to teach her a lesson. He ended up killing her.

I was surprised how fast it came back. The memory of how everything came together to make a great meal. The fragrance of the spices guided my fingers the way no instructions or measurements could.

The men in this area, they insist that their women are virgins and have ten fingers.

According to Tante Atie, each finger had a purpose. It was the way she had been taught to prepare herself to become a woman. Mothering. Boiling. Loving. Baking. Nursing. Frying. Healing. Washing. Ironing. Scrubbing. It wasn't her fault, she said. Her ten fingers had been named for her even before she was born. Sometimes, she even wished she had six fingers on each hand so she could have two left for herself.

I rushed back and forth between the iron pots in the yard. The air smelled like spices that I had not cooked with since I'd left my mother's home two years before.

I usually ate random concoctions: frozen dinners, samples from global cookbooks, food that was easy to put together and brought me no pain. No memories of a past that at times was cherished and at others despised.

By the time we ate, the air was pregnant with rain. Thunder groaned in the starless sky while the lanterns flickered in the hills.

"Well done," Tante Atie said after her fourth serving of my rice and beans. My grandmother chewed slowly as she gave my daughter her bottle.

"If the wood is well carved," said my grandmother, "it teaches us about the carpenter. Atie, you taught Sophie well."

Tante Atie was taken off guard by my grandmother's compliment. She kissed me on the forehead before taking the dishes to the yard to wash. Then, she went into the house, took her notebook, and left for her lesson with Louise.

My grandmother groaned her disapproval. She pulled out a small pouch and packed pinches of tobacco powder into her nose. She inhaled deeply, stuffing more and more into her nostrils.

She had a look of deep concern on her face, as her eyes surveyed the evening clouds.

"*Tandé.* Do you hear anything?" she asked.

There was nothing but the usual night sounds: birds finding their ways in the dark, as they shuffled through the leaves.

Often at night, there were women who travelled long distances, on foot or on mare, to save the car fare to Port-au-Prince.

I strained my eyes to see beyond the tree shadows on the road.

"There is a girl going home," my grandmother said. "You cannot see her. She is far away. Quite far. It is not the distance that is important. If I hear a girl from far away, there is an emotion, something that calls to my soul. If your soul is linked with someone, somehow you can always feel when something is happening to them."

"Is it Tante Atie, the girl on the road?"

"*Non.* It is really a girl. A younger woman."

"Is the girl in danger?"

"That's why you listen. You should hear young feet crushing wet leaves. Her feet make a *swish-swash* when they hit the ground and when she hurries, it sounds like a whip chasing a mule."

I listened closely, but heard no whip.

"When it is dark, all men are black," she said. "There is no way to know anything unless you apply your ears. When you listen, it's *kòm si* you had deafness before and you can hear now. Sometimes you can't fall asleep because the sound of someone crying keeps you awake. A whisper sounds like a roar to your ears. Your ears are witness to matters that do not concern you. And what is worse, you cannot forget. Now, listen. Her feet make a *swish* sound and when she hurries it's like a whip in the wind."

I tried, but I heard no whip.

"It's the way old men cry," she said. "Grown brave men have a special way they cry when they are afraid."

She closed her eyes and lowered her head to concentrate.

"It is Ti Alice," she said.

"Who is Ti Alice?"

"The young child in the bushes, it is Ti Alice. Someone is there with her."

"Is she in danger?"

My grandmother tightened her eyelids.

"I know Ti Alice," she said. "I know her mother."

"Why is she in the bushes?"

"She must be fourteen or fifteen years now."

"Why is she out there?"

"She is rushing back to her mother. She was with a friend, a boy."

I thought I heard a few hushed whispers.

"I think I hear a little," I said, rocking my daughter with excitement.

"Ti Alice and the boy, they are bidding one another goodbye, for the night."

My grandmother wrapped her arms around her body, rocking and cradling herself.

"What is happening now?" I asked.

"Her mother is waiting for her at the door of their hut. She is pulling her inside to test her."

The word sent a chill through my body.

"She is going to test to see if young Alice is still a virgin," my grandmother said. "The mother, she will drag her inside the hut, take her last small finger and put it inside her to see if it goes in. You said the other night that your mother tested you. That is what is now happening to Ti Alice."

I have heard it compared to a virginity cult, our mothers' obsession with keeping us pure and chaste. My mother always listened to the echo of my urine in the toilet, for if it was too loud it meant that I had been deflowered. I learned very early in life that virgins always took small steps when they walked. They never did acrobatic splits, never rode horses or bicycles. They always covered themselves well and, even if their lives depended on it, never parted with their panties.

The story goes that there was once an extremely rich man who married a poor black girl. He had chosen her out of hundreds of prettier girls because she was untouched. For the wedding night, he bought her the whitest sheets and nightgowns he could possibly find. For himself, he bought a can of thick goat milk in which he planned to sprinkle a drop of her hymen blood to drink.

Then came their wedding night. The girl did not bleed. The man had his honor and reputation to defend. He could not face the town if he did not have a blood-spotted sheet to hang in his courtyard the next morning. He did the best he could to make her bleed, but no matter how hard he tried, the girl did not bleed. So he took a knife and cut her between her legs to get some blood to show. He got enough blood for her wedding gown and sheets, an unusual amount to impress the neighbors. The blood kept flowing like water out of the girl. It flowed so much it wouldn't stop. Finally, drained of all her blood, the girl died.

Later, during her funeral procession, her blood-soaked sheets were paraded by her husband to show that she had been a virgin on her wedding night. At the grave site, her husband drank his blood-spotted goat milk and cried like a child.

I closed my eyes upon the images of my mother slipping her hand under the sheets and poking her pinky at a void, hoping that it would go no further than the length of her fingernail.

Like Tante Atie, she had told me stories while she was doing it, weaving elaborate tales to keep my mind off the finger, which I knew one day would slip into me and condemn me. I had learned to *double* while being *tested*. I would close my eyes and imagine all the pleasant things that I had known. The lukewarm noon breeze through our bougainvillea. Tante Atie's gentle voice blowing over a field of daffodils.

There were many cases in our history where our ancestors had *doubled*. Following in the *vaudou* tradition, most of our presidents were actually one body split in two: part flesh and part shadow. That was the only way they could murder and rape so many people and still go home to play with their children and make love to their wives.

After my marriage, whenever Joseph and I were together, I *doubled*.

"The testing? Why do the mothers do that?" I asked my grandmother.

"If a child dies, you do not die. But if your child is disgraced, you are disgraced. And people, they think daughters will be raised trash with no man in the house."

"Did your mother do this to you?"

"From the time a girl begins to menstruate to the time you turn her over to her husband, the mother is responsible for her purity. If I give a soiled daughter to her husband, he can shame my family, speak evil of me, even bring her back to me."

"When you tested my mother and Tante Atie, couldn't you tell that they hated it?"

"I had to keep them clean until they had husbands."

"But they don't have husbands."

"The burden was not mine alone."

"I hated the tests," I said. "It is the most horrible thing that ever happened to me. When my husband is with me now, it gives me such nightmares that I have to bite my tongue to do it again."

"With patience, it goes away."

"No Grandmè Ifé, it does not."

"Ti Alice, she has passed her examination."

The sky reddened with a sudden flash of lightning. "Now you have a child of your own. You must know that everything a mother does, she does for her child's own good. You cannot always carry the pain. You must liberate yourself."

We walked to my room and put my daughter down to sleep.

"I will go soon," I told my grandmother, "back to my husband."

"It is better," she said. "It is hard for a woman to raise girls alone."

She walked into her room, took her statue of Erzulie, and pressed it into my hand.

"My heart, it weeps like a river," she said, "for the pain we have caused you."

I held the statue against my chest as I cried in the night. I thought I heard my grandmother crying too, but it was the rain slowing down to a mere drizzle, tapping on the roof.

The next morning, I went jogging, along the road, through the cemetery plot, and into the hills. The sun had already dried some of the puddles from the drizzle the night before.

Along the way, people stared at me with puzzled expressions on their faces. *Is this what happens to our girls when they leave this place?* They become such frightened creatures that they run like the wind, from nothing at all.

Suggestions for Discussion

1. What does the family name, Caco, mean? Is the name symbolic?

2. What relationships exist between the women of each generation in the Caco family?

3. How has the narrator changed since she first left home?

4. What is the story of the rich man who married the poor black girl? Why does this story, and the "testing" of Ti Alice, resonate so strongly with the narrator?

5. How are the men of Haiti depicted in this story?

Suggestion for Writing

Compare the generational relationships between women in this story to the mother–daughter relationship depicted by Amy Tan in *Waverly Jong: The Rules of the Game* on page 890. What role does culture play in determining the nature of these relationships?

PATRICIA HIGHSMITH

The Trouble with Mrs. Blynn,
the Trouble with the World

Patricia Highsmith (1921–1995), Texas-born author of more than twenty books, lived in France and Switzerland for most of her life. Her classic thrillers, *Strangers on a Train* (1950) and *The Talented Mr. Ripley* (1955), were made into acclaimed motion pictures. She also wrote *Mermaids on the Golf Course* (1985), *The Blunderer* (1966), and *A Dog's Ransom* (1972). *Nothing That Meets the Eye* is a collection of short stories that was published posthumously in 2002.

Mrs. Palmer was dying, there was no doubt of that to her or to anyone else in the household. The household had grown from two, Mrs. Palmer and Elsie the housemaid, to four in the past ten days. Elsie's daughter Liza, age fourteen, had come to help her mother, and had brought their shaggy sheep-dog Princy—who to Mrs. Palmer made a fourth presence in the house. Liza spent most of her time doing things in the kitchen, and slept in the little low-ceilinged room with double-deck bunks down the steps from Mrs. Palmer's room. The cottage was small—a sitting room and dining alcove and kitchen downstairs, and upstairs Mrs. Palmer's bedroom, the room with the two bunks, and a tiny back room where Elsie slept. All the ceilings were low and the door-ways and the ceiling above the stairway even lower, so that one had to duck one's head constantly.

Mrs. Palmer reflected that she would have to duck her head very few times more, as she rose only a couple of times a day, making her way, her lavender dressing gown clutched about her against the chill, to the bathroom. She had leukemia. She was not in any pain, but she was terribly weak. She was sixty-one. Her son Gregory, an officer in the R.A.F., was stationed in the Middle East, and perhaps would come in time and perhaps wouldn't. Mrs. Palmer had purposely not made her telegram urgent, not wanting to upset or inconvenience him, and his telegraphed reply had simply said that he would do his best to get leave to fly to her, and would let her know when. A cowardly telegram hers had been, Mrs. Palmer thought. Why hadn't she had the courage to say outright, "Am going to die in about a week. Can you come to see me?"

"Missus Palmer?" Elsie stuck her head in the door, one floury hand resting against the doorjamb. "Did Missus Blynn say four-thirty or five-thirty today?"

Mrs. Palmer did not know, and it did not seem in the least important. "I think five-thirty."

Elsie gave a preoccupied nod, her mind on what she would serve for five-thirty tea as opposed to four-thirty tea. The five-thirty tea could be less substantial, as Mrs. Blynn would already have had tea somewhere.

"Anything I can get you, Missus Palmer?" she asked in a sweet voice, with a genuine concern.

"No, thank you, Elsie, I'm quite comfortable." Mrs. Palmer sighed as Elsie closed the door again. Elsie was willing, but unintelligent. Mrs. Palmer could not *talk* to her, not that she would have wanted to talk intimately to her, but it would have been nice to have the feeling that she could talk to someone in the house if she wished to.

Mrs. Palmer had no close friends in the town, because she had been here only a month. She had been en route to Scotland when the weakness came on her again and she had collapsed on a train platform in Ipswich. A long journey to Scotland by train or even airplane had been out of the question, so on a strange doctor's recommendation Mrs. Palmer had hired a taxi and driven to a town on the east coast called Eamington, where the doctor knew there was a visiting nurse, and where the air was splendid and bracing. The doctor had evidently thought she needed only a few weeks' rest and she would be on her feet again, but Mrs. Palmer had had a premonition that this wasn't true. She had felt better the first few days in the quiet little town, she had found the cottage called Sea Maiden and rented it at once, but the spurt of energy had been brief. In Sea Maiden she had collapsed again, and Mrs. Palmer had the feeling that Elsie and even a few other acquaintances she had made, like Mr. Frowley the real-estate agent, resented her *faiblesse*. She was not only a stranger come to trouble them, to make demands on them, but her relapse belied the salubrious powers of Eamington air—just now mostly gale-force winds which swept from the northeast day and night, tearing the buttons from one's coat, plastering a sticky, opaque film of salt and spray on the windows of all the houses on the seafront. Mrs. Palmer was sorry to be a burden herself, but at least she could pay for it, she thought. She had rented a rather shabby cottage that would otherwise have stayed empty all winter, since it was early February now, she was employing Elsie at slightly better than average Eamington wages, she paid Mrs. Blynn a guinea per half-hour visit (and most of that half hour was taken up with her tea), and she soon would bring business to the undertaker, the sexton, and perhaps the shop-keeper who sold flowers. She had also paid her rent through March.

Hearing a quick tread on the pavement, in a lull in the wind's roar, Mrs. Palmer sat up a little in bed. Mrs. Blynn was arriving. An anxious frown touched Mrs. Palmer's thin-skinned forehead, but she smiled faintly, too, with beforehand politeness. She reached for the long-handled mirror that lay on her bed table. Her gray face had ceased to shock her or to make her feel shame. Age was age, death was death, and not pretty, but she still had the impulse to do what she could to look nicer for the world. She tucked some hair back into place, moistened her lips, tried a little smile, pulled a shoulder of her night-dress even with the other and her pink cardigan closer about her. Her pallor made the blue of her eyes much bluer. That was a pleasant thought.

Elsie knocked and opened the door at the same time. "Missus Blynn, Ma'am."

"Good afternoon, Mrs. Palmer," Mrs. Blynn said, coming down the two steps from the threshold into Mrs. Palmer's room. She was a full-bodied, dark-blond woman of middle height, about forty-five, and she wore her usual bulky two-piece black suit with a rose-colored floral pin on her left breast. She also wore pale-pink lipstick and rather high heels. Like many women in Eamington, she was a sea widow, and had taken up nursing after she was forty. She was highly thought of in the town as an energetic woman who did useful work. "And how are you this afternoon?"

"Good afternoon. Well as can be expected, I think you'd say," Mrs. Palmer said with an effort at cheerfulness. Already she was loosening the covers, preparatory to pushing them back entirely for her daily injection.

But Mrs. Blynn was standing with an absent smile in the center of the room, hands folded backward on her hips, surveying the walls, gazing out the window. Mrs. Blynn had once lived in this house with her husband, for six months when they were first married, and every day Mrs. Blynn said something about it. Mrs. Blynn's husband had been the captain of a merchant ship, and had gone down with it ten years ago in a collision with a Swedish ship only fifty nautical miles from Eamington. Mrs. Blynn had never married again. Elsie said that her house was filled with photographs of the captain in uniform and of his ship.

"Yes-s, it's a wonderful little house," Mrs. Blynn said, "even if the wind does come in a bit." She looked at Mrs. Palmer with brighter eyes, as if she were about to say, "Well, now, a few more of these injections and you'll be as fit as can be, won't you?"

But in the next seconds Mrs. Blynn's expression changed. She groped in her black bag for the needle and the bottle of clear fluid that would do no good. Her mouth lost its smile and drooped, and deeper lines came at its corners. By the time she plunged the needle into Mrs. Palmer's fleshless body, her bulging green-gray eyes were glassy, as if she saw nothing and did not need to see anything: this was her business, and she knew how to do it. Mrs. Palmer was an object, which paid a guinea a visit. The object was going to die. Mrs. Blynn became apathetic, as if even the cutting off of the guinea in three days or eight days mattered nothing to her, either.

Guineas as such mattered nothing to Mrs. Palmer, but in view of the fact that she was soon quitting this world she wished Mrs. Blynn could show something so human as a desire to prolong the guineas. Mrs. Blynn's eyes remained glassy, even when she glanced at the door to see if Elsie was coming in with her tea. Occasionally the floorboards in the hall cracked from the heat or the lack of it, and so they did when someone walked just outside the door.

The injection hurt today, but Mrs. Palmer did not flinch. It was really such a small thing; she smiled at the slightness of it. "A little sunshine today, wasn't there?" Mrs. Palmer said.

"Was there?" Mrs. Blynn jerked the needle out.

"Around eleven this morning. I noticed it." Weakly she gestured toward the window behind her.

"We can certainly use it," Mrs. Blynn said, putting her equipment back in her bag. "Goodness, we can use that fire, too." She had fastened her bag, and now she chafed her palms, huddling toward the grate.

Princy was stretched full length before the fire, looking like a rolled-up shag rug.

Mrs. Palmer tried to think of something pleasant to say about Mrs. Blynn's husband, their time in this house, the town, anything. She could only think of how lonely Mrs. Blynn's life must be since her husband died. They had had no children. According to Elsie, Mrs. Blynn had worshipped her husband, and took pride in never having remarried. "Have you many patients this time of year?" Mrs. Palmer asked.

"Oh, yes. Like always," Mrs. Blynn said, still facing the fire and rubbing her hands.

Who? Mrs. Palmer wondered. *Tell me about them.* She waited, breathing softly.

Elsie knocked once, by bumping a corner of the tray against the door.

"Come in, Elsie," they both said, Mrs. Blynn a bit louder.

"Here we are," Elsie said, setting the tray down on a hassock made by two massive olive-green pillows, one atop the other. Butter slid down the side of a scone, spread onto the plate, and began to congeal while Elsie poured the tea.

Elsie handed Mrs. Palmer a cup of tea with three lumps of sugar, but no scone, because Mrs. Blynn said they were too indigestible for her. Mrs. Palmer did not mind. She appreciated the sight of well-buttered scones, anyway, and of healthy people like Mrs. Blynn eating them. She was offered a ginger biscuit and declined it. Mrs. Blynn talked briefly to Elsie about her water pipes, about the reduced price of something at the butcher's this week, while Elsie stood with folded arms, leaning against the edge of the door, letting in a frigid draft on Mrs. Palmer. Elsie was taking in all Mrs. Blynn's information about prices. Now it was ketchup at the health store. On sale this week.

"Call me if you'd like something," Elsie said, as usual, ducking out the door.

Mrs. Blynn was sunk in her scones, leaning over so the dripping butter would fall on the stone floor and not on her skirt.

Mrs. Palmer shivered, and drew the covers up.

"Is your son coming?" Mrs. Blynn asked in a loud, clear voice, looking straight at Mrs. Palmer.

Mrs. Palmer did not know what Elsie had told Mrs. Blynn. She had told Elsie that he might come, that was all. "I haven't heard yet. He's probably waiting to tell me the exact time he'll come—or to find out if he can or not. You know how it is in the Air Force."

"Um-m," Mrs. Blynn said through a scone, as if of course she knew, having had a husband who had been in service. "He's your only son and heir, I take it."

"My only one," Mrs. Palmer said.

"Married?"

"Yes." Then, anticipating the next question, "He has one child, a daughter, but she's still very small."

Mrs. Blynn's eyes kept drifting to Mrs. Palmer's bed table, and suddenly Mrs. Palmer realized what she was looking at—her amethyst pin. Mrs. Palmer had worn it for a few days on her cardigan sweater, until she had felt so bad that the pin ceased to lift her spirits and became almost tawdry, and she had removed it.

"That's a beautiful pin," Mrs. Blynn said.

"Yes. My husband gave it to me years ago."

Mrs. Blynn came over to look at it, but she did not touch it. The rectangular amethyst was set in small diamonds. She stood up, looking down at it with alert, bulging eyes. "I suppose you'll pass it on to your son—or his wife."

Mrs. Palmer flushed with embarrassment, or anger. She hadn't thought to whom she would pass it on, particularly. "I suppose my son will get everything, as my heir."

"I hope his wife appreciates it," Mrs. Blynn said, turning on her heel with a smile, setting her cup down in its saucer.

Then Mrs. Palmer realized that for the last few days it was the pin that Mrs. Blynn had been looking at when her eyes drifted over to the bed table. When Mrs. Blynn had gone, Mrs. Palmer picked up the pin and held it in her palm protectively. Her jewel box was across the room. Elsie came in, and Mrs. Palmer said, "Elsie, would you mind handing me that blue box over there?"

"Certainly, Ma'am," Elsie said, swerving from the tea tray to the box on the top of the bookshelf. "This the one?"

"Yes, thank you." Mrs. Palmer took it, opened the lid, and dropped the pin on her pearls. She had not much jewelry, perhaps ten or eleven pieces, but each piece meant a special occasion in her life, or a special period, and she loved them all. She looked at Elsie's blunt, homely profile as she bent over the tray, arranging everything so that it could be carried out at once.

"That Mrs. Blynn," Elsie said, shaking her head, not looking at Mrs. Palmer. "Asked me if I thought your son was coming. How was I to know? I said yes, *I* thought so." Now she stood with the tray, looking at Mrs. Palmer, and she smiled awkwardly, as if she had said perhaps too much. "The trouble with Mrs. Blynn is she's always nosing—if you'll pardon me saying so. Asking questions, you know?"

Mrs. Palmer nodded, feeling too low just at that moment to make a comment. She had no comment, anyway. Elsie, she thought, had passed back and forth by the amethyst pin for days and never mentioned it, never touched it, maybe never even noticed it. Mrs. Palmer suddenly realized how much more she liked Elsie than she liked Mrs. Blynn.

"The trouble with Mrs. Blynn—she means well, but…" Elsie floundered and jiggled the tray in her effort to shrug. "It's too bad. Everyone's always saying it about her," she finished, as if this summed it up, and started out the door. But she turned with the door open. "At tea, for instance. It's always get this and get that for her, as if she were a grand lady or something. A day ahead she tells me. I don't see why she don't bring what she wants from the bakery now and then herself. If you know what I mean."

Mrs. Palmer nodded. She supposed she knew. She knew. Mrs. Blynn was like a nursemaid she had had for a time for Gregory. Like a divorcée she and her husband had known in London. She was like a lot of people.

Mrs. Palmer died two days later. It was a day when Mrs. Blynn came in and out, perhaps six times, perhaps eight. A telegram had arrived that morning from Gregory, saying that he had at last wangled leave and would take off in a matter of hours, landing at a military field near Eamington. Mrs. Palmer did not know if she would see him again or not; she could not judge her strength that far. Mrs. Blynn took her temperature and felt her pulse frequently, then pivoted on one foot in the room, looking about as if she were alone and thinking her own thoughts. Her expression was blankly pleasant, her peaches-and-cream cheeks aglow with health.

"Your son's due today," Mrs. Blynn half said, half asked, on one of her visits.

"Yes," Mrs. Palmer said.

It was then dusk, though it was only four in the afternoon.

That was the last clear exchange she had with anyone, for she sank into a kind of dream. She saw Mrs. Blynn staring at the blue box on the top of the bookshelf, staring at it even as she shook the thermometer down. Mrs. Palmer called for Elsie and had her bring the box to her. Mrs. Blynn was not in the room then.

"This is to go to my son when he comes," Mrs. Palmer said. "All of it. Everything. You understand? It's all written…" But, even though it was all itemized, a single piece like the amethyst pin might be missing and Gregory would never do anything about it, maybe not even notice, maybe think she'd lost it somewhere in the last weeks and not reported it. Gregory was like that. Then Mrs. Palmer smiled at herself, and also reproached herself. *You can't take it with you.* That was very true, and people who tried to were despicable and rather absurd. "Elsie, this is yours," Mrs. Palmer said, and handed Elsie the amethyst pin.

"Oh, Mrs. Palmer! Oh, no, I couldn't take *that!*" Elsie said, not taking it, and in fact retreating a step.

"You've been very good to me," Mrs. Palmer said. She was very tired, and her arm dropped to the bed. "Very well," she murmured, seeing that it was really no use.

Her son came at six that evening, sat with her on the edge of her bed, held her hand and kissed her forehead. But when she died Mrs. Blynn was closest, bending over her with her great round peaches-and-cream face and her green-gray eyes as expressionless as some fantastic reptile's. Mrs. Blynn, to the last, continued to say crisp, efficient things to her, like "Breathe easily. That's it," and "Not chilly, are you? Good." Somebody had mentioned a priest earlier, but this had been overruled by both Gregory and Mrs. Palmer. So it was Mrs. Blynn's eyes that she looked into as her life left her. Mrs. Blynn so authoritative, strong, efficient, one might have taken her for God himself. Especially since when Mrs. Palmer looked toward her son she couldn't really see him, only a vague pale-blue figure in the corner, tall and erect, with a dark spot at the top that was his hair. He was looking at her, but now she was too weak to call him. Anyway, Mrs. Blynn had shooed them all back. Elsie was standing against the closed door, ready to run out for something, ready to take any order. Near her was the smaller figure of Liza, who occasionally whispered something and was shushed by her mother. In an instant, Mrs. Palmer saw her entire life—her carefree childhood and youth, her happy marriage, the blight of the death of her other son at the age of ten, the shock of her husband's death eight years ago—but all in all a happy life, she supposed, though she could wish that her own character had been better, *purer,* that she had never shown temper or selfishness, for instance. All that was past now, but what remained was a feeling that she had been imperfect, wrong, like Mrs. Blynn's presence now, like Mrs. Blynn's faint smile, wrong, wrong for the time and the occasion. Mrs. Blynn did not understand her. Mrs. Blynn did not know her. Mrs. Blynn, somehow, could not comprehend good will. Therein lay the flaw, and the flaw of life itself. Life is a long failure of understanding, Mrs. Palmer thought, a long, mistaken shutting of the heart.

Mrs. Palmer had the amethyst pin in her closed left hand. Hours ago, sometime in the afternoon, she had taken it with an idea of safekeeping, but now she realized the absurdity of that. She had also wanted to give it to Gregory directly, and had forgotten. Her closed hand lifted an inch or so, her lips moved, but no sound came. She wanted to give it to Mrs. Blynn: one positive and generous gesture she could still make to this essence of nonunderstanding, she thought, but now she had not the strength to make her want known—and that was like life, too, everything a little too late. Mrs. Palmer's lids shut on the vision of Mrs. Blynn's glassy, attentive eyes.

Suggestions for Discussion

1. What is "The Trouble with Mrs. Blynn?" What is "The Trouble with the World?" Are the two linked?

2. How does Mrs. Palmer face her coming death? What thoughts fill her mind as she thinks back upon her life?

3. What are Mrs. Palmer's feelings for Elsie?

4. What did Mrs. Palmer want to do with the amethyst pin? What becomes of it at the end of the story? Why does Highsmith end the story in this fashion?

Suggestion for Writing

What is your most valued possession and to whom would you bequeath it? Write about why this item is important to you and why you have chosen this particular person to be your heir.

෧෧෧෧

WILLIAM CARLOS WILLIAMS

The Use of Force

William Carlos Williams (1883–1963) practiced medicine in Rutherford, NJ, the factory town in which he was born. *Selected Poems* appeared in 1949, *Collected Later Poetry* in 1950, and *Collected Poems* in 1951. His long epic poem, *Paterson,* won the National Book Award for Poetry in 1950. *Desert Music* appeared in 1954, *Journey to Love* in 1955. He has also written novels, *White Mule* (1937) and *In the Money* (1940); short stories, *Life Along the Passaic* (1938) and *Selected Essays* (1954); and an *Autobiography* (1951). He received the Bollingen Award for Poetry in 1953. The simple and direct language in this short story, published in 1938, heightens the intensity of the feelings of the doctor, parents, and child.

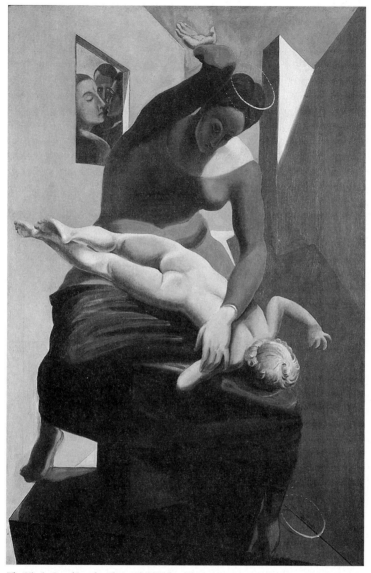

The Virgin Spanking the Christ Child Before Three Witnesses: André Breton, Paul Eluard and the Painter, oil on canvas, Max Ernst, 1926, Museum Ludwig, Cologne.

They were new patients to me, all I had was the name, Olson. Please come down as soon as you can, my daughter is very sick.

When I arrived I was met by the mother, a big startled looking woman, very clean and apologetic who merely said, Is this the doctor? and let me in.

In the back, she added. You must excuse us, doctor, we have her in the kitchen where it is warm. It is very damp here sometimes.

The child was fully dressed and sitting on her father's lap near the kitchen table. He tried to get up, but I motioned for him not to bother, took off my overcoat and started to look things over. I could see that they were all very nervous, eyeing me up and down distrustfully. As often, in such cases, they weren't telling me more than they had to, it was up to me to tell them; that's why they were spending three dollars on me.

The child was fairly eating me up with her cold, steady eyes, and no expression to her face whatever. She did not move and seemed, inwardly, quiet; an unusually attractive little thing, and as strong as a heifer in appearance. But her face was flushed, she was breathing rapidly, and I realized that she had a high fever. She had magnificent blonde hair, in profusion. One of those picture children often reproduced in advertising leaflets and the photogravure sections of the Sunday papers.

She's had a fever for three days, began the father, and we don't know what it comes from. My wife has given her things, you know, like people do, but it don't do no good. And there's been a lot of sickness around. So we tho't you'd better look her over and tell us what is the matter.

As doctors often do I took a trial shot at it as a point of departure. Has she had a sore throat?

Both parents answered me together, No...No, she says her throat don't hurt her.

Does your throat hurt you? added the mother to the child. But the little girl's expression didn't change nor did she move her eyes from my face.

Have you looked?

I tried to, said the mother, but I couldn't see.

As it happens we had been having a number of cases of diphtheria in the school to which this child went during that month and we were all, quite apparently, thinking of that, though no one had as yet spoken of the thing.

Well, I said, suppose we take a look at the throat first. I smiled in my best professional manner and asking for the child's first name I said, come on, Mathilda, open your mouth and let's take a look at your throat.

Nothing doing.

Aw, come on, I coaxed, just open your mouth wide and let me take a look. Look, I said opening both hands wide, I haven't anything in my hands. Just open up and let me see.

Such a nice man, put in the mother. Look how kind he is to you. Come on, do what he tells you to. He won't hurt you.

At that I ground my teeth in disgust. If only they wouldn't use the word "hurt" I might be able to get somewhere. But I did not allow myself to be hurried or disturbed but speaking quietly and slowly I approached the child again.

As I moved my chair a little nearer suddenly with one catlike movement both her hands clawed instinctively for my eyes and she almost reached them too. In fact she knocked my glasses flying and they fell, though unbroken, several feet away from me on the kitchen floor.

Both the mother and father almost turned themselves inside out in embarrassment and apology. You bad girl, said the mother, taking her and shaking her by one arm. Look what you've done. The nice man...

For heaven's sake, I broke in. Don't call me a nice man to her. I'm here to look at her throat on the chance that she might have diphtheria and possibly die of it. But that's nothing to her. Look here, I said to the child, we're going to look at your throat. You're old enough to understand what I'm saying. Will you open it now by yourself or shall we have to open it for you?

Not a move. Even her expression hadn't changed. Her breaths however were coming faster and faster. Then the battle began. I had to do it. I had to have a throat culture for her own protection. But first I told the parents that it was entirely up to them. I explained the danger but said that I would not insist on a throat examination so long as they would take the responsibility.

If you don't do what the doctor says you'll have to go to the hospital, the mother admonished her severely.

Oh yeah? I had to smile to myself. After all, I had already fallen in love with the savage brat, the parents were contemptible to me. In the ensuing struggle they grew more and more abject, crushed, exhausted while she surely rose to magnificent heights of insane fury of effort bred of her terror of me.

The father tried his best, and he was a big man but the fact that she was his daughter, his shame at her behavior, and his dread of hurting her made him release her just at the critical times when I had almost achieved success, till I wanted to kill him. But his dread also that she might have diphtheria made him tell me to go on, go on though he himself was almost fainting, while the mother moved back and forth behind us raising and lowering her hands in an agony of apprehension.

Put her in front of you on your lap, I ordered, and hold both her wrists.

But as soon as he did the child let out a scream. Don't, you're hurting me. Let go of my hands. Let them go I tell you. Then she shrieked terrifyingly, hysterically. Stop it! Stop it! You're killing me!

Do you think she can stand it, doctor? said the mother.

You get out, said the husband to his wife. Do you want her to die of diphtheria?

Come on now, hold her, I said.

Then I grasped the child's head with my left hand and tried to get the wooden tongue depressor between her teeth. She fought, with clenched teeth, desperately! But now I also had grown furious—at a child. I tried to hold myself down but I couldn't. I know how to expose a throat for inspection. And I did my best. When finally I got the wooden spatula behind the last teeth and just the point of it into the mouth cavity, she opened up for an instant but before I could see anything she came down again and gripped the wooden blade between her molars; she reduced it to splinters before I could get it out again.

Aren't you ashamed, the mother yelled at her. Aren't you ashamed to act like that in front of the doctor?

Get me a smooth-handled spoon of some sort, I told the mother. We're going through with this. The child's mouth was already bleeding. Her tongue was cut and she was screaming in wild hysterical shrieks. Perhaps I should have desisted and come back in an hour or more. No doubt it would have been better. But I have seen at least two children lying dead in bed of neglect in such cases, and feeling that I must get a diagnosis now or never I went at it again. But the worst of it was that I too had got beyond reason. I could have torn the child apart in my own fury and enjoyed it. It was a pleasure to attack her. My face was burning with it.

The damned little brat must be protected against her own idiocy, one says to one's self at such times. Others must be protected against her. It is a social necessity. And all these things are true. But a blind fury, a feeling of adult shame, bred of a longing for muscular release are the operatives. One goes on to the end.

In the final unreasoning assault I overpowered the child's neck and jaws. I forced the heavy silver spoon back of her teeth and down her throat till she gagged. And there it was—both tonsils covered with membrane. She had fought valiantly to keep me from knowing her secret. She had been hiding that sore throat for three days at least and lying to her parents in order to escape just such an outcome as this.

Now truly she was furious. She had been on the defensive before but now she attacked. Tried to get off her father's lap and fly at me while tears of defeat blinded her eyes.

Suggestions for Discussion

1. How do you explain the child's resistance to the doctor? What is her relationship to her parents?

2. Account for the doctor's statement: "I had already fallen in love with the savage brat, the parents were contemptible to me." How are the doctor's feelings reflected during the struggle? How does he rationalize them?

3. Comment on the use of force. What alternatives did the doctor have?

4. Look at the image on page 153 carefully. What feelings does this image prompt in you? Surprise? Offense? Is the use of force ever justifiable?

Suggestion for Writing

Create a scene in which there is interaction between the child and her parents.

~~~~~~~~

LOUISE ERDRICH

A Wedge of Shade

Louise Erdrich (b. 1954), of Chippewa extraction, is a leading voice among Native American writers. Born in Minnesota, she received her B.A. from Dartmouth and her M.A. from Johns Hopkins University. She has won the Nelson Algren Award and the National Books Critics Circle Award for fiction and was first on the *New York Times* bestseller list with her novels *The Beet Queen* (1986) and *Tracks* (1988). Her other works include *Baptism of Desire* (1989), *The Crown of Columbus* (1991), *The Blue Jay's Dance* (1995), *Tales of Burning Love* (1996), *The Antelope Wife* (1998), *The Birchbark House* (1999), and *Love Medicine* (2000). This short story, published in 1989, deals with the intensity of family bonds and the difficulty of loosening them to claim one's own life.

Every place that I could name you, in the whole world around us, has better things about it than Argus, North Dakota. I just happened to grow up there for eighteen years, and the soil got to be part of me, the air has something in it that I breathed. Argus water doesn't taste as good as water in the cities. Still, the first thing I do, walking back into my mother's house, is stand at the kitchen sink and toss down glass after glass.

"Are you filled up?" My mother stands behind me. "Sit down if you are."

She's tall and board-square, French-Chippewa, with long arms and big knuckles. Her face is rawboned, fierce, and almost masculine in its edges and planes. Several months ago, a beauty operator convinced her that she should feminize her look with curls. Now the permanent, grown out in grizzled streaks, bristles like the coat of a terrier. I don't look like her. Not just the hair, since hers is salt-and-pepper and mine is a reddish brown, but my build. I'm short, boxy, more like my Aunt Mary. Like her, I can't seem to shake this town. I keep coming back here.

"There's jobs at the beet plant," my mother says.

This rumor, probably false, since the plant is in a slump, drops into the dim, close air of the kitchen. We have the shades drawn because it's a hot June, over a hundred degrees, and we're trying to stay cool. Outside, the water has been sucked from everything. The veins in the leaves are hollow, the ditch grass is crackling. The sky has absorbed every drop. It's a thin whitish-blue veil stretched from end to end over us, a flat gauze tarp. From the depot, I've walked here beneath it, dragging my suitcase.

We're sweating as if we're in an oven, a big messy one. For a week, it's been too hot to clean much or even move, and the crops are stunted, failing. The farmer next to us just sold his field for a subdivision, but the construction workers aren't doing much. They're wearing wet rags on their heads, sitting near the house sites in the brilliance of noon. The studs of wood stand upright over them, but uselessly—nothing casts shadows. The sun has dried them up, too.

"The beet plant," my mother says again.

"Maybe so," I say, and then, because I've got something bigger on my mind, "Maybe I'll go out there and apply."

"Oh?" She is intrigued now.

"God, this is terrible!" I take the glass of water in my hand and tip some onto my head. I don't feel cooler, though; I just feel the steam rising off me.

"The fan broke down," she states. "Both of them are kaput now. The motors or something. If Mary would get the damn tax refund, we'd run out to Pamida, buy a couple more, set up a breeze. Then we'd be cool out here."

"Your garden must be dead," I say, lifting the edge of the pull shade.

"It's sick, but I watered. And I won't mulch; that draws the damn slugs."

"Nothing could live out there, no bug." My eyes smart from even looking at the yard, which is a clear sheet of sun, almost incandescent.

"You'd be surprised."

I wish I could blurt it out, just tell her. Even now, the words swell in my mouth, the one sentence, but I'm scared, and with good reason. There is this about my mother: it is awful to see her angry. Her lips press together and she stiffens herself within, growing wooden, silent. Her features become fixed and remote, she will not speak. It takes a long time, and until she does you are held in suspense. Nothing that she ever says, in the end, is as bad as that feeling of dread. So I wait, half believing that she'll figure out my secret for herself, or drag it out of me, not that she ever tries. If I'm silent, she hardly notices. She's not like Aunt Mary, who forces me to say more than I know is on my mind.

My mother sighs. "It's too hot to bake. It's too hot to cook. But it's too hot to eat anyway."

She's talking to herself, which makes me reckless. Perhaps she is so preoccupied by the heat that I can slip my announcement past her. I should just say it, but I lose nerve, make an introduction that alerts her. "I have something to tell you."

I've cast my lot; there's no going back unless I think quickly. My thoughts hum.

But she waits, forgetting the heat for a moment.

"Ice," I say. "We have to have ice." I speak intensely, leaning toward her, almost glaring, but she is not fooled.

"Don't make me laugh," she says. "There's not a cube in town. The refrigerators can't keep cold enough." She eyes me the way a hunter eyes an animal about to pop from its den and run.

"O.K." I break down. "I really do have something." I stand, turn my back. In this lightless warmth I'm dizzy, almost sick. Now I've gotten to her and she's frightened to hear, breathless.

"Tell me," she urges. "Go on, get it over with."

And so I say it. "I got married." There is a surge of relief, a wind blowing through the room, but then it's gone. The curtain flaps and we're caught again, stunned in an even denser heat. It's now my turn to wait, and I whirl around and sit right across from her. Now is the time to tell her his name, a Chippewa name that she'll know from the papers, since he's notorious. Now is the time to get it over with. But I can't bear the picture she makes, the shock that parts her lips, the stunned shade of hurt in her eyes. I have to convince her, somehow, that it's all right.

"You hate weddings! Just think, just picture it. Me, white net. On a day like this. You, stuffed in your summer wool, and Aunt Mary, God knows…and the tux, the rental, the groom…"

Her head had lowered as my words fell on her, but now her forehead tips up and her eyes come into view, already hardening. My tongue flies back into my mouth.

She mimics, making it a question, "The groom…"

I'm caught, my lips half open, a stuttering noise in my throat. How to begin? I have rehearsed this, but my lines melt away, my opening, my casual introductions. I can think of nothing that would convince her of how much more he is than the captions beneath the photos. There is no picture adequate, no representation that captures him. So I just put my hand across the table and I touch her hand. "Mother," I say, as if we're in a staged drama, "he'll arrive here shortly."

There is something forming in her, some reaction. I am afraid to let it take complete shape. "Let's go out and wait on the steps, Mom. Then you'll see him."

"I do not understand," she says in a frighteningly neutral voice. This is what I mean. Everything is suddenly forced, unnatural—we're reading lines.

"He'll approach from a distance." I can't help speaking like a bad actor. "I told him to give me an hour. He'll wait, then he'll come walking down the road."

We rise and unstick our blouses from our stomachs, our skirts from the backs of our legs. Then we walk out front in single file, me behind, and settle ourselves on the middle step. A scrubby box-elder tree on one side casts a light shade, and the dusty lilacs seem to catch a little breeze on the other. It's not so bad out here, still hot, but not so dim, contained. It is worse past the trees. The heat shimmers in a band, rising off the fields, out of the spars and bones of houses that will wreck our view. The horizon and the edge of town show through the gaps in the framing now, and as we sit we watch the workers move, slowly, almost in a practiced recital, back and forth. Their headcloths hang to their shoulders, their hard hats are dabs of yellow, their white T-shirts blend into the fierce air and sky. They don't seem to be doing anything, although we hear faint thuds from their hammers. Otherwise, except for the whistles of a few birds, there is silence. Certainly we don't speak.

It is a longer wait than I anticipated, maybe because he wants to give me time. At last the shadows creep out, hard, hot, charred, and the heat begins to lengthen and settle. We are going into the worst of the afternoon when a dot at the end of the road begins to form.

Mom and I are both watching. We have not moved our eyes around much, and we blink and squint to try and focus. The dot doesn't change, not for a long while. And then it suddenly springs clear in relief—a silhouette, lost for a moment in the shimmer, reappearing. In that shining expanse he is a little wedge of moving shade. He continues, growing imperceptibly, until there are variations in the outline, and it can be seen that he is large. As he passes the construction workers, they turn and stop, all alike in their hats, stock-still.

Growing larger yet, as if he has absorbed their stares, he nears us. Now we can see the details. He is dark, the first thing. His arms are thick, his chest is huge, and the features of his face are wide and open. He carries nothing in his hands. He wears a black T-shirt, the opposite of the construction workers, and soft jogging shoes. His jeans are held under his stomach by a belt with a star beaded on the buckle. His hair is long, in a tail. I am the wrong woman for him. I am paler, shorter, un-magnificent. But I stand up. Mom joins me, and I answer proudly when she asks, "His name?"

"His name is Gerry—" Even now I can't force his last name through my lips. But Mom is distracted by the sight of him anyway.

We descend one step, and stop again. It is here we will receive him. Our hands are folded at our waists. We're balanced, composed. He continues to stroll toward us, his white smile widening, his eyes filling with the sight of me as mine are filling with him. At the end of the road behind him, another dot has appeared. It is fast-moving and the sun flares off it twice: a vehicle. Now there are two figures—one approaching in a spume of dust from the rear, and Gerry, unmindful, not slackening or quickening his pace, continuing on. It is like a choreography design. They move at parallel speeds in front of our eyes. Then, at the same moment, at the end of our yard, they conclude the performance; both of them halt.

Gerry stands, looking toward us, his thumbs in his belt. He nods respectfully to Mom, looks calmly at me, and half smiles. He raises his brows, and we're suspended. Officer Lovchik emerges from the police car, stooped and tired. He walks up behind Gerry and I hear the snap of handcuffs, then I jump. I'm stopped by Gerry's gaze, though, as he backs away from me, still smiling tenderly. I am paralyzed halfway down the walk. He kisses the air while Lovchik cautiously prods at him, fitting his prize into the car. And then the doors slam, the engine roars, and they back out and turn around. As they move away there is no siren. I think I've heard Lovchik mention questioning. I'm sure it is lots of fuss for nothing, a mistake, but it cannot be denied—this is terrible timing.

I shake my shoulders, smooth my skirt, and turn to my mother with a look of outrage. "How do you like that?" I try.

She's got her purse in one hand, her car keys out.

"Let's go," she says.

"O.K.," I answer. "Fine. Where?"

"Aunt Mary's."

"I'd rather go and bail him out, Mom."

"Bail," she says. "*Bail?*"

She gives me such a look of cold and furious surprise that I sink immediately into the front seat, lean back against the vinyl. I almost welcome the sting of the heated plastic on my back, thighs, shoulders.

Aunt Mary lives at the rear of the butcher shop she runs. As we walk toward the "House of Meats," her dogs are rugs in the dirt, flattened by the heat of the day. Not one of them barks at us to warn her. We step over them and get no more reaction than a whine, the slow beat of a tail. Inside, we get no answers either, although we call Aunt Mary up and down the hall. We enter the kitchen and sit at the table, which holds a half-ruined watermelon. By the sink, in a tin box, are cigarettes. My mother takes one and carefully puts a match to it, frowning. "I know what," she says. "Go check the lockers."

There are two—a big freezer full of labelled meats and rental space, and another, smaller one that is just a side cooler. I notice, walking past the meat display counter, that the red beacon beside the outside switch of the cooler is glowing. That tells you when the light is on inside.

I pull the long metal handle toward me and the thick door swishes open. I step into the cool, spicy air. Aunt Mary is there, too proud to ever register a hint of surprise. She simply nods and looks away as though I've just been out for a minute, although we've not seen one another in six months or more. She is relaxing on a big can of pepper labelled "Zanzibar," reading a scientific-magazine article. I sit down on a barrel of alum. With no warning, I drop my bomb; "I'm married." It doesn't matter how I tell it to Aunt Mary, because she won't be, refuses to be, surprised.

"What's he do?" she simply asks, putting aside the sheaf of paper. I thought the first thing she'd do was scold me for fooling my mother. But it's odd, for two women who have lived through boring times and disasters, how rarely one comes to the other's defense, and how often they are each willing to take advantage of the other's absence. But I'm benefiting here. It seems that Aunt Mary is truly interested in Gerry. So I'm honest.

"He's something like a political activist. I mean he's been in jail and all. But not for any crime, you see; it's just because of his convictions."

She gives me a long, shrewd stare. Her skin is too tough to wrinkle, but she doesn't look young. All around us hang loops of sausages, every kind you can imagine, every color, from the purple-black of blutwurst to the pale-whitish links that my mother likes best. Blocks of butter and headcheese, a can of raw milk, wrapped parcels, and cured bacons are stuffed onto the shelves around us. My heart has gone still and cool inside me, and I can't stop talking.

"He's the kind of guy it's hard to describe. Very different. People call him a free spirit, but that doesn't say it either, because he's very disciplined in some ways. He learned to be neat in jail." I pause. She says nothing, so I go on. "I know it's sudden, but who likes weddings? I hate them—all that mess with the bridesmaids' gowns, getting material to match. I don't have girlfriends. I mean, how embarrassing, right? Who would sing 'O Perfect Love'? Carry the ring?"

She isn't really listening.

"What's he do?" she asks again.

Maybe she won't let go of it until I discover the right answer, like a game with nouns and synonyms.

"He—well, he agitates," I tell her.

"Is that some kind of factory work?"

"Not exactly, no, it's not a nine-to-five job or anything…"

She lets the magazine fall, now, cocks her head to one side, and stares at me without blinking her cold yellow eyes. She has the look of a hawk, of a person who can see into the future but won't tell you about it. She's lost business for staring at customers, but she doesn't care.

"Are you telling me that he doesn't…" Here she shakes her head twice, slowly, from one side to the other, without removing me from her stare. "That he doesn't have regular work?"

"Oh, what's the matter, anyway?" I say roughly. "I'll work. This is the nineteen-seventies."

She jumps to her feet, stands over me—a stocky woman with terse features and short, thin points of gray hair. Her earrings tremble and flash—small fiery opals. Her brown plastic glasses hang crooked on a cord around her neck. I have never seen her become quite so instantly furious, so disturbed. "We're going to fix that," she says.

The cooler immediately feels smaller, the sausages knock at my shoulder, and the harsh light makes me blink. I am as stubborn as Aunt Mary, however, and she knows that I can go head to head with her. "We're married and that's final." I manage to stamp my foot.

Aunt Mary throws an arm back, blows air through her cheeks, and waves away my statement vigorously. "You're a little girl. How old is *he?*"

I frown at my lap, trace the threads in my blue cotton skirt, and tell her that age is irrelevant.

"Big word," she says sarcastically. "Let me ask you this. He's old enough to get a job?"

"Of course he is; what do you think? O.K., he's older than me. He's in his thirties."

"Aha, I knew it."

"Geez! So what? I mean, haven't you ever been in love, hasn't someone ever gotten you *right here?*" I smash my fist on my chest.

We lock eyes, but she doesn't waste a second in feeling hurt. "Sure, sure I've been in love. You think I haven't? I know what it feels like, you smart-ass. You'd be surprised. But he was no lazy son of a bitch. Now, listen…" She stops, draws breath, and I let her. "Here's what I mean by 'fix.' I'll teach the sausage-making trade to him—to you, too—and the grocery business. I've about had it anyway, and so's your mother. We'll do the same as my aunt and uncle—leave the shop to you and move to Arizona. I like this place." She looks up at the burning safety bulb, down at me again. Her face drags in the light. "But what the hell. I always wanted to travel."

I'm stunned, a little flattened out, maybe ashamed of myself. "You hate going anywhere," I say, which is true.

The door swings open and Mom comes in with us. She finds a milk can and balances herself on it, sighing at the delicious feeling of the air, absorbing from the silence the fact that we have talked. She hasn't anything to add, I guess, and as the coolness hits, her eyes fall shut. Aunt Mary's too. I can't help it, either, and my eyelids drop, although my brain is conscious and alert. From the darkness, I can see us in the brilliance. The light rains down on us. We sit the way we have been sitting, on our cans of milk and pepper, upright and still. Our hands are curled loosely in our laps. Our faces are blank as the gods'. We could be statues in a tomb sunk into the side of a mountain. We could be dreaming the world up in our brains.

It is later, and the weather has no mercy. We are drained of everything but simple thoughts. It's too hot for feelings. Driving home, we see how field after field of beets has gone into shock, and even some of the soybeans. The plants splay, limp, burned into the ground. Only the sunflowers continue to struggle upright, bristling but small.

What drew me in the first place to Gerry was the unexpected. I went to hear him talk just after I enrolled at the university, and then I demonstrated when they came and got him off the stage. He always went so willingly, accommodating everyone. I began to visit him. I sold lunar calendars and posters to raise his bail and eventually free him. One thing led to another, and one night we found ourselves alone in a Howard Johnson's coffee shop downstairs from where they put him up when his speech was finished. There were much more beautiful women after him; he could have had his pick of Swedes or Yankton Sioux girls, who are the best-looking of all. But I was different, he says. He liked my slant on life. And then there was no going back once it started, no turning, as though it was meant. We had no choice.

I have this intuition as we near the house, in the fateful quality of light, as in the turn of the day the heat continues to press and the blackness, into which the warmth usually lifts, lowers steadily: We must come to the end of something; there must be a close to this day.

As we turn into the yard we see that Gerry is sitting on the porch stairs. Now it is our turn to be received. I throw the car door open and stumble out before the motor even cuts. I run to him and hold him, as my mother, pursuing the order of events, parks carefully. Then she walks over, too, holding her purse by the strap. She stands before him and says no word but simply looks into his face, staring as if he's cardboard, a man behind glass who cannot see her. I think she's rude, but then I realize that he is staring back, that they are the same height. Their eyes are level.

He puts his hand out. "My name is Gerry."

"Gerry what?"

"Nanapush."

She nods, shifts her weight. "You're from that line, the old strain, the ones…" She does not finish.

"And my father," Gerry says, "was Old Man Pillager."

"Kashpaws," she says, "are my branch, of course. We're probably related through my mother's brother." They do not move. They are like two opponents from the same divided country, staring across the border. They do not shift or blink, and I see that they are more alike than I am like either one of them—so tall, solid, dark-haired. They could be mother and son.

"Well, I guess you should come in," she offers. "You are a distant relative, after all." She looks at me. "Distant enough."

Whole swarms of mosquitoes are whining down, discovering us now, so there is no question of staying where we are. And so we walk into the house, much hotter than outside, with the gathered heat. Instantly the sweat springs from our skin and I can think of nothing else but cooling off. I try to force the windows higher in their sashes, but there's no breeze anyway; nothing stirs, no air.

"Are you sure," I gasp, "about those fans?"

"Oh, they're broke, all right," my mother says, distressed. I rarely hear this in her voice. She switches on the lights, which makes the room seem hotter, and we lower ourselves into the easy chairs. Our words echo, as though the walls have baked and dried hollow.

"Show me those fans," says Gerry.

My mother points toward the kitchen. "They're sitting on the table. I've already tinkered with them. See what you can do."

And so he does. After a while she hoists herself and walks out back to him. Their voices close together now, absorbed, and their tools clank frantically, as if they are fighting a duel. But it is a race with the bell of darkness and their waning energy. I think of ice. I get ice on the brain.

"Be right back," I call out, taking the car keys from my mother's purse. "Do you need anything?"

There is no answer from the kitchen but a furious sputter of metal, the clatter of nuts and bolts spilling to the floor.

I drive out to the Superpumper, a big new gas-station complex on the edge of town, where my mother most likely has never been. She doesn't know about convenience stores, has no credit cards for groceries or gas, pays only with small bills and change. She never has used an ice machine. It would grate on her that a bag of frozen water costs eighty cents, but it doesn't bother me. I take the plastic-foam cooler and I fill it for a couple of dollars. I buy two six-packs of Shasta soda and I plunge them in among the uniform cubes of ice. I drink two myself on the way home, and I manage to lift the whole heavy cooler out of the trunk, carry it to the door.

The fans are whirring, beating the air. I hear them going in the living room the minute I come in. The only light shines from the kitchen. Gerry and my mother have thrown the pillows from the couch onto the living-room floor, and they are sitting in the rippling currents of air. I bring the cooler in and put it near us. I have chosen all dark flavors—black cherry, grape, red berry, cola—so as we drink the darkness swirls inside us with the night air, sweet and sharp, driven by small motors.

I drag more pillows down from the other rooms upstairs. There is no question of attempting the bedrooms, the stifling beds. And so, in the dark, I hold hands with Gerry as he settles down between my mother and me. He is huge as a hill between the two of us, solid in the beating wind.

Suggestions for Discussion

1. What does the metaphor "a wedge of shade" have to do with the relationships between the characters in the story?

2. Erdrich uses light and dark, hot and cold, movement and stillness as ways of making us both respond to and understand what is happening in the story. How does she do this? What feelings are evoked? What do we come to know through these metaphors?

3. What reconciles Mom to Gerry?

Suggestions for Writing

1. Metaphors engage us in what is going on without ever becoming explicit about it. Write about a metaphor that expresses something you want to say about a relationship important to you.

2. Write a brief story about what happens in a family when a stranger enters it to stay.

ELIZABETH SPENCER

Instrument of Destruction

While attending Belhaven College in her native Mississippi, Elizabeth Spencer (b. 1921) befriended Eudora Welty and began to cultivate her lifelong interest in writing. After college, she won a Guggenheim Fellowship and moved to Italy, which became the setting of her novella *The Light in the Piazza* (1960). Though she spent long periods living in Europe and Canada, her Southern roots are apparent in works such as *The Voice at the Back Door* (1956) and *The Night Travelers* (1991). Spencer's short fiction has won five O. Henry prizes and been reproduced in collections such as *The Pushcart Prize.* "Instrument of Destruction" concerns a young boy whose privileged family background protects him from the consequences of his mischievous behavior.

I think that someday I am going to come home and not have to hear anything about the little boy next door. But that may be because he has killed my aunt or she has stopped being a lady long enough to kill him. Of course, what he's been doing in the yard is a shame. He's ruined all the flower beds with his tricycle and now he's starting on the shrubs, breaking the thinner fronds out of the center of the spirea to plait into whips and ropes, and removing blossoms from the crêpe myrtle. Nobody can catch him. He waits till my aunt does her shopping, goes to the grocery, or uptown, or to a church meeting, or to the nursing home.

The reason my aunt doesn't like to make an issue about the boy next door is that she was so glad when he and his folks moved in. They have class and good taste and breeding; they come from an excellent family she has some connection with, down in Columbus, Mississippi, a very aristocratic town. Before they came she had nobody but the most ordinary neighbors, people of no interest to her. One woman—the one on the other side of her still—she really does not like and goes to some pains to avoid. The reason she gives is that the woman looks punished by life. True, the woman's husband is down-at-the-heels, has a low-paying job (night copy-desk editor at the newspaper), sleeps all day, looks unshaven, probably drinks too much, and never speaks. His wife's face reflects all this. Well, of course, it does, I tell her. But my aunt can't agree, can't see things this way.

She has had terrible misfortunes about Uncle Paul's illness, being alone, no one to lean on, yet she keeps everything up to a certain mark. The yard is taken care of; a man comes once a week to clip, weed, and mow. Her dresses are always fresh-looking and smart, her gloves when she goes out are white as snow. Her table is set with the best linen and china, every meal. She feels that life has to reach a certain standard daily, has to be pretty and fresh, or it isn't worth calling life. She was beginning to get discouraged, to feel herself islanded in a world that didn't understand her feelings—I obviously do nothing to suit her, trailing out to class daily at the university in skirts and blouses she wouldn't be caught dead in, and going around with what she would call the dregs of humanity if she would come right out and say so.

Then the McAllisters moved in.

Her heart lifted—I could tell—even before she met them, because the painters came and took the horrible gray trim off the house next door with neat applications of white. The windows got removed and painted as well, and new screens installed. Suddenly there were no cobwebs and the panes were glossy clear. Next the porch got freshly done and touches of iron were covered in black enamel. It went on like that. One afternoon, vans arrived, and shining antiques were lifted out from dim, churchlike interiors padded with green quilted hangings, and were transferred smoothly within, not a scratch on the lot, so far as we could tell. Chests came passing after. It was late afternoon with my aunt in the rocker and me in the swing, out on the front porch. "Don't let's look," said my aunt and we both began to laugh, because we both were drinking it all in, from sheer curiosity. Those chests would have draperies in them, we agreed, and linens and silver. Then came packing boxes, lightly borne: china and ornaments, we bet. The rugs followed, bound with lengths of grass rope and bending supple and velvety in the middle. And last of all, on another day, the people came. We'd seen them before, as buyers and directors of workmen. But that day the car—a dark Buick—stopped in the drive with finality and out came the man, the woman, and the boy, and in they went, and the door closed fast.

I have to hand it to my aunt in a lot of ways. If her sort of standards interested me (they don't), I guess I would want to behave just the way she did. She did not, for one thing, try to talk to the new neighbors over the hedge or across the fence in the back yard. She did not send over a cake or some cookies, with a coy welcome-to-our-street note tucked inside. She did not—God forbid—go to "call." As a matter of fact, she did not seem to notice the new family at all. She came and went in her fresh summer outfits and her snow-white gloves. One day, up at the corner (our street slopes down hill) she ran into the woman next door and she was about to pass with a nod but the woman spoke to her and thus she—my aunt—found herself stopped, greeted, even welcomed, in a way, and asked about things. What did one do about cleaning women, gardeners, groceries, etc.? Wouldn't it be nice to break the ice and get better acquainted? The new family did not know Tennessee at all. They were from Columbus, Mississippi. My aunt let go the name of a family there, an exceptionally good family. Like a charming bird released from its cage, the name circled the heads of those two ladies twice and thrice before it shot singing into the bright blue sky. In a day or so my aunt was invited over for a drink.

That weekend she was happier, more content with life, than I had seen her in a long time. The difference was in her eyes and face, in her walk and her voice, everywhere. They had asked all about her. She had told them about Uncle Paul and about me, her niece at the university, and how she'd never had children. They had understood her, it seemed. They had liked her. The little boy was so sweet, she told me. He had got some paints as a present and had brought them to show her.

The next week she had a better chance than over to see the paints—they were all over the sidewalk. I saw them myself.

"Listen, Auntie," I said, "don't worry. It just means he subscribes to *Mad* magazine. That's where he's copied all that."

"I think he's an awful little midget," she said. "They're pretending he's a little boy."

But she kept on accepting when they asked her over for a drink and one warm lovely twilight, she had them, too, out in her garden. (They had got a sitter for the little boy.) Then, being so continually understood by them and so personally treated, she had them to a dinner with a couple of old friends. She loved to give small parties when Uncle Paul was there with her and now it all came back, the first she'd given since he went to the nursing home; she was both sad and excited. But being sociable at heart, her excitement won out and the dinner was a huge success. (The McAllisters, again, left the child with the baby-sitter.)

I myself am not interested in much social life; it seems to me a waste of time, I know when I graduate I will go on to graduate school in one of the sciences, that I will always know people in groups, we will always like music and books together, sex will be (already is) a pairing off among us, we will do cooking that is interesting and good! Married apartment living or small house living around campuses of research centers is what I see in my future. It is good enough. I don't care much where I live as long as it is humanly habitable. This is me. From about the time I got interested in high school chemistry and physics, I have been like this. I went to live with my aunt because my folks knew she needed money (she lives near the campus). But of course I haven't been any real help to her at all. We don't exchange confidences or ideas or anything. I have long dark hair and go around in sandals till my feet just about freeze. If she thinks I'm going to change, she is mistaken. This is me.

Little at a time, my aunt gave the McAllisters their whole social life in her city. She launched them. Otherwise they wouldn't have known the right people at all. This is what my aunt says, and she may be right. They had her to dinner soon with Mr. McAllister's boss (unimpressive, she said) and his wife (a bore, from a boring family she used to know in the church), and they also asked the couple she had introduced them to. Soon they were going to her church and she was leading them up to people there who had been friends of hers and Uncle Paul's and they were delighted with them all. She let them use her willingly because she had been longing for her own kind near her, people who understood her in a deep way. That was why she didn't raise too big a row when the little boy broke down the back fence. The McAllisters said he was an Imaginative child and was always playing games in which something became something else. The fence was one wall of a fort, for instance, and was attacked and taken. Then the sidewalk was like a concrete tablet for drawing on and my aunt's flowers were enemy children from another planet and her crêpe myrtle blossoms were a secret poison to be cooked in with Irish stew and fed to a visiting Indian chief who was treacherous and meant to attack in the night.

"Do you tell Uncle Paul all this?" I ask my aunt.

"Of course not," she says, "what can he do? I told him about the McAllisters, of course. He's glad I'm so happy with them."

I wonder if she really is. I think she worries. How can she end the trouble with that child? What can she do? I think the child is crazy. He doesn't bother any other house or property but hers. From her front gate he murmurs ugly words, conducts (as long as anybody will listen) a bad dialogue with passers-by. My aunt is afraid of making issues, of telling the whole truth. She is afraid not only of losing the McAllisters but also of losing something else which the McAllisters by recognizing have increased her faith in: that is, her own self-image, her own belief in her unfailing charm and courtesy. So she can't take any steps at all, and something terrible will happen.

Her new friendship, which had opened up so beautifully and which she had given her all to with such whole-hearted skill, is not what she had hoped for. I see she is looking strained again and lonelier than before. I could say I dreamed she was tied to a stake in an Indian village while a child raced round her on a tricycle with a feather stuck through a band around its brow, whooping. But I didn't dream that.

He has started cutting the bark off her trees. He has a knife and removes the bark skillfully, in long strips.

I come home unexpectedly. That day I have a headache from too much formaldehyde in the lab plus my worst day of the month. My aunt is away at the nursing home. The child is working away on her pretty young maple. I walk across the lawn.

"Listen, Buster," I say. "You can get away with that with everybody but me. Now you put up that knife and get the hell on home, *comprenez?*"

He goes into a rage, no kidding. The knife slashes me twice before I can knock him winding, which I do. I'm pretty strong, not bad at tennis, and angry. Shocked, too, from the blood actually starting up out of my arm. I just plain clobber him. Then (it's raining and cold) I am racing in for a tourniquet to save my own life and the child is yelling to wake the dead. I am tearing up a cup towel in my aunt's kitchen and calling a cab to get myself to the hospital out-patient emergency entrance. That little bastard nearly killed me. By the time they stitch me up I'm about passed out but faint thoughts murmur something about the mess in my aunt's kitchen, blood all over the floor and for all I know dripped through the hall, over rugs and tables, staining walk and doorway.

Once a month I make the effort to go out with my aunt to see Uncle Paul. A man with naturally dark skin, he has kept his color better than most people would with what he's got and though emaciated he still has his keen glance. He doesn't make you feel sorry for him. I never knew him very well. I don't know him now.

He sits and plays checkers with some of the patients in the sun parlor every day and sometimes bridge, which amuses him more. He reads. I guess he must have been fun to talk to once and in love with her and all that. She must have loved his wiriness, attractive in a man, and loved the thin blade of his cheekbone pressed to hers. Now they've had their love, at least, and they hold hands. When I'm not there they may cry a little, but with me present they make an occasion of the visit, something they charmingly measure up to. I'm not worth it, I want to say. No. No, not that. Nobody is worth it, I want to say. Yet they are going to do it. They go right ahead, light and conversational, pretending the abyss isn't there.

"What happened to your arm?" Uncle Paul asks me.

How far can I go? I don't want to worry him. "An accident," I say.

"She was cutting a cantaloupe," my aunt says, "with that knife—oh, you remember those knives I had to have, handmade with hickory handles, from way out in the country. You always warned me."

"Get those things too sharp, you've got more than a knife," Uncle Paul says. "You've got an instrument of destruction." He laughs. "Is it okay now?"

"Sure," I say.

"Mighty glad you're with Mary," he tells me. He always says that.

"She's great," I say. I like him.

"Sure she is."

He asks about the McAllisters and she says they're fine.

But relations have certainly cooled with the McAllisters since the day their little boy slashed into me. They don't telephone any more. I feel they're going to have to look back on knowing my aunt as an incident of their first year in the new town. Among the other families on the street, those people my aunt doesn't care to know, the word has got round that the boy has calmed down quite a bit since I knocked hell out of him. My aunt would have a great chance now, if she'd make the slightest effort, to make some real human relationships on that street. They all know all about her, and some are there, mysterious among them, like everywhere, who can hold things up—sustainers in time of need.

But she doesn't want them. She wants friends like the McAllisters are, or would have been, if they hadn't given birth to that awful child.

Suggestions for Discussion

1. The narrator of the story feels that her aunt has outdated views of class. How does she characterize her aunt's views, and how does she challenge them?

2. Describe the relationship between the story's two female protagonists and Uncle Paul.

Suggestion for Writing

"Instrument of Destruction" seems to justify corporal punishment in dealing with a problematic child. Compare the measures the narrator takes with those advocated by William Carlos Williams in *The Use of Force* (p. 152) or Barbara Kingsolver in *Somebody's Baby* (p. 133).

POETRY

BOB DYLAN

It's Alright, Ma (I'm Only Bleeding)

Bob Dylan (b. 1941) is an icon of the cultural revolution of the 1960s and a Grammy-winning member of the Rock and Roll Hall of Fame. Influenced by folk music, rhythm and blues, rock 'n' roll, and gospel music, he has written hundreds of songs, recorded more than forty albums, and has sold more than fifty million copies of his recordings. Born Robert Allan Zimmerman in Duluth, Minnesota, Dylan moved to Greenwich Village in 1961 and composed his groundbreaking antiwar song, "Blowin' in the Wind," in 1963. His albums *Highway 61 Revisited* (1965) and *Blonde on Blonde* (1966) are among his most respected, along with his 1998 Grammy-winning album, *Time Out of Mind*. "Times Have Changed," a song he wrote for the motion picture *Wonder Boys*, won an Academy Award for best song in 2000. His album, *Love and Theft*, was released on September 11, 2001.

The following words were first sung by Bob Dylan and accompanied by instrumental music as part of his 1965 album *Bringing It All Back Home*.

> Darkness at the break of noon
> Shadows even the silver spoon
> The handmade blade, the children's balloon
> Eclipses both the sun and moon
> To understand you know too soon
> There is no sense in trying.
>
> Pointed threats they bluff with scorn
> Suicide remarks are torn
> From the fool's gold mouthpiece
> The hollow horn plays wasted words
> Proves to warn
> That he not busy being born
> Is busy dying.

172

Temptation's page flies out the door
You follow, find yourself at war
Watch waterfalls of pity roar
You feel to moan but unlike before
You discover
That you'd just be
One more person crying.

So don't fear if you hear
A foreign sound to your ear
It's alright Ma, I'm only sighing.

As some warn victory, some downfall
Private reasons great or small
Can be seen in the eyes of those that call
To make all that should be killed to crawl
While others say don't hate nothing at all
Except hatred.

Disillusioned words like bullets bark
As human gods aim for their mark
Made everything from toy guns that spark
To flesh-colored Christs that glow in the dark
It's easy to see without looking too far
That not much
Is really sacred.

While preachers preach of evil fates
Teachers teach that knowledge waits
Can lead to hundred-dollar plates
Goodness hides behind its gates
But even the president of the United States
Sometimes must have
To stand naked.

An' though the rules of the road have been lodged
It's only people's games that you got to dodge
And it's alright, Ma, I can make it.

Advertising signs that con you
Into thinking you're the one
That can do what's never been done
That can win what's never been won
Meantime life outside goes on
All around you.

You lose yourself, you reappear
You suddenly find you got nothing to fear
Alone you stand with nobody near
When a trembling distant voice, unclear
Startles your sleeping ears to hear
That somebody thinks
They really found you.

A question in your nerves is lit
Yet you know there is no answer fit to satisfy
Insure you not to quit
To keep it in your mind and not fergit
That it is not he or she or them or it
That you belong to.

Although the masters make the rules
For the wise men and the fools
I got nothing, Ma, to live up to.

For them that must obey authority
That they do not respect in any degree
Who despise their jobs, their destinies
Speak jealously of them that are free
Cultivate their flowers to be
Nothing more than something
They invest in.

While some on principles baptized
To strict party platform ties
Social clubs in drag disguise
Outsiders they can freely criticize
Tell nothing except who to idolize
And then say God bless him.

While one who sings with his tongue on fire
Gargles in the rat race choir
Bent out of shape from society's pliers
Cares not to come up any higher
But rather get you down in the hole
That he's in.

But I mean no harm nor put fault
On anyone that lives in a vault
But it's alright, Ma, if I can't please him.

Old lady judges watch people in pairs
Limited in sex, they dare
To push fake morals, insult and stare
While money doesn't talk, it swears
Obscenity, who really cares
Propaganda, all is phony.

While them that defend what they cannot see
With a killer's pride, security
It blows the minds most bitterly
For them that think death's honesty
Won't fall upon them naturally
Life sometimes
Must get lonely.

My eyes collide head-on with stuffed graveyards
False gods, I scuff
At pettiness which plays so rough
Walk upside-down inside handcuffs
Kick my legs to crash it off
Say okay, I have had enough
What else can you show me?

And if my thought-dreams could be seen
They'd probably put my head in a guillotine
But it's alright, Ma, it's life, and life only.

Suggestions for Discussion

1. What does the title of this piece mean?

2. How does the speaker feel about "the masters [who] make the rules"?

3. If you have heard the song "It's Alright, Ma (I'm Only Bleeding)" in its original form, how is it different seeing these lyrics in isolation now, as opposed to hearing them interpreted vocally by Dylan? Does the meaning change? Do you prefer reading the lyrics or hearing them sung? Why?

Suggestion for Writing

Write the lyrics to a song that features the mother's response to her son.

DIANE DI PRIMA

To My Father

Diane Di Prima (b. 1934), a member of the Beat movement, has written more than thirty books of poetry and prose, including the 1969 *Memoirs of a Beatnik*. She was born and raised in Brooklyn, New York, and relocated to northern California. Cofounder of the New York Poets Theatre and the Poets Press, and an organizer of the Gold Circle, Di Prima has also worked as a publisher and editor; taught poetry writing at the New College of California, San Francisco; and is a mother of five children. Highlights from her writings, many of which have been translated into a dozen languages, include *Dinners and Nightmares* (1961), *The Calculus of Variation* (1972), *Seminary Poems* (1991), and the plays *Murder Cake* and *Whale Honey*. Recent works include *Recollections of My Life as a Woman* and *Fun with Forms*, both printed in 2001.

In my dreams you stand among roses.
You are still the fine gardener you were.
You worry about mother.
You are still the fierce wind, the intolerable force that almost broke me.
Who forced my young body into awkward and proper clothes
Who spoke of his standing in the community.
And men's touch is still a little absurd to me
because you trembled when you touched me.
What external law were you expounding?
How can I take your name like prayer?
My youngest son has your eyes.
Why are you knocking at the doors of my brain?
You kept all their rules and more.
What were you promised that you cannot rest?
What fierce, angry honesty in the darkness?
What can you hope who had preferred my death
to the birth of my oldest daughter?
O fierce hummer of tunes

Forget, eat the black seedcake.
In my dreams you stand at the door of your house
and weep for your wife, my mother.

Suggestions for Discussion

1. How is the narrator's father a model for her vision of manhood?

2. What role does the narrator's mother play in the poem?

3. What is the tone of this poem?

Suggestion for Writing

Write a poem about your father.

E. E. CUMMINGS

my father moved through dooms of love

Edward Estlin Cummings (1894–1963) was an American whose novel *The Enormous Room* (1922) and whose books of poetry *&* (1925) and *XLI Poems* (1925) established his reputation as an avant-garde writer interested in experimenting with stylistic techniques. Awarded several important prizes for poetry, he also was Charles Eliot Norton Lecturer at Harvard University in 1952 and published *i: six nonlectures* (1953). The theme of wholeness and reconciliation of opposites in the father's character is implicitly expressed in this poem from *50 poems* (1940). Images of death, hate, and decay are counterpointed against images that celebrate life and growth.

> my father moved through dooms of love
> through sames of am through haves of give,
> singing each morning out of each night
> my father moved through depths of height

this motionless forgetful where
turned at his glance to shining here;
that if (so timid air is firm)
under his eyes would stir and squirm

newly as from unburied which
floats the first who, his april touch
drove sleeping selves to swarm their fates
woke dreamers to their ghostly roots

and should some why completely weep
my father's fingers brought her sleep:
vainly no smallest voice might cry
for he could feel the mountains grow.

Lifting the valleys of the sea
my father moved through griefs of joy;
praising a forehead called the moon
singing desire into begin

joy was his song and joy so pure
a heart of star by him could steer
and pure so now and now so yes
the wrists of twilight would rejoice

keen as midsummer's keen beyond
conceiving mind of sun will stand,
so strictly (over utmost him
so hugely) stood my father's dream

his flesh was flesh his blood was blood:
no hungry man but wished him food;
no cripple wouldn't creep one mile
uphill to only see him smile.

Scorning the pomp of must and shall
my father moved through dooms of feel;
his anger was as right as rain
his pity was as green as grain

septembering arms of year extend
less humbly wealth to foe and friend
than he to foolish and to wise
offered immeasurable is

proudly and (by octobering flame
beckoned) as earth will downward climb,

so naked for immortal work
his shoulders marched against the dark

his sorrow was as true as bread:
no liar looked him in the head;
if every friend became his foe
he'd laugh and build a world with snow.

My father moved through theys of we,
singing each new leaf out of each tree
(and every child was sure that spring
danced when she heard my father sing)

then let men kill which cannot share,
let blood and flesh be mud and mire,
scheming imagine, passion willed,
freedom a drug that's bought and sold

giving to steal and cruel kind,
a heart to fear, to doubt a mind,
to differ a disease of same,
conform the pinnacle of am

though dull were all we taste as bright,
bitter all utterly things sweet,
maggoty minus and dumb death
all we inherit, all bequeath

and nothing quite so least as truth
—i say though hate were why men breathe—
because my father lived his soul
love is the whole and more than all

Suggestions for Discussion

1. Study the verbal juxtapositions that seem antithetical: "dooms of love"; "depths of height"; "griefs of joy." How is the theme of wholeness and reconciliation of opposites in the character of the father implicitly expressed?

2. Cite passages in which the natural imagery of life, love, birth, and rebirth is counterpointed against images of death, hate, and decay.

SYLVIA PLATH

Daddy

Sylvia Plath (1932–1963) began her career while still a college student by serving as guest editor of *Mademoiselle.* She studied in both the United States and England, taught at Smith College, and then settled in England, where she lived until her suicide. Her poetry is collected in *The Colossus* (1960), *Ariel* (1965), *Crossing the Water* (1971), and *Winter Trees* (1972), and she contributed to such magazines as *Seventeen, Atlantic,* and *Nation. The Bell Jar,* her only novel, was written about her late-adolescent attempt at suicide and was published posthumously in 1963 under the pseudonym Victoria Lucas. In "Daddy," from the collection *Ariel,* the poet as child recalls the past and reinvokes her brutal image of her father.

You do not do, you do not do
Any more, black shoe
In which I have lived like a foot
For thirty years, poor and white,
Barely daring to breath or Achoo.

Daddy, I have had to kill you.
You died before I had time—
Marble-heavy, a bag full of God,
Ghastly statue with one grey toe
Big as a Frisco seal

And a head in the freakish Atlantic
Where it pours bean green over blue
In the waters off beautiful Nauset.
I used to pray to recover you.
Ach, du.

In the German tongue, in the Polish town
Scraped flat by the roller
Of wars, wars, wars.
But the name of the town is common.

My Polack friend

Says there are a dozen or two.
So I never could tell where you
Put your foot, your root,
I never could talk to you.
The tongue stuck in my jaw.

It stuck in a barb wire snare.
Ich, ich, ich, ich
I could hardly speak.
I thought every German was you.
And the language obscene

An engine, an engine
Chuffing me off like a Jew.
A Jew to Dachau, Auschwitz, Belsen.
I began to talk like a Jew.
I think I may well be a Jew.

The snows of the Tyrol, the clear beer of Vienna
Are not very pure or true.
With my gypsy ancestress and my weird luck
And my Taroc pack and my Taroc pack
I may be a bit of a Jew.

I have always been scared of *you,*
With your Luftwaffe, your gobbledygoo.
And your neat moustache
And your Aryan eye, bright blue.
Panzer-man, panzer-man, O You—

Not God but a swastika
So black no sky could squeak through.
Every woman adores a Fascist,
The boot in the face, the brute
Brute heart of a brute like you.

You stand at the blackboard, daddy,
In the picture I have of you,
A cleft in your chin instead of your foot
But no less a devil for that, no not
Any less the black man who

Bit my pretty red heart in two.
I was ten when they buried you.

At twenty I tried to die
And get back, back, back to you.
I thought even the bones would do.

But they pulled me out of the sack,
And they stuck me together with glue.
And then I knew what to do.
I made a model of you,
A man in black with a Meinkampf look

And a love of the rack and the screw.
And I said I do, I do.
So daddy, I'm finally through.
The black telephone's off at the root,
The voice just can't worm through.

If I've killed one man, I've killed two—
The vampire who said he was you
And drank my blood for a year,
Seven years, if you want to know.
Daddy, you can lie back now.

There's a stake in your fat black heart
And the villagers never liked you.
They are dancing and stamping on you.
They always *knew* it was you.
Daddy, daddy, you bastard, I'm through.

Suggestions for Discussion

1. Discuss the theme and mood of the poem. Comment on the relative maturity or insight the narrator has achieved through the distance of time.

2. What may Sylvia Plath's father have had in common with Diane Di Prima's father?

THEODORE ROETHKE

My Papa's Waltz

Theodore Roethke (1908–1963), American poet, taught during the last years of his life at the University of Washington. *The Waking: Poems, 1933–1953* was the winner of the Pulitzer Prize for Poetry in 1953. He received the Bollingen Award for Poetry in 1958. A collected volume, *Words for the Wind,* appeared in 1958, and *The Far Field* was published posthumously in 1964. The poet remembers his antic father, a gardener, and his own difficult childhood.

> The whiskey on your breath
> Could make a small boy dizzy;
> But I hung on like death:
> Such waltzing was not easy.
>
> We romped until the pans
> Slid from the kitchen shelf;
> My mother's countenance
> Could not unfrown itself.
>
> The hand that held my wrist
> Was battered on one knuckle;
> At every step I missed
> My right ear scraped a buckle.
>
> You beat time on my head
> With a palm caked hard by dirt,
> Then waltzed me off to bed
> Still clinging to your shirt.

Suggestion for Discussion

What images suggest the relationship between the boy and his father?

WILLIAM BUTLER YEATS

A Prayer for My Daughter

William Butler Yeats (1865–1939), the leading poet of the Irish literary revival and a playwright, was born near Dublin and educated in London and Dublin. He wrote plays for the Irish National Theatre Society (later called the Abbey Theatre). For a number of years, he served as a senator of the Irish Free State. His volumes of poetry range from *The Wanderings of Oisin* (1889) to *The Last Poems* (1939). *The Collected Poems of W. B. Yeats* appeared in 1933, 1950, and 1956; *The Collected Plays of W. B. Yeats* was published in 1934 and 1952. From his view of a chaotic, threatening world, the poet prays for the harmony and order he considers requisite to the growth of his daughter.

Once more the storm is howling, and half hid
Under this cradle-hood and coverlid
My child sleeps on. There is no obstacle
But Gregory's wood and one bare hill
Whereby the haystack- and roof-levelling wind,
Bred on the Atlantic, can be stayed;
And for an hour I have walked and prayed
Because of the great gloom that is in my mind.

I have walked and prayed for this young child an hour
And heard the sea-wind scream upon the tower,
And under the arches of the bridge, and scream
In the elms above the flooded stream;
Imagining in excited reverie
That the future years had come,
Dancing to a frenzied drum,
Out of the murderous innocence of the sea.

May she be granted beauty and yet not
Beauty to make a stranger's eye distraught,
Or hers before a looking-glass, for such,
Being made beautiful overmuch,
Consider beauty a sufficient end,

Lose natural kindness and maybe
The heart-revealing intimacy
That chooses right, and never find a friend.

Helen, being chosen, found life flat and dull
And later had much trouble from a fool,
While that great Queen, that rose out of the spray,
Being fatherless, could have her way
Yet chose a bandy-leggèd smith for man.
It's certain that fine women eat
A crazy salad with their meat
Whereby the Horn of Plenty is undone.

In courtesy I'd have her chiefly learned;
Hearts are not had as a gift but hearts are earned
By those that are not entirely beautiful;
Yet many, that have played the fool
For beauty's very self, has charm made wise,
And many a poor man that has roved,
Loved and thought himself beloved,
From a glad kindness cannot take his eyes.

May she become a flourishing hidden tree
That all her thoughts may like the linnet be,
And have no business but dispensing round
Their magnanimities of sound.
Nor but in merriment began a chase,
Nor but in merriment a quarrel.
O may she live like some green laurel
Rooted in one dear perpetual place.

My mind, because the minds that I have loved,
The sort of beauty that I have approved,
Prosper but little, has dried up of late,
Yet knows that to be choked with hate
May well be of all evil chances chief.
If there's no hatred in a mind
Assault and battery of the wind
Can never tear the linnet from the leaf.

An intellectual hatred is the worst,
So let her think opinions are accursed.
Have I not seen the loveliest woman born
Out of the mouth of Plenty's horn,
Because of her opinionated mind

Barter that horn and every good
By quiet natures understood
For an old bellows full of angry wind?

Considering that, all hatred driven hence,
The soul recovers radical innocence
And learns at last that it is self-delighting,
Self-appeasing, self-affrighting,
And that its own sweet will is Heaven's will;
She can, though every face should scowl
And every windy quarter howl
Or every bellows burst, be happy still.

And may her bridegroom bring her to a house
Where all's accustomed, ceremonious;
For arrogance and hatred are the wares
Peddled in the thoroughfares.
How but in custom and in ceremony
Are innocence and beauty born?
Ceremony's a name for the rich horn,
And custom for the spreading laurel tree.

Suggestions for Discussion

1. Is the poet imposing on his daughter a conservative ideal of womanhood?

2. What words or images suggest that he might quarrel with the ideas of feminists today?

3. Discuss: "How but in custom and in ceremony / Are innocence and beauty born?"

4. What seems to be the poet's concept of happiness for a woman?

GWENDOLYN BROOKS

"Life for my child is simple, and is good"

Gwendolyn Brooks (1917–2000) is an American poet who grew up in Chicago's slums. Her works, which focus on contemporary black life in the United States, include *A Street in Bronzeville* (1949); *Annie Allen* (1949), which won a Pulitzer Prize; *The Bean Eaters* (1960); *The Near Johannesburg Boy and Other Poems* (1987); and *Report from Part Two* (1996). In this brief poem, the writer sets forth her hopes for her son's joy and growth.

Life for my child is simple, and is good.
He knows his wish. Yes, but that is not all.
Because I know mine too.
And we both want joy of undeep and unabiding things,
Like kicking over a chair or throwing blocks out of a window
Or tipping over an icebox pan
Or snatching down curtains or fingering an electric outlet
Or a journey or a friend or an illegal kiss.
No. There is more to it than that.
It is that he has never been afraid.
Rather, he reaches out and lo the chair falls with a beautiful crash,
And the blocks fall, down on the people's heads,
And the water comes slooshing sloopily out across the floor.
And so forth.
Not that success, for him, is sure, infallible.
But never has he been afraid to reach.
His lesions are legion.
But reaching is his rule.

Suggestions for Discussion

1. Compare Brooks's hopes for her child with those of Yeats for his daughter.

2. What do the joys of "unabiding things" have in common?

3. What oppositions are posed in the poem, and how are they resolved?

Personal Relationships: Men and Women

⌘⌘⌘

Should I get married? Should I be good?
—GREGORY CORSO, "Marriage"

Her mind only vaguely grasped what she was saying. Her physical being was for the moment predominant. She was not thinking of his words, only drinking in the tones of his voice. She wanted to reach out her hand in the darkness and touch him with the sensitive tips of her fingers upon the face or the lips. She wanted to draw close to him and whisper against his cheek–she did not care what–as she might have done if she had not been a respectable woman.
—KATE CHOPIN, "A Respectable Woman"

Fervor, Shirin Neshat, 2000

LARRY BARNS

Courtesy Gladstone Gallery, New York

NOTEBOOK

LEO BRAUDY

Arms and the Man

Leo Braudy, professor of English at the University of Southern California, has written and lectured extensively on the topics of film criticism, seventeenth- and eighteenth-century English literature, and American culture. His articles have appeared in the *New York Times* and *Harpers,* and his books include *Jean Renoir: The World of His Films* (1972), a finalist for the National Book Award, and *The Frenzy of Renown: Fame and Its History* (1986), winner of the Phi Kappa Prize. This selection is from Braudy's *From Chivalry to Terrorism* (2003), which argues that masculinity has typically been defined as triumph in combat—a problematic notion in the post–9/11 world.

Comfortable Kit, ©Oleg Volk, 2004.

As for the war,
That is for men. . . .

—Hector to Andromache, *The Iliad*

This work contains much about war and men at war, about wounds, weapons, and death, about soldiers and generals, strategy and tactics, the minute details of logistics and the fog of battlefield terror. But war is not its theme. Instead it is an effort to outline a history of the intertwined ideas of war and masculinity since the Middle Ages, especially, but not exclusively, focused on European and American history.

Near the end of the twentieth century the "crisis of masculinity" was seen in the chronic tunnel vision of the present as a phenomenon solely of our own time. On the one hand, boxing champion Mike Tyson was convicted of rape; on the other, newspapers reported drastically lowered sperm counts in various countries around the world. President George Bush promised to "kick Saddam Hussein's ass" for his aggression in Kuwait, while after the war the "Gulf War syndrome" became a national controversy: Were the crippling ailments of veterans caused by chemical and biological weapons, or were they the result of the psychological trauma of being in an unusual wartime situation? Were these soldiers, in other words, warriors injured by governmental deviousness or were they ultrasensitive products of an unmanly age? Male gym memberships were going up. Was it because an improved body image was the only available response to a menaced masculinity? Or because the birth control pill had deprived men of their natural function and all they could do was either hide their heads in shame or jump on the nearest treadmill? Into the new century, in discussions of subjects ranging from wars, natural disasters, and political controversies to tabloid stories like the severing of John Wayne Bobbit's penis by his aggrieved wife, a central national and even international drama was phrased invariably in terms of a dubious masculinity. At times modern masculinity was seen as ineffectual; at others, it was threatened and beset; at still others, aggressive and uncivilized.

Compared with the aroused national purpose in response to the terrorist attacks on New York and Washington in September 2001, many of these stories might seem to be the aimless trivia of a society looking for distraction. But that new threat highlighted the confrontation between one kind of war and another: a society of self-anointed holy warriors bent on preserving the exclusive purity of their culture versus a secular society of democratic inclusiveness committed to progress, technological change, and a world political system that was now finding a new set of heroes among policemen, firemen, and other civil servants.

Most of these stories came down to a solemnly familiar issue: What has happened to heroism? But all also invoke a challenge that lies behind that: What has happened to men? Questions of heroism shade imperceptibly into questions of masculinity, which in turn often point to a deep and ongoing confusion over where we are going as a society. Questions of femininity have been news since the advent of modern feminism in the 1960s and 1970s, but it is now also masculinity that attracts the attention of the national and international audience. Talk of the "glass ceiling" that looms for the aspiring female executive appears in the business section and stories about fairness issues for women appear throughout the paper. But they are now accompanied by other stories of the lost world of male privilege and new male roles in private and public life. That privilege certainly still exists, but many of its supposed beneficiaries nevertheless feel psychologically under siege, and from inside the castle at that. So when an otherwise anonymous young man dives into an icy river to rescue plane crash victims, or when policemen, firefighters, and ordinary citizens spring into action to save lives at the risk of their own, true masculinity appears to be momentarily reborn because men have acted immediately and instinctively to help others.

Some accounts ascribe this erosion in the traditional definition of masculinity to changes in the workplace that have undermined the importance of male labor; others to fear of feminism, feminization, and female power. Still other versions have targeted the effects of technology and mass production or the end of the Cold War.

The technological and cultural pressures on the boundaries and definitions of gender are unprecedented: surgery has been able to shape sexual characteristics in ways that were previously impossible; research into genetics, the mere idea of cloning, has opened up even more chasms in the idea of a stable personal identity. White-collar work and a service economy have expanded enormously, in many communities either replacing or surpassing the industrial and agricultural predominance of the past. At the same time, cultural dichotomies between masculine and feminine have also eroded. The anonymity of the Internet, along with the prevalence of morphing as a technological entertainment device, imply the unsettling possibility that age, gender, and ethnic masquerades that were previously only the fantasies of the scriptwriters of Jekyll-and-Hyde films may now be within the capacity of any eleven-year-old with a computer.

But these undeniably new forces that seem to have changed the nature of masculinity are not the whole story. Instead of considering this "crisis" as predominantly a question of this moment, I want to explore how modern assumptions about what constitutes masculinity, male behavior, and individual male identity have been gradually created over the last few centuries, and how understanding that development might allow us to step back and grasp more firmly what is happening now.

What is masculinity when it is much easier for the computer nerd to get a job and support a family than it is for a brawny factory worker? Who is the ideal man? Who is the common man? Is he muscular and physically powerful, or is he wily and able to map grand strategies? Does he wear a bulletproof vest or jogging clothes? Does he love women or other men or only himself? Is he a friend or a solitary hero? For a good part of the twentieth century, writers and thinkers have been interrogating anthropology, physiology, and primatology especially to answer such questions. Most of them look for some invariable root cause—in the chemical balance of brain circuits, in the activities of cavemen and anthropoid apes, or in unchanging "human nature" however defined—to explain the way we are *now.*

But throughout history the definitions of "man," "manly," and "masculine" have shifted in response to the prevailing social and cultural demands. Ideals, aspirations, and assumptions, conscious or not, are as much part of reality as physiology—and often the less understood they are, the stronger their influence. Instead of being a monolith, the mythical patriarchal society in which men enjoyed total power was a constantly mutating battleground, sometimes crisscrossed with sweeping charges and countercharges, sometimes dug into fixed positions with each square yard fought over ferociously. The medieval warriors in *The Song of Roland* can simultaneously slice an opponent entirely in half with one blow and weep copiously over a dying comrade in a manner that more tight-lipped definitions of masculinity reject. Similarly, the idea that male homosexuals make poor soldiers now seems "natural" to those who want to keep gays out of the military. Like previous efforts in the United States to keep out women, blacks, and, elsewhere, Jews, Gypsies, or other minority groups, the assumption is that they are "feminine." Because they lack the virile qualities necessary to engage the enemy, their mere presence will undermine camaraderie, loyalty, and the fighting will of the heterosexuals who stand in the trenches with them.

Yet many of these martial qualities believed to be so in need of protection are less natural or innate than they are based on ideas formulated in nineteenth- and twentieth-century Europe. The Sacred Band of Theban fighting men, made up entirely of homosexual lovers, were the pride of Greece in the fourth century B.C., until they were targeted and destroyed by the Macedonians under Philip in the Battle of Chaeronea. Many other city-states similarly posted lovers to war together.[*] In the powerful armies of

---

[*]Elis and Boeotia were two of the other city-states that posted lovers (*erastes* and *eromenos*) as soldiers together. See Dover, *Greek Homosexuality* (192). The relation between Achilles and Pattroklos is of course central to the *Iliad*, although their degree of physical relation has been often debated. Catharina Blomberg in *The Heart of the Warrior* says that homosexuality was "virtually the rule in feudal Japan."

Alexander and later those of Rome, the ideal fighting man was often considered to be one of a loving pair who fought bravely for the eminently practical reason that, as Phaedrus argues in Plato's *Symposium,* he was fighting for the greatest glory, the admiration of his closest friend. Homoerotic and even homosexual relationships were a frequent aspect of warrior initiation and training in many military societies, including Sparta, Crete, and feudal Japan, as well as among spiritual warrior communities in monasteries. Even in the early fourteenth century, when the order of the Knights Templar was dissolved on charges of blasphemous and homosexual practices, no one suggested that their sins made them unfit or unable to be warriors. It was exactly their warrior prowess, together with their widespread banking interests, that made them such targets of persecution.

The historian Lynn Hunt, reviewing a history of women in western Europe, once remarked that "no one would write a such a book about 'the history of men' "—because "woman" is the anomalous historical category and men as such don't have to be explained. But neither masculinity nor femininity exists as a concept in itself. Each society has had its own specific definitions of manhood and what cultural values masculinity symbolizes. The fortitude to withstand pain, the ability to interpret a sacred text, the prowess with a special weapon, the willingness to seek revenge for a slight to family: each of these different local accents, often stressed in special rituals, constitutes a particular culture's style of masculinity. Social anthropologists try to define those styles and political activists often seek to change them. Defining masculinity itself, in other words, must interweave with defining masculinity in relation to a multitude of factors, including the context of war, which for so much of human history and in the vast majority of human cultures has been the prime place to define oneself as a man.

Many contemporary psychologists and physiologists conclude that there is now little reason for men and women to behave differently solely because of their biological differences. But throughout the forty-thousand-odd years of human history, there has been a process of myth-making deriving from the imagined or real contrast between male and female. Defining "masculinity" and "femininity" as exemplary standards by which to measure normal human experience have thus been crucial ways for cultures to express their basic values. Masculinity particularly has occupied a position of special privilege because, in most such male-female distinctions, women are characterized as the victims of their biological nature as childbearers. Men, in supposed contrast, are free to escape from (or to express) biology, often in elaborate rituals of competition—for women, for possessions, for position. In this way, male violence, and the "masculinity" it suggests, is both regulated within a society and sanctioned against that society's enemies.

In what follows I will look at some crucial moments in this modern history of masculinity, especially as it has been redefined before, during, and in the aftermath of wrenching wars. Despite the millions of soldiers and civilians who have been wounded or died in war, still only a relative minority of human beings has actually experienced frontline battle. But war in all its protean forms—in news or in fiction, as propaganda or as history, fought by real people or by actors—has made its way inexorably into virtually every stage of learning, official and unofficial, permeating the conscious and unconscious minds of individuals, as well as the explicit and implicit values of whole cultures.

Just as ancient economies more often depended upon war than peace for their operation and expansion, wartime masculinity had an earlier evolution than its peacetime versions. But there is little reason to think that this connection between the history of masculinity and the history of violence, especially as expressed in war, is only something that happened in the primitive past and has now somehow stopped because we are more civilized or modern. The most appreciable difference between the past and the present may actually be the *greater* influence of cultural factors on the basic biology of clashing bodies because of the speed of events, along with their media presentation and representation—the interplay of artistic and literary representations of experience with experience itself. Who can think about World War II without the movies and novels set in it, or about the Gulf War without the way it played on television?

Men at war are on the front line of a more exacting and more one-sided definition of what it means to be a man than ever faces men at peace. By its emphasis on the physical prowess of men enhanced by their machines, by its distillation of national identity into the abrupt contrast between winning and losing, war enforces an extreme version of male behavior as the ideal model for all such behavior. Just as epic formulas focus on the hero with his undying fame, war focuses attention on certain ways of being a man and ignores or arouses suspicions about others. Wartime masculinity is a top-down and bottom-up effort to emphasize a code of masculine behavior more single-minded and more traditional than the wide array of circumstances and personal nature that influences the behavior of men in nonwar situations. With the end of a war—and perhaps with the ending of every war until women become an equal part of the military—an overriding and compelling story of friends and foes, violence and honor, often abruptly disintegrates or at least recedes into the background. The story of war, which until then has defined, tested, and guaranteed a specific form of masculinity, is gone, and other versions take the stage.

But the influence of war and its image of how men should be remains, however diminished. I was born in 1941, part of that generation called war babies, too young for the Korean War and too old, too married, or too antiwar for Vietnam. As a child, I went with my parents to camp on the battlefield at Gettysburg, where we slept under olive-drab shelter halves and dug latrines with army surplus foxhole spades. I was too young to feel the specific pressure of the battle, and the elaborate war memorials in the shape of triumphal arches made the scene seem even more sedate, but the name of Devil's Den still caused chills and roused my effort to imagine the sharpshooters amid the rocks. Nearby there was a tree with a perfectly semicircular curve in its trunk, where I was sure it had been grazed by a cannonball, and in a crevice between two boulders I found a shattered fragment of musket ball, itself only part of a perfect sphere.

That view of Gettysburg and that shattered piece of ancient ammunition were at least tangible evidence, even though half-obscured by the veil of history. But the less material shadow of war began early in my life as well, in the constant publicity of the Cold War, when I was collecting war cards from bubblegum packs, reading war comics, watching war movies, and in junior high school making elaborate lists of all the war novels I had read, carefully organized according to the war they were about and the branch of the service they focused on. When I was in the Boy Scouts, military drill and "policing the campsite" were part of our training. Later, in high school Latin, the words of war came early and often. *Pugno* was the model first-conjugation verb, *bellum* the model neuter noun, and Caesar's *Gallic War* the text we cut our teeth on. While in graduate school in the 1960s, I was against the Vietnam War but still preoccupied by it.

I therefore write simply as an ordinary modern man and citizen, steeped in a never-ending barrage of stories about men and war. It is the perceptions of war, how they trickle into the bloodstream of a culture and into the imaginations of individuals, that is my subject, the intertwined ideas and images that both set the scene for actual wars and later turn their meaning into precepts for how "real" men should live and be.

My prime interest here is not so much the necessities and the fatalities of masculinity and war as their contingencies and accidents. Both war and masculinity are ideas shaped by a long interwoven history. The usual way the question of which comes first is answered is to assume that masculinity is an essentially unchanging absolute and that war is a historical event: men are a certain way and therefore wars must occur. No matter how much we know of changes in masculine clothing, masculine attitudes, or masculine body types, there remains a sense of something invariable beneath the surface. Both nineteenth- and twentieth-century feminism frequently used this supposed bedrock masculinity as a backdrop for its own self-definition: women were made, not born; but men were always the same. Masculinity was thus often a stand-in for the power of patriarchy and other "unchanging" ideas. Or else, for the male supremacist, it was the stable standard in a corrupt world: as men are to women, so real men are to an effete and corrupt civilization.

These different and often contradictory uses to which masculinity has been put indicate something of its instability as a category of understanding. Even as both its partisans and its antagonists assert some immutable firmness, the shifting meanings of what it means to be a man seem more like a phantasmagoria of shapes that appear only to vanish. But these are contradictions only if one assumes some actual unity, some masculine purity from which the modern world has strayed. Part of the problem of dealing with two such general concepts as war and masculinity is the need to determine how to tell the story of their evolving meanings, both in themselves and in relation to each other.

To all appearances, the audience for war, or at least for the spectacle of war, is constantly expanding. Thousands of books have been written and are still being written about the techniques of warfare, as well as about the connection of warfare with politics and social change. Most are written to appeal to a general audience of war buffs and amateur historians who can fervently engage the enigmas of the past by digging into its details and second-guessing its generals. Increasingly in recent years, some members of this wide audience for war have also gone beyond armchair strategy to become participants. Weekend warriors are everywhere. Stockbrokers and plumbers fire multicolored paintballs at one another in war games, while elsewhere men dressed in period costumes and carrying highly polished replicas or authentic imitations of period armament refight some historical battle from the American Revolution or the Civil War—with just as much commitment as a scholarly researcher to discovering over which knoll at what time the original soldiers raised their now skeletal heads.

Wars not only end lives, revise political boundaries, and upset social values. They also require such a focus on one prime way of defining what a man is that the reaction against them is central to either the revision or the bolstering of traditional gender ideas. This result is less tangible and quantifiable than the destruction of lives, property, and institutions, but it is no less significant. Whenever war and competition occupy the national spotlight, the contours of masculinity are thrown into high relief. Usually the study of war's impact on social and political institutions tends to emphasize only one direction: something has been destroyed and now must be rebuilt or swept away. But considering these less material factors reveals the frequently ambiguous relation of historical causes and human effects between those who wish to continue wartime modes of manhood at any cost, and those who would like to see them vanish forever.

When I began this book I found myself reading deeply in the literature of war and warfare, until I could tell a hackbut from a howitzer, and then tramp over the battlefields at Marathon, Agincourt, the Little Big Horn, or the Somme, pointing out the fine points of both grand strategy and improvised tactics. But I soon discovered that most military history, with several distinguished exceptions, was not so much about men or war in general as about strategy and statistics, armament and uniforms. War was not the only place to hunt the most elusive ideas. It may be easier to visit battlefields and reconstruct strategy than it is to understand cultural attitudes, but both belong to history and both give a sense of how we have gotten to where we are now.

Although I came to be very interested in men at war, I was also more interested in the ways men at war had turned into men at peace, and what impact that change had on them *as men*. From its beginnings war has meant mobilization, not just materially but also culturally, not just to fight the enemy but also to define who the enemy is and what the enemy wants to take away. Modern war in particular is a total experience, for soldier and civilian alike, in which the variety and differences of normal life turn into a world in which everything fits together. In a war situation, all people—but especially men—are taken out of normal lives to face a wider world than they are used to. But at the same time, because a good portion of that world is called "the enemy," the expansion of perspective and geography turns into a constriction: your prime purpose is to kill. All questions, all ambiguities, all contradictions in what it means to be a man or a citizen are banished in the creation of the warrior.

Until comparatively recent times, war has been central to the writing of history. Of the two great Greek historians who stand at the fountainhead of Western history, Herodotus takes up a large proportion of his time with the Persian Wars and Thucydides writes entirely about the Peloponnesian War. In literature as well, the early poems of many Indo-European cultures are poems of warriors and war. The most familiar to Europeans and Americans are the two Greek poems of wartime and postwar return to domesticity, the *Iliad* and the *Odyssey*. The poems may have been composed in the eighth century B.C., and they refer to events that may have happened in some form in the thirteenth century B.C. But this is hardly the beginning of a tradition, for some seven hundred years before the presumed date of the Trojan War appeared the Mesopotamian epic of Gilgamesh, whose hero, the warrior king of the city of Uruk, meets in the forest his comrade and mirror self, the natural warrior Enkidu. So too, after the religious poetry of the Vedas (which were first written down c. 1500 B.C.), the early poetry of India also includes two war epics: the *Mahabharata* (c. 400 B.C.), seven times as long as the *Iliad* and the *Odyssey* combined, which tells the story of the warrior-hero Arjuna; and the *Ramayana*, which climaxes in a battle between Rama and Ravana.

At least in light of what texts have come down to us, the Asian tradition is somewhat different from the Indo-European. Unlike Indo-European literature, Chinese, Korean, and Japanese literature do not "begin" with stories of war, although the Confucian *Book of Odes* (c. 1000–600 B.C.) does include some poems about the hardships of war, and one of the classic texts of military strategy is Sun Tzu's *The Art of War* (c. fifth century B.C.). Even in the Heian era in Japan (A.D. 794–1185) in which the *bushi* class of hired warriors rose to fight the court's battles, great literature is represented by

Lady Murasaki's story of court intrigue, the *Tale of Genji.* Only later, at a time comparable to the European Middle Ages, under the warrior rule of the shoguns and their samurai retainers, does a warrior-oriented literature begin to develop.

The fortunes of Western epic heroism are thus particularly tied to war, sometimes in a grand defeat and sometimes in victory, but always triumphs that are inevitably connected to the way war destroys men but makes their memories last—Aeneas, Beowulf, Roland, the heroes of the Icelandic sagas, the warriors of the Celts and the Vikings. Down into the Renaissance, the military hero seems to reign virtually supreme, until John Milton in the seventeenth century condemns epic military heroism in *Paradise Lost* to praise a different kind of hero:

> *Not sedulous by nature to indite*
> *Wars, hitherto the only Argument*
> *Heroic deem'd chief mastery to dissect*
> *With long and tedious havoc fabl'd Knights*
> *In Battles feign'd; the better fortitude*
> *Of Patience and Heroic Martyrdom*
> *Unsung.*

War still goes on, but *Paradise Lost* signals a significant eruption of other streams of thought and feeling, which will interact with military masculinity and inexorably change its shape.

Whatever the questions of global economy, technological advance, and weapons delivery, the language of war, of getting people to fight against a real or imagined enemy, is often still individual. The heroicizing of the aggressive warrior in militia movements, along with the justification of violence in the name of the unborn among some antiabortion activists and other vigilante groups, reflects how since the 1980s the United States itself has gone through similar spasms of wondering what the role of traditional masculinity is in the modern world. Little of this uncertainty has found its way into literature except for the fictions of survivalism and racial superiority. But it has become the matter of popular films. As so many action movies of the past two decades show, at a time when technology lets any nondescript, physically uninspiring person have the power to annihilate many, there is some nostalgic satisfaction in seeing a correlation between body and violence, action and personal will, where the hero—Sylvester Stallone, Arnold Schwarzenegger, Jean Claude Van Damme—has access to both the most advanced technology and his own cuirasslike bare chest and muscled arms. Like paintball wars, extreme sports, and battlefield reenactments, their stories are filled with artificially pumped-up excitement and jeopardy.

Many of these films are mythic efforts to synthesize technology and personal physical prowess in the same spirit as the army's 2001 advertising campaign: "An Army of One."

Since the end of the Vietnam War, American films have been filled with characters in whom the line between the human and the technological is ambiguous. *Robo Cop* represents one sort, the remanufactured man; the androids of films like *Blade Runner* and *Aliens* another, apparent human beings who are actually robots. Indirectly commenting on the use of overwhelming firepower in Vietnam and later wars, such characters raise the question of whether superweaponry is enough. Despite all the "smart bombs," the answer seems to be no. Some recourse to the individual and the primitive is necessary in order to ground the otherwise abstract technology: Rambo emerges from the swamp with his bow and arrows to defeat his enemies, like the Indians triumphing over Braddock at Fort Duquesne. Although sometimes cloaked in Cold War politics, action films are at root about questions of personal honor—the violence of righteous revenge that is beyond the law, like the justifications of dueling that began in the sixteenth century, when the state was assuming the monopoly of violence. The difference now is that the honor dramatized in most action films is not aristocratic but democratic, heroes without family name, whose only resource is themselves. Ironically enough, with September 11, at a time when the United States was indulging in widespread nostalgia about World War II and its citizen soldiers, a full-fledged enemy appears who targets civilians and makes heroes of the policemen and firemen who protect them. At least for the moment, the heroic on the Western side, in the images of the World Trade Center, is defined by the normal person doing his or her job.

Films may still rely on the solitary hero, but the political propaganda of the warrior who will set the corrupt world right by violence now no longer comes out of either official Europe or official Japan but from thwarted and marginalized small groups around the world. Most prominently in the Middle East, it is the revenge of the nomad against the settled, or of the religion of the desert against the values of the city. These recent events underline the relativity of the European view of masculinity and how it has been shaped by the idea of the nation and citizenship. But the resurgent focus on tribal loyalties in the Islamic world also shares some structural resemblances with the conflicts in Bosnia after the death of Tito, the Hutu/Tutsi conflict in Rwanda, and other responses to the end of imperial rule that enforced rather than cultivated cooperation. That civilians are the primary target of many of these attacks further underscores the fact that they mean to destroy morale much more than infrastructure. But in fact, to bring civilians so forcefully into jeopardy in effect often reknits an industrial and mercantile world otherwise more likely to savor its freedoms without paying their preservation too much attention.

Is the most recent form of terrorism thus the last gasp of a militant warrior personality type that has survived the centuries? What, if anything, is valuable in the warrior tradition? What is worth saving, and what has led us into the horrors of the twentieth and twenty-first centuries? In the 1990s the United States saw a brief efflorescence of a mythic and pseudopoetic men's movement, heralded by Robert Bly's *Iron John*, which drew upon the Jungian idea that each man had in him four archetypes—the King, the Magician, the Lover, and the Warrior—and the Warrior was especially in need of nurturance. Like William James's moral equivalent of war, this was the warrior who did not need to kill to prove his prowess, but whose energy and traits of integrity and assertiveness could be turned in more socially useful directions. Here, too, the perceived problem was that the warrior self had either been commercialized, feminized, and technologized into impotence or had been exaggerated and darkened into death and violence. At its best, this movement asked whether the need to rearmor or "rewarrior" oneself was a spiritual battle rather than a physical battle (like the original meaning of jihad), and whether it required a different sort of transformative adventure than war. At its worst, it was a self-indulgent audience of men listening to laments about male vulnerability, unwilling to give up the undeniable historical structures of male privilege but able to play the victim because others resented and caricatured that privilege, instead of just silently assuming it. Either way, the various movements found it hard to resist a suffocating air of self-congratulation, most egregiously in the chant of the Promise Keepers: "Thank God I'm a man!"

The problem with such an effort to renovate positive warrior traits—honor, integrity, self-sacrifice, camaraderie, openness—while purging negative ones is that it continues to be built on a polarized masculinity and femininity, in which any individual woman is considered to be Woman unless proven otherwise, while any individual man is constantly being tested to see whether he is Man or not. Although men may wield social power as Men, individual men have to continue striving and being tested, while each woman can unproblematically claim that identity. Masculinity, in other words, may be pure, but any man needs to constantly prove it by himself and distinguish it from ersatz forms. Once again, we are back in the realm of warriors and the initiation of war.

The questions thus remain: Are there any masculine myths suitable for a settled or global world, or are men doomed to feel insufficient in the face of modernity, women's rights, globalization, technology—whatever you prefer as the prime villain? After a millennium and more of metamorphosis, are the old myths on the verge of a final collapse as men struggle toward some new synthesis? Which myths and traditions and nostalgias actually strengthen masculinity; which undermine it?

My tentative sense is that Europe and the United States in particular are in the aftermath of a period in the histories of both war and masculinity, and that we have moved decisively toward seeing human nature as a larger and more complex whole, in which judgments about individuals need not be based on their sexuality, their religion, or their race. Part of that change, it must be said, is in the weakening of the bonds of nationalism if not nationality. When the warrior tradition becomes imbued with nationalism, it has often been at its worst—self-important and intolerant of others—although the individual warrior tradition also has its faults, when personal integrity turns into solipsism.

But if there has been any positive result from the bloodiest century in history, it has been the visible changes in the definition of being human, particularly in extending it to all races and to women as well as men. We have not reached the egalitarian Utopia, but large portions of the world have certainly changed. Has this been the result of the annihilating violence of twentieth-century war? Will the coming of a worldwide spectrum of political possibility parallel an opening up of a spectrum of sexual possibility? Before the "axis of evil" came onto the scene, the Bush administration had put enormous effort into reassuring both American Muslims and the Islamic world that the American battle was not with them but with a few specific "evil ones." The language of good and evil was invoked time and time again, but the religious and triumphalist tinge it so often had in the past was downplayed. "Unpatriotic," which had previously been the sole criterion of judgment during wartime, now had to be balanced with "insensitive" as a criticism of policy. The negotiation between groups of widely differing backgrounds and agendas that has become a mainstay of national and local politics had international implications as well. There was no repetition of the Japanese deportations and internments of World War II. Muslim men were questioned by the FBI, and there were many reported instances of injustice and mistreatment. But the government also had to be publicly responsive to charges of racial and ethnic profiling.

One of the frequent immediate reactions to the September 11 bombings was to look disdainfully at the American media culture with its incessant gossip about the trivial details of the life of the famous, its breathless hankering after scandal and personal exposure, and say that the attacks had evoked a new seriousness in the United States, as Lloyd George and others thought World War I would bring. Soon enough, though, the media gossip mill was back in full swing, and with its resurgence it might be difficult not to think that the old warrior ethic of austere self-sacrifice and loyalty has in fact been defeated by commercialism and the profit motive.

The truth may be more complex. Certainly, the attack, literally and symbolically, was directly against the commercial moneymaking side of American culture. Reflecting the Taliban destruction of the Buddha statues in

Afghanistan, the Al Qaeda bombers deployed iconoclasm to bring spiritual defeat to a mercantile culture. But gossip and aimless consumerism are on the fringes of a larger battle. Perhaps, as the dour critics of the eighteenth century thought, commerce actually is antiwar in effect. As connections with other nations balance and subdue international hostilities, the imperatives of a consumer society foster an unwillingness to allow death or deprivation for too long. To the warrior society, commerce is without any moral dimension; it is purely about getting and spending. But commerce also fosters a network of interconnections that might supersede national honor with principles that apply to the world.

At home and abroad, the United States is often mocked for trying to be the world's policeman. Yet this urge, however imperfectly, ignorantly, and sometimes cynically it may often be carried out (Rwanda being a prime example), coincides with the United Nations Charter reaffirmation of the Kellogg-Briand pact's outlawing of aggressive war. Military action that is undertaken to implement a world honor, a moral point of view that transcends national boundaries, like human rights, is always subject to often justifiable accusations that it merely protects the interests of the powerful. But in the history of both war and humanity, the invocation of a language of ethical responsibility rather than of national honor or material gain is itself a milestone, of aspiration if not of achievement.

It sounds utopian and foolish to say that we are at the end of a cycle in European history, one that began in the Middle Ages and that defined masculinity, femininity, and society by what they excluded. But the conjunction of a fundamentalist warrior-oriented terrorism and an industrialized world willing to accept a wider spectrum of both male and female possibilities may not be a coincidence at all. Perhaps it is a necessary step in the emancipation of the human race from its own mind-forged manacles.

Certainly there will still be subgroups, gangs of all sorts, that identify themselves more by their enemies and their willingness to fight than by who they are in themselves. But the question remains whether the national states that defined themselves by what they were not might be changing into more comprehensive places, and the restrictive idea of masculinity that went along with that politics of exclusion might be changing as well. The twentieth century began with much talk of the clash between civilization and barbarism. But civilization in that limited sense may be a worn-out and discredited concept that needs to be replaced with something at once more all-embracing and more sensitive to individual difference. Everyone is not only the product of cultural influences but also an exception to them, and a rebuke to their overpowering generality.

Whether the newly globalized world will usher in multiple masculinities as well, and what effect those varieties will have on traditional forms, remains to be seen. Whatever happens, the real need is to feel the currents of old belief in ourselves, like underground streams—not streams that have been there from eternity but those that were laid down a century or more ago in response to circumstances and ideas that have otherwise vanished. We still feel them, and the only way to be free of them is to recognize their existence, to be able to stand back and see how they developed in the course of history rather than as part of some chimerical innate human nature.

Suggestions for Discussion

1. What key observations does Braudy make about the history of men in combat and the image of male heroism?

2. Describe the contemporary "crisis of masculinity." What role has the feminist movement played in this crisis?

3. According to Braudy, what do American action films tell us about our culture's view of manhood?

4. Braudy raises the questions: "What, if anything, is valuable in the warrior tradition? What is worth saving, and what has led us into the horrors of the twentieth and twenty-first centuries?" How does Braudy confront these questions? What are your thoughts on the issue?

5. What possible cause does Braudy cite for the "war on terror" and the September 11 attack on the United States?

6. The photograph accompanying *Arms and the Man* contrasts with many of Leo Braudy's statements. The image itself contains tension: a smiling young face and a potentially lethal weapon. Consider the places where you routinely see weapons as part of your personal life (movies, video games, TV, music videos, and so on). How do you react to these common images of weapons being used? Does gender (both your own and that of the weapon user) play a part in your feelings?

Suggestion for Writing

Compare Braudy's views on the contemporary crisis of masculinity with those that Jared Diamond presents in "What Are Men Good For?" beginning on the following page.

≈≈≈≈

JARED DIAMOND

What Are Men Good For?

Jared Diamond (b. 1937) is a conservationist, author, and a professor of Physiology at the UCLA School of Medicine who has spent years studying ecology and the evolution of birds in New Guinea and its neighboring islands. A MacArthur Foundation Fellowship winner, Diamond is a member of the National Academy of Sciences, the American Academy of Arts and Sciences, and the American Philosophical Society. He was awarded a Pulitzer Prize and a Rhone-Poulenc Science Book Prize for his 1997 book *Guns, Germs, and Steel: The Fates of Human Societies*, and is the author of *The Third Chimpanzee* (1992) and *Collapse: How Societies Choose to Fail or Succeed* (2004). The following essay, from *Why Is Sex Fun?* (1997), offers a thoughtful—and sometimes amusing—examination of the role of the male in contemporary society.

Last year I received a remarkable letter from a professor at a university in a distant city, inviting me to an academic conference. I did not know the writer, and I couldn't even figure out from the name whether the writer was a man or a woman. The conference would involve long plane flights and a week away from home. However, the letter of invitation was beautifully written. If the conference was going to be as beautifully organized, it might be exceptionally interesting. With some ambivalence because of the time commitment, I accepted.

My ambivalence vanished when I arrived at the conference, which turned out to be every bit as interesting as I had anticipated. In addition, much effort had been made to arrange outside activities for me, including shopping, bird-watching, banquets, and tours of archaeological sites. The professor behind this masterpiece of organization and the original virtuoso letter proved to be a woman. In addition to giving a brilliant lecture at the conference and being a very pleasant person, she was among the most stunningly beautiful women I had ever met.

On one of the shopping trips that my hostess arranged, I bought several presents for my wife. The student who had been sent along as my guide evidently reported these purchases to my hostess, because she commented on them when I sat next to her at the conference banquet. To my astonishment, she told me, "My husband never buys me any presents!" She had formerly bought presents for him but eventually stopped when he never reciprocated.

Someone across the table then asked me about my fieldwork on birds of paradise in New Guinea. I explained that male birds of paradise provide no help in rearing the nestlings but instead devote their time to trying to seduce as many females as possible. Surprising me again, my hostess burst out, "Just like men!" She explained that her own husband was much better than most men, because he encouraged her career aspirations. However, he spent most evenings with other men from his office, watched television while at home on the weekend, and avoided helping with the household and with their two children. She had repeatedly asked him to help; she finally gave up and hired a housekeeper. There is, of course, nothing unusual about this story. It stands out in my mind only because this woman was so beautiful, nice, and talented that one might naively have expected the man who chose to marry her to have remained interested in spending time with her.

My hostess nevertheless enjoys much better domestic conditions than do many other wives. When I first began to work in the New Guinea highlands, I often felt enraged at the sight of gross abuse of women. Married couples whom I encountered along jungle trails typically consisted of a woman bent under an enormous load of firewood, vegetables, and an infant, while her husband sauntered along upright, bearing nothing more than his bow and arrow. Men's hunting trips seemed to yield little more than male bonding opportunities, plus some prey animals immediately consumed in the jungle by the men. Wives were bought, sold, and discarded without their consent.

Later, though, when I had children of my own and sensed my feelings as I shepherded my family on walks, I thought that I could better understand the New Guinea men striding beside their families. I found myself striding next to my own children, devoting all my attention to making sure that they did not get run over, fall, wander off, or suffer some other mishap. Traditional New Guinea men had to be even more attentive because of the greater risks facing their children and wives. Those seemingly carefree men strolling along beside a heavily burdened wife were actually functioning as lookouts and protectors, keeping their hands free so that they could quickly deploy their bow and arrow in the event of ambush by men of another tribe. But the men's hunting trips, and the sale of women as wives, continue to trouble me.

To ask what men are good for may sound like a flip one-liner. In fact, the question touches a raw nerve in our society. Women are becoming intolerant of men's self-ascribed status and are criticizing those men who provide better for themselves than for their wives and children. The question also poses a big theoretical problem for anthropologists. By the criterion of services offered to mates and children, males of most mammal species are good for nothing except injecting sperm. They part from the female after copulation, leaving her to bear the entire burden of feeding, protecting, and training the offspring. But human males differ by (usually or often) remaining with their mate and offspring after copulation. Anthropologists widely assume that men's resulting added roles contributed crucially to the evolution of our species' most distinctive features. The reasoning goes as follows.

The economic roles of men and women are differentiated in all surviving hunter-gatherer societies, a category that encompassed all human societies until the rise of agriculture ten thousand years ago. Men invariably spend more time hunting large animals, while women spend more time gathering plant foods and small animals and caring for children. Anthropologists traditionally view this ubiquitous differentiation as a division of labor that promotes the nuclear family's joint interests and thereby represents a sound strategy of cooperation. Men are much better able than women to track and kill big animals, for the obvious reasons that men don't have to carry infants around to nurse them and that men are on the average more muscular than women. In the view of anthropologists, men hunt in order to provide meat to their wives and children.

A similar division of labor persists in modern industrial societies: many women still devote more time to child care than men do. While men no longer hunt as their main occupation, they still bring food to their spouse and children by holding money-paying jobs (as do a majority of American women as well). Thus, the expression "bringing home the bacon" has a profound and ancient meaning.

Meat provisioning by traditional hunters is considered a distinctive function of human males, shared with only a few of our fellow mammal species such as wolves and African hunting dogs. It is commonly assumed to be linked to other universal features of human societies that distinguish us from our fellow mammals. In particular, it is linked to the fact that men and women remain associated in nuclear families after copulation, and that human children (unlike young apes) remain unable to obtain their own food for many years after weaning.

This theory, which seems so obvious that its correctness is generally taken for granted, makes two straightforward predictions about men's hunting. First, if the main purpose of hunting is to bring meat to the hunter's family, men should pursue the hunting strategy that reliably yields the most meat. Hence we should observe that men are on the average bagging more pounds of meat per day by going after big animals than they would bring home by targeting small animals. Second, we should observe that a hunter brings his kill to his wife and kids, or at least shares it preferentially with them rather than with nonrelatives. Are these two predictions true?

Surprisingly for such basic assumptions of anthropology, these predictions have been little tested. Perhaps unsurprisingly, the lead in testing them has been taken by a woman anthropologist, Kristen Hawkes of the

University of Utah. Hawkes's tests have been based especially on quantitative measurements of foraging yields for Paraguay's Northern Aché Indians, carried out jointly with Kim Hill, A. Magdalena Hurtado, and H. Kaplan. Hawkes performed other tests on Tanzania's Hadza people in collaboration with Nicholas Blurton Jones and James O'Connell. Let's consider first the evidence for the Aché.

The Northern Aché used to be full-time hunter-gatherers and continued to spend much time foraging in the forest even after they began to settle at mission agricultural settlements in the 1970s. In accord with the usual human pattern, Aché men specialize in hunting large mammals, such as peccaries and deer, and they also collect masses of honey from bees' nests. Women pound starch from palm trees, gather fruits and insect larvae, and care for children. An Aché man's hunting bag varies greatly from day to day: he brings home food enough for many people if he kills a peccary or finds a beehive, but he gets nothing at all on one-quarter of the days he spends hunting. In contrast, women's returns are predictable and vary little from day to day because palms are abundant; how much starch a woman gets is mainly a function of just how much time she spends pounding it. A woman can always count on getting enough for herself and her children, but she can never reap a bonanza big enough to feed many others.

The first surprising result from the studies by Hawkes and her colleagues concerned the difference between the returns achieved by men's and women's strategies. Peak yields were, of course, much higher for men than for women, since a man's daily bag topped 40,000 calories when he was lucky enough to kill a peccary. However, a man's average daily return of 9,634 calories proved to be lower than that of a woman (10,356), and a man's median return (4,663 calories per day) was much lower. The reason for this paradoxical result is that the glorious days when a man bagged a peccary were greatly outnumbered by the humiliating days when he returned empty-handed.

Thus, Aché men would do better in the long run by sticking to the unheroic "woman's job" of pounding palms than by their devotion to the excitement of the chase. Since men are stronger than women, they could pound even more daily calories of palm starch than can women, if they chose to do so. In going for high but very unpredictable stakes, Aché men can be compared to gamblers who aim for the jackpot: in the long run, gamblers would do much better by putting their money in the bank and collecting the boringly predictable interest.

The other surprise was that successful Aché hunters do not bring meat home mainly for their wives and kids but share it widely with anyone around. The same is true for men's finds of honey. As a result of this widespread sharing, three-quarters of all the food that an Aché consumes is acquired by someone outside his or her nuclear family.

It's easy to understand why Aché women aren't big-game hunters: they can't spend the time away from their children, and they can't afford the risk of going even a day with an empty bag, which would jeopardize lactation and pregnancy. But why does a man eschew palm starch, settle for the lower average return from hunting, and not bring home his catch to his wife and kids, as the traditional view of anthropologists predicts?

This paradox suggests that something other than the best interests of his wife and children lie behind an Aché man's preference for big-game hunting. As Kristen Hawkes described these paradoxes to me, I developed an awful foreboding that the true explanation might prove less noble than the male's mystique of bringing home the bacon. I began to feel defensive on behalf of my fellow men and to search for explanations that might restore my faith in the nobility of the male strategy.

My first objection was that Kristen Hawkes's calculations of hunting returns were measured in calories. In reality, any nutritionally aware modern reader knows that not all calories are equal. Perhaps the purpose of big-game hunting lies in fulfilling our need for protein, which is more valuable to us nutritionally than the humble carbohydrates of palm starch. However, Aché men target not only protein-rich meat but also honey, whose carbohydrates are every bit as humble as those of palm starch. While Kalahari San men ("Bushmen") are hunting big game, San women are gathering and preparing mongongo nuts, an excellent protein source. While lowland New Guinea hunter-gatherer men are wasting their days in the usually futile search for kangaroos, their wives and children are predictably acquiring protein in the form of fish, rats, grubs, and spiders. Why don't San and New Guinea men emulate their wives?

I next began to wonder whether Aché men might be unusually ineffective hunters, an aberration among modern hunter-gatherers. Undoubtedly, the hunting skills of Inuit (Eskimo) and Arctic Indian men are indispensable, especially in winter, when little food other than big game is available. Tanzania's Hadza men, unlike the Aché, achieve higher average returns by hunting big game rather than small game. But New Guinea men, like the Aché, persist in hunting even though yields are very low. And Hadza hunters persist in the face of enormous risks, since on the average they bag nothing at all on twenty-eight out of twenty-nine days spent hunting. A Hadza family could starve while waiting for the husband-father to win his gamble of bringing down a giraffe. In any case, all that meat occasionally bagged by a Hadza or Aché hunter isn't reserved for his family, so the question of whether big-game hunting yields higher or lower returns than alternative strategies is academic from his family's point of view. Big-game hunting just isn't the best way to feed a family.

Still seeking to defend my fellow men, I then wondered: could the purpose of widely sharing meat and honey be to smooth out hunting yields by means of reciprocal altruism? That is, I expect to kill a giraffe only every twenty-ninth day, and so does each of my hunter friends, but we all go off in different directions, and each of us is likely to kill his giraffe on a different day. If successful hunters agree to share meat with each other and their families, all of them will often have full bellies. By that interpretation, hunters should prefer to share their catch with the best other hunters, from whom they are most likely to receive meat some other day in return.

In reality, though, successful Aché and Hadza hunters share their catch with anyone around, whether he's a good or hopeless hunter. That raises the question of why an Aché or Hadza man bothers to hunt at all, since he can claim a share of meat even if he never bags anything himself. Conversely, why should he hunt when any animal that he kills will be shared widely? Why doesn't he just gather nuts and rats, which he can bring to his family and would not have to share with anyone else? There must be some ignoble motive for male hunting that I was overlooking in my efforts to find a noble motive.

As another possible noble motive, I thought that widespread sharing of meat helps the hunter's whole tribe, which is likely to flourish or perish together. It's not enough to concentrate on nourishing your own family if the rest of your tribe is starving and can't fend off an attack by tribal enemies. This possible motive, though, returns us to the original paradox: the best way for the whole Aché tribe to become well nourished is for everybody to humble themselves by pounding good old reliable palm starch and collecting fruit or insect larvae. The men shouldn't waste their time gambling on the occasional peccary.

In a last effort to detect family values in men's hunting, I reflected on hunting's relevance to the role of men as protectors. The males of many territorial animal species, such as songbirds, lions, and chimpanzees, spend much time patrolling their territories. Such patrols serve multiple purposes: to detect and expel intruding rival males from adjacent territories; to observe whether adjacent territories are in turn ripe for intrusion; to detect predators that could endanger the male's mate and offspring; and to monitor seasonal changes in abundance of foods and other resources. Similarly, at the same time as human hunters are looking for game, they too are attentive to potential dangers and opportunities for the rest of the tribe. In addition, hunting provides a chance to practice the fighting skills that men employ in defending their tribe against enemies.

This role of hunting is undoubtedly an important one. Nevertheless, one has to ask what specific dangers the hunters are trying to detect, and whose interests they are thereby trying to advance. While lions and other big carnivores do pose dangers to people in some parts of the world, by far the greatest danger to traditional hunter-gatherer human societies everywhere has been posed by hunters from rival tribes. Men of such societies were involved in intermittent wars, the purpose of which was to kill men of other tribes. Captured women and children of defeated rival tribes were either killed or else spared and acquired as wives and slaves, respectively. At worst, patrolling groups of male hunters could thus be viewed as advancing their own genetic self-interest at the expense of rival groups of men. At best, they could be viewed as protecting their wives and children, but mainly against the dangers posed by other men. Even in the latter case, the harm and the good that adult men bring to the rest of society by their patrolling activities would be nearly equally balanced.

Thus, all five of my efforts to rescue Aché big-game hunting as a sensible way for men to contribute nobly to the best interests of their wives and children collapsed. Kristen Hawkes then reminded me of some painful truths about how an Aché man himself (as opposed to his wife and kids) gets big benefits from his kills besides the food entering his stomach.

To begin with, among the Aché, as among other peoples, extramarital sex is not uncommon. Dozens of Aché women, asked to name the potential fathers (their sex partners around the time of conception) of 66 of their children, named an average of 2.1 men per child. Among a sample of 28 Aché men, women named good hunters more often than poor hunters as their lovers, and they named good hunters as potential fathers of more children.

To understand the biological significance of adultery, recall that the facts of reproductive biology introduce a fundamental asymmetry into the interests of men and women. Having multiple sex partners contributes nothing directly to a woman's reproductive output. Once a woman has been fertilized by one man, having sex with another man cannot lead to another baby for at least nine months, and probably for at least several years under hunter-gatherer conditions of extended lactational amenorrhea. In just a few minutes of adultery, though, an otherwise faithful man can double the number of his own offspring.

Now compare the reproductive outputs of men pursuing the two different hunting strategies that Hawkes terms the "provider" strategy and the "show-off" strategy. The provider hunts for foods yielding moderately high returns with high predictability, such as palm starch and rats. The show-off hunts for big animals; by scoring only occasional bonanzas amid many more days of empty bags, his mean return is lower. The provider brings home on the average the most food for his wife and kids, although he never acquires enough of a surplus to feed anyone else. The show-off on the average brings less food to his wife and kids but does occasionally have lots of meat to share with others.

Obviously, if a woman gauges her genetic interests by the number of children whom she can rear to maturity, that's a function of how much food she can provide them, so she is best off marrying a provider. But she is further well served by having show-offs as neighbors, with whom she can trade occasional adulterous sex for extra meat supplies for herself and her kids. The whole tribe also likes a show-off because of the occasional bonanzas that he brings home for sharing.

As for how a man can best advance his own genetic interests, the show-off enjoys advantages as well as disadvantages. One advantage is the extra kids he sires adulterously. The show-off also gains some advantages apart from adultery, such as prestige in his tribe's eyes. Others in the tribe want him as a neighbor because of his gifts of meat, and they may reward him with their daughters as mates. For the same reason, the tribe is likely to give favored treatment to the show-off's children. Among the disadvantages to the show-off are that he brings home on the average less food to his own wife and kids; this means that fewer of his legitimate children may survive to maturity. His wife may also philander while he is doing so, with the result that a lower percentage of her children are actually his. Is the show-off better off giving up the provider's certainty of paternity of a few kids, in return for the possibility of paternity of many kids?

The answer depends on several numbers, such as how many extra legitimate kids a provider's wife can rear, the percentage of a provider's wife's kids that are illegitimate, and how much a show-off's kids find their chances of survival increased by their favored status. The values of these numbers must differ among tribes, depending on the local ecology. When Hawkes estimated the values for the Aché, she concluded that, over a wide range of likely conditions, show-offs can expect to pass on their genes to more surviving children than can providers. This purpose, rather than the traditionally accepted purpose of bringing home the bacon to wife and kids, may be the real reason behind big-game hunting. Aché men thereby do good for themselves rather than for their families.

Thus, it is not the case that men hunters and women gatherers constitute a division of labor whereby the nuclear family as a unit most effectively promotes its joint interests, and whereby the work force is selectively deployed for the good of the group. Instead, the hunter-gatherer lifestyle involves a classic conflict of interest. What's best for a man's genetic interests isn't necessarily best for a woman's, and vice versa. Spouses share interests, but they also have divergent interests. A woman is best off married to a provider, but a man is not best off being a provider.

Biological studies of recent decades have demonstrated numerous such conflicts of interest in animals and humans—not only conflicts between husbands and wives (or between mated animals), but also between parents and children, between a pregnant woman and her fetus, and between siblings. Parents share genes with their offspring, and siblings share genes with each other. However, siblings are also potentially each other's closest competitors, and parents and offspring also potentially compete. Many animal studies have shown that rearing offspring reduces the parent's life expectancy because of the energy drain and risks that the parent incurs. To a parent, an offspring represents one opportunity to pass on genes, but the parent may have other such opportunities. The parent's interests may be better served by abandoning one offspring and devoting resources to other offspring, whereas the offspring's interests may be best served by surviving at the expense of its parents. In the animal world as in the human world, such conflicts not infrequently lead to infanticide, parricide (the murder of parents by an offspring), and siblicide (the murder of one sibling by another). While biologists explain the conflicts by theoretical calculations based on genetics and foraging ecology, all of us recognize them from experience, without doing any calculations. Conflicts of interest between people closely related by blood or marriage are the commonest, most gut-wrenching tragedies of our lives.

What general validity do these conclusions possess? Hawkes and her colleagues studied just two hunter-gatherer peoples, the Aché and the Hadza. The resulting conclusions await testing of other hunter-gatherers. The answers are likely to vary among tribes and even among individuals. From my own experience in New Guinea, Hawkes's conclusions are likely to apply even more strongly there. New Guinea has few large animals, hunting yields are low, and bags are often empty. Much of the catch is consumed directly by the men while off in the jungle, and the meat of any big animal brought home is shared widely. New Guinea hunting is hard to defend economically, but it brings obvious payoffs in status to successful hunters.

What about the relevance of Hawkes's conclusions to our own society? Perhaps you're already livid because you foresaw that I'd raise that question, and you're expecting me to conclude that American men aren't good for much. Of course that's not what I conclude. I acknowledge that many (most? by far the most?) American men are devoted husbands, work hard to increase their income, devote that income to their wives and kids, do much child care, and don't philander.

But, alas, the Aché findings are relevant to at least some men in our society. Some American men do desert their wives and children. The proportion of divorced men who renege on their legally stipulated child support is scandalously high, so high that even our government is starting to do something about it. Single parents outnumber coparents in the United States, and most single parents are women.

Among those men who remain married, all of us know some who take better care of themselves than of their wives and children, and who devote inordinate time, money, and energy to philandering and to male status symbols and activities. Typical of such male preoccupations are cars, sports, and alcohol consumption. Much bacon isn't brought home. I don't claim to have measured what percentage of American men rate as show-offs rather than providers, but the percentage of show-offs appears not to be negligible.

Even among devoted working couples, time budget studies show that American working women spend on the average twice as many hours on their responsibilities (defined as job plus children plus household) as do their husbands, yet women receive on the average less pay for the same job. When American husbands are asked to estimate the number of hours that they and their wives each devote to children and household, the same time budget studies show that men tend to overestimate their own hours and to underestimate their wife's hours. It's my impression that men's household and child-care contributions are on the average even lower in some other industrialized countries, such as Australia, Japan, Korea, Germany, France, and Poland, to mention just a few with which I happen to be familiar. That's why the question what men are good for continues to be debated within our societies, as well as between anthropologists.

Suggestions for Discussion

1. How does the anecdote about Diamond's host at the beginning of the essay set the tone for the piece as a whole?

2. In Diamond's view, how do modern American men compare to males from a hunter-gatherer society?

3. What role does economics play in determining social roles for men and women?

Suggestion for Writing

A running joke employed by many American television sitcoms is that the housewife is the wisest, most caring, and most effective member of the nuclear family, while the husband is an infantile, unintelligent pleasure-seeker. In *The Simpsons*, for example, Marge Simpson is a far better parent and spouse than her husband, Homer, whose endearing shirking of his domestic duties is one of the main sources of the show's humor. How does a satirical series such as *The Simpsons* reflect or refute what Diamond is saying in this essay? Write your thoughts down in a free-style, journal format.

PERSONAL REMINISCENCES

ANDREW SULLIVAN

If Love Were All

Andrew Sullivan (b. 1963) is a journalist and author based in Washington, DC, who publicly revealed that he was HIV-positive in 1996. A practicing Catholic and political activist, Sullivan writes a weekly column about the United States for the *Sunday Times,* London, and regularly contributes articles for the *New York Times Magazine.* Formerly a senior editor at the *New Republic* (serving between 1991 and 1996), he is the author of *Virtually Normal: An Argument about Homosexuality* (1995) and has edited the book *Same-Sex Marriage: Pro and Con* (1997). In the following excerpt from his 1998 book, *Love Undetectable: Notes on Friendship, Sex, and Survival,* Sullivan draws upon his literary and religious background to define friendship and to extol its virtues while simultaneously honoring his best friend, who died of AIDS.

> And this is what we mean by friends: even when
> they are absent, they are with us; even when
> they lack some things, they have an abundance
> of others; even when they are weak, they are
> strong; and, harder still to say, even when they are
> dead, they are alive.
>
> —CICERO, *De Amicitia*

I don't think I'm alone in thinking that the deepest legacy of the plague years is friendship. The duties demanded in a plague, it turned out, were the duties of friends: the kindness of near strangers, the support that asks the quietest of acknowledgments, the fear that can only be shared with someone stronger than a lover. In this sense, gay men were perhaps oddly well prepared for the trauma, socially primed more than many others to face the communal demands of plague. Denied a recognized family, often estranged from their natural one, they had learned in the few decades of their free existence that friendship was the nourishment that would enable them to survive and flourish. And having practiced such a virtue in good times, they were as astonished as everyone else to see how well they could deploy it in bad.

It certainly came easily to me. For me, friendship has always been the most accessible of relationships—certainly far more so than romantic love. Friendship, I learned, provided a buffer in the interplay of emotions, a distance that made the risk of intimacy bearable, a space that allowed the other person to remain safely another person. So, for most of my life, for a variety of reasons, I found it far simpler to make friends than to find lovers. No doubt, this had something to do with my homosexuality (since friendship is the only gay relationship that is socially acknowledged) and something to do with my haphazard romantic history (for want of a lover, a friend often filled the emotional spaces in my life). But friendship, although it may come more instinctively to some than to others, is not a relationship anyone has a special claim to. Gay men have sustained and nourished it in our culture only by default. And they are good at friendship not because they are homosexual, but because, in the face of a deep and silent isolation, they are human. Insofar as friendship was an incalculable strength of homosexuals during the calamity of AIDS, it merely showed, I think, how great a loss is our culture's general underestimation of this central human virtue.

For, of all our relationships, friendship is the most common and the most natural. In its universality, it even trumps family. Many of us fail to marry, and many more have no children; others never know their mother or father, and plenty have no siblings. But any human being who has ever lived for any time has had a friend. It is a relationship available to and availed by all of us. It is at once the most particular and the most universal relationship there is.

And yet we hardly talk about it. What we know most intimately in practice, we flee from in the abstract. The twentieth century has seen almost no theoretical exploration of friendship, no exposition of what it means, no defense of it, or even attack on it. Those modern writers who have ventured to deal with friendship have often done so in passing—a brief lecture by Kant, a diatribe by Kierkegaard, a sublime interlude by Oakeshott. The first and last serious treatment of the matter was Montaigne's, and even his landmark evocation, "*De l'Amitié*," was a mere essay, and a tiny fraction of his total work. One has to journey far further back, to ancient and medieval times, to glimpse a world where this relationship was given its full due and seen as something worth examining in its own right—as a critical social institution, as an ennobling moral experience, as an immensely delicate but essential interplay of the virtues required to sustain a fully realized human being.

Of course, this modern silence may not be altogether a bad sign. There's something about friendship that lends itself to reticence. Lovers, after all, never stop telling each other about their love; they gabble endlessly about it, tell the world about it, emit excruciating poetry and a constant stream of art to reflect every small aspect of its power and beauty. But friends, more often than not, deflect attention from their friendship. They don't talk about it much. Sometimes, in fact, you can tell how strong the friendship is by the silence that envelops it. Lovers and spouses may talk frequently about their "relationship," but friends tend to let their regard for one another speak for itself or let others point it out.

And a part of this reticence is reflected in the moments when friendship is appreciated. If friendship rarely articulates itself when it is in full flood, it is often only given its due when it is over, especially if its end is sudden or caused by death. Suddenly, it seems, we have lost something so valuable and profound that we have to make up for our previous neglect and acknowledge it in ways that would have seemed inappropriate before. One of the greatest poetic expressions of friendship, perhaps, is Tennyson's "In Memoriam." The deepest essay, Montaigne's, was written about a friend who had been wrenched bitterly away from the author at an early age. Cicero's classic dialogue on the subject was written in honor of a dead friend; so was the most luminescent medieval work, Aelred of Rievaulx's *De Spirituali Amicitia*. Augustine's spasm of grief at the death of a friend is the first time he ever really expressed the friendship he once felt, rather than simply feeling it. And the emergence of friendship as a critical experience during the plague years merely confirms this pattern. It is as if death and friendship enjoy a particularly close relationship, as if it is only when pressed to the extremes of experience that this least extreme of relationships finds its voice, or when we are forced to consider what really matters, that we begin to consider what friendship is.

I found myself reading Augustine on a plane ride after Patrick's memorial service. There's something about the acute, accessible pain in Augustine's writing that has always made me feel less alone in moments of pain. And in the days after Pat's death, the grief had intensified. I had been eclipsed, it felt like, by a sudden sense of loss, a gloom made only more opaque by my confusion about what it actually was that I had lost. I felt as if I was in a dark room, kicking at a door that wasn't there. The darkness went on immeasurably. It had no meaning that I could decipher, and, although I had long anticipated it, it still stung me. Augustine's account of his grief resonated in a way nothing modern ever had. For this man, surely one of the most remarkable men who has ever lived, friendship was "sweet beyond all the sweetnesses of life that I had experienced." Sweeter than love, than sex, than physical pleasure, than all the sweetnesses of a carnal world that he relished but was eventually, reluctantly, to abandon. So when his friend died of a sudden illness, his grief was of an intensity that today we reserve for our family or spouses—not for those with whom we are merely friends. This is how he put it:

> Grief darkened my heart. Everything on which I set my gaze was death. My home town became a torture to me; my father's house a strange world of unhappiness; all that I had shared with my friend was without him transformed into a cruel torment. My eyes looked for him everywhere, and he was not there. I hated everything because they did not have him, nor could they now tell me "look, he is on the way," as used to be the case when he was alive and absent from me....I found myself weighed down by a sense of being tired of living and scared of dying. I suppose the more I loved him, the more hatred and fear I felt for the death which had taken him from me, as if it were my most ferocious enemy. I thought that since death had consumed him, it was suddenly going to engulf all humanity.

It is only, perhaps, when you absorb the notion that someone is truly your equal, truly interchangeable with you, that the death of another makes mortality real. It is as if only in the death of a friend that a true reckoning with mortality is ever fully made, before it is too late, which is why so many theologians for so long saw friendship as an integral and vital part of a truly spiritual life. In that close encounter with the end of life, certain things become clearer before they become opaque again. And it is at these times that the feelings of grief may actually take the place of a friendship itself, providing a focus for attention, a physical and emotional catharsis that alone displaces the experience we recently had. Which is why we cling to it, like a narcotic, and are afraid of a normal future that will only remind us again of the loss that will never go away. With Patrick, death swept away the mystery of our friendship and exposed its raw existence. The friendship articulated itself at the moment that it ceased to exist.

We were as alike as we were unlike. Patrick was a big-boned, apple-cheeked, redheaded bruiser of a man, a Southerner with an immense capacity to charm and infuriate. My first sight of him (before I had ever met him) was watching him stride across Dupont Circle, shirtless, with a huge metal bicycle chain draped around his neck, like a python. I'd been told about him by a mutual friend, who'd known him since college and who thought we would get along. When I eventually got to know him, I began to see why. He had read everything, it seemed. All of Faulkner, twice over at least. Obscure works by Gide, and obscurer historical texts on the Civil War. He had taught himself to play the piano and relaxed listening to Marian McPartland and Arvo Pärt. Obsessed with food, he cooked vast, fatty, floury Southern meals, and knew Rilke in the original German. He laughed mischievously, made up stories, was prone to sudden violent outbursts of temper and hardly ever answered the phone. He was a deeply proud person, and fearless. A rebel who revered authority, a sexual adventurer who treasured love, a traditionalist who rarely gave up a chance to try something new, Patrick struck so many chords within me over the few years I knew him that it seemed truly as if the world were less lonely with him in it.

And to begin with, of course, I fell in love with him. Most of us did. He didn't allow many people into his intimate life, and the few of us who were privileged to be there were soon forced to tolerate some of the worst varieties of emotional manipulation, but we did so gladly. He drew us to him and kept us there, despite indignities, and rudenesses, and peremptory withdrawals. The charm was almost hypnotic, and there was a sweet serenity about it.

I met him in a bookstore, buying a dictionary. He had wandered over, mock sheepish, his shirt hanging out, his baggy khakis sliding down his rump. We struck up some inane conversation and exchanged phone numbers. Over the next few weeks, the courtship blossomed and collapsed. Our first date was an elaborate dinner, cooked in his apartment, accessible only by a fire escape which let into the kitchen itself. We got drunk and stuffed ourselves, and fooled clumsily around until it was time to go. I remember the large, old-fashioned candlewick bedspread he had, the kind my grandparents used to have, and the bric-a-brac he had collected from countless yard sales that was strewn around the place: plastic Madonnas, rural oil prints, a plaster sundial. And none of this was paraded as some sort of kitsch, an ironic statement of 1990s detachment. Everything Patrick collected he collected because it actually affected him, amused him, reflected some small part of a real and funny world he was glad to be a part of. The only thing Patrick was truly ironic about was irony. He would form his hands into the bunny ears of quotation marks and squawk his contempt.

Of course, he was already romantically involved (with more than one person, it turned out). And there came the inevitable moment when he had to tell me that our connection was about friendship not love, and that the kind of attachment I had begun to feel for him was something about which he could feel only ambivalence, not surety. He told me this on the street at night with tears in his eyes, his chubby face choking with sad transparency. In a world in which emotion is increasingly strained through the filter of self-mocking, Patrick never stinted in his feeling. It was direct and real and old. And his love was, at times, overpowering.

That love was no less love for being in the mode of friendship. We have come to dread that moment when a date or a lover turns to us and says, "Let's be friends," but this dread is too often a misplaced one. Patrick, in the first regard, taught me that. We would have been hopeless lovers: far too headstrong to tolerate each other's constant company, far too individual to have merged into one. But as friends, we had space to breathe, to be ourselves, and, by being ourselves in the company of each other, we helped each other ease more deeply into what we thought were our futures. We gave one another confidence, confidence to resist the categories into which society wanted to shoehorn us, confidence to risk too much in exploring our world, confidence to return to our somewhat estranged families and reconcile ourselves to their love.

The friendship had its ups and downs. One memorable explosion occurred when I blurted out the fact that Pat's ex-lover was now seeing someone else. Patrick fumed and then wrote the kind of letter that smokes in the mailbox. "Further, Andrew," his peroration climaxed, in a long and characteristically relentless screed, "your statement was accompanied by a gesture, a peculiarly self-satisfied, shit-eating smirk, clearly intended to vex, annoy, and upset." We didn't speak for a few weeks.

And the friendship had its unremarkable highs. There were many early evenings when, after a long and bruising day at work, I would simply arrive at Pat's, let myself in, lie down on his couch, and listen to a constant rush of increasingly far-fetched stories, about his life, his home-town, or the characters he had come across in his recent travels. These moments of calm, of unspoken informality, of unarticulated ease in each other's worlds, were, I think, characteristic of friendship, at least in its less developed form.

For months and then years, this friendship continued, occasionally fading and sometimes unexpectedly crackling. But then it changed, or slipped into another dimension, or intensified so dramatically that it seemed to take on a qualitatively different form. And it was almost as if we felt it coming. In the summer that I had been diagnosed with HIV, Patrick had momentarily disappeared. This wasn't particularly strange. For days and sometimes weeks at a time, Pat would simply drop out of sight, fail to return calls, or just absent himself from social duties. But this absence had come after a particularly difficult conversation we had just had. We had sat on the floor in my apartment and talked about the disease that stalked both of us. Pat rarely talked about it, and had never gotten tested. I had just gotten my results, and was still in shock. Fearful of telling anyone, I had even kept the news from Patrick. But I needed to be near him and to talk, even in code, about the fear that was consuming me.

I remember how hard it was to lie to him or not to tell him everything. For the first time in our friendship, I kept something back, pinioned by the disease, and the shame, and the terror of exposure, into compromising our mutual honesty, in protecting myself from my friend's protection. But he seemed intuitively to understand and, oddly enough, to talk about his own fears. "Sometimes," he said, "it feels like some bogeyman in the forest, waiting to pounce on my back, and sometimes I wish it would, just because then

I'd know where it was. And I'd know how to fight it. It would be in front of me, and I'd know what to do. I really wish I had it, somehow. It would be less frightening than not knowing."

Within a few weeks of that conversation, Pat was hospitalized with AIDS-related pneumonia. I didn't know about his illness at first, because, like me, he decided to keep it to himself. In this, we both participated in one of the unsung rites of AIDS. Not so much the fear, or the shame, but the fusion of the two, the uniquely isolating and self-punishing crucible in which the disease often announces itself. But after a month or so of not seeing him, or getting my many calls returned, I spotted him in his usual place at Mass and noticed he looked remarkably thinner. When I tried to catch his eye, he bent down in prayer. And after Communion, after my own prayers, when I looked up to go to that part of the church to talk to him, he had suddenly disappeared. He was avoiding me.

Then, a few days later, he called me at my office and said he wanted to talk to me about something. It was serious, he said. I told him I wanted to talk to him too. I too had something difficult to tell him. There had been, for both of us, a slow erosion in the wall of discretion we had constructed between us. We met a few blocks away, at a fountain in a park, and told each other, with mounting disbelief, the same piece of news. And in the muggy haze of a Washington summer afternoon, the friendship began again. Whatever barriers and boundaries there had been between us until that moment suddenly dissolved into something much more like union, solidarity, relief. So much relief. We were at that moment each other's only HIV-positive friend, each other's only confidant in the same tribulation. And what we had previously had in common swiftly seemed trivial in comparison.

Pat wrote me later that summer about how he felt:

> With all that's happened to us—together and apart—I'm inclined to think that somehow we were chosen to know each other, to help sustain each other, and to teach each other about the mysteries of loving, living, dying. After the initial crush of your news, when I had been prepared not to receive but to give a report on my HIV status to you, I found myself strangely grown more attached and connected to you, even protective of you, and I felt an effusion of love and tenderness that, for the first time since I met you, was not constrained by considerations of others, of anything or anyone other than you, and me, and our feelings for one another. Somehow I was able to love you wholly, and this gave me great strength to face the greatest fears I have known. How is it that such news can clear an immediate path between us, sweep away the debris and the impediments...?

I don't know how the letter continued, because he never sent it to me, and that is the only page I have. It was found in his possessions a year or so after his death. Perhaps he felt it unnecessary in the end to say it to me and merely needed to prove it to himself. The reticence of friendship, again. Or perhaps the feeling was powerful and true only for that moment, and seemed excessive in retrospect. But it was, I think, nevertheless real, at least for a moment. And I felt it too.

Suggestions for Discussion

1. How does Sullivan draw upon classical sources to define friendship?

2. According to Sullivan, how does friendship differ from romantic and familial attachments?

3. How has the suffering and death caused by the AIDS virus deepened Sullivan's sense of the value of friendship?

Suggestion for Writing

Write about the history of your relationship with your closest friend while meditating on what friendship means to you.

ESSAYS

~~~~~~~

MARY WOLLSTONECRAFT

A Vindication of the Rights of Woman

Mary Wollstonecraft (1759–1797), mother of *Frankenstein* author Mary Shelley and wife of radical British politician William Godwin, was a schoolteacher, a governess, and a member of a publishing firm. She is the author of two autobiographical novellas, *Mary* (1788) and the posthumously published *Maria: Or, the Wrongs of Woman* (1798). In 1792, Wollstonecraft published *A Vindication of the Rights of Woman*, an extraordinary eighteenth-century landmark in the history of feminist political writings. Wollstonecraft wrote this diatribe against those who would keep women slavishly dependent and hoped to persuade women to become educated, sensible human beings.

My own sex, I hope, will excuse me, if I treat them like rational creatures, instead of flattering their *fascinating* graces, and viewing them as if they were in a state of perpetual childhood, unable to stand alone. I earnestly wish to point out in what true dignity and human happiness consists—I wish to persuade women to endeavor to acquire strength, both of mind and body, and to convince them that the soft phrases, susceptibility of heart, delicacy of sentiment, and refinement of taste, are almost synonymous with epithets of weakness, and that those beings who are only the objects of pity and that kind of love, which has been termed its sister, will soon become objects of contempt.

Dismissing, then, those pretty feminine phrases, which the men condescendingly use to soften our slavish dependence, and despising that weak elegancy of mind, exquisite sensibility, and sweet docility of manners, supposed to be the sexual characteristics of the weaker vessel, I wish to show that elegance is inferior to virtue, that the first object of laudable ambition is to obtain a character as a human being, regardless of the distinction of sex; and that secondary views should be brought to this simple touchstone.

This is a rough sketch of my plan; and should I express my conviction with the energetic emotions that I feel whenever I think of the subject, the dictates of experience and reflection will be felt by some of my readers. Animated by this important object, I shall disdain to cull my phrases or polish my style; I aim at being useful, and sincerity will render me unaffected; for, wishing rather to persuade by the force of my arguments, than dazzle by the elegance of my language, I shall not waste my time in rounding periods, or in fabricating the turgid bombast of artificial feelings, which, coming from the head, never reach the heart. I shall be employed about things, not words! and, anxious to render my sex more respectable members of society, I shall try to avoid that flowery diction which has slided from essays into novels, and from novels into familiar letters and conversation.

These pretty superlatives, dropping glibly from the tongue, vitiate the taste, and create a kind of sickly delicacy that runs away from simple unadorned truth; and a deluge of false sentiments and overstretched feelings, stifling the natural emotions of the heart, render the domestic pleasures insipid, that ought to sweeten the exercise of those severe duties, which educate a rational and immortal being for a nobler field of action.

The education of women has, of late, been more attended to than formerly; yet they are still reckoned a frivolous sex, and ridiculed or pitied by the writers who endeavor by satire or instruction to improve them. It is acknowledged that they spend many of the first years of their lives in acquiring a smattering of accomplishments; meanwhile strength of body and mind are sacrificed to libertine notions of beauty, to the desire of establishing themselves—the only way women can rise in the world—by marriage. And this desire making mere animals of them, when they marry they act as such children may be expected to act—they dress; they paint, and nickname God's creatures. Surely these weak beings are only fit for a seraglio!—Can they be expected to govern a family with judgment, or take care of the poor babes whom they bring into the world?

If then it can be fairly deduced from the present conduct of the sex, from the prevalent fondness for pleasure which takes place of ambition, and those nobler passions that open and enlarge the soul; that the instruction which women have hitherto received has only tended, with the constitution of civil society, to render them insignificant objects of desire—mere propagators of fools!—if it can be proved that in aiming to accomplish them, without cultivating their understandings, they are taken out of their sphere of duties, and made ridiculous and useless when the short-lived bloom of beauty is over,* I presume that *rational* men will excuse me for endeavoring to persuade them to become more masculine and respectable.

Indeed the word masculine is only a bugbear: there is little reason to fear that women will acquire too much courage or fortitude; for their appar-

---

*A lively writer, I cannot recollect his name, asks what business women turned of forty have to do in the world?

ent inferiority with respect to bodily strength, must render them, in some degree, dependent on men in the various relations of life; but why should it be increased by prejudices that give a sex to virtue, and confound simple truths with sensual reveries?

Women are, in fact, so much degraded by mistaken notions of female excellence, that I do not mean to add a paradox when I assert, that this artificial weakness produces a propensity to tyrannize, and gives birth to cunning, the natural opponent of strength, which leads them to play off those contemptible infantine airs that undermine esteem even whilst they excite desire. Let men become more chaste and modest, and if women do not grow wiser in the same ratio, it will be clear that they have weaker understandings. It seems scarcely necessary to say, that I now speak of the sex in general. Many individuals have more sense than their male relatives; and, as nothing preponderates where there is a constant struggle for an equilibrium, without it has naturally more gravity, some women govern their husbands without degrading themselves, because intellect will always govern.

Suggestions for Discussion

1. Why does the author urge women to reject their conventional image of weakness?

2. How does she relate diction and style to the cause of women's rights? The author acknowledges that her feelings are "energetic." How are you made aware of the strength of her conviction? Why is *fascinating* italicized?

3. How does her own use of language affect her purpose and tone?

4. With what details does she convey her view of marriage? How would you characterize her attitude toward members of her own sex?

5. What evidence is there in this brief excerpt that the author is detached from her subject? Deeply involved?

6. According to Wollstonecraft, how does the education of women both reflect and foster the concept of their frivolity and weakness? What does she see as its effect on the family?

7. What causal relationship is established in the last paragraph?

8. How does the concept of self function in the author's argument?

9. What rhetorical devices are used to persuade the reader?

Suggestions for Writing

1. Imagine a dialogue between Mary Wollstonecraft and D. H. Lawrence, whose essay follows. Focus on points of agreement and disagreement.

2. "The first object of laudable ambition is to obtain a character as a human being, regardless of the distinction of sex." Discuss this statement in the light of your reading on the search for self.

3. Defend or refute the comment that the word *masculine,* as applied to women, is "only a bugbear."

∾∾∾∾∾

D . H . L A W R E N C E

Give Her a Pattern

D. H. Lawrence (1885–1930) was a schoolteacher before he turned to writing and became one of the great English novelists of the twentieth century. His best-known novels, which focus on relationships between men and women, include *Sons and Lovers* (1913), *Women in Love* (1920), and *Lady Chatterley's Lover* (1928). He also wrote short stories, essays, poetry, and literary criticism. In "Give Her a Pattern," from *Phoenix II: Uncollected Papers of D. H. Lawrence* (1959), Lawrence castigates men for not accepting women as real human beings of the feminine sex.

The real trouble about women is that they must always go on trying to adapt themselves to men's theories of women, as they always have done. When a woman is thoroughly herself, she is being what her type of man wants her to be. When a woman is hysterical it's because she doesn't quite know what to be, which pattern to follow, which man's picture of woman to live up to.

For, of course, just as there are many men in the world, there are many masculine theories of what women should be. But men run to type, and it is the type, not the individual, that produces the theory, or "ideal" of woman. Those very grasping gentry, the Romans, produced a theory or ideal of the matron, which fitted in very nicely with the Roman property lust. "Caesar's wife should be above suspicion."—So Caesar's wife kindly proceeded to be above it, no matter how far below it the Caesar fell. Later gentlemen like Nero produced the "fast" theory of woman, and later ladies were fast enough for everybody. Dante arrived with a chaste and untouched Beatrice, and chaste and untouched Beatrices began to march self-importantly through the centuries. The Renaissances discovered the learned woman, and learned women buzzed mildly into verse and prose. Dickens invented the child-wife, so child-wives have swarmed ever since. He also fished out his version of the chaste Beatrice, a chaste but marriageable Agnes. George Eliot imitated this pattern, and it became confirmed. The noble woman, the pure spouse, the devoted mother took the field, and was simply worked to death. Our own poor mothers were this sort. So we younger men, having been a bit frightened of our noble mothers, tended to revert to the child-wife. We weren't very inventive. Only the child-wife must be a boyish little thing—that was the new touch we added. Because young men are definitely frightened of the real female. She's too risky a quantity. She is too untidy, like David's Dora. No, let her be a boyish little thing, it's safer. So a boyish little thing she is.

There are, of course, other types. Capable men produce the capable woman ideal. Doctors produce the capable nurse. Business men produce the capable secretary. And so you get all sorts. You can produce the masculine sense of honor (whatever that highly mysterious quantity may be) in women, if you want to.

There is, also, the eternal secret ideal of men—the prostitute. Lots of women live up to this idea: just because men want them to.

And so, poor woman, destiny makes away with her. It isn't that she hasn't got a mind—she has. She's got everything that man has. The only difference is that she asks for a pattern. Give me a pattern to follow! That will always be woman's cry. Unless of course she has already chosen her pattern quite young, then she will declare she is herself absolutely, and no man's idea of women has any influence over her.

Now the real tragedy is not that women ask and must ask for a pattern of womanhood. The tragedy is not, even, that men give them such abominable patterns, child-wives, little-boy-baby-face girls, perfect secretaries, noble spouses, self-sacrificing mothers, pure women who bring forth children in virgin coldness, prostitutes who just make themselves low, to please the men; all the atrocious patterns of womanhood that men have supplied to woman; patterns all perverted from any real natural fullness of a human being. Man is willing to accept woman as an equal, as man in skirts, as an angel, a devil, a baby-face, a machine, an instrument, a bosom, a womb, a pair of legs, a servant, an encyclopaedia, an ideal, or an obscenity; the one thing he won't accept her as, is a human being, a real human being of the feminine sex.

And, of course, women love living up to strange patterns, weird patterns—the more uncanny the better. What could be more uncanny than the present pattern of the Eton-boy girl with flower-like artificial complexion? It is just weird. And for its very weirdness women like living up to it. What can be more gruesome than the little-boy-baby-face pattern? Yet the girls take it on with avidity.

But even that isn't the real root of the tragedy. The absurdity, and often, as in the Dante–Beatrice business, the inhuman nastiness of the pattern— for Beatrice had to go on being chaste and untouched all her life, according to Dante's pattern, while Dante had a cozy wife and kids at home—even that isn't the worst of it. The worst of it is, as soon as a woman has really lived up to the man's pattern, the man dislikes her for it. There is intense secret dislike for the Eton-young-man girl, among the boys, now that she is actually produced. Of course, she's very nice to show in public, absolutely the thing. But the very young men who have brought about her production detest her in private and in their private hearts are appalled by her.

When it comes to marrying, the pattern goes all to pieces. The boy marries the Eton-boy girl, and instantly he hates the *type*. Instantly his mind begins to play hysterically with all the other types, noble Agneses, chaste Beatrices, clinging Doras, and lurid *filles de joie*. He is in a wild welter of confusion. Whatever pattern the poor woman tries to live up to, he'll want another. And that's the condition of modern marriage.

Modern woman isn't really a fool. But modern man is. That seems to me the only plain way of putting it. The modern man is a fool, and the modern young man a prize fool. He makes a greater mess of his women than men have ever made. Because he absolutely doesn't know *what* he wants her to be. We shall see the changes in the woman-pattern follow one another fast and furious now, because the young men hysterically don't know what they want. Two years hence women may be in crinolines—there was a pattern for you!—or a bead flap, like naked negresses in mid-Africa—or they may be wearing brass armor, or the uniform of the Horse Guards. They may be anything. Because the young men are off their heads, and don't know what they want.

The women aren't fools, but they *must* live up to some pattern or other. They *know* the men are fools. They don't really respect the pattern. Yet a pattern they must have, or they can't exist.

Women are not fools. They have their own logic, even if it's not the masculine sort. Women have the logic of emotion, men have the logic of reason. The two are complementary and mostly in opposition. But the woman's logic of emotion is no less real and inexorable than the man's logic of reason. It only works differently.

And the woman never really loses it. She may spend years living up to a masculine pattern. But in the end, the strange and terrible logic of emotion will work out the smashing of that pattern, if it has not been emotionally satisfactory. This is the partial explanation of the astonishing changes in women. For years they go on being chaste Beatrices or child-wives. Then on a sudden—bash! The chaste Beatrice becomes something quite different, the child-wife becomes a roaring lioness! The pattern didn't suffice, emotionally.

Whereas men are fools. They are based on a logic of reason, or are supposed to be. And then they go and behave, especially with regard to women, in a more-than-feminine unreasonableness. They spend years training up the little-boy-baby-face type, till they've got her perfect. Then the moment they marry her, they want something else. Oh, beware, young women, of the young men who adore you! The moment they've got you they'll want something utterly different. The moment they marry the little-boy-baby-face, instantly they begin to pine for the noble Agnes, pure and majestic, or the infinite mother with deep bosom of consolation, or the perfect business woman, or the lurid prostitute on black silk sheets; or, most idiotic of all, a combination of all the lot of them at once. And that is the logic of reason! When it comes to women, modern men are idiots. They don't know what they want, and so they never want, permanently, what they get. They want a cream cake that is at the same time ham and eggs and at the same time porridge. They are fools. If only women weren't bound by fate to play up to them!

For the fact of life is that women *must* play up to man's pattern. And she only gives her best to a man when he gives her a satisfactory pattern to play up to. But today, with a stock of ready-made, worn-out idiotic patterns to live up to, what can women give to men but the trashy side of their emotions? What could a woman possibly give to a man who wanted her to be a boy-baby-face? What could she possibly give him but the dribblings of an idiot?—And, because women aren't fools, and aren't fooled even for very long at a time, she gives him some nasty cruel digs with her claws, and makes him cry for mother dear!—abruptly changing his pattern.

Bah! men are fools. If they want anything from women, let them give women a decent, satisfying idea of womanhood—not these trick patterns of washed-out idiots.

Suggestions for Discussion

1. Consider the title "Give Her a Pattern" in the light of Lawrence's attitude toward women. As he sketches some of the patterns imposed on women by men through the ages, whom does he regard as villain? Is there any evidence that he regards both men and women as victims of their culture?

2. What details provide the basis for the statement that the one thing man "won't accept her as, is a human being, a real human being of the feminine sex"?

3. Observe the repetition of the charge that modern men are fools. What does Lawrence mean by the statement that women are bound by fate to play up to men? How does he suggest that women are not as great fools as men?

4. What is the basis for his fatalistic attitude toward the possibility of real change in relationships between men and women?

5. What relationship does he make between art and nature?

6. How does he lead up to a definition of woman's tragedy?

7. How are comparison and contrast employed to develop his thesis?

8. How do structure, diction, exclamatory sentences, and metaphor contribute to tone and purpose?

9. What rhetorical devices are used to persuade the reader?

Suggestions for Writing

1. Write on modern female stereotypes and the mass media.

2. "Women love living up to strange patterns." What are some of these patterns today?

3. "When it comes to marrying, the pattern goes all to pieces." Can you illustrate?

4. Discuss and illustrate the "terrible logic of emotion" from your own experience.

ᘓᘓᘓᘓᘓ

VIRGINIA WOOLF

The Angel in the House

Virginia Woolf (1882–1941) was an English novelist and critic known for her experimentation with the novel's form. Her works include *The Voyage Out* (1915), *Night and Day* (1919), *Jacob's Room* (1922), *Mrs. Dalloway* (1925), *To the Lighthouse* (1927), *Orlando: A Biography* (1928), *The Waves* (1931), *The Years* (1937), *Between the Acts* (1941), and several collections of essays, including *The Death of the Moth and Other Essays* (1942), in which this essay appeared. With her husband, Leonard Woolf, she founded the Hogarth Press. Although Woolf was able to overcome certain obstacles to honest writing, she states in the following essay that women still have "many ghosts to fight, many prejudices to overcome."

When your secretary invited me to come here, she told me that your Society is concerned with the employment of women and she suggested that

I might tell you something about my own professional experiences. It is true I am a woman; it is true I am employed; but what professional experiences have I had? It is difficult to say. My profession is literature; and in that profession there are fewer experiences for women than in any other, with the exception of the stage—fewer, I mean, that are peculiar to women. For the road was cut many years ago—by Fanny Burney, by Aphra Behn, by Harriet Martineau, by Jane Austen, by George Eliot—many famous women, and many more unknown and forgotten, have been before me, making the path smooth, and regulating my steps. Thus, when I came to write, there were very few material obstacles in my way. Writing was a reputable and harmless occupation. The family peace was not broken by the scratching of a pen. No demand was made upon the family purse. For ten and sixpence one can buy paper enough to write all the plays of Shakespeare—if one has a mind that way. Pianos and models, Paris, Vienna, and Berlin, masters and mistresses, are not needed by a writer. The cheapness of writing paper is, of course, the reason why women have succeeded as writers before they have succeeded in the other professions.

But to tell you my story—it is a simple one. You have only got to figure to yourselves a girl in a bedroom with a pen in her hand. She had only to move that pen from left to right—from ten o'clock to one. Then it occurred to her to do what is simple and cheap enough after all—to slip a few of those pages into an envelope, fix a penny stamp in the corner, and drop the envelope into the red box at the corner. It was thus that I became a journalist; and my effort was rewarded on the first day of the following month—a very glorious day it was for me—by a letter from an editor containing a cheque for one pound ten shillings and sixpence. But to show you how little I deserve to be called a professional woman, how little I know of the struggles and difficulties of such lives, I have to admit that instead of spending that sum upon bread and butter, rent, shoes and stockings, or butcher's bills, I went out and bought a cat—a beautiful cat, a Persian cat, which very soon involved me in bitter disputes with my neighbours.

What could be easier than to write articles and to buy Persian cats with the profits? But wait a moment. Articles have to be about something. Mine, I seem to remember, was about a novel by a famous man. And while I was writing this review, I discovered that if I were going to review books I should need to do battle with a certain phantom. And the phantom was a woman, and when I came to know her better I called her after the heroine of a famous poem. The Angel in the House. It was she who used to come between me and my paper when I was writing reviews. It was she who bothered me and wasted my time and so tormented me that at last I killed her. You who come of a younger and happier generation may not have heard of her—you may not know what I mean by the Angel in the House. I will describe her as shortly as I can. She was intensely sympathetic. She was immensely charm-ing. She was utterly unselfish. She excelled in the difficult arts of family life. She sacrificed herself daily. If there was chicken, she took the leg; if there was a draught she sat in it—in short she was so constituted that she never had a mind or a wish of her own, but preferred to sympathize always with the minds and wishes of others. Above all—I need not say it—she was pure. Her purity was supposed to be her chief beauty—her blushes, her great grace. In those days—the last of Queen Victoria—every house had its Angel. And when I came to write I encountered her with the very first words. The shadow of her wings fell on my page; I heard the rustling of her skirts in the room. Directly, that is to say, I took my pen in hand to review that novel by a famous man, she slipped behind me and whispered: "My dear, you are a young woman. You are writing about a book that has been written by a man. Be sympathetic; be tender; flatter; deceive; use all the arts and wiles of our sex. Never let anybody guess that you have a mind of your own. Above all, be pure." And she made as if to guide my pen. I now record the one act for which I take some credit to myself, though the credit rightly belongs to some excel-lent ancestors of mine who left me a certain sum of money—shall we say five hundred pounds a year?—so that it was not necessary for me to depend solely on charm for my living. I turned upon her and caught her by the throat. I did my best to kill her. My excuse, if I were to be had up in a court of law, would be that I acted in self-defense. Had I not killed her she would have killed me. She would have plucked the heart out of my writing. For, as I found, directly I put pen to paper, you cannot review even a novel without having a mind of your own, without expressing what you think to be the truth about human relations, morality, sex. And all these questions, accord-ing to the Angel in the House, cannot be dealt with freely and openly by women; they must charm, they must conciliate, they must—to put it bluntly—tell lies if they are to succeed. Thus, whenever I felt the shadow of her wing or the radiance of her halo upon my page, I took up the inkpot and flung it at her. She died hard. Her fictitious nature was of great assistance to her. It is far harder to kill a phantom than a reality. She was always creeping back when I thought I had despatched her. Though I flatter myself that I killed her in the end, the struggle was severe; it took much time that had bet-ter have been spent upon learning Greek grammar; or in roaming the world in search of adventures. But it was a real experience; it was an experience that was bound to befall all women writers at that time. Killing the Angel in the House was part of the occupation of a woman writer.

But to continue my story. The Angel was dead; what then remained? You may say that what remained was a simple and common object—a young woman in a bedroom with an inkpot. In other words, now that she had rid herself of falsehood, that young woman had only to be herself. Ah, but what is "herself"? I mean, what is a woman? I assure you, I do not know. I do not believe that you know. I do not believe that anybody can know until she has expressed herself in all the arts and professions open to human skill. That indeed is one of the reasons why I have come here—out of respect for you, who are in process of showing us by your experiments what a woman is, who are in process of providing us, by your failures and successes, with that extremely important piece of information.

But to continue the story of my professional experiences. I made one pound ten and six by my first review; and I bought a Persian cat with the proceeds. Then I grew ambitious. A Persian cat is all very well, I said; but a Persian cat is not enough. I must have a motor car. And it was thus that I became a novelist—for it is a very strange thing that people will give you a motor car if you will tell them a story. It is a still stranger thing that there is nothing so delightful in the world as telling stories. It is far pleasanter than writing reviews of famous novels. And yet, if I am to obey your secretary and tell you my professional experiences as a novelist, I must tell you about a very strange experience that befell me as a novelist. And to understand it you must try first to imagine a novelist's state of mind. I hope I am not giving away professional secrets if I say that a novelist's chief desire is to be as unconscious as possible. He has to induce in himself a state of perpetual lethargy. He wants life to proceed with the utmost quiet and regularity. He wants to see the same faces, to read the same books, to do the same things day after day, month after month, while he is writing, so that nothing may break the illusion in which he is living—so that nothing may disturb or disquiet the mysterious nosings about, feelings round, darts, dashes and sudden discoveries of that very shy and illusive spirit, the imagination. I suspect that this state is the same both for men and women. Be that as it may, I want you to imagine me writing a novel in a state of trance. I want you to figure to yourselves a girl sitting with a pen in her hand, which for minutes, and indeed for hours, she never dips into the inkpot. The image that comes to my mind when I think of this girl is the image of a fisherman lying sunk in dreams on the verge of a deep lake with a rod held out over the water. She was letting her imagination sweep unchecked round every rock and cranny of the world that lies submerged in the depths of our unconscious being. Now came the experience, the experience that I believe to be far commoner with women writers than with men. The line raced through the girl's fingers. Her imagination had rushed away. It had sought the pools, the depths, the dark places where the largest fish slumber. And then there was a smash. There was an explosion. There was foam and confusion. The imagination had dashed itself against something hard. The girl was roused from her dream. She was indeed in a state of the most acute and difficult distress. To speak without figure she had thought of something, something about the body, about the passions which it was unfitting for her as a woman to say. Men, her reason told her, would be shocked. The consciousness of what men will say of a woman who speaks the truth about her passions had roused her from her artist's state of unconsciousness. She could write no more. The trance was over. Her imagination could work no longer. This I believe to be a very common experience with women writers—they are impeded by the extreme conventionality of the other sex. For though men sensibly allow themselves great freedom in these respects, I doubt that they realize or can control the extreme severity with which they condemn such freedom in women.

These then were two very genuine experiences of my own. These were two of the adventures of my professional life. The first—killing the Angel in the House—I think I solved. She died. But the second, telling the truth about my own experiences as a body, I do not think I solved. I doubt that any woman has solved it yet. The obstacles against her are still immensely powerful—and yet they are very difficult to define. Outwardly, what is simpler than to write books? Outwardly, what obstacles are there for a woman rather than for a man? Inwardly, I think, the case is very different; she has still many ghosts to fight, many prejudices to overcome. Indeed it will be a long time still, I think, before a woman can sit down to write a book without finding a phantom to be slain, a rock to be dashed against. And if this is so in literature, the freest of all professions for women, how is it in the new professions which you are now for the first time entering?

Those are the questions that I should like, had I time, to ask you. And indeed, if I have laid stress upon these professional experiences of mine, it is because I believe that they are, though in different forms, yours also. Even when the path is nominally open—when there is nothing to prevent a woman from being a doctor, a lawyer, a civil servant—there are many phantoms and obstacles, as I believe, looming in her way. To discuss and define them is I think of great value and importance; for thus only can the labor be shared, the difficulties be solved. But besides this, it is necessary also to discuss the ends and the aims for which we are fighting, for which we are doing battle with these formidable obstacles. Those aims cannot be taken for granted; they must be perpetually questioned and examined. The whole position, as I see it—here in this hall surrounded by women practising for the first time in history I know not how many different professions—is one of extraordinary interest and importance. You have won rooms of your own in the house hitherto exclusively owned by men. You are able, though not without great labor and effort, to pay the rent. You are earning your five hundred pounds a year. But this freedom is only a beginning; the room is your own, but it is still bare. It has to be furnished; it has to be decorated; it has to be shared. How are you going to furnish it, how are you going to decorate it? With whom are you going to share it, and upon what terms? These, I think, are questions of the utmost importance and interest. For the first time in history you are able to ask them; for the first time you are able to decide for yourselves what the answers should be. Willingly would I stay and discuss those questions and answers—but not tonight. My time is up; and I must cease.

Suggestions for Discussion

1. What are the characteristics of this phantom, the Angel in the House? Do they persist today?

2. Why does the author say she had to kill the Angel?

3. What remaining obstacles to truth did she find? In what ways may women still encounter these obstacles?

4. What are the implications in the concluding paragraph concerning relationships with men?

5. "Ah, but what is 'herself'? I mean, what is a woman?" Discuss these rhetorical questions in relation to purpose and tone.

6. What points of agreement or disagreement might Woolf have with Lawrence?

7. What rhetorical devices are employed to persuade the reader?

Suggestions for Writing

1. Describe an Angel in the House you know.

2. Does this phantom of the Angel still haunt contemporary drama, movies, fiction, advertising?

3. Apply one or more of Woolf's generalizations to a woman poet or writer of fiction.

$$\infty\infty\infty$$

MARGARET ATWOOD

Fiction: Happy Endings

Margaret Atwood (b. 1939) has lived in both the United States and Europe, but her home is in Toronto. She did graduate work at Harvard on a Woodrow Wilson fellowship and has taught at several Canadian

Copyright ©C. Tyler from the book *Late Bloomer,* 2005, Fantagraphics. Originally published in 1990 as the cover for *Wimmen's Comix.*

and American universities. Her novel *The Blind Assassin* (2000) earned a Booker Prize. Among her other books are *The Edible Woman* (1976), *Life Before Man* (1980), *Surfacing* (1981), *The Handmaid's Tale* (1986), *Cat's Eye* (1989), *The Robber Bride* (1993), and *Morning in a Burned House* (1995). A collection of Atwood's essays, *Writing with Intent*, was published in 2005. She has also written short stories, television plays, children's books, criticism, and poetry. In this updated critique of happy endings, from *Good Bones and Simple Murders* (1983), the author comments bitterly upon the relationships of men and women and the vicissitudes of life.

John and Mary meet. What happens next? If you want a happy ending, try A.

ᘉ

A

John and Mary fall in love and get married. They both have worthwhile and remunerative jobs which they find stimulating and challenging. They buy a charming house. Real estate values go up. Eventually, when they can afford live-in help, they have two children, to whom they are devoted. The children turn out well. John and Mary have a stimulating and challenging sex life and worthwhile friends. They go on fun vacations together. They retire. They both have hobbies which they find stimulating and challenging. Eventually they die. This is the end of the story.

ᘉ

B

Mary falls in love with John but John doesn't fall in love with Mary. He merely uses her body for selfish pleasure and ego gratification of a tepid kind. He comes to her apartment twice a week and she cooks him dinner, you'll notice that he doesn't even consider her worth the price of a dinner out, and after he's eaten the dinner he fucks her and after that he falls asleep, while she does the dishes so he won't think she's untidy, having all those dirty dishes lying around, and puts on fresh lipstick so she'll look good when he wakes up, but when he wakes up he doesn't even notice, he puts on his socks and his shorts and his pants and his shirt and his tie and his shoes, the reverse order from the one in which he took them off. He doesn't take off

Mary's clothes, she takes them off herself, she acts as if she's dying for it every time, not because she likes sex exactly, she doesn't but she wants John to think she does because if they do it often enough surely he'll get used to her, he'll come to depend on her and they will get married, but John goes out the door with hardly so much as a good-night and three days later he turns up at six o'clock and they do the whole thing over again.

Mary gets run down. Crying is bad for your face, everyone knows that and so does Mary but she can't stop. People at work notice. Her friends tell her John is a rat, a pig, a dog, he isn't good enough for her, but she can't believe it. Inside John, she thinks, is another John, who is much nicer. This other John will emerge like a butterfly from a cocoon, a Jack from a box, a pit from a prune, if the first John is only squeezed enough.

One evening John complains about the food. He has never complained about the food before. Mary is hurt.

Her friends tell her they've seen him in a restaurant with another woman, whose name is Madge. It's not even Madge that finally gets to Mary: it's the restaurant. John has never taken Mary to a restaurant. Mary collects all the sleeping pills and aspirins she can find, and takes them and half a bottle of sherry. You can see what kind of a woman she is by the fact that it's not even whiskey. She leaves a note for John. She hopes he'll discover her and get her to the hospital in time and repent and then they can get married, but this fails to happen and she dies.

John marries Madge and everything continues as in A.

∾

C

John, who is an older man, falls in love with Mary, and Mary, who is only twenty-two, feels sorry for him because he's worried about his hair falling out. She sleeps with him even though she's not in love with him. She met him at work. She's in love with someone called James, who is twenty-two also and not yet ready to settle down.

John on the contrary settled down long ago: this is what is bothering him. John has a steady respectable job and is getting ahead in his field, but Mary isn't impressed by him, she's impressed by James, who has a motorcycle, being free. Freedom isn't the same for girls, so in the meantime Mary spends Thursday evenings with John. Thursdays are the only days John can get away.

John is married to a woman called Madge and they have two children, a charming house which they bought just before the real estate values went up, and hobbies which they find stimulating and challenging, when they have the time. John tells Mary how important she is to him, but of course he can't leave his wife because a commitment is a commitment. He goes on about this more than is necessary and Mary finds it boring, but older men can keep it up longer so on the whole she has a fairly good time.

One day James breezes in on his motorcycle with some top-grade California hybrid and James and Mary get higher than you'd believe possible and they climb into bed. Everything becomes very underwater, but along comes John, who has a key to Mary's apartment. He finds them stoned and entwined. He's hardly in any position to be jealous, considering Madge, but nevertheless he's overcome with despair. Finally he's middle-aged, in two years he'll be bald as an egg and he can't stand it. He purchases a handgun, saying he needs it for target practice—this is the thin part of the plot, but it can be dealt with later—and shoots the two of them and himself.

Madge, after a suitable period of mourning, marries an understanding man called Fred and everything continues as in A, but under different names.

❧

D

Fred and Madge have no problems. They get along exceptionally well and are good at working out any little difficulties that may arise. But their charming house is by the seashore and one day a giant tidal wave approaches. Real estate values go down. The rest of the story is about what caused the tidal wave and how they escape from it. They do, though thousands drown. Some of the story is about how the thousands drown, but Fred and Madge are virtuous and lucky. Finally on high ground they clasp each other, wet and dripping and grateful, and continue as in A.

❧

E

Yes, but Fred has a bad heart. The rest of the story is about how kind and understanding they both are until Fred dies. Then Madge devotes herself to charity work until the end of A. If you like, it can be "Madge," "cancer," "guilty and confused," and "birdwatching."

❧

F

If you think this is all too bourgeois, make John a revolutionary and Mary a counterespionage agent and see how far that gets you. You'll still end up with A, though in between you may get a lustful brawling saga of passionate involvement, a chronicle of our times, sort of.

You'll have to face it, the endings are the same however you slice it. Don't be deluded by any other endings, they're all fake, either deliberately fake, with malicious intent to deceive, or just motivated by excessive optimism if not by downright sentimentality.

The only authentic ending is the one provided here:

John and Mary die. John and Mary die. John and Mary die.

So much for endings. Beginnings are always more fun. True connoisseurs, however, are known to favor the stretch in between, since it's the hardest to do anything with.

That's about all that can be said for plots, which anyway are just one thing after another, a what and a what and a what.

Now try How and Why.

Suggestions for Discussion

1. In the spare language of *A*, there are simple undeveloped declarative sentences. What is the effect on substance and tone?

2. What is the author saying about men–women relationships in *B* and *C*? What is the significance of the ending in *B* and *C* in which everything continues as in *A*?

3. What does Atwood mean when she says that plots are "just one thing after another, a what and a what and a what"?

4. In her last sentence, the author says "Now try How and Why." What is she saying about plots, about fiction, and about relationships?

Suggestions for Writing

1. In her discussion of Mary and John, the author poses a number of problems in men–women relationships. Discuss them, drawing on illustrations from your observation or experience.

2. Discuss what you believe to be the major areas of disagreement in marriage.

3. Review a book in which you find an illogical happy ending.

FICTION

KATE CHOPIN

A Respectable Woman

Kate Chopin (1851–1904) was an early feminist who did not begin to write until her late thirties. Her first novel, *At Fault* (1890), was followed by two volumes of short stories, *Bayou Folk* (1894) and *A Night in Acadie* (1897), and her masterpiece, *The Awakening* (1899). The "respectable woman" in this piece, published in 1894, undergoes a metamorphosis after her earlier indifference to her husband's friend.

Mrs. Baroda was a little provoked to learn that her husband expected his friend, Gouvernail, up to spend a week or two on the plantation.

They had entertained a good deal during the winter; much of the time had also been passed in New Orleans in various forms of mild dissipation. She was looking forward to a period of unbroken rest, now, and undisturbed tête-à-tête with her husband, when he informed her that Gouvernail was coming up to stay a week or two.

This was a man she had heard much of but never seen. He had been her husband's college friend; was now a journalist, and in no sense a society man or "a man about town," which were, perhaps, some of the reasons she had never met him. But she had unconsciously formed an image of him in her mind. She pictured him tall, slim, cynical; with eye-glasses, and his hands in his pockets; and she did not like him. Gouvernail was slim enough, but he wasn't very tall nor very cynical; neither did he wear eye-glasses nor carry his hands in his pockets. And she rather liked him when he first presented himself.

But why she liked him she could not explain satisfactorily to herself when she partly attempted to do so. She could discover in him none of those brilliant and promising traits which Gaston, her husband, had often assured her that he possessed. On the contrary, he sat rather mute and receptive before her chatty eagerness to make him feel at home and in face of Gaston's frank and wordy hospitality. His manner was as courteous toward her as the most exacting woman could require; but he made no direct appeal to her approval or even esteem.

Once settled at the plantation he seemed to like to sit upon the wide portico in the shade of one of the big Corinthian pillars, smoking his cigar lazily and listening attentively to Gaston's experience as a sugar planter.

"This is what I call living," he would utter with deep satisfaction, as the air that swept across the sugar field caressed him with its warm and scented velvety touch. It pleased him also to get on familiar terms with the big dogs that came about him, rubbing themselves sociably against his legs. He did not care to fish, and displayed no eagerness to go out and kill grosbecs when Gaston proposed doing so.

Gouvernail's personality puzzled Mrs. Baroda, but she liked him. Indeed, he was a lovable, inoffensive fellow. After a few days, when she could understand him no better than at first, she gave over being puzzled and remained piqued. In this mood she left her husband and her guest, for the most part, alone together. Then finding that Gouvernail took no manner of exception to her action, she imposed her society upon him, accompanying him in his idle strolls to the mill and walks along the batture. She persistently sought to penetrate the reserve in which he had unconsciously enveloped himself.

"When is he going—your friend?" she one day asked her husband. "For my part, he tires me frightfully."

"Not for a week yet, dear. I can't understand; he gives you no trouble."

"No. I should like him better if he did; if he were more like others, and I had to plan somewhat for his comfort and enjoyment."

Gaston took his wife's pretty face between his hands and looked tenderly and laughingly into her troubled eyes. They were making a bit of toilet sociably together in Mrs. Baroda's dressing-room.

"You are full of surprises, ma belle," he said to her. "Even I can never count upon how you are going to act under given conditions." He kissed her and turned to fasten his cravat before the mirror.

"Here you are," he went on, "taking poor Gouvernail seriously and making a commotion over him, the last thing he would desire or expect."

"Commotion!" she hotly resented. "Nonsense! How can you say such a thing? Commotion, indeed! But, you know, you said he was clever."

"So he is. But the poor fellow is run down by overwork now. That's why I asked him here to take a rest."

"You used to say he was a man of ideas," she retorted, unconciliated. "I expected him to be interesting, at least. I'm going to the city in the morning to have my spring gowns fitted. Let me know when Mr. Gouvernail is gone; I shall be at my Aunt Octavie's."

That night she went and sat alone upon a bench that stood beneath a live oak tree at the edge of the gravel walk.

She had never known her thoughts or her intentions to be so confused. She could gather nothing from them but the feeling of a distinct necessity to quit her home in the morning.

Mrs. Baroda heard footsteps crunching the gravel; but could discern in the darkness only the approaching red point of a lighted cigar. She knew it was Gouvernail, for her husband did not smoke. She hoped to remain unnoticed, but her white gown revealed her to him. He threw away his cigar and seated himself upon the bench beside her, without a suspicion that she might object to his presence.

"Your husband told me to bring this to you, Mrs. Baroda," he said, handing her a filmy, white scarf with which she sometimes enveloped her head and shoulders. She accepted the scarf from him with a murmur of thanks, and let it lie in her lap.

He made some commonplace observation upon the baneful effect of the night air at that season. Then as his gaze reached out into the darkness, he murmured, half to himself:

"'Night of south winds—night of the large few stars!
Still nodding night—'"

She made no reply to this apostrophe to the night, which indeed, was not addressed to her.

Gouvernail was in no sense a diffident man, for he was not a self-conscious one. His periods of reserve were not constitutional, but the result of moods. Sitting there beside Mrs. Baroda, his silence melted for the time.

He talked freely and intimately in a low, hesitating drawl that was not unpleasant to hear. He talked of the old college days when he and Gaston had been a good deal to each other; of the days of keen and blind ambitions and large intentions. Now there was left with him, at least, a philosophic acquiescence to the existing order—only a desire to be permitted to exist, with now and then a little whiff of genuine life, such as he was breathing now.

Her mind only vaguely grasped what he was saying. Her physical being was for the moment predominant. She was not thinking of his words, only drinking in the tones of his voice. She wanted to reach out her hand in the darkness and touch him with the sensitive tips of her fingers upon the face or the lips. She wanted to draw close to him and whisper against his cheek— she did not care what—as she might have done if she had not been a respectable woman.

The stronger the impulse grew to bring herself near him, the further, in fact, did she draw away from him. As soon as she could do so without an appearance of too great rudeness, she rose and left him there alone.

Before she reached the house, Gouvernail had lighted a fresh cigar and ended his apostrophe to the night.

Mrs. Baroda was greatly tempted that night to tell her husband—who was also her friend—of this folly that had seized her. But she did not yield to the temptation. Beside being a respectable woman she was a very sensible one; and she knew there are some battles in life which a human being must fight alone.

When Gaston arose in the morning, his wife had already departed. She had taken an early train to the city. She did not return till Gouvernail was gone from under her roof.

There was some talk of having him back during the summer that followed. That is, Gaston greatly desired it; but this desire yielded to his wife's strenuous opposition.

However, before the year ended, she proposed, wholly from herself, to have Gouvernail visit them again. Her husband was surprised and delighted with the suggestion coming from her.

"I am glad, chère amie, to know that you have finally overcome your dislike for him; truly he did not deserve it."

"Oh," she told him, laughingly, after pressing a long, tender kiss upon his lips, "I have overcome everything! you will see. This time I shall be very nice to him."

Suggestions for Discussion

1. How do you learn that Mrs. Baroda is ambivalent about Gouvernail?

2. Why do you think Mrs. Baroda left for the city? What precipitated the move?

3. What details suggest to you that this story was written in an earlier era?

4. What is the significance of the title? Relate it to the theme of the story. Is it used ironically?

5. What are you led to surmise is the relationship of Mrs. Baroda to her husband?

6. What do you think will happen on Gouvernail's next visit? How are you prepared for it?

Suggestion for Writing

Write an essay on Question 4 or 6 above.

CARSON McCULLERS

The Sojourner

Carson McCullers (1917–1967), a Southern writer, was awarded
Guggenheim Fellowships in 1942 and in 1946. Her published works
include *The Heart Is a Lonely Hunter* (1940), *The Mortgaged Heart*
(1940), *Reflections in a Golden Eye* (1941), *The Member of the Wedding*
(1946), *The Ballad of the Sad Café and Collected Short Stories* (1951), and
Clock Without Hands (1961). In the following story, from *The Ballad of
the Sad Café,* a rootless man relives and revisits his past, and the experience enables him to acknowledge the waste of his years, the brevity of
life, and his need to reorder his relationships with those close to him.

The twilight border between sleep and waking was a Roman one this
morning: splashing fountains and arched, narrow streets, the golden lavish
city of blossoms and age-soft stone. Sometimes in this semiconsciousness
he sojourned again in Paris, or German war rubble, or a Swiss skiing and a
snow hotel. Sometimes, also, in a fallow Georgia field at hunting dawn.
Rome it was this morning in the yearless region of dreams.

John Ferris awoke in a room in a New York hotel. He had the feeling that
something unpleasant was awaiting him—what it was, he did not know. The
feeling, submerged by matinal necessities, lingered even after he had dressed
and gone downstairs. It was a cloudless autumn day and the pale sunlight
sliced between the pastel skyscrapers. Ferris went into the next-door drug-
store and sat at the end booth next to the window glass that overlooked the
sidewalk. He ordered an American breakfast with scrambled eggs and sausage.

Ferris had come from Paris to his father's funeral which had taken place
the week before in his home town in Georgia. The shock of death had made
him aware of youth already passed. His hair was receding and the veins in
his now naked temples were pulsing and prominent and his body was spare
except for an incipient belly bulge. Ferris had loved his father and the bond
between them had once been extraordinarily close—but the years had somehow unraveled this filial devotion; the death, expected for a long time, had
left him with an unforeseen dismay. He had stayed as long as possible to be
near his mother and brothers at home. His plane for Paris was to leave the
next morning.

Ferris pulled out his address book to verify a number. He turned the pages with growing attentiveness. Names and addresses from New York, the capitals of Europe, a few faint ones from his home state in the South. Faded, printed names, sprawled drunken ones. Betty Wills: a random love, married now. Charlie Williams: wounded in the Hürtgen Forest, unheard of since. Grand old Williams—did he live or die? Don Walker: a B.T.O. in television, getting rich. Henry Green: hit the skids after the war, in a sanitarium now, they say. Cozie Hall: he had heard that she was dead. Heedless, laughing Cozie—it was strange to think that she too, silly girl, could die. As Ferris closed the address book, he suffered a sense of hazard, transience, almost of fear.

It was then that his body jerked suddenly. He was staring out of the window when there, on the sidewalk, passing by, was his ex-wife. Elizabeth passed quite close to him, walking slowly. He could not understand the wild quiver of his heart, nor the following sense of recklessness and grace that lingered after she was gone.

Quickly Ferris paid his check and rushed out to the sidewalk. Elizabeth stood on the corner waiting to cross Fifth Avenue. He hurried toward her meaning to speak, but the lights changed and she crossed the street before he reached her. Ferris followed. On the other side he could easily have overtaken her, but he found himself lagging unaccountably. Her fair hair was plainly rolled, and as he watched her Ferris recalled that once his father had remarked that Elizabeth had a "beautiful carriage." She turned at the next corner and Ferris followed, although by now his intention to overtake her had disappeared. Ferris questioned the bodily disturbance that the sight of Elizabeth aroused in him, the dampness of his hands, the hard heartstrokes.

It was eight years since Ferris had last seen his ex-wife. He knew that long ago she had married again. And there were children. During recent years he had seldom thought of her. But at first, after the divorce, the loss had almost destroyed him. Then after the anodyne of time, he had loved again, and then again. Jeannine, she was now. Certainly his love for his ex-wife was long since past. So why the unhinged body, the shaken mind? He knew only that his clouded heart was oddly dissonant with the sunny, candid autumn day. Ferris wheeled suddenly and, walking with long strides, almost running, hurried back to the hotel.

Ferris poured himself a drink, although it was not yet eleven o'clock. He sprawled out in an armchair like a man exhausted, nursing his glass of bourbon and water. He had a full day ahead of him as he was leaving by plane the next morning for Paris. He checked over his obligations: take luggage to Air France, lunch with his boss, buy shoes and an overcoat. And something—wasn't there something else? Ferris finished his drink and opened the telephone directory.

His decision to call his ex-wife was impulsive. The number was under Bailey, the husband's name, and he called before he had much time for self-debate. He and Elizabeth had exchanged cards at Christmastime, and Ferris had sent a carving set when he received the announcement of her wedding. There was no reason *not* to call. But as he waited, listening to the ring at the other end, misgiving fretted him.

Elizabeth answered; her familiar voice was a fresh shock to him. Twice he had to repeat his name, but when he was identified, she sounded glad. He explained he was only in town for that day. They had a theater engagement, she said—but she wondered if he would come by for an early dinner. Ferris said he would be delighted.

As he went from one engagement to another, he was still bothered at odd moments by the feeling that something necessary was forgotten. Ferris bathed and changed in the late afternoon, often thinking about Jeannine: he would be with her the following night. "Jeannine," he would say, "I happened to run into my ex-wife when I was in New York. Had dinner with her. And her husband, of course. It was strange seeing her after all these years."

Elizabeth lived in the East Fifties, and as Ferris taxied uptown he glimpsed at intersections the lingering sunset, but by the time he reached his destination it was already autumn dark. The place was a building with a marquee and a doorman, and the apartment was on the seventh floor.

"Come in, Mr. Ferris."

Braced for Elizabeth or even the unimagined husband, Ferris was astonished by the freckled red-haired child; he had known of the children, but his mind had failed somehow to acknowledge them. Surprise made him step back awkwardly.

"This is our apartment," the child said politely. "Aren't you Mr. Ferris? I'm Billy. Come in."

In the living room beyond the hall, the husband provided another surprise; he too had not been acknowledged emotionally. Bailey was a lumbering red-haired man with a deliberate manner. He rose and extended a welcoming hand.

"I'm Bill Bailey. Glad to see you. Elizabeth will be in, in a minute. She's finishing dressing."

The last words struck a gliding series of vibrations, memories of the other years. Fair Elizabeth, rosy and naked before her bath. Half-dressed before the mirror of her dressing table, brushing her fine, chestnut hair. Sweet, casual intimacy, the soft-fleshed loveliness indisputably possessed. Ferris shrank from the unbidden memories and compelled himself to meet Bill Bailey's gaze.

"Billy, will you please bring that tray of drinks from the kitchen table?"

The child obeyed promptly, and when he was gone Ferris remarked conversationally, "Fine boy you have there."

"We think so."

Flat silence until the child returned with a tray of glasses and a cocktail shaker of Martinis. With the priming drinks they pumped up conversation: Russia, they spoke of, and the New York rain-making, and the apartment situation in Manhattan and Paris.

"Mr. Ferris is flying all the way across the ocean tomorrow," Bailey said to the little boy who was perched on the arm of his chair, quiet and well behaved. "I bet you would like to be a stowaway in his suitcase."

Billy pushed back his limp bangs. "I want to fly in an airplane and be a newspaperman like Mr. Ferris." He added with sudden assurance, "That's what I would like to do when I am big."

Bailey said, "I thought you wanted to be a doctor."

"I do!" said Billy. "I would like to be both. I want to be a atom-bomb scientist too."

Elizabeth came in carrying in her arms a baby girl.

"Oh, John!" she said. She settled the baby in the father's lap. "It's grand to see you. I'm awfully glad you could come."

The little girl sat demurely on Bailey's knees. She wore a pale pink crepe de Chine frock, smocked around the yoke with rose, and a matching silk hair ribbon tying back her pale soft curls. Her skin was summer tanned and her brown eyes flecked with gold and laughing. When she reached up and fingered her father's horn-rimmed glasses, he took them off and let her look through them a moment. "How's my old Candy?"

Elizabeth was very beautiful, more beautiful perhaps than he had ever realized. Her straight clean hair was shining. Her face was softer, glowing and serene. It was a madonna loveliness, dependent on the family ambiance.

"You've hardly changed at all," Elizabeth said, "but it has been a long time."

"Eight years." His hand touched his thinning hair self-consciously while further amenities were exchanged.

Ferris felt himself suddenly a spectator—an interloper among these Baileys. Why had he come? He suffered. His own life seemed so solitary, a fragile column supporting nothing amidst the wreckage of the years. He felt he could not bear much longer to stay in the family room.

He glanced at his watch. "You're going to the theater?"

"It's a shame," Elizabeth said, "but we've had this engagement for more than a month. But surely, John, you'll be staying home one of these days before long. You're not going to be an expatriate, are you?"

"Expatriate," Ferris repeated. "I don't much like the word."

"What's a better word?" she asked.

He thought for a moment. "Sojourner might do."

Ferris glanced again at his watch, and again Elizabeth apologized. "If only we had known ahead of time—"

"I just had this day in town. I came home unexpectedly. You see, Papa died last week."

"Papa Ferris is dead?"

"Yes, at Johns Hopkins. He had been sick there nearly a year. The funeral was down home in Georgia."

"Oh, I'm so sorry, John. Papa Ferris was always one of my favorite people."

The little boy moved from behind the chair so that he could look into his mother's face. He asked, "Who is dead?"

Ferris was oblivious to apprehension; he was thinking of his father's death. He saw again the outstretched body on the quilted silk within the coffin. The corpse flesh was bizarrely rouged and the familiar hands lay massive and joined above a spread of funeral roses. The memory closed and Ferris awakened to Elizabeth's calm voice.

"Mr. Ferris's father, Billy. A really grand person. Somebody you didn't know."

"But why did you call him *Papa* Ferris?"

Bailey and Elizabeth exchanged a trapped look. It was Bailey who answered the questioning child. "A long time ago," he said, "your mother and Mr. Ferris were once married. Before you were born—a long time ago."

"Mr. Ferris?"

The little boy stared at Ferris, amazed and unbelieving. And Ferris's eyes, as he returned the gaze, were somehow unbelieving too. Was it indeed true that at one time he had called this stranger, Elizabeth, Little Butterduck during nights of love, that they had lived together, shared perhaps a thousand days and nights and—finally—endured in the misery of sudden solitude the fiber by fiber (jealousy, alcohol and money quarrels) destruction of the fabric of married love?

Bailey said to the children, "It's somebody's suppertime. Come on now."

"But Daddy! Mama and Mr. Ferris—I—"

Billy's everlasting eyes—perplexed and with a glimmer of hostility—reminded Ferris of the gaze of another child. It was the young son of Jeannine—a boy of seven with a shadowed little face and knobby knees whom Ferris avoided and usually forgot.

"Quick march!" Bailey gently turned Billy toward the door. "Say good night now, son."

"Good night, Mr. Ferris." He added resentfully, "I thought I was staying up for the cake."

"You can come in afterward for the cake," Elizabeth said. "Run along now with Daddy for your supper."

Ferris and Elizabeth were alone. The weight of the situation descended on those first moments of silence. Ferris asked permission to pour himself another drink and Elizabeth set the cocktail shaker on the table at his side. He looked at the grand piano and noticed the music on the rack.

"Do you still play as beautifully as you used to?"

"I still enjoy it."

"Please play, Elizabeth."

Elizabeth rose immediately. Her readiness to perform when asked had always been one of her amiabilities; she never hung back, apologized. Now as she approached the piano there was the added readiness of relief.

She began with a Bach prelude and fugue. The prelude was as gaily iridescent as a prism in a morning room. The first voice of the fugue, an announcement pure and solitary, was repeated intermingling with a second voice, and again repeated within an elaborated frame, the multiple music, horizontal and serene, flowed with unhurried majesty. The principal melody was woven with two other voices, embellished with countless ingenuities— now dominant, again submerged, it had the sublimity of a single thing that does not fear surrender to the whole. Toward the end, the density of the material gathered for the last enriched insistence on the dominant first motif and with a chorded final statement the fugue ended. Ferris rested his head on the chair back and closed his eyes. In the following silence a clear, high voice came from the room down the hall.

"Daddy, how *could* Mama and Mr. Ferris—" A door was closed.

The piano began again—what was this music? Unplaced, familiar, the limpid melody had lain a long while dormant in his heart. Now it spoke to him of another time, another place—it was the music Elizabeth used to play. The delicate air summoned a wilderness of memory. Ferris was lost in the riot of past longings, conflicts, ambivalent desires. Strange that the music, catalyst for this tumultuous anarchy, was so serene and clear. The singing melody was broken off by the appearance of the maid.

"Miz Bailey, dinner is out on the table now."

Even after Ferris was seated at the table between his host and hostess, the unfinished music still overcast his mood. He was a little drunk.

"*L'improvisation de la vie humaine*," he said. "There's nothing that makes you so aware of the improvisation of human existence as a song unfinished. Or an old address book."

"Address book?" repeated Bailey. Then he stopped, noncommittal and polite.

"You're still the same old boy, Johnny," Elizabeth said with a trace of the old tenderness.

It was a Southern dinner that evening, and the dishes were his old favorites. They had fried chicken and corn pudding and rich, glazed candied sweet potatoes. During the meal Elizabeth kept alive a conversation when the silences were overlong. And it came about that Ferris was led to speak of Jeannine.

"I first knew Jeannine last autumn—about this time of the year—in Italy. She's a singer and she had an engagement in Rome. I expect we will be married soon."

The words seemed so true, inevitable, that Ferris did not at first acknowledge to himself the lie. He and Jeannine had never in that year spoken of marriage. And indeed, she was still married—to a White Russian money-changer in Paris from whom she had been separated for five years. But it was too late to correct the lie. Already Elizabeth was saying: "This really makes me glad to know. Congratulations, Johnny."

He tried to make amends with truth. "The Roman autumn is so beautiful. Balmy and blossoming." He added, "Jeannine has a little boy of six. A curious trilingual little fellow. We go to the Tuileries sometimes."

A lie again. He had taken the boy once to the gardens. The sallow foreign child in shorts that bared his spindly legs had sailed his boat in the concrete pond and ridden the pony. The child had wanted to go in to the puppet show. But there was not time, for Ferris had an engagement at the Scribe Hotel. He had promised they would go to the guignol another afternoon. Only once had he taken Valentin to the Tuileries.

There was a stir. The maid brought in a white-frosted cake with pink candles. The children entered in their night clothes. Ferris still did not understand.

"Happy birthday, John," Elizabeth said. "Blow out the candles."

Ferris recognized his birthday date. The candles blew out lingeringly and there was the smell of burning wax. Ferris was thirty-eight years old. The veins in his temples darkened and pulsed visibly.

"It's time you started for the theater."

Ferris thanked Elizabeth for the birthday dinner and said the appropriate good-byes. The whole family saw him to the door.

A high, thin moon shone above the jagged, dark skyscrapers. The streets were windy, cold. Ferris hurried to Third Avenue and hailed a cab. He gazed at the nocturnal city with the deliberate attentiveness of departure and perhaps farewell. He was alone. He longed for flight-time and the coming journey.

The next day he looked down on the city from the air, burnished in sunlight, toylike, precise. Then America was left behind and there was only the Atlantic and the distant European shore. The ocean was milky pale and placid beneath the clouds. Ferris dozed most of the day. Toward dark he was thinking of Elizabeth and the visit of the previous evening. He thought of Elizabeth among her family with longing, gentle envy and inexplicable regret. He sought the melody, the unfinished air, that had so moved him. The cadence, some unrelated tones, were all that remained; the melody itself evaded him. He had found instead the first voice of the fugue that Elizabeth had played—it came to him, inverted mockingly and in a minor key. Suspended above the ocean the anxieties of transience and solitude no longer troubled him and he thought of his father's death with equanimity. During the dinner hour the plane reached the shore of France.

At midnight Ferris was in a taxi crossing Paris. It was a clouded night and mist wreathed the lights of the Place de la Concorde. The midnight bistros gleamed on the wet pavements. As always after a transocean flight the change of continents was too sudden. New York at morning, this midnight Paris. Ferris glimpsed the disorder of his life: the succession of cities, of transitory loves; and time, the sinister glissando of the years, time always.

"*Vite! Vite!*" he called in terror. "*Dépéchez-vous.*"

Valentin opened the door to him. The little boy wore pajamas and an outgrown red robe. His grey eyes were shadowed and, as Ferris passed into the flat, they flickered momentarily.

"*J'attends Maman.*"

Jeannine was singing in a night club. She would not be home before another hour. Valentin returned to a drawing, squatting with his crayons over the paper on the floor. Ferris looked down at the drawing—it was a banjo player with notes and wavy lines inside a comicstrip balloon.

"We will go again to the Tuileries."

The child looked up and Ferris drew him closer to his knees. The melody, the unfinished music that Elizabeth had played came to him suddenly. Unsought, the load of memory jettisoned—this time bringing only recognition and sudden joy.

"Monsieur Jean," the child said, "did you see him?"

Confused, Ferris thought only of another child—the freckled, family-loved boy. "See who, Valentin?"

"Your dead papa in Georgia." The child added, "Was he okay?"

Ferris spoke with rapid urgency: "We will go often to the Tuileries. Ride the pony and we will go into the guignol. We will see the puppet show and never be in a hurry any more."

"Monsieur Jean," Valentin said. "The guignol is now closed."

Again, the terror, the acknowledgment of wasted years and death. Valentin, responsive and confident, still nestled in his arms. His cheek touched the soft cheek and felt the brush of the delicate eyelashes. With inner desperation he pressed the child close—as though an emotion as protean as his love could dominate the pulse of time.

Suggestions for Discussion

1. In *The Mortgaged Heart*, McCullers suggests that the way by which we master loneliness is "to belong to something larger and more powerful than the weak, lonely self." How is this belief developed in this short story?

2. What do the descriptions in the opening four paragraphs tell you about Ferris? In particular, try to account for his emotional response to the names in his address book.

3. From the moment Ferris catches a glimpse of Elizabeth on the sidewalk outside the restaurant to his flight to Paris and his taxi ride across the city, the reader gains an understanding of Elizabeth and of their relationship. What details clarify your knowledge of Elizabeth? Of Ferris?

4. What is Ferris's response to his evening at the Baileys? How does the playing of the fugue and the second piece he couldn't identify affect Ferris?

5. Why does Ferris lie to Elizabeth about his relationship with Jeannine and Valentin?

6. How are you prepared for Ferris's new relationship with Valentin?

7. What is the meaning of the last sentence? Relate it to what has gone before in Ferris's life.

Suggestions for Writing

1. Discuss the McCullers quotation in Question 1.

2. Write a narrative growing out of your observation or experience about the effects of divorce on the former mates and/or the children.

POETRY

WILLIAM SHAKESPEARE

William Shakespeare (1564–1616) is generally acknowledged to be the greatest playwright in the English language. He was born in Stratford-upon-Avon, England. By 1592, he had become an actor and playwright in London, and in 1599, he helped establish the famous Globe Theatre. Shakespeare's works include historical plays, such as *Henry IV, Henry V,* and *Richard III*; comedies such as *A Midsummer Night's Dream* and *The Taming of the Shrew*; and tragedies such as *Macbeth, Hamlet, King Lear,* and *Othello*. He also wrote a number of love sonnets, two of which follow. First published in a collected edition of poetry in 1609, Shakespeare's sonnets include poignant musings on love, art, death, and parenthood. Critics believe that these sonnets were written for two mysterious recipients—one a treacherous "dark lady" and the other a beloved young man, although the nature of Shakespeare's relationship to these two figures remains a topic of heated debate in academic circles. The self-doubt in Sonnet 29 is resolved with the poet's thoughts of his love. In Sonnet 116, the poet attests to the inviolability and permanence of love.

When in Disgrace with Fortune and Men's Eyes

(Sonnet 29)

When, in disgrace with fortune and men's eyes,
I all alone beweep my outcast state,
And trouble deaf heaven with my bootless cries,
And look upon myself and curse my fate;
Wishing me like to one more rich in hope,
Featured like him, like him with friends possessed,
Desiring this man's art, and that man's scope,
With what I most enjoy contented least;

Yet in these thoughts myself almost despising,
Haply I think on thee, and then my state,
Like to the lark at break of day arising
From sullen earth, sings hymns at heaven's gate;
For thy sweet love remembered such wealth brings
That then I scorn to change my state with kings.

Let Me Not to the Marriage of True Minds

(Sonnet 116)

Let me not to the marriage of true minds
Admit impediments. Love is not love
Which alters when it alteration finds,
Or bends with the remover to remove:
Oh, no! it is an ever-fixed mark,
That looks on tempests and is never shaken;
It is the star to every wandering bark,
Whose worth's unknown, although his height be taken.
Love's not Time's fool, though rosy lips and cheeks
Within his bending sickle's compass come;
Love alters not with his brief hours and weeks,
But bears it out even to the edge of doom.
If this be error and upon me proved,
I never writ, nor no man ever loved.

Suggestions for Discussion

1. How does the imagery in each of the sonnets contribute to its unity?
2. How does dramatic understatement at the end of the second of the two sonnets reinforce the theme?

WILLIAM BLAKE

William Blake (1757–1827), poet and artist, illustrated his poems with his own engravings. His works include *Songs of Innocence* (1789), *Songs of Experience* (1794), *The Marriage of Heaven and Hell* (1790), *The Gates of Paradise* (1793), and *Visions of the Daughters of Albion* (1793). The poems that follow suggest some of the contradictions inherent in concepts of love.

The Clod and the Pebble

"Love seeketh not Itself to please,
　　Nor for itself hath any care,
But for another gives its ease,
　　And builds a Heaven in Hell's despair."

So sung the Clod of Clay,
　　Trodden with the cattle's feet,
But a Pebble in the brook
　　Warbled out these metres meet:

"Love seeketh only Self to please,
　　To bind another to its delight,
Joys in another's loss of ease,
　　And builds a Hell in Heaven's Despite."

The Garden of Love

I went to the Garden of Love,
And I saw what I never had seen:
A Chapel was built in the midst,
Where I used to play on the green.

And the gates of this Chapel were shut,
And "Thou shalt not" writ over the door:
So I turned to the Garden of Love
That so many sweet flowers bore;

And I saw it was filled with graves,
And tomb-stones where flowers should be;
And Priests in black gowns were walking their rounds,
And binding with briars my joys and desires.

Suggestion for Discussion

Both of Blake's poems suggest some of the contradictions inherent in concepts
of "love." What are they, and what seems to be the poet's conclusion?

≈≈≈

W . H . A U D E N

Lay Your Sleeping Head, My Love

Wystan Hugh Auden (1907–1973), English poet educated at Oxford
University, was early recognized as a leader of the poets of his generation. His poetry collections include *The Orators* (1932); *The Double Man*
(1941); *The Age of Anxiety* (1947), which won a Pulitzer Prize in 1948;
The Shield of Achilles (1955); *Homage to Clio* (1960); and *About the House*
(1965). Auden also experimented with drama, and his criticism was collected in *The Dyer's Hand* in 1963. In 1967 he was made a fellow of
Christ College, Oxford. His autobiography, *Certain World: A Commonplace Book,* was published in 1970. The writer speaks of the threats to
love in this poem, from *Collected Poems* (1940), which weaves back and
forth between the present and future, the concrete and abstract.

Lay your sleeping head, my love,
Human on my faithless arm;
Time and fevers burn away
Individual beauty from
Thoughtful children, and the grave

Proves the child ephemeral:
But in my arms till break of day
Let the living creature lie,
Mortal, guilty, but to me
The entirely beautiful.

Soul and body have no bounds:
To lovers as they lie upon
Her tolerant enchanted slope
In their ordinary swoon,
Grave the vision Venus sends
Of supernatural sympathy,
Universal love and hope;
While an abstract insight wakes
Among the glaciers and the rocks
The hermit's sensual ecstasy.
Eye and knocking heart may bless,
Certainty, fidelity
On the stroke of midnight pass
Like vibrations of a bell,
And fashionable madmen raise
Their pedantic boring cry:
Every farthing of the cost,
All the dreaded cards foretell,
Shall be paid, but from this night
Not a whisper, not a thought,
Not a kiss nor look be lost.

Beauty, midnight, vision dies:
Let the winds of dawn that blow
Softly round your dreaming head
Such a day of sweetness show
Eye and knocking heart may bless,
Find the mortal world enough;
Noons of dryness see you fed
By the involuntary powers,
Nights of insult let you pass
Watched by every human love.

Suggestions for Discussion

1. What images are employed by the speaker to suggest the hazards of love?
2. Account for the movement from present to future and from particular to general.

R I T A   D O V E

Beauty and the Beast

Rita Dove (b. 1952) was appointed the first black poet laureate of the United States in 1993. She has an M.F.A. from the University of Iowa and also holds honorary degrees from several universities. Her books of poetry include *The Yellow House on the Corner* (1980), *Museum* (1983), the Pulitzer Prize winner *Thomas and Beulah* (1987), *Grace Notes* (1989), *Selected Poems* (1993), *On the Bus with Rosa Parks* (2000), and *American Smooth* (2004). She has also written a collection of short stories, *Fifth Sunday* (1985), and a novel, *Through the Ivory Gate* (1992). Her verse drama, *The Darker Face of the Earth*, debuted in 1994. "Beauty and the Beast," from *The Yellow House on the Corner*, illustrates how the artist transforms an ever-popular fairy tale into a statement on the human condition.

> Darling, the plates have been cleared away,
> the servants are in their quarters.
> What lies will we lie down with tonight?
> The rabbit pounding in your heart, my
>
> child legs, pale from a life of petticoats?
> My father would not have had it otherwise
> when he trudged the road home with our souvenirs.
> You are so handsome it eats my heart away…
>
> Beast, when you lay stupid with grief
> at my feet, I was too young to see anything
> die. Outside, the roses are folding
> lip upon red lip. I miss my sisters—
>
> they are standing before their clouded mirrors.
> Gray animals are circling under the windows.
> Sisters, don't you see what will snatch you up—
> the expected, the handsome, the one who needs us?

Suggestions for Discussion

1. Who is the speaker in this poem? Try to put together the characteristics of the speaker from suggestions in the poem to describe the nature of the person speaking.

2. Why does the speaker refer to the Beast as lying "stupid with grief / at my feet"? The speaker asks several other questions in the poem. How are they related to each other?

Suggestion for Writing

Write an essay in which you compare and contrast the events of the fairy tale with the remarks of the speaker in the poem. Summarize clearly the significance of the speaker's statements and questions to the Beast and to her sisters.

MAY SWENSON

Women

American poet May Swenson (1919–1989) is best known for *Another Animal* (1954), *A Cage of Spines* (1958), *To Mix with Time* (1963), *Poems to Solve* (1966), and *Half Sun Half Sleep* (1967). She won numerous prizes and grants, including Guggenheim, Ford Foundation, and Rockefeller Foundation fellowships; the National Institute of Arts and Letters Award; and the Shelley Award. In the following poem, which appeared in *Iconographs* (1968), the poet's anger is reflected in the pedestal and rocking horse metaphors.

<pre>
Women   Or they
    should be   should be
        pedestals   little horses
           moving   those wooden
        pedestals   sweet
           moving   oldfashioned
              to the   painted
                 motions   rocking
                    of men   horses
              the gladdest things in the toyroom
</pre>

```
              The                              feelingly
            pegs                              and then
          of their                          unfeelingly
          ears                              To be
        so familiar                        joyfully
       and dear                            ridden
      to the trusting                    rockingly
     fists                              ridden until
   To be chafed                        the restored
 egos dismount and the legs stride away
 Immobile                            willing
    sweetlipped                      to be set
     sturdy                          into motion
      and smiling                    Women
       women                          should be
        should always                pedestals
         be waiting                    to men
```

Suggestions for Discussion

1. How does the central metaphor define the author's point of view? How does it contribute to tone?

2. How does the second extended metaphor contribute to purpose and tone?

3. How do alliteration and repetition function in the poem?

4. Comment on the function of the verbs and adjectives in creating mood and tone.

Suggestion for Writing

Using the same title, write an ironic sketch or poem.

CRININO

GREGORY CORSO

Marriage

Gregory Corso (1930–2001) was a central member of the Beat movement of the 1950s, along with his poetic contemporaries Jack Kerouac, Allen Ginsberg, and Diane Di Prima. His books of poetry include *The Vestal Lady on Brattle* (1955), *Gasoline* (1958), *Happy Birthday of Death* (1960), *Long Live Man* (1962), and *Herald of the Autochthonic Spirit* (1981); he also wrote the novel *The American Express* (1961). In the following poem, written in 1960, Corso turns his wry eye on the institution of marriage and considers whether or not he should take the plunge and get married, as everyone seems to want him to.

Should I get married ? Should I be good ?
Astound the girl next door with my velvet suit and faustus hood ?
Don't take her to movies but to cemeteries
tell all about werewolf bathtubs and forked clarinets
then desire her and kiss her and all the preliminaries
and she going just so far and I understanding why
not getting angry saying You must feel ! It's beautiful to feel !
Instead take her in my arms lean against an old crooked tombstone
and woo her the entire night the constellations in the sky —

When she introduces me to her parents
back straightened, hair finally combed, strangled by a tie,
should I sit knees together on their 3rd degree sofa
and not ask Where's the bathroom ?
How else to feel other than I am,
often thinking Flash Gordon soap —

O how terrible it must be for a young man
seated before a family and the family thinking
We never saw him before ! He wants our Mary Lou !
After tea and homemade cookies they ask What do you do for a
                                                        living ?

Should I tell them ? Would they like me then ?
Say All right get married, we're losing a daughter

but we're gaining a son—
And should I then ask Where's the bathroom ?

O God, and the wedding ! All her family and her friends
and only a handful of mine all scroungy and bearded
just wait to get at the drinks and food —
And the priest! he looking at me as if I masturbated
asking me Do you take this woman for your lawful wedded wife ?
And I trembling what to say say Pie Glue !
I kiss the bride all those corny men slapping me on the back

She's all yours, boy ! Ha-ha-ha !
And in their eyes you could see some obscene honeymoon going

on —

Then all that absurd rice and clanky cans and shoes
Niagara Falls ! Hordes of us ! Husbands ! Wives ! Flowers !

Chocolates !

All streaming into cozy hotels
All going to do the same thing tonight
The indifferent clerk he knowing what was going to happen
The lobby zombies they knowing what
The whistling elevator man he knowing
The winking bellboy knowing
Everybody knowing ! I'd be almost inclined not to do anything !
Stay up all night ! Stare that hotel clerk in the eye !
Screaming: I deny honeymoon ! I deny honeymoon !
running rampant into those almost climactic suites
yelling Radio belly ! Cat shovel !
O I'd live in Niagara forever ! in a dark cave beneath the Falls
I'd sit there the Mad Honeymooner
devising ways to break marriages, a scourge of bigamy
a saint of divorce —

But I should get married I should be good
How nice it'd be to come home to her
and sit by the fireplace and she in the kitchen
aproned young and lovely wanting my baby
and so happy about me she burns the roast beef
and comes crying to me and I get up from my big papa chair
saying Christmas teeth ! Radiant brains ! Apple deaf !
God what a husband I'd make ! Yes, I should get married !
So much to do ! like sneaking into Mr Jones' house late at night
and cover his golf clubs with 1920 Norwegian books
Like hanging a picture of Rimbaud on the lawnmower
like pasting Tannu Tuva postage stamps all over the picket fence
like when Mrs Kindhead comes to collect for the Community Chest

grab her and tell her There are unfavorable omens in the sky !
And when the mayor comes to get my vote tell him
When are you going to stop people killing whales !
And when the milkman comes leave him a note in the bottle
Penguin dust, bring me penguin dust, I want penguin dust —

Yet if I should get married and it's Connecticut and snow
and she gives birth to a child and I am sleepless, worn,
up for nights, head bowed against a quiet window, the past behind
                                             me,
finding myself in the most common of situations a trembling man
knowledged with responsibility not twig-smear nor Roman coin
                                                 soup —

O what would that be like !
Surely I'd give it for a nipple a rubber Tacitus
For a rattle a bag of broken Bach records
Tack Della Francesca all over its crib
Sew the Greek alphabet on its bib
And build for its playpen a roofless Parthenon

No, I doubt I'd be that kind of father
not rural not snow no quiet window
but hot smelly tight New York City
seven flights up, roaches and rats in the walls
a fat Reichian wife screeching over potatoes Get a job !
And five nose running brats in love with Batman
And the neighbors all toothless and dry haired
like those hag masses of the 18th century
all wanting to come in and watch TV
The landlord wants his rent
Grocery store Blue Cross Gas & Electric Knights of Columbus
Impossible to lie back and dream Telephone snow, ghost parking —
No ! I should not get married I should never get married !
But — imagine If I were married to a beautiful sophisticated woman
tall and pale wearing an elegant black dress and long black gloves
holding a cigarette holder in one hand and a highball in the other
and we lived high up in a penthouse with a huge window
from which we could see all of New York and ever farther on
                                            clearer days
No, can't imagine myself married to that pleasant prison dream —

O but what about love ? I forget love
not that I am incapable of love

it's just that I see love as odd as wearing shoes —
I never wanted to marry a girl who was like my mother
And Ingrid Bergman was always impossible
And there's maybe a girl now but she's already married
And I don't like men and —
but there's got to be somebody !
Because what if I'm 60 years old and not married,
all alone in a furnished room with pee stains on my underwear
and everybody else is married ! All the universe married but me !

Ah, yet well I know that were a woman possible as I am possible
then marriage would be possible —
Like SHE in her lonely alien gaud waiting her Egyptian lover
so I wait — bereft of 2,000 years and the bath of life.

Suggestions for Discussion

1. Why does the narrator feel pressured to get married? What are the sources of the pressure? Does he wish to marry?

2. What future does the narrator see for himself if he remains single?

3. What kinds of women does the narrator consider marrying? How does he feel about each of the women and their personalities?

4. What are the narrator's expectations regarding possible fatherhood?

Suggestion for Writing

Write a literary essay examining the vision of the institution of marriage as presented in this poem. If you wish, you may contrast this poem with Mark Strand's poem, *The Marriage,* which follows in this book.

~~~~~~

MARK STRAND

The Marriage

Although he was born on Canada's Prince Edward Island, Mark Strand (b.1934) was chosen as poet laureate of the United States in 1990. He won the 1999 Pulitzer Prize for *Blizzard of One,* a book of poems, and he has since been a MacArthur fellow. In addition to his books of poetry,

Strand has produced several volumes of translations and edited numerous anthologies. His other works include the children's book *Rembrandt Takes a Walk* (1986), *The Golden Ecco Anthology* (1994), and *The Weather of Words* (2000), a book of prose. The following poem was published in *Selected Poems* (1990).

The wind comes from opposite poles,
traveling slowly.

She turns in the deep air.
He walks in the clouds.

She readies herself,
shakes out her hair,

makes up her eyes,
smiles.

The sun warms her teeth,
the tip of her tongue moistens them.

He brushes the dust from his suit
and straightens his tie.

He smokes.
Soon they will meet.

The wind carries them closer.
They wave.

Closer, closer.
They embrace.

She is making a bed.
He is pulling off his pants.

They marry
and have a child.

The wind carries them off
in different directions.

The wind is strong, he thinks
as he straightens his tie.

I like this wind, she says
as she puts on her dress.

The wind unfolds.
The wind is everything to them.

Suggestions for Discussion

1. What is the wind, and why is it everything to the couple in this poem?

2. What do the series of images presented in this poem tell us?

3. How does the story of this romance develop?

Suggestion for Writing

Now that you have read Mark Strand's "The Marriage," read Gregory Corso's poem "Marriage," the previous selection in this book. The poems have nearly identical titles but are very different. Using the title "A Marriage," write your own poem on the theme to make it a poetic trilogy, either responding directly to words written by Strand or Corso, or presenting an entirely different view on the subject.

E. E. CUMMINGS

i like my body when it is with your

e. e. cummings (1894–1962) was an American poet whose book *The Enormous Room* (1922) and poetry *&* and *XLI Poems* (1925) established his reputation as an avant-garde writer interested in experimenting with stylistic techniques. Awarded several important prizes for poetry, he was also Charles Eliot Norton Lecturer at Harvard University in 1952 and wrote *i: six nonlectures* (1953). In the following poem, from *Completer Poems 1904–1962*, the repetitions and typography as well as the sensory detail contribute to cummings's expression of joy in physical love.

> i like my body when it is with your
> body. It is so quite new a thing.
> Muscles better and nerves more.
> i like your body. i like what it does,
> i like its hows. i like to feel the spine
> of your body and its bones, and the trembling
> -firm-smooth ness and which i will
> again and again and again
> kiss, i like kissing this and that of you,
> i like, slowly stroking the, shocking fuzz

of your electric fur, and what-is-it comes
over parting flesh....And eyes big love-crumbs,

and possibly i like the thrill

of under me you so quite new

Suggestions for Discussion

1. Account for the appeal of the poem.
2. How do the repetitions and the typography contribute to the poem's effectiveness? What distinguishes this poem from prose?

ᴄᴠᴄᴠᴄᴠ

R O B E R T   B L Y

After Drinking All Night
with a Friend, We Go Out in a Boat
at Dawn to See Who Can
Write the Best Poem

Robert Bly (b. 1926), from Madison, Minnesota, is a poet, literary scholar, naturalist, and founder of the men's movement of the 1960s; his poetic style is often likened to Latin American and European surrealism. A former naval officer whose education was sponsored by the G.I. Bill, Bly attended Harvard University and earned an M.A. in writing at the University of Iowa. His books of poetry include *Silence in the Snowy Fields* (1962), *The Light around the Body*, which won a National Book Award in 1968, *Loving a Woman in Two Worlds* (1985), *The Night Abraham Called to the Stars* (2001), and *The Insanity of Empire: A Book of Poems Against the Iraq War* (2004).

These pines, these fall oaks, these rocks,
This water dark and touched by wind—
I am like you, you dark boat,
Drifting over water fed by cool springs.

Beneath the waters, since I was a boy,
I have dreamt of strange and dark treasures,
Not of gold, or strange stones, but the true
Gift, beneath the pale lakes of Minnesota.

This morning also, drifting in the dawn wind,
I sense my hands, and my shoes, and this ink—
Drifting, as all of this body drifts,
Above the clouds of the flesh and the stone.

A few friendships, a few dawns, a few glimpses of grass,
A few oars weathered by the snow and the heat,
So we drift toward shore, over cold waters,
No longer caring if we drift or go straight.

Suggestions for Discussion

1. How does the title of the poem influence the way that you read it? Read it again, trying to forget the title, and see if the poem takes on a different meaning.

2. Does it matter that you never get to see the other poem in this contest?

3. How does Bly describe the boat, and what does it mean to him?

Suggestion for Writing

Have a poetry contest, like the one indicated by the title of this poem. Drinking all night before hand is optional.

The Cultural Tradition: Popular Culture

Fast food is heavily marketed to children and prepared by people who are barely older than children. This is an industry that both feeds and feeds off the young.

—ERIC SCHLOSSER, Fast Food Nation

Critics complain that we have reached a point where ignorant blather is considered on a par with informed commentary, where the views of Henry Kissinger carry only a slightly higher price tag than those of "Joe, from Round Rock, Texas."

—DAVID C. BARKER, "Talk Radio, Persuasion, and American
Political Behavior"

Mariko Mori, Birth of a Star, 1996

MIKO NO INORI

Courtesy Deitch Projects

NOTEBOOK

∞∞∞∞

GLORIA STEINEM

Wonder Woman

Gloria Steinem (b. 1934), one of the champions of the contemporary women's movement, is an author, social activist, and pioneering female journalist and editor who won fame as a critic and proponent of reproductive rights for women. She was a cofounder of *New York Magazine* in 1968 and in the 1970s cofounded *Ms.* magazine–the first national women's magazine run by women. She is also the founder of the Coalition of Labor Union Women, the National Women's Political Caucus, and the Ms. Foundation for Women. Born in Toledo, OH, Steinem enrolled in Smith College in 1952 and studied abroad in Switzerland and India. Some of her books include *The Thousand Indias* (1957), *Outrageous Acts and Everyday Rebellions* (1983), the biography *Marilyn: Norma Jean* (1986), *Revolution from Within* (1992), and *Moving Beyond Words* (1994). In the following essay, Steinem explains how her childhood hero Wonder Woman, an iconic comic book feminist with magical powers and superhuman strength, helped inspire her and fuel her self-esteem during her formative years.

Wonder Woman is the only female super-hero to be published continuously since comic books began—indeed, she is one of the few to have existed at all or to be anything other than part of a male super-hero group— but this may strike many readers as a difference without much distinction. After all, haven't comic books always been a little disreputable? Something that would never have been assigned in school? The answer to those questions is yes, which is exactly why they are important. Comic books have power—including over the child who still lives within each of us—because they are *not* part of the "serious" grown-up world.

I remember hundreds of nights reading comic books under the covers with a flashlight; dozens of car trips while my parents told me I was ruining my eyes and perhaps my mind ("brain-deadeners" was what my mother called them); and countless hours spent hiding in a tree or some other inaccessible spot where I could pore over their pages in sweet freedom. Because my family's traveling meant I didn't go to school regularly until I was about twelve, comic books joined cereal boxes and ketchup labels as the primers that taught me how to read. They were even cheap enough to be the first things I bought on my own—a customer who couldn't see over the countertop but whose dignity was greatly enhanced by making a choice, counting out carefully hoarded coins, and completing a grown-up exchange.

I've always wondered if this seemingly innate drive toward independence in children isn't more than just "a movement toward mastery," as psychologists say. After all, each of us is the result of millennia of environment and heredity, a unique combination that could never happen before—or again. Like a seed that contains a plant, a child is already a unique person; an ancient spirit born into a body too small to express itself, or even cope with the world. I remember feeling the greatest love for my parents whenever they allowed me to express my own will, whether that meant wearing an inappropriate hat for days on end, or eating dessert before I had finished dinner.

Perhaps it's our memories of past competence and dreams for the future that create the need for super-heroes in the first place. Leaping skyscrapers in a single bound, seeing through walls, and forcing people to tell the truth by encircling them in a magic lasso—all would be satisfying fantasies at any age, but they may be psychological necessities when we have trouble tying our shoes, escaping a worldview composed mainly of belts and knees, and getting grownups to *pay attention*.

The problem is that the super-heroes who perform magical feats—indeed, even mortal heroes who are merely competent—are almost always men. A female child is left to believe that, even when her body is as big as her spirit, she will still be helping with minor tasks, appreciating the accomplishments of others, and waiting to be rescued. Of course, pleasure is to be found in all these experiences of helping, appreciating, and being rescued; pleasure that should be open to boys, too. Even in comic books, heroes sometimes work in groups or are called upon to protect their own kind, not just helpless females. But the truth is that a male super-hero is more likely to be vulnerable, if only to create suspense, than a female character is to be powerful or independent. For little girls, the only alternative is suppressing a crucial part of ourselves by transplanting our consciousness into a male character—which usually means a white one, thus penalizing girls of color doubly, and boys of color, too. Otherwise, choices remain limited: in the case of girls, to an "ideal" life of sitting around like a Technicolor clotheshorse, getting into jams with villains, and saying things like, "Oh, Superman! I'll always be grateful to you"; in the case of boys of color, to identifying with villains who may be the only ethnic characters with any power; and in the case of girls of color, to making an impossible choice between parts of their identity. It hardly seems worth learning to tie our shoes.

I'm happy to say that I was rescued from this dependent fate at the age of seven or so; rescued (Great Hera!) by a woman. Not only did she have the wisdom of Athena and Aphrodite's power to inspire love, she was also faster than Mercury and stronger than Hercules. In her all-woman home on Paradise Island, a refuge of ancient Amazon culture protected from nosy travelers by magnetic thought-fields that created an area known to the world as the Bermuda Triangle, she had come to her many and amazing powers naturally. Together with her Amazon sisters, she had been trained in them from infancy and perfected them in Greek-style contests of dexterity, strength, and speed. The lesson was that each of us might have unknown powers within us, if we only believed and practiced them. (To me, it always seemed boring that Superman had bulletproof skin, X-ray vision, and the ability to fly. Where was the contest?) Though definitely white, as were all her Amazon sisters, she was tall and strong, with dark hair and eyes—a relief from the weak, bosomy, blonde heroines of the 1940s.

Of course, this Amazon did need a few fantastic gadgets to help her once she entered a modern world governed by Ares, God of War, not Aphrodite, Goddess of Love: a magic golden lasso that compelled all within its coils to obey her command, silver bracelets that repelled bullets, and an invisible plane that carried her through time as well as space. But she still had to learn how to throw the lasso with accuracy, be agile enough to deflect bullets from her silver-encased wrists, and navigate an invisible plane.

Charles Moulton, whose name appeared on each episode as Wonder Woman's writer and creator, had seen straight into my heart and understood the fears of violence and humiliation hidden there. No longer did I have to pretend to like the "POW!" and "SPLAT!" of boys' comic books, from Captain Marvel to the Green Hornet. No longer did I have nightmares after looking at ghoulish images of torture and murder, bloody scenes made all the more realistic by steel-booted Nazis and fang-toothed Japanese who were caricatures of World War II enemies then marching in every newsreel. (Eventually, the sadism of boys' comic books was so extreme that it inspired Congressional hearings, and publishers were asked to limit the number of severed heads and dripping entrails—a reminder that television wasn't the first popular medium selling sadism to boys.) Best of all, I could stop pretending to enjoy the ridicule, bossing-around, and constant endangering of female characters. In these Amazon adventures, only the villains bought the idea that "masculine" meant aggression and "feminine" meant submission.

Only the occasional female accomplice said things like "Girls want superior men to boss them around," and even they were usually converted to the joys of self-respect by the story's end.

This was an Amazon super-hero who never killed her enemies. Instead, she converted them to a belief in equality and peace, to self-reliance, and respect for the rights of others. If villains destroyed themselves, it was through their own actions or some unbloody accident. Otherwise, they might be conquered by force, but it was a force tempered by love and justice.

In short, she was wise, beautiful, brave, and explicitly out to change "a world torn by the hatreds and wars of men."

She was Wonder Woman.

Only much later, when I was in my thirties and modern feminism had begun to explain the political roots of women's status—instead of accepting some "natural" inferiority decreed by biology, God, or Freud—did I realize how hard Charles Moulton had tried to get an egalitarian worldview into comic book form. From Wonder Woman's birth myth as Princess Diana of Paradise Island, "that enlightened land," to her adventures in America disguised as Diana Prince, a be-spectacled army nurse and intelligence officer (a clear steal from Superman's Clark Kent), this female super-hero was devoted to democracy, peace, justice, and "liberty and freedom for all womankind."

One typical story centers on Prudence, a young pioneer in the days of the American Frontier, where Wonder Woman has been transported by the invisible plane that doubles as a time machine. After being rescued from a Perils of Pauline life, Prudence finally realizes her own worth, and also the worth of all women. "From now on," she says proudly to Wonder Woman, "I'll rely on myself, not on a man." Another story ends with Wonder Woman explaining her own long-running romance with Captain Steve Trevor, the American pilot whose crash-landing on Paradise Island was Aphrodite's signal that the strongest and wisest of all the Amazons must answer the call of a war-torn world. As Wonder Woman says of this colleague whom she so often rescues: "I can never love a dominant man."

The most consistent villain is Ares, God of War, a kind of metavillain who considers women "the natural spoils of war" and insists they stay home as the slaves of men. Otherwise, he fears women will spread their antiwar sentiments, create democracy in the world, and leave him dishonored and unemployed. That's why he keeps trying to trick Queen Hippolyte, Princess Diana's mother, into giving up her powers as Queen of the Amazons, thus allowing him to conquer Paradise Island and destroy the last refuge of ancient feminism. It is in memory of a past time when the Amazons did give in to the soldiers of Ares, and were enslaved by them, that Aphrodite requires each Amazon to wear a pair of cufflike bracelets. If captured and bound by them (as Wonder Woman sometimes is in particularly harrowing episodes), an Amazon loses all her power. Wearing them is a reminder of the fragility of female freedom.

In America, however, villains are marked not only by their violence, but by their prejudice and lust for money. Thomas Tighe, woman-hating industrialist, is typical. After being rescued by Wonder Woman from accidental imprisonment in his own bank vault, he refuses to give her the promised reward of a million dollars. Though the money is needed to support Holliday College, the home of the band of college girls who aid Wonder Woman, Tighe insists that its students must first complete impossible tests of strength and daring. Only after Wonder Woman's powers allow them to meet every challenge does Tighe finally admit: "You win, Wonder Woman!... I am no longer a woman hater." She replies: "Then you're the real winner, Mr. Tighe! Because when one ceases to hate, he becomes stronger!"

Other villains are not so easily converted. Chief among them is Dr. Psycho, perhaps a parody of Sigmund Freud. An "evil genius" who "abhors women," the mad doctor's intentions are summed up in this scene-setting preface to an episode called "Battle for Womanhood": "With weird cunning and dark, forbidden knowledge of the occult, Dr. Psycho prepares to change the independent status of modern American women back to the days of the sultans and slave markets, clanking chains and abject captivity. But sly and subtle Psycho reckons without Wonder Woman!"

When I looked into the origins of my proto-feminist super-hero, I discovered that her pseudonymous creator had been a very non-Freudian psychologist named William Moulton Marston. Also a lawyer, businessman, prison reformer, and inventor of the lie-detector test (no doubt the inspiration for Wonder Woman's magic lasso), he had invented Wonder Woman as a heroine for little girls, and also as a conscious alternative to the violence of comic books for boys. In fact, Wonder Woman did attract some boys as readers, but the integrated world of comic book trading revealed her true status: at least three Wonder Woman comic books were necessary to trade for one of Superman. Among the many male super-heroes, only Superman and Batman were to be as long-lived as Wonder Woman, yet she was still a second-class citizen.

Of course, it's also true that Marston's message wasn't as feminist as it might have been. Instead of portraying the goal of full humanity for women and men, which is what feminism has in mind, he often got stuck in the subject/object, winner/loser paradigm of "masculine" versus "feminine," and came up with female superiority instead. As he wrote: "Women represent love; men represent force. Man's use of force without love brings evil and unhappiness. Wonder Woman proves that women are superior to men because they have love in addition to force." No wonder I was inspired but confused by the isolationism of Paradise Island: Did women have to live separately in order to be happy and courageous? No wonder even boys who could accept equality might have felt less than good about themselves in some of these stories: Were there *any* men who could escape the cultural instruction to be violent?

Wonder Woman herself sometimes got trapped in this either/or choice. As she muses to herself: "Some girls love to have a man stronger than they are to make them do things. Do I like it? I don't know, it's sort of thrilling. But isn't it more fun to make a man obey?" Even female villains weren't capable of being evil on their own. Instead, they were hyperfeminine followers of men's commands. Consider Priscilla Rich, the upper-class antagonist who metamorphoses into the Cheetah, a dangerous she-animal. "Women have been submissive to men," wrote Marston, "and taken men's psychology [force without love] as their own."

In those wartime years, stories could verge on a jingoistic, even racist patriotism. Wonder Woman sometimes forgot her initial shock at America's unjust patriarchal system and confined herself to defeating a sinister foreign threat by proving that women could be just as loyal and brave as men in service of their country. Her costume was a version of the Stars and Stripes. Some of her adversaries were suspiciously short, ugly, fat, or ethnic as a symbol of "un-American" status. In spite of her preaching against violence and for democracy, the good guys were often in uniform, and no country but the United States was seen as a bastion of freedom.

But Marston didn't succumb to stereotypes as often as most comic book writers of the 1940s. Though Prudence, his frontier heroine, is threatened by monosyllabic Indians, Prudence's father turns out to be the true villain, who has been cheating the Indians. And the irrepressible Etta Candy, one of Wonder Woman's band of college girls, is surely one of the few fat-girl heroines in comics.

There are other unusual rewards. Queen Hippolyte, for instance, is a rare example of a mother who is good, powerful, and a mentor to her daughter. She founds nations, fights to protect Paradise Island, and is a source of strength to Wonder Woman as she battles the forces of evil and inequality. Mother and daughter stay in touch through a sort of telepathic TV set, and the result is a team of equals who are separated only by experience. In the flashback episode in which Queen Hippolyte succumbs to Hercules, she is even seen as a sexual being. How many girl children grew to adulthood with no such example of a strong, sensual mother—except for these slender stories? How many mothers preferred sons, or believed the patriarchal myth that competition is "natural" between mothers and daughters, or tamed their daughters instead of encouraging their wildness and strength? We are just beginning to realize the sense of anger and loss in girls whose mothers had no power to protect them, or forced them to conform out of fear for their safety, or left them to identify only with their fathers if they had any ambition at all.

Finally, there is Wonder Woman's ability to unleash the power of self-respect within the women around her; to help them work together and support each other. This may not seem revolutionary to male readers accustomed to stories that depict men working together, but for females who are usually seen as competing for the favors of men—especially little girls who may just be getting to the age when girlfriends betray each other for the approval of boys—this discovery of sisterhood can be exhilarating indeed. Women get a rare message of independence, of depending on themselves, not even on Wonder Woman. "You saved yourselves," as she says in one of her inevitable morals at story's end. "I only showed you that you could."

Whatever the shortcomings of William Marston, his virtues became clear after his death in 1947. Looking back at the post-Marston stories I had missed the first time around—for at twelve or thirteen, I thought I had outgrown Wonder Woman and had abandoned her—I could see how little her later writers understood her spirit. She became sexier-looking and more submissive, violent episodes increased, more of her adversaries were female, and Wonder Woman herself required more help from men in order to triumph. Like so many of her real-life sisters in the postwar era of conservatism and "togetherness" of the 1950s, she had fallen on very hard times.

By the 1960s, Wonder Woman had given up her magic lasso, her bullet-deflecting bracelets, her invisible plane, and all her Amazonian powers. Though she still had adventures and even practiced karate, any attractive man could disarm her. She had become a kind of female James Bond, though much more boring because she was denied his sexual freedom. She was Diana Prince, a mortal who walked about in boutique, car-hop clothes and took the advice of a male mastermind named "I Ching."

It was in this sad state that I first rediscovered my Amazon super-hero in 1972. *Ms.* magazine had just begun, and we were looking for a cover story for its first regular issue to appear in July. Since Joanne Edgar and other of its founding editors had also been rescued by Wonder Woman in their childhoods, we decided to rescue Wonder Woman in return. Though it wasn't easy to persuade her publishers to let us put her original image on the cover of a new and unknown feminist magazine, or to reprint her 1940s Golden Age episodes inside, we finally succeeded. Wonder Woman appeared on newsstands again in all her original glory, striding through city streets like a colossus, stopping planes and bombs with one hand and rescuing buildings with the other.

Clearly, there were many nostalgic grown-ups and heroine-starved readers of all ages. The consensus of response seemed to be that if we had all read more about Wonder Woman and less about Dick and Jane, we might have been a lot better off. As for her publishers, they, too, were impressed. Under the direction of Dorothy Woolfolk, the first woman editor of Wonder Woman in all her long history, she was returned to her original Amazon status—golden lasso, bracelets, and all.

One day some months after her rebirth, I got a phone call from one of Wonder Woman's tougher male writers. "Okay," he said, "she's got all her Amazon powers back. She talks to the Amazons on Paradise Island. She even has a Black Amazon sister named Nubia. Now will you leave me alone?"

I said we would.

In the 1970s, Wonder Woman became the star of a television series. As played by Lynda Carter, she was a little blue of eye and large of breast, but she still retained her Amazon powers, her ability to convert instead of kill, and her appeal for many young female viewers. There were some who refused to leave their TV sets on Wonder Woman night. A few young boys even began to dress up as Wonder Woman on Halloween—a true revolution.

In the 1980s, Wonder Woman's story line was revamped by DC Comics, which reinvented its male super-heroes Superman and Batman at about the same time. Steve Trevor became a veteran of Vietnam; he remained a friend, but was romantically involved with Etta Candy. Wonder Woman acquired a Katharine Hepburn–Spencer Tracy relationship with a street-smart Boston detective named Ed Indelicato, whose tough-guy attitude played off Wonder Woman's idealism. She also gained a friend and surrogate mother in Julia Kapatelis, a leading archaeologist and professor of Greek culture at Harvard University who can understand the ancient Greek that is Wonder Woman's native tongue, and be a model of a smart, caring, single mother for girl readers. Julia's teenage daughter, Vanessa, is the age of many readers and goes through all of their uncertainties, trials, and tribulations, but has the joy of having a powerful older sister in Wonder Woman. There is even Myndi Mayer, a slick Hollywood public relations agent who turns Wonder Woman into America's hero, and is also in constant danger of betraying Diana's idealistic spirit. In other words, there are many of the currents of society today, from single mothers to the worries of teenage daughters and a commercial culture, instead of the simpler plots of America's dangers in World War II.

You will see whether Wonder Woman carries her true Amazon spirit into the present. If not, let her publishers know. She belongs to you.

Since Wonder Woman's beginnings more than a half century ago, however, a strange thing has happened: the Amazon myth has been rethought as archaeological relics have come to light. Though Amazons had been considered figments of the imagination, perhaps the mythological evidence of man's fear of woman, there is a tentative but growing body of evidence to support the theory that some Amazon-like societies did exist. In Europe, graves once thought to contain male skeletons—because they were buried with weapons or were killed by battle wounds—have turned out to hold skeletons of females after all. In the jungles of Brazil, scientists have found caves of what appears to have been an all-female society. The caves are strikingly devoid of the usual phallic design and theme; they feature, instead, the triangular female symbol, and the only cave that does bear male designs is believed to have been the copulatorium, where Amazons mated with males from surrounding tribes, kept only the female children, and returned male infants to the tribe. Such archaeological finds have turned up not only along the Amazon River in Brazil, but at the foot of the Atlas Mountains in northwestern Africa, and on the European and Asiatic sides of the Black Sea.

There is still far more controversy than agreement, but a shared supposition of these myths is this: imposing patriarchy on the gynocracy of prehistory took many centuries and great cruelty. Rather than give up freedom and worship only male gods, some bands of women resisted. They formed all-woman cultures that survived by capturing men from local tribes, mating with them, and raising their girl children to have great skills of body and mind. These bands became warriors and healers who were sometimes employed for their skills by patriarchal cultures around them. As a backlash culture, they were doomed, but they may also have lasted for centuries.

Perhaps that's the appeal of Wonder Woman, Paradise Island, and this comic book message. It's not only a child's need for a lost independence, but an adult's need for a lost balance between women and men, between humans and nature. As the new Wonder Woman says to Vanessa, "Remember your *power*, little sister."

However simplified, that is Wonder Woman's message: Remember Our Power.

Suggestions for Discussion

1. According to Steinem, why are children drawn to comic books and super heroes? Why are the various character traits of a superhero—including race, age, and gender—important to a young reader of comic books?

2. What kind of morality does the fictional character of Wonder Woman represent? What critical observations does Steinem make about the positive and negative aspects of the heroine?

3. Why did Steinem come into conflict with DC comics over its changes in the characterization of Wonder Woman? How was the issue resolved? In what other ways has the character changed over the years? You may discuss the more recent depictions of Wonder Woman in comic books, in the *Justice League* cartoon, and on film.

4. How do modern superheroines, including Buffy the Vampire the Slayer, *Kill Bill*'s the Bride (Uma Thurman as Beatrix Kiddo), and *Alias*' Sydney Bristow (Jennifer Garner) compare with Wonder Woman? Might Steinem approve of them?

Suggestions for Writing

1. Think of the fictional character with whom you most strongly identify. Why do you feel such a kinship with a figure who doesn't, in a physical sense, exist in the real world? Do you feel that this character has, in any way, shaped the way you have behaved or viewed yourself or the world around you? Explore the history of your relationship with this character in an essay like the one that Steinem wrote about Wonder Woman.

2. Read Leo Braudy's piece "Arms and the Man" (in *Men and Women*) and compare his observations concerning male heroism with Steinem's concerning female heroism.

≈≈≈≈

MARINA WARNER

Fantasy's Power and Peril

Marina Warner (b. 1946), a feminist historian and cultural critic, has explored the portrayal of women in myths, fairy tales, and Christian iconography in works such as *Alone of Her Sex: The Myth and the Cult of the Virgin Mary* (1976), *Joan of Arc* (1981), and *From the Beast to the Blonde: On Fairy Tales and Their Tellers* (1994). Her novel *The Lost Father* made the short list for the Booker Prize in 1988. A native of London, she is a member of the Department of Literature, Film, and Theatre Studies at the University of Essex.

Myths in which heroic figures are pitted in mortal combat against diabolical enemies have gained fresh energy in popular culture since Sept. 11. The enormous success of the Harry Potter franchise and the drumroll for the imminent release of the film version of J. R. R. Tolkien's "Lord of the Rings" suggest the strong consolatory power of such starkly drawn tales of good conquering evil.

Drawing of invisible Bilbo speaking with the Dragon Smaug from *The Hobbit*, by J. R. R. Tolkien, illustrated by David Waytt (Harper Collins Modern Classics). Sarah Brown Agency.

Boy heroes doing battle with mighty monsters have long been the staple of "bloods," as such adventures were called when they were first published for young people in the 19th century. In modern fairy tales, the dragon-killers have shrunk in size and style: the warriors have shed wings and armor and put on spectacles, morphing into brave hobbits and young lads.

Yet both Tolkien, who published his epic fantasy in the aftermath of World War II, and J. K. Rowling, the author of the Harry Potter series, are writing within an epic tradition that stretches back to ancient Greece. The evil lord Sauron in "The Lord of the Rings" is named after the Greek for dragon; in the Harry Potter stories, the implacable Voldemort's name means Will-to-Death in a kind of mock medieval French.

The strength and familiarity of the good-vs.-evil tale can make the narratives seem inevitable or natural. And children's writers aren't the only ones drawn to such fantasies: the Irish poet Seamus Heaney recently made an eloquent, bleak translation of "Beowulf," the Anglo-Saxon epic that formed Tolkien's life work in his professional capacity is an Oxford professor.

Fantasies of evil and dreams of victory over its agents are increasing in voltage, needless to say, in response to the terrible events of recent times. Osama bin Laden, in fact, appears eerily to be continuing Sauron and Voldemort's legacy (as well as, perhaps, the earlier ambitions of the lethal, foreign antagonists of James Bond).

These ideas have roots in the history of ancient religions. It was in the Middle East, in the thought of the prophet Zoroaster, that the gods worshiped by the ancient Persians were declared to be devils. The prophet Mani, in the middle of the 3rd century in Persia, expanded this ethical interpretation of the continuing struggle between light and dark into a strong form of religious dualism; Manicheans envisaged the clash of forces as a personal, eternal struggle between divine powers of good and evil.

Both Zoroastrianism and Manicheanism have profoundly influenced the extreme warrior visions of Islamic and Judao-Christian thought—Saint Augustine, for example, was a Manichee in his youth and its philosophy colored his deep commitment to the notion of original evil.

The Christian devil, though a bright angel in his beginnings, became a vehicle of irreversible wickedness: the great philosopher Origen is neither a saint nor even a father of the church because he held that the devil could be converted. This was heresy. Wagner's Ring cycle, a direct progenitor of Tolkien's myth, was forged in the same crucible. In many ways, the century that has just ended and the one that has just begun have not experienced the rise of Christian or Islamic fundamentalism so much as the revival of Zoroastrianism.

But this tradition assumes there is only one way to view the world: as a titanic battle between good and evil, with the triumphant goals of destruction, extermination and annihilation. Mythology and history suggest alternatives: fantasies of reconciliation and redemption, for example.

One countervailing fairy-tale tradition that has been sidelined in the epic fantasies of Ms. Rowling and Tolkien is the transformation story. The model of "Beauty and the Beast" structures thousands of fairy tales, ancient and modern. This kind of story, focusing on the possibility of change, imagines the redemption of the monster, his (sometimes her) conversion. To even mention this now seems inappropriate. Yet the fantasy of destruction in itself produces change by another means, and such changes may be more dangerous than before.

Transformation stories are associated with women, for it is Beauty's courage, perseverance and fidelity that accomplish the Beast's metamorphosis. One of the striking features of the current fantasies about evil is their thoroughgoing maleness: Tolkien's work includes examples of female monstrosity (Shelob, a gigantic, malignant spider) but not of female heroism. (In the film, there's a token feminized elf, played by the actress Cate Blanchett.) And the Harry Potter books display little imagination with regard to both young and older female characters.

Another troubling dimension of Pottermania and the Tolkien revival is that they both invest power in talismanic objects that must be controlled, or, if necessary, smashed. Tolkien's ring, Quidditch broomsticks and other magic weapons act as instruments with an instant, direct effect. The association of magical power with weapons of destruction, not with philosophical wisdom, with devices, not with deliberation and negotiation, takes such stories out of the human arena.

Interestingly, for such fantastical tales, they reject enigma, unpredictability and wonder: the students at Hogwarts have only to learn spells, like lessons, or acquire the right brand of weapon, to become lords of creation themselves.

It's always difficult to tell the dancer from the dance in matters of myth and ideology: do box-office megahits reflect anxieties and dreams, or do they shape them, encourage them, even incite them?

The insistence on one kind of narrative can obliterate another. Besides, while the fantasy of the dark lord who can be blamed for all harm and hurt may provide immediate comfort and hope, this kind of story knows it can't settle the matter. It imagines a perpetually recurring struggle with irrepressible forces of evil: in the Harry Potter books, Lord Voldemort comes back to life again and again.

These myths ultimately grant more power to their villains than they can ever take away.

Suggestions for Discussion

1. Write a response to Warner's assertion that mythological stories about "good" fighting "evil" have the power to influence our reaction to real-life conflicts. Cite specific examples of myths and actual events.

2. Like Warner, Leo Braudy draws parallels between representations of male heroism and the modern-day "war on terror." Read Braudy's piece "Arms and the Man" and compare his observations with Warner's.

3. Warner argues that it is better to negotiate with enemies than demonize them, citing "Beauty and the Beast" as an example of a redeeming social myth. Howard Gardner's "Leading Beyond the Nation-State" (p. 711) talks of real-life peacemakers and their methods of reconciliation. Compare what these authors say about the power of storytelling and rhetoric.

Suggestion for Writing

"Fantasy's Power and Peril" references Zoroastrianism, Origen's heresy (sometimes called apokatastasis), and the evolution of the "Beauty and the Beast" fairy tale. Conduct further research on one of these historical allusions and use it as the basis for an informal essay responding to Warner's arguments.

PERSONAL REMINISCENCES

BERNICE REAGON

Black Music in Our Hands

Bernice Reagon (1942), the editor of *Black American Culture and Scholarship* (1985), grew up in Albany, GA, and attended Albany State College and Spelman College before earning her doctorate in black history and music from Howard University in 1975. Having served as a director of the Washington, DC, Black Repertory Company and as consultant in black music to the Smithsonian Institution, she asserts in this essay the importance of "Black music that functions in relation to the people and community who provide the nurturing compost that makes its creation and continuation possible."

In the early 1960s, I was in college at Albany State. My major interests were music and biology. In music I was a contralto soloist with the choir, studying Italian arias and German lieder. The Black music I sang was of three types: (1) Spirituals sung by the college choir. These were arranged by such people as Nathaniel Dett and William Dawson and had major injections of European musical harmony and composition. (2) Rhythm 'n' Blues, music done by and for Blacks in social settings. This included the music of bands at proms, juke boxes, and football game songs. (3) Church music; gospel was a major part of Black church music by the time I was in college. I was a soloist with the gospel choir.

Prior to the gospel choir, introduced in my church when I was twelve, was many years' experience with unaccompanied music—Black choral singing, hymns, lined out by strong song leaders with full, powerful, richly ornate congregational responses. These hymns were offset by upbeat, clapping call-and-response songs.

I saw people in church sing and pray until they shouted. I knew *that* music as a part of a cultural expression that was powerful enough to take people from their conscious selves to a place where the physical and intellectual being worked in harmony with the spirit. I enjoyed and needed that experience. The music of the church was an integral part of the cultural world into which I was born.

286

Outside of church, I saw music as good, powerful sounds you made or listened to. Rhythm and blues—you danced to; music of the college choir—you clapped after the number was finished.

The Civil Rights Movement changed my view of music. It was after my first march. I began to sing a song and in the course of singing changed the song so that it made sense for that particular moment. Although I was not consciously aware of it, this was one of my earliest experiences with how my music was supposed to *function.* This music was to be integrative of and consistent with everything I was doing at that time; it was to be tied to activities that went beyond artistic affairs such as concerts, dances, and church meetings.

The next level of awareness came while in jail. I had grown up in a rural area outside the city limits, riding a bus to public school or driving to college. My life had been a pretty consistent, balanced blend of church, school, and proper upbringing. I was aware of a Black educated class that taught me in high school and college, of taxi cabs I never rode in, and of people who used buses I never boarded. I went to school with their children.

In jail with me were all these people. All ages. In my section were women from about thirteen to eighty years old. Ministers' wives and teachers and teachers' wives who had only nodded at me or clapped at a concert or spoken to my mother. A few people from my classes. A large number of people who rode segregated city buses. One or two women who had been drinking along the two-block stretch of Little Harlem as the march went by. Very quickly, clashes arose: around age, who would have authority, what was proper behavior?

The Albany Movement was already a singing movement, and we took the songs to jail. There the songs I had sung because they made me feel good or because they said what I thought about a specific issue did something. I would start a song and everybody would join in. After the song, the differences among us would not be as great. Somehow, making a song required an expression of that which was common to us all. The songs did not feel like the same songs I had sung in college. This music was like an instrument, like holding a tool in your hand.

I found that although I was younger than many of the women in my section of the jail, I was asked to take on leadership roles. First as a song leader and then in most other matters concerning the group, especially in discussions, or when speaking with prison officials.

I fell in love with that kind of music. I saw that to define music as something you listen to, something that pleases you, is very different from defining it as an instrument with which you can drive a point. In both instances, you can have the same song. But using it as an instrument makes it a different kind of music.

The next level of awareness occurred during the first mass meeting after my release from jail. I was asked to lead the song that I had changed after the first march. When I opened my mouth and began to sing, there was a force and power within myself I had never heard before. Somehow this music—music I could use as an instrument to do things with, music that was mine to shape and change so that it made the statement I needed to make—released a kind of power and required a level of concentrated energy I did not know I had. I liked the feeling.

For several years, I worked with the Movement eventually doing Civil Rights songs with the Freedom Singers. The Freedom Singers used the songs, interspersed with narrative, to convey the story of the Civil Rights Movement's struggles. The songs were more powerful than spoken conversation. They became a major way of making people who were not on the scene feel the intensity of what was happening in the south. Hopefully, they would move the people to take a stand, to organize support groups or participate in various projects.

The Georgia Sea Island Singers, whom I first heard at the Newport Festival, were a major link. Bessie Jones, coming from within twenty miles of Albany, Georgia, had a repertoire and song-leading style I recognized from the churches I had grown up in. She, along with John Davis, would talk about songs that Black people had sung as slaves and what those songs meant in terms of their struggle to be free. The songs did not sound like the spirituals I had sung in college choirs; they sounded like the songs I had grown up with in church. There I had been told the songs had to do with worship of Jesus Christ.

The next few years I spent focusing on three components: (1) The music I had found in the Civil Rights Movement. (2) Songs of the Georgia Sea Island Singers and other traditional groups, and the ways in which those songs were linked to the struggles of Black peoples at earlier times. (3) Songs of the church that now sounded like those traditional songs and came close to having, for many people, the same kind of freeing power.

There was another experience that helped to shape my present-day use of music. After getting out of jail, the mother of the church my father pastored was at the mass meeting. She prayed, a prayer I had heard hundreds of times. I had focused on its sound, tune, rhythm, chant, whether the moans came at the proper pace and intensity. That morning I heard every word that she said. She did not have to change one word of prayer she had been praying for much of her Christian life for me to know she was addressing the issues we were facing at that moment. More than her personal prayer, it felt like an analysis of the Albany, Georgia, Black community.

My collection, study, and creation of Black music has been, to a large extent, about freeing the sounds and the words and the messages from casings in which they have been put, about hearing clearly what the music has to say about Black people and their struggle.

When I first began to search, I looked for what was then being called folk music, rather than for other Black forms, such as jazz, rhythm and blues, or gospel. It slowly dawned on me that during the Movement we had used all those forms. When we were relaxing in the office, we made up songs using popular rhythm and blues tunes; songs based in rhythm and blues also came out of jails, especially from the sit-in movement and the march to Selma, Alabama. "Oh Wallace, You Never Can Jail Us All" is an example from Selma. "You Better Leave Segregation Alone" came out of the Nashville Freedom Rides and was based on a bit by Little Willie John, "You Better Leave My Kitten Alone." Gospel choirs became the major musical vehicle in the urban center of Birmingham, with the choir led by Carlton Reese. There was also a gospel choir in the Chicago work, as well as an instrumental ensemble led by Ben Branch.

Jazz had not been a strong part of my musical life. I began to hear it as I traveled north. Thelonious Monk and Charlie Mingus played on the first SNCC benefit at Carnegie Hall. I heard of and then heard Coltrane. Then I began to pick up the pieces that had been laid by Charlie Parker and Coleman Hawkins and whole lifetimes of music. This music had no words. But, it had power, intensity, and movement under various degrees of pressure; it had vocal texture and color. I could feel that the music knew how it felt to be Black and Angry. Black and Down, Black and Loved, Black and Fighting.

I now believe that Black music exists in every place where Black people run, every corner where they live, every level on which they struggle. We have been here a long while, in many situations. It takes all that we have created to sing our song. I believe that Black musicians/artists have a responsibility to be conscious of their world and to let their consciousness be heard in their songs.

And we need it all—blues, gospel, ballads, children's games, dance, rhythms, jazz, love songs, topical songs—doing what it has always done. We need Black music that functions in relation to the people and community who provide the nurturing compost that makes its creation and continuation possible.

Suggestions for Discussion

1. Analyze the careful structure of Reagon's essay.

2. Discuss the levels of awareness about music that the author describes. What examples does she use to illustrate each?

3. Discuss her assertion that music is "tied to activities that" go "beyond artistic affairs." Are her examples convincing? Explain.

Suggestions for Writing

1. Describe the special significance of certain music in your life.

2. Compare and contrast Bernice Reagon's essay with Aaron Copland's "How We Listen to Music," on page 403.

∾∾∾∾∾

DAVID SEDARIS

The Women's Open

Humorist David Sedaris (b. 1956) came to the public's attention with the 1992 NPR radio essay *The SantaLand Diaries*, based on his experiences working as a Macy's Christmas elf. His books include *Barrel Fever* (1995), *Me Talk Pretty One Day* (2001), and *Dress Your Family in Corduroy and Denim* (2004), which reached number one on the *New York Times* bestseller list for nonfiction. The following story, taken from *Naked* (1997), is an autobiographical account of his father's obsession with golf and its effects on his sister.

My sister Lisa became a woman on the fourteenth hole of the Pinehurst golf course. That's what she was told by the stranger who led her to the women's lounge. "Relax, sugar, you're a woman now."

We had gone unwittingly, shanghaied by our father, who had offered to take Lisa and me for a ride in the secondhand Porsche he'd recently bought. His sherbet-colored pants should have tipped us off, but seeing as there were no clubs in the backseat, we thought we were safe.

"Just a short little jaunt," my father said. He folded back the car's canvas roof and crouched into the driver's seat. "Hell, maybe we'll just tool up to the fairground and back, drive by the correctional center and watch the guys in the exercise yard—you both seem to enjoy that. Maybe we'll go out to the highway and get ourselves some soft ice cream, who knows! Live a little, why don't you? You're not going to experience a thing sitting in the house with your nose pressed up against the TV. It's a beautiful day, let's smell the goddamned flowers."

We shot past the prison so fast, I could barely make out the guards in their gun towers. Both the fairground and the ice cream stand faded in the distance as my father regarded his watch and nervously tapped his fingers against the leather-jacketed steering wheel. He knew exactly where we were headed and had it timed so that we'd arrive just in time for the tee off. "Well, what do you know," he said, pulling off the road and into the crowded golf-course parking lot. "I wonder if there's some kind of a tournament taking place? What do you say we take a quick peek? Gosh, this is a beautiful place, Wait'll you get a look at these fairways."

Lisa and I groaned, cursing our stupidity. Once again we'd been duped. There was nothing worse than spending an afternoon on a golf course. We knew what was in store for us and understood that the next few hours would pass like days or maybe even weeks. Our watches would yawn, the minute and hour hands joining each other in a series of periodic naps. First, our father would push us to the front of a large, gaily dressed crowd. Robbed of their choice spots, these spectators would huff and grumble, whispering insults we would pretend not to hear.

"They're kids," our father would say. "What do you want them to do, stand on my shoulders for Christ's sake? Come on, pal, have a heart."

The big boys were playing that day, men whose names we recognized from the tedious magazines my father kept stacked beside the toilet and heaped in the backseat of his Mustang. We'd seen these players on television and heard their strengths and weaknesses debated by the bronzed maniacs who frequented the pro shop of our country club. These people chipped and parred. They birdied and eagled and double-bogeyed with an urgency that failed to capture our imagination. Seeing the pros in person was no more interesting than eating an ice-cold hamburger, but it meant the world to our father, who hoped their presence might kindle a passion, inciting us to take up our clubs and strive for excellence. This was, for him, an act of love, a misguided attempt to enrich our lives and bring us closer together as a family.

"You kids are so damned lucky." He placed his hands on our shoulders, inching us closer to the front. "These are the best players in the PGA, and here you are with front-row seats."

"What seats?" Lisa asked. "Where?"

We stood on the grassy embankment, watching as the first player teed off.

"Lisa," our father whispered, "go get it. Go get Snead's tee."

When Lisa refused, it was up to me to wander onto the green, searching for the spent wooden peg that might have been whacked anywhere from six to twenty feet from its point of origin. Our father collected these tees as good-luck charms and kept them stored in a goldfish bowl that sat upon his dresser. It was forbidden to wander onto the green during a tournament, so he used us to do his legwork, hoping the officials might see us as enthusiastic upstarts who decorated their rooms with posters of the masters working their way out of sand traps or hoisting trophies over their heads following stunning victories at Pebble Beach. Nothing could have been further from the truth. No matter how hard he tried to motivate us, the members of my family refused to take even the slightest interest in what was surely the dullest game ever invented. We despised golf and everything that went with it, from the mushroom-capped tam-o' shanters right down to the cruel spiked shoes.

"Oh, Lou," my mother would whine, dressed for a cocktail party in her muted, earth-tone caftan. "You're not going to wear *that,* are you?"

"What's wrong with this?" he'd ask. "These pants are brand-new."

"New to you," she'd say. "Pimps and circus clowns have been dressing that way for years."

We never understood how a man who took such pride in his sober tailored suits could spend his weekends in Day-Glo pants patterned with singing tree frogs or wee kilted Scotsmen. You needed sunglasses to open his closer door, what with all the candy-colored sweaters, aggressive madras sports-coats, and painfully bright polo shirts all screaming for attention. Highway workmen wore such shocking colors so that motorists could see them from a distance. It made sense for them, but what perils did these golfers face? There were no jacked-up Firebirds or eighteen-wheelers racing down the fairway threatening to flatten their comfortable little foursomes. We were taught at an early age never to yell or even speak in a normal tone of voice while on the golf course. Denied the full use of their vocal cords, these people let their outlandish clothing do the shouting for them, and the results were often deafening.

"I don't feel so well," Lisa whispered to my father as we marched from the sand trap to the putting green on the eighth hole. "I really think we need to leave."

My father ignored her. "If Trevino bogeys this hole, he's screwed. That last bunker shot pinned his ass right to the wall. Did you see his backswing?"

"I'm concerned right now about *my* back," Lisa said. "It's aching and I want to go home and lie down."

"We'll be just another minute." My father fingered the collection of tees in his pocket. "The problem with both you kids is that you're not paying enough attention to the game. First thing tomorrow morning I'm signing you up for some more lessons, and then you'll see what I'm talking about. Jesus, this game is just so exciting, you won't be able to stand it."

We had serious doubts that it was exciting, but he was right when he said we wouldn't be able to stand it. A tight man with a dollar, our father had signed us up for our first lessons when we could barely hold a rattle. No, we could not have a nude maid, but he was more than happy to give us an expensive set of child-sized clubs, which sat in the dark corners of our bedrooms, the canvas bags clawed and tattered by our cat, who was the only one who seemed to enjoy them. He bought green carpet for the living room and called us in to observe his stance as he sank balls into a coffee can. The driving range, the putt-putt courses—he just didn't get it. We didn't want advice on our swing, we wanted only to be left alone to practice witchcraft, deface fashion dolls, or sit in the privacy of our rooms fantasizing about anything other than golf. He had hoped that caddying might provide us with a better understanding of the game. My sisters and I collapsed beneath the weight of his clubs, barely conscious when he called out for a nine iron or a sand wedge. Caddying was a thankless job, especially in North Carolina, where by mid-March the humidity is fierce enough to curl paper. Ninety-eight degrees on the second hole and we'd crumple to the green, listening as children our own age shouted and splashed in the nearby pool.

The tournament dragged on, and by the time we reached the fourteenth hole, Lisa had begun to bleed, the rust-colored spot visible on her white culottes. She was close to tears, sunburned and frightened when she whispered something into my father's ear.

"We'll just get one of the gals," my father said. "They'll take care of you." He turned to a handsome white-haired woman wearing a lime green visor and a skirt patterned with grinning pandas. "Hey, sweetheart, I wonder if you could help me out with a personal problem." Like my father, this woman had followed these players from hole to hole, taking note of their every move. She had come out that day to bask in the glow of the masters, and now a strange man was asking her to accompany his daughter to the clubhouse and outfit her with a sanitary napkin.

She didn't seem to appreciate being called "sweetheart" and bristled when my father, his eyes never leaving the ball, suggested that if she shake a leg, she might make it back in time for the next tee off. She looked at my father as if he were something she had scraped off the bottom of her shoe. It was a withering gaze that softened once it shifted direction and settled on Lisa, who stood shamefully staring at the ground, her hands cupped to hide the stain. The woman nodded her head and, placing her hand on my sister's shoulder, reluctantly led her toward a distant cluster of buildings. I didn't understand the problem but very much wanted to join them, thinking perhaps we might talk this person into giving us a ride home, away from this grinding monotony and the cruel, remorseless sun. With Lisa gone, it would become my sole responsibility to fetch the splintered tees and pester the contestants for their autographs. "Lou," I would say, holding out my father's scorecard. "My name is Lou."

The game finally over, we returned to the parking lot to find Lisa stretched out in the backseat of the Porsche, her face and lap covered with golf towels.

"Don't say it," she threatened. "Whatever it is, I don't want to hear it."

"All I was going to do was ask you to take your lousy feet off the seat of the car," my father said.

"Yeah, well, why don't you go fuck yourself." The moment she said it, Lisa bolted upright, as if there might still be time to catch the word between her teeth before it reached our father's ears. None of us had ever spoken to him that way, and now he would have no choice but to kill her. Some unprecedented threshold had been passed, and even the crickets stopped their racket, stunned into silence by the word that hung in the air like a cloud of spent gunpowder.

My father sighed and shook his head in disappointment. This was the same way he reacted to my mother when anger and frustration caused her to forget herself. Lisa was not a daughter now but just another female unable to control her wildly shifting emotions.

"Don't mind her," he said, wiping a thin coat of pollen off the windshield. "She's just having lady problems."

Throughout the years our father has continued his campaign to interest us in the sport of golf. When Gretchen, Amy, and Tiffany rejected his advances, he placed his hopes on our brother, Paul, who found the sprawling greens an excellent place to enjoy a hit of acid and overturn the golf carts he borrowed from their parking lot beside the pro shop.

Our father bought a wide screen TV, an enormous model the size of an industrial-sized washing machine, and uses it only to watch and record his beloved tournaments. The top of the set is stacked high with videocassettes marked 94 PGA and 89 U.S. OPEN—UNBELIEVABLE!!!!

Before our mother died, she put together a videotape she thought Lisa might enjoy. The two of them had spent a great deal of time in the kitchen, drinking wine and watching old movies on the black-and-white portable television that sat beside the sink. These were just a few favorites my mother had recorded. "No big deal," she'd said, "just a little something to watch one day when you're bored."

A few weeks after the funeral Lisa searched my parents' house for the tape, finding it on the downstairs bar beside my father's chair. She carried the cassette home but found she needed a bit more time before watching it. For Lisa, these movies would recall private times, just her and our mother perched on stools and reeling off the names of the actors as they appeared on the screen. These memories would be a gift that Lisa preferred to savor before opening. She waited until the initial grief had passed and then, settling onto her sofa with a tray of snacks, slipped in the tape, delighted to find it began with *Double Indemnity*. The opening credits were rolling when suddenly the video skipped and shifted to color. It was a man, squatting on his heels and peering down the shaft of his putter as though it were a rifle. Behind him stood a multitude of spectators shaded by tall pines, their faces tanned and rapt in concentration. "Greg Norman's bogeyed all three par fives," the announcer whispered. "But if he eagles here on the fifteenth, he's still got a shot at the Masters."

Suggestions for Discussion

1. What does the tone of this autobiographical piece tell the reader about Sedaris's views of himself and his family?

2. Do you sympathize with the father's character, even though his sexism and sports obsession make him a somewhat ridiculous figure in the story? Explain.

Suggestion for Writing

Compare Sedaris's brand of humor writing with the style adopted by Dave Barry (p. 299).

ESSAYS

ROGER EBERT

Great Movies

Roger Ebert (b. 1942) is the well-known film critic who popularized the "Two Thumbs Up," "Two Thumbs Down," and "Split Decision" movie review approach with fellow critic Gene Siskel on the television program they began in 1975, *Siskel and Ebert.* Although Siskel died in 1999, Ebert continues the program (now called *Ebert and Roeper*) with critic Richard Roeper. Ebert began his career as the *Chicago Sun-Times'* resident film critic in 1967 and won a 1975 Pulitzer Prize for criticism. Since 1969, Ebert has lectured on film in the University of Chicago's fine arts program. Each year his reviews are collected in a new edition of *The Movie Yearbook*. His other books include *A Kiss Is Still a Kiss* (1985), *Behind the Phantom's Mask* (1993), and *I Hated, Hated, Hated this Movie* (2000). Ebert was inspired to write the essay included below as he neared completion on *The Great Movies* (2002), a book in which he expressed his love for some of the best movies that he has ever seen.

Every other week I visit a film classic from the past and write about it. My "Great Movies" series began in the autumn of 1996 and now reaches a landmark of 100 titles with today's review of Federico Fellini's "8 1/2," which is, appropriately, a film about a film director. I love my job, and this is the part I love the most.

We have completed the first century of film. Too many moviegoers are stuck in the present and recent past. When people tell me that "Ferris Bueller's Day Off" or "Total Recall" are their favorite films, I wonder: Have they tasted the joys of Welles, Bunuel, Ford, Murnau, Keaton, Hitchcock, Wilder or Kurosawa? If they like Ferris Bueller, what would they think of Jacques Tati's "Mr. Hulot's Holiday," also about a strange day of misadventures? If they like "Total Recall," have they seen Fritz Lang's "Metropolis," also about an artificial city ruled by fear?

I ask not because I am a film snob. I like to sit in the dark and enjoy movies. I think of old films as a resource of treasures. Movies have been made for 100 years, in color and black and white, in sound and silence, in wide-screen and the classic frame, in English and every other language. To limit yourself to popular hits and recent years is like being Ferris Bueller but staying home all day.

I believe we are born with our minds open to wonderful experiences, and only slowly learn to limit ourselves to narrow tastes. We are taught to lose our curiosity by the bludgeon-blows of mass marketing, which brainwash us to see "hits," and discourage exploration.

I know that many people dislike subtitled films, and that few people reading this article will have ever seen a film from Iran, for example. And yet a few weeks ago at my Overlooked Film Festival at the University of Illinois, the free kiddie matinee was "Children of Heaven," from Iran. It was a story about a boy who loses his sister's sneakers through no fault of his own, and is afraid to tell his parents. So he and his sister secretly share the same pair of shoes. Then he learns of a footrace where third prize is…a pair of sneakers.

"Anyone who can read at the third-grade level can read these subtitles," I told the audience of 1,000 kids and some parents. "If you can't, it's OK for your parents or older kids to read them aloud—just not too loudly."

The lights went down and the movie began. I expected a lot of reading aloud. There was none. Not all of the kids were old enough to read, but apparently they were picking up the story just by watching and using their intelligence. The audience was spellbound. No noise, restlessness, punching, kicking, running down the aisles. Just eyes lifted up to a fascinating story. Afterward, we asked kids up on the stage to ask questions or talk about the film. What they said indicated how involved they had become.

Kids. And yet most adults will not go to a movie from Iran, Japan, France or Brazil. They will, however, go to any movie that has been plugged with a $30 million ad campaign and sanctified as a "box-office winner." Yes, some of these big hits are good, and a few of them are great. But what happens between the time we are 8 and the time we are 20 that robs us of our curiosity? What turns movie lovers into consumers? What does it say about you if you only want to see what everybody else is seeing?

I don't know. What I do know is that if you love horror movies, your life as a filmgoer is not complete until you see "Nosferatu." I know that once you see Orson Welles appear in the doorway in "The Third Man," you will never forget his curious little smile. And that the life and death of the old man in "Ikiru" will be an inspiration every time you remember it.

I have not written any of the 100 Great Movies reviews from memory. Every film has been seen fresh, right before writing. When I'm at home, I often watch them on Sunday mornings. It's a form of prayer: The greatest films are meditations on why we are here. When I'm on the road, there's no telling where I'll see them. I saw "Written on the Wind" on a cold January night at the Everyman Cinema in Hampstead, north of London. I saw "Last Year at Marienbad" on a DVD on my PowerBook while at the Cannes Film Festival. I saw "2001: A Space Odyssey" in 70mm at Cyberfest, the celebration of HAL 9000's birthday, at the University of Illinois. I saw "Battleship Potemkin" projected on a sheet on the outside wall of the Vickers Theater in Three Oaks, Mich., while three young musicians played the score they had written for it. And Ozu's "Floating Weeds" at the Hawaii Film Festival, as part of a shot-by-shot seminar that took four days.

When people asked me where they should begin in looking at classic films, I never knew what to say. Now I can say, "Plunge into these Great Movies, and go where they lead you."

There's a next step. If you're really serious about the movies, get together with two or three friends who care as much as you do. Watch the film all the way through on video. Then start again at the top. Whenever anyone sees anything they want to comment on, freeze the frame. Talk about what you're looking at. The story, the performances, the sets, the locations. The camera movement, the lighting, the composition, the special effects. The color, the shadows, the sound, the music. The themes, the tone, the mood, the style.

There are no right answers. The questions are the point. They make you an active movie watcher, not a passive one. You should not be a witness at a movie, but a collaborator. Directors cannot make the film without you. Together, you can accomplish amazing things. The more you learn, the quicker you'll know when the director is not doing his share of the job. That's the whole key to being a great moviegoer. There's nothing else to it.

Suggestions for Discussion

1. According to Roger Ebert, what happens to our curiosity level as we get older? Why does this happen?

2. How does Ebert make the case for the greatness of certain older movies and foreign films? How persuasive are his arguments?

3. How does Ebert try to deflect the accusation that he is a film snob?

Suggestions for Writing

1. Watch one of the classic motion pictures that Roger Ebert has cited in this essay and test his theory to see if it is, in actuality, a great movie. Were you inclined not to like the film in advance when you heard that it was an older film or a foreign film? Were you surprised by your reaction when you saw

it? Are you interested in seeing more of the movies he has mentioned on his list? Write down your reactions to the film and try to come to a determination about how you evaluate the relative quality of the movies that you have seen in your life.

2. Make a list of your favorite movies. Compare it with other lists of great films, including those compiled by Roger Ebert, by the American Film Institute, and by the users of the Internet Movie Database (www.imdb.com). What aesthetic taste and artistic criteria seem to be at work in the making of these lists? Are there any other observations that can be made about popular taste and scholarly opinion by examining these lists?

∽∽∽∽

D A V E   B A R R Y

The Internet

Dave Barry (b. 1947), a Pulitzer Prize-winning satirist and author, writes a syndicated column at the *Miami Herald*, where he has worked since 1983. The now-defunct television series *Dave's World* and the Barry Sonnenfeld motion picture *Big Trouble* (2002) were adapted from his writings. He is also the author of *Babies and Other Hazards of Sex* (1984), *Dave Barry's Book of Bad Songs* (1997), *Dave Barry's Complete Guide to Guys* (2000), and the novel *Tricky Business* (2002). In this passage, reprinted from *Dave Barry in Cyberspace* (1997), Barry pokes fun at e-mail, chat rooms, Web sites, and other Internet fixtures.

The Internet is the most important single development in the history of human communications since the invention of "call waiting."

A bold statement? Indeed it is, but consider how the Internet can simplify and enhance our lives. Imagine that you need to do the following chores: (1) make an airline reservation; (2) buy some tickets to a concert; (3) research a question on your income taxes; and (4) help your child gather information for a school report. To accomplish all this fifteen years ago, you could easily have spent an entire day talking on the phone and driving to the library, IRS office, etc. Whereas today, you simply turn on your computer, dial up your local Internet access number, and in less than an instant—thanks to the Internet's global reach and astounding versatility—you're listening to a busy signal!

Yes, it can be difficult to get through to the Internet, because it's so popular. These days it seems as though *everybody* has one of those cryptic little Internet addresses:

Hunchback@NotreDame.com
jhoffa@landfill.r.i.p
millionsofbacteria@yourarmpit.p-u

Why is the Internet so popular? For one thing, it enables you to communicate quickly and easily with people all over the world—even people you don't *want* to communicate with. I know this for a fact, because one time several years ago, when I was new to the Internet, I attempted to send an electronic message to a writer I know in England named Michael Bywater, whom I met when I was on a book tour in London. Michael and I had really hit it off, in part because we share a common philosophical outlook on important economic, social, and political issues, and in part because we consumed an enormous quantity of beer.

So when I got back to the United States, I wrote Michael this chatty little message, which was basically an inside joke that would make sense only to him. It addressed Michael as "Mr. Chuckletrousers"—a name I'd seen in a London newspaper headline—and it contained various sophisticated and extremely subtle humor elements that could look, to the uninformed observer, like bad words.

The problem was that, because of my limited grasp of how the Internet works, instead of sending this message just to Michael, I somehow managed to send (or, in cyberlingo, "post") it to THE WHOLE ENTIRE INTERNET. It immediately became semi-famous. People called it the Chuckletrousers Post, and it spread like wildfire around the Internet, as people made copies and sent them to their friends, who made copies for *their* friends. As far as I can tell, thousands, perhaps *millions* of people ended up seeing it. To this day, I am regularly approached by total strangers who say, "Hi, Mr. Chuckletrousers!" and then walk off, snickering. If there are in fact intelligent beings elsewhere in the universe, I'm pretty sure that the first communication they will receive from our planet will be the Chuckletrousers Post.[1]

The irony is, about a week after the original post, Michael Bywater—remember him?—posted a message on the Internet saying that he'd heard there was some message going around with his name in it, but he hadn't seen it, and could somebody please send it to him? In other words, I had managed to send this hideously embarrassing message to *everybody in the world except the person who was supposed to read it.*

Yes, thanks to the awesome communications capabilities of the Internet, I was able to make an intergalactic fool of myself, and there's no reason why you can't do the same. So get with it! Join the Internet! At first you may

---

[1]If it *is* the first communication they receive, they will immediately vaporize Earth. And they will be right.

be a little confused by some of the jargon, but trust me, after you've spent just a few hours cruising in Cyberspace, you'll be totally lost. To speed this process along, I've prepared the following helpful list of:

Common Questions and Answers About the Internet

Q. *What, exactly, is the Internet?*
A. The Internet is a worldwide network of university, government, business, and private computer systems.

Q. *Who runs it?*
A. A 13-year-old named Jason.

Q. *How can I get on the Internet?*
A. The easiest way is to sign up with one of the popular commercial "on-line" services, such as Prodigy, CompuServe, or America Online, which will give you their program disks for free.[2] Or, if you just leave your house unlocked, they'll sneak in some night and install their programs on your computer when you're sleeping. They *really* want your business.

Q. *What are the benefits of these services?*
A. The major benefit is that they all have simple, "user-friendly" interfaces that enable you—even if you have no previous computer experience—to provide the on-line services with the information they need to automatically put monthly charges on your credit card bill forever.

Q. *What if I die?*
A. They don't care.

Q. *Can't I cancel my account?*
A. Of course! You can cancel your account at any time.

Q. *How?*
A. Nobody has ever been able to find out. Some of us have been trying for *years* to cancel our on-line-service accounts, but no matter what we do, the charges keep appearing on our bills. We're thinking of entering the Federal Witness Protection Program.

Q. *What if I have children?*
A. You'll want an anesthetic, because it *really* hurts.

Q. *No, I mean: What if my children also use my Internet account?*
A. You should just sign your house and major internal organs over to the on-line service right now.

---

[2] I have received Prodigy disks with *airline peanuts*. Really. They weren't bad, although they could have used a little salt.

Q. *Aside from running up charges, what else can I do once I'm connected to an on-line service?*

A. Millions of things! An incredible array of things! No end of things!

Q. *Like what?*

A. You can…ummmm…OK! I have one! You can chat.

Q. *"Chat"?*

A. Chat.

Q. *I can already chat. I chat with my friends.*

A. Yes, but on the Internet, which connects millions of people all over the entire globe, you can chat with *total strangers,* many of whom are boring and stupid!

Q. *Sounds great! How does it work?*

A. Well, first you decide which type of area you wish to chat in. Some areas are just for general chatting, and some are for specific interest groups, such as Teens, Poets, Cat Lovers, Religious People, Gays, Gay Teens Who Read Religious Poetry to Cats, and of course Guys Having Pointless Arguments About Sports. At any given moment, an area can contain anywhere from two to dozens of people, who use clever fake names such as "ByteMe2" so nobody will know their real identities.

Q. *What are their real identities?*

A. They represent an incredible range of people, people of all ages, in all kinds of fascinating fields—from scientists to singers, from writers to wranglers, from actors to athletes—you could be talking to almost anybody on the Internet!

Q. *Really?*

A. No. You're almost always talking to losers and hormone-crazed 13-year-old boys. But they *pretend* to be writers, wranglers, scientists, singers, etc.

Q. *What do people talk about in chat areas?*

A. Most chat-area discussions revolve around the fascinating topic of who is entering and leaving the chat area. A secondary, but equally fascinating, topic is where everybody lives. Also, for a change of pace, every now and then the discussion is interrupted by a hormone-crazed 13-year-old boy wishing to talk dirty to women.

To give you an idea of how scintillating the repartee can be, here's a re-creation of a typical chat-area dialogue (do not read this scintillating repartee while operating heavy machinery):

LilBrisket: Hi everybody

Wazootyman: Hi LilBrisket

TOADSTER: Hi Bris
LUNGFLOOK: Hi B
LILBRISKET: What's going on?
TOADSTER: Not much
LUNGFLOOK: Pretty quiet

[longish pause]

WAZOOTYMAN: Anybody here from Texas?
LILBRISKET: No
TOADSTER: Nope
LUNGFLOOK: Sorry

[longish pause]

UVULABOB: Hi everybody
TOADSTER: Hi UvulaBob
LUNGFLOOK: Hi Uvula
LILBRISKET: Hi UB
WAZOOTYMAN: Hi U
UVULABOB: What's happening?
LILBRISKET: Kinda slow
TOADSTER: Same old same old
LUNGFLOOK: Pretty quiet
JASON56243837: LilBrisket, take off your panties
LILBRISKET: OK, but I'm a man

[longish pause]

WAZOOTYMAN: UvulaBob, are you from Texas?
UVULABOB: No.

[longish pause]

LUNGFLOOK: Well, gotta run.
TOADSTER: 'bye, Lungflook
LILBRISKET: Take 'er easy, Lungster
WAZOOTYMAN: See ya around, Lung
UVULABOB: So long, L

[longish pause]

POLYPMASTER: Hi everybody
LILBRISKET: Hey, PolypMaster
TOADSTER: Yo, Polyp
UVULABOB: Hi, P

POLYPMASTER: What's going on?
LILBRISKET: Not much
TOADSTER: Pretty quiet
UVULABOB: Kinda slow…

And so it goes in the chat areas, hour after riveting hour, where the ideas flow fast and furious, and at any moment you could learn some fascinating nugget of global-network information, such as whether or not PolypMaster comes from Texas.

Q. *I've heard that people sometimes use Internet chat areas to have "cybersex." What exactly is that?*
A. This is when two people send explicitly steamy messages to each other, back and forth, back and forth, faster and faster, hotter and hotter, *faster* and *faster* and *hotter* and *harder* and *harder* until *OHHHH GOD-DDDDDD* they suddenly find that they have a bad case of sticky keyboard, if you get my drift.

Q. *That's disgusting!*
A. Yes.

Q. *Could you give an example?*
A. Certainly:

BORN2BONE: I want you NOW
HUNNIBUNNI: I want YOU now
BORN2BONE: I want to take off your clothes
HUNNIBUNNI: Yes! YES!
BORN2BONE: I'm taking off your clothes
HUNNIBUNNI: OH YESSSS

[longish pause]

HUNNIBUNNI: Is something wrong?
BORN2BONE: I can't unhook your brassiere
HUNNIBUNNI: I'll do it
BORN2BONE: Thanks. Oh my god! I'm touching your, umm, your…
HUNNIBUNNI: Copious bosoms?
BORN2BONE: Yes! Your copious bosoms! I'm touching them!
HUNNIBUNNI: YES!
BORN2BONE: Both of them!
HUNNIBUNNI: YESSS!!
BORN2BONE: I'm taking off your panties!

HUNNIBUNNI: You already did.

BORN2BONE: Oh, OK. You're naked! I'm touching your entire nakedness!

HUNNIBUNNI: YESSSSSS!!!

WAZOOTYMAN: Anybody here from Texas?

BORN2BONE: No

HUNNIBUNNI: No

BORN2BONE: I am becoming turgid in my manfulness!

HUNNIBUNNI: YES! YES YOU ARE!! YOU ARE A BULL! YOU ARE MY GREAT BIG RAGING BULL STALLION!

WAZOOTYMAN: Hey, thanks

HUNNIBUNNI: Not you

BORN2BONE: I AM A STALLION! I AM A RAGING, BULGING BULL STALLION, AND I AM THRUSTING MY...MY...ummm...

HUNNIBUNNI: Your love knockwurst?

BORN2BONE: YES! I AM THRUSTING MY LOVE KNOCKWURST INTO YOUR...YOUR...

HUNNIBUNNI: Promise you won't laugh?

BORN2BONE: Yes

HUNNIBUNNI: My passion persimmon

BORN2BONE: Ha ha!

HUNNIBUNNI: You promised!

BORN2BONE: Sorry. OK, here goes: I AM THRUSTING MY MASSIVE KNOCKWURST OF LOVE INTO YOUR PASSION PERSIMMON!

HUNNIBUNNI: YES! YES! YES!

BORN2BONE: OHHH! IT FEELS SO GOOD!! I FEEL POWERFUL!!

HUNNIBUNNI: YOU ARE POWERFUL, BORN2BONE!! I FEEL YOUR POWER INSIDE ME!!!

BORN2BONE: IT FEELS LIKE, LIKE...

HUNNIBUNNI: Like what?

BORN2BONE: IT FEELS JUST LIKE, OHMIGOD-OHMIGOD...

HUNNIBUNNI: TELL ME BORN2BONE!! TELL WHAT IT FEELS LIKE!!

BORN2BONE: OH GOD IT FEELS LIKE...IT FEELS LIKE WHEN I BREAK A TIE VOTE IN THE SENATE!!!

[pause]

HUNNIBUNNI: What did you say?

BORN2BONE: Whoops

HUNNIBUNNI: It feels like when you break a tie vote in the Senate?

BORN2BONE: Umm, listen, what I meant was...

HUNNIBUNNI: This is you, isn't it, Al? ISN'T IT?? YOU BASTARD!!! YOU TOLD ME YOU WERE ATTENDING A STATE FUNERAL THIS AFTERNOON!!!

BORN2BONE: Tipper?

HUNNIBUNNI: Whoops

Q. *Aside from chatting, what else can I do on the Internet?*
A. You can join one of the thousands of forums wherein people, by posting messages, discuss and debate important scientific, historical, philosophical, and political topics of the day.

Q. *Like what?*
A. Barry Manilow.

Q. *There's a forum for Barry Manilow?*
A. There's a forum for *everything*.

Q. *What happens on these forums?*
A. Well, on the Barry Manilow forum, for example, fans post messages about how much they love Barry Manilow, and other fans respond by posting messages about how much *they* love Barry Manilow, too. And then sometimes the forum is invaded by people posting messages about how much they *hate* Barry Manilow, which in turn leads to angry countermessages and vicious name-calling that can go on for *months*.

Q. *Just like junior high school!*
A. But even more pointless.

Q. *Are there forums about sex?*
A. Zillions of them.

Q. *What do people talk about on those?*
A. Barry Manilow.

Q. *No, really.*
A. OK, they talk about sex, but it is *not* all titillating. Often you'll find highly scientific discussions that expand the frontiers of human understanding.

Q. *Can you give a specific example that you are not making up?*
A. Yes. Strictly for the purpose of researching this book, I checked into one of the sex forums, pretty much at random, and I found a series of related messages, or "thread," on the topic of "How to do the BUZZ!" It turns out that the Buzz is a sexual technique.[3] In the opening message of this thread,

---

[3]Duh.

an enthusiastic advocate—who apparently is a doctor—explains, in semi-clinical detail, how to perform this technique. Here's an excerpt:

> You pucker up your lips to form an O, then buzzzzzzzzz so that your lips are vibrating. You can practice on your finger. When your lips are vibrating on your finger, that's the sensation you are aiming at. It is rather like playing a trumpet when you don't blow but PHEbbbbbbbbbbbbbt.

This message ends with the following warning:

> Women, if you are buzzing a man…NEVER, NEVER, buzz the hole at the top (urethra). Likewise for men doing a woman, NEVER, NEVER, blow or buzz directly into the vaginal opening. It is possible to force air into the circulatory system so that an air bubble will form and can cause a stroke, and brain damage or heart failure. So, suck is OK, but BLOW is not!

Are you starting to see the benefits of the Information Superhighway? Already we have learned an exciting new sexual technique that, if we do it wrong, could kill our partner!

But that's just the beginning of this thread. The next message, apparently from another doctor, strongly disputes the contention that the Buzz poses medical dangers, calling it "unbelievable" and "pseudo-medical hokum."

This statement is in turn disputed by the *next* message, which states, authoritatively, that the original warning is correct, and that "it's documented in any decent medical textbook."

(Think of it: The Buzz is *documented in medical textbooks.*)

This is followed by more authoritative-sounding posts, also apparently from members of the medical profession, concerning the dangers involved in blowing air into people's orifices. Here's another excerpt:

> When I was in practice there had been a number of cases reported in the literature of people forcing air into both the rectum and urethra with very damaging, and in some cases fatal results.… This was usually compressed air from a compressor, or noncompressed air from a vacuum cleaner.

At this point the discussion, as is often the case on Internet forums, branches off in a new direction:

> While we are on a medical topic here is something I've been wondering about: I visit a "hands on" lap-dancing club in San Francisco, and would like to know if there is any medical danger from licking breasts. I'm serious about this—undoubtedly the 22-year-olds I lick have just come from some other guy that's been licking her too. Does spit evaporate or something? Or does it stay on for the next guy to lick up??

The thread ended at this point, but I have no doubt that eventually there were more messages from concerned individuals from all over the world wishing to advance the frontiers of human understanding on the vital topic of diseases transmitted via breast spit.

Q. *It is a beautiful thing, the Internet.*
A. It is.

Q. *What is the "World Wide Web"?*
A. The World Wide Web is the multimedia version of the Internet, where you can get not only text but also pictures and sounds on a semi-infinite range of topics. This information is stored on "Web pages," which are maintained by companies, institutions, and individuals. Using special software, you can navigate to these pages and read, look at, or listen to all kinds of cool stuff. It would not surprise me to learn that, by the time you read these words, somewhere on the Web you can look at an actual electron microscope image of a molecule of breast spit.

Q. *Wow! How can I get on the Web?*
A. It's easy! Suppose you're interested in buying a boat from an Australian company that has a Web page featuring pictures and specifications of its various models. All you have to do is fire up your World Wide Web software and type in the company's Web page address, which will probably be an intuitive, easy-to-remember string of characters like this:

http//:www.fweemer-twirple~.com/heppledork/sockitomesockitome@fee.fie/fo/fum.

Q. *What if I type one single character wrong?*
A. You will launch U.S. nuclear missiles against Norway.

Q. *Ah.*
A. But assuming you type in the correct address, you merely press Enter, and there you are!

Q. *Where?*
A. Sitting in front of your computer waiting for something to happen. It could take weeks. Entire new continents can emerge from the ocean in the time it takes for a Web page to show up on your screen. Contrary to what you may have heard, the Internet does not operate at the speed of light; it operates at the speed of the Department of Motor Vehicles. It might be quicker for you to just go over to Australia and look at the boats in person.

Q. *Does that mean that the World Wide Web is useless?*
A. Heck no! If you're willing to be patient, you'll find that you can utilize the vast resources of the Web to waste time in ways that you never before dreamed possible.

Q. *For example?*

A. For example, recently I was messing around with a "Web browser," which is a kind of software that lets you search all of cyberspace—millions of documents—for references to a specific word or group of words. You can find pretty much everything that anybody has ever written on the Internet about that topic; it's an incredibly powerful research tool. So I decided to do a search on an issue that concerns—or should concern—all of humanity.

Q. *Tapeworms?*

A. Exactly. I entered the word "tapeworm," and the browser came up with a list of hundreds of places on the Web where that word appeared. I started checking them out at random,[4] and eventually I came to a forum in Austin, Texas, devoted to sushi.

Q. *Hey, why not?*

A. Exactly. And in this forum, I found a message, posted by sushi chef Yasuhiro Muramatsu, entitled "A Note About Salmon." Reading it, I was struck by how...*poetic* it sounded. It was like a new, expanded kind of haiku. If you don't mind, I'd like to reproduce it here.

Q. *By all means.*

A. Thank you. Here it is:

A Note About Salmon
Yasuhiro Muramatsu

I am a sushi chef.
I have seen several worms and eggs in salmon fillet.
It is very rare case, but some time salmon has egg of "tapeworm."
It cause serious health problem, if you have it.

We don't eat raw salmon in Japan.
Only one exception is "RUIBE."
It is pre-frozen salmon (must be lower –20c, and more than 12hr).
So, you had better ask your sushi chef it before you order their raw
    salmon.

Salmon is one of the most affordable fish for sushi and sashimi.
And it is also looks good.
Therefore, a lot of Japanese restaurants are serving raw salmon.

I hope none of them does just slice and serve it.
I think you had better don't eat raw salmon except the restaurants
    which you can trust it.

---

[4]This took a lot of time; but, as a writer, I *have* a lot of time.

By the way, I have never eat raw salmon.
I like Norway style marinade salmon "lox."

Q. *That is truly beautiful.*

A. Yes. And it's just one teensy little piece, one infinitesimally tiny fraction, of the gigantic, pulsating, mutating, multiplying mass of stuff out there on the Internet. Sooner or later, *everything* is going to be on there somewhere. You should be on there, too. Don't be afraid! Be like the bold explorer Christopher Columbus,[5] setting out into uncharted waters, fearful of what you might encounter, but also mindful of the old inspirational maritime saying: "If you don't leave the land, then you'll probably never have a chance to get scurvy and develop anemia, spongy gums, and bleeding from the mucous membranes."

So come on! Join me and millions of others on this exciting Cyber-Frontier, with its limitless possibilities for the enhancement of knowledge and the betterment of the human race!

Wazootyman is waiting for you.

Suggestions for Discussion

1. How does Dave Barry use humor to convey genuine points about problems with the Internet?

2. How does Barry describe the reliability of information posted on Internet "Web pages"?

3. What are the advantages and disadvantages of the impersonal nature of the Internet and the anonymity it affords?

4. How does Barry describe "chat rooms"?

5. What is "cybersex"? How does Barry mock it?

6. What is the "Mr. Chuckletrousers" post and what does it say about Internet communication? What other mistakes can someone make while using the Internet?

7. Since this article is a few years old, Barry makes now-dated references to dial-up modems and Vice President Al Gore. How much of this article is still accurate? What has changed?

Suggestions for Writing

1. Have you encountered any of the problems Barry described? Are there any easy solutions? Do you find more merit in the chat rooms than he

---

[5]E-mail address: ChrisCol@nina,pinta&santamaria.ahoy

describes? Do you agree or disagree with his assessment of the quality of "Web pages"?

2. In what way has the information on the Internet proven valuable to you? Have you ever been mislead by information posted on the Internet?

3. Has communicating with strangers through the Internet made it easier to make friends and business contacts? Or do you find more traditional methods of meeting people are still superior?

REBECCA MEAD

You've Got Blog

Prior to becoming a *New Yorker* staff writer in 1997, Rebecca Mead wrote for the *Sunday Times* of London and served as a contributing editor at *New York* magazine. She has received a B.A. from Oxford University and an M.A. from New York University. The following article concerns "blogs," often-intimate Web sites dedicated to news, trivia, and the personal lives of their creators.

Meg Hourihan was in a bad mood. She had nothing major to worry about, but she was afflicted by the triple malaise of a woman in her late twenties: (a) the weather was lousy; (b) she was working too hard; and (c) she didn't have a boyfriend. Nothing, not even eating, seemed very interesting to her. The only thing that did sound appealing was moving to France and finding a hot new French boyfriend, but even when she talked about that idea she struck a sardonic, yeah-right-like-I'm-really-going-to-do-*that* kind of tone.

I know this about Meg because I read it a few months ago on her personal Web site, which is called Megnut.com. I've been reading Megnut for a while now, and so I know all kinds of things about its author, like how much she loved Hilary Swank in "Boys Don't Cry," and how she wishes there were good fish tacos to be had in San Francisco, where she lives. I know she's a feminist, and that she writes short stories, and that she's close to her mom. I know that she's a little dreamy and idealistic, that she fervently believes there is a distinction between "dot-com people," who are involved in the Internet for its I.P.O. opportunities, and "Web people," who are in love with the imaginative possibilities presented by the medium, and that she counts herself among the latter.

Meg is one of the founders of a company called Pyra, which produces an Internet application known as Blogger. Blogger, which can be used free on the Internet, is a tool for creating a new kind of Web site that is known as a "weblog," or "blog," of which Megnut is an example. A blog consists primarily of links to other Web sites and commentary about those links. Having a blog is rather like publishing your own, on-line version of *Reader's Digest,* with daily updates: you troll the Internet, and, when you find an article or a Web site that grabs you, you link to it—or, in weblog parlance, you "blog" it. Then other people who have blogs—they are known as bloggers—read your blog, and if they like it they blog your blog on their own blog.

Blogs often consist of links to articles that readers might otherwise have missed, and thus make for informative reading: it was via an excellent blog called Rebecca's Pocket that I learned, for instance, that the Bangkok transit authority had introduced a ladies-only bus to protect female passengers from straphanging molestation. It also led me to a site devoted to burritos, where I underwent an online burrito analysis, in which my personality type was diagnosed according to my favorite burrito elements: "Your pairing of a meat-free burrito and *all* those fatty toppings indicates a dangerous ability to live with illusions." Blogs often include links to sites that illuminate the matter at hand. For example, when Meg wrote about planning a plumeria cutting, she linked to a site called the Plumeria Place, which included a picture and a description of the plant.

Many bloggers have Internet-related jobs, and so they use their sites to keep other bloggers informed of the latest news in the world of Web design or copyright law. Jason Kottke, a Web designer from Minneapolis who maintains a site called Kottke.org, is widely admired among bloggers as a thoughtful critic of Web culture. (On the strength of the picture transmitted by his Webcam, he is also widely perceived as very cute. If you read around among blogs, you find that Kottke is virtually beset by blogging groupies.) Getting blogged by Kottke, or by Meg Hourihan or one of her colleagues at Pyra, is the blog equivalent of having your book featured on "Oprah": it generally means a substantial boost in traffic—enough, perhaps, to earn the blog a mention on Beebo.org, which has functioned as a blog best-seller list. (An example from a blog called Fairvue.com: "Jason K. linked to Fairvue. My life is now complete.")

The weblog format of links and commentary has been around for some years, but in the early days of weblogging the sites had to be built by hand, one block of code at a time, which meant that they were produced only by a handful of technology mavens. There were a few weblogs that earned a following among non-tech civilians—Jim Romenesko's Medianews, a weblog of stories about the media business, is one; Arts & Letters Daily, a digest of intellectual affairs, is another—but most remained more specialized. A year and a half ago, there were only fifty or so weblogs; now the number has increased to thousands, with blogs like Megnut getting around a thousand visits a day. This growth is due in large part to Blogger, and a couple of other weblogging tools such as Pitas and EditThisPage, which have made launching a personal Web site far simpler.

Most of the new blogs are, like Megnut, intimate narratives rather than digests of links and commentary; to read them is to enter a world in which the personal lives of participants have become part of the public domain. Because the main audience for blogs is other bloggers—blogging etiquette requires that, if someone blogs your blog, you blog his blog back—reading blogs can feel a lot like listening in on a conversation among a group of friends who all know each other really well. Blogging, it turns out, is the CB radio of the Dave Eggers generation. And that is how, when Meg Hourihan followed up her French-boyfriend-depression posting with a stream-of-consciousness blog entry a few weeks later saying that she had developed a crush on someone but was afraid to act on it—"Maybe I've become very good at eluding love but that's not a complaint I just want to get it all out of my head and put it somewhere else," she wrote—her love life became not just her business but the business of bloggers everywhere.

Pyra, the company that produces Blogger, has its offices on the ground floor of a warehouse building on Townsend Street in SoMa, the former industrial district that is now home to many of San Francisco's Internet businesses. The company, which was founded last year by Evan Williams (who has his own blog, Evhead.com) in collaboration with Meg Hourihan, occupies two computer-filled rooms that face each other across an atrium littered with random pieces of office furniture discarded by Internet startups whose fortunes took a dive when the Nasdaq did, last April. Pyra survived the dive, with some help from venture capitalists, and from Mr. and Mrs. Hourihan, Meg's parents. (More recently, Advance Publications, which publishes this magazine, invested in Pyra.) Still, Ev and Meg ruefully talk about how they managed to get through the summer of 1999, the season of implausible I.P.O.s, without becoming rich.

"We first met at a party," Meg explained, as she and I sat on a battered couch. Ev rolled his desk chair over to join us. Meg, who grew up in Boston and graduated from Tufts with a degree in English, is voluble and given to gesticulation. She is tall and athletic-looking, and has cropped spiky hair that last spring she bleached white-blond after polling the readers of her blog about her hairstyling options. Meg and Ev dated for a while before deciding that their shared passion for the Internet did not translate into a shared passion for each other; but then Ev drafted Meg to help him start Pyra, the goal of which was to develop a Web-based tool that would help project managers share information with co-workers. (They have since been joined by four other friends.)

"I knew she was very good at helping me think about ideas," Ev said. Ev comes from Nebraska—he once blogged an aerial photograph of the family farm—and is taciturn and ironic; he has a beetling brow and a Tintin coif. In 1991, he dropped out of the University of Nebraska-Lincoln after a year and launched his first Internet company, for which he still owes his parents money.

Blogger wasn't part of Pyra's original plan; Ev and a colleague, Paul Bausch, built it for fun, and then launched it on the Web one week in the summer of 1999, when Meg was on vacation. That fall, Blogger found plenty of users among geeks who were glad to have a tool that made weblogging easier; only recently, though, did Ev and Meg set aside their other Pyra plans. "It took us a long time to realize what we had with Blogger," Meg said.

That afternoon, Meg sat down with me at her computer—I tried to stay out of the range of the Webcam that is trained on her whenever she sits at her desk—and showed me how Blogger works. To use Blogger, it helps to know a little of the computer language html, but, once you've set up your site, adding new chunks of text is as easy as sending an E-mail. Meg clicked open the Blogger inputting box, typed a few words, and showed me how she could hit one button and send the text to her site. The creators of Blogger think it may make posting items on the Web a little too easy; a new term, "blogorrhea," has been coined to describe the kind of entries—"I'm tired," or "This sucks"—that are the work of the unimaginative blogger.

While I was sitting at Meg's desk, I noticed the bookmarks that she had on her Web browser. Among them were Evhead and Kottke.org. She had also marked Jason Kottke's Webcam. Jason Kottke was the object of the crush that Meg had described in her blog a few months earlier. They met last March, at South by Southwest, an alternative-culture conference that takes place in Austin every spring.

"I recognized him immediately," Meg wrote in an E-mail to me. "He was taller than I thought he'd be, but I knew it was him." She had been reading his blog, Kottke.org, for ages. "I always thought he seemed cool and intelligent...but I thought he was a bit conceited. He was so well-known, and he wrote once about taking some on-line I.Q. tests and he actually posted his results, which I thought was showoffish."

After meeting Jason, Meg changed her mind: "He seemed not at all conceited like I thought, and actually pretty funny and nice, and cute, much cuter than he ever appeared on his Webcam."

Meg made sure she had an excuse to stay in touch—she offered to send Jason a customized version of Blogger code for him to try on Kottke.org. Once she got back to San Francisco, she said, "I wrote on Megnut that I had a crush, and he E-mailed me and said, 'Who's the crush on? Spill it, sister.' So I E-mailed him back and said it was him. He was really surprised." Meg took further electronic action to advance her aims, and altered her Web site so that it included her ICQ number—the number someone would need to send her an instant message, even though the last thing she wanted was to be inundated with instant messages from strangers. A couple of days later,

Jason ICQ'd her for the first time. ("He fell for my trick," she said.) That night, they instant-messaged for three hours. A week later, she shifted technologies again, and called him on the telephone. Then she invited him to San Francisco, and that was that.

Meg and Jason had been dating for two months when I visited San Francisco, and he was due to arrive from Minneapolis for the weekend. Meg told me about a Web device she uses called Flight Tracker: you type in a flight number, and a map is displayed, with an icon representing the location of the airplane. "I always look at it, and think, Oh, he's over Nebraska now," she said.

I already knew that Meg and Jason were involved, because I'd been reading their Web sites; although neither of them had written anything about the relationship, there were hints throughout their recent entries. Those hints had also been under discussion on a Web site called Metafilter. Metafilter is a "community weblog," which means that anyone who is a member can post a link to it. Most of the posts to Metafilter are links to news stories or weird Web sites, but in early June someone named Monkeyboy had linked to a photograph of Meg and Jason looking into Jason's bathroom mirror. The picture was posted on a Web site belonging to a friend of Meg's who collects photographs of the mirrors of Web celebrities. Monkeyboy also linked to Megnut's "crush" entry, and to an entry that Jason had written on Kottke.org about Meg's site design, and he posted them all on Metafilter with the words "So what's up with this? I think there's something going on here." This generated a lively discussion, with some bloggers furthering the gossip by linking to other blogs whose authors had confessed to having crushes on Jason, while others wrote in suggesting it was none of anyone's business.

When I looked back at Jason's blog for the period just after he met Meg, I found no references to a romance. Jason's style is a little more sober. But there was one entry in which he seemed to be examining the boundary between his Web life and his non-Web life. He'd written that there were things going on in his life that were more personal than the stuff he usually wrote about in his weblog. "Why don't I just write it down somewhere private... a Word doc on my computer or in a paper diary?" he asked himself, and his readers. "Somehow, that seems strange to me though....The Web is the place for you to express your thoughts and feelings and such. To put those things elsewhere seems absurd."

One day, I met Meg and Jason for breakfast. Jason, who is twenty-seven, is tall with short hair and sideburns; he was wearing jeans and a Princess Mononoke T-shirt. She ordered a tofu scramble and soy latte, he had real eggs. I asked what it was like to have their private lives discussed among the members of their virtual community, and they said they thought it was funny. I asked whether they ever included hidden messages to each other in their blogs, an idea that seemed to surprise them. "Well, I did once use that word 'tingly,' " Meg said. Jason blushed.

A few days later, they stoked the gossip further by posting identical entries on their Web sites; word-for-word accounts of seeing a young girl on a bicycle in the street, and descriptions of the childhood memories that it triggered. Then a strange thing happened. One by one, several bloggers copied the little-girl entry into their blogs, as if they had seen the child on the bicycle, too. Other bloggers started to write parodies of the little-girl entry. Still other bloggers started to post messages to Metafilter, asking what the hell was going on with all these sightings of little girls. When I sent Meg an E-mail about this outbreak, she wrote back, "I was especially struck by the number of people who thought it was a big prank pulled by the 'popular' kids to make fun of the uncool kids."

There have been some ostentatious retreats from the blogging frenzy: last June, one well-known blogger named Derek Powazek announced in his blog that he wanted no part of it anymore, and that instead of addressing himself to the blogger community at large he would henceforth be writing with only a few friends and family members in mind. This announcement provoked a flurry of postings from neophyte bloggers, who feared they were facing the Twilight of Blogging before they had really had a chance to enjoy the Dawn of Blogging.

The people at Pyra, having generated a blog explosion with their Blogger software, aren't entirely happy about the way blogs have developed. "It's like being frustrated with your kid, when you know he could be doing so much more," Ev told me. He and Meg have been developing different uses for Blogger, including ones from which they might actually make some money. One idea is to install Blogger on the intranets of companies, so that it can be used as a means of letting large groups share information. (Cisco is currently experimenting with using Blogger in-house to keep minutes of project meetings up to date.)

Meanwhile, Meg and Ev have developed a whole new level of celebrity status. Not long ago, a group of bloggers created a community blog called the Pyra Shrine. There are posts about how hot Meg is ("Megnut is da bomb. She's one kewl lady") and whether Ev needs a personal assistant ("You know, to make him coffee and get him stuff. I'd do it. For free, even!"). The whole thing is very silly, and completely irresistible if you're a reader of Megnut or Evhead, or, indeed, if you are the creator of Megnut or Evhead. Meg linked to it on her site recently, and wrote, "O.K., I have to admit, this The Pyra Shrine cracks me up."

It was through the Pyra Shrine that I learned, one day last month, that Jason was moving to San Francisco. ("That's a big sacrifice. He must really love her," one of the Shrine contributors had posted.) I E-mailed Meg, who told me that Jason had taken a new Web-design job and was driving across the country—he was probably in Wyoming at that very moment. I remarked that since he was in a car she couldn't use Flight Tracker to see where he was.

"Oh yeah, it's so bad," she wrote back. "I'm so used to being able to communicate with him, or at least check in in some way all the time (Webcam, Flight Tracker, ICQ, E-mail, etc.) and now there's nothing. Well, except for phone at night, but still, seems like nothing compared with what I've gotten used to."

Later that night, I called Meg, and she sounded excited. "He should be here in three or four days," she said. Having mastered the techniques for having a digital relationship, she was finally ready for an analog one; and she hadn't even had to move to France to get it.

Suggestions for Discussion

1. Respond to Mead's comment that blogs create "a world in which the personal lives of participants have become part of the public domain." What is the value, if any, of putting personal information on-line for strangers to read? Would you be comfortable with compromising your own privacy by writing an intimate blog?

2. According to Mead, Megnut.com is mainly concerned with the details of Meg Hourihan's life and cataloging interesting links such as the burrito personality test. Search the Web for other blogs and compare them with Megnut.com in terms of content, tone, and what you believe you learned (or did not learn) from them.

Suggestion for Writing

Traditional news media sources have faced a stiff challenge from news bloggers who post commentary on current events. Conduct a Web search on news blogs and, after reading blog entries from several sites, evaluate their reliability as sources of information and analysis.

ERIC SCHLOSSER

Fast Food Nation

Manhattan-born Eric Schlosser became a correspondent for the *Atlantic Monthly* in 1996, and he has contributed to the *New Yorker* and *Rolling Stone*. His writing addresses controversial topics; *Reefer Madness* (2003) concerns "underground" enterprises such as migrant labor, pornography, and drugs, and more recently he has investigated the American prison system. This selection is taken from *Fast Food Nation* (2001), which attacks the fast food industry and its influence on society.

~

What We Eat

Over the last three decades, fast food has infiltrated every nook and cranny of American society. An industry that began with a handful of modest hot dog and hamburger stands in southern California has spread to every corner of the nation, selling a broad range of foods wherever paying customers may be found. Fast food is now served at restaurants and drive-throughs, at stadiums, airports, zoos, high schools, elementary schools, and universities, on cruise ships, trains, and airplanes, at K-Marts, Wal-Marts, gas stations, and even at hospital cafeterias. In 1970, Americans spent about $6 billion on fast food; in 2000, they spend more than $110 billion. Americans now spend more money on fast food than on higher education, personal computers, computer software, or new cars. They spend more on fast food than on movies, books, magazines, newspapers, videos, and recorded music—combined.

Pull open the glass door, feel the rush of cool air, walk in, get on line, study the backlit color photographs above the counter, place your order, hand over a few dollars, watch teenagers in uniforms pushing various buttons, and moments later take hold of a plastic tray full of food wrapped in colored paper and cardboard. The whole experience of buying fast food has become so routine, so thoroughly unexceptional and mundane, that it is now taken for granted, like brushing your teeth or stopping for a red light. It has become a social custom as American as a small, rectangular, handheld, frozen, and reheated apple pie.

This is a book about fast food, the values it embodies, and the world it has made. Fast food has proven to be a revolutionary force in American life; I am interested in it both as a commodity and as a metaphor. What people eat (or don't eat) has always been determined by a complex interplay of social, economic, and technological forces. The early Roman Republic was fed by its citizen-farmers; the Roman Empire, by its slaves. A nation's diet can be more revealing than its art or literature. On any given day in the United States about one-quarter of the adult population visits a fast food restaurant. During a relatively brief period of time, the fast food industry has helped to transform not only the American diet, but also our landscape, economy, workforce, and popular culture. Fast food and its consequences have become inescapable, regardless of whether you eat it twice a day, try to avoid it, or have never taken a single bite.

The extraordinary growth of the fast food industry has been driven by fundamental changes in American society. Adjusted for inflation, the hourly wage of the average U.S. worker peaked in 1973 and then steadily declined for the next twenty-five years. During that period, women entered the workforce in record numbers, often motivated less by a feminist perspective than by a need to pay the bills. In 1975, about one-third of American mothers with young children worked outside the home; today almost two-thirds of such mothers are employed. As the sociologists Cameron Lynne Macdonald and Carmen Sirianni have noted, the entry of so many women into the workforce has greatly increased demand for the types of services that housewives traditionally perform: cooking, cleaning, and child care. A generation ago, three-quarters of the money used to buy food in the United States was spent to prepare meals at home. Today about half of the money used to buy food is spent at restaurants—mainly at fast food restaurants.

The McDonald's Corporation has become a powerful symbol of America's service economy, which is now responsible for 90 percent of the country's new jobs. In 1968, McDonald's operated about one thousand restaurants. Today it has about twenty-eight thousand restaurants worldwide and opens almost two thousand new ones each year. An estimated one out of every eight workers in the United States has at some point been employed by McDonald's. The company annually hires about one million people, more than any other American organization, public or private. McDonald's is the nation's largest purchaser of beef, pork, and potatoes—and the second largest purchaser of chicken. The McDonald's Corporation is the largest owner of retail property in the world. Indeed, the company earns the majority of its profits not from selling food but from collecting rent. McDonald's spends more money on advertising and marketing than any other brand. As a result it has replaced Coca-Cola as the world's most famous brand. McDonald's operates more playgrounds than any other private entity in the United States. It is one of the nation's largest distributors of toys. A survey of American schoolchildren found that 96 percent could identify Ronald McDonald. The only fictional character with a higher degree of recognition was Santa Claus. The impact of McDonald's on the way we live today is hard to overstate. The Golden Arches are now more widely recognized than the Christian cross.

In the early 1970s, the farm activist Jim Hightower warned of "the McDonaldization of America." He viewed the emerging fast food industry as a threat to independent businesses, as a step toward a food economy dominated by giant corporations, and as a homogenizing influence on American life. In *Eat Your Heart Out* (1975), he argued that "bigger is *not* better." Much of what Hightower feared has come to pass. The centralized purchasing decisions of the large restaurant chains and their demand for standardized products have given a handful of corporations an unprecedented degree of power over the nation's food supply. Moreover, the tremendous success of the fast food industry has encouraged other industries to adopt similar business methods. The basic thinking behind fast food has become the operating system of today's retail economy, wiping out small businesses, obliterating regional differences, and spreading identical stores throughout the country like a self-replicating code.

America's main streets and malls now boast the same Pizza Huts and Taco Bells, Gaps and Banana Republics, Starbucks and Jiffy-Lubes, Foot Lockers, Snip N' Clips, Sunglass Huts, and Hobbytown USAs. Almost every facet of American life has now been franchised or chained. From the maternity ward at a Columbia/HCA hospital to an embalming room owned by Service Corporation International—"the world's largest provider of death care services," based in Houston, Texas, which since 1968 has grown to include 3,823 funeral homes, 523 cemeteries, and 198 crematoriums, and which today handles the final remains of one out of every nine Americans—a person can now go from the cradle to the grave without spending a nickel at an independently owned business.

The key to a successful franchise, according to many texts on the subject, can be expressed in one word: "uniformity." Franchises and chain stores strive to offer exactly the same product or service at numerous locations. Customers are drawn to familiar brands by an instinct to avoid the unknown. A brand offers a feeling of reassurance when its products are always and everywhere the same. "We have found out...that we cannot trust some people who are nonconformists," declared Ray Kroc, one of the founders of McDonald's, angered by some of his franchisees. "We will make conformists out of them in a hurry...The organization cannot trust the individual; the individual must trust the organization."

One of the ironies of America's fast food industry is that a business so dedicated to conformity was founded by iconoclasts and self-made men, by entrepreneurs willing to defy conventional opinion. Few of the people who built fast food empires ever attended college, let alone business school. They worked hard, took risks, and followed their own paths. In many respects, the fast food industry embodies the best and the worst of American capitalism at the start of the twenty-first century—its constant stream of new products and innovations, its widening gulf between rich and poor. The industrialization of the restaurant kitchen has enabled the fast food chains to rely upon a low-paid and unskilled workforce. While a handful of workers manage to rise up the corporate ladder, the vast majority lack full-time employment, receive no benefits, learn few skills, exercise little control over their workplace, quit after a few months, and float from job to job. The restaurant industry is now America's largest private employer, and it pays some of the lowest wages. During the economic boom of the 1990s, when many American workers enjoyed their first pay raises in a generation, the real value of wages in the restaurant industry continued to fall. The roughly 3.5 million fast food workers are by far the largest group of minimum wage earners in the United States. The only Americans who consistently earn a lower hourly wage are migrant farm workers.

A hamburger and french fries became the quintessential American meal in the 1950s, thanks to the promotional efforts of the fast food chains. The typical American now consumes approximately three hamburgers and four orders of french fries every week. But the steady barrage of fast food ads, full of thick juicy burgers and long golden fries, rarely mentions where these foods come from nowadays or what ingredients they contain. The birth of the fast food industry coincided with Eisenhower-era glorifications of technology, with optimistic slogans like "Better Living through Chemistry" and "Our Friend the Atom." The sort of technological wizardry that Walt Disney promoted on television and at Disneyland eventually reached its fulfillment in the kitchens of fast food restaurants. Indeed, the corporate culture of McDonald's seems inextricably linked to that of the Disney empire, sharing a reverence for sleek machinery, electronics, and automation. The leading fast food chains still embrace a boundless faith in science—and as a result have changed not just what Americans eat, but also how their food is made.

The current methods for preparing fast food are less likely to be found in cookbooks than in trade journals such as *Food Technologist* and *Food Engineering*. Aside from the salad greens and tomatoes, most fast food is delivered to the restaurant already frozen, canned, dehydrated, or freeze-dried. A fast food kitchen is merely the final stage in a vast and highly complex system of mass production. Foods that may look familiar have in fact been completely reformulated. What we eat has changed more in the last forty years than in the previous forty thousand. Like Cheyenne Mountain, today's fast food conceals remarkable technological advances behind an ordinary-looking façade. Much of the taste and aroma of American fast food, for example, is now manufactured at a series of large chemical plants off the New Jersey Turnpike.

In the fast food restaurants of Colorado Springs, behind the counters, amid the plastic seats, in the changing landscape outside the window, you can see all the virtues and destructiveness of our fast food nation. I chose Colorado Springs as a focal point for this book because the changes that have recently swept through the city are emblematic of those that fast food—and the fast food mentality—have encouraged throughout the United States. Countless other suburban communities, in every part of the country, could have been used to illustrate the same points. The extraordinary growth of Colorado Springs neatly parallels that of the fast food industry: during the last few decades, the city's population has more than doubled. Subdivisions, shopping malls, and chain restaurants are appearing in the foothills of Cheyenne Mountain and the plains rolling to the east. The Rocky Mountain region as a whole has the fastest-growing economy in the United States, mixing high-tech and service industries in a way that may define America's workforce for years to come. And new restaurants are opening there at a faster pace than anywhere else in the nation.

Fast food is now so commonplace that it has acquired an air of inevitability, as though it were somehow unavoidable, a fact of modern life. And yet the dominance of the fast food giants was no more preordained than the march of colonial split-levels, golf courses, and manmade lakes across the deserts of the American West. The political philosophy that now prevails in so much of the West—with its demand for lower taxes, smaller government, an unbridled free market—stands in total contradiction to the region's true economic underpinnings. No other region of the United States has been so dependent on government subsidies for so long, from the nineteenth-century construction of its railroads to the twentieth-century financing of its military bases and dams. One historian has described the federal government's 1950s highway-building binge as a case study in "interstate socialism"—a phrase that aptly describes how the West was really won. The fast food industry took root alongside that interstate highway system, as a new form of restaurant sprang up beside the new off-ramps. Moreover, the extraordinary growth of this industry over the past quarter-century did not occur in a political vacuum. It took place during a period when the inflation-adjusted value of the minimum wage declined by about 40 percent, when sophisticated mass marketing techniques were for the first time directed at small children, and when federal agencies created to protect workers and consumers too often behaved like branch offices of the companies that were supposed to be regulated. Ever since the administration of President Richard Nixon, the fast food industry has worked closely with its allies in Congress and the White House to oppose new worker safety, food safety, and minimum wage laws. While publicly espousing support for the free market, the fast food chains have quietly pursued and greatly benefited from a wide variety of government subsidies. Far from being inevitable, America's fast food industry in its present form is the logical outcome of certain political and economic choices.

In the potato fields and processing plants of Idaho, in the ranchlands east of Colorado Springs, in the feedlots and slaughterhouses of the High Plains, you can see the effects of fast food on the nation's rural life, its environment, its workers, and its health. The fast food chains now stand atop a huge food-industrial complex that has gained control of American agriculture. During the 1980s, large multinationals—such as Cargill, ConAgra, and IBP—were allowed to dominate one commodity market after another. Farmers and cattle ranchers are losing their independence, essentially becoming hired hands for the agribusiness giants or being forced off the land. Family farms are now being replaced by gigantic corporate farms with absentee owners. Rural communities are losing their middle class and becoming socially stratified, divided between a small, wealthy elite and large numbers of the working poor. Small towns that seemingly belong in a Norman Rockwell painting are being turned into rural ghettos. The hardy, independent farmers whom Thomas Jefferson considered the bedrock of American democracy are a truly vanishing breed. The United States now has more prison inmates than full-time farmers.

The fast food chains' vast purchasing power and their demand for a uniform product have encouraged fundamental changes in how cattle are raised, slaughtered, and processed into ground beef. These changes have made meatpacking—once a highly skilled, highly paid occupation—into the most dangerous job in the United States, performed by armies of poor, transient immigrants whose injuries often go unrecorded and uncompensated. And the same meat industry practices that endanger these workers have facilitated the introduction of deadly pathogens, such as *E. coli* 0157:H7, into America's hamburger meat, a food aggressively marketed to children. Again and again, efforts to prevent the sale of tainted ground beef have been thwarted by meat industry lobbyists and their allies in Congress. The federal government has the legal authority to recall a defective toaster oven or stuffed animal—but still lacks the power to recall tons of contaminated, potentially lethal meat.

I do not mean to suggest that fast food is solely responsible for every social problem now haunting the United States. In some cases (such as the malling and sprawling of the West) the fast food industry has been a catalyst and a symptom of larger economic trends. In other cases (such as the rise of franchising and the spread of obesity) fast food has played a more central role. By tracing the diverse influences of fast food I hope to shed light not only on the workings of an important industry, but also on a distinctively American way of viewing the world.

Elitists have always looked down at fast food, criticizing how it tastes and regarding it as another tacky manifestation of American popular culture. The aesthetics of fast food are of much less concern to me than its impact upon the lives of ordinary Americans, both as workers and consumers. Most of all, I am concerned about its impact on the nation's children. Fast food is heavily marketed to children and prepared by people who are barely older than children. This is an industry that both feeds and feeds off the young. During the two years spent researching this book, I ate an enormous amount of fast food. Most of it tasted pretty good. That is one of the main reasons people buy fast food: it has been carefully designed to taste good. It's also inexpensive and convenient. But the value meals, two-for-one deals, and free refills of soda give a distorted sense of how much fast food actually costs. The real price never appears on the menu.

The sociologist George Ritzer has attacked the fast food industry for celebrating a narrow measure of efficiency over every other human value, calling the triumph of McDonald's "the irrationality of rationality." Others consider the fast food industry proof of the nation's great economic vitality, a beloved American institution that appeals overseas to millions who admire our way of life. Indeed, the values, the culture, and the industrial arrangements of our fast food nation are now being exported to the rest of the world. Fast food has joined Hollywood movies, blue jeans, and pop music as one of America's most prominent cultural exports. Unlike other commodities, however, fast food isn't viewed, read, played, or worn. It enters the body and becomes part of the consumer. No other industry offers, both literally and figuratively, so much insight into the nature of mass consumption.

Hundreds of millions of people buy fast food every day without giving it much thought, unaware of the subtle and not so subtle ramifications of their purchases. They rarely consider where this food came from, how it was made, what it is doing to the community around them. They just grab their tray off the counter, find a table, take a seat, unwrap the paper, and dig in. The whole experience is transitory and soon forgotten. I've written this book out of a belief that people should know what lies behind the shiny, happy surface of every fast food transaction. They should know what really lurks between those sesame-seed buns. As the old saying goes: You are what you eat.

How to Do It

Congress should ban advertising that preys upon children, it should stop subsidizing dead-end jobs, it should pass tougher food safety laws, it should protect American workers from serious harm, it should fight against dangerous concentrations of economic power. Congress should do all those things, but it isn't likely to do any of them soon. The political influence of the fast food industry and its agribusiness suppliers makes a discussion of what Congress should do largely academic. The fast food industry spends millions of dollars every year on lobbying and billions on mass marketing. The wealth and power of the major chains make them seem impossible to defeat. And yet those companies must obey the demands of one group—consumers—whom they eagerly flatter and pursue. As the market for fast food in the United States becomes increasingly saturated, the chains have to compete fiercely with one another for customers. According to William P. Foley II, the chairman of the company that owns Carl's Jr., the basic imperative of today's fast food industry is "Grow or die." The slightest drop in a chain's market share can cause a large decline in the value of its stock. Even the McDonald's Corporation is now vulnerable to the changing whims of consumers. It is opening fewer McDonald's in the United States and expanding mainly through pizza, chicken, and Mexican food chains that do not bear the company name.

The right pressure applied to the fast food industry in the right way could produce change faster than any act of Congress. The United Students Against Sweatshops and other activist groups have brought widespread attention to the child labor, low wages, and hazardous working conditions in Asian factories that make sneakers for Nike. At first, the company disavowed responsibility for these plants, which it claimed were owned by independent suppliers. Nike later changed course, forcing its Asian suppliers to improve working conditions and pay higher wages. The same tactics employed by the antisweatshop groups can be used to help workers much closer to home—workers in the slaughterhouses and processing plants of the High Plains.

As the nation's largest purchaser of beef, the McDonald's Corporation must be held accountable for the behavior of its suppliers. When McDonald's demanded ground beef free of lethal pathogens, the five companies that manufacture its hamburger patties increased their investment in new equipment and microbial testing. If McDonald's were to demand higher wages and safer working conditions for meat-packing workers, its suppliers would provide them. As the nation's largest purchaser of potatoes, McDonald's could also use its clout on behalf of Idaho farmers. And as the second-largest purchaser of chicken, McDonald's could demand changes in the way poultry growers are compensated by their processors. Small increases in the cost of beef, chicken, and potatoes would raise fast food menu prices by a few pennies, if at all. The fast food chains insist that suppliers follow strict specifications regarding the sugar content, fat content, size, shape, taste, and texture of their products. The chains could just as easily enforce a strict code of conduct governing the treatment of workers, ranchers, and farmers.

McDonald's has already shown a willingness to act quickly when confronted with consumer protests. In the late 1960s, African-American groups attacked the McDonald's Corporation for opening restaurants in minority neighborhoods without giving minority businessmen the opportunity to become franchisees. The company responded by actively recruiting African-American franchisees, a move that defused tensions and helped McDonald's penetrate urban markets. A decade ago, environmentalists criticized the chain for the amount of polystyrene waste it generated. At the time, McDonald's served hamburgers in little plastic boxes that were briefly used and then discarded, making it one of the nation's largest purchasers of polystyrene. In order to counter the criticism, McDonald's formed an unusual alliance with the Environmental Defense Fund in August of 1990 and later announced that the chain's hamburgers would no longer be served in polystyrene boxes. The decision was portrayed in the media as the "greening" of McDonald's and a great victory for the environmental movement. The switch from plastic boxes to paper ones did not, however, represent a sudden and profound change in corporate philosophy. It was a response to bad publicity. McDonald's no longer uses polystyrene boxes in the United States—but it continues to use them overseas, where the environmental harms are no different.

Even the anticipation of consumer anger has prompted McDonald's to demand changes from its suppliers. In the spring of 2000, McDonald's informed Lamb Weston and the J. R. Simplot Company that it would no longer purchase frozen french fries made from genetically engineered potatoes. As a result, the two large processors told their growers to stop planting genetically engineered potatoes—and sales of Monsanto's New Leaf, the nation's only biotech potato, instantly plummeted. McDonald's had stopped serving genetically engineered potatoes a year earlier in Western Europe, where the issue of "Frankenfoods" had generated enormous publicity. In the United States, there was relatively little consumer backlash against genetic engineering. Nevertheless, McDonald's decided to act. Just the fear of controversy swiftly led to a purchasing change with important ramifications for American agriculture.

The challenge of overcoming the fast food giants may seem daunting. But it's insignificant compared to what the ordinary citizens, factory workers, and heavy-metal fans of Plauen once faced. They confronted a system propped up by guns, tanks, barbed wire, the media, the secret police, and legions of informers, a system that controlled every aspect of state power—except popular consent. Without leaders or a manifesto, the residents of a small East German backwater decided to seek the freedom of their forefathers. And within months a wall that had seemed impenetrable fell.

Nobody in the United States is forced to buy fast food. The first step toward meaningful change is by far the easiest: stop buying it. The executives who run the fast food industry are not bad men. They are businessmen. They will sell free-range, organic, grass-fed hamburgers if you demand it. They will sell whatever sells at a profit. The usefulness of the market, its effectiveness as a tool, cuts both ways. The real power of the American consumer has not yet been unleashed. The heads of Burger King, KFC, and McDonald's should feel daunted; they're outnumbered. There are three of them and almost three hundred million of you. A good boycott, a refusal to buy, can speak much louder than words. Sometimes the most irresistible force is the most mundane.

Pull open the glass door, feel the rush of cool air, walk inside, get in line, and look around you, look at the kids working in the kitchen, at the customers in their seats, at the ads for the latest toys, study the backlit color photographs above the counter, think about where the food came from, about how and where it was made, about what is set in motion by every single fast food purchase, the ripple effect near and far, think about it. Then place your order. Or turn and walk out the door. It's not too late. Even in this fast food nation, you can still have it your way.

Suggestions for Discussion

1. Some readers might consider Schlosser's argument an overreaction, and protest that fast food is reasonably good and a helpful time-saving measure. How does Schlosser anticipate these objections, and how successful is he in building his case against the fast food industry?

2. Has the "McDonaldization" of American society standardized tastes, resulting in a loss of uniqueness and individuality? Place your answer in the context of Schlosser's arguments.

Suggestions for Writing

1. Thoreau's "Why I Went Out Into the Woods" recounts his effort to break free of social constraints and assert his individuality. In today's culture of the "Fast Food Nation," how might a similar escape from conformity be attempted?

2. After assessing the problem of fast food in a broad sense, Schlosser suggests a series of steps the American people can take to combat its negative influence. Assess the practicality of these steps in an essay. Do further research.

∾∾∾∾

S A R A H   L Y A L L

Germaine Greer's "Cruelty TV"

Sarah Lyall is the London correspondent for the *New York Times*. In this article, she recounts feminist scholar Germaine Greer's participation in the British reality show *Celebrity Big Brother*. Disgusted by the show's practice of pitting contestants against each other to avoid being "voted out," Greer left the cast prematurely and triggered a controversy over the influence and possible immorality of reality television. Lyall examines the issue from several standpoints, including Greer's attacks on *Celebrity Big Brother* and remarks from its defenders.

Possibly the only thing more surprising than the news that Germaine Greer—the Australian feminist, literary scholar and cultural critic—had joined the cast of the latest "Celebrity Big Brother" series was what she did when she quit, five days later.

Contestants habitually complain about their experiences on reality television shows. It is one of the standard features of the entertainment, like groveling for meals or getting drunk and falling over. But the complaints are usually directed at the other participants. As one said about another in a past season, "If I had stayed in that house a minute longer, I would have murdered Les."

What made the 65-year-old Greer's departure last week so riveting, by contrast, was that her attack was not a personal whining session, but a blistering cultural and literary critique of the show that revealed her as perhaps the only contestant who has ever actually read (or at least admitted reading) George Orwell's "1984," where the whole notion of Big Brother was born.

Greer, still best known for her 1970s feminist manifesto, "The Female Eunuch," compared the show, in which celebrities are confined together as viewers decide who goes and who stays, to "a fascist prison camp" where bullying was encouraged and sensory deprivation used as a weapon of torture.

"The business of the 'Big Brother' house was to bring about a state of abjection among the inhabitants," she told reporters after her departure.

In a furious article in *The Sunday Times* of London, Greer expanded on her theme, complaining that deliberately poor conditions and the withholding of privileges were wearing down the weaker contestants, leading them to turn on one another. When one participant begged to be given a Diet Coke, saying that he could not cope without it, for instance, the program makers distributed it to the other cast members and encouraged them to taunt him.

Food in the house was stale and rancid, Greer said. The kitchen was filthy and contestants had to share towels and bathrobes "crawling with bacteria promiscuously collected from all eight bodies."

Even worse, she said, was the way the program makers would "lock down" the contestants in their bedrooms when technicians entered the set, drawing the blinds but leaving the lights on. During lockdowns, contestants were forbidden to eat or use the bathroom. A shrill, reverberating alarm sounded if they tried to doze off.

"As Mussolini's enforcers found, it is easy to break a prisoner by turning day into night and jumbling their mealtimes," wrote Greer, who during the show had urged her fellow contestants to revolt by stripping and sitting naked. (No one did.) "It would have served Big Brother right if housemates had wet their beds and daubed their walls" with excrement.

To some, it was as if Greer, alone among the parade of contestants present and past, had dared finally to mention the emperor's lack of clothes.

"My personal take on why Greer signed up for 'Big Brother' was that it was a simple, benevolent decision to try to help mankind," the critic Caitlin Moran wrote in *The Times* of London. "In all the reality shows over the past five years, we have never, on a single occasion, had anyone even remotely sane and intelligent on them."

But Greer's attack offended another *Times* columnist, Julie Burchill, a "Big Brother" fan whose article on the matter carried the headline "My Feminist Hero Has Become a Rancid Bore."

"It is rather offensive to those who have spent time in fascist prisons— or even people who have two brain cells to rub together—to compare a game show to a fascist prison." Burchill wrote, accusing Greer of failing to understand "the risibly obvious fact that this 'Big Brother' was not the original oppressive brute, as created by George Orwell," but rather a "pantomime villain toying with a few pampered volunteers."

Greer was certainly the odd one out when she entered the "Celebrity Big Brother" house along a motley crowd of has-beens and would-bes, including Brigitte Nielsen, the Amazonian former wife of Sylvester Stallone, and John McCririck, the eccentric host of television horse-racing programs. McCririck offered a window into his personality when he said of his wife on the show: "Her body's sagging, and in truth I'm fed up with her."

Greer explained that she had joined the show because she wanted money to help rehabilitate her 125 acres, or 50 hectares, of Australian rain forest, as well as to "strike a blow for old ladies." She is said to have received £50,000 ($93,000) for agreeing to participate. Had she won, she said, she would have donated the prize money to Buglife, an invertebrate conservation charity.

Some feminists were upset at what they saw as a betrayal of the cause and distressed by the undignified spectacle of the various tasks Greer had to undergo to win food and privileges: wading through rotting vegetables and cigarette butts; sitting on a revolving merry-go-round that made her vomit repeatedly; dressing like a Victorian serving-wench.

"Germaine is one of the icons of my life, but because of the way culture is, she will now be known for 'Big Brother' rather than for anything else she's done," said Bonnie Greer, a co-panelist with Greer on a BBC arts-review program. (They are not related.)

Greer has constantly defied expectation and never been far from the public eye. In 1994 she publicly opened her house to homeless people, only to discover later that one of her "guests" had in fact been a reporter for a British tabloid researching a tell-all article. She has stripped for magazines, denounced marriage as state-sanctioned slavery for women and written with equal fluency about Shakespeare, the environment and orgasms. She seems unbothered by the latest fuss.

In her *Sunday Times* article, she said that she had remained in the house until she realized that she could not persuade the other housemates to join her in her planned revolt against "Big Brother's" bullying thought police.

"It is now up to the British public to decide what should become of cruelty television," she said, "and to turn their thumbs down."

Suggestions for Discussion

1. Consider how Greer's criticisms of *Celebrity Big Brother* might be applied to other reality shows.

2. Do you believe that people who willingly participate in competitive or embarrassing reality shows deserve whatever treatment they get? Would you be willing to participate in such a program for money, fame, or some other reward?

Suggestion for Writing

Germaine Greer (b. 1939), a standard-bearer for the women's liberation move-ment, is the author of *The Female Eunuch* (1971), *Sex and Destiny: The Politics of Human Fertility* (1984), and *The Whole Woman* (1999). Consider how her feminist standpoint might be related to her negative opinion of reality televi-sion. Do you see a link between her concerns? If possible, reinforce your argu-ment with quotations and ideas taken from her writing.

DAVID C. BARKER

Talk Radio, Persuasion, and American Political Behavior

David C. Barker (b. 1969), a professor of political science at the Univer-sity of Pittsburgh, has written about "talk radio" for the *Journal of Poli-tics, Social Science Quarterly,* and *Political Communication.* The following excerpt, taken from his book *Rushed to Judgment* (2002), discusses how radio programs influence public opinion, legislation, and election results.

We Americans are changing the way we gather political information. Perhaps due to our increased access to information and due to changes in lifestyle, we increasingly seek information that can be obtained conveniently, that doubles as entertainment, or that provides a perspective with which we sympathize. Thus while millions of Americans still peruse a daily newspa-per and/or religiously view the evening network news, millions more book-mark their preferred political websites, watch political news magazines on cable television, or tune in to talk radio during their daily commutes. Such growth in usage of "new media" (Davis and Owen 1998) may have sub-stantial implications for democratic discourse in the "marketplace of ideas." While the traditional media (e.g., newspapers, TV news, and major news magazines such as *Time* and *Newsweek*) attempt to uphold occupational norms of objectivity and equal time in their coverage of political events (Bennett 1988), the new media are not regulated by such canons. Therefore as more Americans receive information from sources whose primary objec-tives are to entertain and persuade, democratic dialogue may become more misinformed, contentious, and polarized—resulting in legislative gridlock and/or restricted policy alternatives.

For political scientists, social psychologists, and communication scholars, the new media may provide fresh opportunities to find evidence of persuasive media influence over audience members' beliefs, opinions, and behavior. However, what analysis of the new media offers on one hand in terms of new opportunity, it takes away with the other, for the new media invite a notoriously self-selected audience. Cognitive dissonance theory posits that individuals may avoid messages that they find potentially distasteful, relying entirely on sources that appear kindred in spirit (Festinger 1957). Thus untangling the reciprocal causality between audience exposure to new media and political behavior poses a heavy analytical challenge.

Political talk radio typifies the new media. Convenient, entertaining, and provocative in its discourse, most political talk radio is unapologetically ideological in message.

Political talk radio may be defined as *radio programs (usually sporting a call-in format) that emphasize the discussion of elections, policy issues, and other public affairs.* Originating in the 1930s, talk radio was a popular outlet for politicians. Of course, Franklin Roosevelt's fireside chats during the Great Depression are legendary. Roosevelt's radio speeches during the 1940 campaign were heard by as much as 39 percent of households owning radio sets (Chase 1942). But political talk radio has never been the exclusive domain of those holding or running for office. Perhaps as a counterweight to Roosevelt, Father Charles Coughlin held an audience of approximately ten million for his weekly broadcasts attacking the New Deal (Tull 1965; Brinkley 1982).

Nationally syndicated radio call-in programs had their genesis in the 1970s. The Larry King Show was the most prominent of these early shows, with more than three hundred affiliates. But political discussion often took a back seat on these shows to entertainment personalities, popular psychology, and the like. Political talk radio as we know it today began in the 1980s and has flourished in the 1990s. (Capella, Turow, and Jamieson 1996; Davis and Owen 1998).

But despite its popularity, talk radio is very controversial. While some hail it as America's new "back fence," fostering pseudocommunities and providing the ultimate arena for free, democratic discourse (Ratner 1995; Levin 1987), others worry that talk radio may foster listeners' basest instincts. Critics complain that we have reached a point where ignorant blather is considered on par with informed commentary (e.g., Dreier and Middleton, 1994), where the views of Henry Kissinger carry only a slightly higher price tag in the political marketplace than those of "Joe, from Round Rock, Texas."

One of the events that paved the way for the success of political talk radio was the Federal Communication Commission's decision in 1985 that the Fairness Doctrine was no longer needed, a decision that was unsuccessfully challenged by Congress and subsequently upheld by a federal Appeals Court in 1989. Adopted in 1949, the Fairness Doctrine had stipulated that broadcasters must provide reasonable balance when airing controversial opinions. With the end of the Fairness Doctrine, broadcasters were free to air ideologically biased programming.

Indeed, as opposed to traditional media, political talk shows are unabashedly biased. While some networks, such as ABC, Major Radio Network, and Westwood One carry both liberal and conservative hosts, and the small Pacifica network is an example of a leftist network, the majority of political talk programs feature conservative, libertarian, or populist hosts (Davis and Owen 1998). In response to challenges of unfairness, some hosts contend that rather than stifling opposing viewpoints, their existence provides needed balance to the mainstream media. Host Blanquitta Cullum argues that "by using the evening news as a left-wing doormat, they [liberals] have created demand for a right-wing product" (Cullum 1994). Similarly, Rush Limbaugh says "…my views and commentary don't need to be balanced by equal time. I am equal time. And the free market has proven my contentions" (Limbaugh 1994).

Hosts also claim that callers offer a different range of perspectives. Limbaugh often brags, "liberals are pushed to the front of the line." But balance is not the goal of such devices. Political talk radio must appeal to the marketplace; hence the primary goal of most shows is entertainment. An open-minded consideration of the various sides of an issue is not entertainment to most listeners. By contrast, verbal conflict that culminates with a clear "winner" spurs interest. As Limbaugh admits, "the primary purpose of a call is to make me look good, not to provide a forum for the public to make speeches" (Limbaugh 1992).

❧

Format

Talk radio programs typically conform to the following script: an opening monologue by the host, sometimes followed by the introduction of a guest or guests, accompanied by interaction between the guest or host and callers. With or without guests, the host is the headliner of the program. Davis and Owen (1998) remark that the host is more like Geraldo Rivera or Oprah Winfrey than Dan Rather or Judy Woodruff. The host's opening monologue carries tremendous import. It sets the tone and agenda for the remainder of the show, establishing the topics that will be up for discussion and the host's (never retreating) position on those issues. Opening monologues can last anywhere from just a few minutes up to half an hour, depending on the host's interests, the presence of guests, and the news cycle. Some hosts supplement opening monologues with shorter monologues at the beginning of each hour. With ten to twenty hours of airtime to fill each week, hosts have time to discuss issues at length. However, just because talk radio hosts have more time to delve into issues does not necessarily translate into a more substantial treatment of those issues than would be found in the mainstream press. Programs often cover a wide range of issues—moving quickly between callers, host pontification, and advertising—which often translates into superficial discussion (Davis and Owen 1998).

Following the opening monologue, the host usually begins taking calls. A call screener answers the phone and conveys information about the caller to the host by typing onto a terminal that the host can read through a computer screen. That information includes the caller's name, approximate age, gender, location, and a brief summary of the point that the caller wants to make. Thus the screener is a filter whose job is to enhance the appeal of the program. That usually means limiting calls from those over fifty years of age, those who cannot effectively articulate their point, or those who are likely to make the host look bad (Davis and Owen 1998). Studies have also found that male callers are more than twice as likely as female callers to achieve airtime.

The majority of callers usually agree with the host, at least when the host is conservative (Davis and Owen 1998). This may be because more people who agree are likely to call, or it may be attributable to the screening process. Conflict spurs interest, so it stands to reason that screeners would want to "put through" callers who disagree with the host. However, as Limbaugh has noted, the primary purpose of a call is to glorify the host. As a consequence, *skilled* callers who disagree may be screened out. Once on the air, callers have a limited amount of time to make their point. Rarely does a host interact with a caller for more than two or three minutes. Women and the elderly, if they get through, are often allotted even less time (Davis and Owen 1998).

☙

Media Portrayal

What is the nature of mainstream media attention to political talk radio? A large-scale content analysis by scholars at the Annenberg School of Communication (Capella, Turow, and Jamieson 1996) found that, in general, the print media's attention to talk radio is narrow and unfavorable. First, the Annenberg scholars' study indicates that a reader of the mainstream print media would find little in-depth investigation of talk radio hosts or their programs. In fact, "the mainstream print media pay little attention to issues discussed on radio's political talk programs" (38). Furthermore, the analysis found that the press tend to describe talk radio as a pernicious force. Fewer than 5 percent of the articles included in the content analysis reflected any degree of positivity toward the mentioned talk radio host or show. Typical examples of print media characterization from the Annenberg analysis include the following:

> Listening in for a day is to be pelted with tales and travails, vehemence and vitriol, paranoia and pettiness, stupidity masquerading as wisdom and, occasionally even vice versa. (Weber 1992)
> There is a meanness in the land. We can hear it in the angry howls on talk radio. As Limbaugh or some other imitator goads his listeners on, the basic message is: we are entitled to our meanness. (Gabler 1995)
> What passes for political debate on many talk shows is often a cacophony of inflammatory rhetoric and half-truths. (Dreier and Middleton 1994)

Moreover, the press tend to portray talk radio as being homogeneous. Most articles that discuss talk radio content provide outrageous and disturbing quotations from Bob Grant or G. Gordon Liddy and then proceed to generalize such comments to talk radio more broadly. They rarely acknowledge that other, more-moderate forms not only exist but dominate the medium. This negative media portrayal may explain why nonlisteners tend to view political talk radio quite negatively (Capella, Turow, and Jamieson 1996).

Finally, the Annenberg scholars found that the press portray political talk radio not only as nefarious but also as a powerful force in American politics. They conclude that those reading story-length accounts of talk radio in the mainstream media would infer that talk radio has been extraordinarily effective in blocking or overturning legislative action, advocating legislation, influencing political behavior, and mobilizing political support (Capella, Turow, and Jamieson 1996).

With regard to deliberative democracy, my colleagues and I sought to understand the effects that call-in political talk radio might have on public levels of information and misinformation. Does the deliberation afforded by the medium lead to a more thoughtful and informed citizenry, or to more demagoguery? We looked at a sample of San Diego residents, comparing talk radio listeners to nonlisteners, and recorded relative levels of information and misinformation. Our results were at once encouraging and somewhat alarming; while talk radio listening is strongly associated with objective information about public affairs, it is also highly correlated with misinformation—the confident holding of information that is objectively false. We found that the distinction depended on whether the information had an ideological dimension. For example, talk radio listeners were more likely than nonlisteners to accurately answer questions involving political information without any kind of ideological element—such as how much of a majority is needed in Congress to override a presidential veto. But those who listened to shows with conservative hosts were also much more likely to inaccurately perceive that the federal budget deficit had grown under the Clinton administration. At the same time, we found that listeners to shows with moderate hosts tended to have the lowest levels of misinformation in the sample.

We do not attribute the high levels of misinformation among conservative-show listeners to lying on the part of conservative talk show hosts, but rather to the tendency on the part of listeners to engage in "inferential reasoning," whereby they receive granules of correct information, combine it with the ideological message they are hearing, and draw inferences about reality. This argument is consistent with the constructionist model of media effects, where media neither powerfully inject the masses with does of propaganda that the masses unwittingly take in, nor do they only have "minimal effects"—much like Plato's allegory of the cave, message receivers take what they learn, fit it into the image of reality that they have based on personal experience, and draw inferences about reality that may or may not be accurate. Hence the same message can produce different effects in the heads of different people.

So does talk radio enhance the prospects of American deliberative democracy? It appears that it has the potential to enhance civic-mindedness and spur listeners to feel as though they can make a difference in the political process, but outside the experimental laboratory, that community spirit only seems to extend to listeners whose opinions are given voice by those achieving airtime on the shows. Those who are not in agreement with the host or the majority of callers may feel isolated and may choose to silence themselves in the political arena. Furthermore, listeners to ideologically charged shows appear to engage in inferential reasoning that seems to lead, in this case, to greater misinformation and demagoguery, which is antithetical to the goals of deliberative democracy. Hence perhaps a talk radio universe governed by the now-extinct Fairness Doctrine and therefore dedicated to objectivity and the equal expression of different points of view would have great promise as an agent of deliberative democracy. But that is not the universe in which we live—where talk radio is dedicated to maintaining an audience and furthering the interests of the host. Like the other forms of the "new media," maintaining an audience means entertaining the audience and often targeting an audience. Objectivity and equal opportunities for expression do not serve those purposes as well as satire, polemic, and otherwise telling the target audience what it wants to hear.

ᘯ

Works Cited

Bennett, L. 1988. *News: The Politics of Illusion,* 2nd ed. New York: Longman.
Brinkley, A. 1982. *Voices of Protest: Huey Long, Father Coughlin, and the Great Depression.* New York: Knopf.

Capella, J. N., J. Turow, and K. H. Jamieson. 1996. "Call-In Political Talk Radio: Background, Content, Audiences, Portrayal in Mainstream Media." A report from the Annenberg Public Policy Center of the University of Pennsylvania.

Chase, F. 1942. *Sound and Fury: An Informal History of Broadcasting.* New York: Harper and Brothers.

Davis, R. and D. Owen. 1998. *New Media and American Politics.* New York: Oxford University Press.

Dreier, P. and W. J. Middleton. 1994. "How Talk Radio Helped GOP's Resurgence." *Chicago Tribune* (21 December): 129.

Festinger, L. 1957. *A Theory of Cognitive Dissonance.* Evanston, Ill.: Row, Peterson.

Gabler, N. 1995. "A Multitude of Meanness." *Los Angeles Times* (1 January): M1.

Levin, M. B. 1987. *Talk Radio and the American Dream.* Lexington, Mass.: Lexington Books.

Limbaugh, R. H. 1992. *The Way Things Ought to Be.* New York: Pocket Books.

———. 1994. "Why Liberals Fear Me." *Policy Review* 70: 4–10.

Ratner, E. 1995. "Talk Radio Responds: Our 'Back Fence.'" *Los Angeles Times* (25 April): B7.

Tull, C. J. 1965. *Father Coughlin and the New Deal.* Syracuse: Syracuse University Press.

Weber, B. 1992. "A Loud Angry World on the Dial." *New York Times* (7 June): 31.

Suggestions for Discussion

1. Do you agree with Barker's assertion that people avoid listening to political arguments that challenge their already established beliefs? How frequently do you seek out the opinion of the "other side," and have you ever been persuaded to change your mind on an important issue?

2. The terms "liberal," "conservative," and "balanced" are often poorly defined and broadly applied, leading to confusion in political debate. How would you define these terms? Do you think your definitions are unbiased?

3. Investigate several sources of news to determine which you feel have a bias (liberal or conservative) and which seem to be impartial. Examine print media, radio, television, and Internet news sources.

Suggestion for Writing

Barker challenges the popular notion of the "liberal media." However, some critics make a strong case for a liberal media bias. Do further research on both sides of the argument to come to your own conclusions about the nature of modern political discourse. Sources you may investigate include:

Eric Alterman, *What Liberal Media?*
Ann Coulter, *Slander: Liberal Lies about the American Right*
Kristina Borjesson, ed., *Into the Buzzsaw*
Bernard Goldberg, *Arrogance: Rescuing America from the Media Elite*
Edward S. Herman, *Manufacturing Consent*
Jim A. Kuypers, *Press Bias and Politics*
Michael Medved, *Hollywood vs. America*
Outfoxed: Rupert Murdoch's War on Journalism (DVD)
John Stossel, *Give Me a Break*

NICK HORNBY

I'm Like a Bird

Nick Hornby (b. 1957), a novelist and pop music critic for the *New Yorker,* is the author of the novels *High Fidelity, Fever Pitch,* and *About a Boy*, all of which were translated to the silver screen. A resident of Highbury, North London, he also wrote *How to Be Good* and *A Long Way Down.* The Academy of Arts and Letters awarded Hornby the E. M. Forster Award in 1999.

Of course I can understand people dismissing pop music. I know that a lot of it, nearly all of it, is trashy, unimaginative, poorly written, slickly produced, inane, repetitive and juvenile (although at least four of these adjectives could be used to describe the incessant attacks on pop that you can still find in posh magazines and newspapers); I know too, believe me, that Cole Porter was "better" than Madonna or Travis, that most pop songs are aimed cynically at a target audience three decades younger than I am, that in any case the golden age was thirty-five years ago and there has been very little of value since. It's just that there's this song I heard on the radio, and I bought the CD, and now I have to hear it ten or fifteen times a day…

That's the thing that puzzles me about those of you who feel that contemporary pop (and I use the word to encompass soul, reggae, country, rock—anything and everything that you might regard as trashy) is beneath you, or behind you, or beyond you—some preposition denoting distance, anyway: does this mean that you never hear, or at least never enjoy, new songs, that everything you sing in the shower was written years, decades, centuries ago? Do you really deny yourselves the pleasure of mastering a new tune (a pleasure, incidentally, that your kind is perhaps the first in the history to forego) because you are afraid it might make you look as if you don't know who Foucault is? I'll bet you're fun at parties.

See, the song that has been driving me potty with pleasure recently is "I'm Like a Bird," by Nelly Furtado. Only history will judge whether Ms Furtado turns out to be any kind of artist, and though I have my suspicions that she will not change the way we look at the world, I can't say that I'm very bothered: I will always be grateful to her for creating in me the narcotic need to hear her song again and again. It is, after all, a harmless need, easily satisfied, and there are few enough of those in the world. I don't even want to make a case for this song, as opposed to any other— although I happen to think that it's a very good pop song, with a dreamy languor and a bruised optimism that immediately distinguishes it from its anaemic and stunted peers. The point is that a few months ago it didn't exist, at least as far as we are concerned, and now here it is, and that, in itself, is a small miracle.

Dave Eggers has a theory that we play songs over and over, those of us who do, because we have to "solve" them, and it's true that in our early relationship with, and courtship of, a new song, there is a stage which is akin to a sort of emotional puzzlement. There's a little bit in "I'm Like a Bird," for example, about halfway through, where the voice is double-tracked on a phrase, and the effect—especially on someone who is not a musician, someone who loves and appreciates music but is baffled and seduced by even the simplest musical tricks—is rich and fresh and addictive.

Sure, it will seem thin and stale soon enough. Before very long I will have "solved" "I'm Like a Bird," and I won't want to hear it very much any more— a three-minute pop song can only withhold its mysteries for so long, after all. So, yes, it's disposable, as if that makes any difference to anyone's perceptions of the value of pop music. But then, shouldn't we be sick of the "Moonlight Sonata" by now? Or the Mona Lisa? Or *The Importance of Being Earnest*? They're empty! Nothing left! We sucked 'em dry! That's what gets me: the very people who are snotty about the disposability of pop will go over and over again to see Lady Bracknell say "A *handbag*?" in a funny voice. You don't think that joke's exhausted itself? Maybe disposability is a sign of pop music's maturity, a recognition of its own limitations, rather than the converse.

A couple of times a year I make myself a tape to play in the car, a tape full of all the new songs I've loved over the previous few months, and every time I finish one I can't believe that there'll be another. Yet there always is, and I can't wait for the next one; you only need a few hundred more things like that, and you've got a life worth living.

Suggestions for Discussion

1. What kind of audience is Nick Hornby addressing in this article? What assumptions is he making about these readers' personal taste in music?

2. What does Dave Eggers mean when he says that we listen to the same song over and over again in an effort to "solve" the song?

3. How does Hornby compare pop music with classical, or high, art?

Suggestion for Writing

Write a defense of something that is dear to you—perhaps a hobby, occupation, or work of art—that you feel has been unfairly criticized or dismissed by the general public.

ᘉᘉᘉᘉ

RANDALL KENNEDY

The Protean N-Word

Randall Kennedy (b. 1954), the author of *Race, Crime, and the Law*, is a faculty member of Harvard Law School who received an undergraduate degree from Princeton and earned his law degree from Yale. A resident of Dedham, MA, Kennedy served as a law clerk to Supreme Court Justice Thurgood Marshall. Kennedy is a member of the American Academy of Arts and Sciences, the American Philosophical Association, and the American Law Institute, and is the author of *Interracial Intimacies: Sex, Marriage, Identity, and Adoption* (2003). In the selection that follows, reprinted from his 2002 book *Nigger: The Strange Career of a Troublesome Word*, Kennedy explores the changing significance of a word that was once considered merely an abominable racial slur but which now appears to have taken on a multitude of entirely new connotations.

If *nigger* represented only an insulting slur and was associated only with racial animus, this book would not exist, for the term would be insufficiently interesting to warrant extended study. *Nigger* is fascinating precisely because it has been put to a variety of uses and can radiate a wide array of meanings. Unsurprisingly, blacks have often used *nigger* for different purposes than racist whites. To lampoon slavery, blacks created the story of the slave

Franklin, oil on canvas. Markus Faust, 2001.

caught eating one of his master's pigs. "Yes, suh, Massa," the slave quipped, "you got less pig now, but you sho' got more nigger." To poke fun at the grisly phenomenon of lynching, African Americans told of the black man who, upon seeing a white woman pass by, said, "Lawd, will I ever?" A white man responded, "No, nigger, never." The black man replied, "Where there's life, there's hope." And the white man declared, "Where there's a nigger, there's a rope." To dramatize the tragic reality of Jim Crow subjugation, African Americans recounted the tale of the Negro who got off a bus down south. Seeing a white policeman, he politely asked for the time. The policeman hit him twice with a club and said, "Two o'clock, nigger. Why?" "No reason, Cap'n," the black man answered. "I's just glad it ain't twelve." And to satirize "legal" disenfranchisement, African Americans told the joke about the black man who attempted to register to vote. After the man answered a battery of questions that were far more difficult than any posed to whites, an official confronted him with a headline in a Chinese paper and demanded a translation. "Yeah, I know what it means," the black man said. "It means that niggers don't vote in Mississippi again this year."

In the 1960s and 1970s, protest became more direct and more assertive. Drafted to fight a "white man's war" in Vietnam, Muhammad Ali refused to be inducted into the U.S. Army, explaining, "No Vietcong ever called me 'nigger.' " Emphasizing the depth of white racism all across the United States, activists joked, "What is a Negro with a Ph.D.?" Their response? "Dr. Nigger."

In his famous "Letter from a Birmingham Jail," Martin Luther King Jr. continued to agitate, listing in wrenching detail the indignities that prompted his impatience with tardy reform. He cited having to sleep in automobiles because of racial exclusion from motels, having to explain to his children why they could not go to amusement parks open to the white public, and being "harried by day and haunted by night by the fact that you are a Negro, living constantly at tip-toe stance never quite knowing what to expect next." Among King's litany of abuses was the humiliating way in which whites routinely addressed blacks: "Your wife and mother," he observed, "are never given the respected title 'Mrs.,' " and under the etiquette of Jim Crow, "your first name becomes 'nigger' and your middle name becomes 'boy' (however old you are) and your last name becomes 'John.' "

For some observers, the only legitimate use of *nigger* is as a rhetorical boomerang against racists. There are others, however, who approvingly note a wide range of additional usages. According to Professor Clarence Major, when *nigger* is "used by black people among themselves, [it] is a racial term with undertones of warmth and good will—reflecting...a tragicomic sensibility that is aware of black history." The writer Claude Brown once admiringly described *nigger* as "perhaps the most soulful word in the world," and journalist Jarvis DeBerry calls it "beautiful in its multiplicity of functions." "I am not aware," DeBerry writes, "of any other word capable of expressing so many contradictory emotions." Traditionally an insult, *nigger* can also be a compliment, as in "He played like a nigger." Historically a signal of hostility, it can also be a salutation announcing affection, as in "This is my main nigger." A term of belittlement, *nigger* can also be a term of respect, as in "James Brown is a straight-up nigger." A word that can bring forth bitter tears in certain circumstances, *nigger* can prompt joyful laughter in others.

A candid portrayal of the N-word's use among African Americans may be found in Helen Jackson Lee's autobiography, *Nigger in the Window*. It was Lee's cousin who first introduced her to *nigger's* possibilities. As Lee remembered it, "Cousin Bea had a hundred different ways of saying *nigger;* listening to her, I learned the variety of meanings the word could assume. How it could be opened like an umbrella to cover a dozen different moods, or stretched like a rubber band to wrap up our family with other colored families....*Nigger* was a piece-of-clay word that you could shape...to express your feelings."

Nigger has long been featured in black folk humor. There is the story, for example, of the young boy inspired by a minister's sermon on loving all of God's creatures. Finding a frozen rattlesnake, he nicely put the animal under his shirt to warm it up. "Nigger, I'm gonna bite the hell out of you!" the snake announced upon its revival. "Mr. Snake," the boy asked, "you mean to say you gonna bite me after I followed the preacher's teaching and took you to my bosom?" "Hell yeah, nigger," the snake replied. "You knew I was a snake, didn't you?"

Before the 1970s, however, *nigger* seldom figured in the routines of professional comedians. It was especially rare in the acts of those who performed for racially mixed audiences. Asserting that unmentionable slurs derived much of their seductive power from their taboo status, the iconoclastic white comedian Lenny Bruce recommended a strategy of subversion through overuse. In a 1963 routine, Bruce suggested with characteristic verve that "if President Kennedy got on television and said, 'Tonight I'd like to introduce the niggers in my cabinet,' and he yelled 'Niggerniggernig-gerniggerniggerniggernigger' at every nigger he saw…till *nigger* didn't mean anything anymore, till *nigger* lost its meaning…you'd never hear any four-year-old nigger cry when he came home from school."

But Bruce was unusual, and in terms of the N-word, he failed to inspire emulation. While the hip comedians of the 1950s and 1960s—Dick Gregory, Nipsey Russell, Mort Sahl, Godfrey Cambridge, Moms Mabley, Redd Foxx—told sexually risqué or politically barbed jokes, *nigger* for the most part remained off-limits.

All that changed with the emergence of Richard Pryor. Through live performances and a string of albums, he brought *nigger* to center stage in stand-up comedy, displaying with consummate artistry its multiple meanings.

Pryor's single best performance may be heard on the aptly titled *That Nigger's Crazy*, winner of the 1974 Grammy Award for best comedy recording. The album explores Pryor's professional fears ("Hope I'm funny…because I know niggers ready to kick ass"), blacks' alleged ability to avoid certain sorts of danger ("Niggers never get burned up in buildings….White folks just panic, run to the door, fall all over each other….Niggers get outside, *then* argue"), black parenting styles ("My father was one of them eleven-o'clock niggers"), comparative sociology ("White folks fuck quiet; niggers make noise"), racial anthropology ("White folks…don't know how to play the dozens"), and social commentary ("Nothin' can scare a nigger after four hundred years of this shit").

The bit that often provokes the most applause from black listeners is Pryor's "Niggers vs. Police":

Cops put a hurtin' on your ass, man, y'know? They really degrade you.

White folks don't believe that shit, don't believe cops degrade you. [They say,] "Oh, c'mon, those people were resisting arrest. I'm tired of this harass-ment of police officers." Police live in [a white] neighborhood, and [all his white neighbors] be knowin' the man as Officer Timson. "Hello, Officer Timson, going bowling tonight? Yes, nice Pinto you have. Ha, ha."

Niggers don't know 'em like that. See, white folks get a ticket, they pull over [and say], "Hey Officer, yes, glad to be of help." Nigger got to be talkin' about "I am reaching into my pocket for my license! 'Cause I don't wanta be no muthafuckin' accident!"

Mel Watkins has rightly maintained that what made Richard Pryor a pathbreaking figure was that he "introduce[d] and popularize[d] that unique, previously concealed or rejected part of African-American humor that thrived in the lowest, most unassimilated portion of the black community." He broke free, at least for a while, of all those—whites and blacks alike—who, sometimes for different reasons, shared an aversion to too much realism. He seemed radically unconcerned with deferring to any social conventions, particularly those that accepted black comedians as clowns but rejected them as satirists. Nothing more vividly symbolized his defiant, risk-taking spirit than his unprecedented playfulness regarding the explosive N-word in performances before racially mixed audiences.

In the years since the release of *That Nigger's Crazy,* the N-word has become a staple in the routine of many black comedians. Among these, the one who most jarringly deploys it is Chris Rock, whose signature skit begins with the declaration "I love black people, but I hate niggers." He goes on:

It's like our own personal civil war.
On the one side, there's black people.
On the other, you've got niggers.
The niggers have got to go. Every time black people want to have a good time, niggers mess it up. You can't do anything without some ignorant-ass niggers fucking it up.
Can't go to a movie the first week it opens. Why? Because niggers are shooting at the screen....
You can't have anything in your house. Why? Because the niggers who live next door will break in, take it all, and then come over the next day and go, "We heard you got robbed."

According to Rock, "niggers always want credit for some shit they're *supposed* to do. They'll say something like 'I took care of my kids.' " Exploding with impatience, Rock interjects:

You're *supposed* to, you dumb motherfucker.
"I ain't never been to jail."
Whaddya want? A cookie? You're not *supposed* to go to jail, you low-expectation-having mother-fucker.

Rock asserts that "the worst thing about niggers is that they love to *not know.*" That's because, he says, "niggers don't read. Books are like Kryptonite to a nigger."

Aware that some may condemn his routine as latter-day minstrelsy, racial betrayal, or a false pandering to antiblack prejudice, Rock exclaims near the end of his performance,

I know what all you black [listeners] think.

"Man, why you got to say that?…It isn't us, it's the *media*. The media has distorted our image to make us look bad. Why must you come down on us like that, brother? It's not us, it's the media."

Please cut the shit. When I go to the money machine at night, I'm not looking over my shoulder for the media.

I'm looking for niggers.

Ted Koppel never took anything from me. Niggers have. Do you think I've got three guns in my house because the media's outside my door trying to bust in?

Rap is another genre of entertainment suffused with instances of *nigger*. A cursory survey just of titles yields Dr. Dre's "The Day the Niggas Took Over," A Tribe Called Quest's "Sucka Nigga," Jaz-Z's "Real Nigger," the Geto Boys' "Trigga Happy Nigga," DMX's "My Niggas," and Cypress Hill's "Killa Hill Nigga." In "Gangsta's Paradise," meanwhile, Coolio declares,

I'm the kind of nigga
little homies want to be like
on their knees in the night
saying prayers in the streetlights.

Ice-T says in one of his songs, "I'm a nigger not a colored man or a black or a Negro or an Afro-American." Ice Cube, for his part, dubs himself "the Nigga ya love to hate," And Beanie Sigel promises

I'ma ride with my niggas
die with my niggas
get high with my niggas
split pies with my niggas
till my body gets hard
soul touch the sky
till my numbers get called
and God shuts my eyes.

One of the seminal influences in gangsta rap called itself NWA, short for "Niggaz Wit Attitude." One of this group's most popular albums was *Efil4zaggin*, which, read backward, is "Niggaz 4 Life." Tupac Shakur proclaimed that for him, *nigga* stood for "Never Ignorant, Gets Goals Accomplished."

Some people—I call them eradicationists—seek to drive *nigger* out of rap, comedy, and all other categories of entertainment even when (perhaps *especially* when) blacks themselves are the ones using the N-word. They see this usage as bestowing legitimacy on *nigger* and misleading those whites who have little direct interaction with African Americans. Eradicationists also maintain that blacks' use of *nigger* is symptomatic of racial self-hatred or the internalization of white racism, thus the rhetorical equivalent of black-on-black crime.

There is something to both of these points. The use of *nigger* by black rappers and comedians has given the term a new currency and enhanced cachet such that many young whites yearn to use the term like the blacks whom they see as heroes or trendsetters. It is undoubtedly true, moreover, that in some cases, blacks' use of *nigger* is indicative of an antiblack, self-hating prejudice. I myself first became aware of the term as a child in an all-black setting—my family household in Columbia, South Carolina—in which older relatives routinely attributed to negritude traits they disparaged, including tardiness, dishonesty, rudeness, impoverishment, cowardice, and stupidity. Such racial disparagement *of* blacks *by* blacks was by no means idiosyncratic. It is a widespread feature of African American culture that has given rise to a distinctive corpus of racial abasement typified by admonishments, epigraphs, and doggerel such as:

> Stop acting like a nigger.
>> I don't want nothing black but a Cadillac.
>> Niggers and flies. Niggers and flies. The more I see niggers, the more I
> like flies.

> *If you're white, you're right,*
> *If you're yellow, you're mellow,*
> *If you're brown, stick around,*
> *If you're black, step back.*

This tendency toward racial self-abnegation has been much diminished since the civil rights revolution. But it still retains a grip on the psyches of many black Americans and is searingly evident in a phrase well known in black circles: "Niggers ain't shit."

Self-hatred, however, is an implausible explanation for why many assertive, politically progressive African Americans continue to say "nigger" openly and frequently in conversations with one another. These are African Americans who, in their own minds at least, use *nigger* not in subjection to racial subordination but in defiance of it. Some deploy a long tradition, especially evident in black nationalist rhetoric, of using abusive criticism to spur action that is intended to erase any factual predicate for the condemnation voiced. An example is writing by the Last Poets, a group established in 1968 that merged poetry, music, and politics in forms that anticipated certain types of rap. A famous item in the Last Poets' repertoire was "Niggers Are Scared of Revolution," in which they charged that:

> Niggers are scared of revolution but niggers shouldn't be scared of revolution because revolution is nothing but change, and all niggers do is change. Niggers come in from work and change into pimping clothes to hit the streets to make some quick change. Niggers change their hair from black to red to blond and hope like hell their looks will change. Niggers kill other niggers just because one didn't receive the correct change....
>
> Niggers shoot dope into their arms. Niggers shoot guns and rifles on New Year's Eve a new year that is coming in where white police will do more shooting at them. Where are niggers when the revolution needs some shot? Yeah...you know, niggers are somewhere shooting the shit. Niggers are scared of revolution.

Describing their intentions, Umar Bin Hassan writes that the poem constituted a "call to arms" because "niggers are human beings lost in somebody else's system of values and morals."

Many blacks also do with *nigger* what other members of marginalized groups have done with slurs aimed at shaming them. They have thrown the slur right back in their oppressors' faces. They have added a positive meaning to *nigger,* just as women, gays, lesbians, poor whites, and children born out of wedlock have defiantly appropriated and revalued such words as *bitch, cunt, queer, dyke, redneck, cracker,* and *bastard.*

Yet another source of allegiance to *nigger* is a pessimistic view of the African American predicament. Many blacks who use *nigger* in public before racially mixed audiences disdain dressing up their colloquial language. They do not even attempt to put their best foot forward for the purpose of impressing whites or eroding stereotypes because they see such missions as lost causes. They like to use *nigger* because it is a shorthand way of reminding themselves and everyone else precisely where they perceive themselves as standing in American society—the message being, "Always remember you's a nigger." As Bruce A. Jacobs observes, "To proclaim oneself a nigger is to declare to the disapproving mainstream, 'You can't fire me. I quit.' Hence the perennial popularity of the word. Among poor black youth who...carry a burning resentment of white society. To growl that one is a nigga is a seductive gesture...that can feel bitterly empowering."

Two additional considerations also warrant notice here, both of them having to do with the power of words to simultaneously create and divide communities. Some blacks use *nigger* to set themselves off from Negroes who refuse to use it. To proclaim oneself a nigger is to identify oneself as real, authentic, uncut, unassimilated, and unassimilable—the opposite, in short, of a Negro, someone whose rejection of *nigger* is seen as part of an effort to blend into the white mainstream. Sprinkling one's language with *niggers* is thus a way to "keep it real."

Roping off cultural turf is another aim of some blacks who continue to use *nigger* in spite of its stigmatized status. Certain forms of black cultural expression have become commercially valuable, and black cultural entrepreneurs fear that these forms will be exploited by white performers who will adopt them and, tapping white-skin privilege, obtain compensation far outstripping that paid to black performers. This is, of course, a realistic fear in light of the long history of white entertainers' becoming rich and famous by marketing in whiteface cultural innovations authored by their underappreciated black counterparts. A counterstrategy is to seed black cultural expression with gestures that are widely viewed as being off-limits to whites. Saying "nigger" is one such gesture. Even whites who immerse themselves in black hip-hop culture typically refrain from openly and unabashedly saying "nigger" like their black heroes or colleagues, for fear that it might be perceived as a sign of disrespect rather than one of solidarity.

Some non-white entertainers have used *nigger* in their acts. John Lennon and Yoko Ono, for example, entitled a song "Woman Is the Nigger of the World," and Patti Smith wrote "Rock 'n' Roll Nigger." But Lennon, Ono, and Smith performed in overwhelmingly white milieus. Rap, by contrast, is dominated by blacks. A few white rappers have achieved commercial success and won the respect of black artists and audiences. I am thinking here especially of the white rapper Eminem, a superstar in the hip-hop culture. Eminem has assumed many of the distinctive mannerisms of his black rap colleagues, making himself into a "brother" in many ways—in his music, his diction, his gait, his clothes, his associations. He refuses to say, however, any version of a word that his black hip-hop colleagues employ constantly as a matter of course; the nonchalance with which he tosses around epithets such as *bitch* and *faggot* does not extend to *nigger*. "That word," he insists, "is not even in my vocabulary."

Eminem is certainly following a prudent course, for many people, white and black alike, disapprove of a white person saying nigger under virtually any circumstance. "When we call each other 'nigger' it means no harm," Ice Cube remarks. "But if a white person uses it, it's something different, it's a racist word." Professor Michael Eric Dyson likewise asserts that whites must know and stay in their racial place when it comes to saying "nigger." He writes that "most white folk attracted to black culture know better than to cross a line drawn in the sand of racial history. *Nigger* has never been cool when spit from white lips."

The race line that Dyson applauds, however, is a specious divide. There is nothing necessarily wrong with a white person saying "nigger," just as there is nothing necessarily wrong with a black person saying it. What should matter is the context in which the word is spoken—the speaker's aims, effects, alternatives. To condemn whites who use the N-word without regard to context is simply to make a fetish of *nigger*. Harriet Beecher Stowe

(*Uncle Tom's Cabin*), Mark Twain (*Huckleberry Finn*), William Dean Howells (*An Imperative Duty*), Edward Sheldon (*The Nigger*), Eugene O'Neill (*All God's Chillun*), Lillian Smith (*Strange Fruit*), Sinclair Lewis (*Kingsblood Royal*), Joyce Carol Oates (*Them*), E. L. Doctorow (*Ragtime*), John Grisham (*A Time to Kill*), and numerous other white writers have unveiled *nigger*-as-insult in order to dramatize and condemn racism's baleful presence.

In 1967, President Lyndon Baines Johnson decided to appoint an African American to the Supreme Court for the first time in American history. First on Johnson's list of candidates was Thurgood Marshall—"Mr. Civil Rights," the hero of *Brown v. Board of Education* and, of course, the man he ended up putting on the Court. But before he announced his selection, Johnson asked an assistant to identify some other possible candidates. The aide mentioned A. Leon Higginbotham, whom Johnson had appointed to the federal trial bench. Reportedly, the president dismissed the suggestion with the comment "The only two people who have ever heard of Judge Higginbotham are you and his momma. When I appoint a nigger to the [Supreme Court], I want everyone to know he's a nigger." Was the use of *nigger* in this context a venting of racial prejudice? Maybe. Johnson had been raised in a thoroughly racist environment, had supported racist policies for a long period, and, as we have seen, casually used *nigger* as part of his private vocabulary before he became president. On this particular occasion, however, it seems likely that he was merely seeking to highlight the racial exclusion against which he was acting, parodying the old regime even as he sought to reform it. If this is an accurate assessment of the situation, I see nothing wrong with what Johnson said, and I applaud what he did.

Can a relationship between a black person and a white one be such that the white person should properly feel authorized, at least within the confines of that relationship, to use the N-word? For me the answer is yes. Carl Van Vechten, for instance, wrote of "niggers" in correspondence with his friend Langston Hughes, and Hughes did not object (though he did once write that *nigger* was a red flag for all Negroes). *Should* Hughes have objected? No. Van Vechten, a key supporter of the Harlem Renaissance, had shown time and again that he abhorred racial prejudice, would do what he could to improve the fortunes of African Americans, and treasured his black friends. It was against this backdrop of achieved trust that Hughes (and other black writers) rightly permitted Van Vechten to use *nigger* as so many African Americans have used it— as an ironic, shorthand spoof on the absurdity of American race relations.

As we have seen, *nigger* can mean many different things, depending upon, among other variables, intonation, the location of the interaction, and the relationship between the speaker and those to whom he is speaking. Generally a reference to people of color, particularly blacks, *nigger* can refer to people of any hue. Senator Robert C. Byrd (D. West Virginia) got into trouble for saying publicly that he "had seen a lot of white niggers in [his] time." But more and more the word is being applied ecumenically.

Sociologist John Hartigan reports that poor whites in Detroit often refer to their white neighbors as *niggers*. Typically they mean the word as an insult. But they do not necessarily mean for it to be a *racial* insult. Responding to an inquiry about a white-on-white deployment of *nigger*, one of the participants in Hartigan's study remarked: "He's a nigger, man, and you know what I mean by that. He's an asshole, and it doesn't matter whether a person's black or white, orange or plaid, he can still be a nigger if he runs his mouth like that asshole." Another white Detroiter observed by Hartigan echoed this sentiment. "You don't have to be black to be a nigger," he declared. "Niggers come in all colors." (Interestingly, he added: "We are all colored….There's about a hundred shades of white.")

The linguist Arthur K. Spears has also discerned an appreciable revision of *nigger*'s racial usage. He writes that "White public school teachers hear themselves referred to as 'that White nigga' or simply 'nigga,' and [that] Asian Americans in San Francisco can be heard, as they navigate high school hallways, to call one another niggas."

More vividly than most words, then, *nigger* illustrates Justice Oliver Wendell Holmes's observation that "a word is not a crystal, transparent and unchanged." A word is instead "the skin of a living thought [that] may vary greatly in color and content according to the circumstances and the time in which it is used."

Suggestions for Discussion

1. How has the meaning of the word "nigger" changed over time?

2. How have recent and modern stand-up comedians and rap musicians used the word?

3. Why might "eradicationists" argue for the elimination of the word "nigger" from existence?

4. The accompanying image, a painting by Markus Faust, shows an African-American male seated at a table. Examine the image carefully— the setting, clothing, posture, hairstyle, facial expression. What do you see and how do you respond to what you are seeing? Does reading Randall Kennedy's thoughts on African-Americans in popular culture make a difference to the way you respond to the image? In what ways?

Suggestion for Writing

What other names, labels, or slang-terms besides "nigger" might be considered offensive or have a different connotation depending on the speaker and the tone? Are the issues that Kennedy explores when dissecting "the protean N-word" applicable to this other term as well? Write an essay on the topic.

POETRY

SONIA SANCHEZ

A Poem for Ella Fitzgerald

Sonia Sanchez (b. 1934), a poet, playwright, and children's fiction writer, was born in Birmingham, AL, and moved to Harlem at the age of nine. She graduated from Hunter College with a political science degree and did graduate work at New York University before going on to become the first college professor to ever offer a course on African American women writers. She is a retired professor of creative writing and Black American literature at Temple University. She is the author of *I've Been a Woman* (1978), *Homegirls and Handgrenades* (1984), *Under a Soprano Sky* (1987), *Wounded in the House of a Friend* (1995), *Does Your House Have Lions?* (1997), *Like the Singing Coming off the Drums* (1998), and *Shake Loose My Skin* (1999).

when she came on the stage, this Ella
there were rumors of hurricanes and
over the rooftops of concert stages
the moon turned red in the sky,
it was Ella, Ella.
queen Ella had come
and words spilled out
leaving a trail of witnesses smiling
amen—amen—a woman—a woman.

she began
this three agèd woman
nightingales in her throat
and squads of horns came out
to greet her.

streams of violins and pianos
splashed their welcome
and our stained glass silences
our braided spaces
unraveled

opened up
said who's that coming?
who's that knocking at the door?
whose voice lingers on
that stage gone mad with
    perdido. perdido. perdido.
    i lost my heart in toledooooooo.

whose voice is climbing
up this morning chimney
smoking with life
carrying her basket of words
    a tisket a tasket
    my little yellow
    basket—i wrote a
    letter to my mom and
    on the way I dropped it—
    was it red…no no no no
    was it green…no no no no
    was it blue…no no no no
    just a little yellow

voice rescuing razor thin lyrics
from hopscotching dreams.

we first watched her navigating
an apollo stage amid high-stepping
yellow legs

we watched her watching us
shiny and pure woman
sugar and spice woman
her voice a nun's whisper
her voice pouring out
guitar thickened blues,
her voice a faraway horn
questioning the wind,
and she became Ella,
first lady of tongues
Ella cruising our veins
voice walking on water
crossed in prayer,
she became holy
a thousand sermons
concealed in her bones
as she raised them in a

symphonic shudder
carrying our sighs into
her bloodstream.

this voice, chasing the
morning waves,
this Ella-tonian voice soft
like four layers of lace.

> when i die Ella
> tell the whole joint
> please, please, don't talk
> about me when i'm gone....

i remember waiting one nite for her appearance
audience impatient at the lateness
of musicians
I remember it was april
and the flowers ran yellow
the sun downpoured yellow butterflies
and the day was yellow and silent
all of spring held us
in a single drop of blood.

when she appeared on stage
she became Nut arching over us
feet and hands placed on the stage
music flowing from her breasts
she swallowed the sun
sang confessions from the evening stars
made earth divulge her secrets
gave birth to skies in her song
remade the insistent air
and we became anointed found
inside her bop

> bop bop dowa
> bop bop doowaaa
> bop bop dooooowaaaa

Lady. Lady. Lady.
be good. be good
to me.

      to you.   to us all
cuz we just some lonesome babes
in the woods
hey lady. sweetellalady
Lady. Lady. Lady. be gooooood
ELLA ELLA ELLALADY
       be good
           gooooood
                goooooood…

Suggestions for Discussion

  1. How does Sanchez describe Ella Fitzgerald?

  2. What is the significance of the religious symbolism in the poem?

Suggestion for Writing

Were you ever moved to heights of emotion by music? Describe the experience in a poem.

The Cultural Tradition:
Art, the Artist, and Society

Reading is the creative center of a writer's life. I take a book with me everywhere I go, and find there are all sorts of opportunities to dip in. The trick is to teach yourself to read in small sips as well as in long swallows.

—STEPHEN KING, *On Writing*

In this sense fiction became the agency of my efforts to answer the questions. Who am I, what am I, how did I come to be? What shall I make of the life around me, what celebrate, what reject, how confront the snarl of good and evil which is inevitable?

—RALPH ELLISON, "On Becoming a Writer"

Self-Portrait on Garbage Can
ANTONY ZITO
Antony Zito Studio Gallery

NOTEBOOK

V. S. NAIPAUL

Two Worlds: Nobel Lecture 2001

V. S. Naipaul (b. 1932) left his native Trinidad in 1950 to attend University College at Oxford. He worked as a freelance journalist and broadcaster for the BBC's "Caribbean Voices" program before dedicating himself to writing. His works include *The Mystic Masseur* (1957), *A House for Mr. Biswas* (1961), *A Bend in the River* (1979), and a collection of letters, *Between Father and Son* (1990). *The Writer and the World* (2002) is a compilation of essays based on his travels throughout Africa, America, and Asia. Naipaul gave the following speech after winning the 2001 Nobel Prize for Literature.

This is unusual for me. I have given readings and not lectures. I have told people who ask for lectures that I have no lecture to give. And that is true. It might seem strange that a man who has dealt in words and emotions and ideas for nearly fifty years shouldn't have a few to spare, so to speak. But everything of value about me is in my books. Whatever extra there is in me at any given moment isn't fully formed. I am hardly aware of it; it awaits the next book. It will—with luck—come to me during the actual writing, and it will take me by surprise. That element of surprise is what I look for when I am writing. It is my way of judging what I am doing—which is never an easy thing to do.

Proust has written with great penetration of the difference between the writer as writer and the writer as a social being. You will find his thoughts in some of his essays in *Against Sainte-Beuve*, a book reconstituted from his early papers.

The nineteenth-century French critic Sainte-Beuve believed that to understand a writer it was necessary to know as much as possible about the exterior man, the details of his life. It is a beguiling method, using the man to illuminate the work. It might seem unassailable. But Proust is able very convincingly to pick it apart. "This method of Sainte-Beuve," Proust writes, "ignores what a very slight degree of self-acquaintance teaches us: that a book is the product of a different self from the self we manifest in our habits, in our social life, in our vices. If we would try to understand that particular self, it is by searching our own bosoms, and trying to reconstruct it there, that we may arrive at it."

Those words of Proust should be with us whenever we are reading the biography of a writer—or the biography of anyone who depends on what can be called inspiration. All the details of the life and the quirks and the friendships can be laid out for us, but the mystery of the writing will remain. No amount of documentation, however fascinating, can take us there. The biography of a writer—or even the autobiography—will always have this incompleteness.

Proust is a master of happy amplification, and I would like to go back to *Against Sainte-Beuve* just for a little. "In fact," Proust writes, "it is the secretions of one's innermost self, written in solitude and for oneself alone that one gives to the public. What one bestows on private life—in conversation...or in those drawing-room essays that are scarcely more than conversation in print—is the product of a quite superficial self, not of the innermost self which one can only recover by putting aside the world and the self that frequents the world."

When he wrote that, Proust had not yet found the subject that was to lead him to the happiness of his great literary labour. And you can tell from what I have quoted that he was a man trusting to his intuition and waiting for luck. I have quoted these words before in other places. The reason is that they define how I have gone about my business. I have trusted to intuition. I did it at the beginning. I do it even now. I have no idea how things might turn out, where in my writing I might go next. I have trusted to my intuition to find the subjects, and I have written intuitively. I have an idea when I start, I have a shape; but I will fully understand what I have written only after some years.

I said earlier that everything of value about me is in my books. I will go further now. I will say I am the sum of my books. Each book, intuitively sensed and, in the case of fiction, intuitively worked out, stands on what has gone before, and grows out of it. I feel that at any stage of my literary career it could have been said that the last book contained all the others.

It's been like this because of my background. My background is at once exceedingly simple and exceedingly confused. I was born in Trinidad. It is a small island in the mouth of the great Orinoco river of Venezuela. So Trinidad is not strictly of South America, and not strictly of the Caribbean. It was developed as a New World plantation colony, and when I was born in 1932 it had a population of about 400,000. Of this, about 150,000 were Indians, Hindus and Muslims, nearly all of peasant origin, and nearly all from the Gangetic plain.

This was my very small community. The bulk of this migration from India occurred after 1880. The deal was like this. People indentured themselves for five years to serve on the estates. At the end of this time they were given a small piece of land, perhaps five acres, or a passage back to India. In 1917, because of agitation by Gandhi and others, the indenture system was abolished. And perhaps because of this, or for some other reason, the pledge of land or repatriation was dishonoured for many of the later arrivals. These people were absolutely destitute. They slept in the streets of Port of Spain, the capital. When I was a child I saw them. I suppose I didn't know they were destitute—I suppose that idea came much later—and they made no impression on me. This was part of the cruelty of the plantation colony.

I was born in a small country town called Chaguanas, two or three miles inland from the Gulf of Paria. Chaguanas was a strange name, in spelling and pronunciation, and many of the Indian people—they were in the majority in the area—preferred to call it by the Indian caste name of Chauhan.

I was thirty-four when I found out about the name of my birthplace. I was living in London, had been living in England for sixteen years. I was writing my ninth book. This was a history of Trinidad, a human history, trying to re-create people and their stories. I used to go to the British Museum to read the Spanish documents about the region. These documents—recovered from the Spanish archives—were copied out for the British government in the 1890s at the time of a nasty boundary dispute with Venezuela. The documents begin in 1530 and end with the disappearance of the Spanish Empire.

I was reading about the foolish search for El Dorado, and the murderous interloping of the English hero, Sir Walter Raleigh. In 1595 he raided Trinidad, killed all the Spaniards he could, and went up the Orinoco looking for El Dorado. He found nothing, but when he went back to England he said he had. He had a piece of gold and some sand to show. He said he had hacked the gold out of a cliff on the bank of the Orinoco. The Royal Mint said that the sand he asked them to assay was worthless, and other people said that he had bought the gold beforehand from North Africa. He then published a book to prove his point, and for four centuries people have believed that Raleigh had found something. The magic of Raleigh's book, which is really quite difficult to read, lay in its very long title: *The Discovery of the Large, Rich, and Beautiful Empire of Guiana, with a relation of the great and golden city of Manoa (which the Spaniards call El Dorado) and the provinces of Emeria, Aromaia, Amapaia, and other countries, with their rivers adjoining.* How real it sounds! And he had hardly been on the main Orinoco.

And then, as sometimes happens with confidence men, Raleigh was caught by his own fantasies. Twenty-one years later, old and ill, he was let out of his London prison to go to Guiana and find the gold mines he said he had found. In this fraudulent venture his son died. The father, for the sake of his reputation, for the sake of his lies, had sent his son to his death. And then Raleigh, full of grief, with nothing left to live for, went back to London to be executed.

The story should have ended there. But Spanish memories were long—no doubt because their imperial correspondence was so slow: it might take up to two years for a letter from Trinidad to be read in Spain. Eight years afterwards the Spaniards of Trinidad and Guiana were still settling their scores with the Gulf Indians. One day in the British Museum I read a letter from the King of Spain to the governor of Trinidad. It was dated 12 October 1625.

"I asked you," the King wrote, "to give me some information about a certain nation of Indians called Chaguanes, who you say number above one thousand, and are of such bad disposition that it was they who led the English when they captured the town. Their crime hasn't been punished because forces were not available for this purpose and because the Indians acknowledge no master save their own will. You have decided to give them a punishment. Follow the rules I have given you; and let me know how you get on."

What the governor did I don't know. I could find no further reference to the Chaguanes in the documents in the Museum. Perhaps there were other documents about the Chaguanes in the mountain of paper in the Spanish archives in Seville which the British government scholars missed or didn't think important enough to copy out. What is true is that the little tribe of over a thousand—who would have been living on both sides of the Gulf of Paria—disappeared so completely that no one in the town of Chaguanas or Chauhan knew anything about them. And the thought came to me in the Museum that I was the first person since 1625 to whom that letter of the king of Spain had a real meaning. And that letter had been dug out of the archives only in 1896 or 1897. A disappearance, and then the silence of centuries.

We lived on the Chaguanes' land. Every day in term time—I was just beginning to go to school—I walked from my grandmother's house—past the two or three main-road stores, the Chinese parlour, the Jubilee Theatre, and the high-smelling little Portuguese factory that made cheap blue soap and cheap yellow soap in long bars that were put out to dry and harden in the mornings—every day I walked past these eternal-seeming things—to the Chaguanas Government School. Beyond the school was sugar-cane, estate land, going up to the Gulf of Paria. The people who had been dispossessed would have had their own kind of agriculture, their own calendar, their own codes, their own sacred sites. They would have understood the Orinoco-fed currents in the Gulf of Paria. Now all their skills and everything else about them had been obliterated.

The world is always in movement. People have everywhere at some time been dispossessed. I suppose I was shocked by this discovery in 1967 about my birthplace because I had never had any idea about it. But that was the way most of us lived in the agricultural colony, blindly. There was no plot by the authorities to keep us in our darkness. I think it was more simply that the knowledge wasn't there. The kind of knowledge about the Chaguanes would not have been considered important, and it would not have been easy

to recover. They were a small tribe, and they were aboriginal. Such people—
on the mainland, in what was called B. G., British Guiana—were known to
us, and were a kind of joke. People who were loud and ill-behaved were
known, to all groups in Trinidad, I think, as *warrahoons*. I used to think it
was a made-up word, made up to suggest wildness. It was only when I began
to travel in Venezuela, in my forties, that I understood that a word like that
was the name of a rather large aboriginal tribe there.

There was a vague story when I was a child—and to me now it is an
unbearably affecting story—that at certain times aboriginal people came
across in canoes from the mainland, walked through the forest in the south
of the island, and at a certain spot picked some kind of fruit or made some
kind of offering, and then went back across the Gulf of Paria to the sodden
estuary of the Orinoco. The rite must have been of enormous importance
to have survived the upheavals of four hundred years, and the extinction of
the aborigines in Trinidad. Or perhaps—though Trinidad and Venezuela
have a common flora—they had come only to pick a particular kind of fruit.
I don't know. I can't remember anyone inquiring. And now the memory is
all lost; and that sacred site, if it existed, has become common ground.

What was past was past. I suppose that was the general attitude. And we
Indians, immigrants from India, had that attitude to the island. We lived for
the most part ritualised lives, and were not yet capable of self-assessment,
which is where learning begins. Half of us on this land of the Chaguanes
were pretending—perhaps not pretending, perhaps only feeling, never formulating it as an idea—that we had brought a kind of India with us, which
we could, as it were, unroll like a carpet on the flat land.

My grandmother's house in Chaguanas was in two parts. The front part,
of bricks and plaster, was painted white. It was like a kind of Indian house,
with a grand balustraded terrace on the upper floor, and a prayer-room on
the floor above that. It was ambitious in its decorative detail, with lotus capitals on pillars, and sculptures of Hindu deities, all done by people working
only from a memory of things in India. In Trinidad it was an architectural
oddity. At the back of this house, and joined to it by an upper bridge room,
was a timber building in the French Caribbean style. The entrance gate was
at the side, between the two houses. It was a tall gate of corrugated iron on
a wooden frame. It made for a fierce kind of privacy.

So as a child I had this sense of two worlds, the world outside that tall
corrugated-iron gate, and the world at home—or, at any rate, the world of
my grandmother's house. It was a remnant of our caste sense, the thing that
excluded and shut out. In Trinidad, where as new arrivals we were a disadvantaged community, that excluding idea was a kind of protection; it
enabled us—for the time being, and only for the time being—to live in our
own way and according to our own rules, to live in our own fading India. It
made for an extraordinary self-centredness. We looked inwards; we lived

out our days; the world outside existed in a kind of darkness; we inquired about nothing.

There was a Muslim shop next door. The little loggia of my grandmother's shop ended against his blank wall. The man's name was Mian. That was all that we knew of him and his family. I suppose we must have seen him, but I have no mental picture of him now. We knew nothing of Muslims. This idea of strangeness, of the thing to be kept outside, extended even to other Hindus. For example, we ate rice in the middle of the day, and wheat in the evenings. There were some extraordinary people who reversed this natural order and ate rice in the evenings. I thought of these people as strangers— you must imagine me at this time as under seven, because when I was seven all this life of my grandmother's house in Chaguanas came to an end for me. We moved to the capital, and then to the hills to the northwest.

But the habits of mind engendered by this shut-in and shutting-out life lingered for quite a while. If it were not for the short stories my father wrote I would have known almost nothing about the general life of our Indian community. Those stories gave me more than knowledge. They gave me a kind of solidity. They gave me something to stand on in the world. I cannot imagine what my mental picture would have been without those stories.

The world outside existed in a kind of darkness; and we inquired about nothing. I was just old enough to have some idea of the Indian epics, the Ramayana in particular. The children who came five years or so after me in our extended family didn't have this luck. No one taught us Hindi. Sometimes someone wrote out the alphabet for us to learn, and that was that; we were expected to do the rest ourselves. So, as English penetrated, we began to lose our language. My grandmother's house was full of religion; there were many ceremonies and readings, some of which went on for days. But no one explained or translated for us who could no longer follow the language. So our ancestral faith receded, became mysterious, not pertinent to our day-to-day life.

We made no inquiries about India or about the families people had left behind. When our ways of thinking had changed, and we wished to know, it was too late. I know nothing of the people on my father's side; I know only that some of them came from Nepal. Two years ago a kind Nepalese who liked my name sent me a copy of some pages from an 1872 gazetteer-like British work about India, *Hindu Castes and Tribes as Represented in Benares;* the pages listed—among a multitude of names—those groups of Nepalese in the holy city of Banaras who carried the name Naipal. That is all that I have.

Away from this world of my grandmother's house, where we ate rice in the middle of the day and wheat in the evenings, there was the great unknown— in this island of only 400,000 people. There were the African or African-derived people who were the majority. They were policemen; they were teachers. One of them was my very first teacher at the Chaguanas Government School; I remembered her with adoration for years. There was the capital, where very soon we would all have to go for education and jobs, and where we would settle permanently, among strangers. There were the white people, not all of them English; and the Portuguese and the Chinese, at one time also immigrants like us. And, more mysterious than these, were the people we called Spanish, 'pagnols, mixed people of warm brown complexions who came from the Spanish time, before the island was detached from Venezuela and the Spanish Empire—a kind of history absolutely beyond my child's comprehension.

To give you this idea of my background, I have had to call on knowledge and ideas that came to me much later, principally from my writing. As a child I knew almost nothing, nothing beyond what I had picked up in my grandmother's house. All children, I suppose, come into the world like that, not knowing who they are. But for the French child, say, that knowledge is waiting. That knowledge will be all around them. It will come indirectly from the conversation of their elders. It will be in the newspapers and on the radio. And at school the work of generations of scholars, scaled down for school texts, will provide some idea of France and the French.

In Trinidad, bright boy though I was, I was surrounded by areas of darkness. School elucidated nothing for me. I was crammed with facts and formulas. Everything had to be learned by heart; everything was abstract for me. Again, I do not believe there was a plan or plot to make our courses like that. What we were getting was standard school learning. In another setting it would have made sense. And at least some of the failing would have lain in me. With my limited social background it was hard for me imaginatively to enter into other societies or societies that were far away. I loved the idea of books, but I found it hard to read them. I got on best with things like Andersen and Aesop, timeless, placeless, not excluding. And when at last in the sixth form, the highest form in the college, I got to like some of our literature texts—Molière, Cyrano de Bergerac—I suppose it was because they had the quality of the fairytale.

When I became a writer those areas of darkness around me as a child became my subjects. The land; the aborigines; the New World; the colony; the history; India; the Muslim world, to which I also felt myself related; Africa; and then England, where I was doing my writing. That was what I meant when I said that my books stand one on the other, and that I am the sum of my books. That was what I meant when I said that my background, the source and prompting of my work, was at once exceedingly simple and exceedingly complicated. You will have seen how simple it was in the country town of Chaguanas. And I think you will understand how complicated it was for me as a writer. Especially in the beginning, when the literary models I had—the models given me by what I can only call my false learning— dealt with entirely different societies. But perhaps you might feel that the material was so rich it would have been no trouble at all to get started and to go on. What I have said about the background, however, comes from the knowledge I acquired with my writing. And you must believe me when I tell you that the pattern in my work has only become clear in the last two months or so. Passages from old books were read to me, and I saw the connections. Until then the greatest trouble for me was to describe my writing to people, to say what I had done.

I said I was an intuitive writer. That was so, and that remains so now, when I am nearly at the end. I never had a plan. I followed no system. I worked intuitively. My aim every time was do a book, to create something that would be easy and interesting to read. At every stage I could only work within my knowledge and sensibility and talent and world-view. Those things developed book by book. And I had to do the books I did because there were no books about those subjects to give me what I wanted. I had to clear up my world, elucidate it, for myself.

I had to go to the documents in the British Museum and elsewhere, to get the true feel of the history of the colony. I had to travel to India because there was no one to tell me what the India my grandparents had come from was like. There was the writing of Nehru and Gandhi; and strangely it was Gandhi, with his South African experience, who gave me more, but not enough. There was Kipling; there were British-Indian writers like John Masters (going very strong in the 1950s, with an announced plan, later abandoned, I fear, for thirty-five connected novels about British India); there were romances by women writers. The few Indian writers who had come up at that time were middle-class people, town-dwellers; they didn't know the India we had come from.

And when that Indian need was satisfied, others became apparent: Africa, South America, the Muslim world. The aim has always been to fill out my world picture, and the purpose comes from my childhood: to make me more at ease with myself. Kind people have sometimes written asking me to go and write about Germany, say, or China. But there is much good writing already about those places; I am willing to depend there on the writing that exists. And those subjects are for other people. Those were not the areas of darkness I felt about me as a child. So, just as there is a development in my work, a development in narrative skill and knowledge and sensibility, so there is a kind of unity, a focus, though I might appear to be going in many directions.

When I began I had no idea of the way ahead. I wished only to do a book. I was trying to write in England, where I stayed on after my years at the university, and it seemed to me that my experience was very thin, was not truly of the stuff of books. I could find in no book anything that came near my background. The young French or English person who wished to write would have found any number of models to set him on his way. I had none. My father's stories about our Indian community belonged to the past. My world was quite different. It was more urban, more mixed. The simple physical details of the chaotic life of our extended family—sleeping rooms or sleeping spaces, eating times, the sheer number of people—seemed impossible to handle. There was too much to be explained, both about my home life and about the world outside. And at the same time there was also too much about us—like our own ancestry and history—that I didn't know.

At last one day there came to me the idea of starting with the Port of Spain street to which we had moved from Chaguanas. There was no big corrugated-iron gate shutting out the world there. The life of the street was open to me. It was an intense pleasure for me to observe it from the verandah. This street life was what I began to write about. I wished to write fast, to avoid too much self-questioning, and so I simplified. I suppressed the child-narrator's background. I ignored the racial and social complexities of the street. I explained nothing. I stayed at ground level, so to speak. I presented people only as they appeared on the street. I wrote a story a day. The first stories were very short. I was worried about the material lasting long enough. But then the writing did its magic. The material began to present itself to me from many sources. The stories became longer; they couldn't be written in a day. And then the inspiration, which at one stage had seemed very easy, rolling me along, came to an end. But a book had been written, and I had in my own mind become a writer.

The distance between the writer and his material grew with the two later books; the vision was wider. And then intuition led me to a large book about our family life. During this book my writing ambition grew. But when it was over I felt I had done all that I could do with my island material. No matter how much I meditated on it, no further fiction would come.

Accident, then, rescued me. I became a traveller. I travelled in the Caribbean region and understood much more about the colonial set-up of which I had been part. I went to India, my ancestral land, for a year; it was a journey that broke my life in two. The books that I wrote about these two journeys took me to new realms of emotion, gave me a world-view I had never had, extended me technically. I was able in the fiction that then came to me to take in England as well as the Caribbean—and how hard that was to do. I was able also to take in all the racial groups of the island, which I had never before been able to do.

This new fiction was about colonial shame and fantasy, a book, in fact, about how the powerless lie about themselves, and lie to themselves, since it is their only resource. The book was called *The Mimic Men*. And it was not about mimics. It was about colonial men mimicking the condition of manhood, men who had grown to distrust everything about themselves.

Some pages of this book were read to me the other day—I hadn't looked at it for more than thirty years—and it occurred to me that I had been writing about colonial schizophrenia. But I hadn't thought of it like that. I had never used abstract words to describe any writing purpose of mine. If I had, I would never have been able to do the book. The book was done intuitively, and only out of close observation.

I have done this little survey of the early part of my career to try to show the stages by which, in just ten years, my birthplace had altered or developed in my writing: from the comedy of street life to a study of a kind of widespread schizophrenia. What was simple had become complicated.

Both fiction and the travel-book form have given me my way of looking; and you will understand why for me all literary forms are equally valuable. It came to me, for instance, when I set out to write my third book about India—twenty-six years after the first—that what was most important about a travel book were the people the writer travelled among. The people had to define themselves. A simple enough idea, but it required a new kind of book; it called for a new way of travelling. And it was the very method I used later when I went, for the second time, into the Muslim world.

I have always moved by intuition alone. I have no system, literary or political. I have no guiding political idea. I think that probably lies with my ancestry. The Indian writer R K Narayan, who died this year, had no political idea. My father, who wrote his stories in a very dark time, and for no reward, had no political idea. Perhaps it is because we have been far from authority for many centuries. It gives us a special point of view. I feel we are more inclined to see the humour and pity of things.

Nearly thirty years ago I went to Argentina. It was at the time of the guerrilla crisis. People were waiting for the old dictator Perón to come back from exile. The country was full of hate. Peronists were waiting to settle old scores. One such man said to me, "There is good torture and bad torture." Good torture was what you did to the enemies of the people. Bad torture was what the enemies of the people did to you. People on the other side were saying the same thing. There was no true debate about anything. There was only passion and the borrowed political jargon of Europe. I wrote, "Where jargon turns living issues into abstractions, and where jargon ends by competing with jargon, people don't have causes. They only have enemies."

And the passions of Argentina are still working themselves out, still defeating reason and consuming lives. No resolution is in sight.

I am near the end of my work now. I am glad to have done what I have done, glad creatively to have pushed myself as far as I could go. Because of the intuitive way in which I have written, and also because of the baffling nature of my material, every book has come as a blessing. Every book has amazed me; up to the moment of writing I never knew it was there. But the greatest miracle for me was getting started. I feel—and the anxiety is still vivid to me—that I might easily have failed before I began.

I will end as I began, with one of the marvellous little essays of Proust in *Against Sainte-Beuve*. "The beautiful things we shall write if we have talent," Proust says, "are inside us, indistinct, like the memory of a melody which delights us though we are unable to recapture its outline. Those who are obsessed by this blurred memory of truths they have never known are the men who are gifted...Talent is like a sort of memory which will enable them finally to bring this indistinct music closer to them, to hear it clearly, to note it down..."

Talent, Proust says. I would say luck, and much labour.

Suggestions for Discussion

1. Why was Naipaul reluctant to give this speech?

2. What does Naipaul mean when he claims to be "the sum of [his] books"?

3. What are the "Two Worlds" referred to by the title of this address?

4. How did Naipaul cultivate a better understanding of his childhood and his native culture as he grew older? From where did this self-awareness come?

5. How has Naipaul's writing style evolved? To what extent have the changes that he has experienced in his own life influenced his writing?

6. According to Naipaul, why isn't the biography of an author an effective key in unlocking the secret meaning of a book? What is "the mystery of writing" that remains?

Suggestion for Writing

Do you feel wiser now than you were when you were younger? Is there some sense of understanding or awareness that you have now that helps you fairly evaluate the events of your childhood and the cultural roots that you have sprung from? Are there still things about yourself that you do not understand? How has the journey that your life has taken affected your work and your hobbies? Write a speech, to be given before your class, in which you consider these questions aloud.

❦

STEPHEN KING

On Writing

Stephen King (b. 1947), the famous horror novelist, has written scores of books in the genre, many of which were made into highly successful motion pictures. Critics have noted that his protagonists, both in his horror works and his dramas, are often children or intellectual young men who find themselves pitted against sinister authority figures. The Bangor, ME, resident is best known for the novels *Carrie, The Shining, 'Salem's Lot, The Stand, Misery, Cujo,* and *The Dead Zone.* King also wrote a book of essays on the gothic genre called *Danse Macabre* (1980), and his most acclaimed forays outside of the supernatural are the dramatic novellas *Rita Hayworth and the Shawshank Redemption* and *Stand By Me* (also known as *The Body*), both of which appeared in his 1982 book *Different Seasons.* His recent works include *From a Buick 8* (2002), *The Colorado Kid* (2005), and *On Writing* (2000), a combination memoir and guidebook to aspiring writers, from which the following passage is reprinted.

If you want to be a writer, you must do two things above all others: read a lot and write a lot. There's no way around these two things that I'm aware of, no shortcut.

I'm a slow reader, but I usually get through seventy or eighty books a year, mostly fiction. I don't read in order to study the craft; I read because I like to read. It's what I do at night, kicked back in my blue chair. Similarly, I don't read fiction to study the art of fiction, but simply because I like stories. Yet there is a learning process going on. Every book you pick up has its own lesson or lessons, and quite often the bad books have more to teach than the good ones.

When I was in the eighth grade, I happened upon a paperback novel by Murray Leinster, a science fiction pulp writer who did most of his work during the forties and fifties, when magazines like *Amazing Stories* paid a penny a word. I had read other books by Mr. Leinster, enough to know that the quality of his writing was uneven. This particular tale, which was about mining in the asteroid belt, was one of his less successful efforts. Only that's too kind. It was terrible, actually, a story populated by paper-thin characters and driven by outlandish plot developments. Worst of all (or so it seemed to me at the time), Leinster had fallen in love with the word *zestful*.

Characters watched the approach of ore-bearing asteroids with *zestful smiles*. Characters sat down to supper aboard their mining ship with *zestful anticipation*. Near the end of the book, the hero swept the large-breasted, blonde heroine into a *zestful embrace*. For me, it was the literary equivalent of a smallpox vaccination: I have never, so far as I know, used the word *zestful* in a novel or a story. God willing, I never will.

Asteroid Miners (which wasn't the title, but that's close enough) was an important book in my life as a reader. Almost everyone can remember losing his or her virginity, and most writers can remember the first book he/she put down thinking: *I can do better than this. Hell, I am doing better than this!* What could be more encouraging to the struggling writer than to realize his/her work is unquestionably better than that of someone who actually got paid for his/her stuff?

One learns most clearly what not to do by reading bad prose—one novel like *Asteroid Miners* (or *Valley of the Dolls, Flowers in the Attic,* and *The Bridges of Madison County,* to name just a few) is worth a semester at a good writing school, even with the superstar guest lecturers thrown in.

Good writing, on the other hand, teaches the learning writer about style, graceful narration, plot development, the creation of believable characters, and truth-telling. A novel like *The Grapes of Wrath* may fill a new writer with feelings of despair and good old-fashioned jealousy—"I'll never be able to write anything that good, not if I live to be a thousand"—but such feelings can also serve as a spur, goading the writer to work harder and aim higher. Being swept away by a combination of great story and great writing—of being flattened, in fact—is part of every writer's necessary formation. You cannot hope to sweep someone else away by the force of your writing until it has been done to you.

So we read to experience the mediocre and the outright rotten; such experience helps us to recognize those things when they begin to creep into our own work, and to steer clear of them. We also read in order to measure ourselves against the good and the great, to get a sense of all that can be done. And we read in order to experience different styles.

You may find yourself adopting a style you find particularly exciting, and there's nothing wrong with that. When I read Ray Bradbury as a kid, I wrote like Ray Bradbury—everything green and wondrous and seen through a lens smeared with the grease of nostalgia. When I read James M. Cain, everything I wrote came out clipped and stripped and hard-boiled. When I read Lovecraft, my prose became luxurious and Byzantine. I wrote stories in my teenage years where all these styles merged, creating a kind of hilarious stew. This sort of stylistic blending is a necessary part of developing one's own style, but it doesn't occur in a vacuum. You have to read widely, constantly refining (and redefining) your own work as you do so. It's hard for me to believe that people who read very little (or not at all in some cases) should presume to write and expect people to like what they have written, but I know it's true. If I had a nickel for every person who ever told me he/she wanted to become a writer but "didn't have time to read," I could buy myself a pretty good steak dinner. Can I be blunt on this subject? If you don't have time to read, you don't have the time (or the tools) to write. Simple as that.

Reading is the creative center of a writer's life. I take a book with me everywhere I go, and find there are all sorts of opportunities to dip in. The trick is to teach yourself to read in small sips as well as in long swallows. Waiting rooms were made for books—of course! But so are theater lobbies before the show, long and boring checkout lines, and everyone's favorite, the john. You can even read while you're driving, thanks to the audiobook revolution. Of the books I read each year, anywhere from six to a dozen are on tape. As for all the wonderful radio you will be missing, come on—how many times can you listen to Deep Purple sing "Highway Star"?

Reading at meals is considered rude in polite society, but if you expect to succeed as a writer, rudeness should be the second-to-least of your concerns. The least of all should be polite society and what it expects. If you intend to write as truthfully as you can, your days as a member of polite society are numbered, anyway.

Where else can you read? There's always the treadmill, or whatever you use down at the local health club to get aerobic. I try to spend an hour doing that every day, and I think I'd go mad without a good novel to keep me company. Most exercise facilities (at home as well as outside it) are now equipped with TVs, but TV—while working out or anywhere else—really is about the last thing an aspiring writer needs. If you feel you must have the news analyst blowhards on CNN while you exercise, or the stock market blowhards on MSNBC, or the sports blowhards on ESPN, it's time for you to question how serious you really are about becoming a writer. You must be prepared to do some serious turning inward toward the life of the imagination, and that means, I'm afraid, that Geraldo, Keith Olbermann, and Jay Leno must go. Reading takes time, and the glass teat takes too much of it.

Once weaned from the ephemeral craving for TV, most people will find they enjoy the time they spend reading. I'd like to suggest that turning off that endlessly quacking box is apt to improve the quality of your life as well as the quality of your writing. And how much of a sacrifice are we talking about here? How many *Frasier* and *ER* reruns does it take to make one American life complete? How many Richard Simmons infomercials? How many whiteboy/fatboy Beltway insiders on CNN? Oh man, don't get me started. Jerry-Springer-Dr.-Dre-Judge-Judy-Jerry-Falwell-Donny-and-Marie, I rest my case.

When my son Owen was seven or so, he fell in love with Bruce Springsteen's E Street Band, particularly with Clarence Clemons, the band's burly sax player. Owen decided he wanted to learn to play like Clarence. My wife and I were amused and delighted by this ambition. We were also hopeful, as any parent would be, that our kid would turn out to be talented, perhaps even some sort of prodigy. We got Owen a tenor saxophone for Christmas and lessons with Gordon Bowie, one of the local music men. Then we crossed our fingers and hoped for the best.

Seven months later I suggested to my wife that it was time to discontinue the sax lessons, if Owen concurred. Owen did, and with palpable relief—he hadn't wanted to say it himself, especially not after asking for the sax in the first place, but seven months had been long enough for him to realize that, while he might love Clarence Clemons's big sound, the saxophone was simply not for him—God had not given him that particular talent.

I knew, not because Owen stopped practicing, but because he was practicing only during the periods Mr. Bowie had set for him: half an hour after school four days a week, plus an hour on the weekends. Owen mastered the scales and the notes—nothing wrong with his memory, his lungs, or his eye–hand coordination—but we never heard him taking off, surprising himself with something new, blissing himself out. And as soon as his practice time was over, it was back into the case with the horn, and there it stayed until the next lesson or practice-time. What this suggested to me was that when it came to the sax and my son, there was never going to be any real play-time; it was all going to be rehearsal. That's no good. If there's no joy in it, it's just no good. It's best to go on to some other area, where the deposits of talent may be richer and the fun quotient higher.

Talent renders the whole idea of rehearsal meaningless; when you find something at which you are talented, you do it (whatever *it* is) until your fingers bleed or your eyes are ready to fall out of your head. Even when no one is listening (or reading, or watching), every outing is a bravura performance, because you as the creator are happy. Perhaps even ecstatic. That goes for reading and writing as well as for playing a musical instrument, hitting a baseball, or running the four-forty. The sort of strenuous reading and writing program I advocate—four to six hours a day, every day—will not seem strenuous if you really enjoy doing these things and have an aptitude for them; in fact, you may be following such a program already. If you feel you need permission to do all the reading and writing your little heart desires, however, consider it hereby granted by yours truly.

The real importance of reading is that it creates an ease and intimacy with the process of writing; one comes to the country of the writer with one's papers and identification pretty much in order. Constant reading will pull you into a place (a mind-set, if you like the phrase) where you can write eagerly and without self-consciousness. It also offers you a constantly growing knowledge of what has been done and what hasn't, what is trite and what is fresh, what works and what just lies there dying (or dead) on the page. The more you read, the less apt you are to make a fool of yourself with your pen or word processor.

Suggestions for Discussion

1. Why does King feel that reading bad books can have a positive effect on a budding writer? What effect can the reading of good writing have?
2. According to King, why is it so necessary to read a lot and to write a lot in order to be a good writer?
3. What kinds of sacrifices does King believe a writer must make if he or she expects to succeed at becoming a good writer?

Suggestion for Writing

Take a dreadful story, poem, play, or screenplay and extensively rewrite it to make it great.

RALPH ELLISON

On Becoming a Writer

Ralph Ellison (1914–1994), the distinguished American writer, was born in Oklahoma City. In the 1930s, he was a student at the Tuskegee Institute, which granted him an honorary Ph.D. in human letters in 1963. He held honorary degrees from other American universities. was a visiting professor of writing in many of them, and was professor emeritus of English at New York University. Ellison is best known for *The Invisible Man* (1952). His other works include *Going to the Territory* (1986) and *Shadow and Act* (1964), a collection of essays from which is taken the following reminiscence of becoming aware of what it means to be an "American Negro."

In the beginning writing was far from a serious matter; it was a reflex of reading, an extension of a source of pleasure, escape, and instruction. In fact, I had become curious about writing by way of seeking to understand the aesthetic nature of literary power, the devices through which literature could command my mind and emotions. It was not, then, the *process* of writing which initially claimed my attention, but the finished creations, the artifacts, poems, plays, novels. The act of learning writing technique was, therefore, an amusing investigation of what seemed at best a secondary talent, an exploration, like dabbling in sculpture, of one's potentialities as a "Renaissance Man." This, surely, would seem a most unlikely and even comic concept to introduce here; and yet, it is precisely because I come from where I do (the Oklahoma of the years between World War I and the Great Depression) that I must introduce it, and with a straight face.

Anything and everything was to be found in the chaos of Oklahoma; thus the concept of the Renaissance Man has lurked long within the shadow of my past, and I shared it with at least a half dozen of my Negro friends. How we actually acquired it I have never learned, and since there is no true sociology of the dispersion of ideas within the American democracy, I doubt if I ever shall. Perhaps we breathed it in with the air of the Negro community of Oklahoma City, the capital of that state whose Negroes were often charged by exasperated white Texans with not knowing their "place." Perhaps we took it defiantly from one of them. Or perhaps I myself picked it up from some transplanted New Englander whose shoes I had shined on a Saturday afternoon. After all, the most meaningful tips do not always come in the form of money, nor are they intentionally extended. Most likely, however, my friends and I acquired the idea from some book or some idealistic Negro teacher, some dreamer seeking to function responsibly in an environment which at its most normal took on some of the mixed character of nightmare and of dream.

One thing is certain, ours was a chaotic community, still characterized by frontier attitudes and by that strange mixture of the naive and sophisticated, the benign and malignant, which makes the American past so puzzling and its present so confusing; that mixture which often affords the minds of the young who grow up in the far provinces such wide and unstructured latitude, and which encourages the individual's imagination—up to the moment "reality" closes in upon him—to range widely and, sometimes, even to soar.

We hear the effects of this in the Southwestern jazz of the 30's, that joint creation of artistically free and exuberantly creative adventurers, of artists who had stumbled upon the freedom lying within the restrictions of their musical tradition as within the limitations of their social background, and who in their own unconscious way have set an example for any Americans, Negro or white, who would find themselves in the arts. They accepted themselves and the complexity of life as they knew it, they loved their art and through it they celebrated American experience definitively in sound. Whatever others thought or felt, this was their own powerful statement, and only non-musical assaults upon their artistic integrity—mainly economically inspired changes of fashion—were able to compromise their vision.

Much of so-called Kansas City jazz was actually brought to perfection in Oklahoma by Oklahomans. It is an important circumstance for me as a writer to remember, because while these musicians and their fellows were busy creating out of tradition, imagination, and the sounds and emotions around them, a freer, more complex, and driving form of jazz, my friends and I were exploring an idea of human versatility and possibility which went against the barbs or over the palings of almost every fence which those who controlled social and political power had erected to restrict our roles in the life of the country. Looking back, one might say that the jazzmen, some of whom we idolized, were in their own way better examples for youth to follow than were most judges and ministers, legislators and governors (we were stuck with the notorious Alfalfa Bill Murray). For as we viewed these pillars of society from the confines of our segregated community we almost always saw crooks, clowns, or hypocrites. Even the best were revealed by their attitudes toward us as lacking the respectable qualities to which they pretended and for which they were accepted outside by others, while despite the outlaw nature of their art, the jazzmen were less torn and damaged by the moral compromises and insincerities which have so sickened the life of our country.

Be that as it may, our youthful sense of life, like that of many Negro children (though no one bothers to note it—especially the specialists and "friends of the Negro" who view our Negro-American life as essentially non-human) was very much like that of Huckleberry Finn, who is universally so praised and enjoyed for the clarity and courage of his moral vision. Like Huck, we observed, we judged, we imitated and evaded as we could the dullness, corruption, and blindness of "civilization." We were undoubtedly comic because, as the saying goes, we weren't supposed to know what it was all about. But to ourselves we were "boys," members of a wild, free, outlaw tribe which transcended the category of race. Rather we were Americans born into the forty-sixth state, and thus, into the context of Negro-American post–Civil War history, "frontiersmen." And isn't one of the implicit functions of the American frontier to encourage the individual to a kind of dreamy wakefulness, a state in which he makes—in all ignorance of the accepted limitations of the possible—rash efforts, quixotic gestures, hopeful testings of the complexity of the known and the given?

Spurring us on in our controlled and benign madness was the voracious reading of which most of us were guilty and the vicarious identification and empathetic adventuring which it encouraged. This was due, in part, perhaps to the fact that some of us were fatherless—my own father had died when I was three—but most likely it was because boys are natural romantics. We were seeking examples, patterns to live by, out of a freedom which for all its being ignored by the sociologists and subtle thinkers, was implicit in the Negro situation. Father and mother substitutes also have a role to play in aiding the child to help create himself. Thus we fabricated our own heroes and ideals catch-as-catch-can; and with an outrageous and irreverent sense of freedom. Yes, and in complete disregard of ideas of respectability or the surreal incongruity of some of our projections. Gamblers and scholars, jazz musicians and scientists, Negro cowboys and soldiers from the Spanish-American and First World Wars, movie stars and stunt men, figures from the Italian Renaissance and literature, both classical and popular, were combined with the special virtues of some local bootlegger, the eloquence of some Negro preacher, the strength and grace of some local athlete, the ruthlessness of some businessman-physician, the elegance in dress and manners of some head-waiter or hotel doorman.

Looking back through the shadows upon this absurd activity, I realize now that we were projecting archetypes, recreating folk figures, legendary heroes, monsters even, most of which violated all ideas of social hierarchy and order and all accepted conceptions of the hero handed down by cultural, religious, and racist tradition. But we, remember, were under the intense spell of the early movies, the silents as well as the talkies; and in our community, life was not so tightly structured as it would have been in the traditional South—or even in deceptively "free" Harlem. And our imaginations processed reality and dream, natural man and traditional hero, literature and folklore, like maniacal editors turned loose in some frantic film-cutting room. Remember, too, that being boys, yet in the play-stage of our development, we were dream-serious in our efforts. But serious nevertheless, for *culturally* play is a preparation, and we felt that somehow the human ideal lay in the vague and constantly shifting figures—sometimes comic but always versatile, picaresque, and self-effacingly heroic—which evolved from our wildly improvisatory projections: figures neither white nor black, Christian nor Jewish, but representative of certain desirable essences, of skills and powers, physical, aesthetic, and moral.

The proper response to these figures was, we felt, to develop ourselves for the performance of many and diverse roles, and the fact that certain definite limitations had been imposed upon our freedom did not lessen our sense of obligation. Not only were we to prepare but we were to perform—not with mere competence but with an almost reckless verve; with, may we say (without evoking the quaint and questionable notion of *négritude*) Negro-American style? Behind each artist there stands a traditional sense of style, a sense of the felt tension indicative of expressive completeness; a mode of humanizing reality and of evoking a feeling of being at home in the world. It is something which the artist shares with the group, and part of our boyish activity expressed a yearning to make any and everything of quality *Negro-American;* to appropriate it, possess it, recreate it in our own group and individual images.

And we recognized and were proud of our group's own style wherever we discerned it, in jazzmen and prize-fighters, ballplayers, and tap dancers; in gesture, inflection, intonation, timbre, and phrasing. Indeed, in all those nuances of expression and attitude which reveal a culture. We did not fully understand the cost of that style, but we recognized within it an affirmation of life beyond all question of our difficulties as Negroes.

Contrary to the notion currently projected by certain specialists in the "Negro problem" which characterizes the Negro-American as self-hating and defensive, we did not so regard ourselves. We felt, among ourselves at least, that we were supposed to be whoever we would and could be and do anything and everything which other boys did, and do it better. Not defensively, because we were ordered to do so; nor because it was held in the society at large that we were naturally, as Negroes, limited—but because we demanded it of ourselves. Because to measure up to our own standards was the only way of affirming our notion of manhood.

Hence it was no more incongruous, as seen from our own particular perspective in this land of incongruities, for young Negro Oklahomans to project themselves as Renaissance men than for white Mississippians to see themselves as ancient Greeks or noblemen out of Sir Walter Scott. Surely our fantasies have caused far less damage to the nation's sense of reality, if for no other reason than that ours were expressive of a more democratic ideal. Remember, too, as William Faulkner made us so vividly aware, that the slaves often took the essence of the aristocratic ideal (as they took Christianity) with far more seriousness than their masters, and that we, thanks to the tight telescoping of American history, were but two generations from that previous condition. Renaissance men, indeed!

I managed, by keeping quiet about it, to cling to our boyish ideal during three years in Alabama, and I brought it with me to New York, where it not only gave silent support to my explorations of what was then an unknown territory, but served to mock and caution me when I became interested in the Communist ideal. And when it was suggested that I try my hand at writing it was still with me.

The act of writing requires a constant plunging back into the shadow of the past where time hovers ghostlike. When I began writing in earnest I was forced, thus, to relate myself consciously and imaginatively to my mixed background as American, as Negro-American, and as a Negro from what in its own belated way was a pioneer background. More important, and inseparable from this particular effort, was the necessity of determining my true relationship to that body of American literature to which I was most attracted and through which, aided by what I could learn from the literatures of Europe, I would find my own voice and to which I was challenged, by way of achieving myself, to make some small contribution, and to whose composite picture of reality I was obligated to offer some necessary modifications.

This was no matter of sudden insight but of slow and blundering discovery, of a struggle to stare down the deadly and hypnotic temptation to interpret the world and all its devices in terms of race. To avoid this was very important to me, and in light of my background far from simple. Indeed, it was quite complex, involving as it did, a ceaseless questioning of all those formulas which historians, politicians, sociologists, and an older generation of Negro leaders and writers—those of the so-called "Negro Renaissance"— had evolved to describe my group's identity, its predicament, its fate, and its relation to the larger society and the culture which we share.

Here the question of reality and personal identity merge. Yes, and the question of the nature of the reality which underlies American fiction and thus the human truth which gives fiction viability. In this quest, for such it soon became, I learned that nothing could go unchallenged; especially that feverish industry dedicated to telling Negroes who and what they are, and which can usually be counted upon to deprive both humanity and culture of their complexity. I had undergone, not too many months before taking the path which led to writing, the humiliation of being taught in a class in sociology at a Negro college (from Park and Burgess, the leading textbook in the field) that Negroes represented the "lady of the races." This contention the Negro instructor passed blandly along to us without even bothering to wash his hands, much less his teeth. Well, I had no intention of being bound by any such humiliating definition of my relationship to American literature. Not even to those works which depicted Negroes negatively. Negro-Americans have a highly developed ability to abstract desirable qualities from those around them, even from their enemies, and my sense of reality could reject bias while appreciating the truth revealed by achieved art. The pleasure which I derived from reading had long been a necessity, and in the *act* of reading, that marvelous collaboration between the writer's artful vision and the reader's sense of life, I had become acquainted with other possible selves; freer, more courageous and ingenuous and, during the course of the narrative at least, even wise.

At the time I was under the influence of Ernest Hemingway, and his description, in *Death in the Afternoon*, of his thinking when he first went to Spain became very important as translated in my own naïve fashion. He was trying to write, he tells us,

> and I found the greatest difficulty aside from knowing truly what you really felt, rather than what you were supposed to feel, and had been taught to feel,

was to put down what really happened in action; what the actual things were which produced the emotion that you experienced....

His statement of moral and aesthetic purpose which followed focused my own search to relate myself to American life through literature. For I found the greatest difficulty for a Negro writer was the problem of revealing what he truly felt, rather than serving up what Negroes were supposed to feel, and were encouraged to feel. And linked to this was the difficulty, based upon our long habit of deception and evasion, of depicting what really happened within our areas of American life, and putting down with honesty and without bowing to ideological expediencies the attitudes and values which give Negro-American life its sense of wholeness and which render it bearable and human and, when measured by our own terms, desirable.

I was forced to this awareness through my struggles with the craft of fiction; yes, and by my attraction (soon rejected) to Marxist political theory, which was my response to the inferior status which society sought to impose upon me (I did not then, now, or ever *consider* myself inferior).

I did not know my true relationship to America—what citizen of the U.S. really does?—but I did know and accept how I felt inside. And I also knew, thanks to the old Renaissance Man, what I expected of myself in the matter of personal discipline and creative quality. Since by the grace of the past and the examples of manhood picked willy-nilly from the continuing-present of my background, I rejected all negative definitions imposed upon me by others, there was nothing to do but search for those relationships which were fundamental.

In this sense fiction became the agency of my efforts to answer the questions, Who am I, what am I, how did I come to be? What shall I make of the life around me, what celebrate, what reject, how confront the snarl of good and evil which is inevitable? What does American society mean when regarded out of my *own* eyes, when informed by my *own* sense of the past and viewed by my *own* complex sense of the present? How, in other words, should I think of myself and my pluralistic sense of the world, how express my vision of the human predicament, without reducing it to a point which would render it sterile before that necessary and tragic—though enhancing—reduction which must occur before the fictive vision can come alive? It is quite possible that much potential fiction by Negro-Americans fails precisely at this point: through the writers' refusal (often through provincialism or lack of courage or through opportunism) to achieve a vision of life and a resourcefulness of craft commensurate with the complexity of their actual situation. Too often they fear to leave the uneasy sanctuary of race to take their chances in the world of art.

Suggestions for Discussion

1. Discuss the significance to Ellison of his experience growing up in Oklahoma.

2. What distinction does Ellison make between "the process of writing" and "the finished creations, the artifacts, poems, plays, novels"?

3. Describe his use of literature to relate himself to American life.

Suggestions for Writing

1. Discuss a piece of fiction that has helped you "answer the questions, Who am I, what am I, how did I come to be?"

2. Relate the importance of where you "come from" to your understanding of yourself.

RICHARD FORD

Where Does Writing Come From?

Richard Ford (b. 1944) is best known for his novel *The Sportswriter* (1986) and its sequel, *Independence Day* (1995), which earned him a Pulitzer Prize. Raised in Jackson, MS, Ford has a reputation for itinerancy, making homes for himself in France, Mexico, and fourteen states in America. He earned his M.F.A. at the University of California in Irvine, where he studied under Oakley Hall and E. L. Doctorow. His other works include *A Piece of My Heart* (1976), *The Ultimate Good Luck* (1981), *Rock Springs* (1987), *Wildlife* (1990), and *A Multitude of Sins* (2002). In this article, published in 1993, Ford meditates on his inspiration as a writer.

Where does writing come from?

I've often been guilty of trying to answer this question. I've done so, I suppose, in the spirit André Breton must've had in mind when he wrote:

Our brains are dulled by the incurable mania of wanting to make the unknown known.

I've done it on public stages after readings, in panel discussions with dozing colleagues, standing before rows of smirking students, at the suggestion of cruel and cynical journalists in hotel rooms at home and abroad. And I believe I can honestly say that I would never spontaneously have asked myself this question had not someone else seemed interested, or had my financial fortunes not seemed (correctly or incorrectly) tied to such speculation. I must've thought I knew the answer, or thought I didn't need to know it. Yet, once the question was asked, I've over the years taken an interest in the answers I've come up with—which is to say, dreamed up—much in the way I take interest in the progress of any piece of fiction I'm writing. This, after all, is what one does, or what I do anyway when I write fiction: pick out something far-fetched or at least previously unthought of by me, something I feel a kind of language-less yen for, and then see what I can dream up about it or around it that's interesting or amusing to myself in the hope that by making it make sense in words I'll make it interesting and important to someone else.

Plenty of writers for plenty of centuries have furrowed their brows over this question—where does it come from, all this stuff you write? An important part of Wordsworth's answer for instance was that '…good poetry is the spontaneous overflow of powerful feelings'. And I've seen no reason I shouldn't just as well get my two cents' worth down on the chance I might actually get to or near the bottom of the whole subject and possibly help extinguish literature once and for all—since that seems to be where the enquiry tends: let's get writing explained and turned into a neat theorem, like a teasing problem in plasma physics, so we can forget about it and get back to watching *Seinfeld*. And failing that, I might at least say something witty or charming that could make a listener or a reader seek out the book I really do care about—the one I've just written and hope you'll love.

It may be that this investigation stays alive in America partly because of that principally American institution, the creative writing course—of which I am a bona fide graduate, and about which Europeans like to roll their eyes. The institution has many virtues—time to write being the most precious. But it also has several faults, one of which is the unproven good of constantly having like-minded colleagues and compatriots around to talk to about what one is doing, as if companionship naturally improved one's important work just when one is doing it. How we do what we do and why we do it may just be a subject a certain kind of anxious person can't help tumbling to at a time in life when getting things written at all is a worry, and when one's body of work is small and not very distinguishable from one's private self, and when one comes to find that the actual thing one is writing is not a very riveting topic of conversation over drinks. Among dedicated novices, the large subject of provenance may be all we have in common and all that will pass for artily abstract speculation of a disinterested kind.

Clearly another socio-literary force which keeps the topic alive is that among many people who are not writers there's occasionally a flighty belief that writers are special people, vergers of some kind, in charge of an important interior any person would be wise to come close to as a way of sidling up to a potent life's essence. Questions about how, why, etc. become just genuflects before the medium. And writers, being generally undercharged in self-esteem and forever wanting more attention for their work, are often quite willing to become their work's exponent if not its actual avatar. I remember an anecdote about a male writer I know who, upon conducting an interested visitor to his desk overlooking the Pacific, is reported to have whispered as they tiptoed into the sacred, sun-shot room, 'Well, here it is. This is where I make the magic.'

Again, nothing's new here: just another instance of supposing an approach upon the writer will reveal the written thing more fully, more truly; or if not that then it's the old mistake of confusing the maker with the made thing—an object which may really have some magical pizazz about it, who knows?

Considering an actual set of mechanical connections that might have brought a piece of writing from nowhere, the 'place' it resided before I'd written it, to its final condition as the book I hope you'll love, actually impresses upon me the romantic view that artistic invention is a kind of casual magic, one which can't be adequately explained the way, say, a train's arrival in Des Moines can nicely be accounted for by tracing the tracks and switches and sidings and tunnels all the way to its origin in Paducah.

You can—and scholars do—try to trace some apparent connections back from the finished work to the original blank mind and page and even to before that ('He used his father's name for the axe-murderer'...hmmm; 'she suffered glaucoma just like the jilted sister who became a Carmelite nun, so how can you argue the whole damn story isn't about moral blindness?'). But of course such a procedure is famously unreliable and even sometimes downright impertinent, since in the first place (and there need not be a second) such investigations start at and take for granted the existence of Des Moines, whereas for the writer (and I mean soon to abandon this train business) Des Moines is not just a city but a word that has to be not merely found, but conjured from nothing. In fact the word may not even have been Des Moines to begin with—it may have been Abilene or Chagrin Falls—but became Des Moines because the writer inadvertently let Abilene slip his mind, or because Des Moines had that nice diphthong in it and looked neat and Frenchy on the page, whereas Abilene had those three clunky syllables, and there was already a dopey country song about it. Anyway, there are at least two Abilenes, one in Texas and another one in Kansas, which is confusing, and neither has rail service.

You can see what I mean: the true connections might never really be traceable because they exist only in that murky, silent but fecund interstellar night where impulse, free association, instinct and error reign. And even if I were faithfully to try explaining the etiological connections in a piece of writing I'd done, I still might lie about them, or I might just be wrong because I forgot. But in any case I'd finally have to make something up pretty much the way a scholar does—though not exactly like a writer does who, as I said before, always starts with nothing.

I remember once a complimentary reviewer of a book I'd written singling out for approval my choice of adjectives, which seemed to him surprising and expansive and of benefit to the story. One sentence he liked contained a phrase in which I'd referred to a character's eyes as 'old': 'He looked on her in an old-eyed way.' Naturally, I was pleased to have written *something* that *somebody* liked. Only, when I was not long afterward packing away manuscripts for the attic, my eyes happened to fall upon the page and the very commended phrase, 'old-eyed', and to notice that somehow in the rounds of fatigued retyping that used to precede a writer's final sign-off on a book in the days before word processors, the original and rather dully hybridized 'cold-eyed' had somehow lost its 'c' and become 'old-eyed', only nobody'd noticed since they both made a kind of sense.

This is my larger point writ, admittedly, small, and it calls to mind the joke about the man from Alabama who couldn't understand how a thermos could keep cold things cold and hot things always hot, and expressed his wonder in a phrase akin to the title of this very essay: 'How do it know?'

Anyone who's ever written a novel or a story or a poem and had the occasion later to converse about it with an agitated or merely interested reader knows the pinchy feel that comes when the reader tries to nail down the connections *linking* the story to some supposed 'source,' either as a way of illuminating the procedures that transform life to shapely art, or else of just plain diminishing an act of creation to some problem of industrial design.

In my case, this enquiry often centres on the potent subject of children, and specifically writing about children, and more prosecutorily on how it is I can write about children to such and such effect without actually having or having had any myself. (My wife and I don't have any.)

It's frequently surprising to whomever I'm speaking to that I can write persuasively about children: although the surprise is often expressed not as pure delight but in a kind of blinkingly suspicious tone whose spirit is either that I do have children (in another county, maybe) and don't want to admit it, or else that somebody in a position of authority needs to come down and take a closer look at my little minor inventions to certify that they're really as finely and truly drawn as they seem.

Myself, I try to stay in happy spirits about such questioning. Some stranger, after all, *has* or seems to have read at least a part of some book I've written and been moved by it, and I'm always grateful for that. He or she could also as easily have been watching *Seinfeld*. And so mostly I just try to smile and chuckle and mumble-mutter something about having been a child once myself, and if that doesn't work I say something about there being children pretty much everywhere for the watchful to study, and that my Jamesian job, after all, is to be a good observer. And finally if that isn't enough I say that if it were so hard to write about children I of all people wouldn't be able to do it, since I'm no smarter than the next guy.

But the actual truth—the one I know to be true and that sustains my stories—is that even though I was once a child, and even though there are a God's own slew of bratty kids around to be studied like lab rats, and even though I'm clearly not the smartest man in the world, I still mostly write about children by making them up. I make them up out of language bits, out of my memories, out of stories in newspapers, out of overheard remarks made by my friends and their kids, out of this and out of that, and sometimes out of nothing at all but the pleasurable will to ascribe something that might be interesting to a child instead of to an adult or to a spaceman or a horse, after which a child, a fictive child, begins to take shape on the page as a willed, moral gesture toward a reader. "'All I want for Christmas is to know the difference between that and which,' said little Johnny, who was just ten years old but already beginning to need some firmer discipline.' Behold: a child is born.

Occasionally if pushed or annoyed I'll come right out and say it: *I make these little buggers up, that's what. So sue me.* But an odd restraint almost always makes me revert to my prior explanations. Some delicacy in me simply doesn't want to say, 'They're invented things, these characters, you can't track them down like rabbits to their holes. They won't be hiding there.' It's as though arguing for invention and its fragile, wondrous efficacy was indelicate, wasn't quite nice. And even though arguing for it wouldn't harm or taint invention's marvels (we all know novels are made-up things; it's part of our pleasure to keep such knowledge in our minds), still I always feel queasy doing it—not like a magician who reluctantly shows a rube how to pull a nickel out of his own ear, but more like a local parish priest who upon hearing a small but humiliating confession from a friend, lets the friend off easy just to move matters on to higher ground.

Wallace Stevens wrote once that 'in an age of disbelief…it is for the poet to supply the satisfactions of belief in his measure and his style'. And that takes in how I feel about invention—invented characters, invented land-scapes, invented breaks of the heart and their subsequent repairs. I believe that there are important made-up things that resist precise tracing back, and that it's a blessing there are, since our acceptance of them in literature (act-ing as a substitute for less acceptable beliefs) suggests that for every human problem, every insoluble, every cul-de-sac, every despair, there's a chance we can conjure up an improvement—Des Moines, where previously there was only a glum Abilene.

Frank Kermode wrote thirty years ago in his wonderful book *The Sense of an Ending* that, 'It is not that we are connoisseurs of chaos, but that we are surrounded by it, and equipped for coexistence with it only by our fictive powers.' To my mind, not to believe in invention, in our fictive powers, to believe that all is traceable, that the rabbit must finally be in the hole waiting is (because it's dead wrong) a certain recipe for the willi-waws of disappointment, and a small but needless reproach to mankind's saving capacity to imagine what could be better and, with good hope then, to seek it.

Suggestions for Discussion

1. According to Richard Ford, what makes it so difficult for a writer to explain the writing process logically?

2. Why are creative writing courses sometimes criticized?

3. How can an author write convincingly about a subject that he or she is not intimately familiar with?

4. What does Ford claim writers have in common with magicians? Should writers be expected to explain their craft?

Suggestions for Writing

1. What happens in your mind when you write? Is there a discernible thought process at work? What inspires you? What helps you improve as a writer? Is there anything that hurts your ability to order your thoughts on paper? If you have ever experienced writer's block, what was the experience like, and what do you think caused it? Consider these issues and compose a thoughtful essay that details your personal experiences as a writer.

2. Write a short story of your own, remaining conscious of how you go about creating character, setting, mood, and conflict. What is the message of your story? What real-life concerns of yours can be found in your writing? Did the story change or evolve as you were working on it? How does the finished tale differ from the one you intended to tell when you first began the project?

❧❧❧❧

DAVID BAYLES AND TED ORLAND

The Nature of the Problem

David Bayles and Ted Orland wrote the book *Art and Fear* in 1993. In it, they explored the artistic process itself as well as the various factors that discourage artists from completing worthwhile creative projects. In the following excerpt, which is the book's opening chapter, Bayles and Orland encourage artists to consider why the creative process is so emotionally draining and why so many artists give up on their art too soon.

> *Life is short, art long, opportunity fleeting, experience*
> *treacherous, judgement difficult.*
>
> —HIPPOCRATES (460–400 B.C.)

Making art is difficult. We leave drawings unfinished and stories unwritten. We do work that does not feel like our own. We repeat ourselves. We stop before we have mastered our materials, or continue on long after their potential is exhausted. Often the work we have not done seems more real in our minds than the pieces we have completed. And so questions arise: *How does art get done? Why, often, does it not get done? And what is the nature of the difficulties that stop so many who start?*

These questions, which seem timeless, may actually be particular to our age. It may have been easier to paint bison on the cave walls long ago than to write this (or any other) sentence today. Other people, in other times and places, had some robust institutions to shore them up: witness the Church, the clan, ritual, tradition. It's easy to imagine that artists doubted their calling less when working in the service of God than when working in the service of self.

Not so today. Today almost no one feels shored up. Today artwork does not emerge from a secure common ground: the bison on the wall is someone else's magic. Making art now means working in the face of uncertainty; it means living with doubt and contradiction, doing something no one much cares whether you do, and for which there may be neither audience nor reward. Making the work you want to make means setting aside these doubts so that you may see clearly what you have done, and thereby see where to go next. Making the work you want to make means finding nourishment within the work itself. This is not the Age of Faith, Truth and Certainty.

Yet even the notion that you have a say in this process conflicts with the prevailing view of artmaking today—namely, that art rests fundamentally upon talent, and that talent is a gift randomly built into some people and not into others. In common parlance, either you have it or you don't—great art is a product of genius, good art a product of near-genius (which Nabokov likened to *Near-Beer*), and so on down the line to pulp romances and paint-by-the-numbers. This view is inherently fatalistic—even if it's true, it's fatalistic—and offers no useful encouragement to those who would make art. Personally, we'll side with Conrad's view of fatalism: namely, that it is a species of fear—the fear that your fate is in your own hands, but that your hands are weak.

But while talent—not to mention fate, luck and tragedy—all play their role in human destiny, they hardly rank as dependable tools for advancing your own art on a day-to-day basis. Here in the day-to-day world (which is, after all, the only one we live in), the job of getting on with your work turns upon making some basic assumptions about human nature, assumptions that place the power (and hence the responsibility) for your actions in your own hands. Some of these can be stated directly:

∾

A Few Assumptions

ARTMAKING INVOLVES SKILLS THAT CAN BE LEARNED. The conventional wisdom here is that while "craft" can be taught, "art" remains a magical gift bestowed only by the gods. Not so. In large measure becoming an artist consists of learning to accept yourself, which makes your work personal, and in following your own voice, which makes your work distinctive. Clearly, these qualities can be nurtured by others. Even talent is rarely distinguishable, over the long run, from perseverance and lots of hard work. It's true that every few years the authors encounter some beginning photography student whose first-semester prints appear as finely crafted as any Ansel Adams might have made. And it's true that a natural gift like that (especially coming at the fragile early learning stage) returns priceless encouragement to its maker. But all that has nothing to do with artistic content. Rather, it simply points up the fact that most of us (including Adams himself!) had to work years to perfect our art.

ART IS MADE BY ORDINARY PEOPLE. Creatures having only virtues can hardly be imagined making art. It's difficult to picture the Virgin Mary painting landscapes. Or Batman throwing pots. The flawless creature wouldn't *need* to make art. And so, ironically, the ideal artist is scarcely a theoretical figure at all. If art is made by ordinary people, then you'd have to allow that the ideal artist would be an ordinary person too, with the whole usual mixed bag of traits that real human beings possess. This is a giant hint about art, because it suggests that our flaws and weaknesses, while often obstacles to our getting work done, are a source of strength as well. Something about making art has to do with overcoming things, giving us a clear opportunity for doing things in ways we have always known we should do them.

MAKING ART AND VIEWING ART ARE DIFFERENT AT THEIR CORE. The sane human being is satisfied that the best he/she can do at any given moment is the best he/she can do at any given moment. That belief, if widely embraced, would make this book unnecessary, false, or both. Such sanity is, unfortunately, rare. Making art provides uncomfortably accurate feedback about the gap that inevitably exists between what you intended to do, and what you did. In fact, if artmaking did not tell you (the maker) so enormously much about yourself, then making art that matters to you would be impossible. To all viewers but yourself, what matters is the product: the finished artwork. To you, and you alone, what matters is the process: the experience of shaping that artwork. The viewers' concerns are not your concerns (although it's dangerously easy to adopt their attitudes). Their job is whatever it is: to be moved by art, to be entertained by it, to make a killing off it, whatever. Your job is to learn to work on your work.

For the artist, that truth highlights a familiar and predictable corollary: artmaking can be a rather lonely, thankless affair. Virtually all artists spend some of their time (and some artists spend virtually all of their time) producing work that no one else much cares about. It just seems to come with the territory. But for some reason—self-defense, perhaps—artists find it tempting to romanticize this lack of response, often by (heroically) picturing themselves peering deeply into the underlying nature of things long before anyone else has eyes to follow.

Romantic, but wrong. The sobering truth is that the disinterest of others hardly ever reflects a gulf in vision. In fact there's generally no good reason why others *should* care about most of any one artist's work. The function of the overwhelming majority of your artwork is simply to teach you how to make the small fraction of your artwork that soars. One of the basic and difficult lessons every artist must learn is that even the failed pieces are essential. X-rays of famous paintings reveal that even master artists sometimes made basic midcourse corrections (or deleted really dumb mistakes) by overpainting the still-wet canvas. The point is that you learn how to make your work *by making your work,* and a great many of the pieces you make along the way will never stand out *as finished art.* The best you can do is make art you care about—and lots of it!

The rest is largely a matter of perseverance. Of course once you're famous, collectors and academics will circle back in droves to claim credit for spotting evidence of genius in every early piece. But until your ship comes in, the only people who will really care about your work are those who care about you personally. Those close to you know that making the work is essential to your well-being. They will always care about your work, if not because it is great, then because it is yours—and this is something to be genuinely thankful for. Yet however much they love you, it still remains as true for them as for the rest of the world: learning to make your work is not their problem.

ARTMAKING HAS BEEN AROUND LONGER THAN THE ART ESTABLISHMENT. Through most of history, the people who made art never thought of themselves as making art. In fact it's quite presumable that art was being made long before the rise of consciousness, long before the pronoun "I" was ever employed. The painters of caves, quite apart from not thinking of themselves as artists, probably never thought of themselves at all.

What this suggests, among other things, is that the current view equating art with "self-expression" reveals more a contemporary bias in our thinking than an underlying trait of the medium. Even the separation of art from craft is largely a post–Renaissance concept, and more recent still is the notion that art transcends what you do, and represents what you are. In the past few centuries Western art has moved from unsigned tableaus of orthodox religious scenes to one-person displays of personal cosmologies. "Artist" has gradually become a form of identity which (as every artist knows) often carries with it as many drawbacks as benefits. Consider that if artist equals self, then when (inevitably) you make flawed art, you are a flawed person, and when (worse yet) you make no art, you are no person at all! It seems far healthier to sidestep that vicious spiral by accepting many paths to successful artmaking—from reclusive to flamboyant, intuitive to intellectual, folk art to fine art. One of those paths is yours.

Suggestions for Discussion

1. According to Bayles and Orland, why is it important to remember that "artmaking involves skills that can be learned" and that "art is made by ordinary people"?
2. Why do the authors believe that it may be harder to produce art now than it was in earlier ages?
3. How is making art different from viewing art?

Suggestion for Writing

In a self-effacing essay, explore your own fears and anxieties about writing, drawing, or "making art." How might you confront these fears and beat them back long enough to finally produce that bit of personal craftsmanship that you've always wanted to?

ESSAYS

∾∾∾∾∾

E. M. FORSTER

Art for Art's Sake

Edward Morgan Forster (1879–1970) was a British novelist educated at King's College, Cambridge. He lived for a time in Italy, was a member of the Bloomsbury Group of writers and artists in London, and spent the major part of his life in Cambridge. His works include *Where Angels Fear to Tread* (1905), *A Room with a View* (1908), and *A Passage to India* (1924). In this essay from *Two Cheers for Democracy* (1951), Forster explains the importance of art as a source of comfort and order in a troubled society.

I believe in art for art's sake. It is an unfashionable belief, and some of my statements must be of the nature of an apology. Sixty years ago I should have faced you with more confidence. A writer or a speaker who chose "Art for Art's Sake" for his theme sixty years ago could be sure of being in the swim, and could feel so confident of success that he sometimes dressed himself in aesthetic costumes suitable to the occasion—in an embroidered dressing-gown, perhaps, or a blue velvet suit with a Lord Fauntleroy collar; or a toga, or a kimono, and carried a poppy or a lily or a long peacock's feather in his mediaeval hand. Times have changed. Not thus can I present either myself or my theme today. My aim rather is to ask you quietly to reconsider for a few minutes a phrase which has been much misused and much abused, but which has, I believe, great importance for us—has, indeed, eternal importance.

Now we can easily dismiss those peacock's feathers and other affectations—they are but trifles—but I want also to dismiss a more dangerous heresy, namely the silly idea that only art matters, an idea which has somehow got mixed up with the idea of art for art's sake, and has helped to discredit it. Many things besides art matter. It is merely one of the things that matter, and high though the claims are that I make for it, I want to keep them in proportion. No one can spend his or her life entirely in the creation or the appreciation of masterpieces. Man lives, and ought to live, in a complex world, full of conflicting claims, and if we simplified them down into the aesthetic he would be sterilised. Art for art's sake does not mean that only art matters and I would also like to rule out such phrases as, "The Life of Art," "Living for Art," and "Art's High Mission." They confuse and mislead.

What does the phrase mean? Instead of generalising, let us take a specific instance—Shakespeare's *Macbeth,* for example, and pronounce the words, "*Macbeth* for *Macbeth*'s sake." What does that mean? Well, the play has several aspects—it is educational, it teaches us something about legendary Scotland, something about Jacobean England, and a good deal about human nature and its perils. We can study its origins, and study and enjoy its dramatic technique and the music of its diction. All that is true. But *Macbeth* is furthermore a world of its own, created by Shakespeare and existing in virtue of its own poetry. It is in this aspect *Macbeth* for *Macbeth*'s sake, and that is what I intend by the phrase "art for art's sake." A work of art—whatever else it may be—is a self-contained entity, with a life of its own imposed on it by its creator. It has internal order. It may have external form. That is how we recognise it.

Take for another example that picture of Seurat's which I saw two years ago in Chicago—"*La Grande Jatte.*" Here again there is much to study and to enjoy: the pointillism, the charming face of the seated girl, the nineteenth-century Parisian Sunday sunlight, the sense of motion in immobility. But here again there is something more; "*La Grande Jatte*" forms a world of its own, created by Seurat and existing by virtue of its own poetry: "*La Grande Jatte*" pour "*La Grande Jatte*": *l'art pour l'art.* Like *Macbeth* it has internal order and internal life.

It is to the conception of order that I would now turn. This is important to my argument, and I want to make a digression, and glance at order in daily life, before I come to order in art.

In the world of daily life, the world which we perforce inhabit, there is much talk about order, particularly from statesmen and politicians. They tend, however, to confuse order with orders, just as they confuse creation with regulations. Order, I suggest, is something evolved from within, not something imposed from without; it is an internal stability, a vital harmony, and in the social and political category, it has never existed except for the convenience of historians. Viewed realistically, the past is really a series of *dis*orders, succeeding one another by discoverable laws, no doubt, and certainly marked by an increasing growth of human interference, but disorders all the same. So that, speaking as a writer, what I hope for today is a disorder which will be more favourable to artists than is the present one, and which will provide them with fuller inspirations and better material conditions. It will not last—nothing lasts—but there have been some advantageous disorders in the past—for instance, in ancient Athens, in Renaissance Italy, eighteenth-century France, periods in China and Persia—and we may do something to accelerate the next one. But let us not again fix our hearts where true joys are not to be found. We were promised a new order after the first world war through the League of Nations. It did not come, nor have I faith in present promises, by whomsoever endorsed. The implacable offensive of Science forbids. We cannot reach social and political stability for the reason that we continue to make scientific discoveries and to apply them, and thus to destroy the arrangements which were based on more elementary discoveries. If Science would discover rather than apply—if, in other words, men were more interested in knowledge than in power—mankind would be in a far safer position, the stability statesmen talk about would be a possibility, there could be a new order based on vital harmony, and the earthly millennium might approach. But Science shows no signs of doing this: she gave us the internal combustion engine, and before we had digested and assimilated it with terrible pains into our social system, she harnessed the atom, and destroyed any new order that seemed to be evolving. How can man get into harmony with his surroundings when he is constantly altering them? The future of our race is, in this direction, more unpleasant than we care to admit, and it has sometimes seemed to me that its best chance lies through apathy, uninventiveness, and inertia. Universal exhaustion might promote that Change of Heart which is at present so briskly recommended from a thousand pulpits. Universal exhaustion would certainly be a new experience. The human race has never undergone it, and is still too perky to admit that it may be coming and might result in a sprouting of new growth through the decay.

I must not pursue these speculations any further—they lead me too far from my terms of reference and maybe from yours. But I do want to emphasize that order in daily life and in history, order in the social and political category, is unattainable under our present psychology.

Where is it attainable? Not in the astronomical category, where it was for many years enthroned. The heavens and the earth have become terribly alike since Einstein. No longer can we find a reassuring contrast to chaos in the night sky and look up with George Meredith to the stars, the army of unalterable law, or listen for the music of the spheres. Order is not there. In the entire universe there seem to be only two possibilities for it. The first of them—which again lies outside my terms of reference—is the divine order, the mystic harmony, which according to all religions is available for those who can contemplate it. We much admit its possibility, on the evidence of the adepts, and we must believe them when they say that it is attained, if attainable, by prayer. "O thou who changest not, abide with me," said one of its poets. "*Ordina questo amor, o tu che m'ami,*" said another: "Set love in order thou who lovest me." The existence of a divine order, though it cannot be tested, has never been disproved.

The second possibility for order lies in the aesthetic category, which is my subject here: the order which an artist can create in his own work, and to that we must now return. A work of art, we are all agreed, is a unique product. But why? It is unique not because it is clever or noble or beautiful or enlightened or original or sincere or idealistic or useful or educational—it may embody any of those qualities—but because it is the only material object in the universe which may possess internal harmony. All the others have been pressed into shape from outside, and when their mold is removed they collapse. The work of art stands up by itself, and nothing else does. It achieves something which has often been promised by society, but always delusively. Ancient Athens made a mess—but the *Antigone* stands up. Renaissance Rome made a mess—but the ceiling of the Sistine got painted. James I made a mess—but there was *Macbeth.* Louis XIV—but there was *Phedre.* Art for art's sake? I should just think so, and more so than ever at the present time. It is the one orderly product which our muddling race has produced. It is the cry of a thousand sentinels, the echo from a thousand labyrinths; it is the lighthouse which cannot be hidden: *c'est le meilleur témoignage que nous puissions donner de notre dignité. Antigone* for *Antigone*'s sake, *Macbeth* for *Macbeth*'s, "*La Grande Jatte*" *pour* "*La Grande Jatte.*"

If this line of argument is correct, it follows that the artist will tend to be an outsider in the society to which he has been born, and that the nineteenth century conception of him as a Bohemian was not inaccurate. The conception erred in three particulars: it postulated an economic system where art could be a full-time job, it introduced the fallacy that only art matters, and it overstressed idiosyncracy and waywardness—the peacock-feather aspect—rather than order. But it is a truer conception than the one which prevails in official circles on my side of the Atlantic—I don't know about yours: the conception which treats the artist as if he were a particularly bright government advertiser and encourages him to be friendly and matey with his fellow citizens, and not to give himself airs.

Estimable is mateyness, and the man who achieves it gives many a pleasant little drink to himself and to others. But it has no traceable connection with the creative impulse, and probably acts as an inhibition on it. The artist who is seduced by mateyness may stop himself from doing the one thing which he, and he alone, can do—the making of something out of words or sounds or paint or clay or marble or steel or film which has internal harmony and presents order to a permanently disarranged planet. This seems worth doing, even at the risk of being called uppish by journalists. I have in mind an article which was published some years ago in the London *Times,* an article called "The Eclipse of the Highbrow," in which the "Average Man" was exalted, and all contemporary literature was censured if it did not toe the line, the precise position of the line being naturally known to the writer of the article. Sir Kenneth Clark, who was at that time director of our National Gallery, commented on this pernicious doctrine in a letter which cannot be too often quoted. "The poet and the artist," wrote Clark, "are important precisely because they are not average men; because in sensibility, intelligence, and power of invention they far exceed the average." These memorable words, and particularly the words "power of invention," are the Bohemian's passport. Furnished with it, he slinks about society, saluted now by a brickbat and now by a penny, and accepting either of them with equanimity. He does not consider too anxiously what his relations with society may be, for he is aware of something more important than that—namely the invitation to invent, to create order, and he believes he will be better placed for doing this if he attempts detachment. So round and round he slouches, with his hat pulled over his eyes, and maybe with a louse in his beard, and—if he really wants one—a peacock's feather in his hand.

If our present society should disintegrate—and who dare prophesy that it won't?—this old-fashioned and démodé figure will become clearer: the Bohemian, the outsider, the parasite, the rat—one of those figures which have at present no function either in a warring or a peaceful world. It may not be dignified to be a rat, but many of the ships are sinking, which is not dignified either—the officials did not build them properly. Myself, I would sooner be a swimming rat than a sinking ship—at all events I can look around me for a little longer—and I remember how one of us, a rat with particularly bright eyes called Shelley, squeaked out, "Poets are the unacknowledged legislators of the world," before he vanished into the waters of the Mediterranean.

What laws did Shelley propose to pass? None. The legislation of the artist is never formulated at the time, though it is sometimes discerned by future generations. He legislates through creating. And he creates through his sensitiveness and power to impose form. Without form the sensitiveness vanishes. And form is as important today, when the human race is trying to ride the whirlwind, as it ever was in those less agitating days of the past, when the earth seemed solid and the stars fixed, and the discoveries of science were made slowly, slowly. Form is not tradition. It alters from generation to generation. Artists always seek a new technique, and will continue to do so as long as their work excites them. But form of some kind is imperative. It is the surface crust of the internal harmony, it is the outward evidence of order.

My remarks about society may have seemed too pessimistic, but I believe that society can only represent a fragment of the human spirit, and that another fragment can only get expressed through art. And I wanted to take this opportunity, this vantage ground, to assert not only the existence of art, but its pertinacity. Looking back into the past, it seems to me that that is all there has ever been: vantage grounds for discussion and creation, little vantage grounds in the changing chaos, where bubbles have been blown and webs spun, and the desire to create order has found temporary gratification, and the sentinels have managed to utter their challenges, and the huntsmen, though lost individually, have heard each other's calls through the impenetrable wood, and the lighthouses have never ceased sweeping the thankless seas. In this pertinacity there seems to me, as I grow older, something more and more profound, something which does in fact concern people who do not care about art at all.

In conclusion, let me summarise the various categories that have laid claim to the possession of Order.

(1) The social and political category. Claim disallowed on the evidence of history and of our own experience. If man altered psychologically, order here might be attainable: not otherwise.

(2) The astronomical category. Claim allowed up to the present century, but now disallowed on the evidence of the physicists.

(3) The religious category. Claim allowed on the evidence of the mystics.

(4) The aesthetic category. Claim allowed on the evidence of various works of art, and on the evidence of our own creative impulses, however weak these may be or however imperfectly they may function. Works of art, in my opinion, are the only objects in the material universe to possess internal order, and that is why, though I don't believe that only art matters, I do believe in Art for Art's Sake.

Suggestions for Discussion

1. Why does Forster make clear that the belief in art for art's sake does not mean a belief that only art matters?

2. Where does art stand, for Forster, in the list of things that matter?

3. Explain Forster's phrase, "*Macbeth* for *Macbeth*'s sake." How does he use it to explain his main argument?

4. Explain Forster's comparison of the order of art with order in life. How does this comparison function in his argument?

5. What does Forster mean by claiming that a work of art is a unique product?

6. Examine Forster's categories that have laid claim to the possession of order. Why does he reject all but the religious and aesthetic categories?

Suggestions for Writing

1. Write a paper explaining Forster's defense of art.

2. Obviously, many people feel differently from Forster about the autonomy of art. In Marxist countries, for example, art is often considered to be a servant of the state. Write a paper in which you argue for or against Forster's position.

Loving Care, Janine Antoni, 1993. Courtesy of the artist and Luhring Augustine, New York.

E. L. DOCTOROW

Ultimate Discourse

Edgar Lawrence Doctorow (b. 1931) was born in New York City, grad-uated with honors in philosophy from Kenyon College, and has received two honorary doctoral degrees. Besides time spent as an editor, Doc-torow has taught English at Sarah Lawrence College; Yale University; University of California, Irvine; and New York University. Among his works are *The Book of Daniel* (1971); *Ragtime* (1975), for which he won the National Book Critics Circle Award; *Drinks Before Dinner* (1979); *Loon Lake* (1980); *Billy Bathgate* (1988); *Lives of the Poets* (1997); *City of God* (2000); and *The March* (2005). In 1990 he won the National Book Critics Circle Award and the PEN/Faulkner Award and was elected to the American Academy and Institute of Arts and Letters. In this brief essay, he explains why fiction occupies a significant place in our lives.

When I was a boy everyone in my family was a good storyteller, my mother and father, my brother, my aunts and uncles and grandparents; all of them were people to whom interesting things seemed to happen. The events they spoke of were of a daily, ordinary sort, but when narrated or acted out they took on great importance and excitement as I listened.

Of course, when you bring love to the person you are listening to, the story has to be interesting, and in one sense the task of a professional writer who publishes books is to overcome the terrible loss of not being someone the reader knows and loves.

But apart from that, the people whose stories I heard as a child must have had a very firm view of themselves in the world. They must have been strong enough as presences in their own minds to trust that people would listen to them when they spoke.

I know now that everyone in the world tells stories. Relatively few people are given to mathematics or physics, but narrative seems to be within everyone's grasp, perhaps because it comes of the nature of language itself.

The moment you have nouns and verbs and prepositions, the moment you have subjects and objects, you have stories.

For the longest time there would have been nothing but stories, and no sharper distinction between what was real and what was made up than between what was spoken and what was sung. Religious arousal and scientific discourse, simple urgent communication and poetry, all burned together in the intense perception of a metaphor—that, for instance, the sun was a god's chariot driven across the heavens.

Stories were as important to survival as a spear or a hoe. They were the memory of the knowledge of the dead. They gave counsel. They connected the visible to the invisible. They distributed the suffering so that it could be borne.

In our era, even as we separate the functions of language, knowing when we speak scientifically we are not speaking poetically, and when we speak theologically we are not speaking the way we do to each other in our houses, and even as our surveys demand statistics, and our courts demand evidence, and our hypotheses demand proof—our minds are still structured for storytelling.

What we call fiction is the ancient way of knowing, the total discourse that antedates all the special vocabularies of modern intelligence.

The professional writer of fiction is a conservative who cherishes the ultimate structures of the human mind. He cultivates within himself the universal disposition to think in terms of conflict and its resolution, and in terms of character undergoing events, and of the outcome of events being not at all sure, and therefore suspenseful—the whole thing done, moreover, from a confidence of narrative that is grounded in our brains as surely as the innate talent to construe the world grammatically.

The fiction writer, looking around him, understands the homage a modern up-to-date world of nonfiction specialists pays to his craft—even as it isolates him and tells him he is a liar. Newsweeklies present the events of the world as installments in a serial melodrama. Weather reports on television are constructed with exact attention to conflict (high-pressure areas clashing with lows), suspense (the climax of tomorrow's prediction coming after the commercial), and the consistency of voice (the personality of the weathercaster). The marketing and advertising of product-facts is unquestionably a fictional enterprise. As is every government's representations of its activities. And modern psychology, with its concepts of *sublimation, repression, identity crisis, complex,* and so on, proposes the interchangeable parts for the stories of all of us; in this sense it is the industrialization of storytelling.

But nothing is as good at fiction as fiction. It is the most ancient way of knowing but also the most modern, managing when it's done right to burn all the functions of language back together into powerful fused revelation. Because it is total discourse it is ultimate discourse. It excludes nothing. It will express from the depth and range of its sources truths that no sermon or experiment or news report can begin to apprehend. It will tell you without shame what people do with their bodies and think with their minds. It will deal evenhandedly with their microbes or their intuitions. It will know their nightmares and blinding moments of moral crisis. You will experience love, if it so chooses, or starvation or drowning or dropping through space or holding a hot pistol in your hand with the police pounding on the door. This is the way it is, it will say, this is what it feels like.

Fiction is democratic, it reasserts the authority of the single mind to make and remake the world. By its independence from all institutions, from the family to the government, and with no responsibility to defend their hypocrisy or murderousness, it is a valuable resource and instrument of survival.

Fiction gives counsel. It connects the present with the past, and the visible with the invisible. It distributes the suffering. It says we must compose ourselves in our stories in order to exist. It says if we don't do it, someone else will do it for us.

Suggestions for Discussion

1. Doctorow suggests that storytelling is basic to everyone, a universal activity. How does he distinguish between the stories people tell to their loved ones and those authors write for publication?

2. What does Doctorow say is the origin of the urge to tell stories? Explain his assertion that storytelling fuses the elements of religion, science, and poetry.

3. Although the fused elements became separate in modern times, how does fiction remain fundamental to all activity? How, for example, is it used by representatives of government and business and by professional psychologists?

4. Doctorow says that "nothing is as good at fiction as fiction." Explain his reasons for this assertion.

Suggestions for Writing

1. Doctorow not only calls fiction the "ultimate discourse," but he says that it is also "democratic." Write an essay in which you explain both of these assertions. Do you agree? Why?

2. Doctorow states that fiction "says we must compose ourselves in our stories in order to exist. It says if we don't do it, someone else will do it for us." Explain what he means by these remarks, particularly the last sentence.

ALEKSANDR SOLZHENITSYN

Playing Upon the Strings of Emptiness

Aleksandr Solzhenitsyn (b. 1918), a Russian writer, was born in Kislovodsk, grew up in Rostov, and studied mathematics at the university there. During World War II, he rose to the rank of captain in the Soviet artillery and was decorated for bravery. While still serving on the German front in 1945, he was arrested for criticizing Stalin and sentenced to eight years in prison, where he became familiar with other political prisoners. Solzhenitsyn's novel *One Day in the Life of Ivan Denisovich* (1962) was published through the intervention of Nikita Khrushchev. Its publication made the author famous. Because his subsequent novels, *The First Circle* (1964) and *Cancer Ward* (1966), were regarded as too critical of the Soviet Union, he was censored and expelled from the Union of Soviet Writers. Solzhenitsyn was awarded the Nobel Prize for Literature in 1970, but, wishing to remain in the

Soviet Union, he refused it. Since he also refused to remain silent about Soviet repression, he was arrested and forcibly deported in 1974. Soon after, he accepted his Nobel Prize. He is perhaps best known for *The Gulag Archipelago* (1973), which records the prison operations of Soviet totalitarianism from 1918 to 1956. Recent works include *November 1916* (1999) and *Solzhenitsyn: A Soul in Exile* (2001). After many years of exile in the United States, Solzhenitsyn returned to Russia after the overturn of the government of the Soviet Union. In 1993 he received the medal of honor of the National Arts Club. His wife received the award on his behalf and read his acceptance speech, printed here, translated by his sons, Ignat and Stephan. The reader, aware of the author's experience with repression in the Soviet Union, should not be surprised by the conservatism of his position in this speech.

There is a long-accepted truth about art that "style is the man" (*"le style est l'homme"*). This means that every work of a skilled musician, artist or writer is shaped by an absolutely unique combination of personality traits, creative abilities and individual, as well as national, experience. And since such a combination can never be repeated, art (but I shall here speak primarily of literature) possesses infinite variety across the ages and among different peoples. The divine plan is such that there is no limit to the appearance of ever new and dazzling creative talents, none of whom, however, negate in any way the works of their outstanding predecessors, even though they may be 500 or 2,000 years removed. The unending quest for what is new and fresh is never closed to us, but this does not deprive our grateful memory of all that came before.

No new work of art comes into existence (whether consciously or unconsciously) without an organic link to what was created earlier. But it is equally true that a healthy conservatism must be flexible both in terms of creation and perception, remaining equally sensitive to the old and to the new, to venerable and worthy traditions, and to the freedom to explore, without which no future can ever be born. At the same time the artist must not forget that creative *freedom* can be dangerous, for the fewer artistic limitations he imposes on his own work, the less chance he has for artistic success. The loss of a responsible organizing force weakens or even ruins the structure, the meaning and the ultimate value of a work of art.

Every age and every form of creative endeavor owes much to those outstanding artists whose untiring labors brought forth new meanings and new rhythms. But in the 20th century the necessary equilibrium between tradition and the search for the new has been repeatedly upset by a falsely understood "avant-gardism"—a raucous, impatient "avant-gardism" at any cost. Dating from before World War I, this movement undertook to destroy all commonly accepted art—its forms, language, features and properties—in its drive to build a kind of "superart," which would then supposedly spawn the New Life itself. It was suggested that literature should start anew "on a blank sheet of paper." (Indeed, some never went much beyond this stage.) Destruction, thus, became the apotheosis of this belligerent avant-gardism. It aimed to tear down the entire centuries-long cultural tradition, to break and disrupt the natural flow of artistic development by a sudden leap forward. This goal was to be achieved through an empty pursuit of novel forms as an end in itself, all the while lowering the standards of craftsmanship for oneself to the point of slovenliness and artistic crudity, at times combined with a meaning so obscured as to shade into unintelligibility.

This aggressive impulse might be interpreted as a mere product of personal ambition, were it not for the fact that in Russia (and I apologize to those gathered here for speaking mostly of Russia, but in our time it is impossible to bypass the harsh and extensive experience of my country), in Russia this impulse and its manifestations preceded and foretold the most *physically* destructive revolution of the 20th century. Before erupting on the streets of Petrograd, this cataclysmic revolution erupted on the pages of the artistic and literary journals of the capital's bohemian circles. It is there that we first heard scathing imprecations against the entire Russian and European way of life, the calls to sweep away all religions or ethical codes, to tear down, overthrow, and trample all existing traditional culture, along with the self-extolment of the desperate innovators themselves, innovators who never did succeed in producing anything of worth. Some of these appeals literally called for the destruction of the Racines, the Murillos and the Raphaels, "so that bullets would bounce off museum walls." As for the classics of Russian literature, they were to be "thrown overboard from the ship of modernity." Cultural history would have to begin anew. The cry was "Forward, forward!"—its authors already called themselves "futurists," as though they had now stepped over and beyond the present, and were bestowing upon us what was undoubtedly the genuine art of the Future.

But no sooner did the revolution explode in the streets, than those "futurists" who only recently, in their manifesto entitled "A Slap in the Face of Public Taste," had preached an "insurmountable hatred toward the existing language"—these same "futurists" changed their name to the "Left Front," now directly joining the revolution at its leftmost flank. It thus became clear that the earlier outbursts of this "avant-gardism" were no mere literary froth, but had very real embodiment in life. Beyond their intent to overturn the entire culture, they aimed to uproot life itself. And when the Communists gained unlimited power (their own battle cry called for tearing the existing world "down to its foundations," so as to build a new Unknown Beautiful World in its stead, with equally unlimited brutality) they not only opened wide the gates of publicity and popularity to this horde of so-called "avant-gardists," but even gave some of them, as to faithful allies, power to administrate over culture.

Granted, neither the ragings of this pseudo-"avant-garde" nor its power over culture lasted long; there followed a general coma of all culture. We in the U.S.S.R. began to trudge, downcast, through a 70-year-long ice age, under whose heavy glacial cover one could barely discern the secret heartbeat of a handful of great poets and writers. These were almost entirely unknown to their own country, not to mention the rest of the world, until much later. With the ossification of the totalitarian Soviet regime, its inflated pseudoculture ossified as well, turning into the loathsome ceremonial forms of so-called "socialist realism." Some individuals have been eager to devote numerous critical analyses to the essence and significance of this phenomenon. I would not have written a single one, for it is outside the bounds of art altogether: the *object* of study, the style of "socialist realism," never existed. One does not need to be an expert to see that it consisted of nothing more than servility, a style defined by "What would you care for?" or "Write whatever the Party commands." What scholarly discussion can possibly take place here?

And now, having lived through these 70 lethal years inside Communism's iron shell, we are crawling out, though barely alive. A new age has clearly begun, both for Russia and for the whole world. Russia lies utterly ravaged and poisoned; its people are in a state of unprecedented humiliation, and are on the brink of perishing physically, perhaps even biologically. Given the current conditions of national life, and the sudden exposure and ulceration of the wounds amassed over the years, it is only natural that literature should experience a pause. The voices that bring forth the nation's literature need time before they can begin to sound once again.

However, some writers have emerged who appreciate the removal of censorship and the new, unlimited artistic freedom mostly in one sense: for allowing uninhibited "self-expression." The point is to *express* one's own perception of one's surroundings, often with no sensitivity toward today's ills and scars, and with a visible emptiness of heart; to express the personality of an author, whether it is significant or not; to express it with no sense of responsibility toward the morals of the public, and especially of the young; and at times thickly lacing the language with obscenities which for hundreds of years were considered unthinkable to put in print, but now seem to be almost in vogue.

The confusion of minds after 70 years of total oppression is more than understandable. The artistic perception of the younger generations finds itself in shock, humiliation, resentment, amnesia. Unable to find in themselves the strength fully to withstand and refute Soviet dogma in the past, many young writers have now given in to the more accessible path of pessimistic relativism. Yes, they say, Communist doctrines were a great lie; but then again, absolute truths do not exist anyhow, and trying to find them is pointless. Nor is it worth the trouble to strive for some kind of higher meaning.

And in one sweeping gesture of vexation, classical Russian literature—which never disdained reality and sought the truth—is dismissed as next to worthless. Denigrating the past is deemed to be the key to progress. And so it has once again become fashionable in Russia to ridicule, debunk, and toss overboard the great Russian literature, steeped as it is in love and compassion toward all human beings, and especially toward those who suffer. And in order to facilitate this operation of discarding, it is announced that the lifeless and servile "socialist realism" had in fact been an organic continuation of full-blooded Russian literature.

Thus we witness, through history's various thresholds, a recurrence of one and the same perilous anti-cultural phenomenon, with its rejection of and contempt for all foregoing tradition, and with its mandatory hostility toward whatever is universally accepted. Before, it burst in upon us with the fanfares and gaudy flags of "futurism"; today the term "post-modernism" is applied. (Whatever the meaning intended for this term, its lexical makeup involves an incongruity: the seeming claim that a person can think and experience *after* the period in which he is destined to live.)

For a post-modernist, the world does not possess values that have reality. He even has an expression for this: "the world as text," as something secondary, as the text of an author's work, wherein the primary object of interest is the author himself in his relationship to the work, his own introspection. Culture, in this view, ought to be directed inward at itself (which is why these works are so full of reminiscences, to the point of tastelessness); it alone is valuable and real. For this reason the concept of play acquires a heightened importance—not the Mozartian playfulness of a Universe overflowing with joy, but a forced playing upon the strings of emptiness, where an author need have no responsibility to anyone. A denial of any and all ideals is considered courageous. And in this voluntary self-delusion, "post-modernism" sees itself as the crowning achievement of all previous culture, the final link in its chain. (A rash hope, for already there is talk of the birth of "conceptualism," a term that has yet to be convincingly defined in terms of its relationship to *art*, though no doubt this too will duly be attempted. And then there is already *post–avant-gardism;* and it would be no surprise if we were to witness the appearance of a "post–post-modernism," or of a "post-futurism.") We could have sympathy for this constant searching, but only as we have sympathy for the suffering of a sick man. The search is doomed by its theoretical premises to forever remaining a secondary or ternary exercise, devoid of life or of a future.

But let us shift our attention to the more complex flow of this process. Even though the 20th century has seen the more bitter and disheartening lot fall to the peoples under Communist domination, our whole world is living through a century of spiritual illness, which could not but give rise to a similar ubiquitous illness in art. Although for other reasons, a similar "post-modernist" sense of confusion about the world has also arisen in the West.

Alas, at a time of an unprecedented rise in the material benefits of civilization and ever-improving standards of living, the West, too, has been undergoing an erosion and obscuring of high moral and ethical ideals. The spiritual axis of life has grown dim, and to some lost artists the world has now appeared in seeming senselessness, as an absurd conglomeration of debris.

Yes, world culture today is of course in crisis, a crisis of great severity. The newest directions in art seek to outpace this crisis on the wooden horse of clever stratagems—on the assumption that if one invents deft, resourceful new methods, it will be as though the crisis never was. Vain hopes. Nothing worthy can be built on a neglect of higher meanings and on a relativistic view of concepts and culture as a whole. Indeed, something greater than a phenomenon confined to art can be discerned shimmering here beneath the surface—shimmering not with light but with an ominous crimson glow.

Looking intently, we can see that behind these ubiquitous and seemingly innocent experiments of rejecting "antiquated" tradition there lies a deep-seated hostility toward any spirituality. This relentless cult of novelty, with its assertion that art need not be good or pure, just so long as it is new, newer, and newer still, conceals an unyielding and long-sustained attempt to undermine, ridicule and uproot all moral precepts. There is no God, there is no truth, the universe is chaotic, all is relative, "the world as text," a text any post-modernist is willing to compose. How clamorous it all is, but also—how helpless.

For several decades now, world literature, music, painting and sculpture have exhibited a stubborn tendency to grow not higher but to the side, not toward the highest achievements of craftsmanship and of the human spirit but toward their disintegration into a frantic and insidious "novelty." To decorate public spaces we put up sculptures that estheticize pure ugliness—but we no longer register surprise. And if visitors from outer space were to pick up our music over the airwaves, how could they ever guess that earthlings once had a Bach, a Beethoven and a Schubert, now abandoned as out of date and obsolete?

If we, the creators of art, will obediently submit to this downward slide, if we cease to hold dear the great cultural tradition of the foregoing centuries together with the spiritual foundations from which it grew—we will be contributing to a highly dangerous fall of the human spirit on earth, to a degeneration of mankind into some kind of lower state, closer to the animal world.

And yet, it is hard to believe that we will allow this to occur. Even in Russia, so terribly ill right now, we wait and hope that after the coma and a period of silence, we shall feel the breath of a reawakening Russian literature, and that we shall witness the arrival of fresh new forces—of our younger brothers.

Suggestions for Discussion

1. Explain Solzhenitsyn's point that God provides the opportunity for many skilled, original, and diverse artists. How does he relate this occurrence to the tradition of literature? What does he mean by "healthy conservatism"?

2. What distinguishes twentieth-century literature from the tradition of the past?

3. What is Solzhenitsyn's reaction to "avant-gardism"? Why does he believe that this art movement differs from any other art movement in previous times? Why does he regard the avant-garde as destructive?

4. What is the tone of this speech? Is it suited to the subject? Does Solzhenitsyn distinguish between the literature of the West and that of Russia? According to the author, what role did communism play in the development of twentieth-century literature?

5. Discuss the author's use of the term *post-modernism.* How does he trace the rise of post-modernism to the loss of spirituality in the West?

Suggestions for Writing

1. Write a paper in which you attempt to summarize and evaluate the author's conservative hostility to twentieth-century literature.

2. T. S. Eliot's essay "Tradition and the Individual Talent" makes several points similar to the one made in this speech. Write a paper in which you compare and contrast the arguments of both authors. (You will find the other essay in the *Collected Essays* of T. S. Eliot.)

❧❧❧

AARON COPLAND

How We Listen to Music

Aaron Copland (1900–1990) studied music in the United States and France. His French teacher, Nadia Boulanger, was the first to conduct his *Symphony for Organ and Orchestra* in 1925. Much of Copland's work reflects the influence of American jazz and folk music; good examples of this are *John Henry* (1940) and his well-known ballets *Billy the Kid* (1938), *Rodeo* (1942), and *Appalachian Spring* (1944). His major symphonic works are *El Salon Mexico* (1936) and *The Third Symphony* (1946); he also composed music for films. Copland was awarded the National Medal for Arts four years before he died, and he continues to be a major influence in contemporary music, decades after his death. Copland also wrote about music. In this essay from *What to Listen for in Music* (1939, 1957), he provides a defense for the difficulty of contemporary music and explains the obligations of the intelligent listener.

We all listen to music according to our separate capacities. But, for the sake of analysis, the whole listening process may become clearer if we break it up into its component parts, so to speak. In a certain sense we all listen to music on three separate planes. For lack of a better terminology, one might name these: (1) the sensuous plane, (2) the expressive plane, (3) the sheerly musical plane. The only advantage to be gained from mechanically splitting up the listening process into these hypothetical planes is the clearer view to be had of the way in which we listen.

The simplest way of listening to music is to listen for the sheer pleasure of the musical sound itself. That is the sensuous plane. It is the plane on which we hear music without thinking, without considering it in any way. One turns on the radio while doing something else and absent-mindedly bathes in the sound. A kind of brainless but attractive state of mind is engendered by the mere sound appeal of the music.

You may be sitting in a room reading this book. Imagine one note struck on the piano. Immediately that one note is enough to change the atmosphere of the room—providing that the sound element in music is a powerful and mysterious agent, which it would be foolish to deride or belittle.

The surprising thing is that many people who consider themselves qualified music lovers abuse that plane in listening. They go to concerts in order to lose themselves. They use music as a consolation or an escape. They enter an ideal world where one doesn't have to think of the realities of everyday life. Of course they aren't thinking about the music either. Music allows them to leave it, and they go off to a place to dream, dreaming because of and apropos of the music yet never quite listening to it. ~~musc primal~~

Yes, the sound appeal of music is a potent and primitive force, but you must not allow it to usurp a disproportionate share of your interest. The sensuous plane is an important one in music, a very important one, but it does not constitute the whole story.

There is no need to digress further on the sensuous plane. Its appeal to every normal human being is self-evident. There is, however, such a thing as becoming more sensitive to the different kinds of sound stuff as used by various composers. For all composers do not use that sound stuff in the same way. Don't get the idea that the value of music is commensurate with its sensuous appeal or that the loveliest sounding music is made by the greatest composer. If that were so, Ravel would be a greater creator than Beethoven. The point is that the sound element varies with each composer, that his usage of sound forms an integral part of his style and must be taken into account when listening. The reader can see, therefore, that a more conscious approach is valuable even on this primary plane of music listening.

The second plane on which music exists is what I have called the expressive one. Here, immediately, we tread on controversial ground. Composers have a way of shying away from any discussion of music's expressive side. Did not Stravinsky himself proclaim that his music was an "object," a "thing," with a life of its own, and with no other meaning than its own purely musical existence? This intransigent attitude of Stravinsky's may be due to the fact that so many people have tried to read different meanings into so many pieces. Heaven knows it is difficult enough to say precisely what it is that a piece of music means, to say it definitely, to say it finally so that everyone is satisfied with your explanation. But that should not lead one to the other extreme of denying to music the right to be "expressive."

My own belief is that all music has an expressive power, some more and some less, but that all music has a certain meaning behind the notes and that the meaning behind the notes constitutes, after all, what the piece is saying, what the piece is about. The whole problem can be stated quite simply by asking, "Is there a meaning to music?" My answer to that would be, "Yes." And "Can you state in so many words what the meaning is?" My answer to that would be, "No." Therein lies the difficulty.

Simple-minded souls will never be satisfied with the answer to the second of these questions. They always want music to have a meaning, and the more concrete it is the better they like it. The more the music reminds them of a train, a storm, a funeral, or any other familiar conception the more expressive it appears to be to them. This popular idea of music's meaning—stimulated and abetted by the usual run of musical commentator—should be discouraged wherever and whenever it is met. One timid lady once confessed to me that she suspected something seriously lacking in her appreciation of music because of her inability to connect it with anything definite. That is getting the whole thing backward, of course.

Still, the question remains, How close should the intelligent music lover wish to come to pinning a definite meaning to any particular work? No closer than a general concept, I should say. Music expresses, at different moments, serenity or exuberance, regrets or triumph, fury or delight. It expresses each of these moods, and many others, in a numberless variety of subtle shadings and differences. It may even express a state of meaning for which there exists no adequate word in any language. In that case, musicians often like to say that it has only a purely musical meaning. They sometimes go further and say that *all* music has only a purely musical meaning. What they really mean is that no appropriate word can be found to express the music's meaning and that, even if it could, they do not feel the need of finding it.

But whatever the professional musician may hold, most musical novices still search for specific words with which to pin down their musical reactions. That is why they always find Tschaikovsky easier to "understand" than Beethoven. In the first place, it is easier to pin a meaning-word on a Tschaikovsky piece than on a Beethoven one. Much easier. Moreover, with the Russian composer, every time you come back to a piece of his it almost always says the same thing to you, whereas with Beethoven it is often quite difficult to put your finger right on what he is saying. And any musician will tell you that that is why Beethoven is the greater composer. Because music which always says the same thing to you will necessarily soon become dull music, but music whose meaning is slightly different with each hearing has a greater chance of remaining alive.

Listen, if you can, to the forty-eight fugue themes of Bach's *Well Tempered Clavichord.* Listen to each theme, one after another. You will soon realize that each theme mirrors a different world of feeling. You will also soon realize that the more beautiful a theme seems to you the harder it is to find any word that will describe it to your complete satisfaction. Yes, you will certainly know whether it is a gay theme or a sad one. You will be able, in other words, in your own mind, to draw a frame of emotional feeling around your theme. Now study the sad one a little closer. Try to pin down the exact quality of its sadness. Is it pessimistically sad or resignedly sad; is it fatefully sad or smilingly sad?

Let us suppose that you are fortunate and can describe to your own satisfaction in so many words the exact meaning of your chosen theme. There is still no guarantee that anyone else will be satisfied. Nor need they be. The important thing is that each one feel for himself the specific expressive quality of a theme or, similarly, an entire piece of music. And if it is a great work of art, don't expect it to mean exactly the same thing to you each time you return to it.

Themes or pieces need not express only one emotion, of course. Take such a theme as the first main one of the *Ninth Symphony,* for example. It is clearly made up of different elements. It does not say only one thing. Yet anyone hearing it immediately gets a feeling of strength, a feeling of power. It isn't a power that comes simply because the theme is played loudly. It is a power inherent in the theme itself. The extraordinary strength and vigor of the theme results in the listener's receiving an impression that a forceful statement has been made. But one should never try to boil it down to "the fateful hammer of life," etc. That is where the trouble begins. The musician, in his exasperation, says it means nothing but the notes themselves, whereas the nonprofessional is only too anxious to hang on to any explanation that gives him the illusion of getting closer to the music's meaning.

Now, perhaps, the reader will know better what I mean when I say that music does have an expressive meaning but that we cannot say in so many words what that meaning is.

The third plane on which music exists is the sheerly musical plane. Besides the pleasurable sound of music and the expressive feeling that it gives off, music does exist in terms of the notes themselves and of their manipulation. Most listeners are not sufficiently conscious of this third plane....

Professional musicians, on the other hand, are, if anything, too conscious of the mere notes themselves. They often fall into the error of becoming so engrossed with their arpeggios and staccatos that they forget the deeper aspects of the music they are performing. But from the layman's standpoint, it is not so much a matter of getting over bad habits on the sheerly musical plane as of increasing one's awareness of what is going on, in so far as the notes are concerned.

When the man in the street listens to the "notes themselves" with any degree of concentration, he is most likely to make some mention of the melody. Either he hears a pretty melody or he does not, and he generally lets it go at that. Rhythm is likely to gain his attention next, particularly if it seems exciting. But harmony and tone color are generally taken for granted, if they are thought of consciously at all. As for music's having a definite form of some kind, that idea seems never to have occurred to him.

It is very important for all of us to become more alive to music on its sheerly musical plane. After all, an actual musical material is being used. The intelligent listener must be prepared to increase his awareness of the musical material and what happens to it. He must hear the melodies, the rhythms, the harmonies, the tone colors in a more conscious fashion. But above all he must, in order to follow the line of the composer's thought, know something of the principles of musical form. Listening to all of these elements is listening on the sheerly musical plane.

Let me repeat that I have split up mechanically the three separate planes on which we listen merely for the sake of greater clarity. Actually, we never listen on one or the other of these planes. What we do is to correlate them— listening in all three ways at the same time. It takes no mental effort, for we do it instinctively.

Perhaps an analogy with what happens to us when we visit the theater will make this instinctive correlation clearer. In the theater, you are aware of the actors and actresses, costumes and sets, sounds and movements. All these give one the sense that the theater is a pleasant place to be in. They constitute the sensuous plane in our theatrical reactions.

The expressive plane in the theater would be derived from the feeling that you get from what is happening on the stage. You are moved to pity, excitement, or gayety. It is this general feeling, generated aside from the particular words being spoken, a certain emotional something which exists on the stage, that is analogous to the expressive quality in music.

The plot and plot development is equivalent to our sheerly musical plane. The playwright creates and develops a character in just the same way that a composer creates and develops a theme. According to the degree of your awareness of the way in which the artist in either field handles his material you will become a more intelligent listener.

It is easy enough to see that the theatergoer never is conscious of any of these elements separately. He is aware of them all at the same time. The same is true of music listening. We simultaneously and without thinking listen on all three planes.

In a sense, the ideal listener is both inside and outside the music at the same moment, judging it and enjoying it, wishing it would go one way and watching it go another—almost like the composer at the moment he composes it; because in order to write his music, the composer must also be inside and outside his music, carried away by it and yet coldly critical of it. A subjective and objective attitude is implied in both creating and listening to music.

What the reader should strive for, then, is a more *active* kind of listening. Whether you listen to Mozart or Duke Ellington, you can deepen your understanding of music only by being a more conscious and aware listener—not someone who is just listening, but someone who is listening *for* something.

Suggestions for Discussion

1. According to Copland, on what different levels do we listen to music?

2. Why does Copland believe that listening to music as an escape is an inadequate response to it?

3. Does Copland believe that a musical composition can have meaning? Does he believe it possible to state that meaning easily?

4. How, according to Copland, is the meaning of a musical composition related to its expressive power? What boundaries does Copland place on the expressive power of music? Explain his use of Bach in this regard.

5. What for Copland are significant differences between Tchaikovsky and Beethoven? Why does he consider Beethoven the greater composer?

6. What are the elements of the third plane of music? How do professional musicians and listeners of music differ about this third plane? What criticism does Copland make of musicians? What obligation does the intelligent listener have to this plane?

7. Explain Copland's analogy between the elements in music and in drama. What important differences exist for the audience in its response to both forms of art?

8. Contrast E. M. Forster's position (Forster's essay, "Art for Art's Sake," is on p. 388) with Copland's in the matter of meaning in the arts. Can you account for their different points of view?

Suggestions for Writing

1. Listen to a composition by Bach and to one by Duke Ellington and, insofar as you can, discuss the music on all three levels.

2. Summarize Copland's argument about the problems of responding to art. Do you find this essay helpful for your own response? Explain your position in detail.

∽∽∽∽

DAVID DUBAL

The Age of Modernism

David Dubal is a pianist, a writer, a Juilliard School professor, and a broadcaster on radio station WQXR. Formerly a program director at the WNCN classical music station in New York, Dubal has won the Peabody Award and an Emmy for the documentary *The Golden Age of the Piano*. Among his books are *Reflections from the Keyboard* (1984), *The Art of the Piano* (1989), *Conversations with Menuhin* (1992), and *Evenings with Horowitz* (1991). The following excerpt from his 2001 book, *The Essential Canon of Classical Music*, is an attempt to make modernist music accessible to those who are intimidated by classical music because they find it too difficult to understand or are unable to relate to it.

It is not possible to declare one perfect turning point into Modernism, a term that has commonly been used for composers living into the twentieth century. When a common language falters, new forms must come into being to provide for new expression; so in the early nineteenth century did rigid Classical forms give way to Romanticism. When Romanticism in turn gave way to

Modernism, composers were reacting not so much against rigid forms (after all, many nineteenth- and twentieth-century composers found the sonata form still valid) as against the tonal system. By the third quarter of the nineteenth century, chords had become clogged with different tones. Composers were constantly modulating, hoping always to refresh the ear. Wagner did this most potently, and most composers writing in his wake felt he had left them little more to accomplish. They were right. But composers are, if anything, creative, and many would successfully find their own style in the new century.

No composer of the late nineteenth century was more aware than Liszt that he was working in an exhausted musical vocabulary. Liszt was the first to realize that the major and minor key tonal system would eventually collapse, and by the mid-1870s he was writing small piano pieces that were tonally ambiguous, even titling one of them *Bagatelle Without Tonality*. Nobody wanted to listen to these pieces, and most thought the great virtuoso had gone mad. At the time of his death in 1886, he was the most radical composer in the world.

Liszt set the stage for Modernism, which began in France. Debussy, even as a youngster, was impatient with rules and with thickly textured Romanticism. At the 1887 Paris Exhibition, he heard a Javanese gamelan orchestra and felt released into an entirely new soundscape. Keenly aware of the Wagnerian dead end, and temperamentally antipathetic to the German tradition, Debussy plunged into Modernism both in form and in harmony. In his *Prélude à l'aprés-midi d'un faune* (1892–1894), the fixed forms of the past were replaced by new forms, which were also reflected in new styles of painting, architecture, and poetry. Regularity and balance no longer mattered. Debussy varied his material in the most original and subtle ways, and his forms left behind almost any resemblance to past procedures. No composer within the scope of traditional instruments had ever developed such a heightened sense of timbre. For the diversity and irregularity of his forms (the word *structure* is too rigid to describe them), Debussy needed a revolutionary harmonic system. He used chords as building blocks, shifting them and juxtaposing them for contrast rather than resolution. His impact on music has been felt throughout the century.

Debussy died in 1918. His radical friend, Erik Satie, lived on until 1925. Satie was a far smaller figure, but he served as a catalyst for many young Moderns. His outlook was a severe but necessary reaction to Wagner and Germanic forms in general. His is a touching art, with neither pretension nor caricature. The writer Laurence Davies commented on "Satie's own terrifying willingness to disrobe, shedding all those aids to beauty which the ordinary composer finds indispensable." With his weird titles and pure whimsy, Satie was a breath of fresh air in an age dominated by Mahler and Strauss.

The first generation of composers truly immersed in Modernism were those born in the 1870s, including Scriabin, Vaughan Williams, Ravel, Ives, and Schoenberg. After 1903 Scriabin broke with his early Romanticism. By 1906 he was immersed in mysticism and composed a kind of mystic impressionism, building his chords in fourths; in the *Sixth Piano Sonata* he dispensed with key signatures and entered a trackless territory of atonality. He was a messianic Theosophist, and his music presents a restless longing to be released from the flesh, to dissolve into the universe.

Ralph Vaughan Williams was an English nationalist who brought new energy to English music as well as some advanced technique. Maurice Ravel, far less progressive than Debussy, was a masterful technician who composed illuminating commentaries on each of the forms he invested with his genius. Charles Ives was a progressive American nationalist who lived in dreadful isolation in a musically conventional environment dominated by the nineteenth-century German tradition. Disillusioned, he stopped composing in 1918. Until that time he was amazingly inventive, using atonality, polytonality, clusters, quarter-tones, and much else. The contemporary use of aleatory music (music characterized by chance), noise, and electronic collage come directly from Ives.

The innovations of Ives still sound pungent, as do those of Arnold Schoenberg. If Debussy's basically nonviolent art was a radical departure from tonality, Schoenberg's far more aggressive (and, to the public at large, ugly and neurotic) art would culminate in a new system of composing altogether. Beginning his career as a Wagnerian, he naturally evolved into atonal expressionism. Through the lean war years, Schoenberg the composer was silent, but the theoretician was hard at work, slowly developing a theory in which all twelve tones of the chromatic scale are equal. It is called the twelve-tone system, or serialism.

The critic Wilfrid Mellers nicely defines the theory of music without tonality: "In chromatic serial music as used by Schoenberg, each note of the composition (chords as well as melodic ideas) must be derived from a pre-ordained sequence, or 'row' of the twelve chromatic semitones, either in the row's original form, or inverted, or backwards, or backwards and inverted. The serial principle is extended by later composers (Boulez, Stockhausen) to rhythm (or rather metrical proportions), dynamic and timbre (the allocation of notes in the series to different instruments)." Naturally, many composers by temperament and conditioning rejected Schoenberg or found this new aesthetic system to be a dreadful error. Debussy, Busoni, Scriabin, and Reger died before Schoenberg's earliest serial works of the mid-1920s, which he wrote when he was already past fifty.

The early 1880s saw the births of Bartók, Webern, Varèse, Berg, and Stravinsky. Bartók in the beginning took from Debussy, Richard Strauss, and

Stravinsky but found his personal style in a dissonant, compelling Hungarian nationalism. He ranks near Stravinsky and Schoenberg in searching creativity and perfection of form, though he did not have quite the same impact on music internationally. Berg well showed the flexibility of Schoenberg's system, which he used in his later works. Berg can be called the twelve-tone system's most advanced Romantic, and his music always conveyed a deeply emotional message. Varèse destroyed his earlier work, up to the orchestral piece *Amériques,* composed about 1920. His work would eventually become sound densities, dispensing with any development of ideas and all directionality. He longed for sounds never previously heard or suspected. In his few later tape and electronic compositions with human voice and instruments, he opened up a new world of musical meaning. Webern wrote a complex serial music that captivated composers in the 1950s and 1960s.

For the twentieth-century musical public, Stravinsky was the major figure. He composed in nearly every genre, inventing new rhythms and a vast array of textures, juxtaposing idioms, creating unique harmonic combinations, and so forth. Always a firm tonalist, in his later years he shocked the musical establishment by refreshing his work through serialism.

The above-mentioned are all major innovators, highlights of twentieth-century composition, but many more composers have contributed to the art as well. In a sense, twentieth-century music was a further development of Romanticism, starting with impressionism and ending with minimalism. The diversity has been astonishing, ranging from Szymanowski, Bloch, Respighi, Prokofiev, Hindemith, Poulenc, Barber, Copland, Shostakovich, Kodály, Walton, Schuman, Carter, Gershwin, Sessions, Schnittke, Glass, Crumb, Stockhausen, Ligeti, Bernstein, Babbitt, Rorem, Maxwell Davies, Henze, Corigliano, Dutilleux, and Zwilich, to name only the most celebrated.

How, then, does the world of "classical" music stand at the beginning of the twenty-first century? Oddly, music, with all of this diversity, has been content with instruments that were invented and perfected long ago. No new sound outlets came about until electronic music, and (surprisingly) this development has not been utilized as much as many thought it would be. Only a few composers have experimented with non-Western instruments. No one has invented a keyboard that goes beyond the semitone— something that would enrich composers' palettes immeasurably.

It seems that presently there can be little that is truly new or important, little that can be built upon. The unprecedented market forces of the twentieth century have shown very little concern with promoting classical music. When promoters do focus on classical music, they awkwardly push, over and over, the few most famous works. Over sixty years ago, Virgil Thomson in his book *The State of Music* wrote, "When music shall have become just another consumer commodity like chewing gum, its grand epoch will be over. Already a great deal of it is designed, like central heating, to be merely present. Keeping the rot peripheral, preventing it from infecting the heart, is not going to be easy. Too many people make money out of it."

In the last fifty years, the young have had an unprecedented amount of money to spend, and they have been taught to spend it on bad music—simplistic lyrics set to simplistic music, simulating an orgiastic beat and giving off a constant noise pollution. The "rot" has been getting ever louder and is ever present. Many young people hear classical music only in shopping malls, where it is played to prevent teenage loitering.

Even worse is the shameless way music has become a slave to advertising. We have long been used to hearing never-ending jingles for products, but now television at all times uses a perpetual sound beat, a boom-boom announcing each segment of news or programming, ostensibly to promote excitement but in fact to tame and numb the audience. Movies these days seldom use orchestras but rather go for cheaper synthesized sound, which they purvey, like drugs, in constantly increasing doses. Crushed forever is the sweet popular dance music of yesteryear's big bands. Since Elvis Presley's death, not a day has passed without his image being broadcast or published. He cannot be avoided. Nothing has emerged to counter the severe damage. Amateur home music-making has all but died out, and the public school system is in a shambles, cutting musical education programs and mostly avoiding any contact with art generally. Indeed, "serious" music has been attacked and is associated with that particularly dangerous word, *elitism*. The white male European product has become the enemy of a multicultural American standard.

The bright side is only this: in a largely uneducated mass and an ever-growing population, there somehow seems to be a place for everything. Classical musicians are now so numerous that they are cultivating a new class of excellent listeners. They teach and are usually aggressive in showing their appreciation of the arts. Looking around the concert halls of the world, I find that audiences are no longer made up only of the elderly. A young lawyer recently asked me, "Who is this Harry Partch? I like his stuff," and people are finally listening to Schoenberg without cringing. Serious composers today—and there are thousands of them—mostly live well from grants, commissions, and university positions, and they continue to pour out their work. Perhaps in the twenty-first century, beauty will make a comeback. For most of human history, it was an integral part of being human. In 1941 the great painting connoisseur Bernard Berenson wrote, "Man is a terrible destroyer, but what a creator! The human past, long before written history begins, is strewn with figured records of his love of beauty and testimonials to his genius as creator. Indeed man seems to have begun as artist and only in the last hundred years has he succeeded in emancipating himself from art completely, exchanging the possible Phidias in him for a Ford."

Suggestions for Discussion

1. What was music like just before "the Age of Modernism," and how did its style change in the new age?

2. Which musicians are the key figures in Dubal's musical history, and why are they important?

3. What does Dubal have to say about the state of music in modern times, especially classical music?

Suggestion for Writing

Compare David Dubal's text to Nick Hornby's article, *I'm Like a Bird,* on page 337. Write an essay examining how their perspectives diverge on the subject of popular music and explain your own feelings about the possible artistic validity of the form.

JULIAN JOHNSON

Who Needs Classical Music?

Julian Johnson (b. 1963), a lecturer in music at the University of Oxford, is the author of *Webern and the Transformation of Nature* (2000). Originally trained as a composer, Johnson has produced new musical works for the BBC Symphony Orchestra and the BBC Singers. In the following selection, taken from *Who Needs Classical Music?* (2002), he discusses the various functions of music.

Music does things for us and to us. We use it in different ways to mediate our experiences of the world and ourselves. Its capacity to shape those experiences and to define our self-awareness is the subject of myth and legend and a fact of everyday life. That such symbolic mediations can have a power and a reality greater than the everyday is an important characteristic of our symbol-dominated culture. My argument is based on the idea that we value music for what it does for us and that our musical choices reflect these values. Individually, we often make different musical choices in different social contexts because we expect music to fulfill a range of functions for us in those contexts. Our judgment about the same piece of music can change completely depending on its context.

A piece of avant-garde music, for example, heard on the radio, might be dismissed as "rubbish" by the same person who finds it "good" (i.e., extremely effective) as the score to a horror film. By the same token, I might find the music to a film thrilling while I watch the film but rather dull presented as autonomous music in a concert hall. I expect music to fulfill quite different functions in the two contexts. We do this all the time. We have little difficulty in identifying music that is "good for" a funeral as opposed to a children's party, background music for a shopping center as opposed to music for a military parade, and so on. Furthermore, we recognize that a certain music is "good" at fulfilling certain functions even if we would not judge the music as "good in itself" if it were removed from that function. In other words, we can appreciate and even enjoy music in certain social contexts but might not use that music privately, in our own domestic space. This is important because it highlights that our musical judgments are much more astute and broad-minded once we are aware of social function. What we might think of as the functionless activity of private listening also constitutes a function of music, but one that we consider so "natural" and ubiquitous that we think its standard could be applied universally.

This is the first and most common barrier to thinking about music and considering the partiality of our judgments. Most everyday uses of music function as background to some other activity. Those who design radio programs understand this very well and select different kinds of music for different times of day. Music aimed at commuters on their way home, for example, is likely to be more mellow and relaxing than the upbeat and energetic music played to the same commuters in the morning. Music played in shopping malls is most effective when it encourages people to take their time and feel at ease and when it suggests an air of classic, rich living. All this is obvious enough. But what about those times when people actively choose a certain kind of music, when listening is a more deliberate activity? Here again, we largely make choices according to function. What we want the music to "do" determines our choice. Most people have a sense of what music they would choose to make them feel a certain way. Or, more accurately, people choose certain music at certain times knowing that they produce certain complex and indefinable effects. So we "feel like" some Billie Holiday now, or some Bach, or some Jimi Hendrix.

In essence, these choices are not so different from the ones we make, or that are made for us, about the background music that surrounds us at home or when we are out shopping. In both cases the music is chosen either to complement and reinforce our existing mood or to help change it. Much background music, particularly music on the radio, is used primarily to fill time. That we use music so often to stave off boredom, to fill temporal space that would otherwise seem empty, suggests that silence makes us anxious, that our culture suffers from a collective *horror vacui*. We often use music to "help time pass"—as if, without music, time would grind to a terrifying halt. This filling of time and manipulation of mood accounts for the majority of music-use in the developed world. It applies to a diverse range of musics and listeners and certainly applies as much to the use of classical music as it does to various popular musics. This function is so overwhelming that many people would find it hard to conceive of any other. It becomes normative in the sense that it comes to define what music is.

This normative definition of what music is *for* obscures the difference between musical judgments made by quite different criteria. What passes for debate under deceptive titles like "Is Mozart better than Madonna?" is usually nonsense because it presumes that these very different kinds of music serve the same function. That they are oriented around different functions is underlined by the fact that they are made differently. Their specific musical differences lend themselves to different functions. Music is thus no more a completely subjective matter than any other symbolic form. While different people, at different times, inevitably respond differently to the same piece of music, this difference is not infinitely variable. The idea of art presumes that the object is prior to the act of reception. People may leave the cinema with a variety of emotional experiences, but *Schindler's List* is not a comedy, is not set in the future, and is not about a giant ape called Kong. It does something different than a Disney cartoon.

And so it is with Mozart and Madonna. They are functionally equivalent only if one treats them in the most general way: they are both "music" just as *Schindler's List* and *Toy Story* are both films. But just as these two films do different things because they are made differently, so do Mozart and Madonna, and for the same reason. Approaches that focus only on reception and social use often ignore this basic fact, taking the functional equivalence of the recorded object as indicative of a wider equivalence. Only in specifically musical terms do their differences become apparent: they are made of different musical materials that are organized in different ways. Neither is understood by the criteria of the other. Mozart is outdated and makes for poor dance music, and Madonna's music lacks the sophistication of phrasing and form found in Mozart.

Suggestions for Discussion

1. What is the importance of context when judging a piece of music?
2. Why does Johnson object to broad statements such as "Mozart is better than Madonna"? How might you change this statement in order to make it a more relevant contribution to a discussion about music?

3. When Johnson writes "the idea of art presumes that the object is prior to the act of reception," what is he saying about the relationship between a work of art and the person who is "receiving" it?

Suggestion for Writing

Write about a piece of music that has the power to affect your mood. How did it take on meaning for you? Has it influenced you in different ways at different times? Make reference to Johnson's theories about the relevance of music and its context.

 ⌇⌇⌇⌇⌇

C R I S T I A N   A M I G O

Intervention #1: Musical Openings

Cristian Amigo (b. 1963) is a New York composer and guitarist with a Ph.D. in ethnomusicology. He has received fellowships and commissions from the American Composers Forum, the Sundance Institute's Film Composer Labs, and the Smithsonian Institution's Center for Folklife and Cultural Heritage. Amigo's work, which has been produced for film, dance, theater, and live performance, combines elements of jazz with electronics and Latin American music. This essay, which includes musical notation for one of Amigo's original compositions, calls for open-mindedness in exploring new forms of music.

Part 1: Intro

Music is a notoriously difficult subject to speak or write about. The first time someone sits down to write about or explain it, their enthusiasm usually hits a wall of silence…itself a kind of music. What is *music,* anyway? We assume its reality and acknowledge its central part in our personal and cultural lives, listen to it every day, and spend a substantial amount of our incomes on it. We identify with it and take offense if our favorite music is slighted, and we know what we like and especially what we dislike. We buy it, download it (legally and illegally), shape it with software, dedicate our lives to it, study its organizing principles, make love to it, teach it, turn it up, call the police about it, vibrate our cars with it, perform it on instruments, express it in song, collect it, and mark our histories and identities with it. We worship with it, marry to it, animate ritual with it, call down the *orishas*, and specify what we want played at our funerals. We tease and harass with it, torture with it, and kill with the pumped up feeling it gives us. We sound it at parades and political events to inspire and express identity, solidarity, and patriotism, and we sing it to denounce war and political positions we find offensive. So what is this *it*, this quasi-object we collect and that we experientially and empirically understand as a fact—a known quantity in the world?

Words fail us. We resort to adjectival expressions (awesome, rocking, dope, astounding, miraculous, pedantic, fucking great, stupid, boring, ecstatic) that intimate how we feel, but nothing about the music itself. We speak of Bowie, Shankar, Björk, Miles, Gardel, and Stravinsky, as channellers or icons of music. We name bands, orchestras, *conjuntos*, styles, genres, places and cultures. We pontificate, circumscribe, limit, and expand upon it. We recognize talent in music and deny the label of music to the "noise" that other people make. But what is *it* we expand upon and deny to Others?

It is a quandary, especially for Westerners, to be unable to express in language something they experience as true or real. Those who claim this sort of knowledge are usually labeled mystics or religious fundamentalists. One difficulty in knowing stems from the seemingly unbridgeable divide between the *thing* music and *talk* about music, a situation the American musicologist Charles Seeger once described as the *musicological juncture*. If you agree this is true and break down the musical experience into the two categories of music and talk, it follows that they are two distinct phenomenological domains. This position emphasizes knowledge of music as experiential, distinctly embodied, and independent of conceptual understanding for its meaning. Further, it implies that music must be understood in its own terms as vibration and experience—not as the formal structure of sound as expressed in Western music theory terms such as counterpoint, melody, and harmony, and definitely not in talk and writing about music which is confused with music itself. Do you find yourself frustrated when talking about music? Do you sense that you never quite get to *it*?

Musicians and composers often take this position and in so doing unfortunately make their work and artistic process mysterious to the nonexpert. Popular musicians generally have a mistrust of musical speculation. They consider academic writing and/or critique spurious, self-serving, and intrusive. At the same time they hope for positive reviews and articles (maybe only negative feedback is spurious). This attitude obscures the interdependent relationship between the artist and the critic, and also feeds into the romantic mythology of the musician as the ever-suffering culture hero whose Orphic skills render him above mere mortals. Just think of all the tantrum-throwing prima donnas in pop music with larger egos than talent, or the sad never-ending cases of self-destructive musicians, and you can see how obnoxious and tragic this myth can be.

Not everyone agrees that there is a divide between music and its description in words, especially academics and writers whose livelihoods are dependent upon their writings "on" music. Writers assume there is a relationship between music and social structures, ideologies, class, ethnicity, race, gender, etc. and that these relationships can be expressed through language. Although stylistically the writing of academics and journalists is usually very different, they both work under the assumption that talk and writing about music are worthwhile and plausible (related to reality) endeavors. Academics, concerned with tying music to the social sciences or humanities, have developed a critical sociology of music and cultural studies types of approaches that reveal the life of music in many different contexts. Journalists still serve their classic function of "thumbs up" or "thumbs down," but the best ones show a subtlety of thought and insight that is a valuable corrective to the stiffness of most academic accounts.

In contrast to their "mythological" counterparts, other musicians and composers, especially academic ones, are so tied to their conceptual apparatus that they have to invent entire metaphysical systems and rationales before they feel they have the authority to sound even one note. They are composers without bodies—just brains, soft pencils, and music notation software. The pressure to give a coherent rationale to artistic creation even infects some of the most gifted improvisers, most of whom have banished the consideration of the embodiedness of talent and intuition from their own accounts of their craft, instead falling back onto a technical language that mimics the intellectual absorption of Western music theory and its absence of bodies. This is partly because the symbol "body" has been historically ascribed onto *bodies* of color in opposition to the supposed superiority of the white Western *mind,* and this symbolic violence has an ongoing affect.

As a working artist, I, like many other contemporary composers and musicians, try to walk a middle ground between oral and written tradition—one that is cognizant of the intercultural and (especially in the U.S.) racial tensions inherent in such a project. It's a hazardous course full of false starts and rabbit holes. With a million possibilities in front of us, we have to make some choices from among them, then work with the elements that we hope will make sense together. Intuition about these choices is becoming increasingly important. Intuition in the service of perfect technique is our impossible but worthwhile goal, and being culturally informed is our responsibility as artist-citizens. Today, everybody is eclectic. What you do not want to be is miscellaneous.

This is all very interesting, or not, but have we strayed from our initial question about the identity of *music*? It seems we have, and that is the point: straying is inevitable. Fortunately, there is no ultimate answer to our question. Nobody can say with certainty what music *is.* Music is mediated by the body through culturally and personally specific concepts, metaphors, and experiences. And music is activated through action: active listening, thinking, creation, and performance. In human life, *music* is about music *as, of, and, in, on, for* and *about* X, and the answers are inextricably linked to personal and cultural *value.* Anthropologist John Blacking's definition of music as "humanly organized sound," is perhaps one of the best open-ended attempts at answering the unanswerable question: "what is music?" His egalitarian definition identifies the two crucial components of *music:* people and sound. Perhaps you have never thought of music this way, or perhaps it is obvious to you? In any case, music is not just about sound and its structure, nor exclusively about music-makers, listeners, and celebrities.

Definitions of music are mostly circumscriptions, impositions, limitations on its scope and importance in our lives. A definition is tied to an agenda. It has something to prove—usually at the expense of others and to the benefit of the definer: "we're the ones who know real music" is the basic assumption. Overly wrought closed definitions limit both sides of the argument in the American culture wars. Both tightly wound conservatives and fussy avant-gardes know what's best, and best for you and me....If only we could understand the question of value as they do....If only we were as intelligent as them. The point is we do understand the question and we are as or more intelligent if only because we entertain the possibility of possibilities.

As an artist and scholar, I hope to open the door to myriad interpretations of, or contexts for, playing, thinking, and talking about music. In a sense we're all experts in music: we've had a lifetime of exposure to it and we know what is good and what sucks. But we have to be careful about the certainty of our knowledge and opinions. As the Zen monk Shunryu Suzuki once said: "In the beginner's mind there are many possibilities; in the expert's mind there are few." I hope this essay inspires some and riles up others who see this as yet another claim to cultural relativism in a time that requires sure knowledge of everything, including music. These people view music and art as "optional" components in a formal education, an innocuous pastime that shouldn't say anything except "buy me" or "let me entertain you," and that is engaged in between "serious" moments such as the production of widgets and reading, 'riting, and 'rithmetic. However, even a cursory examination reveals music as an artistic and cultural resource with the potential to model cooperative forms of sociality, and is thus an important part of a basic education in the contemporary world.

The poet Wallace Stevens writes, "music is feeling, then, not sound." For the Argentinean novelist Julio Cortázar, music (from Latin American boleros to tangos to Louis Armstrong) is the soundtrack and a touchstone for his reminiscences of Paris and Buenos Aires. For the Kaluli people of Papua New Guinea, music is linked to the "acoustic ecology" of the rainforest. The *Oxford Dictionary of Music* does not include a definition for *music* and this is a wise editorial choice. The Webster's Collegiate takes a stab at it and defines music as, "[t]he science or art of ordering tones or sounds in succession, in combination, and in temporal relationships to produce a composition having unity and continuity." Why "succession" instead of a pile or mass of sound? Why ordering instead of disordering or randomness/indeterminacy? Why unity instead of chaos? Why continuity rather than non-linearity?—no reason at all, just convention and the unquestioning assimilation of a life-long truisms about the question: "What is music?"

Part 2 Development:
Musical Exercise

Musicians spend a lifetime working through exercises that build and maintain their technique. The following is a musical exercise designed to build your music culture chops (a geek word meaning music skills). It is an open-ended exercise that I begin but do not conclude. I have compiled a preliminary list of single-words that fit the statement; **music *as, of, and, in, at, on, for* and/or *about* X.** This list is not comprehensive, but it reveals many different paths to thinking about and engaging with music. From this list, I randomly chose terms and annotated them with opinions, quasi-definitions, definitions, and stream of consciousness associations. The possibilities are endless and my own annotations were only limited by the word limit of this essay. The complement to my entries are your own annotations (opinions, quasi-definitions, definitions, and stream of consciousness associations) that will exponentially expand your view of music and give you an invaluable resource from which to draw out ideas and sounds.

Exercise

music *as, of, and, in, at, on, for* and/or *about:*
sound, art, function, commodity, vibration, identity, silence, space, waves, digital, copyright, culture, loop:

> **music *as loop.*** Using a short loop of Cuban percussion may give a digital groove a nice "Cuban," flavor, but if that is the extent of the creator's engagement with Cuban music, she should perhaps refrain from claiming a Cuban influence unless she goes back for more tastes of, or a thorough immersion in, Cuban musical cuisine…a deep art. Contemporary Cuban musicians *do* eat rice and beans and use sampling technology in their own work, but eating rice and beans and using samples does not make you Cuban…¿*entiendes?* How many times can you say Cuban?

thunderous, pompous, plane, plain, rhythm, movement, groove, funky, swing,
adjective, volume, discovery, culture, distraction, commodity:

> **music *as commodity.*** In an increasingly commodified digital age,
> it is easy to assume that owning a computer, a sampler (with a
> couple of sitar samples) and digital recordings (MP3s, CDs, iTunes,
> video), and cultivating a look, automatically makes the consumer
> an artist—the consumer-artist. Corporations know the artists'
> lifestyle is attractive, and they sell the artist-identity to anyone who
> can come up with the purchase price of their hip products. If your
> credit line is high enough you can purchase genius credentials. Of
> course, artists *do* use computers and global influences (and
> samples) for realizing their work, and they, as well as consumer-
> artists, *do* find themselves increasingly engaged in working with
> digital processes that composer Brian Eno describes as "curatorial."
> (i.e. selecting and mixing pre-existing materials as opposed to
> creating sounds and forms from scratch.

thinking, ethnic, form, theory, education:

> **music *in education.*** 1. In America, formal education in music is
> still the Western classical one of conservatories, with the addition
> of a jazz curriculum since the 1970s. Quick, how many of your
> favorite classic, mostly African American jazz artists learned how
> to play in conservatories like these?

musicians, immigrants, artists, color, shape, soundtrack, style, spatial, silence:

> **music *of silence.*** On September 11, 2001 dancers moved to a silent
> *milonga*—unsounded, but heard—in New York City's Central Park.

ritual, television, stage, dirge, opera:

> **music *in opera.*** If the drama isn't sung it isn't opera.

concentration, camp:

> **music *in camp.*** 1. A Jewish women's orchestra is forced to
> accompany the Nazi slaughter at Auschwitz.

history, memory:

> **music *and memory.*** Berkeley-based Chilean composer Quique
> Cruz uses his music and art to critique the Chilean military junta's
> brutality against its own people since 1973.

story, vocal, instrument, weapon:

> **music *as weapon.*** See torture.

depressant, text, written:

> **music *as written.*** A melody of mine from Michael John Garcés'
> play *points of departure.*

oral, polyrhythmic, business, structure, dark, corny, hip hop, metal, violence,
software, instruments, guitar:

> **music *on guitar.*** Jimi Hendrix, Paco de Lucia, and Baden Powell.

composer, orchestra, location, ambience, cage:

> **music *as cage.*** John Cage's experiments with indeterminacy and
> open structures challenged the dominant almost metaphysical
> belief in the evolutional superiority of Western, especially German,
> music, its rational and "scientific" basis, and the teleological
> structure of its melodic and harmonic principles.

emptiness, form, definition:

> **music *in definition.*** Music is the infinite sonic possibility of finite
> beings.

zen, war, other, logic, mind, study:

> **music *as study.*** Acousticians, systematic musicologists, and
> physicists think about music in scientific terms: as waves; as
> envelopes of attack, decay, sustain, and release; as pressure on the
> human body and other materials; as empirical analysis of musical
> perception and cognition; aesthetics; tuning systems; and so on.
> Ethnomusicologists originally focused on non-Western folk and
> classical musics (Hindustani, Balinese, Japanese), but now study all
> forms of "world" and popular music, their primary focus being the
> relationship of music to culture, the latter a concern they inherited
> from anthropology and now share with the rest of the social
> sciences and humanities. Musicologists come in different types and
> sizes. Some of them are still concerned with the three B's (Bach,
> Beethoven, Brahms), but others are interested in heavy metal,
> country, girl groups, queer studies, etc.

theory, power, safe, monks, spheres, myth, nature, motive, fragment, sequence, anger, career, song, voice, tone, timbre, gender, class, poem, copyright:

> **music *and copyright.*** Why do some companies protect copyright while at the same time producing and selling the technology to "infringe" upon said copyright? If we outlaw samplers, then only outlaws will have samplers.

muslim, faith, busy, minimal, maximal, god, broadway, gamelan, stupid, dumb, race, nazi, terror:

> **music *and terror.*** See torture.

baroque, repetition, hope, asia, gay, disco, porn, medium, liquid, beat, dj, platonic:

> **music *as platonic.*** A fantasy universe where music has an objective reality outside of time, space, and the stain of culture—where genius is a humanly transcendent and transparent fact accessible to a reasonable, always Western, usually male, mind.

> **music *as alternative.*** Is alternative a quality or a specific style?

musical, street, soldiers, death, vietnam, baghdad, minorities, expression, over-whelming, healing, airports, autos, silk, wood, bamboo, prayer, happy, joy, infinite:

> **music *as infinite.*** John Coltrane and Charlie Parker knew that music was always one step ahead of their musical efforts—they never controlled it in a way they found completely satisfactory. I once heard Herbie Hancock say that music, if not respected, can "kick your ass." I believe Herbie.

musicology, systematic, major, dope, feeling, texture, grain, leading, magazines, prison, space, gang, entertainment, tradition, new, postmodern, evolution:

> **music *in evolution.*** As late as the mid- to late-nineteenth century, misreadings of Darwin were used to support the evolutionist belief that culture evolved in discrete stages with the European stage forming the apex of the evolutionary triangle. It was thought that by studying the music of "primitives," Europeans might discover something about what their own culture and society was like when it too was "barbaric." Only toward the beginning of the twentieth century was this belief finally discarded through the efforts of the anthropologist Franz Boas and his students. They insisted that since culture(s) evolved differently, cultural manifestations such as music and art needed to be studied in their own cultural contexts.

resistance, gun, witness, torture:

> **music *for torture.*** A 2005 article in the *New York Times* noted that, as a part of normal interrogation procedures, prisoners in Guantánamo, Cuba, were being forced to listen to the music of rap-metal band Rage Against the Machine at physiologically destructive decibel levels.

fame, live, live, recorded, serial, control, german, old, contagion, sin, outrageous, within, children, animals, offices, airports, supermarkets, dance, facile, martial, length, volume, society, ancient, primitive, salvation:

> **music *of salvation.*** Religious music played a central part in the indoctrination of colonial subjects whose own musical expressions were replaced by the music of the Catholic church. In this way. Spaniards in colonial Mexico were able to eliminate most Aztec knowledge of their own music and culture in the span of one generation.

samba, produced, raw, intro, outro, segue, cartoonish, character, foolish, ghoulish, tight, timing, feel, real, jazz, wanting, mambo, gagaku, library, building, additive, subtractive, architecture:

> **music *as architecture.*** Music is talked about *ad infinitum* despite the popularity of sayings such as "talking about music is like dancing to architecture." If you find yourself looking at the Brooklyn Bridge and its rhythm, form, and structure don't physically move you, well…look again.

street, secondary, first, party, groove, ocean, stream, dream, article, subliminal, exotic, flowers, royal, toil, hierarchical, revolution, protest, status:

> **music *and status.*** The Koran regards music as a vice and corrupter of virtue. Does anyone remember the Taliban's proscriptions against music? A low regard for music and musicians is not unique to the Muslim world. Until fairly recently, while considering music a central component of national culture, Latin American society shunned the figure of the popular musician, and considered him (usually a him) a marginal figure whose only function was partying, chasing women, consuming his host's wine, food and resources, and drinking his own life away. His status changed, of course, if he happened to be famous, his success ensuring social approval and adulation from Mexico City to Santiago, Chile.

sloppy, sick, rolling, owned, buddhist, crude, odd, playing, swaying, orphic, per-
functory, obnoxia, enchanting, thrilling, killing, woman, allegro, adagio, tro-
phy, man, crystalline, child, event, school, sports, elite, license, mood,
predictable, incomprehensible, scattered, festival, parade, computer, aid, social,
performance, rational, bolero, cuba:

> **music *as cuba.*** A floating conservatory.

contested, superior, war, movies, suave, trio, quartet, nonet, score:

> **music *as score.*** In Western "serious" or classical music, the written
> score is such a naturalized part of the culture that it is often thought
> of as the music itself rather than as a set of instructions for realizing
> a musical performance.

mystery, talent, electronic, chant, rant, punk, policy, dying, gift, british, phal-
lus, technical, queer, sacred, africa, lecture, popular, collage, science, bit, wave-
form, decadence, sustain, release, relief, meaningful, meaningless, therapy, sex,
love, future, work, drama, theatre, institution:

> **music *as institution.*** Classical music has suffered from dwindling
> public support that makes the future of current musical institutions
> such as orchestras and conservatories uncertain. Often these two,
> the institutions and the music, are conflated, and the death knell of
> the institutions is equated with the end of "music." The reality is
> more complicated, and I am optimistic about the fate of Western
> classical music. Its contribution to the cultural history of the world
> is an unprecedented tradition of artistic accomplishment. Perhaps
> the classical music community will find a way to reanimate its
> relevance in a postmodern world, and in that way keep their jobs
> to their and our mutual benefit. But, the elitism has to go. Nobody
> appreciates being snubbed, especially people who are potential
> patrons. Hopefully, the institutionalizers of jazz will also take heed
> and not tie their futures to a "classical" model that is clearly not
> working.

action, philosophy, literature, strings, transcultural, american, body, formless,
harmless, ponderous, lovely, wicked, vicious, ghetto, thought, energy, impres-
sion, painting, abstract, concrete, dada, luxury, savage, insistent, polyrhyth-
mic, polytonal, polyester, oldies, folk, artifact, process, system, glorious,
enlightenment, maya, mantra, pain, seasonal, mix, muted, math, symbol,
numbers, singing, open, improvisation, closed, chord, dynamic, medium, lan-
guage, hymn, indigenous, drum, line, concert, show, group, notes, growing,
tempo, slowing, stopping, held, list, old, brown, farce, satire, comedy, drama,
ruined, saved, played, fate, book, false, writing, notation, stars, crazy, weak,

shit, tribe, town, radio, tame, game, village, hindu, pop, bomb, misused, commitment, political,...

Part 3: Outro

Music is too large to contain, even for the biggest egos and talents. That is why I do not believe anyone who identifies themself as, or plays, an "expert" on music—it's an exorbitant and unrealistic claim to make. This does not mean that there are not people of wisdom, insight, and experience from whom I can't learn....There are many, and I do learn every day. I try to keep my mind and ears open to suggestions and sounds that often come from unexpected places.

I do not claim "expertise" in all matters musical, and I can only suggest you avoid becoming experts yourselves. That way you don't turn out like those bores who claim to be objective barometers of cultural value. Leave that nonsense to politicians. Instead, try to keep the excitement of a "beginners mind," that active, interested, even naïve part of yourself that always sees things as if for the first time—fresh and new. Trust your insights, but challenge your and others' assumptions about the place of music and art in everyday life. It is always larger than you imagine. And if you can, make some music or noise yourself. Freedom of expression, artistic and otherwise, is our human and American inheritance. It is not given to us by government, and it's not meant to be controlled from without—it's inherently ours—our creativity belongs to us to do with as we see fit. Let's pass it on.

Suggestions for Discussion

1. What is the musicological juncture, and how does it affect conversation about music?
2. What are the dangers of claiming "expertise" in music?

Suggestion for Writing

Compare Amigo's thoughts on music with those presented by Aaron Copland in *How We Listen to Music* (p. 403), David Dubal in *The Age of Modernism* (p. 409), or Julian Johnson in *Who Needs Classical Music?* (p. 414).

ᏨᏬᏙᏜᏙᏜ

MARGARET ATWOOD

Pornography

Margaret Atwood (b. 1939) has lived in both the United States and Europe, but her home is in Toronto. She did graduate work at Harvard on a Woodrow Wilson fellowship and has taught at several Canadian and American universities. Her novel *The Blind Assassin* (2000) earned a Booker Prize. Among her other books are *The Edible Woman* (1976), *Life Before Man* (1980), *Surfacing* (1981), *The Handmaid's Tale* (1986), *Cat's Eye* (1989), *The Robber Bride* (1993), and *Morning in a Burned House* (1995). A collection of Atwood's essays, *Writing with Intent,* was published in 2005. She has also written short stories, television plays, children's books, criticism, and poetry. In this essay, from *Chatelaine* (1988), she attempts to explain why pornography is clearly intolerable and why discussions of its censorship have created much confusion.

When I was in Finland a few years ago for an international writers' conference, I had occasion to say a few paragraphs in public on the subject of pornography. The context was a discussion of political repression, and I was suggesting the possibility of a link between the two. The immediate result was that a male journalist took several large bites out of me. Prudery and pornography are two halves of the same coin, said he, and I was clearly a prude. What could you expect from an Anglo-Canadian? Afterward, a couple of pleasant Scandinavian men asked me what I had been so worked up about. All "pornography" means, they said, is graphic depictions of whores, and what was the harm in that?

Not until then did it strike me that the male journalist and I had two entirely different things in mind. By "pornography," he meant naked bodies and sex. I, on the other hand, had recently been doing the research for my novel *Bodily Harm,* and was still in a state of shock from some of the material I had seen, including the Ontario Board of Film Censors' "outtakes." By "pornography," I meant women getting their nipples snipped off with garden shears, having meat hooks stuck into their vaginas, being disemboweled; little girls being raped; men (yes, there are some men) being smashed to a pulp and forcibly sodomized. The cutting edge of pornography, as far as I could see, was no longer simple old copulation, hanging from the chandelier or otherwise: it was death, messy, explicit and highly sadistic. I explained this to the nice Scandinavian men. "Oh, but that's just the United States," they said. "Everyone knows they're sick." In their country, they said, violent "pornography" of that kind was not permitted on television or in movies; indeed, excessive violence of any kind was not permitted. They had drawn a clear line between erotica, which earlier studies had shown did not incite men to more aggressive and brutal behavior toward women, and violence, which later studies indicated did.

Some time after that I was in Saskatchewan, where, because of the scenes in *Bodily Harm,* I found myself on an open-line radio show answering questions about "pornography." Almost no one who phoned in was in favor of it, but again they weren't talking about the same stuff I was, because they hadn't seen it. Some of them were all set to stamp out bathing suits and negligees, and, if possible, any depictions of the female body whatsoever. God, it was implied, did not approve of female bodies, and sex of any kind, including that practised by bumblebees, should be shoved back into the dark, where it belonged. I had more than a suspicion that *Lady Chatterley's Lover,* Margaret Laurence's *The Diviners,* and indeed most books by most serious modern authors would have ended up as confetti if left in the hands of these callers.

For me, these two experiences illustrate the two poles of the emotionally heated debate that is now thundering around this issue. They also underline the desirability and even the necessity of defining the terms. "Pornography" is now one of those catchalls, like "Marxism" and "feminism," that have become so broad they can mean almost anything, ranging from certain verses in the Bible, ads for skin lotion and sex texts for children to the contents of *Penthouse,* Naughty '90s postcards and films with titles containing the word *Nazi* that show vicious scenes of torture and killing. It's easy to say that sensible people can tell the difference. Unfortunately, opinions on what constitutes a sensible person vary.

But even sensible people tend to lose their cool when they start talking about this subject. They soon stop talking and start yelling, and the name-calling begins. Those in favor of censorship (which may include groups not noticeably in agreement on other issues, such as some feminists and religious fundamentalists) accuse the others of exploiting women through the use of degrading images, contributing to the corruption of children, and adding to the general climate of violence and threat in which both women and children live in this society; or, though they may not give much of a hoot about actual women and children, they invoke moral standards and God's supposed aversion to "filth," "smut" and deviated *perversion,* which may mean ankles.

The camp in favor of total "freedom of expression" often comes out howling as loud as the Romans would have if told they could no longer have innocent fun watching the lions eat up Christians. It too may include segments of the population who are not natural bedfellows: those who proclaim their God-given right to freedom, including the freedom to tote guns, drive when drunk, drool over chicken porn and get off on videotapes of women being raped and beaten, may be waving the same anticensorship banner as responsible liberals who fear the return of Mrs. Grundy, or gay groups for whom sexual emancipation involves the concept of "sexual theatre." *Whatever turns you on* is a handy motto, as is *A man's home is his castle* (and if it includes a dungeon with beautiful maidens strung up in chains and bleeding from every pore, that's his business).

Meanwhile, theoreticians theorize and speculators speculate. Is today's pornography yet another indication of the hatred of the body, the deep mind-body split, which is supposed to pervade Western Christian society? Is it a backlash against the women's movement by men who are threatened by uppity female behavior in real life, so like to fantasize about women done up like outsize parcels, being turned into hamburger, kneeling at their feet in slavelike adoration or sucking off guns? Is it a sign of collective impotence, of a generation of men who can't relate to real women at all but have to make do with bits of celluloid and paper? Is the current flood just a result of smart marketing and aggressive promotion by the money men in what has now become a multibillion-dollar industry? If they were selling movies about men getting their testicles stuck full of knitting needles by women with swastikas on their sleeves, would they do as well, or is this penchant somehow peculiarly male? If so, why? Is pornography a power trip rather than a sex one? Some say that those ropes, chains, muzzles and other restraining devices are an argument for the immense power female sexuality still wields in the male imagination: you don't put these things on dogs unless you're afraid of them. Others, more literary, wonder about the shift from the 19th-century Magic Women or Femme Fatale image to the lollipop-licker, airhead or turkey-carcass treatment of women in porn today. The pro-porners don't care much about theory: they merely demand product. The anti-porners don't care about it in the final analysis either: there's dirt on the street, and they want it cleaned up, now.

It seems to me that this conversation, with its *You're-a-prude/You're-a-pervert* dialectic, will never get anywhere as long as we continue to think of this material as just "entertainment." Possibly we're deluded by the packaging, the format: magazine, book, movie, theatrical presentation. We're used to thinking of these things as part of the "entertainment industry," and we're used to thinking of ourselves as free adult people who ought to be able to see any kind of "entertainment" we want to. That was what the First Choice pay-TV debate was all about. After all, it's only entertainment, right? Entertainment means fun, and only a killjoy would be antifun. What's the harm?

This is obviously the central question: *What's the harm?* If there isn't any real harm to any real people, then the antiporners can tsk-tsk and/or throw up as much as they like, but they can't rightfully expect more legal controls or sanctions. However, the no-harm position is far from being proven.

(For instance, there's a clear-cut case for banning—as the federal government has proposed—movies, photos and videos that depict children engaging in sex with adults: real children are used to make the movies, and hardly anybody thinks this is ethical. The possibilities for coercion are too great.)

To shift the viewpoint, I'd like to suggest three other models for looking at "pornography"—and here I mean the violent kind.

Those who find the idea of regulating pornographic materials repugnant because they think it's Fascist or Communist or otherwise not in accordance with the principles of an open democratic society should consider that Canada has made it illegal to disseminate material that may lead to hatred toward any group because of race or religion. I suggest that if pornography of the violent kind depicted these acts being done predominantly to Chinese, to blacks, to Catholics, it would be off the market immediately, under the present laws. Why is hate literature illegal? Because whoever made the law thought that such material might incite real people to do real awful things to other real people. The human brain is to a certain extent a computer: garbage in, garbage out. We only hear about the extreme cases (like that of American multimurderer Ted Bundy) in which pornography has contributed to the death and/or mutilation of women and/or men. Although pornography is not the only factor involved in the creation of such deviance, it certainly has upped the ante by suggesting both a variety of techniques and the social acceptability of such actions. Nobody knows yet what effect this stuff is having on the less psychotic.

Studies have shown that a large part of the market for all kinds of porn, soft and hard, is drawn from the 16-to-21-year-old population of young men. Boys used to learn about sex on the street, or (in Italy, according to Fellini movies) from friendly whores, or, in more genteel surroundings, from girls, their parents, or, once upon a time, in school, more or less. Now porn has been added, and sex education in the schools is rapidly being phased out. The buck has been passed, and boys are being taught that all women secretly like to be raped and that real men get high on scooping out women's digestive tracts.

Boys learn their concept of masculinity from other men: is this what most men want them to be learning? If word gets around that rapists are "normal" and even admirable men, will boys feel that in order to be normal, admirable and masculine they will have to be rapists? Human beings are enormously flexible, and how they turn out depends a lot on how they're educated, by the society in which they're immersed as well as by their teachers. In a society that advertises and glorifies rape or even implicitly condones it, more women get raped. It becomes socially acceptable. And at a time when men and the traditional male role have taken a lot of flak and men are confused and casting around for an acceptable way of being male (and, in some cases, not getting much comfort from women on that score), this must be at times a pleasing thought.

It would be naïve to think of violent pornography as just harmless entertainment. It's also an educational tool and a powerful propaganda device. What happens when boy educated on porn meets girl brought up on Harlequin romances? The clash of expectations can be heard around the block. She wants him to get down on his knees with a ring, he wants her to get down on all fours with a ring in her nose. Can this marriage be saved?

Pornography has certain things in common with such addictive substances as alcohol and drugs: for some, though by no means for all, it induces chemical changes in the body, which the user finds exciting and pleasurable. It also appears to attract a "hard core" of habitual users and a penumbra of those who use it occasionally but aren't dependent on it in any way. There are also significant numbers of men who aren't much interested in it, not because they're undersexed but because real life is satisfying their needs, which may not require as many appliances as those of users.

For the "hard core," pornography may function as alcohol does for the alcoholic: tolerance develops, and a little is no longer enough. This may account for the short viewing time and fast turnover in porn theatres. Mary Brown, chairwoman of the Ontario Board of Film Censors, estimates that for every one mainstream movie requesting entrance to Ontario, there is one porno flick. Not only the quantity consumed but the quality of explicitness must escalate, which may account for the growing violence: once the big deal was breasts, then it was genitals, then copulation, then that was no longer enough and the hard users had to have more. The ultimate kick is death, and after that, as the Marquis de Sade so boringly demonstrated, multiple death.

The existence of alcoholism has not led us to ban social drinking. On the other hand, we do have laws about drinking and driving, excessive drunkenness and other abuses of alcohol that may result in injury or death to others.

This leads us back to the key question: what's the harm? Nobody knows, but this society should find out fast, before the saturation point is reached. The Scandinavian studies that showed a connection between depictions of sexual violence and increased impulse toward it on the part of male viewers would be a starting point, but many more questions remain to be raised as well as answered. What, for instance, is the crucial difference between men who are users and men who are not? Does using affect a man's relationship with actual women, and, if so, adversely? Is there a clear line between erotica and violent pornography, or are they on an escalating continuum? Is this a "men versus women" issue, with all men secretly siding with the proporners and all women secretly siding against? (I think not;

there *are* lots of men who don't think that running their true love through the Cuisinart is the best way they can think of to spend a Saturday night, and they're just as nauseated by films of someone else doing it as women are.) Is pornography merely an expression of the sexual confusion of this age or an active contributor to it?

Nobody wants to go back to the age of official repression, when even piano legs were referred to as "limbs" and had to wear pantaloons to be decent. Neither do we want to end up in George Orwell's *1984*, in which pornography is turned out by the State to keep the proles in a state of torpor, sex itself is considered dirty and the approved practise is only for reproduction. But Rome under the emperors isn't such a good model either.

If all men and women respected each other, if sex were considered joyful and life-enhancing instead of a wallow in germ-filled glop, if everyone were in love all the time, if, in other words, many people's lives were more satisfactory for them than they appear to be now, pornography might just go away on its own. But since this is obviously not happening, we as a society are going to have to make some informed and responsible decisions about how to deal with it.

Suggestions for Discussion

1. Identify the following in the essay: D. H. Lawrence's *Lady Chatterley's Lover,* Margaret Laurence's *The Diviners,* Mrs. Grundy, the Marquis de Sade.

2. Summarize Atwood's major argument against pornography. What action does she believe society should take against it?

3. How do the Scandinavian countries deal with pornography? How do they define it?

4. Is Atwood too pessimistic about the ability of people who watch or read pornography to resist translating it into action themselves?

Suggestions for Writing

1. Write a paper in which you express your agreement or disagreement with Atwood's definition of pornography.

2. Does Atwood's position result in censorship? Are you opposed to censorship? Write a paper in which you discuss censorship and pornography as defined by Atwood.

3. Is pornography an issue for women or is it important to both sexes? Write a paper in which you explain your opinion.

JOHN BERGER

Uses of Photography

John Berger (b. 1926) is an author of eclectic tastes who has distinguished himself as an art critic, novelist, screenwriter, and documentary

September 11, 2001, 9 PM, © Christian J. Matuschek, 2001 – Photography.

writer. Although originally born in London, Berger now resides in a small French peasant community, which he has used as the setting for a trilogy of books that includes *Pig Earth, Once in Europa,* and *Lilac and Flag.* Also featured in Berger's catalogue of writings are *The Sense of Sight* (1993), *The Success and Failure of Picasso* (1965), and *G* (1992). The following chapter, from his 1980 reflection on art and psychology, *About Looking,* examines photography as an art form and tries to determine the nature of the medium as well as its significance.

For Susan Sontag

I want to write down some of my responses to Susan Sontag's book *On Photography.* All the quotations I will use are from her text. The thoughts are sometimes my own, but all originate in the experience of reading her book.

The camera was invented by Fox Talbot in 1839. Within a mere 30 years of its invention as a gadget for an elite, photography was being used for police filing, war reporting, military reconnaissance, pornography, encyclopedic documentation, family albums, postcards, anthropological records (often, as with the Indians in the United States, accompanied by genocide), sentimental moralising, inquisitive probing (the wrongly named "candid camera"), aesthetic effects, news reporting and formal portraiture. The first cheap popular camera was put on the market, a little later, in 1888. The speed with which the possible uses of photography were seized upon is surely an indication of photography's profound, central applicability to industrial capitalism. Marx came of age the year of the camera's invention.

It was not, however, until the 20th century and the period between the two world wars that the photograph became the dominant and most "natural" way of referring to appearances. It was then that it replaced the word as immediate testimony. It was the period when photography was thought of as being most transparent, offering direct access to the real: the period of the great witnessing masters of the medium like Paul Strand and Walker Evans. It was, in the capitalist countries, the freest moment of photography: it had been liberated from the limitations of fine art, and it had become a public medium which could be used democratically.

Yet the moment was brief. The very "truthfulness" of the new medium encouraged its deliberate use as a means of propaganda. The Nazis were among the first to use systematic photographic propaganda.

"Photographs are perhaps the most mysterious of all the objects that make up and thicken the environment we recognise as modern. Photographs really are experience captured, and the camera is the ideal arm of consciousness in its acquisitive mood."

In the first period of its existence photography offered a new technical opportunity; it was an implement. Now, instead of offering new choices, its usage and its "reading" were becoming habitual, an unexamined part of modern perception itself. Many developments contributed to this transformation. The new film industry. The invention of the lightweight camera—so that the taking of a photograph ceased to be a ritual and became a "reflex." The discovery of photojournalism—whereby the text follows the pictures instead of vice versa. The emergence of advertising as a crucial economic force.

"Through photographs, the world becomes a series of unrelated, freestanding particles; and history, past and present, a set of anecdotes and *faits divers*. The camera makes reality atomic, manageable, and opaque. It is a view of the world which denies interconnectedness, continuity, but which confers on each moment the character of a mystery."

The first mass-media magazine was started in the United States in 1936. At least two things were prophetic about the launching of *Life,* the prophecies to be fully realised in the postwar television age. The new picture magazine was financed not by its sales, but by the advertising it carried. A third of its images were devoted to publicity. The second prophecy lay in its title. This is ambiguous. It may mean that the pictures inside are about life. Yet it seems to promise more: that these pictures *are* life. The first photograph in the first number played on this ambiguity. It showed a newborn baby. The caption underneath read: "Life begins…"

What served in place of the photograph; before the camera's invention? The expected answer is the engraving, the drawing, the painting. The more revealing answer might be: memory. What photographs do out there in space was previously done within reflection.

"Proust somewhat misconstrues that photographs are, not so much an instrument of memory as an invention of it or a replacement."

Unlike any other visual image, a photograph is not a rendering, an imitation or an interpretation of its subject, but actually a trace of it. No painting or drawing, however naturalist, *belongs* to its subject in the way that a photograph does.

"A photograph is not only an image (as a painting is an image), an interpretation of the real; it is also a trace, something directly stencilled off the real, like a footprint or a death mask."

Human visual perception is a far more complex and selective process than that by which a film records. Nevertheless the camera lens and the eye both register images—because of their sensitivity to light—at great speed and in the face of an immediate event. What the camera does, however, and what the eye in itself can never do, is to *fix* the appearance of that event. It removes its appearance from the flow of appearances and it preserves it, not perhaps forever but for as long as the film exists. The essential character of this preservation is not dependent upon the image being static; unedited film rushes preserve in essentially the same way. The camera saves a set of appearances from the otherwise inevitable supercession of further appearances. It holds them unchanging. And before the invention of the camera nothing could do this, except, in the mind's eye, the faculty of memory.

I am not saying that memory is a kind of film. That is a banal simile. From the comparison film/memory we learn nothing about the latter. What we learn is how strange and unprecedented was the procedure of photography.

Yet, unlike memory, photographs do not in themselves preserve meaning. They offer appearances—with all the credibility and gravity we normally lend to appearances—prised away from their meaning. Meaning is the result of understanding functions. "And functioning takes place in time, and must be explained in time. Only that which narrates can make us understand." Photographs in themselves do not narrate. Photographs preserve instant appearances. Habit now protects us against the shock involved in such preservation. Compare the exposure time for a film with the life of the print made, and let us assume that the print only lasts ten years: the ratio for an average modern photograph would be approximately 20,000,000,000: 1. Perhaps that can serve as a reminder of the violence of the fission whereby appearances are separated by the camera from their function.

We must now distinguish between two quite distinct uses of photography. There are photographs which belong to private experience and there are those which are used publicly. The private photograph—the portrait of a mother, a picture of a daughter, a group photo of one's own team—is appreciated and read in a context *which is continuous with that from which the camera removed it.* (The violence of the removal is sometimes felt as incredulousness: "Was that really Dad?") Nevertheless such a photograph remains surrounded by the meaning from which it was severed. A mechanical device, the camera has been used as an instrument to contribute to a living memory. The photograph is a memento from a life being lived.

The contemporary public photograph usually presents an event, a seized set of appearances, which has nothing to do with us, its readers, or with the original meaning of the event. It offers information, but information severed from all lived experience. If the public photograph contributes to a memory, it is to the memory of an unknowable and total stranger. The violence is expressed in that strangeness. It records an instant sight about which this stranger has shouted: Look!

Who is the stranger? One might answer: the photographer. Yet if one considers the entire use-system of photographed images, the answer of "the photographer" is clearly inadequate. Nor can one reply: those who use the photographs. It is because the photographs carry no certain meaning in themselves, because they are like images in the memory of a total stranger, that they lend themselves to any use.

Daumier's famous cartoon of Nadar in his balloon suggests an answer. Nadar is travelling through the sky above Paris—the wind has blown off his hat—and he is photographing with his camera the city and its people below.

Has the camera replaced the eye of God? The decline of religion corresponds with the rise of the photograph. Has the culture of capitalism telescoped God into photography? The transformation would not be as surprising as it may at first seem.

The faculty of memory led men everywhere to ask whether, just as they themselves could preserve certain events from oblivion, there might not be other eyes noting and recording otherwise unwitnessed events. Such eyes they then accredited to their ancestors, to spirits, to gods or to their single deity. What was seen by this supernatural eye was inseparably linked with the principle of justice. It was possible to escape the justice of men, but not this higher justice from which nothing or little could be hidden.

Memory implies a certain act of redemption. What is remembered has been saved from nothingness. What is forgotten has been abandoned. If all events are seen, instantaneously, outside time, by a supernatural eye, the distinction between remembering and forgetting is transformed into an act of judgment, into the rendering of justice, whereby recognition is close to *being remembered,* and condemnation is close to *being forgotten.* Such a presentiment, extracted from man's long, painful experience of time, is to be found in varying forms in almost every culture and religion, and, very clearly, in Christianity.

At first, the secularisation of the capitalist world during the 19th century elided the judgment of God into the judgment of History in the name of Progress. Democracy and Science became the agents of such a judgment. And for a brief moment, photography, as we have seen, was considered to be an aid to these agents. It is still to this historical moment that photography owes its ethical reputation as Truth.

During the second half of the 20th century the judgment of history has been abandoned by all except the underprivileged and dispossessed. The industrialised, "developed" world, terrified of the past, blind to the future, lives within an opportunism which has emptied the principle of justice of all credibility. Such opportunism turns everything—nature, history, suffering, other people, catastrophes, sport, sex, politics—into spectacle. And the implement used to do this—until the act becomes so habitual that the conditioned imagination may do it alone—is the camera.

"Our very sense of situation is now articulated by the camera's interventions. The omnipresence of cameras persuasively suggests that time consists of interesting events, events worth photographing. This, in turn, makes it easy to feel that any event, once underway, and whatever its moral character, should be allowed to complete itself—so that something else can be brought into the world, the photograph."

The spectacle creates an eternal present of immediate expectation: memory ceases to be necessary or desirable. With the loss of memory the continuities of meaning and judgment are also lost to us. The camera relieves us of the burden of memory. It surveys us like God, and it surveys for us. Yet no other god has been so cynical, for the camera records in order to forget.

Susan Sontag locates this god very clearly in history. He is the god of monopoly capitalism.

"A capitalist society requires a culture based on images. It needs to furnish vast amounts of entertainment in order to stimulate buying and anaesthetise the injuries of class, race and sex. And it needs to gather unlimited amounts of information, the better to exploit the natural resources, increase productivity, keep order, make war, give jobs to bureaucrats. The camera's twin capacities, to subjectivise reality and to objectify it, ideally serve these needs and strengthen them. Cameras define reality in the two ways essential to the workings of an advanced industrial society: as a spectacle (for masses) and as an object of surveillance (for rulers). The production of images also furnishes a ruling ideology. Social change is replaced by a change in images."

Her theory of the current use of photographs leads one to ask whether photography might serve a different function. Is there an alternative photographic practice? The question should not be answered naively. Today no alternative professional practice (if one thinks of the profession of photographer) is possible. The system can accommodate any photograph. Yet it may be possible to begin to use photographs according to a practice addressed to an alternative future. This future is a hope which we need now, if we are to maintain a struggle, a resistance, against the societies and culture of capitalism.

Photographs have often been used as a radical weapon in posters, newspapers, pamphlets, and so on. I do not wish to belittle the value of such agitational publishing. Yet the current systematic public use of photography needs to be challenged, not simply by turning round like a cannon and aiming it at different targets, but by changing its practice. How?

We need to return to the distinction I made between the private and public uses of photography. In the private use of photography, the context of the instant recorded is preserved so that the photograph lives in an ongoing continuity. (If you have a photograph of Peter on your wall, you are not likely to forget what Peter means to you.) The public photograph, by contrast, is torn from its context, and becomes a dead object which, exactly because it is dead, lends itself to any arbitrary use.

In the most famous photographic exhibition ever organised, *The Family of Man* (put together by Edward Steichen in 1955), photographs from all over the world were presented as though they formed a universal family album. Steichen's intuition was absolutely correct: the private use of photographs can be exemplary for their public use. Unfortunately the shortcut he took in treating the existing class-divided world as if it were a family, inevitably made the whole exhibition, not necessarily each picture, sentimental and complacent. The truth is that most photographs taken of people are about suffering, and most of that suffering is man-made.

"One's first encounter," writes Susan Sontag, "with the photographic inventory of ultimate horror is a kind of revelation, the prototypically modern revelation: a negative epiphany. For me, it was photographs of Bergen-Belsen and Dachau which I came across by chance in a bookstore in Santa Monica in July 1945. Nothing I have seen—in photographs or in real life—ever cut me as sharply, deeply, instantaneously. Indeed, it seems plausible to me to divide my life into two parts, before I saw those photographs (I was twelve) and after, though it was several years before I understood fully what they were about."

Photographs are relics of the past, traces of what has happened. If the living take that past upon themselves, if the past becomes an integral part of the process of people making their own history, then all photographs would reacquire a living context, they would continue to exist in time, instead of being arrested moments. It is just possible that photography is the prophecy of a human memory yet to be socially and politically achieved. Such a memory would encompass any image of the past, however tragic, however guilty, within its own continuity. The distinction between the private and public uses of photography would be transcended. The Family of Man would exist.

Meanwhile we live today in the world as it is. Yet this possible prophecy of photography indicates the direction in which any alternative use of photography needs to develop. The task of an alternative photography is to incorporate photography into social and political memory, instead of using it as a substitute which encourages the atrophy of any such memory.

The task will determine both the kinds of pictures taken and the way they are used. There can of course be no formulae, no prescribed practice. Yet in recognising how photography has come to be used by capitalism, we can define at least some of the principles of an alternative practice.

For the photographer this means thinking of her or himself not so much as a reporter to the rest of the world but, rather, as a recorder for those involved in the events photographed. The distinction is crucial.

What makes these photographs so tragic and extraordinary is that, looking at them, one is convinced that they were not taken to please generals, to boost the morale of a civilian public, to glorify heroic soldiers or to shock the world press: they were images addressed to those suffering what they depict. And given this integrity towards and with their subject matter, such photographs later became a memorial, to the 20 million Russians killed in the war, for those who mourn them. (See *Russian War Photographs 1941–45*. Text by A. J. P. Taylor, London 1978.) The unifying horror of a total people's war made such an attitude on the part of the war photographers (and even the censors) a natural one. Photographers, however, can work with a similar attitude in less extreme circumstances.

The alternative use of photographs which already exist leads us back once more to the phenomenon and faculty of memory. The aim must be to construct a context for a photograph, to construct it with words, to construct it with other photographs and images. How? Normally photographs are used in a very unilinear way—they are used to illustrate an argument, or to demonstrate a thought which goes like this:

Very frequently also they are used tautologically so that the photograph merely repeats what is being said in words. Memory is not unilinear at all. Memory works radially, that is to say with an enormous number of associations all leading to the same event. The diagram is like this:

If we want to put a photograph back into the context of experience, social experience, social memory, we have to respect the laws of memory. We have to situate the printed photograph so that it acquires something of the surprising conclusiveness of that which *was* and *is*.

What Brecht wrote about acting in one of his poems is applicable to such a practice. For *instant* one can read photography, for *acting* the re-creating of context:

> So you should simply make the instant
> Stand out, without in the process hiding
> What you are making it stand out from.
>   Give your acting
> That progression of one-thing-after-another,
>   that attitude of
> Working up what you have taken on. In this way
> You will show the flow of events and also the course
> Of your work, permitting the spectator
> To experience this Now on many levels, coming from
>   Previously and
> Merging into Afterwards, also having much else Now
> Alongside it. He is sitting not only
> In your theatre but also
> In the world.

There are a few great photographs which practically achieve this by themselves. But any photograph may become such a 'Now' if an adequate context is created for it. In general the better the photograph, the fuller the context which can be created.

Such a context replaces the photograph in time—not its own original time for that is impossible—but in narrated time. Narrated time becomes historic time when it is assumed by social memory and social action. The constructed narrated time needs to respect the process of memory which it hopes to stimulate.

There is never a single approach to something remembered. The remembered is not like a terminus at the end of a line. Numerous approaches or stimuli converge upon it and lead to it. Words, comparisons, signs need to create a context for a printed photograph in a comparable way; that is to say, they must mark and leave open diverse approaches. A radial system has to be constructed around the photograph so that it may be seen in terms which are simultaneously personal, political, economic, dramatic, everyday and historic.

Suggestions for Discussion

1. What is a photograph? How does Berger's text seek to establish a clear and insightful definition of the nature of the photograph? Do you think it is important to find such a definition? Why or why not?

2. According to Berger, how has the invention of the photograph changed the way that people view God? Do you agree with his argument?

3. Examine the photograph on page 434 accompanying Berger's essay carefully, without reading the caption. What do you see? What do you consider its main subject to be? Now, read the caption. Matuschek gives the exact day and time of the photograph. Does this change the way you see this photograph? What do you see as its main subject now?

4. Does this image surprise you in any way? Is it different from other photographs you may have seen recording September 11th? If so, how? What is your emotional response to this particular image? What message does it convey to you? Do you think your response to this image would have been different had you seen it before the September 11th tragedy?

5. Although it was not staged, Matuschek's photograph has an almost composed look to it. Do you see his image more as a work of art or as an historical document? What do you think differentiates photographs taken for artistic reasons from photographs used for historical documentation, propaganda, advertising, and personal enjoyment?

Suggestion for Writing

Reflect on Berger's essay, his take on Sontag's book *On Photography,* as well as on Sontag's essay, *Regarding the Pain of Others,* which appears on page 716 of this book. Using these writings as a guide, analyze Matuschek's photograph (page 434) in a critique that employs some of Berger's and Sontag's theories of art, journalism, politics, and the pain of others.

FICTION

∿∿∿∿

W I L L A   C A T H E R

The Sculptor's Funeral

Willa Cather (1873–1947) was born in Virginia and grew up in Nebraska. On leaving the University of Nebraska, where as an undergraduate she had written for a Lincoln newspaper, she worked in Pittsburgh as a reporter and then as a teacher, and she wrote her first collection of stories, *The Troll Garden* (1905). Her works include *My Ántonia* (1918), *A Lost Lady* (1923), *The Professor's House* (1925), *Death Comes for the Archbishop* (1927), and *Sapphira and the Slave Girl* (1940), which dealt with her native Virginia. In her writing, she celebrated the frontier spirit, whether of art or of action. However, in this story, from *The Troll Garden,* she shows how small-town intolerance and demands for conformity are inimical to artistic impulses and creativity.

A group of the townspeople stood on the station siding of a little Kansas town, awaiting the coming of the night train, which was already twenty minutes overdue. The snow had fallen thick over everything; in the pale starlight the line of bluffs across the wide, white meadows south of the town made soft, smoke-coloured curves against the clear sky. The men on the siding stood first on one foot and then on the other, their hands thrust deep into their trousers pockets, their overcoats open, their shoulders screwed up with the cold; and they glanced from time to time toward the southeast, where the railroad track wound along the river shore. They conversed in low tones and moved about restlessly, seeming uncertain as to what was expected of them. There was but one of the company who looked as though he knew exactly why he was there; and he kept conspicuously apart; walking to the far end of the platform, returning to the station door, then pacing up the track again, his chin sunk in the high collar of his overcoat, his burly shoulders drooping forward, his gait heavy and dogged. Presently he was approached by a tall, spare, grizzled man clad in a faded Grand Army suit, who shuffled out from the group and advanced with a certain deference, craning his neck forward until his back made the angle of a jackknife three-quarters open.

443

"I reckon she's a-goin' to be pretty late agin tonight, Jim," he remarked in a squeaky falsetto. "S'pose it's the snow?"

"I don't know," responded the other man with a shade of annoyance, speaking from out an astonishing cataract of red beard that grew fiercely and thickly in all directions.

The spare man shifted the quill toothpick he was chewing to the other side of his mouth. "It ain't likely that anybody from the East will come with the corpse, I s'pose," he went on reflectively.

"I don't know," responded the other, more curtly than before.

"It's too bad he didn't belong to some lodge or other. I like an order funeral myself. They seem more appropriate for people of some repytation," the spare man continued, with an ingratiating concession in his shrill voice, as he carefully placed his toothpick in his vest pocket. He always carried the flag at the G.A.R. funerals in the town.

The heavy man turned on his heel, without replying, and walked up the siding. The spare man shuffled back to the uneasy group. "Jim's ez full ez a tick, ez ushel," he commented commiseratingly.

Just then a distant whistle sounded, and there was a shuffling of feet on the platform. A number of lanky boys of all ages appeared as suddenly and slimily as eels wakened by the crack of thunder; some came from the waiting-room, where they had been warming themselves by the red stove, or half asleep on the slat benches; others uncoiled themselves from baggage trucks or slid out of express wagons. Two clambered down from the driver's seat of a hearse that stood backed up against the siding. They straightened their stooping shoulders and lifted their heads, and a flash of momentary animation kindled their dull eyes at that cold, vibrant scream, the world-wide call for men. It stirred them like the note of a trumpet; just as it had often stirred the man who was coming home tonight, in his boyhood.

The night express shot, red as a rocket, from out the eastward marsh lands and wound along the river shore under the long lines of shivering poplars that sentineled the meadows, the escaping steam hanging in grey masses against the pale sky and blotting out the Milky Way. In a moment the red glare from the headlight streamed up the snow-covered track before the siding and glittered on the wet, black rails. The burly man with the dishevelled red beard walked swiftly up the platform toward the approaching train, uncovering his head as he went. The group of men behind him hesitated, glanced questioningly at one another, and awkwardly followed his example. The train stopped, and the crowd shuffled up to the express car just as the door was thrown open, the spare man in the G.A.R. suit thrusting his head forward with curiosity. The express messenger appeared in the doorway, accompanied by a young man in a long ulster and traveling cap.

"Are Mr. Merrick's friends here?" inquired the young man.

The group on the platform swayed and shuffled uneasily. Philip Phelps, the banker, responded with dignity: "We have come to take charge of the body. Mr. Merrick's father is very feeble and can't be about."

"Send the agent out here," growled the express messenger, "and tell the operator to lend a hand."

The coffin was got out of its rough box and down on the snowy platform. The townspeople drew back enough to make room for it and then formed a close semicircle about it, looking curiously at the palm leaf which lay across the black cover. No one said anything. The baggage man stood by his truck, waiting to get at the trunks. The engine panted heavily, and the fireman dodged in and out among the wheels with his yellow torch and long oilcan, snapping the spindle boxes. The young Bostonian, one of the dead sculptor's pupils who had come with the body, looked about him helplessly. He turned to the banker, the only one of that black, uneasy, stoop-shouldered group who seemed enough of an individual to be addressed.

"None of Mr. Merrick's brothers are here?" he asked uncertainly.

The man with the red beard for the first time stepped up and joined the group. "No, they have not come yet: the family is scattered. The body will be taken directly to the house." He stooped and took hold of one of the handles of the coffin.

"Take the long hill road up, Thompson, it will be easier on the horses," called the liveryman as the undertaker snapped the door of the hearse and prepared to mount to the driver's seat.

Laird, the red-bearded lawyer, turned again to the stranger: "We didn't know whether there would be anyone with him or not," he explained. "It's a long walk, so you'd better go up in the hack." He pointed to a single battered conveyance, but the young man replied stiffly: "Thank you, but I think I will go up with the hearse. If you don't object," turning to the undertaker, "I'll ride with you."

They clambered up over the wheels and drove off in the starlight up the long, white hill toward the town. The lamps in the still village were shining from under the low, snow-burdened roofs; and beyond, on every side, the plains reached out into emptiness, peaceful and wide as the soft sky itself, and wrapped in a tangible, white silence.

When the hearse backed up to a wooden sidewalk before a naked, weather-beaten frame house, the same composite, ill-defined group that had stood upon the station siding was huddled about the gate. The front yard was an icy swamp, and a couple of warped planks, extending from the sidewalk to the door, made a sort of rickety footbridge. The gate hung on one hinge, and was opened wide with difficulty. Steavens, the young stranger, noticed that something black was tied to the knob of the front door.

The grating sound made by the casket, as it was drawn from the hearse, was answered by a scream from the house; the front door was wrenched open, and a tall, corpulent woman rushed out bareheaded into the snow and flung herself upon the coffin, shrieking: "My boy, my boy! And this is how you've come home to me!"

As Steavens turned away and closed his eyes with a shudder of unutterable repulsion, another woman, also tall, but flat and angular, dressed entirely in black, darted out of the house and caught Mrs. Merrick by the shoulders, crying sharply: "Come, come, mother; you mustn't go on like this!" Her tone changed to one of obsequious solemnity as she turned to the banker: "The parlour is ready, Mr. Phelps."

The bearers carried the coffin along the narrow boards, while the undertaker ran ahead with the coffin rests. They bore it into a large, unheated room that smelled of dampness and disuse and furniture polish, and set it down under a hanging lamp ornamented with jingling glass prisms and before a "Rogers group" of John Alden and Priscilla, wreathed with smilax. Henry Steavens stared about him with the sickening conviction that there had been some horrible mistake, and that he had somehow arrived at the wrong destination. He looked painfully about over the clover-green Brussels, the fat plush upholstery; among the hand-painted china plaques and panels, and vases, for some mark of identification, for something that might once conceivably have belonged to Harvey Merrick. It was not until he recognized his friend in the crayon portrait of a little boy in kilts and curls hanging above the piano, that he felt willing to let any of these people approach the coffin.

"Take the lid off, Mr. Thompson; let me see my boy's face," wailed the elderly woman between her sobs. This time Steavens looked fearfully, almost beseechingly into her face, red and swollen under its masses of strong, black, shiny hair. He flushed, dropped his eyes, and then, almost incredulously, looked again. There was a kind of power about her face—a kind of brutal handsomeness, even, but it was scarred and furrowed by violence, and so coloured and coarsened by fiercer passions that grief seemed never to have laid a gentle finger there. The long nose was distended and knobbed at the end, and there were deep lines on either side of it; her heavy, black brows almost met across her forehead, her teeth were large and square, and set far apart—teeth that could tear. She filled the room; the men were obliterated, seemed tossed about like twigs in an angry water, and even Steavens felt himself being drawn into the whirlpool.

The daughter—the tall, raw-boned woman in crêpe, with a mourning comb in her hair which curiously lengthened her long face—sat stiffly upon the sofa, her hands, conspicuous for their large knuckles, folded in her lap, her mouth and eyes drawn down, solemnly awaiting the opening of the coffin. Near the door stood a mulatto woman, evidently a servant in the house, with a timid bearing and an emaciated face pitifully sad and gentle. She was weeping silently, the corner of her calico apron lifted to her eyes, occasionally suppressing a long, quivering sob. Steavens walked over and stood beside her.

Feeble steps were heard on the stairs, and an old man, tall and frail, odorous of pipe smoke, with shaggy, unkempt grey hair and a dingy beard, tobacco stained about the mouth, entered uncertainly. He went slowly up to the coffin and stood rolling a blue cotton handkerchief between his hands, seeming so pained and embarrassed by his wife's orgy of grief that he had no consciousness of anything else.

"There, there, Annie, dear, don't take on so," he quavered timidly, putting out a shaking hand and awkwardly patting her elbow. She turned with a cry, and sank upon his shoulder with such violence that he tottered a little. He did not even glance toward the coffin, but continued to look at her with a dull, frightened, appealing expression, as a spaniel looks at the whip. His sunken cheeks slowly reddened and burned with miserable shame. When his wife rushed from the room, her daughter strode after her with set lips. The servant stole up to the coffin, bent over it for a moment, and then slipped away to the kitchen, leaving Steavens, the lawyer, and the father to themselves. The old man stood trembling and looking down at his dead son's face. The sculptor's splendid head seemed even more noble in its rigid stillness than in life. The dark hair had crept down upon the wide forehead; the face seemed strangely long, but in it there was not that beautiful and chaste repose which we expect to find in the faces of the dead. The brows were so drawn that there were two deep lines above the beaked nose, and the chin was thrust forward defiantly. It was as though the strain of life had been so sharp and bitter that death could not at once wholly relax the tension and smooth the countenance into perfect peace—as though he were still guarding something precious and holy, which might even yet be wrested from him.

The old man's lips were working under his stained beard. He turned to the lawyer with timid deference: "Phelps and the rest are comin' back to set up with Harve, ain't they?" he asked. "Thank 'ee, Jim, thank 'ee." He brushed the hair back gently from his son's forehead. "He was a good boy, Jim; always a good boy. He was ez gentle ez a child and the kindest of 'em all—only we didn't none of us ever onderstand him." The tears trickled slowly down his beard and dropped upon the sculptor's coat.

"Martin, Martin. Oh, Martin! come here," his wife wailed from the top of the stairs. The old man started timorously: "Yes, Annie, I'm coming." He turned away, hesitated, stood for a moment in miserable indecision; then reached back and patted the dead man's hair softly, and stumbled from the room.

"Poor old man, I didn't think he had any tears left. Seems as if his eyes would have gone dry long ago. At his age nothing cuts very deep," remarked the lawyer.

Something in his tone made Steavens glance up. While the mother had been in the room, the young man had scarcely seen any one else; but now, from the moment he first glanced into Jim Laird's florid face and bloodshot eyes, he knew that he had found what he had been heartsick at not finding before—the feeling, the understanding that must exist in some one, even here.

The man was red as his beard, with features swollen and blurred by dissipation, and a hot, blazing blue eye. His face was strained—that of a man who is controlling himself with difficulty—and he kept plucking at his beard with a sort of fierce resentment. Steavens, sitting by the window, watched him turn down the glaring lamp, still its jangling pendants with an angry gesture, and then stand with his hands locked behind him, staring down into the master's face. He could not help wondering what link there could have been between the porcelain vessel and so sooty a lump of potter's clay.

From the kitchen an uproar was sounding; when the dining-room door opened, the import of it was clear. The mother was abusing the maid for having forgotten to make the dressing for the chicken salad which had been prepared for the watchers. Steavens had never heard anything in the least like it; it was injured, emotional, dramatic abuse, unique and masterly in its excruciating cruelty, as violent and unrestrained as had been her grief of twenty minutes before. With a shudder of disgust the lawyer went into the dining room and closed the door into the kitchen.

"Poor Roxy's getting it now," he remarked when he came back. "The Merricks took her out of the poorhouse years ago; and if her loyalty would let her, I guess the poor old thing could tell tales that would curdle your blood. She's the mulatto woman who was standing in here a while ago, with her apron to her eyes. The old woman is a fury; there never was anybody like her for demonstrative piety and ingenious cruelty. She made Harvey's life a hell for him when he lived at home; he was so sick ashamed of it. I never could see how he kept himself so sweet."

"He was wonderful," said Steavens slowly, "wonderful; but until tonight I have never known how wonderful."

"That is the true and eternal wonder of it, anyway; that it can come even from such a dung heap as this," the lawyer cried, with a sweeping gesture which seemed to indicate much more than the four walls within which they stood.

"I think I'll see whether I can get a little air. The room is so close I am beginning to feel rather faint," murmured Steavens, struggling with one of the windows. The sash was stuck, however, and would not yield, so he sat down dejectedly and began pulling at his collar. The lawyer came over, loosened the sash with one blow of his red fist and sent the window up a few inches. Steavens thanked him, but the nausea which had been gradually climbing into his throat for the last half hour left him with but one desire—a desperate feeling that he must get away from this place with what was left of Harvey Merrick. Oh, he comprehended well enough now the quiet bitterness of the smile that he had seen so often on his master's lips!

He remembered that once, when Merrick returned from a visit home, he brought with him a singularly feeling and suggestive bas-relief of a thin, faded old woman, sitting and sewing something pinned to her knee; while a full-lipped, full-blooded little urchin, his trousers held up by a single gallus, stood beside her, impatiently twitching her gown to call her attention to a butterfly he had caught. Steavens, impressed by the tender and delicate modelling of the thin, tired face, had asked him if it were his mother. He remembered the dull flush that had burned up in the sculptor's face.

The lawyer was sitting in a rocking-chair beside the coffin, his head thrown back and his eyes closed. Steavens looked at him earnestly, puzzled at the line of the chin, and wondering why a man should conceal a feature of such distinction under that disfiguring shock of beard. Suddenly, as though he felt the young sculptor's keen glance, he opened his eyes.

"Was he always a good deal of an oyster?" he asked abruptly. "He was terribly shy as a boy."

"Yes, he was an oyster, since you put it so," rejoined Steavens. "Although he could be very fond of people, he always gave one the impression of being detached. He disliked violent emotion; he was reflective, and rather distrustful of himself—except, of course, as regarded his work. He was sure-footed enough there. He distrusted men pretty thoroughly and women even more, yet somehow without believing ill of them. He was determined, indeed, to believe the best, but he seemed afraid to investigate."

"A burnt dog dreads the fire," said the lawyer grimly, and closed his eyes.

Steavens went on and on, reconstructing that whole miserable boyhood. All this raw, biting ugliness had been the portion of the man whose tastes were refined beyond the limits of the reasonable—whose mind was an exhaustless gallery of beautiful impressions, and so sensitive that the mere shadow of a poplar leaf flickering against a sunny wall would be etched and held there forever. Surely, if ever a man had the magic word in his fingertips, it was Merrick. Whatever he touched, he revealed its holiest secret; liberated it from enchantment and restored to it its pristine loveliness, like the Arabian prince who fought the enchantress spell for spell. Upon whatever he had come in contact with, he had left a beautiful record of the experience—a sort of ethereal signature; a scent, a sound, a colour that was his own.

Steavens understood now the real tragedy of his master's life; neither love nor wine, as many had conjectured; but a blow which had fallen earlier and cut deeper than these could have done—a shame not his, and yet so unescapably his, to hide in his heart from his very boyhood. And without—the frontier warfare; the yearning of a boy, cast ashore upon a desert of newness and ugliness and sordidness, for all that is chastened and old, and noble with traditions.

At eleven o'clock the tall, flat woman in black crêpe entered and announced that the watchers were arriving, and asked them "to step into the dining-room." As Steavens rose, the lawyer said dryly: "You go on—it'll be a good experience for you, doubtless; as for me, I'm not equal to that crowd tonight; I've had twenty years of them."

As Steavens closed the door after him he glanced back at the lawyer, sitting by the coffin in the dim light, with his chin resting on his hand.

The same misty group that had stood before the door of the express car shuffled into the dining room. In the light of the kerosene lamp they separated and became individuals. The minister, a pale, feeble-looking man with white hair and blond chin-whiskers, took his seat beside a small side table and placed his Bible upon it. The Grand Army man sat down behind the stove and tilted his chair back comfortably against the wall, fishing his quill toothpick from his waistcoat pocket. The two bankers, Phelps and Elder, sat off in a corner behind the dinner table, where they could finish their discussion of the new usury law and its effect on chattel security loans. The real estate agent, an old man with a smiling, hypocritical face, soon joined them. The coal and lumber dealer and the cattle shipper sat on opposite sides of the hard coal-burner, their feet on the nickelwork. Steavens took a book from his pocket and began to read. The talk around him ranged through various topics of local interest while the house was quieting down. When it was clear that the members of the family were in bed, the Grand Army man hitched his shoulders and, untangling his long legs, caught his heels on the rounds of his chair.

"S'pose there'll be a will, Phelps?" he queried in his weak falsetto.

The banker laughed disagreeably, and began trimming his nails with a pearl-handled pocketknife.

"There'll scarcely be any need for one, will there?" he queried in his turn.

The restless Grand Army man shifted his position again, getting his knees still nearer his chin. "Why, the ole man says Harve's done right well lately," he chirped.

The other banker spoke up. "I reckon he means by that Harve ain't asked him to mortgage any more farms lately, so as he could go on with his education."

"Seems like my mind don't reach back to a time when Harve wasn't bein' edycated," tittered the Grand Army man.

There was a general chuckle. The minister took out his handkerchief and blew his nose sonorously. Banker Phelps closed his knife with a snap. "It's too bad the old man's sons didn't turn out better," he remarked with reflective authority. "They never hung together. He spent money enough on Harve to stock a dozen cattle farms and he might as well have poured it into Sand Creek. If Harve had stayed at home and helped nurse what little they had, and gone into stock on the old man's bottom farm, they might all have been well fixed. But the old man had to trust everything to tenants and was cheated right and left."

"Harve never could have handled stock none," interposed the cattleman. "He hadn't it in him to be sharp. Do you remember when he bought Sander's mules for eight-year olds, when everybody in town knew that Sander's father-in-law give 'em to his wife for a wedding present eighteen years before, an' they was full-grown mules then."

Every one chuckled, and the Grand Army man rubbed his knees with a spasm of childish delight.

"Harve never was much account for anything practical, and he shore was never fond of work," began the coal and lumber dealer. "I mind the last time he was home; the day he left, when the old man was out to the barn helpin' his hand hitch up to take Harve to the train, and Cal Moots was patchin' up the fence, Harve, he come out on the step and sings out, in his ladylike voice: 'Cal Moots, Cal Moots! please come cord my trunk.'"

"That's Harve for you," approved the Grand Army man gleefully. "I kin hear him howlin' yet when he was a big feller in long pants and his mother used to whale him with a rawhide in the barn for lettin' the cows get foundered in the cornfield when he was drivin' 'em home from pasture. He killed a cow of mine that-a-way onct—a pure Jersey and the best milker I had, an' the ole man had to put up for her. Harve, he was watchin' the sun set acrost the marshes when the anamile got away; he argued that sunset was oncommon fine."

"Where the old man made his mistake was in sending the boy East to school," said Phelps, stroking his goatee and speaking in a deliberate, judicial tone. "There was where he got his head full of trapesing to Paris and all such folly. What Harve needed, of all people, was a course in some first-class Kansas City business college."

The letters were swimming before Steavens's eyes. Was it possible that these men did not understand, that the palm of the coffin meant nothing to them? The very name of their town would have remained forever buried in the postal guide had it not been now and again mentioned in the world in connection with Harvey Merrick's. He remembered what his master had said to him on the day of his death, after the congestion of both lungs had shut off any probability of recovery, and the sculptor had asked his pupil to send his body home. "It's not a pleasant place to be lying while the world is moving and doing and bettering," he had said with a feeble smile, "but it rather seems as though we ought to go back to the place we came from in the end. The townspeople will come in for a look at me; and after they have had their say I shan't have much to fear from the judgment of God. The wings of the Victory, in there"—with a weak gesture toward his studio— "will not shelter me."

The cattleman took up the comment. "Forty's young for a Merrick to cash in; they usually hang on pretty well. Probably he helped it along with whisky."

"His mother's people were not long-lived, and Harvey never had a robust constitution," said the minister mildly. He would have liked to say more. He had been the boy's Sunday-school teacher, and had been fond of him; but he felt that he was not in a position to speak. His own sons had turned out badly, and it was not a year since one of them had made his last trip home in the express car, shot in a gambling house in the Black Hills.

"Nevertheless, there is no disputin' that Harvey frequently looked upon the wine when it was red, also variegated, and it shore made an oncommon fool of him," moralized the cattleman.

Just then the door leading into the parlor rattled loudly and everyone started involuntarily, looking relieved when only Jim Laird came out. His red face was convulsed with anger, and the Grand Army man ducked his head when he saw the spark in his blue, bloodshot eye. They were all afraid of Jim; he was a drunkard, but he could twist the law to suit his client's needs as no other man in all western Kansas could do; and there were many who tried. The lawyer closed the door gently behind him, leaned back against it and folded his arms, cocking his head a little to one side. When he assumed this attitude in the courtroom, ears were always pricked up, as it usually foretold a flood of withering sarcasm.

"I've been with you gentlemen before," he began in a dry, even tone, "when you've sat by the coffins of boys born and raised in this town; and, if I remember rightly, you were never any too well satisfied when you checked them up. What's the matter, anyhow? Why is it that reputable young men are as scarce as millionaires in Sand City? It might almost seem to a stranger that there was some way something the matter with your progressive town. Why did Ruben Sayer, the brightest young lawyer you ever turned out, after he had come home from the university as straight as a die, take to drinking and forge a check and shoot himself? Why did Bill Merrit's son die of the shakes in a saloon in Omaha? Why was Mr. Thomas's son, here, shot in a gambling-house? Why did young Adams burn his mill to beat the insurance companies and go to the pen?"

The lawyer paused and unfolded his arms, laying one clenched fist quietly on the table. "I'll tell you why. Because you drummed nothing but money and knavery into their ears from the time they wore knickerbockers; because you carped away at them as you've been carping here tonight, holding our friends Phelps and Elder up to them for their models, as our grandfathers held up George Washington and John Adams. But the boys, worse luck, were young and raw at the business you put them to; and how could they match coppers with such artists as Phelps and Elder? You wanted them to be successful rascals; they were only unsuccessful ones—that's all the difference. There was only one boy ever raised in this borderland between ruffianism and civilization, who didn't come to grief, and you hated Harvey Merrick more for winning out than you hated all the other boys who got under the wheels. Lord, Lord, how you did hate him! Phelps, here, is fond of saying that he could buy and sell us all out any time he's a mind to; but he knew Harve wouldn't have given a tinker's damn for his bank and all his cattle farms put together; and a lack of appreciation, that way, goes hard with Phelps.

"Old Nimrod, here, thinks Harve drank too much; and this from such as Nimrod and me!

"Brother Elder says Harve was too free with the old man's money—fell short in filial consideration, maybe. Well, we can all remember the very tone in which brother Elder swore his own father was a liar, in the county court; and we all know that the old man came out of that partnership with his son as bare as a sheared lamb. But maybe I'm getting personal, and I'd better be driving ahead at what I want to say."

The lawyer paused a moment, squared his heavy shoulders, and went on: "Harvey Merrick and I went to school together, back East. We were dead in earnest, and we wanted you all to be proud of us some day. We meant to be great men. Even I, and I haven't lost my sense of humour, gentlemen, I meant to be a great man. I came back here to practise, and I found you didn't in the least want me to be a great man. You wanted me to be a shrewd lawyer—oh, yes! Our veteran here wanted me to get him an increase of pension, because he had dyspepsia; Phelps wanted a new country survey that would put the widow Wilson's little bottom farm inside his south line; Elder wanted to lend money at 5 percent a month, and get it collected; old Stark here wanted to wheedle old women up in Vermont into investing their annuities in real-estate mortgages that are not worth the paper they are written on. Oh, you needed me hard enough, and you'll go on needing me; and that's why I'm not afraid to plug the truth home to you this once.

"Well, I came back here and became the damned shyster you wanted me to be. You pretend to have some sort of respect for me; and yet you'll stand up and throw mud at Harvey Merrick, whose soul you couldn't dirty and whose hands you couldn't tie. Oh, you're a discriminating lot of Christians! There have been times when the sight of Harvey's name in some Eastern paper has made me hang my head like a whipped dog; and, again, times when I liked to think of him off there in the world, away from all this hogwallow, doing his great work and climbing the big, clean up-grade he'd set for himself.

"And we? Now that we've fought and lied and sweated and stolen, and hated as only the disappointed strugglers in a bitter, dead little Western town know how to do, what have we got to show for it? Harvey Merrick wouldn't have given one sunset over your marshes for all you've got put together, and you know it. It's not for me to say why, in the inscrutable wisdom of God, a genius should ever have been called from his place of hatred and bitter waters; but I want this Boston man to know that the drivel he's been hearing here tonight is the only tribute any truly great man could ever have from such a lot of sick, side-tracked, burnt-dog, land-poor sharks as the here-present financiers of Sand City—upon which town may God have mercy!"

The lawyer thrust out his hand to Steavens as he passed him, caught up his overcoat in the hall, and had left the house before the Grand Army man had had time to lift his ducked head and crane his long neck about at his fellows.

Next day Jim Laird was drunk and unable to attend the funeral services. Steavens called twice at his office, but was compelled to start East without seeing him. He had a presentiment that he would hear from him again, and left his address on the lawyer's table; but if Laird found it, he never acknowledged it. The thing in him that Harvey Merrick had loved must have gone underground with Harvey Merrick's coffin; for it never spoke again, and Jim got the cold he died of driving across the Colorado mountains to defend one of Phelps's sons who had got into trouble out there by cutting government timber.

Suggestions for Discussion

1. Discuss the details Cather uses to characterize the small Kansas town to which the dead sculptor's body is brought for burial. Why is Steavens repelled by the furnishings in the house of Merrick's mother?

2. The sculptor's mother is overcome by grief. Steavens is disgusted by her outburst of emotion. Why? Explain how Cather arranges details so that we will agree with Steavens.

3. How does Cather contrast Mrs. Merrick with her daughter? What function do both characters have in the story?

4. Why does Cather portray Jim Laird as a heavy drinker? What is his function in the story?

5. What was the real tragedy of the dead sculptor's life? How had it affected his work?

6. What is the theme of Cather's story? Why does she use the long speech by Laird to express it?

Suggestion for Writing

Cather's view of the artist as somehow alienated from his society is illustrated in this story. Write a paper dealing with the issue, using examples of well-known artists. You might make this a research project by investigating the life of Beethoven, Mozart, Baudelaire, or Poe. What about the relation of the artists to society in other cultures, for example, China, India, or Bali?

POETRY

MARIANNE MOORE

Poetry

Marianne Moore (1877–1972) was born in Missouri, graduated from Bryn Mawr College, taught at an Indian school, worked in the New York Public Library, edited *The Dial* between 1925 and 1929, and was a distinguished resident of Brooklyn Heights. Her first collection of poems was published in 1921, her *Collected Poems* in 1951. Among her works are *Predilection* (1955), a volume of critical essays; a poetic translation of La Fontaine's *Fables* (1954); and the volume of poetry *Tell Me, Tell Me* (1967). In the following poem, from *Collected Poems,* as she appears to put poetry in its place and dismisses high-flown theories about art, she affirms the power of the genuine article and the real significance of poetry.

I, too, dislike it: there are things that are important beyond all this fiddle,
  Reading it, however, with a perfect contempt for it, one discovers in
  it after all, a place for the genuine.
     Hands that can grasp, eyes
     that can dilate, hair that can rise
       if it must, these things are important not because a

high-sounding interpretation can be put upon them but because they are
  useful. When they become so derivative as to become unintelligible,
  the same thing may be said for all of us, that we
     do not admire what
     we cannot understand: the bat
       holding on upside down or in quest of something to

eat, elephants pushing, a wild horse taking a roll, a tireless wolf under
  a tree, the immovable critic twitching his skin like a horse that feels a flea,
      the base-
  ball fan, the statistician—
     nor is it valid
       to discriminate against "business documents and

school-books"; all these phenomena are important. One must make a
    distinction
  however: when dragged into prominence by half poets, the result is not
    poetry,
  nor till the poets among us can be
    "literalists of
    the imagination"—above
      insolence and triviality and can present

for inspection, "imaginary gardens with real toads in them," shall we have
  it. In the meantime, if you demand on the one hand,
  the raw material of poetry in
    all its rawness and
    that which is on the other hand
      genuine, you are interested in poetry.

Suggestions for Discussion

1. Why does the poet, on one hand, refer to poetry as "all this fiddle" and, on the other, find in it "a place for the genuine"?

2. What does the poet list as the important parts of poetry? Why does she dismiss the unintelligible in poetry?

3. Moore wants poets to become "literalists of the imagination." Relate this phrase to her belief that the poets must create "imaginary gardens with real toads in them."

Suggestions for Writing

1. Write a paper in which you compare the view of poetry in this poem with the view that poetry is a romantic outburst of pure emotion. What arguments would you use in defense of either position?

2. Rewrite the poem in prose sentences in a paragraph. Write a comment on what you have done with the poem. How have you changed it? Does your change effect a change in defining the piece as a poem?

LI-YOUNG LEE

Persimmons

Li-Young Lee (b. 1957) was born in Jakarta, Indonesia, of Chinese parents. His father, a political prisoner for one year, fled Indonesia with his
family in 1959. They arrived in the United States in 1964, after living in
Hong Kong, Macao, and Japan. Li-Young Lee studied at the University
of Pittsburgh, the University of Arizona, and SUNY at Brockport. He
and his family live in Chicago, where he works as an artist. He is the
author of *Book of My Nights* (2001). His poems in *Rose* (1986), of which
this is one, deal lyrically with the relations between parents and children
and between men and women, as well as the creation of art through
painting or poetry.

In sixth grade Mrs. Walker
slapped the back of my head
and made me stand in the corner
for not knowing the difference
between *persimmon* and *precision.*
How to choose

persimmons. This is precision.
Ripe ones are soft and brown-spotted.
Sniff the bottoms. The sweet one
will be fragrant. How to eat:
put the knife away, lay down newspaper.
Peel the skin tenderly, not to tear the meat.
Chew the skin, suck it,
and swallow. Now, eat
the meat of the fruit,
so sweet,
all of it, to the heart.

Donna undresses, her stomach is white.
In the yard, dewy and shivering
with crickets, we lie naked,
face-up, face-down.
I teach her Chinese.
Crickets: *chin chin.* Dew: I've forgotten.

Naked: I've forgotten.
Ni, wo: you and me.
I part her legs,
remember to tell her
she is beautiful as the moon.

Other words
that got me into trouble were
fight and *fright, wren* and *yarn.*
Fight was what I did when I was frightened,
fright was what I felt when I was fighting.
Wrens are small, plain birds,
yarn is what one knits with.
Wrens are soft as yarn.
My mother made birds out of yarn.
I loved to watch her tie the stuff;
a bird, a rabbit, a wee man.

Mrs. Walker brought a persimmon to class
and cut it up
so everyone could taste
a *Chinese apple.* Knowing
it wasn't ripe or sweet, I didn't eat
but watched the other faces.

My mother said every persimmon has a sun
inside, something golden, glowing,
warm as my face.

Once, in the cellar, I found two wrapped in newspaper,
forgotten and not yet ripe.
I took them and set both on my bedroom windowsill,
where each morning a cardinal
sang, *The sun, the sun.*

Finally understanding
he was going blind,
my father sat up all one night
waiting for a song, a ghost.
I gave him the persimmons,
swelled, heavy as sadness,
and sweet as love.

This year, in the muddy lighting
of my parents' cellar, I rummage, looking
for something I lost.
My father sits on the tired, wooden stairs,

black cane between his knees,
hand over hand, gripping the handle.
He's so happy that I've come home.
I ask how his eyes are, a stupid question.
All gone, he answers.

Under some blankets, I find a box.
Inside the box I find three scrolls.
I sit beside him and untie
three paintings by my father:
Hibiscus leaf and a white flower.
Two cats preening.
Two persimmons, so full they want to drop from the cloth.

He raises both hands to touch the cloth,
asks, *Which is this?*

This is persimmons, Father

Oh, the feel of the wolftail on the silk,
the strength, the tense
precision in the wrist.
I painted them hundreds of times
eyes closed. These I painted blind.
Some things never leave a person:
scent of the hair of one you love,
the texture of persimmons,
in your palm, the ripe weight.

Suggestions for Discussion

1. Discuss the way Lee uses the difficulties he had with English words (*persimmon/precision, fight/fright, wren/yarn*) to create the ideas for this poem.

2. In what ways does the poem reveal the relations between members of the narrator's family? Between the two young lovers? What special bond exists between the narrator in the poem and his father?

3. What statements does the father make about the nature of art in the final stanza of the poem? In the seven-line stanza before the end of the poem?

4. Why has the poet chosen the persimmon as the title for this poem?

Suggestions for Writing

1. Write a paper explaining the structure of the poem. What are its parts? How does the poet help the reader discover them?

2. Write two paragraphs summarizing the poet's ideas on the art of poetry.

C A T E   M A R V I N

Ocean Is a Word in this Poem

Cate Marvin, a professor of creative writing at the College of Staten Island, CUNY, has published poems in the literary journals *Ploughshares, Slate, Verse,* and the *New England Review,* among others. Her first book of poems, *World's Tallest Disaster* (2001), was selected by Robert Pinsky and awarded the Kathryn A. Morton Prize in Poetry. In this poem, Marvin uses a natural scene as a metaphor for a troubled relationship.

One centimeter on the map represents one kilometer on the ground.
River I can cover with a finger, but it's not the water I resent.
Ocean—even the word thinks itself huge, and only because of what it
meant. I remember its lip on a road that ran along the coast of
Portsmouth.

Waves tested a concrete brim where people stood to see how far
the water went. Sky was huge, but I didn't mind why. The sea
was too choppy and gray, a soup thick with salt and distance.
Look, sails are white as wedding dresses, but their cut is much cleaner.

No, I never planned to have a honeymoon by water, knew it'd
tempt me to leave your company, drop in. Ocean may allow boats to
ride its surface, but its word cannot anchor the white slip of this
paper. It cannot swallow the poem. Turbulence is on the wall. The
map—

I would tear it, forget how I learned land's edge exists. I would
sink into the depth of past tense, more treacherous than the murk
into which our vessel went. Now when I pull down the map, eat its
image and paper, I'll swallow what wedding meant. Salt crusts my lips.

Suggestions for Discussion

1. Where is the narrator of this poem?

2. Discuss Marvin's use of the word *ocean.* How are the word and the thing itself related (or not related)?

3. How can the sail's cut be "cleaner" than a wedding dress?

Suggestion for Writing

Attempt to reconstruct the relationship that the narrator reflects upon in this poem.

WALT WHITMAN

Poets to Come

Walt Whitman (1819–1892), regarded by many as the greatest American poet, was born on Long Island, NY. He was a printer, a journalist, and a nurse during the Civil War. Strongly influenced by Ralph Waldo Emerson, he published *Leaves of Grass* in 1855 at his own expense and added sections to new editions over the years. By the time of his death, Whitman had become a major influence on younger poets who were moved by his experiments in free verse and by his transcendental ideas.

Poets to come! orators, singers, musicians to come!
Not to-day is to justify me and answer what I am for,
But you, a new brood, native, athletic, continental, greater than
      before known,
Arouse! for you must justify me.

I myself but write one or two indicative words for the future,
I but advance a moment only to wheel and hurry back in the darkness.

I am a man who, sauntering along without fully stopping, turns a
      casual look upon you and then averts his face,
Leaving it to you to prove and define it,
Expecting the main things from you.

Suggestions for Discussion

1. How will the "poets to come" justify Whitman?

2. Why does Whitman feel he will "hurry back into darkness?"

3. What "main things" does Whitman expect from the future poets?

Suggestion for Writing

Answer Whitman's call and write a poem that he'd be proud to have inspired you to compose.

Science, the Environment, and the Future

❦❦❦

Before the bomb was made, Oppenheimer said, "When you see something that is technically sweet you go ahead and do it."

—GINA KOLATA, "A Clone Is Born"

Fortunately we are spectacularly resistant to brainwashing. No matter how hard their parents or their politicians tell them that smoking is bad for them, young people still take it up. Indeed, it is precisely because grown-ups lecture them about it that it seems so appealing. We are genetically endowed with a tendency to be bloody-minded towards authority, especially in our teens, to guard our own innate character against dictators, teachers, abusing stepparents, or government advertising campaigns.

—MATT RIDLEY, "Free Will"

IT-NOMADE, 6, AUGUST 2000

GUNTER KLÖTZER

©Gunter Klötzer

NOTEBOOK

꩜꩜꩜

HENRY DAVID THOREAU

Why I Went to the Woods

Henry David Thoreau (1817–1862) was a philosopher and poet-naturalist whose independent spirit led him to the famous experiment recorded in *Walden, or Life in the Woods* (1854). Thoreau's passion for freedom and his lifetime resistance to conformity in thought and manners are forcefully present in his famous essay, "On the Duty of Civil Disobedience." In the following essay, Thoreau explains his retreat from civilization to his cabin on Walden Pond.

I went to the woods because I wished to live deliberately, to front only the essential facts of life, and see if I could not learn what it had to teach, and not, when I came to die, discover that I had not lived. I did not wish to

From the series *disConnexion*, Danwen Xing, 2002–2003. ©Danwen Xing.

live what was not life, living is so dear; nor did I wish to practice resignation, unless it was quite necessary. I wanted to live deep and suck out all the marrow of life, to live so sturdily and Spartan-like as to put to rout all that was not life, to cut a broad swath and shave close, to drive life into a corner, and reduce it to its lowest terms, and, if it proved to be mean, why then to get the whole and genuine meanness of it, and publish its meanness to the world; or if it were sublime, to know it by experience, and be able to give a true account of it in my next excursion. For most men, it appears to me, are in a strange uncertainty about it, whether it is of the devil or of God, and have *somewhat hastily* concluded that it is the chief end of man here to "glorify God and enjoy him forever."

Still we live meanly, like ants; though the fable tells us that we were long ago changed into men; like pygmies we fight with cranes; it is error upon error, and clout upon clout, and our best virtue has for its occasion a superfluous and evitable wretchedness. Our life is frittered away by detail. An honest man has hardly need to count more than his ten fingers, or in extreme cases he may add his ten toes, and lump the rest. Simplicity, simplicity, simplicity! I say, let your affairs be as two or three, and not a hundred or a thousand; instead of a million count half a dozen, and keep your accounts on your thumb-nail. In the midst of this chopping sea of civilized life, such are the clouds and storms and quicksands and thousand-and-one items to be allowed for, that a man has to live, if he would not founder and go to the bottom and not make his port at all, by dead reckoning, and he must be a great calculator indeed who succeeds. Simplify, simplify. Instead of three meals a day, if it be necessary eat but one; instead of a hundred dishes, five; and reduce other things in proportion. Our life is like a German Confederacy, made of up petty states, with its boundary forever fluctuating, so that even a German cannot tell you how it is bounded at any moment. The nation itself, with all its so-called internal improvements, which, by the way are all external and superficial, is just such an unwieldy and overgrown establishment, cluttered with furniture and tripped up by its own traps, ruined by luxury and heedless expense, by want of calculation and a worthy aim, as the million households in the lands; and the only cure for it, as for them, is in a rigid economy, a stern and more than Spartan simplicity of life and elevation of purpose. It lives too fast. Men think that it is essential that the *Nation* have commerce, and export ice, and talk through a telegraph, and ride thirty miles an hour, without a doubt, whether *they* do or not; but whether we should live like baboons or like men, is a little uncertain. If we do not get our sleepers, and forge rails, and devote days and nights to the work, but go to tinkering upon our *lives* to improve *them,* who will build railroads? And if railroads are not built, how shall we get to heaven in season? But if we stay at home and mind our business, who will want railroads? We do not ride on the railroad; it rides upon us. Did you ever think what those sleepers are that underlie the railroad? Each one is a man, an Irishman, or a Yankee man. The rails are laid on them, and they are covered with sand, and the cars run smoothly over them. They are sound sleepers, I assure you. And every few years a new lot is laid down and run over; so that, if some have the pleasure of riding on a rail, others have the misfortune to be ridden upon. And when they run over a man that is walking in his sleep, a supernumerary sleeper in the wrong position, and wake him up, they suddenly stop the cars, and make a hue and cry about it, as if this were an exception. I am glad to know that it takes a gang of men for every five miles to keep the sleepers down and level in their beds as it is, for this is a sign that they may sometimes get up again.

Why should we live with such hurry and waste of life? We are determined to be starved before we are hungry. Men say that a stitch in time saves nine, and so they take a thousand stitches to-day to save nine tomorrow. As for *work,* we haven't any of any consequence. We have the Saint Vitus' dance, and cannot possibly keep our heads still. If I should only give a few pulls at the parish bell-rope, as for a fire, that is, without setting the bell, there is hardly a man on his farm in the outskirts of Concord, notwithstanding that press of engagements which was his excuse so many times this morning, nor a boy, nor a woman, I might almost say, but would foresake all and follow that sound, not mainly to save property from the flames, but, if we will confess the truth, much more to see it burn, since burn it must, and we, be it known, did not set it on fire—or to see it put out, and have a hand in it, if that is done as handsomely; yes, even if it were the parish church itself. Hardly a man takes a half-hour's nap after dinner, but when he wakes he holds up his head and asks, "What's the news?" as if the rest of mankind had stood his sentinels. Some give directions to be waked every half-hour, doubtless for no other purpose; and then, to pay for it, they tell what they have dreamed. After a night's sleep the news is as indispensable as the breakfast. "Pray tell me anything new that has happened to a man anywhere on this globe"—and he reads it over his coffee and rolls, that a man has had his eyes gouged out this morning on the Wachito River; never dreaming the while that he lives in the dark unfathomed mammoth cave of this world, and has but the rudiment of an eye himself.

For my part, I could easily do without the post-office. I think that there are very few important communications made through it. To speak critically, I never received more than one or two letters in my life—I wrote this some years ago—that were worth the postage. The penny-post is, commonly, an institution through which you seriously offer a man that penny for his thoughts which is so often safely offered in jest. And I am sure that I never read any memorable news in a newspaper. If we read of one man robbed, or murdered, or killed by accident, or one house burned, or one vessel wrecked, or one steamboat blown up, or one cow run over on the Western Railroad, or one mad dog killed, or one lot of grasshoppers in the winter—we never need read of another. One is enough. If you are acquainted with the principle, what do you care for a myriad instances and applications? To a philosopher all *news,* as it is called, is gossip, and they who edit and read it are old women over their tea. Yet not a few are greedy after this gossip. There was such a rush, as I hear, the other day at one of the offices to learn the foreign news by the last arrival, that several large squares of plate glass belonging to the establishment were broken by the pressure— news which I seriously think a ready wit might write a twelvemonth, or twelve years, beforehand with sufficient accuracy. As for Spain, for instance, if you know how to throw in Don Carlos and the Infanta, and Don Pedro and Seville and Granada, from time to time in the right proportions—they may have changed the names a little since I saw the papers—and serve up a bullfight when other entertainments fail, it will be true to the letter, and give us as good an idea of the exact state or ruin of things in Spain as the most succinct and lucid reports under this head in the newspapers; and as for England, almost the last significant scrap of news from that quarter was the revolution of 1649; and if you have learned the history of her crops for an average year, you never need attend to that thing again, unless your specu- lations are of a merely pecuniary character. If one may judge who rarely looks into the newspapers, nothing new does ever happen in foreign parts, a French revolution not excepted.

What news! how much more important to know what that is which was never old! "Kieou-he-yu (great dignitary of the state of Wei) sent a man to Khoung-tseu to know his news. Khoung-tseu caused the messenger to be seated near him, and questioned him in these terms: What is your master doing? The messenger answered with respect: My master desires to dimin- ish the number of his faults, but he cannot come to the end of them. The messenger being gone, the philosopher remarked: What a worthy messen- ger! What a worthy messenger!" The preacher, instead of vexing the ears of drowsy farmers on their day of rest at the end of the week—for Sunday is the fit conclusion of an ill-spent week, and not the fresh and brave beginning of a new one—with this one other draggle-tail of a sermon, should shout with thundering voice, "Pause! Avast! Why so seeming fast, but deadly slow?"

Shams and delusions are esteemed for soundest truths, while reality is fabulous. If men would steadily observe realities only, and not allow them- selves to be deluded, life, to compare it with such things as we know, would be like a fairy tale and the Arabian Nights' Entertainments. If we respected only what is inevitable and has a right to be, music and poetry would resound along the streets. When we are unhurried and wise, we perceive that only great and worthy things have any permanent and absolute existence, that petty fears and petty pleasures are but the shadow of the reality. This is always exhilarating and sublime. By closing the eyes and slumbering, and consenting to be deceived by shows, men establish and confirm their daily life of routine and habit everywhere, which still is built on purely illusory foundations. Children, who play life, discern its true law and relations more clearly than men, who fail to live it worthily, but who think that they are wiser by experience, that is, by failure. I have read in a Hindoo book, that "there was a king's son, who, being expelled in infancy from his native city, was brought up by a forester, and, growing up to maturity in that state, imagined himself to belong to the barbarous race with which he lived. One of his father's ministers having discovered him, revealed to him what he was, and the misconception of his character was removed, and he knew himself to be a prince. So soul," continues the Hindoo philosopher, "from the circumstances in which it is placed, mistakes its own character, until the truth is revealed to it by some holy teacher and then it knows itself to be *Brahme.*" I perceive that we inhabitants of New England live this mean life that we do because our vision does not penetrate the surface of things. We think that that *is* which *appears* to be. If a man should walk through this town and see only the reality, where, think you, would the "Milldam" go to? If he should give us an account of the realities he beheld there, we should not recognize the place in his description. Look at the meetinghouse, or a courthouse, or a jail, or a shop, or a dwelling-house, and say what that thing really is before a true gaze, and they would all go to pieces in your account of them. Men esteem truth remote, in the outskirts of the system, behind the farthest star, before Adam and after the last man. In eternity there is indeed something true and sublime. But all these times and places and occasions are now and here. God himself culminates in the present moment, and will never be more divine in the lapse of all the ages. And we are enabled to apprehend at all what is sublime and noble only by the perpetual instilling and drenching of the reality that surrounds us. The universe constantly and obediently answers to our conceptions; whether we travel fast or slow, the track is laid for us. Let us spend our lives in conceiving then. The poet or the artist never yet had so fair and noble a design but some of his posterity at least could accomplish it.

Let us spend one day as deliberately as Nature, and not be thrown off the track by every nutshell and mosquito's wing that falls on the rails. Let us rise early and fast, or breakfast, gently and without perturbation; let company come and let company go, let the bells ring and the children cry—determined to make a day of it. Why should we knock under and go with the stream? Let us not be upset and overwhelmed in that terrible rapid and whirlpool called a dinner, situated in the meridian shallows. Weather this danger and you are safe, for the rest of the way is downhill. With unrelaxed nerves, with morning vigor, sail by it, looking another way, tied to the mast like Ulysses. If the engine whistles, let it whistle till it is hoarse for its pains. If the bell rings, why should we run? We will consider what kind of music they are like. Let us settle ourselves and work and wedge our feet downward through the mud and slush of opinion, and prejudice, and tradition, and delusion, and appearance, that alluvion which covers the globe, through Paris and London, through New York and Boston and Concord, through Church and State, through poetry and philosophy and religion, till we come to a hard bottom and rocks in place, which we can call *reality*, and say, This is, and no mistake; and then begin, having a *point d'appui*, below freshet and frost and fire, a place where you might found a wall or a state, or set a lamp-post safely, or perhaps a gauge, not a Nilometer, but a Realometer, that future ages might know how deep a freshet of shams and appearances had gathered from time to time. If you stand right fronting and face to face to a fact, you will see the sun glimmer on both its surfaces, as if it were a cimeter, and feel its sweet edge dividing you through the heart and marrow, and so you will happily conclude your mortal career. Be it life or death, we crave only reality. If we are really dying, let us hear the rattle in our throats and feel cold in the extremities; if we are alive, let us go about our business.

Time is but the stream I go afishing in. I drink at it; but while I drink I see the sandy bottom and detect how shallow it is. Its thin current slides away but eternity remains. I would drink deeper; fish in the sky, whose bottom is pebbly with stars. I cannot count one. I know not the first letter of the alphabet. I have always been regretting that I was not as wise as the day I was born. The intellect is a cleaver; it discerns and rifts its way into the secret of things. I do not wish to be any more busy with my hands than is necessary. My head is hands and feet. I feel all my best faculties concentrated in it. My instinct tells me that my head is an organ for burrowing, as some creatures use their snout and fore paws, and with it I would mine and burrow my way through these hills. I think that the richest vein is somewhere hereabouts; so by the divining-rod and thin rising vapors, I judge; and here I will begin to mine.

Suggestions for Discussion

1. Why did Thoreau go to the woods?

2. With what details does Thoreau support his statement that "we live meanly, like ants"?

3. Interpret Thoreau's rhetorical question in the context of his philosophy: "If you are acquainted with the principle, what do you care for a myriad instances and applications?"

4. With what details does Thoreau illustrate his impatience with man's proclivity for being deluded?

5. How do Thoreau's rhetorical questions, metaphors, and allusions contribute to substance and tone?

6. What aspects of American life do Thoreau repudiate and why?

7. What does he affirm? Paraphrase his last two paragraphs.

Suggestions for Writing

1. Discuss in an essay what you have learned from your observations of nature.

2. Discuss: "Our life is frittered away by detail."

3. Comment on: "Shams and delusions are esteemed for soundless truths, while reality is fabulous."

4. What would Thoreau's impressions be of our current preoccupations?

EDWARD O. WILSON

A Letter to Thoreau

Edward O. Wilson (b. 1929) is a scientist, conservationist, and two-time winner of the Pulitzer Prize, one of which was the Pulitzer Prize for General Non-Fiction in 1979 for his book *On Human Nature.* He was born in Birmingham, AL, and educated at the University of Alabama and Harvard. Now residing in Lexington, MA, Wilson is currently a Pellegrino University Research Professor and Harvard University's Honorary Curator in Entomology of the Museum of Comparative Zoology. Wilson has won many prizes for his research and is a member of the National Academy of Science, a Fellow of the American Academy of Arts and Science, and an honorary member of the Royal Society of London. More recent works include the book that earned him a second Pulitzer Prize, *The Ants* (1990), cowritten with Bert Holldobler; *Naturalist* (1995), a memoir; and *Consilience* (1998), a work on "the unity of knowledge." *The Future of Life* (2002), Wilson's most recent book, is the source for the following passage, in which he writes an open letter to his long-dead naturalist hero, Henry David Thoreau.

Henry!

May I call you by your Christian name? Your words invite familiarity and make little sense otherwise. How else to interpret your insistent use of the first personal pronoun? *I* wrote this account, you say, here are *my* deepest thoughts, and no third person placed between us could ever be so well represented. Although *Walden* is sometimes oracular in tone, I don't read it, the way some do, as an oration to the multitude. Rather, it is a work of art, the testament of a citizen of Concord, in New England, from one place, one time, and one writer's personal circumstance that manages nevertheless to reach across five generations to address accurately the general human condition. Can there be a better definition of art?

You brought me here. Our meeting could have just as well been a woodlot in Delaware, but here I am at the site of your cabin on the edge of Walden Pond. I came because of your stature in literature and the conservation movement, but also—less nobly, I confess—because my home is in Lexington, two towns over. My pilgrimage is a pleasant afternoon's excursion to a nature reserve. But mostly I came because of all your contemporaries you are the one I most need to understand. As a biologist with a modern scientific library, I know more than Darwin knew. I can imagine the measured responses of that country gentleman to a voice a century and a half beyond his own. It is not a satisfying fantasy: the Victorians have for the most part settled into a comfortable corner of our remembrance. But I cannot imagine your responses, at least not all of them. Too many shadowed residues there in your text, too many emotional trip wires. You left too soon, and your restless spirit haunts us still.

Is it so odd to speak apostrophically across 150 years? I think not. Certainly not if the subject is natural history. The wheels of organic evolution turn at a millennial pace, too slowly for evolution to have transformed species from your time to mine. The natural habitats they compose also remain mostly unchanged. Walden Woods around the pond, having been only partly cut and never plowed, looks much the same in my time as in yours, although now more fully wooded. Its ambience can be expressed in similar language.

Anyway, the older I become, the more it makes sense to measure history in units of life span. That pulls us closer together in real time. Had you lived to eighty instead of just forty-four, we might today have a film clip of you walking on Walden Pond beach through a straw-hatted and parasoled crowd on holiday. We could listen to your recorded voice from one of Mr. Edison's wax cylinders. Did you speak with a slight burr, as generally believed? I am seventy-two now, old enough to have had tea with Darwin's last surviving granddaughter at the University of Cambridge. While a Harvard graduate student I discussed my first articles on evolution with Julian Huxley, who as a little boy sat on the knee of his grandfather Thomas Henry Huxley, Darwin's "bulldog" disciple and personal friend. You will know what I am talking about. You still had three years to live when in 1859 *The Origin of Species* was published. It was the talk of Harvard and salons along the Atlantic seaboard. You purchased one of the first copies available in America and annotated it briskly. And here is one more circumstance on which I often reflect: as a child I could in theory have spoken to old men who visited you at Walden Pond when they were children of the same age. Thus only one living memory separates us. At the cabin site even that seems to vanish.

Forgive me, I digress. I am here for a purpose: to become more a Thoreauvian, and with that perspective better to explain to you, and in reality to others and not least to myself, what has happened to the world we both have loved.

The landscape away from Walden Pond, to start, has changed drastically. In your time the forest was almost gone. The tallest white pines had been cut long before and hauled away to Boston to be trimmed into ship masts. Other timber was harvested for houses, railroad ties, and fuel. Most of the swamp cedars had become roof shingles. America, still a wood-powered nation, was approaching its first energy crisis as charcoal and cordwood ran short. Soon everything would change. Then coal would fill the breach and catapult the industrial revolution forward at an even more furious pace.

When you built your little house from the dismantled planks of James Collins's shanty in 1845, Walden Woods was a threatened oasis in a mostly treeless terrain. Today it is pretty much the same, although forest has grown up to fill the farmland around it. The trees are still scraggly second-growth descendants of the primeval giants that clothed the lake banks until the mid-1700s. Around the cabin site, beech, hickory, red maple, and scarlet and white oak push up among half-grown white pines in a bid to reestablish the rightful hardwood domination of southern New England forests. Along the path from your cabin on down to the nearest inlet—now called Thoreau's Cove—these trees give way to an open stand of larger white pines, whose trunks are straight and whose branches are evenly spread and high off the ground. The undergrowth consists of a sparse scattering of saplings and huckleberry. The American chestnut, I regret to report, is gone, done in by an overzealous European fungus. Only a few sprouts still struggle up from old stumps here and there, soon to be discovered by the fungus and killed back. Sprouting their serrate leaves, the doomed saplings are faint reminders of the mighty species that once composed a full quarter of the eastern virgin forest. But all the other trees and shrubs you knew so well still flourish. The red maple is more abundant than in your day. It is more than ever both the jack-of-all-trades in forest regeneration and the crimson glory of the New England autumn.

I can picture you clearly as your sister Sophia sketched you, sitting here on the slightly raised doorstep. It is a cool morning in June, by my tastes the best month of the year in New England. In my imagination I have settled beside you. We gaze idly across this spring-fed lake of considerable size that New Englanders perversely call a pond. Today in this place we speak a common idiom, breathe the same clean air, listen to the whisper of the pines. We scuff the familiar leaf litter with our shoes, pause, look up to watch a circling red-tailed hawk pass overhead. Our talk drifts from here to there but never so far from natural history as to break the ghostly spell and never so intimate as to betray the childish sources of our common pleasure. A thousand years will pass and Walden Woods will stay the same, I think, a flickering equilibrium that works its magic on human emotion in variations with each experience.

We stand up to go a-sauntering. We descend the cordwood path to the lake shore, little changed in contour from the sketch you made in 1846, follow it around, and coming to a rise climb to the Lincoln Road, then circle back to the Wyman Meadow and on down to Thoreau's Cove, completing a round-trip of two miles. We search along the way for the woods least savaged by axe and crosscut saw. It is our intention to work not around but *through* these remnants. We stay within a quarter-mile or so of the lake, remembering that in your time almost all the land outside the perimeter woods was cultivated.

Mostly we talk in alternating monologues, because the organisms we respectively favor are different enough to require cross-explanation. There are two kinds of naturalists, you will agree, defined by the search images that guide them. The first—your tribe—are intent on finding big organisms: plants, birds, mammals, reptiles, amphibians, perhaps butterflies. Big-organism people listen for animal calls, peer into the canopy, poke into tree hollows, search mud banks for scat and spoor. Their line of sight vacillates around the horizontal, first upward to scan the canopy, then down to peer at the ground. Big-organism people search for a single find good enough for the day. You, I recall, thought little of walking four miles or more to see if a certain plant had begun to flower.

I am a member of the other tribe—a lover of little things, a hunter also, but more the snuffling opossum than the questing panther. I think in millimeters and minutes, and am nowhere near patient as I prowl, having been spoiled forever by the richness of invertebrates and quick reward for little effort. Let me enter a tract of rich forest and I seldom walk more than a few hundred feet. I halt before the first promising rotten log I encounter. Kneeling, I roll it over, and always there is instant gratification from the little world hidden beneath. Rootlets and fungal strands pull apart, adhering flakes of bark fall back to earth. The sweet damp musty scent of healthy soil rises like a perfume to the nostrils that love it. The inhabitants exposed are like deer jacklighted on a country road, frozen in a moment of their secret lives. They quickly scatter to evade the light and desiccating air, each maneuvering in the manner particular to its species. A female wolf spider sprints headlong for several body lengths and, finding no shelter, stops and stands rigid. Her brindled integument provides camouflage, but the white silken egg case she carries between her pedipalps and fangs gives her away. Close by, julid millipedes, which were browsing on mold when the cataclysm struck, coil their bodies in defensive spirals. At the far end of the exposed surface a large scolopendrid centipede lies partly concealed beneath decayed bark fragments. Its sclerites are a glistening brown armor, its jaws poison-filled hypodermic needles, its legs downward-curving scythes. The scolopendrid offers no threat unless you pick it up. But who would dare touch this miniature dragon? Instead I poke it with the tip of a twig. *Get out of there!* It writhes, spins around, and is gone in a flash. Now I can safely rake my fingers through the humus in search of less threatening species.

These arthropods are the giants of the microcosm (if you will allow me to continue what has turned into a short lecture). Creatures their size are present in dozens—hundreds, if an ant or termite colony is present. But these are comparatively trivial numbers. If you focus down by a power of ten in size, enough to pick out animals barely visible to the naked eye, the numbers jump to thousands. Nematode and enchytraeid pot worms, mites, springtails, pauropods, diplurans, symphylans, and tardigrades seethe in the underground. Scattered out on a white ground cloth, each crawling speck becomes a full-blown animal. Together they are far more striking and diverse in appearance than snakes, mice, sparrows, and all the other vertebrates hereabouts combined. Their home is a labyrinth of miniature caves and walls of rotting vegetable debris cross-strung with ten yards of fungal threads. And they are just the surface of the fauna and flora at our feet. Keep going, keep magnifying until the eye penetrates microscopic water films on grains of sand, and there you will find ten billion bacteria in a thimbleful of soil and frass. You will have reached the energy base of the decomposer world as we understand it 150 years after your sojourn in Walden Woods.

Untrammeled nature exists in the dirt and rotting vegetation beneath our shoes. The wilderness of ordinary vision may have vanished—wolf, puma, and wolverine no longer exist in the tamed forests of Massachusetts. But another, even more ancient wilderness lives on. The microscope can take you there. We need only narrow the scale of vision to see a part of these woods as they were a thousand years ago. This is what, as a small-organism naturalist, I can tell you.

"Thó-reau." Your family put the emphasis on the first syllable, as in "thorough," did it not? At least that is what your close friend Ralph Waldo

Emerson scribbled on a note found among his papers. Thoreau, thorough naturalist, you would have liked the Biodiversity Day we held in your honor here recently. It was conceived by Peter Alden, a Concord resident and international wildlife tour guide. (Easy name to remember; he is a descendant of John Alden of Pilgrim fame.) On July 4, 1998, the anniversary of the day in 1845 you moved furniture into the Walden cabin, Peter and I were joined by more than a hundred other naturalists from around New England. We set out to list all the wild species of organisms—plants, animals, and fungi— we could find in one day with unaided vision or hand lens within a broad section of Concord and Lincoln around Walden Pond. We aimed for a thousand. The final tally, announced to the thorn-scratched, mosquito-bitten group assembled at an outdoor meal that evening, was 1,904. Well, actually 1,905, to stretch the standards a bit, because the next day a moose *(Alces alces)* came from somewhere and strolled into Concord Center. It soon strolled out again, and evidently departed the Concord area, thus lowering the biodiversity back to the July 4 level.

If you could have come back that Biodiversity Day you might have joined us unnoticed (that is, if you refrained from bringing up President Polk and the Mexican question). Even the 1840s clothing would not have betrayed you, given our own scruffy and eclectic field wear. You would have understood our purpose too. From your last two books, *Faith in a Seed* and *Wild Fruits* (finally rescued from your almost indecipherable notes and published in the 1990s), it is apparent that you were moving toward scientific natural history when your life prematurely ended. It was logical for you to take that turn: the beginning of every science is the description and naming of phenomena. Human beings seem to have an instinct to master their surroundings that way. We cannot think clearly about a plant or animal until we have a name for it; hence the pleasure of bird watching with a field guide in hand. Alden's idea quickly caught on. As I write, in 2001, Biodiversity Days, or "bioblitzes" as they are also called, are being held or planned elsewhere in the United States as well as in Austria, Germany, Luxembourg, and Switzerland. In June 2001 we were joined for a third event in Massachusetts by students from 260 towns over the entire state.

At Walden Pond that first day I met Brad Parker, one of the character actors who play you while giving tours around the reconstructed cabin. He is steeped in Thoreauviana, and eerily convincing. He refused to deviate even one second from your persona as we talked, bless him, and for a pleasant hour I lived in the virtual 1840s he created. Of course, to reciprocate I invited him to peer with me at insects and other invertebrates beneath nearby stones and fallen dead branches. We moved on to a clump of bright yellow mushrooms. Then Neo-Thoreau mentioned a singing wood thrush in the canopy above us, which my deafness in the upper registers prevented me from hearing. We went on like this for a while, with his making nineteenth-century sallies and responses and my struggling to play the part of a time-warped visitor. No mention was made of the thunder of aircraft above us on their approach to Hanscom Field. Nor did I think it anomalous that at sixty-nine I was speaking to a reanimation of you, Henry Real-Thoreau, at thirty. In one sense it was quite appropriate. The naturalists of my generation are you grown older and more knowledgeable, if not wiser.

A case in point on the growth of knowledge. Neo-Thoreau and I talked about the ant war you described in *Walden*. One summer day you found red ants locked in mandible-to-mandible combat with black ants all around your cabin. The ground was littered with the dead and dying, and the ambulatory maimed fought bravely on. It was an ant-world Austerlitz, as you said, a conflict dwarfing the skirmish on the Concord Bridge that started the American Revolution a rifle shot from Walden Pond. May I presume to tell you what you saw? It was a slave raid. The slavers were the red ants, most likely *Formica subintegra*, and the victims were the black ants, probably *Formica subsericea*. The red ants capture the infants of their victims, or more precisely, their cocoon-clad pupae. Back in the red-ant nest the kidnapped pupae complete their development and emerge from their cocoons as adult workers. Then, because they instinctively accept the first workers they meet as nestmates, they enter into voluntary servitude to their captors. Imagine that! A slave raid at the doorstep of one of America's most ardent abolitionists. For millions of years this harsh Darwinian strategy has prevailed, and so will it ever be, with no hope that a Lincoln, a Thoreau, or an Underground Railroad might arise in the formicid world to save the victim colonies.

Now, prophet of the conservation movement, mentor of Gandhi and Martin Luther King Jr., accept this tribute tardily given. Keen observer of the human condition, scourge of the philistine culture, Greek stoic adrift in the New World, you are reborn in each generation and vested with new meaning and nuance. Sage of Concord—Saint Henry, they sometimes call you—you've fairly earned your place in history.

On the other hand, you were not a great naturalist. (Forgive me!) Even had you kept entirely to natural history during your short life, you would have ranked well below William Bartram, Louis Agassiz, and that prodigious collector of North American plants John Torrey, and be scarcely remembered today. With longer life it would likely have been different, because you were building momentum in natural history rapidly when you left us. And to give you full credit, your ideas on succession and other properties of living communities pointed straight toward the modern science of ecology.

That doesn't matter now. I understand why you came to Walden Pond; your words are clear enough on that score. Granted, you chose this spot primarily to study nature. But you could have done that as easily and far more comfortably on daily excursions from your mother's house in Concord Center, half an hour's walk away, where in fact you did frequently repair for a decent meal. Nor was your little cabin meant to be a wilderness hermitage. No wilderness lay within easy reach anyway, and even the woods around Walden Pond had shrunk to their final thin margins by the 1840s. You called solitude your favorite companion. You were not afraid, you said, to be left to the mercy of your own thoughts. Yet you craved humanity passionately, and your voice is anthropocentric in mood and philosophy. Visitors to the Walden cabin were welcomed. Once a group of twenty-five or more crowded into the solitary room of the tiny house, shoulder to shoulder. You were not appalled by so much human flesh pressed together (but I am). You were lonely at times. The whistle of a passing train on the Fitchburg track and the distant rumble of oxcarts crossing a bridge must have given you comfort on cold, rainy days. Sometimes you went out looking for someone, anyone, in spite of your notorious shyness, just to have a conversation. You fastened on them, as you put it, like a bloodsucker.

In short, you were far from the hard-eyed frontiersman bearing pemmican and a long rifle. Frontiersmen did not saunter, botanize, and read Greek. So how did it happen that an amateur naturalist perched in a toy house on the edge of a ravaged woodland became the founding saint of the conservation movement? Here is what I believe happened. Your spirit craved an epiphany. You sought enlightenment and fulfillment the Old Testament way, by reduction of material existence to the fundamentals. The cabin was your cave on the mountainside. You used poverty to purchase a margin of free existence. It was the only method you could devise to seek the meaning in a life otherwise smothered by quotidian necessity and haste. You lived at Walden, as you said (I dare not paraphrase),

> to front only the essential facts of life, and see if I could not learn what it had to teach, and not, when I came to die, discover that I had not lived...to live deep and suck out all the marrow of life, to live so sturdily and Spartan-like as to put to rout all that was not life, to cut a broad swath and shave close, to drive life into a corner, and reduce it to its lowest terms, and, if it proved to be mean, why then to get the whole and genuine meanness of it, and publish its meanness to the world; or if it were sublime, to know it by experience, and be able to give a true account of it in my next excursion.

You were mistaken, I think, to suppose that there are as many ways of life possible as radii that can be drawn from the center of a circle, and your choice just one of them. On the contrary, the human mind can develop along only a very few pathways imaginable. They are selected by satisfactions we instinctively seek in common. The sturdiness of human nature is the reason people plant flowers, gods live on high mountains, and a lake is the eye of the world through which—your metaphor—we can measure our own souls.

It is exquisitely human to search for wholeness and richness of experience. When these qualities are lost among the distracting schedules of everyday life, we seek them elsewhere. When you stripped your outside obligations to the survivable minimum, you placed your trained and very active mind in an unendurable vacuum. And this is the essence of the matter: in order to fill the vacuum, you discovered the human proclivity to embrace the natural world.

Your childhood experience told you exactly where to go. It could not be a local cornfield or gravel pit. Nor the streets of Boston, which, however vibrant as the hub of a growing nation, might cost a layabout his dignity and even his life. It had to be a world both tolerant of poverty and rich and beautiful enough to be spiritually rewarding. Where around Concord could that possibly be but a woodlot next to a lake?

You traded most of the richness of social existence for an equivalent richness of the natural world. The choice was entirely logical, for the following reason. Each of us finds a comfortable position somewhere along the continuum that ranges from complete withdrawal and self-absorption at one end to full civic engagement and reciprocity at the other. The position is never fixed. We fret, vacillate, and steer our lives through the riptide of countervailing instincts that press from both ends of the continuum. The uncertainty we feel is not a curse. It is not a confusion on the road out of Eden. It is just the human condition. We are intelligent mammals, fitted by evolution—by God, if you prefer—to pursue personal ends through cooperation. Our priceless selves and family first, society next. In this respect we are the polar opposite of your cabinside ants, bound together as replaceable parts of a superorganism. Our lives are therefore an insoluble problem, a dynamic process in search of an indefinable goal. They are neither a celebration nor a spectacle but rather, as a later philosopher put it, a predicament. Humanity is the species forced by its basic nature to make moral choices and seek fulfillment in a changing world by any means it can devise.

You searched for essence at Walden and, whether successful in your own mind or not, you hit upon an ethic with a solid feel to it: nature is ours to explore forever; it is our crucible and refuge; it is our natural home; it is all these things. Save it, you said: in wildness is the preservation of the world.

Now, in closing this letter, I am forced to report bad news. (I put it off till the end.) The natural world in the year 2001 is everywhere disappearing before our eyes—cut to pieces, mowed down, plowed under, gobbled up, replaced by human artifacts.

No one in your time could imagine a disaster of this magnitude. Little more than a billion people were alive in the 1840s. They were overwhelmingly agricultural, and few families needed more than two or three acres to survive. The American frontier was still wide open. And far away on continents to the south, up great rivers, beyond unclimbed mountain ranges, stretched unspoiled equatorial forests brimming with the maximum diversity of life. These wildernesses seemed as unattainable and timeless as the planets and stars. That could not last, because the mood of Western civilization is Abrahamic. The explorers and colonists were guided by a biblical prayer: May we take possession of this land that God has provided and let it drip milk and honey into our mouths, forever.

Now, more than six billion people fill the world. The great majority are very poor; nearly one billion exist on the edge of starvation. All are struggling to raise the quality of their lives any way they can. That unfortunately includes the conversion of the surviving remnants of the natural environment. Half of the great tropical forests have been cleared. The last frontiers of the world are effectively gone. Species of plants and animals are disappearing a hundred or more times faster than before the coming of humanity, and as many as half may be gone by the end of this century. An Armageddon is approaching at the beginning of the third millennium. But it is not the cosmic war and fiery collapse of mankind foretold in sacred scripture. It is the wreckage of the planet by an exuberantly plentiful and ingenious humanity.

The race is now on between the technoscientific forces that are destroying the living environment and those that can be harnessed to save it. We are inside a bottleneck of overpopulation and wasteful consumption. If the race is won, humanity can emerge in far better condition than when it entered, and with most of the diversity of life still intact.

The situation is desperate—but there are encouraging signs that the race can be won. Population growth has slowed, and, if the present trajectory holds, is likely to peak between eight and ten billion people by century's end. That many people, experts tell us, can be accommodated with a decent standard of living, but just barely: the amount of arable land and water available per person, globally, is already declining. In solving the problem, other experts tell us, it should also be possible to shelter most of the vulnerable plant and animal species.

In order to pass through the bottleneck, a global land ethic is urgently needed. Not just any land ethic that might happen to enjoy agreeable sentiment, but one based on the best understanding of ourselves and the world around us that science and technology can provide. Surely the rest of life matters. Surely our stewardship is its only hope. We will be wise to listen carefully to the heart, then act with rational intention and all the tools we can gather and bring to bear.

Henry, my friend, thank you for putting the first element of that ethic in place. Now it is up to us to summon a more encompassing wisdom. The living world is dying; the natural economy is crumbling beneath our busy feet. We have been too self-absorbed to foresee the long-term consequences of our actions, and we will suffer a terrible loss unless we shake off our delusions and move quickly to a solution. Science and technology led us into this bottleneck. Now science and technology must help us find our way through and out.

You once said that old deeds are for old people, and new deeds are for new. I think that in historical perspective it is the other way around. You were the new and we are the old. Can we now be the wiser? For you, here at Walden Pond, the lamentation of the mourning dove and the green frog's *t-r-r-oonk!* across the predawn water were the true reason for saving this place. For us, it is an exact knowledge of what that truth is, all that it implies, and how to employ it to best effect. So, two truths. We will have them both, you and I and all those now and forever to come who accept the stewardship of nature.

Affectionately yours,
Edward

Suggestions for Discussion

1. Who is Wilson writing to here, really? Is this a letter to a dead man, an open letter to you and to other readers, or is it, somehow, both a letter to you and a letter to Thoreau?

2. How does Wilson evaluate the significance of Thoreau as a writer, a naturalist, and a historical figure?

3. According to Thoreau, what is the nature of the environmental crisis that we face and why is it important that we remember Thoreau's writings as we search for a solution to the crisis?

4. Read the selection by Thoreau, *Why I Went to the Woods* (see p. 464), and compare the Thoreau you find in those pages to the Thoreau described by Wilson.

Suggestion for Writing

Write a letter to someone who means a lot to you who is no longer alive. Offer up your deepest thoughts and feelings to this person, focusing especially on his/her effect on your life.

PERSONAL REMINISCENCES

FREEMAN DYSON

Can Science Be Ethical?

Freeman Dyson (b. 1923), a native of Berkshire, England, is a physicist and professor emeritus at Cornell University best known for his speculative research into the possible existence of extraterrestrial intelligence. A longtime advocate of the human exploration and colonization of space, Dyson participated in the Orion Project in the 1950s, which endeavored to send a manned spacecraft to Mars. The research team succeeded in testing a working model but the government abandoned the project because of various technical and environmental concerns. *Disturbing the Universe* (1979), *Weapons and Hope* (1984), *Origins of Life* (1985), *Infinite in All Directions* (1988), and *The Sun, The Genome and The Internet* (1999) are among his most famous books. In this article, published in 1997, Dyson explains how science can be used as a tool for both good and evil purposes.

One of my favorite monuments is a statue of Samuel Gompers not far from the Alamo in San Antonio, Texas. Under the statue is a quote from one of Gompers's speeches:

What does labor want?
We want more schoolhouses and less jails,
More books and less guns,
More learning and less vice,
More leisure and less greed,
More justice and less revenge,
We want more opportunities to cultivate our better nature.

Samuel Gompers was the founder and first president of the American Federation of Labor. He established in America the tradition of practical bargaining between labor and management which led to an era of growth and prosperity for labor unions. Now, seventy years after Gompers's death, the unions have dwindled, while his dreams, more books and fewer guns, more leisure and less greed, more schoolhouses and fewer jails, have been tacitly abandoned. In a society without social justice and with a free-market ideology, guns, greed, and jails are bound to win.

When I was a student of mathematics in England fifty years ago, one of my teachers was the great mathematician G. H. Hardy, who wrote a little book, *A Mathematician's Apology,* explaining to the general public what mathematicians do. Hardy proudly proclaimed that his life had been devoted to the creation of totally useless works of abstract art, without any possible practical application. He had strong views about technology, which he summarized in the statement "A science is said to be useful if its development tends to accentuate the existing inequalities in the distribution of wealth, or more directly promotes the destruction of human life." He wrote these words while war was raging around him.

Still, the Hardy view of technology has some merit even in peacetime. Many of the technologies that are now racing ahead most rapidly, replacing human workers in factories and offices with machines, making stockholders richer and workers poorer, are indeed tending to accentuate the existing inequalities in the distribution of wealth. And the technologies of lethal force continue to be as profitable today as they were in Hardy's time. The marketplace judges technologies by their practical effectiveness, by whether they succeed or fail to do the job they are designed to do. But always, even for the most brilliantly successful technology, an ethical question lurks in the background: the question whether the job the technology is designed to do is actually worth doing.

The technologies that raise the fewest ethical problems are those that work on a human scale, brightening the lives of individual people. Lucky individuals in each generation find technology appropriate to their needs. For my father ninety years ago, technology was a motorcycle. He was an impoverished young musician growing up in England in the years before World War I, and the motorcycle came to him as a liberation. He was a working-class-boy in a country dominated by the snobberies of class and accent. He learned to speak like a gentleman, but he did not belong in the world of gentlemen. The motorcycle was a great equalizer. On his motorcycle, he was the equal of a gentleman. He could make the grand tour of Europe without having inherited an upper-class income. He and three of his friends bought motorcycles and rode them all over Europe.

My father fell in love with his motorcycle and with the technical skills that it demanded. He understood, sixty years before Robert Pirsig wrote *Zen and the Art of Motorcycle Maintenance,* the spiritual quality of the motorcycle. In my father's day, roads were bad and repair shops few and far between. If you intended to travel any long distance, you needed to carry your own tool kit and spare parts and be prepared to take the machine apart and put it back together again. A breakdown of the machine in a remote place often required major surgery. It was as essential for a rider to understand the anatomy and physiology of the motorcycle as it was for a surgeon to understand the anatomy and physiology of a patient. It sometimes happened that my father and his friends would arrive at a village where no motorcycle had ever been seen before. When this happened, they would give rides to the village children and hope to be rewarded with a free supper at the village inn. Technology in the shape of a motorcycle was comradeship and freedom.

Fifty years after my father, I discovered joyful technology in the shape of a nuclear fission reactor. That was in 1956, in the first intoxicating days of peaceful nuclear energy, when the technology of reactors suddenly emerged from wartime secrecy and the public was invited to come and play with it. This was an invitation that I could not refuse. It looked then as if nuclear energy would be the great equalizer, providing cheap and abundant energy to rich and poor alike, just as fifty years earlier the motorcycle gave mobility to rich and poor alike in class-ridden England.

I joined the General Atomic Company in San Diego, where my friends were playing with the new technology. We invented and built a little reactor which we called the TRIGA, designed to be inherently safe. Inherent safety meant that it would not misbehave even if the people operating it were grossly incompetent. The company has been manufacturing and selling TRIGA reactors for forty years and is still selling them today, mostly to hospitals and medical centers, where they produce short-lived isotopes for diagnostic purposes. They have never misbehaved or caused any danger to the people who used them. They have only run into trouble in a few places where the neighbors objected to their presence on ideological grounds, no matter how safe they might be. We were successful with the TRIGA because it was designed to do a useful job at a price that a big hospital could afford. The price in 1956 was a quarter of a million dollars. Our work with the TRIGA was joyful because we finished it quickly, before the technology became entangled with politics and bureaucracy, before it became clear that nuclear energy was not and never could be the great equalizer.

Forty years after the invention of the TRIGA, my son George found another joyful and useful technology, the technology of CAD–CAM, computer-aided design and computer-aided manufacturing. CAD–CAM is the technology of the postnuclear generation, the technology that succeeded after nuclear energy failed. George is a boat-builder. He designs seagoing kayaks. He uses modern materials to reconstruct the ancient craft of the

Aleuts, who perfected their boats by trial and error over thousands of years and used them to travel prodigious distances across the northern Pacific. His boats are fast and rugged and seaworthy. When he began his boat-building twenty-five years ago, he was a nomad, traveling up and down the north Pacific coast, trying to live like an Aleut, and built his boats like an Aleut, shaping every part of each boat and stitching them together with his own hands. In those days he was a nature-child, in love with the wilderness, rejecting the urban society in which he had grown up. He built boats for his own use and for his friends, not as a commercial business.

As the years went by George made a graceful transition from the role of rebellious teen-ager to the role of solid citizen. He married, raised a daughter, bought a house in the city of Bellingham, and converted an abandoned tavern by the waterfront into a well-equipped workshop for his boats. His boats are now a business. And he discovered the joys of CAD–CAM.

His workshop now contains more computers and software than sewing needles and hand tools. It is a long time since he made the parts of a boat by hand. He now translates his designs directly into CAD–CAM software and transmits them electronically to a manufacturer who produces the parts. George collects the parts and sells them by mail order to his regular customers with instructions for assembling them into boats. Only on rare occasions, when a wealthy customer pays for a custom-built job, does George deliver a boat assembled in the workshop. The boat business occupies only a part of his time. He also runs a historical society concerned with the history and ethnography of the north Pacific. The technology of CAD–CAM has given George resources and leisure, so that he can visit the Aleuts in their native islands and reintroduce to the young islanders the forgotten skills of their ancestors.

Forty years into the future, which joyful new technology will be enriching the lives of our grandchildren? Perhaps they will be designing their own dogs and cats. Just as the technology of CAD–CAM began in the production lines of large manufacturing companies and later became accessible to individual citizens like George, the technology of genetic engineering may soon spread out from the biotechnology companies and agricultural industries and become accessible to our grandchildren. Designing dogs and cats in the privacy of a home may become as easy as designing boats in a waterfront workshop.

Instead of CAD–CAM we may have CAS–CAR, computer-aided selection and computer-aided reproduction. With the CAS–CAR software, you first program your pet's color scheme and behavior, and then transmit the program electronically to the artificial fertilization laboratory for implementation. Twelve weeks later, your pet is born, satisfaction guaranteed by the software company. When I recently described these possibilities in a public lecture at a children's museum in Vermont, I was verbally assaulted by a young woman in the audience. She accused me of violating the rights of animals. She said I was a typical scientist, one of those cruel people who spend their lives torturing animals for fun. I tried in vain to placate her by saying that I was only speaking of possibilities, that I was not actually myself engaged in designing dogs and cats. I had to admit that she had a legitimate complaint. Designing dogs and cats is an ethically dubious business. It is not as innocent as designing boats.

When the time comes, when the CAS–CAR software is available, when anybody with access to the software can order a dog with pink and purple spots that can crow like a rooster, some tough decisions will have to be made. Shall we allow private citizens to create dogs who will be objects of contempt and ridicule, unable to take their rightful place in dog society? And if not, where shall we draw the line between legitimate animal breeding and illegitimate creation of monsters? These are difficult questions that our children and grandchildren will have to answer. Perhaps I should have spoken to the audience in Vermont about designing roses and orchids instead of dogs and cats. Nobody seems to care so deeply for the dignity of roses and orchids. Vegetables, it seems, do not have rights. Dogs and cats are too close to being human. They have feelings like ours. If our grandchildren are allowed to design their own dogs and cats, the next step will be using the CAS–CAR software to design their own babies. Before that next step is reached, they ought to think carefully about the consequences.

What can we do today, in the world as we find it at the end of the twentieth century, to turn the evil consequences of technology into good? The ways in which science may work for good or evil in human society are many and various. As a general rule, to which there are many exceptions, science works for evil when its effect is to provide toys for the rich, and works for good when its effect is to provide necessities for the poor. Cheapness is an essential virtue. The motorcycle worked for good because it was cheap enough for a poor schoolteacher to own. Nuclear energy worked mostly for evil because it remained a toy for rich governments and rich companies to play with. "Toys for the rich" means not only toys in the literal sense but technological conveniences that are available to a minority of people and make it harder for those excluded to take part in the economic and cultural life of the community. "Necessities for the poor" include not only food and shelter but adequate public health services, adequate public transportation, and access to decent education and jobs.

The scientific advances of the nineteenth century and the first half of the twentieth were generally beneficial to society as a whole, spreading wealth to rich and poor alike with some degree of equity. The electric light, the telephone, the refrigerator, radio, television, synthetic fabrics, antibiotics, vitamins, and vaccines were social equalizers, making life easier and more comfortable for almost everybody, tending to narrow the gap between rich and poor rather than to widen it. Only in the second half of our century has the balance of advantage shifted. During the last forty years, the strongest efforts in pure science have been concentrated in highly esoteric fields remote from contact with everyday problems. Particle physics, low-temperature physics, and extragalactic astronomy are examples of pure sciences moving further and further away from their origins. The intensive pursuit of these sciences does not do much harm, or much good, either to the rich or the poor. The main social benefit provided by pure science in esoteric fields is to serve as a welfare program for scientists and engineers.

At the same time, the strongest efforts in applied science have been concentrated upon products that can be profitably sold. Since the rich can be expected to pay more than the poor for new products, market-driven applied science will usually result in the invention of toys for the rich. The laptop computer and the cellular telephone are the latest of the new toys. Now that a large fraction of high-paying jobs are advertised on the Internet, people excluded from the Internet are also excluded from access to jobs. The failure of science to produce benefits for the poor in recent decades is due to two factors working in combination: the pure scientists have become more detached from the mundane needs of humanity, and the applied scientists have become more attached to immediate profitability.

Although pure and applied science may appear to be moving in opposite directions, there is a single underlying cause that has affected them both. The cause is the power of committees in the administration and funding of science. In the case of pure science, the committees are composed of scientific experts performing the rituals of peer review. If a committee of scientific experts selects research projects by majority vote, projects in fashionable fields are supported while those in unfashionable fields are not. In recent decades, the fashionable fields have been moving further and further into specialized areas remote from contact with things that we can see and touch. In the case of applied science, the committees are composed of business executives and managers. Such people usually give support to products that affluent customers like themselves can buy.

Only a cantankerous man like Henry Ford, with dictatorial power over his business, would dare to create a mass market for automobiles by arbitrarily setting his prices low enough and his wages high enough that his workers could afford to buy his product. Both in pure science and in applied science, rule by committee discourages unfashionable and bold ventures. To bring about a real shift of priorities, scientists and entrepreneurs must assert their freedom to promote new technologies that are more friendly than the old to poor people and poor countries. The ethical standards of scientists must change as the scope of the good and evil caused by science has changed. In the long run, as Haldane and Einstein said, ethical progress is the only cure for the damage done by scientific progress.

The nuclear arms race is over, but the ethical problems raised by non-military technology remain. The ethical problems arise from three "new ages" flooding over human society like tsunamis. First is the Information Age, already arrived and here to stay, driven by computers and digital memory. Second is the Biotechnology Age, due to arrive in full force early in the next century, driven by DNA sequencing and genetic engineering. Third is the Neurotechnology Age, likely to arrive later in the next century, driven by neural sensors and exposing the inner workings of human emotion and personality to manipulation. These three new technologies are profoundly disruptive. They offer liberation from ancient drudgery in factory, farm, and office. They offer healing of ancient diseases of body and mind. They offer wealth and power to the people who possess the skills to understand and control them. They destroy industries based on older technologies and make people trained in older skills useless. They are likely to bypass the poor and reward the rich. They will tend, as Hardy said eighty years ago, to accentuate the inequalities in the existing distribution of wealth, even if they do not, like nuclear technology, more directly promote the destruction of human life.

The poorer half of humanity needs cheap housing, cheap health care, and cheap education, accessible to everybody, with high quality and high aesthetic standards. The fundamental problem for human society in the next century is the mismatch between the three new waves of technology and the three basic needs of poor people. The gap between technology and needs is wide and growing wider. If technology continues along its present course, ignoring the needs of the poor and showering benefits upon the rich, the poor will sooner or later rebel against the tyranny of technology and turn to irrational and violent remedies. In the future, as in the past, the revolt of the poor is likely to impoverish rich and poor together.

The widening gap between technology and human needs can only be filled by ethics. We have seen in the last thirty years many examples of the power of ethics. The worldwide environmental movement, basing its power on ethical persuasion, has scored many victories over industrial wealth and technological arrogance. The most spectacular victory of the environmentalists was the downfall of nuclear industry in the United States and many other countries, first in the domain of nuclear power and more recently in the domain of weapons. It was the environmental movement that closed down factories for making nuclear weapons in the United

States, from plutonium-producing Hanford to warhead-producing Rocky Flats. Ethics can be a force more powerful than politics and economics.

Unfortunately, the environmental movement has so far concentrated its attention upon the evils that technology has done rather than upon the good that technology has failed to do. It is my hope that the attention of the Greens will shift in the next century from the negative to the positive. Ethical victories putting an end to technological follies are not enough. We need ethical victories of a different kind, engaging the power of technology positively in the pursuit of social justice.

If we can agree with Thomas Jefferson that these truths are self-evident, that all men are created equal, that they are endowed with certain inalienable rights, that among these are life, liberty, and the pursuit of happiness, then it should also be self-evident that the abandonment of millions of people in modern societies to unemployment and destitution is a worse defilement of the earth than nuclear power stations. If the ethical force of the environmental movement can defeat the manufacturers of nuclear power stations, the same force should also be able to foster the growth of technology that supplies the needs of impoverished humans at a price they can afford. This is the great task for technology in the coming century.

The free market will not by itself produce technology friendly to the poor. Only a technology positively guided by ethics can do it. The power of ethics must be exerted by the environmental movement and by concerned scientists, educators, and entrepreneurs working together. If we are wise, we shall also enlist in the common cause of social justice the enduring power of religion. Religion has in the past contributed mightily to many good causes, from the building of cathedrals and the education of children to the abolition of slavery. Religion will remain in the future a force equal in strength to science and equally committed to the long-range improvement of the human condition.

In the world of religion, over the centuries, there have been prophets of doom and prophets of hope, with hope in the end predominating. Science also gives warnings of doom and promises of hope, but the warnings and the promises of science cannot be separated. Every honest scientific prophet must mix the good news with the bad. Haldane was an honest prophet, showing us the evil done by science not as inescapable fate but as a challenge to be overcome. He wrote in his book *Daedalus* in 1923, "We are at present almost completely ignorant of biology, a fact which often escapes the notice of biologists, and renders them too presumptuous in their estimates of the present condition of their science, too modest in their claims for its future." Biology has made amazing progress since 1923, but Haldane's statement is still true.

We still know little about the biological processes that affect human beings most intimately—the development of speech and social skills in infants, the interplay between moods and emotions and learning and understanding in children and adults, the onset of aging and mental deterioration at the end of life. None of these processes will be understood within the next decade, but all of them might be understood within the next century. Understanding will then lead to new technologies that offer hope of preventing tragedies and ameliorating the human condition. Few people believe any longer in the romantic dream that human beings are perfectible. But most of us still believe that human beings are capable of improvement.

In public discussions of biotechnology today, the idea of improving the human race by artificial means is widely condemned. The idea is repugnant because it conjures up visions of Nazi doctors sterilizing Jews and killing defective children. There are many good reasons for condemning enforced sterilization and euthanasia. But the artificial improvement of human beings will come, one way or another, whether we like it or not, as soon as the progress of biological understanding makes it possible. When people are offered technical means to improve themselves and their children, no matter what they conceive improvement to mean, the offer will be accepted. Improvement may mean better health, longer life, a more cheerful disposition, a stronger heart, a smarter brain, the ability to earn more money as a rock star or baseball player or business executive. The technology of improvement may be hindered or delayed by regulation, but it cannot be permanently suppressed. Human improvement, like abortion today, will be officially disapproved, legally discouraged, or forbidden, but widely practiced. It will be seen by millions of citizens as a liberation from past constraints and injustices. Their freedom to choose cannot be permanently denied.

Two hundred years ago, William Blake engraved *The Gates of Paradise*, a little book of drawings and verses. One of the drawings, with the title "Aged Ignorance," shows an old man wearing professorial eyeglasses and holding a large pair of scissors. In front of him, a winged child is running naked in the light from a rising sun. The old man sits with his back to the sun. With a self-satisfied smile he opens his scissors and clips the child's wings. With the picture goes a little poem:

> *In Time's Ocean falling drown'd,*
> *In Aged Ignorance profound,*
> *Holy and cold, I clip'd the Wings*
> *Of all Sublunary Things.*

This picture is an image of the human condition in the era that is now beginning. The rising sun is biological science, throwing light of ever-increasing intensity onto the processes by which we live and feel and think. The winged child is human life, becoming for the first time aware of itself and its potentialities in the light of science. The old man is our existing human society, shaped by ages of past ignorance. Our laws, our loyalties, our fears and hatreds, our economic and social injustices, all grew slowly and are deeply rooted in the past. Inevitably the advance of biological knowledge will bring clashes between old institutions and new desires for human self-improvement. Old institutions will clip the wings of new desires. Up to a point, caution is justified and social constraints are necessary. The new technologies will be dangerous as well as liberating. But in the long run, social constraints must bend to new realities. Humanity cannot live forever with clipped wings. The vision of self-improvement, which William Blake and Samuel Gompers in their different ways proclaimed, will not vanish from the earth.

Suggestions for Discussion

1. What is the Hardy view of technology?

2. What examples does Freeman Dyson give of technologies that have been used for both good and evil?

3. How does Dyson believe genetic engineering will impact on our future?

4. What is the great task of technology in the coming century?

Suggestions for Writing

1. What scientific innovation has most benefited the progress of humanity? Have any scientific discoveries proven so destructive that you wish they had never been unearthed?

2. Would you use the advancements in genetic engineering to "design" one of your own children? Is this procedure moral? Who should be allowed access to this technology? What limits, if any, should be placed upon this procedure?

ESSAYS

❀❀❀

ALAN TENNANT

Great Plains of the Arctic

Alan Tennant (b. 1943 in Houston, TX) has led nature expeditions in locations as wide-ranging as Africa, South America, and the Galapagos Islands, and lectured on a variety of subjects from wildlife to literature and film criticism. An expert on reptiles, Tennant wrote a series of field guides to North American snakes and served as president of the Society for the Preservation of Reptiles and Amphibians. His 1980 nonfiction book *The Guadeloupe Mountains of Texas* won both the Southern Book Award and the Western Books Award, and his recent bestseller *On the Wing* (2004) was adapted for the screen by National Geographic Films. Tennant specially wrote the selection that follows for publication in *The Conscious Reader*.

Among the world's magical natural kingdoms—equatorial rain forest, coral reef, cloud forest, savannah grassland and tropical wetland—none embodies the ethereal character of polar tundra. There, at the top of the world, the sweep of sky and horizon that typifies arctic steppe seems to operate in a dimension more transparent than that of other places, because with neither water vapor nor airborne dust to diffuse the clarity of distant views, the land takes on a kind of stereoscopic translucence in which far off details are revealed in the hyper realistic detail of laboratory-altered photographs.

But the most striking thing about this supranatural clarity is that it occurs in the absence of bright sunlight. Although the sun never sets during the polar summer, neither does it rise very far above the horizon—an angle that produces a golden, late-afternoon illumination that, except for occasional clouds, never varies. "In the temperate zone," writes Barry Lopez in *Arctic Dreams,* "each day has a discrete dawn that suggests a new beginning. But in the Far North the day does not start over again every day."

From the crest of a ridge above Alaska's Colville River, where I'd gone to study northern peregrine falcons, the flinty ridges of the Brooks Range lay on the southern horizon. Like much of the Arctic Slope's topography, their orientation seemed askew, for North American mountains generally

491

rise along a north-south axis. Seven or eight thousand feet in elevation, the peaks seemed no more than a dozen miles away, although they were nearer a hundred, but the granite wall they formed conclusively separates the biotic communities of the rest of Alaska from everything that lay around me.

Early European travelers found the country here a wasteland, and indeed, despite all its luminous precision the terrain seemed strangely sterile. Vegetation of only meager height matted its gentle slopes, creating a billiard table prospect, although up close that velvet surface proved astonishingly difficult to traverse. The highest ground was not bad, for bare, reddish soil separated rocks covered with scaly patches of orange, green, gray, and brown lichen. But everywhere else the tundra formed a knee-deep mat of stunted birch, cranberry, blue crowberry, arctic heather, and an assemblage of low sedges so thoroughly entwined that their meshed stems made up a kind of botanical steel wool too flimsy to walk on top of and too snarled to bulldoze through.

Cutting narrow swaths through this wooly matrix were game trails, their muddy surface embossed with the circular prints of caribou. Splayed like big doubled commas, stamped impressions going in opposite directions scribed the herd's daily commutes. Sometimes, though, there was drama. A heavily pocked gravel bar recorded a small band's emergence from the Colville, but as their trail churned silently away from the water another trajectory of tracks suddenly appeared, punched in deadly overlay atop the caribous' suddenly panicked, wide-spaced galloping prints.

Wolves. Three of them, from the different sizes of their paws, running in tandem, focused on the swerving line of the smallest set of caribou hooves. Still in virtual, silent flight and pursuit all four animals vanished into the backside heather, but trying to follow their tracks away from the river, beside a low-growing mass of saxifrage I found only a mélange of confused earthen sign.

With no more trail to decipher, I regarded the plants. The most evident was saxifrage. A welcome sight to native northerners, who eat its buds, *Saxifrage oppositifolia* most often grows on rocky uplands where little besides lichens finds a toehold. With its trailing, leafy stems, saxifrage branches end in single flowers, usually a vibrant purple, although lone white blossoms occasionally appear. All are so crowded together that the local Inuit call the plant "something like blood spots"—which banks of the flowers do resemble, especially in the snow, now in late June melted no more than a few days.

Adapted to region's repeated gales, like other arctic plants saxifrage stays low, dragging its stems and glossy leaves along the radiation-concentrating soil where the temperature is a bit higher than that of the air even a few inches above ground level. Around the saxifrage flourished a bonsai forest of miniature sedges, reindeer lichen, moss campions and mountain avens—some

older that I—that covered the valley's sloping flanks and, on the low hills, fitted snugly into every crevice. From those confined refugia each plant sent
out hardly more than a tendril a season, yet was still so vulnerable to intrusion that with every step I crushed a bouquet of minuscule leaves and stems.

I felt worst about stepping on the blooms. Between the tundra's low
sedges grew yellow arnica, mastodon flowers, Labrador tea, alpine foxtails
and pygmy buttercups. All were tiny, but avoiding the wind and seeking
warmer temperatures wasn't the only reason the tundra's floral mat was so
low. Here, every plant's priority was to make the best of the brevity of sunlight, the lack of nutrients in the thin, acidic soil, and the difficulty in accessing the minimal precipitation of these high latitudes, since every bit of the
region's moisture spends most of the year locked up as ice.

This was vegetation designed—evolved—to contend with bad weather,
for arctic plants live with more restricted energy flows than even desert vegetation, eking out such a slow, careful existence that a spruce thrusting up
a broomstick stem no more than a yard from roots to its topmost needles
could have been constructing that thin trunk for half a century. As in other
xeric regions, less than a dozen annual inches of rain falls in most sub-polar
regions—yet in the melt-water days of summer, tundra becomes the world's
only swampy desert.

It is also North America's last great Serengeti. Before the coming of the
oil camps, the North Slope's more than six thousand square miles comprised
the largest swath of wild grazing land left in North America, filled with the
same great numbers of migrant ungulates and — and in its tundra wolves
and barren ground grizzlies — the same big predators typical of Pleistocene
grasslands everywhere on earth.

Biologically speaking, of course, we are still in the Pleistocene. Humans
have killed almost all the earth's large grazers, as well as their predators, and
uprooted the plants that used to support them both. But other than that no
fundamental epochal change separates us from the period when the big
mammals flourished. Or sets us off from the characteristic variability of
Pleistocene weather. Deep ice cores from Greenland show that the largest of
the Wisconsin Glaciers may have melted in less than a century. According
to many climatologists, however, that colossal thaw could have happened in
as little as a couple of decades; if global warming alters the northward flow
of warm ocean currents like the Gulf Stream that keep the polar chill at bay,
massive ice might return almost as quickly.

For in these lands beside the polar sea, ice is never far away. For millennia, below everything, there has always been ice. Ice that physically supports
the boggy land, shapes its matted mud into the landforms of the topographic
maps, and during the partial summer thaw waters this country's plants
and animals. Deeper, there lies ice too far down to feel the summer thaw:

permanent frost that has not seen the sun since its moisture, some of it, dripped as rain from the backs of shaggy Pleistocene horses, camels, and mammoth, tundra-living elephants.

All of them are still here, held in long-frozen suspension, sometimes not so far below the surface. On earlier trips, my groups have found not only crumbly ivory tusks but, once, an actual mammoth carcass decaying out of frigid riverbank clay — evidence of a flourishing polar prairie entirely unlike the wet tundra that has replaced the dry steppe grass on which the mammoths fed.

Other remnants of this lost time are a few leavings of the people who hunted the great pachyderms. Far to the east, flaked stone tools comparable in design and age to those of European Neanderthals were left by the first American immigrants, people who came across the landlocked Bering Straits into a country as dark and frigid as any on earth. Yet they survived, ultimately begetting the Pre-Dorset, then Dorset cultures, whose stone-ringed house foundations still turn up in sheltered sites across the tundra.

What distinguished their adaptive ecology — as well as that of every high latitude plant and animal species — is the seasonal brevity here, of the active part of every living thing's existence. Only during a few gloriously sunlit summer weeks does the circumpolar continental rim come to life, as a sort of briefly-wakened Brigadoon, before once more slipping back beneath the gray mantle of ice and darkness where it slumbers for most of the year. To survive such climatic extremes requires physiological courage — in our terms, heroism — and every growing plant and joyously feeding, breeding, sleeping-not-at-all animal I see is able to be here only because of a valor unknown to creatures who spend their lives in a single temperate habitat.

To enjoy the summer riches of this far northern Eden means employing one of two almost equally desperate strategies. One of these—that of the endures—is to somehow survive months of almost extraterrestrial cold, although in the green glory of summer it was difficult for me to picture the other side of the year here—a dim other world, lit only by star shine, whipped by gales that dropped the temperature to more than 60 degrees below freezing—though that was exactly the scene, six months before, when I'd stood on this very spot.

Then, the only birds had been ptarmigan, snow grouse molted white as the frozen turf that paved their world, and flurries of snow buntings, gusted up into the swirling flakes of which they seemed an icy part. The only other visible creature was a tiny, ivory-hued fox that skittered like a shadow between the hollows where it, like the buntings and ptarmigan, sheltered from the wind in which no small creature could live for long.

Nothing, it seemed, but a lone arctic gyrfalcon that skimmed low over the Colville bluffs, hunting the dimness with eyes huge as those of an owl, striving to fuel itself with the flesh of its prey. It would still be here, hunting, with the coming of spring, when the subterranean sleepers, arctic ground squirrels and the grizzlies and wolverines that prey on them, emerge to find a land almost devoid of vertebrate life.

Until the migrant birds arrive.

Heroes of a different sort, theirs is the opposite strategy of the endurers. Instead of evolving ways to survive the long months of cold, they have gained—during the long advance and retreat of the glaciers that periodically exposed these lush northern lands—the incredible ability to travel to warmer wintering grounds sometimes halfway across the planet. Then, in millions of individual intercontinental pilgrimages, they have learned to return in time to raise their young in the Arctic's vast summer cornucopia of food, where they also enjoy a relative freedom from predation because few carnivores are able to survive the sub-polar winter. Theirs was an epic journey, a monumental quest for home that, in a small plane, I once followed north.

My company was a radio-tagged female peregrine called Amelia, after long distance aviator Amelia Earhart. Watching the myriad flocks of smaller birds, also Arctic-bound below and around our little Cessna, it gradually became clear with what determination each of those fragile, airborne creatures would fling itself aloft each morning, heading north, fired with the hope of once more seeing its distant place of birth.

As was Amelia. Like other falcons, her devotion was not only to place, but also to a mate, for breeding pairs may spend three-quarters of every year apart, making their trans-continental journeys entirely alone. Yet, as spring moves north across the hemisphere, from thousands of miles apart both partners somehow know to simultaneously dig the samurai blades of their slender wings into the air, faithfully lofting themselves onto the long highway leading back to their nuptial ledge.

Some arrive on the Texas coast, fresh from Central America, then perhaps—like Amelia—follow the Rockies north, going on to Canada or Alaska. There, most will rendezvous with the same, long-remembered partner—a mate they might have last seen under the falling sun of the previous September. In the air before their always sunlit summer cliffs they will once more court, as they may have done each spring of the preceding dozen years, spinning swift Ferris wheels above familial eyries whose lineage of peregrines may stretch back to the Pleistocene.

No predators will seek them here, but in their blood and tissue some of those global wanderers bear traces of agricultural chemicals, including the DDT still employed by village exterminators from the Yucatan to Venezuela. Other falcons carry petroleum residue first ingested by their shorebird prey. Easy kills when sickened after feeding on organochlorine saturated invertebrates picked up beside the open sludge ponds of the Latin

American petrochemical industry, these wading birds concentrate the signature toxins which, in the bodies of their predators burn on, weeks and thousands of miles later, in the far reaches of the Arctic.

Yet as arctic migrants go, peregrines are not among the most heroic travelers. More arduous are the journeys of tiny, flitting wheatears that have flown across the Bering Strait from Central Asia; of godwits and golden plovers arrived from as far away as Argentina; and jaegers, veterans of six thousand miles flown all the way over the vast blue curve of the Pacific from almost inconceivably distant down-under New Zealand.

Everywhere I looked, savannah sparrows flitted through the heather, as focused on the domestic details of their narrow surroundings as if they had not just ridden their stubby wings more than 3,000 miles to get here. Because, to them, it was worth it. Tens of thousands of generations of their kind had prospered by coming to this rich land, where, during summer, from horizon to horizon, spatters of silver paint seem daubed onto the olive-toned heather. Ponds, every one of which houses swarms of soon-to-metamorphose insect larvae waiting to feed every small passerine perched in the surrounding heather. Below them, on the potholes' muddy banks, live myriad small crustaceans, mollusks, and earthworms—a parallel feast for the horned larks, American pipits and Lapland longspurs which, on their long legs, scurried across every bare patch of ground I could see.

Like the longspurs, named for the extended rear claw they use to dig scratch up prey, for the most part the tundra's small passerines stayed as low as its plants, calling from waist-high willow sprouts, the tallest vegetation in sight. But that didn't inhibit what can only be seen as joy—maybe just euphoria at being back on their breeding grounds—where no creatures' enthusiasm matched that of the pipits. Full of whistle-song each male would leap into the air, climbing in a low arc over the sedge where its mate, perhaps already on eggs, sat watching. Lacking the treetop perches their southern counterparts use to broadcast territorial calls, tundra-living songbirds create high, airborne stages from which to shower down the long string of melody that establishes their proprietorship of nesting turf.

That bold display makes them vulnerable to peregrines, but most of arctic birdlife's great vulnerability comes from having to nest on the ground. There they are exposed to every trotting fox or loping wolverine, but what saves the majority of the nesters is both the relative scarcity of such predators and the brooding females' cryptic coloring. Walking even a little way, I passed brooding sparrows, longspurs, and snow buntings, each brown-backed female flattened inconspicuously against her natal cup. Camouflage is less possible with nestlings, but adaptive evolution has given the young of many arctic nesters more highly developed legs than those of comparably aged southern latitude relatives that enable them to scramble out of the nest in as little as a week after hatching.

The shorebirds used a different strategy. Flushing abruptly away from the mottled gravel bars where their speckled eggs or chicks lay hidden, parent plovers so put so much heart into feigning injury that I usually let myself be led away by their desperate display.

That took me to the phalarope. As I reversed course from a plover's hidden scrape a piebald flash caught my eye. It was a red phalarope, a real find because only during midsummer do these little swimming sandpipers venture inland from the arctic seas. Like a miniature bumper car the phalarope scooted and spun across the surface of its front yard-sized pond, but its sudden revolutions were far from random. The partly webbed toes that powered its circular skitters were actually tiny mix-masters, twisting aquatic vortexes that drew larval insects and minute crustaceans up from the muddy bottom, into the reach of its precise, black-spine bill.

For a wading bird—for any bird—the phalarope was spectacular. Its radiant russet waistcoat, snowy cheeks, and a black cap was typically colorful male-display plumage. Yet the gaudily-feathered little sandpiper swimming before me was female. Her mate, who was nowhere to be seen, was less vividly-plumaged, with an only faintly rusty breast and a less contrasting brown-streaked back—for more than 98% of bird species, the definitive plumage of females adapted to camouflage on the nest.

The anomaly was because this female phalarope would not share with her smaller mate the responsibility of raising their young—nor, in all likelihood, would he have even been her exclusive breeding partner. More probably he was one of several males this highly independent female had actively sought and courted, then left with eggs that each of her consorts would now be incubating while she was far away, feeding at sites like the stillwater pond where I'd found her. This week or next, each of those abandoned dads—for every male phalarope is a single parent—would begin tending the hatching chicks their mother would never see, raising them to flight and then accompany them at least part of the way on their first migration south.

Those youngsters were easy to picture. Two days before, on Prudhoe's big tarmac runway I'd answered the wave of one of the flight mechanics who, cradling something of obvious worth, had approached the hangar where I stood waiting for a bush plane. His valuation was correct: cupped in his palms were a pair of alert-eyed phalarope chicks, red-necked subspecies of the female phalarope still whirling like a waterbug in front of me. Downy-beige, with fuzzy mascara eye stripes and wire-like legs, in irritation the babies had pressed the soft points of their sewing needle bills against the big calloused fingers that enclosed them.

"Jet-wash. Blew these right under my truck," their savior confided. "Thought they were scraps of paper. You're the photographer…got any idea where the nest is?"

I did not, but it didn't really matter. These two were already entering the free-swimming developmental stage during which, until their encounter with a landing airliner, they'd been learning the delicate skill of aquatic larvae-snatching from their nowhere-to-be-seen father. His absence didn't auger well, but I eased them back into the multi-channeled ditch that ran alongside the runway: if their dad was going to find them, it would be here, though I knew the chances of these two being recovered were next to nothing.

Predators, storms, just plain bad luck have always taken a toll of such adolescents, and to an animal death is just death, whether it comes in the talons of a diving peregrine or as the result of a jet's hurricane destruction of a parental bond. But overall it matters...matters when technology obliterates not just the life but the ineffable symmetry of something as perfect as these gem-like little beings.

In a skitter of chocolate-and-white wings the red female phalarope took off from our hidden pool, and as I watched her skim like a skipping rock across the surface I thought of where she would be in a few weeks, after she'd left this northern tundra, and of whether my lost chicks from Prudhoe, maybe still alive, might be there too. Because for both sorts of phalarope, with the season's change an entirely new life was about to begin.

By then, that cavalier, multi-husbanded mother would have molted away her striking summer cinnamon and in its place would wear the gray of autumn. Far from her placid summer pond, she, along with all her kind, would be paddling in a wild place of ocean wind, riding big jade-green waves far out on the Chukchi Sea. There, she would spend the autumn tracking the titanic undulations of migrating humpback whales which, crossing coastal shoals churn to the surface the same sort of minuscule invertebrates that on the tundra she herself had gently stirred from the floor of her quiet wetland pools.

And, had they not run afoul of Alaska Airlines' turbines—maybe even in spite of having done so—the chicks I'd released at Prudhoe could also be nearby, for every pod of southward forging humpbacks was attended, along with northern fulmars, blacklegged kittiwakes, and diving murres, by flocks of both types of small swimming sandpipers. Rusty brown in the fledging plumage that had already carried them far from the still pools where they were born, the adolescent phalaropes would also be dancing over heaving alps of water and whale flesh. Some would be paddling alongside their dads, with whom they might then ride long-traveling ocean swells past the western tip of North America, south through the Bering Strait, then far down into the Pacific where, tiny as chips of wood, they would spend the winter probing for plankton along floating weed-lines, bobbing on the open sea a thousand miles from land.

Next spring, the surviving phalaropes would make the long flight home. They would come because of their devotion to this far northern plain: an inbred geographic memory of this ancestral place of glistening still-water ponds just released from the ice. But they would also come because they have no place else to go.

Since the continental glaciers retreated the tundra has lain, remote and untouched, at the top of the world. Yet now that final bastion of arctic purity is vanishing, as even this remote, sub-polar Eden is in the process of being decimated by the most pervasive of all mankind's environmental assaults.

Cores taken from the floor of Arctic lakes have shown a steady increase in warm water-living microorganisms, montane glaciers are pulling back everywhere on earth, and by 2004, the low walls of ice and frozen soil that had formerly bordered the rivers here were crumbling. In their place lay a crumpled rug of displaced tundra, its roots dangling into the arid, empty space where for eons there had lain the support of sustaining permafrost.

Until recently, that frozen substrate underlay—held in place—every square mile of the Arctic Plain. Now, much of it is gone, with more melting every year during the longer, warmer summers brought on by mankind's greenhouse gas emissions. In its place an alien floral community has taken root. As the southern tree-line advances toward the pole, a newly grown willow/scrub ecosystem is developing, a habitat in whose bankside thickets moose—found nowhere north of the Brooks Range as recently as thirty years ago, but now a competitor with caribou for the role of dominant ungulate—stare out at me from leafy bowers nearly every time I go ashore.

It is the cruelest irony that a portion of the hydrocarbon soot—which on a global level is warming the atmosphere enough to destroy this ecosystem—comes partly from burning the petroleum now being extracted from virtually underfoot.

Late in the summer of 2004, as I left Umiat, remnant of an old Distant Early Warning radar camp midway along the Colville, the sandhill cranes that nest on its riparian flats were taking to the air. Ordinarily, most of the adults would have been followed by fawn brown young, trying the newly flighted wings soon to carry them down distant aerial pathways to the Gulf of Mexico.

This year many of the parents were alone. Seemingly one of the most pristine spots in North America, the valley around Umiat—long proposed as part of a Colville Wilderness Corridor—was recently declared a toxic waste site. Its very soil oozes an oily residue, contaminated by PCBs and oil drilling effluent spread by petroleum production platforms dating back to the 1940s. As I loaded my skiff to head upriver, a trio of husky Inupiat, brought in by the Bureau of Land Management and the Alaska Department of Transportation as cleanup workers, came over to visit.

Best job they'd ever had, they reported. Plenty to eat, especially with a cook sent all the way out here just for them. And no big hurry: all they had to do was bake, for sixteen days, the contaminated dirt they scooped up with a backhoe, packing it into one of the DEW Line Quonset huts they'd converted into an oven. After that, they were supposed to spread the soil back on the ground. Their three-man team had been at work for five months, during which they had managed to give a sixteen-day bake to the dirt covering an area about the size of two football fields. The Umiat valley is over a mile wide and many miles in length, but to the Inupiat this project was no more absurd than anything else that Naluaqmiu, the white man, does all the time.

Far from being mostly a matter of cleaning up decades-old spills, in this country the expansion of Big Oil is a current, ever-growing threat. At Prudhoe's enormous supply depot, equipment supplier to the largest petrochemical complex outside the Middle East, seismic survey helicopters were leaving daily for exploration in the National Petroleum Reserve. Along the Colville they were almost constantly overhead, while back in Prudhoe mapping crews were readying drilling site surveys for upcoming forays into the even richer fields of the heretofore entirely protected Arctic National Wildlife Refuge while grousing about having to wait until after the November election to begin work.

Their employers' ambitions were almost universally shared here, because in the Far North nearly everyone either works for an oil company or earns his living serving their employees. And because oil exploration on the Arctic Slope takes place far from public view, its impact is almost invisible—a fact that has both made the drilling easy to rationalize in the corridors of far-off power and has allowed it to remain at the top of the Bush Administration's energy objectives.

By the spring of 2005, drilling in the Arctic National Wildlife Refuge—long cherished by conservationists as the most pristine bit of untouched tundra, while at the same time Big Oil's greatest symbol of pro-drilling lobbying power—had been approved, 51 to 49, by the U.S. Senate. That means that within the next few years the unseen avian heroes of ten million annual journeys to the Far North are likely to find their homeland irreparably changed. Every bit of lost tundra involves a wealth of biological detail: layer upon layer of discrete habitats—linked neighborhoods of plants and animals that together make up an integrated nearctic ecosystem, a system now being sacrificed to satisfy a few months' worth of our prodigious appetite for oil.

It is not worth it.

We have already lost most of North America's native birdlife. Displaced by human encroachment, much of this huge segment of our natural heritage now finds itself with no place left to go: Eastern songbirds, winging back from ever more deforested tropical winter ranges, find their nesting woodlands bulldozed into shopping malls and parking lots, while shorebirds arriving on their ancestral feeding flats see only oceanfront condominiums. Prairie-living species look down from their arrival flights each spring to find their grassland nest sites occupied by just-framed residential rooftops.

Expanded arctic drilling would be even more destructive, obliterating one of the earth's few remaining stages large enough to display the essential optimism of life itself. It is a proscenium now solely in our American hands since much of the northern tier of Europe and Asia is contaminated with effluent from decades of unregulated Russian petroleum production. If similar environmental impacts occur here, with the sacrifice of America's last Great Plain will go our final chance to discover the frozen bodies of Pleistocene megafauna, stumble across Dorset Culture ruins, or to participate in the vitality—in the grandeur—of the small, airborne lives that every spring struggle back, with so much heart, to reach their birthplace here.

Suggestions for Discussion

1. What is Tennant's basis for calling the migrant birds heroes?

2. What threats do humankind pose to the ecosystem that Tennant describes? Consider both small scale and large scale effects of human encroachment on the tundra.

Suggestion for Writing

Conduct further research on the issue of arctic oil drilling and write a letter to a politician, advocating either Tennant's position or an alternate position you have adopted after doing this research. Send the letter if you choose, but it is not mandatory.

∾∾∾

GINA KOLATA

A Clone Is Born

Gina Kolata (b. 1948), a science reporter for the *New York Times* since 1988, is the author of *The Baby Doctors: Probing the Limits of Fetal Medicine* (1990), *Clone: The Road to Dolly and the Path Ahead* (1998) (from which the following excerpt is reprinted), and *Ultimate Fitness: The Quest for Truth About Health and Exercise* (2003). Kolata earned a bachelor's degree in molecular biology from the Massachusetts Institute of Technology and a master's degree in mathematics from the University of Maryland. Probably as a result of her background in journalistic writing (a style that, ideally, encourages objectivity), Kolata adopts a somewhat impartial air in this essay, chronicling several conflicting attitudes toward the morally ambiguous issue of cloning while minimizing the presence of her own authorial voice and opinions.

Many people wonder if this is a miracle for which we can thank
God, or an ominous new way to play God ourselves.

—Nancy Duff, Princeton Theological Seminary

On a soft summer night, July 5, 1996, at 5:00 P.M., the most famous lamb in history entered the world, head and forelegs first. She was born in a shed, just down the road from the Roslin Institute in Roslin, Scotland, where she was created. And yet her creator, Ian Wilmut, a quiet, balding fifty-two-year-old embryologist, does not remember where he was when he heard that the lamb, named Dolly, was born. He does not even recall getting a telephone call from John Bracken, a scientist who had monitored the pregnancy of the sheep that gave birth to Dolly, saying that Dolly was alive and healthy and weighed 6.6 kilograms, or 14.5 pounds.

It was a moment of remarkable insouciance. No one broke open champagne. No one took pictures. Only a few staff members from the institute and a local veterinarian who attended the birth were present. Yet Dolly, a fluffy creature with grayish-white fleece and a snow-white face, who looked for all the world like hundreds of other lambs that dot the rolling hills of Scotland, was soon to change the world.

When the time comes to write the history of our age, this quiet birth, the creation of this little lamb, will stand out. The events that change history are few and unpredictable. In the twentieth century, there was the discovery of the quantum theory, the revolutionary finding by physicists that the normal rules of the visible world do not apply in the realm of the atom. There was Einstein's theory of general relativity, saying that space and time can be warped. There was the splitting of the atom, with its promise of good and evil. There was the often-overlooked theorem of mathematician Kurt Gödel, which said that there are truths that are unknowable, theorems that can be neither proved nor disproved. There was the development of computers that transformed Western society.

In biology and medicine, there was the discovery of penicillin in the 1940s, and there was James Watson and Francis Crick's announcement, in 1953, that they had found the structure of DNA, the genetic blueprint. There was the conquest of smallpox that wiped the ancient scourge from the face of the earth, and the discovery of a vaccine that could prevent the tragedy of polio. In the 1980s, there was the onslaught of AIDS, which taught us that plagues can afflict us still.

In politics, there were the world wars, the rise and fall of communism, and the Great Depression. There is the economic rise of Asia in the latter part of the century, and the ever-shifting balance of the world's powers.

But events that alter our very notion of what it means to be human are few and scattered over the centuries. The birth of Dolly is one of them. "Analogies to Copernicus, to Darwin, to Freud, are appropriate," said Alan Weisbard, a professor of law and medical ethics at the University of Wisconsin. The world is a different place now that she is born.

Dolly is a clone. She was created not out of the union of a sperm and an egg but out of the genetic material from an udder cell of a six-year-old sheep. Wilmut fused the udder cell with an egg from another sheep, after first removing all genetic material from the egg. The udder cell's genes took up residence in the egg and directed it to grow and develop. The result was Dolly, the identical twin of the original sheep that provided the udder cells, but an identical twin born six years later. In a moment of frivolity, as a wry joke, Wilmut named her Dolly after Dolly Parton, who also was known, he said, for her mammaries.

Until Dolly entered the world, cloning was the stuff of science fiction. It had been raised as a possibility decades ago, then dismissed, relegated to the realm of the kooky, the fringy, something that serious scientists thought was simply not going to happen anytime soon.

Yet when it happened, even though it involved but one sheep, it was truly fantastic, and at the same time horrifying in a way that is hard to define. In 1972, when Willard Gaylin, a psychiatrist and the founder of the Hastings Center, an ethics think tank, mistakenly thought that science was on the verge of cloning, he described its awesome power: "One could imagine taking a single sloughed cell from the skin of a person's hand, or even from the hand of a mummy (since cells are neither 'alive' nor 'dead,' but merely intact or not intact), and seeing it perpetuate itself into a sheet of skin tissue. But could one really visualize the cell forming a finger, let alone a hand, let alone an embryo, let alone another Amenhotep?"

And what if more than one clone is made? Is it even within the realm of the imaginable to think that someday, perhaps decades from now, but someday, you could clone yourself and make tens, dozens, hundreds of genetically identical twins? Is it really science fiction to think that your cells could be improved beforehand, genetically engineered to add some genes and snip out others? These ideas, that so destroy the notion of the self, that touch on the idea of the soul, of human identity, seemed so implausible to most scientists that they had declared cloning off-limits for discussion.

Even ethicists, those professional worriers whose business it is to raise alarms about medicine and technology, were steered away from talk of cloning, though they tried to make it a serious topic. In fact, it was one of the first subjects mentioned when the bioethics field came into its own in the late 1960s and early 1970s. But scientists quashed the ethicists' ruminations, telling them to stop inventing such scary scenarios. The ethicists were informed that they were giving science a bad name to raise such specters as if they were real possibilities. The public would be frightened, research grants might dry up, scientists would be seen as Frankensteins, and legitimate studies that could benefit humankind could be threatened as part of an anti-science backlash.

Daniel Callahan, one of the founders of the bioethics movement and the founder, with Gaylin, of the Hastings Center, recalled that when he and others wanted to talk about cloning, scientists pooh-poohed them. They were told, he said, that "there was no real incentive for science to do this and it was just one of those scary things that ethicists and others were talking about that would do real harm to science."

Now, with the birth of Dolly, the ethicists were vindicated. Yes, it was a sheep that was cloned, not a human being. But there was nothing exceptional about sheep. Even Wilmut, who made it clear that he abhorred the very idea of cloning people, said that there was no longer any theoretical reason why humans could not clone themselves, using the same methods he had used to clone Dolly. "There is no reason in principle why you couldn't do it." But, he added, "all of us would find that offensive."

The utterly pragmatic approach of Wilmut and many other scientists, however, ignores the awesome nature of what was accomplished. Our era is said to be devoted to the self, with psychologists and philosophers battling over who can best probe the nature of our identities. But cloning pares the questions down to their essence, forcing us to think about what we mean by the self, whether we are our genes or, if not, what makes us *us*. "To thine own self be true" goes the popular line from Shakespeare—but what is the self?

We live in an age of the ethicist, a time when we argue about pragmatism and compromises in our quest to be morally right. But cloning forces us back to the most basic questions that have plagued humanity since the dawn of recorded time: What is good and what is evil? And how much potential for evil can we tolerate to obtain something that might be good? We live in a time when sin is becoming one of those quaint words that we might hear in church but that has little to do with our daily world. Cloning, however, with its possibilities for creating our own identical twins, brings us back to the ancient sins of vanity and pride: the sins of Narcissus, who so loved himself, and of Prometheus, who, in stealing fire, sought the powers of God. In a time when we hear rallying cries of reproductive freedom, of libertarianism and the rights of people to do what they want, so long as they hurt no one else, cloning, by raising the possibility that people could be made to order like commodities, places such ideas against the larger backdrop of human dignity.

So before we can ask why we are so fascinated by cloning, we have to examine our souls and ask, What exactly so bothers many of us about trying to replicate our genetic selves? Or, if we are not bothered, why aren't we?

We want children who resemble us. Even couples who use donor eggs because the woman's ovaries have failed or because her eggs are not easily fertilized, or who use donor sperm because the man's sperm is not viable, peruse catalogs of donors to find people who resemble themselves. We want to replicate ourselves. Several years ago, a poem by Linda Pastan, called "To a Daughter Leaving Home," was displayed on the walls of New York subways. It read:

Knit two, purl two,
I make of small boredoms
a fabric
to keep you warm.
Is it my own image
I love so
in your face?
I lean over your sleep,
Narcissus over
his clear pool,
ready to fall in—
to drown for you
if necessary.

Yet if we so love ourselves, reflected in our children, why is it so terrifying to so many of us to think of seeing our exact genetic replicas born again, identical twins years younger than we? Is there a hidden fear that we would be forcing God to give us another soul, thereby bending God to our will, or, worse yet, that we would be creating soul-less beings that were merely genetic shells of humans? After all, in many religions, the soul is supposed to be present from the moment of conception, before a person is born and shaped by nurture as well as nature. If a clone is created, how could its soul be different from the soul of the person who is cloned? Is it possible, as molecular biologist Gunther Stendt once suggested, that "a human clone would nor consist of real persons but merely of Cartesian automata in human shape"?

Or is it one thing for nature to form us through the vagaries of the genetic lottery, and another for us to take complete control, abandoning all thoughts of somehow, through the mixing of genes, having a child who is like us, but better? Normally, when a man and a woman have a child together, the child is an unpredictable mixture of the two. We recognize that, of course, in the hoary old joke in which a beautiful but dumb woman suggests to an ugly but brilliant man that the two have a child. Just think of how wonderful the baby would be, the woman says, with my looks and your brains. Aha, says the man. But what if the child inherited my looks and your brains?

Theologians speak of the special status of a child, born of an act of love between a man and a woman. Of course, we already routinely employ infertility treatments, like donor eggs, semen banks, and frozen embryos, that have weakened these ties between the parents and the child. But, said Gilbert Meilaender, a Lutheran theologian, cloning would be "a new and decisive turn on this road." Cloning entails the production, rather than the creation, of a child. It is "far less a surrender to the mystery of the genetic lottery," he said, and "far more an understanding of the child as a product of human will."

Elliott Dorff, a rabbi at the University of Judaism in Los Angeles, said much the same thing. "Each person involved has to get out of himself or herself in order to make and have a child." But if a person can be reproduced through cloning, that self-surrender is lost, and there is danger of self-idolization.

Cloning also poses a danger to our notion of mortality, Dorff said. The biblical psalm says, "Teach us to number our days so that we can obtain a heart of wisdom," he recalled. "The sense that there is a deadline, that there is an end to all this, forces us to make good use of our lives."

In this age of entertainment, when philosophical and theological questions are pushed aside as too difficult or too deep, cloning brings us face-to-face with our notion of what it means to be human and makes us confront both the privileges and limitations of life itself. It also forces us to question the powers of science. Is there, in fact, knowledge that we do not want? Are there paths we would rather not pursue?

The time is long past when we can speak of the purity of science, divorced from its consequences. If any needed reminding that the innocence of scientists was lost long ago, they need only recall the comments of J. Robert Oppenheimer, the genius who was a father of the atomic bomb and who was transformed in the process from a supremely confident man, ready to follow his scientific curiosity, to a humbled and stricken soul, wondering what science had wrought.

Before the bomb was made, Oppenheimer said, "When you see something that is technically sweet you go ahead and do it." After the bomb was dropped on Hiroshima and Nagasaki, in a chilling speech at the Massachusetts Institute of Technology in 1947, he said: "In some sort of crude sense which no vulgarity, no humor, no overstatement can quite extinguish, the physicists have known sin; and this is a knowledge which they cannot lose."

As with the atom bomb, cloning is complex, multilayered in its threats and its promises. It offers the possibility of real scientific advances that can improve our lives and save them. In medicine, scientists dream of using cloning to reprogram cells so we can make our own body parts for transplantation. Suppose, for example, you needed a bone-marrow transplant. Some deadly forms of leukemia can be cured completely if doctors destroy your own marrow and replace it with healthy marrow from someone else. But the marrow must be a close genetic match to your own. If not, it will lash out at you and kill you. Bone marrow is the source of the white blood cells of the immune system. If you have someone else's marrow, you'll make their white blood cells. And if those cells think you are different from them, they will attack.

Today, if you need marrow, you have to hope that a sister, brother, parent, or child happens to have bone-marrow cells that are genetically compatible with your own. If you have no relative whose marrow matches yours, you can search in computer databases of people who have volunteered to donate their marrow, but your chances of finding someone who matches you are less than one in twenty thousand—or one in a million if your genetic type is especially rare.

But suppose, instead, that scientists could take one of your cells—any cell—and merge it with a human egg. The egg would start to divide, to develop, but it would not be permitted to divide more than a few times. Instead, technicians would bathe it in proteins that direct primitive cells, embryo cells, to become marrow cells. What started out to be a clone of you could grow into a batch of your marrow—the perfect match.

More difficult, but not inconceivable, would be to grow solid organs, like kidneys or livers, in the same way.

Another possibility is to create animals whose organs are perfect genetic matches for humans. If you needed a liver, a kidney, or even a heart, you might be able to get one from a pig clone that was designed so it had human proteins on the surface of its organs. The reason transplant surgeons steer away from using animal organs in humans, even though there is a dire shortage of human organs, is that animals are so genetically different from people. A pig kidney transplanted into a human is just so foreign that the person's immune system will attack it and destroy it. But cloning offers a different approach. Scientist could take pig cells, for example, and add human genes to them in the laboratory, creating pig cells that were coated with human proteins. Then they could make cloned pigs from those cells. Each pig would have organs that looked, to a human immune system, for all the world like a human organ. These organs could be used for transplantation.

Cloning could also be used to make animals that are living drug factories—exactly the experiment that Ian Wilmut's sponsor, a Scottish company called PPL Therapeutics, Ltd., wants to conduct. Scientists could insert genes into laboratory cells that would force the cells to make valuable drugs, like clotting factors for hemophiliacs. Then they could clone animals from those cells and create animals that made the drugs in their milk. The only step remaining would be to milk the clones and extract the drugs.

Another possibility would be to clone prize dairy cows. The average cow produces about fifteen thousand pounds of milk annually, but world champion milk producers make as much as forty thousand pounds of milk a year. The problem for breeders is that there are, apparently, so many genes involved in creating one of these phenomenal cows that no one has learned how to breed them the old-fashioned way. But if you had a cow that produced forty thousand pounds of milk a year, you could clone her and make a herd.

Zoologists might clone animals that are on the verge of extinction, keeping them alive and propagating when they might otherwise have vanished from the earth.

The possibilities are limitless, scientists say, and so, some argue, we should stop focusing on our hypothetical fears and think about the benefits that cloning could bring.

Others say that cloning is far from business as usual, far from a technical advance, and that we should be wary of heading down such a brambly path.

But was the cloning of Dolly really such a ground-shifting event? After all, the feat came as a climax to years of ever more frightening, yet dazzling, technological feats, particularly in the field of assisted reproduction. Each step, dreaded by some, cursed by others, welcomed by many more, soon grew to be part of the medical landscape, hardly worthy of comment. And so, with this history as background, some asked why, and how, anyone thought cloning could be controlled—or why anyone would want to. Besides, some asked, why was cloning any different in principle from some of the more spectacular infertility treatments that are accepted with hardly a raised eyebrow?

The infertility revolution began in 1978, when Louise Brown was born in England, the world's first test-tube baby. After more than a decade of futile efforts, scientists finally had learned to fertilize women's eggs outside their bodies, allowing the first stages of human life to begin in a petri dish in a laboratory. The feat raised alarms at the time. It was, said Moshe Tendler, a professor of medical ethics and chair of the biology department at Yeshiva University, "matchmaking at its most extreme, two reluctant gametes trying to be pushed together whether they liked it or not."

But in vitro fertilization flourished despite its rocky start, nourished by the plaintive cries of infertile couples so unjustly condemned to be barren, and justified by the miracle babies—children who were wanted so badly that their parents were willing to spend years in doctors' offices, take out loans for tens of thousands of dollars, and take their chances of finally, ultimately, failing and losing all hope of having a child who bore their genes. The doctors who ran the clinics soothed the public's fears. In vitro fertilization was not horrifying, they said. It was just a way to help infertile couples have babies.

The federal government quickly got out of the business of paying for any research that even peripherally contributed to the manipulation of human embryos, but in vitro fertilization clinics simply did research on their own, with money from the fees they charged women for infertility treatments, and so the field advanced, beyond the purview of university science, with its federal grants and accompanying strict rules and regulations.

"There are no hard-and-fast rules; there is no legislation," said Arthur Wisot, the executive director of the Center for Advanced Reproductive Care in Redondo Beach, California. "This whole area of medicine is totally unregulated. We don't answer to anyone but our peers."

Nearly every year, the fertility clinics would take another step. Recently, they began advertising something they called intercytoplasmic sperm injection, or I.C.S.I., in which they could get usable sperm even from men who seemed to make none, or whose sperm cells were misshapen or immotile and simply unable to fertilize an egg. The scientists would insert a needle into a man's testicle and remove immature sperm, which were little more than raw genes. They would inject these nascent sperm into an egg to create an embryo. Medical scientists later discovered that many of these men had such feeble sperm because the genes that controlled their sperm production were mutated. When the sperm, carrying the mutated gene, were used to make a baby boy, the boy would grow up with the same mutations and he, too, would need I.C.S.I. to have a baby. Some scientists worried that there might be other consequences of such a mutation.

But the infertility doctors and many infertile couples were unconcerned by the possibility that this technique might be less of an unqualified boon than it at first appeared. And the I.C.S.I. advertisements continued unabated.

Infertility doctors also learned to snip a cell from a microscopic embryo and analyze it for genetic defects, selecting only healthy embryos to implant in a woman's womb. They learned that there is no age barrier to pregnancy: Women who had passed the age of menopause could still carry a baby if they used eggs from a younger woman, fertilized in a laboratory. Even women in their early sixties have gotten pregnant, and while some doctors have said they do not want to participate in creating such pregnancies, others say that it is really up to the women whether they want to become mothers at such an advanced age.

Infertility clinics are even learning to do the ultimate prenatal testing: fishing fetal cells out of a pregnant woman's blood and analyzing them for genetic defects. It is, said Tendler, "the perfect child syndrome. We can now take 5 cc of a woman's blood when she is seven to nine weeks pregnant, do 191 genetic probes on that cell, and decide whether that baby is going to make it or not."

The latest development involves methods to sort sperm, separating those sperm with Y chromosomes, which would create boys, from those with X chromosomes, which would create girls. Soon parents can have the ultimate control over the sex of their babies.

At the same time, molecular biologists learned to snip genes out of cells and to sew others in, engineering cells to order. Infertility clinics expect, before long, to be able to add genes to human embryos—or delete genes that could cause disease or disability—creating a perfect child before even implanting an embryo into a woman's womb.

At first, the feats of reproductive scientists were the objects of controversy and shock. But we have become accustomed to their achievements. And it is hard to argue against the cries that couples have a right to reproductive freedom. Many have suffered for years, yearning for a child of their own. If they want to create babies, and are paying with their own money, who has the right to tell them no?

These days, when infertility doctors introduce a new method to the public, or when their techniques disrupt what we have thought of as the natural order, there is, at first, a ripple of surprise, or sometimes dismay, but then that reaction fades and all we remember is that there seemed to be reports of one more incredible technological trick.

Even newspapers are becoming blasé. One Sunday in April, about six weeks after the cloning of Dolly was announced, I was attending a meeting of a federal commission that was assessing cloning. I crept out of the meeting to call a national news editor at *The New York Times* and inform him of the meeting's progress. He said there was something else he wanted to ask me about. There was a story out of Florida, he said, about a woman who just gave birth to her own grandchild. Was that news, he asked me?

I assured him that it was not news. Several years ago, another woman had done the same thing, and we'd reported it on page 1. The woman's daughter had been born with ovaries but not a uterus, so the mother carried the baby for the daughter. That story had come and gone, no longer even worth a raised eyebrow.

So when Dolly was born, in this age of ever-more-disarming scientific advances, some worried that her birth might be greeted with a brief shiver, then forgotten, like the woman who gave birth to her own grandchild. Leon Kass, a biochemist turned philosopher, at the University of Chicago, warned that to react as though cloning were just another infertility treatment would be to miss the point of Dolly. He worried that we may be too jaded by previous triumphs of technological wizardry to take cloning as seriously as we should. He quoted Raskolnikov, the protagonist of Fyodor Dostoyevsky's *Crime and Punishment*: "Man gets used to everything—the beast."

It is true, of course, that the revolution in infertility treatments set the stage for people to think about cloning a human. Were it not for the proficiency of doctors in manipulating human eggs and sperm, it would not be feasible to even think of transferring the chromosomes of an adult cell into a human egg. But there is an intellectual chasm between methods that result in a baby with half its genes from the mother and half from the father and cloning, which would result in a baby whose genes are identical to those of an adult who was cloned.

Human cloning, Kass said, would be "something radically new, both in itself and in its easily foreseeable consequences. The stakes here are very high indeed." Until now "we have benefited mightily from the attitude, let technology go where it will and we can fix any problems that might arise later." But, he said, "that paradigm is open to question." Now we are "threatened with really major changes in human life, even human nature." And even if an absolute prohibition on cloning cannot be made effective, "it would at least place the burden on the other side to show the necessity" of taking this awesome step.

What is at issue, Kass said, "is nothing less than whether human procreation is going to remain human, whether children are going to be made rather than begotten, and whether it is a good thing, humanly speaking, to say yes to the road which leads, at best, to the dehumanized rationality of *Brave New World*." And so "What we have here is not business as usual, to be fretted about for a while and then given our seal of approval, not least because it appears to be unusual." Instead, he said, "the future of humanity may hang in the balance."

The cloning debate, Kass said, is so much more than just an argument about one more step in assisted reproduction. "This is really one of those critical moments where one gets a chance to think about terribly important things. Not just genetics and what is the meaning of mother and father and kinship, but also the whole relationship between science and society and attitudes toward technology." Cloning, he said, "provides the occasion as well as the urgent necessity of deciding whether we shall be slaves of unregulated progress and ultimately its artifacts or whether we shall remain free human beings to guide our technique towards the enhancement of human dignity."

He quoted the theologian Paul Ramsey: "Raise the ethical questions with a serious and not a frivolous conscience. A man of frivolous conscience announces that there are ethical quandaries ahead that we must urgently consider before the future catches up with us. By this he often means that we need to devise a new ethics that will provide the rationalization for doing in the future what men are bound to do because of the new actions and interventions science will have made possible. In contrast, a man of serious conscience means to say in raising urgent ethical questions that there may be some things that men should never do. The good things that men do can be made complete only by the things they refuse to do."

Yet if there is one lesson of cloning it is that there is no uniformly accepted way to think about the ethical questions that it elicits, and no agreement, even among the most thoughtful and well-informed commentators, about what is right and what is wrong. Many—but by no means all—theologians tended to condemn the notion of human cloning. Many ethicists were similarly repelled, but others asked instead, who would be harmed, and why are we so sure that harm would ensue? While theologians cited religious traditions and biblical proscriptions, lawyers cited reproductive rights and said it would be very hard to argue that it was illegal to clone oneself. In the meantime, some ethicists said they'd heard from in vitro fertilization clinics, which—operating already outside the usual rules that bind scientists, and looking for paying customers—were extremely interested in investigating cloning.

The diversity of opinions extended even to interpretations of identical passages from the Bible. One priest and Catholic theologian argued from Genesis that cloning would be against God's will. An orthodox rabbi and theologian argued from the same passage that cloning should not be proscribed.

The priest, Albert Moraczewski, of the National Conference of Catholic Bishops, was invited to explain the Catholic point of view by a presidential commission that was asked to make recommendations on whether cloning should be permitted. He began by saying that the cloning of humans would be an affront to human dignity. Then he spoke of the familiar story of Adam and Eve, told in the Book of Genesis, in which God gave humans dominion "over the creatures that swim in the sea, that fly in the air, or that walk the earth." And he spoke of God's order. "The Lord God gave man this order: 'You are free to eat from any of the trees of the garden except the tree of knowledge of good and bad.' "

Moraczewski explained that according to the Catholic interpretation, "Adam and Eve were given freedom in the garden but with one limitation, which if transgressed would lead to death. Accordingly, human beings have been granted intelligence and free will so that human beings can search for, and recognize, the truth and freely pursue the good."

Cloning, he said, would exceed "the limits of the delegated dominion given to the human race. There is no evidence that humans were given the power to alter their nature or the manner in which they come into existence."

He added that couples who clone a child would be dehumanizing the act of procreating and treating their child as an object, attempting to "design and control the very identity of the child."

Moraczewski concluded by quoting John Paul II: "The biological nature of every person is untouchable."

The next day, Moshe Tendler, an Orthodox Jewish rabbi, spoke to the commission. He, too, started with Genesis, and with the same quotation. But his interpretation of it, from the Jewish tradition, was very different.

"This knowledge of good and evil has always confused theologians and certainly the layman," Tendler said. "If Adam and Eve did not know of good and evil, how could they have sinned? They knew good and evil. The tree of good and evil is the tree that allows you to think that you can reevaluate, you can set another yardstick for what is good and what is evil."

The Jewish tradition says that humans are obliged to help master our world, according to Tendler, as long as they do not transgress into areas where they would attempt to contravene God. It would not be in character with the Jewish tradition to have a technology that could have outcomes that are good—like preserving the family line of a Holocaust survivor who had no other living relatives—and decide, ahead of time, not to use it for fear of its evil consequences. "We are bound by good and evil as given to us by divine imperative. And we knew pretty well in most areas what is good and what is evil until cloning came along and now we are not so sure what is good and what is evil.

"So, cloning, it is not intrinsically good or evil," Tendler said. The question, really, is whether particular applications of cloning might be a transgression by humans into the domain of God.

"I will give you a simile or metaphor of a guest invited to your house," Tendler said. "You ask them to be comfortable, help themselves, there is cake in the cake box and fruits in the refrigerator, and coffee in the coffeemaker." When you wake up, he continued, you're pleased to see that your guest did as you suggested. "But if he should move your sofa to the other side of the wall because he thought that that is where it really belongs, you will not invite him again."

God, Tendler added, says, "Make yourselves comfortable in my world, but you are guests in my house, do not act as if you own the place. Don't you rearrange my furniture."

He spoke also of a metaphor from the Talmud. "The question was posed, 'Is there not a time when you say to the bee, neither your honey nor your sting'?" And so, he asked, are we really prepared to ban cloning, to give up the honey, because we are so afraid of the sting?

On the other hand, some wonder whether we might not want to squash the bee. Nancy Duff, a theologian at the Princeton Theological Seminary, argued from Protestant tradition that, at the very least, all thoughts of human cloning should be put on hold. "Many people wonder if this is a miracle for which we can thank God, or an ominous new way to play God ourselves," she said. "At the very least, it represents the ongoing tension between faith and science."

But there is also a secular point of view, one that asks how persuasive, after all, are the hypothetical harms of cloning, and whether they are great enough to override the right that people have to reproductive freedom. John Robertson, a law professor at the University of Texas in Austin, who specializes in ethics and reproductive law, said he is unconvinced by those who argue that cloning is somehow too unnatural, too repugnant, too contrary to the laws of God, to proceed with. "In assessing harm, deviation from traditional methods of reproduction, including genetic selection of offspring characteristics, is not in itself a compelling reason for restriction when tangible harm to others is not present." He argued that cloning is not significantly different from other methods our society now accepts as ethical, and which are now being actively studied in research laboratories throughout the world. He referred to methods for adding genes or correcting faulty ones, in an attempt to cure diseases like muscular dystrophy or cystic fibrosis, which, although not yet possible, is expected to occur before too long.

"Cloning enables a child with the genome of another embryo or person to be born," Robertson said. "The genome is taken as it is. Genetic alteration, on the other hand, will change the genome of a person who could have been born with their genome intact." So what is the greater intervention? Given a choice of a child who is a clone or no child at all—a choice that could befall infertile couples—how bad is it to allow them to have a clone? Robertson asked. "If a loving family will rear the child, it is difficult to see why cloning for genetic selection is per se unacceptable."

A compelling argument, said Daniel Brock, a philosopher and ethicist at Brown University, is the right to clone part of our right to reproductive freedom? he asked. He said that although he is not certain that cloning could be protected in this way because it is not, strictly speaking, reproduction, it might nonetheless fall into that broad category. And, he added, if the right to have yourself cloned is treated as a reproductive right, "that creates the presumption that it should be available to people who want to use it without government control."

Brock, for one, thinks that the public reaction to cloning is overblown. "The various harms are usually speculative," he said. "It is difficult to make the claim that these harms are serious enough and well-enough established to justify overriding the claim that cloning should be available." The public, he said, "has a tendency to want to leap ahead to possibilities that we're not even sure are possible."

Ruth Macklin, an ethicist at Albert Einstein College of Medicine, raised similar questions about whether fears of cloning are reasonable. "One incontestable ethical requirement is that no adult person should be cloned without his or her consent," Macklin said. "But if adult persons sought to have themselves cloned, would the resulting individual be harmed by being brought into existence in this way? One harm that some envisage is psychological or emotional distress to a person who is an exact replica of another. Some commentators have elevated this imagined harm to the level of a right: the right to control our own individual genetic identity. But it is not at all clear why the deliberate creation of an individual who is genetically identical to another living being (but separated in time) would violate anyone's rights."

After all, Macklin said, if the cloned person was not created from the cell of another, he or she would not have been born. Is it really better never to have existed than to exist as a clone? "Evidence, not mere surmise, is required to conclude that the psychological burdens of knowing that one was cloned would be of such magnitude that they would outweigh the benefits of life itself."

Macklin even took on those who argued that cloning violates human dignity. Those who hold that view, she said, "owe us a more precise account of just what constitutes a violation of human dignity if no individuals are harmed and no one's rights are violated. Dignity is a fuzzy concept and appeals to dignity are often used to substitute for empirical evidence that is lacking or sound arguments that cannot be mustered."

Kass argued, however, that such utterly pragmatic language obscures the moral significance of what is being contemplated. He quoted Bertrand Russell: "Pragmatism is like that warm bath that heats up so imperceptibly that you don't know when to scream."

The clashing viewpoints, said Ezekiel J. Emanuel, a doctor and ethicist at the Dana-Farber Cancer Institute in Boston, who was a member of the president's commission that was studying cloning, seem to indicate "a moral values gap." And so, he added, how people react to cloning "depends a lot on one's world outlook, as it were. How much you might weigh these other values depends a lot on how you understand yourself and your place in the world."

And that, in the end, is what cloning brings to the fore. Cloning is a metaphor and a mirror. It allows us to look at ourselves and our values and to decide what is important to us, and why.

It also reflects the place of science in our world. Do we see science as a threat or a promise? Are scientists sages or villains? Have scientists changed over the years from natural philosophers to technologists focused on the next trick that can be played on nature?

Freud once said that, sometimes, a cigar is just a cigar. But so far, we have not reached a point where a clone is just a clone. As the social and cultural history of cloning continues, the questions and the insights into who we are, who we are becoming, and who we want to be grow ever deeper. Dolly, it now seems, is more a beginning than an end.

Suggestions for Discussion

1. Why has the birth of Dolly, the cloned lamb, forced us to reexamine our views on sin and our definitions of what is good and what is evil? Why are

some religious thinkers in favor of the use of cloning technology and why are some against it?

2. How and why is this technological innovation likened to the invention of the atomic bomb? Is such a comparison valid?

3. What are some of the possible practical applications of the developing technology?

Suggestion for Writing

Write a fictional story about an infertile couple that considers cloning a child. During the course of the tale, you should tackle some of the moral issues explored in Kolata's article. You may give your work an ideological slant, in which you directly express your views on human cloning, or you may leave the issues unresolved and morally gray.

෬෬෬෬

M A T T   R I D L E Y

Free Will

Matt Ridley (b. 1958) is an expert on the research that led to the mapping of the human genome, arguably the most important scientific discovery of our time, and he wrote a 1999 book, *Genome*, which detailed his theories concerning the repercussions of this discovery. A British writer dubbed an heir to the late Lewis Thomas by the *Washington Post*, Ridley is a former science editor, U.S. editor, and Washington correspondent of *The Economist*. He is the author of *The Red Queen: Sex and the Evolution of Human Nature*, *The Origins of Virtue: Human Instincts and the Evolution of Cooperation*, and the 2004 paperback *The Agile Gene: How Nature Turns on Nurture*.

> *Hume's fork: Either our actions are determined, in which case we are not responsible for them, or they are the result of random events, in which case we are not responsible for them.*
>
> —*Oxford Dictionary of Philosophy*

As the first draft of this book was being completed, a few months before the end of the millennium, there came news of a momentous announcement. At the Sanger Centre, near Cambridge, the complete sequence of chromosome 22 had been finished, the first human chromosome to be read from beginning to end. All 11 million "words" in the twenty-second chapter of the human autobiography have therefore been read and written down in English letters: 33.4 million As, Cs, Gs and Ts.

Near the tip of the long arm of chromosome 22 there lies a massive and complicated gene, pregnant with significance, known as *HFW*. It has fourteen exons, which together spell out a text more than 6,000 letters long. That text is severely edited after transcription by the strange process of RNA splicing to produce a highly complicated protein that is expressed only in a small part of the prefrontal cortex of the brain. The function of the protein is, generalising horribly, to endow human beings with free will. Without *HFW*, we would have no free will.

The preceding paragraph is fictional. There is no *HFW* gene on chromosome 22 nor on any other. After twenty-two chapters of relentless truth, I just felt like deceiving you. I cracked under the strain of being a non-fiction writer and could no longer resist the temptation to make something up.

But who am "I"? The I who, overcome by a silly impulse, decided to write a fictional paragraph? I am a biological creature put together by my genes. They prescribed my shape, gave me five fingers on each hand and thirty-two teeth in my mouth, laid down my capacity for language, and defined about half of my intellectual capacity. When I remember something, it is they that do it for me, switching on the CREB system to store the memory. They built me a brain and delegated responsibility for day-to-day duties to it. They also gave me the distinct impression that I am free to make up my own mind about how to behave. Simple introspection tells me there is nothing that I "cannot help myself" doing. There is equally nothing that says that I must do one thing and not something else. I am quite capable of jumping in my car and driving to Edinburgh right now and for no other reason than that I want to, or of making up a whole paragraph of fiction. I am a free agent, equipped with free will.

Where did this free will come from? It plainly could not have come from my genes, or else it would not be free will. The answer, according to many, is that it came from society, culture and nurture. According to this reasoning, freedom equals the parts of our natures not determined by our genes, a sort of flower that blooms after our genes have done their tyrannical worst. We can rise above our genetic determinism and grasp that mystic flower, freedom.

There has been a long tradition among a certain kind of science writer to say that the world of biology is divided into people who believe in genetic determinism and people who believe in freedom. Yet these same writers have rejected genetic determinism only by establishing other forms of biological determinism in its place—the determinism of parental influence or social conditioning. It is odd that so many writers who defend human dignity against the tyranny of our genes seem happy to accept the tyranny of our surroundings. I was once criticised in print for allegedly saying (which I had not) that all behaviour is genetically determined. The writer went on to give an example of how behaviour was not genetic: it was well known that child abusers were generally abused themselves as children and this was the cause of their later behaviour. It did not seem to occur to him that this was just as deterministic and a far more heartless and prejudicial condemnation of people who had suffered enough than anything I had said. He was arguing that the children of child abusers were likely to become child abusers and there was little they could do about it. It did not occur to him that he was applying a double standard: demanding rigorous proof for genetic explanations of behaviour while easily accepting social ones.

The crude distinction between genes as implacable programmers of a Calvinist predestination and the environment as the home of liberal free will is a fallacy. One of the most powerful environmental sculptors of character and ability is the sum of conditions in the womb, about which you can do nothing. As I argued in the chapter on chromosome 6, some of the genes for intellectual ability are probably genes for appetite rather than aptitude: they set their possessor on a course of willing learning. The same result can be achieved by an inspiring teacher. Nature, in other words, can be much more malleable than nurture.

Aldous Huxley's *Brave New World*, written at the height of eugenic enthusiasm in the 1920s, presents a terrifying world of uniform, coerced control in which there is no individuality. Each person meekly and willingly accepts his or her place in a caste system—alphas to epsilons—and obediently does the tasks and enjoys the recreations that society expects of him or her. The very phrase 'brave new world' has come to mean such a dystopia brought into being by central control and advanced science working hand-in-hand.

It therefore comes as something of a surprise to read the book and discover that there is virtually nothing about eugenics in it. Alphas and epsilons are not bred, but are produced by chemical adjustment in artificial wombs followed by Pavlovian conditioning and brainwashing, then sustained in adulthood by opiate-like drugs. In other words, this dystopia owes nothing to nature and everything to nurture. It is an environmental, not a genetic, hell. Everybody's fate is determined, but by their controlled environment, not their genes. It is indeed biological determinism, but not genetic determinism. Aldous Huxley's genius was to recognise how hellish a world in which nurture prevailed would actually be. Indeed, it is hard to tell whether the extreme genetic determinists who ruled Germany in the 1930s caused more suffering than the extreme environmental determinists who ruled Russia at the same time. All we can be sure of is that both extremes were horrible.

Fortunately we are spectacularly resistant to brainwashing. No matter how hard their parents or their politicians tell them that smoking is bad for them, young people still take it up. Indeed, it is precisely because grown-ups lecture them about it that it seems so appealing. We are genetically endowed with a tendency to be bloody-minded towards authority, especially in our teens, to guard our own innate character against dictators, teachers, abusing step-parents or government advertising campaigns.

Besides, we now know that virtually all the evidence purporting to show how parental influences shape our character is deeply flawed. There is indeed a correlation between abusing children and having been abused as a child, but it can be entirely accounted for by inherited personality traits. The children of abusers inherit their persecutor's characteristics. Properly controlled for this effect, studies leave no room for nurture determinism at all. The step-children of abusers, for instance, do not become abusers.

The same, remarkably, is true of virtually every standard social nostrum you have ever heard. Criminals rear criminals. Divorcees rear divorcers. Problem parents rear problem children. Obese parents rear obese children. Having subscribed to all of these assertions during a long career of writing psychology textbooks, Judith Rich Harris suddenly began questioning them a few years ago. What she discovered appalled her. Because virtually no studies had controlled for heritability, there was no proof of causation at all in any study. Not even lip service was being paid to this omission: correlation was being routinely presented as causation. Yet in each case, from behaviour genetics studies, there was new, strong evidence against what Rich Harris calls 'the nurture assumption'. Studies of the divorce rate of twins, for example, reveal that genetics accounts for about half of the variation in divorce rate, non-shared environmental factors for another half and shared home environment for nothing at all. In other words, you are no more likely to divorce if reared in a broken home than the average—unless your biological parents divorced. Studies of criminal records of adoptees in Denmark revealed a strong correlation with the criminal record of the biological parent and a very small correlation with the criminal record of the adopting parent—and even that vanished when controlled for peer-group effects, whereby the adopting parents were found to live in more, or less, criminal neighbourhoods according to whether they themselves were criminals.

Indeed, it is now clear that children probably have more non-genetic effect on parents than vice versa. As I argued in the chapter on chromosomes X and Y, it used to be conventional wisdom that distant fathers and overprotective mothers turn sons gay. It is now considered much more likely to be the reverse: perceiving that a son is not fully interested in masculine concerns, the father retreats; the mother compensates by being overprotective. Likewise, it is true that autistic children often have cold mothers; but this is an effect, not a cause: the mother, exhausted and dispirited by years of unrewarding attempts to break through to an autistic child, eventually gives up trying.

Rich Harris has systematically demolished the dogma that has lain, unchallenged, beneath twentieth-century social science: the assumption that parents shape the personality and culture of their children. In Sigmund Freud's psychology, John Watson's behaviourism and Margaret Mead's anthropology, nurture-determinism by parents was never tested, only assumed. Yet the evidence, from twin studies, from the children of immigrants and from adoption studies, is now staring us in the face: people get their personalities from their genes and from their peers, not from their parents.

In the 1970s, after the publication of E. O. Wilson's book *Sociobiology*, there was a vigorous counter-attack against the idea of genetic influences on behaviour led by Wilson's Harvard colleagues, Richard Lewontin and Stephen Jay Gould. Their favourite slogan, used as a title for one of Lewontin's books, was uncompromisingly dogmatic: "Not in our genes!" It was at the time still just a plausible hypothesis to assert that genetic influences on behaviour were slight or non-existent. After twenty-five years of studies in behavioural genetics, that view is no longer tenable. Genes do influence behaviour.

Yet even after these discoveries, environment is still massively important—probably in total more important than genes in nearly all behaviours. But a remarkably small part in environmental influence is played by parental influence. This is not to deny that parents matter, or that children could do without them. Indeed, as Rich Harris observes, it is absurd to argue otherwise. Parents shape the home environment and a happy home environment is a good thing in its own right. You do not have to believe that happiness determines personality to agree that it is a good thing to have. But children do not seem to let the home environment influence their personality outside the home, nor to let it influence their personality in later life as an adult. Rich Harris makes the vital observation that we all keep the public and private zones of our lives separate and we do not necessarily take the lessons or the personality from one to the other. We easily 'code-switch' between them. Thus we acquire the language (in the case of immigrants) or accent of our peers, not our parents, for use in the rest of our lives. Culture is transmitted autonomously from each children's peer group to the next and not from parent to child—which is why, for example, the move towards greater adult sexual equality has had zero effect on willing sexual segregation in the playground. As every parent knows, children prefer to imitate peers than parents. Psychology, like sociology and anthropology, has been dominated by those with a strong antipathy to genetic explanations; it can no longer sustain such ignorance.

My point is not to rehearse the nature–nurture debate, which I explored in the chapter on chromosome 6, but to draw attention to the fact that even if the nurture assumption had proved true, it would not have reduced determinism one iota. As it is, by stressing the powerful influence that conformity to a peer group can have on personality, Rich Harris lays bare just how much more alarming social determinism is than genetic. It is brainwashing. Far from leaving room for free will, it rather diminishes it. A child who expresses her own (partly genetic) personality in defiance of her parents' or her siblings' pressures is at least obeying endogenous causality, not somebody else's.

So there is no escape from determinism by appealing to socialisation. Either effects have causes or they do not. If I am timid because of something that happened to me when I was young, that event is no less deterministic than a gene for timidity. The greater mistake is not to equate determinism with genes, but to mistake determinism for inevitability. Said the three authors of *Not in Our Genes,* Steven Rose, Leon Kamin and Richard Lewontin, "To the biological determinists the old credo 'You can't change human nature' is the alpha and omega of the human condition." But this equation—determinism equals fatalism—is so well understood to be a fallacy that it is hard to find the straw men that the three critics indict.

The reason the equation of determinism with fatalism is a fallacy is as follows. Suppose you are ill, but you reason that there is no point in calling the doctor because either you will recover, or you won't: in either case, a doctor is superfluous. But this overlooks the possibility that your recovery or lack thereof could be caused by your calling the doctor, or failure to do so. It follows that determinism implies nothing about what you can or cannot do. Determinism looks backwards to the causes of the present state, not forward to the consequences.

Yet the myth persists that genetic determinism is a more implacable kind of fate than social determinism. As James Watson has put it, 'We talk about gene therapy as if it can change someone's fate, but you can also change someone's fate if you pay off their credit card.' The whole point of genetic knowledge is to remedy genetic defects with (mostly non-genetic) interventions. Far from the discoveries of genetic mutations leading to fatalism, I have already cited many examples where they have led to redoubled efforts to ameliorate their effects. As I pointed out in the chapter on chromosome 6, when dyslexia was belatedly recognised as a real, and possibly genetic, condition, the response of parents, teachers and governments was not fatalistic. Nobody said that because it was a genetic condition dyslexia was therefore incurable and from now on children diagnosed with dyslexia would be allowed to remain illiterate. Quite the reverse happened: remedial education for dyslexics was developed, with impressive results. Likewise, as I argued in the chapter on chromosome 11, even psychotherapists have found genetic explanations of shyness helpful in curing it. By reassuring shy people that their shyness is innate and 'real,' it somehow helps them overcome it.

Nor does it make sense to argue that biological determinism threatens the case for political freedom. As Sam Brittan has argued, 'the opposite of freedom is coercion, not determinism.' We cherish political freedom because it allows us freedom of personal self-determination, not the other way around. Though we pay lip service to our love of free will, when the chips are down we cling to determinism to save us. In February 1994 an American named Stephen Mobley was convicted of the murder of a pizza-shop manager, John Collins, and sentenced to death. Appealing to have the sentence reduced to life imprisonment, his lawyers offered a genetic defence. Mobley came, they said, from a long pedigree of crooks and crim-inals. He probably killed Collins because his genes made him do it. 'He' was not responsible; he was a genetically determined automaton.

Mobley was happy to surrender his illusion of free will; he wanted it to be thought that he had none. So does every criminal who uses the defence of insanity or diminished responsibility. So does every jealous spouse who uses the defence of temporary insanity or justifiable rage after murdering an unfaithful partner. So does the unfaithful partner when justifying the infidelity. So does every tycoon who uses the excuse of Alzheimer's disease when accused of fraud against his shareholders. So indeed does a child in the playground who says that his friend made him do it. So does each one of us when we willingly go along with a subtle suggestion from the thera-pist that we should blame our parents for our present unhappiness. So does a politician who blames social conditions for the crime rate in an area. So does an economist when he asserts that consumers are utility maximisers. So does a biographer when he tries to explain how his subject's character was forged by formative experiences. So does everybody who consults a horoscope. In every case there is a willing, happy and grateful embracing of determinism. Far from loving free will, we seem to be a species that posi-tively leaps to surrender it whenever we can.

Full responsibility for one's actions is a necessary fiction without which the law would flounder, but it is a fiction all the same. To the extent that you act in character you are responsible for your actions; yet acting in character is merely expressing the many determinisms that caused your character. David Hume found himself impaled on this dilemma, subsequently named Hume's fork. Either our actions are determined, in which case we are not responsible for them, or they are random, in which case we are not respon-sible for them. In either case, common sense is outraged and society impos-sible to organise.

Christianity has wrestled with these issues for two millennia and the-ologians of other stripes for much longer. God, almost by definition, seems to deny free will or He would not be omnipotent. Yet Christianity in par-ticular has striven to preserve a concept of free will because, without it, human beings cannot be held accountable for their actions. Without accountability, sin is a mockery and Hell a damnable injustice from a just

God. The modern Christian consensus is that God has implanted free will in us, so that we have a choice of living virtuously or in sin.

Several prominent evolutionary biologists have recently argued that religious belief is an expression of a universal human instinct—that there is in some sense a group of genes for believing in God or gods. (One neuro-scientist even claims to have found a dedicated neural module in the temporal lobes of the brain that is bigger or more active in religious believers; hyper-religiosity is a feature of some types of temporal-lobe epilepsy.) A religious instinct may be no more than a by-product of an instinctive super-stition to assume that all events, even thunderstorms, have wilful causes. Such a superstition could have been useful in the Stone Age. When a boul-der rolls down the hill and nearly crushes you, it is less dangerous to sub-scribe to the conspiracy theory that it was pushed by somebody than to assume it was an accident. Our very language is larded with intentionality. I wrote earlier that my genes built me and delegated responsibility to my brain. My genes did nothing of the sort. It all just happened.

E. O. Wilson even argues, in his book *Consilience,* that morality is the codified expression of our instincts, and that what is right is indeed—despite the naturalistic fallacy—derived from what comes naturally. This leads to the paradoxical conclusion that belief in a god, being natural, is therefore correct. Yet Wilson himself was reared a devout Baptist and is now an agnostic, so he has rebelled against a deterministic instinct. Likewise, Steven Pinker, by remaining childless while subscribing to the theory of the selfish gene, has told his selfish genes to 'go jump in a lake.'

So even determinists can escape determinism. We have a paradox. Unless our behaviour is random, then it is determined. If it is determined, then it is not free. And yet we feel, and demonstrably are, free. Charles Dar-win described free will as a delusion caused by our inability to analyse our own motives. Modern Darwinists such as Robert Trivers have even argued that deceiving ourselves about such matters is itself an evolved adaptation. Pinker has called free will 'an idealisation of human beings that makes the ethics game playable.' The writer Rita Carter calls it an illusion hard-wired into the mind. The philosopher Tony Ingram calls free will something that we assume other people have—we seem to have an inbuilt bias to ascribe free will to everybody and everything about us, from recalcitrant outboard motors to recalcitrant children equipped with our genes.

I would like to think that we can get a little closer to resolving the para-dox than that. Recall that, when discussing chromosome 10, I described how the stress response consists of genes at the whim of the social environment, not vice versa. If genes can affect behaviour and behaviour can affect genes, then the causality is circular. And in a system of circular feedbacks, hugely unpredictable results can follow from simple deterministic processes.

This kind of notion goes under the name of chaos theory. Much as I hate to admit it, the physicists have got there first. Pierre-Simon de LaPlace, the great French mathematician of the eighteenth century, once mused that if, as a good Newtonian, he could know the positions and the motions of every atom in the universe, he could predict the future. Or rather, he suspected that he could not know the future, but he wondered why not. It is fashionable to say that the answer lies at the subatomic level, where we now know that there are quantum-mechanical events that are only statistically predictable and the world is not made of Newtonian billiard balls. But that is not much help because Newtonian physics is actually a pretty good description of events at the scale at which we live and nobody seriously believes that we rely, for our free will, on the probabilistic scaffolding of Heisenberg's uncertainty principle. To put the reason bluntly: in deciding to write this chapter this afternoon, my brain did not play dice. To act randomly is not the same thing as to act freely—in fact, quite the reverse.

Chaos theory provides a better answer to LaPlace. Unlike quantum physics, it does not rest on chance. Chaotic systems, as defined by mathematicians, are determined, not random. But the theory holds that even if you know all the determining factors in a system, you may not be able to predict the course it will take, because of the way different causes can interact with each other. Even simply determined systems can behave chaotically. They do so partly because of reflexivity, whereby one action affects the starting conditions of the next action, so small effects become larger causes. The trajectory of the stock market index, the future of the weather and the 'fractal geometry' of a coastline are all chaotic systems: in each case, the broad outline or course of events is predictable, but the precise details are not. We know it will be colder in winter than summer, but we cannot tell whether it will snow next Christmas Day.

Human behaviour shares these characteristics. Stress can alter the expression of genes, which can affect the response to stress and so on. Human behaviour is therefore unpredictable in the short term, but broadly predictable in the long term. Thus at any instant in the day, I can choose not to consume a meal. I am free not to eat. But over the course of the day it is almost a certainty that I will eat. The timing of my meal may depend on many things—my hunger (partly dictated by my genes), the weather (chaotically determined by myriad external factors), or somebody else's decision to ask me out to lunch (he being a deterministic being over whom I have no control). This interaction of genetic and external influences makes my behaviour unpredictable, but not undetermined. In the gap between those words lies freedom.

We can never escape from determinism, but we can make a distinction between good determinisms and bad ones—free ones and unfree ones. Suppose that I am sitting in the laboratory of Shin Shimojo at the California

Institute of Technology and he is at this very moment prodding with an electrode a part of my brain somewhere close to the anterior cingulate sulcus. Since the control of 'voluntary' movement is in this general area, he might be responsible for me making a movement that would, to me, have all the appearance of volition. Asked why I had moved my arm, I would almost certainly reply with conviction that it was a voluntary decision. Professor Shimojo would know better (I hasten to add that this is still a thought experiment suggested to me by Shimojo, not a real one). It was not the fact that my movement was determined that contradicted my illusion of freedom; it was the fact that it was determined from outside by somebody else.

The philosopher A. J. Ayer put it this way:

> If I suffered from a compulsive neurosis, so that I got up and walked across the room, whether I wanted to or not, or if I did so because somebody else compelled me, then I should not be acting freely. But if I do it now, I shall be acting freely, just because these conditions do not obtain; and the fact that my action may nevertheless have a cause is, from this point of view, irrelevant.

A psychologist of twins, Lyndon Eaves, has made a similar point:

> Freedom is the ability to stand up and transcend the limitations of the environment. That capacity is something that natural selection has placed in us, because it's adaptive...If you're going to be pushed around, would you rather be pushed around by your environment, which is not you, or by your genes, which in some sense is who you are.

Freedom lies in expressing your own determinism, not somebody else's. It is not the determinism that makes a difference, but the ownership. If freedom is what we prefer, then it is preferable to be determined by forces that originate in ourselves and not in others. Part of our revulsion at cloning originates in the fear that what is uniquely ours could be shared by another. The single-minded obsession of the genes to do the determining in their own body is our strongest bulwark against loss of freedom to external causes. Do you begin to see why I facetiously flirted with the idea of a gene for free will? A gene for free will would not be such a paradox because it would locate the source of our behaviour inside us, where others cannot get at it. Of course, there is no single gene, but instead there is something infinitely more uplifting and magnificent: a whole human nature, flexibly preordained in our chromosomes and idiosyncratic to each of us. Everybody has a unique and different, endogenous nature. A self.

Suggestions for Discussion

1. Why does Ridley begin his discussion of free will with the fictional example of chromosome 22?

2. How does Ridley juggle religious, scientific, and psychological theories about free will?

3. According to Ridley, do we have free will? What are the limits of free will?

Suggestion for Writing

What biological, social, or economic force most conspires to curtail our free will? Explain.

☙☙☙☙☙

NILES ELDREDGE

Creationism Isn't Science

Niles Eldredge (b. 1925), a scientist from Brooklyn, NY, who was educated as an undergraduate and graduate at Columbia University, is the curator of the Department of Invertebrates at the American Museum of Natural History in New York. The author of a number of books, including *Time Frame* (1985), *Life Pulse* (1987), and *Miner's Canary* (1991), his more recent works include *The Triumph of Evolution* (2001) *The Fossil Factory* (2002), and *Why We Do It* (2004). Eldredge is a scientist deeply concerned about Darwinism and other theories of evolution that derive from Charles Darwin's *On the Origin of Species* (1859). Following the publication of Darwin's book, a violent argument ensued between science and religion that appeared to come to a close after the Scopes trial in 1925. In recent years, however, with the rise of fundamentalist religion in the United States, an argument has flowered that creationism has as much validity as a theory as Darwin's theory of evolution. Eldredge attempts to show in this essay (published in 1981) why the two theories are not equal and how the zeal of creationists is undermining the teaching of science in the schools.

Despite this country's apparent modernism, the creationist movement once again is growing. The news media proclaimed a juryless trial in California as "Scopes II" and those who cling to the myth of progress wonder how the country could revert to the primitive state it was in when Darrow and Bryan battled it out in the hot summer of 1925 in Dayton, Tennessee. But the sad truth is that we have not progressed. Creationism never com-

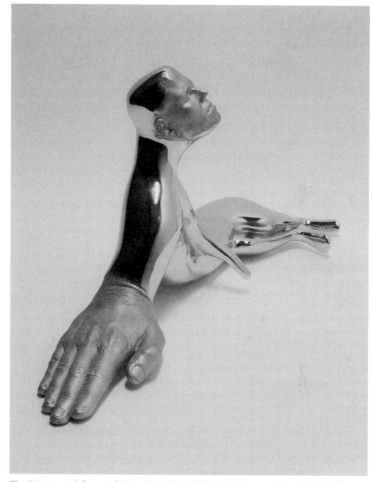

Pine Marten, stainless steel, Rona Pondick, 2000–2001. Courtesy Sonnabend Gallery, New York.

pletely disappeared as a political, religious, and educational issue. Scopes was convicted of violating the Tennessee statute forbidding the teaching of the evolutionary origins of mankind (although in fact he was ill and never really did teach the evolution segment of the curriculum). The result was a drastic cutback in serious discussion of evolution in many high school texts until it became respectable again in the 1960s.

Although technological advances since 1925 have been prodigious, and although science news magazines are springing up like toadstools, the American public appears to be as badly informed about the real nature of science as it ever was. Such undiluted ignorance, coupled with the strong anti-intellectual tradition in the U.S., provides a congenial climate for creationism to leap once more to the fore, along with school prayer, sex education, Proposition 13, and the other favorite issues of the populist, conservative movement. Much of the success of recent creationist efforts lies in a prior failure to educate our children about science—how it is done, by whom, and how its results are to be interpreted.

Today's creationists usually cry for "equal time" rather than for actually substituting the Genesis version of the origin of things for the explanations preferred by modern science. (The recent trial in California is an anachronism in this respect because the plaintiff simply affirmed that his rights of religious freedom were abrogated by teaching him that man "descended from apes.") At the heart of the creationists' contemporary political argument is an appeal to the time-honored American sense of fair play. "Look," they say, "evolution is only a theory. Scientists cannot agree on all details either of the exact course of evolutionary history, or how evolution actually takes place." True enough. Creationists then declare that many scientists have grave doubts that evolution actually has occurred—a charge echoed by Ronald Reagan during the campaign, and definitely false. They argue that since evolution is only a theory, why not, in the spirit of fair play, give equal time to equally plausible explanations of the origin of the cosmos, of life on earth, and of mankind? Why not indeed?

The creationist argument equates a biological, evolutionary system with a non-scientific system of explaining life's exuberant diversity. Both systems are presented as authoritarian, and here lies the real tragedy of American science education: the public is depressingly willing to see merit in the "fair play, equal time" argument precisely because it views science almost wholly in this authoritarian vein. The public is bombarded with a constant stream of oracular pronouncements of new discoveries, new truths, and medical and technological innovations, but the American education system gives most people no effective choice but to ignore, accept on faith, or reject out of hand each new scientific finding. Scientists themselves promote an Olympian status for their profession; it's small wonder that the public has a tough time deciding which set of authoritarian pronouncements to heed. So why not present them all and let each person choose his or her own set of beliefs?

Of course, there has to be some willingness to accept the expertise of specialists. Although most of us "believe" the earth is spherical, how many of us can design and perform an experiment to show that it must be so? But to stress the authoritarianism of science is to miss its essence. Science is the enterprise of comparing alternative ideas about what the cosmos is, how it works, and how it came to be. Some ideas are better than others, and the criterion for judging which are better is simply the relative power of different ideas to fit our observations. The goal is greater understanding of the natural universe. The method consists of constantly challenging received ideas, modifying them, or, best of all, replacing them with better ones.

So science is ideas, and the ideas are acknowledged to be merely approximations to the truth. Nothing could be further from authoritarianism— dogmatic assertions of what is true. Scientists deal with ideas that appear to be the best (the closest to the truth) given what they think they know about the universe at any given moment. If scientists frequently act as if their ideas *are* the truth, they are simply showing their humanity. But the human quest for a rational coming-to-grips with the cosmos recognizes imperfection in observation and thought, and incorporates the frailty into its method. Creationists disdain this quest, preferring the wholly authoritarian, allegedly "revealed" truth of divine creation as an understanding of our beginnings. At the same time they present disagreement among scientists as an expression of scientific failure in the realm of evolutionary biology.

To the charge that "evolution is *only* a theory," we say "all science is theory." Theories are ideas, or complex sets of ideas, which explain some aspect of the natural world. Competing theories sometimes coexist until one drives the other out, or until both are discarded in favor of yet another theory. But it is true that one major theory usually holds sway at any one time. All biologists, including biochemists, molecular geneticists, physiologists, behaviorists, and anatomists, see a pattern of similarity interlocking the spectrum of millions of species, from bacteria to timber wolves. Darwin finally convinced the world that this pattern of similarity is neatly explained by "descent with modification." If we imagine a genealogical system where an ancestor produces one or more descendants, we get a pattern of progressive similarity. The whole array of ancestors and descendants will share some feature inherited from the first ancestor; as each novelty appears, it is shared only with later descendants. All forms of life have the nucleic acid RNA. One major branch of life, the vertebrates, all share backbones. All mammals have three inner ear bones, hair, and mammary glands. All dogs share features not found in other carnivores, such as cats. In other words, dogs share similarities among themselves in addition to having general mammalian features, plus general vertebrate features, as well as anatomical and biochemical similarities shared with the rest of life.

How do we test the basic notion that life has evolved? The notion of evolution, like any scientific idea, should generate predictions about the natural world, which we can discover to be true or false. The grand prediction of evolution is that there should be one basic scheme of similarities interlocking all of life. This is what we have consistently found for over 100 years, as thousands of biologists daily compared different organisms. Medical experimentation depends upon the interrelatedness of life. We test drugs on rhesus monkeys and study the effects of caffeine on rats because we cannot experiment on ourselves. The physiological systems of monkeys are more similar to our own than to rats. Medical scientists know this and rely on this prediction to interpret the significance of their results in terms of human medicine. Very simply, were life not all interrelated, none of this would be possible. There would be chaos, not order, in the natural world. There is no competing, rational biological explanation for this order in nature, and there hasn't been for a long while.

Creationists, of course, have an alternative explanation for this order permeating life's diversity. It is simply the way the supernatural creator chose to pattern life. But any possible pattern could be there, including chaos—an absence of any similarity among the "kinds" of organisms on earth—and creationism would hold that it is just what the creator made. There is nothing about this view of life that smacks of prediction. It tells us nothing about what to expect if we begin to study organisms in detail. In short, there is nothing in this notion that allows us to go to nature to test it, to verify or reject it.

And there is the key difference. Creationism (and it comes in many guises, most of which do not stem from the Judeo–Christian tradition) is a belief system involving the supernatural. Testing an idea with our own experiences in the natural universe is simply out of bounds. The mystical revelation behind creationism is the opposite of science, which seeks rational understanding of the cosmos. Science thrives on alternative explanations, which must be equally subject to observational and experimental testing. No form of creationism even remotely qualifies for inclusion in a science curriculum.

Creationists have introduced equal-time bills in over 10 state legislatures, and recently met with success when Governor White of Arkansas signed such a bill into law on March 19 (reportedly without reading it). Creationists also have lobbied extensively at local school boards. The impact has been enormous. Just as the latest creationist bill is defeated in committee, and some of their more able spokesmen look silly on national TV, one hears of a local school district in the Philadelphia environs where some of the teachers have adopted the "equal time" or "dual model" approach to discussing "origins" in the biology curriculum on their own initiative. Each creationist "defeat" amounts to a Pyrrhic victory for their opponents. Increasingly, teachers are left to their own discretion, and whether out of personal conviction, a desire to be "fair," or fear of parental reprisal, they are teaching creationism along with evolution in their biology classes. It is simply the path of least resistance.

Acceptance of equal time for two alternative authoritarian explanations is a startling blow to the fabric of science education. The fundamental notion a student should get from high school science is that people can confront the universe and learn about it directly. Just one major inroad against this basic aspect of science threatens all of science education. Chemistry, physics, and geology—all of which spurn biblical revelation in favor of direct experience, as all science must—are jeopardized every bit as much as biology. That some creationists have explicitly attacked areas of geology, chemistry, and physics (in arguments over the age of the earth, for example) underscores the more general threat they pose to all science. We must remove science education from its role as authoritarian truthgiver. This view distorts the real nature of science and gives creationists their most potent argument.

The creationists' equal-time appeal maintains that evolution itself amounts to a religious belief (allied with a secular humanism) and should not be included in a science curriculum. But if it is included, goes the argument, it must appear along with other religious notions. Both are authoritarian belief systems, and neither is science, according to this creationist ploy.

The more common creationist approach these days avoids such sophistry and maintains that both creationism and evolution belong in the realm of science. But apart from some attempts to document the remains of Noah's Ark on the flanks of Mt. Ararat, creationists have been singularly unsuccessful in posing testable theories about the origin, diversity, and distribution of plants and animals. No such contributions have appeared to date either in creationism's voluminous literature or, more to the point, in the professional biological literature. "Science creationism" consists almost exclusively of a multipronged attack on evolutionary biology and historical geology. No evidence, for example, is presented in favor of the notion that the earth is only 20,000 years old, but many arguments attempt to poke holes in geochemists' and astronomers' reckoning of old Mother Earth's age at about 4.6 billion years. Analysis of the age of formation of rocks is based ultimately on the theories of radioactive decay in nuclear physics. (A body of rock is dated, often by several different means, in several different laboratories. The results consistently agree. And rocks shown to be roughly the same age on independent criteria [usually involving fossils] invariably check out to be roughly the same age when dated radiometrically. The system, although not without its flaws, works.) The supposed vast age of any particular rock can be shown to be false, but not by quoting Scripture.

All of the prodigious works of "scientific creationism" are of this nature. All can be refuted. However, before school boards or parent groups, creationists are fond of "debating" scientists by bombarding the typically ill-prepared biologist or geologist with a plethora of allegations, ranging from the second law of thermodynamics (said to falsify evolution outright) to the supposed absence of fossils intermediate between "major kinds." No scientist is equally at home in all realms of physics, chemistry, geology, and biology in this day of advanced specialization. Not all the proper retorts spring readily to mind. Retorts there are, but the game is usually lost anyway, as rebuttals strike an audience as simply another set of authoritarian statements they must take on faith.

Although creationists persist in depicting both science and creationism as two comparable, monolithic belief systems, perhaps the most insidious attack exploits free inquiry in science. Because we disagree on specifics, some of my colleagues and I are said now to have serious doubts that evolution has occurred. Distressing as this may be, the argument actually highlights the core issue raised by creationism. The creationists are acknowledging that science is no monolithic authoritarian belief system. But even though they recognize that there are competing ideas within contemporary biology, the creationists see scientific debate as a sign of weakness. Of course, it really is a sign of vitality.

Evolutionary theory since the 1940s (until comparatively recently) has focused on a single coherent view of the evolutionary process. Biologists of all disciplines agree to a remarkable degree on the outlines of this theory, the so-called "modern synthesis." In a nutshell, this was a vindication of Darwin's original position: that evolution is predominantly an affair of gradual progressive change. As environmental conditions changed, natural selection (a culling process similar to the "artificial" selection practiced by animal breeders) favored those variants best suited to the new conditions. Thus evolutionary change is fundamentally adaptive. The modern synthesis integrated the newly arisen science of genetics with the Darwinian view and held that the entire diversity of life could be explained in these simple terms.

Some biologists have attacked natural selection itself, but much of the current uproar in evolutionary biology is less radical in implication. Some critics see a greater role for random processes. Others, like me, see little evidence of gradual, progressive change in the fossil record. We maintain that the usual explanation—the inadequacy of the fossil record—is itself inadequate to explain the non-change, the maintenance of status quo which lasts in some cases for 10 million years or more in our fossil bones and shells. In this view, change (presumably by natural selection causing adaptive modifications) takes place in bursts of a few thousand years, followed usually by immensely longer periods of business as usual.

Arguments become heated. Charges of "straw man," "no evidence," and so on are flung about—which shows that scientists, like everyone, get their egos wrapped up in their work. They believe passionately in their own ideas, even if they are supposed to be calm, cool, dispassionate, and able to evaluate all possibilities evenly. (It is usually in the collective process of argument that the better ideas win out in science; seldom has anyone single-handedly evinced the open-mindedness necessary to drop a pet idea.) But nowhere in this *sturm und drang* has any of the participants come close to denying that evolution has occurred.

So the creationists distort. An attack on some parts of Darwin's views is equated with a rejection of evolution. They conveniently ignore that Darwin merely proposed one of many sets of ideas on *how* evolution works. The only real defense against such tactics lies in a true appreciation of the scientific enterprise—the trial-and-error comparison of ideas and how they seem to fit the material universe. If the public were more aware that scientists are expected to disagree, that what a scientist writes today is not the last word, but a progress report on some very intensive thinking and investigation, creationists would be far less successful in injecting an authoritarian system of belief into curricula supposedly devoted to free, open rational inquiry into the nature of natural things.

Suggestions for Discussion

1. Eldredge refers to the "Scopes II" trial in California. What was the first Scopes trial in Tennessee about? What issues about evolution were raised in 1925 by the trial, and how are they relevant today?

2. What does Eldredge have to say about the relationship between the populist–conservative movement and creationism? How do you define *creationism*?

3. Explain Eldredge's response to the claim that because Darwinian evolution is only a theory, equal time in the schools should be given to the proponents of creationism.

4. For Eldredge, what are the dangers of accepting the authoritarianism of science? What does he believe the real function of the scientific enterprise to be? How do creationists, according to Eldredge, misunderstand the meaning of the constant debates raging in the scientific community?

5. What causes one major scientific theory to predominate for a given period of time? Summarize Eldredge's explanation of why Darwin's theory has held the support of scientists for such a long period.

6. Why does Eldredge believe that creationism does not lend itself to testing? What is the significance of testing theories?

7. For Eldredge, what is the most significant danger of the struggle by creationists for equal time in the schools? How do creationists take advantage, according to Eldredge, of scientific authoritarianism? Why does Eldredge believe that debates among scientists are a sign of vitality?

8. Summarize Eldredge's description of recent debates among evolutionists and his claim that these debates are distorted by creationists.

Suggestions for Writing

1. Write a paper in which you explain how one may believe in God without accepting the position of the creationists. Document your argument with examples.

2. Do you believe that creationists should be allowed equal time with biologists in the schools? If you do, explain your position.

3. Write a paper in which you summarize Eldredge's position and contrast it with arguments by a creationist. State why you agree with one side of the argument or the other.

4. Describe the sculpture on page 527 in as detailed a manner as possible. How would you characterize its facial expression? Its posture? What feeling does Pondick's fusion of human and animalistic castings evoke in you, and why? Speculate: How might this work of art be different if the figure was painted instead of sculpted? Consider: Is the medium of sculpture part of the work's message? Is its texture? Its material? What is the message of the work—metamorphosis? Evolution? Genetic engineering? Or something else? Ponder your projection.

᠅᠅᠅᠅

S H E R R Y   T U R K L E

Seeing Through Computers

Sherry Turkle, a licensed clinical psychologist and one of the foremost authorities on computers and the Internet, has focused her psychoanalytic studies on the relationship between humans and technology. Turkle has made numerous television and radio appearances, and her research has received wide coverage in the popular and academic media. An affiliate member of the Boston Psychoanalytic Society and a professor of the sociology of science at the Massachusetts Institute of Technology, Turkle received her joint doctorate in sociology and personality psychology from Harvard University in 1976. The National Science Foundation, the Guggenheim Foundation, and the Rockefeller Foundation have all funded her research. Her books include *Psychoanalytic Politics: Jacques Lacan and Freud's French Revolution* (1978), *The Second Self: Computers and the Human Spirit* (1984), and *Life on the Screen: Identity in the Age of the Internet* (1995). The following piece, published in 1997, explores the impact computers have had on the field of education.

Today nearly everyone is certain that schools and universities should teach students about computers, but exactly what they should teach isn't so clear. The ideal of computer literacy, of an empowering relationship with the computer, has changed dramatically since educators and their critics first began worrying about making Americans computer literate two decades ago. Originally, the goal was teaching students how computers worked and how to write programs; if students could understand what was going on "inside" the computer, they would have mastery over it. Now the goal is to teach students how to use computer applications, on the premise that if they can work with the computer, they can forget what's inside and still be masters of the technology. But is that enough? And might it be too much in some fields of education where using computers is almost too easy a substitute for hands-on learning?

The uncertainty about what students (and the rest of us) need to know reflects a more general cultural change in the understanding of computers. When I first studied programming at Harvard in 1978, the professor introduced the computer to the class by calling it a giant calculator. No matter how complicated a computer might seem, what happened inside it could be mechanically unpacked. Programming, the professor reassured us, was a cut-and-dried technical activity whose rules were crystal clear.

These reassurances captured the essence of the computer in a culture of calculation. Computers were thought to be "transparent" when the users could look beyond the magic to the mechanism. The first personal computers of the 1970s and early 1980s, like the mainframes and minicomputers, required users to know how to issue exact instructions. Someone who knew programming could handle the challenge more easily. By the mid-1980s, increased processing power made it possible to build graphical user interfaces, commonly known by the acronym GUI, which hid the bare machine from its user. The new opaque interfaces—the first popular one on the mass market was the 1984 Macintosh—represented more than a technical change. The Macintosh "desktop" introduced a way of thinking about the computer that put a premium on the manipulation of a surface simulation. The desktop's interactive objects, its dialogue boxes in which the computer "spoke" to its user, pointed toward new kinds of experience in which people did not so much command machines as enter into conversations with them. In personal relationships, we often interact without understanding what is going on within the other person; similarly, when we take things at (inter)face value in the culture of simulation, if a system performs for us, it has all the reality it needs.

In 1980, most computer users who spoke of transparency were referring to a transparency analogous to that of traditional machines, an ability to "open the hood" and poke around. But when users of the Macintosh talked about its transparency, they were talking about seeing their documents and programs represented by attractive and easy-to-interpret icons. They were referring to an ability to make things work without needing to go below the screen surface. Today, the word "transparency" has taken on its Macintosh meaning in both computer talk and colloquial language. In a culture of simulation, when people say that something is transparent, they mean that they can see how to make it work, not that they know how it works.

Most people over 30 years old (and even many younger ones) have had an introduction to computers similar to the one I received in my first programming course. But children growing up with computers today are dealing with objects that suggest that the fundamental lessons of computing that I was taught are wrong. The lessons of computing today have little to do with calculation and rules; instead they concern simulation, navigation, and interaction. The very image of the computer as a giant calculator has become quaint. Of course, there is still "calculation" going on within the computer, but it is no longer widely considered to be the important or interesting level to focus on. But then, what is the interesting and important level?

Through the mid-1980s, when educators wanted to make the mechanism transparent, they taught about the logical processes of the computer's inner workings, typically beginning with an introduction to binary numbers, and instructed children in programming languages that would make computational processes transparent to them. In the highly influential *Mindstorms: Children, Computers, and Powerful Ideas,* published in 1980, Seymour Papert of the Massachusetts Institute of Technology wrote that learning about the computer should mean learning about the powerful ideas that the computer carries. In the Logo programming language he developed, children were taught to give explicit commands to a screen cursor known as a Turtle: FORWARD 100; RIGHT TURN 90. The commands cause the Turtle to trace geometric patterns that could be defined as programs. The idea behind the exercise went beyond the actual programs; Papert hoped that the process of writing these programs would teach children how to "think like a computer." The goal of the exercise was to experience procedural thinking and to understand how simple programs could be used as building blocks for more complex ones.

Although Logo is still in use, educators now most often think of computer literacy as the ability to use the computer as an information appliance for such purposes as running simulations, accessing CD–ROMs, and navigating the Internet. There is certainly nothing wrong and much that is right with students having those skills. But many teachers question whether mastery of those skills should be the goal of "computer education" or "computer literacy."

"It's not my job to instruct children in the use of an appliance and then to leave it at that," says an unhappy seventh-grade teacher at a June 1996 meeting of the Massachusetts chapter of an organization of "Computer Using Educators," a group known as MassCUE. Most of the 80 or so teachers present have been in computer education for over a decade. In the 1980s, many of them saw their primary job as teaching the Logo programming language because they believed that it communicated important thinking skills. One teacher describes those days: "Logo was not about relating to the hardware of the computer, so it wasn't about how the computer 'worked' in any literal sense, but its claim was that it could teach about procedural thinking. It could teach about transparency at its level."

Another adds, reflecting on Logo: "The point was not that children needed to understand things about the simplest level of how the hardware worked, but that things needed to be translated down to an appropriate level, I mean, a relevant level." Someone asks how she knows what is relevant. She stumbles, and looks around to her fellow teachers questioningly. A colleague tries to offer some help: "You have to offer children some model of how a computer works because the computer needs to be demystified. Children need to know that it is a mechanism, a mechanism that they control."

By now, the conversation is animated. Several teachers disagree, arguing that teaching that the computer is a controllable mechanism is not enough. One says: "Children know that the telephone is a mechanism and that they control it. But it's not enough to have that kind of understanding about the computer. You have to know how a simulation works. You have to know what an algorithm is." The problem, however, may be that a new generation no longer believes they have to know what an algorithm is.

The changing exhibits at Boston's Computer Museum illustrate the evolution of ideas about how to present computers and the dilemmas that educators now face. Oliver Strimpel, the museum's current director, proposed the idea for a "Walk-Through Computer" exhibit in 1987 when he was director of exhibits. Strimpel describes his original idea in the language of a computer transparent to its users: "I wanted to blow up the computer so that its invisible processes could be made visible. I wanted people to understand the computer from the bottom up." The exhibit opened in 1990, its trademark a room-size computer keyboard, a keyboard kids could play on.

At that time, the exhibit began by introducing the visitor to a computer program that charted the shortest route between two cities, *World Traveller*. All that followed was designed to help the visitor trace how a keyboard command to *World Traveller* was translated to lower and lower levels in the machine—all the way down to the changing patterns of electrons on a computer chip. "The key to my thinking," says Strimpel, "was the idea of levels, of layers. We worked very hard to show several levels of how a computer worked, trying to take visitors along the long conceptual path from the behavior of a program to the anatomy of the hardware and low-level software that made it all work. We built 'viewports' that attempted to give people a look inside key components such as the CPU, disk, and RAM."

By 1995, it was time to update the exhibit. The museum's studies of visitor reaction to the original exhibit had shown that many people went through the exhibit without understanding the notion of layering or the message of the viewports. In focus groups conducted by the staff, children said they wanted to know what "happened" when you touched a key on a computer. Their question encouraged Strimpel to go into the first planning meetings committed to a new exhibit that would show the translation of a keyboard stroke into a meaningful signal—the connection between the user's action and the computer's response. He imagined that with improved technology and more exhibit experience, a new version of the walk-through computer could communicate layering in a more sophisticated way.

But Strimpel, in his forties, a member of the "culture of calculation," did not prevail. The people on his staff, mostly in their twenties, were products of the culture of simulation. "What seemed important to them when we went to our second version," says Strimpel wistfully, "was explaining the functionalities—what a disk drive does, what a CD-ROM player does, not how the chip worked. The revised exhibit does not attempt to give explanations at different levels." In the culture of simulation one does not dwell on how the computer solves "its" problems. What is important is that it solves your problems. Strimpel had insisted that the original walk-through computer stress the notion of algorithm. "You could look into a blow-up of how information was passed from one part of the program to another as it attacked the problem of finding the shortest distance between two points," says Strimpel. "In the second exhibit, the idea of algorithm dropped out."

In the revised exhibit, the presentation of a giant, walk-through machine was maintained, updated now to look more like a modern desktop PC. The walk-through computer had quickly become the museum's trademark. But its function was now purely iconic. As Strimpel puts it, "The giant keyboard became a piece of sculpture."

Boston-area schoolteachers regularly take their students to the Computer Museum. They praise the richness of its special exhibits, the many chances it offers for students to try out computer applications to which they would not otherwise have access. Students learn how buildings and cars and turnpikes are designed. They play with voice recognition and artificial intelligence. Teachers praise the museum's Internet exhibits; their students can go online at speeds and with display technology that they cannot even demonstrate in their schools.

But at the MassCUE meeting, the very mention of the walk-through computer provokes heated debate. Several teachers remark that children get excited by the exhibit, but other teachers are skeptical. One comments: "Sometimes, the fifth graders go through that and ask, 'What were we supposed to learn?' But what's worse is that lots of them don't even ask what they were supposed to learn. They're used to the computer as a black box, something you take 'as-is.'" Another teacher says: "When you look in a microscope at a cell and the cell gets bigger and bigger, you are learning that you can see more structure when you change the scale. With the walk-through computer, you get a keyboard big enough to sit on. For these kids, it's just part of taking for granted that you can make a computer bigger and bigger but that doesn't mean that you can see it better."

At the MassCUE discussion, one currently popular position about computer literacy is underrepresented. This is the view that computer literacy should no longer be about the computer at all but rather about the application programs you can run on it. The arguments for this position are strong. One is grounded in practical, economic concerns. Entering today's workforce requires fluency with software. Word processors, spreadsheets, databases, Internet search engines, computer-aided design programs—these are the tools of contemporary trades. Learning to use these tools demands a new kind of craftsmanship, one that confers a competitive edge. Additionally, like all craftsmanship, there is a thin line between craft and artistry. These tools, artfully used, enable users to discover new solutions to old problems and to explore problems that were never previously envisaged.

Another argument for software fluency as an educational goal goes beyond such practicalities to a more philosophical point. The computer is a simulation machine. The world of simulation is the new stage for playing out our fantasies, both emotional and intellectual. The walk-through computer is its theater, its perfect icon. From this point of view, what children need to know is how to play on this new stage, how to sort out the complex relationship between the simulated and the "real," between representations of the world and the world itself. The "hands-on" manipulation of software may bring these heady issues down to earth. An eleven-year-old child who spends an afternoon manipulating images on Adobe *Photoshop*, creating landscapes that exist only within the computer, may use the software as an object-to-think-with for thinking through issues at the center of contemporary cultural debate. And yet it is often the case—too often the case—that experiences with simulation do not open up questions but close them down.

In the 1980s, the controversy in the world of computers and education was about whether computer literacy should be about programming. Would an emphasis on programming skills in the curriculum teach something important, or would it, as some feared in the parlance of the time, turn children into "linear thinkers"? Today, the debate about computers in education centers around the place of educational software and simulations in the curriculum.

"Your orgot is being eaten up," flashes the message on the screen. It is a rainy Sunday afternoon and I am with Tim, 13. We are playing *SimLife*, Tim's favorite computer game, which sets its users the task of creating a functioning ecosystem. "What's an orgot?" I ask Tim. He doesn't know. "I just ignore that," he says confidently. "You don't need to know that kind of stuff to play." I suppose I look unhappy, haunted by a lifetime habit of not proceeding to step two before I understand step one, because Tim tries to appease me by coming up with a working definition of orgot. "I think it is sort of like an organism. I never read that, but just from playing, I would say that's what it is."

A few minutes later the game informs us: "Your fig orgot moved to another species." I say nothing, but Tim reads my mind and shows compassion: "Don't let it bother you if you don't understand. I just say to myself that I probably won't be able to understand the whole game any time soon. So I just play." I begin to look through dictionaries in which orgot is not listed and finally find a reference to it embedded in the game itself, in a file called READ ME. The text apologizes for the fact that orgot has been given several and in some ways contradictory meanings in this version of *SimLife*, but one of them is close to organism. Tim was right—enough.

Tim's approach to *SimLife* is highly functional. He says he learned his style of play from video games: "Even though *SimLife*'s not a video game, you can play it like one." By this he means that in *SimLife*, like video games, one learns from the process of play. You do not first read a rule book or get your terms straight. Tim is able to act on an intuitive sense of what will work without understanding the rules that underlie the game's behavior. His response to *SimLife*—comfort at play, without much understanding of the model that underlies the game—is precisely why educators worry that students may not be learning much when they use learning software.

Just as some teachers do not want to be "reduced" to instructing children in a computer "appliance," many resent providing instruction in a learning environment that often strikes them as an overblown video game. The question of simulation is posed from preschool through the college years. Why should four-year-olds manipulate virtual magnets to pick up virtual pins? Why should seven-year-olds add virtual ballast to virtual ships? Why should fifteen-year-olds pour virtual chemicals into virtual beakers? Why should eighteen-year-olds do virtual experiments in virtual physics laboratories? The answer to these questions is often: because the simulations are less expensive; because there are not enough science teachers. But these answers beg a large question: Are we using computer technology not because it teaches best but because we have lost the political will to fund education adequately?

Even at MIT, the effort to give students ready access to simulation tools has provoked an intense and long-lived debate. In the School of Architecture and Planning, for example, there was sharp disagreement about the impact of computer-aided design tools. Some faculty said that computers were useful insofar as they compensated for a lack of drawing skills; others complained that the results had a lower aesthetic value, making the architect more of an engineer and less of an artist. Some claimed that computers encouraged flexibility in design. Others complained that they made it easier for students to get lost in a multitude of options. Some faculty believed that computer-aided design was producing novel solutions to old problems. Others insisted that these solutions were novel and sterile. Most faculty agreed that the computer helped them generate more precise drawings, but many described a loss of attachment to their work. One put it this way:

> I can lose this piece of paper in the street and if [a day later] I walk on the street and see it, I'll know that I drew it. With a drawing that I do on the computer… I might not even know that it's mine.

Another architecture professor felt that simulation not only encourages detachment from one's work, but detachment from real life:

> Students can look at the screen and work at it for a while without learning the topography of a site, without really getting it in their head as clearly as they would if they knew it in other ways, through traditional drawing for example.… When you draw a site, when you put in the contour lines and the trees, it becomes ingrained in your mind. You come to know the site in a way that is not possible with the computer.

In the physics department, the debate about simulation was even sharper. Only a small subset of real-world physics problems can be solved by purely mathematical, analytical techniques. Most require experimentation in which one conducts trials, evaluates results, and fits a curve through the resulting data. Not only does the computer make such inductive solutions easier, but as a practical matter, it also makes many of them possible for the first time. As one faculty member put it:

> A student can take thousands of curves and develop a feeling for the data. Before the computer, nobody did that because it was too much work. Now, you can ask a question and say, "Let's try it." The machine does not distance students from the real, it brings them closer to it.

But Victor Weisskopf, an emeritus professor who had for many years been chair of MIT's physics department, provided a resonant slogan for the anticomputer group. When colleagues showed him their computer printouts, Weisskopf was fond of saying, "When you show me that result, the computer understands the answer, but I don't think you understand the answer." Physicists in the anticomputer camp speak reverently of the power of direct, physical experiences in their own introductions to science, of "learning Newton's laws by playing baseball." For one, simulation is the enemy of good science. "I like physical objects that I touch, smell, bite into," he said. "The idea of making a simulation…excuse me, but that's like masturbation."

There is general agreement that since you can't learn about the quantum world by playing baseball, only a computer simulation can provide visual intuitions about what it would look like to travel down a road at nearly the speed of light. But beyond that, simulations are controversial. The pro-simulation faculty stresses that computers make it possible to play with different parameters and see how systems react in real time, giving students an experience of "living physics," but the opposing camp thinks that using simulation when you could directly measure the real world is close to blasphemy. One puts it this way:

> My students know more and more about computer reality, but less and less about the real world. And they no longer even really know about computer reality, because the simulations have become so complex that people don't build them any more. They just buy them and can't get beneath the surface. If the assumptions behind some simulation were flawed, my students wouldn't even know where or how to look for the problem. So I'm afraid that where we are going here is towards *Physics: The Movie.*

Of course, both sides of the debating faculty at MIT are right. Simulations, whether in a game like *SimLife* or in a physics laboratory or computer-aided-design application, do teach users how to think in an active way about complex phenomena as dynamic, evolving systems. And they also get people accustomed to manipulating a system whose core assumptions they may not understand and that may or may not be "true." Simulations enable us to abdicate authority to the simulation; they give us permission to accept the opacity of the model that plays itself out on our screens.

Writing in *American Prospect* ["Seductions of Sim: Policy as a Simulation Game," Spring 1994], Paul Starr has pointed out that this very abdication of authority (and acceptance of opacity) corresponds to the way simulations are sometimes used in the real worlds of politics, economics, and social planning. Perhaps screen simulations on our personal computers can be a form of consciousness-raising. Starr makes it clear that while it is easy to criticize such games as *SimCity* and *SimHealth* for their hidden assumptions, we tolerate opaque simulations in other spheres. Social policymakers regularly deal with complex systems that they seek to understand through computer models that are used as the basis for actions. Policymaking, says Starr, "inevitably re[lies] on imperfect models and simplifying assumptions that the media, the public, and even policymakers themselves generally don't understand." He adds, writing about Washington and the power of the Congressional Budget Office, America's "official simulator," "We shall be working and thinking in *SimCity* for a long time." So, simulation games are not just objects for thinking about the real world but also cause us to reflect on how the real world has itself become a simulation game.

The seduction of simulation invites several possible responses. One can accept simulations on their own terms, the stance that Tim encouraged me to take, the stance that Starr was encouraged to take by Washington colleagues who insisted that even if the models are wrong, he needed to use the official models to get anything done. This might be called simulation resignation. Or one can reject simulations to whatever degree possible, the position taken by the MIT physicists who saw them as a thoroughly destructive force in science education. This might be called simulation denial.

But one can imagine a third response. This would take the cultural pervasiveness of simulation as a challenge to develop a new social criticism. This new criticism would discriminate among simulations. It would take as its goal the development of simulations that help their users understand and challenge their model's built-in assumptions.

I think of this new criticism as the basis for a new class of skills: readership skills for the culture of simulation. On one level, high school sophomores playing *SimCity* for two hours may learn more about city planning than they would pick up from a textbook, but on another level they may not know how to think about what they are doing. When I interview a tenth grader named Marcia about *SimCity,* she boasts of her prowess and reels off her "top ten most useful rules of Sim." Among these, number six grabs my attention: "Raising taxes always leads to riots."

Marcia seems to have no language for discriminating between this rule of the game and the rules that operate in a "real" city. She has never programmed a computer. She has never constructed a simulation. She has no language for asking how one might write the game so that increased taxes led to increased productivity and social harmony. And she certainly does not see herself as someone who could change the rules. Like Tim confronted with the orgot, she does not know how to "read" a simulation. Marcia is like someone who can pronounce the words in a book but doesn't understand what they mean. She does not know how to measure, criticize, or judge what she is learning. We are back to the idea over which the MassCUE teacher stumbled when trying to describe the notion of an "appropriate" level at which to understand computers and the programs that animate them. When Oliver Strimpel talked about wanting to use the computer museum as a place to teach the power of a transparent understanding of the layers of the machine, he was talking about understanding the "naked" computer. As we face computers and operating systems of an increasingly dizzying size and complexity, this possibility feels so remote that it is easy to dismiss such yearnings as old-fashioned. But Marcia's situation—she is a fluent "user" but not a fluent thinker—re-poses the question in urgent terms. Marcia may not need to see the registers on her computer or the changing charges on a computer chip, but she needs to see something. She needs to be working with simulations that teach her about the nature of simulation itself, that teach her enough about how to build her own simulation that she becomes a literate "reader" of the new medium.

Increasingly, understanding the assumptions that underlie simulation is a key element of political power. People who understand the distortions imposed by simulations are in a position to call for more direct economic and political feedback, new kinds of representation, more channels of information. They may demand greater transparency in their simulations; they may demand that the games we play (particularly the ones we use to make real-life decisions) make their underlying models more accessible.

We come to written text with centuries-long habits of readership. At the very least, we have learned to begin with the journalist's traditional questions: who, what, when, where, why, and how. Who wrote these words, what is their message, why were they written, how are they situated in time and place, politically and socially? A central goal for computer education must now be to teach students to interrogate simulations in much the same spirit. The specific questions may be different but the intent is the same: to develop habits of readership appropriate to a culture of simulation.

Walt Whitman once wrote: "There was a child went forth every day. And the first object he look'd upon, that object he became." We make our technologies, our objects, but then the objects of our lives shape us in turn. Our new objects have scintillating, pulsating surfaces; they invite playful exploration; they are dynamic, seductive, and elusive. They encourage us to move away from reductive analysis as a model of understanding. It is not clear what we are becoming when we look upon them—or that we yet know how to see through them.

Suggestions for Discussion

1. How have the goals of computer literacy changed?

2. What impact do computers have on child psychology?

3. What are the advantages and disadvantages of using computers to teach architecture and physics?

4. What is the danger of "linear thinking"?

Suggestion for Writing

Can a computer ever be an adequate substitute for a human teacher? Explain the virtues and defects of both kinds of instruction. Which would you prefer to have as a tutor?

∾∾∾∾∾

A N D R E W   G R O S S O

The Individual in the New Age

Andrew Grosso, the chair of the Association for Computer Machinery's Committee on Law and Technology, is an attorney based in Washington, DC. A 1980 law graduate from the University of Notre Dame, Grosso also earned degrees in physics and computer science from Rensselaer Polytechnic Institute. The law firm he founded in 1994 specializes in civil and criminal litigation as well as electronic commerce issues. In the following article, published in 2001, Grosso draws upon his background in both the fields of law and technology to examine the ways in which modern technology can encroach upon our human rights and civil liberties.

I want to be an individual.

This is a proud statement to make. In many countries, in many times, people have been persecuted for this ideal and for their attempts to live up to it. Many are still persecuted today. What worries me is the real danger that, in the age of computing and the Internet, this ideal may be quietly facing a final stand. And it may not survive.

First I define what I mean by being an individual. To me, it means the right to separate myself from others, and particularly the right to stand separate from the state. It is this latter characteristic that most concerns me.

We are familiar with the debate on privacy. The words "Clipper Chip," "CALEA," "encryption," and "Carnivore" are hot-button topics in the computer professional community. Yet, privacy is but one aspect of what it means to be an individual. Remove privacy, and one can still be an individual, albeit at great risk of ridicule and retribution. However, remove the concept of the individual and privacy becomes meaningless: there can be no right to keep private what belongs to the state; if I am not an individual, what I am and what I do belongs not to me, but to the state.

So why is this distinction important? Because it rephrases the debate. Dilution of privacy can be justified on many grounds, usually in the name of law enforcement, security, and safety; the U.S. Constitution permits "reasonable" invasions of privacy. Dilution of the individual, however, is more serious, and more rarely permitted. Witness the "beyond a reasonable doubt" standard in criminal cases. Since we are, in fact, engaged in a war over the right of the individual to remain separate from the state, we must frame the question correctly, to take back the quarter given when mere privacy is the issue.

∾

The Wrong Question

Has the question been wrongly framed? Yes. Take as a case study the CALEA (Communications Assistance for Law Enforcement Act) and Clipper Chip controversies of the last decade. In both instances, adversaries to these initiatives opposed them as intrusions on the people's right to privacy. Let us examine this approach.

Liberty can no more survive anarchy than it can despotism, except perhaps in name only. Thus, Western jurisprudence permits intrusions on "private communications." Granted, burdens must be met; criminal conduct must be suspected; probable cause must be established, usually by investigation; court orders must be obtained; procedures must be followed. However, once these burdens are met, surreptitious monitoring of a "private communication" is authorized and endorsed to satisfy urgent societal needs. In a system where people live and interact together, such intrusions are necessary to ensure order.

The emphasis in Western jurisprudence is on recognizing that what is occurring is an intrusion. We allow an individual to take actions that would give him or her an expectation of privacy. That is, we recognize that an individual has a right to seek protections for his or her "private" communications. Also, we (simultaneously) recognize the right of the state to try to overcome these protections. This becomes a game, and there are no absolutes. The individual has no absolute expectation of privacy, as the state may always figure out a technological means to legally overcome the protections he or she has implemented. On the other side of the ledger, the state can never be certain it has uncovered all the communications made by a targeted individual, and can never be sure that it can overcome all the technological means a target may use to protect communications. The important factor here is that the state is not preventing a person from attempting to protect his or her communications; it is, rather, merely trying to listen in.

This game is more than just a game. As long as it is organic—that is, active and evolving—there is a meaningful independence of the individual from the state, and a means to ensure that the individual will not devolve to a mere appendage of the state.

Let us return to CALEA and the Clipper Chip. What did they propose? It was more than simple intrusion. It was the elimination of the necessity for intrusion, as they removed the ability of individuals to attempt to protect themselves. Clipper would have forbade, as a legal matter, the use of effective encryption by private individuals. A government would always have access to the keys for any encryption a person might legally use. CALEA, which is now law, mandates that all telecommunications facilities transmit to an off-site, government location any communication that passes through those facilities, upon U.S. government request. Our commercial telecommunications facilities serve as ears for the state, and I am not allowed to avoid them if I wish to use local or global telephone lines.

What is so offensive about Clipper and CALEA is not that they contradict society's notions of fair intrusion on private communications, it is that they remove the ability of the individual from acting as an individual in trying to protect his or her communications. The rules of this game permit but one player.

~

Anonymity vs. Accountability

David Brin, a popular science fiction writer (and a trained scientist) wrote *The Transparent Society* (1998). The premise of this book is that privacy can no longer be protected, and, for that reason, we must turn to the opposite of privacy so society can function. In Brin's world, everyone's actions are observable by everyone else, all the time—full accountability for all.

Brin's idea might work, after a fashion, if the concept of the state did not exist, and if every person was on equal footing in terms of resources, power, and, most importantly, ethics. This, however, is not reality. People in power and the state itself will always be able to shield what they want from the prying eyes of the masses. Those masses will then be left to account to the state. With such full accountability, the individual could no more stand up to the state than could an inmate stand up to a prison warden. The rules of the new game are not fair if only one player can make use of all the rules.

~

Quantity to Quality

I now turn to Whitfield Diffie and Susan Laundau, mathematicians both. They authored their own book entitled *Privacy on the Line: The Politics of Wiretapping and Encryption* (1998). A major tenet in their book is that technology's increasing ability to analyze available information has produced qualitative changes in what U.S. courts perceive to be reasonable surveillance. Let us examine this observation.

There is a principle in law that what is available to the public is not accorded privacy protections vis-à-vis the state. Here is an obvious example: Suppose I walk outside of my home, down the street, and visit a neighbor. Assume the local police are watching me, and videotape my every move. The police have not intruded upon my privacy. By stepping outside, by consenting to be seen by the public-at-large, the courts hold that I have no expectation of privacy in my journey.

Let us take another example. Suppose it is the day I was born. Medical records are maintained, in a computer database. I grow up. Scholastic records are maintained by computers. I start a career, marry, and have children. More records are maintained, by computers. I travel, use credit cards, use ATM machines, make telephone calls, file court cases, send email, surf the Web. More records are maintained, by computers. All of these records can be stored, retrieved, transferred, merged, and correlated—globally. Everything I have done since I was born can be retroactively tracked by the state. Is the state intruding upon my privacy?

The classical answer is no: by performing each of the these actions in the public arena, the courts would hold that I had no expectation of privacy in any of them. However, this doctrine was established before the technology advanced to the point where it was feasible for massive databases to be maintained, before it was feasible for people to use electronic media to conduct innocuous transactions, and before it was feasible for databases to be merged, correlated, and used to produce a day-by-day profile of my life from birth to death.

What has happened is that a quantitative change in the amount of public data the state can obtain and analyze has produced a qualitative change in the way the game is played between the individual and the state. I am accountable to the state, and I cannot hide as long as I wish to be part of normal society.

Technology's role in this debate is not yet done. Now, I wish to be alone. I stay indoors, in my home, behind my walls. Do I have an expectation of privacy? Years ago the walls of my own home would shut out prying eyes and ears. Today, thermal imaging and sound detection reduce their value as protectors. The heat and sound that escape from my house are in the public domain. So, I ask, do I retain an expectation of privacy in my own home?

Federal courts have already ruled on this question. The case concerned a defendant who admittedly was growing marijuana in his own home, and was using heat lamps to do so. The U.S. Department of Justice took the position that use of thermal imaging to identify these lamps did not intrude on any reasonable expectation of privacy, that its law enforcement agents merely "passively detected and recorded heat that escaped from the house." The U.S. Court of Appeals for the Ninth Circuit ruled in favor of the government, and the issue is now before the U.S. Supreme Court.

Such "escaped heat" was not detectable when classic definitions of privacy were adopted. Should the Ninth Circuit's ruling stand, it would mean the following: the state will be able to continuously update its means of detecting our activities, while legislating away the legality of our attempts to conceal our activities, à la CALEA and Clipper.

The game has now drifted in one direction.

❦

Whence Now?

I am not without hope. As an attorney, I seek the use of laws. There is no need to look too far: the enumeration in the Constitution, of certain rights, shall not be construed to deny or disparage others retained by the people.

These words were written more than 200 years ago. They comprise the Ninth Amendment of the U.S. Constitution.

What these words mean is the rights comprising liberty are not granted by the state to the people, but arise from the people and must be honored by the state. In simpler language, they are a concise mandate for the primacy of the individual over the state, depicting the wall that separates the two. Somewhere, among the varied and numerous rights with which each person is vested from birth, there lies one allowing the individual to separate from the state, and to take those steps reasonable and necessary to protect oneself from its modern means of intrusion. If nothing more, the U.S. Constitution, and its Ninth Amendment, show us that law was intended to serve the individual as well as the desires of government.

Somehow it is fitting that a refuge of liberty in this age of technological surveillance should be a single sentence from the pen of those who could not have conceived of a computer, let alone an Internet. But, then, the concept of liberty is self-evident and eternal, and its expression should be simple. The authors of the U.S. Constitution told us we can use law as a means to ensure the liberty of the individual whatever each age may bring. We need only now find the will to do so in our own age.

Suggestions for Discussion

1. According to Grosso, why is individuality so difficult a goal in the modern era?

2. In Grosso's view, how much privacy do we really have, whether in our own home or outside?

3. Despite his fears, Grosso says he is "not without hope." Why?

Suggestion for Writing

One of the most common subjects in science fiction is the speculative future in which all individuality is erased by an oppressive, technology-driven regime. The novel *1984*, the television series *The Prisoner,* and the movie *The Matrix* are just a few examples of this kind of tale, which has often been dismissed as paranoid and defeatist. But where does fantasy end and reality begin? Given Grosso's concerns, how close are we to realizing one of these realities in our own time? Or do we already live in one? Detail your thoughts on this issue in an essay.

∾∾∾∾

BARBARA GOLDSMITH

Obsessive Genius: The Inner World of Marie Curie

Feminist author and historian Barbara Goldsmith is a regular contributor to the *New York Times* and *Architectural Digest,* and a founding editor
of *New York* magazine. Her publications include *Little Gloria…Happy at
Last* (1980) and *Johnson v. Johnson* (1987). She is a trustee of the New York
Public Library and a member of the President's Commission on the Celebration of Women in American History.

Paris, April 20, 1995: the white carpet stretched block after block down
the rue Soufflot ending in front of the Panthéon, which was draped in tri-
color banners that extended from the dome to the pavement. To the tune of
the "Marseillaise," the Republican Guardsmen moved along the white
expanse. The thousands who lined the streets were unusually quiet; some
tossed flowers as the cortège moved by. Faculty from the Curie Institute were
followed by Parisian high school students who held aloft four-foot blue,
white, and red letters—the Greek symbols for alpha, beta, and gamma rays.

As the marchers approached the Panthéon, they fanned out and stared
up at a platform under the grand dome on which were seated such lumi-
naries as President François Mitterrand. Suffering from cancer, in the last
weeks of his fourteen-year presidency, he had decided to dedicate his final
speech to the "women of France" and in a dramatic gesture to place the
ashes of Madame Curie and her husband, Pierre, in the Panthéon, thus making Marie (Marya Salomee Sklodowska) Curie the first woman to be buried
there for her own accomplishments. The Curies had been exhumed from
their graves in the suburb of Sceaux to join such French immortals as
Honoré-Gabriel Riqueti (Comte de Mirabeau), Jean-Jacques Rousseau,
Émile Zola, Victor Hugo, Voltaire (François-Marie Arouet), Jean-Baptiste
Perrin, and Paul Langevin.

Seated beside Mitterrand was Lech Walesa, the president of Poland,
Madame Curie's native country. Finally, there were the families of the two
scientists being enshrined: their daughter Eve, and the children of their

deceased daughter Irène and her husband Frédéric Joliot-Curie—Hélène Langevin-Joliot and Pierre Joliot, both distinguished scientists.

Pierre-Gilles de Gennes—the director of the School of Industrial Physics and Chemistry of the City of Paris (EPCI), where Marie and Pierre had discovered radioactivity, radium, and polonium—spoke first, saying that the Curies represented "the collective memory of the people of France and the beauty of self-sacrifice." Lech Walesa spoke of Marie Curie's Polish origins and termed her a patriot both of Poland and France. François Mitterrand then rose:

> This transfer of Pierre and Marie Curie's ashes to our most sacred sanctuary is not only an act of remembrance, but also an act in which France affirms her faith in science, in research, and we affirm our respect for those whom we consecrate here, their force and their lives. Today's ceremony is a deliberate outreach on our part from the Panthéon to the first lady of our honored history. It is another symbol that captures the attention of our nation and the exemplary struggle of a woman who decided to impose her abilities in a society where abilities, intellectual exploration, and public responsibility were reserved for men.

Above Mitterrand's head, as he spoke these words, one could read the inscription on the Panthéon's façade: TO GREAT MEN FROM A GRATEFUL COUNTRY. The irony is apparent.

After the speeches, a deafening ovation echoed down the streets. The modest Pierre Curie, who wanted to be buried in Sceaux because he abhorred "noise and ceremonies," would have hated this display. But, like it or not, the Curies, especially Marie, had been deified. Madame Curie was now an icon for the ages and an inspiration to women who saw in her the fulfillment of their own dreams and aspirations, however vague. I was among them.

As a teenager, I tacked up, among the detritus on my bulletin board, between a reproduction of Van Gogh's *Starry Night* and my Friday night bowling card, a photograph of Marie Curie sitting under an elm tree, her arms stretched out to encircle the waists of her daughters, two year old Eve, and nine year old Irène. I don't know why I was drawn to this photograph, but it wasn't about science. Madame Curie was my idol, and like other idols you don't have to know what they did to worship them. Perhaps I found comfort in what I took to be Marie's protective embrace since, at the time, my own mother was far away in a hospital, having been critically injured in an automobile accident. Who knows?

In the photograph there are none of the usual smiling faces. All three look ineffably sad. I didn't know why then. Now I do. Under the picture I had placed two of Madame Curie's quotations: "Nothing in life is to be feared. It is only to be understood," and "It is important to make a dream of life and of a dream reality." It was only while researching this book that I found that Pierre Curie, not Marie, wrote the latter.

In any case, there is little doubt that Marie Curie's life was truly inspirational. She was rare as a unicorn in the field of science. She came from an impoverished Polish family and worked for eight years to earn enough money to study at the Sorbonne. She overcame incredible hardships. In 1893, Marie Curie became the first woman to secure a degree in physics at the Sorbonne. The following year she received a second degree, in mathematics. She was the first woman to be appointed a professor at the Sorbonne, and the first woman to receive not only one but two Nobel Prizes: the first in physics along with her husband, Pierre, and Henri Becquerel (for the discovery of radioactivity); the second, eight years later, in chemistry (for the isolation of the elements polonium and radium). She was the first woman to be elected to the 224-year-old French Academy of Medicine. In addition to having a spectacular career, Marie raised two daughters largely as a single mother and saw that they were well educated, physically strong, and independent.

These are the facts of Madame Curie's life. But, they have become shrouded in a romantic myth constructed to suit the beliefs and proclivities of many people—journalists, scientists, medical practitioners, feminists, businessmen, industrialists, and even Madame Curie herself. She is remembered as a scientific Joan of Arc. Paris streets are named after Madame Curie and her husband, Pierre; the French 500-franc note (now a collector's item) is imprinted with her face and her so-called "miserable shed" laboratory, as well as several scenes from her life. Stamps and coins bear her image. The World War I automobiles that were refitted to contain X-ray equipment were known as "Les Petites Curie." Semi-documentaries and feature films contribute to her legend. As a child, I was entranced with Greer Garson as Marie and Walter Pidgeon as her husband, Pierre, in the 1943 film *Madame Curie.* I remember the movie-star Marie, her face glistening with sweat as she stirs a vat of boiling ore. I will never forget the scene in the dark of the night, when Marie and Pierre enter her laboratory to see a tiny luminous stain congealed in a dish. "Oh Pierre! Could it be? Could this be it?" exclaims Marie, as tears roll down her cheeks. Yes, this was it—Radium!

Many years have passed since a foolish girl was inspired by a Hollywood heroine. Now it is women, and the mores and history of the time in which they lived, that constitute a major theme in my writing. Why are some women trapped in their environment while others escape, or circumvent, or ignore these obstacles? How did society and family affect their aspirations? Why do some women seek independence while others want to tread a prescribed path? And, what common chord did Madame Curie strike in the psyche, particularly of women? These were a few of the questions that intrigued me.

My own obsession lies in an investigation of the vast disparity between image and reality. The mythical Madame Curie remains perhaps the most famous woman scientist in the world. Radium is thought to be her colossal discovery and has been given an enormous importance in the cure of cancers through radiation therapy. But in reality, is this true, and was this her major contribution to science? There is no doubt that over the last century Madame Curie's life has evolved into an image of towering perfection. But behind this image there was a real woman. It was this person that I wished to pursue.

Suggestions for Discussion

1. Why did Goldsmith choose to begin an account of Marie Curie's life with a description of her reburial in 1995?
2. Consider Goldsmith's statement, "Madame Curie was my idol, and like other idols you don't have to know what they did to worship them." What is she saying about the nature of fame and influence?

Suggestion for Writing

Relate Goldsmith's portrait of Marie Curie to Howard Gardner's discussion of great leaders in *Leading Beyond the Nation-State* (p. 711). In what ways did Curie provide inspirational leadership? How is she similar to the figures described by Gardner, and how is she different?

∽∾∽∾∽

S H I R E E N   L E E

The New Girls Network: Women, Technology, and Feminism

After facing discrimination during her career as an engineer, Shireen Lee became an advocate for women's rights in the workplace. She is a founding member of SportsBridge, a nonprofit organization dedicated to improving the status of young women, and in 2001, she served as an advisor for the Asian Pacific American Women's Leadership Institute. Lee has also worked extensively with the United Nations, helping to start the Youth Caucus of the UN Commission on the Status of Women. "The New Girls Network" is a call for women to study "hard" research-oriented sciences and use modern technology to promote feminism and social transformation.

In history, we have seen technology out of our control: when the United States during the Second World War dropped atom bombs on Hiroshima and Nagasaki, killing thousands of people and destroying worlds, even the scientists who had helped create the bomb were dumbfounded by the results of their work. Soon after terrorists killed thousands of people by flying airplanes into the World Trade Center and the Pentagon on September 11, 2001, Americans experienced further panic when the biological agent anthrax started showing up in the mail, making some severely ill and killing others. But our technological future does not have to continue in the same way.

"Imagine," writes Anita Borg, president of the nonprofit Institute for Women and Technology, "a world in which information technology (IT) was used to its highest potential, being an engine for an efficient, ecological economy and providing new opportunities for more people based on more available knowledge. Imagine a political system based on open access to information, better education, more communication, and equal participation. Imagine connecting people around the world in the spirit of positive internationalism, where social goals such as universal literacy, basic education, and health care are achieved."

Technology could help us reimagine societies, communities, and futures that move beyond the binaries—white-black; male-female; straight-gay; First World–Third World; future-past; technological-organic; work-play— of our contemporary world. As they achieve certain credentials in technology, women are participating in these reimaginings. But there continue to be barriers to women getting the right credentials, and to the careers where they can use them.

I grew up in Malaysia, where single-sex education is the norm. I benefited from being able to develop intellectually and physically in an environment free from the consuming social pressures of girl-boy interaction. Throughout my schooling I focused on math and science, and excelled. It seemed natural that I would become an engineer.

In Canada, where I attended college, graduating engineers are each presented with an iron ring in a secret ceremony designed by Rudyard Kipling and dating back to 1922. Engineers wear their rings on the little fingers of their working hands after taking an oath of ethics. At the age of twenty-three, I took off my iron ring when I stopped working at oil refineries, but I did not turn my back on technology.

An Environmental Scan

In 2001, the Bureau of Labor Statistics projected that between 2000 and 2010, eight of the ten fastest-growing occupations would be computer related, with computer engineers topping the list. Yet, according to the National Council for Research on Women, women's share of bachelor's degrees in computer science dropped to fewer than 20 percent in 1999, after having reached a high of 37 percent in 1984. A look at these numbers from the supply side suggests that the gap between male and female participation in the technology workforce, instead of closing, will actually widen in the near future. We are simply not graduating enough women to fill tomorrow's technological jobs: information technologists, computer applications specialists, games programmers, code writers in software development, and systems programmers, among others. The Information Technology Association of America predicts that, by 2010, 60 percent of American jobs will require technological skills. Contrast this demand with the following current statistics: women leave engineering jobs—ranging from electrical and mechanical engineering positions to computer-related engineering jobs, such as hardware engineering—at double the rate of men, and women are more likely to leave technological occupations altogether.

The mantra of second wave feminists was "Let us in!" Their success opened the doors to educational opportunities and brought women into schools and the workforce in unprecedented numbers. The women of that generation butted up against centuries-old traditions of patriarchal governance and belief systems to gain financial and reproductive independence. What does the world look like today for the daughters of those 1970s feminists?

Gender and racial discrimination at the end of the twentieth and beginning of the twenty-first century is subtle yet still pervasive. It stems largely from unconscious ways of thinking that have been socialized into all of us, men and women alike. In the realm of technology, its influence spans the pipeline from girls in school to women in the job market.

The Education-Career Discontinuity

Back in 1992, the American Association of University Women (AAUW) published *The AAUW Report: How Schools Shortchange Girls,* which claimed that there was a dearth of women in technology careers because girls were not taking math and science classes in school. The approach to the problem at the time can be summed up as follows: If we can get girls to take the classes and excel in them, they will naturally choose corresponding careers. Nearly a decade later, Patricia Campbell, coauthor of the report and an expert on educating girls and people of color in math and science, reiterated the original premise of the report and took it a step further, when she said "Achievement is necessary but not sufficient."

Campbell and Beatriz Chu Clewell, leading researchers in the field, tell us that girls, particularly those in the middle-class socioeconomic sphere, are now taking math and science classes in the same numbers as boys, and in some cases excelling in them. But they are *still* not choosing technology careers to the extent anticipated ten years ago. Girls do not seem to be making the link between math and science education and technology careers. Campbell believes that many girls place greater importance than do boys on making a positive difference in the larger world. Girls apparently do not see the connection between technology jobs, which tend to be highly specialized and solitary endeavors, and changing the world. Katie Wheeler, executive director of the Girls' Coalition of Greater Boston, a consortium of nonprofits, funders, and researchers interested in girls' issues, agrees. "Girls perceive technology and the hard sciences like physics as not involving people. They don't see in technology the potential to help people in the world. That's why most girls and women end up in the life sciences like biology rather than in high tech." Compounding an already unfavorable situation, research by the Congressional Commission on the Advancement of Women and Minorities in Science, Engineering and Technology Development (CAWMSET) confirms what most people already suspect. Many girls do not see themselves reflected in the role models, men *or* women, in technology careers. The general image of technology workers and engineers as unusually intelligent, socially inept, and absentminded "geeks" or "nerds" is often a deterrent.

For low-income young people of color, especially African-Americans, Latinos and Latinas, and Native Americans, the question of gender is moot— among them the overriding bartier is economic. Lack of educational resources in inner-city schools, where the majority of students are blacks and Latinos and Latinas, affects participation and achievement in math and science for both girls *and* boys. In Massachusetts, for example, tenth graders are required to take the Massachusetts Comprehensive Assessment System test, or MCAS, in a variety of subjects, including math and science. In low-income areas such as Springfield, Holyoke, and sections of Boston where a majority of the students are of color, the rate of failure is startling. In Springfield, in the year 2000, 94 percent of tenth-grade Latinos and Latinas and 91 percent of black students failed the math section; in Holyoke, 95 percent of Latinos and Latinas failed; and in Boston, 86 percent of Latinos and Latinas failed, as did 82 percent of black students. Deficient inner-city public school systems make it almost impossible for students to consider fields in technology because they aren't even getting the basic education needed to participate fully in society. Many women and girls of color must fight prejudices against their race, gender, and class that keep them from entering any number of career fields.

Yet there is hope. Many companies that seek to promote ethnic and racial diversity in the workplace have begun to fund training programs which benefit people of color. These programs may not have an impact on a large scale, but they are making a difference in particular neighborhoods. In Washington, D.C., Edgewood Terrace, an 884-unit apartment complex, was once so crime-ridden that the local media referred to it as Little Beirut.

After the Community Preservation and Development Corporation, a non-profit organization, began work to make Edgewood a better place to live, good things started to happen. It created EdgeNet, an intranet-style system that networks users together and hopes to help residents gain computer literacy. The Gateway @ Edgewood Terrace, a CPDC computer learning center that has more that sixty workstations and four networked labs, began to help residents get logged on. In addition, the Gateway center offers classes in computer skills and applications and will offer network management and beginning Microsoft Certified Systems Engineers courses.

Feminism has opened doors for those women who do not have to contend with race and class barriers, especially in fields such as medicine and law. In spring 2001, the *New York Times* reported that for the first time, incoming female students would outnumber male students in law schools across the country. In engineering, however, men dominate: of all engineering bachelor's degrees awarded in 2000, 47,320 went to men and only 12,216 to women. According to Campbell's research, even in colleges with the strongest outreach and support for women engineering students, enrollment of incoming female students has plateaued at about 20 percent over the last few years. A similar pattern is evident in the workforce. In an article in the *San Francisco Chronicle,* Karen Calo, vice president of human resources for the IBM Software Group in New York, observed that although women now make up 30 percent of lawyers and doctors, fewer than 10 percent of engineers are women. Even fewer are women of color. Technology is still very much a pale male profession.

Subtle Messages, Major Barriers

A historical lack of women in technology careers has resulted in work cultures that have developed without them. According to Sokunthear Sy, a young female engineer at Accenture (formerly Andersen Consulting), there are more informal support structures for men. Male-dominated work environments do a poor job of retaining women once they begin working in industry. "Subtle things like golfing that happen socially because that's the thing to do…[to] hang out after hours. Most women don't golf. And women with families can't hang out. Relationships that form outside of work influence decisions at work especially when reviews come around." A recent survey by Women of Silicon Valley, a joint project of the Community Foundation of Silicon Valley and the strategic advising group Collaborative Economics, confirms that 41 percent of women who work in technology, compared with only 23 percent of women not in technology jobs, feel that they have to "fit into a masculine workplace" to advance.

The subtle messages that women don't belong extends even to seemingly trivial elements, like clothing. As a chemical engineer I had to visit oil refineries several days a week. Attire mandated by safety regulations included steel-toe boots and Nomex fire-resistant overalls, which back then came only in men's sizes. On my first day of work I was forced to show up in boots that were two sizes too big and overalls with sleeves and pant legs rolled up multiple times. I looked like I was playing dress up in my father's clothes—not the image that one wants to project walking into a control room that is 100 percent male workers. But these are details that no one tells a newly graduated female engineer.

Today overt gender discrimination in schools and the workplace is rarely tolerated, so most people, both male and female, believe that women are on equal footing with men. After-school and mentoring programs to support girls and women in technology are thus often viewed by girls, women, and their male peers as remedial. Sy maintains that "there is a fear that if you get involved in specialized groups, people will think, Oh, you need extra help. You can't do it on your own. For example, if you are in a women's mentoring group and you get promoted, people will say that's why." Support programs can reinforce the stereotype that women are not as capable as men and need a leg up.

Programs targeted at groups that have historically been discriminated against, such as students of color in universities, or women in technology careers, serve to move us along a path of greater equity. It is not the *programs* themselves that need to be eliminated but rather people's *perceptions* of them. Contrast the opposition to affirmative action programs for women and people of color with the G.I. Bill, which provided higher education grants to veterans. The G.I. Bill, after all, can be viewed as a national, federally initiated affirmative action program—benefiting mainly young white men. According to Michael Haydock in an article for *American History,* "By the time the last American World War II veteran was graduated in 1956, the United States was richer by 450,000 engineers, 238,000 teachers, 91,000 scientists, 67,000 doctors, 22,000 dentists." Would the country also benefit from similar increases of women and/or people of color in these professions? This point seems particularly salient in the high-tech sector, where, according to CAWMSET, the demand for skilled American workers will continue to outstrip supply. With the G.I. Bill as a model, one can imagine a grants program that could provide badly needed science and math resources for low-income girls and young women of color in urban public schools. Think of the possibilities—if political will is forthcoming.

Redefining Our Position: Women as Technology Innovators

The challenges facing women in technology fields are nothing new. Most commentary on women and technology—academic and otherwise—makes this clear. However, the focus is often on what women are *not* doing. That vantage point perpetuates a deficit model—women seem perpetually to fall short of expectations. Such an approach can become a self-fulfilling prophecy.

The spotlight rarely shines on what women are doing *right*. They are redefining their involvement with technology and using technology to empower and advance themselves and other women. Problems still exist, but there are many women who have adapted to their environment and found ways to succeed.

Nowhere is this more apparent than in the high-tech sector. Here are the numbers we typically see: There are just three female CEOs among the Fortune 500 and only seven in the Fortune 1000; women hold only 4 percent of the top management positions in Fortune 500 companies. No surprise. What the media usually don't tell us is that women account for 45 percent of the highest ranking corporate officers in Internet companies, and 6 percent of Internet companies financed by venture capital firms in 1999 have female CEOs.

If you read only half the story, you see only a partial picture. Rather than butting heads with patriarchal corporate America, women are using a different leverage point—smaller, newer companies. That these startling statistics show up in the high-tech sector, an industry that burst into prominence after the feminist era of the 1970s, is probably no accident. High-tech has become the nexus for minirevolutions—linking women's leadership in small businesses and global women's activism to create a new form of feminist activism.

Women Business Owners: Today's Feminists

Women in general are no longer just banging on the doors of corporations saying, "Let us in!" We are taking matters into our own hands and creating new centers of power. Women are starting their own businesses in unprecedented numbers. Between 1992 and 1997, according to the National Federation of Women Business Owners (NFWBO), the number of women-owned firms increased two and a half times faster than all U.S. businesses. As of 1996, one in eight women-owned firms in the United States was owned by a woman of color, and the number of these firms has increased three times faster than the overall rate of business growth in the past ten years. What about younger women? Ta'chelle Herron, of San Francisco, is a twenty-one-year-old woman of color, a product of the urban public school system. She insists that women *can* use technology for their advancement. "Start your own business! Once you learn the fundamentals of how the systems work, you can switch that around and use it for yourself—to make money. I started my own graphic design business." A 2001 survey on women in Silicon Valley confirms this trend. It found that many women in technology are leaving the corporate workplace. About 10 percent of women in Silicon Valley are independent contractors, and another 20 percent said they planned to start their own businesses in the next three years. The U.S. Small Business Administration tells us that women now own a staggering 9 million companies—38 percent of all U.S. enterprises. They employ over 27.5 million people.

Further, women are breaking down the binaries associated with pleasure and work, activism and work; they are living their activism in ways that they find fulfilling. Feminism, once synonymous with marching in the streets, is now part of the economic engine of the country. Thanks in part to what those marching women accomplished, contemporary women are making change from within institutions. Looking at her peers, Rebecca Tadikonda, a twenty-eight-year-old recent MBA graduate from Stanford University, observes, "Amongst high-tech start-ups where there is a women CEO or where there are more women on the management team, there are more women in the company overall. If there aren't women or if there are fewer women on the management team, there are fewer women in the company overall." This point seems consistent with recent research by the Stanford Graduate School of Business. According to the report, "Gender and the Organization-Building Process in Young, High-Tech Firms," women's early representation in core scientific and technical roles has decisive consequences for how emerging companies evolve. This presence in turn could have positive implications for the development of women-friendly workplace cultures. As alluded to earlier, long-established male-centric cultures in large companies are often deterrents to women's advancement. Increasing numbers of women in leadership positions in high-tech companies will inevitably offer a more diverse array of role models for young girls and help them see that people in technology careers can be like them. Whether they are conscious of it or not, women leaders are also acting as activists and role models by paving the way for other women. Feminist activism may not look like it did thirty years ago, but it is definitely alive and thriving.

The High-Tech Sector

Women in the high-tech sector in particular are reimagining the possibilities for work, activism, empowerment, technology, and our future. Why? David Brooks gives a compelling argument for a new "bobo" ethos that has its ground zero in the high-tech industry. *Bobo* means "bourgeois bohemian"—a melding of capitalist bourgeois values and bohemian egalitarian ideals. Old society, with its insular isms—sexism, racism, ageism— has been displaced by educated, antiestablishment people with scuffed shoes who embrace change, welcome experimentation, challenge convention, and thirst for the new. Bobos resist conventional ways of doing things. Women in high-tech are among the forces creating this new environment and are redefining capitalism in a more human way.

The Women's Technology Cluster is an incubator for women-owned high-tech start-ups in San Francisco. Founded by Catherine Muther, a feminist and former head of marketing for Cisco Systems, the cluster provides its companies with a cadre of advisers, partners, and peers who can make connections to funding and other resources. Built into this business model is a unique giveback component. Each business that enters the Women's Technology Cluster commits a small percentage of its equity to the charitable Venture Philanthropy Fund, which over time assists female entrepreneurs and helps sustain other women-owned companies in the cluster. This new collaborative business model embodies the feminist ideals of philanthropy and social equity. Hillary Clinton, in a tongue-in-cheek poke at the "old boys network," dubbed this movement the "new girls network."

Despite their potential, women-owned high-tech start-ups still have a notoriously difficult time raising venture capital, a key source of funding for new companies. Venture capitalists provide financial backing and management assistance to new, fast-growing businesses. Unlike banks, which give loans that have to be repaid as debt, venture capitalists get a portion of the company that they invest in. In 1999 women-led companies received less than 5 percent of the $36 billion invested by venture capitalists. This is not surprising since venture capitalists typically review proposals submitted by people whom they know, whom they know of, or who are like them—the old boys network in action.

In response, women have once again mobilized. In 2000, the National Women's Business Council launched Springboard, an annual series of forums to help women gain access to venture capital. In cities across the country, specially selected groups of women-led companies were coached to present their business plans to hundreds of corporate, individual, and venture investors during daylong events. In just one year Springboard companies raised a total of $450 million in venture capital. According to Denise Brosseau, president of the Forum for Women Entrepreneurs, which cosponsored two Springboard forums in the San Francisco Bay Area, the long-term goal of showcasing women entrepreneurs is to put them on the venture capital map—essentially to give them a jump start into the venture capitalists' network.

In 1994 there was another development just as ground-breaking as Springboard, perhaps even more so. Inroads Capital Partners started the first-ever venture capital fund targeting women entrepreneurs. Today four other funds—Women's Growth Capital Fund, Milepost Ventures (formerly Viridian Capital), Fund Isabella, and Axxon Capital—have followed suit. These funds, all managed *and* founded by women, focus investments on early-stage companies that are led, founded, or owned by women, as well as companies that sell products or services catering primarily to women. Willa

Seldon, cofounder and general partner of Milepost Ventures, recalls. "When we first started our fund, a number of people said, 'Why would you even think about doing that?' " Seldon and her peers must feel an enormous sense of satisfaction (and validation) since increasing visibility for women entrepreneurs has translated into real dollars. "There is direct investment [by VC firms] of course," she continues. "But it usually ends up being more after you take into account angel investors [wealthy individuals—women or men—who invest directly in start-up companies, business incubators for women, and additional resources like educational workshops]. Women VC firms have driven larger community backing."

Full participation in a capitalist society is contingent upon private ownership—of money, property, and assets. The relationship is straightforward: ownership grants participation. This is a dynamic from which women have historically been, for the most part, excluded. In the past, legislation curtailed women's rights to ownership of property. Even since (white) American women received legal rights to personal property in the nineteenth century, their participation has been restricted by a culture that views men as the purveyors of monetary and economic matters. Many women continue to face limitations on their ability to participate fully in capitalist society. Yet women with money who invest in women-owned businesses are supporting women's empowerment on many levels. Women can take charge of their own assets. They can invest with an eye toward empowering other women who are in turn starting their own businesses. All these women have the potential to be role models and philanthropists (not merely earners) for the next generation of women.

Virtual Organizing, Global Activism

After I left engineering, I joined a group of women who use technology for feminist empowerment. I bought a one-way train ticket from Toronto to San Francisco to help start a nonprofit organization for girls. Five years later, while I am fully immersed in local, national, and international advocacy for girls and young women, technology remains an integral part of my work, but like other women, I have redefined my involvement with it. Now, as one of the cofounders of the Youth Caucus of the United Nations Commission on the Status of Women, I use Internet technologies to fight for women's rights. In a sense, I have come full circle. I left a job in technology because there was no gender awareness or sensitivity there, and I now use the Internet to organize young women activists from around the world.

The Internet has revolutionized the way we organize. While e-mail, websites, Listservs, search engines, and newsgroups have improved communications for all groups, they have been particularly effective in serving a women's political agenda. All over the world, women's groups tend to be small, helping communities on a local, grassroots level. Historically they have worked in isolation, having little communication with one another. In the past three years, as access to the Internet worldwide has grown exponentially, this circumstance has changed drastically. Even in poor rural communities women may now have access to a computer with an online connection, albeit not with the frequency that we take for granted in the United States. Nonetheless, even sporadic access has globally facilitated information-sharing and coalition-building among women's groups in unprecedented numbers. Through Listservs that help build online communities, young women activists from Nigeria and Bosnia share learning about peer education models in HIV-AIDS prevention, and youth activists from Kenya and India exchange information about the state of girls' and young women's education in their countries.

The Internet offers possibilities for inclusion, diversity, and transparency that feminists have always aspired to but have sometimes had difficulty achieving. New technologies have sped up our communications, allowed us to share information on a grand scale, and given an immediacy to what we do. My favorite image of these new practices remains the computer room set up for the thousands of women's activists who converged on the UN in June 2000 for the Special Session of the General Assembly, also known as Beijing + 5. At each of the twenty or so computer terminals sat a women's rights activist from a different country e-mailing the latest information about the negotiations in New York back to her colleagues at home while hearing feedback on lobbying strategy from the dozens of activists from her country who could not be at the United Nations. If information is power, then that little room was power central.

The Internet has also changed how we interact with government, making it easier for us to influence legislation, demand accountability, and promote democratic participation. Women who have been reluctant to take a visible role in the women's movement now have the option of being "armchair activists" who can have an impact without leaving their homes or sacrificing anonymity. Rebecca Tadikonda epitomizes this new breed of women's activist. "I got an e-mail from a friend of mine about [the appointment of Attorney General John] Ashcroft and clicked on to the website," she says. "It only took five minutes—I wouldn't have done it if it was longer. I ended up forwarding the e-mail to a bunch of my women friends. Then I got another activist e-mail from another woman friend that I had forwarded the e-mail to. It creates networks and is an easy and personal way to get people involved in political activism—*especially* if the e-mail comes from someone you know."

The Internet has definitely brought more women into the political process. According to Jennifer Pozner, founder and executive director of Women In Media News (WIMN), a media watchdog group, since President George W. Bush's inauguration, women have been embracing technology as a means of activism like never before. When President Bush reinstated the "global gag rule," which prevents government agencies from giving funds to private family planning programs outside the United States even if the money is not going to be used for abortion, Patt Morrison wrote a column in the *Los Angeles Times* denouncing it. Morrison sent the president a card that read, "President George W. Bush. In honor of President's Day, a donation has been made to Planned Parenthood in your name." People began forwarding the column via e-mail, asking that donations to Planned Parenthood be made in Bush's name. The e-mail spread like wildfire, and Planned Parenthood received $500,000.

Toward an Empowered Future

When we think of technology, we often think more of the *use* of technology—using computers, e-mail, cell phones—and less of the *creation* of technology—designing computer software and hardware. The distinction is important because women now relate to technology much differently than men do. Women tend to be users more than creators of technology, whereas men are as much creators as they are users. Women have clearly used technology to their advantage in their activist work and business lives, but they are often shut out from creating the technology. Being good at using technology and adapting it for our political activism and financial independence is a huge step forward. But women must also play an integral part in creating the technology. To ensure that women are not left behind, we must develop ways to educate and graduate more women engineers and computer scientists and facilitate their participation in the workforce. Bridging this gap will ensure that future generations of feminists will not only express their activism from the outside, through existing technology, but also from within, through new technologies that are created with a gender lens and communities of color in mind.

How exactly will creating technology benefit women? Let's imagine. Thanks to new communications technologies, working from home at least part of the time is a growing phenomenon. This arrangement benefits women, particularly those with families, more than any other demographic group. Could this flexible approach to work have come about even earlier if women were responsible for designing the computers, networks, and faxes that make it all possible? Does it surprise anyone that when more women entered the medical profession, we started seeing more research on the impact of diseases on women and using women subjects rather than the male standard?

According to the Institute for Women and Technology, most product designers create products with themselves in mind. As a result, most new products reflect the desires of the single, eighteen- to thirty-five-year-old men who design them. What if women were at the forefront of creating technology? We can imagine a spectrum of changes from the trivial—keyboards to fit women's smaller hands—to products with broad societal consequences. Will women engineers choose to perpetuate the multibillion-dollar military industry that keeps us locked in war games all over the globe? Or will they apply their intelligence and expertise to solving more pressing global problems?

As a movement, young feminists must continue to fight for meaningful representation and participation in the technology workforce and, equally important, continue to create their own workforces. But there is much work to be done. Gender equity in computer access, knowledge, and use cannot be measured solely by how many women send e-mail, surf the Net, or perform basic functions on the computer. The new benchmark should emphasize computer fluency—being able to interpret the information that technology makes available, mastering analytical skills and computer concepts, employing technology proactively, and imagining innovative uses for technology across a wide range of problems and subjects.

Suggestions for Discussion

1. According to Lee, what role do women play in scientific research? How much progress have they made toward equality in the field?

2. What is the "New Girls Network"? How do goals of research, activism, and empowerment shape the Network's agenda?

3. Lee describes technology as a force with the potential to create not only great benefits but also great harm. Compare her discussion of this issue with Freeman Dyson's in "Can Science Be Ethical?"

Suggestion for Writing

Read Barbara Goldsmith's essay "Obsessive Genius: The Inner World of Marie Curie" (p. 550). Relate Goldsmith's study of Curie, an iconic female scientist of the past, to Lee's discussion of the current and future role of women in the sciences.

POETRY

WALT WHITMAN

When I Heard the Learn'd Astronomer

Walt Whitman (1819–1892), regarded by many as the greatest American poet, was born on Long Island, NY. He was a printer, a journalist, and a nurse during the Civil War. Strongly influenced by Ralph Waldo Emerson, he published *Leaves of Grass* in 1855 at his own expense. Whitman added new section to the work over the years as new editions were published. By the time of his death, he had become a major influence on younger poets who were moved by his experiments in free verse and by his transcendental ideas. In "When I Heard the Learn'd Astronomer," impatient with explanations of abstract science, he turns instead to silent contemplation of nature which, he implies, provides a profounder insight than do the "charts and diagrams" of science.

When I heard the learn'd astronomer,
When the proofs, the figures, were ranged in columns before me,
When I was shown the charts and diagrams, to add, divide, and measure
    them,
When I sitting heard the astronomer where he lectured with much
    applause in the lecture-room,
How soon unaccountable I became tired and sick,
Till rising and gliding out I wander'd off by myself,
In the mystical moist night-air, and from time to time,
Look'd up in perfect silence at the stars.

Suggestions for Discussion

1. Notice that this poem is contained in one sentence. How does Whitman organize the sentence to lead to the climax of the last line?

2. What is the poet's attitude toward the scientist? Why does he reject the scientific method of looking at nature? Why is his response "unaccountable"?

3. What is the significance of the phrase "perfect silence" in the last line?

Suggestion for Writing

Write an essay in which you explain not only the idea in the poem but how the idea is developed. Your essay should consider how a prose statement of the idea would differ.

❧❧❧

AFFONSO ROMANO DE SANT'ANNA

Letter to the Dead

The works of writer, professor, and literary critic Affonso Romano De Sant'Anna (b. 1937) explore the cultural and political landscapes of his native Brazil. His book *Popular Music and Modern Brazilian Poetry* (1978) acknowledges the artistry and influence of popular music lyrics, and in *Loving Cannibalism* (1984), De Sant'Anna offers an analysis of love poetry undertaken from a psychological standpoint. In his 1980 poem "What Kind of Nation Is This?" De Sant'Anna challenged the Brazilian government's policy of censorship, charging that it harmed the national sense of identity. His talent for social commentary is evident in the following poem, translated from the original Portuguese by Mark Strand and published in the *New Yorker* in 2000.

Friends, nothing has changed
in essence.

Wages don't cover expenses,
wars persist without end,
and there are new and terrible viruses,
beyond the advances of medicine.
From time to time, a neighbor

falls dead over questions of love.
There are interesting films, it is true,
and, as always, voluptuous women
seducing us with their mouths and legs,
but in matters of love
we haven't invented a single position that's new.

Some astronauts stay in space
six months or more, testing
equipment and solitude.
In each Olympics new records are predicted
and in the countries social advances and setbacks.
But not a single bird has changed its song
with the times.

We put on the same Greek tragedies,
reread "Don Quixote," and spring
arrives on time each year.

Some habits, rivers, and forests are lost.
Nobody sits in front of his house anymore
or takes in the breezes of afternoon,
but we have amazing computers
that keep us from thinking.

On the disappearance of the dinosaurs
and the formation of galaxies
we have no new knowledge.
Clothes come and go with the fashions.
Strong governments fall, others rise,
countries are divided,
and the ants and the bees continue
faithful to their work.

Nothing has changed in essence.

We sing congratulations at parties,
argue football on street corners,
die in senseless disasters,
and from time to time
one of us looks at the star-filled sky
with the same amazement we had
when we looked at caves.
And each generation, full of itself,
continues to think
that it lives at the summit of history.

Suggestions for Discussion

1. If "nothing has changed in essence" then why does each generation "think that it lives at the summit of history"?

2. Are the narrator's feelings about the continuity of human experience clearly defined or ambivalent?

3. Doesn't De Sant'Anna admit that technology creates change when the narrator notes "we have amazing computers that keep us from thinking"?

Suggestion for Writing

Compare De Sant'Anna's *Letter to the Dead* to Edward O. Wilson's *Letter to Thoreau* (p. 470). How does each writer preach a message to the living while employing the artistic conceit of a missive to the deceased? Analyze the effectiveness of this technique as a form of persuasive writing.

Freedom and Human Dignity

Tell me, then, whether you agree with and assent to my first principle, that neither injury nor retaliation nor warding off evil by evil is ever right.

—PLATO, "The Crito"

The history of mankind is a history of repeated injuries and usurpations on the part of man toward woman, having in direct object the establishment of an absolute tyranny over her.

—ELIZABETH CADY STANTON and
LUCRETIA COFFIN MOTT, "Seneca Falls Convention"

Deployment

IMKE LASS, 2003

NOTEBOOK

MARTIN LUTHER KING, JR.

I Have a Dream

Martin Luther King, Jr. (1929–1968), the charismatic leader of the civil
rights movement of the 1950s and 1960s, was assassinated in 1968 in
Memphis, TN. He led sit-ins and demonstrations throughout the South
and was president of the Southern Christian Leadership Conference as
well as pastor of a large church in Atlanta. He followed the principles of
nonviolent resistance put forth by Gandhi and Thoreau in all of his public actions and utterances. The following speech, which King delivered
at a centennial celebration of the Emancipation Proclamation in front
of the Lincoln Memorial, moves the reader as deeply today as it did his
enormous crowd of listeners then. It points the way to a world free from
the burden of racism.

Five score years ago, a great American, in whose symbolic shadow we
stand, signed the Emancipation Proclamation. This momentous decree
came as a great beacon light of hope to millions of Negro slaves who had
been seared in the flames of withering injustice. It came as a joyous daybreak to end the long night of captivity.

But one hundred years later, we must face the tragic fact that the Negro
is still not free. One hundred years later, the life of the Negro is still sadly
crippled by the manacles of segregation and the chains of discrimination.
One hundred years later, the Negro lives on a lonely island of poverty in the
midst of a vast ocean of material prosperity. One hundred years later, the
Negro is still languished in the corners of American society and finds himself an exile in his own land. So we have come here today to dramatize an
appalling condition.

In a sense we have come to our nation's Capital to cash a check. When
the architects of our republic wrote the magnificent words of the Constitution and the Declaration of Independence, they were signing a promissory
note to which every American was to fall heir. This note was a promise that
all men would be guaranteed the unalienable rights of life, liberty, and the
pursuit of happiness.

It is obvious today that America has defaulted on this promissory note insofar as her citizens of color are concerned. Instead of honoring this sacred obligation, America has given the Negro people a bad check; a check which has come back marked "insufficient funds." But we refuse to believe that the bank of justice is bankrupt. We refuse to believe that there are insufficient funds in the great vaults of opportunity of this nation. So we have come to cash this check—a check that will give us upon demand the riches of freedom and the security of justice. We have also come to this hallowed spot to remind America of the fierce urgency of *now*. This is no time to engage in the luxury of cooling off or to take the tranquilizing drug of gradualism. *Now* is the time to make real the promises of Democracy. *Now* is the time to rise from the dark and desolate valley of segregation to the sunlit path of racial justice. *Now* is the time to open the doors of opportunity to all of God's children. *Now* is the time to lift our nation from the quicksands of racial injustice to the solid rock of brotherhood.

It would be fatal for the nation to overlook the urgency of the moment and to underestimate the determination of the Negro. This sweltering summer of the Negro's legitimate discontent will not pass until there is an invigorating autumn of freedom and equality. 1963 is not an end, but a beginning. Those who hope that the Negro needed to blow off steam and will now be content will have a rude awakening if the nation returns to business as usual. There will be neither rest nor tranquillity in America until the Negro is granted his citizenship rights. The whirlwinds of revolt will continue to shake the foundations of our nation until the bright day of justice emerges.

But there is something that I must say to my people who stand on the warm threshold which leads into the palace of justice. In the process of gaining our rightful place we must not be guilty of wrongful deeds. Let us not seek to satisfy our thirst for freedom by drinking from the cup of bitterness and hatred. We must forever conduct our struggle on the high plane of dignity and discipline. We must not allow our creative protest to degenerate into physical violence. Again and again we must rise to the majestic heights of meeting physical force with soul force. The marvelous new militancy which has engulfed the Negro community must not lead us to a distrust of all white people, for many of our white brothers, as evidenced by their presence here today, have come to realize that their destiny is tied up with our destiny and their freedom is inextricably bound to our freedom. We cannot walk alone.

And as we walk, we must make the pledge that we shall march ahead. We cannot turn back. There are those who are asking the devotees of civil rights, "When will you be satisfied?" We can never be satisfied as long as the Negro is the victim of the unspeakable horrors of police brutality. We can never be satisfied as long as our bodies, heavy with fatigue of travel, cannot gain lodging in the motels of the highways and the hotels of the cities. We cannot be satisfied as long as the Negro's basic mobility is from a smaller ghetto to a larger one. We can never be satisfied as long as a Negro in Mississippi cannot vote and a Negro in New York believes he has nothing for which to vote. No, no, we are not satisfied, and we will not be satisfied until justice rolls down like waters and righteousness like a mighty stream.

I am not unmindful that some of you have come here out of great trials and tribulations. Some of you have come fresh from narrow jail cells. Some of you have come from areas where your quest for freedom left you battered by the storms of persecution and staggered by the winds of police brutality. You have been the veterans of creative suffering. Continue to work with the faith that unearned suffering is redemptive.

Go back to Mississippi, go back to Alabama, go back to South Carolina, go back to Georgia, go back to Louisiana, go back to the slums and ghettos of our northern cities, knowing that somehow this situation can and will be changed. Let us not wallow in the valley of despair.

I say to you today, my friends, that in spite of the difficulties and frustrations of the moment I still have a dream. It is a dream deeply rooted in the American dream.

I have a dream that one day this nation will rise up and live out the true meaning of its creed: "We hold these truths to be self-evident; that all men are created equal."

I have a dream that one day on the red hills of Georgia the sons of former slaves and the sons of former slaveowners will be able to sit down together at the table of brotherhood.

I have a dream that one day even the state of Mississippi, a desert state sweltering with the heat of injustice and oppression, will be transformed into an oasis of freedom and justice.

I have a dream that my four little children will one day live in a nation where they will not be judged by the color of their skin but by the content of their character.

I have a dream today.

I have a dream that one day the state of Alabama, whose governor's lips are presently dripping with the words of interposition and nullification, will be transformed into a situation where little black boys and black girls will be able to join hands with little white boys and white girls and walk together as sisters and brothers.

I have a dream today.

I have a dream that one day every valley shall be exalted, every hill and mountain shall be made low, the rough places will be made plains, and the crooked places will be made straight, and the glory of the Lord shall be revealed, and all flesh shall see it together.

This is our hope. This is the faith with which I return to the South. With this faith we will be able to hew out of the mountain of despair a stone of hope.

With this faith we will be able to transform the jangling discords of our nation into a beautiful symphony of brotherhood. With this faith we will be able to work together, to pray together, to struggle together, to go to jail together, to stand up for freedom together, knowing that we will be free one day.

This will be the day when all of God's children will be able to sing with new meaning

> My country, 'tis of thee,
> Sweet land of liberty,
>   Of thee I sing:
> Land where my fathers died,
> Land of the pilgrims' pride,
> From every mountainside
>   Let freedom ring.

And if America is to be a great nation this must become true. So let freedom ring from the prodigious hilltops of New Hampshire. Let freedom ring from the mighty mountains of New York. Let freedom ring from the heightening Alleghenies of Pennsylvania!

Let freedom ring from the snowcapped Rockies of Colorado!

Let freedom ring from the curvacious peaks of California!

But not only that; let freedom ring from Stone Mountain of Georgia.

Let freedom ring from Lookout Mountain of Tennessee!

Let freedom ring from every hill and molehill of Mississippi. From every mountainside, let freedom ring.

When we let freedom ring, when we let it ring from every village and every hamlet, from every state and every city, we will be able to speed up that day when all of God's children, black men and white men, Jews and Gentiles, Protestants and Catholics, will be able to join hands and sing in the words of the old Negro spiritual, "Free at last! free at last! thank God almighty, we are free at last!"

Suggestions for Discussion

1. What role does repetition play in this speech?

2. Discuss Martin Luther King's use of the Bible, the spiritual song, and the Declaration of Independence in this speech. How is each source dependent upon the other?

3. It is clear that this selection was designed as an oration. What are its oratorical qualities?

4. Why does King stress pacifism as a means in the struggle for civil rights?

Suggestions for Writing

1. What do you think has been the outcome of King's dream? Write an essay in which you discuss where the dream has been fulfilled and where it has remained unfulfilled.

2. Write a paragraph about the effective use of repetition in King's oration.

❧❧❧❧❧

DOROTHY DAY

Martin Luther King

Dorothy Day (1897–1980) studied the works of Tolstoy and Sinclair at the University of Illinois at Urbana; it fueled her lifelong passion for social justice. After moving to New York in 1916, she wrote in support of women's suffrage, birth control, and pacifism in articles that often appeared in Marxist journals such as the *Liberator*. Her 1927 conversion to Catholicism alienated her husband but led to a close relationship with activist Peter Maurin, who helped her found the charitable Catholic Worker Movement in 1933. Day dedicated the remainder of her life to fighting poverty and died in poverty herself. In the following piece, written in April 1968, Day reacts to the news of Martin Luther King, Jr.'s assassination.

Just three weeks ago Martin Luther King was shot as he stood on the balcony of a motel in Memphis, Tennessee. I was sitting in the kitchen of one of the women's apartments on Kenmare Street watching the television when the news flash came. I sat there stunned, wondering if he was suffering a superficial wound, as James Meredith did on his Mississippi walk to overcome fear, that famous march on which the cry "Black Power" was first shouted. Martin Luther King wrote about it in his last book. *Where Do We Go from Here?*—a book which all of us should read because it makes us understand what the words "Black Power" really mean. Dr. King was a man of the deepest and most profound spiritual insights.

These were the thoughts which flashed through my mind as I waited, scarcely knowing that I was waiting, for further news. The dreaded words were spoken almost at once. "Martin Luther King is dead." The next day was

Good Friday, the day commemorated by the entire Christian world as the day when Jesus Christ, true God and true Man, shed His blood.

"Unless the grain of wheat fall into the ground and die, it remains alone. But if it die it produces much fruit." Martin Luther King died daily, as St. Paul said. He faced death daily and said a number of times that he knew he would be killed for the faith that was in him. The faith that men could live together as brothers. The faith in the Gospel teaching of nonviolence. The faith that man is capable of change, of growth, of growing in love.

Cynics may say that many used nonviolence as a tactic. Many may scoff at the outcry raised at his death, saying that this is an election year and all candidates had to show honor to a fallen Black hero. But love and grief were surely in the air those days of mourning, and all that was best in the country—in the labor movement, the civil rights movement, and the peace movement—cast aside all their worldly cares and occupations to go to Memphis to march with the sanitation union men, on whose behalf, during whose strike, Martin Luther King had given himself; and to Atlanta, where half a million people gathered to walk in the funeral procession, to follow the farm cart and the two mules which drew the coffin of the dead leader.

Always, I think, I will weep when I hear the song "We Shall Overcome," and when I read the words "Free at last, Free at last, Great God Almighty, Free at last."

Suggestions for Discussion

1. According to Day, what would cynics say about Martin Luther King's death?

2. How do you think Martin Luther King is thought of today, and how do modern-day politicians evoke his name?

3. Compare Day's portrayal of Martin Luther King with your own impression of him after reading the speech "I Have a Dream" (p. 572).

Suggestion for Writing

Think of an important public figure who has died during your lifetime, and write about how this person's death affected you.

PERSONAL REMINISCENCES

⧼෴⧽

A R N I E   K A N T R O W I T Z

Growing Up Gay

Arnie Kantrowitz (b. 1940) is a writer, educator, and gay activist from Newark, NJ, who served as the chair of the English department at the College of Staten Island, CUNY. A regular contributor to *The Advocate* and *Christopher Street,* his essays have also appeared in numerous anthologies, including *Personal Dispatches: Writers Respond to AIDS* (1990), *Hometowns* (1991), *Leatherfolk* (1991), *A Member of the Family* (1992), *Friends and Lovers* (1995), and *Gay and Lesbian Heritage* (1995). Kantrowitz also wrote *Walt Whitman,* a biography of the American poet and transcendentalist, for the Chelsea House series *Lives of Notable Gay Men and Lesbians.* He graduated from Rutgers in 1961 and earned a master's degree from New York University in 1963. The following passage, which relates Kantrowitz's experiences "coming out" to friends, family members, and colleagues, is from his 1977 autobiography, *Under the Rainbow.*

I didn't open the closet door to an all singing, all dancing, all Technicolor welcome. It took many months and a lot of encouragement from my new friends. Surrounded by each other, it seemed that if we told the truth together, the world would change. "Just tell the truth," my mother had taught me. No longer alone, I was less afraid. So I set about becoming honest and changing at least my corner of the world, and I assumed that the Emerald City was not far off.

Coming out was a little different with each person. The women were generally easier to tell, expressing their relief with responses like "Thank goodness you're something. I never heard of you going out with anyone, and I thought you were asexual!"

The men were a little more intimidating, but I didn't let that stop me. One of my colleagues answered my declaration with, "I thought there were some queers in the department. Do you know any others?" But his tone was sympathetic.

"If I did, I wouldn't tell you," I answered. "They'll have to do it themselves. And the word isn't 'queers.' It's 'homosexuals.' Try to remember that."

When I made my announcement to Herb, he said with concern, "What are you trying to do? Destroy yourself? Why do you have to tell everyone your secrets? Do you want them to hate you?"

I answered, "Do you hate me, Herb? Do you hate me because I'm gay?"

"You're my friend," he said simply.

There was sporadic hassling after that, when he would inadvertently drop words like "cocksucker" in my presence, but a little rage cleared that habit up.

My childhood friend Gerry, at whose wedding I had been the best man, confessed it made him uncomfortable. "It's just an emotional reaction. Give me some time to get used to it." I gave it. He got used to it. I told his parents. His father received it as a civil rights issue. His mother didn't much like the fact, but she loved me, and welcomed me in her home as always.

From other old friends there were confused silences, unanswered letters, doubts and qualms from people who I thought knew me so well that no such news could alter our relationships. One friend, Louis, told me it was fine with him. I had driven his wife to the hospital when she was in labor, and I was his daughter's godfather. But the first time he saw me kiss a man hello, he fled the apartment in embarrassed confusion, tripping over his own excuses.

"I was paranoid," he explained on the phone a few days later. "It touched something inside of me that I don't want to know about. I'm really sorry. We'll get together again." I haven't seen him since.

But I had no time for everyone else's pain. I worked on the premise that anyone who couldn't deal with the fact that I was gay never really knew me in the first place, liked only part of me, and all of me was going to be up front from then on, ready or not.

Approaching my mother about the subject for the second time wasn't easy. I didn't want any more salt on my head, and her repugnance for the topic had put it in a class with leprosy. I hadn't seen much of her lately. The dream life she had forged for herself had begun to crumble. The heavies were muscling in on my step-father's numbers territory. At the same time, with startling regularity, customers were winning their numbers bets, forcing him to pay out what would have been his profits. My mother and he had invested their earnings in stocks, but the market was in a slump, and instead of being able to pull out their investment, they lost tens of thousands of dollars, money that might have gone to save the business. The rest had been spent on the house that crested Athens Road in Short Hills. The house had become a millstone, until it seemed worth consideration to insure it heavily and fire-bomb it. Instead, Frank borrowed money from the underworld and then found he couldn't pay it back. The Mafia had been known to strike at home and family to intimidate its debtors. They had to flee. They sold the house and went into hiding in southern New Jersey, not answering the phone, receiving mail at an anonymous post office box. The furniture—rugs and silver and crystal and paintings, the lavender brocades, the statues and busts, the silk chairs and the seventeen-foot couch—all went into storage without insurance. There was a fire in the warehouse. Nothing remained but ashes and memories of grandeur and a return to bitterness. The Cadillacs were aging, the furs were looking worn around the edges, and the eleven-carat diamond ring that was my mother's most precious possession was in a pawnbroker's shop. They needed the money for food. Frank had lost all of his incentive and sat around waiting for something to happen. Occasionally he played solitaire.

So my mother was in none too receptive a mood when her older son declared that he liked being a homosexual. "I've found out that homosexuality isn't a sickness after all," I announced. "It's no different from being left-handed in a world that's full of right-handed people. It's not a question of failure on your part; it's just the way some people are, and they can...*we* can be as happy as anyone else. I mean, I don't think I want to kill myself over it. I'll just be healthy my own way, like my friends."

"If that's what makes you happy," she said, leveling her gaze at me like an antiaircraft gun from the chair where she sat. "But you wasted all that money being psychoanalyzed for nothing." The subject was closed.

My brother's response was more equivocal. "I guess I always knew it," he said quietly, "even if I never said it to myself in so many words."

"Then it's okay with you?" I asked, not seeking approval but friendship.

"I won't condemn it, but I can't condone it," he answered.

But I wouldn't accept mere impartiality. "It's not up to you to judge me," I said. "That's not offering very much."

"What do you want me to do? Throw my arms around you and be glad you're my brother?"

Fifteen minutes later I thought of an answer. "I won't ask you to throw your arms around me," I said with steel determination, "but is it too much to expect you to be glad I'm your brother?"

"Don't get excited. I'm glad. I'm glad," he answered. He looked at me in a new light. "It's just that I have to think about it."

I told my father next. I had heard stories of fathers disowning their gay sons, breaking their arms with wrenches, committing them to asylums. But talking to him on the phone one time, I simply let it happen. I had been telling him about an argument I was having with my mother.

"Don't let your mother rule your life," he counseled. "You have to live by your own rules."

"I do live by my own rules, Dad. But I'm not sure you would approve of them either."

"I know what you are," he said to my amazement. "I see how you live." (I had never thought of my pork-chop life as especially exotic, but Greenwich Village spoke for itself in his New Jersey mind.) "And I still say live by your own rules," he finished, "as long as you're not hurting anybody."

What an easy relief. Why hadn't this happened earlier? But I had to be sure we were talking about the same thing. It wouldn't be a genuine coming out if I didn't say the words loud and clear. "I'd rather have you know I'm a homosexual than have to hide it," I asserted. "And you'd know sooner or later anyway, because I've become very active in the gay liberation movement."

"Can't you keep your name a secret?" he asked worriedly. "What about your job? The situation is such, you understand, that you have a lot to lose. Let somebody else do the demonstrating, somebody who doesn't have a career like yours." This was in accord with his general "Don't make waves" school of political apathy.

"There is nobody else," I answered. "It's my struggle. We all have something to lose—and something to gain. Don't worry about me: I'll survive. My self-respect is more important to me than my job anyway."

Remembering my father's admonition awhile later, I was a little nervous when President Birenbaum of Staten Island Community College showed up at an English Department party. I knew I was wearing my lambda button as I went up to greet my boss, but principle came before security. The first thing he said, pointing to the button, was "And what's this?"

"It's a lambda," I replied cavalierly. "It's the symbol of gay liberation. I'm a homosexual, and I'm working in the gay movement."

He looked a little startled, but suppressed it almost before I could notice it. Then he touched my cheek gently with his hand. "Good luck," he said.

Suggestions for Discussion

1. When Kantrowitz came out to friends and family members, what were some of their reactions?

2. How did these various reactions affect Kantrowitz?

3. Why does President Birenbaum wish Kantrowitz "Good luck" at the end of the selection?

Suggestion for Writing

Have you ever had a secret that you felt you needed to reveal to your friends and loved ones, but you feared what their reaction might be? Write an autobiographical story in which you relate the nature of the conflict you faced, and how (or if) it was resolved.

W . E . B .   D U   B O I S

On Being Crazy

William Edward Burghardt Du Bois (1868–1963) was born in Massachusetts. In the course of his life, he became a major influence on American blacks. By 1903 he had written *The Souls of Black Folk,* which stated his major objections to the attitudes found in the writings of Booker T. Washington, the most influential black figure in the early twentieth century. In 1909 Du Bois helped found the National Association for the Advancement of Colored People (NAACP). He edited *Crisis,* the magazine of the NAACP, and also founded the influential quarterly *Phylon* at Atlanta University. In this brief sketch (1907), Du Bois, in a series of conversations, touches ironically on the insanity of the relations between blacks and whites in the early days of the twentieth century.

It was one o'clock and I was hungry. I walked into a restaurant, seated myself, and reached for the bill of fare. My table companion rose.

"Sir," said he, "do you wish to force your company on those who do not want you?"

No, said I, I wish to eat.

"Are you aware, sir, that this is social equality?"

Nothing of the sort, sir, it is hunger—and I ate.

The day's work done, I sought the theatre. As I sank into my seat, the lady shrank and squirmed.

I beg pardon, I said.

"Do you enjoy being where you are not wanted?" she asked coldly.

Oh no, I said.

"Well you are not wanted here."

I was surprised. I fear you are mistaken, I said, I certainly want the music, and I like to think the music wants me to listen to it.

"Usher," said the lady, "this is social equality."

"No, madame," said the usher, "it is the second movement of Beethoven's Fifth Symphony."

After the theatre, I sought the hotel where I had sent my baggage. The clerk scowled.

"What do you want?"

Rest, I said.

"This is a white hotel," he said.

I looked around. Such a color scheme requires a great deal of cleaning, I said, but I don't know that I object.

"We object," said he.

Then why, I began, but he interrupted.

"We don't keep niggers," he said, "we don't want social equality."

Neither do I, I replied gently, I want a bed.

I walked thoughtfully to the train. I'll take a sleeper through Texas. I'm a little bit dissatisfied with this town.

"Can't sell you one."

I only want to hire it, said I, for a couple of nights.

"Can't sell you a sleeper in Texas," he maintained. "They consider that social equality."

I consider it barbarism, I said, and I think I'll walk.

Walking, I met another wayfarer, who immediately walked to the other side of the road, where it was muddy. I asked his reason.

"Niggers is dirty," he said.

So is mud, said I. Moreover, I am not as dirty as you—yet.

"But you're a nigger, ain't you?" he asked.

My grandfather was so called.

"Well then!" he answered triumphantly.

Do you live in the South? I persisted, pleasantly.

"Sure," he growled, "and starve there."

I should think you and the Negroes should get together and vote out starvation.

"We don't let them vote."

We? Why not? I said in surprise.

"Niggers is too ignorant to vote."

But, I said, I am not so ignorant as you.

"But you're a nigger."

Yes, I'm certainly what you mean by that.

"Well then!" he returned, with that curiously inconsequential note of triumph. "Moreover," he said, "I don't want my sister to marry a nigger."

I had not seen his sister, so I merely murmured, let her say no.

"By God, you shan't marry her, even if she said yes."

But—but I don't want to marry her, I answered, a little perturbed at the personal turn.

"Why not!" he yelled, angrier than ever.

Because I'm already married and I rather like my wife.

"Is she a nigger?" he asked suspiciously.

Well, I said again, her grandmother was called that.

"Well then!" he shouted in that oddly illogical way.

I gave up.

Go on, I said, either you are crazy or I am.

"We both are," he said as he trotted along in the mud.

Suggestions for Discussion

1. Why has Du Bois chosen these specific scenes for his conversations with white people?

2. In what way is the final conversation different from those preceding it?

3. Discuss some of the examples of Du Bois's use of irony.

Suggestion for Writing

Write an essay in which you examine the areas of racism dealt with in this selection from today's perspective. What significant differences would you find? What similarities? In what way is "On Being Crazy" relevant for our time?

~~~~~

RICHARD WRIGHT

The Ethics of Living Jim Crow

A major American black writer, Richard Wright (1908–1960) wrote stories, novels, an autobiography, and other books about America's racial problems. His best-known works are *Native Son* (1940), *Black Boy* (1945), and *White Man, Listen* (1957). The following autobiographical account of his education in race relations in a totally segregated South is from *Uncle Tom's Children* (1938).

~

I

My first lesson in how to live as a Negro came when I was quite small. We were living in Arkansas. Our house stood behind the railroad tracks. Its skimpy yard was paved with black cinders. Nothing green ever grew in that yard. The only touch of green we could see was far away, beyond the tracks, over where the white folks lived. But cinders were good enough for me and I never missed the green growing things. And anyhow cinders were fine weapons. You could always have a nice hot war with huge black cinders. All you had to do was crouch behind the brick pillars of a house with your hands full of gritty ammunition. And the first woolly black head you saw pop out from behind another row of pillars was your target. You tried your very best to knock it off. It was great fun.

I never fully realized the appalling disadvantages of a cinder environment till one day the gang to which I belonged found itself engaged in a war with the white boys who lived beyond the tracks. As usual we laid down our cinder barrage, thinking that this would wipe the white boys out. But they replied with a steady bombardment of broken bottles. We doubled our cinder barrage, but they hid behind trees, hedges, and the sloping embankments of their lawns. Having no such fortifications, we retreated to the brick pillars of our homes. During the retreat a broken milk bottle caught me behind the ear, opening a deep gash which bled profusely. The sight of blood pouring over my face completely demoralized our ranks. My fellow-combatants left me standing paralyzed in the center of the yard, and scurried for their homes. A kind neighbor saw me and rushed me to a doctor, who took three stitches in my neck.

I sat brooding on my front steps, nursing my wound and waiting for my mother to come from work. I felt that a grave injustice had been done me. It was all right to throw cinders. The greatest harm a cinder could do was leave a bruise. But broken bottles were dangerous; they left you cut, bleeding, and helpless.

When night fell, my mother came from the white folks' kitchen. I raced down the street to meet her. I could just feel in my bones that she would understand. I knew she would tell me exactly what to do next time. I grabbed her hand and babbled out the whole story. She examined my wound, then slapped me.

"How come yuh didn't hide?" she asked me. "How come yuh awways fightin'?"

I was outraged, and bawled. Between sobs I told her that I didn't have any trees or hedges to hide behind. There wasn't a thing I could have used as a trench. And you couldn't throw very far when you were hiding behind the brick pillars of a house. She grabbed a barrel stave, dragged me home, stripped me naked, and beat me till I had a fever of one hundred and two. She would smack my rump with the stave, and, while the skin was still smarting, impart to me gems of Jim Crow wisdom. I was never to throw cinders any more. I was never to fight any more wars. I was never, never, under any conditions, to fight *white* folks again. And they were absolutely right in clouting me with the broken milk bottle. Didn't I know she was working hard every day in the hot kitchens of the white folks to make money to take care of me? When was I ever going to learn to be a good boy? She couldn't be bothered with my fights. She finished by telling me that I ought to be thankful to God as long as I lived that they didn't kill me.

All that night I was delirious and could not sleep. Each time I closed my eyes I saw monstrous white faces suspended from the ceiling, leering at me.

From that time on, the charm of my cinder yard was gone. The green trees, the trimmed hedges, the cropped lawns grew very meaningful, became a symbol. Even today when I think of white folks, the hard, sharp outlines of white houses surrounded by trees, lawns, and hedges are present somewhere in the background of my mind. Through the years they grew into an overreaching symbol of fear.

It was a long time before I came in close contact with white folks again. We moved from Arkansas to Mississippi. Here we had the good fortune not to live behind the railroad tracks, or close to white neighborhoods. We lived in the very heart of the local Black belt. There were black churches and black preachers; there were black schools and black teachers; black groceries and black clerks. In fact, everything was so solidly black that for a long time I did not even think of white folks, save in remote and vague terms. But this could not last forever. As one grows older one eats more. One's clothing costs more. When I finished grammar school I had to go to work. My mother could no longer feed and clothe me on her cooking job.

There is but one place where a black boy who knows no trade can get a job, and that's where the houses and faces are white, where the trees, lawns, and hedges are green. My first job was with an optical company in Jackson, Mississippi. The morning I applied I stood straight and neat before the boss, answering all his questions with sharp yessirs and nosirs. I was very careful to pronounce my *sirs* distinctly, in order that he might know that I was polite, that I knew where I was, and that I knew he was a *white* man. I wanted that job badly.

He looked me over as though he were examining a prize poodle. He questioned me closely about my schooling, being particularly insistent about how much mathematics I had had. He seemed very pleased when I told him I had had two years of algebra.

"Boy, how would you like to try to learn something around here?" he asked me.

"I'd like it fine, sir," I said, happy. I had visions of "working my way up." Even Negroes have those visions.

"All right," he said. "Come on."

I followed him to the small factory.

"Pease," he said to a white man of about thirty-five, "this is Richard. He's going to work for us."

Pease looked at me and nodded.

I was then taken to a white boy of about seventeen.

"Morrie, this is Richard, who's going to work for us."

"Whut yuh sayin' there, boy!" Morrie boomed at me.

"Fine!" I answered.

The boss instructed these two to help me, teach me, give me jobs to do, and let me learn what I could in my spare time.

My wages were five dollars a week.

I worked hard, trying to please. For the first month I got along O.K. Both Pease and Morrie seemed to like me. But one thing was missing. And I kept thinking about it. I was not learning anything and nobody was volunteering to help me. Thinking they had forgotten that I was to learn something about the mechanics of grinding lenses, I asked Morrie one day to tell me about the work. He grew red.

"Whut yuh tryin' t' do, nigger, get smart?" he asked.

"Naw; I ain't tryin t' git smart," I said.

"Well, don't, if yuh know whut's good for yuh!"

I was puzzled. Maybe he just doesn't want to help me, I thought. I went to Pease.

"Say, are yuh crazy, you black bastard?" Pease asked me, his gray eyes growing hard.

I spoke out, reminding him that the boss had said I was to be given a chance to learn something.

"Nigger, you think you're *white*, don't you?"

"Naw, sir!"

"Well, you're acting mighty like it!"

"But, Mr. Pease, the boss said…"

Pease shook his fist in my face.

"This is a *white* man's work around here, and you better watch yourself!"

From then on they changed toward me. They said good-morning no more. When I was just a bit slow in performing some duty, I was called a lazy black son-of-a-bitch.

Once I thought of reporting all this to the boss. But the mere idea of what would happen to me if Pease and Morrie should learn that I had "snitched" stopped me. And after all the boss was a white man, too. What was the use?

The climax came at noon one summer day. Pease called me to his workbench. To get to him I had to go between two narrow benches and stand with my back against a wall.

"Yes, sir," I said.

"Richard, I want to ask you something," Pease began pleasantly, not looking up from his work.

"Yes, sir," I said again.

Morrie came over, blocking the narrow passage between the benches. He folded his arms, staring at me solemnly.

I looked from one to the other, sensing that something was coming.

"Yes, sir," I said for the third time.

Pease looked up and spoke very slowly.

"Richard, *Mr.* Morrie here tells me you called me *Pease.*"

I stiffened. A void seemed to open up in me. I knew this was the showdown.

He meant that I had failed to call him Mr. Pease. I looked at Morrie. He was gripping a steel bar in his hands. I opened my mouth to speak, to protest, to assure Pease that I had never called him simply *Pease,* and that I had never had any intentions of doing so, when Morrie grabbed me by the collar, ramming my head against the wall.

"Now, be careful, nigger!" snarled Morrie, baring his teeth. "*I* heard yuh call 'im *Pease!*" 'N' if yuh say yuh didn't yuh're callin' me a *lie,* see?" He waved the steel bar threateningly.

If I had said: No, sir, Mr. Pease, I never called you *Pease,* I would have been automatically calling Morrie a liar. And if I had said: Yes, sir, Mr. Pease, I called you *Pease,* I would have been pleading guilty to having uttered the worst insult that a Negro can utter to a southern white man. I stood hesitating, trying to frame a neutral reply.

"Richard, I asked you a question!" said Pease. Anger was creeping into his voice.

"I don't remember calling you *Pease,* Mr. Pease," I said cautiously. "And if I did, I sure didn't mean…"

"You black son-of-a-bitch! You called me *Pease,* then!" he spat, slapping me till I bent sideways over a bench. Morrie was on top of me, demanding:

"Didn't yuh call 'im *Pease*? If yuh say yuh didn't, I'll rip yo' gut string loose with this bar, yuh black granny dodger! Yuh can't call a white man a liar 'n' git erway with it, you black son-of-a-bitch!"

I wilted. I begged them not to bother me. I knew what they wanted. They wanted me to leave.

"I'll leave," I promised. "I'll leave right *now.*"

They gave me a minute to get out of the factory. I was warned not to show up again, or tell the boss.

I went.

When I told the folks at home what had happened, they called me a fool. They told me that I must never again attempt to exceed my boundaries. When you are working for white folks, they said, you got to "stay in your place" if you want to keep working.

∾

II

My Jim Crow education continued on my next job, which was portering in a clothing store. One morning, while polishing brass out front, the boss and his twenty-year-old son got out of their car and half dragged and half kicked a Negro woman into the store. A policeman standing at the corner looked on, twirling his night-stick. I watched out of the corner of my eye, never slackening the strokes of my chamois upon the brass. After a few minutes, I heard shrill screams coming from the rear of the store. Later the woman stumbled out, bleeding, crying, and holding her stomach. When she reached the end of the block, the policeman grabbed her and accused her of being drunk. Silently, I watched him throw her into a patrol wagon.

When I went to the rear of the store, the boss and his son were washing their hands at the sink. They were chuckling. The floor was bloody and strewn with wisps of hair and clothing. No doubt I must have appeared pretty shocked, for the boss slapped me reassuringly on the back.

"Boy, that's what we do to niggers when they don't want to pay their bills," he said, laughing.

His son looked at me and grinned.

"Here, hava cigarette," he said.

Not knowing what to do, I took it. He lit his and held the match for me. This was a gesture of kindness, indicating that even if they had beaten the poor old woman, they would not beat me if I knew enough to keep my mouth shut.

"Yes, sir," I said, and asked no questions.

After they had gone, I sat on the edge of a packing box and stared at the bloody floor till the cigarette went out.

That day at noon, while eating in a hamburger joint, I told my fellow Negro porters what had happened. No one seemed surprised. One fellow, after swallowing a huge bite, turned to me and asked:

"Huh! Is tha' all they did t' her?"

"Yeah. Wasn't tha' enough?" I asked.

"Shucks! Man, she's a lucky bitch!" he said, burying his lips deep into a juicy hamburger. "Hell, it's a wonder they didn't lay her when they got through."

❧

III

I was learning fast, but not quite fast enough. One day, while I was delivering packages in the suburbs, my bicycle tire was punctured. I walked along the hot, dusty road, sweating and leading my bicycle by the handlebars.

A car slowed at my side.

"What's the matter, boy?" a white man called.

I told him my bicycle was broken and I was walking back to town.

"That's too bad," he said. "Hop on the running board."

He stopped the car. I clutched hard at my bicycle with one hand and clung to the side of the car with the other.

"All set?"

"Yes, sir," I answered. The car started.

It was full of young white men. They were drinking. I watched the flask pass from mouth to mouth.

"Wanna drink, boy?" one asked.

I laughed as the wind whipped my face. Instinctively obeying the freshly planted precepts of my mother, I said:

"Oh, no!"

The words were hardly out of my mouth before I felt something hard and cold smash me between the eyes. It was an empty whisky bottle. I saw stars, and fell backwards from the speeding car into the dust of the road, my feet becoming entangled in the steel spokes of my bicycle. The white men piled out and stood over me.

"Nigger, ain' yuh learned no better sense'n tha' yet?" asked the man who hit me. "Ain' yuh learned t' say *sir* t' a white man yet?"

Dazed, I was pulled to my feet. My elbows and legs were bleeding. Fists doubled, the white man advanced, kicking my bicycle out of the way.

"Aw, leave the bastard alone. He's got enough," said one.

They stood looking at me. I rubbed my shins, trying to stop the flow of blood. No doubt they felt a sort of contemptuous pity, for one asked:

"Yuh wanna ride t' town now, nigger? Yuh reckon yuh know enough t' ride now?"

"I wanna walk," I said, simply.

Maybe it sounded funny. They laughed.

"Well, walk, yuh black son-of-a-bitch!"

When they left they comforted me with:

"Nigger, yuh sho better be damn glad it wuz us yuh talked t' tha' way. Yuh're a lucky bastard, 'cause if yuh'd said tha' t' somebody else, yuh might've been a dead nigger now."

∽

IV

Negroes who had lived in the South know the dread of being caught alone upon the streets in white neighborhoods after the sun has set. In such a simple situation as this the plight of the Negro in America is graphically symbolized. While white strangers may be in these neighborhoods trying to get home, they can pass unmolested. But the color of a Negro's skin makes him easily recognizable, makes him suspect, converts him into a defenseless target.

Late one Saturday night I made some deliveries in a white neighborhood. I was pedaling my bicycle back to the store as fast as I could, when a police car, swerving toward me, jammed me into the curbing.

"Get down and put up your hands!" the policemen ordered.

I did. They climbed out of the car, guns drawn, faces set, and advanced slowly.

"Keep still!" they ordered.

I reached my hands higher. They searched my pockets and packages. They seemed dissatisfied when they could find nothing incriminating. Finally, one of them said:

"Boy, tell your boss not to send you out in white neighborhoods after sundown."

As usual, I said:

"Yes, sir."

∾

V

My next job was a hall-boy in a hotel. Here my Jim Crow education broadened and deepened. When the bell-boys were busy, I was often called to assist them. As many of the rooms in the hotel were occupied by prostitutes, I was constantly called to carry them liquor and cigarettes. These women were nude most of the time. They did not bother about clothing, even for bell-boys. When you went into their rooms, you were supposed to take their nakedness for granted, as though it startled you no more than a blue vase or a red rug. Your presence awoke in them no sense of shame, for you were not regarded as human. If they were alone, you could steal sidelong glimpses at them. But if they were receiving men, not a flicker of your eyelids could show. I remember one incident vividly. A new woman, a huge, snowy-skinned blonde, took a room on my floor. I was sent to wait upon her. She was in bed with a thick-set man; both were nude and uncovered. She said she wanted some liquor and slid out of bed and waddled across the floor to get her money from a dresser drawer. I watched her.

"Nigger, what in hell you looking at?" the white man asked me, raising himself upon his elbows.

"Nothing," I answered, looking miles deep into the blank wall of the room.

"Keep your eyes where they belong, if you want to be healthy!" he said.
"Yes, sir."

∾

VI

One of the bell-boys I knew in this hotel was keeping steady company with one of the Negro maids. Out of a clear sky the police descended upon his home and arrested him, accusing him of bastardy. The poor boy swore he had had no intimate relations with the girl. Nevertheless, they forced him to marry her. When the child arrived, it was found to be much lighter in complexion than either of the two supposedly legal parents. The white men around the hotel made a great joke of it. They spread the rumor that some white cow must have scared the poor girl while she was carrying the baby. If you were in their presence when this explanation was offered, you were supposed to laugh.

⌒

VII

One of the bell-boys was caught in bed with a white prostitute. He was castrated and run out of town. Immediately after this all the bell-boys and hall-boys were called together and warned. We were given to understand that the boy who had been castrated was a "mighty, mighty lucky bastard." We were impressed with the fact that next time the management of the hotel would not be responsible for the lives of "trouble-makin' niggers." We were silent.

⌒

VIII

One night, just as I was about to go home, I met one of the Negro maids. She lived in my direction, and we fell in to walk part of the way home together. As we passed the white night-watchman, he slapped the maid on her buttock. I turned around, amazed. The watchman looked at me with a long, hard, fixed-under stare. Suddenly he pulled his gun and asked:

"Nigger, don't yuh like it?"

I hesitated.

"I asked yuh don't yuh like it?" he asked again, stepping forward.

"Yes, sir," I mumbled.

"Talk like it, then!"

"Oh, yes, sir!" I said with as much heartiness as I could muster.

Outside, I walked ahead of the girl, ashamed to face her. She caught up with me and said:

"Don't be a fool! Yuh couldn't help it!"

This watchman boasted of having killed two Negroes in self-defense.

Yet, in spite of all this, the life of the hotel ran with an amazing smoothness. It would have been impossible for a stranger to detect anything. The maids, the hall-boys, and the bell-boys were all smiles. They had to be.

∾

IX

I had learned my Jim Crow lessons so thoroughly that I kept the hotel job till I left Jackson for Memphis. It so happened that while in Memphis I applied for a job at a branch of the optical company. I was hired. And for some reason, as long as I worked there, they never brought my past against me.

Here my Jim Crow education assumed quite a different form. It was no longer brutally cruel, but subtly cruel. Here I learned to lie, to steal, to dissemble. I learned to play that dual role which every Negro must play if he wants to eat and live.

For example, it was almost impossible to get a book to read. It was assumed that after a Negro had imbibed what scanty schooling the state furnished he had no further need for books. I was always borrowing books from men on the job. One day I mustered enough courage to ask one of the men to let me get books from the library in his name. Surprisingly, he consented. I cannot help but think that he consented because he was a Roman Catholic and felt a vague sympathy for Negroes, being himself an object of hatred. Armed with a library card, I obtained books in the following manner: I would write a note to the librarian, saying: "Please let this nigger boy have the following books." I would then sign it with the white man's name.

When I went to the library, I would stand at the desk, hat in hand, looking as unbookish as possible. When I received the books desired I would take them home. If the books listed in the note happened to be out, I would sneak into the lobby and forge a new one. I never took any chances guessing with the white librarian about what the fictitious white man would want to read. No doubt if any of the white patrons had suspected that some of the volumes they enjoyed had been in the home of a Negro, they would not have tolerated it for an instant.

The factory force of the optical company in Memphis was much larger than that in Jackson, and more urbanized. At least they liked to talk, and would engage the Negro help in conversation whenever possible. By this means I found that many subjects were taboo from the white man's point of view. Among the topics they did not like to discuss with Negroes were the following: American white women; the Ku Klux Klan; France, and how Negro soldiers fared while there; French women; Jack Johnson; the entire northern part of the United States; the Civil War; Abraham Lincoln; U. S. Grant; General Sherman; Catholics; the Pope; Jews; the Republican Party; slavery; social equality; Communism; Socialism; the 13th and 14th Amendments to the Constitution; or any topic calling for positive knowledge or manly self-assertion on the part of the Negro. The most accepted topics were sex and religion.

There were many times when I had to exercise a great deal of ingenuity to keep out of trouble. It is a southern custom that all men must take off their hats when they enter an elevator. And especially did this apply to us blacks with rigid force. One day I stepped into an elevator with my arms full of packages. I was forced to ride with my hat on. Two white men stared at me coldly. Then one of them very kindly lifted my hat and placed it upon my armful of packages. Now the most accepted response for a Negro to make under such circumstances is to look at the white man out of the corner of his eye and grin. To have said: "Thank you!" would have made the white man *think* that you *thought* you were receiving from him a personal service. For such an act I have seen Negroes take a blow in the mouth. Finding the first alternative distasteful, and the second dangerous, I hit upon an acceptable course of action which fell safely between these two poles. I immediately—no sooner than my hat was lifted—pretended that my packages were about to spill, and appeared deeply distressed with keeping them in my arms. In this fashion I evaded having to acknowledge his service, and, in spite of adverse circumstances, salvaged a slender shred of personal pride.

How do Negroes feel about the way they have to live? How do they discuss it when alone among themselves? I think this question can be answered in a single sentence. A friend of mine who ran an elevator once told me:

"Lawd, man! Ef it wuzn't fer them polices 'n' them ol' lynch-mobs, there wouldn't be nothin' but uproar down here!"

Suggestions for Discussion

1. Analyze Wright's sketch in terms of (a) structure, (b) progression and unity in nine segments, (c) expository-narrative style, and/or (d) themes.

2. How does Wright's title contribute to the development of the major themes of the sketch? Why does he use *ethics* and *living*?

3. Discuss his use of personal experiences to illustrate his themes.

4. Discuss his use of violence in the sketch. Is it believable? Significant? Explain.

Suggestions for Writing

1. Analyze the motivation behind an incident of discrimination that you have observed or experienced.

2. Analyze the dramatic irony in the last line and its climactic effect as the final comment on the whole sketch.

ESSAYS

THOMAS JEFFERSON

The Declaration of Independence

The Continental Congress, assembled in Philadelphia in 1776, delegated to Thomas Jefferson (1743–1826) the task of writing a declaration of independence from Great Britain, which the Congress amended and adopted on July 4 of that year. In its theory as well as in its style, the Declaration of Independence is a typical eighteenth-century view of man's place in society, which included the right to overthrow a tyrannical ruler. After the Revolution, Jefferson was elected governor of Virginia and, in 1801, he was elected the third president of the United States. He was the father of what became known as "Jeffersonian democracy," which exceeded the democracy then advocated by either George Washington or Jefferson's rival, Alexander Hamilton. After leaving the presidency, he founded the University of Virginia as a place where truth could assert itself in free competition with other ideas.

When in the course of human events, it becomes necessary for one people to dissolve the political bands which have connected them with another, and to assume among the powers of the earth, the separate and equal station to which the Laws of Nature and of Nature's God entitle them, a decent respect to the opinions of mankind requires that they should declare the causes which impel them to the separation.

We hold these truths to be self-evident, that all men are created equal, that they are endowed by their Creator with certain inalienable rights, that among these are life, liberty, and the pursuit of happiness. That to secure these rights, governments are instituted among men, deriving their just powers from the consent of the governed. That whenever any form of government becomes destructive of these ends, it is the right of the people to alter or to abolish it, and to institute new government, laying its foundation on such principles and organizing its powers in such form, as to them shall seem most likely to effect their safety and happiness. Prudence, indeed, will dictate that governments long established should not be changed for light and transient causes; and accordingly all experience hath shown, that mankind are more disposed to suffer, while evils are sufferable, than to right themselves by abolishing the forms to which they are accustomed. But when a long train of abuses and usurpations, pursuing invariably the same object, evinces a design to reduce them under absolute despotism, it is their right, it is their duty, to throw off such government, and to provide new guards for their future security. Such has been the patient sufferance of these Colonies; and such is now the necessity which constrains them to alter their former systems of government. The history of the present King of Great Britain is a history of repeated injuries and usurpations, all having in direct object the establishment of an absolute tyranny over these States. To prove this, let facts be submitted to a candid world.

He has refused his assent to laws, the most wholesome and necessary for the public good.

He has forbidden his Governors to pass laws of immediate and pressing importance, unless suspended in their operation till his assent should be obtained; and when so suspended, he has utterly neglected to attend to them.

He has refused to pass other laws for the accommodation of large districts of people, unless those people would relinquish the right of representation in the legislature, a right inestimable to them and formidable to tyrants only.

He has called together legislative bodies at places unusual, uncomfortable, and distant from the depository of their public records, for the sole purpose of fatiguing them into compliance with his measures.

He has dissolved representative houses repeatedly, for opposing with manly firmness his invasions on the rights of the people.

He has refused for a long time, after such dissolutions, to cause others to be elected; whereby the legislative powers, incapable of annihilation, have returned to the people at large for their exercise; the State remaining in the meantime exposed to all the dangers of invasion from without and convulsions within.

He has endeavoured to prevent the population of these states; for that purpose obstructing the laws for naturalization of foreigners; refusing to pass others to encourage their migration hither, and raising the conditions of new appropriations of lands.

He has obstructed the administration of justice, by refusing his assent to laws for establishing judiciary powers.

He has made judges dependent on his will alone, for the tenure of their offices, and the amount and payment of their salaries.

He has erected a multitude of new offices, and sent hither swarms of officers to harass our people, and eat out their substance.

He has kept among us, in times of peace, standing armies without the consent of our legislatures.

He has affected to render the military independent of and superior to the civil power.

He has combined with others to subject us to a jurisdiction foreign of our constitution, and unacknowledged by our laws; giving his assent to their acts of pretended legislation:

For quartering large bodies of armed troops among us:

For protecting them, by a mock trial, from punishment for any murders which they should commit on the inhabitants of these States:

For cutting off our trade with all parts of the world:

For imposing taxes on us without our consent:

For depriving us in many cases of the benefits of trial by jury:

For transporting us beyond seas to be tried for pretended offences:

For abolishing the free system of English laws in a neighbouring Province, establishing therein an arbitrary government, and enlarging its boundaries so as to render it at once an example and fit instrument for introducing the same absolute rule into these Colonies:

For taking away our Charters, abolishing our most valuable laws, and altering fundamentally the forms of our governments:

For suspending our own legislatures, and declaring themselves invested with power to legislate for us in all cases whatsoever.

He has abdicated government here, by declaring us out of his protection and waging war against us.

He has plundered our seas, ravaged our coasts, burnt our towns, and destroyed the lives of our people.

He is at this time transporting large armies of foreign mercenaries to complete the works of death, desolation, and tyranny, already begun with circumstances of cruelty and perfidy scarcely paralleled in the most barbarous ages, and totally unworthy the head of a civilized nation.

He has constrained our fellow citizens taken captive on the high seas to bear arms against their country, to become the executioners of their friends and brethren, or to fall themselves by their hands.

He has excited domestic insurrections amongst us, and has endeavoured to bring on the inhabitants of our frontiers, the merciless Indian savages, whose known rule of warfare, is an undistinguished destruction of all ages, sexes, and conditions.

In every stage of these oppressions we have petitioned for redress in the most humble terms: our repeated petitions have been answered only by repeated injury. A prince whose character is thus marked by every act which may define a tyrant is unfit to be the ruler of a free people.

Nor have we been wanting in attention to our British brethren. We have warned them from time to time of attempts by their legislature to extend an unwarrantable jurisdiction over us. We have reminded them of the circumstances of our emigration and settlement here. We have appealed to their native justice and magnanimity, and we have conjured them by the ties of our common kindred to disavow these usurpations, which would inevitably interrupt our connections and correspondence. They too have been deaf to the voice of justice and of consanguinity. We must, therefore, acquiesce in the necessity, which denounces our separation, and hold them, as we hold the rest of mankind, enemies in war, in peace friends.

We, therefore, the Representatives of the United States of America, in General Congress assembled, appealing to the Supreme Judge of the world for the rectitude of our intentions, do, in the name, and by authority of the good people of these Colonies, solemnly publish and declare, That these United Colonies are, and of right ought to be, Free and Independent States; that they are absolved from all allegiance to the British Crown, and that all political connection between them and the state of Great Britain, is and ought to be totally dissolved; and that as Free and Independent States, they have full power to levy war, conclude peace, contract alliances, establish commerce, and to do all other acts and things which Independent States may of right do. And for the support of this declaration, with a firm reliance on the protection of Divine Providence, we mutually pledge to each other our lives, our fortunes, and our sacred honor.

Suggestions for Discussion

1. What is the basis for Jefferson's belief that "all men are created equal"?

2. In the eighteenth century, the notion of the "divine right" of kings was still popular. How does Jefferson refute that notion?

3. Discuss the list of tyrannical actions that Jefferson attributes to the King of Great Britain. Account for the order in which he lists them.

4. This essay has been called a "model of clarity and precision." Explain your agreement with this statement. How does Jefferson balance strong feeling with logical argument?

Suggestion for Writing

Jefferson asserts that "all men are created equal," and yet he does not include black slaves as equals. In Jefferson's *Autobiography*, he wrote that a clause "reprobating the enslaving the inhabitants of Africa" was omitted in the final draft "in complaisance to South Carolina and Georgia." Was Jefferson merely opportunistic in agreeing to strike this clause? Write an essay in which you relate the ideas of the Declaration to the ideas in Lincoln's Gettysburg Address (see p. 607). Show how one set of ideas leads to the other.

The Declaration of the Rights of Man

Soon after the fall of the Bastille on July 14, 1789, a day celebrated in France as July 4th is celebrated in the United States, the French National Assembly was asked to provide a declaration that would correspond to the American Declaration of Independence. The Assembly appointed a committee of five to draft the document. After several weeks of debate and compromise, the completed declaration was approved and proclaimed on August 27, 1789. Although a number of phrases resemble the American model, the Declaration of the Rights of Man is derived more particularly from the English Bill of Rights of 1689. Ironically, the basis for democratic government embodied in this document was to be subverted by a leader of the new republic who would declare himself Emperor. This leader was Napoléon Bonaparte, and he ruled from 1804 until 1815.

The representatives of the French people, gathered in the National Assembly, believing that ignorance, neglect, and disdain of the rights of men are the sole causes of public misfortunes and of the corruption of governments, have resolved to set forth, in solemn declaration, the natural, inalienable, and sacred rights of men, in order that this Declaration, held always before the members of the body social, will forever remind them of their rights and duties; that the acts of legislative and executive power, always identifiable with the ends and purposes of the whole body politic, may be more fully respected; that the complaints of citizens, founded henceforth on simple and incontrovertible principles, may be turned always to the maintaining of the Constitution and to the happiness of all.

The National assembly therefore recognizes and declares, in the presence and under the auspices of the Supreme Being, the following rights of Man and of citizen:

1. Men are born and will remain free and endowed with equal rights. Social distinctions can be based only upon usefulness to the common weal.

2. The end and purpose of all political groups is the preservation of the natural and inalienable rights of Man. These rights are Liberty, the Possession of Property, Safety, and Resistance to Oppression.

3. The principle of all sovereignty will remain fundamentally in the State. No group and no individual can exercise authority which does not arise expressly from the State.

4. Liberty consists in being able to do anything which is not harmful to another or to others; therefore, the exercise of the natural rights

of each individual has only such limits as will assure to other members of society the enjoyment of the same rights. These limits can be determined only by the Law.

5. The Law has the right to forbid only such actions as are harmful to society. Anything not forbidden by the Law can never be forbidden; and none can be forced to do what the Law does not prescribe.

6. The Law is the expression of the will of the people. All citizens have the right and the duty to concur in the formation of the Law, either in person or through their representatives. Whether it punishes or whether it protects, the Law must be the same for all. All citizens, being equal in the eyes of the Law, are to be admitted equally to all distinctions, ranks, and public employment, according to their capacities, and without any other discrimination than that established by their individual abilities and virtues.

7. No individual can be accused, arrested, or detained except in cases determined by the Law, and according to the forms which the Law has prescribed. Those who instigate, expedite, execute, or cause to be executed any arbitrary or extralegal prescriptions must be punished; but every citizen called or seized through the power of the Law must instantly obey. He will render himself culpable by resisting.

8. The Law should establish only those penalties which are absolutely and evidently necessary, and none can be punished except through the power of the Law, as already established and proclaimed for the public good and legally applied.

9. Every individual being presumed innocent until he has been proved guilty, if it is considered necessary to arrest him, the Law must repress with severity any force which is not required to secure his person.

10. None is to be persecuted for his opinions, even his religious beliefs, provided that his expression of them does not interfere with the order established by the Law.

11. Free communication of thought and opinion is one of the most precious rights of Man; therefore, every citizen can speak, write, or publish freely, except that he will be required to answer for the abuse of such freedom in cases determined by the Law.

12. The guarantee of the rights of Man and of the citizen makes necessary a Public Force and Administration; this Force and Administration has therefore been established for the good of all, and not for the particular benefit of those to whom it has been entrusted.

13. For the maintaining of this Public Force and Administration, and for the expense of administering it, a common tax is required; it must be distributed equally among the people, in accordance with their ability to pay.

14. All citizens have the right and duty to establish, by themselves or by their representatives, the requirements of a common tax, to consent to it

freely, to indicate its use, and to determine its quota, its assessment, its collection, and its duration.

15. Society has the right and duty to demand from every public servant an accounting of his administration.

16. No society in which the guarantee of rights is not assured nor the distinction of legal powers determined can be said to have a constitution.

17. The possession of property being an inviolable and sacred right, none can be deprived of it, unless public necessity, legally proved, clearly requires the deprivation, and then only on the necessary condition of a previously established just reparation.

Suggestions for Discussion

1. What is the major purpose of setting forth the principles enunciated in this declaration?

2. The declaration refers to a "Supreme Being." Why did not the writers of the declaration refer simply to God?

3. How do the seventeen "rights of Man and of citizen" define the relationship between the individual person and the state?

4. How does the declaration define the function of the law and of the state?

5. How does the declaration propose to guarantee freedom of speech?

6. Can you explain why the declaration says that the possession of property is an "inviolable and sacred right"? How does this statement basically differ from modern revolutionary thought?

7. On what principles is this declaration based?

Suggestions for Writing

1. Write an essay about the similarities and differences between this declaration and both the United States Declaration of Independence and the Bill of Rights of the United States Constitution.

2. Examine the English Bill of Rights of 1689 and write an essay in which you explain the close relationship between the French and English declarations.

ELIZABETH CADY STANTON AND LUCRETIA COFFIN MOTT

Seneca Falls Convention

On July 19–20, 1848, around two hundred delegates (women and men) representing suffragist, abolitionist, and temperance groups met in Seneca Falls, NY, at a convention to discuss women's rights. The Declaration of Sentiments and Resolutions was written by Elizabeth Cady Stanton and Lucretia Coffin Mott, assisted by the delegates present. The first major document that sought to define the issues and goals of the nineteenth-century women's movement, it was modeled after the Declaration of Independence to suggest the natural line of development from the American Revolution. Consequently, it stated women's demands for legal, political, economic, and social equality. The only resolution that created an objection was the one on women's suffrage, but after debate it too was included. Sixty-eight women and thirty-two men signed the declaration.

When, in the course of human events, it becomes necessary for one portion of the family of man to assume among the people of the earth a position different from that which they have hitherto occupied, but one to which the laws of nature and of nature's God entitle them, a decent respect to the opinions of mankind requires that they should declare the causes that impel them to such a course.

We hold these truths to be self-evident: that all men and women are created equal; that they are endowed by their Creator with certain inalienable rights; that among these are life, liberty, and the pursuit of happiness; that to secure these rights governments are instituted, deriving their just powers from the consent of the governed. Whenever any form of government becomes destructive of these ends, it is the right of those who suffer from it to refuse allegiance to it, and to insist upon the institution of a new government, laying its foundation on such principles, and organizing its powers in such form, as to them shall seem most likely to effect their safety and happiness. Prudence, indeed, will dictate that governments long established should not be changed for light and transient

Taking Liberty, Homeland Security, 2002, Patricia S. Levey, 2002. Copyright Patricia Levey. Courtesy of Photo-Eye Gallery, Santa Fe, NM.

causes; and accordingly all experience hath shown that mankind are more disposed to suffer, while evils are sufferable, than to right themselves by abolishing the forms to which they were accustomed. But when a long train of abuses and usurpations, pursuing invariably the same object, evinces a design to reduce them under absolute despotism, it is their duty to throw off such government, and to provide new guards for their future security. Such has been the patient sufferance of the women under this government, and such is now the necessity which constrains them to demand the equal station to which they are entitled.

The history of mankind is a history of repeated injuries and usurpations on the part of man toward woman, having in direct object the establishment of an absolute tyranny over her. To prove this, let facts be submitted to a candid world.

He has never permitted her to exercise her inalienable right to the elective franchise.

He has compelled her to submit to laws, in the formation of which she had no voice.

He has withheld from her rights which are given to the most ignorant and degraded men—both natives and foreigners.

Having deprived her of this first right of a citizen, the elective franchise, thereby leaving her without representation in the halls of legislation, he has oppressed her on all sides.

He has made her, if married, in the eye of the law, civilly dead.

He has taken from her all right in property, even to the wages she earns.

He has made her, morally, an irresponsible being, as she can commit many crimes with impunity, provided they be done in the presence of her husband. In the covenant of marriage, she is compelled to promise obedience to her husband, he becoming to all intents and purposes, her master—the law giving him power to deprive her of her liberty, and to administer chastisement.

He has so framed the laws of divorce, as to what shall be the proper causes, and in case of separation, to whom the guardianship of the children shall be given, as to be wholly regardless of the happiness of women—the law, in all cases, going upon a false supposition of the supremacy of man, and giving all power into his hands.

After depriving her of all rights as a married woman, if single, and the owner of property, he has taxed her to support a government which recognizes her only when her property can be made profitable to it.

He has monopolized nearly all the profitable employments, and from those she is permitted to follow, she receives but a scanty remuneration. He closes against her all the avenues to wealth and distinction which he considers most honorable to himself. As a teacher of theology, medicine, or law, she is not known.

He has denied her the facilities for obtaining a thorough education, all colleges being closed against her.

He allows her in Church, as well as State, but a subordinate position, claiming Apostolic authority for her exclusion from the ministry, and, with some exceptions, from any public participation in the affairs of the Church.

He has created a false public sentiment by giving to the world a different code of morals for men and women, by which moral delinquencies which exclude women from society, are not only tolerated, but deemed of little account in man.

He has usurped the prerogative of Jehovah himself, claiming it as his right to assign for her a sphere of action, when that belongs to her conscience and to her God.

He has endeavored, in every way that he could, to destroy her confidence in her own powers, to lessen her self-respect, and to make her willing to lead a dependent and abject life.

Now, in view of this entire disfranchisement of one-half the people of this country, their social and religious degradation—in view of the unjust laws above mentioned, and because women do feel themselves aggrieved, oppressed, and fraudulently deprived of their most sacred rights, we insist that they have immediate admission to all the rights and privileges which belong to them as citizens of the United States.

In entering upon the great work before us, we anticipate no small amount of misconception, misrepresentation, and ridicule; but we shall use every instrumentality within our power to effect our object. We shall employ agents, circulate tracts, petition the State and National legislatures, and endeavor to enlist the pulpit and the press in our behalf. We hope this Convention will be followed by a series of Conventions embracing every part of the country.

Whereas, The great precept of nature is conceded to be, that "man shall pursue his own true and substantial happiness." Blackstone in his Commentaries remarks, that this law of Nature being coeval with mankind, and dictated by God himself, is of course superior in obligation to any other. It is binding over all the globe, in all countries and at all times; no human laws are of any validity if contrary to this, and such of them as are valid, derive all their force, and all their validity, and all their authority, mediately and immediately, from this original; therefore,

Resolved, That such laws as conflict, in any way, with the true and substantial happiness of woman, are contrary to the great precept of nature and of no validity, for this is "superior in obligation to any other."

Resolved, That all laws which prevent woman from occupying such a station in society as her conscience shall dictate, or which place her in a position inferior to that of man, are contrary to the great precept of nature, and therefore of no force or authority.

Resolved, That woman is man's equal—was intended to be so by the Creator, and the highest good of the race demands that she should be recognized as such.

Resolved, That the women of this country ought to be enlightened in regard to the laws under which they live, that they may no longer publish their degradation by declaring themselves satisfied with their present position, nor their ignorance, by asserting that they have all the rights they want.

Resolved, That inasmuch as man, while claiming for himself intellectual superiority, does accord to woman moral superiority, it is pre-eminently his duty to encourage her to speak and teach, as she has an opportunity, in all religious assemblies.

Resolved, That the same amount of virtue, delicacy, and refinement of behavior that is required of woman in the social state, should also be required of man, and the same transgressions should be visited with equal severity on both man and woman.

Resolved, That the objection of indelicacy and impropriety, which is so often brought against woman when she addresses a public audience, comes with a very ill-grace from those who encourage, by their attendance, her appearance on the stage, in the concert, or in feats of the circus.

Resolved, That woman has too long rested satisfied in the circumscribed limits which corrupt customs and a perverted application of the Scriptures have marked out for her, and that it is time she should move in the enlarged sphere which her great Creator has assigned her.

Resolved, That it is the duty of the women of this country to secure to themselves their sacred right to the elective franchise.

Resolved, That the equality of human rights results necessarily from the fact of the identity of the race in capabilities and responsibilities.

Resolved, therefore, That, being invested by the Creator with the same capabilities, and the same consciousness of responsibility for their exercise, it is demonstrably the right and duty of woman, equally with man, to promote every righteous cause by every righteous means; and especially in regard to the great subjects of morals and religion, it is self-evidently her right to participate with her brother in teaching them, both in private and in public, by writing and by speaking, by any instrumentalities proper to be used, and in any assemblies proper to be held; and this being a self-evident truth growing out of the divinely implanted principles of human nature, any custom or authority adverse to it, whether modern or wearing the hoary sanction of antiquity, is to be regarded as a self-evident falsehood, and at war with mankind.

Resolved, That the speedy success of our cause depends upon the zealous and untiring efforts of both men and women, for the overthrow of the monopoly of the pulpit, and for the securing to woman an equal participation with men in the various trades, professions, and commerce.

Suggestions for Discussion

1. Compare the Declaration of Independence with the Seneca Falls Declaration and discuss their parallel structure. Note particularly the basis, the "whereas" statement, for the resolutions that follow.

2. Examine and discuss the preliminary list of grievances that lead to the need for the resolutions.

3. How might a contemporary declaration on the rights of women differ from this one? What other resolutions might appear at a similar convention today?

4. Why was there objection to women's suffrage?

5. The convention was attended by abolitionists and members of the temperance movement. How were these causes compatible with a convention on women's rights?

Suggestions for Writing

1. Write a paper comparing the Declaration of Independence with the Seneca Falls Declaration. What was missing from the first of these declarations?

2. Write a paper in which you discuss how a contemporary convention might stress different grievances. Be specific. Try to write some contemporary resolutions.

ABRAHAM LINCOLN

The Gettysburg Address

Abraham Lincoln (1809–1865), the sixteenth president of the United States, is generally regarded, along with Thomas Jefferson, to be one of the greatest American prose stylists. On November 19, 1863, he traveled to Gettysburg in southern Pennsylvania to dedicate the cemetery for the soldiers killed there the previous July. The simple words he composed form the most famous speech ever delivered in America. A close reading reveals why it continues to hold meaning for Americans today.

Four score and seven years ago our fathers brought forth on this continent, a new nation, conceived in Liberty, and dedicated to the proposition that all men are created equal.

Now we are engaged in a great civil war, testing whether that nation, or any nation so conceived and so dedicated, can long endure. We are met on a great battlefield of that war. We have come to dedicate a portion of that field, as a final resting place for those who here gave their lives that that nation might live. It is altogether fitting and proper that we should do this.

But, in a larger sense, we can not dedicate—we can not consecrate—we can not hallow—this ground. The brave men, living and dead, who struggled here, have consecrated it, far above our poor power to add or detract. The world will little note nor long remember what we say here, but it can never forget what they did here. It is for us the living, rather, to be dedicated here to the unfinished work which they who fought here have thus far so nobly advanced. It is rather for us to be here dedicated to the great task remaining before us—that from these honored dead we take increased devotion to that cause for which they gave the last full measure of devotion—that we here highly resolve that these dead shall not have died in vain—that this nation, under God, shall have a new birth of freedom—and that government of the people, by the people, for the people, shall not perish from the earth.

Suggestions for Discussion

1. How is the proposition "that all men are created equal" related to the issues of the Civil War?

2. Why does Lincoln not simply begin his essay, "Eighty-seven years ago"? What would he lose in tone if he had done so?

3. In paragraph three, Lincoln says, "The world will little note, nor long remember what we say here." How do you account for the fact that he was wrong? Why did he make this statement? What function does it serve?

4. How does Lincoln use the verbs *dedicate, consecrate, hallow*? Could one easily change the order of these words?

5. How does Lincoln connect the first paragraph of his speech to the last?

6. What was the "unfinished work" of the soldiers who died at the Battle of Gettysburg?

Suggestion for Writing

Write an essay in which you relate the power of this speech to the simplicity of its language.

WILLIAM FAULKNER

Nobel Prize Award Speech

William Faulkner (1897–1962) lived most of his life in Oxford, MS. After a year at the University of Mississippi, he joined the Royal Canadian Air Force, eager to participate in World War I. His novels set in the fictional Yoknapatawpha County, Mississippi, include *The Sound and the Fury* (1929), *Light in August* (1932), *Absalom, Absalom!* (1936), and *The Hamlet* (1940). In his speech accepting the Nobel Prize for Literature in 1949, Faulkner states his belief in the significance and dignity of humankind and the need for the writer to reassert the universal truths of "love and honor and pity and pride and compassion and sacrifice."

I feel that this award was not made to me as a man but to my work—a life's work in the agony and sweat of the human spirit, not for glory and least of all for profit, but to create out of the materials of the human spirit something which did not exist before. So this award is only mine in trust. It will not be difficult to find a dedication for the money part of it commensurate with the purpose and significance of its origin. But I would like to do the same with the acclaim too, by using this moment as a pinnacle from which I might be listened to by the young men and women already dedicated to the same anguish and travail, among whom is already that one who will some day stand here where I am standing.

Our tragedy today is a general and universal physical fear so long sustained by now that we can even bear it. There are no longer problems of the spirit. There is only the question: When will I be blown up? Because of this, the young man or woman writing today has forgotten the problems of the human heart in conflict with itself which alone can make good writing because only that is worth writing about, worth the agony and the sweat.

He must learn them again. He must teach himself that the basest of all things is to be afraid; and, teaching himself that, forget it forever, leaving no room in his workshop for anything but the old verities and truths of the heart, the old universal truths lacking which any story is ephemeral and doomed—love and honor and pity and pride and compassion and sacrifice. Until he does so, he labors under a curse. He writes not of love but of lust, of defeats in which nobody loses anything of value, of victories without hope and, worst of all, without pity or compassion. His griefs grieve on no universal bones, leaving no scars. He writes not of the heart but of the glands.

Until he relearns these things, he will write as though he stood alone and watched the end of man. I decline to accept the end of man. It is easy enough to say that man is immortal simply because he will endure; that when the last ding-dong of doom has clanged and faded from the last worthless rock hanging tideless in the last red and dying evening, that even then there will still be one more sound: that of his puny inexhaustible voice, still talking. I refuse to accept this. I believe that man will not merely endure: he will prevail. He is immortal, not because he alone among creatures has an inexhaustible voice but because he has a soul, a spirit capable of compassion and sacrifice and endurance. The poet's, the writer's, duty is to write about these things. It is his privilege to help man endure by lifting his heart, by reminding him of the courage and honor and hope and pride and compassion and pity and sacrifice which have been the glory of his past. The poet's voice need not merely be the record of man, it can be one of the props, the pillars to help him endure and prevail.

Suggestions for Discussion

1. Do you agree with Faulkner's optimistic statement about man's ability to "endure and prevail"? Explain.

2. Do you think Faulkner's speech too brief for a major occasion such as the Nobel Prize Awards? Explain your answer.

3. Discuss whether or not man still lives in that state of general and universal physical fear to which Faulkner refers.

Suggestions for Writing

1. Summarize your own opinions about man's ability to survive the challenges of the next hundred years.

2. Prepare a formal speech in which you accept an international prize for literature or some other accomplishment.

GEORGE ORWELL

The Principles of Newspeak

George Orwell (1903–1950), pseudonym of Eric Arthur Blair, a British writer with socialist sympathies, wrote essays and novels based on his experiences as a British imperial policeman in Burma, as an impoverished writer in Paris and London, and as a volunteer in the republican army in the Spanish Civil War. He was for a few years the editor of the magazine of the British Labour Party. Although his essays and letters are considered masterpieces of prose style, he is probably best known for the satirical anti-communist fable *Animal Farm* (1945) and for the novel *1984* published in 1949. Orwell conceived a terrifying vision of a future where mechanized language and thought have become the tools of a totalitarian society. This essay, written as an appendix to *1984*, presents "Newspeak," the official language of Oceania, as the logical outcome and instrument of a repressive government. It also suggests that Newspeak has its basis in what Orwell considered our degradation of the English language.

Newspeak was the official language of Oceania and had been devised to meet the ideological needs of Ingsoc, or English Socialism. In the year 1984 there was not as yet anyone who used Newspeak as his sole means of communication, either in speech or writing. The leading articles in the *Times* were written in it, but this was a tour de force which could only be carried out by a specialist. It was expected that Newspeak would have finally superseded Oldspeak (or Standard English, as we should call it) by about the year 2050. Meanwhile it gained ground steadily, all Party members tending to use Newspeak words and grammatical constructions more and more in their everyday speech. The version in use in 1984, and embodied in the Ninth and Tenth Editions of the Newspeak dictionary, was a provisional one, and contained many superfluous words and archaic formations which were due to be suppressed later. It is with the final, perfected version, as embodied in the Eleventh Edition of the dictionary, that we are concerned here.

The purpose of Newspeak was not only to provide a medium of expression for the world-view and mental habits proper to the devotees of Ingsoc, but to make all other modes of thought impossible. It was intended that

Left Speechless—Convention 04, © Christian J. Matuschek – Photography.

when Newspeak had been adopted once and for all and Oldspeak forgotten, a heretical thought—that is, a thought diverging from the principles of Ingsoc—should be literally unthinkable, at least so far as thought is dependent on words. Its vocabulary was so constructed as to give exact and often very subtle expression to every meaning that a Party member could properly wish to express, while excluding all other meanings and also the possibility of arriving at them by indirect methods. This was done partly by the invention of new words, but chiefly by eliminating undesirable words and by stripping such words as remained of unorthodox meanings, and so far as possible of all secondary meanings whatever. To give a single example. The word *free* still existed in Newspeak, but it could only be used in such statements as "This dog is free from lice" or "This field is free from weeds." It could not be used in its old sense of "politically free" or "intellectually free," since political and intellectual freedom no longer existed even as concepts, and were therefore of necessity nameless. Quite apart from the suppression of definitely heretical works, reduction of vocabulary was regarded as an end in itself, and no word that could be dispensed with was allowed to survive. Newspeak was designed not to extend but to *diminish* the range of thought, and this purpose was indirectly assisted by cutting the choice of words down to a minimum.

Newspeak was founded on the English language as we now know it, though many Newspeak sentences, even when not containing newly created words, would be barely intelligible to an English-speaker of our own day. Newspeak words were divided into three distinct classes, known as the A vocabulary, the B vocabulary (also called compound words), and the C vocabulary. It will be simpler to discuss each class separately, but the grammatical peculiarities of the language can be dealt with in the section devoted to the A vocabulary, since the same rules held good for all three categories.

The A vocabulary. The A vocabulary consisted of the words needed for the business of everyday life—for such things as eating, drinking, working, putting on one's clothes, going up and down stairs, riding in vehicles, gardening, cooking, and the like. It was composed almost entirely of words that we already possess—words like *hit, run, dog, tree, sugar, house, field*—but in comparison with the present-day English vocabulary, their number was extremely small, while their meanings were far more rigidly defined. All ambiguities and shades of meaning had been purged out of them. So far as it could be achieved, a Newspeak word of this class was simply a staccato sound expressing *one* clearly understood concept. It would have been quite impossible to use the A vocabulary for literary purposes or for political or philosophical discussion. It was intended only to express simple, purposive thoughts, usually involving concrete objects or physical actions.

The grammar of Newspeak had two outstanding peculiarities. The first of these was an almost complete interchangeability between different parts of speech. Any word in the language (in principle this applied even to very abstract words such as *if* or *when*) could be used either as verb, noun, adjective, or adverb. Between the verb and the noun form, when they were of the same root, there was never any variation, this rule of itself involving the destruction of many archaic forms. The word *thought,* for example, did not exist in Newspeak. Its place was taken by *think,* which did duty for both noun and verb. No etymological principle was involved here; in some cases it was the original noun that was chosen for retention, in other cases the verb. Even where a noun and a verb of kindred meaning were not etymologically connected, one or other of them was frequently suppressed. There was, for example, no such word as *cut,* its meaning being sufficiently covered by the noun-verb *knife.* Adjectives were formed by adding the suffix *-ful* to the noun-verb, and adverbs by adding *-wise.* Thus, for example, *speedful* meant "rapid" and *speedwise* meant "quickly." Certain of our present-day adjectives, such as *good, strong, big, black, soft,* were retained, but their total number was very small. There was little need for them, since almost any adjectival meaning could be arrived at by adding *-ful* to a noun-verb. None of the now-existing adverbs was retained, except for a very few already ending in *-wise;* the *-wise* termination was invariable. The word *well,* for example, was replaced by *goodwise.*

In addition, any word—this again applied in principle to every word in the language—could be negatived by adding the affix *un-,* or could be strengthened by the affix *plus-,* or, for still greater emphasis, *doubleplus-.* Thus, for example, *uncold* meant "warm," while *pluscold* and *doublepluscold* meant, respectively, "very cold" and "superlatively cold." It was also possible, as in present-day English, to modify the meaning of almost any word by prepositional affixes such as *ante-, post-, up-, down-,* etc. By such methods it was found possible to bring about an enormous diminution of vocabulary. Given, for instance, the word *good,* there was no need for such a word as bad, since the required meaning was equally well—indeed, better—expressed by *ungood.* All that was necessary, in any case where two words formed a natural pair of opposites, was to decide which of them to suppress. *Dark,* for example, could be replaced by *unlight,* or *light* by *undark,* according to preference.

The second distinguishing mark of Newspeak grammar was its regularity. Subject to a few exceptions which are mentioned below, all inflections followed the same rules. Thus, in all verbs the preterite and the past participle were the same and ended in *-ed.* The preterite of *steal* was *stealed,* the preterite of *think* was *thinked,* and so on throughout the language, all such forms as *swam, gave, brought, spoke, taken,* etc., being abolished. All plurals were made by adding *-s* or *-es* as the case might be. The plurals of *man, ox, life* were *mans, oxes, lifes.* Comparison of adjectives was invariably made by adding *-er, -est* (*good, gooder, goodest*), irregular forms and the *more, most* formation being suppressed.

The only classes of words that were still allowed to inflect irregularly were the pronouns, the relatives, the demonstrative adjectives, and the auxiliary verbs. All of these followed their ancient usage, except that *whom* had been scrapped as unnecessary, and the *shall, should* tenses had been dropped, all their uses being covered by *will* and *would.* There were also certain irregularities in word-formation arising out of the need for rapid and easy speech. A word which was difficult to utter, or was liable to be incorrectly heard, was held to be ipso facto a bad word; occasionally therefore, for the sake of euphony, extra letters were inserted into a word or an archaic formation was retained. But this need made itself felt chiefly in connection with the B vocabulary. *Why* so great an importance was attached to ease of pronunciation will be made clear later in this essay.

The B vocabulary. The B vocabulary consisted of words which had been deliberately constructed for political purposes: words, that is to say, which not only had in every case a political implication, but were intended to impose a desirable mental attitude upon the person using them. Without a full understanding of the principles of Ingsoc it was difficult to use these words correctly. In some cases they could be translated into Oldspeak, or even into words taken from the A vocabulary, but this usually demanded a long paraphrase and always involved the loss of certain overtones. The B words were a sort of verbal shorthand, often packing whole ranges of ideas into a few syllables, and at the same time more accurate and forcible than ordinary language.

The B words were in all cases compound words.* They consisted of two or more words, or portions of words, welded together in an easily pronounceable form. The resulting amalgam was always a noun-verb, and inflected according to the ordinary rules. To take a single example: the word *goodthink,* meaning, very roughly, "orthodoxy," or, if one chose to regard it as a verb, "to think in an orthodox manner." This inflected as follows: noun-verb, *goodthink;* past tense and past participle, *goodthinked;* present participle, *goodthinking;* adjective, *goodthinkful;* adverb, *goodthinkwise;* verbal noun, *goodthinker.*

The B words were not constructed on any etymological plan. The words of which they were made up could be any parts of speech, and could be placed in any order and mutilated in any way which made them easy to pronounce while indicating their derivation. In the word *crimethink* (thoughtcrime), for instance, the *think* came second, whereas in *thinkpol* (Thought Police) it came first, and in the latter word police had lost its second syllable. Because of the greater difficulty in securing euphony, irregular formations were commoner in the B vocabulary than in the A vocabulary. For example, the adjectival forms of *Minitrue, Minipax,* and *Miniluv* were, respectively, *Minitruthful, Minipeaceful,* and *Minilovely,* simply because *-trueful, paxful,* and *loveful* were slightly awkward to pronounce. In principle, however, all B words could inflect, and all inflected in exactly the same way.

Some of the B words had highly subtilized meanings, barely intelligible to anyone who had not mastered the language as a whole. Consider, for

---

*Compound words such as *speakwrite* were of course to be found in the A vocabulary, but these were merely convenient abbreviations and had no special idological color.

example, such a typical sentence from a *Times* leading article as *Oldthinkers unbellyfeel Ingsoc.* The shortest rendering that one could make of this in Old-speak would be: "Those whose ideas were formed before the Revolution cannot have a full emotional understanding of the principles of English Socialism." But this is not an adequate translation. To begin with, in order to grasp the full meaning of the Newspeak sentence quoted above, one would have to have a clear idea of what is meant by *Ingsoc.* And, in addition, only a person thoroughly grounded in Ingsoc could appreciate the full force of the word *bellyfeel,* which implied a blind, enthusiastic acceptance difficult to imagine today; or of the word *oldthink,* which was inextricably mixed up with the idea of wickedness and decadence. But the special function of certain Newspeak words, of which *oldthink* was one, was not so much to express meanings as to destroy them. These words, necessarily few in number, had had their meanings extended until they contained within themselves whole batteries of words which, as they were sufficiently covered by a single comprehensive term, could now be scrapped and forgotten. The greatest difficulty facing the compilers of the Newspeak dictionary was not to invent new words, but, having invented them, to make sure what they meant: to make sure, that is to say, what ranges of words they canceled by their existence.

As we have already seen in the case of the word *free,* words which had once borne a heretical meaning were sometimes retained for the sake of convenience, but only with the undesirable meanings purged out of them. Countless other words such as *honor, justice, morality, internationalism, democracy, science,* and *religion* had simply ceased to exist. A few blanket words covered them, and, in covering them, abolished them. All words grouping themselves round the concepts of liberty and equality, for instance, were contained in the single word *crimethink,* while all words grouping themselves round the concepts of objectivity and rationalism were contained in the single word *oldthink.* Greater precision would have been dangerous. What was required in a Party member was an outlook similar to that of the ancient Hebrew who knew, without knowing much else, that all nations other than his own worshiped "false gods." He did not need to know that these gods were called Baal, Osiris, Moloch, Ashtaroth, and the like; probably the less he knew about them the better for his orthodoxy. He knew Jehovah and the commandments of Jehovah; he knew, therefore, that all gods with other names or other attributes were false gods. In somewhat the same way, the Party member knew what constituted right conduct, and in exceedingly vague, generalized terms he knew what kinds of departure from it were possible. His sexual life, for example, was entirely regulated by the two Newspeak words *sexcrime* (sexual immorality) and *goodsex* (chastity). *Sexcrime* covered all sexual misdeeds whatever. It covered fornication, adultery, homosexuality, and other perversions, and in addition, normal intercourse practiced for its own sake. There was no need to enumerate them separately, since they were all equally culpable, and, in principle, all punishable by death. In the C vocabulary, which consisted of scientific and technical words, it might be necessary to give specialized names to certain sexual aberrations, but the ordinary citizen had no need of them. He knew what was meant by *goodsex*— that is to say, normal intercourse between man and wife, for the sole purpose of begetting children, and without physical pleasure on the part of the woman; all else was *sexcrime*. In Newspeak it was seldom possible to follow a heretical thought further than the perception that it *was* heretical; beyond that point the necessary words were nonexistent.

No word in the B vocabulary was ideologically neutral. A great many were euphemisms. Such words, for instance, as *joycamp* (forced-labor camp) or *Minipax* (Ministry of Peace, i.e., Ministry of War) meant almost the exact opposite of what they appeared to mean. Some words, on the other hand, displayed a frank and contemptuous understanding of the real nature of Oceanic society. An example was *prolefeed*, meaning the rubbishy entertainment and spurious news which the Party handed out to the masses. Other words, again, were ambivalent, having the connotation "good" when applied to the Party and "bad" when applied to its enemies. But in addition there were great numbers of words which at first sight appeared to be mere abbreviations and which derived their ideological color not from their meaning but from their structure.

So far as it could be contrived, everything that had or might have political significance of any kind was fitted into the B vocabulary. The name of every organization, or body of people, or doctrine, or country, or institution, or public building, was invariably cut down into the familiar shape; that is, a single easily pronounced word with the smallest number of syllables that would preserve the original derivation. In the Ministry of Truth, for example, the Records Department, in which Winston Smith worked, was called *Recdep*, the Fiction Department was called *Ficdep*, the Teleprograms Department was called *Teledep*, and so on. This was not done solely with the object of saving time. Even in the early decades of the twentieth century, telescoped words and phrases had been one of the characteristic features of political language; and it had been noticed that the tendency to use abbreviations of this kind was most marked in totalitarian countries and totalitarian organizations. Examples were such words as *Nazi, Gestapo, Comintern, Inprecorr, Agitprop*. In the beginning the practice had been adopted as it were instinctively, but in Newspeak it was used with a conscious purpose. It was perceived that in thus abbreviating a name one narrowed and subtly altered its meaning, by cutting out most of the associations that would otherwise cling to it. The words *Communist International*, for instance, call up a composite picture of universal human brotherhood, red flags, barricades, Karl Marx, and the Paris Commune. The word *Comintern*, on the other hand, suggests merely a tightly knit organization and a well-defined body of doctrine. It refers to something almost as easily recognized, and as limited in purpose, as a chair or a table. *Comintern* is a word that can be uttered almost without taking thought, whereas *Communist International* is a phrase over which one is obliged to linger at least momentarily. In the same way, the associations called up by a word like *Minitrue* are fewer and more controllable than those called up by *Ministry of Truth*. This accounted not only for the habit of abbreviating whenever possible, but also for the almost exaggerated care that was taken to make every word easily pronounceable.

In Newspeak, euphony outweighed every consideration other than exactitude of meaning. Regularity of grammar was always sacrificed to it when it seemed necessary. And rightly so, since what was required, above all for political purposes, were short clipped words of unmistakable meaning which could be uttered rapidly and which roused the minimum of echoes in the speaker's mind. The words of the B vocabulary even gained in force from the fact that nearly all of them were very much alike. Almost invariably these words—*goodthink, Minipax, prolefeed, sexcrime, joycamp, Ingsoc, bellyfeel, thinkpol,* and countless others—were words of two or three syllables, with the stress distributed equally between the first syllable and the last. The use of them encouraged a gabbling style of speech, at once staccato and monotonous. And this was exactly what was aimed at. The intention was to make speech, and especially speech on any subject not ideologically neutral, as nearly as possible independent of consciousness. For that purpose of everyday life it was no doubt necessary, or sometimes necessary, to reflect before speaking, but a Party member called upon to make a political or ethical judgment should be able to spray forth the correct opinions as automatically as a machine gun spraying forth bullets. His training fitted him to do this, the language gave him an almost foolproof instrument, and the texture of the words, with their harsh sound and a certain willful ugliness which was in accord with the spirit of Ingsoc, assisted the process still further.

So did the fact of having very few words to choose from. Relative to our own, the Newspeak vocabulary was tiny, and new ways of reducing it were constantly being devised. Newspeak, indeed, differed from almost all other languages in that its vocabulary grew smaller instead of larger every year. Each reduction was a gain, since the smaller the area of choice, the smaller the temptation to take thought. Ultimately it was hoped to make articulate speech issue from the larynx without involving the higher brain centers at all. This aim was frankly admitted in the Newspeak word *duckspeak,* meaning "to quack like a duck." Like various other words in the B vocabulary, *duckspeak* was ambivalent in meaning. Provided that the opinions which were quacked out were orthodox ones, it implied nothing but praise, and when the *Times* referred to one of the orators of the Party as a *double-plus-good duckspeaker* it was paying a warm and valued compliment.

The C vocabulary. The C vocabulary was supplementary to the others and consisted entirely of scientific and technical terms. These resembled the scientific terms in use today, and were constructed from the same roots, but the usual care was taken to define them rigidly and strip them of undesirable meanings. They followed the same grammatical rules as the words in the other two vocabularies. Very few of the C words had any currency either in everyday speech or in political speech. Any scientific worker or technician could find all the words he needed in the list devoted to his own speciality, but he seldom had more than a smattering of the words occurring in the other lists. Only a very few words were common to all lists, and there was no vocabulary expressing the function of Science as a habit of mind, or a method of thought, irrespective of its particular branches. There was, indeed, no word for "Science," any meaning that it could possibly bear being already sufficiently covered by the word *Ingsoc.*

From the foregoing account it will be seen that in Newspeak the expression of unorthodox opinions, above a very low level, was well-nigh impossible. It was of course possible to utter heresies of a very crude kind, a species of blasphemy. It would have been possible, for example, to say *Big Brother is ungood.* But this statement, which to an orthodox ear merely conveyed a self-evident absurdity, could not have been sustained by reasoned argument, because the necessary words were not available. Ideas inimical to Ingsoc could only be entertained in a vague wordless form, and could only be named in very broad terms which lumped together and condemned whole groups of heresies without defining them in doing so. One could, in fact, only use Newspeak for unorthodox purposes by illegitimately translating some of the words back into Oldspeak. For example, *All mans are equal* was a possible Newspeak sentence, but only in the same sense in which *All men are redhaired* is a possible Oldspeak sentence. It did not contain a grammatical error, but it expressed a palpable untruth, i.e., that all men are of equal size, weight, or strength. The concept of political equality no longer existed, and the secondary meaning had accordingly been purged out of the word *equal.* In 1984, when Oldspeak was still the normal means of communication, the danger theoretically existed that in using Newspeak words one might remember their original meanings. In practice it was not difficult for any person well grounded in *doublethink* to avoid doing this, but within a couple of generations even the possibility of such a lapse would have vanished. A person growing up with Newspeak as his sole language would no more know that *equal* had once had the secondary meaning of "politically equal," or that *free* had once meant "intellectually free," than, for instance, a person who had never heard of chess would be aware of the secondary meanings attaching to *queen* and *rook.* There would be many crimes and errors which it would be beyond his power to commit, simply because they were nameless and therefore unimaginable. And it was to be foreseen that with the passage of time the distinguishing characteristics of Newspeak would become more and more pronounced—its words growing fewer and fewer, their meanings more and more rigid, and the chance of putting them to improper uses always diminishing.

When Oldspeak had been once and for all superseded, the last link with the past would have been severed. History had already been rewritten, but fragments of the literature of the past survived here and there, imperfectly censored, and so long as one retained one's knowledge of Oldspeak it was possible to read them. In the future such fragments, even if they chanced to survive, would be unintelligible and untranslatable. It was impossible to translate any passage of Oldspeak into Newspeak unless it either referred to some technical process or some very simple everyday action, or was already orthodox (*goodthinkful* would be the Newspeak expression) in tendency. In practice this meant that no book written before approximately 1960 could be translated as a whole. Prerevolutionary literature could only be subjected to ideological translation—that is, alteration in sense as well as language. Take for example the well-known passage from the Declaration of Independence:

> We hold these truths to be self-evident, that all men are created equal, that they are endowed by their Creator with certain inalienable rights, that among these are life, liberty and the pursuit of happiness. That to secure these rights, Governments are instituted among men, deriving their powers from the consent of the governed. That whenever any form of Government becomes destructive of those ends, it is the right of the People to alter or abolish it, and to institute new Government...

It would have been quite impossible to render this into Newspeak while keeping to the sense of the original. The nearest one could come to doing so would be to swallow the whole passage up in the single word *crimethink*. A full translation could only be an ideological translation, whereby Jefferson's words would be changed into a panegyric on absolute government.

A good deal of the literature of the past was, indeed, already being transformed in this way. Considerations of prestige made it desirable to preserve the memory of certain historical figures, while at the same time bringing their achievements into line with the philosophy of Ingsoc. Various writers, such as Shakespeare, Milton, Swift, Byron, Dickens, and some others were therefore in process of translation; when the task had been completed, their original writings, with all else that survived of the literature of the past, would be destroyed. These translations were a slow and difficult business, and it was not expected that they would be finished before the first or second decade of the twenty-first century. There were also large quantities of merely utilitarian literature—indispensable technical manuals and the like—that had to be treated in the same way. It was chiefly in order to allow time for the preliminary work of translation that the final adoption of Newspeak had been fixed for so late a date as 2050.

Suggestions for Discussion

1. Explain Orwell's statement that Newspeak was designed to "*diminish* the range of thought." How does he demonstrate this statement by the use of the word *free*?

2. Summarize the uses of the A vocabulary. Contrast it with present-day English and discuss the former's use of the parts of speech. Why are verbs usually suppressed? Why were most existing adverbs abolished? Why were all noun plurals formed by adding *-s* or *-es*?

3. Define the B vocabulary. What were its uses? Discuss the examples given, particularly the sentence, "*Oldthinkers unbellyfeel Ingsoc.*"

4. What difficulties faced the compilers of the Newspeak dictionary?

5. What are the precedents for Newspeak word combinations such as *Recdep* and *Ficdep*? What comment on current standard English does Orwell make here?

6. How does the word *duckspeak* symbolize the purpose of Newspeak?

7. What are the uses of the C vocabulary? Why did the word "Science" cease to exist?

8. Discuss the sentences "*Big Brother is ungood*" and "*All mans are equal*" as examples of Newspeak.

9. What is the Newspeak equivalent of the opening passage of the Declaration of Independence? Discuss Orwell's reasons for inventing this translation. Relate the translation to the entire essay.

Suggestions for Writing

1. Examine your local newspaper for examples of words that resemble Newspeak and write an essay discussing the reasons for your choice.

2. Write an essay explaining how Newspeak is an instrument of power. Why is it a necessary ideal of Oceania? Discuss some words or sentences from contemporary political speeches or essays that come close to Newspeak.

3. Ponder the "defaced" picture on p. 612. How does the image speak to you? What significance might the picture have paired with Orwell? Why scratch away part of an image rather than rip away the whole poster? Picture the political arena and reflect upon freedom of speech. Enter into a discussion.

✺✺✺

HARRIET JACOBS

The Women

Harriet Jacobs (1818–1896) describes the effects of Nat Turner's Rebellion in *Incidents in the Life of a Slave Girl* (1861). The following selection, from *Black Slave Narratives* (1970), pinpoints with simple clarity the moral dilemmas that face a young female slave caught between her owner's desires and his wife's jealousy.

I would ten thousand times rather that my children should be the half-starved paupers of Ireland than to be the most pampered among the slaves of America. I would rather drudge out my life on a cotton plantation, till the grave opened to give me rest, than to live with an unprincipled master and a jealous mistress. The felon's home in a penitentiary is preferable. He may repent, and turn from the error of his ways, and so find peace, but it is not so with a favorite slave. She is not allowed to have any pride of character. It is deemed a crime in her to wish to be virtuous.

Mrs. Flint possessed the key to her husband's character before I was born. She might have used this knowledge to counsel and to screen the young and the innocent among her slaves; but for them she had no sympathy. They were the objects of her constant suspicion and malevolence. She watched her husband with unceasing vigilance; but he was well practiced in means to evade it. What he could not find opportunity to say in words he manifested in signs. He invented more than were ever thought of in a deaf and dumb asylum. I let them pass, as if I did not understand what he meant; and many were the curses and threats bestowed on me for my stupidity. One day he caught me teaching myself to write. He frowned, as if he was not well pleased; but I suppose he came to the conclusion that such an accomplishment might help to advance his favorite scheme. Before long, notes were often slipped into my hand. I would return them, saying, "I can't read them, sir." "Can't you?" he replied; "then I must read them to you." He always finished the reading by asking, "Do you understand?" Sometimes he would complain of the heat of the tea room, and order his supper to be placed on a small table in the piazza. He would seat himself there with a well-satisfied smile, and tell me to stand by and brush away the flies. He would eat very slowly, pausing between the mouthfuls. These intervals were employed in describing the happiness I was so foolishly throwing away, and in threatening me with the penalty that finally awaited my stubborn disobedience. He boasted much of the forbearance he had exercised toward me, and reminded me that there was a limit to his patience. When I succeeded in avoiding opportunities for him to talk to me at home, I was ordered to come to his office, to do some errand. When there, I was obliged to stand and listen to such language as he saw fit to address to me. Sometimes I so openly expressed my contempt for him that he would become violently enraged, and I wondered why he did not strike me. Circumstanced as he was, he probably thought it was better policy to be forebearing. But the state of things grew worse and worse daily. In desperation I told him that I must and would apply to my grandmother for protection. He threatened me with death, and worse than death, if I made my complaint to her. Strange to say, I did not despair. I was naturally of a buoyant disposition, and always I had a hope of somehow getting out of his clutches. Like many a poor, simple slave before me, I trusted that some threads of joy would yet be woven into my dark destiny.

I had entered my sixteenth year, and every day it became more apparent that my presence was intolerable to Mrs. Flint. Angry words frequently passed between her and her husband. He had never punished me himself, and he would not allow anybody else to punish me. In that respect, she was never satisfied; but, in her angry moods, no terms were too vile for her to bestow upon me. Yet I, whom she detested so bitterly, had far more pity for her than he had, whose duty it was to make her life happy. I never wronged her, or wished to wrong her; and one word of kindness from her would have brought me to her feet.

After repeated quarrels between the doctor and his wife, he announced his intention to take his youngest daughter, then four years old, to sleep in his apartment. It was necessary that a servant should sleep in the same room, to be on hand if the child stirred. I was selected for that office, and informed for what purpose that arrangement had been made. By managing to keep within sight of people, as much as possible, during the daytime, I had hitherto succeeded in eluding my master, though a razor was often held to my throat to force me to change this line of policy. At night I slept by the side of my great aunt, where I felt safe. He was too prudent to come into her room. She was an old woman, and had been in the family many years. Moreover, as a married man, and a professional man, he deemed it necessary to save appearances in some degree. But he resolved to remove the obstacle in the way of his scheme; and he thought he had planned it so that he should evade suspicion. He was well aware how much I prized my refuge by the side of my old aunt, and he determined to dispossess me of it. The first night the doctor had the little child in his room alone. The next morning, I was ordered to take my station as nurse the following night. A kind Providence interposed in my favor. During the day Mrs. Flint heard of this new arrangement, and a storm followed. I rejoiced to hear it rage.

After a while my mistress sent for me to come to her room. Her first question was, "Did you know you were to sleep in the doctor's room?"

"Yes, ma'am."

"Who told you?"

"My master."

"Will you answer truly all the questions I ask?"

"Yes, ma'am."

"Tell me, then, as you hope to be forgiven, are you innocent of what I have accused you?"

"I am."

She handed me a Bible, and said, "Lay your hand on your heart, kiss this holy book, and swear before God that you tell me the truth."

I took the oath she required, and I did it with a clear conscience.

"You have taken God's holy word to testify your innocence," said she. "If you have deceived me, beware! Now take this stool, sit down, look me directly in the face, and tell me all that has passed between your master and you."

I did as she ordered. As I went on with my account her color changed frequently, she wept, and sometimes groaned. She spoke in tones so sad, that I was touched by her grief. The tears came to my eyes; but I was soon convinced that her emotions arose from anger and wounded pride. She felt that her marriage vows were desecrated, her dignity insulted; but she had no compassion for the poor victim of her husband's perfidy. She pitied herself as a martyr; but she was incapable of feeling for the condition of shame and misery in which her unfortunate, helpless slave was placed.

Yet perhaps she had some touch of feeling for me; for when the conference was ended, she spoke kindly, and promised to protect me. I should have been much comforted by this assurance if I could have had confidence in it; but my experiences in slavery had filled me with distrust. She was not a very refined woman, and had not much control over her passions. I was an object of her jealousy, and, consequently, of her hatred; and I knew I could not expect kindness or confidence from her under the circumstances in which I was placed. I could not blame her. Slaveholders' wives feel as other women would under similar circumstances. The fire of her temper kindled from small sparks, and now the flame became so intense that the doctor was obliged to give up his intended arrangement.

I knew I had ignited the torch, and I expected to suffer for it afterward; but I felt too thankful to my mistress for the timely aid she rendered me to care much about that. She now took me to sleep in a room adjoining her own. There I was an object of her especial care, though not of her especial comfort, for she spent many a sleepless night to watch over me. Sometimes

I woke up, and found her bending over me. At other times she whispered in my ear, as though it was her husband who was speaking to me, and listened to hear what I would answer. If she startled me, on such occasions, she would glide stealthily away; and the next morning she would tell me I had been talking in my sleep, and ask who I was talking to. At last I began to be fearful for my life. It had been often threatened; and you can imagine, better than I can describe, what an unpleasant sensation it must produce to wake up in the dead of night and find a jealous woman bending over you. Terrible as this experience was, I had fears that it would give place to one more terrible.

My mistress grew weary of her vigils; they did not prove satisfactory. She changed her tactics. She now tried the trick of accusing my master of crime, in my presence, and gave my name as the author of the accusation. To my utter astonishment, he replied, "I don't believe it; but if she did acknowledge it, you tortured her into exposing me." Tortured into exposing him! Truly, Satan had no difficulty in distinguishing the color of his soul! I understood his object in making this false representation. It was to show me that I gained nothing by seeking the protection of my mistress; that the power was still all in his own hands. I pitied Mrs. Flint. She was a second wife, many years the junior of her husband; and the hoary-headed miscreant was enough to try the patience of a wiser and better woman. She was completely foiled, and knew not how to proceed. She would gladly have had me flogged for my supposed false oath; but, as I have already stated, the doctor never allowed anyone to whip me. The old sinner was politic. The application of the lash might have led to remarks that would have exposed him in the eyes of his children and grandchildren. How often did I rejoice that I lived in a town where all the inhabitants knew each other! If I had been on a remote plantation, or lost among the multitude of a crowded city, I should not be a living woman at this day.

The secrets of slavery are concealed like those of the Inquisition. My master was, to my knowledge, the father of eleven slaves. But did the mothers dare to tell who was the father of their children? Did the other slaves dare to allude to it, except in whispers among themselves? No, indeed! They knew too well the terrible consequences.

My grandmother could not avoid seeing things which excited her suspicions. She was uneasy about me, and tried various ways to buy me; but the never-changing answer was always repeated: "Linda does not belong to *me*. She is my daughter's property, and I have no legal right to sell her." The conscientious man! He was too scrupulous to *sell* me; but he had no scruples whatever about committing a much greater wrong against the helpless young girl placed under his guardianship, as his daughter's property. Sometimes my persecutor would ask me whether I would like to be sold. I told him I would rather be sold to anybody than to lead such a life as I did. On such occasions he would assume the air of a very injured individual, and reproach me for my ingratitude. "Did I not take you into the house, and make you the companion of my own children?" he would say. "Have I ever treated you like a Negro? I have never allowed you to be punished, not even to please your mistress. And this is the recompense I get, you ungrateful girl!" I answered that he had reasons of his own for screening me from punishment, and that the course he pursued made my mistress hate me and persecute me. If I wept, he would say, "Poor child! Don't cry! don't cry! I will make peace for you with your mistress. Only let me arrange matters in my own way. Poor, foolish girl! you don't know what is for your own good. I would cherish you. I would make a lady of you. Now go, and think of all I have promised you."

I did think of it.

Reader, I draw no imaginary pictures of southern homes. I am telling you the plain truth. Yet when victims make their escape from this wild beast of Slavery, northerners consent to act the part of bloodhounds, and hunt the poor fugitive back into his den, "full of dead men's bones, and all uncleanness." Nay, more, they are not only willing, but proud, to give their daughters in marriage to slaveholders. The poor girls have romantic notions of a sunny clime, and of the flowering vines that all the year round shade a happy home. To what disappointments are they destined! The young wife soon learns that the husband in whose hands she has placed her happiness pays no regard to his marriage vows. Children of every shade of complexion play with her own fair babies, and too well she knows that they are born unto him of his own household. Jealousy and hatred enter the flowery home, and it is ravaged of its loveliness.

Southern women often marry a man knowing that he is the father of many little slaves. They do not trouble themselves about it. They regard such children as property, as marketable as the pigs on the plantation; and it is seldom that they do not make them aware of this by passing them into the slave-trader's hands as soon as possible, and thus getting them out of their sight. I am glad to say there are some honorable exceptions.

I have myself known two southern wives who exhorted their husbands to free those slaves toward whom they stood in a "parental relation"; and their request was granted. These husbands blushed before the superior nobleness of their wives' natures. Though they had only counseled them to do that which it was their duty to do, it commanded their respect, and rendered their conduct more exemplary. Concealment was at an end, and confidence took the place of distrust.

Though this bad institution deadens the moral sense, even in white women, to a fearful extent, it is not altogether extinct. I have heard southern ladies say of Mr. Such-a-one, "He not only thinks it no disgrace to be the father of those little niggers, but he is not ashamed to call himself their master. I declare, such things ought not to be tolerated in any decent society!"

Suggestions for Discussion

1. Discuss the effectiveness of Harriet Jacobs's narrative method. Compare it with that used by Richard Wright in "The Ethics of Living Jim Crow" on p. 584.

2. How successfully does Jacobs communicate her desperation? How does she do so?

Suggestion for Writing

Write a newspaper editorial commenting on the events reported by Harriet Jacobs.

·························

C H I E F   J O S E P H

His Message of Surrender

Chief Joseph, one of the leaders of the Nez Percé tribes, fought against the destruction of his people in a manner that made him a hero (along with other chiefs, such as Tecumseh, Crazy Horse, and Sitting Bull) in the eyes of white settlers in Montana and Idaho. As part of an effort to drive the Plains Indians off their lands and onto reservations, the army commissioners decided that Joseph's Nez Percé should be moved to join others on the Lapwai Reservation in Montana. When Joseph resisted, a series of battles followed, and the Nez Percé attempted to cross the Bitterroot Mountains to Idaho. In the skirmishes that followed, most of the Nez Percé were killed. After four months of fighting and a journey of thirteen hundred miles, they were stopped in a battle a short distance from the Canadian border. Chief Joseph persuaded the approximately 120 remaining warriors to surrender and sent a message to General Howard, the American officer in command. The following brief passage is an extract from a larger message and is taken from an article, "Chief Joseph, the Nez Percé," by C. E. S. Wood in the *Century Monthly Illustrated* magazine (May 1884).

Hear Me, My Warriors

Hear me, my warriors; my heart is sick and sad.
Our chiefs are killed,
The old men are all dead
It is cold, and we have no blankets;
The little children are freezing to death.
Hear me, my warriors; my heart is sick and sad.
From where the sun now stands I will fight no more forever!

Suggestions for Discussion

1. Although Chief Joseph's message is addressed to General Howard, it seems to have a larger audience. How do you imagine that wider audience reacted? The interpreter of the message is reported to have wept as he delivered it. The original message was not in the form of a poem.

2. Examine several history books that describe the destruction of the Plains Indians and give a full account of Chief Joseph's defeat. Organize a group discussion of the incident. Attempt to interpret the meaning of the episode in American history. How does this brief document relate to the theme of freedom and human dignity?

Suggestion for Writing

Find and read the lengthier message in an account of the Nez Percé. Then write a paper on the differences between it and the extract printed in this text.

CHIEF SEATTLE

Speech on the Signing of the Treaty of Port Elliott

Chief Seattle (1786–1866) of the Suquamish and Dewamish tribes, was a significant figure among Native Americans of the Pacific Northwest. The city of Seattle was named in his honor. He was one of several chiefs in the Northwest who maintained peaceful relations with the continually encroaching white settlers. This speech, translated by a doctor named Henry Smith, acknowledges the defeat of the Native Americans and their willingness to live on a reservation in the state of Washington, provided that the American government agrees to treat them humanely and to respect the differences in their culture.

Yonder sky that has wept tears of compassion upon my people for centuries untold, and which to us appears changeless and eternal, may change. Today is fair. Tomorrow may be overcast with clouds. My words are like the stars that never change. Whatever Seattle says the great chief at Washington can rely upon with as much certainty as he can upon the return of the sun or the seasons. The White Chief says that Big Chief at Washington sends us greetings of friendship and goodwill. That is kind of him for we know he has little need of our friendship in return. His people are many. They are like the grass that covers vast prairies. My people are few. They resemble the scattering trees of a storm-swept plain. The great, and—I presume—good, White Chief sends us word that he wishes to buy our lands but is willing to allow us enough to live comfortably. This indeed appears just, even generous, for the Red Man no longer has rights that he need respect, and the offer may be wise also, as we are no longer in need of an extensive country.... I will not dwell on, nor mourn over, our untimely decay, nor reproach our paleface brothers with hastening it, as we too may have been somewhat to blame.

Youth is impulsive. When our young men grow angry at some real or imaginary wrong, and disfigure their faces with black paint, it denotes that their hearts are black, and then they are often cruel and relentless, and our old men and old women are unable to restrain them. Thus it has ever been. Thus it was when the white men first began to push our forefathers westward. But let us hope that the hostilities between us may never return. We would have everything to lose and nothing to gain. Revenge by young men is considered gain, even at the cost of their own lives, but old men who stay at home in times of war, and mothers who have sons to lose, know better.

Our good father at Washington—for I presume he is now our father as well as yours, since King George has moved his boundaries further north—our great good father, I say, sends us word that if we do as he desires he will protect us. His brave warriors will be to us a bristling wall of strength, and his wonderful ships of war will fill our harbors so that our ancient enemies far to the northward—the Hydas and Tsimpsians—will cease to frighten our women, children, and old men. Then in reality will he be our father and we his children. But can that ever be? Your God is not our God! Your God loves your people and hates mine. He folds his strong and protecting arms lovingly about the paleface and leads him by the hand as a father leads his infant son—but He has forsaken His red children—if they really are his. Our God, the Great Spirit, seems also to have forsaken us. Your God makes your people wax strong every day. Soon they will fill the land. Our people are ebbing away like a rapidly receding tide that will never return. The white man's God cannot love our people or He would protect them. They seem to be orphans who can look nowhere for help. How then can we be brothers? How can your God become our God and renew our prosperity and awaken in us dreams of returning greatness? If we have a common heavenly father He must be partial—for He came to his paleface children. We never saw Him. He gave you laws but He had no word for His red children whose teeming multitudes once filled this vast continent as stars fill the firmament. No; we are two distinct races with separate origins and separate destinies. There is little in common between us.

To us the ashes of our ancestors are sacred and their resting place is hallowed ground. You wander far from the graves of your ancestors and seemingly without regret. Your religion was written upon tables of stone by the iron finger of your God so that you could not forget. The Red Man could never comprehend nor remember it. Our religion is the traditions of our ancestors—the dreams of our old men, given them in solemn hours of night by the Great Spirit; and the visions of our sachems; and it is written in the hearts of our people.

Your dead cease to love you and the land of their nativity as soon as they pass the portals of the tomb and wander way beyond the stars. They are soon forgotten and never return. Our dead never forget the beautiful world that gave them being.

Day and night cannot dwell together. The Red Man has ever fled the approach of the White Man, as the morning mist flees before the morning sun. However, your proposition seems fair and I think that my people will accept it and will retire to the reservation you offer them. Then we will dwell apart in peace, for the words of the Great White Chief seem to be the words of nature speaking to my people out of dense darkness.

It matters little where we pass the remnant of our days. They will not be many. A few more moons; a few more winters—and not one of the descendants of the mighty hosts that once moved over this broad land or lived in happy homes, protected by the Great Spirit, will remain to mourn over the graves of a people once more powerful and hopeful than yours. But why should I mourn at the untimely fate of my people? Tribe follows tribe, and nation follows nation, like the waves of the sea. It is the order of nature, and regret is useless. Your time of decay may be distant, but it will surely come, for even the White Man whose God walked and talked with him as friend with friend, cannot be exempt from the common destiny. We may be brothers after all. We will see.

We will ponder your proposition, and when we decide we will let you know. But should we accept it, I here and now make this condition that we will not be denied the privilege without molestation of visiting at any time the tombs of our ancestors, friends and children. Every part of this soil is sacred in the estimation of my people. Every hillside, every valley, every plain and grove, has been hallowed by some sad or happy event in days long vanished.... The very dust upon which you now stand responds more lovingly to their footsteps than to yours, because it is rich with the blood of our ancestors and our bare feet are conscious of the sympathetic touch.... Even the little children who lived here and rejoiced here for a brief season will love these somber solitudes and at eventide they greet shadowy returning spirits. And when the last Red Man shall have perished, and the memory of my tribe shall have become a myth among the White Men, these shores will swarm with the invisible dead of my tribe, and when your children's children think themselves alone in the field, the store, the shop, upon the highway, or in the silence of the pathless woods, they will not be alone.... At night when the streets of your cities and villages are silent and you think them deserted, they will throng with the returning hosts that once filled and still love this beautiful land. The White Man will never be alone.

Let him be just and deal kindly with my people, for the dead are not powerless. Dead, did I say? There is no death, only a change of worlds.

Suggestions for Discussion

1. Discuss the figurative language that Chief Seattle uses in the speech. How are similes and metaphors used to characterize white settlers and Native Americans?

2. What is the tone of the speech? How does its tone fit Chief Seattle's purposes?

3. Experts have argued that this translation by Dr. Smith reflects a stereotypical picture of the Native American. What examples can you find in support of this claim? Why might this have occurred despite Dr. Smith's fluency in tribal languages?

4. Identify some ironic aspects of the speech. How might Americans of the mid-nineteenth century have responded to Chief Seattle's predictions?

Suggestions for Writing

1. Chief Seattle's speech refers to Native American enemies from whom he expects the government to protect his tribes. Write a short research paper in which you explain who those enemies were and the grounds for their enmity.

2. Write a paper comparing and contrasting the poetic nature of this speech with that of the Gettysburg Address. How do the two speeches reflect not only the differences between the two speakers and the occasions for their speeches but cultural differences as well?

3. Chief Seattle converted to Christianity in the 1830s. Does this speech reflect his conversion? Write a paper in which you contrast the fact of his conversion with what he says about God in the speech.

᰾᰾᰾᰾

P L A T O

The Crito

Translated by Benjamin Jowett, revised by Peter White

Plato (428–348 B.C.), born of a noble family, lived in Athens during troubled political times. After the defeat of Athens in the Peloponnesian War, an autocratic and repressive government replaced the democracy, and it, in turn, was succeeded by a regime more demagogic than democratic. Under this government in 399 B.C., Socrates was prosecuted, tried, and condemned to death for subversive activities. In the *Apology* and the *Crito* (neither of them typical Platonic dialogues), Plato undertook the task of rehabilitating Socrates' reputation. Although the historian Xenophon has provided a somewhat different version of Socrates' trial, Plato's portrait of Socrates explains why he regarded him as the best of men. The *Crito* (and the *Phaedo*) presents Socrates in prison as he awaits execution. Crito, a wealthy Athenian, whose primary loyalty in this case is to his friend rather than to the state, urges Socrates to accept his help in escaping. In the course of the dialogue, Socrates leads Crito to agree that a respect for the law and a belief in personal integrity demand that Socrates accept his execution with dignity. Toward the end of the *Crito*, Plato personifies the laws of Athens to explain Socrates' decision to obey them.

Plato also uses the persona of Socrates to argue his own positions on ethics, politics, and other philosophical issues in *Republic*, which Plato wrote after *Crito*, and other dialogues. Soon after his fortieth year, Plato founded the Academy, the first institute for the purpose of educating suitable rulers for Athens, a school that became a model for many that followed.

SOCRATES: Why have you come at this hour, Crito? It must be quite early?

CRITO: Yes, certainly.

SOCRATES: What is the exact time?

CRITO: The dawn is breaking.

SOCRATES: I wonder that the keeper of the prison would let you in.

CRITO: He knows me, because I often come, Socrates; moreover, I have done him a kindness.

SOCRATES: And are you only just arrived?

CRITO: I came some time ago.

SOCRATES: Then why did you sit and say nothing instead of at once awakening me?

CRITO: That I could never have done, Socrates. I only wish I were not so sleepless and distressed myself. I have been looking at you, wondering how you can sleep so comfortably, and I didn't wake you on purpose, so that you could go on sleeping in perfect comfort. All through your life, I have often thought you were favored with a good disposition, but I have never been so impressed as in the present misfortune, seeing how easily and tranquilly you bear it.

SOCRATES: Why, Crito, when a man has reached my age he ought not to be repining at the approach of death.

CRITO: And yet other old men find themselves in similar misfortunes, and age does not prevent them from repining.

SOCRATES: That is true. But you have not told me why you come at this early hour.

CRITO: I come with a message which is painful—not, I expect, to you, but painful and oppressive for me and all your friends, and I think it weighs most heavily of all on me.

SOCRATES: What? Has the ship come from Delos, on the arrival of which I am to die?*

CRITO: No, the ship has not actually arrived, but she will probably be here today, as persons who have come from Sunium tell me that they left her there; and therefore tomorrow, Socrates, will be the last day of your life.

SOCRATES: Very well, Crito; if such is the will of the gods, I am willing; but my belief is that there will be a day's delay.

CRITO: Why do you think so?

*Once every year Athens sent a state ship on a ceremonial pilgrimage to the island of Delos; no executions could be carried out between its departure and return.

SOCRATES: I will tell you. I am to die on the day after the arrival of the ship.

CRITO: Yes; that is what the authorities say.

SOCRATES: But I do not think that the ship will be here until tomorrow; this I infer from a vision which I had last night, or rather only just now, when you fortunately allowed me to sleep.

CRITO: And what was the nature of the vision?

SOCRATES: There appeared to me the likeness of a woman, fair and comely, clothed in bright raiment, who called to me and said: O Socrates,

"The third day hence to fertile Phthia shalt thou come."*

CRITO: What a singular dream, Socrates!

SOCRATES: There can be no doubt about the meaning, Crito, I think.

CRITO: Yes; the meaning is only too clear. But, oh! my beloved Socrates, let me entreat you once more to take my advice and escape. For if you die, I shall not only lose a friend who can never be replaced, but there is another evil: people who do not know you and me will believe that I might have saved you if I had been willing to give money but that I did not care. Now, can there be a worse disgrace than this—that I should be thought to value money more than the life of a friend? For the many will not be persuaded that I wanted you to escape and that you refused.

SOCRATES: But why, my dear Crito, should we care about the opinion of the many? Good men, and they are the only persons who are worth considering, will think of these things truly as they occurred.

CRITO: But you see, Socrates, that the opinion of the many must be regarded, for what is now happening shows that they can do the greatest evil to anyone who has lost their good opinion.

SOCRATES: I only wish it were so, Crito, and that the many could do the greatest evil; for then they would also be able to do the greatest good— and what a fine thing this would be! But in reality they can do neither; for they cannot make a man either wise or foolish, and whatever result they produce is the result of chance.

CRITO: Well, I will not dispute with you; but please tell me, Socrates, whether you are not acting out of regard to me and your other friends: Are you not afraid that, if you escape from prison, we may get into trouble with the informers for having stolen you away and lose either the whole or a great part of our property—or that even a worse evil may happen to us? Now, if you fear on our account, be at ease; for in order to save you, we ought surely to run this or even a greater risk; be persuaded, then, and do as I say.

*The apparition borrows the words in which Achilles contemplated a return from Troy to his home, Iliad 9.36.3.

SOCRATES: Yes, Crito, that is one fear which you mention, but by no means the only one.

CRITO: Fear not—there are persons who are willing to get you out of prison at no great cost; and as for the informers, they are far from being exorbitant in their demands—a little money will satisfy them. My means, which are certainly ample, are at your service; and if, out of solicitude about me, you hesitate to use mine, there are non-Athenians here who will give you the use of theirs; and one of them, Simmias the Theban, has brought a large sum of money for this very purpose; and Cebes and many others are prepared to spend their money in helping you to escape. Therefore do not hesitate to save yourself because you are worried about this, and do not say, as you did in the court, that you will have difficulty in knowing what to do with yourself anywhere else. For men will love you in other places to which you may go, and not in Athens only; there are friends of mine in Thessaly, if you would like to go to them, who will value and protect you, and no Thessalian will give you any trouble. Nor can I think that you are at all justified, Socrates, in betraying your own life when you might be saved. You are only working to bring about what your enemies, who want to destroy you, would and did in fact work to accomplish. And further, I should say that you are deserting your own children; for you might bring them up and educate them, instead of which you go away and leave them, and they will have to take their chances; and if they do not meet with the usual fate of orphans, there will be small thanks to you. No man should bring children into the world who is unwilling to persevere to the end in their nurture and education. But you appear to be choosing the easier part, not the better and manlier, which would have been more becoming in one who has professed a life-long concern for virtue, like yourself. And indeed, I am ashamed not only of you but of us, who are your friends, when I reflect that the whole business will be attributed entirely to our want of courage. The trial need never have come on or might have been managed differently. And now it may seem that we have made a ridiculous bungle of this last chance, thanks to our lack of toughness and courage, since we failed to save you and you failed to save yourself, even though it was possible and practicable if we were good for anything at all. So, Socrates, you must not let this turn into a disgrace as well as a tragedy for yourself and us. Make up your mind then, or rather have your mind already made up; for the time of deliberation is over, and there is only one thing to be done, which must be done this very night, and, if we delay at all, it will be no longer practicable or possible; I beseech you therefore, Socrates, be persuaded by me, and do not be contrary.

SOCRATES: My dear Crito, your solicitude is invaluable if it is rightly directed, but otherwise, the more intense, the more difficult it is to deal with. And so we should consider whether I ought to follow this course or not. You know it has always been true that I paid no heed to any consideration I was aware of except that argument which, on reflection, seemed best to me. I cannot throw over the arguments I used to make in times past just because this situation has arisen: they look the same to me as before, and I respect and honor them as much as ever. You must therefore understand that if, on the present occasion, we cannot make better arguments, I will not yield to you—not even if the power of the people conjures up the bugaboos of imprisonment and death and confiscation, as though we could be scared like little children. What will be the fairest way of considering the question? Shall I return to your old argument about the opinions of men? We were saying that some of them are to be regarded, and others not. Now were we right in maintaining this before I was condemned? And has the argument which was once good now proved to be talk for the sake of talking—mere childish nonsense? That is what I want to consider with your help, Crito: whether, under my present circumstances, the argument will appear to be in any way different or not, and whether we shall subscribe to it or let it go. That argument, which, as I believe, is maintained by many persons of authority, was to the effect, as I was saying, that the opinions of some men are to be regarded, and of other men not to be regarded. Now you, Crito, are not going to die tomorrow—at least, there is no human probability of this—and therefore you are disinterested and not liable to be deceived by the circumstances in which you are placed. Tell me, then, whether I am right in saying that some opinions, and the opinions of some men only, are to be valued and that other opinions, and the opinions of other men, are not to be valued. I ask you whether I was right in maintaining this?

CRITO: Certainly.

SOCRATES: The good opinions are to be regarded, and not the bad?

CRITO: Yes.

SOCRATES: And the opinions of the wise are good, and the opinions of the unwise are bad?

CRITO: Certainly.

SOCRATES: Now what was the argument about this: does the serious athlete attend to the praise and blame and opinion of every man or of one man only—his physician or trainer, whoever he may be?

CRITO: Of one man only.

SOCRATES: And he ought to fear the censure and welcome the praise of that one only, and not of the many?

CRITO: Clearly so.

SOCRATES: And he ought to act and train and eat and drink in the way which seems good to his single master, who has understanding, rather than according to the opinion of all other men put together?

CRITO: True.

SOCRATES: And if he disobeys and disregards the opinion and approval of the one, and regards the opinion of the many who have no understanding, will he not suffer harm?

CRITO: Certainly he will.

SOCRATES: And what will the harm be: where will it be localized, and what part of the disobedient person will it affect?

CRITO: Clearly, it will affect the body; that is what is destroyed.

SOCRATES: Very good, and is not this true, Crito, of other things, which we need not separately enumerate? In questions of just and unjust, fair and foul, good and evil, which are the subjects of our present consultation, ought we to follow the opinion of the many, and to fear them, or the opinion of the one man who has understanding? Ought we not to fear and reverence him more than all the rest of the world, and, if we desert him, shall we not ruin and mutilate that principle in us which is improved by justice and deteriorated by injustice—there is such a principle?

CRITO: Certainly there is, Socrates.

SOCRATES: Take a parallel instance: if, ignoring the advice of those who have understanding, we destroy that which is improved by health and is deteriorated by disease, would life be worth having? and that which has been destroyed is—the body?

CRITO: Yes.

SOCRATES: Would life be worth living with an evil and corrupted body?

CRITO: Certainly not.

SOCRATES: And will life be worth living if that faculty which injustice damages and justice improves is ruined? Do we suppose that principle—whatever it may be in man which has to do with justice and injustice—to be inferior to the body?

CRITO: Certainly not.

SOCRATES: More honorable than the body?

CRITO: Far more.

SOCRATES: Then, my friend, we must not regard what the many say of us but what he, the one man who has understanding of just and unjust, will say and what the truth will say. And therefore you begin in error when you advise that we should regard the opinion of the many about just and unjust, good and evil, honorable and dishonorable. "Well," someone will say, "but the many can kill us."

CRITO: That is plain, and a person might well say so. You are right, Socrates.

SOCRATES: But dear Crito, the argument which we have gone over still seems as valid as before. And I should like to know whether I may say the same of another proposition—that not life, but a good life, is to be chiefly valued?

CRITO: Yes, that also remains unshaken.

SOCRATES: And a good life is equivalent to an honorable and just one— that holds also?

CRITO: Yes, it does.

SOCRATES: From these premises I proceed to argue the question whether I am justified in trying to escape without the consent of the Athenians; and if I am clearly right in escaping, then I will make the attempt, but, if not, I will abstain. The other considerations which you mention—of money and loss of character and the duty of educating one's children— are, I fear, only the doctrines of the multitude, who, if they could, would restore people to life as readily as they put them to death—and with as little reason. But since we have been forced this far by the logic of our argument, the only question which remains to be considered is whether we shall do right in giving money and thanks to those who will rescue me, and in taking a direct role in the rescue ourselves, or whether in fact we will be doing wrong. And if it appears that we will be doing wrong, then neither death nor any other calamity that follows from staying and doing nothing must be judged more important than that.

CRITO: I think that you are right, Socrates. How then shall we proceed?

SOCRATES: Let us consider the matter together, and you, either refute me if you can, and I will be convinced, or else cease, my dear friend, from repeating to me that I ought to escape against the wishes of the Athenians. It is most important to me that I act with your assent and not against your will. And now please consider whether my starting point is adequately stated, and also try to answer my questions as you think best.

CRITO: I will.

SOCRATES: Are we to say that we are never intentionally to do wrong, or that in one way we ought and in another we ought not to do wrong? Or is doing wrong always evil and dishonorable, as we often concluded in times past? Or have all those past conclusions been thrown overboard during the last few days? And have we, at our age, been earnestly discoursing with one another all our life long only to discover that we are no better than children? Or, in spite of the opinion of the many, and in spite of consequences, whether better or worse, shall we insist on the truth of what was then said, that injustice is always an evil and a dishonor to him who acts unjustly? Shall we say so or not?

CRITO: Yes.

SOCRATES: Then we must do no wrong?

CRITO: Certainly not.

SOCRATES: Nor, when injured, injure in return, as the many imagine; for we must injure no one at all?

CRITO: Clearly not.

SOCRATES: Again, Crito, may we do evil?

CRITO: Surely not, Socrates.

SOCRATES: And what of doing evil in return for evil, which is the morality of the many—is that just or not?

CRITO: Not just.

SOCRATES: For doing evil to another is the same as injuring him?

CRITO: Very true.

SOCRATES: Then we ought not to retaliate or render evil for evil to anyone, whatever evil we may have suffered from him. But I would have you consider, Crito, whether you really mean what you are saying. For this opinion has never been held, and never will be held, by any considerable number of persons; and those who are agreed and those who are not agreed upon this point have no common ground and can only despise one another when they see how widely they differ. Tell me, then, whether you agree with and assent to my first principle, that neither injury nor retaliation nor warding off evil by evil is ever right. And shall that be the premise of our argument? Or do you decline and dissent from this? For so I have ever thought, and continue to think; but, if you are of another opinion, let me hear what you have to say. If, however, you remain of the same mind as formerly, I will proceed to the next step.

CRITO: You may proceed, for I have not changed my mind.

SOCRATES: The next thing I have to say, or, rather, my next question, is this: Ought a man to do what he admits to be right, or ought he to betray the right?

CRITO: He ought to do what he thinks right.

SOCRATES: In light of that, tell me whether or not there is some victim— a particularly undeserving victim—who is hurt if I go away without persuading the city. And do we abide by what we agree was just or not?

CRITO: I cannot answer your question, Socrates, because I do not see what you are getting at.

SOCRATES: Then consider the matter in this way: imagine that I am about to run away (you may call the proceeding by any name which you like), and the laws and the government come and interrogate me: "Tell us, Socrates," they say; "what are you up to? are you not going by an act of yours to destroy us—the laws, and the whole state—as far as in you lies? Do you imagine that a state can subsist and not be overthrown in which the decisions of law have no power but are set aside and trampled upon by individuals?" What will be our answer, Crito, to questions like these? Anyone, and especially a rhetorician, would have a good deal to say against abrogation of the law that requires a sentence to be carried out. He will argue that this law should not be set aside. Or shall we retort, "Yes; but the state has injured us and given an unjust sentence." Suppose I say that?

CRITO: Very good, Socrates.

SOCRATES: "And was that our agreement with you?" the laws would answer; "or were you to abide by the sentence of the state?" And if I were to express my astonishment at their talking this way, they would probably add: "Take control of your astonishment and answer, Socrates—you are in the habit of asking and answering questions. Tell us: What complaint have you to make against us which justifies you in attempting to destroy us and the state? In the first place, did we not bring you into existence? Your father married your mother by our aid and brought you into the world. Say whether you have any objection to urge against those of us who regulate marriage." None, I should reply. "Or against those of us who after birth regulate the nurture and education of children, in which you also were trained? Were not the laws, which have the charge of education, right in commanding your father to train you in music and athletics?" Right, I should reply. "Well then, since you were brought into the world and nurtured and educated by us, can you deny in the first place that you are our child and slave, as your fathers were before you? And if this is true, do you really think you have the same rights as we do and that you are entitled to do to us whatever we do to you? Would you have any right to strike or revile or do any other evil to your father or your master, if you had one, because you had been struck or reviled by him or received some other evil at his hands?—you would not say this? And because we think it right to destroy you, do you think that you have any right to destroy us in return, and your country, as far as in you lies? Will you, O professor of true virtue, pretend that you are justified in this? Has a philosopher like you failed to discover that our country is more to be valued and higher and holier far more than mother or father or any ancestor, and more to be regarded in the eyes of the gods and of men of understanding? Also to be soothed and gently and reverently entreated when angry, even more than a father, and either to be persuaded or, if not persuaded, to be obeyed? And when we are punished by her, whether with imprisonment or beatings, the punishment is to be endured in silence; and if she leads us to wounds or death in battle, there we follow as is right; neither may anyone yield or retreat or leave his rank, but whether in battle, or in a court of law, or in any other place, he must do what his city and his country order him, or he must change their view of what is just; and if he may do no violence to his father or mother, much less may he do violence to his country." What answer shall we make to this, Crito? Do the laws speak truly, or do they not?

CRITO: I think that they do.

SOCRATES: Then the laws will say, "Consider, Socrates, if we are speaking truly that in your present attempt you are going to do us an injury. For, having brought you into the world, and nurtured and educated you, and given you and every other citizen a share in every good which we had to give, we further proclaim to any Athenian, by the liberty which we allow him, that if he does not like us when he has come of age and has seen the ways of the city and made our acquaintance, he may go where he pleases and take his goods with him. None of us laws will stand in the way if any of you who are dissatisfied with us and the city want to go to a colony or to move anywhere else. None of us forbids anyone to go where he likes, taking his property with him. But he who has experience of the manner in which we order justice and administer the state, and still remains, has entered into an implied contract that he will do as we command him. And he who disobeys us is, as we maintain, thrice wrong: first, because in disobeying us he is disobeying his parents; secondly, because we are the authors of his education; thirdly, because he has made an agreement with us that he will duly obey our commands, but he neither obeys them nor convinces us that our commands are unjust. We show flexibility. We do not brutally demand his compliance but offer him the choice of obeying or persuading us; yet he does neither.

"These are the sorts of accusations to which, as we were saying, you, Socrates, will be exposed if you accomplish your intentions; you, above all other Athenians." Suppose now I ask, why I rather than anybody else? They might reasonably take me to task because I above all other men have acknowledged the agreement. "There is clear proof," they will say, "Socrates, that we and the city were not displeasing to you. Of all Athenians you have been the most constant resident in the city, which, as you never leave it, you may be supposed to love. For you never went out of the city either to see the games, except once, when you went to the

Isthmus, or to any other place unless when you were on military service; nor did you travel as other men do. Nor had you any curiosity to know other states or their laws: your affections did not go beyond us and our state; we were your special favorites, and you acquiesced in our government of you; and here in this city you had your children, which is a proof of your satisfaction. Moreover, you might in the course of the trial, if you had liked, have fixed the penalty at banishment, and then you could have done with the city's consent what you now attempt against its will. But you pretended that you preferred death to exile and that you were not unwilling to die. And now you do not blush at the thought of your old arguments and pay no respect to us, the laws, of whom you are the destroyer, and are doing what only a miserable slave would do, running away and turning your back on the compacts and agreements by which you agreed to act as a citizen. And, first of all, answer this very question: Are we right in saying that by your actions if not in words you agreed to our terms of citizenship? Is that true or not?" How shall we answer, Crito? Must we not assent?

CRITO: We cannot help it, Socrates.

SOCRATES: Then will they not say: "You, Socrates, are breaking the covenants and agreements which you made with us. You were not compelled to agree, or tricked, or forced to make up your mind in a moment, but had a period of seventy years during which you were free to depart if you were dissatisfied with us and the agreements did not seem fair. You did not pick Sparta or Crete, whose fine government you take every opportunity to praise, or any other state of the Greek or non-Greek world. You spent less time out of Athens than men who are crippled or blind or otherwise handicapped. That shows how much more than other Athenians you valued the city and us too, its laws (for who would value a city without laws?). And will you not now abide by your agreements? You will if you listen to us, Socrates, and you will not make yourself ridiculous by leaving the city.

"For just consider: if you transgress and err in this sort of way, what good will you do either to yourself or to your friends? That your friends will be driven into exile and deprived of citizenship or will lose their property is tolerably certain. And you yourself, if you go to one of the neighboring cities, like Thebes or Megara (both being well-ordered states, of course), will come as an enemy of their government, and all patriotic citizens will eye you suspiciously as a subverter of the laws, and you will confirm in the minds of the judges the justice of their own condemnation of you. For he who is a corrupter of the laws is more than likely to be a corrupter of the young and foolish portion of mankind. Will you then flee from well-ordered cities and law-abiding men? And will life be worth living if you do that? Or will you approach them and discourse unashamedly about—about what, Socrates? Will you discourse as you did here, about how virtue and justice and institutions and laws are the best things among men? Don't you think that such behavior coming from Socrates will seem disgusting? Surely one must think so. But if you go away from well-governed states to Crito's friends in Thessaly, where there is great disorder and license, they will be charmed to hear the tale of your escape from prison, set off with ludicrous particulars of the manner in which you were wrapped in a goatskin or some other disguise and metamorphosed in the usual manner of runaways. But will there be no one to comment that in your old age, when in all probability you had only a little time left to live, you were not ashamed to violate the most sacred laws from the greedy desire of a little more life? Perhaps not, if you keep them in good temper; but if they are out of temper, you will hear many degrading things. You will live as the flatterer and slave of all men, achieving what else but the chance to feast in Thessaly, as though you had gone abroad in order to get a meal? And where will the old arguments be, about justice and virtue? Say that you wish to live for the sake of your children—you want to bring them up and educate them—will you take them into Thessaly and deprive them of Athenian citizenship? Is this the benefit which you will confer upon them? Or are you under the impression that they will be better cared for and educated here if you are still alive, although absent from them; for your friends will take care of them? Do you fancy that, if you move to Thessaly, they will take care of them but that, if you move into the other world, they will not take care of them? No, if those who call themselves friends are good for anything, they will—to be sure, they will.

"Listen, then, Socrates, to us who have brought you up. Think not of life and children first and of justice afterwards but of justice first, so that you may defend your conduct to the rulers of the world below. For neither will you nor any that belong to you be happier or holier or juster in this life, or happier in another, if you do as Crito bids. Now you depart in innocence, a sufferer and not a doer of evil; a victim, not of the laws but of men. But if you escape, returning evil for evil and injury for injury, breaking the covenants and agreements which you have made with us and wronging those you ought least of all to wrong—that is to say, yourself, your friends, your country, and us—we shall be angry with you while you live, and our brethren, the laws in the world below, will receive you in no kindly spirit; for they will know that you have done your best to destroy us. Listen, then, to us and not to Crito."

This, dear Crito, is the voice I seem to hear murmuring in my ears, like the sound of the flute in the ears of the mystic; that voice, I say, is humming in my ears and prevents me from hearing any other. You must realize that you will be wasting your time if you speak against the convictions I hold at the moment. But if you think you will get anywhere, go ahead.

CRITO: No, Socrates, I have nothing to say.

SOCRATES: Then be resigned, Crito, and let us follow this course, since this is the way the god points out.

Suggestions for Discussion

1. What arguments do Crito use to urge Socrates to escape? To what extent do you agree with his position? How does Socrates counter his arguments?

2. Why does Socrates say that one should only consider the opinion of good people?

3. What qualities of character do Plato create for both Crito and Socrates? Which of the two men is more like most of us?

4. Explain Socrates' use of the analogy of the athlete and his trainer and the parallel question of whether life is worth living in a corrupted body.

5. How does Socrates distinguish between the value of "life" and "a good life"?

6. Socrates persuades Crito that a good man should never intentionally commit a wrong act. How does he relate this assertion to the issue of whether he should attempt to escape from prison?

7. Why does Socrates summon up the laws of Athens to discuss his strict obedience to them? What arguments do they offer?

8. Why does Socrates say that he must listen to the voice of the god? How does he connect the laws of the state to the god?

Suggestions for Writing

1. Socrates' arguments for obeying the laws of the state have not always found universal agreement. In modern times, civil disobedience has moved men such as Henry David Thoreau, Mahatma Gandhi, and Martin Luther King, Jr. In a research paper of five pages, compare and contrast the writings of Thoreau, Gandhi, and King with this dialogue by Plato.

2. Have you ever broken the law or been tempted to do so? What reasons have restrained you or otherwise guided your behavior? Write a paper of five hundred words in which you analyze your own motives as Socrates analyzes his.

MARY GORDON

A Moral Choice

Mary Gordon (b. 1949) was born on Long Island, NY, and educated at Barnard College and the University of Syracuse. She has taught English at Dutchess County Community College, Amherst College, and Barnard College and has published short stories, poems, and novels that have received critical and popular success. Among her works are *Final Payments* (1978); *The Company of Women* (1981); *Men and Angels* (1985); *The Other Side* (1989); a collection of stories, *Temporary Shelter* (1990); *The Rest of Life* (1993); and *Spending: A Utopian Divertimento* (1998). Her recent works include *Joan of Arc: Penguin Lives* (2000), *Seeing Through Places: Reflections on Geography and Identity* (2000), and *Pearl* (2005). In this essay, published in 1990, she calls for clear definitions of the moral issues surrounding abortion and explains why she has taken a pro-choice position.

I am having lunch with six women. What is unusual is that four of them are in their seventies, two of them widowed, the other two living with husbands beside whom they've lived for decades. All of them have had children. Had they been men, they would have published books and hung their paintings on the walls of important galleries. But they are women of a certain generation, and their lives were shaped around their families and personal relations. They are women you go to for help and support. We begin talking about the latest legislative act that makes abortion more difficult for poor women to obtain. An extraordinary thing happens. Each of them talks about the illegal abortions she had during her young womanhood. Not one of them was spared the experience. Any of them could have died on the table of whatever person (not a doctor in any case) she was forced to approach, in secrecy and in terror, to end a pregnancy that she felt would blight her life.

I mention this incident for two reasons: first as a reminder that all kinds of women have always had abortions; second because it is essential that we remember that an abortion is performed on a living woman who has a life in which a terminated pregnancy is only a small part. Morally speaking, the decision to have an abortion doesn't take place in a vacuum. It is connected to other choices that a woman makes in the course of an adult life.

Anti-choice propagandists paint pictures of women who choose to have abortions as types of moral callousness, selfishness, or irresponsibility. The woman choosing to abort is the dressed-for-success yuppie who gets rid of her baby so that she won't miss her Caribbean vacation or her chance for promotion. Or she is the feckless, promiscuous ghetto teenager who couldn't bring herself to just say no to sex. A third, purportedly kinder, gentler picture has recently begun to be drawn. The woman in the abortion clinic is there because she is misinformed about the nature of the world. She is having an abortion because society does not provide for mothers and their children, and she mistakenly thinks that another mouth to feed will be the ruin of her family, not understanding that the temporary truth of family unhappiness doesn't stack up beside the eternal verity that abortion is murder. Or she is the dupe of her husband or boyfriend, who talks her into having an abortion because a child will be a drag on his life-style. None of these pictures created by the anti-choice movement assumes that the decision to have an abortion is made responsibly, in the context of a morally lived life, by a free and responsible moral agent.

◌◌

The Ontology of the Fetus

How would a woman who habitually makes choices in moral terms come to the decision to have an abortion? The moral discussion of abortion centers on the issue of whether or not abortion is an act of murder. At first glance it would seem that the answer should follow directly upon two questions: Is the fetus human? and Is it alive? It would be absurd to deny that a fetus is alive or that it is human. What would our other options be—to say that it is inanimate or belongs to another species? But we habitually use the terms "human" and "live" to refer to parts of our body—"human hair," for example, or "live red-blood cells"—and we are clear in our understanding that the nature of these objects does not rank equally with an entire personal existence. It then seems important to consider whether the fetus, this alive human thing, is a *person*, to whom the term "murder" could sensibly be applied. How would anyone come to a decision about something so impalpable as personhood? Philosophers have struggled with the issue of personhood, but in language that is so abstract that it is unhelpful to ordinary people making decisions in the course of their lives. It might be more productive to begin thinking about the status of the fetus by examining the language and customs that surround it. This approach will encourage us to focus on the choosing, acting woman, rather than the act of abortion—as if the act were performed by abstract forces without bodies, histories, attachments.

This focus on the acting woman is useful because a pregnant woman has an identifiable, consistent ontology, and a fetus takes on different ontological identities over time. But common sense, experience, and linguistic usage point clearly to the fact that we habitually consider, for example, a seven-week-old fetus to be different from a seven-month-old one. We can tell this by the way we respond to the involuntary loss of one as against the other. We have different language for the experience of the involuntary expulsion of the fetus from the womb depending upon the point of gestation at which the experience occurs. If it occurs early in the pregnancy, we call it a miscarriage; if late, we call it a stillbirth.

We would have an extreme reaction to the reversal of those terms. If a woman referred to a miscarriage at seven weeks as a stillbirth, we would be alarmed. It would shock our sense of propriety; it would make us uneasy; we would find it disturbing, misplaced—as we do when a bag lady sits down in a restaurant and starts shouting, or an octogenarian arrives at our door in a sailor suit. In short, we would suspect that the speaker was mad. Similarly, if a doctor or a nurse referred to the loss of a seven-month-old fetus as a miscarriage, we would be shocked by that person's insensitivity: could she or he not understand that a fetus that age is not what it was months before?

Our ritual and religious practices underscore the fact that we make distinctions among fetuses. If a woman took the bloody matter—indistinguishable from a heavy period—of an early miscarriage and insisted upon putting it in a tiny coffin and marking its grave, we would have serious concerns about her mental health. By the same token, we would feel squeamish about flushing a seven-month-old fetus down the toilet—something we would quite normally do with an early miscarriage. There are no prayers for the matter of a miscarriage, nor do we feel there should be. Even a Catholic priest would not baptize the issue of an early miscarriage.

The difficulties stem, of course, from the odd situation of a fetus's ontology: a complicated, differentiated, and nuanced response is required when we are dealing with an entity that changes over time. Yet we are in the habit of making distinctions like this. At one point we know that a child is no longer a child but an adult. That this question is vexed and problematic is clear from our difficulty in determining who is a juvenile offender and who is an adult criminal and at what age sexual intercourse ceases to be known as statutory rape. So at what point, if any, do we on the pro-choice side say that the developing fetus is a person, with rights equal to its mother's?

The anti-choice people have one advantage over us; their monolithic position gives them unity on this question. For myself, I am made uneasy by third-trimester abortions, which take place when the fetus could live outside the mother's body, but I also know that these are extremely rare and often performed on very young girls who have had difficulty comprehending the realities of pregnancy. It seems to me that the question of late abortions should be decided case by case, and that fixation on this issue is a deflection from what is most important: keeping early abortions, which are in the majority by far, safe and legal. I am also politically realistic enough to suspect that bills restricting late abortions are not good-faith attempts to make distinctions about the nature of fetal life. They are, rather, the cynical embodiments of the hope among anti-choice partisans that technology will be on their side and that medical science's ability to create situations in which younger fetuses are viable outside their mothers' bodies will increase dramatically in the next few years. Ironically, medical science will probably make the issue of abortion a minor one in the near future. The RU-486 pill, which can induce abortion early on, exists, and whether or not it is legally available (it is not on the market here, because of pressure from anti-choice groups), women will begin to obtain it. If abortion can occur through chemical rather than physical means, in the privacy of one's home, most people not directly involved will lose interest in it. As abortion is transformed from a public into a private issue, it will cease to be perceived as political; it will be called personal instead.

❧

An Equivocal Good

But because abortion will always deal with what it is to create and sustain life, it will always be a moral issue. And whether we like it or not, our moral thinking about abortion is rooted in the shifting soil of perception. In an age in which much of our perception is manipulated by media that specialize in the sound bite and the photo op, the anti-choice partisans have a twofold advantage over us on the pro-choice side. The pro-choice moral position is more complex, and the experience we defend is physically repellent to contemplate. None of us in the pro-choice movement would suggest that abortion is not a regrettable occurrence. Anti-choice proponents can offer pastel photographs of babies in buntings, their eyes peaceful in the camera's gaze. In answer, we can't offer the material of an early abortion, bloody, amorphous in a paper cup, to prove that what has just been removed from the woman's body is not a child, not in the same category of being as the adorable bundle in an adoptive mother's arms. It is not a pleasure to look at the physical evidence of abortion, and most of us don't get the opportunity to do so.

The theologian Daniel Maguire, uncomfortable with the fact that most theological arguments about the nature of abortion are made by men who have never been anywhere near an actual abortion, decided to visit a clinic and observe abortions being performed. He didn't find the experience easy, but he knew that before he could in good conscience make a moral judgment on abortion, he needed to experience through his senses what an aborted fetus is like: he needed to look at and touch the controversial entity. He held in his hand the bloody fetal stuff; the eight-week-old fetus fit in the palm of his hand, and it certainly bore no resemblance to either of his two children when he had held them moments after their birth. He knew at that point what women who have experienced early abortions and miscarriages know: that some event occurred, possibly even a dramatic one, but it was not the death of a child.

Because issues of pregnancy and birth are both physical and metaphorical, we must constantly step back and forth between ways of perceiving the world. When we speak of gestation, we are often talking in terms of potential, about events and objects to which we attach our hopes, fears, dreams, and ideals. A mother can speak to the fetus in her uterus and name it; she and her mate may decorate a nursery according to their vision of the good life; they may choose for an embryo a college, a profession, a dwelling. But those of us who are trying to think morally about pregnancy and birth must remember that these feelings are our own projections onto what is in reality an inappropriate object. However charmed we may be by an expectant father's buying a little football for something inside his wife's belly, we shouldn't make public policy based on such actions, nor should we force others to live their lives conforming to our fantasies.

As a society, we are making decisions that pit the complicated future of a complex adult against the fate of a mass of cells lacking cortical development. The moral pressure should be on distinguishing the true from the false, the real suffering of living persons from our individual and often idiosyncratic dreams and fears. We must make decisions on abortion based on an understanding of how people really do live. We must be able to say that poverty is worse than not being poor, that having dignified and meaningful work is better than working in conditions of degradation, that raising a child one loves and has desired is better than raising a child in resentment and rage, that it is better for a twelve-year-old not to endure the trauma of having a child when she is herself a child.

When we put these ideas against the ideas of "child" or "baby," we seem to be making a horrifying choice of life-style over life. But in fact we are telling the truth of what it means to bear a child, and what the experience of abortion really is. This is extremely difficult, for the object of the discussion is hidden, changing, potential. We make our decisions on the basis of approximate and inadequate language, often on the basis of fantasies and fears. It will always be crucial to try to separate genuine moral concern from phobia, punitiveness, superstition, anxiety, a desperate search for certainty in an uncertain world.

One of the certainties that is removed if we accept the consequences of the pro-choice position is the belief that the birth of a child is an unequivocal good. In real life we act knowing that the birth of a child is not always a good thing: people are sometimes depressed, angry, rejecting, at the birth of a child. But this is a difficult truth to tell; we don't like to say it, and one of the fears preyed on by anti-choice proponents is that if we cannot look at the birth of a child as an unequivocal good, then there is nothing to look toward. The desire for security of the imagination, for typological fixity, particularly in the area of "the good," is an understandable desire. It must seem to some anti-choice people that we on the pro-choice side are not only murdering innocent children but also murdering hope. Those of us who have experienced the birth of a desired child and felt the joy of that moment can be tempted into believing that it was the physical experience of the birth itself that was the joy. But it is crucial to remember that the birth of a child itself is a neutral occurrence emotionally: the charge it takes on is invested in it by the people experiencing or observing it.

∽

The Fear of Sexual Autonomy

These uncertainties can lead to another set of fears, not only about abortion but about its implications. Many anti-choice people fear that to support abortion is to cast one's lot with the cold and technological rather than with the warm and natural, to head down the slippery slope toward a brave new world where handicapped children are left on mountains to starve and the old are put out in the snow. But if we look at the history of abortion, we don't see the embodiment of what the anti-choice proponents fear. On the contrary, excepting the grotesque counterexample of the People's Republic of China (which practices forced abortion), there seems to be a real link between repressive anti-abortion stances and repressive governments. Abortion was banned in Fascist Italy and Nazi Germany; it is illegal in South Africa and in Chile. It is paid for by the governments of Denmark, England, and the Netherlands, which have national health and welfare systems that foster the health and well-being of mothers, children, the old, and the handicapped.

Advocates of outlawing abortion often refer to women seeking abortion as self-indulgent and materialistic. In fact these accusations mask a discomfort with female sexuality, sexual pleasure, and sexual autonomy. It is possible for a woman to have a sexual life unriddled by fear only if she can be confident that she need not pay for a failure of technology or judgment (and who among us has never once been swept away in the heat of a sexual moment?) by taking upon herself the crushing burden of unchosen motherhood.

It is no accident, therefore, that the increased appeal of measures to restrict maternal conduct during pregnancy—and a new focus on the physical autonomy of the pregnant woman—have come into public discourse at precisely the time when women are achieving unprecedented levels of economic and political autonomy. What has surprised me is that some of this new anti-autonomy talk comes to us from the left. An example of this new discourse is an article by Christopher Hitchens that appeared in *The Nation* last April, in which the author asserts his discomfort with abortion. Hitchens's tone is impeccably British: arch, light, we're men of the left.

> Anyone who has ever seen a sonogram or has spent even an hour with a textbook on embryology knows that the emotions are not the deciding factor. In order to terminate a pregnancy, you have to still a heartbeat, switch off a developing brain, and whatever the method, break some bones and rupture some organs. As to whether this involves pain on the "Silent Scream" scale, I have no idea. The "right to life" leadership, again, has cheapened everything it touches.

"It is a pity," Hitchens goes on to say, "that...the majority of feminists and their allies have stuck to the dead ground of 'Me Decade' possessive individualism, an ideology that has more in common than it admits with the prehistoric right, which it claims to oppose but has in fact encouraged." Hitchens proposes, as an alternative, a program of social reform that would make contraception free and support a national adoption service. In his opinion, it would seem, women have abortions for only two reasons: because they are selfish or because they are poor. If the state will take care of the economic problems and the bureaucratic messiness around adoption, it remains only for the possessive individuals to get their act together and walk with their babies into the communal utopia of the future. Hitchens would allow victims of rape or incest to have free abortions, on the grounds that since they didn't choose to have sex, the women should not be forced to have the babies. This would seem to put the issue of volition in a wrong and telling place. To Hitchens's mind, it would appear, if a woman chooses to have sex, she can't choose whether or not to have a baby. The implications of this are clear. If a woman is consciously and volitionally sexual, she should be prepared to take her medicine. And what medicine must the consciously sexual male take? Does Hitchens really believe, or want us to believe, that every male who has unintentionally impregnated a woman will be involved in the lifelong responsibility for the upbringing of the engendered child? Can he honestly say that he has observed this behavior—or, indeed, would want to see it observed—in the world in which he lives?

༄

Real Choices

It is essential for a moral decision about abortion to be made in an atmosphere of open, critical thinking. We on the pro-choice side must accept that there are indeed anti-choice activists who take their position in good faith. I believe, however, that they are people for whom childbirth is an emotionally overladen topic, people who are susceptible to unclear thinking because of their unrealistic hopes and fears. It is important for us in the pro-choice movement to be open in discussing those areas involving abortion which are nebulous and unclear. But we must not forget that there are some things that we know to be undeniably true. There are some undeniable bad consequences of a woman's being forced to bear a child against her will. First is the trauma of going through a pregnancy and giving birth to a child who is not desired, a trauma more long-lasting than that experienced by some (only some) women who experience an early abortion. The grief of giving up a child at its birth—and at nine months it is a child whom one has felt move inside one's body—is underestimated both by anti-choice partisans and by those for whom access to adoptable children is important. This grief should not be forced on any woman—or, indeed, encouraged by public policy.

We must be realistic about the impact on society of millions of unwanted children in an overpopulated world. Most of the time, human beings have sex not because they want to make babies. Yet throughout history sex has resulted in unwanted pregnancies. And women have always aborted. One thing that is not hidden, mysterious, or debatable is that making abortion illegal will result in the deaths of women, as it has always done. Is our historical memory so short that none of us remember aunts, sisters, friends, or mothers who were killed or rendered sterile by septic abortions? Does no one in the anti-choice movement remember stories or actual experiences of midnight drives to filthy rooms from which aborted women were sent out, bleeding, to their fate? Can anyone genuinely say that it would be a moral good for us as a society to return to those conditions?

Thinking about abortion, then, forces us to take moral positions as adults who understand the complexities of the world and the realities of human suffering, to make decisions based on how people actually live and choose, and not on our fears, prejudices, and anxieties about sex and society, life and death.

Suggestions for Discussion

1. What is the function of the personal episode Mary Gordon uses in the opening paragraph of the essay?

2. What reasons for abortion do anti-choice people ascribe to those who want abortions? What are Gordon's responses to those reasons?

3. How does Gordon deal with the issue of whether a fetus is live and human? Is her discussion of this issue valid or persuasive? Do you agree with the distinctions she makes between the terms "miscarriage" and "stillbirth"?

4. What does Gordon mean by the term "the ontology of the fetus"? How does this term become crucial to her argument in favor of choice?

5. For the author, what are the real moral choices surrounding a woman's decision to have an abortion? How complex does she believe the issue to be?

6. Gordon objects to the positions of the political left and right on this issue. Explain.

Suggestions for Writing

1. Write a paper in which you argue for or against Gordon's position on abortion. Summarize her argument and try to agree or disagree with it by reference to the points she makes.

2. Look at the last three paragraphs of Gordon's essay. Do you agree or disagree with her conclusions? Write an essay in which you state your position clearly and concretely.

～～～～

G A R R Y   W I L L S

The Dramaturgy of Death

Garry Wills (b. 1934) is a historian and writer for the *New York Review of Books* who won a Pulitzer Prize for his 1993 book, *Lincoln at Gettysburg*. A practicing Roman Catholic who champions church reforms, Wills is also the author of *Saint Augustine* (1999), *Papal Sin* (2000), and *Why I Am A Catholic* (2002). Wills, has won two National Book Critics Circle Awards and the 1998 National Medal for the Humanities. Recent works include *Henry Adams and the Making of America* (2005) and *The Rosary* (2005). In the following essay, published in 2001, Wills details the historical justifications for capital punishment and explains why he himself is opposed to the death penalty.

❦

1. Capital Punishment:
The Rationales

A slight perusal of the laws by which the measures of vindictive
and coercive justice are established will discover so many
disproportions between crimes and punishments, such capricious
distinctions of guilt, and such confusion of remissness and severity
as can scarcely be believed to have been produced by public
wisdom, sincerely and calmly studious of public happiness.

—Samuel Johnson, *Rambler* 114

Nietzsche denied that capital punishment ever arose from a single or consistent theory of its intent or effect. It erupted from a tangle of overlapping yet conflicting urges, which would be fitted out with later rationalizations. The only common denominator he found in the original urges was some form of grievance (he used the French term *ressentiment*).[1] One can expand his own list of such urges:

Killing as exclusion. This occurs when society does not want to admit any responsibility for persons considered outsiders. Abandonment of wounded or captured people one does not want to feed or support is an example, or exposure of unwanted children, or exiling the defenseless (as the blind and old Oedipus was extruded from Thebes), or "outlawing"—leaving people without protection to any predators on them. Outlawing was an English practice continued in our colonies. In fact, Thomas Jefferson, when he revised the laws of Virginia for the new republic, left certain categories of offenders "out of the protection of the laws"—freed slaves who either enter the state or refuse to leave it, a white woman bearing a black child who does not leave the state within a year. [2]

These could be killed or mistreated in any way without remedy at law. The ancient Greeks denied offenders recourse to law by the penalty of *atimia* (loss of rights). There were lesser degrees of this, but the full degree of "*atimia*…and condemnation to death are interchangeable."[3] Nietzsche calls this "Punishment as the expulsion of a degenerate element…as a means of preserving the purity of a race or maintaining a social type."

---

[1] Friedrich Nietzsche, *On the Genealogy of Morals* 2.11–14, translated by Walter Kaufmann, in *Basic Writings of Nietzsche* (Modern Library, 1992), pp. 509–518.
[2] *The Papers of Thomas Jefferson*, Vol. 2, edited by Julian P. Boyd (Princeton University Press, 1950), p. 471.
[3] A. R. W. Harrison, *The Law of Athens*, Vol. 2: *Procedure* (Oxford University Press, 1971), p. 170.

Killing as cleansing. Outlawing abandons people to possible or probable death but does not directly bring it about. Other forms of extrusion require society's purification by *destruction* of a polluted person. Unless society or its agents effect this purification, the pollution continues to taint them. Lesser pollutions can be robbed of their effect by simply driving away the affected person. But deeper taints are removed only by accompanying the expulsion with something like stoning the polluter to death or throwing him off a cliff. Plato said that the murderer of anyone in his own immediate family was to be killed by judicial officers and magistrate, then "thrown down naked on a designated crossroads outside the city; whereupon every official present must throw his own stone at the head of the corpse, to cleanse the whole city, and finally must take him beyond the land's outer boundaries and cast him out, all rites of burial denied" (*Laws* 873b–c).

Killing as execration. Sometimes the community must thrust away contamination by ritual curses (*arai*), joining the punitive cry of the Furies, who are also called Arai (Aeschylus, *Eumenides* 417). When Prometheus is punished by exposure as the penalty of theft, Brute Force (Bia) tells the technician clamping him to the rock (Hephaistos) that he should curse as well as immobilize him (Aeschylus, *Prometheus* 38, 67–68). Southern lynch mobs stayed to curse with fury their hanged victim from a similar impulse.

Killing to maintain social order. Superiors dramatize their dominance by showing that it is easy for those higher in the social scale to kill those lower, but harder for the lower to kill the higher. Plato's legal code devised a penalty for a slave who kills a free man—public scourging to death before the free man's tomb and family—that had no symmetrical penalty for a free man who kills a slave (*Laws* 872b–c). In Jefferson's legal code, slaves could not testify against whites, but whites could testify against slaves.[4]

In parts of this country still, a black killing a white is far more likely to receive a death sentence than a white killing a black. Nietzsche calls this "Punishment as a means of inspiring fear of those who determine and execute the punishment."

Killing to delegitimize a former social order. Revolutionary tribunals execute officials of an overthrown regime. Even without a coup, critics of Athenian democracy claimed that mass juries were too ready to condemn their leaders. When the Turkish general Lala Mustafa Pasha captured Cyprus from the Venetians in 1570, the podestà who had held out against him, Marcantonio Bragadin, was mutilated (nose and ears cut off), dragged around the city walls, dangled from a ship's mast, tied naked to a post, skinned alive, beheaded, and "quartered" (his four limbs cut off). Then his skin, stuffed with straw, was tied to a cow and led through the streets of the Famagusta, before being returned as a victory prize to Constantinople.

[4]*The Papers of Thomas Jefferson*, Vol. 2, p. 471.

Venetian rule was pulverized in its representative. Nietzsche calls this "Punishment as a festival, namely as the rape and mockery of a finally defeated enemy."

Killing as posthumous delegitimation. Some inquisitors tried dead men and symbolically executed them.[5] The leaders of the Gowrie Plot that tried to supplant King James VI of Scotland in 1600 were tried posthumously and their corpses were hanged, drawn (eviscerated), and quartered. In 897, Pope Formosus had the corpse of his predecessor, Stephen VI, exhumed, propped up in his papal garb, tried and condemned for usurpation, stripped of his vestments, his head (that had borne the tiara) cut off, along with the three fingers of his right hand used in benediction, and head, fingers, and body then thrown in the Tiber—all to declare Stephen's consecration of bishops and ordination of priests invalid.

Killing as total degradation. The previous three forms of execution punished an offender as a member of a class (lower or higher); but other humiliating deaths are contrived to deprive a person of humanity as such. Public torture before death was one means for this—scourging that makes the offender scream and writhe, losing dignity along with his composure. The Greek punishment for theft was *apotympanismos,* the beating of a naked man clamped down in a crouched position before he was left to die of exposure (it is the punishment given to Prometheus in his play, though he cannot die).[6] The death for traitors in Elizabethan England was an elaborate piece of theater. First the offender was dragged backward on a hurdle to the place of execution—signifying, said the Attorney General Sir Edward Coke, that the man was "not worthy any more to tread upon the face of the earth whereof he was made; also for that he hath been retrograde to nature, therefore is he drawn backward at a horse-tail."[7] Then the man (it was a male punishment) was stripped, hanged, cut down living, castrated, disemboweled, his heart and viscera thrown in boiling water, decapitated, quartered, and his head exposed on Tower Bridge. When Jesuit priests were hanged, drawn, and quartered, their head, members, torso, and clothes were hidden away to prevent the taking of relics.

Killing and posthumous degradation. Refusal of burial led the ancient Greeks to let bodies be exposed for ravaging by dogs and kites (Creon's treat-

---

[5]Robert Adams, *The Abuses of Punishment* (St. Martin's, 1998), p. 156.

[6]For the *apotympanismos* of Prometheus, see Louis Gernet, *The Anthropology of Ancient Greece,* translated by John Hamilton, S. J., and Blaise Nagy (Johns Hopkins University Press, 1968), pp. 242–244. Plato has Protagoras identify Prometheus' crime as, precisely, theft (of fire) at *Protagoras* 322e.

[7]Coke quoted in Leon Radzinowicz, *A History of English Criminal Law and Its Administration from 1750,* Vol. 1 (Macmillan, 1899), pp. 221–222.

ment of Polyneices in Sophocles' *Antigone*). Romans let crucified bodies hang to be pecked at and decompose. Florentines in the Renaissance dangled the corpses of criminals from the high windows of the Bargello till they rotted, and commissioned artists like Andrea del Sarto to depict them there, prolonging the shame after they were gone.[8] Joan of Arc was killed by a slow fire that consumed her clothes and skin, then the flames were raked away, to expose her body as a woman's and to show that no demon had spirited her away. Then intense fire was mounted to burn her down to ashes for scattering in the Seine, to prevent any collection of relics.[9]

Killing by ordeal. In this punishment, the innocent were supposed to be protected if subjected to ordeal by combat, ordeal by fire (walking through it, as Saint Francis is supposed to have done in Egypt), or ordeal by water. The latter was especially reserved for suspected witches, who would sink only if innocent. A less lethal form of this punishment survived in the "ducking stool" for immersing witches. Jefferson's revised code says this: "All attempts to delude the people, or to abuse their understanding by exercise of the pretended [claimed] arts of witchcraft, conjuration, enchantment, or sorcery or by pretended prophecies, shall be punished by ducking and whipping at the discretion of a jury, not exceeding 15 stripes."[10]

Threatened killing as inducement to remorse. Refusal to undergo trial by ordeal could be taken as a confession, leading to a lesser penalty than death. Recanting could have the same effect. Joan of Arc, when first brought out to the stake with its kindling, renounced her voices as "idolatry" (devil worship), and was given life imprisonment. Only when she abjured her recantation was she actually put to the stake. Scaffold repentance could reduce the sentence to less than death—or, at the least, make officials perform a "merciful" (a swifter, not a lingering) execution—e.g., letting a man die in the noose before being cut down for disemboweling. Nietzsche calls this punishment for the "improvement" of the criminal.

Killing as repayment. The *lex talionis,* as it exacts "an eye for an eye," must exact a life for a life. We say, "You're going to *pay* for this." Jefferson followed the logic of his state's *lex talionis*:

> Whosoever shall be guilty of Rape, Polygamy, or Sodomy with man or woman shall be punished, if a man, by castration, if a woman, by cutting thro' the cartilage of her nose a hole of one half inch diameter at the least.... Whosoever on purpose and of malice fore-thought shall maim another, or

---

[8]Samuel Y. Edgerton Jr., *Pictures and Punishment: Art and Criminal Prosecution During the Florentine Renaissance* (Cornell University Press, 1985), pp. 112–123.

[9]*A Parisian Journal, 1405–1449,* translated by Janet Shirley (Clarendon Press/Oxford University Press, 1968).

[10]*The Papers of Thomas Jefferson,* Vol. 2, p. 502.

shall disfigure him, by cutting out or disabling the tongue, slitting or cutting off a nose, lip or ear, branding, or otherwise, shall be maimed or disfigured in like sort: or if that cannot be for want of the same part, then as nearly as may be in some other part of at least equal value and estimation in the opinion of a jury, and moreover shall forfeit one half of his lands and goods to the sufferer.[11]

Taking a life for a life on this principle is called by Nietzsche "Punishment as recompense to the injured party for the harm done."

Killing as repayment-plus. In Athenian law, repayment was of equal value if the crime was unintentional, but of double if it was intentional.[12] On that principle, death has not been reserved only for taking a life, but can be considered an added penalty for crimes like major theft, rape, treasonous speech, and the like.

Killing as victim therapy. The Attic orator Antiphon has the father of a son killed by accident plead that the unintentional killer must be punished; the death leaves the father aggrieved (*epithymion*—much like Nietzsche's *ressentiment*).[13] The grievance, of course, would be even greater if the killing were intentional. Soothing this sense of grievance is now called "giving closure" to the ordeal of victims.

Killing as a form of pedagogy. We say that punishing a man will "teach him a lesson." More important, it may teach others the consequence of crime, deterring anyone who contemplates a similar offense. Kant said that the person should be treated as his own end, not as a means for others' advantage. But the person executed is, by this theory, turned into a teaching instrument for the benefit of others.

∾

2. Public Execution

> *Experience of past times gives us little reason to hope that any reformation will be effected by a periodical havoc of our fellow beings.*
>
> —Samuel Johnson, *Rambler* 114

The fourteen types of capital punishment listed above do not exhaust all the possible urges expressed in our havocking of others. And as Nietzsche said, they are not neat little separate rationales. They conflict with each other at an intellectual level, but they reinforce each other at the emotional level. They

---

[11]*The Papers of Thomas Jefferson,* Vol. 2, pp. 497–498.
[12]Demosthenes, *Against Meidias* 43.
[13]Antiphon, *Tetralogy* 2.1.2.

are more powerful for certain people in certain combinations. But they have one thing in common: *they all demand, in logic, maximum display and publicity*. The outlaw's status must be proclaimed for people to act on it. The other effects sought—whether cleansing, order enforcement, delegitimation, humiliation, repayment, therapy, deterrence—can only be achieved if an audience sees what is being done to satisfy, intimidate, soothe, or instruct it.

In fact, various means to dramatize the process, to make its meaning clear, to show the right way to "read" it, were invented. Those going to the scaffold often had their crimes blazoned on their backs. Joan of Arc wore a fool's cap with her four crimes printed on it. A crucified man had his crime posted on the cross. Lesser criminals were branded to sustain the memory of their crime. Ingenious means of execution were invented to express society's horror, anger, power, and the like. Any punishment that fits the crime should be *seen* to fit the crime. Indeed, the only urges that people now commonly admit to—the last four in the above list (repayment of two kinds, "closure," and deterrence)—are closely linked with publicity. The repayment is to *us,* to society as well as to the victims, the therapy is for the victims' contemplation, and an act meant to deter should vividly catch the attention of those who might benefit from it. How can they "learn their lesson" if it is not spelled out for them?

Our unconfessed difficulty is that we have given up whatever logic there was to the death penalty, since we have become unable to embrace most of the practices of the past. We no longer believe in a divine miasma to be purged, or divine guidance to be revealed in survival by ordeal. We have given up the desecration of corpses, killing as a reinforcement of class distinctions, torture, maiming, evisceration, and all the multiple methods used to reduce the criminal to a *corpus vile*. Even Jefferson wavered on the *lex talionis* when it came to blinding an offender (he could go as far as a nose for a nose, but not as far as an eye for an eye). Our Constitution forbids cruel and unusual punishment, and we take that to mean that there will be no gratuitous humiliation of the convict—we do not even put people in the stocks anymore, much less invite the public to see a condemned man being strapped onto a gurney. We want painless executions, so we have recurred to one of the few humane-looking methods of the Greeks—lethal injection (hemlock), though among the many deterrents to becoming a philosopher, Socrates' quiet (and self-chosen) death in his seventies has never ranked very high.

So far from stigmatizing or humiliating the inmate of death row, we now provide him with a long and costly process meant to ascertain guilt, with free legal aid if he cannot afford his own, with counseling and family visits, with reading of his choice and TV, a last meal to his specifications, a last request, religious attendance, guaranteed burial, a swift and nearly painless death. We shut up his last hours from the general public, and act as if this secret rite will deter by some magic of mere occurrence. We treat the killing as a dirty little secret, as if we are ashamed of it. Well, we should be ashamed. Having given up on most of the previous justifications for the death penalty, we cling to a mere vestige of the practice, relying most urgently on one of the least defensible defenses of it.

ᨒ

3. Deterrence

The gibbet, indeed, certainly disables those who die upon it from infesting the community; but their death seems not to contribute more to the reformation of their associates than any other method of separation.

—Samuel Johnson, *Rambler* 114

The bad faith of the process shows in the insistence on using the deterrence argument when it has been discredited by all the most reputable studies. This is an old story. In the eighteenth century, Samuel Johnson, who liked to defend any tradition he could, discovered no deterrent effect following on traditional executions, though they were far more numerous and far more public than they are now (factors, some people think, that add to deterrent effect). In the middle of the twentieth century, Arthur Koestler could refer to a strong scholarly record on the matter:

> This belief in the irreplaceable deterrent value of the death-penalty has been proved to be a superstition by the long and patient inquiries of the Parliamentary Select Committee of 1930 and the Royal Commission on Capital Punishment of 1948; yet it pops up again and again. Like all superstitions, it has the nature of a Jack-in-the-box; however often you hit it over the head with facts and statistics, it will solemnly pop up again, because the hidden spring inside it is the unconscious and irrational power of traditional beliefs. [14]

Present and former presidents of the most prestigious criminological societies, polled in 1995, overwhelmingly said they did not think the death penalty significantly reduces the homicide rate (94 percent), and they knew of no empirical evidence that would support such a claim (94.1 percent).[15] They held (79.2 percent) that execution causes no reduction in crime—a finding confirmed by the fact that states with the death penalty have higher murder rates than those without (the region with the highest number of

---

[14]Arthur Koestler, *Reflections on Hanging* (Macmillan, 1957), p. 6.
[15]Michael L. Radelet and Ronald L. Akers, "Deterrence and the Death Penalty: The View of the Experts," *Journal of Criminal Law and Criminology* (Fall 1996), p. 14 (sun.soci.niu.edu/~crit-crim/dp/dppapers/mike.deterence).

homicides, the South, accounts for over 80 percent of the nation's executions).[16] Furthermore, countries in Europe that have given up the death penalty have far lower murder rates than does the United States (since those countries *do* have gun control laws).[17] Disbelief in the deterring power of execution is also expressed, though not so overwhelmingly, by police chiefs and sheriffs—not a far-left part of the community—surveyed by Peter D. Hart Research Associates in 1995. They did not think (67 percent) that executions significantly reduce homicides. In fact, New York's former police chief Patrick V. Murphy responded that "the flimsy notion that the death penalty is an effective law enforcement tool is being exposed as mere political puffery."[18]

Expert criminologists said (100 percent, joined in this by 85 percent of the police chiefs) that politicians support the death penalty for symbolic reasons, to show they are tough on crime, though that distracts them (86.6 percent of the criminologists, 56 percent of the police chiefs) from addressing better methods of reducing the homicide rate. The police listed five things that would be more effective in fighting crime, including longer sentences, more police, and gun control. It takes little observation of actual politicians to confirm that politicians support the death penalty for electoral reasons. Now-Senator Dianne Feinstein, who had opposed capital punishment as a very active member of the California parole board, embraced it in 1990 when she ran for governor. When I asked her during that campaign what had made her change her position, she said that she had become convinced that executions do deter other criminals. I said that most studies I had seen denied this, but she told me she had read new and better research, though she could not name it for me. "I'll send it to you," she promised—but she never did. The only empirical evidence that mattered to her was her knowledge of the way Rose Bird had been resoundingly defeated for reelection as the chief justice of the Supreme Court of California because she opposed capital punishment.

When Andrew Young ran for governor of Georgia in 1990, he too abandoned his earlier opposition to the death penalty (though his daughter remained an activist opponent of it, because of its disproportionate rate among blacks—the NAACP Legal Defense Fund discovered that a black's chance of being executed in Georgia was eleven times that of a white). I asked Young if he too had been convinced that executions deter. He said that he had

---

[16]See "Facts About Deterrence and the Death Penalty" at the Web site for the Death Penalty Information Center, www.deathpenaltyinfo.org/deter.html.

[17] "Facts About Deterrence and the Death Penalty."

[18]Radelet and Akers, "Deterrence and the Death Penalty," p. 5.

not, but that as mayor of Atlanta he had listened to police tell him that it discouraged them to catch criminals and see them escape execution—"I did it for their morale." (He did it, though, only when he was leaving the mayor's office and addressing a much whiter constituency in his race for governor.)

Other politicians obviously look to the polls, not to policy studies, when taking their stand on executions. Campaigning to become the senator from New York, Hillary Clinton knew how much support the state's former governor, Mario Cuomo, had lost because of his resolute stand against executions. William Weld, while he was still governor of Massachusetts, said that he relied not on studies but on "my gut": "My gut is that...capital punishment is deterrent."[19] The deft use of the death penalty issue by Bob Graham as governor of Florida and in his 1986 race for the Senate is studied in a book that Timothy McVeigh is known to have read in prison.[20] In 1984, Graham dismissed scholarly studies on the death penalty by saying, "This is an issue that is inherently beyond what empirical research can validate," making him another gut-truster like Weld.[21] But if we cannot know the deterrent effect, we are certainly killing one man for a hypothetical effect on others that is uncertain.

Actually, the deterrent theory of capital punishment, always weak, is especially flimsy now, when a rash of cases—some involving DNA evidence—has proved that some innocent men are on death row. The evidence of incompetent defenses, faked evidence, and negligent procedures has led to announced or informal moratoria on executions.[22] In Oklahoma alone, where Timothy McVeigh's crime was committed, the evidence in approximately three thousand cases is now tainted by the defective lab work of one technician, Joyce Gilchrist.[23] The execution of the innocent is not a new issue, but widespread public awareness of it is. The British study by the Select Committee on Capital Punishment, cited by Arthur Koestler, found cases of mistaken executions, including "many" reported by the governor of Sing Sing in America.[24]

Some try to separate the problem of killing the *right* person from the question of whether we should execute *any* person at all. But since the principal prop of the death penalty is deterrence theory, that prop is knocked

[19]Radelet and Akers, "Deterrence and the Death Penalty," p. 2.

[20]David Von Drehle, *Among the Lowest of the Dead: The Culture of Death Row* (Times Books, 1995), pp. 13–15, 293, 325–326.

[21]Radelet and Akers, "Deterrence and the Death Penalty," p. 5.

[22]Richard C. Dieter, *Innocence and the Death Penalty: The Increasing Danger of Executing the Innocent* (Death Penalty Information Center, www.death-penaltyinfo.org/inn.html, 1997).

[23]Jim Yardley, "Inquiry Focuses on Scientist Employed by Prosecutors," *The New York Times*, May 2, 2001, p. A14.

[24]Adams, *The Abuses of Punishment*, p. 170.

out when uncertainty of guilt enters the national consciousness. Even if we were to grant that executions deter, they may not deter people who think it is a random matter whether the right person is caught. If they might get off while guilty, or be killed while innocent, that fact is not a very stable basis for forswearing a particular homicide. And executing the mentally defective or marginally juvenile, like the disproportionate killing of blacks, cannot much intimidate a would-be murderer who is mentally sound, of mature age, or white.

These considerations join longer-term flaws in the deterrence argument. Juries are readiest to convict people for crimes of passion, sexually charged rape-murders, child-abuse murders, or serial killings. To see these offenders caught will not necessarily affect the person most likely to have the coolness and calculation that deterrence requires. And obviously they do not affect other people in the grip of obsessions, mental instability, or drug- or alcohol-induced frenzy. Plato was against executing those guilty of a crime of passion (*Laws* 867–d), but our juries reflect more the anger of society than the didactic strategies of deterrence. In doing this, the juries fail to make the calculations that we are told future murderers will make. The whole theory is senseless.

ᴄᴧ

4. "Closure"

> [People come] in thousands to the legal massacre and look with
> carelessness, perhaps with triumph, on the utmost exacerbations
> of human misery.
>
> —Samuel Johnson, *Rambler* 114

"Closure" has become a buzzword, not only for discussing the death penalty but for addressing any kind of social discontent. When the unmarried mother of Jesse Jackson's child sued Rev. Jackson, it was not about anything so crass as money, it was to find "closure" for herself and her child.[25] Who can deprive a grieving person of solace? This is the argument Antiphon's prosecutor made when he demanded emotional relief for the loss of his child to an accident. Attorney General John Ashcroft endorsed the argument by arranging for the families of Timothy McVeigh's victims to see him die. This conflicts with the logic of deterrence, since the families are not viewing the event to deter them from becoming mass murderers. If the real

---

[25]Don Terry and Monica Davey, " 'I'm Not a Blackmailer,' Mother of Jesse Jackson's Child Says," *Chicago Tribune,* May 8, 2001.

point of executions is to act *in terrorem* for other criminals, the Oklahoma families are the least appropriate audience.

Ashcroft's response to the hot pressures of the McVeigh case is just that of Dianne Feinstein or Andrew Young to less emotionally charged instances of capital punishment, where no mass murder is involved. McVeigh, the cold killer revealed in *American Terrorist*, by Lou Michel and Dan Herbeck,[26] triggers all the upsurges of emotion Nietzsche described. We feel that the very existence of a McVeigh is an affront to society, a pollutant of our life, a thing we cannot be clean of without execration. But the politician does not want to be seen ministering to atavistic reactions in their raw state. So he invokes deterrence where it does not apply, or says that humane consideration of the victims' sympathies trumps all other considerations. Seeing the murderer die, we are told, will just help the families to "close a chapter of their lives."

But is this really likely? The aim of emotional healing is to bring inflamed emotions of loss and *ressentiment* back into a manageable relationship with other parts of one's life. Does that happen when, for many years in most cases (six years so far in McVeigh's case), a victim's survivors focus on seeing that someone pays for his or her loss? This tends to reenact the outrage in a person's mind, rather than to transcend it. It prolongs the trauma, delaying and impeding the healing process. When I asked Sister Helen Prejean, the author of *Dead Man Walking*,[27] what she has observed, she said that families are asked by prosecutors to attend the trial of a relative's murderer, but to show no emotion lest they cause a mistrial. "They learn new details of the crime, and with each new turn of the trial and its aftermath the media call them to get a reaction." This is less like healing than like tearing scabs open again and again. Some relatives who want to escape this process are accused by their own of not loving the victim, says Sister Helen: "I have seen families torn apart over the death penalty."

What's more, the sterile, anodyne, and bureaucratic procedures of a modern execution can baffle the desire for revenge encouraged before its performance. Sister Helen recalls a man who said he wished to see more suffering, and who comes with pro-death demonstrators to all later executions. This is hardly one who has found "closure." The eeriness of the closure language was revealed when McVeigh himself, through his lawyer, Rob Nigh, expressed sympathy for the relatives' "disappointment" after his execution was delayed.[28] He is more the manipulator of these grieving people than an offering to them.

Emotional counselors work toward reconciliation with the facts, as religious leaders recommend forgiveness. Many church bodies oppose the death

[26]Regan Books, 2001.
[27]Vintage, 1996.
[28]Helen Kennedy, "McVeigh Execution," New York *Daily News,* May 12, 2001, p. 3.

penalty, drawing on rich traditions in the various faiths. Saint Augustine resisted the killing of murderers, even of two men who had murdered one of his own priests, arguing that the fate of souls is in God's hands (Letters 133, 134). It is true that Thomas Aquinas likened the killing of murderers to the amputation of a limb for the good of the whole body, but his fellow Dominican Niceto Blázquez points out how defective this argument is: Thomas was drawing an analogy with the excommunication of sinners from the Church, the body of Christ—but that is a move meant to promote reunion, to rescue a person from the death of his soul, not to impose a death on the body.[29]

Conservative Catholics, who are aghast at fellow believers' willingness to ignore the Pope on matters like contraception, blithely ignore in their turn papal pleas to renounce the death penalty (addressed most recently to the McVeigh case). And I have not seen Bible-quoting fundamentalists refer to the one place in the Gospels where Jesus deals with capital punishment. At John 8:3–11, he interrupts a legal execution (for adultery) and tells the officers of the state that their own sinfulness deprives them of jurisdiction. Jesus himself gives up any jurisdiction for this kind of killing: "Neither do I condemn you." George W. Bush said during the campaign debates of last year that Jesus is his favorite philosopher—though he did not hesitate to endorse the execution of 152 human beings in Texas, where half of the public defenders of accused murderers were sanctioned by the Texas bar for legal misbehavior or incompetence. Mr. Bush clearly needs some deeper consultation with the philosopher of his choice.

Suggestions for Discussion

1. Describe one of the rationales for the death penalty that Wills explores. How valid is this rationale?

2. How does Wills build upon classic historical, literary, and philosophical texts to make his argument about the death penalty?

Suggestion for Writing

As an exercise in critical-thinking and in developing strong debate tactics, write a response to Wills's essay in which you take the opposite view of the issue. Be sure to respond directly to key facts and arguments put forward by Wills in formulating both your thesis and the body of your essay.

[29]James J. Megivern, *The Death Penalty: An Historical and Theological Survey* (Paulist Press, 1997), pp. 118–120.

FICTION

∾∾∾∾∾

WILLIAM FAULKNER

Dry September

William Faulkner (1897–1962) lived most of his life in Oxford, MS. After a year at the University of MS, he joined the Royal Canadian Air Force, eager to participate in World War I. His novels set in the fictional Yoknapatawpha County in Mississippi include *The Sound and the Fury* (1929); *Light in August* (1932); *Absalom, Absalom!* (1936); and *The Hamlet* (1940). This story, taken from the section of Faulkner's *Collected Stories* (1950) called "The Village," offers an acute social and psychological analysis of life in a small Southern town after World War I. Notice how Faulkner focuses on the gentle barber, the hysterical spinster, and the brutal ex-soldier to provide social commentary.

∾

I

Through the bloody September twilight, aftermath of sixty-two rainless days, it had gone like a fire in dry grass—the rumor, the story, whatever it was. Something about Miss Minnie Cooper and a Negro. Attacked, insulted, frightened: none of them, gathered in the barber shop on that Saturday evening where the ceiling fan stirred, without freshening it, the vitiated air, sending back upon them, in recurrent surges of stale pomade and lotion, their own stale breath and odors, knew exactly what had happened.

"Except it wasn't Will Mayes," a barber said. He was a man of middle age; a thin, sand-colored man with a mild face, who was shaving a client. "I know Will Mayes. He's a good nigger. And I know Minnie Cooper, too."

"What do you know about her?" a second barber said.

"Who is she?" the client said. "A young girl?"

"No," the barber said. "She's about forty, I reckon. She ain't married. That's why I dont believe—"

"Believe, hell!" a hulking youth in a sweat-stained silk shirt said. "Wont you take a white woman's word before a nigger's?"

"I dont believe Will Mayes did it," the barber said. "I know Will Mayes."

"Maybe you know who did it, then. Maybe you already got him out of town, you damn niggerlover."

"I dont believe anybody did anything. I dont believe anything happened. I leave it to you fellows if them ladies that get old without getting married dont have notions that a man cant—"

"Then you are a hell of a white man," the client said. He moved under the cloth. The youth had sprung to his feet.

"You dont?" he said. "Do you accuse a white woman of lying?"

The barber held the razor poised above the half-risen client. He did not look around.

"It's this durn weather," another said. "It's enough to make a man do anything. Even to her."

Nobody laughed. The barber said in his mild, stubborn tone: "I aint accusing nobody of nothing. I just know and you fellows know how a woman that never—"

"You damn niggerlover!" the youth said.

"Shut up, Butch," another said. "We'll get the facts in plenty of time to act."

"Who is? Who's getting them?" the youth said. "Facts, hell! I—."

"You're a fine white man," the client said. "Aint you?" In his frothy beard he looked like a desert rat in the moving pictures. "You tell them, Jack," he said to the youth. "If there aint any white men in this town, you can count on me, even if I aint only a drummer and a stranger."

"That's right, boys," the barber said. "Find out the truth first. I know Will Mayes."

"Well, by God!" the youth shouted. "To think that a white man in this town—"

"Shut up, Butch," the second speaker said. "We got plenty of time."

The client sat up. He looked at the speaker. "Do you claim that anything excuses a nigger attacking a white woman? Do you mean to tell me you are a white man and you'll stand for it? You better go back North where you came from. The South dont want your kind here."

"North what?" the second said. "I was born and raised in this town."

"Well, by God!" the youth said. He looked about with a strained, baffled gaze, as if he was trying to remember what it was he wanted to say or to do. He drew his sleeve across his sweating face. "Damn if I'm going to let a white woman—"

"You tell them, Jack," the drummer said. "By God, if they—"

The screen door crashed open. A man stood in the floor, his feet apart and his heavy-set body poised easily. His white shirt was open at the throat; he wore a felt hat. His hot, bold glance swept the group. His name was

McLendon. He had commanded troops at the front in France and had been decorated for valor.

"Well," he said, "are you going to sit there and let a black son rape a white woman on the streets of Jefferson?"

Butch sprang up again. The silk of his shirt clung flat to his heavy shoulders. At each armpit was a dark halfmoon. "That's what I been telling them! That's what I—"

"Did it really happen?" a third said. "This aint the first man scare she ever had, like Hawkshaw says. Wasn't there something about a man on the kitchen roof, watching her undress, about a year ago?"

"What?" the client said. "What's that?" The barber had been slowly forcing him back into the chair; he arrested himself reclining, his head lifted, the barber still pressing him down.

McLendon whirled on the third speaker. "Happen? What the hell difference does it make? Are you going to let the black sons get away with it until one really does it?"

"That's what I'm telling them!" Butch shouted. He cursed, long and steady, pointless.

"Here, here," a fourth said. "Not so loud. Dont talk so loud."

"Sure," McLendon said; "no talking necessary at all. I've done my talking. Who's with me?" He poised on the balls of his feet, roving his gaze.

The barber held the drummer's face down, the razor poised. "Find out the facts first, boys. I know Willy Mayes. It wasn't him. Let's get the sheriff and do this thing right."

McLendon whirled upon him his furious, rigid face. The barber did not look away. They looked like men of different races. The other barbers had ceased also above their prone clients. "You mean to tell me," McLendon said, "that you'd take a nigger's word before a white woman's? Why, you damn niggerloving—"

The third speaker rose and grasped McLendon's arm; he too had been a soldier. "Now, now. Let's figure this thing out. Who knows anything about what really happened?"

"Figure out hell!" McLendon jerked his arm free. "All that're with me get up from there. The ones that aint—" He roved his gaze, dragging his sleeve across his face.

Three men rose. The drummer in the chair sat up. "Here," he said, jerking at the cloth about his neck; "get this rag off me. I'm with him. I dont live here, but by God, if our mothers and wives and sisters—" He smeared the cloth over his face and flung it to the floor. McLendon stood in the floor and cursed the others. Another rose and moved toward him. The remainder sat uncomfortable, not looking at one another, then one by one they rose and joined him.

The barber picked the cloth from the floor. He began to fold it neatly. "Boys, dont do that. Will Mayes never done it. I know."

"Come on," McLendon said. He whirled. From his hip pocket protruded the butt of a heavy automatic pistol. They went out. The screen door crashed behind them reverberant in the dead air.

The barber wiped the razor carefully and swiftly, and put it away, and ran to the rear, and took his hat from the wall. "I'll be back as soon as I can," he said to the other barbers. "I cant let—" He went out, running. The two other barbers followed him to the door and caught it on the rebound, leaning out and looking up the street after him. The air was flat and dead. It had a metallic taste at the base of the tongue.

"What can he do?" the first said. The second one was saying "Jees Christ, Jees Christ" under his breath. "I'd just as lief be Will Mayes as Hawk, if he gets McLendon riled."

"Jees Christ, Jees Christ," the second whispered.

"You reckon he really done it to her?" the first said.

II

She was thirty-eight or thirty-nine. She lived in a small frame house with her invalid mother and a thin, sallow, unflagging aunt, where each morning between ten and eleven she would appear on the porch in a lace-trimmed boudoir cap, to sit swinging in the porch swing until noon. After dinner she lay down for a while, until the afternoon began to cool. Then, in one of the three or four new voile dresses which she had each summer, she would go downtown to spend the afternoon in the stores with the other ladies, where they would handle the goods and haggle over the prices in cold, immediate voices, without any intention of buying.

She was of comfortable people—not the best in Jefferson, but good people enough—and she was still on the slender side of ordinary looking, with a bright, faintly haggard manner and dress. When she was young she had had a slender, nervous body and a sort of hard vivacity which had enabled her for a time to ride upon the crest of the town's social life as exemplified by the high school party and church social period of her contemporaries while still children enough to be unclassconscious.

She was the last to realize that she was losing ground; that those among whom she had been a little brighter and louder flame than any other were beginning to learn the pleasure of snobbery—male—and retaliation—female. That was when her face began to wear that bright, haggard look. She still carried it to parties on shadowy porticoes and summer lawns, like a mask or a flag, with that bafflement of furious repudiation of truth in her eyes. One evening at a party she heard a boy and two girls, all schoolmates, talking. She never accepted another invitation.

She watched the girls with whom she had grown up as they married and got homes and children, but no man ever called on her steadily until the children of the other girls had been calling her "aunty" for several years, the while their mothers told them in bright voices about how popular Aunt Minnie had been as a girl. Then the town began to see her driving on Sunday afternoons with the cashier in the bank. He was a widower of about forty—a high-colored man, smelling always faintly of the barber shop or of whisky. He owned the first automobile in town, a red runabout; Minnie had the first motoring bonnet and veil the town ever saw. Then the town began to say: "Poor Minnie." "But she is old enough to take care of herself," others said. That was when she began to ask her old schoolmates that their children call her "cousin" instead of "aunty."

It was twelve years now since she had been relegated into adultery by public opinion, and eight years since the cashier had gone to a Memphis bank, returning for one day each Christmas, which he spent at an annual bachelors' party at a hunting club on the river. From behind their curtains the neighbors would see the party pass, and during the over-the-way Christmas day visiting they would tell her about him, about how well he looked, and how they heard that he was prospering in the city, watching with bright, secret eyes her haggard, bright face. Usually by that hour there would be the scent of whisky on her breath. It was supplied her by a youth, a clerk at the soda fountain: "Sure; I buy it for the old gal. I reckon she's entitled to a little fun."

Her mother kept to her room altogether now; the gaunt aunt ran the house. Against that background Minnie's bright dresses, her idle and empty days, had a quality of furious unreality. She went out in the evenings only with women now, neighbors, to the moving pictures. Each afternoon she dressed in one of the new dresses and went downtown alone, where her young "cousins" were already strolling in the late afternoons with their delicate, silken heads and thin, awkward arms and conscious hips, clinging to one another or shrieking and giggling with paired boys in the soda fountain when she passed and went on along the serried store fronts, in the doors of which the sitting and lounging men did not even follow her with their eyes any more.

∿

III

The barber went swiftly up the street where the sparse lights, insect-swirled, glared in rigid and violent suspension in the lifeless air. The day had died in a pall of dust; above the darkened square, shrouded by the spent dust, the sky was as clear as the inside of a brass bell. Below the east was a rumor of the twice-waxed moon.

When he overtook them McLendon and three others were getting into a car parked in an alley. McLendon stooped his thick head, peering out beneath the top. "Changed your mind, did you?" he said. "Damn good thing; by God, tomorrow when this town hears about how you talked tonight—"

"Now, now," the other ex-soldier said. "Hawkshaw's all right. Come on, Hawk; jump in."

"Will Mayes never done it, boys," the barber said. "If anybody done it. Why, you all know well as I do there ain't any town where they got better niggers than us. And you know how a lady will kind of think things about men when there aint any reason to, and Miss Minnie anyway—"

"Sure, sure," the soldier said. "We're just going to talk to him a little; that's all."

"Talk hell!" Butch said. "When we're through with the—"

"Shut up, for God's sake!" the soldier said. "Do you want everybody in town—"

"Tell them, by God!" McLendon said. "Tell every one of the sons that'll let a white woman—"

"Let's go; let's go: here's the other car." The second car slid squealing out of a cloud of dust at the alley mouth. McLendon started his car and took the lead. Dust lay like fog in the street. The street lights hung nimbused as in water. They drove on out of town.

A rutted lane turned at right angles. Dust hung above it too, and above all the land. The dark bulk of the ice plant, where the Negro Mayes was night watchman, rose against the sky. "Better stop here, hadn't we?" the soldier said. McLendon did not reply. He hurled the car up and slammed to a stop, the headlights glaring on the blank wall.

"Listen here, boys," the barber said, "if he's here, dont that prove he never done it? Dont it? If it was him, he would run. Dont you see he would?" The second car came up and stopped. McLendon got down; Butch sprang down beside him. "Listen, boys," the barber said.

"Cut the lights off!" McLendon said. The breathless dark rushed down. There was no sound in it save their lungs as they sought air in the parched dust in which for two months they had lived; then the diminishing crunch of McLendon's and Butch's feet, and a moment later McLendon's voice:

"Will!... Will!"

Below the east the wan hemorrhage of the moon increased. It heaved above the ridge, silvering the air, the dust, so that they seemed to breathe, live, in a bowl of molten lead. There was no sound of nightbird nor insect, no sound save their breathing and a faint ticking of contracting metal about the cars. Where their bodies touched one another they seemed to sweat dryly, for no more moisture came. "Christ!" a voice said; "let's get out of here."

But they didn't move until vague noises began to grow out of the darkness ahead; then they got out and waited tensely in the breathless dark. There was another sound: a blow, a hissing expulsion of breath and McLendon cursing in undertone. They stood a moment longer, then they ran forward. They ran in a stumbling clump, as though they were fleeing something. "Kill him, kill the son," a voice whispered. McLendon flung them back.

"Not here," he said. "Get him into the car." "Kill him, kill the black son!" the voice murmured. They dragged the Negro to the car. The barber had waited beside the car. He could feel himself sweating and he knew he was going to be sick at the stomach.

"What is it, captains?" the Negro said. "I aint done nothing. 'Fore God, Mr. John." Someone produced handcuffs. They worked busily about the Negro as though he were a post, quiet, intent, getting in one another's way. He submitted to the handcuffs, looking swiftly and constantly from dim face to dim face. "Who's here, captains?" he said, leaning to peer into the faces until they could feel his breath and smell his sweaty reek. He spoke a name or two. "What you all say I done, Mr. John?"

McLendon jerked the car door open. "Get in!" he said.

The Negro did not move. "What you all going to do with me, Mr. John? I aint done nothing. White folks, captains, I aint done nothing: I swear 'fore God." He called another name.

"Get in!" McLendon said. He struck the Negro. The others expelled their breath in a dry hissing and struck him with random blows and he whirled and cursed them, and swept his manacled hands across their faces and slashed the barber upon the mouth, and the barber struck him also. "Get him in there," McLendon said. They pushed at him. He ceased struggling and got in and sat quietly as the others took their places. He sat between the barber and the soldier, drawing his limbs in so as not to touch them, his eyes going swiftly and constantly from face to face. Butch clung to the running board. The car moved on. The barber nursed his mouth with his handkerchief.

"What's the matter, Hawk?" the soldier said.

"Nothing," the barber said. They regained the highroad and turned away from town. The second car dropped back out of the dust. They went on, gaining speed; the final fringe of houses dropped behind.

"Goddamn, he stinks!" the soldier said.

"We'll fix that," the drummer in front beside McLendon said. On the running board Butch cursed into the hot rush of air. The barber leaned suddenly forward and touched McLendon's arm.

"Let me out, John," he said.

"Jump out, niggerlover," McLendon said without turning his head. He drove swiftly. Behind them the sourceless lights of the second car glared in the dust. Presently McLendon turned into a narrow road. It was rutted with disuse. It led back to an abandoned brick kiln—a series of reddish mounds and weed- and vine-choked vats without bottom. It had been used for pasture once, until one day the owner missed one of his mules. Although he prodded carefully in the vats with a long pole, he could not even find the bottom of them.

"John," the barber said.

"Jump out, then," McLendon said, hurling the car along the ruts. Beside the barber the Negro spoke:

"Mr. Henry."

The barber sat forward. The narrow tunnel of the road rushed up and past. Their motion was like an extinct furnace blast: cooler, but utterly dead. The car bounded from rut to rut.

"Mr. Henry," the Negro said.

The barber began to tug furiously at the door. "Look out, there!" the soldier said, but the barber had already kicked the door open and swung onto the running board. The soldier leaned across the Negro and grasped at him, but he had already jumped. The car went on without checking speed.

The impetus hurled him crashing through dust-sheathed weeds, into the ditch. Dust puffed about him, and in a thin, vicious crackling of sapless stems he lay choking and retching until the second car passed and died away. Then he rose and limped on until he reached the highroad and turned toward town, brushing at his clothes with his hands. The moon was higher, riding high and clear of the dust at last, and after a while the town began to glare beneath the dust. He went on, limping. Presently he heard cars and the glow of them grew in the dust behind him and he left the road and crouched again in the weeds until they passed. McLendon's car came last now. There were four people in it and Butch was not on the running board.

They went on; the dust swallowed them; the glare and the sound died away. The dust of them hung for a while, but soon the eternal dust absorbed it again. The barber climbed back onto the road and limped on toward town.

∾

IV

As she dressed for supper on that Saturday evening, her own flesh felt like fever. Her hands trembled among the hooks and eyes, and her eyes had a feverish look, and her hair swirled crisp and crackling under the comb. While she was still dressing the friends called for her and sat while she donned her sheerest underthings and stockings and a new voile dress. "Do you feel strong enough to go out?" they said, their eyes bright too, with a dark glitter. "When you have had time to get over the shock, you must tell us what happened. What he said and did; everything."

In the leafed darkness, as they walked toward the square, she began to breathe deeply, something like a swimmer preparing to dive, until she ceased trembling, the four of them walking slowly because of the terrible heat and out of solicitude for her. But as they neared the square she began to tremble again, walking with her head up, her hands clenched at her sides, their voices about her murmurous, also with that feverish, glittering quality of their eyes.

They entered the square, she in the center of the group, fragile in her fresh dress. She was trembling worse. She walked slower and slower, as children eat ice cream, her head up and her eyes bright in the haggard banner of her face, passing the hotel and the coatless drummers in chairs along the curb looking around at her: "That's the one: see? The one in pink in the middle." "Is that her? What did they do with the nigger? Did they—?" "Sure. He's all right." "All right, is he?" "Sure. He went on a little trip." Then the drug store, where even the young men lounging in the doorway tipped their hats and followed with their eyes the motions of her hips and legs when she passed.

They went on, passing the lifted hats of the gentlemen, the suddenly ceased voices, deferent, protective. "Do you see?" the friends said. Their voices sounded like long, hovering sighs of hissing exultation. "There's not a Negro on the square. Not one."

They reached the picture show. It was like a miniature fairyland with its lighted lobby and colored lithographs of life caught in its terrible and beautiful mutations. Her lips began to tingle. In the dark, when the picture began, it would be all right; she could hold back the laughing so it would not waste away so fast and so soon. So she hurried on before the turning faces, the undertones of low astonishment, and they took their accustomed places where she could see the aisle against the silver glare and the young men and girls coming in two and two against it.

The lights flicked away; the screen glowed silver, and soon life began to unfold, beautiful and passionate and sad, while still the young men and girls entered, scented and sibilant in the half dark, their paired backs in silhouette delicate and sleek, their slim, quick bodies awkward, divinely young, while beyond them the silver dream accumulated, inevitably on and on. She began to laugh. In trying to suppress it, it made more noise than ever; heads began to turn. Still laughing, her friends raised her and led her out, and she stood at the curb, laughing on a high, sustained note, until the taxi came up and they helped her in.

They removed the pink voile and the sheer underthings and the stockings, and put her to bed, and cracked ice for her temples, and sent for the doctor. He was hard to locate, so they ministered to her with hushed ejaculations, renewing the ice and fanning her. While the ice was fresh and cold she stopped laughing and lay still for a time, moaning only a little. But soon the laughing welled again and her voice rose screaming.

"Shhhhhhhhhh! Shhhhhhhhhhhhh!" they said, freshening the icepack, smoothing her hair, examining it for gray; "poor girl!" Then to one another: "Do you suppose anything really happened?" their eyes darkly aglitter, secret and passionate. "Shhhhhhhhhh! Poor girl! Poor Minnie!"

V

It was midnight when McLendon drove up to his neat new house. It was trim and fresh as a birdcage and almost as small, with its clean, green-and-white paint. He locked the car and mounted the porch and entered. His wife rose from a chair beside the reading lamp. McLendon stopped in the floor and stared at her until she looked down.

"Look at that clock," he said, lifting his arm, pointing. She stood before him, her face lowered, a magazine in her hands. Her face was pale, strained, and weary-looking. "Haven't I told you about sitting up like this, waiting to see when I come in?"

"John," she said. She laid the magazine down. Poised on the balls of his feet, he glared at her with his hot eyes, his sweating face.

"Didn't I tell you?" He went toward her. She looked up then. He caught her shoulder. She stood passive, looking at him.

"Don't, John. I couldn't sleep…The heat; something. Please, John. You're hurting me."

"Didn't I tell you?" He released her and half struck, half flung her across the chair, and she lay there and watched him quietly as he left the room.

He went on through the house, ripping off his shirt, and on the dark, screened porch at the rear he stood and mopped his head and shoulders with the shirt and flung it away. He took the pistol from his hip and laid it on the table beside the bed, and sat on the bed and removed his shoes, and rose and slipped his trousers off. He was sweating again already, and he stooped and hunted furiously for the shirt. At last he found it and wiped his body again, and, with his body pressed against the dusty screen, he stood panting. There was no movement, no sound, not even an insect. The dark world seemed to lie stricken beneath the cold moon and the lidless stars.

Suggestions for Discussion

1. Faulkner tells this story of a lynching in five parts. Discuss the relation of the parts to each other.

2. What is the function of Hawkshaw? Why is it appropriate for the story to open in a barber shop? Explain the discussion between the barbers and the customers.

3. In what ways is John McLendon different from the other men? What explains his power over them?

4. Explain the significance of the scene in which Will Mayes hits Hawkshaw in the mouth.

5. How do you know that nothing has happened to Miss Minnie Cooper? What aspects of her character make clear that she has invented an affront?

6. Explain the title of the story. How does Faulkner use weather as a force in the story? What has weather to do with the lynching?

Suggestions for Writing

1. Write an essay in which you explain how this story is an eloquent attack on lynching. Does Faulkner permit himself to comment on what has occurred?

2. Write an essay in which you explain how the characters in this story provide a comment on the relation between the races.

POETRY

REYNOLDS PRICE

Tom, Dying of AIDS

Macon, NC, native Reynolds Price (b. 1933) has taught at his alma mater, Duke University, since 1958, and has published more than thirty volumes of fiction, drama, essays, poetry, and translations. A member of the American Academy of Arts and Letters and a James B. Duke Professor of English, Price was a Rhodes Scholar who began a three-year period of study at Merton College, Oxford, in 1955. Nineteen-sixty-two saw the publication of his first novel, *A Long and Happy Life,* which won the William Faulkner Award and has never been out of print. Some of his more recent works include *Kate Vaiden* (which won the National Book Critics Circle Award in 1986), *A Singular Family* (1999), *A Serious Way of Wondering* (2003), and *The Good Priest's Son* (2005).

> In seven years you took my picture
> A thousand times—in New York mainly
> Ringed by gawkers, muggers, geeks—
> And you as high as any bystander:
> Lobbing me jokes like booby-trapped balls,

Chairs of sorrow: Mo(u)rning chairs in a Parisian park, Bernd Brandenburg, Summer 2001. ©Brandenburg@lovestoryofberlin.de

677

Tying your limbs in sheepshank knots
To break my pose and make me yield
Or asking me questions God will blush
To ask at Judgment. I'd laugh and answer;
You'd click and brush my hair aside
Or turn to a geek, "Ain't this boy
Fine?"
        I always came out
Looking like me. Others complained
(Nobody likes the you you like), but
You agreed—*It's you. I just* found *you.*
    Today I hear you're nearly lost,
Under a hundred pounds, eyes out,
Hid from all you saw and served.
      But Tom, I find you—see you still
In parks, up alleys, wrenching your face,
Your wiry limbs, into clowns and monkeys:
Finding *me.*

Suggestions for Discussion

1. What snapshots are taken in this poem?

2. What is the difference between an image summoned purely by memory and one that has been immortalized by film?

3. How does this poem compare with Andrew Sullivan's piece, *If Love Were All* (which is reprinted on p. 215), in its depiction of the effects of the AIDS virus?

Suggestion for Writing

Write a poem in honor of a friend you have not seen in many years but for whom you still have strong sentimental feelings.

M A T T H E W   A R N O L D

Dover Beach

Matthew Arnold (1822–1888), son of Thomas Arnold, the famous head-master of Rugby (a British public school), was first a poet, but he later abandoned poetry to become a lecturer, a critic of life and literature, and an inspector of schools. His *Collected Poems* appeared in 1869, *Essays in Criticism* in 1865 and 1888, *Culture and Anarchy* in 1869, *Friendship's Garland* in 1879, and *Mixed Essays* in 1879. In "Dover Beach," the speaker at a moment of emotional crisis, talking to one he loves, raises the question of whether humans can find any peace or joy or release from pain in a world of conflict.

> The sea is calm tonight.
> The tide is full, the moon lies fair
> Upon the straits; on the French coast the light
> Gleams and is gone; the cliffs of England stand,
> Glimmering and vast, out in the tranquil bay.
> Come to the window, sweet is the night-air!
> Only, from the long line of spray
> Where the sea meets the moon-blanched land,
> Listen! you hear the grating roar
> Of pebbles which the waves draw back, and fling,
> At their return, up the high strand,
> Begin, and cease, and then again begin,
> With tremulous cadence slow, and bring
> The eternal note of sadness in.
>
> Sophocles long ago
> Heard it on the Aegean, and it brought
> Into his mind the turbid ebb and flow
> Of human misery; we
> Find also in the sound a thought,
> Hearing it by this distant northern sea.
> The Sea of Faith
> Was once, too, at the full, and round earth's shore
> Lay like the folds of a bright girdle furled.
> But now I only hear
> Its melancholy, long, withdrawing roar,
> Retreating, to the breath
> Of the night-wind, down the vast edges drear
> And naked shingles of the world.
>
> Ah, love, let us be true
> To one another! for the world, which seems
> To lie before us like a land of dreams,
> So various, so beautiful, so new,
> Hath really neither joy, nor love, nor light,
> Nor certitude, nor peace, nor help for pain;
> And we are here as on a darkling plain
> Swept with confused alarms of struggle and flight,
> Where ignorant armies clash by night.

Suggestions for Discussion

1. How does the sea symbolize modern life?
2. What is the speaker seeking, and what values does he affirm? Exercise your imagination and rewrite this poem from the perspective of the beach as it regards the speaker.

CNCNCN

MARK LEVINE

About Face

(A Poem Called "Dover Beach")

Mark Levine, born in Toronto, was educated at Brown University and the University of Iowa, where he received his M.F.A. In addition to *Debt* (1993), from which "About Face" is taken, he has written *Enola Gay* (2000), and his poetry was included in *Best Poems of 1991*. This poem uses the frame of Matthew Arnold's Victorian work "Dover Beach" to make a powerful commentary about the violence of our contemporary world.

It's dead out here. The sea is calm tonight.
Just me, the sand, the sand-like
things, wriggling like wet pockets.
I cover my eyes with some fingers; I have fingers
to spare. I open my mouth and hear the medicine
splashing on my tongue. The cliffs of England stand.

Behind enemy lines? Yes. Toujours. The Sea of Faith
was once, too, at the full. The barricades are stacked
like empty chairs after tonight's performance.
Is tonight's performance over?
I'm dragging bodies along as decoys, a dozen
well-dressed bodies, greasy, glazed with red sauce. Tonight's menu:
Peking duck. My stench is making me hungry.
Commander, may I have a body too?

Is someone quaking in my boots? To fear? Perchance, to flee.
Out here "advance" looks a lot like "retreat."

My wheels kick up sand as they spin.
Listen! you hear the grating.
My gears are caught. No use hurrying.
Time's nearly up. And I have
thoughts to collect, faces to grow.

My instructions read: "Come as you
were, leave as you are." Only, from the long
line of spray—
Commander, can you hear me?
I'm waiting for my answer.

Come to the window. Sweet is the night air.
My guests are here, clamoring to be let in.
I am here, clamoring to be let in.
In. Where is that? Come to the window.
Knocking twice, I greet myself at the door and am surprised.

Oh naked shingles of the world. My enemy's skin is bad
from eating boiled soap and scrubbing with potatoes.
My enemy's parts are detachable.
He is having a reaction to his medicine:
pain-free, confused. Am I

my enemy's enemy? My enemy's keeper? My
enemy? Ah, love, let us be true.
We're all a bit tired
to be killing so much, but we continue.
The tickets were bought through the mail long ago so why not.
No time to save face.

Action. Action.
A cardboard bomber flies by with its flaming nets.
We are here as on a darkling plain.
Make me an offer. I'm going fast.
The theater is so crowded no one can be sure
if the fire is in their hair
or in their wigs.

Suggestions for Discussion

1. Why does Levine choose to set what he has to say within the frame of Matthew Arnold's "Dover Beach"?

2. "Am I / my enemy's enemy? My enemy's keeper? My / enemy?…" Who or what is the enemy in the poem?

3. There is a sense in Levine's poem that the despair that undergirds Arnold's poem has evolved in our time into the enactment of a death and destruction that overflows everything. If this is the case, what has brought it about?

4. The author uses theatrical metaphors throughout his poem. Why? What do they help us to understand?

Suggestions for Writing

1. A poet works not by explication but by exemplification. Create ten images, or verbal pictures, that show to your reader something you want to convey. Try not to use modifiers. Nouns and verbs are most powerful by themselves.

2. War is a common subject of poetry. So is love. Find two other poems, on either of these topics, that say different things about the subject, and discuss them in an essay.

ANTHONY HECHT

The Dover Bitch

Anthony Hecht (1923–2004) was inspired to become a poet after reading T. S. Eliot and W. H. Auden at Bard College in New York. World War II forced him to postpone his artistic career, but many of his later poems were based on his experiences fighting in Europe. His books of poetry include *A Summoning of Stones* (1954), Pulitzer Prize winner *The Hard Hours* (1967), *Millions of Strange Shadows* (1977), and *The Transparent Man* (1990). Hecht also wrote a detailed study of Auden called *The Hidden Law* (1993) and, with Helen Bacon, produced a translation of Aeschylus' *Seven Against Thebes* (1975). This poem, like Mark Levine's "About Face," is a reaction to Matthew Arnold's "Dover Beach."

So there stood Matthew Arnold and this girl
With the cliffs of England crumbling away behind them,
And he said to her, "Try to be true to me,

And I'll do the same for you, for things are bad
All over, etc., etc."
Well now, I knew this girl. It's true she had read
Sophocles in a fairly good translation
And caught that bitter allusion to the sea,
But all the time he was talking she had in mind
The notion of what his whiskers would feel like
On the back of her neck. She told me later on
That after a while she got to looking out
At the lights across the channel, and really felt sad,
Thinking of all the wine and enormous beds
And blandishments in French and the perfumes.
And then she got really angry. To have been brought
All the way down from London, and then be addressed
As a sort of mournful cosmic last resort
Is really tough on a girl, and she was pretty.
Anyway, she watched him pace the room
And finger his watch-chain and seem to sweat a bit,
And then she said one or two unprintable things.
But you mustn't judge her by that. What I mean to say is,
She's really all right. I still see her once in a while
And she always treats me right. We have a drink
And I give her a good time, and perhaps it's a year
Before I see her again, but there she is,
Running to fat, but dependable as they come.
And sometimes I bring her a bottle of Nuit d'Amour.

Suggestions for Discussion

1. Why does the girl lose patience with Matthew Arnold?

2. What is the nature of the narrator's relationship with the girl? Do you believe he is truly happy when he is with her?

3. Does this poem change your attitude toward "Dover Beach" and its sentiments?

Suggestion for Writing

Explore the relationship between "Dover Beach," "About Face," and "The Dover Bitch." After comparing their different tones, structures, and concerns, identify which poem resonated with you the most and discuss why you find it is more relevant than the others.

Globalism, Nationalism, and Cultural Identity

Even the president of the United States
Sometimes must have
To stand naked.

—BOB DYLAN, "It's Alright, Ma (I'm Only Bleeding)"

It has always annoyed me to hear from the mouths of certain arbiters of blackness that middle-class blacks should "reach back" and pull up those blacks less fortunate than they—as though middle-class status were an unearned and essentially passive condition in which one needed a large measure of noblesse oblige to occupy one's time. My own image is of reaching back from a moving train to lift on board those who have no tickets.

— SHELBY STEELE, "On Being Black and Middle Class"

Musical Chairs

PETER GOURFAIN, 2004

©Peter Gourfain

NOTEBOOK

ADAM GOPNIK

The City and the Pillars

Adam Gopnik, art critic, travel writer, and regular contributor to the *New Yorker,* describes himself as a "comic-sentimental" essayist. *Paris to the Moon* (2001) collects articles and journal entries he produced while living in France. He wrote *High and Low: Modern Art and Popular Cul-*

Floating Memorial, Folded Street, watercolor on inkjet printer, Steven Holl, 2001. Courtesy Steven Holl Architects, New York.

ture (with Kirk Varnedoe, in 1990) and edited *Americans in Paris: A Literary Anthology* (2004). The following essay, published in the *New Yorker* shortly after the destruction of the World Trade Center, depicts Manhattan before and after the attack on September 11, 2001.

On the morning of the day they did it, the city was as beautiful as it had ever been. Central Park had never seemed so gleaming and luxuriant— the leaves just beginning to fall, and the light on the leaves left on the trees somehow making them at once golden and bright green. A bird-watcher in the Ramble made a list of the birds he saw there, from the northern flicker and the red-eyed vireo to the rose-breasted grosbeak and the Baltimore oriole. "Quite a few migrants around today," he noted happily.

In some schools, it was the first day, and children went off as they do on the first day, with the certainty that, this year, we will have fun again. The protective bubble that for the past decade or so had settled over the city, with a bubble's transparency and bright highlights, still seemed to be in place above us. We always knew that that bubble would burst, but we imagined it bursting as bubbles do: no one will be hurt, we thought, or they will be hurt only as people are hurt when bubbles burst, a little soap in your mouth. It seemed safely in place for another day as the children walked to school. The stockbroker fathers delivered—no, inserted—their kids into school as they always do, racing downtown, their cell phones already at work, like cartoons waiting for their usual morning caption: "Exasperated at 8 A.M."

A little while later a writer who happened to be downtown saw a flock of pigeons rise, high and fast, and thought. Why are the pigeons rising? It was only seconds before he realized that the pigeons had felt the wave of the concussion before he heard the sound. In the same way, the shock wave hit us before the sound, the image before our understanding. For the lucky ones, the day from then on was spent in a strange, calm, and soul-emptying back and forth between the impossible images on television and the usual things on the street.

Around noon, a lot of people crowded around a lamppost on Madison, right underneath a poster announcing the Wayne Thiebaud show at the Whitney: all those cakes, as if to signal the impotence of our abundance. The impotence of our abundance! In the uptown supermarkets, people began to shop. It was a hoarding instinct, of course, though oddly not brought on by any sense of panic; certainly no one on television or radio was suggesting that people needed to hoard. Yet people had the instinct to do it, and, in any case, in New York the instinct to hoard quickly seemed to shade over into the instinct to consume, shop for anything, shop because it might be a comfort. One woman emerged from a Gristede's on Lexington with a bottle of olive oil and said, "I had to get *something*." Mostly people

bought water—bottled water, French and Italian—and many people, waiting in the long lines, had Armageddon baskets: the Manhattan version, carts
filled with steaks, Häagen-Dazs, and butter. Many of the carts held the goods
of the bubble decade, hothouse goods: flavored balsamics and cappellini
and arugula. There was no logic to it, as one man pointed out in that testy,
superior, patient tone: "If trucks can't get through, the Army will take over
and give everybody K rations or some crazy thing; if they do, this won't matter." Someone asked him what was he doing uptown? He had been down
there, got out before the building collapsed, and walked up.

People seemed not so much to suspend the rituals of normalcy as to
carry on with them in a kind of bemusement—as though to reject the image
on the screen, as though to say, That's there, we're here, they're not here yet,
it's not here yet. "Everything turns away quite leisurely from the disaster,"
Auden wrote, about a painting of Icarus falling from the sky; now we know
why they turned away—they saw the boy falling from the sky, sure enough,
but they did not know what to do about it. If we do the things we know how
to do, New Yorkers thought, then what has happened will matter less.

The streets and parks were thinned of people, but New York is so
dense—an experiment in density, really, as Venice is an experiment in
water—that the thinning just produced the normal density of Philadelphia
or Baltimore. It added to the odd calm. 'You wouldn't put it in a book," a
young man with an accent said to a girl in the Park, and then he added, "Do
you like to ski?" Giorgio Armani was in the Park—Giorgio Armani? Yes,
right behind the Metropolitan Museum, with his entourage, beautiful Italian boys and girls in tight white T-shirts. "*Cinema,*" he kept saying, his
hands moving back and forth like an accordion player's. "*Cinema.*"

Even urban geography is destiny, and New York, a long thin island, cuts
downtown off from uptown, west side off from east. (And a kind of moral
miniaturization is always at work, as we try unconsciously to seal ourselves
from the disaster: people in Europe say "America attacked" and people in
America say "New York attacked" and people in New York think, Downtown
attacked.) For the financial community, this was the Somme; it was impossible not to know someone inside that building, or thrown from it. Whole companies, tiny civilizations, an entire Zip Code vanished. Yet those of us outside
that world, hovering in midtown, were connected to the people dying in the
towers only by New York's uniquely straight lines of sight—you looked right
down Fifth Avenue and saw that strange, still neat package of white smoke.

The city has never been so clearly, so surreally, sectioned as it became
on Wednesday and Thursday. From uptown all the way down to Fourteenth
Street, life is almost entirely normal—fewer cars, perhaps one note quieter
on the street, but children and moms and hot-dog vendors on nearly every
corner. In the flower district, the wholesalers unpack autumn branches from
the boxes they arrived in this morning. "That came over the bridge?" some-

one asks, surprised at the thought of a truck driver waiting patiently for hours just to bring in blossoming autumn branches. The vendor nods.

At Fourteenth Street, one suddenly enters the zone of the missing, of mourning not yet acknowledged. It is, in a way, almost helpful to walk in that strange new village, since the concussion wave of fear that has been sucking us in since Tuesday is replaced with an outward ripple of grief and need, something human to hold on to. The stanchions and walls are plastered with homemade color-Xerox posters, smiling snapshots above, a text below, searching for the missing: "Roger Mark Rasweiler. Missing, One WTC, 100th floor." "We Need Your Help: Giovanna 'Gennie' Gambale." "We're Looking for Kevin M. Williams, 104th Fl. WTC." "Have You Seen Him? Robert 'Bob' Dewitt." "Ed Feldman—Call Ross." "Millan Rustillo— Missing WTC." Every lost face is smiling, caught at Disney World or Miami Beach, on vacation. Every poster lovingly notes the missing person's height and weight to the last ounce and inch. "Clown tattoo on right shoulder," one says. On two different posters there is an apologetic note along with the holiday snap: "Was Not Wearing Sunglasses on Tuesday."

Those are the ones who've gone missing. On television, the reporters keep talking about the World Trade Center as a powerful symbol of American financial power. And yet it was, in large part, the back office of Wall Street. As Eric Darton showed in his fine social history of the towers, they were less a symbol of America's financial might than a symbol of the Port Authority's old inferiority complex. It was not the citadel of capitalism but, according to the real order of things in the capitalist world, just a come-on— a desperate scheme dreamed up in the late fifties to bring businesses back downtown. In later years, of course, downtown New York became the center of world trade, for reasons that basically had nothing to do with the World Trade Center, so that now Morgan Stanley and Cantor Fitzgerald were there, but for a long time it was also a big state office building, where you went to get a document stamped or a license renewed. No one loved it save children, who took to it because it was iconically so simple, so tall and two. When a child tried to draw New York, he would draw the simplest available icons: two rectangles and an airplane going by them.

Near Washington Square, the streets empty out, and the square itself is beautiful again. "I saw it coming," a bicycle messenger says. "I thought it was going to take off the top of that building." He points to the little Venetian-style campanile on Washington Square South. The Village seems like a village. In a restaurant on Washington Place at ten-thirty, the sous-chefs are quietly prepping for lunch, with the chains still on all the tables and the front door open and unguarded. "We're going to try and do dinner today," one of the chefs says. A grown woman rides a scooter down the middle of LaGuardia Place. Several café owners, or workers, go through the familiar act of hosing down the sidewalk. With the light pall of smoke hanging over everything, this everyday job becomes somehow cheering, cleansing. If you enter one of the open cafés and order a meal, the familiar dialogue—"And a green salad with that." "You mean a side salad?" "Yeah, that'd be fine....What kind of dressing do you have?—feels reassuring, too, another calming routine.

Houston Street is the dividing line, the place where the world begins to end. In SoHo, there is almost no one on the street. No one is allowed on the streets except residents, and they are hidden in their lofts. Nothing is visible, except the cloud of white smoke and soot that blows from the dense stillness below Canal. An art critic and a museum curator watched the explosions from right here. "It was a sound like two trucks crashing on Canal, no louder than that, than something coming by terribly fast, and the building was struck," the critic said. "I thought, This is it, mate, the nuclear attack. I'm going to die. I was peaceful about it, thought. But then the flame subsided, and then the building fell." The critic and the curator watched it fall together. Decades had passed in that neighborhood where people insisted that now everything was spectacle, nothing had meaning. Now there was a spectacle, and it *meant*.

The smell, which fills the empty streets of SoHo from Houston to Canal, blew uptown on Wednesday night, and is not entirely horrible from a reasonable distance—almost like the smell of smoked mozzarella, a smell of the bubble time. Closer in, it becomes acrid, and unbreathable. The white particulate smoke seems to wreathe the empty streets—to wrap right around them. The authorities call this the "frozen zone." In the "Narrative of A. Gordon Pym," spookiest and most cryptic of Poe's writings, a man approaches the extremity of existence, the pole beneath the Southern Pole. "The whole ashy material fell now continually around us," he records in his diary, "and in vast quantities. The range of vapor to the southward had arisen prodigiously in the horizon, and began to assume more distinctness of form. I can liken it to nothing but a limitless cataract, rolling silently into the sea from some immense and far-distant rampart in the heaven. The gigantic curtain ranged along the whole extent of the southern horizon. It emitted no sound." Poe, whose house around here was torn down not long ago, is a realist now.

More than any other city, New York exists at once as a city of symbols and associations, literary and artistic, and as a city of real things. This is an emotional truth, of course—New York is a city of wacky dreams and of disillusioning realities. But it is also a plain, straightforward architectural truth, a visual truth, a material truth. The city looks one way from a distance, a skyline full of symbols, inviting pilgrims and Visigoths, and another way up close, a city full of people. The Empire State and Chrysler Buildings exist as symbols of thirties materialism and as abstract ideas of skyscrapers and as big dowdy office buildings—a sign and then a thing and then a sign and then a thing and then a sign, going back and forth all the time. (It is possible to transact business in the Empire State Building, and only then nudge yourself and think, Oh, yeah, this is the Empire State Building.) The World Trade Center existed both as a thrilling double exclamation point at the end of the island and as a rotten place to have to go and get your card stamped, your registration renewed.

The pleasure of living in New York has always been the pleasure of living in both cities at once: the symbolic city of symbolic statements (this is big, I am rich, get me) and the everyday city of necessities, MetroCards and coffee shops and long waits and longer trudges. On the afternoon of that day, the symbolic city, the city that the men in the planes had attacked, seemed much less important than the real city, where the people in the towers lived. The bubble is gone, but the city beneath—naked now in a new way, not startling but vulnerable—seemed somehow to increase in our affection, our allegiance. On the day they did it, New Yorkers walked the streets without, really, any sense of "purpose" or "pride" but with the kind of tender necessary patriotism that lies in just persisting.

New York, E. B. White wrote in 1949, holds a steady, irresistible charm for perverted dreamers of destruction, because it seems so impossible. "The intimation of mortality is part of New York now," he went on to write, "in the sound of jets overhead." We have heard the jets now, and we will probably never be able to regard the city with quite the same exasperated, ironic affection we had for it before. Yet on the evening of the day, one couldn't walk through Central Park, or down Seventh Avenue, or across an empty but hardly sinister Times Square—past the light on the trees, or the kids on their scooters, or the people sitting worried in the outdoor restaurants with menus, frowning, as New Yorkers always do, as though they had never seen a menu before—without feeling a surprising rush of devotion to the actual New York, Our Lady of the Subways, New York as it is. It is the symbolic city that draws us here, and the real city that keeps us. It seems hard but important to believe that that city will go on, because we now know what it would be like to lose it, and it feels like losing life itself.

Suggestions for Discussion

1. How does Gopnik re-create the atmosphere in New York City as it was mere hours before the attack on September 11, 2001? According to Gopnik, how did that atmosphere change as soon as the planes struck the World Trade Center?

2. What is Gopnik saying when he suggests that the World Trade Center was a relatively unimportant building before it was destroyed, beloved only by children who enjoyed drawing it?

3. In Gopnik's view, what will life in New York City be like from now on?

4. The drawing on p. 686 is an architect's vision for a new structure to be built at Ground Zero, the former site of the World Trade Center. Another plan has since been adopted, so there is no real-world application for this drawing. In your opinion, do you consider this vision to be practical? How do practicality and vision affect or impede each other? In small groups, discuss this issue of vision versus practicality. Since the drawing does not represent a possible future, what significance might it still have? As art?

Suggestion for Writing

Compare the two views of Manhattan on September 11, 2001: Gopnik's written account and Matsuchek's photograph on p. 434. How do the two representations differ in focus and in the feelings they evoke? What message does the torn flag convey in Matuschek's photographic moment? Reflect on the changes of meaning of ordinary things and happenstances, through extraordinary events, by our projections.

∾∾∾∾∾

ANTHONY SHADID

Legacy of the Prophet

Anthony Shadid is a foreign correspondent for the *Washington Post*. His coverage of the Iraq war earned him the 2004 Pulitzer Prize for International Reporting and provided the basis for his book *Night Draws Near: Iraq's People in the Shadow of America's War* (2005). This selection is from the second edition of *Legacy of the Prophet* (2000, 2002), Shadid's exploration of contemporary Islamic politics and its ties to American foreign policy.

His words came suddenly, delivered with righteousness. His concern was Osama bin Ladin. "A hero, that's the feeling of the people right now, that he's fighting to save the Muslim world," Mohammed Abdullah said. "When he dies, he'll be a martyr." His sentiments, unadulterated by sensitivity, left me with a sense I had felt often as a journalist in the Muslim world. In October 2001, as smoke continued to rise from the rubble of the World Trade Center and the ugly gash in the Pentagon lay bare, I traveled to Cairo, one of the Muslim world's greatest cities, to cover one aspect of a story that, by then, had become sadly familiar to me. Off and on, for nearly ten years, I had reported and written about the attacks, the strife and the bombings that had come to define, for much of the world, the face of political Islam. Similar circumstances brought me here again, and much remained familiar. There was grief at the shedding of innocents' blood in the attacks of September 11 and over the death of more innocents in the war that followed in Afghanistan. There was disbelief at the spectacle that terrorism can unleash. And, no less troubling, there was the same misunderstanding, the same yawning gulf in perceptions that seemed to follow the scars left by the attacks.

Abdullah, I soon learned, was not alone in his beliefs. To the young men that had gathered around me at a sprawling bus stop in Cairo, their beards suggesting a fervent devotion, the Saudi militant exiled in Afghanistan was a symbol of an embattled religion, the very personification of the men's own frustrations at a faith overwhelmed by an omnipotent West. Their issue was justice, or a lack of it. Bin Ladin, they said, spoke of defending Palestinians, of ending sanctions on Iraq, of curtailing near-total U.S. sway over the region. An older man in a white peasant gown spoke up, raising his voice over the square's circus of vendors hawking fruit and buses barreling down the street, their exhaust stirring the dust carried by Egypt's desert winds. "He's a man who defends his rights," the man insisted, as others nodded in agreement. "If someone tries to hit me, I have to defend myself. He's defending his land, his religion, his rights and himself."

How had we reached this point? As I stood amid Cairo's thriving chaos, I began to think about the divide that made two cultures, both defined to a great extent by religion, almost incomprehensible to each other. Many Muslims, whose disenchantment with the United States evoked an almost nihilist disdain, seemed to cast bin Ladin as militant rather than terrorist, dissident rather than executioner. His defiance of the West had assumed the mantle of heroic resistance. The world's affairs here were defined not by liberty, not by freedom, but instead by justice, a concept that takes on greater importance to those without it. To the men at the bus stop, the United States and, by default, the West were the instruments for depriving justice across the Muslim world, a vast territory embracing one billion people who make up a majority in some forty-five countries.

Passions were no less ardent in the West. The attacks of September 11 were the latest, most persuasive evidence of modern-day Islam's seeming penchant for senseless butchery. Before much of the world, and in a frighteningly short time, one of history's most sublime prophetic messages had become a faith defined not by the omnipotence of God and the need for generosity and justice but by a darker, more menacing side of human nature. Lost were memories of Islam's proud past: the Ottoman Empire's centuries of glory, Arab accomplishments in mathematics, astronomy and medicine, the conquests of an Islamic army whose domain stretched from Central Asia to southwestern France and Islam's heritage in preserving, tailoring and then transmitting Greek philosophy to medieval Europe. Instead, a new legacy had evolved in our lifetimes, and the messages of Islamic militants scrawled in blood were poised to leave a more lasting impression. The result, it seems, is yet another repetition of the fear, misunderstanding and hostility that have defined relations between Islam and the West since before Pope Urban II launched the crusades to liberate the Holy Land in the eleventh century.

From 1979 on, U.S. policy toward the Muslim world has been dangerous and remarkably flawed. Typically, it has been content to view political Islam as inherently threatening or as a target of sometimes cynical opportunity. The approach has helped bring about nearly two decades of enmity with Iran and conflict with Sudan. In Saudi Arabia, our blind support for the monarchy—and, by default, its corruption and repression—has cultivated an Islamic opposition that today threatens both U.S. troops and access to the world's largest oil reserves. U.S. policy toward Israel and the Palestinian authority has inflamed activists there, embroiling the United States in a conflict that need not be our own. In distant Afghanistan, on the cultural and political periphery of the Muslim world, the United States opportunistically armed and supported militias that drew on Islam to fight the Soviet Union in the 1980s. Today, many of those same militants are sworn enemies of America. Bin Ladin, of course, became their most influential graduate.

There is an alternative, one that will require a particular element of courage in the wake of the attacks of September 11 and the war in Afghanistan. The United States and the West face a strategic choice, and that choice will go far in determining the course of politics in much of the Muslim world. Egypt again may be enlightening. Since the Arab world's largest country signed a peace treaty with Israel in 1979, the United States has acted as its patron, wielding substantial, almost colonial, influence over its internal and foreign affairs. This influence, however, has not entailed pressure on its authoritarian government to enact democratic reform. Both Egypt and the United States recognize that such changes, in time, would give rise to an already popular Islamic current in Egypt's political life. That policy is shortsighted and clearly untenable. Repression has already failed in Iran and is soon to fail in the Persian Gulf and in countries like Egypt, where time and again the government has failed to stamp out the substantial support political Islam enjoys, giving rise instead to a generation of militants whose exploits still scar New York, Washington, Luxor, Islamabad and beyond. That leaves one viable alternative: The West must encourage democracy in places like Egypt with the realization that it is, in effect, encouraging Islamism by making room for its growth. It means governments might be elected that have no love for the United States. On the other hand, America's support for those same movements—the Center Party, for instance—could bring forth a new relationship in which U.S. policy and political Islam find common ground. To do so, the West must take further steps in ending the isolation of traditional enemies, giving countries like Iran an opportunity to evolve into more democratic states. In nations like Turkey, Jordan, Kuwait and Yemen, where democratic Islamic movements are now emerging or already in place, the United States must seek to make clear that their assumption of power is not in itself an adverse development. The choice is not sentimental, and without question, the risk of such policies is great. But the potential benefits are myriad—stability in an oil-rich region, democracy in authoritarian countries, a more viable weapon against the scourge of terrorism and the first step in ending a cultural conflict that, today more than ever, threatens to escalate. Both sides must take the journey together.

Suggestions for Discussion

1. How does Shadid present the different perspectives of the West and the Islamic world? Do you think he is successful in creating sympathy for both?

2. What factors does Shadid cite as causes for the rift between the American and Muslim cultures? Explain why you do or do not agree with his assessment, and cite other factors that might be responsible for encouraging conflict.

3. Why do you think Shadid puts so much effort into describing the bus stop scene in Cairo?

Suggestion for Writing

Contrast Shadid's idea of America's role in world politics with the viewpoint presented by Elie Wiesel in the next reading, *The America I Love*. Which vision of foreign policy do you find more persuasive? Cite specific arguments used by both authors.

ELIE WIESEL

The America I Love

Elie Wiesel (b. 1928 in Sighet, Transylvania) was deported to the Nazi concentration camps at the age of fifteen, where he lost his parents and his younger sister. After World War II, he moved to Paris and became a journalist. His memoir *Night*, recounting his experiences in the camps, was published in 1958. Wiesel has since written more than forty books and served as an advocate for human rights around the world. He has been awarded the Congressional Gold Medal, the Presidential Medal of Freedom, and the Medal of Liberty Award. In 1986, he won the Nobel Peace Prize and established the Elie Wiesel Foundation for Humanity in collaboration with his wife, Marion. In this article, Wiesel recalls the intense patriotism he felt upon becoming an American citizen in 1963 and defends America against criticisms that it started the Iraq war for selfish reasons.

The day I received American citizenship was a turning point in my life. I had ceased to be stateless. Until then, unprotected by any government and unwanted by any society, the Jew in me was overcome by a feeling of pride mixed with gratitude.

From that day on, I felt privileged to belong to a country which, for two centuries, has stood as a living symbol of all that is charitable and decent to victims of injustice everywhere—a country in which every person is entitled to dream of happiness, peace and liberty; where those who have are taught to give back.

In America, compassion for the refugee and respect for the other still have biblical connotations.

Grandiloquent words used for public oratory? Even now, as America is in the midst of puzzling uncertainty and understandable introspection because of tragic events in Iraq, these words reflect my personal belief. For I cannot forget another day that remains alive in my memory: April 11, 1945.

That day I encountered the first American soldiers in the Buchenwald concentration camp. I remember them well. Bewildered, disbelieving, they walked around the place, hell on each, where our destiny had been played out. They looked at us, just liberated, and did not know what to do or say. Survivors snatched from the dark throes of death, we were empty of all hope—too weak, too emaciated to hug them or even speak to them. Like lost children, the American soldiers wept and wept with rage and sadness. And we received their tears as if they were heartrending offerings from a wounded and generous humanity.

Ever since that encounter, I cannot repress my emotion before the flag and the uniform—anything that represents American heroism in battle. That is especially true on July Fourth. I reread the Declaration of Independence, a document sanctified by the passion of a nation's thirst for justice and sovereignty, forever admiring both its moral content and majestic intonation. Opposition to oppression in all its forms, defense of all human liberties, celebration of what is right in social intercourse: All this and much more is in that text, which today has special meaning.

Granted, U.S. history has gone through severe trials, of which antiblack racism was the most scandalous and depressing. I happened to witness it in the late Fifties, as I traveled through the South. What did I feel? Shame. Yes, shame for being white. What made it worse was the realization that, at that time, racism was the law, thus making the law itself immoral and unjust.

Still, my generation was lucky to see the downfall of prejudice in many of its forms. True, it took much pain and protest for that law to be changed, but it was. Today, while fanatically stubborn racists are still around, some of them vocal, racism as such has vanished from the American scene. That is true of anti-Semitism too. Jew-haters still exist here and there, but organized anti-Semitism does not—unlike in Europe, where it has been growing with disturbing speed.

As a great power, America has always seemed concerned with other people's welfare, especially in Europe. Twice in the 20th century, it saved the "Old World" from dictatorship and tyranny.

America understands that a nation is great not because its economy is flourishing or its army invincible but because its ideals are loftier. Hence America's desire to help those who have lost their freedom to conquer it again. America's credo might read as follows: For an individual, as for a nation, to *be* free is an admirable duty—but to help others *become* free is even more admirable.

Some skeptics may object: But what about Vietnam? And Cambodia? And the support some administrations gave to corrupt regimes in Africa or the Middle East? And the occupation of Iraq? Did we go wrong—and if so, where?

And what are we to make of the despicable, abominable "interrogation methods" used on Iraqi prisoners of war by a few soldiers (but even a few are too many) in Iraqi military prisons?

Well, one could say that no nation is composed of saints alone. None is sheltered from mistakes or misdeeds. All have their Cain and Abel. It takes vision and courage to undergo serious soul-searching and to favor moral conscience over political expediency. And America, in extreme situations, is endowed with both. America is always ready to learn from its mishaps. Self-criticism remains its second nature.

Not surprising, some Europeans do not share such views. In extreme left-wing political and intellectual circles, suspicion and distrust toward America is the order of the day. They deride America's motives for its military interventions, particularly in Iraq. They say: It's just money. As if America went to war only to please the oil-rich capitalists.

They are wrong. America went to war to liberate a population too long subjected to terror and death.

We see in newspapers and magazines and on television screens the mass graves and torture chambers imposed by Saddam Hussein and his accomplices. One cannot but feel grateful to the young Americans who leave their families, some to lose their lives, in order to bring to Iraq the first rays of hope—without which no people can imagine the happiness of welcoming freedom.

Hope is a key word in the vocabulary of men and women like myself and so many others who discovered in America the strength to overcome cynicism and despair.

Remember the legendary Pandora's box? It is filled with implacable, terrifying curses. But underneath, at the very bottom, there is hope. Now as before, now more than ever, it is waiting for us.

Suggestions for Discussion

1. Do you agree with Wiesel's assertion that America started the Iraq war for unselfish reasons? Justify your position.

2. Wiesel maintains that racism and anti-Semitism have vanished from mainstream American society. Do you believe this is an accurate assessment? And do you think there are other forms of prejudice thriving in our culture today, or has America truly, as Wiesel asserts, learned "from its mishaps" of the past?

Suggestion for Writing

Compare Wiesel's concept of America's role in the global community with the views presented by Anthony Shadid in *Legacy of the Prophet* (p. 692).

PERSONAL REMINISCENCES

∾∾∾∾∾

RICHARD RODRIGUEZ

Hispanic

Richard Rodriguez (b. 1944) earned his B.A. at Stanford and his M.A. at Columbia, and he has done further graduate work at the University of California, Berkeley, and the Warburg Institute, London. He has been a Fulbright fellow, held an NEH Fellowship, won the Commonwealth Gold Medal for *Hunger for Memory: The Education of Richard Rodriguez* (1982), and was awarded the Anisfield-Wolf Award for Race Relations. In 1992 he published a biography of his father, *Days of Obligation: An Argument with My Mexican Father*. The following text, reprinted from *Brown: The Last Discovery of America* (2002), is an examination of the cultural label "Hispanic" and its connotations.

Hi.spa´.nick. 1. Spanish, *adjective*. 2. Latin American, *adjective*. 3. His-pano, *noun*. An American citizen or resident of Spanish descent. 4. Duck-ing under the cyclone fence, *noun*. 5. Seen running from the scene of the crime, *adjective*. Clinging to a raft off the Florida coast. Elected mayor in New Jersey. Elevated to bishop or traded to the San Diego Padres. Awarded the golden pomegranate by the U.S. Census Bureau: "most fertile." Soon, an oxymoron: America's largest minority. An utter absurdity: "destined to out-number blacks." A synonym for the future (salsa having replaced catsup on most American kitchen tables). Madonna's daughter. Sammy Sosa's son. Lit-tle Elián and his Great Big Family. A jillarioso novel about ten sisters, their sorrows and joys and intrauterine devices. The new face of American Protes-tantism: Evangelical minister, tats on his arms; wouldn't buy a used car from. Highest high school dropout rate; magical realism.

The question remains: Do Hispanics exist?

I tell myself, on mornings like this—the fog has burned off early—that I am really going to give it up. Hispanicism cannot interest me anymore. My desk a jumble of newspaper clippings. Look at all this! Folders. It looks like a set for *The Makropolous Case*. I will turn instead to the death agony of a moth, the gigantic shuddering of lantern-paper wings. Or I will count the wrinkles on Walden Pond. I will write some of those constipated, low-paying, fin de siècle essays about the difficulty of *saying* anything in this, our age. *Visi d'arte,* from now on, as Susan Sontag sang so memorably from the chapel of Sant'Andrea della Valle.

For years now I have pursued Hispanicism, as a solitary, self-appointed inspector in an old Hitchcock will dog some great hoax; amassing data; abstractedly setting down his coffee cup at a precarious angle to its saucer, to the stack of papers and books and maps on which it rests, because he is drawn to some flash-lit, spyglassed item in the morning paper. I am catching them up, slowly, inexorably, confident of the day—soon—when I shall publish my findings.

Soon. I take my collapsible double-irony on tour to hotel ballroom conferences and C-SPAN-televised luncheons and "Diversity Week" lectures at universities. For a fee, I rise to say I am not Latin American, because I am Hispanic. I am Hispanic because I live in the United States. *Thank you.* (For a larger fee, I will add there is no such thing as a Hispanic. *Thank you.*)

But this morning I have decided, after all, to join the hoax.

Hispanic has had its way with me. I suspect also with you. The years have convinced me that Hispanic is a noun that can't lose. An adjective with legs. There is money in it.

Hispanic (the noun, the adjective) has encouraged the Americanization of millions of Hispanics. But at the same time, Hispanic—the ascending tally announced by the U.S. Census Bureau—has encouraged the Latinization of non-Hispanics.

As a Hispanic, as a middle-aged noun, like Oscar Wilde descending to gaol, I now take my place in the booth provided within that unglamorous American fair devised by the Richard Nixon administration in 1973 (O.M.B. Statistical Directive 15). Within the Nixonian fair are five exposition halls:

BLACK;
WHITE;
ASIAN/PACIFIC ISLANDER;
NATIVE AMERICAN/ESKIMO;
HISPANIC.

They aren't much, these drafty rooms—about what you'd expect of government issue. Nixon's fair attempted to describe the world that exists by portraying a world that doesn't. Statisticians in overalls moved India— *ouffff*—that heavy, spooled and whirligigged piece of Victorian mahogany, over beneath the green silk tent of Asia. Mayan Indians from the Yucatán were directed to the Hispanic pavilion (Spanish colonial), which they must share with Argentine tangoistas, Colombian drug dealers, and Russian Jews who remember Cuba from the viewpoint of Miami. Of the five ports, Hispanic has the least reference to blood. There is no such thing as Hispanic blood. *(Do I not bleed?)* Though I meet young Hispanics who imagine they descend from it.

Nixon's fair does at least succeed in portraying the United States in relation to the world. One can infer a globe from a pentagram.

Over my head, as I write these words, a New World Indian is singing in the language of the conquistador. (A Korean contractor, hired by my landlord, has enlisted a tribe of blue-jumpered Mexican Indians to reroof the apartment building where I live.) In trustworthy falsetto, the young man lodges a complaint against an intangible mistress unfond, as high above him as the stars, and as cold. Yesterday, as he was about to hoist a roll of tar paper, this same young man told me the choir of roofers, excepting "*el patron,*" originate from a single village in a far state of Mexico. And a few minutes ago, I overheard them all—the Mexicans and the Korean contractor—negotiating their business in pidgin (Spanish, curiously; I would have expected English). Then my ceiling shook with their footfalls. And with bolts of tar paper flung upon it. My library leapt in its shelves—those ladies and gentlemen, so unaccustomed.

Tomorrow, having secured my abstractions against the rainy season, the Mexican Indians will fly away to some other rooftop in the city, while I must remain at this desk.

Why must I? Because my literary agent has encouraged from me a book that answers a simple question: *What do Hispanics mean to the life of America?* He asked me that question several years ago in a French restaurant on East Fifty-seventh Street, as I watched a waiter approach our table holding before him a shimmering *îles flottantes*.

But those were palmier days. Before there were Hispanics in America, there was another fictitious, inclusive genus: the Latin Lover. The Latin Lover was male counterpart to the vamp. He specialized in the inarticulate—"dark"—passions; perhaps a little cruel. He was mascaraed, mute, prepotent. Phantom, sheikh, or matador, he was of no philosophy but appetite. His appetite was blond.

White America's wettest perdition fantasy has always been consanguinity with some plum-colored thigh. The Latin Lover was a way of meeting the fantasy halfway. This was not a complicated scenario. Nor was Hollywood fussy about casting it. Ramon Navarro, Rudolph Valentino, Ezio Pinza, Rossano Brazzi, Ricardo Montalban, Prince Rainier, George Chakiris, all descended from the dusky isles of Cha-Cha.

Probably the last unironic Latin Lover conscripted into American fantasy was Omar Sharif, hired to seduce Peter O'Toole.

But, by then, Lucille Ball had undermined the fantasy by domesticating the Latin Lover. In the 1950s, Lucille Ball insisted upon casting her real-life husband as her fictional husband, against the advice of CBS Television executives. Desi Arnaz was not mute, nor were his looks smoldering. In fact his eyes bulged with incredulity at *la vida loca* with Lucy. Curiously, Lucy was the madcap for having married a Cuban bandleader in the first place. Curiously, Desi was the solid American citizen (though he did wear a smoking jacket at home). Soon, millions of Americans began a Monday night vigil, awaiting the birth of Little Ricky, the first Hispanic.

By the time *I Love Lucy* went to divorce court, Desi Arnaz had been replaced on our television screens by Fidel Castro. Castro was a perverted hot-blood—he was a cold warrior—as was his Byronic sidekick, Ché. Our fantasy toyed for a time with what lay beneath the beards. When we eventually got a translation, we took fright. *Bad wolf!* Rhetoric too red for our fantasy.

The red wolf ripped away the Copacabana curtain—all the nightclub gaity of Latin America in old black-and-white movies—to reveal a land of desperate want.

In the early 1960s, Mexican Americans were described by American liberals as an "invisible minority." Americans nevertheless saw farmworkers in the Central Valley of California singing and praying in Spanish. Americans later saw angry Chicanos on TV imitating the style of black militancy.

By the 1970s, even as millions of Latin Americans came north, seeking their future as capitalists, the Latin Lover faded from America's imagination.

Surviving Chicanos (one still meets them) scorn the term Hispanic, in part because it was Richard Nixon who drafted the noun and who made the adjective uniform. Chicanos resist the term, as well, because it reduces the many and complicated stories of the Mexican in America to a mere chapter of a much larger saga that now includes Hondurans and Peruvians and Cubans. Chicanos resent having to share mythic space with parvenus and numerically lesser immigrant Latin American populations. After all, Mexican Americans number more than seventy percent of the nation's total Hispanics. And, Chicanos say, borrowing a tabula rasa from American Indians, we are not just another "immigrant" population in the United States. We were here before the *Mayflower*. Which is true enough, though "we" and "here" are blurred by imprecision. California was once Mexico, as were other parts of the Southwestern United States. So we were here when here was there. In truth, however, the majority of Mexican Americans, or our ancestors, crossed a border.

One meets Hispanics who refuse Hispanic because of its colonial tooling. Hispanic, they say, places Latin America (once more) under the rubric of Spain. An alternate noun the disaffected prefer is "Latino," because they imagine the term locates them in the Americas, which the term now does in all revised American dictionaries, because Latinos insist that it does. (What is language other than an agreement, like Greenwich Mean Time?) In fact, Latino commits Latin America to Iberian memory as surely as does Hispanic. And Latino is a Spanish word, thus also paying linguistic obeisance to Spain. For what, after all, does "Latin" refer to, if not the imperial root system?

Hispanicus sui.

My private argument with Latino is no more complicated than my dislike for a dictation of terms. I am Latino against my will: I write for several newspapers—the *Los Angeles Times* most often—papers that have chosen to warrant "Latino" over "Hispanic" as correct usage. The newspaper's computer becomes sensitive, not to say jumpy, as regards correct political usage. Every Hispanic the computer busts is digitally repatriated to Latino. As I therefore also become.

In fact, I do have a preference for Hispanic over Latino. To call oneself Hispanic is to admit a relationship to Latin America in English. *Soy* Hispanic is a brown assertion.

Hispanic nativists who, of course, would never call themselves Hispanic, nonetheless have a telling name for their next-door neighbors who are not Hispanic. The word is "Anglo." Do Irish Americans become Anglos? And do you suppose a Chinese American or an African American is an Anglo? Does the term define a group of Americans by virtue of a linguistic tie to England or by the lack of a tie to Spain? (Come now, think. Did no one in your family take a Spanish course? In high school?) In which case, the more interesting question becomes whether Hispanics who call Anglos Anglo are themselves Anglo?

Nevertheless, in a Texas high school, according to the *Dallas Morning News,* a gang of "Anglos" and a gang of "Hispanics" shed real blood in a nonfictional cafeteria, in imitation of a sixteenth-century sea battle the students doubtlessly never heard of. Who could have guessed that a European rivalry would play itself out several hundred years after Philip's Armada was sunk by Elizabeth's navy? And here? No other country in the world has been so confident of its freedom from memory. Yet Americans comically (because unknowingly) assume proxy roles within a centuries-old quarrel of tongues.

Englande and España divided much of the Americas between them. England gave her colonial territories a remarkable code of civil law, a spectacular literature, a taste for sweeties, and the protean pronoun that ushered in the modern age—"I"—the lodestar for Protestant and capitalist and Hispanic memoirist. Counter-Reformation Spain gave its New World possessions *nosotros*—the cupolic "we"—an assurance of orthodoxy, baroque, fugue, smoke, sunglasses, and a piquant lexicon for miscegenation. Every combination of races is accounted for in New World Spanish. (Except Hispanic.) (Or Latino.)

The numerical rise of the Hispanic in the United States occasioned language skirmishes, especially in those parts of the country where the shadow of Philip's crown once crossed Elizabeth's scepter. On the one hand, in the 1960s, Chicano neo-nationalists attempted to make "bilingual education" the cornerstone of their political agenda, since little other than tongue (and not even that oftentimes) united Hispanics. Anglo nativists distributed ballots to establish English as "the official language of the United States." In truth, America is a more complicated country than either faction dares admit.

Americans do not speak "English." Even before our rebellion against England, our tongue tasted of Indian—*succotash, succotash,* we love to say it; *Mississippi,* we love to spell. We speak American. Our tongue is not something slow and mucous that plods like an oyster through its bed in the sea, afearing of taint or blister. Our tongue sticks out; it is a dog's tongue, an organ of curiosity and science.

The history of a people—their hungers, weathers, kinships, humors, erotic salts and pastimes—gets told by turns of phrase. Which is why the best history of the United States I ever read is not a history of battles and presidents and such, but H. L. Mencken's *The American Language,* an epic of nouns and verbs and proverbs; things we pick up or put down by name.

By 1850, William C. Fowler was describing "American dialects." Nine years later, John Russell Bartlett offered a glossary of "words and phrases usually regarded as peculiar to the United States": archaisms, et cetera. The American tongue created what Russell called "negroisms"—cadences, inflections, parodies, refusals. Our lewd tongue partook of everything that washed over it; everything that it washed—even a disreputable history. That is how young Walt Whitman heard America singing in the nineteenth century, heard the varied carols of trade in old New York harbor, heard young fellows, robust, friendly, singing with open mouths.

Nativists who want to declare English the official language of the United States do not understand the omnivorous appetite of the language they wish to protect. Neither do they understand that their protection would harm our tongue. (A restaurant in my neighborhood advertises "Harm on Rye.") Those Americans who would build a fence around American English to forestall the Trojan burrito would turn American into a frightened tongue, a shrinking little oyster tongue, as French has lately become, priested over by the Ancients of the Académie, who fret so about *le weekend.*

In an essay published in *Harper's* of April 1917, an immigrant son, M. E. Ravage, complained about the way Americans lick the oak leaves and acorns off the old monikers, so that they became "emasculated and devoid of either character or meaning. Mordecai—a name full of romantic association—had been changed to the insipid monosyllable Max. Rebecca—mother of the race—was in America Becky. Samuel had been shorn to Sam, Abraham to Abe, Israel to Izzy."

How Ricardo became rich: When I was new to this tongue I now include myself in, I learned some things that were true about America from its corn, its speed, its disinclination to be tied down, pretty much; its inclination toward shortcuts, abbreviations, sunwise turns. I learned from "hi" and "nope" and "OK." We Americans like the old, rubbed phrases; we like better the newest, sassiest, most abbreviated: Y2K. The most bubbulous American word I learned early on was the unexpected word for one's father (though not mine) and soda and what the weasel goes: pop.

I observed parents laughing over their children's coinages. I inferred the burden and responsibility of each adolescent generation to come up with neat subversions; to reinvent adolescence in a patois inscrutable to adults. The older generation expected it.

But not in my family. My mother and father (with immigrant pragmatism) assumed the American tongue would reinvent their children. Just so did several immigrant Hispanic mothers in Southern California recently remark their children's reluctance to join America. These mothers feared their children were not swimming in the American current—not in the swifts and not in the depths; not even in the pop. They blamed "bilingual education," a leaky boat theorem ostensibly designed to sink into the American current. (In fact, the theorem became a bureaucracy preoccupied with prolonging itself.) These few mothers organized an opposition to bilingual education and eventually they sank the Armada in California. Theirs was an American impulse: to engage the American flow directly and to let their children be taken by it.

But the American current always fears itself going dry—it longs, always, for a wetter wah-wah (there used to be a night club called "King Tut's Wah-Wah Hut"); yearns now to swizzle Latin America in its maw. Spanish is becoming unofficially but truly the second language of the United States. Moreover, Yankee pragmatism accomplishes the romance of the American tongue. By the 1980s, advertising executives in L.A. and Miami were the first to describe the United States as "the fifth-largest Spanish-speaking market in the world." Pragmatism made Spanish the language of cheap labor from fishing villages in Alaska to Chinese restaurants in Georgia to my rooftop here in San Francisco.

Thus does official America now communicate in at least two "voices," like a Tuva singer; three in Eurasian San Francisco. And if it isn't entirely English, it is nevertheless entirely American.

Press ONE, if you wish to continue in English. Pragmatism leads to Spanish signage at government offices, hospitals, parking lots, bus stops, polls. Telephone instructions, prescription instructions, microwave instructions— virtually all instructions in America are in Spanish as well as English. American politicians, too, begin to brush up their Yanqui-Dudel.

I remain skeptical of the effect pragmatic Spanish might have on the assimilation of Latin American immigrants. Working-class newcomers from Latin America do not suffer the discontinuity that previous generations used to propel themselves into the future tense. But middle-class Americans, friends of mine, composites of friends of mine, of a liberal bent, nice people, OK people, see nothing wrong with bilingual education. In fact, they wish their own children to be bilingual. In fact, they send their kids to French schools. In fact, they ask if I know of a housekeeper who might inadvertently teach their children Spanish while she dusts under the piano.

Nope.

But I marvel at the middle-class American willingness to take Spanish up. Standing in the burrito line in a Chinese neighborhood, I notice how many customers know the chopsticks of Spanish: "carnitas" and "guacamole" and "sí," "gracias," "refritos," and "caliente," and all the rest of what they need to know. And it occurs to me that the Chinese-American couple in front of me, by speaking Spanish, may actually be speaking American English.

On an American Airlines flight to New York, I listen to the recorded bilingual safety instructions. "She" speaks in cheerful, speedo, gum-scented American English. "He" partners her every unlikely event in Spanish; makes tragedy sound a tad less unlikely. (The Latin Lover speaks, I think to myself.)

Some years ago, I stood on a bluff on the San Diego side of the U.S.–Mexico border, watching Latin American peasants bent double and yet moving rapidly through the dark. I experienced something like the confounding stasis one dislikes in those Escher prints where the white birds fly east as the black birds fly west and the gray birds seem unformed daubs of marzipan. Was I watching the past become the future or the future becoming the past?

Back in the 1960s, Chicano activists referred to the "reconquista" of the United States, by which they meant the Southwest was becoming, again, Spanish-speaking, as it had been in the 1840s (history, therefore, a circle, and not, as America had always insisted, a straight line). Then again I might be watching an advance of the Spanish crown—Latin American peasants as cannon fodder for the advance of King Philip II; spies in cloaks who will insinuate themselves into Anglo households to whisper Ave Marias into baby's shell-like ear.

Sitting on American Airlines flight 64, I am not so sure. The numbers of Latin American immigrants making their way into the United States more truly honor England. Millions of Latin Americans, my parents among them, have come to the United States because of the enduring failures of Father Spain. Their coming honors England.

Her face painted white, she receives the passenger list into her gem-encrusted hand, but does not look upon it.

The Armada sank, ma'am.

There is glint in her simian eye. Lips recede from tallow teeth to speak:

They are trumped, then, My Lord Admiral.

The airplane shudders down the runway, hoisting sail.

What did Nixon know? Did he really devise to rid himself of a bunch of spic agitators by officially designating them a minority, entitled to all rights, honors, privileges, and obligations thereto appertaining: rhetorical flatteries, dollars, exploding cigars? (Maybe, by the same token, he could put blacks on notice that they were no longer such a hot ticket.)

A young Bolivian in Portland giggled, oh quite stupidly, at my question, her hand patting her clavicle as if she held a fan. I had asked her whether she had yet become Hispanic. Perhaps she didn't understand the question.

In *The Next American Nation*, Michael Lind observes that "real Hispanics think of themselves not as generic Hispanics, but as Mexicans, or Puerto Ricans or Cubans or Chileans." Lind is wrong. Well, he is right in the past tense; he is wrong in the future. You won't find Hispanics in Latin America (his point)— not in the quickening cities, not in the emasculated villages. You need to come to the United States to meet Hispanics (my point). What Hispanic immigrants learn within the United States is to view themselves in a new way, as belonging to Latin America entire—precisely at the moment they no longer do.

America's brilliance is a lack of subtlety. Most Americans are soft on geography. We like puzzles with great big pieces, piecrust coasts. And we're not too fussy about the midlands. But American obliviousness of the specific becomes a gift of prophesy regarding the approaching mass. Our impatience has created the map of the future. Many decades before Germans spoke of the EEC or the French could imagine buying french fries with Euros, Americans spoke of "Europe" (a cloud bank, the Eiffel Tower, the Colosseum, any decorative ormolu, inventing the place in novels and government reports, blurring borders and tongues and currencies and Prussians and Talleyrands into an abstraction, the largest unit, the largest parenthesis that can yet contain onion domes, Gothic spires, windmills, gondolas, bidets, and the *Mona Lisa*).

Many European men, such as the gondolier in Venice, come home from work to eat their noonday meals (according to an American social studies textbook, c. 1959).

Similarly, and for many generations, slaves and the descendants of slaves in America invented a homeland called "Africa"—a land before slave ships, a prelapsarian savanna whereupon the provocatively dressed gazelle could stroll safely after dark. Perhaps someday Africa will exist, in which case it will have been patented by African Americans in the U.S.A. from the example of the American Civil Rights movement. Yes, and lately I have begun to meet people in the United States who call themselves "Asians." A young woman (a Vietnamese immigrant) tells me, for instance, she will only "date Asian." Asians do not exist anywhere in Asia. The lovely brown woman who has cared for my parents, a Mormon born on an island in a turtle-green sea (I've guessed the Philippines or Samoa), will only admit to "Pacific Islander." A true daughter of Nixon.

It is not mere carelessness that makes Americans so careless, it is also that Americans think more about the future than the past. The past is vague to us. Tribal feuds may yet hissle and spit on the stoves of somebody's memory, but we haven't got time for that. The entry guard at Ellis Island didn't have time for that. The INS official at LAX doesn't have time for that. He is guarding the portal to individualism, the greatest abstraction the world has ever known: *One at a time, one at a time—back up, sir!* Only America could create Hispanics, Asians, Africans, Americans.

The Chinese people are like Americans in many ways. They like to laugh and be happy and play games. (Same American social studies textbook, c. 1959.)

It was only when it came to the landmass extending from Tierra del Fuego to the Aleutians that Americans refused to think in terms of hemispheric or historical mass. America (the noun) became our border against all that lay to the south and north—much to the annoyance of Mexicans, for example, or Canadians. "We are Americans, too," they said. No you're not, you are Mexicans. And you are Canadians. We are Americans©.

Whereas Miss Bolivia, having gotten over herspanic and now surreptitiously refreshing her lip gloss, does, as it turns out, understand my question. She is not Hispanic. Ha ha no. What is she then?

Her eyes flash. I mean, what do you consider yourself to be?

¡*Bolivian*!

Of course, but I protest she is destined for Hispanicity. Because you live in the United States, you see.

¿ ?

You will know more Colombians and Nicaraguans as friends, fellow religionists, than you would have known had you never left Bolivia. Spanish-language radio and TV, beamed at immigrants of provincial memory, will parlay soccer scores from an entire hemisphere. You will hear weather reports from Valparaiso to Anchorage borne on a dolphin-headed breeze. Listen, chaste Miss Bolivia: All along the dial, north and south, on Spanish-language radio stations, you can already hear a new, North American Spanish accent—akin to "accentless" California TV English—meant to be decipherable (and inoffensive) alike to Cubans, Mexicans, Dominicans, and blonds like you, because it belongs to none.

Hispanic Spanish is hybrid, uniform. Colorless, yes. I do not deplore it. If I were Miss Bolivia, I might deplore it. One should deplore any loss of uniquity in a world that has so little. But I take the bland transparent accent as an anabranch of the American tongue. We bid fond farewell to Miss Bolivia. Who's our next contestant, Johnny?

The Cuban grandfather in Miami, Dick, who persists in mocking Mexicans because we are Indians, less European than he is, the old frog. We've put him in a soundproof booth so his Hispanic grandson can mimic for us the old man's Caribbean Spanish, filigreed as a viceroy's sleeve.

I think Richard Nixon would not be surprised to hear that some of my Hispanic nieces and nephews have Scottish or German surnames. Nixon intended his Spanish'd noun to fold Hispanics into America. By the time the Sunday supplements would begin writing about the political ascendancy of a Hispanic generation, the American children of that generation would be disappearing into America. But Nixon might be surprised to hear that my oldest nephew, German-surnamed, has a restaurant in Oakland dedicated to classic Mexican cooking; the majority of his customers are not Hispanic.

In generations past, Americans regarded Latin America as an "experiment in democracy," meaning the brutish innocence of them, the negligent benevolence of us, as defined by the Monroe Doctrine. We installed men with dark glasses to overthrow men with dark glasses.

As a result of Nixon's noun, our relationship to Latin America became less remote. Within our own sovereign borders, crested with eagles, twenty-five million became twenty-seven million Hispanics; became thirty-five million. The Census Bureau began making national predictions: By the year 2040 one in three Americans will declare herself Hispanic. Leaving aside the carbonated empiricism of such predictions, they nevertheless did convince many Americans that Latin America is no longer something "down there," like an adolescent sexual abstraction. By the reckoning of the U.S. Census Bureau, the United States has become one of the largest Latin American nations in the world.

And every day and every night poor people trample the legal fiction that America controls its own destiny. There is something of inevitability, too, in what I begin hearing in America from businessmen—a hint of Latin American fatalism, a recognition of tragedy that is simply the verso of optimism, but descriptive of the same event: *You can't stop them coming* becomes *the necessity to develop a Spanish-language ad strategy*.

The mayor of San Diego, speaking to me one morning several years ago about her city's relationship to Tijuana, about the proximity of Tijuana to San Diego, used no future tense—*Here we are,* she said. She used no hand gesture to indicate "they" or "there" or "here." The mayor's omission of a demonstrative gesture in that instance reminded me of my father's nonchalance. My father never expected to escape tragedy by escaping Mexico, by escaping poverty, by coming to the United States. Nor did he. Such sentiments—the mayor's, my father's—are not, I remind you, the traditional sentiments of an "I" culture, which would formulate the same proximity as "*right up to here.*" For my father, as for the mayor, the border was missing.

In old cowboy movies, the sheriff rode hell-for-leather to capture the desperados before they crossed the Rio Grande. It is an old idea, more Protestant than Anglo-Saxon: that Latin America harbors outlaws.

Some Americans prefer to blame the white-powder trail leading from here to there on the drug lords of Latin America. More Americans are beginning to attribute the rise of drug traffic to American addiction. Tentative proposals to legalize drugs, like tentative proposals to open the border, bow to the inevitable, which is, in either case, the knowledge that there is no border.

The other day I read a survey that reported a majority of Americans believe most Hispanics are in the United States illegally. Maybe. Maybe there is something inherently illegal about all of us who are Hispanics in the United States, gathered under an assumed name, posing as one family. Nixon's categorical confusion brings confusion to all categories.

Once the United States related millions of its citizens into the family Hispanic—which as a legality exists only within U.S. borders—then that relation extends back to our several origins and links them. At which juncture the U.S.A. becomes the place of origin for all Hispanics. The illegal idea now disseminated southward by the U.S. is the idea that all Latin Americans are Hispanic.

The United States has illegally crossed its own border.

Suggestions for Discussion

1. According to Rodriguez, what are the various mental images conjured up by the word "Hispanic"?

2. What role does Richard Nixon play in Rodriguez's essay?

3. According to Rodriguez, how does language shape identity?

4. How has the United States illegally crossed its own border?

Suggestion for Writing

Compare Rodriguez's treatment of the word "Hispanic" with Randall Kennedy's dissection of the word "Nigger" in *The Protean N-Word* (see p. 339).

ESSAYS

∽∽∽∽

HOWARD GARDNER

Leading Beyond the Nation-State

Howard Gardner (b. 1943) is a professor of education at the Harvard
Graduate School of Education and codirector of Harvard Project Zero,
a long-term study of human intellectual and creative development. He
is the author of more than twenty books, including *Frames of Mind: The
Theory of Multiple Intelligences* (1985), *Creating Minds* (1993), *The Disciplined Mind: Beyond Facts and Standardized Tests* (2000), and
Intelligence Reframed (2000). In this selection, from *Changing Minds*
(2004), Gardner profiles three leaders who have exerted positive influences through persuasive storytelling.

Although relatively few positions exist for leaders of entities larger than
a single nation, the topic is well worth exploring in any effort to understand
how minds are changed. Sometimes, such a transnational position has a pre-
determined constituency; for example, the secretary-general of the United
Nations or the head of the World Health Organization. The leader of the
Catholic Church, or of other religious bodies, may well have influence that
extends beyond a single land. And indeed, Pope John Paul II stands out
among the popes of recent times because he has exerted influence not only
over the members of his far-flung church but also, in some matters, over
non-Catholics as well. Far more than his immediate predecessors, with the
exception of John XXIII, John Paul II has been able both to fashion stories
about political and personal values and to embody them in the impressive
life that he has lived. Pope John XXIII, operating in the 1960s, was an
avowedly simple pastor who called for a liberalization of the church and a
decentralization of power; in partial reaction two decades later. John Paul
II embraced the traditional conservative values of the church and located
the reins of power squarely within the Vatican. At the same time, however,
John Paul II is the most traveled and international of Popes, one who has
forged a special tie with the young of different lands, and one who has been
credited with an indispensable role in the collapse of Communism in Eastern Europe.

On rare occasions, individuals with neither vast armies nor vast congregations have succeeded in exerting influence well beyond national boundaries. Like the successful leaders of nations that we've already examined, they have done so because of the persuasiveness of their stories and the steadfastness with which they have reinforced those stories through their manner of living. In the twentieth century, three men stand out as exemplars in this category: Mohandas (Mahatma) Gandhi, Nelson Mandela, and Jean Monnet.

Perhaps the most well-known is Gandhi. Growing up in undistinguished surroundings in late-nineteenth-century colonial India, Gandhi spent time in England as a young man and then lived for twenty years in South Africa. There he was horrified by the mistreatment by European colonizers of Indians and other "colored persons": he read widely in philosophy and religion; and he became involved in various protests. Returning to his native India at the start of the World War I, Gandhi perfected methods of satyagraha—peaceful (nonviolent) protest (or resistance). Alongside his devoted countrymen, Gandhi led a series of strikes and protest marches, destined to throw into sharp relief the differences between the brutal English masters—who sought to hold power at any cost—and the nonbelligerent Indians. These protests were choreographed to underscore the nobility of the native cause and the reasonableness with which Indians were striving to express their goals. Gandhi's overt message was: "We do not seek to make war or shed blood. We only want to be treated as fellow human beings. Once we have achieved the status of equals, we have no further claims."

In one sense, Gandhi's message could not have been simpler: It can be traced back to Christ and to other religious leaders. Yet, it also clashed with an entrenched counterstory: that one can only attain an equal status vis-à-vis one's colonizers if—like the United States in the late eighteenth century or South America in the early nineteenth century—one is willing to go to war. Moreover, Gandhi did not only have a simple linguistic message; he also developed an integrated program of prayer, fasting, and facing one's opponents without weapons, even willing to do so until death. His embodiment of the message could not have been more dramatic; it went well beyond verbal expression, to include a whole range of evocative formats, such as his squatting on the ground and operating a simple machine for spinning cloth.

Gandhi's story reverberated around the world. While annoying some (Churchill memorably disparaged him as that "half-naked fakir"), it inspired many leaders and ordinary citizens—ranging from Martin Luther King Jr. in the American South in the early 1960s, to the students who rallied for greater democracy in Tiananmen Square in Beijing in 1989.

Like Gandhi, Nelson Mandela embodied a message that resonated on a level far beyond the borders of his own South Africa. Indeed, of all the leaders in recent years, Mandela is widely considered one of the most impressive and influential. A lawyer by training, Mandela became actively involved in resistance as part of the African National Congress. At first, he embraced nonviolent resistance, but after a series of frustrating and degrading encounters, he joined a paramilitary group. Narrowly escaping death by combat or judicial sentence, Mandela was imprisoned for twenty-seven years. Although such an experience would likely have demoralized, radicalized, or marginalized most other persons—especially since it occurred at middle age, often considered the apogee of an individual's personal power—imprisonment seemed only to fortify Mandela. On his release, he rejected any effort to engage in armed conflict; instead he worked with his political opponent F.W. de Klerk to set up democratic institutions, and in 1994 he went on to win the presidency of a post-apartheid South Africa.

Rather than seeking revenge against his opponents and jailers, Mandela called for reconciliation. He was convinced—and was able to convince others—that South Africa could not function as a society unless it could put its wrenching history behind it. Under the leadership of Nobel Peace Prize winner Archbishop Desmond Tutu, Mandela convened a Commission of Truth and Reconciliation. The Gandhian idea behind this commission was that it would seek to establish what actually happened during the years of apartheid but would not attempt to sit in ultimate judgment. The truth having been established as well as it could be, citizens of varying persuasions could come to terms with the past and commit their future energies to the buildup of a new and more fully representative society. A master of nonverbal as well as verbal forms, Mandela asked his one-time jailer to sit in the first row during his presidential inaugural ceremony.

Mandela succeeded in changing the minds not only of millions of his otherwise diverse fellow citizens but equally of millions of observers around the world—few of whom would have predicted that South Africa could become a new nation without decades of bloodshed. Ideas like the Commission on Truth and Reconciliation have traveled across national boundaries. The tipping points for Mandela's success entail both his exemplary behavior after his release from jail and the willingness of the entrenched South African leadership to negotiate with him—both examples reflecting Mandela's personal resonance, among other things.

A third figure of global importance worked largely behind the scenes; the French economist and diplomat Jean Monnet, born in 1888. When his comfortable life was shattered by the events of World War I, Monnet—a careful and reflective student of history—pondered why it was necessary for European countries to continue to go to war, as they had intermittently since the time of Charlemagne more than a thousand years before. He began to work toward the creation of institutions that could bring about a united Europe. After the trauma of World War I, the collapse of the League of Nations, the rise of fascism, and the unprecedented warfare of World War II, a lesser person would have concluded that attempts to build a European community were futile. Monnet, however, was a firm believer in his own oft-repeated slogan: "I regard every defeat (or every challenge) as an opportunity." Amid the physical and psychological ruins of war-torn Europe, Monnet envisioned—and proceeded to sow—the seeds of a larger European polity.

Like Gandhi and Mandela, Monnet had been pursuing his mission for half a century and was well into his seventies by the time of his greatest impact. During the post–World War II period, he played a catalytic role in setting up a number of institutions, including the European Coal and Steel Community, the Action Committee of the United States of Europe, and the European common market. He was opposed nearly every step of the way, most notably by General Charles de Gaulle, the charismatic advocate of French autonomy, and by other nationalists of the Thatcher stripe. Yet while de Gaulle may have prevailed with the French electorate in the 1960s, Monnet's vision has ultimately triumphed on the Continent. After Monnet's death in 1979, the European Union was well launched, the euro was adopted in twelve countries, and, as of this writing, the United States of Europe are closer to a reality than at any time since the Napoleonic era.

Unlike a president, a pope, or the leader of an international organization such as the United Nations, neither Gandhi, nor Mandela, nor Monnet had a dedicated, guaranteed audience. They had to create their constituencies from scratch, with neither financial inducements nor coercive political weapons. They had to identify and speak to an opposition that held power; leaders of South Africa and colonial India, in Gandhi's case; the defenders of apartheid in Mandela's case; and the entrenched national interests of Europe in Monnet's case. At the same time they had to address and convince a lay constituency. Neither Gandhi nor Mandela could have led the fight for independence without an "army" of ordinary followers, who, in the extreme, were prepared to die nonviolently for their cause. And while Monnet worked significantly behind the scenes in the manner of what I term an "indirect" leader, his vision of Europe ultimately has had to triumph at the ballot box. Indeed, it has still not triumphed in nations such as Switzerland and Norway, which (surprisingly) remain outside of the Union.

As leaders addressing heterogeneous audiences, these men had available only the weapons of persuasion and embodiment. They had to tell their stories over and over again, tell them well, and embody their stories in appropriate life actions and evocative symbolic elements. They had to recognize, acknowledge, and ultimately undermine the regnant counter-stories. And it is here that they showed their genius.

Hard as it is to mobilize a heterogeneous audience, the established way of doing so is to fashion and articulate a story that is serene in its simplicity. Indeed, the bitter lesson of the first half of the twentieth century is that the simplest and most awful stories generally triumph: The goal of politics is to attain power and to use it toward selfish ends; Might makes right; The state is all-powerful—one must do what it says or perish. These simple stories led to the triumph of terrifying "isms" of the left and the right: fascism, nazism, bolshevism, communism. One might even say that the hateful policies of Hitler, Mussolini, Tojo, Lenin, Stalin, and Mao Zedong convinced the majority of their countrymen; their popularity only waned when military defeat was imminent or starvation threatened. It appeared that in most of the world's nations, these "isms" were more appealing than democracy. Churchill well described this enigma in his oft-quoted comment that "democracy is the worst form of Government except for all those other forms that have been tried from time to time."

Gandhi, Mandela, and Monnet did not, however, take the easy way out. They did not just tell a simple, familiar story more effectively. Rather, they took on a far more daunting task: to develop a new story, tell it well, embody it in their lives, and help others understand why it deserves to triumph over the simpler counterstory. Moreover, they drew continually and imaginatively on several other levers of mind change: reason, multiple modes of representation, and resonance with the experiences of those whom they sought to influence. At the same time, they attempted to mollify the resistances that they encountered; they took advantage of real world events; and they marshaled whatever resources they had at their disposal. On a personal note, these three men are my own chosen heroic leaders. They took a more complex, less familiar story, a story that was more "inclusive," and succeeded in giving that story life in institutions that continued beyond their own moments in the limelight.

Suggestions for Discussion

1. How does Gardner distinguish Gandhi, Mandela, and Monnet from leaders with guaranteed audiences, such as presidents and popes?

2. What qualities do Gardner's "chosen heroic leaders" share, and in what ways are they different?

3. What are the various forms of expression—both verbal and nonverbal—employed by Gandhi, Mandela, and Monnet? Cite at least one specific example for each.

Suggestion for Writing

Compare Gardner's ideas about leadership with the philosophy of Niccolò Machiavelli's *Of Cruelty and Clemency* (p. 748).

∞∞∞∞

S U S A N   S O N T A G

Regarding the Pain of Others

Social commentator, author, and director Susan Sontag (1933–2004) is
best known for writing incisive philosophical examinations of contemporary issues. The native New Yorker earned M.A.s in English literature
and philosophy from Harvard University in 1954 and 1955 and published her first novel, *The Benefactor,* in 1963. Other works include
Against Interpretation (1966), *On Photography* (1977), *Illness as Metaphor*
(1978), *AIDS and Its Metaphors* (1988), and *In America* (2002), winner
of the National Book Award. Sontag won the Montblanc de la Culture
Award for her humanitarian efforts in Sarajevo and was listed as one of
Life magazine's "Women Who Shook the World." The following reflections are drawn from *Regarding the Pain of Others* (2003).

One can feel obliged to look at photographs that record great cruelties
and crimes. One should feel obliged to think about what it means to look
at them, about the capacity actually to assimilate what they show. Not all
reactions to these pictures are under the supervision of reason and conscience. Most depictions of tormented, mutilated bodies do arouse a pruri-
ent interest. (*The Disasters of War* is notably an exception: Goya's images
cannot be looked at in a spirit of prurience. They don't dwell on the beauty
of the human body; bodies are heavy, and thickly clothed.) All images that
display the violation of an attractive body are to a certain degree, pornographic. But images of the repulsive can also allure. Everyone knows that
what slows down highway traffic going past a horrendous car crash is not
only curiosity. It is also, for many, the wish to see something gruesome. Calling such wishes "morbid" suggests a rare aberration, but the attraction to
such sights is not rare, and is a perennial source of inner torment.

Indeed, the very first acknowledgment (as far as I am aware) of the
attraction of mutilated bodies occurs in a founding description of mental
conflict. It is a passage in *The Republic,* Book IV, where Plato's Socrates
describes how our reason may be overwhelmed by an unworthy desire,
which drives the self to become angry with a part of its nature. Plato has
been developing a tripartite theory of mental function, consisting of reason, anger or indignation, and appetite or desire—anticipating the Freudian

schema of superego, ego, and id (with the difference that Plato puts reason on top and conscience, represented by indignation, in the middle). In the course of this argument, to illustrate how one may yield, even if reluctantly; to repulsive attractions, Socrates relates a story he heard about Leontius, son of Aglaion:

> On his way up from the Piracus outside the north wall, he noticed the bodies of some criminals lying on the ground, with the executioner standing by them. He wanted to go and look at them, but at the same time he was disgusted and tried to turn away. He struggled for some time and covered his eyes, but at last the desire was too much for him. Opening his eyes wide, he ran up to the bodies and cried, "There you are, curse you, feast yourselves on this lovely sight."

Declining to choose the more common example of an inappropriate or unlawful sexual passion as his illustration of the struggle between reason and desire, Plato appears to take for granted that we also have an appetite for sights of degradation and pain and mutilation.

Surely the undertow of this despised impulse must also be taken into account when discussing the effect of atrocity pictures.

At the beginning of modernity, it may have been easier to acknowledge that there exists an innate tropism toward the gruesome. Edmund Burke observed that people like to look at images of suffering. "I am convinced we have a degree of delight, and that no small one, in the real misfortunes and pains of others," he wrote in *A Philosophical Enquiry into the Origin of Our Ideas of the Sublime and Beautiful* (1757). "There is no spectacle we so eagerly pursue, as that of some uncommon and grievous calamity." William Hazlitt, in his essay on Shakespeare's Iago and the attraction of villainy on the stage, asks, "Why do we always read the accounts in the newspapers of dreadful fires and shocking murders?" Because, he answers, "love of mischief," love of cruelty, is as natural to human beings as is sympathy.

One of the great theorists of the erotic, Georges Bataille, kept a photograph taken in China in 1910 of a prisoner undergoing "the death of a hundred cuts" on his desk, where he could look at it every day. (Since become legendary, it is reproduced in the last of Bataille's books published during his lifetime, in 1961, *The Tears of Eros*.) "This photograph," Bataille wrote, "had a decisive role in my life. I have never stopped being obsessed by this image of pain, at the same time ecstatic and intolerable." To contemplate this image, according to Bataille, is both a mortification of the feelings and a liberation of tabooed erotic knowledge—a complex response that many people must find hard to credit. For most, the image is simply unbearable: the already armless sacrificial victim of several busy knives, in the terminal stage of being flayed—a photograph, not a painting; a real Marsyas, not a mythic one—and still alive in the picture, with a look on his upturned face as ecstatic as that of any Italian Renaissance Saint Sebastian. As objects of contemplation, images of the atrocious can answer to several different needs. To steel oneself against weakness. To make oneself more numb. To acknowledge the existence of the incorrigible.

Bataille is not saying that he takes pleasure at the sight of this excruciation. But he is saying that he can imagine extreme suffering as something more than just suffering, as a kind of transfiguration. It is a view of suffering, of the pain of others, that is rooted in religious thinking, which links pain to sacrifice, sacrifice to exaltation—a view that could not be more alien to a modern sensibility, which regards suffering as something that is a mistake or an accident or a crime. Something to be fixed. Something to be refused. Something that makes one feel powerless.

What to do with such knowledge as photographs bring of faraway suffering? People are often unable to take in the sufferings of those close to them. (A compelling document on this theme is Frederick Wiseman's film *Hospital.*) For all the voyeuristic lure—and the possible satisfaction of knowing, This is not happening to *me,* I'm not ill, I'm not dying, I'm not trapped in a war—it seems normal for people to fend off thinking about the ordeals of others, even others with whom it would be easy to identify.

A citizen of Sarajevo, a woman of impeccable adherence to the Yugoslav ideal, whom I met soon after arriving in the city the first time in April 1993, told me: "In October 1991 I was here in my nice apartment in peaceful Sarajevo when the Serbs invaded Croatia, and I remember when the evening news showed footage of the destruction of Vukovar, just a couple of hundred miles away, I thought to myself, 'Oh, how horrible,' and switched the channel. So how can I be indignant if someone in France or Italy or Germany sees the killing taking place here day after day on their evening news and says, 'Oh, how horrible,' and looks for another program. It's normal. It's human." Wherever people feel safe—this was her bitter, self-accusing point—they will be indifferent. But surely a Sarajevan might have another motive for shunning images of terrible events taking place in what was then, after all, another part of her own country than did those abroad who were turning their backs on Sarajevo. The dereliction of the foreigners, to whom she was so charitable, was also a consequence of the feeling that nothing could be done. Her unwillingness to engage with these premonitory images of nearby war was an expression of helplessness and fear.

People can turn off not just because a steady diet of images of violence has made them indifferent but because they are afraid. As everyone has observed, there is a mounting level of acceptable violence and sadism in mass culture: films, television, comics, computer games. Imagery that would have had an audience cringing and recoiling in disgust forty years ago is watched without so much as a blink by every teenager in the multiplex. Indeed, mayhem is entertaining rather than shocking to many people in most modern cultures. But not all violence is watched with equal detachment. Some disasters are more apt subjects of irony than others.*

It is because, say, the war in Bosnia didn't stop, because leaders claimed it was an intractable situation, that people abroad may have switched off the terrible images. It is because a war, any war, doesn't seem as if it can be stopped that people become less responsive to the horrors. Compassion is an unstable emotion. It needs to be translated into action, or it withers. The question is what to do with the feelings that have been aroused, the knowledge that has been communicated. If one feels that there is nothing "we" can do—but who is that "we"?—and nothing "they" can do either—and who are "they"?—then one starts to get bored, cynical, apathetic.

And it is not necessarily better to be moved. Sentimentality, notoriously, is entirely compatible with a taste for brutality and worse. (Recall the canonical example of the Auschwitz commandant returning home in the evening, embracing his wife and children, and sitting at the piano to play some Schubert before dinner.) People don't become inured to what they are shown—if that's the right way to describe what happens—because of the *quantity* of images dumped on them. It is passivity that dulls feeling. The states described as apathy, moral or emotional anesthesia, are full of feelings; the feelings are rage and frustration. But if we consider what emotions would be desirable, it seems too simple to elect sympathy. The imaginary proximity to the suffering inflicted on others that is granted by images suggests a link between the faraway sufferers—seen close-up on the television screen—and the privileged viewer that is simply untrue, that is yet one more mystification of our real relations to power. So far as we feel sympathy, we feel we are not accomplices to what caused the suffering. Our sympathy proclaims our innocence as well as our impotence. To that extent, it can be (for all our good intentions) an impertinent—if not an inappropriate—response. To set aside the sympathy we extend to others beset by war and murderous politics for a reflection on how our privileges are located on the same map as their suffering, and may—in ways we might prefer not to imagine—be linked to their suffering, as the wealth of some may imply the destitution of others, is a task for which the painful, stirring images supply only an initial spark.

---

*Tellingly, that connoisseur of death and high priest of the delights of apathy, Andy Warhol, was drawn to news reports of a variety of violent deaths (car and plane crashes, suicides, executions). But his silk-screened transcriptions excluded death in war. A news photo of an electric chair and a tabloid's screaming front page, "129 Die in Jet," yes. "Hanoi Bombed," no. The only photograph Warhol silk-screened that refers to the violence of war is one that had become iconic; that is, a cliché: the mushroom cloud of an atomic bomb, repeated as on a sheet of postage stamps (like the faces of Marilyn, Jackie, Mao) to illustrate its opaqueness, its fascination, its banality.

Suggestions for Discussion

1. Discuss your response to a gruesome scene depicted on television. Why was your curiosity raised? Analyze your responses to the event and the coverage.

2. Discuss Sontag's assertion that passivity dulls feeling.

Suggestions for Writing

1. Consider Edmund Burke's observation that we "have a degree of delight… in the real misfortunes and pains of others."

2. What does Sontag mean when she writes that compassion "needs to be translated into action, or it withers"?

ᘛᘛᘛᘛᘛ

A L I C E   K A P L A N

War on Trial

Alice Kaplan, a scholar of the culture and history of post–World War II France, is the author of *Reproductions of Banality: Fascism, Literature, and French Intellectual Life* (1986); *French Lessons: A Memoir* (1993); and *The Collaborator: The Trial and Execution of Robert Brasillach* (2000). A member of the usage panel for the *American Heritage Dictionary,* Kaplan is also a professor of Romance studies and literature at Duke University and is director-elect of Duke's new Institute for French and Francophone Studies. In this article, published in 1997, Kaplan analyzes the legacy of the Nuremberg trials and their impact on the politics of warfare since World War II.

In a classroom in Richland, Washington, a teacher named James Campbell makes the Nuremberg trials come to life. Campbell conducts a mock war-crimes tribunal at the Hanford High School as part of a social studies course called War–Peace Studies. He begins the term by asking his students to consider the fragility of democracy, and he studies with them not only the rise of the Nazis but the tendency in all societies toward demagoguery and scapegoating. He asks his students to consider how race can be manipulated and applied in a political situation. One dilemma Campbell faces as a teacher is how rough to be.

"I don't want to blow these kids' idealism out of the water," he says, "but at the same time, I want to arm them with an understanding of human nature." After learning about Nazi atrocities, Campbell's students want to know how the Holocaust could have happened. The mock trial becomes a drama of accountability. As the class comes to understand the enormity of the Nazi crimes and familiarizes itself with the excuses of the major defendants—"I was only following orders" and "I didn't know what was happening"—the political issues become moral ones. What does it mean to resist, to take risks, in Richland, Washington? What did it mean during the American civil-rights movement? What did it mean in Nazi Germany?

There were 21 men in the dock at Nuremberg. In the mock trial at Hanford High, there are two defendants: Reichsmarschall Hermann Göring and Minister of Armaments Albert Speer. Göring, second in command to Hitler and the ringleader of the defendants, is the wily, barefaced liar who outfoxes the prosecution. Speer, by contrast, is an elegant technocrat who expresses regret with eloquence and charm, arguing, "I was just doing my job and wasn't aware of the political implications of what I was doing. I was a patriot and wanted to see my country win the war."

That's a compelling argument in Richland, where, in the 1940s, workers for the Manhattan Project produced the plutonium for the bomb that was dropped on Nagasaki. Campbell doesn't have to question what moral authority the Americans had to prosecute Germans for war crimes after what we did: His students raise the issue themselves. It's hard to forget the atomic bomb when a mushroom cloud graces the rival Richland High football team's helmet. Another local issue comes up regularly during the mock Nuremberg trial, because Japanese-Americans living in the Richland area were interned in camps during World War II. The students know that one of their favorite teachers, Mr. Yamamoto, was interned as a little boy.

Campbell has been a teacher for 31 years. When he started teaching about Nuremberg, it was 1972 and he was talking to his classes about the My Lai massacre and Lieutenant Calley. His students had older brothers and sisters in Vietnam. Richland was still a bomb factory. Today, it's Bosnia that links Nuremberg to the present. The students discuss ethnic strife and stage a session of the UN Security Council; they debate sending troops to Bosnia and taking captured war criminals to The Hague.

If teachers like Campbell keep coming back to the Nuremberg trials as the setting for this sort of education, it is because for more than 50 years, Nuremberg has shaped our perception of war, justice and the fragile boundaries separating human from inhuman behavior. Thinking about Nuremberg means thinking about the consequences of individual and group actions, about responsibility for the survival of humankind.

This is true not only because Nuremberg formed our understanding of the central events of the 20th century—World War II and the Holocaust— but because it continues to shape our understanding of the events of our own time. I met James Campbell at a recent conference at the Library of Congress marking the 50th anniversary of the trial's end. There, topics ranged from the memories of Nuremberg prosecutors to the current political difficulties in establishing a permanent international war-crimes tribunal.

In 1945, war was still considered a fathomable narrative event, with declarations, fronts, actions, battles, a beginning and an end. There were the European and Pacific theaters; there was the Nazi advance across Europe; there were D-Day, V-E Day, V-J Day. The decades since the Nuremberg war-crimes trials in 1945 and 1946 have seen the end of war as we once knew it—as a regular, though tragic, occurrence in the life of nations. Although the atom bomb made us wonder if war might become so technologized that it would be reduced to one massively destructive moment, in fact it's the opposite of this *Dr. Strangelove* scenario that has come to pass. War in our global society lacks coherence—which makes it more dangerous, not less.

Who can say when the war in Bosnia was declared? Conflicts in Northern Ireland, in Israel and the Occupied Territories, in Rwanda, also feel permanent, impossible to resolve. With the Cold War and its binary structure at an end, the world has broken out in undeclared and local wars. They take place in remote "trouble spots," with no obvious connection to the rest of the world.

Yet many of the old moral and political issues that the world contended with in 1945 persist. Today, two tribunals are undertaking the first effort since Nuremberg to enforce humanitarian justice on an international scale, by seeking out those responsible for crimes of genocide, ethnic cleansing and rape in Bosnia and Rwanda. This attempt is hampered not only by its ad hoc nature but by the fact that many of those accused of the crimes remain in power or out of the reach of justice. In Rwanda, more than 100,000 people await trial in prisons and detention centers. The huge number of murder suspects makes individual justice almost impossible to imagine. In Bosnia, victims whose stories are essential to a successful prosecution are reluctant to come forward. War criminals receive government protection; they don't even bother to hide. The tribunals themselves are badly funded, so that debates about morality are overshadowed by debates about money. The proceedings drag on. In the trials, as in the wars themselves, there's no sense of a discrete event, no narrative satisfaction. Nuremberg, in contrast, was the trial of the century, a day of reckoning that lasted 11 intense months.

Although the Holocaust tends to overshadow our thinking about Nuremberg, the Allied powers were far more concerned with the war as a whole—and especially with condemning the German policy of waging "aggressive war." Their attempt to outlaw a certain kind of war has a pre–Nuremberg history in our century. At the end of World War I, the Treaty of Versailles included a clause asking that the Kaiser and certain members of the German military be charged with war crimes and violation of international treaties. The Kaiser was never tried because the Dutch refused to extradite him. The Germans themselves were put in charge of the remaining indictments, with the idea that the nation must punish its own wrongdoers. The results were negligible: Six Germans received minor sentences. Nazi crimes in World War II went so far beyond what had been known in the history of modern warfare that they made the slaughter in the trenches of World War I seem almost sane. When it came to trying the Nazis, the fact that the victorious Allies were judging the vanquished was almost beside the point. Who else was going to try them?

It would have been far easier—and certainly understandable—if the Allies had simply lined up the German high command in front of a military firing squad and killed them in a final act of war. The Nuremberg effort, declared the chief prosecutor, was an unsurpassed example of restraint: "That four great nations, flushed with victory and stung with injury, stay the hand of vengeance and voluntarily submit their captive enemies to the judgment of the law is one of the most significant tributes that Power has ever paid to Reason."

The author of those words was Justice Robert H. Jackson, a dignified, bookish man who had risen to the Supreme Court without ever having gone to college. In his opening statement, Jackson also spoke in chilling terms of the imperative to bring the Nazis to justice: "The wrongs which we seek to condemn and punish have been so calculated, so malignant and so devastating," he warned, "that civilization cannot tolerate their being ignored, because it cannot survive their being repeated."

It is tempting to look back on the Nuremberg trials, and on World War II itself, as the last moment when good and evil were easily distinguishable and punishable. Nothing could be more straightforward than the Allied struggle against the genocidal enemy; nothing could be clearer than the need for justice in 1945. But the Nuremberg effort was far from simple and was certainly not an instance of justice free of politics.

The idea of Nuremberg was born in a series of meetings between the Allies beginning in January 1942, as reports of Hitler's brutality were proliferating. By the summer of 1945, President Harry Truman had put Jackson in charge of the groundwork for the trial, and representatives from each Allied nation met in London to devise a protocol. The Soviets wanted to hold the trials in the Nazi capital, Berlin, which was in their zone of occupation. But that city, along with much of Germany, was in ruins. Only Nuremberg had an intact palace of justice with a jail next to it, so the trials took place there, in the American zone.

But even in Nuremberg, there were thousands of bodies buried under rubble. The stench of death was everywhere. Social life for the tribunal's numerous personnel centered on the Grand Hotel, entire sections of which had been destroyed by bombs. The trials of the major Nazi war criminals took place from November 1945 until October 1946. In subsequent trials, bankers, industrialists and doctors who had helped implement the Final Solution were put on the stand.

The Allied indictment against the principal defendants comprised four counts. Count One charged the Nazis with having a "Common Plan or Conspiracy" to commit the subsequent counts: Crimes against Peace, War Crimes and Crimes against Humanity. Count Two, Crimes against Peace, concerned violations of specific treaties in the initiation of "aggressive war." Count Three, War Crimes, concerned Nazi violation of the laws and customs of war, such as the murder of hostages and the torture and murder of civilians in occupied territory. Count Four, Crimes against Humanity, focused on the death camps, on the murder, extermination, enslavement and deportation of civilian populations. It specified the mass murder of the Jews and named persecution on political, racial or religious grounds as a criterion for crimes against humanity.

Jackson declared that the moral standards set at Nuremberg must thenceforth bind all civilized societies—not just the vanquished but also the victors. If the judges turned the process into a mere show trial or punished the Nazis for breaking rules that the Allies would not themselves obey, they would ultimately undo all they had set out to accomplish. His metaphor was haunting: "We must never forget," Jackson said, "that the record on which we judge these defendants today is the record on which history will judge us tomorrow. To pass these defendants a poisoned chalice is to put it to our own lips as well."

Jackson's evocation of the poisoned chalice remains the most important statement made at Nuremberg, the most lasting admonition. It made Nuremberg not only a reckoning with the past but a contract for the future. That vigilance, that double consciousness of responsibility for the crimes of others and for one's own misdeeds, is at the heart of the trial's legacy.

And yet none of the Allied nations came to Nuremberg with a clear conscience; not one has had a perfect record since. In one particularly chilling incident during pretrial negotiations among the prosecutors, the Soviets wanted to blame their massacre of Polish officers in the Katyn Forest on the Nazis. Justice Jackson's son William (who assisted his father at the trials) recently acknowledged that the Americans already knew from intelligence reports that the Soviets had been the killers at Katyn. Rather than jeopardizing the trials over one incident, the Americans told the Soviets it was up to them to prove their case. The Katyn massacre was listed in the indictment as follows: "In September 1941, 11,000 Polish officers, who were prisoners of war, were killed in the Katyn Forest in Smolensk." Soviet responsibility for Katyn was eventually revealed and remains a blot on the trial.

Nor, in the end, was justice always served. Ten major war criminals were hanged, seven sentenced to prison and three acquitted. (German-run courts tried and convicted those three soon thereafter.) Göring escaped the noose by committing suicide the morning of his scheduled execution. The charming, eloquent Speer got off with a prison sentence, while the proletarian Fritz Sauckel—Speer's underling in the administration of slave labor—was condemned to death; class prejudice clearly played a role. U.S. chief prosecutor Telford Taylor, looking back after 50 years, thinks that it was probably unfair to condemn newspaperman Julius Streicher to death for crimes against humanity based solely on his hate propaganda in *Der Stürmer.*

While the Allies were busy judging the defendants, American intelligence agents were on the lookout for former Nazis who could help in the incipient Cold War. One of them, Klaus Barbie, head of the Gestapo in Lyons, was wanted by the French for a variety of crimes, including the torture and murder of the French resistance hero Jean Moulin. Barbie was spirited away to Bolivia in 1951 with American assistance. Forty years later, Allan Ryan, special investigator for the Justice Department, revealed the American complicity in Barbie's escape from Europe. At Ryan's insistence, the U.S. government apologized to France for delaying justice in the Barbie case for 40 years. Klaus Barbie the murderer, the torturer of resistance heroes, was apparently a good, solid informant. For the people involved in recruiting him, the end justified the means.

When Barbie was finally brought to trial in 1987, his defense lawyer, Jacques Vergès, argued that France had no moral standing to judge Barbie in light of its own crimes in Algeria: In the 1950s and 1960s, French generals who had themselves been tortured by the Gestapo not many years earlier used torture on the Algerian nationalists. By Vergès's logic, all French actions since 1945 could be taken into consideration in a trial concerning events that took place before 1945. His argument made no legal sense but was troubling nonetheless, because it evoked a genuine national tragedy.

The biblical injunction about sinners casting stones cannot hold true with crimes as great as the Nazis'. And yet Vergès's revelation of his country's moral hypocrisy points to an important problem. It *is* arbitrary to try some nations but not others, to outlaw some wars and not others. What's missing are the standards by which we must judge. Those standards are exactly what the victors who gathered at Nuremberg 50 years ago hoped to establish once and for all.

Nuremberg insisted on the idea that you could not hold the entire German civilization accountable for Nazi crimes, only specific individuals and organizations. This distinction became manifest in one dramatic moment at the trial, when prosecutors began screening films of Nazi atrocities. Madeleine Jacob, the fierce legal correspondent for France's *Franc-Tireur,* recounts in her memoirs how, just as the courtroom was plunged into darkness and she was regretting that she wouldn't be able to observe the Nazi leaders' faces, "a beam of light appeared from beneath the tables where the defendants were seated, lighting up each face in the dock. There before us were 21 masks—yes, masks, because all we could see were the faces. What a hallucination." Spectators in the courtroom didn't focus on the films themselves; they were far more interested in the reactions of the defendants as they watched their crimes projected on the screen. The overwhelming question at Nuremberg was not so much What happened? as Who could have done these deeds? The lighting, like the trial itself, was designed to spotlight the theme of individual responsibility.

The idea of agency went along with the entire philosophical climate of the postwar period: the climate of European existentialism, with its emphasis on personal responsibility. Individual agency was an ethical and legal touchstone, not only at Nuremberg but at trials of Nazi collaborators throughout Europe. In January 1945, Robert Brasillach, a French fascist newspaper editor, went on trial in Paris for having collaborated with the Nazis. The existentialist philosopher Simone de Beauvoir reported on the trial for the journal she had founded with Jean-Paul Sartre, *Les Temps Modernes.* Beauvoir's understanding of the Brasillach trial was paradoxical: She approved of the fact that he took responsibility for his actions, but she refused to sign a petition in his favor. It is precisely because he had taken responsibility for his life that he must go to his death, she wrote. In acknowledging his actions, in being willing to die for them, she added, Brasillach had dignity. And so, by implication, did humanity.

The other great legacy of Nuremberg is the concept that certain deeds are so heinous that they can be deemed "crimes against humanity." The idea that an individual can commit crimes that pose a threat to humanity itself was so new when the trial opened that Janet Flanner, writing for *The New Yorker,* dismissed it as "the most nebulous possible charge." The Allies had a hazy awareness that the Nazis' deeds had been different from simple war crimes, not just in their scale but in their basic nature. Still, no one could explain exactly why. In his eloquent opening statement, the French prosecutor Francis de Menthon mentioned the persecution of the Jews only once, concentrating instead on what he called—in the universal language of philosophy—"crimes against the human condition." The term *genocide* had been coined as early as 1933 to refer to the liquidation of an ethnic group, and the word did appear in the Nuremberg indictment. But the concept never took hold during the trials. The prosecution's definition of crimes against humanity blended racial extermination, political persecution and the wartime killing of civilians—acts only vaguely distinguishable from general war crimes. It was only two decades later, when Adolf Eichmann went on trial in Israel for his role in administering the death camps, that the crucial idea of genocide came into its own.

Flanner was right: Nuremberg had coined a key phrase without knowing what to do with it. Nonetheless, the concept of crimes against humanity has remained the most vital part of the Nuremberg legacy, both because of what we have learned and understood about Nazi genocide since 1945 and because such crimes still threaten our world. French philosopher Alain Finkielkraut marks Nuremberg's invention of crimes against humanity as an event in civilization's understanding of itself. Until then, he says, we knew that individuals could die but assumed that humanity would go on, from generation to generation. "In 1945," he writes in *Remembering in Vain,* "civilization discovered...that humanity is their responsibility, that they are its guardians. The notion of crimes against humanity is the legal evidence of this realization."

While the crimes-against-humanity charge continues to inform philosophical and political debates, the prosecution of the Nazis on the grounds of "aggressive war" has been largely forgotten by the public in recent years. Today, the world too often reacts to crimes against humanity in isolation from political questions. Every massacre, every instance of genocide, is fueled by complex power struggles and ideological factors. Aggression cannot be neglected, because it is the political ground on which crimes against humanity grow.

American prosecutors at Nuremberg thought the crime of aggression was the crux of the case; they were only beginning to absorb the evidence of the Holocaust. It is important to put 1945 in the context of 1918. World War I, which all the prosecutors had experienced as children or young people, was supposed to be the war to end all wars. It must have seemed in 1945 as though, unless such conflicts were somehow banned, there was going to be a new world war every 25 years.

As the centerpiece of the Nuremberg prosecution, the aggressive-war charge did not involve Nazi racial policy per se, but questions of Nazi domination and conquest. The Americans and British in charge of prosecuting this aspect of the case painstakingly traced Hitler's rise to power, his violation of treaties, his occupation of Europe. In their view, all other crimes stemmed from this initial Nazi plan.

At the height of the Vietnam War, discussions of the aggressive-war charge returned with vehemence. In 1968, filmmaker Marcel Ophuls released his documentary *Memories of Justice,* which contrasts footage of Nuremberg with a harsh critique of the American role in Vietnam. Telford Taylor visited Hanoi with an antiwar delegation after publishing a controversial book, *Nuremberg and Vietnam* (1970), asking whether Nuremberg's lessons could be applied to the present crisis. On two facing pages, he contrasted an eye-witness account of the killing of Jews by the SS in the Ukraine with an eye-witness account of the U.S. Army massacre of Vietnamese civilians at My Lai.

Ironically, U.S. Secretary of State Dean Rusk had himself accused North Vietnam of aggressive war, citing Nuremberg precedent in order to justify military intervention. Taylor concluded *Nuremberg and Vietnam* by excoriating the American government for this: "The anti-aggression spirit of Nuremberg and the United Nations Charter is invoked to justify our venture in Vietnam, where we have smashed the country to bits, and will not even take the trouble to clean up the blood and rubble....Somehow, we failed ourselves to learn the lessons we undertook to teach at Nuremberg, and that failure is today's American tragedy." (Throughout the Vietnam era, war resisters attempted to use the "Nuremberg defense" in court, arguing that they were morally bound not to participate in an aggressive war. The comparison failed to convince American judges.)

A quarter century after Taylor's powerful polemic, Jonathan Bush, a research fellow at the U.S. Holocaust Museum, argues passionately that the aggressive-war charge is as necessary in international law today as it was in 1946 and 1966. The charter for the international tribunal weighing crimes against humanity in the former Yugoslavia does not mention aggression. We can only imagine what would have happened in Bosnia if an effective forum for bringing aggressive-war crimes to trial had existed in 1991.

The aggressive-war charge invariably raises the specter of politics. It requires examining how wars begin, what powers promote them, who is ultimately responsible. The Nuremberg prosecutors had to take a hard look at the crises and betrayals of the 1930s as well as the industrialized killing of the 1940s. In struggling to understand today's fragmented Europe, we must look back at the prewar era, before the continent was frozen into East and West, and then at the end of the Cold War, when political power was again up for grabs. Providing this context is the most difficult imperative of all—which is precisely why we must undertake it.

When Justice Jackson closed the American prosecution of Nazi war criminals at Nuremberg, he referred to Shakespeare's *Richard III* and to Gloucester, the self-hating villain who murdered his way to power, denying all his deeds. The Nazi leaders, he said,

> ...now ask this Tribunal to say that they are not guilty of planning, executing, or conspiring to commit this long list of crimes and wrongs. They stand before the record of this trial as blood-stained Gloucester stood by the body of his slain king. He begged of the widow, as they beg of you: "Say I slew them not." And the queen replied, "Then say they were not slain. But dead they are..." If you were to say of these men that they are not guilty, it would be as true to say that there has been no war, there are no slain, there has been no crime.

After Jackson finished speaking, there was a stunned silence in the courtroom. He was pleading for a future in which the facts of Nazi war crimes would be irrefutable. And he had delivered a warning.

Half a century after Nuremberg, the event that was to have set a lasting precedent, there is still no permanent international court to enforce the tenets of humanitarian law, and the aggressive-war charge has fallen by the wayside. Now, as in 1945, we are haunted by the horror of war crimes, by the knowledge that civilization is fragile and we are the guardians of humanity, and yet we are incapable of acting on that knowledge.

With only months to prepare the trial of the century, the prosecutors and judges at Nuremberg did their work well—as far as history is concerned. The evidence they gathered and the categories they invented to organize that evidence in a way we can still study and debate make it impossible for any sane person to pretend that there was no Nazi crime. When it came to safeguarding the future, they were less successful, and Jackson's closing words remain far too relevant. The students in James Campbell's class at Hanford High School have new wars and new war crimes to add to their curriculum every year.

Suggestions for Discussion

1. How has the nature of war changed since 1945?

2. What precedent were the Allies attempting to set during the Nuremberg trials? According to Alice Kaplan, did they succeed?

3. Was justice served at Nuremberg?

4. Why is it so difficult to prosecute war criminals?

5. What problems does the teacher in this article face in educating children about the history and nature of war atrocities?

Suggestions for Writing

1. At what age should children learn about the Holocaust? What is the importance of such an education?

2. In a well-developed essay, explore the possible reasons why some people find it so difficult to rebel against an order they believe is immoral. Have you ever been ordered to perform an action you believed was unjust? Did you follow that order against your better judgment, or did you refuse as a matter of principle? Do any such experiences help you to better understand or judge the actions of the war criminals tried at Nuremberg? Explain.

CRCRCRCRCR

JAMES BALDWIN

The Discovery of What It Means to Be an American

James Baldwin (1924–1987) was born in New York of Southern, deeply religious, and poor parents. At fourteen, he became a preacher in the Fireside Pentecostal Church in Harlem. His first novel, *Go Tell It on the Mountain* (1953), reflects his experience as a preacher and, together with *Another Country* (1962), a novel about sex and race, established his reputation as a writer. Since the publication of a lengthy essay, *The Fire Next Time* (1962), he has taken a place as an important spokesman for blacks. He wrote significant autobiographical essays, and this essay from *Nobody Knows My Name* (1961) examines the ways in which his sojourn in Paris contributed to his understanding both of himself and of America.

"It is a complex fate to be an American," Henry James observed, and the principal discovery an American writer makes in Europe is just how complex this fate is. America's history, her aspirations, her peculiar triumphs, her even more peculiar defeats, and her position in the world—yesterday and today—are all so profoundly and stubbornly unique that the very word "America" remains a new, almost completely undefined and extremely controversial proper noun. No one in the world seems to know exactly what it describes, not even we motley millions who call ourselves Americans.

I left America because I doubted my ability to survive the fury of the color problem here. (Sometimes I still do.) I wanted to prevent myself from becoming *merely* a Negro; or, even, merely a Negro writer. I wanted to find in what way the *specialness* of my experience could be made to connect me with other people instead of dividing me from them. (I was as isolated from Negroes as I was from whites, which is what happens when a Negro begins, at bottom, to believe what white people say about him.)

In my necessity to find the terms on which my experience could be related to that of others, Negroes and whites, writers and non-writers, I proved, to my astonishment, to be as American as any Texas G.I. And I found my experience was shared by every American writer I knew in Paris. Like me, they had been divorced from their origins, and it turned out to make very little difference that the origins of white Americans were European and mine were African—they were no more at home in Europe than I was.

The fact that I was the son of a slave and they were the sons of free men meant less, by the time we confronted each other on European soil, than the fact that we were both searching for our separate identities. When we had found these, we seemed to be saying, why, then, we would no longer need to cling to the shame and bitterness which had divided us so long.

It became terribly clear in Europe, as it never had been here, that we knew more about each other than any European ever could. And it also became clear that, no matter where our fathers had been born, or what they had endured, the fact of Europe had formed us both was part of our identity and part of our inheritance.

I had been in Paris a couple of years before any of this became clear to me. When it did, I, like many a writer before me upon the discovery that his props have all been knocked out from under him, suffered a species of breakdown and was carried off to the mountains of Switzerland. There, in that absolutely alabaster landscape, armed with two Bessie Smith records and a typewriter, I began to try to re-create the life that I had first known as a child and from which I had spent so many years in flight.

It was Bessie Smith, through her tone and her cadence, who helped me to dig back to the way I myself must have spoken when I was a pickaninny, and to remember the things I had heard and seen and felt. I had buried them very deep. I had never listened to Bessie Smith in America (in the same way that, for years, I would not touch watermelon), but in Europe she helped to reconcile me to being a "nigger."

I do not think that I could have made this reconciliation here. Once I was able to accept my role—as distinguished, I must say, from my "place"—in the extraordinary drama which is America, I was released from the illusion that I hated America.

The story of what can happen to an American Negro writer in Europe simply illustrates, in some relief, what can happen to any American writer there. It is not meant, of course, to imply that it happens to them all, for Europe can be very crippling, too; and, anyway, a writer, when he has made his first breakthrough, has simply won a crucial skirmish in a dangerous, unending and unpredictable battle. Still, the breakthrough is important, and the point is that an American writer, in order to achieve it, very often has to leave this country.

The American writer, in Europe, is released, first of all, from the necessity of apologizing for himself. It is not until he *is* released from the habit of flexing his muscles and proving that he is just a "regular guy" that he realizes how crippling this habit has been. It is not necessary for him, there, to pretend to be something he is not, for the artist does not encounter in Europe the same suspicion he encounters here. Whatever the Europeans may actually think of artists, they have killed enough of them off by now to know that they are as real—and as persistent—as rain, snow, taxes or businessmen.

Of course, the reason for Europe's comparative clarity concerning the different functions of men in society is that European society has always been divided into classes in a way that American society never has been. A European writer considers himself to be part of an old and honorable tradition—of intellectual activity, of letters—and his choice of a vocation does not cause him any uneasy wonder as to whether or not it will cost him all his friends. But this tradition does not exist in America.

On the contrary, we have a very deep-seated distrust of real intellectual effort (probably because we suspect that it will destroy, as I hope it does, that myth of America to which we cling so desperately). An American writer fights his way to one of the lowest rungs on the American social ladder by means of pure bull-headedness and an indescribable series of odd jobs. He probably *has* been a "regular fellow" for much of his adult life, and it is not easy for him to step out of that lukewarm bath.

We must, however, consider a rather serious paradox: though American society is more mobile than Europe's, it is easier to cut across social and occupational lines there than it is here. This has something to do, I think, with the problem of status in American life. Where everyone has status, it is also perfectly possible, after all, that no one has. It seems inevitable, in any case, that a man may become uneasy as to just what his status is.

But Europeans have lived with the idea of status for a long time. A man can be as proud of being a good waiter as of being a good actor, and, in neither case, feel threatened. And this means that the actor and the waiter can have a freer and more genuinely friendly relationship in Europe than they are likely to have here. The waiter does not feel, with obscure resentment, that the actor has "made it," and the actor is not tormented by the fear that he may find himself, tomorrow, once again a waiter.

This lack of what may roughly be called social paranoia causes the American writer in Europe to feel—almost certainly for the first time in his life—that he can reach out to everyone, that he is accessible to everyone and open to everything. This is an extraordinary feeling. He feels, so to speak, his own weight, his own value.

It is as though he suddenly came out of a dark tunnel and found himself beneath the open sky. And, in fact, in Paris, I began to see the sky for what seemed to be the first time. It was borne in on me—and it did not make me feel melancholy—that this sky had been there before I was born and would be there when I was dead. And it was up to me, therefore, to make of my brief opportunity the most that could be made.

I was born in New York, but have lived only in pockets of it. In Paris, I lived in all parts of the city—on the Right Bank and the Left, among the bourgeoisie and among *les misérables,* and knew all kinds of people, from pimps and prostitutes in Pigalle to Egyptian bankers in Neuilly. This may sound extremely unprincipled or even obscurely immoral: I found it healthy. I love to talk to people, all kinds of people, and almost everyone, as I hope we still know, loves a man who loves to listen.

This perpetual dealing with people very different from myself caused a shattering in me of preconceptions I scarcely knew I held. The writer is meeting in Europe people who are not American, whose sense of reality is entirely different from his own. They may love or hate or admire or fear or envy this country—they see it, in any case, from another point of view, and this forces the writer to reconsider many things he had always taken for granted. This reassessment, which can be very painful, is also very valuable.

This freedom, like all freedom, has its dangers and its responsibilities. One day it begins to be borne in on the writer, and with great force, that he is living in Europe as an American. If he were living there as a European, he would be living on a different and far less attractive continent.

This crucial day may be the day on which an Algerian taxi-driver tells him how it feels to be an Algerian in Paris. It may be the day on which he passes a café terrace and catches a glimpse of the tense, intelligent and troubled face of Albert Camus. Or it may be the day on which someone asks him to explain Little Rock and he begins to feel that it would be simpler—and, corny as the words may sound, more honorable—to *go* to Little Rock than sit in Europe, on an American passport, trying to explain it.

This is a personal day, a terrible day, the day to which his entire sojourn has been tending. It is the day he realizes that there are no untroubled countries in this fearfully troubled world; that if he has been preparing himself for anything in Europe, he has been preparing himself—for America. In short, the freedom that the American writer finds in Europe brings him, full circle, back to himself, with the responsibility for his development where it always was: in his own hands.

Even the most incorrigible maverick has to be born somewhere. He may leave the group that produced him—he may be forced to—but nothing will efface his origins, the marks of which he carries with him everywhere. I think it is important to know this and even find it a matter for rejoicing, as the strongest people do, regardless of their station. On this acceptance, literally, the life of a writer depends.

The charge has often been made against American writers that they do not describe society, and have no interest in it. Of course, what the American writer is describing is his own situation. But what is *Anna Karenina* describing if not the tragic fate of the isolated individual, at odds with her time and place?

The real difference is that Tolstoy was describing an old and dense society in which everything seemed—to the people in it, though not to

Tolstoy—to be fixed forever. And the book is a masterpiece because Tolstoy was able to fathom, and make us see, the hidden laws which really governed this society and made Anna's doom inevitable.

American writers do not have a fixed society to describe. The only society they know is one in which nothing is fixed and in which the individual must fight for his identity. This is a rich confusion, indeed, and it creates for the American writer unprecedented opportunities.

That the tensions of American life, as well as the possibilities, are tremendous is certainly not even a question. But these are dealt with in contemporary literature mainly compulsively; that is, the book is more likely to be a symptom of our tension than an examination of it. The time has come, God knows, for us to examine ourselves, but we can only do this if we are willing to free ourselves of the myth of America and try to find out what is really happening here.

Every society is really governed by hidden laws, by unspoken but profound assumptions on the part of the people, and ours is no exception. It is up to the American writer to find out what these laws and assumptions are. In a society much given to smashing taboos without thereby managing to be liberated from them, it will be no easy matter.

It is no wonder, in the meantime, that the American writer keeps running off to Europe. He needs sustenance for his journey and the best models he can find. Europe has what we do not have yet, a sense of the mysterious and inexorable limits of life, a sense, in a word, of tragedy. And we have what they sorely need: a new sense of life's possibilities.

In this endeavor to wed the vision of the Old World with that of the New, it is the writer, not the statesman, who is our strongest arm. Though we do not wholly believe it yet, the interior life is a real life, and the intangible dreams of people have a tangible effect on the world.

Suggestions for Discussion

1. How does Baldwin's discovery of what it means to be an American relate to his search for identity?

2. How did his Paris sojourn contribute to his sense of self?

3. In what ways did his life in Paris enable him to "find in what way the *specialness* of my experience could be made to connect me with other people instead of dividing me from them"?

4. How did the Bessie Smith records contribute to Baldwin's search?

5. Compare the attitudes of Americans and Europeans toward writers and toward status.

6. How do the allusions to the Algerian taxi driver, Camus, and the questioner regarding Little Rock relate to Baldwin's understanding of himself and of America?

7. What does the author regard as the responsibility of the writer?

8. What does the author mean when he states that "the interior life is a real life"?

Suggestions for Writing

1. Refer to the text and develop an answer to the third Suggestion for Discussion.

2. Baldwin believes that America has a "new sense of life's possibilities." What are some of these possibilities?

3. Shelley labeled poets "the potential legislators of the world." Baldwin states that it is the writer, not the statesman, who is our strongest arm in wedding "the vision of the Old World with that of the New." What is your view?

SHELBY STEELE

On Being Black and Middle Class

Shelby Steele was born in Cedar Rapids, IA, in 1946. He has degrees from Coe College, the University of Southern Illinois, and the University of Utah. A frequent contributor to the national debate on race relations, Steele won a National Book Critics Circle Award and created a stir of controversy for *The Content of Our Character: A New Vision of Race* (1990), in which he claims African-Americans suffer from self-doubt and need to move beyond the issues of race. He also wrote *A Dream Deferred: The Second Betrayal of Black Freedom in America* (1998). The following essay, which originally appeared in the journal *Commentary* in 1988, examines the tensions and dilemmas facing a successful member of the black middle class who wants to retain his ethnic heritage.

Not long ago a friend of mine, black like myself, said to me that the term "black middle class" was actually a contradiction in terms. Race, he insisted, blurred class distinctions among blacks. If you were black, you were just black and that was that. When I argued, he let his eyes roll at my naiveté. Then he went on. For us, as black professionals, it was an exercise in self-flattery, a pathetic pretension, to give meaning to such a distinction. Worse, the very idea of class threatened the unity that was vital to the black community as a whole. After all, since when had white America taken note of anything but color when it came to blacks? He then reminded me of an old

Malcolm X line that had been popular in the sixties. Question: What is a black man with a Ph.D.? Answer: A nigger.

For many years I had been on my friend's side of this argument. Much of my conscious thinking on the old conundrum of race and class was shaped during my high school and college years in the race-charged sixties, when the fact of my race took on an almost religious significance. Progressively, from the mid-sixties on, more and more aspects of my life found their explanation, their justification, and their motivation in race. My youthful concerns about career, romance, money, values, and even styles of dress became a subject to consultation with various oracular sources of racial wisdom. And these ranged from a figure as ennobling as Martin Luther King, Jr., to the underworld elegance of dress I found in jazz clubs on the South Side of Chicago. Everywhere there were signals, and in those days I considered myself so blessed with clarity and direction that I pitied my white classmates who found more embarrassment than guidance in the fact of *their* race. In 1968, inflated by my new power, I took a mischievous delight in calling them culturally disadvantaged.

But now, hearing my friend's comment was like hearing a priest from a church I'd grown disenchanted with. I understood him, but my faith was weak. What had sustained me in the sixties sounded monotonous and off the mark in the eighties. For me, race had lost much of its juju, its singular capacity to conjure meaning. And today, when I honestly look at my life and the lives of many other middle-class blacks I know, I can see that race never fully explained our situation in American society. Black though I may be, it is impossible for me to sit in my single-family house with two cars in the driveway and a swing set in the back yard and *not* see the role class has played in my life. And how can my friend, similarly raised and similarly situated, not see it?

Yet despite my certainty I felt a sharp tug of guilt as I tried to explain myself over my friend's skepticism. He is a man of many comedic facial expressions and, as I spoke, his brow lifted in extreme moral alarm as if I were uttering the unspeakable. His clear implication was that I was being elitist and possibly (dare he suggest?) anti-black—crimes for which there might well be no redemption. He pretended to fear for me. I chuckled along with him, but inwardly I did wonder at myself. Though I never doubted the validity of what I was saying, I felt guilty saying it. Why?

After he left (to retrieve his daughter from a dance lesson) I realized that the trap I felt myself in had a tiresome familiarity and, in a sort of slow-motion epiphany, I began to see its outline. It was like the suddenly sharp vision one has at the end of a burdensome marriage when all the long-repressed incompatibilities come undeniably to light.

What became clear to me is that people like myself, my friend, and middle-class blacks generally are caught in a very specific double bind that keeps two equally powerful elements of our identity at odds with each other.

The middle-class values by which we were raised—the work ethic, the importance of education, the value of property ownership, of respectability, of "getting ahead," of stable family life, of initiative, of self-reliance, etc.—are, in themselves, raceless and even assimilationist. They urge us toward participation in the American mainstream, toward integration, toward a strong identification with the society—and toward the entire constellation of qualities that are implied in the word "individualism." These values are almost rules for how to prosper in a democratic, free-enterprise society that admires and rewards individual effort. They tell us to work hard for ourselves and our families and to seek our opportunities whenever they appear, inside or outside the confines of whatever ethnic group we may belong to.

But the particular pattern of racial identification that emerged in the sixties and that still prevails today urges middle-class blacks (and all blacks) in the opposite direction. This pattern asks us to see ourselves as an embattled minority, and it urges an adversarial stance toward the mainstream, an emphasis on ethnic consciousness over individualism. It is organized around an implied separatism.

The opposing thrust of these two parts of our identity results in the double bind of middle-class blacks. There is no forward movement on either plane that does not constitute backward movement on the other. This was the familiar trap I felt myself in while talking with my friend. As I spoke about class, his eyes reminded me that I was betraying race. Clearly, the two indispensable parts of my identity were a threat to each other.

Of course when you think about it, class and race are both similar in some ways and also naturally opposed. They are two forms of collective identity with boundaries that intersect. But whether they clash or peacefully coexist has much to do with how they are defined. Being both black and middle class becomes a double bind when class and race are defined in sharply antagonistic terms, so that one must be repressed to appease the other.

But what is the "substance" of these two identities, and how does each establish itself in an individual's overall identity? It seems to me that when we identify with any collective we are basically identifying with images that tell us what it means to be a member of that collective. Identity is not the same thing as the fact of membership in a collective; it is, rather, a form of self-definition, facilitated by images of what we wish our membership in the collective to mean. In this sense, the images we identify with may reflect the aspirations of the collective more than they reflect reality, and their content can vary with shifts in those aspirations.

But the process of identification is usually dialectical. It is just as necessary to say what we are *not* as it is to say what we are—so that finally identification comes about by embracing a polarity of positive and negative images. To identify as middle class, for example, I must have both positive and negative images of what being middle class entails; then I will know what I should and should not be doing in order to be middle class. The same goes for racial identity.

In the racially turbulent sixties the polarity of images that came to define racial identification was very antagonistic to the polarity that defined middle-class identification. One might say that the positive images of one lined up with the negative images of the other, so that to identify with both required either a contortionist's flexibility or a dangerous splitting of the self. The double bind of the black middle class was in place.

The black middle class has always defined its class identity by means of positive images gleaned from middle- and upper-class white society, and by means of negative images of lower-class blacks. This habit goes back to the institution of slavery itself, when "house" slaves both mimicked the whites they served and held themselves above the "field" slaves. But in the sixties the old bourgeois impulse to dissociate from the lower classes (the "we–they" distinction) backfired when racial identity suddenly called for the celebration of this same black lower class. One of the qualities of a double bind is that one feels it more than sees it, and I distinctly remember the tension and strange sense of dishonesty I felt in those days as I moved back and forth like a bigamist between the demands of class and race.

Though my father was born poor, he achieved middle-class standing through much hard work and sacrifice (one of his favorite words) and by identifying fully with solid middle-class values—mainly hard work, family life, property ownership, and education for his children (all four of whom have advanced degrees). In his mind these were not so much values as laws of nature. People who embodied them made up the positive images in his class polarity. The negative images came largely from the blacks he had left behind because they were "going nowhere."

No one in my family remembers how it happened, but as time went on, the negative images congealed into an imaginary character named Sam, who, from the extensive service we put him to, quickly grew to mythic proportions. In our family lore he was sometimes a trickster, sometimes a boob, but always possessed of a catalogue of sly faults that gave up graphic images of everything we should not be. On sacrifice: "Sam never thinks about tomorrow. He wants it now or he doesn't care about it." On work: "Sam doesn't favor it too much." On children: "Sam likes to have them but not to raise them." On money: "Sam drinks it up and pisses it out." On fidelity: "Sam has to have two or three women." On clothes: "Sam features loud clothes. He likes to see and be seen." And so on. Sam's persona amounted to a negative instruction manual in class identity.

I don't think that any of us believed Sam's faults were accurate representations of lower-class black life. He was an instrument of self-definition, not of sociological accuracy. It never occurred to us that he looked very much like the white racist stereotype of blacks, or that he might have been a manifestation of our own racial self-hatred. He simply gave us a counterpoint against which to express our aspirations. If self-hatred was a factor, it was not, for us, a matter of hating lower-class blacks but of hating what we did not want to be.

Still, hate or love aside, it is fundamentally true that my middle-class identity involved a dissociation from images of lower-class black life and a corresponding identification with values and patterns of responsibility that are common to the middle class everywhere. These values sent me a clear message: be both an individual and a responsible citizen; understand that the quality of your life will approximately reflect the quality of effort you put into it; know that individual responsibility is the basis of freedom and that the limitations imposed by fate (whether fair or unfair) are no excuse for passivity.

Whether I live up to these values or not, I know that my acceptance of them is the result of lifelong conditioning. I know also that I share this conditioning with middle-class people of all races and that I can no more easily be free of it than I can be free of my race. Whether all this got started because the black middle class modeled itself on the white middle class is no longer relevant. For the middle-class black, conditioned by these values from birth, the sense of meaning they provide is as immutable as the color of his skin.

I started the sixties in high school feeling that my class-conditioning was the surest way to overcome racial barriers. My racial identity was pretty much taken for granted. After all, it was obvious to the world that I was black. Yet I ended the sixties in graduate school a little embarrassed by my class background and with an almost desperate need to be "black." The tables had turned. I knew very clearly (though I struggled to repress it) that my aspirations and my sense of how to operate in the world came from my class background, yet "being black" required certain attitudes and stances that made me feel secretly a little duplicitous. The inner compatibility of class and race I had known in 1960 was gone.

For blacks, the decade between 1960 and 1969 saw racial identification undergo the same sort of transformation that national identity undergoes in times of war. It became more self-conscious, more narrowly focused, more prescribed, less tolerant of opposition. It spawned an implicit party line, which tended to disallow competing forms of identity. Race-as-identity was lifted from the relative slumber it knew in the fifties and pressed into service in a social and political war against oppression. It was redefined along sharp adversarial lines and directed toward the goal of mobilizing the great mass of black Americans in this warlike effort. It was imbued with a strong moral authority, useful for denouncing those who opposed it and for celebrating those who honored it as a positive achievement rather than as a mere birthright.

The form of racial identification that quickly evolved to meet this challenge presented blacks as a racial monolith, a singular people with a common experience of oppression. Differences within the race, no matter how ineradicable, had to be minimized. Class distinctions were one of the first such differences to be sacrificed, since they not only threatened racial unity but also seemed to stand in contradiction to the principle of equality which was the announced goal of the movement for racial progress. The discomfort I felt in 1969, the vague but relentless sense of duplicity, was the result of a historical necessity that put my race and class at odds, that was asking me to cast aside the distinction of my class and identify with a monolithic view of my race.

If the form of this racial identity was the monolith, its substance was victimization. The civil rights movement and the more radical splinter groups of the late sixties were all dedicated to ending racial victimization, and the form of black identity that emerged to facilitate this goal made blackness and victimization virtually synonymous. Since it was our victimization more than any other variable that identified and unified us, moreover, it followed logically that the purest black was the poor black. It was images of him that clustered around the positive pole of the race polarity; all other blacks were, in effect, required to identify with him in order to confirm their own blackness.

Certainly there were more dimensions to the black experience than victimization, but no other had the same capacity to fire the indignation needed for war. So, again out of historical necessity, victimization became the overriding focus of racial identity. But this only deepened the double bind for middle-class blacks like me. When it came to class we were accustomed to defining ourselves against lower-class blacks and identifying with at least the values of middle-class whites; when it came to race we were now being asked to identify with images of lower-class blacks and to see whites, middle class or otherwise, as victimizers. Negative lining up with positive, we were called upon to reject what we had previously embraced and to embrace what we had previously rejected. To put it still more personally, the Sam figure I had been raised to define myself against had now become the "real" black I was expected to identify with.

The fact that the poor black's new status was only passively earned by the condition of his victimization, not by assertive, positive action, made little difference. Status was status apart from the means by which it was achieved, and along with it came a certain power—the power to define the terms of access to that status, to say who was black and who was not. If a lower-class black said you were not really "black"—a sellout, an Uncle Tom—the judgment was all the more devastating because it carried the authority of his status. And this judgment soon enough came to be accepted by many whites as well.

In graduate school I was once told by a white professor, "Well, but…you're not really black. I mean, you're not disadvantaged." In his mind my lack of victim status disqualified me from the race itself. More recently I was complimented by a black student for speaking reasonably correct English, "proper" English as he put it. "But I don't know if I really want to talk like that," he went on. "Why not?" I asked. "Because then I wouldn't be black no more," he replied without a pause.

To overcome his marginal status, the middle-class black had to identify with a degree of victimization that was beyond his actual experience. In college (and well beyond) we used to play a game called "nap matching." It was a game of one-upmanship, in which we sat around outdoing each other with stories of racial victimization, symbolically measured by the naps of our hair. Most of us were middle class and so had few personal stories to relate, but if we could not match naps with our own biographies, we would move on to those legendary tales of victimization that came to us from the public domain.

The single story that sat atop the pinnacle of racial victimization for us was that of Emmett Till, the Northern black teenager who, on a visit to the South in 1955, was killed and grotesquely mutilated for supposedly looking at or whistling at (we were never sure which, though we argued the point endlessly) a white woman. Oh, how we probed his story, finding in his youth and Northern upbringing the quintessential embodiment of black innocence, brought down by a white evil so portentous and apocalyptic, so gnarled and hideous, that it left us with a feeling not far from awe. By telling his story and others like it, we came to *feel* the immutability of our victimization, its utter indigenousness, as a thing on this earth like dirt or sand or water.

Of course, these sessions were a ritual of group identification, a means by which we, as middle-class blacks, could be at one with our race. But why were we, who had only a moderate experience of victimization (and that offset by opportunities our parents never had), so intent on assimilating or appropriating an identity that in so many ways contradicted our own? Because, I think, the sense of innocence that is always entailed in feeling victimized filled us with a corresponding feeling of entitlement, or even license, that helped us endure our vulnerability on a largely white college campus.

In my junior year in college I rode to a debate tournament with three white students and our faculty coach, an elderly English professor. The experience of being the lone black in a group of whites was so familiar to me that I thought nothing of it as our trip began. But then halfway through the trip the professor casually turned to me and, in an isn't-the-world-funny sort of tone, said that he had just refused to rent an apartment in a house he owned to a "very nice" black couple because their color would "offend" the white couple who lived downstairs. His eyebrows lifted helplessly over his hawkish nose, suggesting that he too, like me, was a victim of America's racial farce. His look assumed a kind of comradeship: he and I were above this grimy business of race, though for expediency we had occasionally to concede the world its madness.

My vulnerability in this situation came not so much from the professor's blindness to his own racism as from his assumption that I would participate in it, that I would conspire with him against my own race so that he might remain comfortably blind. Why did he think I would be amenable to this? I can only guess that he assumed my middle-class identity was so complete and all-encompassing that I would see his action as nothing more than a trifling concession to the folkways of our land, that I would in fact applaud his decision not to disturb propriety. Blind to both his own racism and to me—one blindness serving the other—he could not recognize that he was asking me to betray my race in the name of my class.

His blindness made me feel vulnerable because it threatened to expose my own repressed ambivalence. His comment pressured me to choose between my class identification, which had contributed to my being a college student and a member of the debating team, and my desperate desire to be "black." I could have one but not both; I was double-bound.

Because double binds are repressed there is always an element of terror in them: the terror of bringing to the conscious mind the buried duplicity, self-deception, and pretense involved in serving two masters. This terror is the stuff of vulnerability, and since vulnerability is one of the least tolerable of all human feelings, we usually transform it into an emotion that seems to restore the control of which it has robbed us; most often, that emotion is anger. And so, before the professor had even finished his little story, I had become a furnace of rage. The year was 1967, and I had been primed by endless hours of nap-matching to feel, at least consciously, completely at one with the victim-focused black identity. This identity gave me the license, and the impunity, to unleash upon this professor one of those volcanic eruptions of racial indignation familiar to us from the novels of Richard Wright. Like Cross Damon in *Outsider*, who kills in perfectly righteous anger, I tried to annihilate the man. I punished him not according to the measure of his crime but according to the measure of my vulnerability, a measure set by the cumulative tension of years of repressed terror. Soon I saw that terror in *his* face, as he stared hollow-eyed at the road ahead. My white friends in the back seat, knowing no conflict between their own class and race, were astonished that someone they had taken to be so much like themselves could harbor a rage that for all the world looked murderous.

Though my rage was triggered by the professor's comment, it was deepened and sustained by a complex of need, conflict, and repression in myself of which I had been wholly unaware. Out of my racial vulnerability I had developed the strong need of an identity with which to defend myself. The only such identity available was that of me as victim, him as victimizer. Once in the grip of this paradigm, I began to do far more damage to myself than he had done.

Seeing myself as a victim meant that I clung all the harder to my racial identity, which, in turn, meant that I suppressed my class identity. This cut me off from all the resources my class values might have offered me. In those values, for instance, I might have found the means to a more dispassionate response, the response less of a victim attacked by a victimizer than of an individual offended by a foolish old man. As an individual I might have reported this professor to the college dean. Or I might have calmly tried to reveal his blindness to him, and possibly won a convert. (The flagrancy of his remark suggested a hidden guilt and even self-recognition on which I might have capitalized. Doesn't confession usually signal a willingness to face oneself?) Or I might have simply chuckled and then let my silence serve as an answer to his provocation. Would not my composure, in any form it might take, deflect into his own heart the arrow he'd shot at me?

Instead, my anger, itself the hair-trigger expression of a long-repressed double bind, not only cut me off from the best of my own resources, it also distorted the nature of my true racial problem. The righteousness of this anger and easy catharsis it brought buoyed the delusion of my victimization and left me as blind as the professor himself.

As a middle-class black I have often felt myself *contriving* to be "black." And I have noticed this same contrivance in others—a certain stretching away from the natural flow of one's life to align oneself with a victim-focused black identity. Our particular needs are out of sync with the form of identity available to meet those needs. Middle-class blacks need to identify racially; it is better to think of ourselves as black and victimized than not black at all; so we contrive (more unconsciously than consciously) to fit ourselves into an identity that denies our class and fails to address the true source of our vulnerability.

For me this once meant spending inordinate amounts of time at black faculty meetings, though these meetings had little to do with my real racial anxieties or my professional life. I was new to the university, one of two blacks in an English department of over seventy, and I felt a little isolated and vulnerable, though I did not admit it to myself. But at these meetings we discussed the problems of black faculty and students within a framework of victimization. The real vulnerability we felt was covered over by all the adversarial drama the victim/victimized polarity inspired, and hence went unseen and unassuaged. And this, I think, explains our rather chronic ineffectiveness as a group. Since victimization was not our primary problem—the university had long ago opened its doors to us—we had to contrive to make it so, and there is not much energy in contrivance. What I got at these meetings was ultimately an object lesson in how fruitless struggle can be when it is not grounded in actual need.

At our black faculty meetings, the old equation of blackness with victimization was ever present—to be black was to be a victim; therefore, not to be a victim was not to be black. As we contrived to meet the terms of this formula there was an inevitable distortion of both ourselves and the larger university. Through the prism of victimization the university seemed more impenetrable than it actually was, and we more limited in our powers. We fell prey to the victim's myopia, making the university an institution from which we could seek redress but which we could never fully join. And this mind-set often led us to look more for compensations for our supposed victimization than for opportunities we could pursue as individuals.

The discomfort and vulnerability felt by middle-class blacks in the sixties, it could be argued, was a worthwhile price to pay considering the progress achieved during that time of racial confrontation. But what may have been tolerable then is intolerable now. Though changes in American society have made it an anachronism, the monolithic form of racial identification that came out of the sixties is still very much with us. It may be more loosely held, and its power to punish heretics has probably diminished, but it continues to catch middle-class blacks in a double bind, thus impeding not only their own advancement but even, I would contend, that of blacks as a group.

The victim-focused black identity encourages the individual to feel that his advancement depends almost entirely on that of the group. Thus he loses sight not only of his own possibilities but of the inextricable connection between individual effort and individual advancement. This is a profound encumbrance today, when there is more opportunity for blacks than ever before, for it reimposes limitations that can have the same oppressive effect as those the society has only recently begun to remove.

It was the emphasis on mass action in the sixties that made the victim-focused black identity a necessity. But in the eighties and beyond, when racial advancement will come only through a multitude of individual advancements, this form of identity inadvertently adds itself to the forces that hold us back. Hard work, education, individual initiative, stable family life, property ownership—these have always been the means by which ethnic groups have moved ahead in America. Regardless of past or present victimization, these "laws" of advancement apply absolutely to black Americans also. There is no getting around this. What we need is a form of racial identity that energizes the individual by putting him in touch with both his possibilities and his responsibilities.

It has always annoyed me to hear from the mouths of certain arbiters of blackness that middle-class blacks should "reach back" and pull up those blacks less fortunate than they—as though middle-class status were an unearned and essentially passive condition in which one needed a large measure of noblesse oblige to occupy one's time. My own image is of reaching back from a moving train to lift on board those who have no tickets. A noble enough sentiment—but might it not be wiser to show them the entire structure of principles, effort, and sacrifice that puts one in a position to buy a ticket any time one likes? This, I think, is something members of the black middle class can realistically offer to other blacks. Their example is not only a testament to possibility but also a lesson in method. But they cannot lead by example until they are released from a black identity that regards that example as suspect, that sees them as "marginally" black, indeed that holds *them* back by catching them in a double bind.

To move beyond the victim-focused black identity we must learn to make a difficult but crucial distinction: between actual victimization, which we must resist with every resource, and identification with the victim's status. Until we do this we will continue to wrestle more with ourselves than with the new opportunities which so many paid so dearly to win.

Suggestions for Discussion

1. How has Shelby Steele's personal history brought him into conflict with the political movement to overcome racism?
2. Steele identifies and explains what it means to be a member of the middle class. Discuss his definition.
3. What is the negative consequence, for Steele, of seeing himself as a victim of racism?
4. Discuss the episode related by Steele of his anger with a white professor as they travel to a debating match.

Suggestions for Writing

1. Write an essay in which you evaluate Steele's statement of his dilemma both as student and professor. Do you sympathize with him? Do you agree or disagree with his position? Explain your position.
2. Take the part of a white or black student, and write a paper in which you discuss the double bind Steele describes. Try to examine carefully your own relation with a member of the opposite race.
3. Write a paper in which you evaluate Steele's solution to what he sees as the problem of being a member of the black middle class.

∽∽∽∽

CARSON MCCULLERS

Loneliness...an American Malady

Carson McCullers (1917–1967), a Southern writer, was awarded Guggenheim Fellowships in 1942 and in 1946. Her published works include *The Heart Is a Lonely Hunter* (1940), *Reflections in a Golden Eye* (1941), *The Member of the Wedding* (1946), *The Ballad of the Sad Café* (1951), and *Clock Without Hands* (1961). This excerpt from *The Mortgaged Heart* (1971) suggests that the way by which we master loneliness is "to belong to something larger and more powerful than the weak, lonely self."

This city, New York—consider the people in it, the eight million of us. An English friend of mine, when asked why he lived in New York City, said that he liked it here because he could be so alone. While it was my friend's desire to be alone, the aloneness of many Americans who live in cities is an involuntary and fearful thing. It has been said that loneliness is the great American malady. What is the nature of this loneliness? It would seem essentially to be a quest for identity.

To the spectator, the amateur philosopher, no motive among the complex ricochets of our desires and rejections seems stronger or more enduring than the will of the individual to claim his identity and belong. From infancy to death, the human being is obsessed by these dual motives. During our first weeks of life, the question of identity shares urgency with the need for milk. The baby reaches for his toes, then explores the bars of his crib; again and again he compares the difference between his own body and the objects around him, and in the wavering, infant eyes there comes a pristine wonder.

Consciousness of self is the first abstract problem that the human being solves. Indeed, it is this self-consciousness that removes us from lower animals. This primitive grasp of identity develops with constantly shifting emphasis through all our years. Perhaps maturity is simply the history of those mutations that reveal to the individual the relation between himself and the world in which he finds himself.

After the first establishment of identity there comes the imperative need to lose this new-found sense of separateness and to belong to something larger and more powerful than the weak, lonely self. The sense of moral isolation is intolerable to us.

In *The Member of the Wedding* the lonely 12-year-old girl, Frankie Addams, articulates this universal need: "The trouble with me is that for a long time I have just been an *I* person. All people belong to a *We* except me. Not to belong to a *We* makes you too lonesome."

Love is the bridge that leads from the *I* sense to the *We*, and there is a paradox about personal love. Love of another individual opens a new relation between the personality and the world. The lover responds in a new way to nature and may even write poetry. Love is affirmation; it motivates the *yes* responses and the sense of wider communication. Love casts out fear, and in the security of this togetherness we find contentment, courage. We no longer fear the age-old haunting questions: "Who am I?" "Why am I?" "Where am I going?"—and having cast out fear, we can be honest and charitable.

For fear is a primary source of evil. And when the question "Who am I?" recurs and is unanswered, then fear and frustration project a negative attitude. The bewildered soul can answer only: "Since I do not understand 'Who I am,' I only know what I am *not*." The corollary of this emotional incertitude is snobbism, intolerance, and racial hate. The xenophobic individual can only reject and destroy, as the xenophobic nation inevitably makes war.

The loneliness of Americans does not have its source in xenophobia; as a nation we are an outgoing people, reaching always for immediate contacts, further experience. But we tend to seek out things as individuals, alone. The European, secure in his family ties and rigid class loyalties, knows little of the moral loneliness that is native to us Americans. While the European artists tend to form groups or aesthetic schools, the American artist is the eternal maverick—not only from society in the way of all creative minds, but within the orbit of his own art.

Thoreau took to the woods to seek the ultimate meaning of his life. His creed was simplicity and his *modus vivendi* the deliberate stripping of external life to the Spartan necessities in order that his inward life could freely flourish. His objective, as he put it, was to back the world into a corner. And in that way did he discover "What a man thinks of himself, that it is which determines, or rather indicates, his fate."

On the other hand, Thomas Wolfe turned to the city, and in his wanderings around New York he continued his frenetic and lifelong search for the lost brother, the magic door. He too backed the world into a corner, and as he passed among the city's millions, returning their stares, he experienced "That silent meeting [that] is the summary of all the meetings of men's lives."

Whether in the pastoral joys of country life or in the labyrinthine city, we Americans are always seeking. We wander, question. But the answer waits in each separate heart—the answer of our own identity and the way by which we can master loneliness and feel that at last we belong.

Suggestion for Discussion

How does the author establish the connections between loneliness and identity? Between *I* and *We*? Between lack of a sense of identity and fear? Between fear and hatred or destruction?

Suggestions for Writing

1. Develop or challenge Thoreau's belief, "What a man thinks of himself, that it is which determines, or rather indicates, his fate."

2. Develop an essay in which you argue that country life is or is not more conducive to the development of a sense of self than city life.

ᘓᘓᘓᘓ

NICCOLÒ MACHIAVELLI

Of Cruelty and Clemency, and Whether It Is Better to Be Loved or Feared

Niccolò Machiavelli (1469–1527) was a Florentine statesman. His best-known work, *The Prince,* written in 1513, is an astute analysis of the contemporary political scene. The work was first translated into English in 1640. This selection from *The Prince,* translated by Luigi Ricci and revised by E. R. P. Vincent, explains by examples from history why the prince must rely on the fear he creates rather than the love he might generate. Machiavelli explains also why the prince, though causing fear, must avoid incurring hatred.

Proceeding to the other qualities before named, I say that every prince must desire to be considered merciful and not cruel. He must, however, take care not to misuse this mercifulness. Cesare Borgia was considered cruel, but his cruelty had brought order to the Romagna, united it, and reduced it to peace and fealty. If this is considered well, it will be seen that he was really much more merciful than the Florentine people, who, to avoid the name of cruelty, allowed Pistoia to be destroyed. A prince, therefore, must not mind incurring the charge of cruelty for the purpose of keeping his subjects united and faithful; for, with a very few examples, he will be more merciful than those who, from excess of tenderness, allow disorders to arise, from whence spring bloodshed and rapine; for these as a rule injure the whole community, while the executions carried out by the prince injure only individuals. And of all princes, it is impossible for a new prince to escape the reputation of cruelty, new states being always full of dangers. Wherefore Virgil through the mouth of Dido says:

> Res dura, et regni novitas me talia cogunt
>   Moliri, et late fines custode tueri.*

Nevertheless, he must be cautious in believing and acting, and must not be afraid of his own shadow, and must proceed in a temperate manner with

*Our harsh situation and the newness of our kingdom compel me to contrive such measure: and to guard our territory far and wide. (Dido offers this explanation to the newly landed Trojans of why her guards received them with hostile and suspicious measures.)

prudence and humanity, so that too much confidence does not render him incautious, and too much diffidence does not render him intolerant.

From this arises the question whether it is better to be loved more than feared, or feared more than loved. The reply is, that one ought to be both feared and loved, but as it is difficult for the two to go together, it is much safer to be feared than loved, if one of the two has to be wanting. For it may be said of men in general that they are ungrateful, voluble dissemblers, anxious to avoid danger, and covetous of gain; as long as you benefit them, they are entirely yours; they offer you their blood, their goods, their life, and their children, as I have before said, when the necessity is remote; but when it approaches, they revolt. And the prince who has relied solely on their words, without making other preparations, is ruined; for the friendship which is gained by purchase and not through grandeur and nobility of spirit is bought but not secured, and at a pinch is not to be expended in your service. And men have less scruple in offending one who makes himself loved than one who makes himself feared; for love is held by a chain of obligation which, men being selfish, is broken whenever it serves their purpose; but fear is maintained by a dread of punishment which never fails.

Still, a prince should make himself feared in such a way that if he does not gain love, he at any rate avoids hatred; for fear and the absence of hatred may well go together, and will be always attained by one who abstains from interfering with the property of his citizens and subjects or with their women. And when he is obliged to take the life of anyone, let him do so when there is proper justification and manifest reason for it; but above all he must abstain from taking the property of others, for men forget more easily the death of their father than the loss of their patrimony. Then also pretexts for seizing property are never wanting, and one who begins to live by rapine will always find some reason for taking the goods of others, whereas causes for taking life are rarer and more fleeting.

But when the prince is with his army and has a large number of soldiers under his control, then it is extremely necessary that he should not mind being thought cruel; for without this reputation he could not keep an army united or disposed to any duty. Among the noteworthy actions of Hannibal is numbered this, that although he had an enormous army, composed of men of all nations and fighting in foreign countries, there never arose any dissension either among them or against the prince, either in good fortune or in bad. This could not be due to anything but his inhuman cruelty, which together with his infinite other virtues, made him always venerated and terrible in the sight of his soldiers, and without it his other virtues would not have sufficed to produce that effect. Thoughtless writers admire on the one hand his actions, and on the other blame the principal cause of them.

And that it is true that his other virtues would not have sufficed may be seen from the case of Scipio (famous not only in regard to his own times, but all times of which memory remains), whose armies rebelled against him in Spain, which arose from nothing but his excessive kindness, which allowed more licence to the soldiers than was consonant with military discipline. He was reproached with this in the senate by Fabius Maximus, who called him a corrupter of the Roman militia. Locri having been destroyed by one of Scipio's officers was not revenged by him, nor was the insolence of that officer punished, simply by reason of his easy nature; so much so, that some one wishing to excuse him in the senate, said that there were many men who knew rather how not to err, than how to correct the errors of others. This disposition would in time have tarnished the fame and glory of Scipio had he persevered in it under the empire, but living under the rule of the senate this harmful quality was not only concealed but became a glory to him.

I conclude, therefore, with regard to being feared and loved, that men love at their own free will, but fear at the will of the prince, and that a wise prince must rely on what is in his power and not on what is in the power of others, and he must only contrive to avoid incurring hatred, as has been explained.

Suggestions for Discussion

1. How does Machiavelli show that Cesare Borgia, known for his cruelty, was more merciful than the people of Florence?

2. Explain the use of the quotation from Virgil.

3. Explain Machiavelli's argument that the prince cannot rely on the love of his subjects.

4. What attitudes does Machiavelli express when he says that "men forget more easily the death of their father than the loss of their patrimony"?

5. Compare and contrast the actions of Scipio and Hannibal. How does Machiavelli explain their actions to prove his point about the need of the prince to inspire fear?

Suggestion for Writing

Write an essay in which you comment on the ideas in this selection that may be brilliant but not admirable. What aspects of life does the author ignore? Why? Why does this selection not express the concern for freedom and human dignity that characterizes most of the selections in this section?

∾∾∾∾

THOMAS MERTON

Love Can Be Kept Only by Being Given Away

Thomas Merton (1915–1968), a social critic and revered Roman Catholic theologian, was a Trappist monk of the Cistercian Abbey of Gethsemani near Bardstown, KY, from 1941 until his death in Bangkok, Thailand. His 1948 autobiography, *The Seven Storey Mountain*, was a best-seller and is considered a spiritual classic. His other works include *The Waters of Siloe* (1949), *The Ascent to Truth* (1951), and *The Road to Joy* (posthumous 1989) as well as several posthumously published letters, journals, and essays. Merton lived as a hermit in his order's monastery between 1965 and 1968 and wrote often about the Eastern religious tradition and its relationship to Christianity; he was also concerned about issues of peace, war, international politics, and revolution. The following passage, from *No Man Is an Island* (1955) is about the importance of selfless love.

1. A happiness that is sought for ourselves alone can never be found: for a happiness that is diminished by being shared is not big enough to make us happy.

There is a false and momentary happiness in self-satisfaction, but it always leads to sorrow because it narrows and deadens our spirit. True happiness is found in unselfish love, a love which increases in proportion as it is shared. There is no end to the sharing of love, and, therefore, the potential happiness of such love is without limit. Infinite sharing is the law of God's inner life. He has made the sharing of ourselves the law of our own being, so that it is in loving others that we best love ourselves. In disinterested activity we best fulfill our own capacities to act and to be.

Yet there can never be happiness in compulsion. It is not enough for love to be shared: it must be shared freely. That is to say it must be given, not merely taken. Unselfish love that is poured out upon a selfish object does not bring perfect happiness: not because love requires a return or a reward for loving, but because it rests in the happiness of the beloved. And if the one loved receives love selfishly, the lover is not satisfied. He sees that his love has failed to make the beloved happy. It has not awakened his capacity for unselfish love.

Hence the paradox that unselfish love cannot rest perfectly except in a love that is perfectly reciprocated: because it knows that the only true peace is found in selfless love. Selfless love consents to be loved selflessly for the sake of the beloved. In so doing, it perfects itself.

The gift of love is the gift of the power and the capacity to love, and, therefore, to give love with full effect is also to receive it. So, love can only be kept by being given away, and it can only be given perfectly when it is also received.

2. Love not only prefers the good of another to my own, but it does not even compare the two. It has only one good, that of the beloved, which is, at the same time, my own. Love shares the good with another not by dividing it with him, but by identifying itself with him so that his good becomes my own. The same good is enjoyed in its wholeness by two in one spirit, not halved and shared by two souls. Where love is really disinterested, the lover does not even stop to inquire whether he can safely appropriate for himself some part of the good which he wills for his friend. Love seeks its whole good in the good of the beloved, and to divide that good would be to diminish love. Such a division would not only weaken the action of love, but in doing so would also diminish its joy. For love does not seek a joy that follows from its effect: its joy is in the effect itself, which is the good of the beloved. Consequently, if my love be pure I do not even have to seek for myself the satisfaction of loving. Love seeks one thing only: the good of the one loved. It leaves all the other secondary effects to take care of themselves. Love, therefore, is its own reward.

3. To love another is to will what is really good for him. Such love must be based on truth. A love that sees no distinction between good and evil, but loves blindly merely for the sake of loving, is hatred, rather than love. To love blindly is to love selfishly, because the goal of such love is not the real advantage of the beloved but only the exercise of love in our own souls. Such love cannot seem to be love unless it pretends to seek the good of the one loved. But since it actually cares nothing for the truth, and never considers that it may go astray, it proves itself to be selfish. It does not seek the true advantage of the beloved or even our own. It is not interested in the truth, but only in itself. It proclaims itself content with an apparent good: which is the exercise of love for its own sake, without any consideration of the good or bad effects of loving.

When such love exists on the level of bodily passion it is easily recognized for what it is. It is selfish, and, therefore, it is not love. Those whose love does not transcend the desires of their bodies, generally do not even bother to deceive themselves with good motives. They follow their passions. Since they do not deceive themselves, they are more honest, as well as more miserable, than those who pretend to love on a spiritual plane without realizing that their "unselfishness" is only a deception.

4. Charity is neither weak nor blind. It is essentially prudent, just, temperate, and strong. Unless all the other virtues blend together in charity, our love is not genuine. No one who really wants to love another will consent to love him falsely. If we are going to love others at all, we must make up our minds to love them well. Otherwise our love is a delusion.

The first step to unselfish love is the recognition that our love may be deluded. We must first of all purify our love by renouncing the pleasure of loving as an end in itself. As long as pleasure is our end, we will be dishonest with ourselves and with those we love. We will not seek their good, but our own pleasure.

5. It is clear, then, that to love others well we must first love the truth. And since love is a matter of practical and concrete human relations, the truth we must love when we love our brothers is not mere abstract speculation: it is the moral truth that is to be embodied and given life in our own destiny and theirs. This truth is more than the cold perception of an obligation, flowing from moral precepts. The truth we must love in loving our brothers is the concrete destiny and sanctity that are willed for them by the love of God. One who really loves another is not merely moved by the desire to see him contented and healthy and prosperous in this world. Love cannot be satisfied with anything so incomplete. If I am to love my brother, I must somehow enter deep into the mystery of God's love for him. I must be moved not only by human sympathy but by that divine sympathy which is revealed to us in Jesus and which enriches our own lives by the outpouring of the Holy Spirit in our hearts.

The truth I love in loving my brother cannot be something merely philosophical and abstract. It must be at the same time supernatural and concrete, practical and alive. And I mean these words in no metaphorical sense. The truth I must love in my brother is God Himself, living in him. I must seek the life of the Spirit of God breathing in him. And I can only discern and follow that mysterious life by the action of the same Holy Spirit living and acting in the depths of my own heart.

6. Charity makes me seek far more than the satisfaction of my own desires, even though they be aimed at another's good. It must also make me an instrument of God's Providence in their lives. I must become convinced and penetrated by the realization that without my love for them they may perhaps not achieve the things God has willed for them. My will must be the instrument of God's will in helping them create their destiny. My love must be to them the "sacrament" of the mysterious and infinitely selfless love God has for them. My love must be for them the minister not of my own spirit but of the Holy Spirit. The words I speak to them must be no other than the words of Christ Who deigns to reveal Himself to them in me.

Such a conception of charity is, above all, proper to a priest. It is an aspect of the grace of Orders. It is, so to speak, inseparable from the priesthood, and a priest cannot be at peace with himself or with God unless he is trying to love others with a love that is not merely his but God's own love. Only this charity which is as strong and as sure as the Spirit of God Himself can save us from the lamentable error of pouring out on others a love that leads them into error and urges them to seek happiness where it can never be found.

7. In order to love others with perfect charity I must be true to them, to myself, and to God.

The true interests of a person are at once perfectly his own and common to the whole Kingdom of God. That is because these interests are all centered in God's designs for his soul. The destiny of each one of us is intended, by the Lord, to enter into the destiny of His entire Kingdom. And the more perfectly we are ourselves the more we are able to contribute to the good of the whole Church of God. For each person is perfected by the virtues of a child of God, and these virtues show themselves differently in everyone, since they come to light in the lives of each one of the saints under a different set of providential circumstances.

If we love one another truly, our love will be graced with a clear-sighted prudence which sees and respects the designs of God upon each separate soul. Our love for one another must be rooted in a deep devotion to Divine Providence, a devotion that abandons our own limited plans into the hands of God and seeks only to enter into the invisible work that builds His Kingdom. Only a love that senses the designs of Providence can unite itself perfectly to God's providential action upon souls. Faithful submission to God's secret working in the world will fill our love with piety, that is to say with supernatural awe and respect. This respect, this piety, gives our love the character of worship, without which our charity can never be quite complete. For love must not only *seek* the truth in the lives of those around us; it must *find* it there. But when we find the truth that shapes our lives we have found more than an idea. We have found a Person. We have come upon the actions of One Who is still hidden, but Whose work proclaims Him holy and worthy to be adored. And in Him we also find ourselves.

8. A selfish love seldom respects the rights of the beloved to be an autonomous person. Far from respecting the true being of another and granting his personality room to grow and expand in its own original way, this love seeks to keep him in subjection to ourselves. It insists that he conform himself to us, and it works in every possible way to make him do so. A selfish love withers and dies unless it is sustained by the attention of the beloved. When we love thus, our friends exist only in order that we may love them. In loving them we seek to make pets of them, to keep them tame. Such love fears nothing more than the escape of the beloved. It requires his subjection because that is necessary for the nourishment of our own affections.

Selfish love often appears to be unselfish, because it is willing to make any concession to the beloved in order to keep him prisoner. But it is supreme selfishness to buy what is best in a person, his liberty, his integrity, his own autonomous dignity as a person, at the price of far lesser goods. Such selfishness is all the more abominable when it takes a complacent pleasure in its concessions, deluded that they are all acts of selfless charity.

A love, therefore, that is selfless, that honestly seeks the truth, does not make unlimited concessions to the beloved.

May God preserve me from the love of a friend who will never dare to rebuke me. May He preserve me from the friend who seeks to do nothing but change and correct me. But may He preserve me still more from one whose love is only satisfied by being rebuked.

If I love my brothers according to the truth, my love for them will be true not only to them but to myself.

I cannot be true to them if I am not true to myself.

"The Lord trieth the just and the wicked, but he that loveth iniquity hateth his own soul" (Psalm 10:6).

"Iniquity" is inequality, injustice, which seeks more for myself than my rights allow and which gives others less than they should receive. To love myself more than others is to be untrue to myself as well as to them. The more I seek to take advantage of others the less of a person will I myself be, for the anxiety to possess what I should not have narrows and diminishes my own soul.

Therefore the man who loves himself too much is incapable of loving anyone effectively, including himself. How then can he hope to love another?

"An unjust man allureth his friend and leadeth him into a way that is not good" (Proverbs 16:29).

9. Charity must teach us that friendship is a holy thing, and that it is neither charitable nor holy to base our friendship on falsehood. We can be, in some sense, friends to all men because there is no man on earth with whom we do not have something in common. But it would be false to treat too many men as intimate friends. It is not possible to be intimate with more than very few, because there are only very few in the world with whom we have practically everything in common.

Love, then, must be true to the ones we love and to ourselves, and also to its own laws. I cannot be true to myself if I pretend to have more in common than I actually have with someone whom I may like for a selfish and unworthy reason.

There is, however, one universal basis for friendship with all men: we are all loved by God, and I should desire them all to love Him with all their power. But the fact remains that I cannot, on this earth, enter deeply into the mystery of their love for Him and of His love for them.

Great priests, saints like the Curé d'Ars, who have seen into the hidden depths of thousands of souls, have, nevertheless, remained men with few intimate friends. No one is more lonely than a priest who has a vast ministry. He is isolated in a terrible desert by the secrets of his fellow men.

10. When all this has been said, the truth remains that our destiny is to love one another as Christ has loved us. Jesus had very few close friends when He was on earth, and yet He loved and loves all men and is, to every soul born into the world, that soul's most intimate friend. The lives of all the men we meet and know are woven into our own destiny, together with the lives of many we shall never know on earth. But certain ones, very few,

are our close friends. Because we have more in common with them, we are able to love them with a special selfless perfection, since we have more to share. They are inseparable from our own destiny, and, therefore, our love for them is especially holy: it is a manifestation of God in our lives.

11. Perfect charity gives supreme praise to the liberty of God. It recognizes His power to give Himself to those who love Him purely without violating the purity of their love. More than that: selfless charity, by receiving from God the gift of Himself, becomes able, by that fact alone, to love with perfect purity. For God Himself creates the purity and the love of those who love Him and one another with perfect charity.

His charity must not be represented as hunger. It is the banquet of the Kingdom of Heaven, to which many were invited by the great King. Many could not come to the banquet because they desired something beyond it, something for themselves—a farm, a wife, a yoke of oxen. They did not know that if they had sought first the banquet and the Kingdom they would have received everything else besides.

Charity is not hungry. It is the *juge convivium*—the perpetual banquet where there is no satiety, a feast in which we are nourished by serving others rather than by feeding ourselves. It is a banquet of prudence also, in which we know how to give to each other his just measure.

"And the Lord said: Who, thinkest thou, is the faithful and wise steward, whom his lord setteth over his family, to give them their measure of wheat in due season? Blessed is that servant, whom when his lord shall come, shall find him so doing" (Luke 12:43–44).

But to feed others with charity is to feed them with the Bread of Life, Who is Christ, and to teach them also to love with a love that knows no hunger.

"I am the Bread of Life: he who comes to Me shall not hunger, and he who believes in Me shall never thirst" (John 6:35).

Suggestions for Discussion

1. According to Merton, when does love become selfish or twisted into a form of hatred? How might one know the difference between real love and selfish love?

2. What role does charity play in Merton's view of love? And why must love be based on truth?

3. Although Merton ultimately frames his thoughts on love in religious terms by linking love as a general concept to a love of Christ, what might a non-Catholic or a nonreligious person glean from Merton's overall view of love?

Suggestion for Writing

Define love in a thoughtful, philosophical essay.

POETRY

WILFRED OWEN

Dulce et Decorum Est

Wilfred Owen (1893–1918) was born in Shropshire, England, and educated at Birkenhead Institute. Among the most celebrated of the English war poets, he was killed in action in World War I. Another war poet, Siegfried Sassoon, collected Owen's poems, which were first published in 1920. Other collections followed, as did critical studies and memoirs. From *The Complete Poems and Fragments of Wilfred Owen,* published in 1984, comes "Dulce et Decorum Est" (taken from Horace's statement, "It is sweet and fitting to die for one's country"); it opposes vivid and devastating images of the casualties of war with statements of sentimental patriotism. It shows war as the ultimate insult to human dignity.

Bent double, like old beggars under sacks,
Knock-kneed, coughing like hags, we cursed through
    sludge,
Till on the haunting flares we turned our backs,
And towards our distant rest began to trudge.
Men marched asleep. Many had lost their boots,
But limped on, blood-shod. All went lame, all blind;
Drunk with fatigue; deaf even to the hoots
Of gas-shells dropping softly behind.

Gas! Gas! Quick, boys!—An ecstasy of fumbling,
Fitting the clumsy helmets just in time,
But someone still was yelling out and stumbling
And flound'ring like a man in fire or lime.—
Dim through the misty panes and thick green light,
As under a green sea, I saw him drowning.
In all my dreams before my helpless sight
He plunges at me, guttering, choking, drowning.

If in some smothering dreams, you too could pace
Behind the wagon that we flung him in,
And watch the white eyes writhing in his face,

His hanging face, like a devil's sick of sin,
If you could hear, at every jolt, the blood
Come gargling from the froth-corrupted lungs
Bitter as the cud

Of vile, incurable sores on innocent tongues,—
My friend, you would not tell with such high zest
To children ardent for some desperate glory,
The old lie: *Dulce et decorum est*
Pro patria mori.

Suggestions for Discussion

1. In the first two stanzas, Owen presents two connected scenes of war. How are these two stanzas related to the final one?

2. Discuss the use of irony in the poem. Show why Owen uses the quotation from Horace.

3. Examine the series of images that Owen uses to describe war. Do they progress through the poem? Show why one cannot interchange the first two stanzas.

Suggestion for Writing

Owen's picture of the destruction of lives constitutes a poetic statement against war. Does this poem lead you to a belief in pacifism? Are there "just" and "unjust" wars? Try to sort out your attitudes and write an essay explaining under what conditions, if any, you might be willing to fight for your country. Support your statements with detailed arguments.

W. H. AUDEN

The Unknown Citizen

Wystan Hugh Auden (1907–1973), born in England and educated at Oxford University, was early recognized as a leader of the poets of his generation. His volumes of poetry include *The Orators* (1932), *The Double Man* (1941), and *The Age of Anxiety* (1947), which won a Pulitzer Prize in 1948. Auden came to the United States at the outbreak of World War II. His autobiography, *Certain World: A Commonplace Book,* published in 1970, traces his return from leftist agnostic to the Church of England. In 1967 he was made a fellow of Christ Church, Oxford. In the following poem, published in 1940, Auden comments satirically on the behavior of a good citizen in a totalitarian state that resembles not only fascist Italy and Nazi Germany but democratic America and Britain as well.

∽

(To JS/07/M/378 This Marble Monument Is Erected by the State)

He was found by the Bureau of Statistics to be
One against whom there was no official complaint,
And all the reports on his conduct agree
That, in the modern sense of an old-fashioned word, he was a saint,
For in everything he did he served the Greater Community.
Except for the War till the day he retired
He worked in a factory and never got fired,
But satisfied his employers, Fudge Motors Inc.
Yet he wasn't a scab or odd in his views,
For his Union reports that he paid his dues,
(Our report on his Union shows it was sound)
And our Social Psychology workers found
That he was popular with his mates and liked to drink.
The Press are convinced that he bought a paper every day
And that his reactions to advertisements were normal in every way.
Policies taken out in his name prove that he was fully insured,
And his Health-card shows he was once in a hospital but left it cured,
Both Producers Research and High-Grade Living declare
He was fully sensible to the advantages of the Installment Plan
And had everything necessary to the Modern Man,
A phonograph, a radio, a car and a frigidaire.
Our researchers into Public Opinion are content
That he held the proper opinions for the time of year;
When there was peace, he was for peace; when there was war, he went.
He was married and added five children to the population,
Which our Eugenist says was the right number for a parent of his
    generation,
And our teachers report that he never interfered with their education.
Was he free? Was he Happy? The question is absurd:
Had anything been wrong, we should certainly have heard.

Suggestions for Discussion

1. Discuss reasons for the state to bother erecting such a monument.

2. Analyze the strengths and weaknesses of the society described by the narrator.

3. Discuss Auden's use of irony in the poem. Find specific examples.

Suggestions for Writing

1. Write a sketch describing and evaluating a typical day in the life of the unknown citizen.

2. Provide an alternative inscription for the monument.

❧❧❧

TED KOOSER

Prisoners from the Front

Former life insurance executive Ted Kooser (b. 1939) was appointed Poet Laureate of the United States in 2004. His poetry collections include *Sure Signs* (1980), *One World at a Time* (1985), *Weather Central* (1994), and *Braided Creek: A Conversation in Poetry* (2003), a collaboration with longtime friend Jim Harrison. Kooser has been awarded two National Endowment for the Arts fellowships in poetry and a Pushcart Prize, and his *Local Wonders: Seasons in the Bohemian Alps* (2002) won the Nebraska Book Award for Nonfiction. He has taught English at the University of Nebraska-Lincoln. This poem, based on a Civil War painting by Winslow Homer, comes from the Pulitzer Prize–winning book *Delights and Shadows* (2004).

Three Confederate soldiers awaiting their disposition by a Union general

The youngest captive wears full
butternut regalia, is handsome
with long red hair, his field cap
cocked, one hand on his hip, a man

not ready to be immortalized
under yellowing varnish. An old man
stands next in line, bearded
and wearing a ragged brown coat.
He slumps like the very meaning
of surrender, but his jaw is set
and his eyes are like flashes
from distant cannon (we have waited
a hundred and forty years
to hear those reports). The third
is hot and young and ornery,
wearing a floppy hat, brim up,
his military coat unbuttoned,
hands stuffed in his pockets,
his mouth poised to spit.
It would be he who would ruin
the Union general's moment,
this formal military portrait,
that neat blue uniform, the cavalry
saber and fancy black hat. He would
surely do something to spoil it
if the painter would give him the chance.

Suggestions for Discussion

1. How might the prisoner spoil the Union general's "moment," and how might the painter stop him?

2. Who has been waiting 140 years to hear the cannon's report?

3. Why has Kooser re-created a painting as a poem?

Suggestion for Writing

Find a reproduction of the Winslow Homer painting *Prisoners from the Front* and compare it with Kooser's poem. Does the painting match the expectations you had based on reading the poem? Do you share Kooser's sentiments about the painting, or do you have another set of interpretations?

KATHA POLLITT

Night Subway

Katha Pollitt (b. 1949), a political analyst, literary critic, and poet, is the author of *Antarctic Traveler* (1982), winner of the National Book Critics Circle Award; *Reasonable Creatures: Essays on Women and Feminism* (1994); and *Subject to Debate: Sense and Dissents on Women, Politics, and Culture* (2001). Her column for *The Nation*, "Subject to Debate," has tackled such controversial issues as abortion, welfare, and the literary canon. In "Night Subway," Pollitt combines two seemingly unrelated subjects—a subway scene and a reference from Herodotus' account of the Persian war.

The nurse coming off her shift at the psychiatric ward
nodding over the *Post*, her surprisingly delicate legs
shining darkly through the white hospital stockings,

Subway, New York USA, Robert Huber, 1999. Robert Huber/www.Lookatonline.com

and the Puerto Rican teens, nuzzling, excited
after heavy dates in Times Square, the girl with green hair,
the Hasid from the camera store, who mumbles
over his prayerbook the nameless name of God,
sitting separate, careful no woman should touch him,
even her coat, even by accident,
the boy who squirms on his seat to look out the window
where signal lights wink and flash like the eyes of dragons
while his mother smokes, each short, furious drag
meaning *Mens no good they tell you anything*—

How not think of Xerxes, how he reviewed his troops
and wept to think that of all those thousands of men
in their brilliant armor, their spearpoints bright in the sun,
not one would be alive in a hundred years?

O sleepers above us, river
rejoicing in the moon, and the clouds passing over the moon.

Suggestions for Discussion

1. How does Pollitt make each of the subway riders seem unique? How does
   she create contrasts between them?

2. The second stanza describes Xerxes, king of Persia, reviewing his troops
   prior to the invasion of Greece. Why do you think Pollitt chose to place this
   seemingly unrelated scene alongside her description of the subway?

3. How does the nature imagery in the final stanza relate to the rest of the poem?

Suggestion for Writing

Write a poem or detailed paragraph describing a public place.

DRAMA

~~~

TONY KUSHNER

Homebody/Kabul

Tony Kushner (b. 1956) is the author of the two-part, Pulitzer Prize–winning play *Angels in America* (1992). An affirmed socialist and gay rights activist, Kushner is often critically praised for his ability to make large-scale political conflicts accessible to a contemporary stage audience by having them viewed through the eyes of "everyday" characters. Born in New York City and raised in Louisiana, Kushner earned his bachelor's degree from Columbia University and did postgraduate work at New York University. Other plays by Kushner include *Stella* (1987), *A Bright Room Called Day* (1987), and *Slavs!* (1994).

Kushner's *Homebody/Kabul* (2001) was initially conceived as a monologue for actress Kika Markham but was later expanded into a three-act play. The play, about a British woman in her midforties who makes a fateful trip to Afghanistan, was inspired by a book Kushner came across by accident in the New York University library in 1997—*An Historical Guide to Kabul,* by Nancy Hatch Dupree.

The action of the play takes place in London, England, and Kabul, Afghanistan, just before and just after the American bombardment of suspected terrorist training camps in Khost, Afghanistan, in August 1998. Written prior to the terrorist attacks that took place in New York City and Washington, DC, on September 11, 2001, the play has since been called "eerily prescient" by numerous commentators. A revised, post–9/11 version of the play opened at the Brooklyn Academy of Music in 2005, featuring Linda Emond as the Homebody and Maggie Gyllenhaal as Priscilla. Kushner has said that his "greatest hope for a play is always that it might prove generative of thought, contemplation, discussion—important components of what I think we want from our entertainments."

ACT ONE

SCENE 1

A woman is sitting in a comfortable chair, in a pleasant room in her home in London. A table stands nearby, a lamp on the table. On the floor near her chair, a shopping bag. She is reading from a small book:

THE HOMEBODY: "Our story begins at the very dawn of history, circa 3,000 B.C...."

(Interrupting herself:)

I am reading from an outdated guidebook about the city of Kabul. In Afghanistan. In the valleys of the Hindu Kush mountains. A guidebook to a city which as we all know, has...undergone change.

My reading, my research is moth-like. Impassioned, fluttery, doomed. A subject strikes my fancy: Kabul—you will see why, that's the tale I'm telling—but then, I can't help myself, it's almost perverse, in libraries, in secondhand bookshops, I invariably seek out not The Source but all that which was dropped by the wayside on the way to The Source, outdated guidebooks—this was published in 1965, and it is now 1998, so the book is a vestige superannuated by some...thirty-three years, long enough for Christ to have been born and die on the cross—old magazines, hysterical political treatises written by an advocate of some long-since defeated or abandoned or transmuted cause; and I find these irrelevant and irresistible, ghostly, dreamy, the knowing what *was* known before the more that has since become known overwhelms...As we are, many of us, overwhelmed, and succumbing to luxury...

(She reads from the guidebook:)

"Our story begins at the very dawn of history, circa 3,000 B.C., when the Aryans, not in armies but in family groups, traveled south from beyond the River Oxus, to cross the Hindu Kush mountains on their way to northern India. This crossing must have made a great impression for, nearly two thousand years later, when the Rigveda, the great hymnic epic poem of the Aryan peoples, is written down, several verses retain the memory of the serene beauty of the valleys of the Kabul River."

(She looks up from the guidebook)

Several months ago I was feeling low and decided to throw a party and a party needs festive hats. So I took the tube to _____, *(She gestures)* where there are shops full of merchandise from exotic locales, wonderful things made by people who believe, as I do not, as *we* do not, in magic; or who used to believe in magic, and not so long ago, whose grandparents believed in magic, believed that some combination of piety, joy, ecstasy, industry, brought to bear on the proper raw materials, wood for instance known to be the favored nesting place of a certain animus or anima possessed of powers released, enlisted in beneficent ways towards beneficent ends when carved, adorned, adored just so...Before colonization and the savage stripping away of such beliefs. For magic beliefs are immensely strong, I think, only if their essential fragility is respected. It's a paradox. If such beliefs, magic beliefs, are untouched, they endure. And who knows? Work magic, perhaps. If they are untouched; and that is hard, for such is the expansive nature of these times that every animate and inanimate thing, corporeal or incorporeal, actual or ideational, real or imagined, every, every discrete unit of...of *being*: if a thing can be said to *be*, to *exist*, then such is the nature of these expansive times that this thing which is must suffer to be *touched*. Ours is a time of connection; the private, and we must accept this, and it's a hard thing to accept, the private is *gone*. All must be touched. All touch corrupts. All must be corrupted. And if you're thinking how awful these sentiments are, you are perfectly correct, these are awful times, but you must remember as well that *this* has always been the chiefest characteristic of The Present, to everyone living through it; always, throughout history, and so far as I can see for all the days and years to come until the sun and the stars fall down and the clocks have all ground themselves to expiry and the future has long long shaded away into Time Immemorial: The Present is *always* an awful place to be. And it remains awful to us, the scene of our crime, the place of our shame, for at least Oh, let's say three full decades of recession—by which word, recession, I am to be taken to mean recedence, not recession as in two consecutive quarters of negative growth in gross domestic product. For a three-decades regnum of imperceptible but mercifully implacable recedency we shudder to recall the times through which we have lived, the Recent Past, about which no one wants to think; and then, have you noticed? Even the most notorious decade three or four decades later is illumined from within. Some light inside is switched on. The scenery becomes translucent, beautifully lit; features of the landscape glow; the shadows are full of agreeable color. Cynics will attribute this transformation to senescence and nostalgia; I who am optimistic, have you noticed? attribute this inner illumination to understanding. It is wisdom's hand which switches on the light within. Ah, now I see what that was all about. Ah, now, now I see why we suffered so back then, now I see what we went through. I understand.

(She reads from the guidebook:)

"Nothing is known of the Aryan passage through the valleys of the Hindu Kush, no writing or significant structure remains from the Aryan settlements which undoubtedly existed on the banks of the Kabul River, one of which would eventually grow into the city of Kabul. The first contemporaneous account to mention the city is recorded circa 520 B.C. when Darius the Great, Achaemenid Persian conqueror and builder of Persepolis, annexed twenty-nine countries to the Persian empire, parts of India, all of what we now know as Afghanistan, including the Kabul Valley. In the summer of 329 B.C., Alexander the Macedonian, having trampled the Achaemenid imperium in his victorious march through Persia, makes camp in the Hindu Kush city of Khandahar, and orders the building of the city of Alexandria-ad-Caucasum."

(She looks up from the guidebook)

Oh I love the world! I love love love love the world! Having said so much, may I assume most of you will have dismissed me as a simpleton? I cannot hope to contravene your peremptory low estimation, which may for all its peremptoriness nevertheless be exactly appropriate. I live with the world's mild censure, or would do were it the case that I ever strayed far enough from my modesty, or should I say my essential surfeit of inconsequence, to so far attract the world's attention as to provoke from it its mild censure; but I have never strayed so far from the unlit to the spotlight, and so should say rather that I live with the world's utter indifference, which I have always taken to be a form of censure-in-potentia.

I speak...I can't help myself. Elliptically. Discursively. I've read too many books, and that's not boasting, for I haven't read *many* books, but I've read too many, exceeding I think my capacity for syncresis—is that a word?—straying rather into syncresis, which is a word. So my diction, my syntax, well, it's so *irritating,* I apologize, I do, it's very hard, I know. To listen. I blame it on the books, how else to explain it? My parents don't speak like this; no one I know does; no one does. It's an *alien influence,* and my borders have only ever been broached by books. Sad to say.

Only ever been broached by books. Except once, briefly. Which is I suppose the tale I'm telling, or rather, trying to tell.

You must be patient. There is an old Afghan saying, which, in rough translation from the Farsi, goes: "*The man who has patience has roses.*

The man who has no patience has no trousers." I am not fluent in Farsi, of course, I read this, and as I say it must be a rough translation.

(She reads from the guidebook:)

"Alexander the Great summoned to the Kabul Valley a mighty army comprising tens of thousands of soldiers from Egypt, Persia and Central Asia and went on to conquer India. When Alexander's own troops grew weary of battle, in 325 B.C., they forced their commander to desist from further conquest. Alexander died in 323 B.C., just as he was planning a return to the Hindu Kush to oversee the Grecianization of this most remarkable land."

(She pauses her reading)

My husband cannot bear my…the sound of me and has threatened to leave on this account and so I rarely speak to him anymore. We both take powerful antidepressants. His pills have one name and mine another. I frequently take his pills instead of mine so I can know what he's feeling. I keep mine in a glass bowl next to the bathroom sink, a nice wide-mouthed bowl, very wide, wide open, like an epergne, but so far as I know he never takes my pills but ingests only his own, which are yellow and red, while mine are green and creamy-white; and I find his refusal to sample dull. A little dull.

(She resumes, from the guidebook:)

"By 322 B.C., only a year after Alexander's death, his vast Macedonian empire had disassembled. Herodotus tells us that the hill tribes of the Kabul Valley were among the first and the most ferocious in rejecting Macedonian authority. Seleucus Nicator, Alexander's successor in the east, attempted to regain the Hindu Kush but was daunted when he encountered, in 305 B.C., in the passes of the Hindu Kush, the armed forces of the Maurya Dynasty which had come to rule India. In exchange for the hand of the daughter of the Maurya emperor, Chandragupta, and for five hundred elephants, the Kabul Valley passed for the first time under Indian suzerainty."

(She puts the guidebook down)

A party needs hats. I had no hope that this would be a good party. My parties are never good parties. This party was intended to celebrate my husband's having completed some joyless task at his place of business, which has something to do with the routing of multiple-y expressive electronic tone signals at extraordinary speeds across millions upon millions of kilometers of wire and cable and fiber and space; I understand none of it and indeed it's quite impossible imagining my husband having to do in any real way with processes so…speedy, myriad, nervous, miraculous. But that parti-colored cloud of gas there, in that galaxy there so far away, that cloud there so hot and blistered by clustering stars, exhaling protean scads of infinitely irreducible fiery data in the form of energy pulses and streams of slicing, shearing, unseeable light—does that nebula know it nebulates? Most likely not. So my husband. It knows nothing, its *nature* is to stellate and constellate and nebulate and add its heft and vortices and frequencies to the Universal Drift, un-self-consciously effusing, effusing, gaseously effusing, and so my husband, and so not I, who seem forever to be imploding and collapsing and am incapable it would seem of lending even this simple tale to the Universal Drift, of telling this simple tale without supersaturating my narrative with maddeningly infuriating or more probably irritating synchitic expegeses.

Synchitic expegeses. Jesus.

A party needs hats and in my mind's eye I remembered quite remarkable hats, not as tall as fezzes nor yet as closely cleaving to the curve of the skull as a skullcap, but really rather pillboxy as ladies wore hats in the early '60s; but these mind's-eye hats were made of tough brilliant dyed wools and scraps of elaborate geometrically arabesqued carpet into which sequins and diamantines and carbuncles and glassene beading had been sewn to dazzling, charming premodern effect. I could see these hats perched on top of the heads of the family members and friends who usually appear at my parties, lovely lovely people all of them but when we assemble we rather…affect one another, one might even say *afflict* one another, in baleful ways and tend to dampen one another's festive spirits, there's no…I suppose one would like something combustible at a party, something catalytic, some fizz, each element triggering transformation in all the other elements till all elements, which is to say, *guests,* are…surprising to themselves and return home feeling less…less certain of…those certainties which*Because* of which, for example, powerful antidepressants are consumed.

(She reads from the guidebook:)

"The third century B.C. was a prosperous time for the Kabul Valley, situated midway between the empires of the Seleucids and the Mauryas, profiting thusly from an extensive trade with both which must have included furs from Central Asia and a recent discovery of the Chinese, silk. By the end of the third century the far-flung Mauryan empire had disappeared and a period of disorder, migration and tribal unrest follows, for which the records are clouded and confused."

(She looks up from the guidebook)

My antidepressant is called…something, a made-up word, a portmanteau chemical cocktail word confected by punning psychopharmacologists but I can never remember precisely what to ask for when I…My husband explains to me with bitter impacted patience each time I request it of him the workings of…Ameliorate-za-pozulac, its workings upon my brain; I cannot retain his bitter impacted explanation, but I believe it's all to do with salt somehow. I believe in fact this drug is a kind of talented salt. And so I imagine my brain floating in a salt bath, frosted with a rime of salt, a pickle-brine brain, pink-beige walnut-wrinkled nutmeat within a crystalliform quartzoid ice-white hoarfrost casing, a gemmy shell, gemmiparous: budding. How any of this is meant to counteract depression is more than I can say.

Perhaps it is the sufficient pleasing image which cheers one and makes life's burdens less difficult to bear.

(She reads from the guidebook:)

"In the middle of the second century B.C., during the Greco-Bactrian confusion, a Chinese tribe, the Hsiung-Nu, attacked a rival tribe, the Yueh-Chih, and drove them from their homes to what is now southern Afghanistan. Then the Hsiung-Nu, displaced from their new homes by another Chinese tribe, also migrated to Afghanistan and once again displaced the Yueh-Chih, who emigrated to the Kabul Valley. As the first century B.C. dawns, the Valley, populated by Indo-Greeks, Mauryas and Macedonians, is now surrounded by the restless nomadic kingdoms of the Yueh-Chih.

"By 48 B.C. the Chinese tribes are united under the banner of their largest clan, the Kushans. From the city of Kapisa, the Kushan court came to rival the Caesars in Rome." And I'd never *heard* of the Kushans, have you? Nor for that matter the Greco-Bactrian Confusion! Though it *feels* familiar, does it not, the Greco-Bactrian Confusion? When did it end? The guidebook does not relate. *Did* it end? Are we perhaps still in it? Still *in* the Greco-Bactrian Confusion? Would it surprise you, really, to learn that we are? Don't you feel it would I don't know *explain* certain things? "Ah yes it is hard I know, to *understand* but you see it's the Greco-Bactrian Confusion, which no one ever actually bothered clearing up, and, well here we are."

But let us return to the Kushans:

"From the city of Kapisa, the Kushan court came to rival the Caesars in Rome. Buddhism, Hinduism, Grecian and Persian deities are gathered into the valleys of the Hindu Kush where a remarkable cross-fertilization takes place."

(She puts the guidebook down)

In my mind's eye, yet from memory: I had seen these abbreviated fez-like pillboxy attenuated yarmulkite millinarisms, um, *hats,* I'm sorry I *will* try to stop, *hats,* yes, in a crowded shop on ⎯⎯⎯⎯⎯ *(Gesture)* which I must have passed and mentally noted on my way towards God knows what, who cares, a dusty shop crowded with artifacts, relics, remnants, little…doodahs of a culture once aswarm with spirit matter, radiant with potent magic the disenchanted dull detritus of which has washed up upon our culpable shores, its magic now shriveled into the safe container of *aesthetic,* which is to say, *consumer* appeal. You know, Third World junk. As I remember, as my mind's eye saw, through its salt crust, Afghan junk. That which was once Afghan, which we, having waved our credit cards in its general direction, have made into junk. I remembered the shop, where I thought it was, what its windows were like, sure I'd never find it again and yet there it was in my mind's eye and I traveled to the spot my mind's eye had fixed upon and I was correct! Took the tube, chewed my nails, there was the shop! Precisely as my salt-wounded mind's eye's corneal rotogravured sorry sorry. I found the shop. It was run by Afghan refugees.

And here are the hats. There are ten. They cost three ninety-nine each.

(She displays the hats, removing them one by one from the shopping bag and putting them on the table)

Looking at the hat we imagine not bygone days of magic belief but the suffering behind the craft, this century has taught us to direct our imagination however fleetingly toward the hidden suffering: evil consequence of evil action taken long ago, conjoining with relatively recent wickedness and wickedness perpetuated now, in August 1998, now now now even as I speak and speak and speak…But whether the product of starveling-manned sweatshop or remote not-on-the-grid village, poor yet still resisting the onslaught of modernity, touched, of course, yet not, though it is only a matter of time, isn't it? not corrupted; whether removed from the maker by the middleman to the merchant by filch or swindle or gunpoint or even murder; whether, for that matter, even Afghan in origin; and not Pakistani; or Peruvian; if not in point of fact made in London by children, aunts and elderly uncles in the third-floor flat above the shop on ⎯⎯⎯⎯⎯ *(Gesture)*: the hats are beautiful; relatively inexpensive; sinister if you've a mind to see them that way; and sad. As dislocations are. And marvelous, as dislocations are. Always bloody.

This one is particularly nice.

(She puts a hat on her head, and reads from the guidebook:)

"Severe economic crises throughout the region in the second century A.D. made it easy for the Sassanians, a purely Iranian Persian dynasty, to claim the Hindu Kush Valley as a semi-independent satrapy. The inhabitants of Kabul from the Kushano-Sassanian period appear to have remained Buddhist, while their Sassanian overlords were obstreperous worshipers of Zoroaster." *(She looks up from the book)* "Obstreperous worshipers of Zoroaster"! For that phrase alone I deem this book a worthy addition to my pickpenny library of remaindered antilegomenoi. *(Back to the book)* "Sassanian hegemony—" *(Up from the book)* Antilegomenoi are volumes of castoff or forgotten knowledge, in case you were wondering. *(Back to the book)* "Sassanian hegemony was toppled by the Hephthalites, or white Huns, who commenced a reign of legendary destructiveness around 400 A.D., savagely persecuting the indigenous worship of Buddha—Buddhism having found many adherents among Hindu Kush peoples as its monks carried news of the Buddha from India through Afghanistan to China. Apart from their fabled viciousness, almost nothing is known about the Hephthalites."

(She looks up from the guidebook)

Nothing when this book was written, and it is rather old. Perhaps more is known now though archaeology in the area has been interrupted. Very little digging, except recently, did you read this, the bodies of two thousand Taliban soldiers were found in a mass grave in northern Afghanistan, prisoners who were executed, apparently by soldiers loyal to the overthrown government of Burhanuddin Rabbani. So someone is digging, and perhaps more now is known about the Hephthalites.

(She reads from the guidebook:)

"Hephthalite rule ended in 531 A.D. after which a state of anarchy prevailed over the entire region, each town protected by an independent chieftain, and the remaining Hephthalite princes"—who, you will remember, made their appearance just one paragraph previous, razing Buddhist temples—"the remaining Hephthalite princes having by this time *converted to Buddhism.*"

And made a great vulgar noise about it, I shouldn't wonder. I find myself disliking intensely the Hepthalites.

"Meanwhile, in 642, the banner of Islam"—Islam at last!—"carried forth from the deserts of Arabia, halted its eastern progress when its armies tried to penetrate the heart of what is now Afghanistan; for every hill and town was defended by fierce tribal warriors. Several hundred years were to pass before Kabul would fully surrender to Islam."

(Turning pages, summarizing:)

This brings us to the end of the millennium, 1023. Kabul over the next three or four hundred years will be conquered by first this empire builder and then that one. Genghis Khan swam through the area on a river of blood. The Great Tamurlaine, a Timurid, wounded his foot during a battle near Kabul, says the guidebook, and whatever it was he was named before (the book is not helpful on this) he was henceforth and forevermore known as Timur-I-Lang, Timur Who Limps. Timur-I-Lang, Tamurlaine. Kabul re-baptised him.

(She puts the guidebook down)

And this is what happened, and it's all there is to my little tale, really: the hats were in a barrel which could be seen through the window; puppets hung from the ceiling, carved freestanding figurines, demiurges, attributes, symbols, carven abstractions representing metaphysical principles critical to the governance of perfect cosmologies now lost to all or almost all human memory; amber beads big as your baby's fists, armor plates like pangolin scales strung on thick ropey catgut cordage meant to be worn by rather large rather ferocious men, one would imagine, or who knows; hideous masks with great tusks and lolling tongues and more eyes than are usual, mind's eyes I suppose and revolving wire racks filled with postcards depicting the severed heads of The Queen and Tony Blair, well not *severed* necessarily but with no body appended; Glaswegian *A to Zed Guides* and newspapers in Arabic, in Urdu, in Pushtu, video-cassettes of rock balladeers from Benares: well why go on and on, sorry I'm sorry, we've all been in these sorts of shops, no bigger than from here to there, haven't we? As if a many-cameled caravan, having roamed across the entire postcolonial not-yet-developed world, crossing the borders of the rainforested kingdoms of Kwashiorkor and Rickets and Untreated Gum Disease and High Infant Mortality Rates, gathering with desperate indiscriminateness—is that the word?—on the mudpitted unpaved trade route its bits and boodle, had finally beached its great heavy no longer portable self in a narrow coal-scuttle of a shop on _____ *(Gesture),* here, here, caravanseraied here, in the developed and overdeveloped and over-overdeveloped paved wasted now deliquescent post–First World postmodern city of London; all the camels having flopped and toppled and fallen here and died of exhaustion, of shock, of the heartache of refugees, the goods simply piled high upon their dromedary bones, just where they came to rest, and set up shop atop the carcasses, and so on.

I select ten hats, thread my way through the musty heaps of swag and thrownaway and offcast and godforsaken sorry sorry through the merchandise to the counter where a man, an Afghan man, my age I think, perhaps a bit older, stands smiling eager to ring up my purchases and make an imprint of my credit card, and as I hand the card to him I see that three fingers on his right hand have been hacked off, following the line of a perfect clean diagonal from middle to ring to little finger, which, the last of the three fingers in the diagonal cut's descent, by, um, hatchet blade? was hewn off almost completely—like this, you see?

(She demonstrates)

But a clean line, you see, not an accident, a measured surgical cut, but not surgery as we know it for what possible medicinal purpose might be served? I tried, as one does, not to register shock, or morbid fascination, as one does my eyes unfocused my senses fled startled to the roof of my skull and then off into the ether like a rapid vapor indifferent to the obstacle of my cranium WHOOSH, clean slate, tabula rasa, terra incognita, where am I yet still my mind's eye somehow continuing to record and detail that poor ruined hand slipping my MasterCard into the…you know, that thing, that roller press thing which is used to…Never mind. Here, in London, that poor ruined hand.

Imagine.

I know nothing of this hand, its history, of course, nothing. I did know, well I have learnt since through research that Kabul, which is the ancient capital of Afghanistan, and where once the summer pavilion of Amir Abdur Rahman stood shaded beneath two splendid old chinar trees, beloved of the Moghuls, Kabul, substantial portions of which are now great heaps of rubble, was it was claimed by the Moghul Emperor Babur founded by none other than Cain himself. Biblical Cain. Who is said to be buried in Kabul, in the gardens south of Bala-Hissar in the cemetery known as Shohada-I-Salehin.

I should like to see that. The Grave of Cain. Murder's Grave. Would you eat a potato plucked from *that* soil?

(She reads from the guidebook:)

"The mighty Moghul emperors, who came to rule the Hindu Kush and all of India, adored Kabul and magnified and exalted it. By the eighteenth century the Moghuls, ruling from Delhi and Agra, succumbed to luxury"—that's what it says, they succumbed to luxury. "Modern Afghanistan is born when, in 1747, heretofore warring Afghan tribal chiefs forge for themselves a state, proclaiming Ahmed Shah Durrani, age twenty-five, King of the Afghans."

(She looks up from the guidebook)

And so the Great Game begins. The Russians seize Khazakstan, the British seize India, Persia caves in to the Russians, the first Anglo-Afghan war is fought, the bazaar in Kabul is burnt and many many people die, Russia seizes Bokhara, the second Anglo-Afghan war, the First World War, the October Revolution, the third Anglo-Afghan war, also known as the Afghanistan War of Independence, Afghanistan sovereignty first recognized by the Soviet Union in 1921, followed by aid received from the Soviet Union, followed by much of the rest of the twentieth century, Afghanistan is armed by the U.S.S.R. against the Pakistanis, the U.S. refuses assistance, militant Islamic movements form the seed of what will become the Mujahideen, the U.S. begins sending money, much civil strife, approaching at times a state of civil war, over liberal reforms such as the unveiling of and equal rights for women, democratic elections held, martial law imposed, the Soviet Union invades, the Mujahideen are armed, at first insufficiently, then rather handsomely by the U.S., staggering amounts of firepower, some captured from the Soviets, some purchased, some given by the West, missiles and anti-aircraft cannon and etc. etc., the Soviets for ten years do their best to outdo the Hephthalites in savagery, in barbarism, then like so many other empires traversing the Hindu Kush the U.S.S.R. is swept away, and now the Taliban, and…Well.

(She closes the guidebook and puts it down)

Afghanistan is one of the poorest countries in the world. With one of the world's most decimated infrastructures. No tourism. Who in the world would wish to travel there? In Afghanistan today I would be shrouded entirely in a *burqa,* I should be subject to *hejab, I* should live in terror of the *sharia hudud,* or more probably dead, unregenerate chatterer that I am. While I am signing the credit card receipt I realize all of a sudden I am able to speak perfect Pushtu, and I ask the man, who I now notice is very beautiful, not on account of regularity of features or smoothness of the skin, no, his skin is broken by webs of lines inscribed by hardships, siroccos and strife, battle scars, perhaps, well certainly the marks of some battle, some life unimaginably more difficult than my own; I ask him to tell me what had happened to his hand. And he says: I was with the Mujahideen, and the Russians did this. I was with the Mujahideen, and an enemy faction of Mujahideen did this. I was with the Russians, I was known to have assisted the Russians, I did informer's work for Babrak Karmal, my name is in the files if they haven't been destroyed, the names I gave are in the files, there are no more files, I stole bread for my starving family, I stole bread *from* a starving family, I profaned, betrayed, according to some stricture I erred and they chopped off the fingers of my hand. *Look, look at my country, look at my Kabul, my city, what is left of my city? The streets are as bare as the mountains now, the buildings are as ragged as mountains and as bare and empty of life, there is no life here only fear, we do not live in the buildings now, we live in terror in the cellars in the caves in the mountains, only God can save us now, only order can save us now, only God's Law harsh and strictly administered can save us now, only The Department for the Promotion of Virtue and the Prevention of Vice can save us now, only terror can save us from ruin, only neverending war, save us from terror and neverending war, save my wife they are stoning my wife, they are chasing her with sticks, save my wife save my daughter from punishment by God, save us from God, from war, from exile, from oil exploration, from no oil exploration, from the West, from the children with rifles, carrying stones, only children with rifles, carrying stones, can save us now.* You will never understand. It is hard, it was hard work to get into the U.K. I am happy here in the U.K. I am terrified I will be made to leave the U.K. I cannot wait to leave the U.K. I despise the U.K. I voted for John Major. I voted for Tony Blair. I did not, I cannot vote, I do not believe in voting, the people who ruined my hand were right to do so, they were wrong to do so, my hand is most certainly ruined, *you will never understand,* why are you buying so many hats?

(Little pause)

We all romp about, grieving, wondering, but with rare exception we mostly remain suspended in the Rhetorical Colloidal Forever that agglutinates between Might and Do. "Might do, might do." I have a friend who says that. "Off to the cinema, care to come?" "Might do." "Would you eat a potato plucked from that soil?" "Might do." Jesus wants you hot or cold but she will hedge her every bet, and why should she not? What has this century taught the civilized if not contempt for those who merely contemplate; the lockup and the lethal injection for those who Do. Awful times, as I have said, our individual degrees of culpability for said awfulness being entirely bound-up in our correspondent degrees of action, malevolent or not, or in our correspondent degrees of inertia, which can be taken as a form of malevolent action if you've a mind to see it that way. I do. I've such a mind. My husband…Never mind. We shall most of us be adjudged guilty when we are summoned before the Judgment Seat. But guilt? Personal guilt? *(Wringing hands)* Oh, oh…No more morally useful or impressive than adult nappy rash, and nearly as unsightly, and ought to be kept as private, ought guilt, as any other useless unimpressive unsightly inflammation. Not suitable for public exchange. And all conversation such as we are having, and though you've said nothing whatsoever we are still conversing, I think, since what I say is driven by fear of you, sitting there before me, by absolute terror of your censure and disdain, and so you need say nothing, you would only weaken your position, whatever it may be, whatever you may be making of this, by speaking, I mean, look at me, look at what I am doing, to myself, to what you must think of me, if ever you chance upon me on _____ *(Gesture)*, out shopping, what will you think? Avoid! Her! All conversation constitutes public exchange was my point, and there are rules of engagement, and skin rash should be displayed in public only for medicinal restorative purposes, inviting the healing rays of the sun and the drying authority of the fresh crisp breeze, and not for the garnering of admiration and the harvesting of sympathy. For most of us deserve neither, and I include myself in that harsh judgment, no matter how guilty we are or feel ourselves to be, my optimism notwithstanding.

I watch as he puts the ten hats in a carrier-bag and feel no surprise when he informs someone in the back of the shop, in Pushto, in which language as I mentioned I now find myself fluent, he's taking the rest of the afternoon off, and he offers me his right hand. I take it and we go out of the shop but no longer on _____ *(Gesture)*, we are standing on a road, a road in Kabul. I hold on tight to his ruined right hand, and he leads me on a guided tour through his city. There are the mountains, unreal as clouds; it is shamelessly sweet, the wreckage rack and ruination all there of course, it's ineffaceable now, this holocaustal effacement, but the gardens of Babur Shah are there too, just like the outdated guidebook promises, and the room in which handsome Shah Shujah, about thirty years of age, of olive complexion and thick black beard, puppet monarch of the British Mission, detested and soon to be murdered by his own insurgent people, displays himself to breathtaking effect, his visitors imagining him at first to be dressed in an armor of jewels, how impractical *that* would be, but actually he wears a green tunic over which are worked flowers of gold and a breast plate of diamonds, shaped like flattened fleurs-de-lis, ornaments of the same kind on each thigh, emeralds above the elbows, diamonds on each wrist, strings of pearls like cross belts but loose, a crown not encrusted with jewels but apparently entirely formed of those precious materials, the whole so complicated and dazzling it is difficult to understand and impossible to describe, and the throne is covered with a cloth adorned with pearls…

(She cries softly)

And the scent of the hat merchant takes me by surprise, toasted almonds, and he smiles a broader shy smile which shatters his face into a thousand shards and near a place called Bemaru, thought to be the grave of Bibi Mahru, the Moon-Faced Lady, who died of grief when her betrothed was reported slain on the battlefield, but he wasn't slain, he'd only lost his hand, near her grave, visited by mothers with ailing children, even today, *especially today* when there are many many such cases, many ailing children—demurely hidden from the sight of the ailing and the destitute and war ravaged we, the hat merchant and I, make love beneath a chinar tree, which is it is my guess a kind of plane tree, beloved of the Moghuls. We kiss, his breath is very bitter, he places his hand inside me, it seems to me his whole hand inside me, and it seems to me a whole hand. And there are flocks of pigeons the nearby villagers keep banded with bronze rings about their legs, and they are released each afternoon for flight, and there is frequently, in the warmer months, kite flying to be seen on the heights of Bemaru.

(Pause)

I sign the receipt, I have paid, he hands me the carrier-bag stuffed with my purchase and with his smile indicates we are done and I should depart. And a chill wind blows up my bones and I long to be back in the safety of my kitchen and I leave the shop pondering the possibility that my prescribed dosage of…Mealy-aza-opzamene is too strong, or that sampling my husband's pills…perhaps these two chemicals are immiscible.

And yes in fact I do have children, well, *one*. A child. For whom alas nothing ever seems to go well. The older she gets. My fault entirely I'm sure or at least so I am told by my husband the near-mute purveyor of reproachful lids-lowered glances. But this is neither here nor there. We all loved one another, once, but today it simply isn't so or isn't what it used to be, it's…well, love.

I love the world. I know how that sounds, inexcusable and vague, but it's all I can say for myself, I love the world, really I do…*Love*. Not the vast and unembraceable and orbicular world, this is no gigantine rhapsodic—for all that one might suspect a person who uses words like gigantine—God!—of narcissism, my love is not that overstretched self-aggrandizing hyperinflated sort of adulation which seeks in the outsized and the impossible-to-clearly-comprehend a reflection commensurate with its own oceanic…of, well, I suppose of the extent to which the soul excuse me I mean the self is always an insoluble mystery to the narcissist who flatters herself that feeling of vagueness always hanging about her which not a salt in the world can cure is something grand, oceanic, titanically erotic while of course what it really is is nothing more than an inadequately shaped unsteady incoherent…quaggy sort of bubble where the solid core ought to be.

I love…this guidebook. Its foxed unfingered pages, forgotten words: "Quizilbash." Its sorrowing supercessional displacement by all that has since occurred. So lost; and also so familiar. The home *(She makes the gesture)* away from home. *Recognizable:* not how vast but how *crowded* the world is, consequences to *everything:* the Macedonians, marching east; one tribe displacing another; or one moment in which the heart strays from itself and love is…gone?

What after all is a child but the history of all that has befallen her, a succession of displacements, bloody, beautiful? How could any mother not love the world? What else is love but recognition? Love's nothing to do with happiness. Power has to do with happiness. Love has only to do with home.

(Little pause)

Where stands the homebody, safe in her kitchen, on her culpable shore, suffering uselessly watching others perishing in the sea, wringing her plump little maternal hands, oh, oh. Never *joining* the drowning. Her feet, neither rooted nor moving. The ocean is deep and cold and erasing. But how dreadful, really unpardonable, to remain dry.

Look at her, look at her, she is so unforgivably dry. Neither here nor there. She does not drown, she…succumbs. To Luxury. She sinks. Terror-struck, down, down into…um, the dangerous silent spaces, or rather places, with gravity and ground, down into the terrible silent gardens of the private, in the frightening echoing silence of which a grieving voice might be heard, chattering away, keening, rocking, shrouded, trying to express that which she lacks all power to express but which she knows must be expressed or else…death. And she would sound I suppose rather like what I sound like now:

(Whispers:)

Avoid! Her!

And now my daughter. Come home as one does. She must have and may not budge, and I understand, I am her mother, she is…starving. I…withhold my touch.

The touch which does not understand is the touch which corrupts, the touch which does not understand that which it touches is the touch which corrupts that which it touches, and which corrupts itself.

And so yes, when unexpectedly a curtain I'd not noticed before is parted by a ruined hand, which then beckons, I find myself improbably considering…

(Pause)

The hats at the party are a brilliant success. My guests adore them. They are hard to keep on the head, made for smaller people than the people we are and so they slip off, which generates amusement, and the guests exchange them while dancing, kaleidoscopic and self-effacing and I think perhaps to our surprise in some small way meltingly intimate, someone else's hat atop your head, making your scalp stiffen at the imagined strangeness; and to a select group in the kitchen I tell about the merchant who sold them to me, and a friend wisely asks, how do you even know he's Afghan, and of course that's a good question, and the fact is I don't. And I wonder for an instant that I didn't ask. "Would you make love to a stranger with a mutilated hand if the opportunity was offered you?" "Might do," she says. Frank Sinatra is playing: such an awful awful man, such perfect perfect music! A paradox!

(Frank Sinatra starts to sing "It's Nice to Go Trav'ling." She sings the first two verses with him, putting the hats back in the shopping bag, one by one:)

It's very nice to go trav'ling
To Paris, London and Rome
It's oh so nice to go trav'ling,
But it's so much nicer yes it's so much nicer
To come home.
It's very nice to just wander
The camel route to Iraq,
It's oh so nice to just wander
But it's so much nicer yes it's oh so nice
To wander back...

(The music fades. The Homebody stands, takes the coat draped over the back of the empty chair, and puts it on. Buttoning the coat, she says:)

In the seventeenth century the Persian poet Sa'ib-I-Tabrizi was summoned to the court of the Moghul emperors in Agra, and on his way he passed, as one does, Kabul, the city in the Hindu Kush, and he wrote a poem, for he had been touched by its strangeness and beauty, moved only as one may be moved through an encounter with the beautiful and strange; and he declared he would never be the same again:

(She picks up the guidebook, but does not open it)

Oh the beautiful city of Kabul wears a rugged mountain skirt,
And the rose is jealous of its lash-like thorns.
The dust of Kabul's blowing soil smarts lightly in my eyes,
But I love her, for knowledge and love both come from her dust.

I sing bright praises to her colorful tulips,
The beauty of her trees makes me blush.
Every street in Kabul fascinates the eye.
In the bazaars, Egypt's caravans pass by.
No one can count the beauteous moons on her rooftops,
And hundreds of lovely suns hide behind her walls.
Her morning laugh is as gay as flowers,
Her dark nights shine like beautiful hair.
Her tuneful nightingales sing with flame in their throats,
Their fiery songs fall like burning leaves.
I sing to the gardens of Kabul;
Even Paradise is jealous of their greenery.

SCENE 2

A hotel room in Kabul, luxurious by Kabuli standards. Two single beds. MILTON CEILING *is seated on one bed,* MULLAH AFTAR ALI DURRANNI *is seated on the other.* DOCTOR QARI SHAH *is standing beside and slightly behind the* MULLAH; QUANGO TWISTLETON *is standing behind* MILTON.

PRISCILLA CEILING is seated in a chair behind a bedsheet which has been hung across one corner of the room. There's a lamp on a small table behind her; her shadow is cast on the bedsheet.
A burqa is draped over the arm of a chair.
It's early morning. The mood in the room is very grim.
DOCTOR QARI SHAH *is speaking, occasionally consulting a notebook.*

DOCTOR QARI SHAH: The conoid tubercle of the left clavicle was found to have been traumatically separated from the conacoid process of the left scapula following severe damage to the conoid ligament, and also the infra spinous fossa quite, ah, shattered by a heavy blow, most probably as the woman was dragged—your wife—by her upper limb, arm that is to say, up and down rubble-strewn streets over piles of bomb debris. After dislocation of the humerus from the glenohumeral joint, there was separation and consequent calamitous exsanguination from the humeral stump. The flexor digitori sublimus and profundus of the middle three phalanges are absent and indicate…trauma also, perhaps occurring as the wife attempts self-defense. *(He holds his left hand in front of his face as if warding off a blow)* The, ah, right gynglymus and enarthrodial joints are found to have been twisted to nonanatomical ninety-degree positions and the arm…separated by dull force. The right side of the os innominatum is also crushed. Her left leg, the tibia separated by dull force from the femur, snapping cleanly below the lesser trochanter, it may be surmised from the severity of the dermal abrading and bruisings having been caught between two large bits of concrete jetsam and ah, pinched clean off. She is being beaten repeatedly with wooden planks and stakes and rusted iron rebar rods, remember. From the surmisable positions of the assailants and so forth, we believe there were ten persons implicit, approximately so.

My English. I have study medicine in Edinburgh, but long ago. I apologize.

(He pauses. No one moves or says anything. He resumes:)

The axillary fascia of the right, ah, hemispherical eminence, um, mamma, um, *breast,* torn from the axilla, from the sternum, torn off in fact, either by force of a blow or as the corpus is dragged. Her left eye having been enucleated, the left orbit vacant, and canines, molars, incisors absent both her superior and inferior maxillaries, and from dull force many of the skull's two and twenty bones are found to have been compromised, the occiput sheared cleanly off. And consequently to which, spillage of, ah, contents.

It may be ventured there seems to have been no forcible invasion of the introitus. She was not dishonored. Your wife.

(Silence.)

MULLAH AFTAR ALI DURRANI: She have been torn up. The lady, she, ah…Torn *apart*. She have been torn apart to pieces.

MILTON: *(Very softly)* Oh my God.

QUANGO: Bloody, bloody hell.

MULLAH AFTAR ALI DURRANI: She have wandered through Cheshme Khedre, where undetonated land mines are. She wander alone by the…Way ran nee-hah? *(To* DOCTOR QARI SHAH*)* How it's said?

DOCTOR QARI SHAH: Ruins.

MULLAH AFTAR ALI DURRANI: Yes, *ruins* by Cheshme Khedre, where nobody live there any longer, why she was there? In these bad times, why this lady your wife come to Kabul? She have been informed upon to have not clad in decent attire for street, not wearing burqa, uncovered. Attack such as this, have never happen before in Kabul, never in Afghanistan.

Since President Clinton have bombed the people in Khost, many killed, the people are very angry against Western aggression-disregard-disrespect for Afghanistan. And also she have been carrying openly this thing:

(From a paper sack he removes a yellow discman, headphones attached, and he hands it to MILTON. MILTON *opens the lid of the discman, looks at the CD inside, closes it.)*

MULLAH AFTAR ALI DURRANI: Impious music which is an affront to Islam, to dress like so and then the music, these are regrettable.

PRISCILLA: *(From behind the bedsheet)* What is it? May I see?

*(*MILTON *steps behind the bedsheet and hands the discman to* PRISCILLA. *She holds it, then puts on the headphones and pushes the play button. All this is in lamplit silhouette against the bedsheet.*
     MILTON *returns, sits on the bed.*
     From behind the bedsheet, PRISCILLA *listens to the music and cries softly.*
     The men listen to her cry.)

MILTON: It's, ah, Frank Sinatra. "Come Fly with Me."

MULLAH AFTAR ALI DURRANI: We search for the criminals who have done this thing, and when they are seized they shall be put to death. Rough boys, criminals, and also perhaps they believe incorrectly she is American.

QUANGO: They've come to claim her body, Minister Durranni.

MULLAH AFTAR ALI DURRANI: This we cannot know. Where it is.

(Little pause.)

QUANGO: You lost her body?

MULLAH AFTAR ALI DURRANI: In Cheshme Khedre where these rough boys kill her there is nearby the UNESCO hospital but this is closed. So she is taken to the Ladies Hospital though already she is dead. Here Doctor Qari Shah inspected her remains. For some cause, she is then transported to Ibn Sena—you say "Avicenna"—Hospital on Sipah Salar Muhhamad Nadir Kahn Wat. In Ladies Hospital there are almost no suture, antibiotics, medicines of this sort; but as she is dead, this lady, that ought not to have been considered. Also as well at Abdullah Ibn Sena there is no medicine, anywhere, anywhere in Afghanistan. But this morning hearing you have arrived from Peshawar, coming to call for the dead lady at Ibn Sena, she is found not to be there. Information regrettably is scarce. We are searching now for where she is. You shall stay here. Or return home.

QUANGO: May I ask. With respect. *(In Dari)* Baw tamawmay eht'rawm. Chirah bahroyaheen haw zaroozee-bood kehgosh baydehand… um…*(With respect. Why…was it necessary for these people to listen to this…)* impenetrable litany of medical horrors? To frighten them?

(Ignoring this, the MULLAH *stands. He turns to* MILTON.*)*

MULLAH AFTAR ALI DURRANI: To you and your daughter, every Afghan heart laments for the mother. Death we know. Kabul is not a city for Western tourist women, we do not want them. In sha' Allah. No thing may be made or unmade unless Allah wills it. He fills our hearts with griefs, to see if we shall be strong. You are kaafer, you do not understand, but this is Allah's way.

(Little pause)

MILTON: Yes, yes…I see. Thank you.

DOCTOR QARI SHAH: I have studied medicine in Edinburgh. I apologize if my English is…impenetrable. *(To* MILTON*)* I am truly sorry.

MILTON: No, it's…quite good.

MULLAH AFTAR ALI DURRANI: These also were hers.

(He reaches in the sack and removes three hats, rough wool berets, not like the ones in Scene 1, and a book.)

MULLAH AFTAR ALI DURRANI: Several fine pacooli. Perhaps gifts for you, her husband.

(The MULLAH *hands the book to* DOCTOR QARI SHAH, *who reads the cover:)*

DOCTOR QARI SHAH: *An Historical Guide to the City of Kabul.*

MULLAH AFTAR ALI DURRANI: But in Kabul now there is no history. There is only God. This is no more a city for…*(To* DOCTOR QARI SHAH*)* Kattel ow tama sha kawol?

DOCTOR QARI SHAH: Sightseeing.

MULLAH AFTAR ALI DURRANI: Precisely. No.

*(*MULLAH DURRANNI *stands, nods to* MILTON, *who nods back, vaguely; the* MULLAH *leaves the room, followed by* DOCTOR QARI SHAH. QUANGO *lingers.*

*   *PRISCILLA *pulls the bedsheet down and stays seated, holding the sheet in one hand, the discman in the other.* MILTON *looks at* QUANGO, *speechless.)*

QUANGO: You'll want to be left alone now.

PRISCILLA: *(Holding out the discman)* You'd think a thing like this would be of some value, wouldn't you, on the black market? They'd have nicked it, her assailants, it's what I'd have done if I'd no money.

QUANGO: Music, it's contra Islam, as the Taliban read it. They read it unlike anyone else in the—

PRISCILLA: Yes, and these were very *pious* boys who beat her to death, do you think? All those rusted iron rebar rods, flailing away, and it hasn't a scratch.

MILTON: Japanese plastics, durable stuff.

She's killed herself.

QUANGO: Oh. No, I...Shouldn't think so.

(MILTON *begins to sob.*)

QUANGO: *(To* PRISCILLA*)* I should like to help. I shall make inquiries about...The body. And I'll...call again, if I might, or...

(PRISCILLA *nods, lights a cigarette.*
   QUANGO *leaves.*)

PRISCILLA: He works for the government? Doesn't seem...governmental, what was his name?

MILTON: Twistleton? Bingo? Pongo? Pongo Twistleton? Can that be? In some semi-official capacity, apparently. There's no embassy, so...

PRISCILLA: Do you think she screamed?

I don't know what she'd sound like if she did.

(*They both cry.*)

MILTON: She loved you. She did, Priss, she did. We both did. We'll go home. We'll miss her, dreadfully, but you're young and I'm not so old and there is the fact of resilience. I shall try to be for you what she was.

(*Little pause*)

PRISCILLA: Yet in this newborn lachrymosity of yours there's nothing I know of the maternal, which never manifest itself in mummy in fluid epiphora but rather in fluency, in that sempiternal dyscrasic fluxion of logorrheic blatherskite beneath the weight of which so much was...crushed.

MILTON: *(Amused, unnerved)* Hah. That's...very like her. Sempiternal. Didn't know you could do...that.

(*Little pause.* MILTON *points to the discman:*)

MILTON: It's all ultimately explained by high-impact polystyrenes.

PRISCILLA: *(Tenderly)* You've no mystery in your soul, Dad.

MILTON: None. I left that to your mother.

PRISCILLA: What are you going to do now?

MILTON: See it all more clearly, I suppose.

(*He starts to cry again.*)

PRISCILLA: You're safe in the hotel room, surely.

MILTON: I didn't say I felt unsafe.

Christ I'd kill for a drink.

PRISCILLA: Alcohol is illegal here. And Pongo Twistleton is a character in a P. G. Wodehouse novel.

I've never seen you cry before.

MILTON: Yes, well, this is what it looks like.

(*He takes off one shoe, then cradles it, still crying*) I told you we should never have come! People remain at home when tragedies happen and the government arranges things like shipping bodies.

PRISCILLA: The government couldn't even tell us if she was alive.

We still don't *know*.

MILTON: Don't know…?

What?

PRISCILLA: We don't know she's dead.

(*Little pause.* MILTON *collects himself.*)

MILTON: You're a bright young woman, Priss. You'll rally yourself. We shall respond to this tragedy by growing, growing close…

PRISCILLA: (*Overlapping*) I'm no spaewife, I've no recourse to the extispiscene but I doubt somehow that your confidence in a father-daughter entelechy—

MILTON: Please stop that.

PRISCILLA: Entelechy. It means growth. But people don't grow close from tragedy. They wither is all, Dad, that's all.

MILTON: How did you get so grim? You never used to be so grim, as a little girl you were—

PRISCILLA: It seemed ludicrous to me, all that. "Os innominatum"? What's that, the, the…*nameless bone*? What the fuck is *that*? And where's her body then? Something's wrong.

MILTON: What are you—

PRISCILLA: Maybe she's kidnapped. Maybe she's hurt, in a hospital, and they're hiding her for some reason. Maybe she's hiding. From us.

MILTON: Oh that's…SHE IS DEAD! *Reuters* has reported it!

PRISCILLA: I'm going out for a bit.

MILTON: Out?

PRISCILLA: Yes.

MILTON: *Out…SIDE?!* You're joking.

PRISCILLA: I'll…lose it utterly. I'm going to find her. There are hospitals on this map.

(She picks up the discman, and the guidebook, and starts for the door.)

MILTON: It's *extremely dangerous* out there. Am I to take two bodies home?

PRISCILLA: Better than none.

MILTON: And think, Priscilla, what she must, um, *look* like. You can't want to see that.

PRISCILLA: I don't know. I might.

(She sees the burqa. She picks it up, examining it.)

MILTON: Oh so *here, here* you're choosing to become adventurous? Are you completely *insane*?

I was being rhetorical. Please don't go.

(She puts the burqa over her head.)

PRISCILLA: *(Looking around, through the face-grille:)* It's as if I've contracted an exotic ophthalmological condition. A chiasmata.

Or strabismus.

(She removes the burqa)

I mean, Milton, for fucksake, she's my mother, she…

Oh God.

(Little pause. Suddenly she screams:)

MUMMY!

(He tries to comfort her. She shakes him off.)

PRISCILLA: Sit here, with you, crying, just waiting, for for nothing, no, can't do that. You stay here, make calls, call the British Aid man.

MILTON: The bloody telephone probably doesn't work.

PRISCILLA: Of course it—

MILTON: Nothing works here! This is not London! Where's her body? *They ate it,* for all we know, this place is that bad it is! And *you may not go out into the—*

PRISCILLA: She isn't dead! I know when I'm being lied to. Prevarication/ evasion expert, me. I have been trained.

You ought never to have had kids you two, you really and truly deserved me.

I'll find her. And if they have ripped her open at least I'll finally get to see her fucking secrets.

(She puts on the burqa again and exits. MILTON *picks up the phone.)*

MILTON: It works, it...

(He jiggles the receiver)

Dead.

(Calling after PRISCILLA*:)*

DEAD! DEAD! DEAD!

Suggestions for Discussion

1. Why do you think Kushner wrote the first scene as one long monologue for the Homebody? How would the play have been different had we actually seen the Homebody interact with her husband and daughter instead of hearing her account of her familial relationships?

2. How does the play contrast the small-scale details of domestic life, such as the "hat" party, with large-scale political conflicts and the grand sweep of history?

3. How do the characters reveal themselves in their use of language and vocabulary?

4. What attitude does the Homebody seem to have toward modern technology and medicine?

5. Is the Homebody talking about Priscilla, Kabul, or something else altogether when she says, "What after all is a child but the history of all that has befallen her, a succession of displacements, bloody, beautiful"?

6. What kind of transformation does Priscilla undergo at the end of Scene Two?

7. The transition between Scene One and Scene Two is arguably jarring on a number of levels. How has Kushner's storytelling style changed? What do we know about what has happened between the two acts? What do we not know?

8. This play was written before the September 11 attacks on the United States. Do you feel that you would have had a different reaction to this play had you read it or seen it performed before September 11 than the reaction you have had to it now?

Suggestions for Writing

1. How does this play examine the violent culture clashes between Western civilization and the Islamic world? What is the nature of this struggle? Does Kushner offer any kind of hope for a resolution to the conflict?

2. Have you ever been confronted with a mystery that you were never able to solve? If so, relate the incident in an essay and explain how it affected you and your outlook on life.

3. Develop or challenge Priscilla's belief that people "don't grow close from tragedy. They wither is all...."

〜〜〜〜

RIC OQUITA

The History of Latin America

Ric Oquita (b. 1961) is a playwright, actor, and teaching artist currently developing plays with students in New York City public schools. His theater collaborations include *goldenfear* (2002), *Descanso* (2003), and *Ecos del Nuevo Mundo* (2005), the source of the following selection. In this two-person play, Oquita explores the volatile history of Latin America and the Caribbean through the eyes of two young sisters of Haitian/Chilean descent who are propelled through time by the magic from their grandmother's trunk.

PLACE: A plaza in Santiago, Chile
TIME: July 24, 1783

(Two Troubadours. LA SEÑORA TROVADORA and EL COMPAÑERO PREGONERO, vie for the audience's attention and for a prime performing spot on the plaza.)

Bateristas do Lampiao, Andreas Rühlow, 1997. ©Andreas Rühlow / www.foto-lounge.de.

EL COMPAÑERO PREGONERO   *Vete al carajo!*

LA SEÑORA TROVADORA   *Rete!*

EL COMPAÑERO PREGONERO   *Nunca!*

LA SEÑORA TROVADORA   *Basta!* (Pause) This is a public plaza and I have work to do.

EL COMPAÑERO PREGONERO   So do I. Your wig is crooked.

LA SEÑORA TROVADORA   *Desgraciado!* (LA SEÑORA TROVADORA glares at her brother and then turns to the audience.) *Bienvenidos.*

EL COMPAÑERO PREGONERO   *Bem-vindo.*

LA SEÑORA TROVADORA   ...which means...

EL COMPAÑERO PREGONERO   *Bon Bini, Byenvini, Purintaxa, Xicalaquican,...*

LA SEÑORA TROVADORA   *Welcome* to The History of Latin America.

EL COMPAÑERO PREGONERO   (overlap) The *Real* History of Latin America...

LA SEÑORA TROVADORA   (overlap) The *Revisionist's* History of Latin America…

EL COMPAÑERO PREGONERO   (overlap) The *Colonialist's* History of Latin America…

LA SEÑORA TROVADORA   *América Latina.*

EL COMPAÑERO PREGONERO   Y el *Caribe.*

LA SEÑORA TROVADORA   *Caribe?* Carribean?

EL COMPAÑERO PREGONERO   Is there an echo in here?

LA SEÑORA TROVADORA   *Ecos…del Nuevo Mundo. Les Échos du monde nouveau. Ecos do mundo novo.*

EL COMPAÑERO PREGONERO   (aside) Echoes from the New World?

LA SEÑORA TROVADORA   (aside) That's the name of my amusement.

EL COMPAÑERO PREGONERO   (aside) Clever title. What's amusing about it?

LA SEÑORA TROVADORA   Latin America is a region rich in paradox, displaying startling contrasts—rich and poor, urban and rural, learned and illiterate. We will take you backward and forward through more than 500 years of our family history. On this travel through time you will meet our grandparents, our aunts and uncles, brothers, mothers and fathers, nephews and nieces and our great-nieces, Cecile and Juana, two sisters from your day who are just about to open their Grandmother's trunk.

EL COMPAÑERO PREGONERO   No previous knowledge of Latin American history is required for this trip. Just hum *La Bamba,* spell Cantinflas, shake like Shakira, whip up a plate of *huevos rancheros* and you'll be on your way.

LA SEÑORA TROVADORA   Look into the wonderful history of Latin America to understand not only what happened but where it is going.

EL COMPAÑERO PREGONERO   Slavery, machismo, political revolutions, economic transformations, U.S. intervention. *La Migra…*

LA SEÑORA TROVADORA   (aside) Shoo! You're scaring away my customers. (to the audience) Hey you! In the year 2020 which Chilean will cross El Rio Grande and become the first female *presidente* of *los Estados Unidos*? Maybe it's you! (LA SEÑORA TROVADORA curtsies to the audience, elegantly displaying her fan.) Esteemed audience, I am pleased and most delighted to bring you this elegant entertainment, which has been favored by Kings and Queens, nobles and royals…

EL COMPAÑERO PREGONERO   (Interrupting her, EL COMPAÑERO PREGONERO mimics her bow, spinning a tattered kerchief.) Honest *campesinos,* my ragtag sideshow has given joy and pleasure to paupers, beggars and whores.

LA SEÑORA TROVADORA   Gentle public, I am a Troubadour, a traveling balladeer, who has come a great distance to embroider the past with dulcet melodies and sentimental sonnets. (She catches the audience's eyes and winks.) Your time with me, La Señora Trovadora, will be poetically sweet and enchantingly fanciful, God willing. I hope to delight your company with vignettes of love, chivalry and honor.

EL COMPAÑERO PREGONERO   (Overlapping) Simple commoners, I am a *Pregonero,* an unadorned herald pulling my cart from ghetto to barrio, peddling my wares while singing the praises of untold histories and unrecognized heroes. My news is to the point. Time is precious and I won't waste yours. I hope to inspire you with anthems of oppression, injustice and revolution. *¡Ojala que sí!*

(Background RENNAISANCE MUSIC begins.)

LA SEÑORA TROVADORA   I play Mayan Gods. (as Mother Sky) "Who is there to praise me?" (to the audience) Conquistadors. (as Francisco Pizarro) "I laugh in the face of death!" (to the audience) and Queens! (as Queen Isabela) "I'm the Queen of the Prom! I'm the Queen of the World!"

EL COMPAÑERO PREGONERO   (aside) Why don't you just be yourself? Or have you forgotten who that is?

LA SEÑORA TROVADORA   (Curt) Enough. All you can play is victims. "Poor me. Mixed-up Mestizo." (To the audience with charm.) I am a Criolla not a Mestiza. I have pure Spanish blood.

EL COMPAÑERO PREGONERO   Ha! Take a good look at yourself!

LA SEÑORA TROVADORA   I speak the romance languages as well as English.

EL COMPAÑERO PREGONERO   The language of colonizers, *Señora.*

LA SEÑORA TROVADORA   So is Spanish, *Compañero.*

EL COMPAÑERO PREGONERO   Let us speak so that we can be understood.

LA SEÑORA TROVADORA   Very well.

(LA SEÑORA TROVADORA AND EL COMPAÑERO PREGONERO *dance a minuet.)*

EL COMPAÑERO PREGONERO   *Señora,* shall we brush up on our history before we begin?

LA SEÑORA TROVADORA   Trivia is not my favorite past time, *Compañero.*

EL COMPAÑERO PREGONERO   J Lo is in the audience.

LA SEÑORA TROVADORA   *Azucar!*

EL COMPAÑERO PREGONERO   Name three significant Women in Latin American History.

LA SEÑORA TROVADORA   Me…uh…La Malinche and…J Lo!

EL COMPAÑERO PREGONERO   Who are Cécile Fatiman and Sor Juana Inez de La Cruz?

LA SEÑORA TROVADORA   I have never heard of them.

EL COMPAÑERO PREGONERO   You will. (They dance, circling each other) Tell me, what is the date today?

LA SEÑORA TROVADORA   July 24, 1783. What does that have to do with history?

EL COMPAÑERO PREGONERO   Who was born today in Caracas, Venezuela?

LA SEÑORA TROVADORA   How would I know? I live in Santiago, Chile. I'm tired of these riddles.

EL COMPAÑERO PREGONERO   This newborn will make history, fight for the liberation of Latin America, have a country named after him and die of tuberculosis, poor and hated.

LA SEÑORA TROVADORA   I am an artiste, not an academic. (LA SEÑORA TROVADORA whisks her fan and gestures grandly.) You're standing in my light.

(They dance a Cha-cha as EL COMPAÑERO PREGONERO mischievously circles LA SEÑORA TROVADORA like a Matador.)

EL COMPAÑERO PREGONERO   What year in Mexico will this sound be heard? (EL COMPAÑERO PREGONERO lets out the cry of Mexican independence, *el grito de Dolores.*)

LA SEÑORA TROVADORA   Please, don't ever do that in public again.

EL COMPAÑERO PREGONERO   (They dance a Merengue.) Did you know the word *Ojalá* meaning "I hope" has roots in the Arabic word *Inshallah or* "May Allah Grant"? 800 years of Muslim rule in Spain, *Señora.* 710 to 1492. An Islamic echo.

LA SEÑORA TROVADORA   Who cares? This dance is over. (She moves towards the audience with a flourish.) It gives me pleasure to lift these lace curtains and guide you on a pageant through time. Three cheers for entertainment! *Olé!*

EL COMPAÑERO PREGONERO   (overlapping) Did you know the word *Olé* is also an entreaty to Allah? (LA SEÑORA glares at her brother. He continues to the audience.) I present the truth hidden behind these lace curtains. Bravo for education!

LA SEÑORA TROVADORA   A salute to magic and mirrors! I bow to a glorious past.

EL COMPAÑERO PREGONERO   I pray for a promising future.

LA SEÑORA TROVADORA   I beg you not to judge the past, *hermano*. I beg you.

EL COMPAÑERO PREGONERO   It's time to go forward, *hermana*. Are you ready?

LA SEÑORA TROVADORA   *Sí.*

∞

Translations

Note: Many words and phrases in the text are generally understood or are translated by the characters.

El Compañero Pregonero y La Señora Trovadora (Spanish)—The Fellow Herald and the Lady Troubadour

Ecos del Nuevo Mundo (Spanish), *Les Échos du monde nouveau* (French), *Ecos do mundo novo* (Portuguese)—Echoes from the New World

Vete al carajo! (Spanish)—Go to hell!

Rete! (Creole)—Stop!

Nunca! (Spanish)—Never!

Basta! (Spanish, Italian)—Enough!

Desgraciado (Spanish)—Despicable person

Bienvenidos (Spanish), *Bem-vindo* (Portuguese), *Bon Bini* (Papiamentu), *Byenvini* (Creole), *Purintaxa* (Aymará), *Xicalaquican* (Náhuatl)—Welcome

Huevos rancheros (Spanish)—"Rancher's" or "Country-style" eggs, Mexican breakfast dish

La Migra (Spanish)—Immigration Police

Presidente of los Estados Unidos (Spanish)—President of the United States

Campesinos (Spanish)—country folk, farmers

¡Ojala que sí! (Spanish)—Hopefully so!

¡Azucar! (Spanish)—Sugar! (an expression popularized by Celia Cruz)

Hermano (Spanish)—brother

Hermana (Spanish)—sister

Suggestions for Discussion

1. What is Oquita saying about history—particularly Latin American history?

2. How do the characters embody the identity of Latin America?

3. Why does Oquita use contemporary references in a play about history?

Suggestion for Writing

Write an essay comparing Oquita's work with the following selection, Ping Chong's *L'Histoire Chinoise*. Analyze their different theatrical presentation styles and perspectives on history.

∿∿∿∿

PING CHONG

L'Histoire Chinoise

Ping Chong (b. 1946 in Toronto, Canada) studied graphic design and film at the School of Visual Arts and the Pratt Institute. After joining Meredith Monk's theatrical company the House Foundation, he staged his first production, *Lazarus* (1972). His other works include *Humbolt's Current*, *Nosferatu*, and *Undesirable Elements*. Chong has received six NEA Fellowships, an Obie Award, a Guggenheim Fellowship, and—in conjunction with Monk—the 1986 Outstanding Achievement in Music Theatre Award. In this selection, from the dance-theatre work *After Sorrow* (1997), a Chinese woman from another century recalls the day her father sold her.

This first segment of After Sorrow *is performed in an open dance space. The floor is black. The back wall is a projection screen. It is lit bright blue. The rest of the stage is dark. The sound of a stream is heard.*

Four Chinese drum stools are placed in an are stage right. A musician with a pipa (a traditional Chinese stringed instrument) sits on a stool. On another stool rests a framed photograph of a young Chinese man.

A Chinese Woman dressed in black, in the fashion of a moderately well-to-do lady of one hundred years ago, enters from downstage right and crosses slowly to center. As she reaches the drum stools, a light comes up on her. She sits down, her back to us. The sound of the stream fades out. Through a voice-over, we hear the Woman speak:

CHINESE WOMAN *(Voice-over):* The day my father sold me, my mother rose even before the roosters in our village. When I opened my eyes. I saw her gazing at me in the half light, gently stroking my hair. She had a curious, sad smile on her face but I didn't notice at the time. My mother said in a very quiet voice that I must get up, that I was going to my beloved grandmother's house. Only in retrospect, in the marrow of a child's worst nightmare, in the endless, deadening days and nights of

my adulthood to come, did I replay this moment over and over again:
the memory of my mother hovering over me, stroking my thick, black
hair, sadly smiling in the indigo half light of a spring dawn.

*(The Woman slowly spins around on her stool, and now speaks to the audience.
As she continues, seven circles of light slowly come up, one on each stool and three
on the floor, which continue the curved pattern of the stools. The circle of light
stage left forms a lattice-work pattern.)*

The day my father sold me, my mother washed my hair with unusual
care. This was Servant 3's business, but on this day Mother did it herself.
I didn't notice at the time. Then she braided my hair with the warm,
familiar crisscrossing rhythms I had learned to take for granted over and
over again. Before my reflection in the mirror she added a hibiscus blos-
som in my hair, and a garment of embroidered satin embraced my person. Then she looked at me for a long, long time. A mother with a child
in a mirror. A mother with a child in a mirror for the last time. I was her
only child. I was a girl. This made my mother the least favored wife in the
household. She was constantly reminded by my father's other wives that a
wife should be producing sons not daughters. *(Opens a fan sharply and
begins fanning herself)* That day when my worthless father sold me, my
mother brought me a bowl of hot rice porridge, which I had every day, but
on this day something special came with it: two flaky melon cakes stud-
ded with cubes of pork fat, which I loved to eat. It was Servant 3's business
to bring me breakfast, but on this day Mother did it herself. I didn't notice
at the time. Then my father came into the room. He said we were going to
my beloved grandmother's house; that we had to hurry to catch the ferry.
My mother began to sob uncontrollably. Then without looking at me she
handed me a sack of dragon eye fruit and more melon cakes, I said, "Don't
cry, Mother, I'm just going to see Grandmother. I'll be back very soon."

On the day my gambler father sold me, my mother was standing at the
open gate to our home with Servant 3. Neither Father's other wives nor
any of my brothers or sisters, nor the other servants came to see me off. It
was the last time I was to see my mother. It was the last time I was to hear
her voice. When we arrived at the ferry landing, a man with rotten teeth
met us onboard and looked me over. He nodded approvingly. My father
locked me in a cabin of the ferry and then negotiated a price for my sale.
I was sold for ninety dollars—ten dollars for every year of my life. I kicked
and screamed for my father to open the door. I banged the cabin door until
my fists were bloody pulp. I cried and cried and cried but to no avail. Then
I felt the ferry glide out into the river's thrust. The inlaid mother-of-pearl
and mahogany furniture, the translucent Ming dynasty porcelain, the ivory
tusk with an entire village meticulously carved along its curve, the blue-
and-white delftware from the Netherlands, the gilded German clock, the
scholar rock in my father's studio—even the rock was worth more than a
daughter's life. When I was finally let out of the cabin, I ran round and

round the ferry screaming for my father but both my father and the man who negotiated for me were gone. At the water's edge silhouetted against the shimmering light of noon, a young man stood all alone. I remember it very well, he stood silent and still staring at me while the overpowering stench of fermented shrimps attacked me and flies strafed the air. He would become my beloved. He would become my other heart.

(*The pipa player plays. The sound of the stream is heard as the pipa music ends. The Woman gets up from the stool and dances. She pulls a red silk scarf from her sleeve and dances with it. As the dance ends, the Woman tucks the scarf back into her sleeve. The lights come down, until just one tight circle remains on the framed photo: it is the Woman's husband. The Woman picks up the photo, then faces the audience, displaying her husband's portrait. As the same time, a full body image of her husband is projected. His image slowly comes into focus as the continues.*)

PROJECTION:

Full image of the man in the photo in America

I see you and you see me. I see you and you see me across the chasm of time. My eyes mirror your face. Your eyes reflect my sorrow. Reflections in mirrors across time. I may be different from you. I may have ways you could never hope to understand. And yet, beneath the necessary evils of our respective social norms, our feelings are the same. I too feel pain when pierced. I too feel the ecstasy of a lover's embrace. I too am warm to the touch. Never doubt for a minute that I am capable of feeling these selfsame things even from the distance of a hundred years which set us apart. Never doubt for a minute that you and I are bound by the ticking of time across time over and over again. And now, if I may, let me ask you one question. One question alone while time permits. Has anyone seen this man, my beloved husband, my lover, my other heart, in the vast reaches of the Western land, these many, many years?

(*The light on the Woman fades while she holds the image of her husband for all the world to see, until only the image of her husband in her hand is lit. Then it too fades along with the projected image of him and the sound of the stream.*)

Suggestions for Discussion

1. What does this play say about memory and how it changes our perception of past events?

2. Why does the woman still feel rage against her father for selling her when she ultimately grew to love her husband?

Suggestion for Writing

Compare the Chinese Woman's monologue with the Homebody's from Tony Kushner's *Homebody/Kabul* (p. 764). Focus on characterization, what the characters reveal about their respective cultures, or the stage technique of sustained narration by a single character.

The Examined Life: Education

I who am blind can give one hint to those who see—one admonition to those who would make full use of the gift of sight: Use your eyes as if tomorrow you would be stricken blind.

—HELEN KELLER, "Three Days to See"

A classic does not necessarily teach us anything we did not know before. In a classic we sometimes discover something we have always known (or thought we knew), but without knowing that this author said it first, or at least is associated with it in a special way. And this, too, is a surprise that gives a lot of pleasure, such as we gain from the discovery of an origin, a relationship, an affinity.

—ITALO CALVINO, "Why Read the Classics?"

LE HONG PHONG SCHOOL, SAIGON, VIETNAM, KHOA, 17

NOTEBOOK

MALCOLM X

A Homemade Education

Malcolm X (1925–1965), born Malcolm Little, became a Muslim while serving a prison sentence and was an early minister of the Nation of Islam's mosque in New York. Before his assassination, he was a spiritual leader, writer, lecturer, and political activist who worked for worldwide African-American unity and equality. The following selection is taken from his powerful *Autobiography of Malcolm X* (1965).

It was because of my letters that I happened to stumble upon starting to acquire some kind of a homemade education.

I became increasingly frustrated at not being able to express what I wanted to convey in letters that I wrote, especially those to Mr. Elijah Muhammad. In the street, I had been the most articulate hustler out there—I had commanded attention when I said something. But now, trying to write simple English, I not only wasn't articulate, I wasn't even functional. How would I sound writing in slang, the way I would say it, something such as, "Look, daddy, let me pull your coat about a cat, Elijah Muhammad—"

Many who today hear me somewhere in person, or on television, or those who read something I've said, will think I went to school far beyond the eighth grade. This impression is due entirely to my prison studies.

It had really begun back in the Charlestown Prison, when Bimbi first made me feel envy of his stock of knowledge. Bimbi had always taken charge of any conversations he was in, and I had tried to emulate him. But every book I picked up had few sentences which didn't contain anywhere from one to nearly all of the words that might as well have been in Chinese. When I just skipped those words, of course, I really ended up with little idea of what the book said. So I had come to the Norfolk Prison Colony still going through only book-reading motions. Pretty soon, I would have quit even these motions, unless I had received the motivation that I did.

I saw that the best thing I could do was get hold of a dictionary—to study, to learn some words. I was lucky enough to reason also that I should try to improve my penmanship. It was sad. I couldn't even write in a straight line. It was both ideas together that moved me to request a dictionary along with some tablets and pencils from the Norfolk Prison Colony school.

I spent two days just riffling uncertainly through the dictionary's pages. I'd never realized so many words existed! I didn't know which words I needed to learn. Finally, just to start some kind of action, I began copying.

In my slow, painstaking, ragged handwriting, I copied into my tablet everything printed on that first page, down to the punctuation marks.

I believe it took me a day. Then, aloud, I read back, to myself, everything I'd written on the tablet. Over and over, aloud, to myself, I read my own handwriting.

I woke up the next morning, thinking about those words—immensely proud to realize that not only had I written so much at one time, but I'd written words that I never knew were in the world. Moreover, with a little effort, I also could remember what many of these words meant. I reviewed the words whose meanings I didn't remember. Funny thing, from the dictionary first page right now, that "aardvark" springs to my mind. The dictionary had a picture of it, a long-tailed, long-eared, burrowing African mammal, which lives off termites caught by sticking out its tongue as an anteater does for ants.

I was so fascinated that I went on—I copied the dictionary's next page. And the same experience came when I studied that. With every succeeding page, I also learned of people and places and events from history. Actually the dictionary is like a miniature encyclopedia. Finally the dictionary's A section had filled a whole tablet—and I went on into the B's. That was the way I started copying what eventually became the entire dictionary. It went a lot faster after so much practice helped me to pick up handwriting speed. Between what I wrote in my tablet, and writing letters, during the rest of my time in prison I would guess I wrote a million words.

I suppose it was inevitable that as my word-base broadened, I could for the first time pick up a book and read and now begin to understand what the book was saying. Anyone who has read a great deal can imagine the new world that opened. Let me tell you something: from then until I left that prison, in every free moment I had, if I was not reading in the library, I was reading on my bunk. You couldn't have gotten me out of books with a wedge. Between Mr. Muhammad's teachings, my correspondence, my visitors—usually Ella and Reginald—and my reading of books, months passed without my even thinking about being imprisoned. In fact, up to then, I never had been so truly free in my life.

The Norfolk Prison Colony's library was in the school building. A variety of classes was taught there by instructors who came from such places as Harvard and Boston universities. The weekly debates between inmate teams were also held in the school building. You would be astonished to know how worked up convict debaters and audiences would get over subjects like "Should Babies Be Fed Milk?"

Available on the prison library's shelves were books on just about every general subject. Much of the big private collection that Parkhurst had willed to the prison was still in crates and boxes in the back of the library—thousands of old books. Some of them looked ancient: covers faded; old-time parchment-looking binding. Parkhurst, I've mentioned, seemed to have been principally interested in history and religion. He had the money and the special interest to have a lot of books that you wouldn't have in general circulation. Any college library would have been lucky to get that collection.

As you can imagine, especially in a prison where there was heavy emphasis on rehabilitation, an inmate was smiled upon if he demonstrated an unusually intense interest in books. There was a sizable number of well-read inmates, especially the popular debaters. Some were said by many to be practically walking encyclopedias. They were almost celebrities. No university would ask any student to devour literature as I did when this new world opened to me, of being able to read and understand.

I read more in my room than in the library itself. An inmate who was known to read a lot could check out more than the permitted maximum number of books. I preferred reading in the total isolation of my own room.

When I had progressed to really serious reading, every night at about ten P.M. I would be outraged with the "lights out." It always seemed to catch me right in the middle of something engrossing.

Fortunately, right outside my door was a corridor light that cast a glow into my room. The glow was enough to read by, once my eyes adjusted to it. So when "lights out" came, I would sit on the floor where I could continue reading in that glow.

At one-hour intervals the night guards paced past every room. Each time I heard the approaching footsteps, I jumped into bed and feigned sleep. And as soon as the guard passed, I got back out of bed onto the floor area of that light-glow, where I would read for another fifty-eight minutes—until the guard approached again. That went on until three or four every morning. Three or four hours of sleep a night was enough for me. Often in the years in the streets I had slept less than that.

The teachings of Mr. Muhammad stressed how history had been "whitened"—when white men had written history books, the black man simply had been left out. Mr. Muhammad couldn't have said anything that would have struck me much harder. I had never forgotten how when my class, me and all of those whites, had studied seventh-grade United States history back in Mason, the history of the Negro had been covered in one paragraph, and the teacher had gotten a big laugh with his joke, "Negroes' feet are so big that when they walk, they leave a hole in the ground."

This is one reason why Mr. Muhammad's teachings spread so swiftly all over the United States, among all Negroes, whether or not they became followers of Mr. Muhammad. The teachings ring true—to every Negro. You can hardly show me a black adult in America—or a white one, for that matter—who knows from the history books anything like the truth about the black man's role. In my own case, once I heard of the "glorious history of the black man," I took special pains to hunt in the library for books that would inform me on details about black history.

I can remember accurately the very first set of books that really impressed me. I have since bought that set of books and I have it at home for my children to read as they grow up. It's called *Wonders of the World*. It's full of pictures of archaeological finds, statues that depict, usually, non-European people.

I found books like Will Durant's *Story of Civilization*. I read H. G. Wells' *Outline of History*. *Souls of Black Folk* by W. E. B. Du Bois gave me a glimpse into the black people's history before they came to this country. Carter G. Woodson's *Negro History* opened my eyes about black empires before the black slave was brought to the United States, and the early Negro struggles for freedom.

J. A. Rogers' three volumes of *Sex and Race* told about race-mixing before Christ's time; about Aesop being a black man who told fables; about Egypt's Pharaohs; about the great Coptic Christian Empires; about Ethiopia, the earth's oldest continuous black civilization, as China is the oldest continuous civilization.

Mr. Muhammad's teaching about how the white man had been created led me to *Findings in Genetics* by Gregor Mendel. (The dictionary's G section was where I had learned what "genetics" meant.) I really studied this book by the Austrian monk. Reading it over and over, especially certain sections, helped me to understand that if you started with a black man, a white man could be produced; but starting with a white man, you never could produce a black man—because the white chromosome is recessive. And since no one disputes that there was but one Original Man, the conclusion is clear.

During the last year or so, in the *New York Times*, Arnold Toynbee used the word "bleached" in describing the white man. (His words were: "White [i.e., bleached] human beings of North European origin....") Toynbee also referred to the European geographic area as only a peninsula of Asia. He said there is no such thing as Europe. And if you look at the globe, you will see for yourself that America is only an extension of Asia. (But at the same time Toynbee is among those who have helped to bleach history. He won't write that again. Every day now, the truth is coming to light.)

I never will forget how shocked I was when I began reading about slavery's total horror. It made such an impact upon me that it later became one of my favorite subjects when I became a minister of Mr. Muhammad's. The world's most monstrous crime, the sin and the blood on the white man's hands, are almost impossible to believe. Books like the one by Frederick Olmstead opened my eyes to the horrors suffered when the slave was landed in the United States. The European woman, Fannie Kimball, who had married a Southern white slaveowner, described how human beings were degraded. Of course I read *Uncle Tom's Cabin*. In fact, I believe that's the only novel I have ever read since I started serious reading.

Parkhurst's collection also contained some bound pamphlets of the Abolitionist Anti-Slavery Society of New England. I read descriptions of atrocities, saw those illustrations of black slave women tied up and flogged with whips; of black mothers watching their babies being dragged off, never to be seen by their mothers again; of dogs after slaves, and of the fugitive slave catchers, evil white men with whips and clubs and chains and guns. I read about the slave preacher Nat Turner, who put the fear of God into the white slavemaster. Nat Turner wasn't going around preaching pie-in-the-sky and "nonviolent" freedom for the black man. There in Virginia one night in 1831, Nat and seven other slaves started out at his master's home and through the night they went from one plantation "big house" to the next, killing, until by the next morning 57 white people were dead and Nat had about 70 slaves following him. White people, terrified for their lives, fled from their homes, locked themselves up in public buildings, hid in the woods, and some even left the state. A small army of soldiers took two months to catch and hang Nat Turner. Somewhere I have read where Nat Turner's example is said to have inspired John Brown to invade Virginia and attack Harper's Ferry nearly thirty years later, with thirteen white men and five Negroes.

I read Herodotus, "the father of History," or, rather, I read about him. And I read the histories of various nations, which opened my eyes gradually, then wider and wider, to how the whole world's white men had indeed acted like devils, pillaging and raping and bleeding and draining the whole world's non-white people. I remember, for instance, books such as Will Durant's *The Story of Oriental Civilization,* and Mahatma Gandhi's accounts of the struggle to drive the British out of India.

Book after book showed me how the white man had brought upon the world's black, brown, red, and yellow peoples every variety of the sufferings of exploitation. I saw how since the sixteenth century, the so-called "Christian trader" white man began to ply the seas in his lust for Asian and African empires, and plunder, and power. I read, I saw, how the white man never has gone among the non-white peoples bearing the Cross in the true manner and spirit of Christ's teachings—meek, humble, and Christlike.

I perceived, as I read, how the collective white man had been actually nothing but a piratical opportunist who used Faustian machinations to make his own Christianity his initial wedge in criminal conquests. First, always "religiously," he branded "heathen" and "pagan" labels upon ancient non-white cultures and civilizations. The stage thus set, he then turned upon his non-white victims his weapons of war.

I read how, entering India—half a billion deeply religious brown people—the British white man, by 1759, through promises, trickery and manipulations, controlled much of India through Great Britain's East India Company. The parasitical British administration kept tentacling out to half of the subcontinent. In 1857, some of the desperate people of India finally mutinied—and, excepting the African slave trade, nowhere has history recorded any more unnecessary bestial and ruthless human carnage than the British suppression of the non-white Indian people.

Over 115 million African blacks—close to the 1930s population of the United States—were murdered or enslaved during the slave trade. And I read how when the slave market was glutted, the cannibalistic white powers of Europe next carved up, as their colonies, the richest areas of the black continent. And Europe's chancelleries for the next century played a chess game of naked exploitation and power from Cape Horn to Cairo.

Ten guards and the warden couldn't have torn me out of those books. Not even Elijah Muhammad could have been more eloquent than those books were in providing indisputable proof that the collective white man had acted like a devil in virtually every contact he had with the world's collective non-white man. I listen today to the radio, and watch television, and read the headlines about the collective white man's fear and tension concerning China. When the white man professes ignorance about why the Chinese hate him so, my mind can't help flashing back to what I read, there in prison, about how the blood forebears of this same white man raped China at a time when China was trusting and helpless. Those original white "Christian traders" sent into China millions of pounds of opium. By 1839, so many of the Chinese were addicts that China's desperate government destroyed twenty thousand chests of opium. The first Opium War was promptly declared by the white man. Imagine! Declaring war upon someone who objects to being narcotized! The Chinese were severely beaten, with Chinese-invented gunpowder.

The Treaty of Nanking made China pay the British white man for the destroyed opium: forced open China's major ports to British trade; forced China to abandon Hong Kong; fixed China's import tariffs so low that cheap British articles soon flooded in, maiming China's industrial development.

After a second Opium War, the Tientsin Treaties legalized the ravaging opium trade, legalized a British–French–American control of China's customs. China tried delaying that Treaty's ratification; Peking was looted and burned.

"Kill the foreign white devils!" was the 1901 Chinese war cry in the Boxer Rebellion. Losing again, this time the Chinese were driven from Peking's choicest areas. The vicious, arrogant white man put up the famous signs, "Chinese and dogs not allowed."

Red China after World War II closed its doors to the Western white world. Massive Chinese agricultural, scientific, and industrial efforts are described in a book that *Life* magazine recently published. Some observers inside Red China have reported that the world never has known such a hate-white campaign as is now going on in this non-white country where, present birthrates continuing, in fifty more years Chinese will be half the earth's population. And it seems that some Chinese chickens will soon come home to roost, with China's recent successful nuclear tests.

Let us face reality. We can see in the United Nations a new world order being shaped, along color lines—an alliance among the non-white nations. America's U.N. Ambassador Adlai Stevenson complained not long ago that in the United Nations "a skin game" was being played. He was right. He was facing reality. A "skin game" is being played. But Ambassador Stevenson sounded like Jesse James accusing the marshal of carrying a gun. Because who in the world's history ever has played a worse "skin game" than the white man?

Mr. Muhammad, to whom I was writing daily, had no idea of what a new world had opened up to me through my efforts to document his teachings in books.

When I discovered philosophy, I tried to touch all the landmarks of philosophical development. Gradually, I read most of the old philosophers, Occidental and Oriental. The Oriental philosophers were the ones I came to prefer; finally, my impression was that most Occidental philosophy had largely been borrowed from the Oriental thinkers. Socrates, for instance, traveled in Egypt. Some sources even say that Socrates was initiated into some of the Egyptian mysteries. Obviously Socrates got some of his wisdom among the East's wise men.

I have often reflected upon the new vistas that reading opened to me. I knew right there in prison that reading had changed forever the course of my life. As I see it today, the ability to read awoke inside me some long dormant craving to be mentally alive. I certainly wasn't seeking any degree, the way a college confers a status symbol upon its students. My homemade education gave me, with every additional book that I read, a little bit more sensitivity to the deafness, dumbness, and blindness that was afflicting the black race in America. Not long ago, an English writer telephoned me from London, asking questions. One was, "What's your alma mater?" I told him, "Books." You will never catch me with a free fifteen minutes in which I'm not studying something I feel might be able to help the black man.

Yesterday I spoke in London, and both ways on the plane across the Atlantic I was studying a document about how the United Nations proposes to insure the human rights of the oppressed minorities of the world. The American black man is the world's most shameful case of minority oppression. What makes the black man think of himself as only an internal United States issue is just a catch-phrase, two words, "civil rights." How is the black man going to get "civil rights" before first he wins his human rights? If the American black man will start thinking about his human rights, and then start thinking of himself as part of one of the world's great peoples, he will see he has a case for the United Nations.

I can't think of a better case! Four hundred years of black blood and sweat invested here in America, and the white man still has the black man begging for what every immigrant fresh off the ship can take for granted the minute he walks down the gangplank.

But I'm digressing. I told the Englishman that my alma mater was books, a good library. Every time I catch a plane, I have with me a book that I want to read—and that's a lot of books these days. If I weren't out here every day battling the white man, I could spend the rest of my life reading, just satisfying my curiosity—because you can hardly mention anything I'm not curious about. I don't think anybody ever got more out of going to prison than I did. In fact, prison enabled me to study far more intensively than I would have if my life had gone differently and I had attended some college. I imagine that one of the biggest troubles with colleges is there are too many distractions, too much panty-raiding, fraternities, and boola-boola and all of that. Where else but in a prison could I have attacked my ignorance by being able to study intensely sometimes as much as fifteen hours a day?

Suggestions for Discussion

1. Discuss the significance of the essay's title, "A Homemade Education."

2. Explain how Malcolm X used his dictionary to improve his education.

3. Discuss his observation that "the ability to read awoke inside me some long dormant craving to be mentally alive."

4. Comment on his assertion that his "alma mater was books."

5. What details help make clear his passion for learning?

Suggestions for Writing

1. Compare and contrast "A Homemade Education" with another section of Malcolm X's *Autobiography*.

2. Write about one or more books that have played an important role in shaping your thinking, attitudes, and behavior.

ANTON CHEKHOV

The Bet

Translated by Constance Garnett

Anton Chekhov (1860–1904), Russian short-story writer and playwright, practiced medicine briefly before devoting himself to literature. Among his plays are *The Sea Gull* (1896), *Uncle Vanya* (1900), *The Three Sisters* (1901), and *The Cherry Orchard* (1904). His stories, translated by Constance Garnett, were published as *The Tales of Chekhov* (1916–1923). In the following story, the drama of the lawyer's solitary existence constitutes the central action. The story culminates in his walking out of the lodge a few hours before fulfilling the conditions of the bet, and it reaches its highest point of intensity, and its resolution, in the letter the lawyer writes that passionately expresses his nihilism and supreme contempt for his fellow men.

∽

I

It was a dark autumn night. The old banker was pacing from corner to corner of his study, recalling to his mind the party he gave in the autumn fifteen years before. There were many clever people at the party and much interesting conversation. They talked among other things of capital punishment. The guests, among them not a few scholars and journalists, for the most part disapproved of capital punishment. They found it obsolete as a means of punishment, unfitted to a Christian State and immoral. Some of them thought that capital punishment should be replaced universally by life imprisonment.

"I don't agree with you," said the host. "I myself have experienced neither capital punishment nor life imprisonment, but if one may judge *a priori,* then in my opinion capital punishment is more moral and more humane than imprisonment. Execution kills instantly, life imprisonment kills by degrees. Who is the more humane executioner, one who kills you in a few seconds or one who draws the life out of you incessantly, for years?"

"They're both equally immoral," remarked one of the guests, "because their purpose is the same, to take away life. The State is not God. It has no right to take away that which it cannot give back, if it should so desire."

Among the company was a lawyer, a young man of about twenty-five. On being asked his opinion, he said:

"Capital punishment and life imprisonment are equally immoral; but if I were offered the choice between them, I would certainly choose the second. It's better to live somehow than not to live at all."

There ensued a lively discussion. The banker who was then younger and more nervous suddenly lost his temper, banged his fist on the table, and turning to the young lawyer, cried out:

"It's a lie. I bet you two millions you wouldn't stick in a cell even for five years."

"If you mean it seriously," replied the lawyer, "then I bet I'll stay not five but fifteen."

"Fifteen! Done!" cried the banker. "Gentlemen, I stake two millions."

"Agreed. You stake two millions, I my freedom," said the lawyer.

So this wild, ridiculous bet came to pass. The banker, who at that time had too many millions to count, spoiled and capricious, was beside himself with rapture. During supper he said to the lawyer jokingly:

"Come to your senses, young man, before it's too late. Two millions are nothing to me, but you stand to lose three or four of the best years of your life. I say three or four, because you'll never stick it out any longer. Don't forget either, you unhappy man, that voluntary is much heavier than enforced imprisonment. The idea that you have the right to free yourself at any moment will poison the whole of your life in the cell. I pity you."

And now the banker, pacing from corner to corner, recalled all this and asked himself:

"Why did I make this bet? What's the good? The lawyer loses fifteen years of his life and I throw away two millions. Will it convince people that capital punishment is worse or better than imprisonment for life? No, no! all stuff and rubbish. On my part, it was the caprice of a well-fed man; on the lawyer's, pure greed of gold."

He recollected further what happened after the evening party. It was decided that the lawyer must undergo his imprisonment under the strictest observation, in a garden wing of the banker's house. It was agreed that during the period he would be deprived of the right to cross the threshold, to see living people, to hear human voices, and to receive letters and newspapers. He was permitted to have a musical instrument, to read books, to write letters, to drink wine, and smoke tobacco. By the agreement he could communicate, but only in silence, with the outside world through a little window specially constructed for this purpose. Everything necessary, books, music, wine, he could receive in any quantity by sending a note through the window. The agreement provided for all the minutest details, which made the confinement strictly solitary, and it obliged the lawyer to remain exactly fifteen years from twelve o'clock of November 14th, 1870 to twelve o'clock of November 14th, 1885. The least attempt on his part to violate the conditions, to escape if only for two minutes before the time freed the banker from the obligation to pay him the two millions.

During the first year of imprisonment, the lawyer, as far as it was possible to judge from his short notes, suffered terribly from loneliness and boredom. From his wing day and night came the sound of the piano. He ·rejected wine and tobacco. "Wine," he wrote, "excites desires, and desires are the chief foes of a prisoner; besides, nothing is more boring than to drink good wine alone, and tobacco spoils the air in his room." During the first year the lawyer was sent books of a light character; novels with a complicated love interest, stories of crime and fantasy, comedies, and so on.

In the second year the piano was heard no longer and the lawyer asked only for classics. In the fifth year, music was heard again, and the prisoner asked for wine. Those who watched him said that during the whole of that year he was only eating, drinking, and lying on his bed. He yawned often and talked angrily to himself. Books he did not read. Sometimes at nights he would sit down to write. He would write for a long time and tear it all up in the morning. More than once he was heard to weep.

In the second half of the sixth year, the prisoner began zealously to study languages, philosophy, and history. He fell on these subjects so hungrily that the banker hardly had time to get books enough for him. In the space of four years about six hundred volumes were brought at his request. It was while that passion lasted that the banker received the following letter from the prisoner: "My dear gaoler, I am writing these lines in six languages. Show them to experts. Let them read them. If they do not find one single mistake, I beg you to give orders to have a gun fired off in the garden. By the noise I shall know that my efforts have not been in vain. The geniuses of all ages and countries speak in different languages; but in them all burns the same flame. Oh, if you knew my heavenly happiness now that I can understand them!" The prisoner's desire was fulfilled. Two shots were fired in the garden by the banker's order.

Later on, after the tenth year, the lawyer sat immovable before his table and read only the New Testament. The banker found it strange that a man who in four years had mastered six hundred erudite volumes, should have spent nearly a year in reading one book, easy to understand and by no means thick. The New Testament was then replaced by the history of religions and theology.

During the last two years of his confinement the prisoner read an extraordinary amount, quite haphazard. Now he would apply himself to the natural sciences, then he would read Byron or Shakespeare. Notes used to come from him in which he asked to be sent at the same time a book on chemistry, a text-book of medicine, a novel, and some treatise on philosophy or theology. He read as though he were swimming in the sea among broken pieces of wreckage, and in his desire to save his life was eagerly grasping one piece after another.

ॐ

II

The banker recalled all this, and thought:

"To-morrow at twelve o'clock he receives his freedom. Under the agreement, I shall have to pay him two millions. If I pay, it's all over with me. I am ruined for ever...."

Fifteen years before he had too many millions to count, but now he was afraid to ask himself which he had more of, money or debts. Gambling on the Stock-Exchange, risky speculation, and the recklessness of which he could not rid himself even in old age, had gradually brought his business to decay; and the fearless, self-confident, proud man of business had become an ordinary banker, trembling at every rise and fall in the market.

"That cursed bet," murmured the old man clutching his head in despair.... "Why didn't the man die? He's only forty years old. He will take away my last farthing, marry, enjoy life, gamble on the Exchange, and I will look on like an envious beggar and hear the same words from him every day: 'I'm obliged to you for the happiness of my life. Let me help you.' No, it's too much! The only escape from bankruptcy and disgrace—is that the man should die."

The clock had just struck three. The banker was listening. In the house every one was asleep, and one could hear only the frozen trees whining outside the windows. Trying to make no sound, he took out of his safe the key of the door which had not been opened for fifteen years, put on his overcoat, and went out of the house. The garden was dark and cold. It was raining. A damp, penetrating wind howled in the garden and gave the trees no rest. Though he strained his eyes, the banker could see neither the ground, nor the white statues, nor the garden wing, nor the trees. Approaching the garden wing, he called the watchman twice. There was no answer. Evidently the watchman had taken shelter from the bad weather and was now asleep somewhere in the kitchen or the greenhouse.

"If I have the courage to fulfill my intention," thought the old man, "the suspicion will fall on the watchman first of all."

In the darkness he groped for the steps and the door and entered the hall of the garden-wing, then poked his way into a narrow passage and struck a match. Not a soul was there. Some one's bed, with no bedclothes on it, stood there, and an iron stove loomed dark in the corner. The seals on the door that led into the prisoner's room were unbroken.

When the match went out, the old man, trembling from agitation, peeped into the little window.

In the prisoner's room a candle was burning dimly. The prisoner himself sat by the table. Only his back, the hair on his head and his hands were visible. Open books were strewn about on the table, the two chairs, and on the carpet near the table.

Five minutes passed and the prisoner never once stirred. Fifteen years' confinement had taught him to sit motionless. The banker tapped on the window with his finger, but the prisoner made no movement in reply. Then the banker cautiously tore the seals from the door and put the key into the lock. The rusty lock gave a hoarse groan and the door creaked. The banker expected instantly to hear a cry of surprise and the sound of steps. Three minutes passed and it was as quiet inside as it had been before. He made up his mind to enter.

Before the table sat a man, unlike an ordinary human being. It was a skeleton, with tight-drawn skin, with long curly hair like a woman's, and a shaggy beard. The colour of his face was yellow, of an earthy shade; the cheeks were sunken, the back long and narrow, and the hand upon which he leaned his hairy head was so lean and skinny that it was painful to look upon. His hair was already silvering with grey, and no one who glanced at the senile emaciation of the face would have believed that he was only forty years old. On the table, before his bended head, lay a sheet of paper on which something was written in a tiny hand.

"Poor devil," thought the banker, "he's asleep and probably seeing millions in his dreams. I have only to take and throw this half-dead thing on the bed, smother him a moment with the pillow, and the most careful examination will find no trace of unnatural death. But, first, let us read what he has written here."

The banker took the sheet from the table and read:

"Tomorrow at twelve o'clock midnight, I shall obtain my freedom and the right to mix with people. But before I leave this room and see the sun I think it necessary to say a few words to you. On my own clear conscience and before God who sees me I declare to you that I despise freedom, life, health, and all that your books call the blessings of the world.

"For fifteen years I have diligently studied earthly life. True, I saw neither the earth nor the people, but in your books I drank fragrant wine, sang songs, hunted deer and wild boar in the forests, loved women.... And beautiful women, like clouds ethereal, created by the magic of your poets' genius, visited me by night, and whispered to me wonderful tales, which made my head drunken. In your books I climbed the summits of Elbruz and Mont Blanc and saw from there how the sun rose in the morning, and in the evening suffused the sky, the ocean and the mountain ridges with a purple gold. I saw from there how above me lightnings glimmered cleaving the clouds; I saw green forests, fields, rivers, lakes, cities; I heard sirens singing, and the playing of the pipes of Pan; I touched the wings of beautiful devils who came flying to me to speak of God.... In your books I cast myself into bottomless abysses, worked miracles, burned cities to the ground, preached new religions, conquered whole countries....

"Your books gave me wisdom. All that unwearying human thought created in the centuries is compressed to a little lump in my skull. I know that I am cleverer than you all.

"And I despise your books, despise all worldly blessings and wisdom. Everything is void, frail, visionary and delusive as a mirage. Though you be proud and wise and beautiful, yet will death wipe you from the face of the earth like the mice underground; and your posterity, your history, and the immorality of your men of genius will be as frozen slag, burnt down together with the terrestrial globe.

"You are mad, and gone the wrong way. You take falsehood for truth and ugliness for beauty. You would marvel if suddenly apple and orange trees should bear frogs and lizards instead of fruit, and if roses should begin to breathe the odour of a sweating horse. So do I marvel at you, who have bartered heaven for earth. I do not want to understand you.

"That I may show you in deed my contempt for that by which you live, I waive the two millions of which I once dreamed as of paradise, and which I now despise. That I may deprive myself of my right to them, I shall come out from here five minutes before the stipulated term, and thus shall violate the agreement."

When he had read, the banker put the sheet on the table, kissed the head of the strange man, and began to weep. He went out of the wing. Never at any other time, not even after his terrible losses on the Exchange, had he felt such contempt for himself as now. Coming home, he lay down on his bed, but agitation and tears kept him a long time from sleeping....

The next morning the poor watchman came running to him and told him that they had seen the man who lived in the wing climb through the window into the garden. He had gone to the gate and disappeared. The banker instantly went with his servants to the wing and established the escape of his prisoner. To avoid unnecessary rumours he took the paper with the renunciation from the table and, on his return, locked it in his safe.

Suggestions for Discussion

1. If you agree that "The Bet" is primarily the lawyer's story, why is our view of the lawyer filtered through the reminiscences and observations of the banker? Why are we permitted to see the lawyer directly only twice? What artistic purposes are served by the use of hearsay and notes and letters, and by the sparseness and flatness of the account of the lawyer's years of confinement?

2. Trace the changes in the lawyer's activities as they mark the development and resolution of the action. What are the implications as to his ultimate fate?

3. How do the shifts in time contribute to suspense and tone?

4. Find examples of irony and paradox.

5. How do you reconcile the lawyer's nihilism with his lyrical assertion that he has known the beauty of earth and love, has seen nature in her glory and tempestuousness, and has achieved wisdom—"All that unwearying human thought created"? What evidence can you find that Chekhov's vision of life extends beyond negation of all values?

Suggestions for Writing

1. Chekhov has said, "When you depict sad or unlucky people and want to touch the reader's heart, try to be colder—it gives their grief, as it were, a background against which it stands out in greater relief.... You must be unconcerned when you write pathetic stories,...the more objective, the stronger will be the effect." Write an evaluation of Chekhov's theories in relation to the characters of the banker and the lawyer, the tone of the story, and its denouement.

2. Write a position paper on the lawyer's (or the banker's) "examined life."

3. Write your own preferred conclusion to "The Bet," or describe the lawyer's next fifteen years, or recount a conversation in which the banker tells his story the next morning.

PERSONAL REMINISCENCES

∽∽∽∽∽

EDWARD HOAGLAND

A Last Look Around

Edward Hoagland is an essayist and novelist whose works focus on wildlife and natural phenomena and their relationship to human civilization. *The Peacock's Tail* (1965), *Seven River's West* (1986), *The Courage of Turtles* (1971), and *Walking the Dead Diamond River* (1973) are among his most prominent works. *Tigers and Ice: Reflections on Nature and Life* and *In the Country of the Blind* both appeared in 1999. He also wrote *Hoagland on Nature* (2003). In the following piece, published in 1997, Hoagland writes about how he has coped with growing old.

We age at different rates, just as our pacing in adolescence and later is different. Hampered by a stutter and mute with girls, for instance, I was instead precocious as a writer and published my first novel before I had lost my virginity. In fact, the publisher had to fly me east for a last-minute consultation because their lawyer, in reading the proofs of the book, discovered a passage where I seemed to be describing a sexual act that could not be depicted in 1955—only to realize in interrogating me, of course, that I had never heard or even conceived of the practice of cunnilingus. He forbore explaining, and I was drafted into the army, and my twenties became like other people's teens as far as sexual experimentation was concerned. Thus my thirties probably corresponded to their twenties, and my forties were naturally rather like their thirties: in that aspect of life perhaps my prime. It seems to make it easier now to be in my sixties, because I don't have to look back in memory very far to uncommon adventures.

Sex is hardly the only form love takes, however, and most of us become better parents, better friends as we mature. The ripening thirties and forties bring some patience and perspective. You learn to make the most of an hour with your daughter at the zoo, or lunch with an old classmate who's resettling and needs to find a job. Dawn in June, when you're my age, 64, with the songbirds singing, and a mother merganser flies over an otter swimming ahead of your canoe, and suddenly dodges as a duck hawk sweeps out of the trees—she had been decoying you away from her knot of half a dozen bobbing babies. But down she splashes into the river, imme-

814

The Activist, oil on canvas, John Currin, 2000. Courtesy the Gagosian Gallery.

diately diving to escape the falcon, and succeeds. Great swamp maples and willows; a wood turtle; a mallard family that appears to have eluded the falcon's notice—he's gone after a blue jay. You're with a friend who is saddled with heart trouble, and this is just the kind of spectacle that concentrates your minds. Not only the glee that you two felt when you were young and predatory like the otter and the falcon, or the mercurial delight of being alive with the sun and a breeze on the water, but the wistful awe of knowing you won't always be outdoors in a canoe during the spring in what looks awfully like God's best heaven. If it isn't, then what is?

Summer won't be endless now; nor episodes of drama and romance. The well takes longer to refill. Even walking, I pant when going uphill—a nice healthy sort of pant in my case, I hope, because I think that, in our day, our life spans, unless we drive like maniacs, are determined by our genes. My father died at just 63, my mother is 94, and I've always felt closer to her. People tend to gain in tolerance and grow more generous-spirited as they get older, but on the other hand, we often lose connectedness and some degree of interest in what's going on. So our generosity or tolerance is not all that expensive to us. Bring a cruel conundrum to our attention and we will certainly sympathize, but we are quite inured to the impossibility of combating injustice and to the corruption of the sort of powerful people who otherwise might try. And much as our backs slip out of whack at some small sidewise tug, so do our minds skid off the point when fatigued a little or short-circuited by a spark. I've been publishing books for 40 years, and I don't have a fastball any more, just a knuckleball, spitball and other Satchel Paigey stuff.

You're only as old as you feel is a refrain one hears enough that it must have some truth to it, though your oncologist might disagree. The remissions he sees uplifting the spirits of so many dying people a week short of death—when they think they are going to live on for years—could be interpreted as the exuberance of fetal angels confused by a passage toward ecstasy, or as an aspect of the anesthetic that commonly tranquilizes creatures that are being engulfed by death, whether a wildebeest in the jaws of a lion or a frog in the mouth of a snake. While in the army, I worked in a morgue and noticed that most dead people smile.

Yet we are, indeed, in some respects as young as we feel. Life is moments, day by day, not a chronometer or a contractual commitment by God. The digits of one's age do not correspond to the arrhythmia of one's heart or to the secret chemistry in our lymph nodes that, mysteriously going rancid, can betray us despite all of the surgery, dentistry and other codger-friendly amenities that money buys. Good works don't keep you off the undertaker's slab, either. But cheeriness, maybe yes. Cheery, lean, little guys do seem to squeeze an extra decade out of the miser up above, as if feeling young were not as important as having a peppy metabolism and appreciating being alive.

Blurry eyesight, fragile knees, broken sleep, the need to pee a dozen times a day (when somebody honks at my car, parked at the side of the interstate, I assume it's a man my own age) are not inherently fun, however, though the smoothing out of temperament does help you cope. Your ingenuity, your curiosity must find a new focus, not simply exploring the world as a kid does. When I watch from my canoe a tall blue heron stalking field mice through the grass, then washing them down with minnows and tadpoles, I don't experience the surge of ambition to be a zoologist I would have felt when I was 15. I just want to go on seeing these intricate things next year.

Among my friends who have been notified that they were terminally ill, those who died least miserably, most gracefully, were people who could be intrigued and absorbed by the peculiar changes their bodies underwent. They didn't stop observing the incongruous handicaps, the bemusing treatments they were subjected to. The music they loved, snatches from books that had meant a lot, the news of friends who stopped in to visit, the civil war afflicting their bodies, the total novelty of dying—comprehending such a crush of sensations took all their waking time (a last hearing of the *Children's Corner* suite!) and emotional resilience. It was a voyage they stayed on deck for.

During a spell of semiblindness a few years ago, I found myself, too, registering the dismally curious stages of what was happening to me, as I gave up driving, lost the capacity to see birds in the sky, then gradually the crowns of the loveliest trees, and my friends' faces close at hand, a fascinating catastrophe. Surgery saved and rejuvenated me; I felt like Lazarus. But I learned how life itemizes exactly what you are losing. With binoculars around my neck, and then a telescope at the window, I put off curtain time. (The moon you can watch endlessly, or a lilac branch bounce in the wind, but people object to being gazed at.) As my daughter dropped in, and the leaves outside turned yellow, I was scrambling to improvise solutions: how to get a particular errand done, how to read three paragraphs by closing one eye and focusing the other ever closer. But would I see her face again? I was reviewing a day at the beach I had had 10 years before in San Francisco with the love of my life, stripping the rubber band out of her hair and kissing a pimple she tried to hide with her free hand, as the purple underbelly of a rainstorm rolled in, but reminded myself that since things hadn't worked out, she wasn't really the love of my life. Or was she?

Life is minutiae, and aging progresses by two steps forward and then one back, jerky as one's legs become. And though I was rejuvenated by millennium-type eye surgery (when nature had had it fixed for eons that people my age should quietly go blind or have heart attacks without bypasses, thus decently getting offstage and leaving enough space for younger people and other mammalians), my memory kept slipping out of gear, as if a cog were chipped, at the same time that I had more to remember in a lengthening life, and my temper grew crankier, though in fact my true balance was becoming more benign. While less in a hurry to get places, I drove worse because my mind was absent. My eyesight had been sharpened with plastic implants, but my mind coughed like an old car's motor and I would pull out into traffic without using my eyes.

My chest ached afterward a little when this happened, as it does when my waking dreams go wandering into uncataloged drawers of my memory where they have no pleasant business being. Yet I don't glance back and notice missed opportunities. Wanting so passionately to be a writer, I grabbed what I saw as the main chance at every turn, avoiding offers to become a tenured professor or a media editorialist in favor of staying freelance. Living frugally came naturally to me as a stutterer who had wondered how it would be possible to earn a living anyway. The only regret that accompanied this choice was not feeling free to have and educate more than one child, instead of the three or four I would have liked to raise if I had had more income. I've never treated anybody scurvily, at least by my lights, and don't experience chagrin of that sort, looking back. But of course I debate my two marriages, and the crossed wires that sometimes threw sparks, or other friendships that lived or lapsed. At parties, you recognize why old-fashioned women tended to be matchmakers. Couples seem so much happier than single people above a certain age. You rarely meet a widow or widower who is sighing with relief.

Marriage as the long-term pairing of men and women is such a hunter-gatherer sort of idea that its durability testifies to how primeval we still are, despite the voltage and velocities of our compression-chamber days. Our guns and murders do too, and the over-the-mountain infidelities that entertain us, our greed for swapping stacks of greenbacks ("frogskins," they used to be called) for goodies, and the special appetite for travel that seizes us, young and old. We hit the road as kids, and then again as old scouts, furloughed from the city, we retire to cruise ships or Winnebagos 40 years later, feeling we've been bottled up, and forage in foreign markets, roaming for the sake of roving, watching the sun's progress as immemorial theater across the sky.

My work enabled me to travel even during my breadwinning years, in Europe or close to the Arctic or below the Sahara. I found the more you do, the more you're up to doing. Camping in the Rockies prepares you for Alaska, and Alaska for Africa. As you grow relaxed about the procedures of distant travel, you get resourceful about the details, locating a tuning fork within yourself that hears the same note in other people wherever you go. Even in war or famine or dictatorship—because we are not speaking of pollyanna travel—your intuitions are valid because all of us have a rendezvous with death, however humble and anticlimactic that may finally be, and exotic disasters should not be incomprehensible. Like Mobutu or Mussolini, we've been cruel and grandiose, have strutted, lied and postured, known sneaky lust and shifty theft and opportunistic betrayal. The spectrum of behavior we witness in going abroad is seldom all that foreign to us.

The eye surgeon had warned me in 1992 that my blindness was going to recur and I should see whatever of the world I wanted to take in rather soon. So, at around 60, I visited India and Antarctica, each for the first time, and returned to Africa twice. It was different because in the case of India and Antarctica I was treated to blue-ribbon, well-financed wilderness tours of sights I could never have reached when my legs were young and strong. And in Africa I was already known for a book I had written 16 years before. The day after arriving in Nairobi, I got a call at the New Stanley Hotel from a stranger named Rob Rose, who was with the Catholic Relief Services agency and asked if I would like to accompany him the next day on a two-week trip into guerrilla territory in the civil war raging in the southern Sudan, where roughly 2 million people have died.

We set off by Land Rover for Kampala, in Uganda, spent a night, then ventured off quickly through disputed territory in that country's own separate, simmering civil war, up to the town of Gulu, with only one car breakdown. Next morning, we continued north through the hamlet of Atiak and choppy, evacuated grasslands and acacia forests and two military outposts to no man's land and finally the Sudanese village of Nimule. Famine country was just beyond. The Dinka and Nuer had been allied against the Arab government in Khartoum, but now, alas, were fighting against each other as well. Their positions had consequently been shattered, their cattle and grain supplies destroyed. They'd fled to Ethiopia, been defeated there again, and retreated in starving condition back to the Nile. But the aid agencies that had been feeding them, frightened by the lethal infighting—in which three relief workers and a journalist had been shot—had pulled out.

I felt sheepish for not having foreseen more than a hint of these developments during my previous trip. Yet I was white-haired now, which changed the character of my reception, even allowing for the impact of the emergency. One elder thought I must be a "king." When I said America didn't have kings, he amended that to "millionaire," looking at my hiking boots; he was barefoot. A white-haired white man, to have come so far, must be at least a high official of the United Nations who had heard 100,000 people were starving here. Pathetic, short, hand-contoured little mounds paralleled the networks of footpaths where we walked the next day. Each was marked by ragged tokens of the famished body newly buried, a broken doll, a tiny skirt or holey sweater that had been laid on top. Dysentery or pneumonia might have abbreviated the child's suffering, but surely a potent senior figure like me, beholding such a tragedy, might intervene.

My friend Rob, half my age, by dint of sleepless and dynamic initiatives, had indeed brought 58 truckloads of corn from the Catholic Relief Services warehouse in the Kenyan port of Mombasa, the first food delivery in a couple of months to the refugee encampments we visited. In my eyes, he was a genuine hero, braving the dangers here and the U.N.'s tacit boycott. But at Aswa, Amei and Ateppi, smiling desperate children by the many hundreds ran to me, a mere itinerant journalist, to touch my hands and cheer me in the Dinka language as the godfather or patriarch who seemed to have arrived to save their lives. If only more food came!—it may have been the most poignant moment in my life. Some of them, boys and girls of six or 12, had already shrunk to skeletal wraiths, monkey-faced from malnutrition, and I saw newborns who would die without ever tasting milk. Their mothers, stretched beside them on the ground, were themselves dying and, prompted by our guides, partly raised their bodies to show me their flat breasts.

Seven women were said to have been grabbed by crocodiles on the bank of the Nile, where they had gone to try to harvest lily roots or fetch water or spear a fish. Wild dates and nuts and the tufts of ricey wild plants had long since been exhausted, the rats smoked from their holes, the grasshoppers roasted. The local streams had been finger-sieved for shiners and crustaceans, and every songbird slingshotted. The very air smelled burnt.

But lives were being saved by our trip. Even divided among 100,000 souls, 58 truckloads of corn staved off the agony of hunger pangs awhile, and my white pate was winning me more credit than I deserved. The hospital was the worst place, ringed by hungry irregular troops, the famished patients lying bedless on concrete, rationed to one cup of cornmeal per day. The nurses were so weakened they could scarcely function and were distracted by their own children's frantic straits. It seemed shameful for a well-fed man from Vermont to be touring this furnace unscathed, with boys and women rushing to him to intercede in Washington and bring it to an end. I did write about what I had seen, and did at the time shout at the guerrilla general who was thought to have helped precipitate this immediate calamity by setting up the killing of the relief workers (not realizing that white people are as tribal as anybody else), as I would not have had the confidence to do when I was young. At roadblocks I was more at ease when ordered out of the car by teenagers with Kalashnikovs; less edgy when we broke down in Uganda in lion and bandit country. I knew that mines are more of a danger than lions, and malaria more than mortar shells or the kids at a roadblock who are looking for other African teenagers to kill, not a cautious and courteous white man.

Aging is not a serene occupation. You stumble physically and tire quickly, maybe even indoors, and your mind can be tricked by threadbare circuitry into surreal or simple confusions, like the proverbial second childhood, when for a moment you don't know where you are. Not in Africa, though: You're on your toes. And I don't think of travel as a vacation. I'd love to see Venice again, but doubt I have anything to say about it that hasn't been better said. So I turn to the new phenomena of the Third World for trips, barely scratched by various hassled travel writers. I want to work out toward the brink of what I think is going to happen—the widespread death of nature, the approaching holocaust of famines, while Westerners retreat in veiled panic into what they prefer to regard as the realer world of cyberspace. (Old age will not be an enemy, in that event.)

The distractions, ruses, nostrums you used to employ to foil depression, such as sexual flings or mountain climbing, are not in the repertoire of most old guys; and their suicide rate can nearly approximate the febrile teens'. But they're also freer of sexual unease and self-esteem or money compulsions. They may lack money, yet not care as much; can better do without. And "seniors," after all, are living on borrowed time—borrowed from the unborn whose world they're using up. I'm almost twice as old as an average American's life expectancy in Colonial times. Just 100 years ago, I'd be blind, crippled with hernias, if not already dead from asthma, appendicitis or parathyroid disease and other stuff I've had before.

And money can be an equalizer. On a ferryboat from Martha's Vineyard to Cape Cod last summer, I noticed with some sympathy an oldish man standing on the deck, who the whole way across the water, and as if for dear life, hugged a sturdy, gaunt, blond, young-fortyish woman. Balancing uncomfortably against the boat's rock, she patiently allowed him to do as he wished, nursely in manner if not in fact. The two young boys traveling with them looked on, amused or embarrassed, though it was not clear whose kids they originally were, his or hers. From his clinging hunger and needy passion—stock-still on the deck hugging her for 45 minutes, except when she excused herself to go to the bathroom—she was a new and important acquisition for him. He felt thankful and lucky. Though of normal build, he looked frail and unsteady, as if he might have just had a major health scare, and was not making her a spectacle for the sake of the other passengers, but his own. Though she didn't care for the compulsive, public part, on the other hand, like a good sport and with a kind of good-hearted, working-class honesty, she appeared to recognize that it was part of the deal. If you become the third wife of an ailing businessman 25 years older and very much richer than you, and he's recuperating from surgery at his summer home, you let him hug you round-the-clock, with or without an audience.

In my fifties, I had a sizable love affair with a woman 17 years younger than me, a nurse who took me all over Alaska on her supervisory rounds. In chartered Cessnas, we flew to remote Eskimo or Indian villages, sleeping on the floor of the health clinic or school gym while she consulted with patients and the local nurse. Frigid, wild places where in January my eyes sometimes froze shut and I would not have gone by myself, but with her felt both bold and safe, knowing that whatever happened to me, I would not be alone. And somehow, like the Eskimos', her eyelids did not get sealed by the frosts. Nor was she winded or chilled on our strenuous walks. Whatever risks we met, surely she could wiggle me out. I remember hugging her intensely for her sex and youth, and like a lifeline to safety and my own youth. Sometimes she would pull my head next to hers and look in the mirror to see how others visualized us—was I conspicuously wrinkly and gray?—but decided no. We made love extensively every night for weeks, and the age disparity seemed to add spice. A tutor indoors, a dependent outside, I clung and pumped as if doubling my luck, my vanishing span on earth; and if I died I would be in her arms, which would make it all right. Now, I couldn't possibly do the things we did, in bed or out, flying all over Alaska, landing on rivers at hamlets where a white man was not welcome unless he couldn't be ejected because he was with the head nurse. It was delicious to bask in my friend's protection, a further frisson to fanciful sex. And chums who are 80 tell me how much more I'll lose by 70, not to mention at their age, of the physical capacity I had at 53.

But did we—we tend to wonder—capture the spirit of our times? Did we grasp a piece and participate? We know how a composer such as George Gershwin captured the expatriate zest of the 1920s with *An American in Paris* and then in the democratic 1930s wrote *Porgy and Bess*. Aaron Copland, too, not a weather vane, spoke for the thumb-your-nose 1930s with *Billy the Kid* and then did *Appalachian Spring* in the patriotic, heal-the-wounds mid-1940s. Our telescoping century, from the Edwardians through two world wars to cyberspace (my mother, who is still alive, saw the first electric lights and automobiles come to her town), has made it hard to keep current. One wouldn't even *want* to have been a flapper in 1929, a red-hunter a quarter century later, and then a bond salesman in the fabulous 1980s.

I left the city for the country in the 1980s, preferring at that point, I guess, to watch the carnival at one remove, and haven't shifted from typewriting essays to word-processing screenplays, as so many good folks have.

Indeed my politics and style of dress (both shabby Ivy) have scarcely changed since I left college. I pounded cross-country during the 1950s; heard Martin Luther King deliver his radiant speech at the Lincoln Memorial in 1963; protested against Vietnam; and saw ticker-tape parades for FDR, Truman, Eisenhower, Kennedy, Johnson and Nixon, plus King George VI and Charles de Gaulle. Didn't do drugs, but saw action enough, and didn't drop out of the domestic brouhaha until 10 years ago.

I wanted to know shadbush from elderberry, dogwood from choke-cherry, bluebirds from indigo buntings, yellowthroats from yellow warblers, the French horn from an English horn, a trombone from a sousaphone, Red Grange from Red Barber, and Newt Gingrich from Joe McCarthy. We opt for what we want as daily conversation in the privacy of our minds, and whether on most days we get to watch the sunrise and listen to a snatch of the genius of Bach. It's not expensive to pay attention to the phases of the moon, to transplant lemon lilies and watch a garter snake birthing 40 babies and a catbird grabbing some, or listen to the itchy-britches of the Canada geese as autumn waxes. We will be motes in the ocean again soon, leached out of the soil of some graveyard, and everlastingly rocking.

That is my sense of an afterlife and my comfort. The hurly-burly of streambed turmoil will be our last rush-hour traffic—thocketing through boulders, past perch pools and drift logs. Enough, we will say, reaching tide-water. We saw enough.

Suggestions for Discussion

1. According to Edward Hoagland, how does growing older change a person for the better? What are some of the negative aspects of aging?

2. How did Hoagland's period of blindness change his life?

3. What importance does the author place on connecting with nature?

4. How does the author look back on his relationships with women?

Suggestions for Writing

1. If a doctor told you that you would soon go blind, what special sights would you be sure to see before you lost your vision? Why would you pick these particular sights?

2. Some people live their lives thinking primarily of the past; others live only for the present, and still others live with their gaze fixed on the future. How do you tend to live your life? Describe.

∿∿∿∿

HELEN KELLER

Three Days to See

Helen Keller (1880–1968) was deaf and blind from the age of nineteen months. Through her teacher, Annie Sullivan, she learned to communicate by using sign language and later through voice lessons. She graduated from Radcliffe College with honors and wrote a critically acclaimed autobiography, *Story of My Life* (1902). Other books are *Optimism* (1903), *The World I Live In* (1908), and *Out of the Dark* (1913). In this essay, Keller movingly describes the delights she would experience were she to have three days to see.

All of us have read thrilling stories in which the hero had only a limited and specified time to live. Sometimes it was as long as a year; sometimes as short as twenty-four hours. But always we were interested in discovering just how the doomed man chose to spend his last days or his last hours. I speak, of course, of free men who have a choice, not condemned criminals whose sphere of activities is strictly delimited.

Such stories set us thinking, wondering what we should do under similar circumstances. What events, what experiences, what associations should we crowd into those last hours as mortal beings? What happiness should we find in reviewing the past, what regrets?

Sometimes I have thought it would be an excellent rule to live each day as if we should die tomorrow. Such an attitude would emphasize sharply the values of life. We should live each day with a gentleness, a vigor, and a keenness of appreciation which are often lost when time stretches before us in the constant panorama of more days and months and years to come. There are those, of course, who would adopt the epicurean motto of "Eat, drink, and be merry," but most people would be chastened by the certainty of impending death.

In stories, the doomed hero is usually saved at the last minute by some stroke of fortune, but almost always his sense of values is changed. He becomes more appreciative of the meaning of life and its permanent spiritual values. It has often been noted that those who live, or have lived, in the shadow of death bring a mellow sweetness to everything they do.

Most of us, however, take life for granted. We know that one day we must die, but usually we picture that day as far in the future. When we are in buoyant health, death is all but unimaginable. We seldom think of it. The days stretch out in an endless vista. So we go about our petty tasks, hardly aware of our listless attitude toward life.

The same lethargy, I am afraid, characterizes the use of all our faculties and senses. Only the deaf appreciate hearing, only the blind realize the manifold blessings that lie in sight. Particularly does this observation apply to those who have lost sight and hearing in adult life. But those who have never suffered impairment of sight or hearing seldom make the fullest use of these blessed faculties. Their eyes and ears take in all sights and sounds hazily, without concentration and with little appreciation. It is the same old story of not being grateful for what we have until we lose it, of not being conscious of health until we are ill.

I have often thought it would be a blessing if each human being were stricken blind and deaf for a few days at some time during his early adult life. Darkness would make him more appreciative of sight; silence would teach him the joys of sound.

Now and then I have tested my seeing friends to discover what they see. Recently I was visited by a very good friend who had just returned from a long walk in the woods, and I asked her what she had observed. "Nothing in particular," she replied. I might have been incredulous had I not been accustomed to such responses, for long ago I became convinced that the seeing see little.

How was it possible, I asked myself, to walk for an hour through the woods and see nothing worthy of note? I who cannot see find hundreds of things to interest me through mere touch. I feel the delicate symmetry of a leaf. I pass my hands lovingly about the smooth skin of a silver birch, or the rough shaggy bark of a pine. In spring I touch the branches of trees hopefully in search of a bud, the first sign of awakening Nature after her winter's sleep. I feel the delightful, velvety texture of a flower, and discover its remarkable convolutions; and something of the miracle of Nature is revealed to me. Occasionally, if I am fortunate, I place my hand gently on a small tree and feel the happy quiver of a bird in full song. I am delighted to have the cool waters of a brook rush through my open fingers. To me a lush carpet of pine needles or spongy grass is more welcome than the most luxurious Persian rug. To me the pageant of seasons is a thrilling and unending drama, the action of which streams through my finger tips.

At times my heart cries out with longing to see all these things. If I can get so much pleasure from mere touch, how much more beauty must be revealed by sight. Yet, those who have eyes apparently see little. The panorama of color and action which fills the world is taken for granted. It is human, perhaps, to appreciate little that which we have and to long for that which we have not, but it is a great pity that in the world of light the gift of sight is used only as a mere convenience rather than as a means of adding fullness to life.

If I were the president of a university I should establish a compulsory course in "How to Use Your Eyes." The professor would try to show his pupils how they could add joy to their lives by really seeing what passes unnoticed before them. He would try to awake their dormant and sluggish faculties.

Perhaps I can best illustrate by imagining what I should most like to see if I were given the use of my eyes, say, for just three days. And while I am imagining, suppose you, too, set your mind to work on the problem of how you would use your own eyes if you had only three more days to see. If with the oncoming darkness of the third night you knew that the sun would never rise for you again, how would you spend those three precious intervening days? What would you most want to let your gaze rest upon?

I, naturally, should want most to see the things which have become dear to me through my years of darkness. You, too, would want to let your eyes rest long on the things that have become dear to you so that you could take the memory of them with you into the night that loomed before you.

If by some miracle I were granted three seeing days, to be followed by a relapse into darkness, I should divide the period into three parts.

On the first day, I should want to see the people whose kindness and gentleness and companionship have made my life worth living. First I should like to gaze long upon the face of my dear teacher, Mrs. Anne Sullivan Macy, who came to me when I was a child and opened the outer world to me. I should want not merely to see the outline of her face, so that I could cherish it in my memory, but to study that face and find in it the living evidence of the sympathetic tenderness and patience with which she accomplished the difficult task of my education. I should like to see in her eyes that strength of character which has enabled her to stand firm in the face of difficulties, and that compassion for all humanity which she has revealed to me so often.

I do not know what it is to see into the heart of a friend through that "window of the soul," the eye. I can only "see" through my finger tips the outline of a face. I can detect laughter, sorrow, and many other obvious emotions. I know my friends from the feel of their faces. But I cannot really picture their personalities by touch. I know their personalities, of course, through other means, through the thoughts they express to me, through whatever of their actions are revealed to me. But I am denied that deeper understanding of them which I am sure would come through sight of them, through watching their reactions to various expressed thoughts and circumstances, through noting the immediate and fleeting reactions of their eyes and countenance.

Friends who are near to me I know well, because through the months and years they reveal themselves to me in all their phases; but of casual friends I have only an incomplete impression, an impression gained from a handclasp, from spoken words which I take from their lips with my finger tips, or which they tap into the palm of my hand.

How much easier, how much more satisfying it is for you who can see to grasp quickly the essential qualities of another person by watching the subtleties of expression, the quiver of a muscle, the flutter of a hand. But does it ever occur to you to use your sight to see into the inner nature of a friend or acquaintance? Do not most of you seeing people grasp casually the outward features of a face and let it go at that?

For instance, can you describe accurately the faces of five good friends? Some of you can, but many cannot. As an experiment, I have questioned husbands of long standing about the color of their wives' eyes, and often they express embarrassed confusion and admit that they do not know. And, incidentally, it is a chronic complaint of wives that their husbands do not notice new dresses, new hats, and changes in household arrangements.

The eyes of seeing persons soon become accustomed to the routine of their surroundings, and they actually see only the startling and spectacular. But even in viewing the most spectacular sights the eyes are lazy. Court records reveal every day how inaccurately "eyewitnesses" see. A given event will be "seen" in several different ways by as many witnesses. Some see more than others, but few see everything that is within the range of their vision.

Oh, the things that I should see if I had the power of sight for just three days!

The first day would be a busy one. I should call to me all my dear friends and look long into their faces, imprinting upon my mind the outward evidences of the beauty that is within them. I should let my eyes rest, too, on the face of a baby, so that I could catch a vision of the eager, innocent beauty which precedes the individual's consciousness of the conflicts which life develops.

And I should like to look into the loyal, trusting eyes of my dogs—the grave, canny little Scottie, Darkie, and the stalwart, understanding Great Dane, Helga, whose warm, tender, and playful friendships are so comforting to me.

On that busy first day I should also view the small simple things of my home. I want to see the warm colors in the rugs under my feet, the pictures on the walls, the intimate trifles that transform a house into home. My eyes would rest respectfully on the books in raised type which I have read, but they would be more eagerly interested in the printed books which seeing people can read, for during the long night of my life the books I have read and those which have been read to me have built themselves into a great shining lighthouse, revealing to me the deepest channels of human life and the human spirit.

In the afternoon of that first seeing day, I should take a long walk in the woods and intoxicate my eyes on the beauties of the world of Nature, trying desperately to absorb in a few hours the vast splendor which is constantly unfolding itself to those who can see. On the way home from my woodland jaunt my path would lie near a farm so that I might see the patient horses plowing in the field (perhaps I should see only a tractor!) and the serene content of men living close to the soil. And I should pray for the glory of a colorful sunset.

When dusk had fallen, I should experience the double delight of being able to see by artificial light, which the genius of man has created to extend the power of his sight when Nature decrees darkness.

In the night of that first day of sight, I should not be able to sleep, so full would be my mind of the memories of the day.

The next day—the second day of sight—I should arise with the dawn and see the thrilling miracle by which night is transformed into day. I should behold with awe the magnificent panorama of light with which the sun awakens the sleeping earth.

This day I should devote to a hasty glimpse of the world, past and present. I should want to see the pageant of man's progress, the kaleidoscope of the ages. How can so much be compressed into one day? Through the museums, of course. Often I have visited the New York Museum of Natural History to touch with my hands many of the objects there exhibited, but I have longed to see with my eyes the condensed history of the earth and its inhabitants displayed there—animals and the races of men pictured in their native environment; gigantic carcasses of dinosaurs and mastodons which roamed the earth long before man appeared, with his tiny stature and powerful brain, to conquer the animal kingdom; realistic presentations of the processes of evolution in animals, in man, and in the implements which man has used to fashion for himself a secure home on this planet; and a thousand and one other aspects of natural history.

I wonder how many readers of this article have viewed this panorama of the face of living things as pictured in that inspiring museum. Many, of course, have not had the opportunity, but I am sure that many who *have* had the opportunity have not made use of it. There, indeed, is a place to use your eyes. You who see can spend many fruitful days there, but I, with my imaginary three days of sight, could only take a hasty glimpse, and pass on.

My next stop would be the Metropolitan Museum of Art, for just as the Museum of Natural History reveals the material aspects of the world, so does the Metropolitan show the myriad facets of the human spirit. Throughout the history of humanity the urge to artistic expression has been almost as powerful as the urge for food, shelter, and procreation. And here, in the vast chambers of the Metropolitan Museum, is unfolded before me the spirit of Egypt, Greece, and Rome, as expressed in their art. I know well through my hands the sculptured gods and goddesses of the ancient Nile-land. I have felt copies of Parthenon friezes, and I have sensed the rhythmic beauty of charging Athenian warriors. Apollos and Venuses and the Winged Victory of Samothrace are friends of my finger tips. The gnarled, bearded features of Homer are dear to me, for he, too, knew blindness.

My hands have lingered upon the living marble of Roman sculpture as well as that of later generations. I have passed my hands over a plaster cast of Michelangelo's inspiring and heroic Moses; I have sensed the power of

Rodin; I have been awed by the devoted spirit of Gothic wood carving. These arts which can be touched have meaning for me, but even they were meant to be seen rather than felt, and I can only guess at the beauty which remains hidden from me. I can admire the simple lines of a Greek vase, but its figured decorations are lost to me.

So on this, my second day of sight, I should try to probe into the soul of man through his art. The things I knew through touch I should now see. More splendid still, the whole magnificent world of painting would be opened to me, from the Italian Primitives, with their serene religious devotion, to the Moderns, with their feverish visions. I should look deep into the canvases of Raphael, Leonardo da Vinci, Titian, Rembrandt. I should want to feast my eyes upon the warm colors of Veronese, study the mysteries of El Greco, catch a new vision of Nature from Corot. Oh, there is so much rich meaning and beauty in the art of the ages for you who have eyes to see!

Upon my short visit to this temple of art I should not be able to review a fraction of that great world of art which is open to you. I should be able to get only a superficial impression. Artists tell me that for a deep and true appreciation of art one must educate the eye. One must learn through experience to weigh the merits of line, of composition, of form and color. If I had eyes, how happily would I embark upon so fascinating a study! Yet I am told that, to many of you who have eyes to see, the world of art is a dark night, unexplored and unilluminated.

It would be with extreme reluctance that I should leave the Metropolitan Museum, which contains the key to beauty—a beauty so neglected. Seeing persons, however, do not need a Metropolitan to find this key to beauty. The same key lies waiting in smaller museums, and in books on the shelves of even small libraries. But naturally, in my limited time of imaginary sight, I should choose the place where the key unlocks the greatest treasures in the shortest time.

The evening of my second day of sight I should spend at a theater or at the movies. Even now I often attend theatrical performances of all sorts, but the action of the play must be spelled into my hand by a companion. But how I should like to see with my own eyes the fascinating figure of Hamlet, or the gusty Falstaff amid colorful Elizabethan trappings! How I should like to follow each movement of the graceful Hamlet, each strut of the hearty Falstaff! And since I could see only one play, I should be confronted by a many-horned dilemma, for there are scores of plays I should want to see. You who have eyes can see any you like. How many of you, I wonder, when you gaze at a play, a movie, or any spectacle, realize and give thanks for the miracle of sight which enables you to enjoy its color, grace, and movement?

I cannot enjoy the beauty of rhythmic movement except in a sphere restricted to the touch of my hands. I can envision only dimly the grace of a Pavlova, although I know something of the delight of rhythm, for often I can sense the beat of music as it vibrates through the floor. I can well imagine that cadenced motion must be one of the most pleasing sights in the world. I have been able to gather something of this by tracing with my fingers the lines in sculptured marble; if this static grace can be so lovely, how much more acute must be the thrill of seeing grace in motion.

One of my dearest memories is of the time when Joseph Jefferson allowed me to touch his face and hands as he went through some of the gestures and speeches of his beloved Rip Van Winkle. I was able to catch thus a meager glimpse of the world of drama, and I shall never forget the delight of that moment. But, oh, how much I must miss, and how much pleasure you seeing ones can derive from watching and hearing the interplay of speech and movement in the unfolding of a dramatic performance! If I could see only one play, I should know how to picture in my mind the action of a hundred plays which I have read or had transferred to me through the medium of the manual alphabet.

So, through the evening of my second imaginary day of sight, the great figures of dramatic literature would crowd sleep from my eyes.

The following morning, I should again greet the dawn, anxious to discover new delights, for I am sure that, for those who have eyes which really see, the dawn of each day must be a perpetually new revelation of beauty.

This, according to the terms of my imagined miracle, is to be my third and last day of sight. I shall have no time to waste in regrets or longings; there is too much to see. The first day I devoted to my friends, animate and inanimate. The second revealed to me the history of man and Nature. Today I shall spend in the workaday world of the present, amid the haunts of men going about the business of life. And where can one find so many activities and conditions of men as in New York? So the city becomes my destination.

I start from my home in the quiet little suburb of Forest Hills, Long Island. Here, surrounded by green lawns, trees, and flowers, are neat little houses, happy with the voices and movements of wives and children, havens of peaceful rest for men who toil in the city. I drive across the lacy structure of steel which spans the East River, and I get a new and startling vision of the power and ingenuity of the mind of man. Busy boats chug and scurry about the river—racy speed boats, stolid, snorting tugs. If I had long days of sight ahead, I should spend many of them watching the delightful activity upon the river.

I look ahead, and before me rise the fantastic towers of New York, a city that seems to have stepped from the pages of a fairy story. What an awe-inspiring sight, these glittering spires, these vast banks of stone and steel—structures such as the gods might build for themselves! This animated picture is a part of the lives of millions of people every day. How many, I wonder, give it so much as a second glance? Very few, I fear. Their eyes are blind to this magnificent sight because it is so familiar to them.

I hurry to the top of one of those gigantic structures, the Empire State Building, for there, a short time ago, I "saw" the city below through the eyes of my secretary. I am anxious to compare my fancy with reality. I am sure I should not be disappointed in the panorama spread out before me, for to me it would be a vision of another world.

Now I begin my rounds of the city. First, I stand at a busy corner, merely looking at people, trying by sight of them to understand something of their lives. I see smiles, and I am happy. I see serious determination, and I am proud. I see suffering, and I am compassionate.

I stroll down Fifth Avenue. I throw my eyes out of focus so that I see no particular object but only a seething kaleidoscope of color. I am certain that the colors of women's dresses moving in a throng must be a gorgeous spectacle of which I should never tire. But perhaps if I had sight I should be like most other women—too interested in styles and the cut of individual dresses to give much attention to the splendor of color in the mass. And I am convinced, too, that I should become an inveterate window shopper, for it must be a delight to the eye to view the myriad articles of beauty on display.

From Fifth Avenue, I make a tour of the city—to Park Avenue, to the slums, to factories, to parks where children play. I take a stay-at-home trip abroad by visiting the foreign quarters. Always my eyes are open wide to all the sights of both happiness and misery so that I may probe deep and add to my understanding of how people work and live. My heart is full of the images of people and things. My eye passes lightly over no single trifle; it strives to touch and hold closely each thing its gaze rests upon. Some sights are pleasant, filling the heart with happiness; but some are miserably pathetic. To these latter I do not shut my eyes, for they, too, are part of life. To close the eye on them is to close the heart and mind.

My third day of sight is drawing to an end. Perhaps there are many serious pursuits to which I should devote the few remaining hours, but I am afraid that on the evening of that last day I should again run away to the theater, to a hilariously funny play, so that I might appreciate the overtones of comedy in the human spirit.

At midnight my temporary respite from blindness would cease, and permanent night would close in on me again. Naturally in those three short days I should not have seen all I wanted to see. Only when darkness had again descended upon me should I realize how much I had left unseen. But my mind would be so crowded with glorious memories that I should have little time for regrets. Thereafter the touch of every object would bring a glowing memory of how that object looked.

Perhaps this short outline of how I should spend three days of sight does not agree with the program you would set for yourself if you knew that you were about to be stricken blind. I am, however, sure that if you actually faced that fate your eyes would open to things you had never seen before, storing up memories for the long night ahead. You would use your eyes as never before. Everything you saw would become dear to you. Your eyes would touch and embrace every object that came within your range of vision. Then, at last, you would really see, and a new world of beauty would open itself before you.

I who am blind can give one hint to those who see—one admonition to those who would make full use of the gift of sight: Use your eyes as if tomorrow you would be stricken blind. And the same method can be applied to the other senses. Hear the music of voices, the song of a bird, the mighty strains of an orchestra, as if you would be stricken deaf tomorrow. Touch each object you want to touch as if tomorrow your tactile sense would fail. Smell the perfume of flowers, taste with relish each morsel, as if tomorrow you could never smell and taste again. Make the most of every sense; glory in the facts of pleasure and beauty which the world reveals to you through the several means of contact which Nature provides. But of all the senses, I am sure that sight must be the most delightful.

Suggestions for Discussion

1. With what details does Keller suggest the manifold things she observes, feels, and touches after an hour's walk through the woods?

2. What were Keller's criteria for her choices for the first day of seeing? What does she feel she loses in her understanding of her friends because of her lack of sight?

3. What desires and curiosities would be satisfied on Keller's second day?

4. What aspects of the theater does Keller miss in not being able to see?

5. What are Keller's goals in her visit to New York City?

6. What is significant about her plan for the evening of the last day?

7. How would you sum up Keller's values as reflected in her priorities for the three days of seeing?

Suggestions for Writing

1. How would you live each day (or a particular day) if you were to die tomorrow?

2. Write an essay discussing some of the things you take for granted.

3. If you were creating a compulsory course on "How to Use Your Eyes," what assignments would you make?

4. Should you have only three more days to see, how would you spend them?

ESSAYS

༄༅

BRUNO BETTELHEIM

The Child's Need for Magic

Bruno Bettelheim (1903–1990) was born in Vienna and educated at the University of Vienna. Having survived the Nazi Holocaust, he became an American psychoanalyst and educator and was director of the remarkable University of Chicago Sonia Shankman Orthogenic School from 1944 to 1973. He wrote many penetrating works on parents and children and the significance of the Holocaust. In this excerpt from *The Uses of Enchantment* (1976), the author believes that fairy tales provide answers to the child's pressing questions about his identity and his world.

Myths and fairy stories both answer the eternal questions: What is the world really like? How am I to live my life in it? How can I truly be myself? The answers given by myths are definite, while the fairy tale is suggestive; its messages may imply solutions, but it never spells them out. Fairy tales leave to the child's fantasizing whether and how to apply to himself what the story reveals about life and human nature.

The fairy tale proceeds in a manner which conforms to the way a child thinks and experiences the world; this is why the fairy tale is so convincing to him. He can gain much better solace from a fairy tale than he can from an effort to comfort him based on adult reasoning and viewpoints. A child trusts what the fairy story tells, because its world view accords with his own.

Whatever our age, only a story conforming to the principles underlying our thought processes carries conviction for us. If this is so for adults, who have learned to accept that there is more than one frame of reference for comprehending the world—although we find it difficult if not impossible truly to think in any but our own—it is exclusively true for the child. His thinking is animistic.

Like all preliterate and many literate people, "the child assumes that his relations to the inanimate world are of one pattern with those to the animate world of people: he fondles as he would his mother the pretty thing that pleased him; he strikes the door that has slammed on him." It should be added that he does the first because he is convinced that this pretty thing loves to be petted as much as he does; and he punishes the door because he is certain that the door slammed deliberately, out of evil intention.

As Piaget has shown, the child's thinking remains animistic until the age of puberty. His parents and teachers tell him that things cannot feel and act; and as much as he may pretend to believe this to please these adults, or not to be ridiculed, deep down the child knows better. Subjected to the rational teachings of others, the child only buries his "true knowledge" deeper in his soul and it remains untouched by rationality; but it can be formed and informed by what fairy tales have to say.

To the eight-year-old (to quote Piaget's examples), the sun is alive because it gives light (and, one may add, it does that because it wants to). To the child's animistic mind, the stone is alive because it can move, as it rolls down a hill. Even a twelve-and-a-half-year-old is convinced that a stream is alive and has a will, because its water is flowing. The sun, the stone, and the water are believed to be inhabited by spirits very much like people, so they feel and act like people.

To the child, there is no clear line separating objects from living things; and whatever has life has life very much like our own. If we do not understand what rocks and trees and animals have to tell us, the reason is that we are not sufficiently attuned to them. To the child trying to understand the world, it seems reasonable to expect answers from those objects which arouse his curiosity. And since the child is self-centered, he expects the animal to talk about the things which are really significant to him, as animals do in fairy tales, and as the child himself talks to his real or toy animals. A child is convinced that the animal understands and feels with him, even though it does not show it openly.

Since animals roam freely and widely in the world, how natural that in fairy tales these animals are able to guide the hero in his search which takes him into distant places. Since all that moves is alive, the child can believe that the wind can talk and carry the hero to where he needs to go, as in "East of the Sun and West of the Moon." In animistic thinking, not only animals feel and think as we do, but even stones are alive; so to be turned into stone simply means that the being has to remain silent and unmoving for a time. By the same reasoning, it is entirely believable when previously silent objects begin to talk, give advice, and join the hero on his wanderings. And since everything is inhabited by a spirit similar to all other spirits (namely, that of the child who has projected his spirit into all these things), because of this inherent sameness it is believable that man can change into animal, or the other way around, as in "Beauty and the Beast" or "The Frog King." Since there is no sharp line drawn between living and dead things, the latter, too, can come to life.

When, like the great philosophers, children are searching for the solutions to the first and last questions—"Who am I? How ought I to deal with life's problems? What must I become?"—they do so on the basis of their animistic thinking. But since the child is so uncertain of what his existence consists, first and foremost comes the question "Who am I?"

As soon as a child begins to move about and explore, he begins to ponder the problem of his identity. When he spies his mirror image, he wonders whether what he sees is really he, or a child just like him standing behind this glassy wall. He tries to find out by exploring whether this other child is really, in all ways, like him. He makes faces, turns this way or that, walks away from the mirror and jumps back in front of it to ascertain whether this other one has moved away or is still there. Though only three years old, the child is already up against the difficult problem of personal identity.

The child asks himself: "Who am I? Where did I come from? How did the world come into being? Who created man and all the animals? What is the purpose of life?" True, he ponders these vital questions not in the abstract, but mainly as they pertain to him. He worries not whether there is justice for individual man, but whether *he* will be treated justly. He wonders who or what projects him into adversity, and what can prevent this from happening to him. Are there benevolent powers in addition to his parents? Are his parents benevolent powers? How should he form himself, and why? Is there hope for him, though he may have done wrong? Why has all this happened to him? What will it mean for his future? Fairy tales provide answers to these pressing questions, many of which the child becomes aware of only as he follows the stories.

From an adult point of view and in terms of modern science, the answers which fairy stories offer are fantastic rather than true. As a matter of fact, these solutions seem so incorrect to many adults—who have become estranged from the ways in which young people experience the world—that they object to exposing children to such "false" information. However, realistic explanations are usually incomprehensible to children, because they lack the abstract understanding required to make sense of them. While giving a scientifically correct answer makes adults think they have clarified things for the child, such explanations leave the young child confused, overpowered, and intellectually defeated. A child can derive security only from the conviction that he understands now what baffled him before—never from being given facts which create *new* uncertainties. Even as the child accepts such an answer, he comes to doubt that he has asked the right question. Since the explanation fails to make sense to him, it must apply to some unknown problem—not the one he asked about.

It is therefore important to remember that only statements which are intelligible in terms of the child's existing knowledge and emotional preoccupations carry conviction for him. To tell a child that the earth floats in space, attracted by gravity into circling around the sun, but that the earth doesn't fall to the sun as the child falls to the ground, seems very confusing to him. The child knows from his experience that everything has to rest on something, or be held up by something. Only an explanation based on that knowledge can make him feel he understands better about the earth in space. More important, to feel secure on earth, the child needs to believe that this world is held firmly in place. Therefore he finds a better explanation in a myth that tells him that the earth rests on a turtle, or is held up by a giant.

If a child accepts as true what his parents tell him—that the earth is a planet held securely on its path by gravity—then the child can only imagine that gravity is a string. Thus the parents' explanation has led to no better understanding or feeling of security. It requires considerable intellectual maturity to believe that there can be stability to one's life when the ground on which one walks (the firmest thing around, on which everything rests) spins with incredible speed on an invisible axis; that in addition it rotates around the sun; and furthermore hurtles through space with the entire solar system. I have never yet encountered a prepubertal youngster who could comprehend all these combined movements, although I have known many who could repeat this information. Such children parrot explanations which according to their own experience of the world are lies, but which they must believe to be true because some adult has said so. The consequence is that children come to distrust their own experience, and therefore themselves and what their minds can do for them.

In the fall of 1973, the comet Kohoutek was in the news. At that time a competent science teacher explained the comet to a small group of highly intelligent second- and third-graders. Each child had carefully cut out a paper circle and had drawn on it the course of the planets around the sun; a paper ellipse, attached by a slit to the paper circle, represented the course of the comet. The children showed me the comet moving along at an angle to the planets. When I asked them, the children told me that they were holding the comet in their hands, showing me the ellipse. When I asked how the comet which they were holding in their hands could also be in the sky, they were all nonplussed.

In their confusion, they turned to their teacher, who carefully explained to them that what they were holding in their hands, and had so diligently created, was only a model of the planets and the comet. The children all agreed that they understood this, and would have repeated it if questioned further. But whereas before they had regarded proudly this circle-cum-ellipse in their hands, they now lost all interest. Some crumpled the paper up, others dropped the model in the wastepaper basket. When the pieces of paper had been the comet to them, they had all planned to take the model home to show their parents, but now it no longer had meaning for them.

In trying to get a child to accept scientifically correct explanations, parents all too frequently discount scientific findings of how a child's mind works. Research on the child's mental processes, especially Piaget's, convincingly demonstrates that the young child is not able to comprehend the two vital abstract concepts of the permanence of quantity, and of reversibility—for instance, that the same quantity of water rises high in a narrow receptacle and remains low in a wide one; and that subtraction reverses the process of addition. Until he can understand abstract concepts such as these, the child can experience the world only subjectively.

Scientific explanations require objective thinking. Both theoretical research and experimental exploration have shown that no child below school age is truly able to grasp these two concepts, without which abstract understanding is impossible. In his early years, until age eight or ten, the child can develop only highly personalized concepts about what he experiences. Therefore it seems natural to him, since the plants which grow on this earth nourish him as his mother did from her breast, to see the earth as a mother or a female god, or at least as her abode.

Even a young child somehow knows that he was created by his parents; so it makes good sense to him that, like himself, all men and where they live were created by a superhuman figure not very different from his parents— some male or female god. Since his parents watch over the child and provide him with his needs in his home, then naturally he also believes that something like them, only much more powerful, intelligent, and reliable— a guardian angel—will do so out in the world.

A child thus experiences the world order in the image of his parents and of what goes on within the family. The ancient Egyptians, as a child does, saw heaven and the sky as a motherly figure (Nut) who protectively bent over the earth, enveloping it and them serenely. Far from preventing man from later developing a more rational explanation of the world, such a view offers security where and when it is most needed—a security which, when the time is ripe, allows for a truly rational world view. Life on a small planet surrounded by limitless space seems awfully lonely and cold to a child—just the opposite of what he knows life ought to be. This is why the ancients needed to feel sheltered and warmed by an enveloping mother figure. To depreciate protective imagery like this as mere childish projections of an immature mind is to rob the young child of one aspect of the prolonged safety and comfort he needs.

True, the notion of a sheltering sky-mother can be limiting to the mind if clung to for too long. Neither infantile projections nor dependence on imaginary protectors—such as a guardian angel who watches out for one when one is asleep, or during Mother's absence—offers true security; but as long as one cannot provide complete security for oneself, imaginings and projections are far preferable to no security. It is such (partly imagined) security which, when experienced for a sufficient length of time, permits the child to develop that feeling of confidence in life which he needs in order to trust himself—a trust necessary for his learning to solve life's problems through his own growing rational abilities. Eventually the child recognizes that what he has taken as literally true—the earth as a mother—is only a symbol.

A child, for example, who has learned from fairy stories to believe that what at first seemed a repulsive, threatening figure can magically change into a most helpful friend is ready to believe that a strange child whom he meets and fears may also be changed from a menace into a desirable companion. Belief in the "truth" of the fairy tale gives him courage not to withdraw because of the way this stranger appears to him at first. Recalling how the hero of many a fairy tale succeeded in life because he dared to befriend a seemingly unpleasant figure, the child believes he may work the same magic.

I have known many examples where, particularly in late adolescence, years of belief in magic are called upon to compensate for the person's having been deprived of it prematurely in childhood, through stark reality having been forced on him. It is as if these young people feel that now is their last chance to make up for a severe deficiency in their life experience; or that without having had a period of belief in magic, they will be unable to meet the rigors of adult life. Many young people who today suddenly seek escape in drug-induced dreams, apprentice themselves to some guru, believe in astrology, engage in practicing "black magic," or who in some other fashion escape from reality into daydreams about magic experiences which are to change their life for the better, were prematurely pressed to view reality in an adult way. Trying to evade reality in such ways has its deeper cause in early formative experiences which prevented the development of the conviction that life can be mastered in realistic ways.

What seems desirable for the individual is to repeat in his life span the process involved historically in the genesis of scientific thought. For a long time in his history man used emotional projections—such as gods—born of his immature hopes and anxieties to explain man, his society, and the universe; these explanations gave him a feeling of security. Then slowly, by his own social, scientific, and technological progress, man freed himself of the constant fear for his very existence. Feeling more secure in the world, and also within himself, man could now begin to question the validity of the images he had used in the past as explanatory tools. From there man's "childish" projections dissolved and more rational explanations took their place. This process, however, is by no means without vagaries. In intervening periods of stress and scarcity, man seeks for comfort again in the "childish" notion that he and his place of abode are the center of the universe.

Translated in terms of human behavior, the more secure a person feels within the world, the less he will need to hold on to "infantile" projections—mythical explanations or fairy-tale solutions to life's eternal problems—and the more he can afford to seek rational explanations. The more secure a man is within himself, the more he can afford to accept an explanation which says his world is of minor significance in the cosmos. Once man feels truly significant in his human environment, he cares little about the importance of his planet within the universe. On the other hand, the more insecure a man is in himself and his place in the immediate world, the more he withdraws into himself because of fear, or else moves outward to conquer for conquest's sake. This is the opposite of exploring out of a security which frees our curiosity.

For these same reasons a child, as long as he is not sure his immediate human environment will protect him, needs to believe that superior powers, such as a guardian angel, watch over him, and that the world and his place within it are of paramount importance. Here is one connection between a family's ability to provide basic security and the child's readiness to engage in rational investigations as he grows up.

As long as parents fully believed that Biblical stories solved the riddle of our existence and its purpose, it was easy to make a child feel secure. The Bible was felt to contain the answers to all pressing questions: the Bible told man all he needed to know to understand the world, how it came into being, and how to behave in it. In the Western world the Bible also provided prototypes for man's imagination. But rich as the Bible is in stories, not even during the most religious of times were these stories sufficient for meeting all the psychic needs of man.

Part of the reason for this is that while the Old and New Testaments and the histories of the saints provided answers to the crucial questions of how to live the good life, they did not offer solutions for the problems posed by the dark sides of our personalities. The Biblical stories suggest essentially only one solution for the asocial aspects of the unconscious: repression of these (unacceptable) strivings. But children, not having their ids in conscious control, need stories which permit at least fantasy satisfaction of these "bad" tendencies, and specific models for their sublimation.

Explicitly and implicitly, the Bible tells of God's demands on man. While we are told that there is greater rejoicing about a sinner who reformed than about the man who never erred, the message is still that we ought to live the good life, and not, for example, take cruel revenge on those whom we hate. As the story of Cain and Abel shows, there is no sympathy in the Bible for the agonies of sibling rivalry—only a warning that acting upon it has devastating consequences.

But what a child needs most, when beset by jealousy of his sibling, is the permission to feel that what he experiences is justified by the situation he is in. To bear up under the pangs of his envy, the child needs to be encouraged to engage in fantasies of getting even someday; then he will be able to manage at the moment, because of the conviction that the future will set things aright. Most of all, the child wants support for his still very tenuous belief that through growing up, working hard, and maturing he will one day be the victorious one. If his present sufferings will be rewarded in the future, he need not act on his jealousy of the moment, the way Cain did.

Like Biblical stories and myths, fairy tales were the literature which edified everybody—children and adults alike—for nearly all of man's existence. Except that God is central, many Bible stories can be recognized as very similar to fairy tales. In the story of Jonah and the whale, for example, Jonah is trying to run away from his superego's (conscience's) demand that he fight against the wickedness of the people of Nineveh. The ordeal which tests his moral fiber is, as in so many fairy tales, a perilous voyage in which he has to prove himself.

Jonah's trip across the sea lands him in the belly of a great fish. There, in great danger, Jonah discovers his higher morality, his higher self, and is wondrously reborn, now ready to meet the rigorous demands of his superego. But the rebirth alone does not achieve true humanity for him: to be a slave neither to the id and the pleasure principle (avoiding arduous tasks by trying to escape from them) nor to the superego (wishing destruction upon the wicked city) means true freedom and higher selfhood. Jonah attains his full humanity only when he is no longer subservient to either institution of his mind, but relinquishes blind obedience to both id and superego and is able to recognize God's wisdom in judging the people of Nineveh not according to the rigid structures of Jonah's superego, but in terms of their human frailty.

Suggestions for Discussion

1. How does Bettelheim distinguish myths from fairy tales? The Bible from fairy tales?

2. Who is Piaget? How has he influenced current thought regarding the way children think and learn?

3. Explain Bettelheim's reference to children as "animistic thinkers." How does this description of them relate to their need for fairy tales?

4. What similarities does the author see between the child and the philosopher? How do they differ?

5. Explain why Bettelheim believes it is a mistake to deprive children of fairy tales. How does he relate their need for fairy tales to the difficulties they have in comprehending scientific ideas?

Suggestions for Writing

1. Using one or more familiar fairy tales , write an essay explaining how magical elements might serve to explain the universe to a child.

2. Write a comparison between a fairy tale and one of the popular children's stories about ordinary life.

ᔕᔕᔕᔕ

REYNOLDS PRICE

The Great Imagination Heist

Macon, NC, native Reynolds Price (b. 1933) has taught at his alma mater, Duke University, since 1958, and has published more than thirty volumes of fiction, drama, essays, poetry, and translations. A member of the American Academy of Arts and Letters and a James B. Duke Professor of English, Price was a Rhodes Scholar who began a three-year period of study at Merton College, Oxford, in 1955. Nineteen-sixty-two saw the publication of his first novel, *A Long and Happy Life*, which won the William Faulkner Award and has never been out of print. Some of his more recent works include *Kate Vaiden* (which won the National Book Critics Circle Award in 1986), *A Singular Family* (1999), *A Serious Way of Wondering* (2003), and *The Good Priest's Son* (2005). The following passage, from *Feasting the Heart* (2000), is the transcription of one of Price's National Public Radio monologues, part of a series of commentaries that he began broadcasting in July of 1995.

The statistics are famous and unnerving. Most high-school graduates have spent more time watching television than they've spent in school. That blight has been overtaking us for fifty years, but it's only in the past two decades that I've begun to notice its greatest damage to us—the death of personal imagination.

In all the millennia before humans began to read, our imaginations were formed from first-hand experiences of the wide external world and especially from the endless flow of stories passed down in cultures founded on face-to-face narrative conversation. Most of those cultures were succeeded by widespread literacy; and the ensuing torrent of printed information, recordings, and films grew large in making our individual imaginations.

Among the blessings of my past, I'm especially grateful for the fact that I was twenty years old before my parents brought television into our home. Till then, I'd only glimpsed it in store windows and had never missed its brand of time-killing. Like millions in my generation, I was hardly unique in having spent hundreds of childhood hours reading a mountain of books and seeing one or two movies in a public theater each week. Like our ancient ancestors, too, I had the big gift of a family who were steady sources of gripping and delightful stories told at every encounter.

I, and my lucky contemporaries then, had our imaginations fed by an external world, yet a world of nuance and suggestion that was intimately related to our early backgrounds of family and friends. That feeding left us free to remake those stories in accordance with our growing secret needs and natures. Only the movies offered us images and plots that tried to hypnotize us—to channel our fantasies in one direction only—but two to four hours of movies per week were hardly tyrannical.

To say that is not to claim that people who matured before the triumph of TV possessed imaginations that were inevitably free, rich, and healthy. It is to claim that an alarming number of younger Americans have had the early shoots of a personal fantasy life blighted by a dictatorial daylong TV exposure. And not merely blighted—many young Americans have had their native fantasy life removed and replaced by the imaginations of the producers of American television and video games.

My gauge for measuring this massive imagination heist has been my experience with college students in the composition classes I've taught through four decades. When I remove the lenses of nostalgia, I won't claim that the quality of most undergraduate narrative prose in the 1950s was brilliant; but I'm convinced that the imaginations of my present students have suffered badly. When you asked a student of the fifties to write a story, he or she was likely to give you an account that involved personal feeling—a scene from Grandmother's funeral, the death of a pet, the rupture of a marriage, and often family happiness.

Ask the same of students now, and you're likely to get a story that amounts to an airless synopsis of a made-for-TV movie—a stereotypical situation of violence or outlandish adventure that races superficially along, then resolves in emotionless triumph for the student's favorite character. Instead of a human narration, you get a commercially controlled and commercially intended product. *Sit still; buy this.*

How bad is that? Awful—for our public and private safety as well as for most of the arts. What can we do about it? Short of destroying all television sets, computer screens, and video games, I'd suggest at least one countervailing therapy: good reading, vast quantities of active or passive reading—and reading which is, in part, guided by a child's caretakers. No other available resource has such a record of benign influence on maturation. Give every child you cherish good books—human stories—at every conceivable opportunity. If they fail to read them, offer bribes—or whatever other legal means—to help them grow their own imaginations in the slow solitude and silence that makes for general sanity.

Suggestions for Discussion

1. Why does Price feel that people's imaginations have been harmed by television?

2. What differentiates stories written by Price's students in the 1950s from those stories penned by students in more recent times?

3. How does Price suggest that we reclaim our ability to imagine?

Suggestions for Writing

1. Do all movies and television shows stunt imaginative growth, or might the best stories that each medium has to offer inspire the mind to greater heights of creativity? Does Price go too far in his condemnation of the media? What are your views?

2. Write the most original story you can to try to stretch your imagination to its limits.

NOEL PERRIN

Science Fiction: Imaginary Worlds and Real-Life Questions

Noel Perrin (1927–2004) was a professor of English and environmental studies at Dartmouth College, a Vermont farmer, and a frequent contributor to the *New Yorker* and other periodicals. He wrote *A Passport Secretly Green* (1961), *First Person Rural: Essays of a Sometime Farmer* (1980), *Third Person Rural* (1981), *Last Person Rural* (1991), and *Solo: Life with an Electric Car* (1992). This personal account of his role in making science fiction respectable at Dartmouth also claims that it is an art form demanding serious consideration.

Fourteen years ago I began to teach a course in science fiction at Dartmouth College. Spaceships figured in the reading, along with faster-than-light travel, telepathic robots and in one story some bright orange aliens who rather resembled tennis balls on legs.

Not all my colleagues in the English department were embarrassed by the new course, just most. Say, 25 out of 30. In general, they knew just enough about science fiction—without, perhaps, having read any except those two special cases, *Brave New World* and *Nineteen Eighty-four*—to know that it was a formula genre, like the murder mystery, and not worthy of attention in the classroom. But they were powerless to stop the new course, or at least it would have taken a concerted effort. I was chairman of the department at the time, and my last year in office I spent such credit as I had left on getting the science fiction course approved.

Why did I want a science fiction course? It is not self-evident that Dartmouth students need to hear about tennis-ball-shaped aliens. Was I maybe pandering to popular taste, as chairmen often do when they want to build enrollment? (If so, it worked. About 160 students signed up that first year, and still more would have if we hadn't quickly closed the course.)

If I was pandering, it certainly wasn't conscious. I wanted the course for what seemed to me the very highest of reasons. I thought that the most important questions of the 20th century got more attention in works of science fiction than anywhere else. Fairly often they even got answers.

Some of these questions are quite specific. What might it feel like to live in the age after a nuclear war? Just how possible will it be, perhaps in the not so distant future, to turn all work over to robots? Since we can splice genes, what kind of creatures will we make of ourselves? Others are as broad as questions can get. What is the good life for human beings? What are our duties, if any, to other life-forms? If we can, should we abolish death? (That's a genuine issue. Some scientists think a form of immortality is no more than a century away.)

Philosophers once used to ask some of the same questions. A few of them still do. But to most philosophers the broad questions seem naïve, the product of an outdated metaphysics, and the narrow ones demand a range of technical knowledge most philosophers don't have.

More recently, novelists pondered many of the more metaphysical issues—until both they and critics realized that literature is self-referential and not much of a guide to the real world. Mainstream fiction now mostly flows in more private directions.

But science fiction, immensely sophisticated about technology, has stayed naïve about metaphysics—naïve in the sense that most science fiction writers continue to suppose that questions of value can be meaningfully discussed. (I suppose that, too. If I didn't, I would probably resign my job.) In fact, science fiction has become the chief refuge for metaphysics. It is where you go in literature if you want to hear people openly and seriously talking about meaning, and especially meaning in a world increasingly made and controlled by ourselves.

That is the main reason I wanted a science fiction course, but it is not the only one. There is also the question of literary merit. I support as much as any of my colleagues the notion that a genre needs to have attained a high level of distinction before it deserves to be taught in a course. I also think science fiction has attained that level. But it is not amazing that most professors of English failed to perceive that in 1975.

To begin with, though science fiction was well out of its infancy in 1975—was in fact about a hundred years old—it still seemed new. For example, with rare exceptions, it attained the dignity of being published in hard cover only in the 1960's. More serious science fiction was (and is) hard to distinguish from a couple of seedy cousins. If you were to pose the three for a group picture, you would put science fiction in the middle, clean-faced and intelligent. On one side, wearing stage armor, would be the sword-and-sorcery novel. On the other, holding a couple of laser pistols and wearing a gaudy helmet, space opera. Both these genres *are* formulaic, derivative, unworthy of being taught. And both are so interactive with science fiction that they can sometimes inhabit the same book. But science fiction is a much more serious genre, which, instead of trafficking in pure fantasy, attempts to be scientifically and logically responsible to the real universe.

Frank Herbert's *Dune,* for example, is part sword-and-sorcery—though in his case I prefer the politer name of heroic fantasy. There are witches in the book, prophecies, much hand-to-hand combat. But the book is also full of spaceships, personal atomic weapons and advanced ecology, and is partly science fiction.

Or take Larry Niven and Jerry Pournelle's book *The Mote in God's Eye,* once described by Robert A. Heinlein, one of the eminences of the field, as possibly the finest science fiction novel he'd ever read. The half of the book devoted to the alien creatures called Moties is indeed major science fiction. But the other half! That takes place aboard a starship of the Imperial Space Navy (I can see my colleagues grinning at the very name), and it reeks of space opera.

I doubt if any of my colleagues had read or even heard of *The Mote in God's Eye* in 1975. But they had certainly picked up on its vibes, as one would have said back then. They knew about space opera, and they erroneously thought that no science fiction existed without it.

In fact, enough science fiction of high literary quality, pure and unmixed with either space opera or fantasy, already existed to fill two or three courses. Easy to assert, hard to prove. What I shall do is name a few of the ones I actually used. The one that gave me the most private amusement was a novella written back in 1909. The author, an Englishman, had been reading H. G. Wells and had been so put off by what he saw as Wells's mindless faith in technology that he wrote his own work of science fiction as a riposte. Thus it came about that in the spring of 1975 one member of the department was teaching E. M. Forster's *Passage to India* in the 20th-century British novel course while I was simultaneously teaching *The Machine Stops* by the same E. M. Forster in the new science fiction course. It fitted in nicely. Just as Forster had written in response to Wells, so Arthur C. Clarke much later was moved to answer Forster in *The City and the Stars;* and that brooding novel—it deals with earthly immortality—was also in the course.

But there are not a lot of Huxleys, Orwells and Forsters who once or twice in their lives come trailing clouds of respectability into science fiction. Most of the good work (and virtually all of the bad) is by people who start out in science fiction, and who, along with all their books, were invisible to my colleagues in 1975. Such were three of the other works I taught.

The star of the course was undoubtedly Walter Miller's extraordinary novel, *A Canticle for Leibowitz.* It's the best and wisest of all novels about the world after a nuclear war, and also the most exhilarating to read. You didn't know a novel about a radioactive world *could* be exhilarating? You haven't read *Canticle* then.

Then I had Samuel R. Delany's story "We, in Some Strange Power's Employ, Move on a Rigorous Line." It's about employees of the one great power company that serves the whole planet, maybe 60 years from now, when the remotest Tibetan village is guaranteed access to electricity. It's also about what constitutes the good life, and about destiny, and about ambition. It operates on more levels than William Empson could have counted, including one on which the story plays off Spenser's *Faerie Queene,* though so unobtrusively that no Dartmouth student has yet noticed. Mr. Delany is the first major black science fiction writer to emerge, not that I knew that in 1975. I just knew that he had written a classic story.

And I also taught Ursula K. Le Guin's *Left Hand of Darkness,* a novel that goes so far beyond either feminism or male chauvinism as to leave people attached to either gender gasping in the dust. One way I know the book's power is that it has consistently stimulated good papers from students—some of the best papers I have ever got in any course.

A book focused on sex and gender is, of course, bound to be deeply interesting to 20-year-olds. I mean, even more interesting than to the rest of us. But *Left Hand* does more than speculate on what human beings would be like if all of us belonged to both sexes and were likely to be active in a male phase one month and female the next. It tells a heroic story. It develops rounded characters, most of them two-sexed inhabitants of the planet Gethen, but one a male visitor from Earth. (His nickname among Gethenians is "the pervert.") It brings a whole imagined world into plenary existence. There is nothing of formula here. There is high literature.

Three student generations have passed since those books were picked. (Not that I mean to claim pioneer status for the course. The first regular science fiction course seems to have been given at Colgate University in 1962.) If much good literature was available back then, vastly more is now. The late 20th century has been the golden age of science fiction.

In this country, writer after fine writer has emerged. I think of Michael Bishop, whose novella *Death and Designation Among the Asadi* gives so powerful a sense of what it would really be like to encounter—and not to understand—an alien intelligence that one understands even Columbus differently after reading it. I think of Alice Sheldon, the woman who wrote as James

Tiptree, Jr. Her depiction of life aboard a United Nations starship in the novella *A Momentary Taste of Being* is to the Niven-Pournelle account of the Imperial Space Navy as a real horse is to a child's drawing. I think of Judith Moffett, who just two or three years ago turned from a successful career as a poet to a still more successful one as a writer of science fiction. Her first novel, *Pennterra,* the only work of Quaker science fiction I know, already establishes her as a presence in the field. It's as interesting ecologically as literarily.

Meanwhile, translation of major work from other parts of the world has proceeded rapidly. The most impressive examples have come from the Soviet Union and its satellites. Science fiction has its Borges in the person of Stanislaw Lem of Poland. I'm thinking especially of *The Cyberiad,* his mock-epic about cybers—that is, cybernetic beings, or robots. Mr. Lem's elaborate fantasies are less *outré* than the reader first supposes. In the real world, computer science students at the Massachusetts Institute of Technology are already wondering—as he has in this fiction—whether it will constitute murder when someone first unplugs a self-aware robot.

Among the Eastern Europeans, I particularly admire Arkady and Boris Strugatsky, Russian brothers whose jointly written novels dominate Soviet science fiction and are among the best in the world. If American publishers had the decency to keep them in print, I would always have had one in the course—most often, probably, *Roadside Picnic,* despite the bad translation in which it comes to us. The concept of the book is wonderful—that at some point a few years hence a group of aliens pauses briefly on Earth without our ever noticing and carelessly leaves a little debris behind when they go, like sandwich bags and soda cans after a picnic. We, like, ants, find it. And it is as mysterious to us as a soda can to an ant, which doesn't even know what Nutrasweet *is,* let alone its risks.

In 1989 I don't suppose that more than half the department is embarrassed by the existence of the course. Maybe less. But not many of my colleagues see it as important, either. I no longer teach the course. (I burn out on any course after a few years—13 with science fiction is my record for longevity.) The department's response has been to "bracket" the course. It will stay in the catalogue, but for now at least it will not be taught.

I admit that some of my colleagues' literary misgivings have been justified. Not about the books, but about me. I have found the metaphysics too tempting. Once a colleague came across a copy of my final exam. There was a perfectly decent question or two about narrational mode and so on, but there was also a question that asked simply, "If it were in your power to air-condition this planet, would you?"

Of course I can see why a literary theorist might shudder at such an exam. And I would be perfectly happy to have the department hire a replacement who would deal with science fiction in more rigorous and analytical ways. Such is the power of the genre that the metaphysics would come through anyway.

Suggestions for Discussion

1. What is Perrin's basic argument for including a course in science fiction in the English department curriculum? Does he make a good case? How?

2. What distinction does Perrin make between science fiction on one hand and the sword-and-sorcery novel and space opera on the other? With what works of space opera are you familiar?

3. Discuss Perrin's reasons for describing works by Miller, Delany, Le Guin, and others as profound works of fiction. Have you read any of the works he mentions? Does his description of them make you want to read them? Why?

4. What is the tone of this essay? How does Perrin establish it? Why does he disparage his final examination question that he quotes?

5. Discuss Perrin's statement that if he did not believe questions of value can be meaningfully discussed, he would give up teaching.

Suggestions for Writing

1. Write a paper in which you explain whether you think a work of science fiction has significance as literature. Notice how Perrin presents his evaluations and attempt to follow his example in your own essay.

2. Write an essay in which you discuss the proposition that what Perrin calls sword-and-sorcery works and space opera are not serious works of literature. Use as many examples, including film, as you think necessary to persuade your reader.

∽∾∽∾

JOAN E. HARTMAN

What We Did and Why We Did It

Joan E. Hartman (b. 1930) is professor emerita of English at the College of Staten Island, CUNY. She has written about early modern women writers, women in the profession, and women's studies. In this essay, she looks back at changes in the academy and explains why these days it is a better place than it was for women—students as well as faculty.

"I'm not a feminist," my women students are likely to say. I hear them, and I know what they mean. I tell them that I am a feminist and have worked, over the past thirty-five or more years, to bring about changes that make women's lives better. If they inquire, I talk a bit about what things were like "back then." The subject of women's lives "back then" is likely to arise in my classes, for, after all, I teach literature. Often students are surprised to discover how restricted and oppressed women were "back then" and how, in addition to the virulent misogyny (that is, hatred of women) present in some literature, a sort of casual misogyny easily surfaces. Women are represented as intellectually deficient, incapable of abstract thought and rational behavior; frivolous, silly, unreliable, materialistic, extravagant; preoccupied with domesticity and gossip; and sexually provocative, whether unchaste or cruelly chaste, whores or virgins.

Why should women in college be feminists? They have benefited from changes that I take credit for helping to make. When the second women's movement began, back in the late 1960s and early 1970s, today's younger college women were yet unborn; older women now returning to college or starting it for the first time were then bearing and raising children. That women constitute more than half the college students now, that older women who did not go to college feel empowered to attend now, that many of their professors are women because women attend graduate school in increasing numbers now (earning more than half the doctorates awarded in some disciplines)—all these changes are the result of the second women's movement. When I was in college, while we didn't wear bustles and high-buttoned shoes, we didn't take higher education for granted either.

Education has always been important to women, and it still is. Our foremothers, at a time when higher education was restricted to men, argued for and worked to provide more education for women. Mary Wollstonecraft, for example, discussed its importance in *A Vindication of the Rights of Woman* (1792), its title an ironic paraphrase of Thomas Paine's *The Rights of Man*. If men refuse to educate women, she inquired, why should they not be intellectually deficient, frivolous, and preoccupied with domesticity? She saw education, then, as the key to greater equality for women. So did the women (and men) who founded women's colleges in the nineteenth century and saw to it that women were admitted to (at least a few) coeducational institutions. I read to my students, when I can, some of the dire consequences that medical doctors, writing in the nineteenth century, predicted in consequence of permitting women to attend college: shriveled ovaries (the result of redirecting blood from their reproductive systems to their brains), unhealthy children, and emotional and sexual maladjustment.

My students expect their education to equip them to do the world's work. It will. Nevertheless, they will continue to lag behind the men they are educated alongside of in their pay. Measuring it in relation to men's pay is statistically complicated; I'll take, for my argument, that women's pay has now risen to eighty cents to men's dollar, which is better than it used to be but hardly equal. Defenders of the status quo may argue for differences in pay as legitimate on grounds that women are biologically different in brains and consequently deficient in aptitudes that fit them for high-paying careers involving mathematics and science. They may argue for differences in pay as legitimate on grounds that women lack ambition to choose challenging careers. They may argue, with evidence, that women stop working to have and to raise children and, more often than men, work part-time. But my women students, having demonstrated their abilities in college, are more likely to encounter differences in pay and feel their injustice after they graduate from college. They are more likely to become feminists then.

The *we* of my title, the doers, are academic feminists, feminists in a number of disciplines, not just mine, literature. We experienced the gendered arrangements of the academy with particular acuteness after leaving graduate school and entering it as professionals. Obviously feminists outside the academy working for women's rights in the early days of the second women's movement encouraged us, nourished our sense of injustice, and gave us hope that change was possible. Some of us thought that the war in Vietnam and civil rights at home should take precedence and that our agenda for women should wait. But we pressed on. And, it must be said, change in the academy has been more possible than change in society at large, though, of course, there has been change there too.

Women in the academy, stirred by events outside the academy, started talking to each other about our lives in ways that we had not done before. This talk, called consciousness-raising then, existed in many forms, sometimes organized, sometimes disorganized and spontaneous. It took place locally, in our own institutions, and nationally, in our professional societies. It gave us a sense of who we were and, more important, a sense that we were not alone in our problems and difficulties and not at individual fault. There were mismatches between us and our work and many of them weren't necessary. We agreed that the academy should and could be changed and, acting in concert, began to change it. We learned how institutions and professions worked and where power lay; we brainstormed strategies to get some of it for ourselves. We propped each other up and took risks that gave us a heady sense of doing important things. We also knew that, out there, other women were doing similar things. Before xeroxing, not to mention the internet, we relied on primitive technologies such as mimeographing and dittoing to keep each other informed: many a call to action or a syllabus for a women's studies course came in the purple print of a ditto.

Whatever differences divided us from each other as a we—and there were some, often intense—we were united in three endeavors: we wanted to look out for ourselves and women colleagues, we wanted to improve the academic experiences of women students (with some consciousness-raising thrown in), and, simultaneously, we wanted to change our disciplines and, eventually, to establish a new field, women's studies. At the time these enterprises seemed to be seamlessly interconnected. We didn't categorize them: one thing led to the next, to the next, and on to the next. Only later did it become clear that we were advancing a single project on several fronts.

Our talking with each other clarified our sense of how the academy sorts faculty and students by gender. Men were hired by first-tier institutions, that is, by major research universities and the elite men's colleges. Women were hired by second- and third-tier institutions, that is, by smaller, less wealthy and less research-oriented universities, women's colleges, coeducational colleges, and two-year colleges. Men taught fewer and better-trained undergraduate students than women, instructed graduate students, were awarded time for research and writing, and were paid more than women. Not all men, of course, benefited from this sorting, but "back then," when I entered the profession, it was even possible for first-tier public institutions with coeducational student bodies not to interview women for positions, much less hire them, and to avow their policy openly. There were also many more single-sex colleges then than there are now; it was considered appropriate for women in women's colleges to be taught by men, singularly inappropriate for men in men's colleges to be taught by women.

A survey of faculty in my field in 1972–1973 showed that men were substantially represented at universities and four-year colleges (41 percent of them at universities, 42 percent at four-year colleges) and lightly represented at two-year colleges (only 17 percent of them). Women, on the other hand, were underrepresented at universities (only 28 percent of them), about equally represented at four-year colleges (44 percent of them), and overrepresented at two-year colleges (28 percent of them). Wherever they taught, however, the pattern was the same: men were to be found at the top of the heap with respect to both rank and salary, women at the bottom. This pattern was of course repeated in most professions and occupations—and still is, though more women are now to be found in the middle of the heap. But it's a pattern that's easy to document in academe, first, because there's a standard terminology for designating rank—lecturer or instructor, assistant professor, associate professor, professor—and second, because the American Association of University Professors publishes an annual survey of academic ranks and salaries. National statistics were empowering to me and my women colleagues: they ratified our sense that women at our institution got bad deals.

When other issues not related to gender surfaced in my department we were able, with the help of equally unhappy male colleagues, to stage a palace revolution. We elected a woman chair and made the proceedings of the department—course assignments, schedules, and personnel decisions—as open as we could. (The dethroned men were certainly unhappy at their loss of power, but we were careful not to retaliate against them.) Women in my department also became active in the governance of the college and made it our business to meet women in other departments. Gradually our projects became college-wide: we agitated for an affirmative action officer and served on the committee that chose her, we supported women faculty who were having difficulty with reappointment, tenure, and promotion, we looked for women faculty in a variety of disciplines to teach courses with a focus on women, and we joined with students we met in these classes to work for a women's center, which we eventually got.

We also joined with women at other institutions in The City University of New York to create an umbrella organization, the CUNY Women's Coalition, that did university-wide some of the things we were doing locally. It also did what was difficult to do locally: it sued the university for discrimination against women in a class-action suit, that is, a suit on behalf of all women faculty in the university. The suit, filed with the Equal Employment Opportunity Commission in 1972 and in federal court in 1973, was finally decided in 1984, in our favor. Women employed by CUNY and women who had been employed by CUNY were awarded money in recognition that, equally accomplished as their male colleagues at all ranks, they had been promoted more slowly and paid less; in addition, it became a matter of record that CUNY had discriminated against women.

As these things were happening at my own institution, I was also asked to join my profession's Commission on the Status of Women, organized under the aegis of the Modern Language Association. One of the Commission's important tasks was to collect information about the unequal status of women and make recommendations to remedy it. Their studies make dry reading—but the statistics mattered: they demonstrated the extent to which women were tracked into institutions that denied them access to the perquisites that enabled men to amass substantial publication records and reputations. The remedies were obvious: to hire women in full-time, tenure-track positions in numbers that approximated their earning doctorates; to make their salaries commensurate with those of men with similar qualifications; to put in place flexible policies that accommodated the facts of women's lives such as childbearing; and to abolish antinepotism rules (that is, rules that kept couples from being hired by the same institution). What was impressive about these studies was how much women had managed to accomplish in spite of the limitations placed upon them by their gender.

So much for improving our own academic experiences: what we wanted was quite straightforward. What we wanted to improve our students' academic experiences was more complicated—it always is complicated to wish for someone else without foisting one's own desires off on them. We tried to engage students in articulating their own desires. Inevitably, however, we came up against differences in power. We were more articulate than they were, we understood the academy better than they did, and we had some power to change it. Our impulses were to change it in ways that would have made it more encouraging and comfortable for us when we were, as undergraduates, aspiring academics. Yet few of our students were aspiring academics; many were not and would not be, no matter how encouraging and comfortable they found the academy.

Changing institutional arrangements to acknowledge the presence of women as students, faculty, and even administrators was uncomplicated. We made practically everyone self-conscious about sexist language. We insisted on department *chairpersons* (instead of department *chairmen*) and taught the virtues of pluralizing: *students* and *they* instead of the *student* and *he*. Of course chairperson was cumbersome and ugly; so what? It called attention to our point, that chairing departments was also women's work. We looked at course titles and descriptions when courses came up for review. I recollect challenging the title of an environmental studies course called "Man and Nature" on the floor of the college council. The title came back as "The Environment and the Biosphere," as cumbersome and ugly as could be. I suspected that the (male) faculty had come up with it on purpose to embarrass me but I didn't challenge it again. Our business was to remind male colleagues that there were women in their classes, by count, over half the student body. While they might be supportive of women students woman by woman, conventional attitudes to women as a group slipped into their language and, undoubtedly, into their behavior. Altering their language was possible; we hoped, in consequence, for altered behavior. We managed our linguistic crusades with good temper. Probably there were grumbles about us as thought police, but I for one wasn't challenged face-to-face.

The policies against sexual harassment we implemented were more controversial than the policies about sexist language. Happily, at my institution, we didn't have to write our own policies, for discussions about what does and does not constitute sexual harassment are fraught with tension; CUNY formed a university-wide committee and wrote one for the entire university. We know that sexual harassment exists. Teaching can be a sexy business, especially when older men with power and authority instruct younger, attractive women. (There have also been instances in which women with power and authority have been accused: see Jane Gallop's *Feminist Accused of Sexual Harassment* [1997]. These get considerable publicity.) But possibilities for false accusations and the need to protect the rights of the accused as well as those of the accuser are enormously complex. The structures for adjudicating complaints at my institution (and most institutions) are now in place and known; whether they are sufficient or used as much as they ought to be isn't clear. At least sexual harassment in colleges and universities is no longer a dirty little secret.

Changes in our classrooms and, in general, changes in our relations with our women students were more complicated than either changing sexist language or implementing policies against sexual harassment. What we tried to do in our women's studies courses was, on the one hand, to decenter our own authority as teachers and, on the other hand, to make students more active participants in their own learning. Many of us were trying to shift our emphasis from teaching to learning in other courses as well: feminist pedagogy overlaps and meshes with two other kinds of pedagogy we were working on "back then," constructionist teaching and collaborative learning. I've written on their interrelationships elsewhere (see *(En)Gendering Knowledge: Feminists in Academe* [1991]): let me sketch them out here. Constructionist teaching looks at how knowledge is made as well as at knowledge itself, it presents knowledge as contingent, made by persons with individual identities, not by abstract and ideal knowers. Individual knowers can be expected to recognize the ways their personal histories affect their investigations; distortions ensue when they imagine they have no personal histories to scrutinize. Collaborative learning asks students to teach each other, to foreground how they make knowledge, to share it, to contest it, and, in consequence, to become more self-reliant learners.

Feminist pedagogy adds to constructionist teaching and collaborative learning a common gender. My feminist colleagues and I talked a lot with each other about our own educations and what it took for us to think of ourselves as makers of knowledge instead of just receivers of knowledge made by others. We weren't born with the confidence that we could make knowledge and we remembered looking at those who seemed to have been born with it—boys, usually, in elementary and high school, young men in college and graduate school—with awe. Of course we'd been socialized to be insecure about our intellectual authority. We shared the routes we'd taken ourselves to become more confident and the strategies we'd been using, even before feminism had articulated our commitments to women students, to pass on to them what had helped us, to restage for them moments that had been important to us in staking out our own authority. We recounted instances in which we'd been able to construct fresh arguments. We invented assignments in which we thought students could construct fresh arguments. We set students to teaching each other. We resisted their looking to us for approval: "You decide," we told them. Collaborative learning works particularly well with women, who by and large don't use collaboration to show off and to put each other down. (Not all men use it to show off—I don't like to engage in gender stereotyping—but they are often socialized to compete with each other and their socialization plays out in the classroom.)

All of us who began to teach women's studies had some marvelously intense and productive courses. We couldn't restrict them to women, not at a public institution, but they were always composed predominantly of women, sometimes exclusively of women. Women students, for the first time—unless they'd attended single-sex schools—heard lots of women's voices and experienced women taking charge of discussions. I did my first women's studies teaching in the evening session, to a group of older women, when an imaginative (woman) dean put together paired courses two nights a week, one a course in the Sociology of Women, the other a course in novels by and about women, which I taught. I sometimes sat in on the sociology course as well. I can't remember whether or not students were required to take both courses; most of them did. They had come with an interest in what they were hearing about the second women's movement; many of them had talked about it with friends and relations and had been rebuffed. They quickly built a community around issues in their lives that connected with the material they were studying. They were capable of and motivated to do the reading. They wanted to discuss it, or most of it, and when they were tuned out they deferred to those who were tuned in. It was a lovely experience to teach them. And certainly, by the evidence of their papers, they learned a lot from the reading they did and also came to write more clearly and incisively than they had when they began the course.

I've had other women's studies courses that went equally as well and some that were difficult. Students took the course because it fit in their schedules, not because they were interested. The intimacy of the discussions generated antagonisms. I still remember with distress one course in which I thought the students were angry with me most of the time. As it turned out, they weren't as angry with me as they were with each other. Also constructivist pedagogy and collaborative learning demand a lot of work from students; it's easier for them to sit back, memorize what professors say, and repeat it. I own to demanding a lot of work from my students; they will complain that it's too much (though some of them will also admit to a kind of pride at having met my expectations). And what I take to be my decentered authority can still seem to them heavy-handed—or else no authority at all. I try to distinguish between the authority that comes from speaking for an "interpretive community" (Stanley Fish's term for an academic community that upholds agreed-on interpretations; see *Is There A Text in This Class?* [1980]) and the lesser authority that comes from speaking for myself.

Which brings me to academic feminists' third endeavor, to change our disciplines and establish a new field, women's studies. My discipline, literature, was open to feminist change on two fronts. We weren't out to banish the works of Dead White Males from the curriculum, as some would luridly have had it—after all, our love for their works led us to study and teach literature in the first place. But we did read canonical male writers with new, more critical eyes, looking at the ways they reflected their culture's assumptions about the nature of women and women's place in society. And we also began to study and teach more women writers, looking at the ways they conformed to or challenged their culture's assumptions about women and women's place in society. We considered their biographies: how did they manage to write? How did they overcome what was often their own reluctance to make themselves visible? How did publishers come to print their works?

There have always some canonical women writers, mostly nineteenth-century British novelists: Jane Austen (who published, anonymously, as "a Lady") and three who published under male pseudonyms, Charlotte Broönte (as Currer Bell), Emily Brontë (as Ellis Bell), and Maryann Evans (as George Eliot). We discovered neglected women writers whose works we thought remarkably interesting and included them on our syllabi. Let me mention some in my own area, British literature of the sixteenth and seventeenth centuries. While we still read, of course, Shakespeare and Sidney, Spenser and Milton, we also read Aphra Behn, Elizabeth Carey, Lucy Hutchinson, Aemilia Lanyer, Katharine Philips, Mary Sidney, and Mary Wroth, to mention a few. (Notice that I don't have to identify Shakespeare as William but do have to identify Behn as Aphra.) We edited their works to make them available. We wrote their biographies. We investigated the mechanisms that consigned them to oblivion while their male contemporaries made it into literary histories, were written about by literary scholars and critics, and got themselves included on syllabi. Consulting the 1789–1815 volume of the Oxford History of English literature (published in 1963) that should have included Mary Wollstonecraft in order to check her dates, I found no individual entry for her, though I did for find individual entries for her husband William Godwin and, in the next volume, for their daughter Mary Godwin Shelley, the author of *Frankenstein* and wife of the poet Shelley. There's a new multi-volume Oxford history in preparation; I warrant Mary Wollstonecraft will get her own space in it. She, like other previously neglected women writers we discovered, is now included in graduate school syllabi and taught in undergraduate courses by practically everyone.

We also established a new field, women's studies. It began in the classroom: feminists in many disciplines began teaching courses that focused on women and calling into question the masculinist constructs of their disciplines. They talked to each other, across disciplines, about what they were doing. They shared syllabi. They read what was being written in disciplines not their own. The pattern replicates that of the first women's studies course I taught in tandem with a course taught by a sociologist; we learned from each other.

In colleges and universities segmented by disciplines and organized by departments, interdisciplinary studies are difficult, both older interdisciplinary studies such as Medieval Studies and Eighteenth-Century Studies, for example, and newer interdisciplinary studies such as African-American Studies, Gay and Lesbian Studies, and Women's Studies. Most faculty remain in traditional departments, reluctant to teach outside the discipline in which they are certified specialists. Interdisciplinary teaching within the confines of a single course is often a collaboration of two or more faculty—and expensive. A few institutions offer advanced degrees in Women's Studies; most often it is a specialty added on to a degree in a traditional discipline. But there are interdisciplinary conferences and interdisciplinary journals that cross disciplines and blur their boundaries. We borrow from each other; we scavenge from each other.

Back in 1991 Ellen Messer-Davidow and I put together a collection of essays called *(Ex) Gendering Knowledge: Feminists in Academe.* We wanted to investigate how feminism was altering various disciplines and also whether Women's Studies was a discipline with its own subject and methods or a place where feminists dispersed among disciplines met. She held it to be a discipline in its own right; I held it to be an interdisciplinary administrative arrangement that brought together dispersed feminists. As I recollect, we even diagrammed our conceptions, she drawing a dome with a cupola, I a grid.

(Ex) Gendering Knowledge showed our disagreement to be oversimple. Across disciplines, we and our contributes discovered, we share a set of beliefs, practices, and values. We believe that knowers—us—are located in particular situations rather than being detached and Olympian, above it all. We are alike in our feminist commitments but different according to our age, class, race, sexual orientation, and the discipline we have chosen. We come to feminism with different life experiences. Nevertheless, we choose our disciplinary projects among the range of possibilities offered by our disciplines because they matter to us. We choose our investigative strategies because they are congenial to us and productive of consequences we like. We value accuracy and completeness in our research; we also value women, compassion, and social justice. We think knowledge makes things happen and we look carefully at the consequences of the knowledge we make. These beliefs, practices, and values are not limited to Women's Studies but they are specific to it. One reviewer of *(En) gendering Knowledge* commented (justly): "Some of what these essays say may be familiar to their authors' colleagues, but the overviews they offer are fascinating and their juxtapositions are provocative: the reader comes to see that feminist scholarship is doing a wide variety of things but that it is also doing related things."

This, then, is what we did and why we did it. If someone had predicted, back in the grey Eisenhower years when I was in college and in graduate school, that the academy would change in the ways that I've described and that I'd have a hand in changing it, I'd have stared at them in disbelief. But now it is a better place for women, both faculty and students, than it was, and I look to the next generation of I'm-not-a-feminist feminists to keep it a better place.

Suggestions for Discussion

1. Why might today's students, female and male, be reluctant to identify themselves as feminists?

2. What challenges did the second women's movement face, and how were they met?

3. How does Hartman answer her own question, "Why should women in college be feminists?"

Suggestion for Writing

Hartman identifies herself as a member of the *second* women's movement. Compare her description of this movement's goals with pioneering feminist tracts such as Mary Wollstonecraft's *A Vindication of the Rights of Woman* (p. 223) and Elizabeth Cady Stanton and Lucretia Coffin Mott's *Seneca Falls Convention* (p. 602).

∿∿∿∿

FRANCINE PROSE

Bad Behavior

Francine Prose (b. 1947) earned degrees from both Radcliffe College and Harvard University. She has taught creative writing at Harvard, the University of Arizona, the Breadloaf Writers Conference, and Warren Wilson College. Prose has written several books, including *The Peaceable Kingdom* (1993), *Guided Tours of Hell* (1997), *Blue Angel* (2000), *The Lives of the Muses* (2002), and *A Changed Man* (2005). She has won the Jewish Book Council Award, the Mile Award, and the Edgar Lewis Wallant Award for her fiction. This article, published in 1995, challenges us to examine our understanding of the nature of sexual harassment.

Five men and women from the university community were convened in a campus conference room to decide if my friend Stephen Dobyns—a distinguished poet and novelist and a tenured creative-writing professor— was guilty of sexual harassment and should be dismissed from his job. The tone was one of such civility and high moral seriousness that I could only assume I was the only person in the room tuned in to the disturbing static beneath all this calm inquiry: the only one hearing echoes of Victorian melodrama, of badly overacted student productions of Arthur Miller's play *The Crucible.*

Perhaps my alienation came from my peculiar role—as a character witness for the alleged sexual harasser. I think of myself as a feminist. I write about "women's issues." I teach in writing programs and am painfully aware of the pressures facing young (and older) female writers. I find myself more often than not taking the woman's side. I believed Anita Hill.

Two months before the hearing, at a graduate-student party, an argument erupted—and my friend splashed a drink in the face of a student who had heard him make a remark about her breasts. (Witnesses say he told another writer to "stop looking at her breasts.") The student filed a formal complaint, and two others have come forward to say that his harassment has destroyed their ability to function in the classroom and at the writing desk.

Clearly, my friend is guilty—but only of bad behavior. You don't go throwing drinks in a student's face and talking about her breasts. Since the drink-throwing incident, my friend has been sober and regularly attends A.A. meetings, but a drinking problem used to exaggerate his confrontational personality. He has spoken without considering the feelings of his audience; he sometimes connects with other men with fairly crude talk about sex. But that's not sexual harassment as I understand it.

No one suggests that he offered to trade good grades for sex. He is not accused of sleeping with or propositioning students—one says he tried to kiss her at a drunken party—or of the focused protected hectoring we might call "harassment." The allegations all concern language: specifically, what the committee calls "salty language" used outside the classroom at graduate-student parties. They involve attempts to be funny, and to provoke. There was one cruel remark about a professor who wasn't present, and the suggestion that another might benefit from a "salty" term for a satisfactory sexual encounter.

Is this sexual harassment? Not in any clear sense, but those clear borders have been smudged by university policies that refer to "a hostile workplace," to "patterns of intimidation." "Hostile" and "intimidation" are subjectively defined, as they were by the student who testified (hilariously, I thought, though, again, no one seemed to notice) that he felt intimidated by my friend's use of a "salty" phrase. He felt he was being asked to condone a locker-room atmosphere that might offend the women present.

There was much talk of protecting women from blunt mentions of sex. And the young women who testified were in obvious need of protection. They gulped, trembled and wept, describing how my friend yelled at them in class or failed to encourage their work. Victorian damsels in distress, they used 19th-century language: they had been "shattered" by his rude, "brutish" behavior. After testifying, they seemed radiant, exalted, a state of being that, like so much else, recalled *The Crucible,* which used the Salem witch trials as a metaphor for the Army–McCarthy hearings.

Are these the modern women feminists had in mind? Victorian girls, Puritan girls, crusading against dirty thoughts and loose speech? I thought of all the salty words I have used in class—words that could apparently cost me my job—and of my own experience with sexual harassment: the colleague who told me that his department only hired me because I was a woman; if they could have found a black woman, they would have hired her. Such words were more damaging than anything he could have said about my breasts. But no one could have accused him of harassment: he didn't make a pass at me or refer to a sexual act.

Finally, I thought of students, men and women whose lives were changed by studying with Dobyns, an excellent teacher who cares about writing, who takes women seriously and is interested in their work and not (like many male teachers who are not, strictly speaking, guilty of sexual harassment) annoyed by female intelligence and bored by the subject of female experience. But these facts were irrelevant to the discussion of whether or not my friend got drunk and said this or that dirty word.

Soon after the hearing, he was informed that he had been found guilty of making five sexually harassing remarks. The committee recommended that he be suspended from his job without pay for two years, banned from campus except to use the library, required to perform 200 hours of community service and to pay one of his accusers $600 to compensate for the wages she lost because of the mental suffering he caused her.

It's as if a nasty bubble of Puritanism has risen to the surface and burst. There's been a narrowing of parameters—not of what can be done, but of what can be *said* by writers whose subject (one might think) is language. In an effort to protect the delicate ears of the gentle sex, a career has been damaged with casual glee. Feminists, academics, intellectuals—those who stand to lose the most from restrictions on free expression—are ignoring the possible consequences of the precedent they are setting. They must be choosing not to imagine the terrible swift ease with which our right to free speech can simply crumble away, gathering momentum as the erosion process begins—until human rights and women's rights are subjects too salty to mention.

Suggestions for Discussion

1. Do you consider throwing a drink in a student's face and talking about her breasts simply an example of "bad behavior"?

2. Francine Prose refers to "university policies that refer to 'a hostile workplace,' to 'patterns of intimidation.'" In fact, these policies are not peculiar to her institution but are outlined in Title 7 of the Equal Employment Opportunities Commission and were affirmed by the Supreme Court in 1986. Do you believe that they should be amended so as not to penalize people such as the professor described in this article?

3. The distinction between what is done and what is said is a critical one in terms of sexual harassment, according to Prose. Do you agree?

Suggestions for Writing

1. Describe an instance of sexual harassment you or someone you know has experienced.

2. Many people believe that, except in rare cases, the lines of sexual harassment are too blurred to be subject to legal action. Do you agree? State your opinion and support it in a well-formulated essay.

3. What has concern about sexual harassment done to relations between the sexes? Depict this in a story or essay.

ITALO CALVINO

Why Read the Classics?

Italo Calvino (1923–1984) is a world-renowned novelist, essayist, and theorist best known for his ability to craft entertaining and intellectually playful fantasy stories with contemporary sensibilities. This Cuban-born activist, who spent most of his life in Italy, drew upon his sense of humor, his knowledge of the sciences, and his passion for politics when writing. Among his books are *The Baron in the Trees* (1957), *Cosmicomics* (1965), *Invisible Cities* (1972), *Under the Jaguar Sun* (1985), *The Castle of Crossed Destinies* (1973), *If on a winter's night a traveler....* (1979) and *Italian Folktales, Selected and Retold by Italo Calvino* (1956). A collection of his literary criticism—the following essay (1978) included—was compiled in a book, *The Uses of Literature* (1986).

L'Espresso (Rome), June 28, 1981.

Let us begin with a few suggested definitions.

(1) The classics are the books of which we usually hear people say, "I am rereading…" and never "I am reading…."

This happens at least among those who consider themselves "very well read." It does not hold good for young people at the age when they first encounter the world, and the classics as a part of that world.

The reiterative prefix before the verb "read" may be a small hypocrisy on the part of people ashamed to admit they have not read a famous book. To reassure them, we need only observe that, however vast any person's basic reading may be, there still remain an enormous number of fundamental works that he has not read.

Hands up, anyone who has read the whole of Herodotus and the whole of Thucydides! And Saint-Simon? And Cardinal de Retz? But even the great nineteenth-century cycles of novels are more often talked about than read. In France they begin to read Balzac in school, and, judging by the number of copies in circulation, one may suppose that they go on reading him even after that, but if a Gallup poll were taken in Italy, I'm afraid that Balzac would come in practically last. Dickens fans in Italy form a tiny elite; as soon as its members meet, they begin to chatter about characters and episodes as if they were discussing people and things of their own acquaintance. Years ago, while teaching in America, Michel Butor got fed up with being asked about Emile Zola, whom he had never read, so he made up his mind to read the entire Rougon-Macquart cycle. He found it was completely different from what he had thought: a fabulous mythological and cosmogonical family tree, which he went on to describe in a wonderful essay.

In other words, to read a great book for the first time in one's maturity is an extraordinary pleasure, different from (though one cannot say greater or lesser than) the pleasure of having read it in one's youth. Youth brings to reading, as to any other experience, a particular flavor and a particular sense of importance, whereas in maturity one appreciates (or ought to appreciate) many more details and levels and meanings. We may therefore attempt the next definition:

(2) We use the word "classics" for books that are treasured by those who have read and loved them; but they are treasured no less by those who have the luck to read them for the first time in the best conditions to enjoy them.

In fact, reading in youth can be rather unfruitful, due to impatience, distraction, inexperience with the product's "instructions for use," and inexperience in life itself. Books read then can be (possibly at one and the same time) formative, in the sense that they give a form to future experiences, providing models, terms of comparison, schemes for classification, scales of value, exemplars of beauty—all things that continue to operate even if a book read in one's youth is almost or totally forgotten. If we reread the book at a mature age, we are likely to rediscover these constants, which by this time are part of our inner mechanisms, but whose origins we have long forgotten. A literary work can succeed in making us forget it as such, but it leaves its seed in us. The definition we can give is therefore this:

(3) The classics are books that exert a peculiar influence, both when they refuse to be eradicated from the mind and when they conceal themselves in the folds of memory, camouflaging themselves as the collective or individual unconscious.

There should therefore be a time in adult life devoted to revisiting the most important books of our youth. Even if the books have remained the same (though they do change, in the light of an altered historical perspective), we have most certainly changed, and our encounter will be an entirely new thing.

Hence, whether we use the verb "read" or the verb "reread" is of little importance. Indeed, we may say:

(4) Every rereading of a classic is as much a voyage of discovery as the first reading.

(5) Every reading of a classic is in fact a rereading. Definition 4 may be considered a corollary of this next one:

(6) A classic is a book that has never finished saying what it has to say.

Whereas definition 5 depends on a more specific formula, such as this:

(7) The classics are the books that come down to us bearing the traces of readings previous to ours, and bringing in their wake the traces they themselves have left on the culture or cultures they have passed through (or, more simply, on language and customs).

All this is true both of the ancient and of the modern classics. If I read the *Odyssey* I read Homer's text, but I cannot forget all that the adventures of Ulysses have come to mean in the course of the centuries, and I cannot help wondering if these meanings were implicit in the text, or whether they are incrustations or distortions or expansions. When reading Kafka, I cannot avoid approving or rejecting the legitimacy of the adjective "Kafkaesque," which one is likely to hear every quarter of an hour, applied indiscriminately. If I read Turgenev's *Fathers and Sons* or Dostoyevsky's *The Possessed,* I cannot help thinking how the characters have continued to be reincarnated right down to our own day.

The reading of a classic ought to give us a surprise or two vis-á-vis the notion that we had of it. For this reason, I can never sufficiently highly recommend the direct reading of the text itself, leaving aside the critical biography, commentaries, and interpretations as much as possible. Schools and universities ought to help us understand that no book that talks *about* a book says more than the book in question, but instead they do their level best to make us think the opposite. There is a very widespread topsy-turviness of values whereby the introduction, critical apparatus, and bibliography are used as a smokescreen to hide what the text has to say and, indeed, can say only if left to speak for itself without intermediaries who claim to know more than the text does. We may conclude that:

(8) A classic does not necessarily teach us anything we did not know before. In a classic we sometimes discover something we have always known (or thought we knew), but without knowing that this author said it first, or at least is associated with it in a special way. And this, too, is a surprise that gives a lot of pleasure, such as we always gain from the discovery of an origin, a relationship, an affinity. From all this we may derive a definition of this type:

(9) The classics are books which, upon reading, we find even fresher, more unexpected, and more marvelous than we had thought from hearing about them.

Naturally, this only happens when a classic really works as such—that is, when it establishes a personal rapport with the reader. If the spark doesn't come, that's a pity; but we do not read the classics out of duty or respect, only out of love. Except at school. And school should enable you to know, either well or badly, a certain number of classics among which—or in reference to which—you can then choose *your* classics. School is obliged to give you the instruments needed to make a choice, but the choices that count are those that occur outside and after school.

It is only by reading without bias that you might possibly come across the book that becomes *your* book. I know an excellent art historian, an extraordinarily well-read man, who out of all the books there are has focused his special love on *Pickwick Papers;* at every opportunity he comes up with some quip from Dickens's book, and connects each and every event in life with some Pickwickian episode. Little by little he himself, and true philosophy, and the universe, have taken on the shape and form of the *Pickwick Papers* by a process of complete identification. In this way we arrive at a very lofty and demanding notion of what a classic is:

(10) We use the word "classic" of a book that takes the form of an equivalent to the universe, on a level with the ancient talismans. With this definition we are approaching the idea of the "total book," as Mallarmé conceived of it.

But a classic can establish an equally strong rapport in terms of opposition and antithesis. Everything that Jean-Jacques Rousseau thinks and does is very dear to my heart, yet everything fills me with an irrepressible desire to contradict him, to criticize him, to quarrel with him. It is a question of personal antipathy on a temperamental level, on account of which I ought to have no choice but not to read him; and yet I cannot help numbering him among *my* authors. I will therefore say:

(11) *Your* classic author is the one you cannot feel indifferent to, who helps you to define yourself in relation to him, even in dispute with him.

I think I have no need to justify myself for using the word "classic" without making distinctions as to age, style, or authority. What distinguishes the classic, in the argument I am making, may be only an echo effect that holds good both for an ancient work and for a modern one that has already achieved its place in a cultural continuum. We might say:

(12) A classic is a book that comes before other classics; but anyone who has read the others first, and then reads this one, instantly recognizes its place in the family tree.

At this point I can no longer put off the vital problem of how to relate the reading of the classics to the reading of all the other books that are anything but classics. It is a problem connected with such questions as "Why read the classics rather than concentrate on books that enable us to understand our own times more deeply?" or "Where shall we find the time and peace of mind to read the classics, overwhelmed as we are by the avalanche of current events?"

We can, of course, imagine some blessed soul who devotes his reading time exclusively to Lucretius, Lucian, Montaigne, Erasmus, Quevedo, Marlowe, the *Discourse on Method, Wilhelm Meister,* Coleridge, Ruskin, Proust, and Valéry, with a few forays in the direction of Murasaki or the Icelandic Sagas. And all this without having to write reviews of the latest publications, or papers to compete for a university chair, or articles for magazines on tight deadlines. To keep up such a diet without any contamination, this blessed soul would have to abstain from reading the newspapers, and never be tempted by the latest novel or sociological investigation. But we have to see how far such rigor would be either justified or profitable. The latest news may well be banal or mortifying, but it nonetheless remains a point at which to stand and look both backward and forward. To be able to read the classics, you have to know "from where" you are reading them; otherwise both the book and the reader will be lost in a timeless cloud. This, then, is the reason why the greatest "yield" from reading the classics will be obtained by someone who knows how to alternate them with the proper dose of current affairs. And this does not necessarily imply a state of imperturbable inner calm. It can also be the fruit of nervous impatience, of a huffing-and-puffing discontent of mind.

Maybe the ideal thing would be to hearken to current events as we do to the din outside the window that informs us about traffic jams and sudden changes in the weather, while we listen to the voice of the classics sounding clear and articulate inside the room. But it is already a lot for most people if the presence of the classics is perceived as a distant rumble far outside a room that is swamped by the trivia of the moment, as by a television at full blast. Let us therefore add:

(13) A classic is something that tends to relegate the concerns of the moment to the status of background noise, but at the same time this background noise is something we cannot do without.

(14) A classic is something that persists as a background noise even when the most incompatible momentary concerns are in control of the situation.

There remains the fact that reading the classics appears to clash with our rhythm of life, which no longer affords long periods of time or the spaciousness of humanistic leisure. It also conflicts with the eclecticism of our culture, which would never be capable of compiling a catalogue of things classical such as would suit our needs.

These latter conditions were fully realized in the case of Leopardi, given his solitary life in his father's house (his "*paterno ostello*"), his cult of Greek and Latin antiquity, and the formidable library put at his disposal by his father, Monaldo. To which we may add the entire body of Italian literature and French literature, with the exception of novels and the "latest hits" in general, which were left to beguile the leisure of his sister Paolina ("*your Stendhal*," he wrote her once). Even with his intense interest in science and history, he was often willing to rely on texts that were not entirely up-to-date, taking the habits of birds from Buffon, the mummies of Fredrik Ruysch from Fontanelle, the voyage of Columbus from Robertson.

In these days a classical education like the young Leopardi's is unthinkable; above all, Count Monaldo's library has multiplied explosively. The ranks of the old titles have been decimated, while new ones have proliferated in all modern literatures and cultures. There is nothing for it but for all of us to invent our own ideal libraries of classics. I would say that such a library ought to be composed half of books we have read and that have really counted for us, and half of books we propose to read and presume will come to count—leaving a section of empty shelves for surprises and occasional discoveries.

I realize that Leopardi is the only name I have cited from Italian literature—a result of the explosion of the library. Now I ought to rewrite the whole article to make it perfectly clear that the classics help us to understand who we are and where we stand, a purpose for which it is indispensable to compare Italians with foreigners and foreigners with Italians. Then I ought to rewrite it yet again, lest anyone believe that the classics ought to be read because they "serve any purpose" whatever. The only reason one can possibly adduce is that to read the classics is better than not to read the classics.

And if anyone objects that it is not worth taking so much trouble, then I will quote Cioran (who is not yet a classic but will become one): "While they were preparing the hemlock, Socrates was learning a tune on the flute. 'What good will it do you,' they asked, 'to know this tune before you die?' "

Suggestions for Discussion

1. Why does Calvino begin his discussion with "a few suggested definitions"?

2. How do classics change in meaning as you read and reread them over time?

3. According to Calvino, why is it necessary for readers to compare classics from his/her own culture with classic works produced by other cultures?

Suggestion for Writing

Consider a story or a work of art that you have been familiar with for many years. How has the meaning of that story changed for you as you have evaluated it during different periods in your life? Write an informal, journal-style piece in which you consider these thoughts.

ROLAND BARTHES

The Death of the Author

Literary critic, writer, and social thinker Roland Barthes (1915–1980) is (along with anthropologist Claude Levi-Strauss) one of the fathers of the structuralist intellectual movement in France in the 1950s. Structuralism is a philosophy that asserts that nothing can be properly understood when examined in isolation but only within the context of the larger (social) structure it inhabits. Educated in the classics at the University of Paris, Barthes' first major published work was *Writing Degree Zero* (1953). He also wrote *Mythologies* (1957); *Elements of Semiology* (1964); and the "anti-autobiography," *Roland Barthes by Roland Barthes* (1975). After he was killed in a car accident in 1980, Susan Sontag published a posthumous volume of his work, *A Barthes Reader* (1982). The following essay, published in 1968, is a classic example of Barthes' philosophy of reading, which departed drastically from traditional literary scholarship in its insistence that the reader gives a piece of writing its true meaning.

In his tale *Sarrasine*, Balzac, speaking of a castrato disguised as a woman, writes this sentence: "She was Woman, with her sudden fears, her inexplicable whims, her instinctive fears, her meaningless bravado, her defiance, and her delicious delicacy of feeling." Who speaks in this way? Is it the hero of the tale, who would prefer not to recognize the castrato hidden beneath the "woman"? Is it Balzac the man whose personal experience has provided him with a philosophy of Woman? Is it Balzac the author, professing certain "literary" ideas about femininity? Is it universal wisdom? Romantic psychology? We can never know, for the good reason that writing is the destruction of every voice, every origin. Writing is that neuter, that composite, that obliquity into which our subject flees, the black-and-white where all identity is lost, beginning with the very identity of the body that writes.

No doubt it has always been so: once a fact is *recounted*—for intransitive purposes, and no longer to act directly upon reality, i.e., exclusive of any function except that exercise of the symbol itself—this gap appears, the voice loses its origin, the author enters into his own death, writing begins. However, the affect of this phenomenon has been variable; in ethnographic societies, narrative is never assumed by a person but by a mediator, shaman, or reciter, whose "performance" (i.e., has mastery of the narrative code) can be admired, but never his "genius." The *author* is a modern character, no doubt produced by our society as it emerged from the Middle Ages, influenced by English empiricism, French rationalism, and the personal faith of the Reformation, thereby discovering the prestige of the individual, or, as we say more nobly, of the "human person." Hence, it is logical that in literary matters it should be positivism, crown and conclusion of capitalist ideology, which has granted the greatest importance to the author's "person." The *author* still reigns in manuals of literary history, in biographies of writers, magazine interviews, and in the very consciousness of litterateurs eager to unite, by means of private journals, their person and their work; the image of literature to be found in contemporary culture is tyrannically centered on the author, his person, his history, his tastes, his passions; criticism still largely consists in saying that Baudelaire's oeuvre is the failure of the man Baudelaire, Van Gogh's is his madness, Tchaikovsky's his vice: *explanation* of the work is still sought in the person of its producer, as if, through the more or less transparent allegory of fiction, it was always, ultimately, the voice of one and the same person, the author, which was transmitting his "confidences."

Though the Author's empire is still very powerful (the new criticism has quite often merely consolidated it), we know that certain writers have already tried to subvert it. In France, Mallarmé, no doubt the first, saw and foresaw in all its scope the necessity to substitute language itself for the subject hitherto supposed to be its owner; for Mallarmé, as for us, it is language which speaks not the author; to write is to reach, through a preliminary impersonality—which we can at no moment identify with the realistic novelist's castrating "objectivity"—that point where not "I" but only language functions, "performs": Mallarmé's whole poetics consists in suppressing the author in favor of writing (and thereby restoring, as we shall see, the reader's place). Valéry, entangled in a psychology of the ego, greatly edulcorated Mallarmean theory, but led by a preference for classicism to conform to the lessons of Rhetoric, he continued to cast the Author into doubt and derision, emphasized the linguistic and "accidental" nature of his activity, and throughout his prose works championed the essentially verbal condition of literature, as opposed to which any resort to the writer's interiority seemed to him pure superstition. Proust himself, despite the apparently psychological character of what is called his *analyses,* visibly undertook to blur by an extreme subtilization the relation of the writer and his characters: by making the narrator not the one who has seen or felt, or even the one who writes, but the one who *is going to write* (the young man of the novel—but, as a matter of fact, how old is he and *who* is he?—wants to write but cannot, and the novel ends when writing finally becomes possible), Proust has given modern writing its epic: by a radical reversal, instead of putting his life into his novel, as is so often said, he made his life itself a work of which his own book was the model, so that it is quite clear to us that it is not Charlus who imitates Montesquiou, but Montesquiou, in his anecdotal, historical reality, who is only a secondary, derived fragment of Charlus. Finally Surrealism, to keep to this prehistory of modernity, could doubtless not attribute a sovereign place to language; since language is system, and what this movement sought was, romantically, a direct subversion of the codes—an illusory subversion, moreover, for a code cannot be destroyed, only "flouted"; yet, by constantly striving to disappoint expected meanings (this was the famous surrealist "shock"), by urging the hand to write as fast as possible what the head was unaware of (this was automatic writing), by accepting the principle and the experiment of collective writing, Surrealism helped desacralize the image of the Author. Last, outside literature itself (in fact, such distinctions are becoming quite dated), linguistics furnishes the destruction of the Author with a precious analytic instrument, showing that the speech-act in its entirety is an "empty" process, which functions perfectly without its being necessary to "fill" it with the person of the interlocutors: linguistically, the author is nothing but the one who writes, just as *I* is nothing but the one who says *I*: language knows a "subject," not a "person," and this subject, empty outside of the very speech-act which defines it, suffices to "hold" language, i.e., to exhaust it.

The removal of the Author (with Brecht, we might speak here of a veritable *distancing,* the Author diminishing like a figure at the far end of the literary stage) is not only a historical fact or an act of writing: it utterly transforms the modern text (or—which is the same thing—the text is henceforth produced and read so that the author absents himself from it at every level). Time, first of all, is no longer the same. The Author, when we believe in him, is always conceived as the past of his own book: book and author are voluntarily placed on one and the same line, distributed as a *before* and an *after:* the Author is supposed to *feed* the book, i.e., he lives before it, thinks, suffers, lives for it; he has the same relation of antecedence with his work that a father sustains with his child. Quite the contrary, the modern *scriptor* is born *at the same time* as his text; he is not furnished with a being which precedes or exceeds his writing, he is not the subject of which his book would be the predicate; there is no time other than that of the speech-act, and every text is written eternally *here* and *now.* This is because (or it follows that) *writing* can no longer designate an operation of recording, of observation, of representation, of "painting" (as the Classics used to say), but instead what the linguists, following Oxfordian philosophy, call a performative, a rare verbal form (exclusively found in the first person and in the present), in which the speech-act has no other content (no other statement) than the act by which it is uttered: something like the *I declare* of kings or the *I sing* of the earliest poets; the modern *scriptor,* having buried the Author, can therefore no longer believe, according to the pathos of his predecessors, that his hand is slower than his passion and that in consequence, making a law of necessity, he must emphasize this delay and endlessly "elaborate" his form; for him, on the contrary, his hand, detached from any voice, borne by a pure gesture of inscription (and not of expression), traces a field without origin—or at least with no origin but language itself, i.e., the very thing which ceaselessly calls any origin into question.

We know now that a text consists not of a line of words, releasing a single "theological" meaning (the "message" of the Author-God), but of a multi-dimensional space in which are married and contested several writings, none of which is original: the text is a fabric of quotations, resulting from a thousand sources of culture. Like Bouvard and Pécuchet, those eternal copyists, at once sublime and comical, whose profound absurdity *precisely* designates the truth of writing, the writer can only imitate an ever anterior, never original gesture, his sole power is to mingle writings, to counter some by others, so as never to rely on just one; if he seeks to *express himself,* at least he knows that the interior "thing" he claims to "translate" is itself no more than a ready-made lexicon, whose words can be explained only through other words, and this ad infinitum: an adventure which exemplarily befell young Thomas De Quincey, so versed in his Greek that in order to translate certain absolutely modern ideas and images into this dead language, Baudelaire tells us, "he had a dictionary made for himself, one much more complex and extensive than the kind produced by the vulgar patience of purely literary themes" *(Les Paradis artificiels);* succeeding the Author, the *scriptor* no longer contains passions, moods, sentiments, impressions, but that immense dictionary from which he draws a writing which will be incessant: life merely imitates the book, and this book itself is but a tissue of signs, endless imitation, infinitely postponed.

Once the Author is distanced, the claim to "decipher" a text becomes entirely futile. To assign an Author to a text is to impose a brake on it, to furnish it with a final signified, to close writing. This conception is quite suited to criticism, which then undertakes the important task of discovering the Author (or his hypostases: society, history, the psyche, freedom) beneath the work: once the Author is found, the text is "explained," the critic has won; hence, it is hardly surprising that historically the Author's empire has been the Critic's as well, and also that (even new) criticism is today unsettled at the same time as the Author. In multiple writing, in effect, everything is to be *disentangled*, but nothing *deciphered*, structure can be followed, "threaded" (as we say of a run in a stocking) in all its reprises, all its stages, but there is no end to it, no bottom; the space of writing is to be traversed, not pierced; writing constantly posits meaning, but always in order to evaporate it: writing seeks a systematic exemption of meaning. Thereby, literature (it would be better, from now on, to say *writing*), by refusing to assign to the text (and to the world-as-text) a "secret" i.e., an ultimate meaning, liberates an activity we may call countertheological, properly revolutionary, for to refuse to halt meaning is finally to refuse God and his hypostases, reason, science, the law.

To return to Balzac's sentence. No one (i.e., no "person") says it: its source, its voice is not the true site of writing, it is reading. Another very specific example will help us here: recent investigations (J.-P. Vernant) have shed some light on the constitutively ambiguous nature of Greek tragedy, whose text is "woven" of words with double meanings, words which each character understands unilaterally (this perpetual misunderstanding is precisely what we call the "tragic"); there is, however, someone who understands each word in its duplicity, and further understands, one may say, the very deafness of the characters speaking in his presence, this "someone" is precisely the reader (or here the listener). Here we discern the total being of writing: a text consists of multiple writings, proceeding from several cultures and entering into dialogue, into parody, into contestation; but there is a site where this multiplicity is collected, and this site is not the author, as has hitherto been claimed, but the reader: the reader is the very space in which are inscribed, without any of them being lost, all the citations out of which a writing is made; the unity of a text is not in its origin but in its destination, but this destination can no longer be personal: the reader is a man without history, without biography, without psychology; he is only that *someone* who holds collected into one and the same field all of the traces from which writing is constituted. That is why it is absurd to hear the new writing condemned in the name of a humanism which hypocritically claims to champion the reader's rights. Classical criticism has never been concerned with the reader; for that criticism, there is no other man in literature than the one who writes. We are no longer so willing to be the dupes of such antiphrases, by which a society proudly recriminates in favor of precisely what it discards, ignores, muffles, or destroys; we know that in order to restore writing to its future, we must reverse the myth: the birth of the reader must be requited by the death of the Author.

Suggestions for Discussion

1. Why does Barthes criticize readers who attempt to determine what authorial intent shaped the books that they read?

2. How does Barthes' argument empower readers?

3. What objections might one raise to Barthes' ideas?

Suggestion for Writing

What are the limits of interpretation of a work? Is any classroom teacher who accepts Barthes' ideas as sound instantly trapped into granting validity to every unusual or absurd reading that students offer? Can a professor who embraces Barthes' views ever justify telling a student that his or her reading is too far-fetched? Explain.

LEWIS THOMAS

Humanities and Science

Lewis Thomas (1913–1993) was a physician whose medical career centered on the Sloan Kettering Cancer Care Center in New York, the city of his birth. He wrote for medical journals at the same time that he wrote popular essays to present science and the scientist's view of the world to the lay public. He won the National Book Award in 1974 for *The Lives of a Cell: Notes of a Biology Watcher*. Other collections include

More Notes of a Biology Watcher (1979), *The Youngest Science: Notes of a Medicine-Watcher* (1983), *Late Night Thoughts on Listening to Mahler's Ninth* (1984), and *The Fragile Species* (1992). In the following essay, from *Late Night Thoughts on Listening to Mahler's Ninth,* Thomas advocates open discussion of what science does not yet know or understand.

Lord Kelvin was one of the great British physicists of the late nineteenth century, an extraordinarily influential figure in his time, and in some ways a paradigm of conventional, established scientific leadership. He did a lot of good and useful things, but once or twice he, like Homer, nodded. The instances are worth recalling today, for we have nodders among our scientific eminences still, from time to time, needing to have their elbows shaken.

On one occasion, Kelvin made a speech on the overarching importance of numbers. He maintained that no observation of nature was worth paying serious attention to unless it could be stated in precisely quantitative terms. The numbers were the final and only test, not only of truth but about meaning as well. He said, "When you can measure what you are speaking about, and express it in numbers, you know something about it. But when you cannot—your knowledge is of a meagre and unsatisfactory kind."

But, as at least one subsequent event showed, Kelvin may have had things exactly the wrong way round. The task of converting observations into numbers is the hardest of all, the last task rather than the first thing to be done, and it can be done only when you have learned, beforehand, a great deal about the observations themselves. You can, to be sure, achieve a very deep understanding of nature by quantitative measurement, but you must know what you are talking about before you can begin applying the numbers for making predictions. In Kelvin's case, the problem at hand was the age of the earth and solar system. Using what was then known about the sources of energy and the loss of energy from the physics of that day, he calculated that neither the earth nor the sun were older than several hundred million years. This caused a considerable stir in biological and geological circles, especially among the evolutionists. Darwin himself was distressed by the numbers; the time was much too short for the theory of evolution. Kelvin's figures were described by Darwin as one of his "sorest troubles."

T. H. Huxley had long been aware of the risks involved in premature extrapolations from mathematical treatment of biological problems. He said, in an 1869 speech to the Geological Society concerning numbers, "This seems to be one of the many cases in which the admitted accuracy of mathematical processes is allowed to throw a wholly inadmissible appearance of authority over the results obtained by them....As the grandest mill in the world will not extract wheat flour from peascods, so pages of formulas will not get a definite result out of loose data."

The trouble was that the world of physics had not moved fast enough to allow for Kelvin's assumptions. Nuclear fusion and fission had not yet been dreamed of, and the true age of the earth could not even be guessed from the data in hand. It was not yet the time for mathematics in this subject.

There have been other examples, since those days, of the folly of using numbers and calculations uncritically. Kelvin's own strong conviction that science could not be genuine science without measuring things was catching. People in other fields of endeavor, hankering to turn their disciplines into exact sciences, beset by what has since been called "physics envy," set about converting whatever they knew into numbers and thence into equations with predictive pretensions. We have it with us still, in economics, sociology, psychology, history, even, I fear, in English-literature criticism and linguistics, and it frequently works, when it works at all, with indifferent success. The risks of untoward social consequences in work of this kind are considerable. It is as important—and as hard—to learn *when* to use mathematics as *how* to use it, and this matter should remain high on the agenda of consideration for education in the social and behavioral sciences.

Of course, Kelvin's difficulty with the age of the earth was an exceptional, almost isolated instance of failure in quantitative measurement in the nineteenth-century physics. The instruments devised for approaching nature by way of physics became increasingly precise and powerful, carrying the field through electromagnetic theory, triumph after triumph, and setting the stage for the great revolution of twentieth-century physics. There is no doubt about it: measurement works when the instruments work, and when you have a fairly clear idea of what it is that is being measured, and when you know what to do with the numbers when they tumble out. The system for gaining information and comprehension about nature works so well, indeed, that it carries another hazard: the risk of convincing yourself that you know everything.

Kelvin himself fell into this trap toward the end of the century. (I don't mean to keep picking on Kelvin, who was a very great scientist; it is just that he happened to say a couple of things I find useful for this discussion.) He stated, in a summary of the achievements of nineteenth-century physics, that it was an almost completed science; virtually everything that needed knowing about the material universe had been learned; there were still a few anomalies and inconsistencies in electromagnetic theory, a few loose ends to be tied up, but this would be done within the next several years. Physics, in these terms, was not a field any longer likely to attract, as it previously had, the brightest and most imaginative young brains. The most interesting part of the work had already been done. Then, within the next decade, came radiation, Planck, the quantum, Einstein, Rutherford, Bohr, and all the rest—quantum mechanics—and the whole field turned over and became a brand-new sort of human endeavor, still now, in the view of many physicists, almost a full century later, a field only at its beginnings.

But even today, despite the amazements that are turning up in physics each year, despite the jumps taken from the smallest parts of nature—particle physics—to the largest of all—the cosmos itself—the impression of science that the public gains is rather like the impression left in the nineteenth-century public mind by Kelvin. Science, in this view, is first of all a matter of simply getting all the numbers together. The numbers are sitting out there in nature, waiting to be found, sorted and totted up. If only they had enough robots and enough computers, the scientists could go off to the beach and wait for their papers to be written for them. Second of all, what we know about nature today is pretty much the whole story: we are very nearly home and dry. From here on, it is largely a problem of tying up loose ends, tidying nature up, getting the files in order. The only real surprises for the future—and it is about those that the public is becoming more concerned and apprehensive—are the technological applications that the scientists may be cooking up from today's knowledge.

I suggest that the scientific community is to blame. If there are disagreements between the world of the humanities and the scientific enterprise as to the place and importance of science in a liberal-arts education, and the role of science in twentieth-century culture, I believe that the scientists are themselves responsible for a general misunderstanding of what they are really up to.

Over the past half century, we have been teaching the sciences as though they were the same academic collection of cut-and-dried subjects as always, and—here is what has really gone wrong—as though they would always be the same. The teaching of today's biology, for example, is pretty much the same kind of exercise as the teaching of Latin was when I was in high school long ago. First of all, the fundamentals, the underlying laws, the essential grammar, and then the reading of texts. Once mastered, that is that: Latin is Latin and forever after will be Latin. And biology is precisely biology, a vast array of hard facts to be learned as fundamentals, followed by a reading of the texts.

Moreover, we have been teaching science as though its facts were somehow superior to the facts in all other scholarly disciplines, more fundamental, more solid, less subject to subjectivism, immutable. English literature is not just one way of thinking, it is all sorts of ways. Poetry is a moving target. The facts that underlie art, architecture, and music are not really hard facts, and you can change them any way you like by arguing about them, but science is treated as an altogether different kind of learning: an unambiguous, unalterable, and endlessly useful display of data needing only to be packaged and installed somewhere in one's temporal lobe in order to achieve a full understanding of the natural world.

And it is, of course, not like this at all. In real life, every field of science that I can think of is incomplete, and most of them—whatever the record of accomplishment over the past two hundred years—are still in the earliest stage of their starting point. In the fields I know best, among the life sciences, it is required that the most expert and sophisticated minds be capable of changing those minds, often with a great lurch, every few years. In some branches of biology the mind-changing is occurring with accelerating velocities. The next week's issue of any scientific journal can turn a whole field upside down, shaking out any number of immutable ideas and installing new bodies of dogma, and this is happening all the time. It is an almost everyday event in physics, in chemistry, in materials research, in neurobiology, in genetics, in immunology. The hard facts tend to soften overnight, melt away, and vanish under the pressure of new hard facts, and the interpretations of what appear to be the most solid aspects of nature are subject to change, now more than at any other time in history. The conclusions reached in science are always, when looked at closely, far more provisional and tentative than are most of the assumptions arrived at by our colleagues in the humanities.

The running battle now in progress between the sociobiologists and the antisociobiologists is a marvel for students to behold, close up. To observe, in open-mouthed astonishment, the polarized extremes, one group of highly intelligent, beautifully trained, knowledgeable, and imaginative scientists maintaining that all sorts of behavior, animal and human, are governed exclusively by genes, and another group of equally talented scientists saying precisely the opposite and asserting that all behavior is set and determined by the environment, or by culture, and both sides brawling in the pages of periodicals such as *The New York Review of Books,* is an educational experience that no college student should be allowed to miss. The essential lesson to be learned has nothing to do with the relative validity of the facts underlying the argument, it is the argument itself that is the education: we do not yet know enough to settle such questions.

It is true that at any given moment there is the appearance of satisfaction, even self-satisfaction, within every scientific discipline. On any Tuesday morning, if asked, a good working scientist will gladly tell you that the affairs of the field are nicely in order, that things are finally looking clear and making sense, and all is well. But come back again, on another Tuesday, and he may let you know that the roof has just fallen in on his life's work, that all the old ideas—last week's ideas in some cases—are no longer good ideas, that something strange has happened.

It is the very strangeness of nature that makes science engrossing. That ought to be at the center of science teaching. There are more than seven-times-seven types of ambiguity in science, awaiting analysis. The poetry of Wallace Stevens is crystal-clear alongside the genetic code.

I prefer to turn things around in order to make precisely the opposite case. Science, especially twentieth-century science, has provided us with a glimpse of something we never really knew before, the revelation of human ignorance. We have been used to the belief, down one century after another, that we more or less comprehend everything bar one or two mysteries like the mental processes of our gods. Every age, not just the eighteenth century, regarded itself as the Age of Reason, and we have never lacked for explanations of the world and its ways. Now, we are being brought up short, and this has been the work of science. We have a wilderness of mystery to make our way through in the centuries ahead, and we will need science for this but not science alone. Science will, in its own time, produce the data and some of the meaning in the data, but never the full meaning. For getting a full grasp, for perceiving real significance when significance is at hand, we shall need minds at work from all sorts of brains outside the fields of science, most of all the brains of poets, of course, but also those of artists, musicians, philosophers, historians, writers in general.

It is primarily because of this need that I would press for changes in the way science is taught. There is a need to teach the young people who will be doing the science themselves, but this will always be a small minority among us. There is a deeper need to teach science to those who will be needed for thinking about it, and this means pretty nearly everyone else, in hopes that a few of these people—a much smaller minority than the scientific community and probably a lot harder to find—will, in the thinking, be able to imagine new levels of meaning that are likely to be lost on the rest of us.

In addition, it is time to develop a new group of professional thinkers, perhaps a somewhat larger group than the working scientists, who can create a discipline of scientific criticism. We have had good luck so far in the emergence of a few people ranking as philosophers of science and historians and journalists of science, and I hope more of these will be coming along, but we have not yet seen a Ruskin or a Leavis or an Edmund Wilson. Science needs critics of this sort, but the public at large needs them more urgently.

I suggest that the introductory courses in science, at all levels from grade school through college, be radically revised. Leave the fundamentals, the so-called basics, aside for a while, and concentrate the attention of all students on the things that are *not* known. You cannot possibly teach quantum mechanics without mathematics, to be sure, but you can describe the strangeness of the world opened up by quantum theory. Let it be known, early on, that there are deep mysteries, and profound paradoxes, revealed in their distant outlines, by the quantum. Let it be known that these can be approached more closely, and puzzled over, once the language of mathematics has been sufficiently mastered.

Teach at the outset, before any of the fundamentals, the still imponderable puzzles of cosmology. Let it be known, as clearly as possible, by the youngest minds, that there are some things going on in the universe that lie beyond comprehension, and make it plain how little is known.

Do not teach that biology is a useful and perhaps profitable science; that can come later. Teach instead that there are structures squirming inside all our cells, providing all the energy for living, that are essentially foreign creatures, brought in for symbiotic living a billion or so years ago, the lineal descendants of bacteria. Teach that we do not have the ghost of an idea how they got there, where they came from, or how they evolved to their present structure and function. The details of oxidative phosphorylation and photosynthesis can come later.

Teach ecology early on. Let it be understood that the earth's life is a system of interliving, interdependent creatures, and that we do not understand at all how it works. The earth's environment, from the range of atmospheric gases to the chemical constituents of the sea, has been held in an almost unbelievably improbable state of regulated balance since life began, and the regulation of stability and balance is accomplished solely by the life itself, like the internal environment of an immense organism, and we do not know how *that* one works, even less what it means. Teach that.

Go easy, I suggest, on the promises sometimes freely offered by science. Technology relies and depends on science these days, more than ever before, but technology is nothing like the first justification for doing research, nor is it necessarily an essential product to be expected from science. Public decisions about what to have in the way of technology are totally different problems from decisions about science, and the two enterprises should not be tangled together. The central task of science is to arrive, stage by stage, at a clearer comprehension of nature, but this does not mean, as it is sometimes claimed to mean, a search for mastery over nature. Science may provide us, one day, with a better understanding of ourselves, but never, I hope, with a set of technologies for doing something or other to improve ourselves. I am made nervous by assertions that human consciousness will someday be unraveled by research, laid out for close scrutiny like the workings of a computer, and then, *and then!* I hope with some fervor that we can learn a lot more than we now know about the human mind, and I see no reason why this strange puzzle should remain forever and entirely beyond us. But I would be deeply disturbed by any prospect that we might use the new knowledge in order to begin doing something about it, to improve it, say. This is a different matter from searching for information to use against schizophrenia or dementia, where we are badly in need of technologies, indeed likely one day to be sunk without them. But the ordinary, everyday, more or less normal human mind is too marvelous an instrument ever to be tampered with by anyone, science or no science.

The education of humanists cannot be regarded as complete, or even adequate, without exposure in some depth to where things stand in the various branches of science, and particularly, as I have said, in the areas of our ignorance. This does not mean that I know how to go about doing it, nor am I unaware of the difficulties involved. Physics professors, most of them, look with revulsion on assignments to teach their subject to poets. Biologists, caught up by the enchantment of their new power, armed with flawless instruments to tell the nucleotide sequences of the entire human genome, nearly matching the physicists in the precision of their measurements of living processes, will resist the prospect of broad survey courses;

each biology professor will demand that any student in his path must master every fine detail within that professor's research program. The liberal-arts faculties, for their part, will continue to view the scientists with suspicion and apprehension. "What do the scientists want?" asked a Cambridge professor in Francis Cornford's wonderful *Microcosmographia Academica.* "Everything that's going," was the quick answer. That was back in 1912, and universities haven't much changed.

The worst thing that has happened to science education is that the great fun has gone out of it. A very large number of good students look at it as slogging work to be got through on the way to medical school. Others look closely at the premedical students themselves, embattled and bleeding for grades and class standing, and are turned off. Very few see science as the high adventure it really is, the wildest of all explorations ever undertaken by human beings, the chance to catch close views of things never seen before, the shrewdest maneuver for discovering how the world works. Instead, they become baffled early on, and they are misled into thinking that bafflement is simply the result of not having learned all the facts. They are not told, as they should be told, that everyone else—from the professor in his endowed chair down to the platoons of postdoctoral students in the laboratory all night—is baffled as well. Every important scientific advance that has come in looking like an answer has turned, sooner or later—usually sooner—into a question. And the game is just beginning.

An appreciation of what is happening in science today, and of how great a distance lies ahead for exploring, ought to be one of the rewards of a liberal-arts education. It ought to be a good in itself, not something to be acquired on the way to a professional career but part of the cast of thought needed for getting into the kind of century that is now just down the road. Part of the intellectual equipment of an educated person, however his or her time is to be spent, ought to be a feel for the queernesses of nature, the inexplicable things.

And maybe, just maybe, a new set of courses dealing systematically with ignorance in science might take hold. The scientists might discover in it a new and subversive technique for catching the attention of students driven by curiosity, delighted and surprised to learn that science is exactly as Bush described it: an "endless frontier." The humanists, for their part, might take considerable satisfaction watching their scientific colleagues confess openly to not knowing everything about everything. And the poets, on whose shoulders the future rests, might, late nights, thinking things over, begin to see some meanings that elude the rest of us. It is worth a try.

Suggestions for Discussion

1. Summarize Thomas's complaints about "the impression of science that the public gains."

2. How would he have science taught?

3. What advantages might there be in "a new set of courses dealing systematically with ignorance in science"?

Suggestions for Writing

1. Discuss one or more unanswered questions that you have encountered in your study of science.

2. Tell about an experience in which you had to change your mind because of new information.

∾∾∾∾∾

KEVIN FINNERAN

The Merits of Meritocracy

Kevin Finneran is the editor of *Issues in Science and Technology,* a magazine that acts as a forum for the discussion of public policy related to science, medicine, and engineering. In this article, published in 1999, Finneran laments the lack of proper grading standards in the current American education system.

On May 17, 1999, the *Wall Street Journal* reported on the disappearing valedictorian. One of the side effects of high-school grade inflation and a complex system of extra credit for some demanding courses is that it is not unusual for a graduating class to have a dozen or more students with straight-A (or better!) averages. How does one pick a valedictorian? Some schools have simply eliminated the honor; others spread it thin. Eaglecrest High School in Aurora, Colorado, had 18 valedictorians this year. Vestavia High School near Birmingham, Alabama, typically allows 5 percent of the graduating class to claim the number one ranking. But in these litigious days, no solution is safe. Last year, an Oklahoma teenager sued to prevent two other students from sharing the title with her.

The problem does not end with the top students. Some schools object to ranking any students. College admissions officers cited in the story estimate that half or more of the applications they receive do not have a class rank for the student. Because grading systems can vary widely from school to school, how does a potential employer or a college admissions officer know how to interpret a transcript that does not reveal how a student performed relative to other students? Perhaps they all have straight-A averages.

Admissions officials who cannot use class standing as a way of differentiating students are likely to put more weight on standardized test scores, but they are also under attack. One problem is that the tests are a useful but far from perfect indicator of who will succeed in school. Another is that African American and Latino students on average receive lower scores than do their white and Asian counterparts. Although the test score gap has closed somewhat in recent decades, it is still sizable; and although all would agree that the best solution is to eliminate the gap completely, it has become clear that this will not happen quickly. In the meantime, because these tests influence not only college admissions but the courses students are able to take in high school, they have the power to close the door to many professional career options.

There is some irony in this, because standardized testing was originally promoted as a way to break down class barriers and open opportunities for capable young people from the lower rungs of the social ladder. For many successful people who came from poor families, these tests are a symbol of the U.S. meritocracy—a sign that what you know matters more than who you know or where you come from. With the widespread recognition that we live in a knowledge-based economy in which well-educated workers are the most valuable resource, the thought that the society would de-emphasize the importance of school grades and standardized test scores is profoundly disturbing. Particularly in the fields of science and engineering, there is a strong belief that some individuals perform better than others and that this performance can be evaluated objectively.

Is it time to be alarmed? No. There should be no doubt that admission to the elite science and engineering college programs is fiercely competitive and that grades and test scores are critical criteria. Likewise, job competition for scientific and technical workers is rigorously meritocratic. The majority of college officials, employers, and ambitious students support the use of these criteria, in no small part because they achieved their own positions because of good grades and high test scores.

A greater threat than the elimination of standardized testing is the misuse of these tests, particularly in the lower grades. A 1999 National Research Council report, *High Stakes: Testing for Tracking, Promotion, and Graduation,* found that critical decisions about individual students are sometimes made on the basis of a test score even when the test was not designed for that purpose. The report finds that standardized tests can be very valuable in making decisions, but only when the student has been taught what is being tested, the test is relevant to the decision being made, and the test score is used in combination with other criteria. What worries the committee that prepared the report is the situation in which a student entering middle school is given a math test on material that was not taught in his elementary school. As a result of a poor score, that student could be tracked into a curriculum that includes no demanding math courses and that virtually eliminates the possibility that the student will ever make it into a science or engineering program or into any college program.

Grades do matter. Test scores do matter. We have a shared societal interest in identifying which individuals are best qualified to do the jobs that are important to all of us. The fact that someone wants to be an engineer or a physician does not mean that we have to let that person design our passenger planes or perform our bypass operations. Course grades and test scores help us identify those most likely to perform well in demanding jobs. If some groups in the society are not performing well on the tests, let's use the tests to identify the problem early in life and to intervene in ways that enable members of these groups to raise their scores. We should remember that these tests are designed to evaluate individuals, not groups. We cannot expect everyone to score well. The very purpose of grades and tests is to differentiate among individuals.

That said, it's worth noting the point made by journalist Nicholas Lemann in several articles about the development and use of standardized tests and the evolution of the meritocracy. The winners in the academic meritocratic sweepstakes, who are well represented among the upper ranks of university faculty and government leaders, tend to exaggerate the importance of academic success (as their stressed-out children will testify). Lemann argues that success in school and standardized testing is not the only or necessarily the best criterion for predicting success in life. The skills and qualities that we need in our society are more numerous and varied than what appears on the college transcript.

In spite of the extensive public attention paid to academic measures, the society seems to have enough collective wisdom to look beyond academics in making important decisions about people. We all know the difference between "book smart," "street smart," and "people smart" and recognize that different jobs and different situations call for various mixes of these and other skills. We do need grades and test scores to identify the academically gifted and accomplished, but we also need the good sense to recognize that academic prowess is only one of many qualities we should be looking for in our researchers, business leaders, and public officials. The people who make the most notable contributions to the quality of our society are the trailblazing inventors, artists, entrepreneurs, and activists, not only or primarily the valedictorians.

Suggestions for Discussion

1. What is meritocracy?

2. What factors make it difficult for modern schools to chose valedictorians?

3. What are Kevin Finneran's feelings about academic rankings?

4. Do grades predict how a student will perform in "the real world" after graduation?

5. How does "book smart" differ from "street smart" and "people smart"?

Suggestions for Writing

1. Write an essay in which you argue for or against the virtue of grading students.

2. If grades and standardized tests were eliminated from the school system, how would a student's progress be evaluated? Would any new system be free of accusations of elitism?

❧❧❧❧

G E O F F R E Y   N U N B E R G

Teaching Students to Swim in the Online Sea

Geoffrey Nunberg, a columnist, radio personality, and consulting professor of linguistics at Stanford University, is the author of *The Way We Talk Now* (2001) and *Going Nucular* (2004). Nunberg hosts a language feature on the National Public Radio program *Fresh Air*, and his column "Topic…Comment" has appeared regularly in *National Language and Linguistic Theory*. The following article, from the February 13, 2005 edition of the *New York Times,* suggests guidelines for helping students evaluate the reliability of on-line sources.

Information literacy seems to be a phrase whose time has come. Last month, the Educational Testing Service announced that it had developed a test to measure students' ability to evaluate online material. That suggested an official recognition that the millions spent to wire schools and universities is of little use unless students know how to retrieve useful information from the oceans of sludge on the Web.

Clearly, "computer skills" are not enough. A teacher of Scandinavian literature at Berkeley recently described how students used the Web to research a paper on the Vikings: "They're Berkeley students, so, of course, they have the sense to restrict their searches to 'vikings NOT minnesota.' But they're perfectly willing to believe a Web site that describes early Viking settlements in Oklahoma."

That trusting nature is partly a legacy of the print age. If we tend to give the benefit of the doubt to the things we read in library books, it is because they have been screened twice: first by a publisher, who decided they were worth printing, and then by the librarian who acquired them or the professor who requested their purchase.

The Web imposes no such filters, even as it allows users to examine subjects people would never have gone to a traditional library to research, like buying a printer or a cheap airline ticket. Many adolescents use the Internet to get information about issues they are reluctant to discuss with parents or teachers, like sexual behavior, sexual identity, drug use or depression and suicide.

But there is a paradox in the way people think of the Web. Everyone is aware that it teems with rotten information, but most people feel confident that they can sort out the dross. In a survey released last month by the Pew Project on the Internet and American Life, 87 percent of search-engine users said they found what they were looking for all or most of the time.

That level of confidence may not be justified, particularly when a search for information requires judging a Web site's credibility. According to the Pew survey, only 38 percent of search-engine users were aware of the difference between unpaid and sponsored search results, and only 18 percent could tell which was which.

A 2002 study directed by BJ Fogg, a Stanford psychologist, found that people tend to judge the credibility of a Web site by its appearance, rather than by checking who put it up and why. But it is much easier to produce a professional-looking Web site than a credible-looking book. The BBC was recently duped by a fake Dow Chemical site into broadcasting an interview with an environmentalist posing as a company spokesman.

Then, too, search engines make it all too easy to filter information in ways that reinforce pre-existing biases. A Google search on "voting machine fraud," for example, will turn up popular Web pages that feature those words prominently, most of which will support the view that voting machines make election fraud easier; opposing sites won't tend to feature that language, so will be missed in the search. A researcher exploring the same topic in a library would be more likely to encounter diverse points of view.

Up to now, librarians have taken the lead in developing information literacy standards and curriculums. There's a certain paradox in that, because a lot of people assumed that the digital age would require neither libraries nor librarians. But today, students have only limited contact with librarians, particularly because they do most of their online information-seeking at home or in the dorm.

More important, leaving information literacy to librarians alone suggests a failure to understand the scope of the problem.

Part of it lies in the word "literacy" itself. No other language has a word that covers such a broad swath of territory, from reading and writing skills, to a familiarity with culture, to elementary competence in subjects like math or geography. To many, "information literacy" suggests a set of basic ABC's that can be consigned to information 101.

One can list some basic principles of information literacy, like "Recognize an information need"; "Evaluate sources critically"; and "Check to see if the site sponsor is reputable." But those precepts are only of limited help with all that people now use online resources to do.

Last fall, for example, I co-taught a graduate course on "Information Quality" at Berkeley's School of Information Management and Systems. The students were highly sophisticated about search engines and knew their way around the Web.

But even they had difficulty with exercises that involved evaluating information in unfamiliar areas, like using the Web to decide which online degree program to recommend to a friend.

Still, given more time, those students would have known where to go for more accurate maps of the territory they were exploring. Unlike most students, they knew that "what's out there" doesn't end with what comes up on Google: University librarians complain that students tend to confine their online research to Web searches, ignoring other resources that the libraries have access to, like old newspaper archives, map collections and census data.

No less important, the students in our course would have known to use an even more basic technique: asking the right person. E-mail turns the Web into a vast digital help desk; user groups are teeming with people who will gladly explain the finer points of espresso machines or the history of English slang. But most people rarely think to make use of them.

In the end, then, instruction in information literacy will have to pervade every level of education and every course in the curriculum, from university historians' use of collections of online slave narratives to middle-school home economics teachers showing their students where to find reliable nutrition information on the Web.

Even then, it is true, most people will fall back on perfunctory techniques for finding and evaluating information online. As Professor Fogg observes, people tend to be "cognitive misers," relying on superficial cues whenever they can get away with it.

Only when confronting a question that is personally important—a health problem, a major purchase—are most people motivated to dig deeper. But that is reason enough to make sure that people have the skills they will need.

Suggestions for Discussion

1. According to Nunberg, what problems might arise when people search for information on the Web?

2. How might Web surfers more accurately assess the credibility of Web sites?

Suggestion for Writing

Compare Nunberg's treatment of the problems and possibilities of the Internet with Dave Barry's *The Internet* (p. 299) or Rebecca Mead's *You've Got Blog* (p. 311).

∽∽∽∽

CATHARINE R. STIMPSON

Learning to See the Miraculous

Catharine R. Stimpson has published more than 150 stories, essays, and reviews in venues such as *Transatlantic Review, Nation, New York Times Book Review,* and *Critical Inquiry.* She has edited numerous books and is the author of *Where the Meanings Are: Feminism and Cultural Spaces* (1988) and *Class Notes* (1979), a novel. Educated at Bryn Mawr College, Cambridge University, and Columbia University, Stimpson is dean of the Graduate School of Arts and Sciences at New York University. She has also served as chairwoman of New York State Humanities Council and the National Council for Research on Women, as president of the Modern Language Association, and as a member of the board of PBS. In this article from *Civilization* magazine, published in 1998, Stimpson explains how she can still find miracles in a relentlessly rational modern world.

Humanism was born of the exultant promise that "man is the measure of all things"; posthumanism mourns that "men are nothing but things to be measured." I rather dislike the term "posthumanism": It is vague; it is modish; and it falsely implies that history is a series of stages that everyone experiences in the same way. Such a scheme proposes that in the beginning, there was prehumanism—a period of Plato, paganism, Peter and Paul; next came humanism—the revival, really, of classical learning, joy in the individual and delight in human powers and possibilities; and now—posthumanism, wherein technologies are either transforming Man into Cyborg or stripping Man of the freedom, dignity and capacities of earlier periods.

Yet "posthumanism" is a useful bit of shorthand for my late-20th-century awareness—both exultant and edgy—that my sense of being a person has morphed from what it was when I first read Plato in the mid-20th century. Something is different, and it needs a name. In part, feminism has made the difference. But feminism, which supports the freedom and dignity and capacities of women, is the daughter of classical humanism. In far greater part, the

Moai, Study 16, Ahu Tongariki, Easter Island, Michael Kenna, 2000. ©Michael Kenna.

difference arises from the invention and distribution of our new technologies for reading nature and human nature, communicating and storing information, and manipulating life's genetic materials. I now casually use e-mail to exchange fascinated messages with actual and virtual friends about a cloned sheep in a Scottish pasture or a man with a pig's heart in a California suburb.

Famously, these technologies present us with a paradox. Human beings have dreamt up and created things that seem to change the very meaning of being human—an accomplishment that provokes contradictory feelings among and within us. I celebrate the surges of human creativity that the invention and use of new technologies represent. I was thrilled when novel techniques of brain-scanning showed surgeons where their micro-instruments should go as they repaired the scarred cerebral cortex of a beloved niece. My feelings of gratitude and relief are responses to the exercise of human powers that humanism lauds.

At the same time, I am deeply anxious. I fear both the reduction of persons to the status of things and the surveillance and control of us "things" that the new technologies permit. The political and psychological need to control surges of human creativity and action is old, but these days it is agog with happiness because of the freshly forged tools at its disposal. The brain scans of psychologists, neurologists and cognitive scientists provide blueprints for someone to mess with—and mess up—a cerebral cortex. My feelings of apprehension are responses to the exercise of human powers that help define posthumanism.

What am I to do with this contradictory set of emotions, this tension between delight and dread? And with this contradictory set of ideas, this tension between a perdurable humanism and the posthumanism that batters it? I have looked for an overarching concept that might help me cope with these oppositions. Somewhat to my surprise, because of my humanistic disdain for dank, rank superstition, I have come to experiment with the idea of…miracles. Yes, miracles.

Traditionally, a miracle is a violation of natural law, an intrusion of the supernatural into history. In this sense, miracles testify to our human yearning to believe in powerful worlds, powerful deities and powerful actors who will rescue us from our dangers and trespasses. Or a miracle might be an incomprehensible event, a mystery, which later generations might manage to rationally decipher. In this sense, a miracle demonstrates the need to recognize that we cannot understand everything the moment it happens. For those of us who fear being controlled, either sort of miracle explosively opens up our sense of possibility. It defies conventional wisdom and bullying regimes, be they of state or society.

The belief in miracles is historically pervasive. Is there any culture or any religion that lacks a story about raising the dead to life, or about making the barren fertile, or about a religious figure ascending to heaven? Contemporary America has its own abundance of miraculous stories. Some are the still-vibrant legacies of long-established religions: Think of the throngs who drive to a suburban home in New Jersey to glimpse a vision of the Virgin Mary. Others are hybrid minglings of old beliefs and current secular practices. Think of the phrase "miracle cure," both an allusion to faith healing and a tribute to the skills of modern medicine—a phrase that suits my niece's recovery but is also doubtless being used today by thousands of men who take Viagra. Then there are the TV sitcoms about angels doing good on earth or TV psychics who advertise 1–900 lines.

However, there is a radically different way to imagine the miraculous. Indeed, this way, which is a fundamental legacy of humanism, reverses our accepted definitions. If a traditional miracle represents the eruption of the supernatural into natural life and of the superhuman into human life, this different sort of miracle can be seen in nature and humanity themselves. What if the stuff of life itself—molecules and men, wavelengths and women, fractals and furry things—is as powerful, beautiful, grand, creative, delightful and surprising as any traditional miracle? What if life itself is as radiant as the divine?

This apprehension and appreciation of miracles was celebrated by Walt Whitman, who supported himself as a printer, teacher, journalist and doer of odd jobs and immersed himself in the realities of life around him. In his poem "Miracles" he sings:

> *Why, who makes much of a miracle?*
> *As to me I know of nothing else but miracles,*
> *Whether I walk the streets of Manhattan,*
> *Or dart my sight over the roofs of houses toward the sky,*
> *Or wade with naked feet along the beach just at the edge of the water,*
>
> *Or stand under trees in the woods,*
> *Or talk by day with any one I love, or sleep in the bed at night with any one*
>   *I love,…*

Later, he revels:

> *To me every hour of the light and dark is a miracle,*
> *Every cubic inch of space is a miracle,…*

He then ends:

> *To me the sea is a continual miracle,*
> *The fishes that swim—the rocks—the motion of the waves—the ships with*
>   *men in them,*
> *What stranger miracles are there?*

To imagine that our relations with nature and with others pulsate with the literally extraordinary energy of miracles—this is indeed an exalted, exhilarating leap of consciousness. But such imaginings can also be dangerous in at least three ways. First, the person who perpetually sees miracles must live in a state of perpetual ecstasy, of constant highs without the rest stops of the low. Such a delirious condition soon burns itself out. Second, much in life is not miraculous. Much in life is sordid, callous, grubby, cruel and murderous. Life can run the gamut from Dilbert's supervisors to Pol Pot, the genocidal ruler of Cambodia who finally died in 1998. A beaten child is not a miracle. An abused woman is not a miracle. An illiterate refugee woman stumbling through the mud with a hungry child on her back is not a miracle. A tortured prisoner in a totalitarian jail is not a miracle. If we see only miracles and marvels, we blind ourselves to social and political and psychological realities that we must sweat and struggle to improve. Third, many religious believers wish to maintain a separation between the powerful, unique realm of the sacred and that of the mundane, the secular. They fear that unless these two realms are held to be distinct, the sacred cannot occasionally surprise the secular, disrupting its ordinary laws. The sacred cannot flex its specialness. That is why the keepers of the sacred realm claim, and at the same time are afraid of, miracles.

Despite these dangers, to see the ordinary natural and human world as a miraculous place is to combine and recombine humanism with posthumanism. Such visionary perceptions enhance our capacity for wonder, our apprehension of the natural and human world as full of mysteries, complexities, intricacies, imagination and enchantments. They provoke pleasure in the structure of DNA, in a shaft of light, in an old house, in the images on a computer screen, in the shape of a hand. They enhance a recognition of the natural and human world not as a place to be measured and manipulated but as a place to be respected, enjoyed and treasured. Doing so, they burnish humanism's delight in human creativity and creations while warning us against a posthumanistic peril: the use of technology to flatten and organize people as if they were quantifiable data on a screen.

In addition, the recognition of the miraculous within nature and ourselves is the source of vital modern social movements that extend the moral legacy of humanism and provide posthumanism with much of its moral energy. One is the environmental movement, which values the preciousness of nature. The second is the interwoven movement for human rights and civil rights, which values the preciousness of every individual and her/his rights. A third movement is the expansion of education, which values the preciousness of every individual's mind and capacity for growth.

A posthumanist with religious yearnings may choose to believe that God or gods or goddesses can interrupt and change the laws that normally govern us. A posthumanist with parapsychic leanings may choose to punch the telephone keypad for a psychic hotline or surf the web to find a psychic's home page. And a posthumanist with no interest at all in the para-real, with full-hearted delight in us people and our world, may find miracles right around the house. No matter what we believe or do, we cannot dismiss the humanistic possibility that we dwell each day with miracles—the miracles of being on this earth, together, with each other and with nature and with our technologies, at once coiled with danger and shimmering with hope, in the flux and sea of human time.

Suggestions for Discussion

1. What is the traditional definition of a miracle?
2. How does Catharine Stimpson define miracles?

3. What are the advantages and disadvantages of finding miracles in the everyday or the commonplace?

4. In what ways does technology invite "delight and dread"?

5. Look at Michael Kenna's image on page 885 and its caption. What does the dramatic caption evoke in you? Is it puzzling? Does it spark your curiosity? Why? Now explore the background of this ancient site—Easter Island? *Ahu Tongariki? Moai?*—on the Internet. Having done some research, what is your response now? Has it altered your view on the image? If so, how? If not, why do you think your response did not change? What might Stimpson say about how we react to such sights?

Suggestions for Writing

1. Has scientific advancement harmed our ability to believe in the miraculous? Has our imagination or our faith in religion suffered as a consequence? Write an essay in response to Stimpson's.

2. Describe a time you have witnessed a miraculous event in your own life. Are there any miracles you believe occurred although you did not experience them firsthand? Why or why not?

FICTION

❦❦❦

A M Y   T A N

Waverly Jong: Rules of the Game

Amy Tan (b. 1952) was born in Oakland, CA, several years after her mother and father immigrated to the San Francisco Bay area from China. Following the death of her father and brother, Tan spent much of her teenage years journeying throughout Europe before settling in Montreux, Switzerland, where she graduated from high school in her junior year. Before turning to writing novels, Tan was a freelance business writer specializing in corporate communications for companies such as AT&T and IBM. Amy Tan's first novel, *The Joy Luck Club,* was published in 1989; it was nominated for multiple awards and won both the Commonwealth Gold Award and the Bay Area Book Reviewers Award, and was adapted into a feature film in 1994, for which Tan wrote the screenplay. The following excerpt is taken from that book, and is told from the perspective of a girl named Waverly Jong. Other books by Tan include *The Kitchen God's Wife* (1991), *The Hundred Secret Senses* (1995), *The Bonesetter's Daughter* (2001), and *The Opposite of Fate* (2003). Tan is also the author of numerous short stories and essays and is a member of the literary garage band, the Rock Bottom Remainders, along with fellow authors Stephen King and Dave Barry.

I was six when my mother taught me the art of invisible strength. It was a strategy for winning arguments, respect from others, and eventually, though neither of us knew it at the time, chess games.

"Bite back your tongue," scolded my mother when I cried loudly, yanking her hand toward the store that sold bags of salted plums. At home, she said, "Wise guy, he not go against wind. In Chinese we say, Come from South, blow with wind—poom!—North will follow. Strongest wind cannot be seen."

The next week I bit back my tongue as we entered the store with the forbidden candies. When my mother finished her shopping, she quietly plucked a small bag of plums from the rack and put it on the counter with the rest of the items.

My mother imparted her daily truths so she could help my older brothers and me rise above our circumstances. We lived in San Francisco's Chinatown. Like most of the other Chinese children who played in the back alleys of restaurants and curio shops, I didn't think we were poor. My bowl was always full, three five-course meals every day, beginning with a soup full of mysterious things I didn't want to know the names of.

We lived on Waverly Place, in a warm, clean, two-bedroom flat that sat above a small Chinese bakery specializing in steamed pastries and dim sum. In the early morning, when the alley was still quiet, I could smell fragrant red beans as they were cooked down to a pasty sweetness. By daybreak, our flat was heavy with the odor of fried sesame balls and sweet curried chicken crescents. From my bed, I would listen as my father got ready for work, then locked the door behind him, one-two-three clicks.

At the end of our two-block alley was a small sandlot playground with swings and slides well-shined down the middle with use. The play area was bordered by wood-slat benches where old-country people sat cracking roasted watermelon seeds with their golden teeth and scattering the husks to an impatient gathering of gurgling pigeons. The best playground, however, was the dark alley itself. It was crammed with daily mysteries and adventures. My brothers and I would peer into the medicinal herb shop, watching old Li dole out onto a stiff sheet of white paper the right amount of insect shells, saffron-colored seeds, and pungent leaves for his ailing customers. It was said that he once cured a woman dying of an ancestral curse that had eluded the best of American doctors. Next to the pharmacy was a printer who specialized in gold-embossed wedding invitations and festive red banners.

Farther down the street was Ping Yuen Fish Market. The front window displayed a tank crowded with doomed fish and turtles struggling to gain footing on the slimy green-tiled sides. A hand-written sign informed tourists, "Within this store, is all for food, not for pet." Inside, the butchers with their blood-stained white smocks deftly gutted the fish while customers cried out their orders and shouted, "Give me your freshest," to which the butchers always protested, "All are freshest." On less crowded market days, we would inspect the crates of live frogs and crabs which we were warned not to poke, boxes of dried cuttlefish, and row upon row of iced prawns, squid, and slippery fish. The sanddabs made me shiver each time; their eyes lay on one flattened side and reminded me of my mother's story of a careless girl who ran into a crowded street and was crushed by a cab. "Was smash flat," reported my mother.

At the corner of the alley was Hong Sing's, a four-table café with a recessed stairwell in front that led to a door marked "Tradesmen." My brothers and I believed the bad people emerged from this door at night. Tourists never went to Hong Sing's, since the menu was printed only in Chinese. A Caucasian man with a big camera once posed me and my playmates in front of the restaurant. He had us move to the side of the picture window so the photo would capture the roasted duck with its head dangling from a juice-covered rope. After he took the picture, I told him he should go into Hong Sing's and eat dinner. When he smiled and asked me what they served, I shouted, "Guts and duck's feet and octopus gizzards!" Then I ran off with my friends, shrieking with laughter as we scampered across the alley and hid in the entryway grotto of the China Gem Company, my heart pounding with hope that he would chase us.

My mother named me after the street that we lived on: Waverly Place Jong, my official name for important American documents. But my family called me Meimei, "Little Sister." I was the youngest, the only daughter. Each morning before school, my mother would twist and yank on my thick black hair until she had formed two tightly wound pigtails. One day, as she struggled to weave a hard-toothed comb through my disobedient hair, I had a sly thought.

I asked her, "Ma, what is Chinese torture?" My mother shook her head. A bobby pin was wedged between her lips. She wetted her palm and smoothed the hair above my ear, then pushed the pin in so that it nicked sharply against my scalp.

"Who say this word?" she asked without a trace of knowing how wicked I was being. I shrugged my shoulders and said, "Some boy in my class said Chinese people do Chinese torture."

"Chinese people do many things," she said simply. "Chinese people do business, do medicine, do painting. Not lazy like American people. We do torture. Best torture."

My older brother Vincent was the one who actually got the chess set. We had gone to the annual Christmas party held at the First Chinese Baptist Church at the end of the alley. The missionary ladies had put together a Santa bag of gifts donated by members of another church. None of the gifts had names on them. There were separate sacks for boys and girls of different ages.

One of the Chinese parishioners had donned a Santa Claus costume and a stiff paper beard with cotton balls glued to it. I think the only children who thought he was the real thing were too young to know that Santa Claus was not Chinese. When my turn came up, the Santa man asked me how old I was. I thought it was a trick question; I was seven according to the American formula and eight by the Chinese calendar. I said I was born on March 17, 1951. That seemed to satisfy him. He then solemnly asked if I had been a very, very good girl this year and did I believe in Jesus Christ and obey my parents. I knew the only answer to that. I nodded back with equal solemnity.

Having watched the other children opening their gifts, I already knew that the big gifts were not necessarily the nicest ones. One girl my age got a large coloring book of biblical characters, while a less greedy girl who selected a smaller box received a glass vial of lavender toilet water. The sound of the box was also important. A ten-year-old boy had chosen a box that jangled when he shook it. It was a tin globe of the world with a slit for inserting money. He must have thought it was full of dimes and nickels, because when he saw that it had just ten pennies, his face fell with such undisguised disappointment that his mother slapped the side of his head and led him out of the church hall, apologizing to the crowd for her son who had such bad manners he couldn't appreciate such a fine gift.

As I peered into the sack, I quickly fingered the remaining presents, testing their weight, imagining what they contained. I chose a heavy, compact one that was wrapped in shiny silver foil and a red satin ribbon. It was a twelve-pack of Life Savers and I spent the rest of the party arranging and rearranging the candy tubes in the order of my favorites. My brother Winston chose wisely as well. His present turned out to be a box of intricate plastic parts; the instructions on the box proclaimed that when they were properly assembled he would have an authentic miniature replica of a World War II submarine.

Vincent got the chess set, which would have been a very decent present to get at a church Christmas party, except it was obviously used and, as we discovered later, it was missing a black pawn and a white knight. My mother graciously thanked the unknown benefactor, saying, "Too good. Cost too much." At which point, an old lady with fine white, wispy hair nodded toward our family and said with a whistling whisper, "Merry, merry Christmas."

When we got home, my mother told Vincent to throw the chess set away. "She not want it. We not want it," she said, tossing her head stiffly to the side with a tight, proud smile. My brothers had deaf ears. They were already lining up the chess pieces and reading from the dog-eared instruction book.

I watched Vincent and Winston play during Christmas week. The chess board seemed to hold elaborate secrets waiting to be untangled. The chessmen were more powerful than Old Li's magic herbs that cured ancestral curses. And my brothers wore such serious faces that I was sure something was at stake that was greater than avoiding the tradesmen's door to Hong Sing's.

"Let me! Let me!" I begged between games when one brother or the other would sit back with a deep sigh of relief and victory, the other annoyed, unable to let go of the outcome. Vincent at first refused to let me play, but when I offered my Life Savers as replacements for the buttons that filled in for the missing pieces, he relented. He chose the flavors: wild cherry for the black pawn and peppermint for the white knight. Winner could eat both.

As our mother sprinkled flour and rolled out small doughy circles for the steamed dumplings that would be our dinner that night, Vincent explained the rules, pointing to each piece. "You have sixteen pieces and so do I. One king and queen, two bishops, two knights, two castles, and eight pawns. The pawns can only move forward one step, except on the first move. Then they can move two. But they can only take men by moving crossways like this, except in the beginning, when you can move ahead and take another pawn."

"Why?" I asked as I moved my pawn. "Why can't they move more steps?"

"Because they're pawns," he said.

"But why do they go crossways to take other men. Why aren't there any women and children?"

"Why is the sky blue? Why must you always ask stupid questions?" asked Vincent. "This is a game. These are the rules. I didn't make them up. See. Here. In the book." He jabbed a page with a pawn in his hand. "Pawn. P-A-W-N. Pawn. Read it yourself."

My mother patted the flour off her hands. "Let me see book," she said quietly. She scanned the pages quickly, not reading the foreign English symbols, seeming to search deliberately for nothing in particular.

"This American rules," she concluded at last. "Every time people come out from foreign country, must know rules. You not know, judge say, Too bad, go back. They not telling you why so you can use their way go forward. They say, Don't know why, you find out yourself. But they knowing all the time. Better you take it, find out why yourself." She tossed her head back with a satisfied smile.

I found out about all the whys later. I read the rules and looked up all the big words in a dictionary. I borrowed books from the Chinatown library. I studied each chess piece, trying to absorb the power each contained.

I learned about opening moves and why it's important to control the center early on; the shortest distance between two points is straight down the middle. I learned about the middle game and why tactics between two adversaries are like clashing ideas; the one who plays better has the clearest plans for both attacking and getting out of traps. I learned why it is essential in the endgame to have foresight, a mathematical understanding of all possible moves, and patience; all weaknesses and advantages become evident to a strong adversary and are obscured to a tiring opponent. I discovered that for the whole game one must gather invisible strengths and see the endgame before the game begins.

I also found out why I should never reveal "why" to others.

A little knowledge withheld is a great advantage one should store for future use. That is the power of chess. It is a game of secrets in which one must show and never tell.

I loved the secrets I found within the sixty-four black and white squares. I carefully drew a handmade chessboard and pinned it to the wall next to my bed, where at night I would stare for hours at imaginary battles. Soon I no longer lost any games or Life Savers, but I lost my adversaries. Winston and Vincent decided they were more interested in roaming the streets after school in their Hopalong Cassidy cowboy hats.

On a cold spring afternoon, while walking home from school, I detoured through the playground at the end of our alley. I saw a group of old men, two seated across a folding table playing a game of chess, others smoking pipes, eating peanuts, and watching. I ran home and grabbed Vincent's chess set, which was bound in a cardboard box with rubber bands. I also carefully selected two prized rolls of Life Savers. I came back to the park and approached a man who was observing the game.

"Want to play?" I asked him. His face widened with surprise and he grinned as he looked at the box under my arm.

"Little sister, been a long time since I play with dolls," he said, smiling benevolently. I quickly put the box down next to him on the bench and displayed my retort.

Lau Po, as he allowed me to call him, turned out to be a much better player than my brothers. I lost many games and many Life Savers. But over the weeks, with each diminishing roll of candies, I added new secrets. Lau Po gave me the names. The Double Attack from the East and West Shores. Throwing Stones on the Drowning Man. The Sudden Meeting of the Clan. The Surprise from the Sleeping Guard. The Humble Servant Who Kills the King. Sand in the Eyes of Advancing Forces. A Double Killing Without Blood.

There were also the fine points of chess etiquette. Keep captured men in neat rows, as well-tended prisoners. Never announce "Check" with vanity, lest someone with an unseen sword slit your throat. Never hurl pieces into the sandbox after you have lost a game, because then you must find them again, by yourself, after apologizing to all around you. By the end of the summer, Lau Po had taught me all he knew, and I had become a better chess player.

A small weekend crowd of Chinese people and tourists would gather as I played and defeated my opponents one by one. My mother would join the crowds during these outdoor exhibition games. She sat proudly on the bench, telling my admirers with proper Chinese humility, "Is luck."

A man who watched me play in the park suggested that my mother allow me to play in local chess tournaments. My mother smiled graciously, an answer that meant nothing. I desperately wanted to go, but I bit back my tongue. I knew she would not let me play among strangers. So as we walked home I said in a small voice that I didn't want to play in the local tournament. They would have American rules. If I lost, I would bring shame on my family.

"Is shame you fall down nobody push you," said my mother.

During my first tournament, my mother sat with me in the front row as I waited for my turn. I frequently bounced my legs to unstick them from the cold metal seat of the folding chair. When my name was called, I leapt up. My mother unwrapped something in her lap. It was her *chang*, a small tablet of red jade which held the sun's fire. "Is luck," she whispered, and tucked it into my dress pocket. I turned to my opponent, a fifteen-year-old boy from Oakland. He looked at me, wrinkling his nose.

As I began to play, the boy disappeared, the color ran out of the room, and I saw only my white pieces and his black ones waiting on the other side. A light wind began blowing past my ears. It whispered secrets only I could hear.

"Blow from the South," it murmured. "The wind leaves no trail." I saw a clear path, the traps to avoid. The crowd rustled. "Shhh! Shhh!" said the corners of the room. The wind blew stronger. "Throw sand from the East to distract him." The knight came forward ready for the sacrifice. The wind hissed, louder and louder. "Blow, blow, blow. He cannot see. He is blind now. Make him lean away from the wind so he is easier to knock down."

"Check," I said, as the wind roared with laughter. The wind died down to little puffs, my own breath.

My mother placed my first trophy next to a new plastic chess set that the neighborhood Tao society had given to me. As she wiped each piece with a soft cloth, she said, "Next time win more, lose less."

"Ma, it's not how many pieces you lose," I said. "Sometimes you need to lose pieces to get ahead."

"Better to lose less, see if you really need."

At the next tournament, I won again, but it was my mother who wore the triumphant grin.

"Lost eight piece this time. Last time was eleven. What I tell you? Better off lose less!" I was annoyed, but I couldn't say anything.

I attended more tournaments, each one farther away from home. I won all games, in all divisions. The Chinese bakery downstairs from our flat displayed my growing collection of trophies in its window, amidst the dust-covered cakes that were never picked up. The day after I won an important regional tournament, the window encased a fresh sheet cake with whipped-cream frosting and red script saying, "Congratulations, Waverly Jong, Chinatown Chess Champion." Soon after that, a flower shop, headstone engraver, and funeral parlor offered to sponsor me in national tournaments. That's when my mother decided I no longer had to do the dishes. Winston and Vincent had to do my chores.

"Why does she get to play and we do all the work," complained Vincent.

"Is new American rules," said my mother. "Meimei play, squeeze all her brains out for win chess. You play, worth squeeze towel."

By my ninth birthday, I was a national chess champion. I was still some 429 points away from grand-master status, but I was touted as the Great American Hope, a child prodigy and a girl to boot. They ran a photo of me in *Life* magazine next to a quote in which Bobby Fischer said, "There will never be a woman grand master." "Your move, Bobby," said the caption.

The day they took the magazine picture I wore neatly plaited braids clipped with plastic barrettes trimmed with rhinestones. I was playing in a large high school auditorium that echoed with phlegmy coughs and the squeaky rubber knobs of chair legs sliding across freshly waxed wooden floors. Seated across from me was an American man, about the same age as Lau Po, maybe fifty. I remember that his sweaty brow seemed to weep at my every move. He wore a dark, malodorous suit. One of his pockets was stuffed with a great white kerchief on which he wiped his palm before sweeping his hand over the chosen chess piece with great flourish.

In my crisp pink-and-white dress with scratchy lace at the neck, one of two my mother had sewn for these special occasions, I would clasp my hands under my chin, the delicate points of my elbows poised lightly on the table in the manner my mother had shown me for posing for the press. I would swing my patent leather shoes back and forth like an impatient child riding on a school bus. Then I would pause, suck in my lips, twirl my chosen piece in midair as if undecided, and then firmly plant it in its new threatening place, with a triumphant smile thrown back at my opponent for good measure.

I no longer played in the alley of Waverly Place. I never visited the playground where the pigeons and old men gathered. I went to school, then directly home to learn new chess secrets, cleverly concealed advantages, more escape routes.

But I found it difficult to concentrate at home. My mother had a habit of standing over me while I plotted out my games. I think she thought of herself as my protective ally. Her lips would be sealed tight, and after each move I made, a soft "Hmmmmph" would escape from her nose.

"Ma, I can't practice when you stand there like that," I said one day. She retreated to the kitchen and made loud noises with the pots and pans. When the crashing stopped, I could see out of the corner of my eye that she was standing in the doorway. "Hmmmmph!" Only this one came out of her tight throat.

My parents made many concessions to allow me to practice. One time I complained that the bedroom I shared was so noisy that I couldn't think. Thereafter, my brothers slept in a bed in the living room facing the street. I said I couldn't finish my rice; my head didn't work right when my stomach was too full. I left the table with half-finished bowls and nobody complained. But there was one duty I couldn't avoid. I had to accompany my mother on Saturday market days when I had no tournament to play. My mother would proudly walk with me, visiting many shops, buying very little. "This my daughter Wave-ly Jong," she said to whoever looked her way.

One day, after we left a shop I said under my breath, "I wish you wouldn't do that, telling everybody I'm your daughter." My mother stopped walking. Crowds of people with heavy bags pushed past us on the sidewalk, bumping into first one shoulder, then another.

"Aiii-ya. So shame be with mother?" She grasped my hand even tighter as she glared at me.

I looked down. "It's not that, it's just so obvious. It's just so embarrassing."

"Embarrass you be my daughter?" Her voice was cracking with anger.

"That's not what I meant. That's not what I said."

"What you say?"

I knew it was a mistake to say anything more, but I heard my voice speaking. "Why do you have to use me to show off? If you want to show off, then why don't you learn to play chess."

My mother's eyes turned into dangerous black slits. She had no words for me, just sharp silence.

I felt the wind rushing around my hot ears. I jerked my hand out of my mother's tight grasp and spun around, knocking into an old woman. Her bag of groceries spilled to the ground.

"Aii-ya! Stupid girl!" my mother and the woman cried. Oranges and tin cans careened down the sidewalk. As my mother stooped to help the old woman pick up the escaping food, I took off.

I raced down the street, dashing between people, not looking back as my mother screamed shrilly, "Meimei! Meimei!" I fled down an alley, past dark curtained shops and merchants washing the grime off their windows. I sped into the sunlight, into a large street crowded with tourists examining trinkets and souvenirs. I ducked into another dark alley, down another street, up another alley. I ran until it hurt and I realized I had nowhere to go, that I was not running from anything. The alleys contained no escape routes.

My breath came out like angry smoke. It was cold. I sat down on an upturned plastic pail next to a stack of empty boxes, cupping my chin with my hands, thinking hard. I imagined my mother, first walking briskly down one street or another looking for me, then giving up and returning home to await my arrival. After two hours, I stood up on creaking legs and slowly walked home.

The alley was quiet and I could see the yellow lights shining from our flat like two tiger's eyes in the night. I climbed the sixteen steps to the door, advancing quietly up each so as not to make any warning sounds. I turned the knob; the door was locked. I heard a chair moving, quick steps, the lock turning—click! click! click!—and then the door opened.

"About time you got home," said Vincent. "Boy, are you in trouble."

He slid back to the dinner table. On a platter were the remains of a large fish, its fleshy head still connected to bones swimming upstream in vain escape. Standing there waiting for my punishment, I heard my mother speak in a dry voice.

"We not concerning this girl. This girl not have concerning for us."

Nobody looked at me. Bone chopsticks clinked against the inside of bowls being emptied into hungry mouths.

I walked into my room, closed the door, and lay down on my bed. The room was dark, the ceiling filled with shadows from the dinnertime lights of neighboring flats.

In my head, I saw a chessboard with sixty-four black and white squares. Opposite me was my opponent, two angry black slits. She wore a triumphant smile. "Strongest wind cannot be seen," she said.

Her black men advanced across the plane, slowly marching to each successive level as a single unit. My white pieces screamed as they scurried and fell off the board one by one. As her men drew closer to my edge, I felt myself growing light. I rose up into the air and flew out the window. Higher and higher, above the alley, over the tops of tiled roofs, where I was gathered up by the wind and pushed up toward the night sky until everything below me disappeared and I was alone.

I closed my eyes and pondered my next move.

Suggestions for Discussion

1. How did Waverly's mother teach her "the art of invisible strength"?

2. What does chess mean to Waverly?

Suggestion for Writing

Write a story, fiction or nonfiction, in which you employ a game or a sport as a metaphor for the tale's central dramatic conflict.

POETRY

LANGSTON HUGHES

Theme for English B

Langston Hughes (1902–1962), a prominent black poet, was born in Missouri and educated at Lincoln University in Pennsylvania. Often using dialect and jazz rhythms, his work expresses the concerns and feelings of American blacks. His collections of poetry include *The Weary Blues* (1926) and *Shakespeare in Harlem* (1940); his novels include *Not Without Laughter* (1930) and *The Best of Simple* (1950). In "Theme for English B," Hughes clearly expresses the chasm between the races that exists even in the college classroom.

The instructor said,

> *Go home and write*
> *a page tonight.*
> *And let that page come out of you—*
> *Then, it will be true.*

I wonder if it's that simple?
I am twenty-two, colored, born in Winston-Salem.
I went to school there, then Durham, then here
to this college on the hill above Harlem.
I am the only colored student in my class.
The steps from the hill lead down into Harlem,
through a park, then I cross St. Nicholas,
Eighth Avenue, Seventh, and I come to the Y,
the Harlem Branch Y, where I take the elevator
up to my room, sit down, and write this page:

It's not easy to know what is true for you or me
at twenty-two, my age. But I guess I'm what
I feel and see and hear, Harlem, I hear you:
hear you, hear me—we two—you, me, talk on this page.
(I hear New York, too.) Me—who?

Well, I like to eat, sleep, drink, and be in love.
I like to work, read, learn, and understand life.
I like a pipe for a Christmas present,
or records—Bessie, bop, or Bach.
I guess being colored doesn't make me *not* like
the same things other folks like who are other races.
So will my page be colored that I write?
Being me, it will not be white.

But it will be
a part of you, instructor.
You are white—
yet a part of me, as I am a part of you.
That's American.
Sometimes perhaps you don't want to be a part of me.
Nor do I often want to be a part of you.
But we are, that's true!
As I learn from you,
I guess you learn from me—
Although you're older—and white—
and somewhat more free.

This is my page for English B.

Suggestions for Discussion

1. With what details does Hughes convey a strong sense of identity?

2. How does Hughes reveal his feelings about composition, learning, Harlem, his racial background, and his instructor?

Suggestion for Writing

Write an essay in which you attempt to convey some of your feelings about your own background, your likes and dislikes. Try to focus on details as Hughes has done in his poem.

TED HUGHES

Hear It Again

Ted Hughes (1930–2002) was a poet and scholar who made a study of world literature, shamanism, primitive poetry, and multicultural literature. Hughes was also the husband of Sylvia Plath, a fellow poet and a legendary figure in the history of women writers. He was born in Mytholmroyd, West Yorkshire, and attended Pembroke College in Cambridge. Among his books of poetry are *The Hawk in the Rain* (1957), *Crow* (1971), *Cave Birds* (1978), *Flowers and Insects* (1986), and *Wolfwatching* (1991). Hughes has also written plays, short stories, and children's literature and has translated several ancient Greek texts into modern English, most notably Aeschylus' Orestes trilogy.

> *'For out of olde feldes, as men seyth,*
> *Cometh of this newe come yer by yere,*
> *And out of olde bokes, in good feyth,*
> *Cometh of this newe science that men lere.'*

> —CHAUCER: *The Parlement of Foules*

Fourteen centuries have learned,
From charred remains, that what took place
When Alexandria's library burned
Brain-damaged the human race.

> *Whatever escaped*
> *Was hidden by bookish monks in their damp cells*
> *Hunted by Alfred dug for by Charlemagne*
> *Got through the Dark Ages little enough but enough*
> *For Dante and Chaucer sitting up all night*
> *   looking for light.*

A Serbian Prof's insanity,
Commanding guns, to split the heart,
His and his people's, tore apart

The Sarajevo library.

> *Tyrants know where to aim*
> *As Hitler poured his petrol and tossed matches*
> *Stalin collected the bards…*
> *In other words the mobile and only libraries…*
> > *of all those enslaved peoples from the Black to*
> > *the Bering Sea*
> *And made a bonfire*
> *Of the mainsprings of national identities to melt*
> > *the folk into one puddle*
> *And the three seconds of the present moment*
> *By massacring those wordy fellows whose memories were*
> > *bigger than armies.*

Where any nation starts awake
Books are the memory. And it's plain
Decay of libraries is like
Alzheimer's in the nation's brain.

> *And in my own day in my own land*
> *I have heard the fiery whisper: 'We are here*
> *To destroy the Book*
> *To destroy the rooted stock of the Book and*
> *The Book's perennial vintage, destroy it*
> *Not with a hammer not with a sickle*
> *And not exactly according to Mao who also*
> *Drained the skull of adult and adolescent*
> *To build a shining new society*
> *With the empties…'*

For this one's dreams and that one's acts,
For all who've failed or aged beyond
The reach of teachers here are found
The inspiration and the facts.

> *As we all know and have heard all our lives*
> *Just as we've heard that here.*

Even the most misfitting child
Who's chanced upon the library's worth,
Sits with the genius of the Earth
And turns the key to the whole world.

> *Hear it again.*

Suggestions for Discussion

1. What series of historical events is Hughes cataloguing, and how are they thematically linked?
2. Explain why Hughes feels that the "Decay of libraries is like/Alzheimer's in the nation's brain."
3. What is Hughes calling us to hear again?

Suggestion for Writing

How might your life have been different if your favorite book, play, movie, religious text, political treatise, or scientific tome were burned or banned by censors? Imagine what you know now that you would not know in that alternate reality, and consider the ramifications of this loss in a personal essay.

GLOSSARY

Abstraction, levels of   Distinguished in two ways: in the range between the general and the specific and in the range between the abstract and the concrete.

A general word refers to a class, genus, or group; a specific word refers to a member of that group. *Ship* is a general word, but *ketch, schooner, liner,* and *tugboat* are specific. The terms *general* and *specific* are relative, however, not absolute. On the one hand, *ketch* is more specific than *ship,* because a ketch is a kind of ship. But on the other hand, *ketch* is more general than *Tahiti ketch,* because a Tahiti ketch is a kind of ketch.

The distinction between the abstract and the concrete also is relative. Ideas, qualities, and characteristics that do not exist by themselves are abstract; physical things such as *house, shoes,* and *horse* are concrete. Concrete words can range not only further into the specific (*bungalow, moccasin,* and *stallion*) but also back toward the general (*domicile, clothing,* and *horses*). These distinctions between the abstract and the concrete and between the general and the specific do not imply that good writing should be specific and concrete and that poor writing is general and abstract. Most good writing constantly moves from the general to the specific and from the abstract to the concrete as the situation demands.

Allusion   Reference to a familiar person, place, or thing, whether real or imaginary: Woodrow Wilson or Zeus evoke leadership and male power, Siam or Atlantis evoke exotic locales, kangaroo or phoenix evoke a comtemplation of the wonder of wildlife. The allusion is an economical way to evoke an atmosphere, a historical era, or an emotion.

Analogy   In exposition, usually a comparison of some length in which the unknown is explained in terms of the known, the unfamiliar in terms of the familiar, the remote in terms of the immediate.

In argument, an analogy consists of a series of likenesses between two or more dissimilar things, demonstrating that they are either similar or identical in other respects; however, these types of analogies can be flawed, because two things alike in many respects are not necessarily alike in all (for example, lampblack and diamonds are both pure carbon; they differ only in their crystal structure. Although analogy never *proves* anything, its dramatic quality, its assistance in establishing tone, and its vividness make it one of the writer's most valuable techniques.

Analysis　A method of exposition by logical division, applicable to anything that can be divided into component parts: an object, such as an automobile or a watch; an institution, such as a college; or a process, such as mining coal or writing a poem. These parts or processes may be described technically and factually or impressionistically and selectively. In the latter method, the parts are organized in relation to a single governing idea so that the mutually supporting function of each of the components in the total structure becomes clear to the reader. For example, the actors, director, script, music score, and special effects are all part of a whole motion picture. Parts may be explained in terms of their characteristic function. Analysis may also be concerned with the connection of events; for example, given this condition or series of conditions, what effects will follow? For example, if a country in a recession, with high taxes and high unemployment, goes to war, what will happen to the economy?

Argument　Often contains the following parts: the *proposition,* an assertion that leads to the issue; the *issue,* what the writer is attempting to prove and the question on which the whole argument rests; and the *evidence,* the facts and opinions that the author offers as testimony. The evidence can be ordered *deductively,* by proceeding logically from certain premises and reaching a conclusion, or *inductively,* by generalizing from several instances and drawing a conclusion. Informal arguments frequently make greater use of the methods of exposition than they do of formal logic—for example, employing statistics, scientific theorems, or laws to further their case. See Analogy, Deductive Reasoning, and Inductive Reasoning.

It is possible to distinguish between argument and persuasion by the means (argument appeals to reason; persuasion, to emotions) or the ends (argument can change a mind; persuasion can lead to action). These distinctions, however, are more academic than functional, for in practice, argument and persuasion are not discrete entities. Yet the proof in argument rests largely upon the objectivity of evidence; the proof in persuasion, upon the heightened use of language.

Assumption　That part of an argument that is unstated because it is either taken for granted by the reader and writer or it is undetected by them. For example, author are not always aware of their prejudices or gaps in knowledge, and it hurts their arguments when these flaws go undetected. When the reader consciously disagrees with an assumption, the writer has misjudged his audience by assuming what the reader refuses to concede. An example of this is a writer, who assumes that British men are stuffy and sexist, writes an essay that British men (and those who disagree with the notion that all members of a single group can be described as all alike) are unlikely to agree with or enjoy.

Audience   For the writer, his expected readers. When the audience is unknown, and the subject matter is closely related to the writer's opinions, preferences, attitudes, and tastes, then the writer's relationship to his audience is his relationship to himself. The writer who distrusts the intelligence of his audience or adapts his material to what he assumes are the tastes and interests of his readers has disguised his authorial voice to the point where it is hard for the reader to feel as close a kinship with him as with a writer with more confessional and less commercialized (or mediated) style.

"It is now necessary to warn the writer that his concern for the reader must be pure; he must sympathize with the reader's plight (most readers are in trouble about half the time) but never seek to know his wants. The whole duty of a writer is to please and satisfy himself, and the true writer always plays to an audience of one. Let him start sniffing the air, or glancing at the Trend Machine, and he is as good as dead although he may make a nice living." Strunk and White, *The Elements of Style* (Macmillan).

On the other hand, when the audience is known (a college class, for example), and the subject matter is factual information, the writer should consider the education, interests, and tastes of her audience. Unless she keeps a definite audience in mind, the beginner is apt to shift levels of usage, employ inappropriate diction, and lose the readers if she does not appeal to any of their interests.

Cause and Effect   A seemingly simple method of development in which a connection is drawn between an event and its trigger. However, because of the philosophical difficulties surrounding causality, the writer should be cautious in ascribing causes. For the explanation of most effects, it is probably safer to proceed in a sequential order, using transitional words to indicate the order of the process. For example, it is a fact that the American Civil War followed the election of President Lincoln, but it is not necessariliy true to say that the election of Lincoln caused the Civil War.

Classification   The division of a whole into the classes that compose it, or the placement of a subject into its appropriate whole. See Analysis and Definition.

Coherence   Literally, a sticking together; therefore, the joining or linking of one point to another. It is the writer's obligation to make clear to the reader the relationship of sentence to sentence and paragraph to paragraph. There are several ways to do this. A writer can achieve coherence by putting the parts in a sequence that is meaningful and relevant—logical sequence, chronological order, order of importance. Or a writer can obtain coherence between parts by using transitional words—*but, however, yet*—to inform the reader that what is to follow contrasts with what went before; and *furthermore, moreover, in addition to* continue or expand what went before.

Another basic way of achieving coherence is to enumerate ideas to remind the reader of the development—*first, second, third.* A more subtle transition is to repeat at the beginning of a paragraph a key word or idea from the end of the preceding paragraph. Such a transition reminds readers of what has gone before and simultaneously prepares them for what is to come.

Comparison and Contrast   The presentation of a subject by indicating similarities between two or more things (comparison) or by indicating differences (contrast). Often comparison and contrast are used in definition and other methods of exposition.

Concreteness   See Abstraction, levels of.

Connotation   All that the word suggests or implies in addition to its literal meaning. For example, the word "odor" technically can suggest any scent, but common usage has led the listener to assume that is means (or connotes) a foul smell.

Contrast   See Comparison and Contrast.

Coordination   Elements of similar importance in similar grammatical construction. More important elements should be placed in grammatically dominant positions. This arrangement makes writing easier to understand and enjoy because the work is organized logically and flows. See Parallelism and Subordination.

Deductive Reasoning   In logic, the application of a generalization to a particular; in rhetoric, development that moves from the general to the specific.

Definition   In logic, the placing of the word to be defined in a general class and then showing how it differs from other members of the class. In rhetoric, the meaningful extension (usually enriched by the use of detail, concrete illustration, anecdote, metaphor) of a logical definition to answer fully, clearly, and often implicitly the question, "What is—?"

Denotation   The literal meaning of a word. See Connotation.

Description   Presenting factual information about an object or experience (objective description); or reporting the impression or evaluation of an object or experience (subjective description). Most description combines the two purposes. For example, *It was a frightening night:* an evaluation with which others might disagree; *The wind blew the shingles off the north side of the house and drove the rain under the door:* two facts about which there can be little disagreement.

Discourse, forms of   Traditionally, exposition, argument, description, and narration. See entries under each. These four kinds of traditional discourse are rarely found in a pure form. Argument and exposition may be interfused in the most complex fashion. Exposition often employs narration and description for purposes of illustration. In an effective piece of writing, the use of more than one form of discourse is never accidental; it always serves the author's central purpose.

Diction   Style as determined by choice of words. Good diction is character-ized by accuracy and appropriateness to subject matter; weak diction, by the use of inappropriate, vague, or trite words. The relationship between the kinds of words a writer selects and his subject matter in large part determines tone. The deliberate use of inappropriate diction is a frequent device of satire.

Emphasis   The arrangement of the elements in a piece of writing so that the important meanings occur in structurally important parts of the work. Rep-etition, order of increasing importance, exclamation points, rhetorical ques-tions, and figures of speech are all devices to achieve emphasis.

Evidence   That part of argument or persuasion that involves proof. It usually takes the form of facts, particulars deduced from general principles, or opin-ions of authorities.

Exposition   That form of discourse that explains or informs. Most papers required of college students are expository. The methods of exposition pre-sented in *The Conscious Reader* are identification, definition, classification, illustration, comparison and contrast, and analysis. See separate entries in the glossary.

Figure of Speech   A form of expression in which the meanings of words are extended beyond the literal. The common figures of speech are metaphor, simile, and analogy.

Generalization   A broad conception or principle derived from particulars. Often, simply a broad statement. See Abstraction, levels of.

Grammar   A systematic description of a language. The organizing principle of a language that gives it shape and provides rules for proper usage.

Identification   A process preliminary to definition of a subject. For the writer, it is that important period preliminary to writing when, wrestling with inchoate glimmerings, she begins to select and shape her materials. As a method of exposition, it brings the subject into focus by describing it.

Illustration   A particular member of a class used to explain or dramatize a class, a type, a thing, a person, a method, an idea, or a condition. The idea explained may be either stated or implied. For purposes of illustration, the individual member of a class must be a fair representation of the dis-tinctive qualities of the class. The use of illustrations, examples, and spe-cific instances adds to the concreteness and vividness of writing. See Narration.

Image   A word or statement that makes an appeal to the senses—sense impres-sions. Thus, there are visual images, auditory images, and so on. Because the most direct experience of the world is through the senses, writing that uses unexpected examples of sense impressions can be unusually effective.

Inductive Reasoning   In logic, the formulation of a conclusion after the observation of an adequate number of particular instances; in rhetoric, the development of an idea or concept that moves from the particular to the general.

Intention   The reason a piece of writing was first written—its goal. For example, some works are written to convince; others, to entertain; others, to teach; and others, to provoke thought or action. It is often wise to try to determine a work's intent to best understand your reaction to it.

Irony   At its simplest, involves a discrepancy between literal and intended meaning; at its most complex, it involves an utterance more meaningful (and usually meaningful in a different way) to the listener than to the speaker. For example, the audience understands Oedipus' remarks about discovering the murderer of the king in a way Oedipus himself cannot understand. The satirist frequently feigns the inability to grasp the full implications of his own remarks.

Issue   Limiting the general proposition to the precise point on which the argument rests. Defeating this point—the issue—defeats the argument. Typically the main proposition of an argument will raise at least one issue for discussion and controversy.

Limitation of Subject   Restriction of the subject to one centralizing subject or idea that can be adequately developed with reference to audience and purpose.

Metaphor   An implied comparison between two things that are seemingly different; a compressed analogy. Effectively used, metaphors increase clarity, interest, vividness, and concreteness.

Narration   A form of discourse that tells a story. If a story is significant in itself, and the particulars appeal to the imagination, it is *narration*. If a story illustrates a point in exposition or argument, it is *illustrative narration*. If a story outlines a process step by step, the particulars appealing to the understanding, it is *expository narration*.

Organization, methods of   Varies with the form of discourse. Exposition uses in part, in whole, or in combination the organizational methods identification, definition, classification, illustration, comparison and contrast, and analysis. Argument and persuasion often use the method of organization of inductive or deductive reasoning, or analogy. Description is often organized around a dominant idea or object. Narration, to give two examples, may be organized chronologically or in terms of point of view.

Paradox   An assertion or sentiment seemingly self-contradictory, or opposed to common sense, that may yet be true. For example, Thomas Jefferson was a slave owner who wrote that "all men are created equal."

Paragraph   A division of writing that serves to discuss one topic or one aspect of a topic. The central thought is either implied or expressed in a topic sentence, and the rest of the paragraph describes that thought. Most pieces of writing are composed of several paragraphs that are organized in some coherent scheme. See Coherence.

Parallelism   Elements of similar rhetorical importance in similar grammatical patterns. See Coordination.

Parody   Mimicking the language and style of another in a gently humorous or critical style. For example, the Austin Powers movies faithfully recreate characters, scenes, and dialogue from the James Bond films—the better to mock James Bond. The same technique is used in literature when Mark Twain writes like James Fenimore Cooper in order to illustrate why he feels that Cooper is a poor novelist.

Perspective   The vantage point chosen by the writer to achieve his purpose, his strategy. It is reflected in his close scrutiny of, or distance from, his subject; his objective representation or subjective interpretation of it. For example, a writer describing a football game may objectively describe both teams' feelings and actions fairly, or subjectively cast one team as heroic and another a villainous. See Diction, Purpose, Tone.

Persuasion   A rhetorical technique that often uses heightened language designed to appeal to the emotions or prompt the listener to take action. See Argument.

Point of View   In description, the position from which the observer looks at the object described; in narration, the person who sees the action, who tells the story; in exposition, the ideological starting point of the composition. First person or third person are the most commonly used points of view.

Proposition   See Argument.

Purpose   What the writer wants to accomplish with a particular piece of writing.

Rhetoric   The art of using language effectively.

Rhetorical Question   A question asked to induce thought and to provide emphasis rather than to evoke an answer.

Rhythm   In poetry and prose, patterned emphasis.

Satire   The attempt to effect reform by exposing an object to laughter. For example, Charles Dickens convinced the government to pass laws protecting children by satirizing in his novels a Victorian England that mistreated the young. Satire makes frequent recourse to irony, wit, ridicule, and parody. It is usually classified under such categories as social satire, personal satire, and literary satire.

Style   "The essence of a sound style is that it cannot be reduced to rules—that it is a living and breathing thing, with something of the demoniacal in it— that it fits its proprietor tightly and yet ever so loosely, as his skin fits him. It is, in fact, quite as securely an integral part of him as that skin is…. In brief, a style is always the outward and visible symbol of a man, and it cannot be anything else." H. L. Mencken, from *On Style*.

"Young writers often suppose that style is a garnish for the meat of prose, a sauce by which a dull dish is made palatable. Style has no such separate entity; it is nondetachable, unfilterable. The beginner should approach style warily, realizing that it is himself he is approaching, no other; and he should begin by turning resolutely away from all devices that are popularly believed to indicate style—all mannerisms, tricks, adornments. The approach to style is by way of plainness, simplicity, orderliness, sincerity." Strunk and White from *The Elements of Style* (Macmillan).

Subordination   Less important rhetorical elements in grammatically subordinate positions. See Coordination and Parallelism.

Syllogism   In formal logic, a deductive argument in three steps: a major premise, a minor premise, and a conclusion. The major premise states a quality of a class (All men are mortal); the minor premise states that X is a member of the class (Socrates is a man); the conclusion states that the quality of a class is also a quality of a member of the class (Socrates is mortal). In rhetoric, the full syllogism is rarely used; instead, one of the premises is usually omitted. "You can rely on her; she is independent" is an abbreviated syllogism. Major premise: Independent people are reliable; minor premise: She is independent; conclusion: She is reliable. Constructing the full syllogism frequently reveals flaws in reasoning, such as the above, which has an error in the major premise.

Symbol   A concrete image that suggests a meaning beyond itself. For example, a cross symbolizes Christianity; a peace symbol symbolizes the hippie movement of the 1960s; and a dove often symbolizes purity, divinity, or peace.

Tone   The manner in which the writer communicates his feelings or ideas about the materials he is presenting. Diction is the most obvious means of establishing tone. Satire and connotation are others. See Diction.

Topic Sentence   The thesis that the paragraph as a whole develops, encapsulated in one concise statement. Some paragraphs do not have topic sentences, but the thesis is implied through tone or arrangement of relevant information.

Transition   The linking together of sentences, paragraphs, and larger parts of the composition to achieve coherence by making logical connections (thematic and/or grammatical) between them. See Coherence.

Unity   The relevance of selected material to the central theme of an essay. See Coherence.

CREDITS

Cristian Amigo. "Intervention #1: Musical Openings." Reprinted by permission of the author.

Margaret Atwood, "Happy Endings" from *Good Bones and Simple Murders*. Copyright © 1983, 1992, 1994 by O.W. Toad Ltd. A Nan A. Talese Book. Used by permission of Doubleday, a division of Random House, Inc.

Margaret Atwood, "Pornography" from *Chatelaine*. Copyright © 1988 by Margaret Atwood. Reprinted with the permission of the author.

W. H. Auden, (1.) "Lullaby" ("Lay Your Sleeping Head, My Love") and (2.) "The Unknown Citizen" from *W. H. Auden: The Collected Poems,* edited by Edward Mendelson. Copyright © 1972 by W. H. Auden. Used by permission of Random House, Inc.

James Baldwin, "The Discovery of What It Means to Be an American" from *Nobody Knows My Name*. Copyright © 1959, 1961 by James Baldwin, renewed 1989. Published by Vintage Books. Reprinted with the permission of the James Baldwin Estate.

David C. Barker, "Rushed to Judgment: Talk Radio, Persuasion, and American Political Behavior." Copyright © 2002 by Columbia University Press and Oxford University Press. Reprinted with the permission of the publishers.

Dave Barry, "The Internet" from *Dave Barry in Cyberspace*. Copyright © 1996 by Dave Barry. Reprinted with the permission of Crown Publishers, a division of Random House, Inc.

Roland Barthes, "The Death of the Author," from *Image/Music/Text,* translated by Stephen Heath. English translation copyright © 1977 by Stephen Heath. Reprinted by permission of Hill and Wang, a division of Farrar, Straus and Giroux, LLC.

David Bayles and Ted Orland, "The Nature of the Problem" from *Art and Fear*. Copyright © 1993 by David Bayles and Ted Orland. Reprinted by permission of Image Continuum Press.

John Berger, "Uses of Photography" from *About Looking*. Copyright © 1980 by John Berger. Used by permission of Pantheon Books, a division of Random House, Inc.

Bruno Bettelheim, "The Child's Need for Magic" from *The Uses of Enchantment*. Copyright © 1975, 1976 by Bruno Bettelheim. Used by permission of Alfred A. Knopf, a division of Random House, Inc.

Robert Bly, "After Drinking All Night with a Friend, We Go Out in a Boat at Dawn to See Who Can Write the Best Poem" from *Silence in the Snowy Fields*. Copyright

ᜒᜒᜒᜒ

Photo Credits

Page 18: From *The Mystery Play* © 1994 Grant Morrison & Jon J. Muth. All Rights Reserved. Used with Permission

Page 21, *top:* Tobias Prasse Photography

Page 21, *bottom:* Tobias Prasse/Zefa-Corbis

Page 29: Don Bachardy, Santa Monica, CA.

Page 63: Alex Webb/Magnum Photos, Inc.

Page 87: © Christian J. Matuschek – Photography

Page 99: Veit Mette/Fotobuero

Page 111: © 2005 Paul Seller/Filmmuseum, Potsdam

Page 153: Museum Ludwig, Cologne, Germany

Page 189: Copyright Shirin Neshat 2000. Photo: Larry Barns, courtesy Gladstone Gallery, New York

Page 190: © Oleg Volk

Page 236: © C. Tyler from the book *Late Bloomer,* 2005, Fantagraphics. Originally published in 1990 as the cover for *Wimmen's Comix.* Website: www. bloomerland.com

Page 271: Courtesy Deitch Projects

Page 282: Sarah Brown Agency

Page 340: Markus Faust

Page 355: Antony Zito Studio Gallery

Page 394: Courtesy of the artist and Luhring Augustine, New York

Page 423: Cristian Amigo

Page 434: © Christian J. Matuschek – Photography

Page 463: Gunter Klötzer

Page 464 *(left and right):* Danwen Xing

Page 527: Courtesy Sonnabend Gallery, New York

Page 571: © Imke Lass

Page 603: Copyright © Patricia Levey. Courtesy of Photo-Eye Gallery, Santa Fe, NM

Page 612: © Christian J. Matuschek – Photography

Page 677: © BerndBrandenburg@love storyofberlin.de

Page 685: Peter Gourfain

Page 686: Courtesy Steven Holl Architects, New York

Page 762: Robert Huber/www.Lookatonline.com

Page 790: © Andreas Rühlow / www.foto-lounge.de

Page 799: © Irmy Wolz

Page 815: Courtesy the Gagosian Gallery

Page 885: © Michael Kenna

AUTHOR/ARTIST
AND
TITLE INDEX